Victoria Crosses on the Western Front Continuation of the German 1918 Offensives

Victoria Crosses on the Western Front Continuation of the German 1918 Offensives

24 March–24 July 1918

Paul Oldfield

Pen & Sword
MILITARY

First published in Great Britain in 2019 by
Pen & Sword Military
an imprint of
Pen & Sword Books Ltd
47 Church Street
Barnsley
South Yorkshire
S70 2AS

ISBN 978 1 47382 710 3

A CIP catalogue record for this book is available from the British Library

Typeset in Ehrhardt by
Mac Style
Printed and bound in the UK by TJ International Ltd, Padstow, Cornwall

Pen & Sword Books Ltd incorporates the imprints of Pen & Sword Archaeology, Atlas, Aviation, Battleground, Discovery, Family History, History, Maritime, Military, Naval, Politics, Railways, Select, Social History, Transport, True Crime, and Claymore Press, Frontline Books, Leo Cooper, Praetorian Press, Remember When, Seaforth Publishing and Wharncliffe.

For a complete list of Pen & Sword titles please contact
PEN & SWORD BOOKS LIMITED
47 Church Street, Barnsley, South Yorkshire, S70 2AS, England
E-mail: enquiries@pen-and-sword.co.uk
Website: www.pen-and-sword.co.uk

Contents

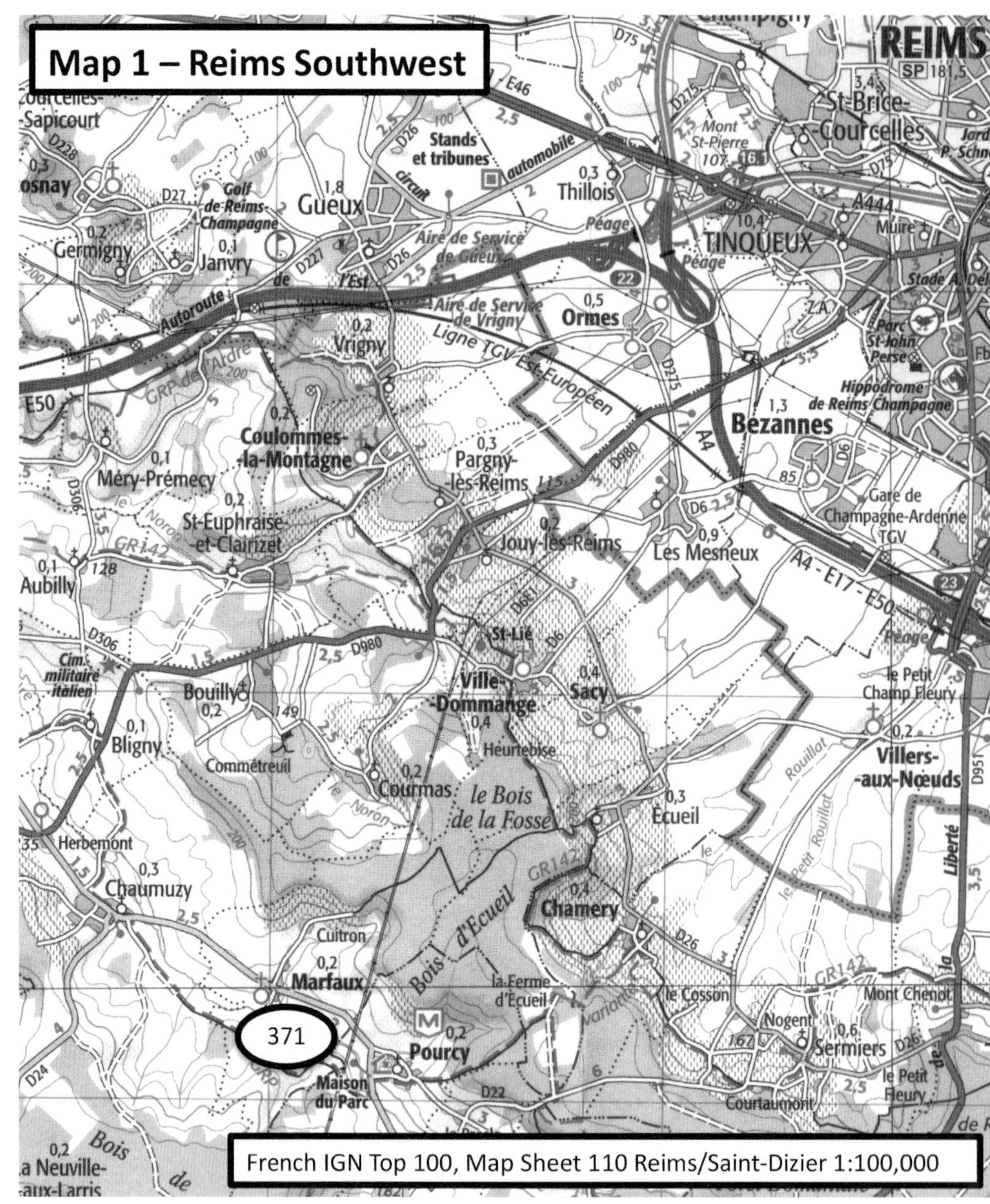
Map 1 – Reims Southwest
REIMS
St-Brice-Courcelles
Stands et tribunes
circuit automobile
Thillois
Gueux
Golf de Reims-Champagne
Germigny
Janvry
TINQUEUX
Muire
Aire de Service de Gueux
Autoroute de l'Est
Aire de Service de Vrigny
Ormes
Vrigny
Ligne TGV Est-Européen
Parc St-John Perse
Hippodrome de Reims Champagne
Bezannes
Coulommes-la-Montagne
Méry-Prémecy
Pargny-lès-Reims
St-Euphraise-et-Clairizet
Jouy-lès-Reims
Les Mesneux
Gare de Champagne-Ardenne TGV
A4-E17-E50
Aubilly
Cim. militaire italien
St-Lié
Ville-Dommange
Sacy
Bouilly
Bligny
Heurtebise
le Petit Champ Fleury
Villers-aux-Nœuds
Commétreuil
Courmas
le Bois de la Fosse
Écueil
Herbemont
Chaumuzy
Chamery
Bois d'Ecueil
Cuitron
Marfaux
la Ferme d'Écueil
le Cosson
Mont Chenot
371
Pourcy
Maison du Parc
Nogent
Sermiers
le Petit Fleury
Courtaumont
La Neuville-aux-Larris
French IGN Top 100, Map Sheet 110 Reims/Saint-Dizier 1:100,000

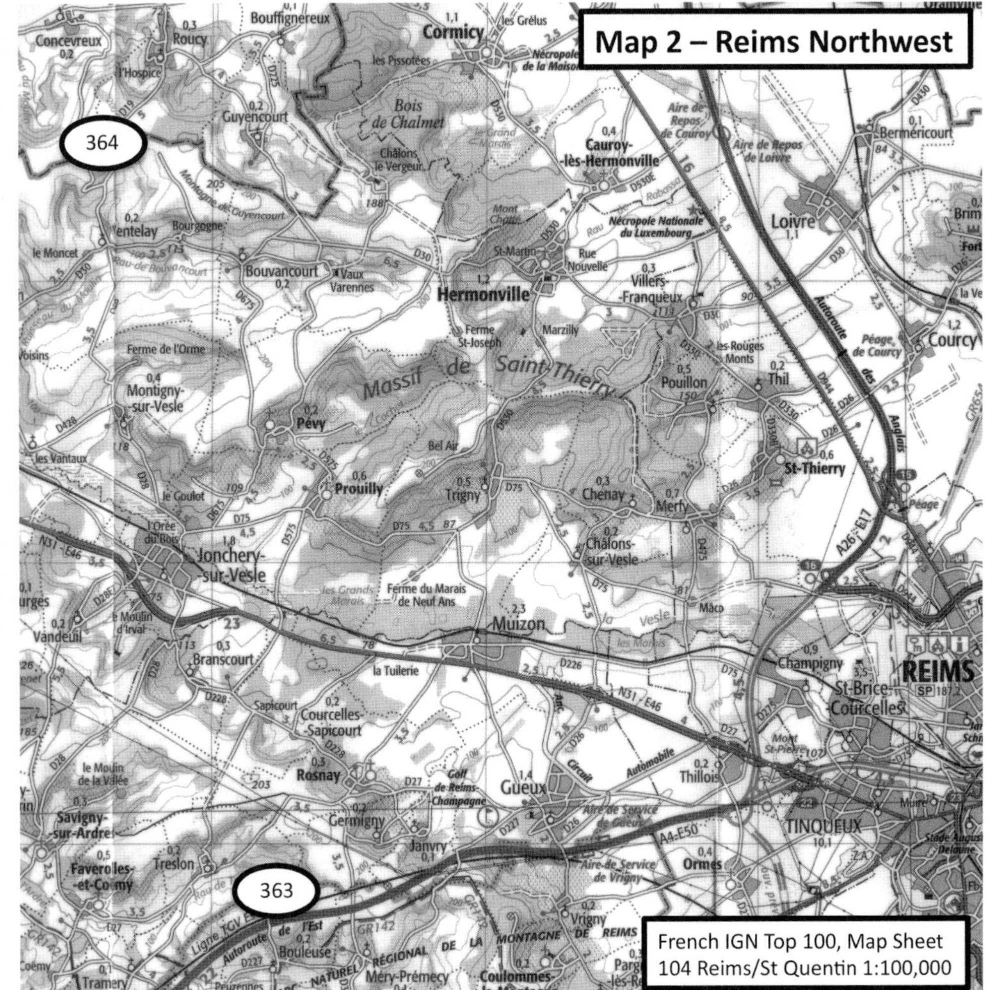
Map 2 – Reims Northwest
364
363
French IGN Top 100, Map Sheet 104 Reims/St Quentin 1:100,000
Cormicy
Hermonville
Massif de Saint-Thierry
Jonchery-sur-Vesle
Muizon
Gueux
REIMS
TINQUEUX
Loivre
Courcy
St-Thierry
Pévy
Prouilly
Trigny
Chenay
Merfy
Thil
Pouillon
Châlons-sur-Vesle
Champigny
St-Brice-Courcelles
Thillois
Ormes
Rosnay
Germigny
Janvry
Vrigny
Bouleuse
Méry-Prémecy
Coulommes-la-Montagne
Savigny-sur-Ardres
Faverolles-et-Coemy
Treslon
Courcelles-Sapicourt
Branscourt
Vandeuil
Montigny-sur-Vesle
Ventelay
Bouvancourt
Guyencourt
Roucy
Concevreux
Bouffignereux
Cauroy-lès-Hermonville
Villers-Franqueux
Bermericourt

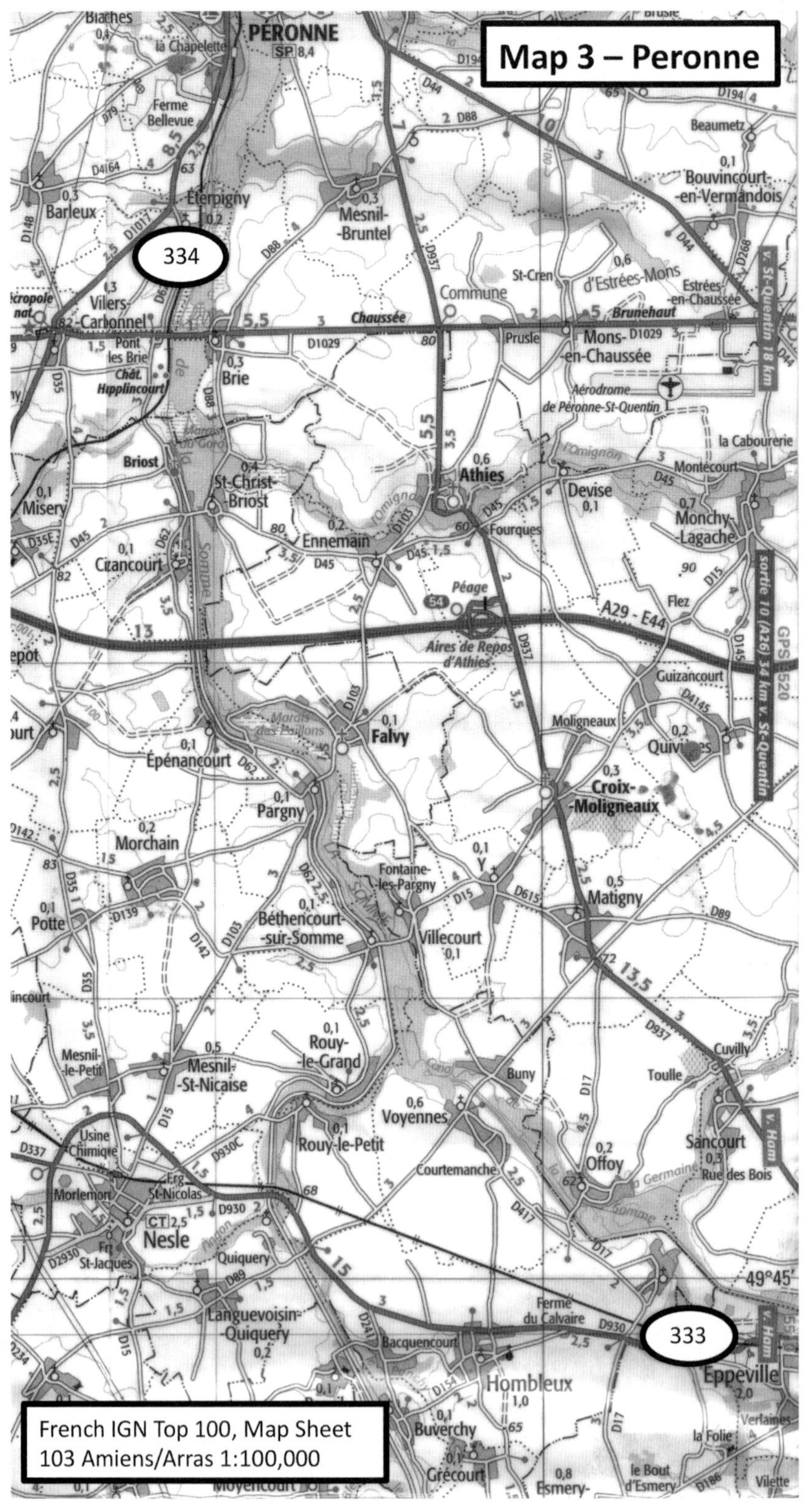

Map 3 – Peronne
334
333
PÉRONNE
Athies
Falvy
Croix-Moligneaux
Nesle
Hombleux
Eppeville
Matigny
Voyennes
A29 - E44
French IGN Top 100, Map Sheet
103 Amiens/Arras 1:100,000

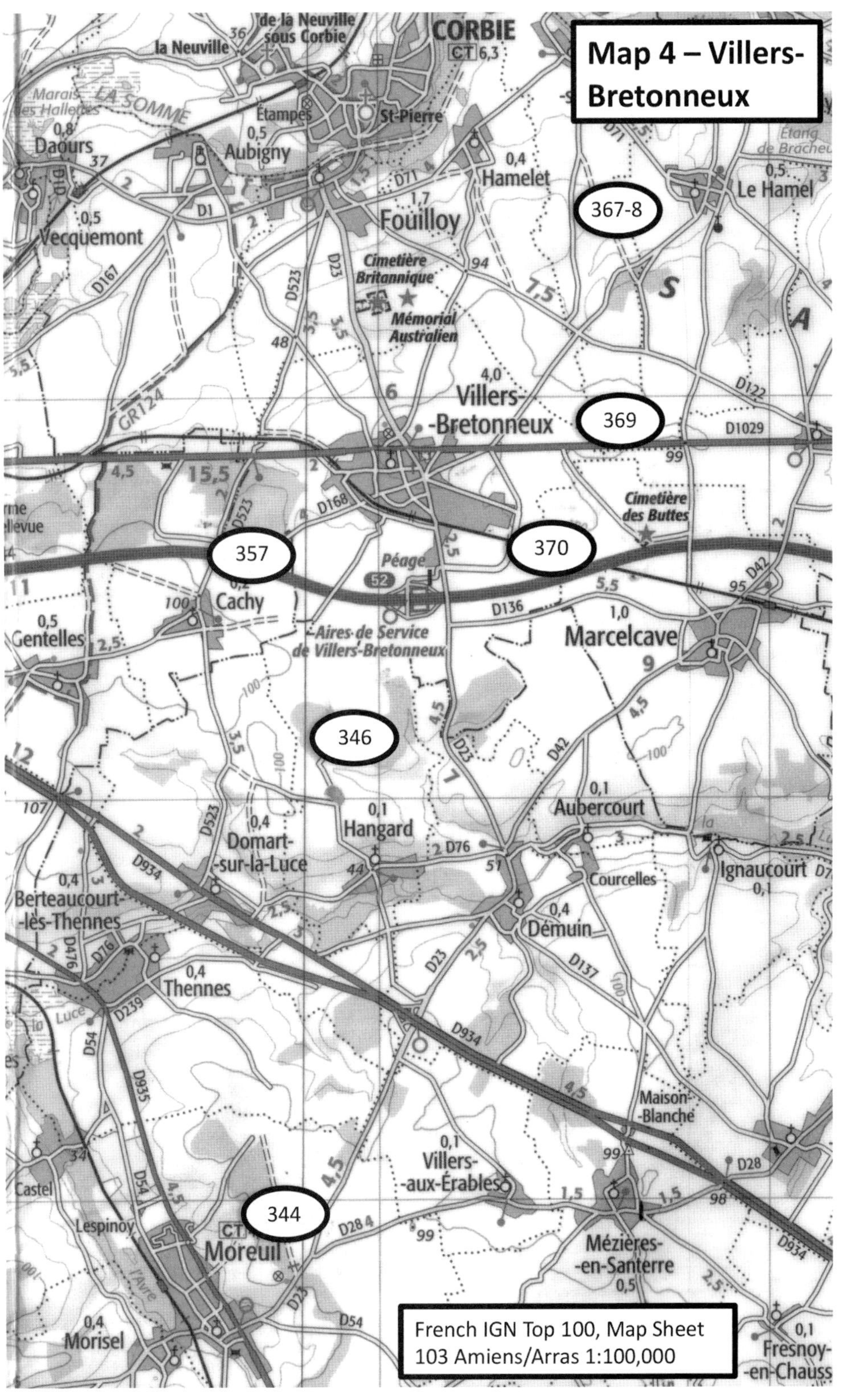
Map 4 – Villers-Bretonneux
367-8
369
370
357
346
344
French IGN Top 100, Map Sheet 103 Amiens/Arras 1:100,000
CORBIE
de la Neuville sous Corbie
la Neuville
Marais des Hallettes
LA SOMME
Daours
Aubigny
Étampes
St-Pierre
Hamelet
Le Hamel
Étang de Bracheux
Vecquemont
Fouilloy
Cimetière Britannique
Mémorial Australien
Villers-Bretonneux
Cimetière des Buttes
Péage
Cachy
Gentelles
Aires de Service de Villers-Bretonneux
Marcelcave
Aubercourt
Hangard
Domart-sur-la-Luce
Ignaucourt
Courcelles
Berteaucourt-lès-Thennes
Démuin
Thennes
Maison-Blanche
Villers-aux-Érables
Castel
Lespinoy
Moreuil
Mézières-en-Santerre
Morisel
Fresnoy-en-Chauss
D1029
D168
D136
D934
D523
D23
D42
D122
D76
D137
D239
D935
D54
D28
D476
D167
D71
GR124

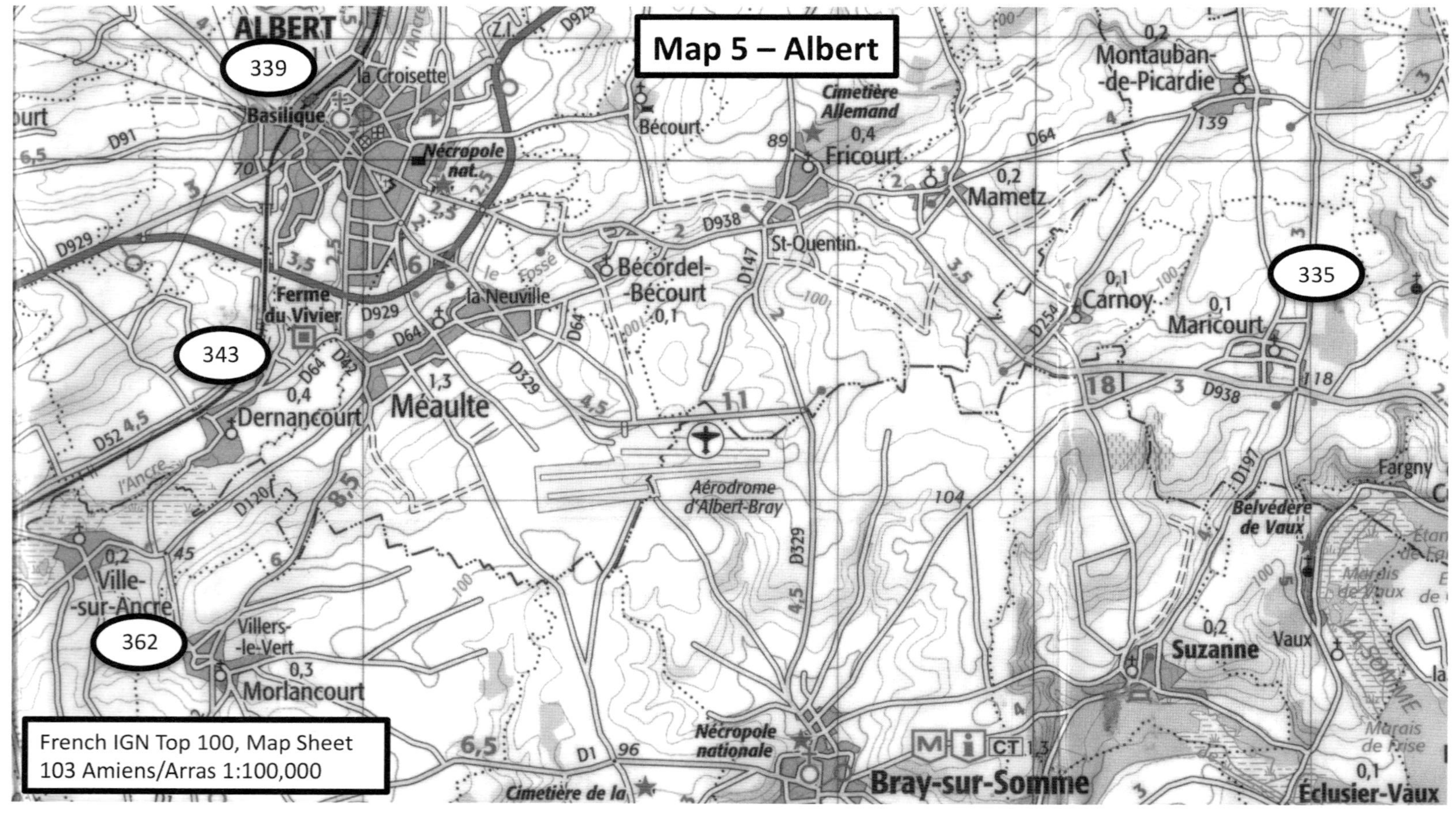

Map 5 – Albert
ALBERT
339
la Croisette
Basilique
Nécropole nat.
Ferme du Vivier
343
Dernancourt
Méaulte
la Neuville
Bécourt
Bécordel-Bécourt
Cimetière Allemand
Fricourt
St-Quentin
Mametz
Montauban-de-Picardie
Carnoy
Maricourt
335
Aérodrome d'Albert-Bray
Fargny
Belvédère de Vaux
Marais de Vaux
Suzanne
Vaux
LA SOMME
Marais de Frise
Éclusier-Vaux
Bray-sur-Somme
Nécropole nationale
Cimetière de la
Ville-sur-Ancre
362
Villers-le-Vert
Morlancourt
l'Ancre
French IGN Top 100, Map Sheet
103 Amiens/Arras 1:100,000

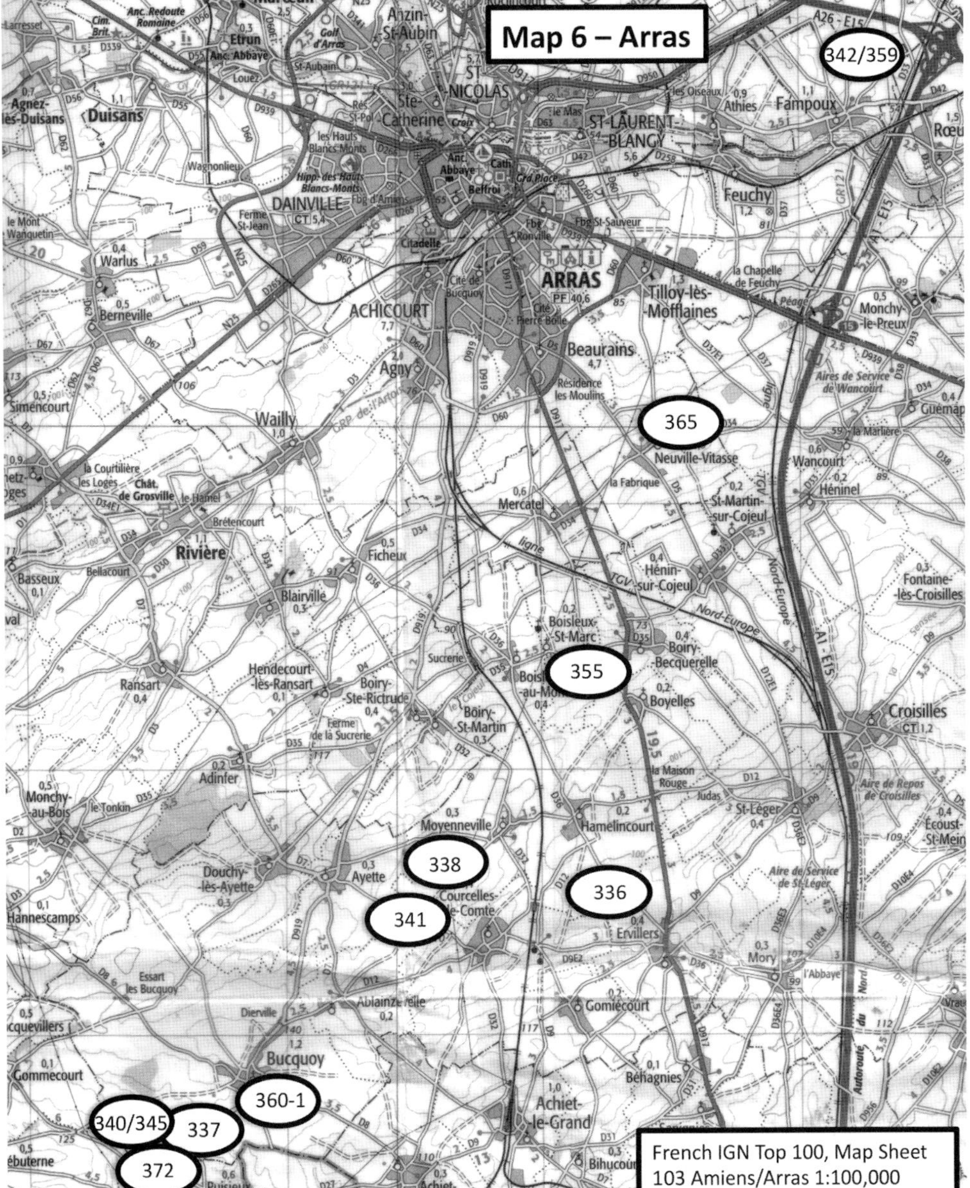
Map 6 – Arras
342/359
365
355
338
336
341
360-1
340/345
337
372
French IGN Top 100, Map Sheet
103 Amiens/Arras 1:100,000
ARRAS
ACHICOURT
DAINVILLE
ST-NICOLAS
ST-LAURENT-BLANGY
Ste-Catherine
Anzin-St-Aubin
Marœuil
Etrun
Duisans
Agnez-lès-Duisans
Athies
Fampoux
Feuchy
Tilloy-lès-Mofflaines
Monchy-le-Preux
Beaurains
Agny
Warlus
Berneville
Simencourt
Wailly
Rivière
Ficheux
Mercatel
Neuville-Vitasse
Wancourt
Héninel
St-Martin-sur-Cojeul
Hénin-sur-Cojeul
Fontaine-lès-Croisilles
Blairville
Boisleux-St-Marc
Boiry-Becquerelle
Boyelles
Croisilles
Basseux
Ransart
Hendecourt-lès-Ransart
Boiry-Ste-Rictrude
Boiry-St-Martin
Adinfer
Monchy-au-Bois
Moyenneville
Hamelincourt
St-Léger
Écoust-St-Mein
Douchy-lès-Ayette
Ayette
Courcelles-le-Comte
Ervillers
Mory
Hannescamps
Essart
Ablainzevelle
Gomiécourt
Bucquoy
Gommecourt
Béhagnies
Achiet-le-Grand
Bihucourt
Puisieux
Achiet-

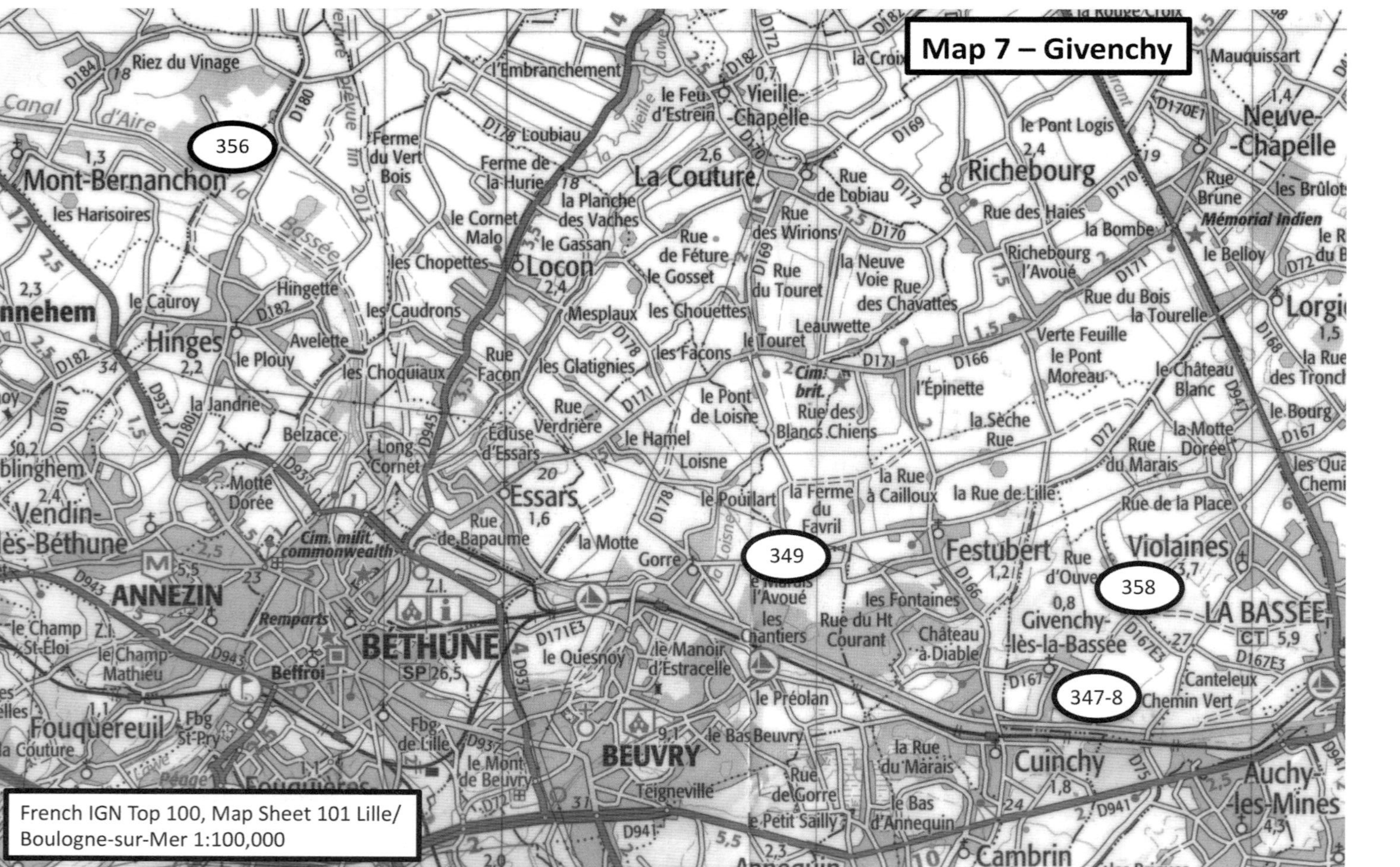
Map 7 – Givenchy
356
349
358
347-8
Mont-Bernanchon
Riez du Vinage
Canal d'Aire
les Harisoires
Hinges
le Cauroy
Hingette
Avelette
le Plouy
la Jandrie
Belzace
Motte Dorée
Vendin-lès-Béthune
ANNEZIN
Fouquereuil
le Champ St-Éloi
le Champ Mathieu
Fbg St-Pry
la Couture
BÉTHUNE
Beffroi
Remparts
Cim. milit. commonwealth
Fbg de Lille
le Mont de Beuvry
BEUVRY
Teigneville
le Bas Beuvry
le Quesnoy
le Manoir d'Estracelle
Essars
Rue de Bapaume
Écluse d'Essars
Long Cornet
les Choquiaux
les Caudrons
les Chopettes
le Cornet Malo
Ferme du Vert Bois
Ferme de la Hurie
Loubiau
l'Embranchement
Locon
le Gassan
la Planche des Vaches
La Couture
le Feu d'Estrein
Vieille-Chapelle
la Croix
Rue de Lobiau
Rue des Wirions
Rue de Féture
le Gosset
Mesplaux
les Glatignies
Rue Facon
Rue Verdrière
le Hamel
Loisne
le Pont de Loisne
les Façons
les Chouettes
Rue du Touret
le Touret
Leauwette
Cim. brit.
Rue des Blancs Chiens
la Neuve Voie
Rue des Chavattes
le Pouilart
la Ferme du Favril
la Motte
Gorre
le Marais
l'Avoué
les Chantiers
Rue du Ht Courant
les Fontaines
Château à Diable
le Préolan
la Rue du Marais
Rue de Gorre
le Petit Sailly
le Bas d'Annequin
Cambrin
Cuinchy
Festubert
la Rue à Cailloux
la Rue de Lille
la Sèche Rue
l'Épinette
Verte Feuille
le Pont Moreau
Rue du Bois
la Tourelle
Richebourg l'Avoué
Rue des Haies
la Bombe
Richebourg
le Pont Logis
Neuve-Chapelle
Mauquissart
Rue Brûne
Mémorial Indien
le Belloy
Lorgi
les Brûlots
le Château Blanc
la Motte Dorée
Rue du Marais
le Bourg
Rue de la Place
Violaines
Rue d'Ouve
Givenchy-lès-la-Bassée
LA BASSÉE
Canteleux
Chemin Vert
Auchy-les-Mines
French IGN Top 100, Map Sheet 101 Lille/ Boulogne-sur-Mer 1:100,000

Map 8 – Bailleul

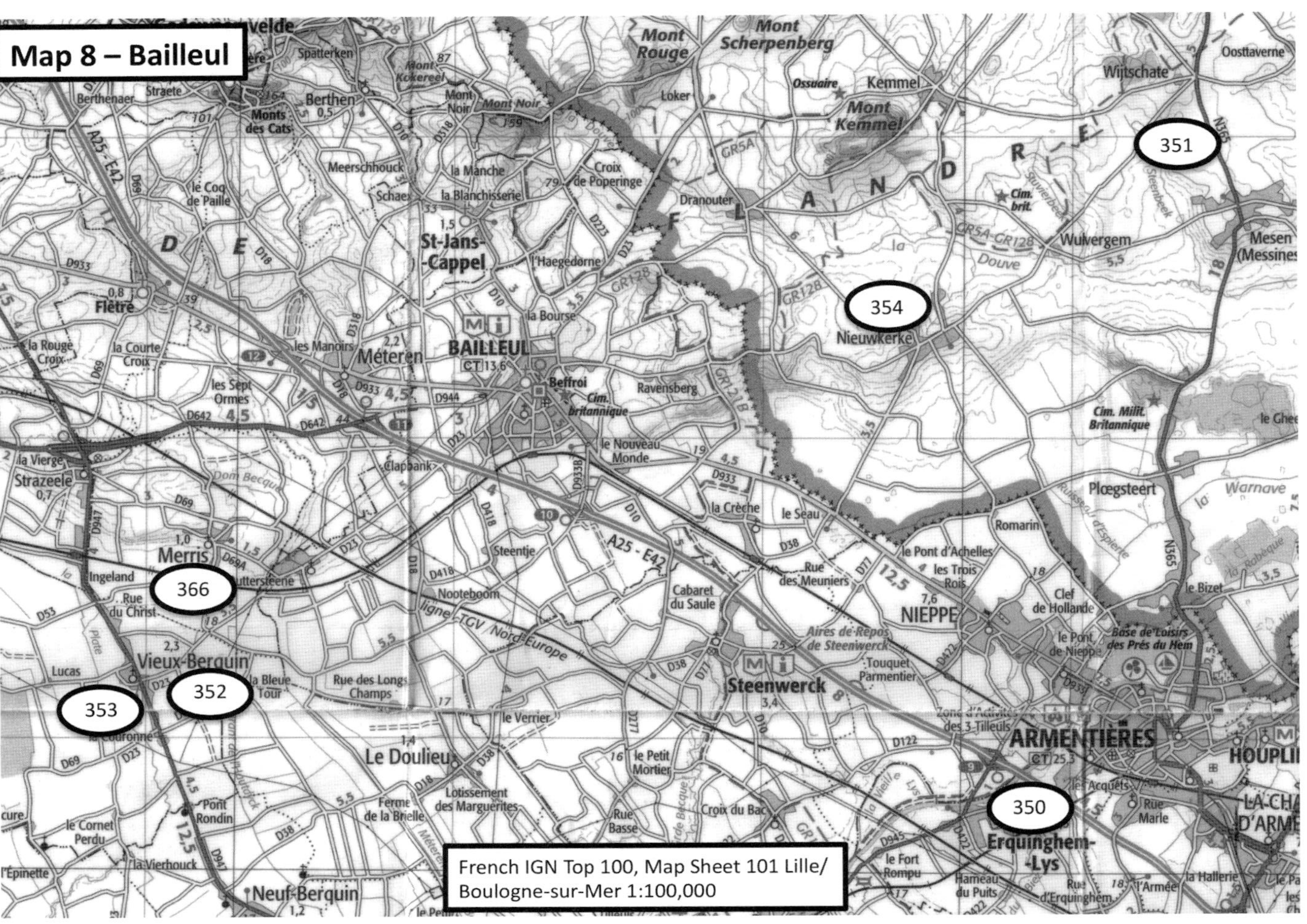

French IGN Top 100, Map Sheet 101 Lille/ Boulogne-sur-Mer 1:100,000

Abbreviations

AA	Anti-Aircraft
AA & QMG	Assistant Adjutant & Quartermaster General
ADC	Aide-de-Camp
ADS	Advanced Dressing Station
AFC	Australian Flying Corps
AIF	Australian Imperial Force
AMBIM	Associate Member of the British Institute of Managers
AMF(L)	ACE (Allied Command Europe) Mobile Force (Land)
AMICE	Associate Member of the Institution of Civil Engineers
AMIMechE	Associate Member of the Institution of Mechanical Engineers
AO	Order of Australia
AOC-in-C	Air Officer Commander-in-Chief
ASC	Army Service Corps
ASDIC	Anti-Submarine Detection Investigation Committee
ATS	Auxiliary Territorial Service
Att'd	Attached
AWOL	Absent without leave
BA	Batchelor of Arts
BAOR	British Army of the Rhine
BEF	British Expeditionary Force
BM	Brigade Major
BMA	British Medical Association
Brig-Gen	Brigadier-General
Bty	Battery (artillery unit of 4–8 guns)
Capt	Captain
CB	Companion of the Order of the Bath
CB	Confined to Barracks
CBE	Commander of the Order of the British Empire
CCF	Combined Cadet Force
CCS	Casualty Clearing Station
CD	Canadian Forces Decoration
CEF	Canadian Expeditionary Force
CFA	Canadian Field Artillery
CFB	Canadian Forces Base

CH	Companion of Honour
CIE	Companion of the Order of the Indian Empire
CIGS	Chief of the Imperial General Staff
C-in-C	Commander-in-Chief
CMG	Companion of the Order of St Michael & St George
CO	Commanding Officer
Col	Colonel
Cpl	Corporal
CQMS	Company Quartermaster Sergeant
CRA	Commander Royal Artillery
CRE	Commander Royal Engineers
CSgt	Colour Sergeant
CSEF	Canadian Siberian Expeditionary Force
CSI	Companion of the Order of the Star of India
CSM	Company Sergeant Major
CStJ	Commander of the Most Venerable Order of the Hospital of Saint John of Jerusalem
Cty	Cemetery
CVO	Commander of the Royal Victorian Order
CWGC	Commonwealth War Graves Commission
DAA&QMG	Deputy Assistant Adjutant & Quartermaster General
DAAG	Deputy Assistant Adjutant General
DAMS	Deputy Assistant Military Secretary
DAQMG	Deputy Assistant Quartermaster General
DBE	Dame Commander of the Order of the British Empire
DCL	Doctor of Civil Law
DCM	Distinguished Conduct Medal
DCNZM	Distinguished Companion of the New Zealand Order of Merit
DCO	Draft Conducting Officer
DFC	Distinguished Flying Cross
DL	Deputy Lieutenant
DLI	Durham Light Infantry
DSC	Distinguished Service Cross
DSO	Distinguished Service Order
Dvr	Driver
ENT	Ear, Nose and Throat
FInstCE	Fellow of the Institution of Civil Engineers
FM	Field Marshal
FRAS	Fellow of the Royal Astronomical Society
FRCP	Fellow of the Royal College of Physicians
FRCS	Fellow of the Royal College of Surgeons
FRCSE	Fellow of the Royal College of Surgeons of England

FRS	Fellow of the Royal Society
FRSA	Fellow of the Royal Society of Arts
FRSM	Fellow of the Royal Society of Medicine
FSA	Fellow of the Society of Actuaries
GBE	Knight/ Dame Grand Cross of the British Empire
GC	George Cross
GCB	Knight Grand Cross of the Order of the Bath
GCMG	Knight Grand Cross of the Order of St Michael & St George
GCVO	Knight/Dame Grand Cross of the Royal Victorian Order
Gen	General
GHQ	General Headquarters
GNZM	Knight/Dame Grand Companion New Zealand Order of Merit
GOC	General Officer Commanding
GOC-in-C	General Officer Commanding in Chief
GSO1, 2 or 3	General Staff Officer Grade 1 (Lt Col), 2 (Maj) or 3 (Capt)
HAC	Honourable Artillery Company
HE	High Explosive
HMAT	Her/His Majesty's Australian Transport/Troopship
HMHS	Her/His Majesty's Hospital Ship
HMNZT	Her/His Majesty's New Zealand Transport/Troopship
HMS	Her/His Majesty's Ship
HMT	Her/His Majesty's Transport/Troopship/Hired Military Transport
HRH	His/Her Royal Highness
HS	Hospital Ship
IAAG	Institute of Accountants and Actuaries in Glasgow
IWGC	Imperial War Graves Commission
JP	Justice of the Peace
KBE	Knight Commander of the Most Excellent Order of the British
KCB	Knight Commander of the Order of the Bath
KCIE	Knight Commander of the Order of the Indian Empire
KCMG	Knight Commander of St Michael and St George
KCVO	Knight Commander of the Royal Victorian Order
Kia	Killed in action
KJStJ	Knight of Justice of the Most Venerable Order of the Hospital of Saint John of Jerusalem
Kms	Kilometres
KOSB	King's Own Scottish Borderers
KOYLI	King's Own Yorkshire Light Infantry
KRRC	King's Royal Rifle Corps
KStJ	Knight of the Most Venerable Order of the Hospital of Saint John of Jerusalem
LCpl	Lance Corporal

LDV	Local Defence Volunteers (predecessor of Home Guard)
LG	London Gazette
LLD	Legum Doctor (Doctor of Law)
Lt	Lieutenant
Lt Col	Lieutenant Colonel
Lt Gen	Lieutenant General
LTh	Licentiate in Theology
Maj	Major
Maj Gen	Major General
MA	Master of Arts
MB	Bachelor of Medicine
MB BCh	Bachelor of Medicine, Bachelor of Surgery (also MBChB MBBS MBBChir)
MBE	Member of the Order of the British Empire
MC	Military Cross
MCh	Master of Surgery
MD	Medical Doctor
MELF	Middle East Land Forces
MGC	Machine Gun Corps
MID	Mentioned in Despatches
M.Inst.CE	Member of the institute of Civil Engineers
MM	Military Medal
MMM	Member of the Order of Military Merit (Canada)
MNZM	Member of the New Zealand Order of Merit
MO	Medical Officer
MOD	Ministry of Defence
MP	Member of Parliament
MRCP	Member of the Royal College of Physicians
MSM	Meritorious Service Medal
MT	Motor Transport
MVO	Member of the Royal Victorian Order
NSPCC	National Society for the Prevention of Cruelty to Children
NSW	New South Wales
NZEF	New Zealand Expeditionary Force
OBE	Officer of the Order of the British Empire
OC	Officer Commanding
ONZ	Order of New Zealand
OP	Observation Post
OStJ	Officer of the Most Venerable Order of the Hospital of Saint John of Jerusalem
OTC	Officers' Training Corps
PC	Police Constable

PC	Privy Counsellor
PoW	Prisoner of War
Pte	Private
ptsc	passed technical staff college
QSO	Companion of the Queen's Service Order (New Zealand)
RA	Royal Artillery
RAAF	Royal Auxiliary Air Force/ Royal Australian Air Force
RAC	Royal Agricultural College
RAC	Royal Armoured Corps
RAF	Royal Air Force
RAFVR	Royal Air Force Volunteer Reserve
RAMC	Royal Army Medical Corps
RAN	Royal Australian Navy
RAP	Regimental Aid Post
RASC	Royal Army Service Corps
RCT	Royal Corps of Transport
RE	Royal Engineers
REME	Royal Electrical and Mechanical Engineers
RETC	Royal Engineers Training Centre
RFA	Royal Field Artillery
RFC	Royal Flying Corps
RGA	Royal Garrison Artillery
RHA	Royal Horse Artillery
RLC	Royal Logistic Corps
RMA	Royal Military Academy
RMC	Royal Military College
RMO	Regimental Medical Officer
RMS	Royal Mail Ship/Steamer
RN	Royal Navy
RNLI	Royal National Lifeboat Institution
RNR	Royal Naval Reserve
RSL	Returned and Services League
RSM	Regimental Sergeant Major
RSPCA	Royal Society for the Prevention of Cruelty to Animals
RTO	Railway Transport Officer
SAI	South African Infantry
Sgt	Sergeant
SMLE	Short Magazine Lee Enfield
SNCO	Senior non-commissioned officers
SOE	Special Operations Executive
Spr	Sapper
SS	Steam Ship

TA	Territorial Army
TD	Territorial Decoration
TF	Territorial Force
TMB	Trench Mortar Battery
Tr	Trench
TSO	Technical Staff Officer
VAD	Voluntary Aid Detachment
VC	Victoria Cross
VD	Volunteer Decoration
VIP	Very Important Person
WAAC	Women's Auxiliary Army Corps
WAAF	Women's Auxiliary Air Force
WG	Welsh Guards
WO1 or 2	Warrant Officer Class 1 or 2
YMCA	Young Men's Christian Association

Introduction

The seventh book in this series covers the German offensives on the Somme and the Lys from 24th March 1918 until the resumption of offensive operations by the BEF in July at Le Hamel and Villers-Bretonneux. Forty VCs were awarded in this period, including thirteen to Australians, Canadians and a New Zealander.

The war entered a new phase with operations becoming more fluid and, as a result, confusing to follow. During the German offensives, BEF units were often falling back under extreme pressure and incurring huge casualties. Formations and units were mixed up and overlapped, ad hoc units were formed and positions changed a number of times daily, usually at short notice. Orders were issued to occupy new positions that were cancelled before they could be implemented and other positions were occupied instead, often without accurate records being kept. Officers who knew these details frequently became casualties and their knowledge was lost. As a result war diaries at this time may lack the same degree of precision as in previous phases of the war, when lines were more static and operations tended to be pre-planned and well defined. It has therefore proved difficult to locate the sites of some VC actions with the same accuracy as in previous books in the series.

As with previous volumes in the series, it is written for the battlefield visitor as well as the armchair reader. Each account provides background information to explain the broad strategic and tactical situation, before focusing on the VC action in detail. Each is supported by a map to allow a visitor to stand on, or close to, the spot and at least one photograph of the site. Detailed biographies help to understand the man behind the Cross.

As far as possible chapters and sections within them follow the titles of battles, actions and affairs as decided by the post-war Battle Nomenclature Committee. VCs are numbered chronologically 333, 334, 335 etc from 24th March 1918. As far as possible they are described in the same order, but when a number of actions were fought simultaneously, the VCs are covered out of sequence on a geographical basis in accordance with the official battle nomenclature.

Refer to the master maps to find the general area for each VC. If visiting the battlefields it is advisable to purchase maps from the respective French and Belgian 'Institut Géographique National'. The French IGN Top 100 and Belgian IGN Provinciekaart at 1:100,000 scale are ideal for motoring, but 1:50,000, 1:25,000 or 1:20,000 scale maps are necessary for more detailed work, e.g. French IGN

Serie Bleue and Belgian IGN Topografische Kaart. They are obtainable from the respective IGN or through reputable map suppliers on-line.

Ranks are as used on the day. Grave references have been shortened, e.g. 'Plot II, Row A, Grave 10' will appear as 'II A 10'. There are some abbreviations, many in common usage, but if unsure refer to the list provided.

I endeavour to include memorials to each VC in their biographies. However, two groups have been omitted. First, every VC is commemorated in the VC Diary and on memorial panels at the Union Jack Club, Sandell Street, Waterloo, London. To include this in every biography would be unnecessarily repetitive. Second, commemorative paving stones have been laid in every VC's birthplace in the British Isles on, or close to, the 100th anniversary of their VC action. Most of the dedication ceremonies took place after the volume was finalised, so it has not been possible to include all of them.

Thanks are due to too many people and organisations to mention here. They are acknowledged in 'Sources' and any omissions are my fault and not intentional. However, I would like to pay a particular tribute to fellow members of the 'Victoria Cross Database Users Group', Doug and Richard Arman, without whom I simply could not complete these books.

Paul Oldfield
Wiltshire
October 2018

Chapter One

First Battles of the Somme 1918– Subsequent Operations

Actions at the Somme Crossings

333 Cpl John Davies, 11th South Lancashire (Pioneers) (30th Division), near Eppeville, France
334 Capt Alfred Toye, 2nd Middlesex (23rd Brigade, 8th Division), Éterpigny, France

24th March 1918

On 21st March 1918 the Germans launched their expected spring offensive on the Somme front against the British Fifth and Third Armies. By 24th March units in Fifth Army were completely intermingled; one CO had 900 men from eleven different units under command. Everything was in short supply and many men were on the point of collapse. On the right of Fifth Army the French relieved III Corps north of the Oise but were themselves also in retreat. The line of the Somme was lost in the south but was maintained from north of Ham to Péronne. The situation was so uncertain that 14th Division was withdrawn to cover the crossings over the Canal du Nord.

On the right of XVIII Corps, 36th Division, with 61st Brigade (20th Division) attached, was in a dangerous salient. The Germans were also driving a wedge between 36th Division and 30th Division to the north but help was at hand. During the night elements of the French 9th and 10th Divisions took up positions behind 30th and 36th Divisions. Two other French divisions were within ten kilometres of the front and the depleted British 61st Division was in reserve.

There were no early attacks against 36th Division but at 11 a.m., when 61st Brigade (20th Division) began to withdraw from the head of the salient, the enemy turned the right flank of 109th Brigade. The two brigades fell back on the French 9th and British 14th Divisions. However, two battalions did not receive the message to retire and were overwhelmed. The Germans pushed the infantry back on Villeselve. With the French also being driven back the position was hopeless. 36th Division pulled back to a line prepared by the French but the retirement was not yet over. When the 9th French Division pulled back, so did the 10th. A threat to the 9th in its new position forced another retirement and 36th Division had to comply by pulling back to the line Quesmy – Guiscard – Hospital Farm, where it joined with

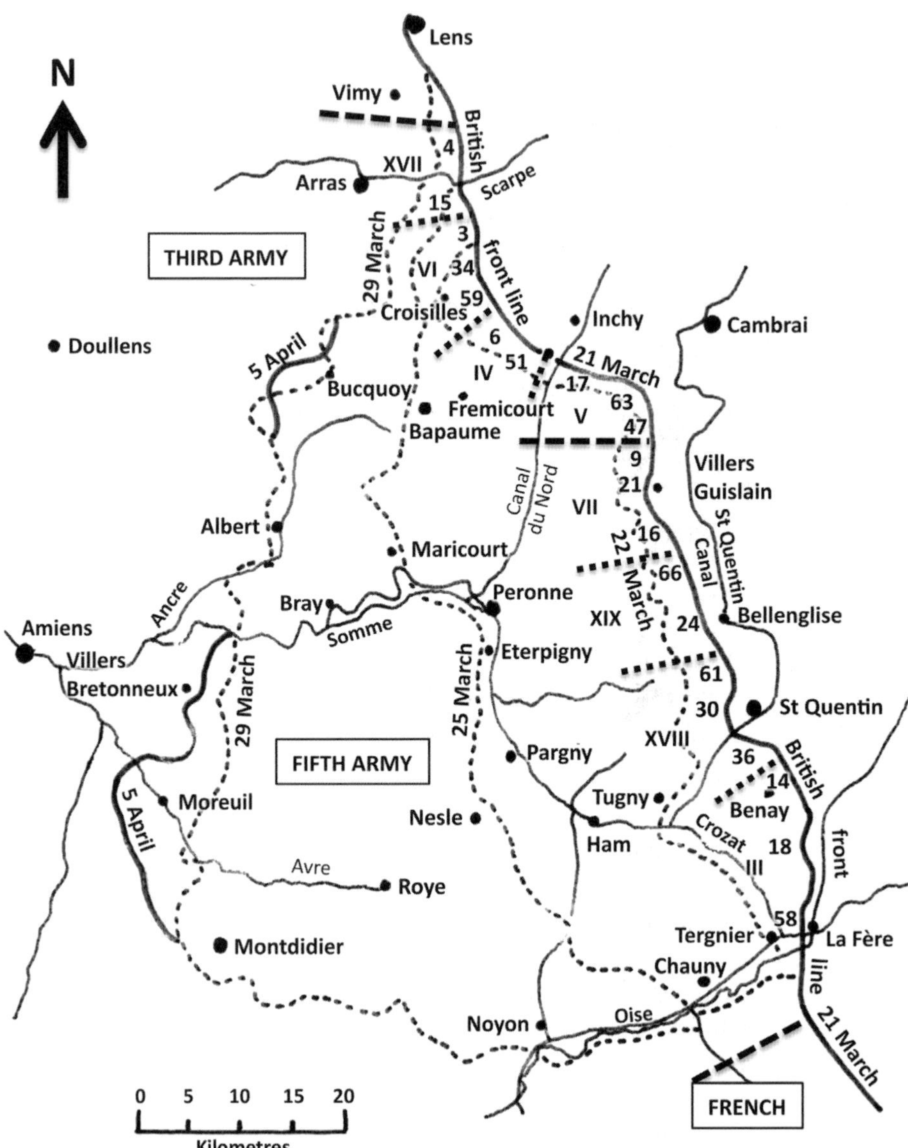

The Third and Fifth Army front from 21st March until 5th April 1918, showing the stages of the German advance. This book covers the events in this area from 24th March onwards. The opening of the German offensive, from 21st March until 23rd March inclusive, is covered in the previous volume in this series – *Cambrai to the Battle of St Quentin*. British corps and divisions are shown as at dawn on 21st March.

the French 62nd Division. By 11 p.m. the French held a continuous thin line and 36th Division, less 61st Brigade, was withdrawn into reserve.

Going back to the morning of the 22nd, the Corps Commander sent 400 men from the Corps Reinforcement Camp and a party of Corps Cyclists to man the Somme

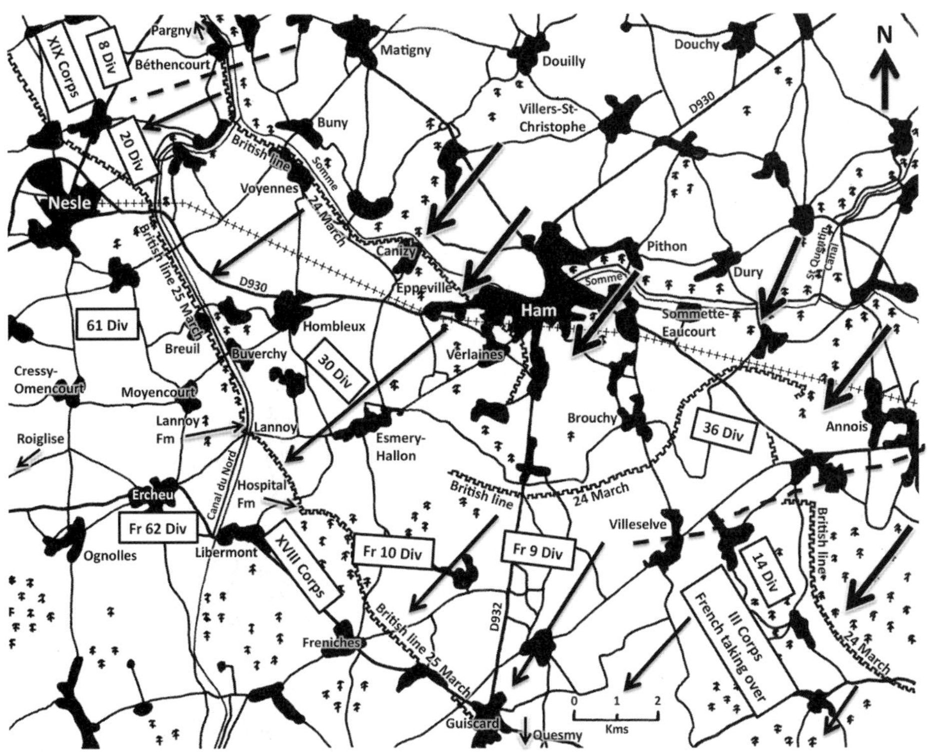

XVIII Corps' area on 24th March 1918.

bridgeheads at Ham, Pithon and Dury. At 11 a.m., 21st and 23rd Entrenching Battalions came under command of 30th Division for the defence of the canal line from Sommette Eaucourt to Canizy, a frontage of about ten kilometres, including the Ham bridgehead. The Division's three engineer field companies began work on the defences about 2 p.m. The positions were weak and had just a single barbed wire fence to the front. East of Ham the canal was dry and presented no obstacle but to the northwest it was not fordable. 89th Brigade was responsible for the defence, reinforced by the two entrenching battalions, detachments of tunnelling companies RE, a composite battalion from the Corps Reinforcement Camp and Corps Cyclists, a total of about 1,000 men. At 7 p.m. orders were issued to pull back to the new positions.

The reinforcements to 89th Brigade were to be withdrawn on 23rd March. Accordingly 21st and 90th Brigades were warned to take over their sectors by midday on 24th March. At 12.45 a.m. reports arrived that the Germans had broken through and were heading directly for Ham along the main road. The line along the canal was held, except for a gap south of Ham, where the troops fell back towards Verlaines. The Ham bridgehead was driven in. However, a brigade of 20th Division filled the gap. The remainder of the 23rd was relatively quiet.

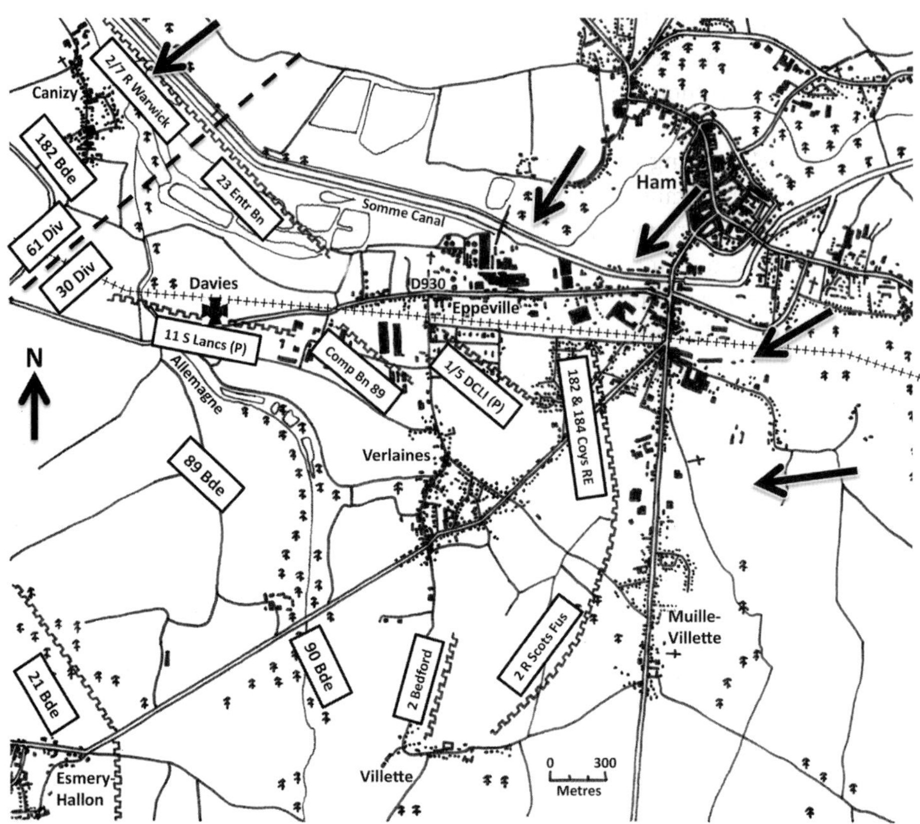

30th Division's front on 24th March. Leave Eppeville westwards on the D930. Cross the railway and after 850m pull in on the right at the entrance to an old dump with a locked barrier. One hundred metres on down the hill is the Allemagne stream. Walk back along the road towards Eppeville to the highest point for a view towards the railway, the high ground held by 11th South Lancashire and the stream over which they escaped covered by the Lewis gunners.

The right of 30th Division's front was badly mixed up but the left was more orderly, with the troops still in formed units. Meanwhile, behind the front, 21st Brigade and some sappers set to work constructing a new line east of Esmery-Hallon. A party under CO 19th King's was tasked with digging another along the Canal du Nord. The night passed without major incident.

11th South Lancashire (Pioneers) took up position southwest of Eppeville. On the left contact was made with 19th King's and 23rd Entrenching Battalion but the right flank beyond Verlaines was wide open. Patrols failed to make contact with British or enemy troops. During the afternoon the open right flank came under pressure and the right company fell back to the trenches occupied by the rest of the Battalion. At 6 p.m. a composite battalion of 89th Brigade came up on the right to cover the exposed flank. At about 9.30 p.m. 11th South Lancashire reorganised its line with two companies on the railway embankment. When the Battalion tried to establish contact with 182nd Brigade on the left, it was discovered that the junction point was held by the Germans. The embankment came under heavy machine gun, artillery and trench mortar fire but the Battalion clung on all night, despite heavy casualties.

Early on the morning of 24th March, 11th South Lancashire discovered that 23rd Entrenching Battalion was not where it was expected to be on the left. It was also clear that the position occupied by the Battalion during the night was untenable in daylight. It was too late to dig another line to link up with the remnants of 89th Brigade. The reserve company was about to be sent to fill the gap, when the situation was overtaken by other events.

After a heavy bombardment from 7 a.m. to 8 a.m., the enemy advanced from the Ham bridgehead against the centre of 30th Division. They also crossed the Somme at Canizy and attacked on the left. Troops on the flanks of 11th South Lancashire were seen to be in retreat and by 8.30 a.m. the two forward companies were almost surrounded. Escape lay over a deep stream (the rather ironically named Allemagne), which was barricaded with barbed wire. The retreat was covered by the Lewis gunners, who fought on until all were killed or wounded. **Corporal John Davies** mounted the parapet in full view of the enemy, who were surging forward in pursuit, in order to obtain a better field of fire for his Lewis gun. He kept his gun in action to the last, causing the enemy many casualties and holding them back, while his comrades got away. It was believed that he had been killed but in May news came through that he had been captured.

Counterattacks were ineffective and by 9 a.m. the left and centre of 30th Division were retreating towards 21st Brigade's line at Esmery-Hallon. The right flank conformed. They rallied on 21st Brigade and a stand was made but, around 10.30 a.m., the withdrawal continued. By 2 p.m. the Division had crossed the Canal du Nord at Lannoy Farm, where the French 62nd Division was in position. 30th Division was to hold the line from Libermont to Buverchy and at 5.10 p.m. the French took over command of the line from Lannoy Farm southwards. From there northwards was held by 90th Brigade to Buverchy, where it was in contact with 20th

From the high point on the D930 looking west. On the left the line of trees and bushes marks the Allemagne stream and the hedge line on the right follows the railway line. John Davies was in action to the left of the road in the field in the centre.

Division. 89th Brigade was in support at Moyencourt. The opportunity was taken to reorganise the mixed units and bring up food, water and ammunition.

The remnants of 11th South Lancashire made their way over the Canal du Nord and at 6.30 p.m. were ordered to occupy a line between Moyencourt and Cressy. Later it was sent to Roiglise, where next morning it formed part of a Divisional composite battalion.

Frontal attacks on 20th Division were repulsed and a defensive right flank was established when 30th Division fell back. The Germans crossed the Somme in XIX Corps' area, sweeping away the left of 20th Division. By 2.30 p.m. they were near the Canal du Nord, enveloping the right flank and a general retirement behind the Canal followed. A counterattack by 61st Division failed and it withdrew behind the Canal. The greatest anxiety was on the left flank of 20th Division where a gap of three kilometres had resulted from the withdrawal of 8th Division (XIX Corps).

In XIX Corps the fighting went largely the British way, but on the right the Germans succeeded in crossing north of Béthencourt and at Pargny. It proved impossible to maintain contact with 20th Division. VII Corps was forced into an orderly retirement. A composite mounted force was sent to hold the 4,600m gap between Fifth and Third Armies until the early hours of the 25th, when elements of 17th Division (Third Army) arrived.

Further north Third Army lost heavily and the situation was confused. There were gaps everywhere and only in the north was a firm line established. V Corps escaped from the Flesquières salient but was still 3,650m ahead of its flanking corps. The right flank lost contact with Fifth Army and V Corps had to pull back further. VI Corps maintained a good position but, overall, Third Army was disorganised, its line was unstable and its men were very tired. However, it was managing to hold and the enemy had yet to make a breakthrough.

Haig met Pétain. The latter expected the Germans to attack in Champagne and did not have sufficient forces to support the British also. Pétain directed General Fayolle to fall back towards Paris if he came under too much pressure. Haig was alarmed that the French priority was their capital, rather than maintaining contact with their ally.

25th March 1918

Early on 25th March the Somme west of Péronne became the boundary between the British and French forces. All troops in VII Corps north of the Somme transferred to Third Army, while those south of the river transferred to XIX Corps. At the same time, south of the Somme III, XVIII and XIX Corps (Fifth Army) came under command of the French Group of Armies of the Reserve under General Fayolle.

The mist cleared at 7.30 a.m. but, despite the advantages of observation and reinforcement by the French, the British were again pushed back. The French relieved III Corps south of the Oise, except for 58th Division and a brigade of

18th Division. Despite this respite, ground was still lost north of the river. In XVIII Corps, 30th and 20th Divisions resisted for most of the day. However, in the afternoon they were shelled from the right rear by German units pushing back the French 62nd Division. They had to retire through the French 22nd Division, suffering many casualties on the way. The French also retired but to the southwest, thus opening a gap. 20th Division was ordered to comply with French movements

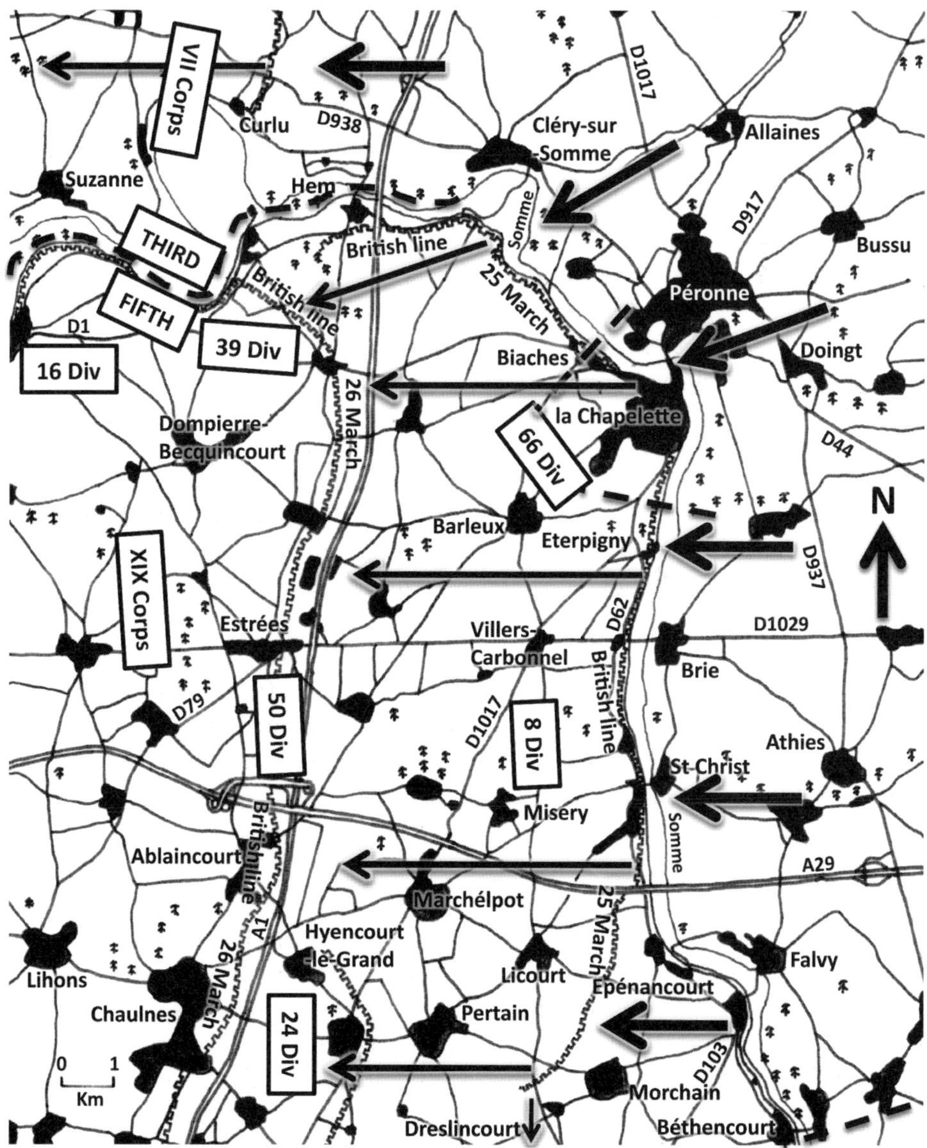

XIX Corps' area on 25th March 1918. The Corps line ran mainly along the Somme Canal west of the river.

until it reached Roye. It was then to turn northwest in order to fill the gap between the two Armies.

XIX Corps held the front from Béthencourt to Hem with 8th, 66th and 39th Divisions. Both flanks were thrown back. That of 8th Division in the south had a one and a half kilometres gap between it and XVIII Corps, which was partly covered by 24th Division (XVIII Corps) five kilometres to the rear.

23rd Brigade (8th Division) held the line west of the Somme from St Christ to Éterpigny. On its right was 24th Brigade and to the left was 197th Brigade (66th Division). In 23rd Brigade, 2nd Devonshire was right forward, with particular responsibility for the crossings at St Christ. 2nd West Yorkshire was left forward, with its main task being to secure the crossings at Brie and Éterpigny. The latter was a military bridge, there being no bridge at Éterpigny pre-war, or indeed today. 2nd Middlesex was in reserve. Each forward battalion had three companies in the line, with the fourth in reserve for counterattacks, and two mortars attached from the Brigade Trench Mortar Battery. The other four mortars were held with the reserve battalion. The main strength was at the canal crossings, with the intervals between covered by widely spaced posts. A Company, 8th Battalion Machine Gun Corps was attached with its sixteen Vickers machine guns. The front was to be dominated by fire from higher ground, but where this was not possible the canal bank was to be occupied.

Early on 24th March it was discovered that there was a gap of about 900m on the left of 23rd Brigade. 2nd West Yorkshire was ordered to cover this and gain contact with 66th Division. Later the gap was filled by 1/7th Durham Light Infantry (Pioneers) from 50th Division. That afternoon 24th Brigade on the right was attacked and forced back. However, the left battalion, 1st Sherwood Foresters, hung on to its positions along the river. During the night the Germans made three determined efforts to force the St Christ crossing. They were repulsed by 2nd Devonshire and 1st Sherwood Foresters after severe hand to hand fighting.

That night 2nd Middlesex relieved 2nd West Yorkshire on the left of 23rd Brigade. 24th Division and elements of 8th Division were ordered to counterattack with the French. However, the Germans anticipated this and attacked at 8 a.m., taking Dreslincourt. 24th Division was dangerously exposed on the right, where the French failed to appear, but managed to hold and inflict heavy casualties. However, at about 1 p.m. the enemy gained Pertain in the north. With both flanks turned the Division had to withdraw.

8th Division's 24th and 25th Brigades were to take part in the counterattack to recapture the west bank of the Somme at Épénancourt. However, the enemy attack at 8 a.m. forced back the British line and a stand was made to the east of Pertain. 25th Brigade slipped sideways and joined 17th Brigade (24th Division) near Dreslincourt. Later both brigades retired into support northeast of Chaulnes. 24th Brigade was exposed by the retirement of 25th Brigade and the right and centre were forced back gradually. By 10.30 a.m. Licourt was in German hands.

24th Brigade retired north to the railway behind Marchélepot, where it joined 151st Brigade (50th Division), while 150th Brigade fell back to cover Misery. The left of 24th Brigade held the riverbank around St Christ and formed a defensive flank for the retirement. In the afternoon 24th, 150th and 151st Brigades held a new position from Hyencourt-le-Grand, in touch with 24th Division, along the railway to in front of Misery. However, at 5 p.m. 150th Brigade was pulled back to the railway line behind Misery, leaving the left of 24th Brigade isolated.

Meanwhile 23rd Brigade held the river line with, from the south, 2nd Devonshire, 2nd Middlesex and 1/7th Durham Light Infantry (Pioneers) (attached from 50th Division). At 7 a.m. the Germans rushed Éterpigny bridge on the left of 2nd Middlesex, held by C Company. **Captain Alfred Toye**, the company commander, quickly organised a counterattack to recapture the bridge. It was lost and retaken again before 7.30 a.m. At 8 a.m. the Germans crossed the river north of the bridge and drove 1/7th Durham Light Infantry back to the high ground 800m west of Barleux. They also entered the north of Éterpigny and surrounded C Company. A reserve platoon, under Second Lieutenant Francis George Edward Mahany (MC

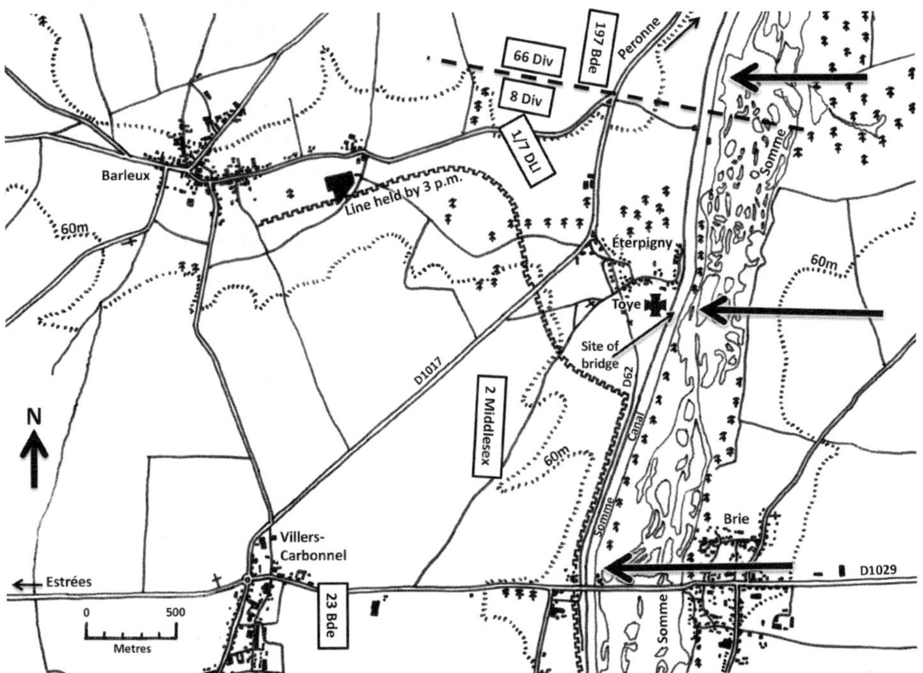

In Éterpigny follow the D62 southwards until it converges with the canal bank. There are plenty of places to pull over here. Climb the bank on the northwest side of the road for a view towards the canal and the scene of Alfred Toye's VC action. Then return through the village and turn left, signed for the communal cemetery. Just before it, turn right and follow this lane to the junction with the D1017. Park on the left just before the major road. The line held by 3 p.m. was astride the D1017 about 175m behind you down the hill.

From the road bank on the D62 looking over the Canal and the area defended by C Company.

for this action), fought its way into the village to relieve the beleaguered garrison. Only three men got through. Just Toye, another officer and six soldiers managed to fight their way out.

Toye collected seventy men of 1/7th Durham Light Infantry and counterattacked, barring the Villers-Carbonnel – Éterpigny road until reinforcements arrived from the brigade reserve (2nd West Yorkshire). These filled the gap between the left of 2nd Middlesex and 50th Division. A counterattack by two companies of 2nd West Yorkshire was brought to a standstill as it reached the edge of the high ground overlooking the river. However, a line was established and efforts by the Germans to seize the high ground were held off all day. Meanwhile B and D Companies, 2nd Middlesex defended Brie bridge under heavy pressure from the front and also from enemy moving down the west bank of the river from Éterpigny.

The Germans crossed in force at Éterpigny and advanced up the valley towards Barleux. 66th Division threw back a defensive flank to the north. About 1 p.m. 66th Division was driven from the canal to the high ground on the edge of the Somme valley. Meanwhile the French, having failed to counterattack in the morning, withdrew to the southwest, which increased the gap on the right.

On the left was VII Corps (Third Army), which had started the day almost ten kilometres behind XIX Corps. It was also driven back and this left XIX Corps with no alternative other than to retire under cover of darkness. 24th Division was already falling back when the orders were received. Elements of 8th Division started

The line held later in the day, looking northeast.

at 7 p.m. and 24th, 150th and 151st Brigades began their move at 8 p.m., covered by 1/8th Durham Light Infantry. 23rd Brigade (2nd Devonshire and the remnants of 2nd Middlesex) continued to hold out on the Villers-Carbonnel – Éterpigny road and along the canal. However, a withdrawal commenced at 8 p.m. to the general line Estrées – Ablaincourt.

Elements of 23rd Brigade had to bayonet charge through Misery to get away. 2nd Middlesex received the order too late, except for one company that moved back with 2nd Devonshire. The rest of the Battalion was partly surrounded and a series of local counterattacks was required to break out. Despite this many were overwhelmed. Eleven of the sixteen rifle platoons were lost; all four in C Company at Éterpigny, three each in B and D Companies and one of A Company.

2nd Devonshire and 1st Sherwood Foresters found their line of retreat intercepted by small parties of the enemy. Resolute action with the bayonet was required to open the line of withdrawal. That night all three battalions in the Brigade were in the line, from right to left – 2nd Devonshire, 2nd Middlesex and 2nd West Yorkshire.

Toye's VC was also awarded for the rearguard actions at Rosières on 26th-27th March and at Caix on the 28th. In command of a composite company, he moved through the village ahead of the Battalion to clear the enemy. On 31st March, at Moreuil Wood, he took command of all 23rd Brigade details and supported 2nd Devonshire, holding the Wood until relieved by the French on the night of 1st/2nd April. Finally, at Villers-Bretonneux on 24th April, he commanded a mixed force of the Brigade and re-established a line that had been abandoned before his arrival. He was wounded twice in a ten-day period but remained at duty throughout.

First Battle of Bapaume

335 Lt Col William Anderson, 12th Highland Light Infantry (106th Brigade, 35th Division), Maricourt, France

336 LCpl Arthur Cross, 40th Battalion Machine-Gun Corps (40th Division), Ervillers, France

337 Pte Thomas Young, 1/9th Durham Light Infantry (Pioneers, 62nd Division), Bucquoy, France

25th March 1918

Since the opening of the German offensive, Third Army had pivoted on its left flank. By 25th March the northernmost troops were almost all in their 21st March positions, but the right flank had pulled back about twenty-seven kilometres. The line was mostly continuous, with some gaps in the centre. Although the British were weak, the Germans were slowing and growing more cautious as their casualties mounted. Orders were issued to fall back fighting to the old British line of July 1916, which was to be occupied by reserves, whilst awaiting French assistance.

In VII Corps, 35th Division was relatively intact, but 9th and 21st Divisions were badly battered. 1st Dismounted Brigade was attached. The Corps' left flank was out of contact with V Corps. The latter sent 51st Brigade (only 600 strong), which, with two regiments of 1st Dismounted Brigade and most of 26th Brigade, filled the gap and formed a defensive flank. However, the left remained a source of concern all day as Germans streamed into Mametz Wood.

On 24th March, 106th Brigade was ordered to Maricourt, where 35th Division was assembling. 12th Highland Light Infantry arrived at Bray-sur-Somme at 3 a.m. and marched to Maricourt by 7 a.m. The brigade commander made a reconnaissance of the area east of Maurepas and Bois de Hem. At 9.30 a.m. the Germans attacked Cléry-sur-Somme and Bois Marrières. 17th Royal Scots was sent to support 105th Brigade, moving to assembly positions near Bois de Hem. 12th Highland Light Infantry came under command of 9th Division in preparation for a counterattack north of Maurepas.

At 2 p.m. 35th Division was ordered to withdraw to the line Hardecourt-au-Bois – Curlu, with the main line of resistance being Trônes Wood – Bois Faviere – Curlu. 106th Brigade came under command of HQ 9th Division at 2 p.m. 18th Highland Light Infantry moved to positions along the Briqueterie – Maricourt road in support of VII Corps Reinforcement Companies, that were holding the main line of resistance just west of Bois Faviere. 12th Highland Light Infantry and a composite battalion held an outpost line from the southern edge of Bernafay Wood to Hardecourt. At the same time 19th Northumberland Fusiliers (Pioneers) and No.4 Composite Battalion came under command of HQ 106th Brigade and they were ordered to reserve positions at Talus Boisé.

105th and 106th Brigades and a battalion of Hunt's Force (VII Corps Entrenching Battalions) were in the front line, with three battalions of Hunt's Force and 18th Highland Light Infantry (106th Brigade) in support. Two regiments of 1st Dismounted Brigade held the defensive flank on the left. In the afternoon Headlam's Force, based on 64th Brigade (21st Division), was ordered to support 35th Division and arrived at Maricourt at 7 p.m. The rest of 21st Division was ordered back to Chipilly on the Somme.

At 8.45 p.m. 12th Highland Light Infantry, astride the Hardecourt – Maricourt road, was attacked on the right and outflanked. It was forced to pull back about 700m, suffering heavy losses. At 11.15 a.m. the outpost line was withdrawn to the eastern edge of Bois Faviere.

Most attacks on 25th March were against 35th Division, which put up a magnificent defence against five enemy divisions. Attacks began at 7.45 a.m. against the whole front and left flank from the direction of Hardecourt. The outpost line and part of Bois Faviere were lost, but a brilliant counterattack by 18th Highland Light Infantry and 12th Highland Light Infantry restored the situation. **Lieutenant Colonel William Anderson** led 12th Highland Light Infantry in recovering the lost ground, capturing twelve machine guns and seventy prisoners. The left flank was slightly pushed in and

19th Northumberland Fusiliers (Pioneers) reinforced it. At 10 a.m. 105th Brigade on the right suffered such heavy casualties from artillery fire that it pulled back to the second line. The composite battalion of Hunt's Force fell back to Maricourt, where it was rallied by 203rd Field Company RE and took up a position between 17th and 18th Lancashire Fusiliers (104th Brigade) in the reserve line.

At 11 a.m. the left was attacked again and 8th Hussars was hard pressed near Bernafay Wood. Despite the pressure, Montauban was held by dismounted cavalry and infantry for the rest of the day. However, to escape envelopment Anderson ordered 12th Highland Light Infantry to fall back to the trenches northeast of Maricourt held by the sappers. It appeared that a breakthrough was about to take place and 12th Highland Light Infantry was forced to withdraw through Maricourt Wood, separating into three groups in the process. One group was commanded by Anderson, the others by Majors Dixon and Cox. Counterattacks

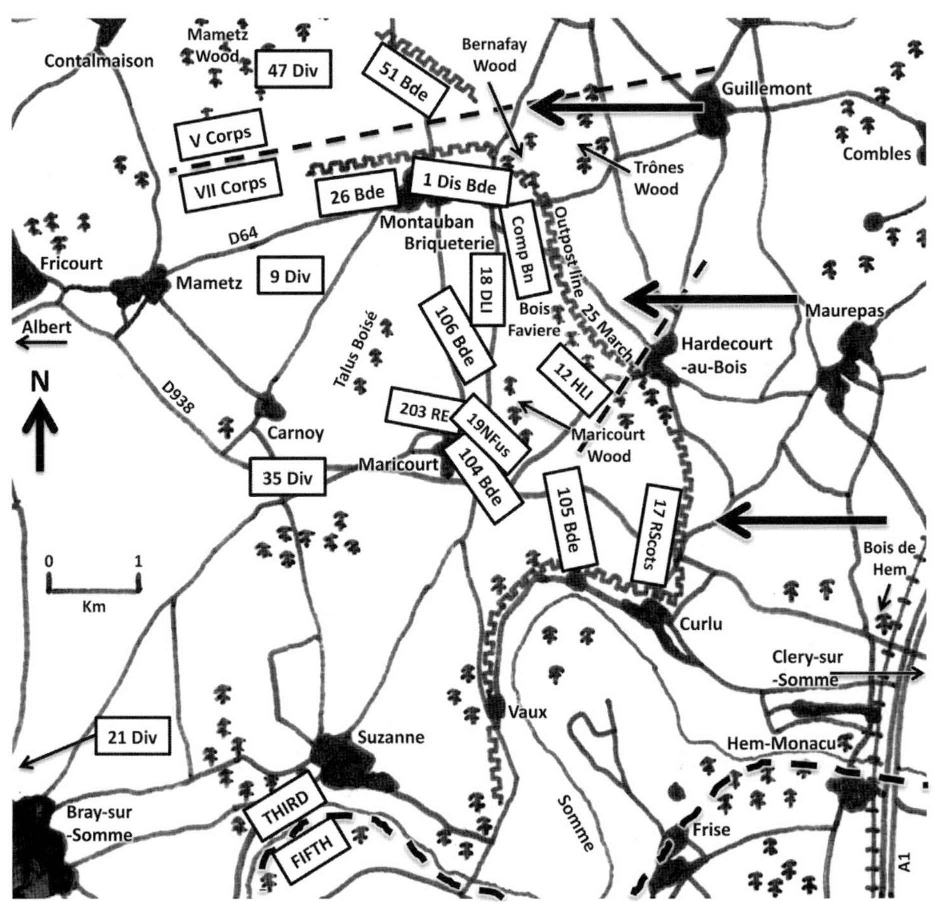

VII Corps' situation on 25th March. For clarity, not all units are shown on this and the following map.

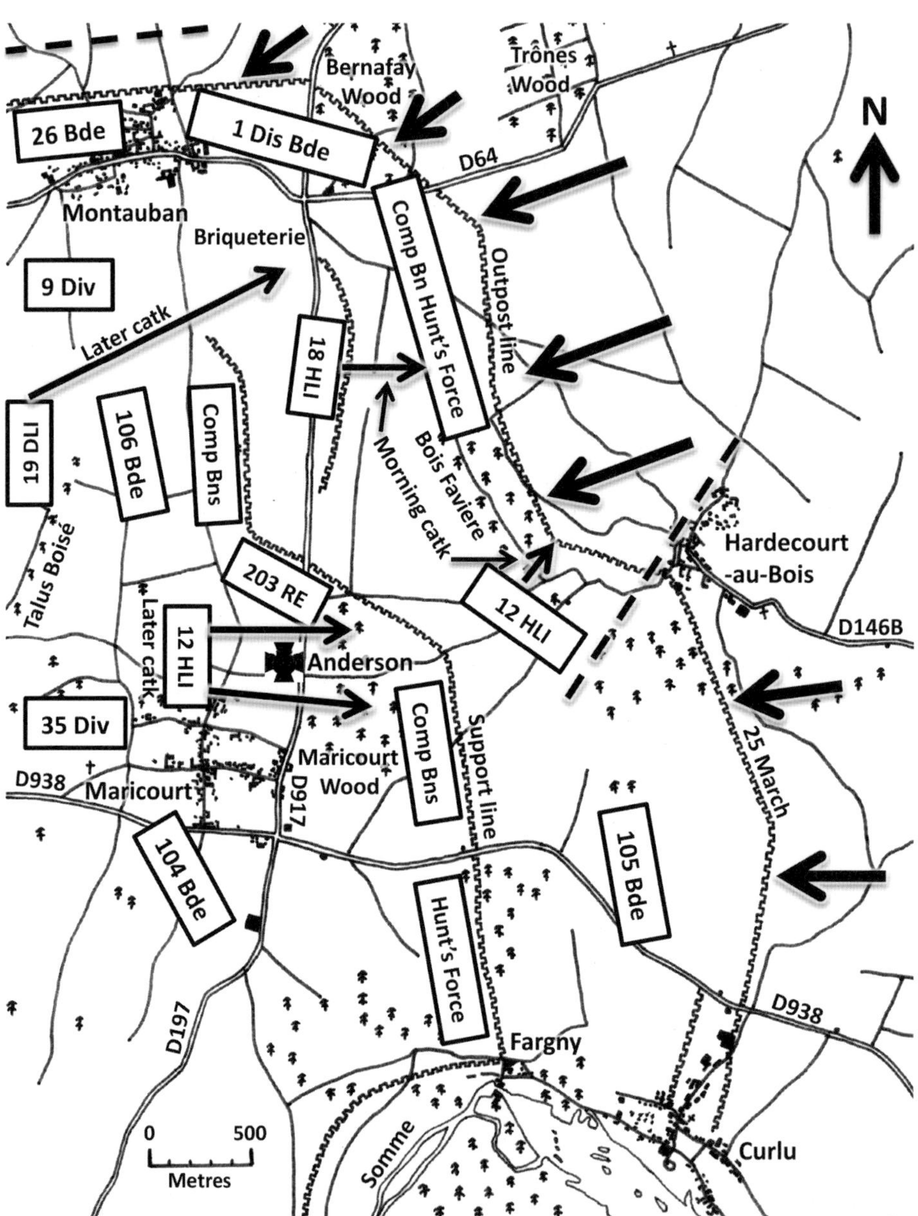

Approach Maricourt from the west along the D938. Pass Péronne Road Cemetery on the left, where William Anderson is buried and also Fred Schofield, brother of John Schofield VC. Continue into the village and 450m after the cemetery, turn left onto the D197 heading northwards. After 1,100m there is a memorial to the junction between the British and French on 1st July 1916. Park here and look back towards Maricourt. The road you have just driven along was crossed from west to east at the start of the counterattack at 4.30 p.m. into Maricourt Wood on the left. At the memorial turn right and pass the northern tip of Maricourt Wood on the right after one hundred metres. Continue for another one hundred metres and stop at the northeast corner of the Wood to overlook the scene of the counterattack at Bois Faviere earlier in the day. On the map counterattack has been shortened to 'catk'.

by two companies each from 104th and 105th Brigades restored the line after three hours' hard fighting.

At 11.30 a.m. the Germans were reported to be advancing westwards along the valley north of Montauban, which endangered the left flank again. 19th Northumberland Fusiliers (Pioneers) was ordered to Montauban to form a defensive flank on the left. A company of 17th Royal Scots and details of 18th Highland Light Infantry moved to extend the front of 19th Northumberland Fusiliers (Pioneers) and a line was established north of Montauban (Bernafay Wood – Briqueterie – Bois Faviere).

Further German attacks at 2.30 p.m. against the left front and flank at Bernafay Wood and north of Bois Faviere failed, but they came on again at 4.30 p.m. between 18th Highland Light Infantry and 1st Dismounted Brigade just south of Bernafay Wood. 106th Brigade's situation was critical. 19th Durham Light Infantry (attached from 104th Brigade) moved from Talus Boisé to counterattack with No.6 Composite Battalion. This attack recovered the lost ground and almost two hundred metres beyond it from Briqueterie – Maricourt Road – eastern edge of Maricourt Wood.

12th Highland Light Infantry, with 17th Entrenching Battalion on the right, also attacked. Anderson seized the opportunity to clear Maricourt Wood and a nearby timber yard, which was packed with enemy machine guns. With no other troops available, HQ 104th Brigade formed up on the right of Anderson and charged alongside. The attack began around 4.30 p.m. from the road running north from Maricourt, moved through the timber yard onto a light railway line, where the troops took cover from heavy fire and then continued to the objective in the northern portion of Maricourt Wood. The attack was entirely successful, although Anderson was killed close to the final objective. By then the Battalion was split into two main groups, one in the north of Maricourt Wood and the other in the southeast of Maricourt.

The Germans fell back 900m but recovered and attacked again at 7 p.m. The situation had to be restored by another counterattack. Meanwhile 12th Division was beginning to arrive. 37th Brigade was sent to Contalmaison to gain touch with 47th Division (V Corps) on the left, while 35th and 36th Brigades were sent to Maricourt and Montauban respectively, under command of 35th Division. At midnight orders were received by HQ 106th Brigade to withdraw to the line Albert – Bray. The move was completed by 3.30 a.m. on 26th March. When 12th Highland Light Infantry was relieved in Maricourt, it formed the Brigade rearguard with 18th Highland Light Infantry.

The battered V Corps held a broken front on the morning of the 25th. Orders were issued to hold the general line Montauban – Martinpuich – Butte de Warlencourt but by 1 p.m. most of the Corps was withdrawing. By 2 p.m. a thin line had been established with numerous gaps. Thinking that the British were in full retreat, the Germans abandoned caution and rushed forward in mass to be cut to

Scene of the first counterattack led by William Anderson on 25th March. The objective, Bois Faviere, is on the left. The attack swept in from right of centre through the low ground, along which the Maricourt – Hardecourt road runs out of sight. On the right is Maricourt Wood.

pieces by field artillery and small arms fire. However, weight of numbers told and V Corps was soon retreating again.

IV Corps faced fifteen German divisions. The previous day 42nd Division had arrived from First Army to take over 40th Division's sector (VI Corps). The enemy started slowly and built in intensity as they tried to exploit gaps in the line, particularly at the junction with V Corps. During the afternoon the Corps' right was thrust back by overwhelming numbers. By the end of the day the front was facing southeast and a gap of five kilometres had opened between it and V Corps on the right.

The second counterattack led by William Anderson, in which he was killed, was launched from this road from right to left into Maricourt Wood on the left. Maricourt village is in the right distance. Just out of picture at the road/track junction on the extreme left is the 1st July 1916 memorial at the junction point between British and French forces.

On the right, 19th Division was attacked at 9 a.m. and was pushed back. Grévillers was held until 11 a.m., but shortly thereafter all three brigades were falling back on 51st Division. At the same time the remnants of 41st Division and elements of 25th Division north of Bapaume were also forced back.

Further north elements of 40th Division were still in the line in 42nd Division's sector. Fighting started at 7.30 a.m., particularly around Sapignies and Behagnies. There were losses but the only ground ceded was between Behagnies and Ervillers, where 120th and 177th (59th Division, VI Corps) Brigades were pushed back slightly in a surprise rush. 42nd Division's right flank was guarded by machine guns, while preparations were made to relieve the tired units of other divisions. It appeared at that time that the Corps line would hold until 62nd Division could be brought up. However, continuous German pressure on 19th Division drove it northwestwards, through the left of 51st Division east of Loupart Wood. At 1.30 a.m., 56th and 58th Brigades were sent back to the Pys–Bihucourt line, covered by 57th Brigade, to

Movements in this area in the period 24th-26th March are very confusing. Units were completely intermingled and gaps were being plugged anyhow. Only the main formations mentioned in the account are therefore shown. The precise location of 4 Section, C Company is not known, so the location shown is the best estimate of the position where Arthur Cross recovered the two machine guns on 25th March.

prolong the line held by 51st Division and attempt to get in touch with 25th and 41st Divisions.

Late on 24th March, 40th Division's right flank had been ordered to withdraw. While this was taking place the Germans attacked and took Mory. A new general line was established east of the Arras – Bapaume road and in front of Ervillers. The Germans continued to attack at Ervillers and an advanced post of two machine

Ervillers, on the high ground right of centre, from the German perspective. The D9 Ervillers – St Léger road runs across the foreground from right to left. Arthur Cross' VC action was somewhere on the high ground in front of the village.

guns (4 Section, C Company, 40th Battalion Machine Gun Corps, attached to 119th Brigade) was surrounded and rushed. **Lance Corporal Arthur Cross** escaped with the remaining two guns and was determined to recover those lost. Early next morning he gained Sergeant Brennan's (believed to be 27690 Sergeant Christopher Brennan – MID for this action and MM for a later action, LG 6th August 1918) permission to search for them. Moving forward carefully, and armed only with a revolver, he found the two guns in the hands of seven German soldiers. Although outnumbered Cross had the advantage of surprise and leapt up with his revolver to demand their surrender. They did and he marched them to the rear, carrying the machine guns and ammunition. Having handed over the prisoners, Cross brought the guns into action against a massed German attack. At 9.30 p.m. Ervillers was evacuated by 1/10th Manchester and a new position was taken up some 900m back.

Following the retirement of 19th Division, the enemy was halted temporarily by 51st Division but, at about 1 p.m., the flanking movement on the right increased in tempo. Large numbers of Germans were seen moving towards Pys and soon afterwards they attacked 2nd Division in the Pys – Coucelette position. The two brigades on the right swung back to form a flank guard but were forced back to the high ground east of Irles. As a result they separated from the third brigade. Further north 25th and 41st Divisions fell back on the Irles – Bihucourt ridge, where 51st Division and a brigade of 41st Division were already established. Bihucourt was lost at 1 p.m. but a counterattack on the German northern flank brought them to a halt for an hour. 42nd Division slowed the German advance, but the fall of Bihucourt changed the situation. The line wheeled back, pivoting on Ervillers, to the Gomiécourt – Ervillers ridge. Three brigades were in position about 3.45 p.m. and another prolonged the line to the right.

At 5.15 p.m. IV Corps ordered a retirement to a shorter front to allow the relief of tired divisions. The two fresh formations, 62nd Division on the right and 42nd Division on the left, were to hold the new line. The remnants of 40th, 41st and 51st Divisions were to withdraw and reorganise, while 19th and 25th Divisions formed a defensive right flank in touch with 62nd Division. Before the retirement began, 51st Division was forced to retire to the south of the position it was planned to occupy. 19th, 25th, 40th and 41st Divisions fell back independently but the Germans were

too exhausted to pursue them. At nightfall 62nd and 42nd Divisions held the enemy on the line Achiet le Petit – Logeast Wood – Ervillers.

VI Corps had a comparatively quiet day. Only 31st Division was attacked and the enemy made no gains. However, the loss of Sapignies and Behagnies to the south caused concern as the VI Corps front was becoming a salient and plans were made for a retirement.

26th March 1918

Late on the afternoon of 25th March, 62nd Division arrived from First Army and came under command of IV Corps. Initially 185th and 186th Brigades deployed east of Achiet-le-Petit and were in position by 3 p.m. 42nd Division was on the left flank. During the early evening, 19th, 25th, 41st and 51st Divisions withdrew through the 42nd and 62nd Divisions. Meanwhile 1/9th Durham Light Infantry (Pioneers) had reached Bucquoy and began digging a new line to the east of the village.

The 62nd Division took over the front from 41st Division at 7 p.m. and during the night pulled back from the exposed covering positions east of Achiet-le-Petit. 186th Brigade took up positions in front of Bucquoy on the right flank of 185th Brigade. 1/9th Durham Light Infantry occupied some old trenches 275m west of the Puisieux – Bucquoy road. 187th Brigade was in reserve around Biez Wood, with one battalion taking over the trenches dug by 1/9th Durham Light Infantry to the east of Bucquoy. All brigades were in position by 8 a.m. on the 26th. The left flank was well covered by 42nd Division but on the right touch had been lost with V Corps. The Germans had every intention of taking advantage of this situation.

The battle began at 8 a.m. when the Germans advanced out of Achiet-le-Petit. Although they were stopped, the whole front of 62nd Division was engaged by enfilade machine gun fire and artillery. However, on the right flank there was a gap of six kilometres to the south and German mounted troops were reported to be west of Hébuterne. These were just patrols but, without authority from HQ 62nd Division, the transport based there pulled back and it took many hours to recover it. Meanwhile attacks on the right flank continued throughout the day.

On the right flank, 5th Duke of Wellington's (2/5th until 1st February 1918, when it became simply 5th) was reinforced by a section of the Machine Gun Battalion. The Germans were reported to be in Puisieux and the right company of 5th Duke of Wellington's was drawn back to form a defensive flank. 1/9th Durham Light Infantry was in support in this area. The enemy came on and the front held, despite a determined effort to outflank 5th Duke of Wellington's around 11.30 a.m. Inevitably ground was surrendered and the right flank was swung back in conjunction with D Company, 1/9th Durham Light Infantry to a new position just north of the Gommecourt – Puisieux road from the southeastern corner of Rossignol Wood. 2/7th Duke of Wellington's in front was unaware that the 5th Battalion was behind

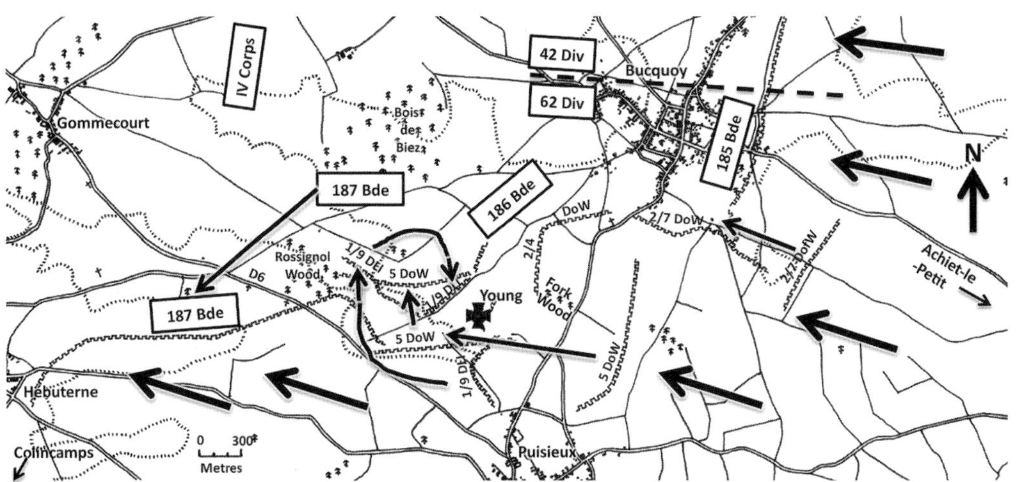

It is difficult to be certain where Thomas Young carried out his rescues. However, a likely site is shown on the map. To overlook the line held by 1/9th Durham Light Infantry, pass Rossignol Wood on the left on the D6 Gommecourt–Puisieux road. Just after cresting the rise, take the left turning onto a solid track heading northeast. It drops into a wide re-entrant and just as it begins to climb again there is a track junction on the left underneath a high bank. Park here and look back. 1/9th Durham Light Infantry held the line of the track you just drove along at the top of the opposite hillside. Thomas Young was probably very active in the area to the left of the track.

and also threw out a defensive right flank. This Battalion had to withdraw, but was ordered back into its former positions by Brigade. Three companies of 2/4th Duke of Wellington's (186th Brigade reserve) were moved opposite Fork Wood to fill a gap between 5th and 2/7th Battalions. The right flank was still wide open and the New Zealand Division, which was rushing to fill it, could not get there until mid-afternoon. The enemy hurled eight attacks at 62nd Division, which had been reinforced by the Machine Gun School. Horrific casualties were inflicted and the attacks were repelled.

At 7 p.m., 4th Australian Brigade began to arrive and took over the defence of Hébuterne from 19th Division. The Germans attacked again at 8 p.m. 2/4th King's Own Yorkshire Light Infantry (2/4th York & Lancaster in some accounts), in 187th Brigade took up a defensive flank from Hébuterne, where it was in contact with 4th Australian Brigade, to the west of Rossignol Wood. Its left flank was in touch with 5th Duke of Wellington's. The rest of 187th Brigade remained in reserve. As dusk was falling the enemy made another effort against the right flank of 186th Brigade between Bucquoy and Rossignol Wood. The right company of 5th Duke of Wellington's was driven back but the situation was restored by a counterattack, supported by eleven tanks. At 10.45 p.m. the leading New Zealand brigade began to arrive to occupy the high ground east of Colincamps and fill the gap between 62nd Division and V Corps.

Looking southwest from the bank above the track junction. 1/9th Durham Light Infantry held the line of the track on the high ground and this is a likely location for some of Thomas Young's rescues.

Over the following days the Germans continued to attack and at times counterattacks had to be launched to restore the situation. The Germans made use of the numerous old trenches in the area to infiltrate close to the defence lines. However, the line remained essentially as it was late on the 26th. Gradually the gap to the south of 62nd Division was filled by Australian and New Zealand brigades. Meanwhile nothing was being done to remedy the situation at the highest level. The French were still obsessed by the possibility of another offensive being opened by the Germans in Champagne.

During the period 25th-31st March, **Private Thomas Young**, a stretcher-bearer in 1/9th Durham Light Infantry, saved nine men in broad daylight. Very little is known beyond the bare facts set out in the citation. Each rescue was under very heavy fire directed at him personally. Some of the men were so badly injured that he had to dress their wounds in the open before bringing them in unaided. When not making these rescues, he worked tirelessly for five days evacuating the wounded from seemingly impossible situations.

338 Sgt Albert Mountain, 15th/17th West Yorkshire (93rd Brigade, 31st Division), Moyenneville, France

26th March 1918

On 26th March the right of Fifth Army fell back in conjunction with the French south of the Somme. On the left, XIX Corps pulled back to conform with the right flank of Third Army, which was five kilometres to the rear at Bray. Due to a misunderstanding, VII Corps, on Third Army's right, also pulled back at the same time and instead of the gap being closed it increased to eight kilometres. Apart from that, Third Army generally held its line and 26th March marked the end of the immediate crisis. The Germans had outstripped their support and were exhausted by continuous fighting and the strain of having to cross the old Somme battlefields.

There would be more hard fighting and territory would be lost but there was no longer a danger of a breakthrough.

Further north in VI Corps, 31st Division had been falling back by stages. On the night of 25th March, 15th/17th West Yorkshire (93rd Brigade) withdrew to the Boyelles – Ervillers road and then, according to the Battalion war diary, to the area of the cemetery at Hamelincourt. However, 31st Division was ordered to conform to the line to the south, by pulling back to the general line Ablainzevelle – Moyenneville, further west than Hamelincourt.

The orders issued by HQ 93rd Brigade early on the morning of 26th March, placed 15th/17th West Yorkshire on the right, southwest of Moyenneville, about two kilometres west of the cemetery at Hamelincourt. 13th York & Lancaster was to be on the left, extending the line north-easterly through Moyenneville, and 18th Durham Light Infantry was to be in support. 92nd Brigade was on the right and 2nd Guards Brigade (Guards Division) on the left. However, about 11 a.m. a 1,350m wide gap was discovered between 31st and Guards Divisions. This was due to 13th York & Lancaster and 18th Durham Light Infantry being misdirected in the dark by the acting Brigade Major, Captain BV Ramsden, who was disorientated, having been blown off his horse by a shell. As a result they did not take up their intended positions and fell back to about 900m east of Adinfer. HQ 93rd Brigade was unaware of this initially and, to add to the confusion, the COs of both battalions were casualties.

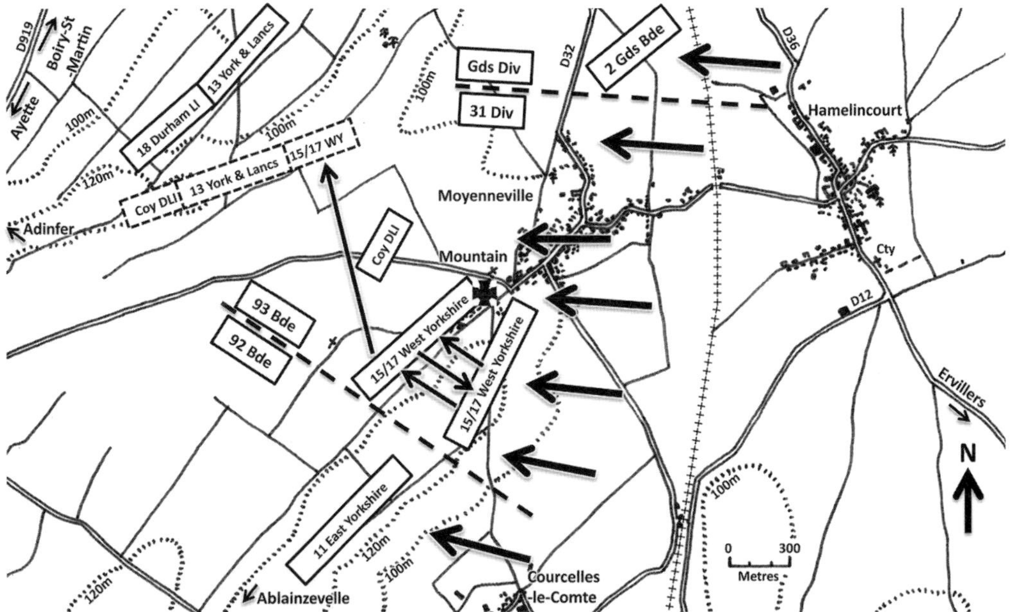

Positions held by 93rd Brigade on 26th March are in solid boxes. The positions held the following day are in dashed boxes. On that day most of 18th Durham Light Infantry was north of Ayette.

From the original position held by 15th/17th West Yorkshire on 26th March looking towards Moyenneville in the centre. The exposed nature of this position to fire from the village is apparent. The road to which the Battalion fell back is marked by the line of trees on the left. On the extreme right is the church in Hamelincourt, about two kilometres away. Albert Mountain's VC action was in the area to the right of the communications mast in the centre of the picture.

According to the Battalion war diary and *The West Yorkshire Regiment in the War*, 15th/17th West Yorkshire was dug in along a sunken lane close to Hamelincourt village cemetery. However, the more detailed war diary kept by HQ 93rd Brigade is clear that 15th/17th West Yorkshire was in its correct position on the ridge running south from Moyenneville, as ordered, but with its left flank in the air. Interestingly there was, and still is, a cemetery to the south of Hamelincourt but no cemetery appears to the south of Moyenneville on contemporary maps, although there is one there today. Despite this, the weight of evidence points strongly to the Battalion being south of Moyenneville rather than Hamelincourt.

The 15th/17th West Yorkshire position was exposed to heavy enfilade machine-gun from Moyenneville. An attempt to extend the line to the left to meet up with the Guards Division failed. The enemy attacked at 11 a.m. and the Battalion fell back to the road running southwest from Moyenneville. In B Company, Second Lieutenant William Stephen Wharram DCM (MC for this action), called for volunteers to protect the flank, while he led a counterattack to restore the situation,

15th/17th West Yorkshire's position later on 26th March along the road running southwest from Moyenneville. The previous position was on top of the ridge to the right.

prior to pulling back. **Sergeant Albert Mountain** came forward with his party of ten men. They moved out to the flank and, with a Lewis gun and their rifles, enfiladed a strong German patrol of about 200 men, killing about one hundred of them. B Company counterattacked and mopped up the rest of the patrol.

The enemy then attempted to move around the Battalion's left flank and two companies were ordered to make an outflanking counterattack. As a result the German advance was halted, a platoon cleared the village and the original position was restored. About thirty-five prisoners were taken and a machine gun was rendered unusable. However, the enemy wounded had to be abandoned as the Battalion had no facilities for them. At 12.30 p.m. the Germans attacked again, forcing the Battalion back to the sunken road southwest of Moyenneville. During this attack Mountain's party wavered but he rallied them and covered the withdrawal of his company. Having held up 600 Germans for half an hour, he retired with only four men. At 8.30 p.m. a counterattack attempted to regain the lost position but the men were exhausted and it was abandoned about halfway to the objective. They fell back to the sunken road again. The situation remained quiet for the rest of the night.

Meanwhile the HQ 93rd Brigade Intelligence Officer and the officers commanding 13th York & Lancaster and 18th Durham Light Infantry attempted to close the gap. However, this proved impossible to achieve in daylight, under very heavy machine gun fire from Moyenneville, but they managed to make up some of the lost ground towards their intended positions. A counterattack by 13th York & Lancaster to retake Moyenneville was cancelled and both battalions were ordered to dig in as close to the west of the village as possible. These orders arrived very late and, with the exception of one company of 18th Durham light Infantry, little digging took place. Before dawn the remainder had to withdraw to the south of Boiry-St-Martin and dug in on the high ground northwest of Moyenneville.

27th March 1918

The strain of recent operations resulted in Commander 93rd Brigade, Brigadier General JG Ingles DSO, and the acting Brigade Major, Captain BV Ramsden, both being evacuated sick. Lieutenant Colonel Gurney DSO took over temporary command of the Brigade and Captain Williams, both East Yorkshire Regiment, became the Brigade Major. Gurney was replaced by Colonel Temple DSO the following day and Williams by Captain JH Stafford MC on the 29th.

The day was quiet until around 12.30 p.m., when the main body of the enemy appeared and attacked the whole front of 31st Division. The brunt of the attack fell on 15th/17th West Yorkshire. Mountain commanded an isolated flank post in this position for twenty-seven hours. The rest of 93rd Brigade was ordered to withdraw to the Purple Line near Adinfer Wood, but the staff officer dispatched to warn 15th/17th West Yorkshire became a casualty and the message never got through. In the absence of orders, the Battalion clung to its position. The Germans had no other opposition and by 4 p.m. they had worked around both flanks and were bringing enfilade machine gun fire to bear. Heavy losses were suffered and at 5 p.m. an attempt was made to retire by platoons under covering fire. Due to the weight of enemy fire this proved to be impossible and at 5.15 p.m. the enemy broke into the positions. Having held for thirty-six hours, the Battalion was overwhelmed. Only four officers and forty men got away. The order to withdraw never reached Mountain's party. Only a few escaped to rejoin the Battalion, including Mountain himself. At least two men, Privates Barlow and Worrall, were captured.

A Company, 18th Durham Light Infantry, 600m west of Moyenneville, also played a gallant part in this action. Although surrounded it managed to fight its way back and rejoined the main body of the Brigade. However, it suffered almost one hundred casualties in so doing.

When it was eventually relieved on 30th March, 93rd Brigade had suffered 1,108 casualties since 22nd March, with 15th/17th West Yorkshire's share being 617, of whom 511 were missing. However, the magnificent stand made by the Battalion enabled the rest of 31st Division to escape and establish a new position east of Ayette.

339 Lt Col John Collings-Wells, 4th Bedfordshire (190th Brigade, 63rd Division), Albert, France

27th March 1918

At a conference at Doullens on 26th March, Marshal Foch was authorised to coordinate the French and British Armies in Flanders. His first order was to cease retirement and to hold the enemy. At the same time, the British Armies bearing the brunt of the German attacks received much needed reinforcements. 5th Division arrived from Italy and three Australian and the New Zealand divisions were despatched. The Germans also reviewed their plans. Ludendorff ordered operations around Amiens to continue, with the aim of forming a barrier facing southwest, while pressure was maintained at Arras and a new offensive was opened in Flanders.

The British had already suffered 74,000 casualties since the German offensives began and replacements had to be found urgently. Reducing the minimum age for foreign service from nineteen to eighteen and a half produced 50,000 trained men, of which 27,000 were available for drafting immediately. Forty thousand men reached France within four days of the offensive opening and arrangements were made to bring another division from Italy and a large quantity of artillery. Eventually two divisions were sent from Palestine. Materiel stocks lost in the retreat were made good by the end of March.

South of the Somme, in spite of Foch's orders, the enemy continued to make progress. XVIII Corps pulled back its right in response to the French falling back from Montdidier. The Germans took advantage of the almost ten kilometres wide

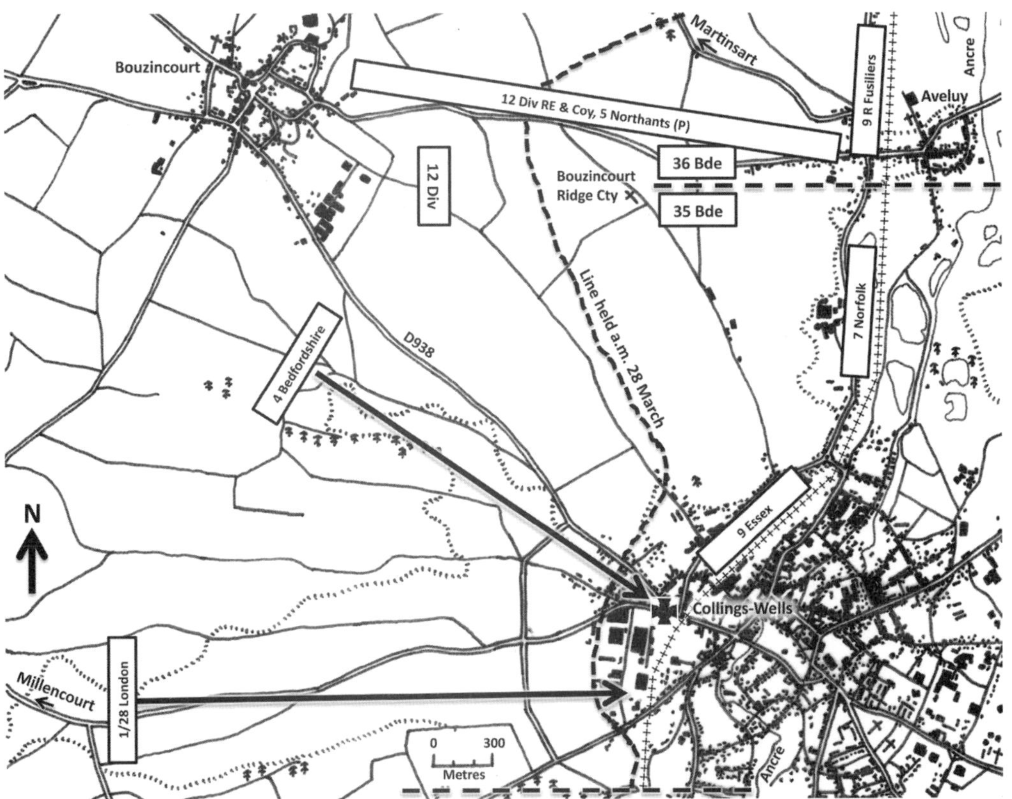

A distant overview of the attack by 4th Bedfordshire on 27th March can be had from Bouzincourt Ridge Cemetery, where John Collings-Wells is buried. For a closer view drive towards Albert from Bouzincourt on the D938 and pull over on the roadside at a suitable viewing point (there are a number of options), without interfering with the traffic on what is often a fast and busy route.

From Bouzincourt Ridge Cemetery with the Basilique in Albert on the left. 4th Bedfordshire advance from right to left along the low ground into Albert.

gap left by the retirement of VII Corps the previous day. This left XVIII Corps and XIX Corps threatened on both flanks. Attacks on Third Army were heavy throughout the day, except on the extreme left (XVII Corps). There were heavy casualties on both sides. Two brigades were forced back north of Moyenneville and the Germans gained a footing in the line west of Serre. Rossignol Wood was lost but overall the enemy gains were insignificant in comparison to their losses. North of Albert the Germans threw five divisions into enlarging their gains west of the Ancre at Aveluy.

4th Bedfordshire had had no respite in the previous six days, falling back fighting all the way. On the 25th it reinforced 189th Brigade near High Wood, which was being very heavily pressed and was in danger of being surrounded. The CO, **Lieutenant Colonel John Collings-Wells**, called for volunteers to form a rearguard, while the remainder of the Battalion escaped. He held the position for an hour and a half. Only when all ammunition had been expended, did he lead them away to safety. Throughout this action he moved about freely under heavy fire to encourage his men. The Battalion withdrew to Thiepval, where it rejoined 190th Brigade in a new position on the ridge. Next day the Brigade marched to Aveluy Wood, destroying the bridges over the Ancre having crossed to the west. It was relieved by 12th Division and withdrew to Martinsart initially but during the afternoon moved into billets in a wood west of Englebelmer.

From the D938 looking along the axis of 4th Bedfordshire's attack towards Albert.

The rest was short lived. At 7 p.m., 190th Brigade was ordered to hold a defensive flank between Aveluy and Bouzincourt against a breakout north from Albert. On arrival it came under command of 35th Brigade (12th Division), which was being gradually pushed back from Albert. It became clear that the enemy would break out unless something was done. At 7.30 a.m. on 27th March a counterattack by two exhausted battalions of 190th Brigade was launched along adjacent parallel valleys converging on Albert. 1/28th London (Artists' Rifles) advanced from Millencourt and 4th Bedfordshire from Bouzincourt. Their objective was to restore the line of the railway running around the west of Albert.

4th Bedfordshire was exhausted after days of continuous fighting, so Collings-Wells placed himself at the head. He was wounded twice in both arms during the advance but refused aid and continued to urge his men on. By his example and determination the Battalion reached its objective, halted the enemy advance and

4th Bedfordshire's objective, the railway crossing the main road into Albert from the west. The road to Bouzincourt comes in from the left and the road from Millencourt from the right.

re-established a line. He had to be almost dragged to a dugout to have his wounds dressed, as he was reluctant to leave his men. Moments later the dugout received a direct hit from a mortar bomb and Collings-Wells was killed, as was his second-in-command, Major George Paterson Nunneley MC (Ovillers Military Cemetery – I C 30) and two other officers.

At the same time a hurried withdrawal took place from Albert towards Bouzincourt. 7th Royal Fusiliers in reserve rushed to a position east of Bouzincourt and restored the situation there. The Brigade was relieved during the night and withdrew to Senlis.

First Battle of Arras 1918

340 Lt Col Oliver Watson, London Yeomanry att'd attached 5th King's Own Yorkshire Light Infantry (187th Brigade, 62nd Division), Rossignol Wood, France

341 2Lt Basil Horsfall, 11th East Lancashire (92nd Brigade, 31st Division) between Moyenneville and Ablainzevelle, France

27th March 1918

IV Corps held a salient against which the Germans made persistent efforts. The most serious threat was to the New Zealanders on the southern face. Before noon the enemy was held by artillery fire but later they came on in greater strength. A determined attack was made on IV Corps' right flank at Bucquoy. 62nd Division had 185th Brigade on the left, east of Bucquoy, and 186th Brigade on the right, between Bucquoy and Rossignol Wood. 187th Brigade had one battalion (2/4th King's Own Yorkshire Light Infantry) on the high ground between Rossignol Wood and the east of Hébuterne. The remainder of the Brigade was in reserve.

Using the cover of shell holes, the machine gunners shot down most of the enemy, while the artillery destroyed many more. German artillery continued to fall on Bucquoy for two more hours but failed to dislodge the defenders. The Germans attacked continuously throughout the afternoon near Rossignol Wood and at Bucquoy. Covered by concentrated artillery fire and aircraft, they used the network of old trenches in the area to close to grenade range with the British. Contemporary accounts of what happened next are quite clear about which units did what and when. However, they are more vague about precise locations and directions.

At 5.15 p.m. A and B Companies, on the left of 2/4th King's Own Yorkshire Light Infantry, were driven from the high ground east of Hébuterne. A company of 2/4th York & Lancaster was also evicted from Rossignol Wood. Loss of the high ground east of Hébuterne opened a gap between the right of 186th Brigade, held by 5th Duke of Wellington's, and 4th Australian Brigade in Hébuterne. Two

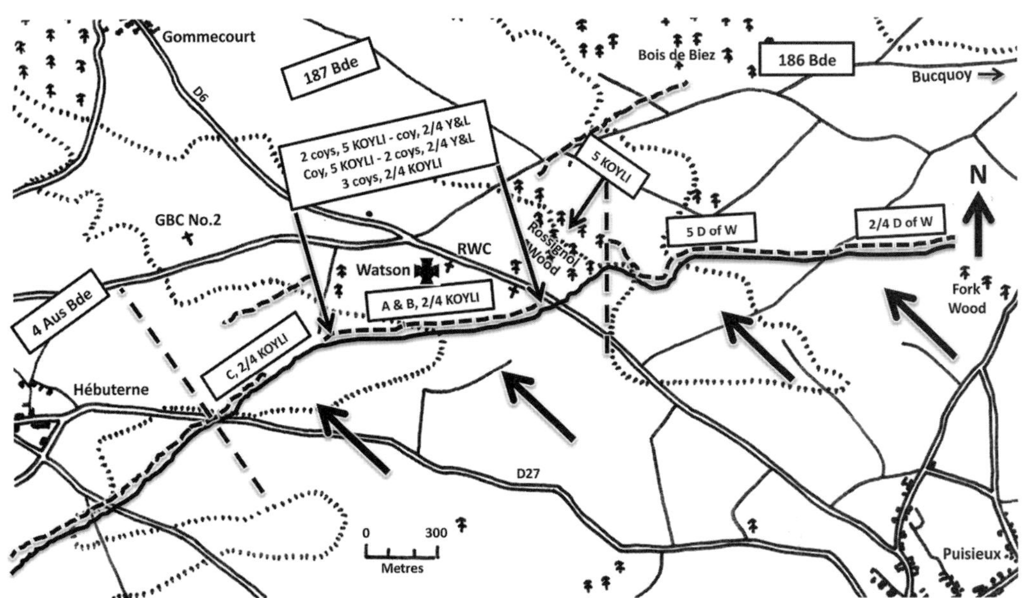

Leave Gommecourt on the D6 southeast towards Puisieux. A track on the right is signed for Gommecourt British Cemetery No.2. Turn left here towards Rossignol Wood and park at the western tip. Turn round to look back over the ground covered in the counterattack. The solid line runs along the approximate front line on 27th March. The dashed lines are those held on 28th March. RWC = Rossignol Wood Cemetery and GBC No.2 = Gommecourt British Cemetery No.2.

companies of 5th King's Own Yorkshire Light Infantry were sent to reinforce 2/4th King's Own Yorkshire Light Infantry by extending the line to the right. Orders were issued for 4th Australian Brigade to block on the right, while 187th Brigade counterattacked. Four tanks, supported by 5th King's Own Yorkshire Light Infantry, attacked the northeast side of Rossignol Wood. They discovered that the Wood had been evacuated but, due to a misunderstanding, 5th King's Own Yorkshire Light Infantry did not occupy it and returned at 10 a.m. 187th Brigade was then ordered to re-establish the line held by 2/4th King's Own Yorkshire Light Infantry before dawn.

The attack was launched in three waves at 4.15 a.m. on the 28th. The first wave consisted of three companies of 2/4th King's Own Yorkshire Light Infantry, the remnants of A and B Companies on the left and D Company on the right. The second wave had two companies of 2/4th York & Lancaster on the left and a company of 5th King's Own Yorkshire Light Infantry on the right. The third wave had a company of 2/4th York & Lancaster on the left and two companies of 5th King's Own Yorkshire Light Infantry in the centre and on the right. On the right, D Company, 2/4th King's Own Yorkshire Light Infantry in the first wave and all the 5th King's Own Yorkshire Light Infantry companies gained their objectives. Three trenches were taken in the darkness. However, at Rossignol Wood they came

The counterattack led by Oliver Watson swept down this slope between the two arrows.

up against strongly held German outposts, including two abandoned British tanks in the southeast corner being used as strongpoints.

Immediate action was needed and the CO of 5th King's Own Yorkshire Light Infantry, **Lieutenant Colonel Oliver Watson**, gathered his small reserve, organised them into bombing parties and led them forward in a series of attacks. When it was clear that they were outnumbered, Watson ordered his men back. By daylight 5th King's Own Yorkshire Light Infantry was holding a line facing southeast, with a road and a light railway line between it and the Wood. At daylight more bombs were brought up in preparation for another effort but, with the sun in their eyes, the British could just make out the enemy advancing in large numbers on the left.

The Germans made use of old communications trenches to surround three companies of 5th King's Own Yorkshire Light Infantry and D Company, 2/4th King's Own Yorkshire Light Infantry from the rear. At 5.30 a.m. Watson was left with only his reserve company to reinforce his line but he hung on for a while longer. He was killed holding the enemy back, whilst personally covering the withdrawal down a communication trench. The remaining men from the two battalions held their flanks against further attacks for the rest of the day and the Australians linked up with them from the south.

VI Corps had 31st, Guards and 3rd Divisions in the line, with 40th Division resting. By this time a Purple Line had been organised to the rear and other systems were under construction behind the British front. 31st Division, on the Corps' right, had 92nd Brigade on the right and 93rd Brigade on the left. 4th Guards Brigade was in a support line, about 2,000m behind the forward brigades, astride Ayette. To 31st Division's left was 2nd Guards Brigade (Guards Division) and to the right was 126th Brigade (42nd Division, IV Corps).

In the early hours of 26th March, 92nd Brigade fell back to a new position between Moyenneville and Ablainzevelle. On the right, 11th East Lancashire occupied the

line from 450m northeast of Ablainzevelle to the crossroads on the Courcelles-le-Comte – Ayette road. Three companies were in the front line (from right to left – W, Y, X), with the fourth (Z) in reserve. Each company had three platoons forward and one in support. 11th East Yorkshire held the remainder of the Brigade frontage on the left, with 10th East Yorkshire in reserve. The two forward battalions pushed outposts forward about 300m onto a ridge. By 7.30 a.m. the forward troops were in position followed, about ninety minutes later, by the reserve battalion, 92nd Trench

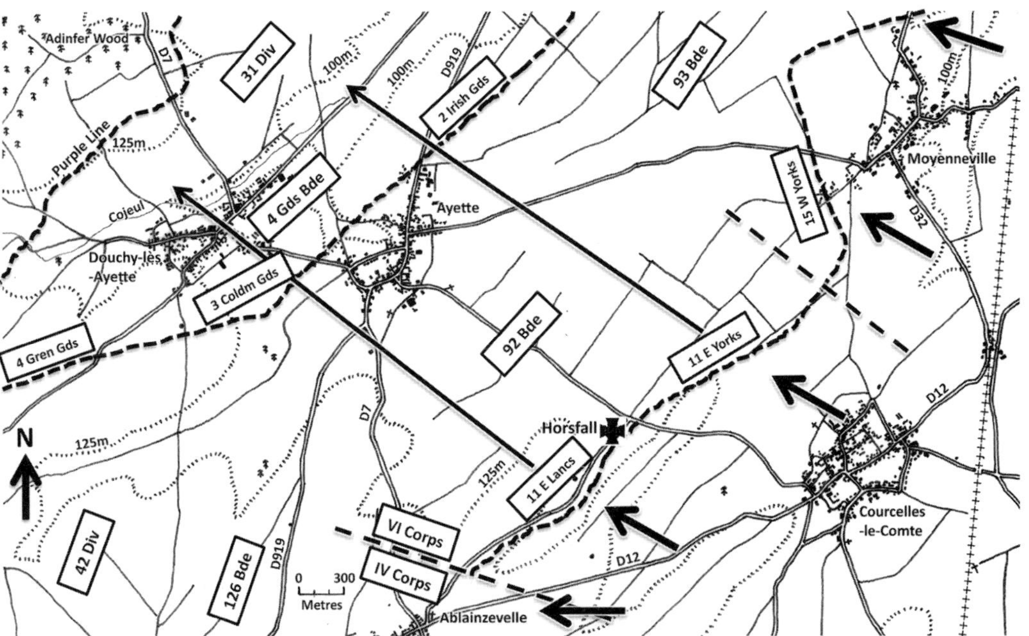

Drive southeast on the unclassified road from Ayette to Courcelles-le-Comte for about two kilometres, to where the road climbs up a small ridge. This is where the forward posts of X Company 11th East Lancashire were sited on 27th March.

Mortar Battery and A Company, 31st Machine Gun Battalion. Although dumps of ammunition were formed in the new positions, there was no wire to deploy to the front.

At 9.45 a.m. there was no sign of 126th Brigade on the right, which was expected to prolong the line to the south. There was some enemy shelling and the situation worsened considerably when the British artillery fell short. To the south, where the flank was open, enemy concentrations were dealt with by SOS fire missions and did not develop into attacks. A patrol in the afternoon again found no sign of 126th Brigade. During the night, the right company of 11th East Lancashire extended its front 1,100m to the south, reinforced by a company of 10th East Yorkshire from the Brigade reserve.

With the right flank still shaky, news was received at 6 p.m. from 93rd Brigade on the left that Moyenneville had fallen. As a result the line held by 93rd Brigade was echeloned behind the left of 92nd Brigade, which then found itself ahead of both neighbouring formations.

At 11.20 a.m. on 27th March the whole of 92nd Brigade's front was hit by an intense bombardment. At noon the German infantry attack commenced and the SOS signals were fired to bring down protective artillery fire. 15th West Yorkshire (93rd Brigade) on the left flank appeared to have fallen back and 11th East Yorkshire came under enfilade machine gun fire. There was desperate fighting until the original position was recovered in a counterattack. The Germans forced 11th East Yorkshire back again but the line was restored once more at 1.15 p.m.

With Ablainzevelle on the right flank in enemy hands, 11th East Lancashire also came under enfilade fire. The Germans were able to attack at the vulnerable junction point between the two brigades. Although the Germans made a few gains in 11th East Lancashire's line, they were quickly ejected at bayonet point. Another attack was launched at noon and another, at 12.20 p.m., was supported by low flying aircraft. Although 11th East Lancashire held the enemy, it was at considerable cost, particularly on the left in X Company. Except for one company, the whole of 10th East Yorkshire in reserve was used to maintain 92nd Brigade's line. The defence involved at least four counterattacks.

The ridge running along the centre of the picture is the one held by 11th East Lancashire on 27th March. Basil Horsfall's platoon was in position to the right of the road. The church in Courcelles can be seen to the left of the copse on the extreme left. Ablainzevelle is out of shot to the right.

Second Lieutenant Basil Horsfall commanded the centre platoon in X Company on the Ablainzevelle – Moyenneville ridge, close to the Courcelles-le-Comte – Ayette road. However, in a letter to Horsfall's father, the CO of 11th East Lancashire wrote that he commanded the left platoon. In the initial attack Horsfall's three forward sections were driven back and he was severely wounded in the head. Despite this, he organised an immediate counterattack and recovered the position. He refused to leave to have his wound dressed, as the three other officers in the company were either dead or badly wounded. Later his platoon had to pull back to avoid heavy shelling but, as soon as it had lifted, he made a second counterattack and restored the position again.

At 1.30 p.m. the enemy advanced in large numbers from Ablainzevelle and a company of 10th East Yorkshire reinforced 11th East Lancashire's right flank. A platoon sent to assist W Company was prevented from reaching the front line due to heavy machine gun fire from the village. The ridge was still held at 2 p.m. but with very few men and the whole defence began to break down. At 3 p.m., 11th East Yorkshire retired to the support line, by which time X Company, 11th East Lancashire had suffered 135 casualties amongst the 180 men committed to the battle.

Events then moved very quickly. The Germans established a strongpoint on top of the ridge on the Ayette – Courcelles road. Communication with HQ 92nd Brigade was lost but arrangements had been made for this eventuality. The senior battalion commander, Lieutenant Colonel Arthur Wilmot Rickman DSO, CO 11th East Lancashire, had been given authority by Brigade HQ to act on his own initiative if communications failed. At 4.25 p.m. he received reports that both flanks of the Brigade had been driven in. Having made a quick reconnaissance of the situation he confirmed that the flanks were by then behind his Battalion HQ. Wires to Brigade HQ had been cut and visual signalling was not possible in the mist. Rickman quickly consulted the other unit commanders, including the CO of 15th West Yorkshire. 165th and 170th Brigades RFA were down to only twelve rounds per gun. The only option was to retire through 4th Guards Brigade (commanded temporarily by Lieutenant Colonel Harold Alexander DSO MC, later Field Marshal, 1st Earl Alexander of Tunis) holding the Ayette line. Rickman issued instructions for 11th East Lancashire, less W Company, to fall back to the high ground southeast of Ayette and for 10th East Yorkshire, less two companies, to fall back to the high ground northeast of Ayette. The companies remaining formed a rearguard under command of an East Yorkshire officer. 10th East Yorkshire provided a detachment to defend Ayette under command of 4th Guards Brigade. The initial retirement was to the south bank of the Cojeul River, which was carried out in good order but not without further losses. Horsfall was the last to leave his platoon's position and he was killed as he attempted to fall back.

Both battalions reformed at the Cojeul and fell back through 4th Guards Brigade to Adinfer Wood. 92nd Brigade reformed there and took up positions in the Purple Line. Enemy troops poised to pursue were broken up by artillery fire and the fighting died down. 92nd Brigade's newly formed composite battalion of Category B men was brought forward from Bienvillers to Brigade HQ. By 6 p.m. 92nd Brigade's line was held, from south to north, by 92nd Trench Mortar Battery, 10th East Yorkshire and 11th East Yorkshire. 11th East Lancashire was in support in Adinfer Wood. About 120 men of the composite battalion were sent forward to support 2nd Irish Guards, which had an open right flank south of Ayette. Other Category B men reinforced their parent battalions.

The resistance put up during the day was sufficient to remove the steam from the enemy offensive and the west of Ayette was as far as the Germans reached. The Guards Division extended southwards to cover 6,300m of frontage. Two battalions of 93rd Brigade were brought up on the left of 31st Division. In the early hours of the 28th the leading elements of 32nd Division began to arrive to take over the line. 11th East Lancashire was relieved by 1st Dorset (14th Brigade).

28th March 1918

342 2Lt Bernard Cassidy, 2nd Lancashire Fusiliers (12th Brigade, 4th Division) near Gavrelle, France

343 Sgt Stanley McDougall, 47th Battalion, AIF (12th Australian Brigade, 4th Australian Division), Dernancourt, France

On 28th March German attacks were repulsed, except in the extreme south, where the British were utterly exhausted and the French were still building their strength. The situation at the junction of the French and British Armies remained critical. On the same day the Germans tried to reinvigorate their offensive by launching a new attack east of Arras, at the junction of Third and First Armies, codenamed Mars. The left of VI Corps (3rd Division) and the right of XVII Corps (15th Division) had not yet been attacked seriously and swung back their flanks in the Battle Zone to keep in contact with the rest of Third Army to the south. North of the Scarpe the left of XVII Corps (4th Division) and First Army still held the original Forward Zone.

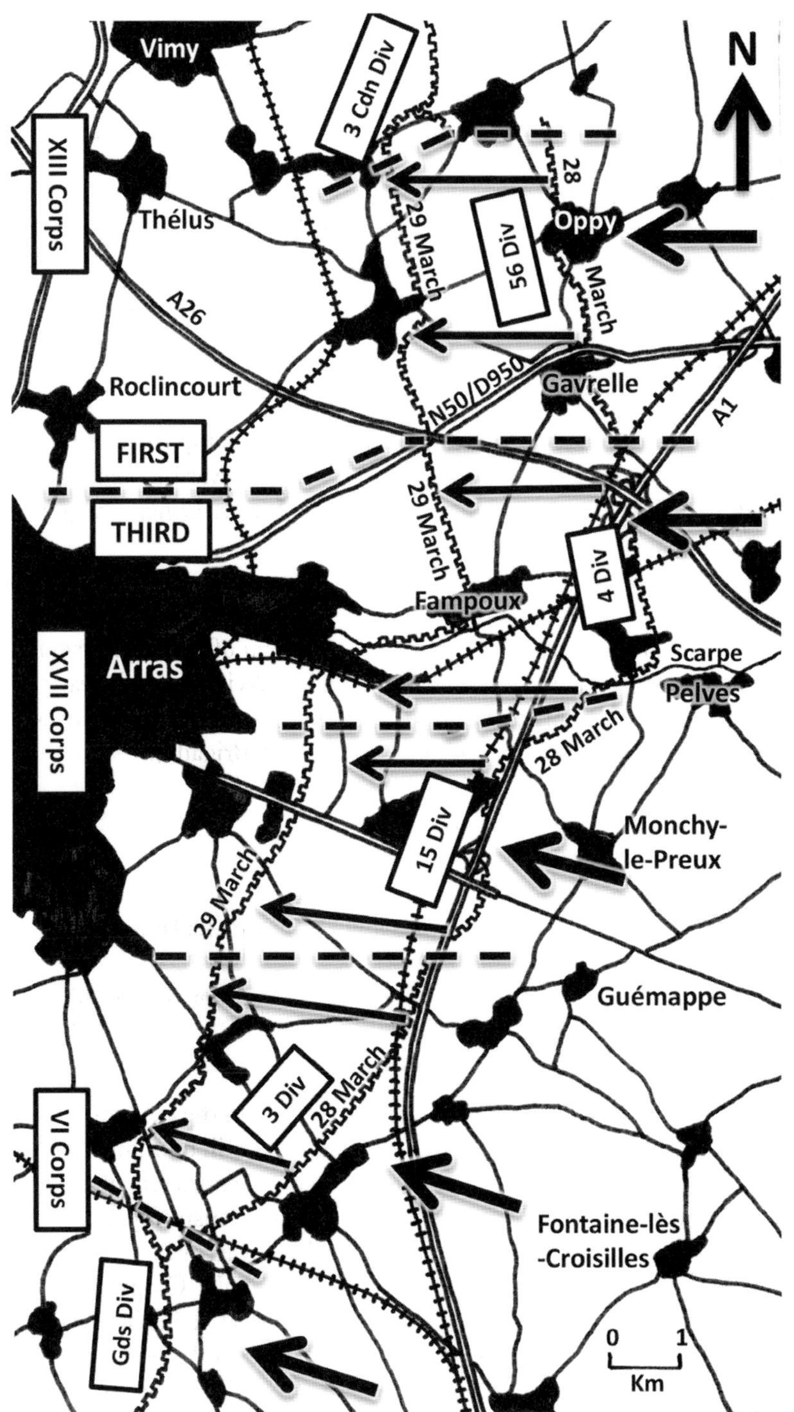

The German Mars offensive on 28th March.

At 3 a.m. a massive bombardment fell on the fronts of VI, XVII (Third Army) and XIII Corps (First Army). The rear areas were hit systematically, including mustard gas on the gun batteries. On the right of VI Corps, 31st Division inflicted massive casualties but lost its forward posts. The Guards Division broke up two large attacks.

3rd, 15th and 4th Divisions in Third Army and 56th Division in First Army were attacked by nine German divisions. These high quality British divisions were occupying well-prepared defences but there were no reserves. The night preceding the attack was quiet until the artillery preparation began. At 5.15 a.m. the bombardment south of the Scarpe (3rd and 15th Divisions) lifted and the enemy made determined, but unsuccessful, efforts to break in. The exception was at 7 a.m. on the right of 15th Division, when the enemy got behind 44th and 45th Brigades and forced them back to the rear line of the Battle Zone. Half an hour later the right and centre of 3rd Division was broken into and by 8.30 a.m. almost the whole front of 3rd and 15th Divisions had been lost. However, by 3 p.m. these divisions were complete on the Green Line and by 5 p.m. the German attack was over. Mars South had failed.

The German effort north of the Scarpe was more concentrated. At the junction of Third and First Armies, 4th and 56th Divisions faced seven German divisions. During the four and a half hours bombardment the front line posts that had not already been abandoned were obliterated. The enemy attack soon after 7 a.m. was held up and lost the creeping barrage. The attackers fought their way forward slowly but came under heavy machine gun fire and were caught up in old trenches.

4th Division had all three brigades in the line and an attack seemed imminent from 5 a.m. onwards. The three engineer companies and the pioneer battalion were formed into an ad hoc reserve brigade. A composite battalion was also made up of transport and other rear details to hold the Red Line west of Arras. The forward battalion in 10th Brigade on the right, 2nd Seaforth Highlanders, was isolated when the troops south of the Scarpe fell back, and it also had to retire. In the centre, 1st Hampshire was the forward battalion in 11th Brigade. When it was attacked in the flank and frontally, it was also forced to fall back. By 9.30 a.m. it was established partly in the front of the Battle Zone and partly in the reserve line of the Forward Zone. 1st Somerset Light Infantry (11th Brigade reserve) formed a defensive flank along the north bank of the Scarpe.

On the left of 4th Division was 12th Brigade, with 2nd Essex forward and 2nd Lancashire Fusiliers in support. Two companies of 1st King's Own in reserve were brought forward to Mississippi and Missouri Trenches. At 7.35 a.m. the two other companies moved up to Logic Trench and Stoke Avenue. 2nd Essex was overwhelmed from the south at the same time as the enemy forced their way into the valley on the Battalion's northern flank. The remnants of the Battalion fell back to Harry and Humid Trenches. 2nd Lancashire Fusiliers reported that it was in Humid Trench but nothing could be seen of the enemy, who were shelling Humid and Harry. At 8.45 a.m. CO 2nd Essex reached HQ 2nd Lancashire Fusiliers and reported that the Germans had broken through on the right. Over 600 men from the Battalion were missing but fortunately the Germans followed more slowly. HQ 12th Brigade ordered 2nd Essex and 2nd Lancashire Fusiliers to hold Humid and Harry Trenches. At about the same time 169th Brigade (56th Division), on the left, reported that the situation there was unclear but understood that the Germans had broken through on the right.

By 9.30 a.m. 2nd Lancashire Fusiliers was holding the line Humid – Harry – Hussar – Hyderabad and was in contact with 11th Brigade in the second system on the right. Germans were seen coming over Greenland Hill in large numbers and were concentrating in a valley southwest of Gavrelle. They were also bombing along Naval Trench.

2nd Lancashire Fusiliers had A Company on the left, occupying Civil Avenue and Humid Trench, and D Company on the right. The Battalion also deployed C Company, 1st King's Own into Hyderabad Support Trench to counter the threat on the right. Enemy bombers advanced down Civil, Caledonian and Chili Avenues. At about 10 a.m. they reached the junction of Humid and Harry Trenches, where they cut A Company off from the rear and from D Company. An attempt to throw the Germans back failed but the two companies fought on. D Company erected a barricade in Hussar Trench, preventing the Germans from making more progress in that direction.

The situation at 11.30 a.m. found 2nd Lancashire Fusiliers and fifty men of 2nd Essex holding Trent and Hyderabad. 1st King's Own was holding Mississippi, Missouri, Logic and Stoke Avenue. A small party of 2nd Lancashire Fusiliers was

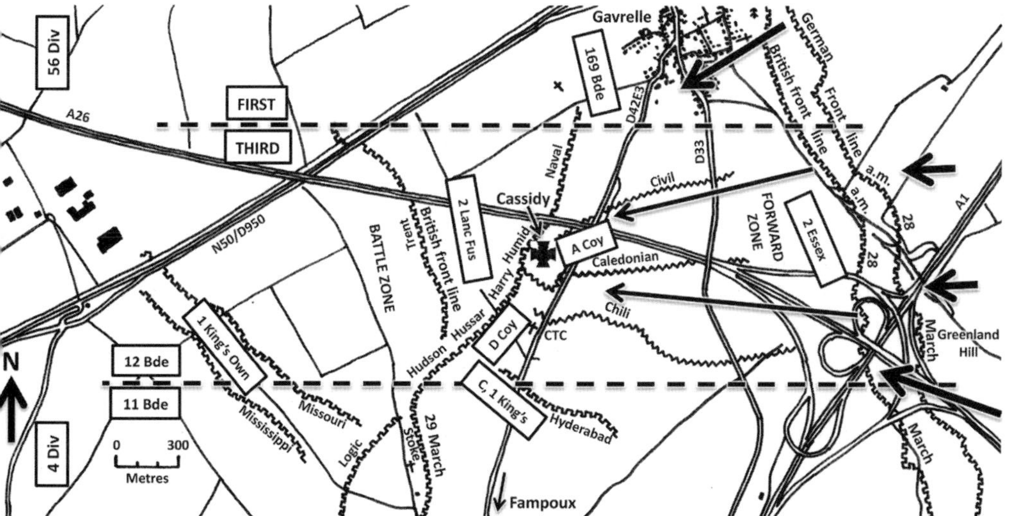

To overlook the action fought by 12th Brigade on 28th March, park at Chili Trench Cemetery (CTC) on the west side of the D42E3 Fampoux–Gavrelle road. Numerous other trenches, many disused and abandoned, have been omitted from the map for clarity.

From the north wall of Chili Trench Cemetery looking north. The trench lines are approximate.

believed to be holding out in Harry. At 1.20 p.m. contact was established with 169th Brigade in Trent and Mississippi but 4th Division remained under considerable pressure. 11th and 12th Brigades fell back and reached the Battle Zone about 1.45 p.m.

A Company, 2nd Lancashire Fusiliers was commanded by **Second Lieutenant Bernard Cassidy**. It was short of ammunition but Cassidy rallied his men repeatedly and drove the enemy out of their trenches on a number of occasions. The only escape lay over the open to Trent Trench and the enemy held both flanks. Cassidy was in telephone contact with the CO throughout the action until his final message, *Here they are, right on me*, followed by silence. Cassidy was killed and the two other officers in the Company were also casualties. A Company was overwhelmed and only six men escaped uninjured. However, the Company had saved the Division's left flank and averted a disaster. B and D Companies repulsed further bombing attacks along Hussar Trench, assisted by C Company, 1st King's Own.

The Germans were discouraged by the fierce resistance and, although attacks continued into the afternoon and evening, they lost impetus. Mars North had also failed but there was still danger in the Scarpe valley. 10th Brigade attacked at 6.30 p.m. to prevent 11th and 12th Brigades from being outflanked. By 8 p.m. the line had moved forward about 700m and the enemy had fallen back into the old Battle Zone. However, this was not enough and, after dark, 11th and 12th Brigades were ordered to pivot on the left and swing back their right. This reduced the flank along the north bank of the Scarpe to 900m, which was well covered by an impenetrable swamp.

HQ 12th Brigade issued orders at 6.30 p.m. for this move. The front line was to run along Trent from the Brigade left boundary to the junction with Hudson, then along Hudson to Stoke Avenue and along it to the Brigade right boundary. 2nd

Lancashire Fusiliers and details of 2nd Essex were in the front Line. 1st King's Own was in support in Mississippi – Missouri – Logic. The new positions were consolidated by 2 a.m. on 29th March.

The right of 56th Division had retired to the front line of the Battle Zone by 9.30 a.m., having taken a heavy toll of the massed Germans. The left was forced back to the Forward Zone reserve trenches. The Germans also forced their way up the swampy valley that formed the boundary with 4th Division to the south and turned the inner flanks. The right of 56th Division was in danger and at 10.30 a.m. it was ordered to retire into the Battle Zone. The left complied and by 1 p.m. the whole of 56th Division was in or behind the Battle Zone front line.

At the end of the day Ludendorff realised that Mars had failed and closed the attack down. He cancelled the Valkerie attack and ordered a fresh offensive (Georgette) against Hazebrouck. However, it would take some time to transfer the artillery north before this new offensive could be launched.

Meanwhile on 28th March, a smaller battle developed to the south of Albert and north of the Ancre. 12th Australian Brigade had spent three days moving and marching to various locations. It was already exhausted when, on 27th March, it was ordered to take up a line south of Albert and relieve 9th Division. 48th Battalion was on the left and 47th Battalion on the right. They advanced at 12.30 p.m. and at 4 p.m. were ordered to advance another 700m. 47th Battalion carried this out, although with some casualties as the Battalion moved into position down a gradual, exposed slope. Two men were killed and a few more were wounded by British aircraft when they mistook them for Germans. By 5 p.m. the Battalion was in position. 48th Battalion avoided casualties by delaying the final approach until after dark. It was in contact with 106th Brigade (35th Division) on the right. From 47th Battalion's war diary it is known that the unit was well up to strength on 26th March, with thirty-seven

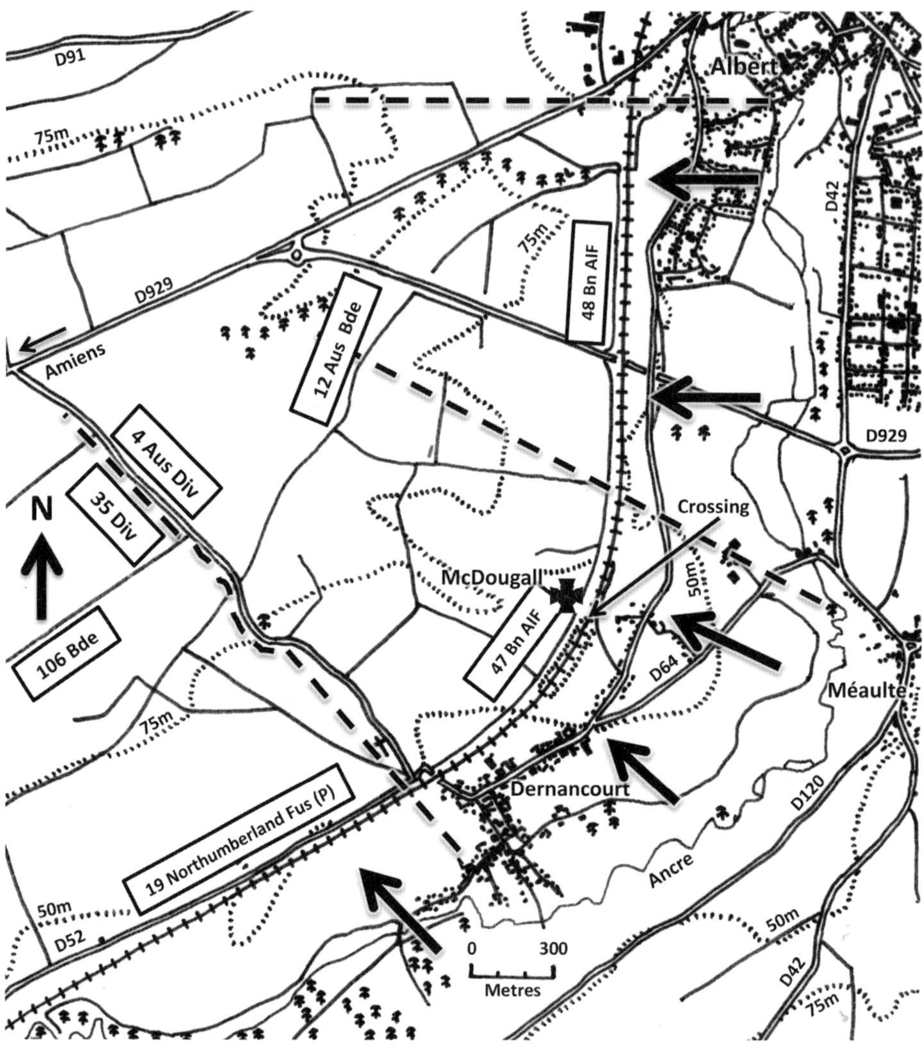

Drive through Dernancourt on the D64 southwestwards. Go under the railway and turn immediately right into a single-track lane. Follow it for 1,150m parallel with the railway line on your right. In the dip there is a rough track turning on the left where you can park but please be aware that agricultural vehicles may need access. The level crossing, marked by an information board, was a few metres back up the hill where the railway emerges from the cutting to the south.

officers and 741 other ranks, plus another eleven officers and 116 other ranks on courses, leave, sick etc.

Dernancourt had been abandoned during the day in favour of holding the line of the railway. However, this formed a salient as the line curved round the hill to the west of the village. Although this position offered excellent observation, it was tactically weak and very exposed. The only prepared defences along the railway were single man scrapes in the embankment. During the night a support line was dug 270m to the rear and on the crest of the hill was Pioneer Trench, well sited with commanding views.

The relief was not completed until 1.30 a.m. on 28th March because of the disorganisation amongst the battered British units of the three brigades in the line. Six platoon posts per battalion were established on the railway as an outpost line. The gaps between were covered by small sentry groups. Due to the shape of the ground, 48th Battalion was forced to employ three companies along the railway, with only one in support. 47th Battalion used two companies along the railway, with the other two in support.

In the middle of 47th Battalion was a level crossing. The right company (Lieutenant William Goodsall) had a platoon in the cutting to the south of the crossing. The right platoon of D Company on the left (Captain Charles Arundel Symons) held a low bank north of the crossing, but there was no garrison on the embankment itself. Two Lewis gunners were positioned at the crossing, with **Sergeant Stanley McDougall** and two men watching it from the embankment immediately to the north.

During the night the Germans occupied Dernanacourt and their artillery and machine guns were very active, particularly along the railway line. At 2.30 a.m. 12th Australian Brigade's reserve, 45th Battalion, moved forward into a support position.

Early on the morning of the 28th it was quiet and McDougall allowed his two men to stand down and snatch some sleep at the foot of the bank, while he kept watch. About 4.30 a.m., in the dim light of approaching dawn, Lieutenant George Crowe Reid (MC for his actions on 5th April), the Battalion Intelligence Officer, and Lieutenant Edward Robinson (MC for this action) came along on their rounds. They passed McDougall and headed north behind the embankment. Through the mist in front McDougall heard the sounds of bayonet scabbards flapping on thighs. He alerted his two sleeping men. Reid heard him and shouted, *Is that you Mac?* He replied, *Yes, come up here quick. I think they're coming at us.* Having confirmed that the Germans were advancing, McDougall and his two men ran off to the north

Overlooking the former crossing site with the railway on the right. In the right distance is the Basilique in Albert.

to alert the nearest platoon of their own company. As McDougall ran along the railway he saw through the mist the Germans advancing towards him. He reached the platoon and with the seven nearest men rushed south again along the railway, intending to line the unoccupied embankment.

The Lewis gunners with him were hit by a grenade. Undaunted McDougall charged the second wave of the German attackers with his rifle and bayonet. Having killed several, he picked up an enemy light machine gun (some accounts say it was the Lewis gun in his own party) and turned it on the attacking force, firing from the hip. He was well ahead of the rest of the party, of whom three or four were killed or wounded almost immediately. Two enemy light machine-gun teams were crossing the embankment no more than seven metres away. McDougall switched his fire onto them and shot all seven of them, the first man having half his head blown away. These machine guns were later recovered by the Battalion. Other Germans, who tried to cross the railway, were either shot or forced back. He inflicted heavy casualties, caused utter confusion and broke up the formation, which dispersed. McDougall then looked over the forward edge of the embankment and saw twenty Germans crouching there in shell holes, awaiting the order to advance. He opened fire, hitting some and the rest fled. When the ammunition ran out, he used the bayonet again.

Meanwhile Reid and Robinson had organised the defence by bringing forward troops onto the embankment. The southern flank of the crossing was still open. The Lewis gunner there was surprised and captured. The Germans turned south along the railway. In the cutting to the south, 2021 Sergeant Alfred Ernest Morris, 12th Australian Machine Gun Company, saw a light flicker and sent 4259 Private Albert Richard Booth Casey to investigate. Casey was captured but the sentry in the cutting received no reply from his challenge and opened fire. Casey escaped later in the ensuing confusion. About fifty Germans in the first wave of the attack had crossed the railway. They were heading southwest behind the right company but came under fire from three directions before they could attack the company in the rear.

Having dealt with the second wave, McDougall picked up a Lewis gun and poured fire into the first wave, which by then had gone beyond the crossing, from as close as ten metres away. The barrel became so hot that his left hand was badly blistered. 2206 Sergeant James Charles Lawrence (MM for his actions on 5th April and MSM later) held the gun while McDougall fired it one-handed. Lawrence and another sergeant then moved across the open behind the embankment. As they did so, a German officer stood up behind them and leveled a pistol. McDougall shouted a warning. Lawrence swung round and fired his rifle but tripped and fell. The German thus missed him and was shot dead by the other sergeant.

A German officer rushed at him with a bayonet but McDougall bayoneted him instead. At one time the enemy rushed him with bombs but he held them off with his pistol until fresh magazines for the Lewis gun arrived.

On the left, 48th Battalion was also attacked frontally in strength. On its right, Lieutenant Mitchell became aware that there were also troops to his right rear. Were they men from 47th Battalion retiring or Germans? He raced towards them to find out and, realising that they were enemy, shouted and cursed at them. This appears to be the same group that McDougall had engaged. Meanwhile the soldiers on the embankment were cursing Mitchell for being in their line of fire. He thrust his pistol into the face of an officer, who was unbuckling his equipment. The German apologised in a mixture of English, French and German, explaining that there was beer and socks in his pack. This party had already lost two officers and twenty other ranks. McDougall's final act was to bayonet a German who was just about to fire on Lieutenant Robinson from the rear. Although wounded, Robinson charged the enemy and killed an officer and three other men. As a result of McDougall's and Robinson's actions, the remaining officer and twenty-nine other ranks of the first wave, surrendered. Robinson also wrested a machine gun from a German gunner and used it to effect on the retreating enemy.

Other groups of enemy were then seen debussing in two areas and were dealt with by the artillery. The Germans poured heavy artillery fire into the support and rear areas, including gas shells. In addition the exposed positions along the railway were subjected to heavy enfilade machine gun fire. The CO of 47th Battalion, Lieutenant Colonel AP Imlay, sent two platoons of the right support company to reinforce the right forward company. Another platoon was sent to reinforce the left. Later he sent a party with urgently required bombs and rifle grenades. All of these moves had to cross an open slope and there were losses.

About 9.30 a.m. the Germans attacked 12th Australian Brigade and 35th Division. The latter massed all its machine guns to counter the attack, which was driven off in some disorder. At the junction of 12th Australian and 106th Brigades the attack was anticipated. Although outnumbered, about one hundred men of 19th Northumberland Fusiliers, 35th Division's pioneer battalion, launched a pre-emptive bayonet charge, supported by some 12th Australian Machine Gun Company gunners armed with their pistols. The bluff worked and six Germans were captured, plus four machine guns, one of which turned out to be a Lewis gun. Elsewhere the Germans were held by firepower alone. They fell back to Dernancourt, where 12th Australian Machine Gun Company and the artillery kept them under fire.

The Germans resorted to shelling the British lines. Two companies of Highland Light Infantry, sent to reinforce 19th Northumberland Fusiliers on the right, suffered heavily moving forward but reached the railway. At noon the Germans appeared to be preparing another attack on the left of 47th Battalion. The CO moved two platoons from support to reinforce the left company but the attack did not materialise. Another party of enemy machine gunners and infantrymen was dispersed by small arms fire with heavy losses. Although the Battalion was suffering casualties, it was inflicting double or more on the enemy.

At 1 p.m. 47th Battalion was ordered to cooperate with 19th Northumberland Fusiliers in an attack on Dernancourt at 2 p.m. If 19th Northumberland Fusiliers succeeded, 47th Battalion was to move its right company forward. A company of 45th Battalion sent to replace it suffered forty-eight casualties in the move forward.

As early as 1.40 p.m. that day the CO of 47th Battalion recommended Sergeant McDougall and Lieutenants Reid and Robinson for awards in a message to Brigade HQ. At 2 p.m. 19th Northumberland Fusiliers sent forward strong patrols against Dernancourt. They were driven back by heavy machine gun fire to the railway. As a result 47th Battalion made no move and the company of 45th Battalion reinforced the right flank instead.

In all there were nine enemy attacks during the day, each preceded by a heavy artillery and mortar bombardment. As the day progressed, 48th Battalion gradually extended its line to the right to allow 47th Battalion to do the same. The bombs arrived in the evening, allowing the last German posts on the embankment to be cleared.

On the left of 47th Battalion the enemy appeared to be threatening another attack and preparations were made to meet it. However, it rained heavily and no attack took place. At 6 p.m. orders were issued for 47th Battalion to send strong patrols into Dernancourt at 10 p.m. to ascertain if it was held or not, and, if not, to retake it. At 10 p.m. a patrol came under heavy machine gun fire from Dernancourt and no further action was taken.

To the south the Germans made three attacks against the line from Marett Wood to Treux held by 35th Division. Reinforcements from 10th Australian Brigade (3rd Australian Division) arrived to help defeat the third German attack. 3rd Australian Division was ordered to support an attack by 1st Cavalry Division south of the Somme, by advancing its right flank. It was then to advance its whole line. 11th and 10th Australian Brigades attacked at 3.40 p.m. but met strong resistance. However, by 8.30 p.m. they had pushed forward 550m on the right and 1,075m on the left.

On 29th March it rained and there was poor visibility. There was little activity and 45th Battalion relieved 47th Battalion in the front line. 47th Battalion's casualties over the two days, 27th-28th March, were twenty-nine killed or died of wounds and 118 wounded.

Battle of Rosières

344 Lt Gordon Flowerdew, Lord Strathcona's Horse CEF, Bois de Moreuil, France

30th March 1918

Late in March 1918 Ludendorff sensed that the Allied line was weakest in front of Amiens and redirected the main thrust of the offensive against it. If successful this would gain an important rail centre for the Germans and also split the French from the British. The French Third and First Armies were driven back by up to 2,700m in places and counterattacks seemed to have little effect. The northern part of the German thrust came up against the British XIX Corps, which included fragments of five battered infantry divisions, part of 1st Cavalry Division and Carey's Force. Despite being under severe pressure, only 1,800m was yielded in the right centre near Démuin. The rest of the line held and the British extended to the right to take over the Moreuil sector from the French. Standing at the southern end of the Santerre Plain, the Moreuil Ridge was an important feature, overlooking the Avre, the last serious obstacle before Amiens. Moreuil Wood was two kilometres long from south to north and about 1,500m wide at the northern end, tapering to a point at the southern end. The vegetation consisted mainly of ash, not yet in leaf, with heavy undergrowth between the trees.

At 4.30 a.m. on 30th March, 20th Division reported that the Germans were passing men into Moreuil Wood from the southeast. French commanders seemed

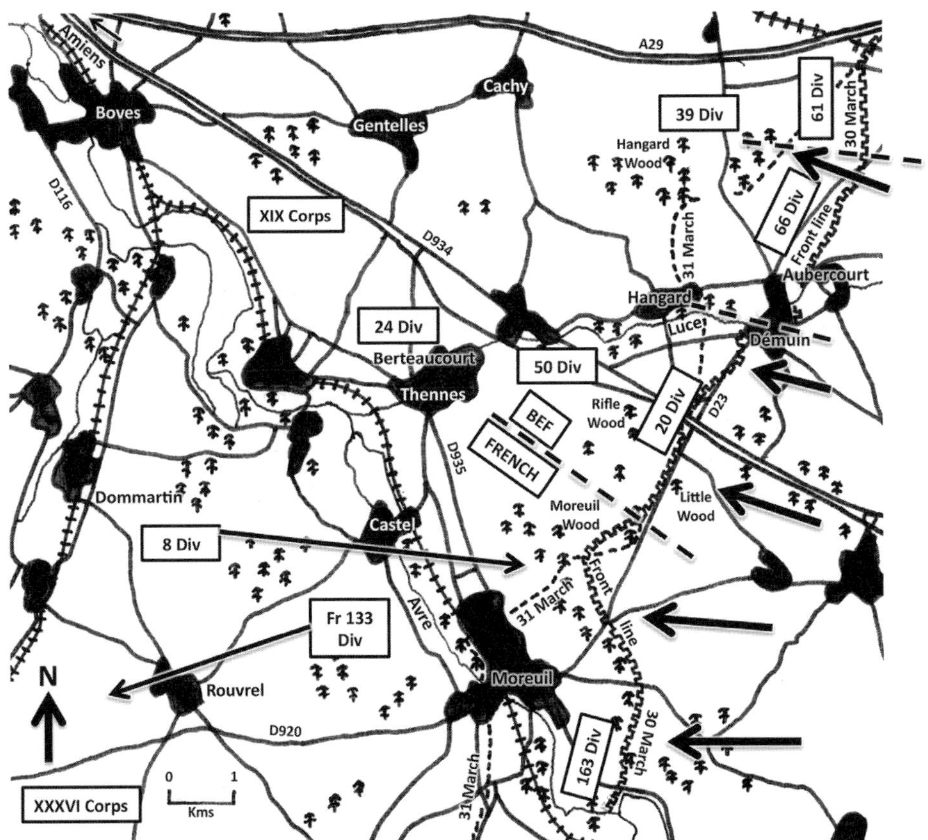

The general situation at the junction of the British and French forces east of the Avre on 30th March.

unaware of what was happening and initially did not know that Moreuil and Moreuil Wood had been evacuated. A five kilometres wide gap had opened in the Allied line. HQ XIX Corps ordered 8th Division to hold the crossings over the Avre at Castel and for 24th Division to hold the crossings over the Luce at Thennes and Berteaucourt. At 2.00 a.m. 2nd Cavalry Division near Boves, southeast of Amiens, was ordered to be ready to move at 6.30 a.m., later delayed until 8.30 a.m. At that hour the commander of the Canadian Cavalry Brigade, Brigadier General John 'Jack' Edward Bernard Seely CB CMG DSO (former Secretary of State for War 1912–14 and later Lord Mottistone), met GOC 2nd Cavalry Division. Seely was ordered to cross the Avre as quickly as possible and delay the enemy advance. This would involve clearing up the situation in Moreuil Wood and securing the line without delay. The two closest brigades (3rd and Canadian Cavalry Brigades) were ordered to work together and safeguard the line of the Moreuil – Démuin road, including Moreuil Wood. Whichever brigade arrived first was to make for the high ground northwest of the road.

Following an eighty minutes bombardment, the Germans advanced north of Moreuil Wood at 8 a.m., supported by squadrons of low flying aircraft. Although the German troops had been in action for nine days and were low on supplies, they were still determined. They entered the unoccupied Moreuil Wood in force and turned the right flank of 20th Division. This formation had all three brigades in the front line, each organised as a battalion, plus a few men of the French 133rd Division. The even weaker 50th Division was in support. As a result, 60th Brigade was forced back.

The Canadian Cavalry Brigade was the closest to Moreuil and already saddled. It moved off in the order Royal Canadian Dragoons, Lord Strathcona's Horse, Brigade Machine Gun Squadron and Fort Garry Horse. At the crossroads at Castel, Seely met a French general, who told him that the Germans were advancing in overwhelming force and that he had sent his men back across the Avre. Seely persuaded him to stay there and to support the Canadian Cavalry Brigade while it counterattacked the ridge to the east.

Seely issued simple orders to his Brigade Major, Major Charles 'Con' Connolly DSO, who was responsible for briefing the units as they arrived at the bridge at Castel. One squadron of Royal Canadian Dragoons was to occupy the southeast corner of the Wood by advancing around the northeast corner, while two squadrons seized the northern edge. One squadron of Lord Strathcona's Horse was to gallop round the northeast end to charge enemy reinforcements pouring into the Wood. It was then to occupy the eastern edge. Meanwhile two other squadrons of Lord Strathcona's Horse were to pass through the Royal Canadian Dragoons and fight through the Wood from north to south, while sections of the Brigade Machine Gun Squadron provided covering fire on the flanks.

By 9.30 a.m. the Canadians were approaching the Wood, which, due to the shape of the ground to the west, allowed them to close to within 200m unseen. However,

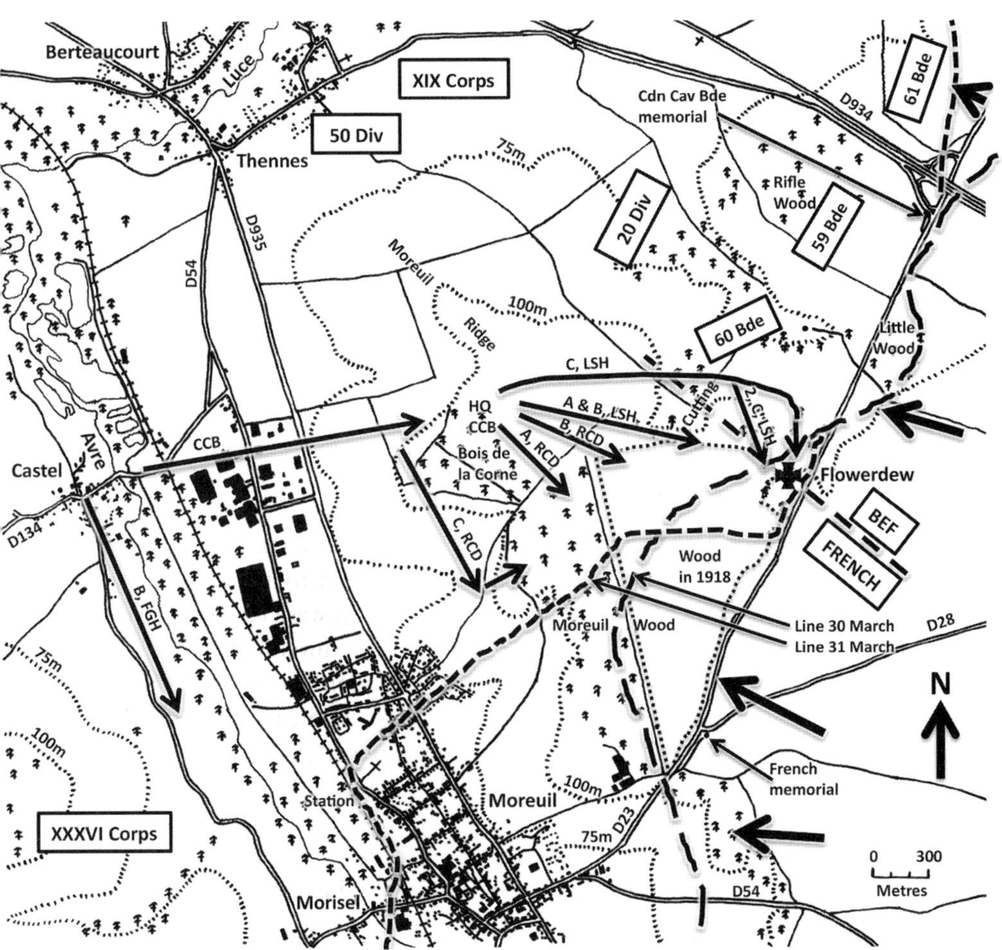

Approach Moreuil from the northeast along the D23 from Demuin. On the way visit the Canadian Cavalry Brigade memorial just south of the D934 on the west side of the D23. The memorial overlooks the whole of the battlefield albeit at some distance, with some parts obscure by trees. In Moreuil turn right at the crossroads with traffic lights and follow the D935 for 1,250m to a roundabout and turn right. There are signs from here for 'Moreuil Wood' with Canadian, British and French flags. Turn immediately left and then right and follow the road up the hill. It passes between Bois de la Corne on the left and Moreuil Wood on the right. Continue for a few hundred metres and park, then walk on until the track peters out. Look eastwards from here over the cutting from where the charge commenced. There is a café at the crossroads in the square in Moreuil. A number of abbreviations appear on the map – CCB = Canadian Cavalry Brigade, RCD = Royal Canadian Dragoons, FGH = Fort Garry Horse and LSH = Lord Strathcona's Horse.

heavy fire was coming from the northern side. Seely went forward with an ADC, orderly and twelve men of the Brigade Signal Troop to establish his HQ at the northern tip of Bois de la Corne.

The Royal Canadian Dragoons moved mounted against the southwest, northwest and northeast corners. A Squadron, commanded by Captain Roy Nordheimer, rode past Brigade HQ to the northwest corner of the Wood. Heavy machine gun and rifle fire forced the Squadron to dismount and advance with fixed bayonets. Nordheimer was shot through the right knee but the Squadron continued and the enemy in this area were driven back.

B Squadron, under Major Reginald Symonds Timmis, was about half strength (eighty as opposed to 150). It was to seize the easternmost corner but, as it moved along the north face of the Wood, it came under a hail of machine gun fire. Some survivors dismounted and got into the Wood in small parties, while others remained mounted and straggled back towards Brigade HQ. Without assistance it was clear that B Squadron could not secure the northeast corner.

C Squadron, under Captain Newcomen, headed for the southwest corner, where it was to make contact with the French in Moreuil. However, as it crested a rise it came under heavy small arms and artillery fire from as little as 400m away and wheeled left into the Wood. There were heavy casualties and many rider-less horses continued to the German gunners. They made very welcome replacements for the poor quality German horses. Seely sent B Squadron, Fort Garry Horse in reserve back across the bridge at Castel and south along the west bank of the Avre. From there it was able to bring fire to bear on the enemy flank in the southwest tip of the Wood.

Lord Strathcona's Horse formed up north of the Wood. The CO, Lieutenant Colonel Donald John MacDonald DSO MC (DSO Bar for this action), had been instructed to attack dismounted. The Brigade Machine Gun Squadron was to provide covering fire, while A and B Squadrons advanced on foot. They had just set off when the order came to provide a mounted squadron. Seely was convinced that the original plan would work if a mounted squadron swept around the northeast corner to secure it and cut off the German's escape. This task fell to **Lieutenant Gordon Flowerdew**'s C Squadron. He was briefed by the CO and BM; once the enemy had been cut off, he was to occupy the edge of the Wood facing southeast.

The northern end of Moreuil Wood, the eastern half of which no longer exists. You can drive most of the way to this point to consider the action by the Canadian Cavalry Brigade on 30th March.

Close up of the final stages of the charge by C Squadron, Lord Strathcona's Horse.

Flowerdew observed the Germans occupying the northeastern tip of the Wood. In order to gain some natural cover as the Squadron approached the objective, he planned to head for a cutting to the north of the northeastern corner of the Wood. Accordingly he ordered Lieutenant Frederick Maurice Harvey VC (MC for this action) to lead 2nd Troop to secure that point, while he followed with the other three troops. Seely rode up alongside Flowerdew to ensure that his instructions were fully understood and to offer moral support. Seely told Flowerdew that his was the most adventurous task of all, but he was confident of success. Flowerdew smiled and said, *I know, sir, I know, it is a splendid moment. I will try not to fail you.* Seely then bade him farewell and watched C Squadron ride away into the mist.

By the time that Flowerdew caught up with 2nd Troop, the first clash had already occurred. Some Germans had been caught unawares while looting a French

transport wagon and had been dealt with by sabres from horseback. Harvey's troop came under fire from the edge of the Wood and dismounted just as the rest of the Squadron arrived. Flowerdew ordered Harvey to attack, *Go ahead and we will go around the end mounted and catch them when they come out.*

Flowerdew led the remaining three troops, about seventy-five men, up a steep bank out of the cutting and into the open. As they crested the rise, they expected to find a disorganised enemy fleeing from Harvey's bayonet attack. Instead there was a steady line of Germans, possibly hundreds strong, with artillery (150mm howitzers and trench mortars) and a machine gun section, less than 300m away. The Germans were no less surprised. They had been warned to expect an attack by tanks, not cavalry, and one company had been placed to the east of the Wood. Behind were most of a battalion, a gun battery and a machine gun company.

An attack on such a well-armed and alert enemy was suicidal. However, to retreat in full view at such close range was liable to be as costly. Flowerdew did not hesitate and half-turned in his saddle to shout, *It's a charge, boys, it's a charge*. The Squadron surged forward in a blur of speed and fury. 551136 Trooper Reginald George Longley had no time to blow the call on his trumpet before he was killed (Canadian National Vimy Memorial, France). The machine gun fire was intense. 551138 Sergeant Thomas Mackay MM, leading 1st Troop, is reputed to have had fifty-nine bullet holes in one leg. The bullet holes in the other leg could not be counted as they were too close together.

Precisely what happened next remains the subject of conjecture. Some versions portray the attack as a miniature Charge of the Light Brigade, with the cavalrymen chopping their way through two lines of Germans about 200m apart, then wheeling and galloping against them from the rear. Survivors recall chaos and carnage, with the horses becoming unmanageable and bolting. British accounts mention that initially the Germans did not waver, but the charge had a great moral effect. Once inside the Wood the cavalry had an unsettling effect on the Germans. Survivors of the Royal Canadian Dragoons noticed the enemy beginning to give way. One effect was to forestall an attack by another German battalion on Moreuil, which, if successful, would have secured a crossing over the Avre and possibly opened the way to Amiens. Only one horseman made it through both enemy lines; 6098 Sergeant Frederick Arthur Wooster (MM for this action) of 1st Troop found himself alone with another party of German troops to his front. He wisely turned about and retraced his steps all the way to Brigade HQ, where he described to Seely what had happened. Wooster then returned to join Harvey's 2nd Troop, which was also augmented by the remnants of B Squadron, Royal Canadian Dragoons. German accounts seem to agree that the charge was halted 200m from the German line and achieved very little. Whatever the truth, there were heavy casualties on both sides. Whatever effect the charge may have had, in the end it proved to be little more than a delaying action.

Flowerdew was hit by two bullets in his chest and also had serious wounds to both thighs. According to Seely, he still had the strength to shout encouragement to his men as they surged past him. Lieutenant Robert Hamilton Harrower and a sergeant recovered Flowerdew from the tree line. They carried him into the Wood, where a burst of machine gun fire struck Harrower in the foot. Flowerdew said, *You had better get under cover Hammy, or they will shoot your head off next*. Four men then took Flowerdew back to a field ambulance.

C Squadron lost about seventy percent of its strength, mainly killed and wounded by rifle and machine gun fire directed from the front and both flanks. Meanwhile the Royal Canadian Dragoons had broken into the Wood and there was fierce hand-to-hand fighting. The outcome was in doubt so Seely committed his last reserves, A and C Squadrons, Fort Garry Horse. The Germans resisted strongly but were eventually forced back, with the assistance of three squadrons of British aircraft, to the eastern edge. The Germans then bombarded the Wood heavily. The Fort Garry Horse and part of 4th Hussars (3rd Cavalry Brigade) reinforced the position and by 11 a.m. the whole of the northern part of the Wood had been secured.

The southern half was still held by the Germans. The Canadian Cavalry Brigade, weakened by heavy casualties, was unable to continue the advance. 3rd Cavalry Brigade arrived on the right, with the remainder of 4th Hussars and 16th Lancers and, later, 5th Lancers. 16th Lancers joined the right flank of the Royal Canadian Dragoons. About 3 p.m., 4th Hussars and 16th Lancers advanced dismounted with about one hundred men of 2nd West Yorkshire (8th Division). The Wood was cleared to the eastern edge but with heavy losses. A German counterattack just after 4 p.m. regained the southern end. As night fell the line ran diagonally across the Wood from northeast to southwest and then to the railway station on the outskirts of Moreuil. The infantry of 23rd and 24th Brigades (8th Division), organised into three battalions under Brigadier General George Grogan (VC 27th-29th May 1918), took over from the cavalry about 8.30 p.m. 5th Lancers remained in support. The Canadian Cavalry Brigade was relieved at 2.30 a.m. on 31st March and moved back to Bois de Sencat. It had lost over 300 men and 800 horses. Lord Strathcona's Horse casualties amounted to forty-two killed and 120 wounded out of the 350 who set out, including horse-holders.

To the north, 20th Division's 59th Brigade lost Rifle Wood. A counterattack by 20th and 50th Divisions regained Rifle and Little Woods at about 3 p.m. However, at 4 p.m. the Germans retook Little Wood and entered Rifle Wood, only to be ejected again later. Another counterattack at 7 p.m. recovered the whole of the old line and re-established contact with 8th Division in Moreuil Wood. North of the Luce, 66th and 61st Divisions held the line, with 39th Division in support. The Germans forced 66th Division back towards Hangard, Bois de Hangard and Lancer Wood, where 39th Division was dug in. Elements of 116th and 117th Brigades counterattacked at 1 p.m. and advanced 500m. However, they could not hold the gains and fell back. 61st Division was shelled but was not attacked and swung back its right to confirm with 66th Division. A counterattack by two fresh battalions of 9th Australian Brigade later was supported on the right by 12th Lancers. Although unable to reach the final objective, the moral effect was great and ensured the safety of the line held by 39th Division, which had been in action for ten days continuously.

At the end of the day XIX Corps had held its own, except close to the Luce where Démuin and Aubercourt were lost, resulting in a dent in the line. On the 31st the Germans recaptured most of Moreuil Wood and occupied Rifle Wood. During the afternoon this was retaken, but only temporarily. A further attack that evening partially restored the situation but Rifle Wood and all but the northwest corner of Moreuil Wood remained in German hands. On the morning of 1st April, dismounted units of 2nd Cavalry Division attacked and the Canadian Cavalry Brigade cleared Rifle Wood. That night small parties of French troops reoccupied Moreuil.

Battle of the Avre

346 Lt Percy Storkey, 19th Battalion, AIF (5th Australian Brigade, 2nd Australian Division), Hangard Wood, France

7th April 1918

On 5th April the German March offensive came to a halt before Amiens. Astride the Somme, the exhausted XIX Corps staff was relieved by HQ III Corps at 8 p.m. By then the whole front from the junction with the French northwards to just short of Albert was held by Australian formations. They had gradually relieved tired British formations, which had borne the brunt of the German onslaught since 21st March. Rawlinson, Commander Fourth Army, commented in his diary, *'I feel happier about the general situation and I now have three brigades of Australians in reserve, so I think we shall be able to keep the Boche out of Amiens'*. Although the Germans had been halted, the Allies lacked the strength to launch a counter-offensive. Despite this, the British and French launched a series of counterattacks either side of the Luce. Meanwhile the Germans had not given up hope completely of seizing Amiens, although they were unable to make a further serious attempt until late in the month.

Foch wishing to launch the French Third and First and British Fourth Armies to clear the Moreuil – Montdidier sector, but needed forty-one divisions for such an enterprise. There were only thirty available. Any action would therefore have to be limited to First French and Fourth British Armies in two steps. The first step involved two minor operations. One by the French was to clear the Germans from the west side of the Avre and another, by the British, was to clear the woods and ravine north and northeast of Hangard. The main step would be a combined offensive to regain the line Moreuil – Démuin – Aubercourt – Warfusée.

On 4th April the Germans took Lancer Wood, the eastern part of Hangard Wood and the ravine from 18th Division. The line held by 18th Division next morning

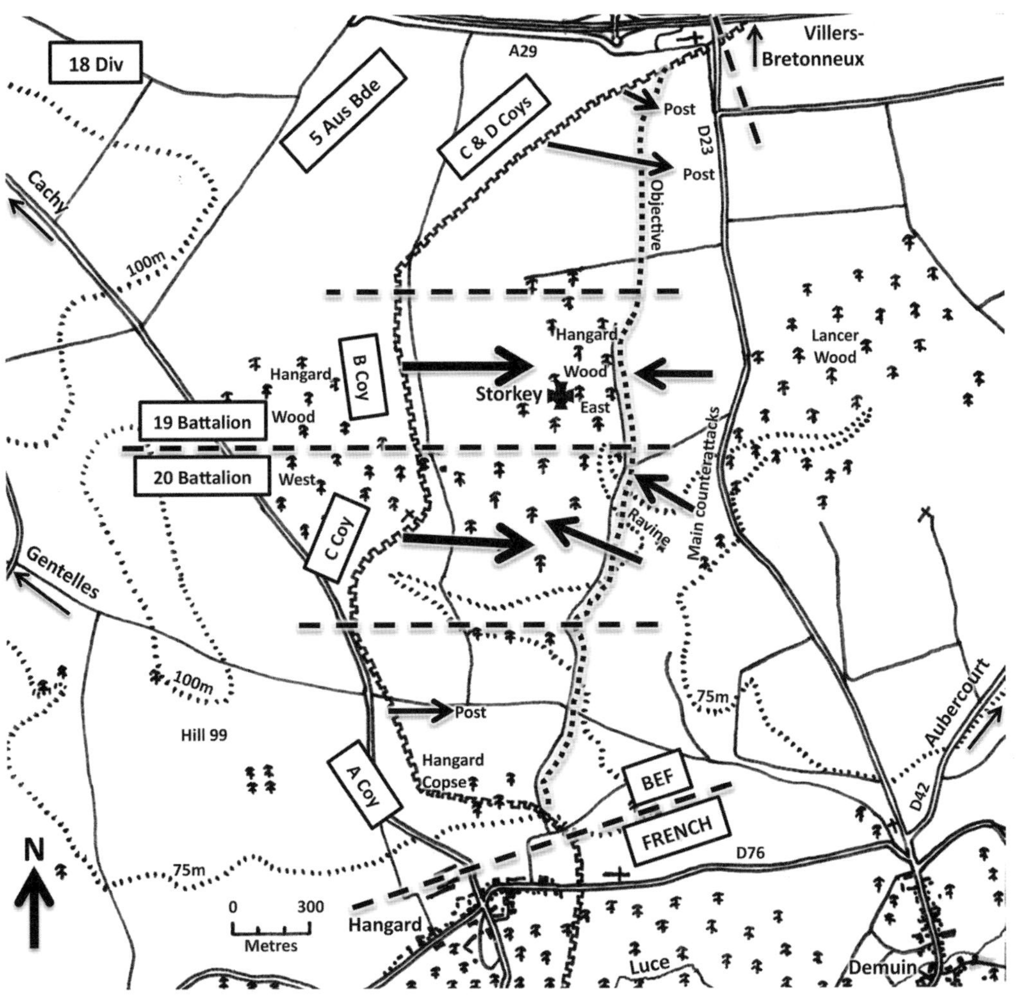

Enter Hangard from the west on the D76. At the church turn left signed for Hangard Wood British Cemetery. The Cemetery is on the right after 1,800m. Park there and walk on for another 300m until you are clear of the woods. The attack started from the left side of the track and headed into the woods to the right. The whole wooded area is private and should not be entered. Sadly this is as close as you can get to the site of Percy Storkey's VC action.

ran through the western part of the Wood, with a short right arm joining the French at Hangard Copse on Hill 99. On the afternoon of 5th April the Germans forced the French out of the cemetery east of Hangard and 6th Northamptonshire out of its posts on Hill 99. They counterattacked and succeeded in recovering the losses. However, the 6th Northamptonshire position was untenable due to enfilade machine gun fire from the German held part of Hangard Wood.

It was decided to relieve the exhausted troops of 18th Division (53rd and 54th Brigades) and 9th Australian Brigade. 5th Australian Brigade took over the line on the night of 5th/6th April, alongside the French First Army. All four battalions were in the line, from the south, 20th, 19th, 18th and 17th. 19th Battalion's strength was thirty-nine officers and 951 other ranks. It was the last to report that the relief had been complete at 5.35 a.m. on 6th April. The relief was particularly difficult, as fighting was still going on and some of the guides got lost. 10th Essex (53rd Brigade) remained available to 5th Australian Brigade for a counterattack if necessary. It was replaced by 7th Royal West Kent next day. By then the whole III Corps front was held by Australian infantry. North of the Roman road was held by 5th Australian Division, as far north as the Somme. South of the Roman road was 5th Australian Brigade under command of HQ 18th Division.

Even while the relief was in progress, orders were issued to seize the eastern part of Hangard Wood by 7th April. This was one of the minor steps envisaged in Foch's plan. 15th Australian Brigade was to advance to gain ground towards Hamel as a diversion. Although 5th Australian Brigade was fresh, the troops were already tired, having spent the previous two nights in the slow process of taking over, firstly, the Aubigny Line, and then the outposts held by 18th Division.

6th April was quiet and preparations for the attack on the eastern part of Hangard Wood were finalised. On the right (southern) flank a platoon of A Company, 20th Battalion was to push forward from the southern end of the re-entrant on Hill 99 to form a flank. Hangard Wood was to be attacked by two companies. On the right was C Company, 20th Battalion under Captain Victor B Portman MC. On the left was B Company, 19th Battalion under Captain Clarence Wallach MC. Both companies had some machine guns attached. To the north two platoons, one each from C and D Companies, 19th Battalion, were to push forward to form the left flank of the attack.

The assault troops were told that air reconnaissance showed that the Wood was held lightly. In reality it was held by two battalions (II & III/133rd Infantry Regiment, 24th (Saxon) Reserve Division). The aim was to push through the Wood and before dawn to dig in just beyond the road on the far side, where they would find *a clear field of fire for 400 yards*. They were to hold all day. The following night both battalions would move forward into the new line.

The southeastern corner of Hangard Wood East looking north into the ravine. The thick vegetation facing Storkey's men is apparent.

The assault companies assembled on a white tape laid by 7th Field Company, Australian Engineers with infantry assistance in the early hours of 7th April. There was no enemy interference. The men were so tired that some fell asleep on the start line. No contact was made between the attacking companies on their inside flanks before 4.55 a.m., when the barrage started. It was rather ragged and almost no shells fell in front of 19th Battalion. Captain Wallach waited a minute, in case of a mistake in timing but there was still no artillery support, just a few intermittent shells.

Wallach's second in command, **Lieutenant Percy Storkey**, had fallen asleep and awoke to find the Company had already advanced seventy metres. They were crossing 350m of open ground before the Wood and he hurried to catch up. There was no opposition from the front but enfilade machine gun fire from the ridge east of Hangard on the right flank caused great loss. As the Wood was entered Wallach was shot through both knees and two junior officers were killed. About a quarter of Wallach's company were hit before reaching the Wood. Clarence Wallach died of his wounds on 22nd April as a result of blood poisoning setting in (Étretat Churchyard Extension, France – II D 1).

Clarence Wallach, one of six brothers who enlisted despite the family being of German origin, played Rugby Union for Australia in five test matches in 1913–14 and another five non-test matches. He and a number of his brothers were members of the Eastern Suburbs Rugby Club. He also played ten matches for New South Wales. Clarence served in 19th Battalion at Gallipoli from September 1915 and later in France. He was on leave with the AIF Football Team in England from December 1917 until February 1918. In April he was severely wounded at Hangard Wood and, although evacuated to hospital, died of his wounds a few weeks later. His possessions were lost when the transport SS *Barunga* was torpedoed by U-*108*.

Storkey took command. He had four men with him and Lieutenant Fred N Lipscomb (MC for this action) had another six. They plunged into the undergrowth of head high saplings and were continually held up by telephone wires. The intention was to get behind the machine guns that had hit them while crossing the open ground in front of the Wood.

They made their way eastwards and then south until reaching a clearing (probably a track) heading south. Along its western side, in six short sections of trench, were a number of machine gun teams and about one hundred Germans with their backs to them. They were still engaging parts of Wallach's company as they struggled forward. Storkey ordered a charge, as if the rest of the Battalion was behind him. He was on one flank and Lipscomb was on the

B Company 19th Battalion attacked from the right of this track into the trees on the left, Hangard Wood East. The track leads to Hangard Wood British Cemetery and ultimately back to Hangard village. Percy Storkey's VC action was about in the centre of this picture, but inside the tree line and is not visible from the track.

other, with the ten men between them. Before the first Germans realised what was happening, Storkey's men were in the trenches with bombs, pistols and bayonets. The Germans in the nearest trench surrendered immediately but those further away hesitated. Storkey called on them to surrender and, when nothing happened, he climbed out of the trench and shot three with his revolver, which then jammed. Some of his men threw in a couple of grenades and about thirty Germans were killed. Three officers and fifty men surrendered. They were sent to the rear with a two man escort, who carried away one of the machine guns (now at the Australian War Memorial, Canberra).

Opposition to the advance practically ceased and Storkey's men pushed on through the Wood to the road running along the eastern edge. They could not see the promised *clear field of fire*. Indeed the Wood continued beyond the road to the bottom of the ravine and from ground level little could be seen. About 350m in front was an open area with a trench line, where at least two companies of Germans were deploying to counterattack.

Storkey had a dilemma. If he went forward into the thinner vegetation he would be in the bottom of the valley with the Germans above him. If he stayed where he was, his men had no field of fire. With no other options available, Storkey decided to pull back to the start line. Before retiring he spoke to a platoon commander of 20th Battalion to ensure that Portman was aware of the changed situation. The Company had suffered sixty-eight casualties, including four officers.

In 20th Battalion, Portman's company was not in position at zero hour. It ran into a thin chain of machine gun posts, each post containing two guns. These were overcome relatively easily, some crews being killed, while others fled. They pressed on, extending the flank to the left to try to contact 19th Battalion, and emerged on

the eastern side of the Wood, where the ground dipped suddenly to the ravine. On the southeastern corner the growth was sparse and the bare slope fell into the branch ravine separating the Wood from Hill 99. The advance made little further headway against enfilade machine gun fire from the far side of the valley. The Company was held up sixty metres inside the edge of the Wood.

Portman was in a better position than Storkey. The Company was high up on the edge of a spur and the thin scrub allowed a good field of fire. However, it was exposed to German fire from the spur opposite and the ravine was almost impossible to see into, providing the enemy with a covered approach for a counterattack.

Several hundred Germans appeared on the spur screening Aubercourt and, at 6 a.m., they attacked from the ravine against Portman's right, covered by intense machine gun fire. The extreme right of the company was annihilated but the Germans did not press on. Portman reinforced that flank with a sergeant and six

Hangard Wood from the south-southwest on Hill 99. There is a noticeable dip between the eastern and western portions. Just to the left of the dip is Hangard Wood British Cemetery.

men. He learned that 19th Battalion was falling back on the left but there was no immediate threat on that flank, so he set some men digging in on the right, facing south. Their entrenching tools had made little impression on the chalk by 7 a.m. when the Germans were seen assembling in the depression ahead. However, the Lewis gunners twice countered German frontal attacks and inflicted huge casualties.

The German came on again on the right. A machine gun caused heavy casualties to the Australians and a corporal and two men were sent to stalk and destroy it with rifle grenades. The machine gun fell silent but others, from the direction of Hangard, swept the crest. As a result the Germans began to infiltrate round the right flank. Portman pulled back this flank and he was reinforced by the left company (D) of the Battalion.

By noon 20th Battalion held a zig-zag line south of and through Hangard Wood. 19th Battalion was back in the original line, leaving two advanced posts in front. With his right flank threatened and his left flank wide open, Portman eventually had no option other than to pull back to the start positions. The sergeant and six men on the right were eventually overcome. Portman and some of his men stayed on the western edge of the Wood for some time, shooting down Germans as they tried to advance and covering the retirement of the wounded. The final withdrawal took place at 8.30 p.m.

The 20th Battalion platoon on the far right did not reach its objective and dug in short of it. The two platoons of 19th Battalion on the left flank encountered little opposition and dug in with good fields of fire.

Storkey reported to his CO, Major Jack Walker, at about 8.30 a.m. and was ordered to go back and reoccupy the abandoned positions. Storkey refused, explaining that he had almost no men left and the impossible nature of the task due to the shape of the ground. Storkey said he would go back but asked to speak to the brigade commander first to explain the situation. Walker was exasperated by Storkey but, when he saw the fifty-three German prisoners being escorted to the rear, realised that Storkey's attack had been partially successful. Storkey was not sent forward again and briefed Brigadier General Smith at Brigade HQ at Gentelles. Smith accepted Storkey's assessment of the situation. Storkey spent the rest of the day bringing in the wounded, who were lying in shell holes west of the Wood. When the remnants of the Company reoccupied their old positions, they were hit by a German bombardment. Storkey was badly shaken, Lipscomb was wounded and 4358 Private Albert Barling, a signaller, was killed (Hangard Communal Cemetery Extension – I J 18).

So the attack failed. The northern half could only have been held by advancing another 360m to where the enemy counterattack force was seen assembling. The southern half, although successful, could not be maintained in isolation. The total cost was 151 casualties. To succeed, any future attack must include an advance south of Hangard to deal with the enfilade machine gun fire. A much larger attack was planned for 9th April to retake Moreuil and Hangard and Lancer Woods but it

Albert Barling was with Percy Storkey when a heavy shell hit their trench. Albert was killed and is buried in Hangard Communal Cemetery Extension on the D76 Démuin road east of Hangard village.

was cancelled on a number of occasions because the French were not ready. A new German offensive on the Lys on 9th April meant that reserves were sent north and ended any hope of launching this attack.

On the evening of 9th April, the Germans captured Hangard, which the French, with British support, retook that night. Operations on 11th-15th April retook more ground but the French line did not move appreciably. The British right flank remained open to observation and fire. Rawlinson protested to Haig that he had received nothing but promises from the French. They did attack on 18th April and gained some ground but the situation remained unsatisfactory, with the open flank threatening the Cachy plateau and Villers Bretonneux.

Battle of the Ancre 1918

345 Capt The Rev'd Theodore Hardy, Royal Army Chaplains' Department att'd 8th Lincolnshire (63rd Brigade, 37th Division), Rossignol Wood, Bucquoy & Gommecourt, France

5th & 25th-27th April 1918

By 30th March the German advance had effectively ended. Although severe fighting continued, little further progress was made. Ludendorff's main objective was to secure Amiens but he postponed further operations until 4th April, in order to allow for rest and preparation. Some local actions continued. Foch issued his first General Directive: the Allies were to check the enemy, remain in close touch and retain free use of Amiens. The front was to be maintained on the existing line, while a strong reserve was formed to stem further enemy attacks or to take the offensive. At midnight on 1st April, Fifth Army returned to Haig's command.

The British knew that the Germans were preparing another offensive, possibly as far north as Ypres. Haig believed that they would concentrate on knocking out the British first. However, initially he did not know if this meant a renewal of the Picardy offensive (Michael), or a new strike against Armentières (George I) or Ypres (George II). He had only one intact division in reserve (57th). Other divisions that were not in the line were exhausted and reconstituting. The situation was so critical that Haig warned General Plumer to be prepared to abandon the Ypres Salient, in order to shorten the line. Intelligence reports began to indicate that the enemy was concentrating between Lens and the La Bassée Canal. On 3rd April, Foch issued his second General Directive, which tasked the French with launching an offensive at Montdidier, while the British attacked between the Luce and the Ancre to free Amiens.

In the meantime, the final phase of the German offensive in Picardy commenced on 4th April with a last effort to reach Amiens. The intention was to bring heavy artillery within range of the city in order to support the final attack the following day. However, the operations on the 4th came nowhere near achieving their objective.

On 5th April a general offensive was ordered against Third Army but it amounted to little more than a series of local actions. These aimed to extend the shallow bridgehead over the Ancre from Buire to Hamel, to break in south of Hébuterne and to capture Bucquoy. The bombardment opened at 7 a.m. but the British, who replied forcibly, were well prepared. VII Corps lost a narrow strip of land and V Corps sustained a few losses in the afternoon, inconsequential in comparison with German casualties.

IV Corps had three divisions in the line facing more than six enemy divisions. From south to north these were the New Zealand, 37th (with 4th Australian Brigade attached) and 42nd. The New Zealanders absorbed five separate attacks and only lost la Signy Farm.

63rd Brigade (37th Division) had relieved 187th Brigade (62nd Division) and a battalion of 125th Brigade (42nd Division) in the Rossignol Wood sector on the night of 1st/2nd April. The following night the Brigade extended its right to take over another 900m of front from 4th Australian Brigade. On 4th April orders were issued for an attack to straighten out the line and improve the Brigade's position. 8th Lincolnshire was to attack on the right and 8th Somerset light Infantry on the left. Each battalion was to be preceded by six tanks from A Company, 10th Battalion Tank Corps. Their move forward to the start positions was to be covered by intermittent artillery and machine gun fire. Battalions were to advance with two companies leading, each with one platoon forward. A third company was in close support and the fourth was held in reserve. Two mortars of 63rd Trench Mortar Battery were to accompany each assault battalion to suppress any strongpoints encountered. 4th Middlesex, in reserve, was to move two companies forward to occupy the start positions of the assault battalions in Cod Trench after zero hour.

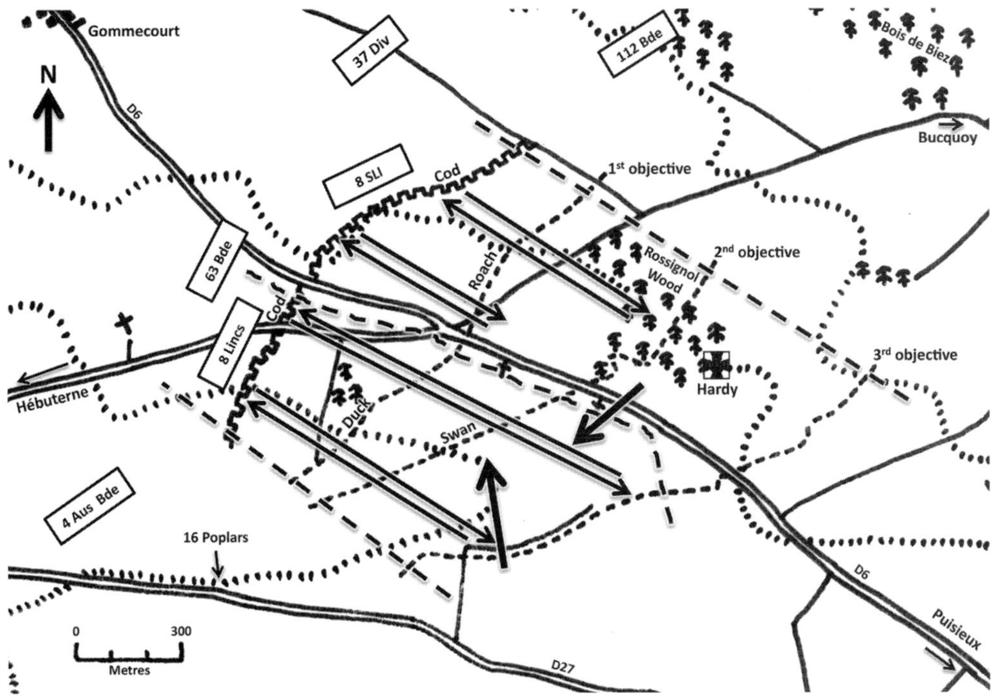

Leave Gommecourt on the D6 southeast towards Puisieux. Pass Rossignol Wood and the quarry on the left and then find somewhere to park on the right side of the road, where there are usually places to pull over. Look back to the edge of Rossignol Wood from where Theodore Hardy and George Radford rescued the wounded soldier.

The attack was supported by six artillery brigades for the creeping barrage, while four batteries of howitzers provided a smoke screen and fifteen heavy batteries fired on trenches, approaches and strongpoints. Fifty machine guns were to engage targets in depth. Another seven machine gun teams were to advance with the infantry to cover consolidation and engage targets of opportunity.

16th Battalion AIF was to cooperate by advancing on the right. On the left, 6th Bedfordshire (112th Brigade) was to withdraw by one hour prior to zero. 1st Essex was to cooperate on this flank and join up with 8th Somerset Light Infantry on the final objective. 1st Essex and 13th Royal Fusiliers were also to demonstrate with small arms fire and smoke candles (wind allowing) to divert German attention and also to screen the attack area from the high ground around Serre. At the end of the attack 1st Essex would be in contact with 63rd Brigade on the right and with 13th Royal Fusiliers on its left. 6th Bedfordshire would have fallen back into support.

The attack was to be launched at 5.30 a.m. on 5th April. Conditions were appalling as the troops assembled in pitch darkness and heavy rain. One company of 8th Somerset Light Infantry took four hours to reach its start line. 8th Lincolnshire's supporting tanks were not able to advance and its right was suffering heavy casualties within fifty metres of leaving the start line. The left platoon was also hit by enemy machine guns after covering 135m. However, the first objective was reached at 5.45 a.m. and about one hundred prisoners were taken and up to ninety enemy were killed or wounded. There was less resistance in the second objective but machine gun fire from both flanks continued. There was heavy bombing on the right in the fight for the final objective in a sunken road 1,100m from the start line. The objective was taken except for two strongpoints on the right and, by 7.45 a.m., consolidation was in progress. The carrying platoon and a blocking party came forward and joined the assault troops in the line. However, there was no contact with 8th Somerset Light Infantry on the left or with the Australians on the right.

At 9 a.m. German reinforcements were seen approaching Rossignol Wood in lorries. Pressure mounted and the small garrison in Swan Trench was driven south into the main trench system. At 1 p.m. the Germans advanced in strength from the area of the strongpoints on the right and cut 8th Lincolnshire in two. For the next three hours the Battalion, outnumbered and short of bombs, fought its way back in good order, inflicting heavy casualties on the enemy. Around 3 p.m. about 200 Germans advanced out of the south side of Rossignol Wood. They were severely handled by machine guns at 16 Poplars and small arms fire. The Battalion reached the original front line by 5.30 p.m. 4th Australian Brigade sent a party to establish a post at 16 Poplars on the right of 63rd Brigade but, when only thirty metres from the objective, news arrived that 8th Lincolnshire had already retired and the party withdrew as well.

On the left, 8th Somerset Light Infantry hesitated when its supporting tanks did not appear and the barrage was lost. Nevertheless the first objective fell with little resistance and about fifty prisoners were taken. The second wave leapfrogged the first and met no real opposition until reaching the western edge of Rossignol Wood. There the attack faltered, particularly on the right, due to a lack of any form of cover. Repeated attempts to get forward merely added to the casualty list.

Due to the thickness of the Wood, the left company lost contact with the right company and was heavily counterattacked by enemy bombers and machine gun parties. This failed to dislodge the company but it was then shelled and suffered heavy casualties. It threw back a defensive right flank but lack of bombs and reduced strength forced its withdrawal to the north side of the Wood. The company reorganised in Hook Trench, (not identified) collected some bombs and made a further attempt to seize the objective. It regained the edge of the Wood but was still out of contact on the right and, having suffered further heavy casualties, it was unable to hold the second objective. On the left, close to the Wood, the Germans surrounded and captured an officer and twenty men.

The company on the right reached the first objective with many casualties and it was counterattacked. The Germans also suffered heavy losses. With its left in the air, a retirement to Roach and Cod Trenches became inevitable.

4th Middlesex sent forward rifle grenades for 8th Lincolnshire at 8.45 a.m. At 10.30 a.m. one and a half platoons with a Lewis gun were sent forward to hold Roach Trench, while an officer and twenty men reinforced 8th Somerset light Infantry in Rossignol Wood. The platoon in Roach Trench stopped an enemy bombing attack from the south and counterattacked to drive it back. The reserve company supplied carrying parties to bring forward bombs, trench mortar rounds and ammunition. The remainder of that company moved up to Cod Trench at 12.30 p.m. to cover the withdrawal of the assault battalions.

The brigade commander was going to use two companies of 4th Middlesex to launch a deliberate attack from north of Rossignol Wood. However, he could only do this if a reserve battalion was put at his disposal to secure his own line first. On the left of IV Corps, the Germans attacked the Bucquoy salient at 9 a.m., striking the left of 37th and the right of 42nd Divisions. The first attack was held off but, at 10.40 a.m., the Germans broke in and took the northeast and east of Bucquoy. At 12.20 p.m. HQ 37th Brigade learned that at least part of Bucquoy had been lost and the plan to attack with 4th Middlesex was abandoned.

37th Brigade had found the Germans to be in far greater strength than expected due to their own impending attack. Failure could also be attributed in part to a shortage of bombs and mud-clogged rifles. Brigade HQ reported the following casualties – forty-four killed or died of wounds, 187 wounded and 104 missing.

Elsewhere the fighting went on all day and the northeast corner of Bucquoy was recovered, but the Germans held on to the eastern half. With this the German offensive in Picardy came to an end, leaving them with a dilemma. Their attacks had gradually diverged, lost concentration and outran their supply chain. The gains were mainly the devastated areas from the 1916 fighting on the Somme. They had failed to secure vital railheads and their losses in men and horses had been enormous.

The south-eastern edge of Rossignol Wood is on the right, with the D6 Gommecourt road on the left. This was the boundary between 8th Somerset Light Infantry on the right and 8th Lincolnshire on the left, both attacking towards the camera position. There is nothing more threatening in the area today than a few curious but docile cows.

Sergeant George Radford, who assisted Theodore Hardy on 5th April, was killed on 21st August and is buried in Gommecourt British Cemetery No.2, near Hébuterne. His grave is fourth from the left in the front row. Rossignol Wood is beyond on the skyline.

By 27th March Prince Rupprecht believed that they had lost the war. The Germans had three options – stop and rest, carry on regardless or try elsewhere. They chose the latter and halted this offensive on 5th April in order to launch a new offensive to the north.

When the assault troops of 63rd Brigade fell back, **Reverend Theodore Hardy** stayed with a wounded man only ten metres from a German occupied pillbox on the south-eastern edge of Rossignol Wood. Hardy remained until dusk and then went to seek assistance. He surprised the troops in a forward post, as they believed everyone in front had withdrawn. 7209 Sergeant George Radford (8th Somerset Light Infantry) agreed to accompany Hardy. The wounded man was too weak to stand but, between them, they managed to drag him back to the British lines. Radford was awarded the DCM for his actions that day in capturing a pillbox and two machine guns.

Remarkable though Hardy's efforts were for a man in his fifties, he went on to perform further outstanding deeds of bravery. 63rd Brigade was in Corps Reserve until it relieved 187th Brigade on 23rd/24th April in the Bucquoy – Biez Wood sector. The main activity during this tour was extensive patrolling. On 25th April a patrol attacked an enemy post in a ruined village. Hardy was at company HQ when he heard an outbreak of firing and followed the patrol. About 350m in front of the front line he found a badly wounded officer whom he was unable to move. There was a great deal of firing and at one time the Germans were between Hardy and the front line, where they captured three soldiers. Eventually Hardy managed to get assistance and the wounded officer was recovered.

On 26th April a shell exploded in a post at Bucquoy and Hardy went to assist, despite the heavy shell and mortar fire. He set to work rescuing those buried under the rubble and succeeded in freeing one man who had been buried completely. Another man he tried to rescue was found to be dead before he could be dug out. Throughout this action Hardy was in imminent danger of being crushed by a dangerously overhanging wall.

Chapter Two

Battles of the Lys

Battle of Estaires

347 2Lt Joseph Collin, 1/4th King's Own (Royal Lancaster) (164th Brigade, 55th Division), Givenchy, France
348 2Lt John Schofield, 2/5th Lancashire Fusiliers (164th Brigade, 55th Division), Givenchy, France
349 Pte Richard Masters, Army Service Corps att'd 141st Field Ambulance RAMC (1st Division), Gorre, near Béthune, France

9th April 1918

During the Michael offensive in Picardy in March the Germans continued to prepare for operations further north. Various combinations of attacks were considered until, on 24th March, planning began for a modified George I (La Bassée Canal to Armentières) and George II (Ypres) offensive, known as Georgette. The initial thrust was to be towards Hazebrouck, spreading next day to Messines Ridge. On 2nd April it became clear to the British that the Germans were about to attack somewhere north of Arras, where there was a maximum of eighty kilometres between the British lines and the coast. Even a short retreat there would bring vital base areas and ports within range of German guns. Giving up large tracts of ground to absorb the attack was not an option.

Intelligence indicated that the enemy wished to secure Vimy Ridge from Arras (Mars) and from Lens (Valkyrie) simultaneously. There was also strong evidence that an attack would be mounted against the Portuguese north of the La Bassée Canal. By early April the Germans had thirty-one fresh divisions and sixteen of these were in the area between the Oise and Lille. Haig requested French assistance but Foch insisted that an offensive by the French First and British Fourth Armies between the Avre and Somme rivers on 8th April should take priority. Haig pointed out that any success gained by that offensive would not make up for a disaster further north. Foch stuck to his plan. On 6th April the Germans attacked the French at La Fère (Archangel) to draw attention away from the north. Meanwhile German

The opening of the German offensive on 9th April 1918.

artillery preparations indicated that the attack would fall between the La Bassée Canal and Fleurbaix. This was confirmed late on 8th April, when enemy movement was detected opposite the Portuguese.

The German offensive on 9th April fell on the left and centre of First Army and extended into the right of Second Army on the 10th. In First Army the attack frontage was held by XI Corps (55th and 2nd Portuguese Divisions, with 51st Division in reserve), on the right, and XV Corps (40th and 34th Divisions, with 50th Division in reserve), on the left. 55th Division had been resting since Cambrai in November but all the other formations had been in the March battles. However, the defences were good as the British had been in this area since the first winter of the war.

The Portuguese on the left of XI Corps were weak, morale was low and they were not expected to withstand an attack. Accordingly they were allocated the Quinque Rue – Picantin sector, which in previous years had been so wet as to preclude offensive action before May. However, it had been a dry winter and it was therefore decided to man most of the Forward Zone in XI Corps' area with the Portuguese, while British troops manned the Battle Zone behind. Plans to relieve the Portuguese on the night of 9th/10th April by 50th Division and 166th Brigade (55th Division) were forestalled by the German offensive.

55th Division on the right of XI Corps held the Givenchy front, with the La Bassée Canal as its right flank. 164th Brigade was on the right and 165th Brigade was on the left, with 166th Brigade in reserve. This position was crucial as it dominated the British rear areas. The defences were well constructed, with some shelters twelve metres deep and tunnels allowed access to various parts of the line. A Line of Resistance was selected, running along the front line on the right but on the left, where breastworks had been constructed due to the wet ground, it ran along the front of the Battle Zone. Known as the Village Line, it ran along the front of the villages of Le Plantin and Festubert. Further north a series of switches continued the Line of Resistance along the rear of the Forward Zone. The defence was based upon platoon posts, well protected with wire to channel the attackers into killing zones. These posts were to be held regardless of what happened around them. The remaining platoons were to launch immediate counterattacks.

At 4.15 a.m. on 9th April a gas and high explosives bombardment fell on the rear areas, from the La Bassée Canal northwards for twenty-four kilometres, to Frelinghien, northeast of Armentières. It was heaviest in the Givenchy – Laventie sector (55th and 2nd Portuguese Divisions). The Portuguese had three weak brigades in the line facing four German divisions. British mounted troops were prepared to cover any gaps that may result until relieved by 51st Division. 50th Division sent a brigade to occupy the line Bout Deville – Cockshy House in the Portuguese Battle Zone.

At 6 a.m. the bombardment slackened and switched to the front line before 7 a.m., returning to full strength at 8 a.m. German patrols pressed forward and at 7.30 a.m. the Portuguese began to drift to the rear. At 8.45 a.m. the German main body attacked and by 10 a.m. most of the Portuguese had passed through the British manning the Battle Zone. The speed of the Portuguese collapse surprised even those who had predicted it. However, 55th Division had anticipated this and the codeword 'Bustle' was issued at 4.30 a.m. for units to move to pre-planned covering positions. On the right, HQ 164th Brigade ordered the support company of 2/5th Lancashire Fusiliers at Gorre to move forward to Tuning Fork and Le Preol North. At the same time the Battalion HQ moved up to the Village Line, close to Pont Fixe, to take command of its three companies there. It arrived at 7.10 a.m. On the left, two companies of 6th Kings (165th Brigade) and a company of 4th South Lancashire (Pioneers) occupied the posts at Route A Keep and Tuning Fork,

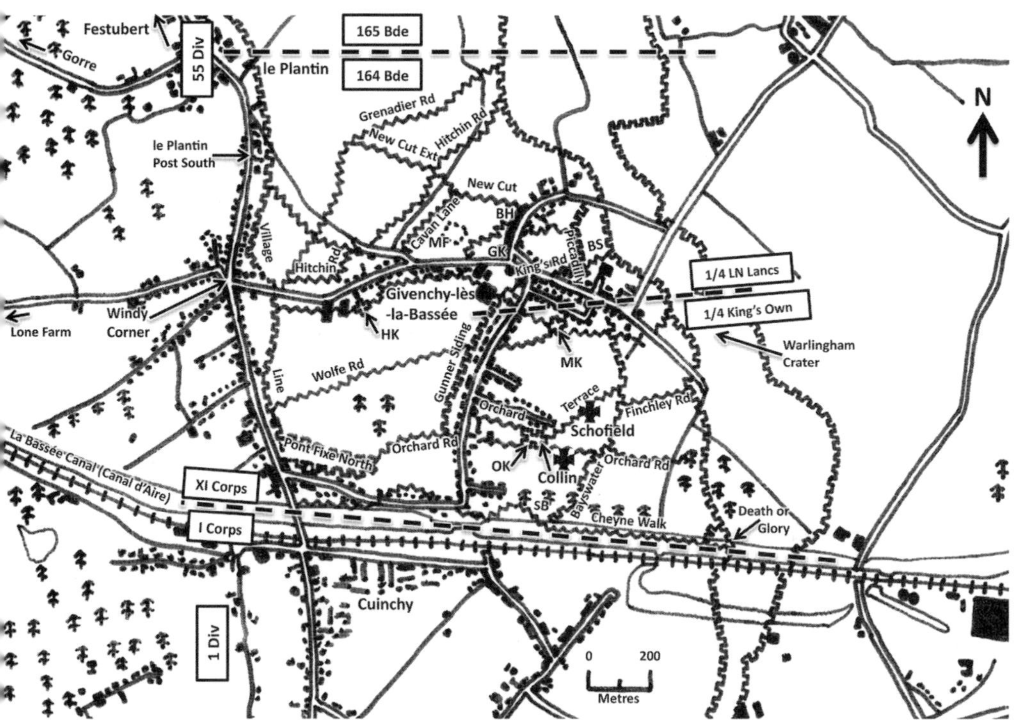

The La Bassée Canal (Canal d'Aire) was widened in the 1960s, so defences that were on its north bank in 1918, such as Cheyne Walk, appear in the waterway on the map. A number of abbreviations are used – OK = Orchard Keep, MK = Mairie Keep, MF = Moat Farm, GK = Givenchy Keep, HK = Herts Keep, BS = Berkeley Street, WC = Windy Corner, BH = Bunny Hutch and SB = Spoil Bank. A good view of the battle area can be had from the corner of the track leading from Givenchy communal cemetery to the canal, at the point where Finchley Road reached the front line. Also from the southern end of the cemetery. Drive south from the centre of Givenchy towards the canal and after 400m turn left into Rue des Fontenelles, which runs parallel with and just north of the former Orchard Road trench. Drive to the eastern end of the road to be close to the sites of both VC actions. Return to the main north-south road and continue southwards. Just before the road swings right to run parallel with the canal, turn left into Rue du Moulin. Drive to the end, where there is ample parking space, and walk onto the Spoil Bank. Views to the north over the area of the battle on 9th April 1918 are restricted by dense vegetation but there are a few gaps and gaining the extra elevation is worth the effort.

covering the left of the Line of Resistance. At 7 a.m., 10th King's (166th Brigade in support) was sent to Tuning Fork to extend the line to the northwest.

Thus even before the German attack began, a defensive flank had been established in depth, which was fortuitous as three German divisions attacked 55th Division at 8.45 a.m. They closed to within twenty metres of the advanced posts under cover of fog and the creeping barrage. However, the British troops were ready and willing to resist. At 9.40 a.m. XI Corps ordered 154th Brigade (51st Division) to Locon on the boundary of 55th and 2nd Portuguese Divisions in the Green (Army) Line, close to 152nd Brigade, leaving 153rd Brigade as the only reserve in the Corps.

In 164th Brigade, on the right of 55th Division, 1/4th King's Own had taken over the right of the Brigade's front on 1st April, from the canal bank at Death or Glory Sap to Warlingham Crater. Three companies held the front line (from the right A, B and D) and C Company was in support holding Gunner Siding and Orchard and Mairie Keeps. The bombardment destroyed the front line and Battalion HQ had numerous casualties but the advanced posts there, and throughout 164th Brigade's area, held out and inflicted enormous casualties. At 9.40 a.m. the Germans reached the Battalion HQ.

On the left was 1/4th Loyal North Lancashire. At 8.40 a.m. the Germans practically surrounded Moat Farm and Givenchy Keep, penetrated into the northeast of Givenchy and set up a machine gun near the church. Ten minutes later they surrounded the Battalion HQ, which held on. A machine gun post in a concrete emplacement, at the junction of Cavan Lane and New Cut Extension, carried on firing. This was despite the enemy entering the rear compartment, where they were checked by the crew with their revolvers. Herts Keep poured heavy fire into the enemy in Hitchin Road and prevented a breakthrough there. However, the Germans succeeded in breaking through on the left and captured the forward posts. A defensive right flank was established in Berkeley Street. By 9.45 a.m. Piccadilly Trench was surrounded. Later the defensive flank fell back to King's Road and Piccadilly Trench was lost.

Meanwhile, soon after 8.30 a.m. in 1/4th King's Own's position on the right, Death or Glory Sap was encircled by the Germans under cover of thick fog. They got into Cheyne Walk to the west, but the Sap held. They surged on and got into Gunner Siding at the junction with Orchard Road, but were held there. They also penetrated Bayswater in several places and established a machine gun post in Orchard Keep. Spoil Bank and Mairie Keep held out. During the early part of the fighting **Second Lieutenant Joseph Collin** held Orchard Keep with sixteen

Looking north from Spoil Bank towards Givenchy with the approximate lines of the various trenches involved in the Joseph Collin and John Schofield VC actions on 9th April.

men of 12 Platoon. The enemy was upon them quickly and Collin ordered rapid fire. He leapt onto the parapet and personally shot three of the attackers. While Collin's party fought off a vastly superior force to their front, a party of at least fifty Germans passed them on the right heading along Orchard Road.

At 10 a.m. the situation became critical as the Germans penetrated to the Cuinchy road near the Canal, at Windy Corner and at Le Plantin Post South. One patrol reached as far as Lone Farm. It was destroyed there by a section of 276th Brigade RFA being pulled out of its emplacement and engaging the enemy at point blank range. The Germans were threatening to separate 164th and 165th Brigades. However, this was to be the high water mark of their advance. From then on commanders from section up to battalion began to restore the situation with counterattacks. Elements of 1/4th Loyal North Lancashire relieved the situation around the Battalion HQ and cleared the Germans from around the pillbox at the junction of Cavan Lane and New Cut at 10.30 a.m.

At 12.55 p.m., when his party had been reduced to only five men, Collin organised a slow fighting withdrawal of about 100m to just in front of Gunner Siding. Having been reinforced there by 9 Platoon and a few men from B Company, a stand was made. The Germans brought up a machine gun, which Collin went after on his own. He fired the contents of his revolver into the enemy crew and then threw a grenade, killing four of them, wounding two or three others and putting the gun out of action. Seeing another machine gun, he set up a Lewis gun on a high point on the parapet and kept the enemy at bay until he was mortally wounded. The party fell back to Gunner Siding, where it reorganised and bombed forward again. This, combined with rifle fire from Marie Keep, Wolfe Road and Gunner Siding, succeeded in forcing the Germans to retreat. By 3.35 p.m. C Company, including the few survivors of 12 Platoon under Lance Sergeant GJ Moon, had recaptured Orchard Keep. Lance Corporal J Pollitt, who was wounded and taken prisoner by the Germans, managed to kill his escort and made his way back. Pollitt is reputed to have been involved in two other VC actions (probably Tom Mayson on 31st July 1917 and James Hewitson on 26th April 1918).

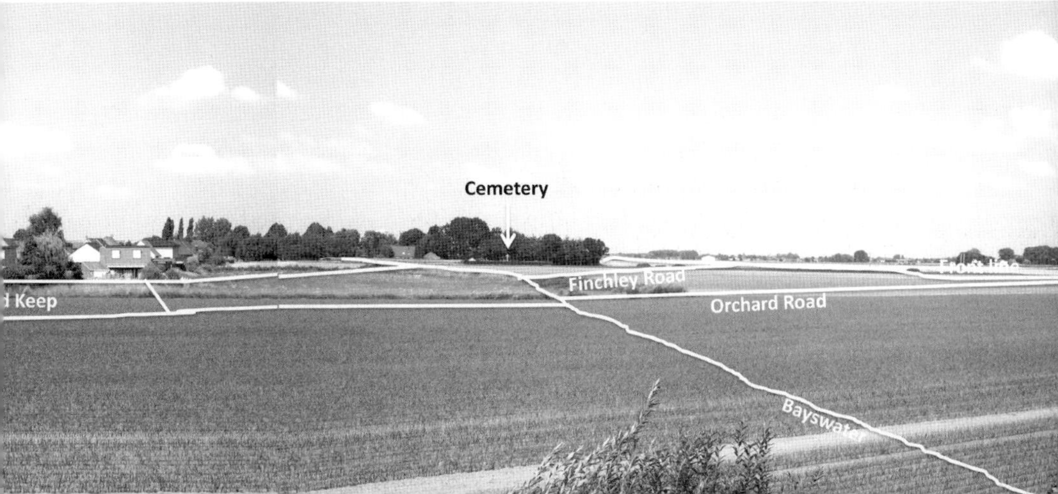

The same ground as in the previous picture but from the eastern end of Rue des Fontenelles. Givenchy cemetery is on the far left and Spoil Bank on the far right.

Elsewhere the posts in the rear held firm and platoon counterattacks drove the enemy out again. By midday only a few houses near Windy Corner were still held by the Germans. Assistance also came from south of the Canal where 1st Gloucestershire (1st Division) lined the south bank and batteries were pulled from their shelters to fire into 55th Division's area. During the afternoon the German gains were gradually recovered. The right company of 1/4th King's Own cleared Cheyne Walk and relieved Death and Glory Sap. At 5 p.m. only Warlingham Crater and Lower Finchley Road were still held by the Germans. A company each from 2/5th Lancashire Fusiliers and 5th South Lancashire (166th Brigade) reinforced the Battalion's line. By 12.30 a.m. on 10th April the Battalion held its original front line again.

2/5th Lancashire Fusiliers was the support battalion in 164th Brigade. Before the battle commenced, A, C and D Companies were in the Village Line along the Cuinchy – Festubert road, under the second in command, with B Company and Battalion HQ in reserve at Gorre. At 5.15 a.m. HQ 164th Brigade had ordered B Company to move to the Tuning Fork – Le Preol Line, running north-south through a wood about 1,600m east of Gorre. The Company moved at 6.25 a.m., at about the same time as Battalion HQ moved to its Forward HQ at Pont Fixe.

The Battalion Chaplain (Captain REG Newman MC) escaped from German captivity and at 10 a.m. reported to Battalion HQ that the enemy had seized Windy Corner. The CO ordered D Company to form a defensive flank on the left, with C Company supporting it. 1/4th King's Own on the right reported that the Germans were advancing through its centre along Orchard Road communication trench and requested reinforcements. A platoon of C Company was all that could be spared as the main threat at that time was at Windy Corner, where the enemy was held by D Company.

B Company then moved forward and ran into a large party of Germans in the gap between the two Brigades, probably displaced there by a counterattack by 165th Brigade at Le Plantin South. The Germans were driven back and B Company sent two platoons to the aid of 1/4th Loyal North Lancashire on the left. They worked their way up Grenadier Road and Hitchin Road communication trenches from Windy Corner, cutting off and capturing many Germans, before taking up positions in New Cut Extension and the old British line. A Company withdrew to Pont Fixe North, having sustained heavy casualties.

The two remaining platoons of B Company were ordered to move up Wolfe Road and Orchard Road communication trenches in the left and centre of 1/4th King's Own's position. **Second Lieutenant John Schofield** led the platoon in Orchard Road. CSM R Walker of B Company, 1/4th King's Own, met Schofield in Orchard Terrace, having advanced with two NCOs along Orchard Road from Bayswater. Schofield told Walker that the Germans still occupied the front line and they put together a party of Lancashire Fusiliers to bomb the trench held by the enemy. While leading nine men against a defended strongpoint, Schofield was attacked by a group of one hundred Germans, who were heavily armed with bombs. He quickly deployed his men and opened such effective rifle and Lewis gun fire, that the enemy was forced into the cover of nearby dugouts. 1078 Private C McGill climbed onto the parapet and began firing at the enemy whilst under heavy fire, killing several Germans and throwing the remainder into confusion. Schofield personally captured twenty and went on with other parties to clear the whole area. Having reformed his team, he set off with ten men towards the front line, having first ensured that his CO was informed of the situation. He ran into large numbers of Germans in the trench, and in a drain to the left and right, who opened rapid fire. Undeterred, Schofield climbed onto the parapet in the face of point blank machine gun fire and forced them to surrender. In total Schofield's actions led to the capture of 123 prisoners. He was killed a few minutes later. Schofield was assisted throughout by

Private McGill, who was awarded the DCM. Both platoons succeeded in gaining the front line.

On the left, in the improving visibility at noon, 1/4th Loyal North Lancashire retook Piccadilly Trench and re-established its front line. However, the Germans hung on around the Battalion HQ and other Germans were retiring from Windy Corner. They were all cut off by a counterattack from Bunny Hutch and were either mopped up or taken prisoner.

At 2.40 p.m. HQ 2/5th Lancashire Fusiliers moved forward into the same dugout as HQ 1/4th King's Own. Later in the day, as they became available, 2/5th Lancashire Fusiliers sent small parties to the front line to help the forward battalions to re-establish their original trenches. The Battalion suffered 169 casualties.

In the afternoon, HQ 164th Brigade reinforced each forward battalion with a company of 5th South Lancashire. Other reinforcements arrived, mainly men of the Brigade returning from detachments to other units, all bringing forward ammunition and grenades. Expenditure of ammunition had been high, with many men firing 150–200 rounds each. The anti-tank gun at Gunner Siding had fired 150 rounds and the Stokes mortars had averaged more than 100 rounds per gun. The Brigade machine guns had also been boldly handled, despite the poor visibility. By 3.45 p.m. the Brigade HQ was reporting to Division that the main line of resistance had been restored, along with most of the forward saps, although a few could not be reached in daylight as the approaches had been destroyed. By 4.30 p.m. contact had been re-established with the right of 165th Brigade in the Village Line. At 2.45 a.m. on the 10th HQ 164th Brigade was able to report that its front line was as held on 8th April before the German attack commenced. Six hundred and forty-one prisoners were taken, including a band that was to play the troops into Béthune, and at least fifty machine guns. Casualties suffered by 164th Brigade totalled 659 (1/4th King's Own – 298, 2/5th Lancashire Fusiliers – 145, 4th Loyal North Lancashire – 202 and 164th Brigade Trench Mortar Battery – 14).

On the left of 55th Division, 165th Brigade fought all the way back to the Line of Resistance. The situation was complicated by its left flank being exposed when the Portuguese collapsed. Soon after Windy Corner had been secured, 165th Brigade counterattacked at Le Plantin South. This resulted in large numbers of Germans being driven south towards Windy Corner into the left flank of 164th Brigade. By midday 165th Brigade was well established, although desperate fighting lay ahead. Reinforcements from 154th and 166th Brigades and divisional troops arrived and, by evening, two firm lines had been established, except where Route A Keep had been lost.

When XI Corps received confirmation of the Portuguese retirement about 11.30 a.m., the last reserve, 153rd Brigade, was sent to Pacaut, south of Merville. 51st Division then had all three brigades in line behind the right sector of the old Portuguese front, while 50th Division (XV Corps) did the same behind the left sector. The Portuguese were ordered to hold the Lawe crossings, which almost

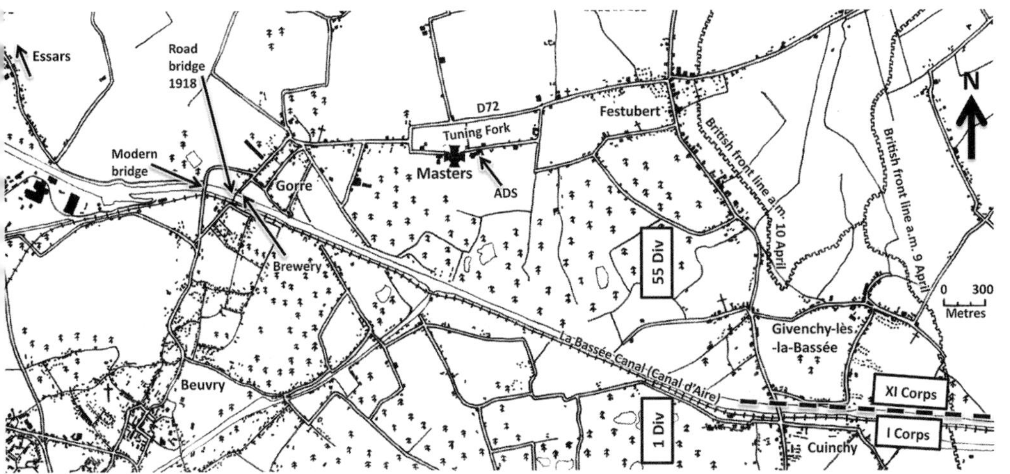

Approach Gorre from the east along the southern leg of the Tuning Fork, Rue du Marais L'Avoue. The northern leg is the main D72 Festubert – Gorre road and is much busier. The former brewery is at the southern end of Rue Jules Bailleul, which is a dead end. The road used to continue over the canal at this point by a drawbridge. Today there is only a footbridge.

coincided with the 10th April front line between Lestrem and Vielle Chapelle, and to keep the roads west of the river clear.

XV Corps covered its right flank before the attack began against the probability of a Portuguese collapse. The main attack in this area fell on 40th Division, already weak from the March fighting. Attacked in flank and rear from the Portuguese area, the Division managed to extricate itself and establish a new front north of Fleurbaix facing south.

The action on 9th April produced one of the rare VCs awarded to support troops. **Private Richard Masters** was an ambulance driver with 141st Field Ambulance (1st Division) at Beuvry, south of the La Bassée Canal. The ambulances were parked on the square in the centre of the town, which was shelled during the opening bombardment by the Germans. Masters and another driver had just moved their ambulances when a shell landed where they had been parked. The road from Gorre to the Tuning Fork was reported to be impassable but there were large numbers of wounded from 55th Division at Givenchy awaiting evacuation. About 1 p.m. Masters volunteered to get through and set off alone. Immediately after crossing the La Bassée Canal by a small bridge by the brewery in Gorre, a shell burst in front of his vehicle and killed eight men making their way to the front. He pulled their mangled remains off the road and continued until a shell hole almost the width of the road blocked his way. Masters packed sandbags from a nearby disused sentry position along one side of the hole to make a causeway wide enough for the ambulance. Shelling of the road continued and it was constantly swept by machine guns. Masters reached the wounded and, with help, loaded four stretchers and nine

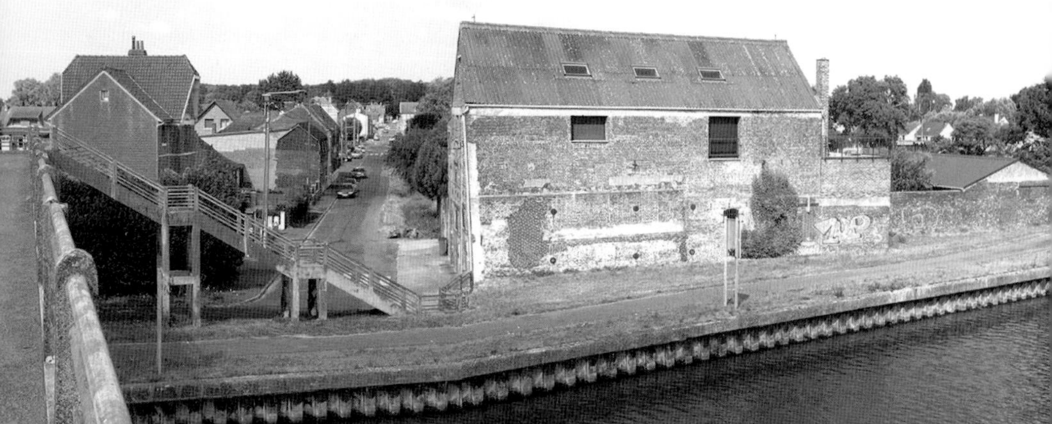

From the footbridge on the site of the drawbridge in 1918. The large building on the right is the former brewery.

The brewery building in this old photograph is understand to have been demolished when the canal was widened post-war. The existing building, with its distinctive curved window tops, is just visible on the extreme left of picture. Note the drawbridge in the foreground. This was lifted off its mountings in the open position on 18th April. As a result Richard Masters conducted a dangerous reconnaissance to find an alternative crossing over the canal.

Comparison with the 1918 picture. An extra storey seems to have been added and the roof realigned. It was on the road here that Masters had to remove the remains of eight soldiers killed by a shell burst in front of his ambulance.

sitting wounded. The ambulance was designed for four stretchers plus two sitting and the extra weight caused a puncture on the return journey, which he had to repair under fire. He was then attacked by a British aircraft, which dropped one of its bombs in front of the ambulance and killed one man on the road. Fortunately the vehicle was undamaged and he managed to return the wounded to the main dressing station, which had moved out of Beuvry due to the heavy shelling.

Due to the large number of wounded, an advanced dressing station was set up in a building close to the sentry position. Masters worked all day bringing back casualties. Until 5 p.m. his was the only ambulance working this route and he was responsible for evacuating the majority of the 200 cases cleared from the area. He also made one very hazardous journey along the road from Gorre to Essars, between the canal and the front line, with the British field artillery firing over his head from a parallel road. While assisting in removing wounded from the cellars of a house, he was gassed but, after being given a gargle at the main dressing station, returned to duty until 9 p.m., when he had to go to hospital himself. When praised for his outstanding efforts that day, he merely commented, *It's all in a day's work you know*. During the course of the day, 251 wounded cases were admitted to 141st Field Ambulance.

The handle of the Tuning Fork looking west towards Gorre church. Gorre British and Indian Cemetery is on the right.

By 18th April Master was back at duty and in the thick of it again, this time attached to 1st Field Ambulance at Fouquières-lès-Béthune. Although not part of the citation for the VC, on that day he was detailed for duty at the dressing station in the brewery cellars at Gorre. The route was very difficult but he arrived there

The southern leg of the Tuning Fork looking east. Masters covered this route repeatedly on 9th April to the ADS, which was amongst the buildings in the distance on the right.

and parked the ambulance under the archway leading into the brewery yard (this can be seen in the 1918 photograph). The MO would not allow any wounded to be cleared due to the route being overlooked by a German observation balloon. Masters sat outside on some bags of coke watching shells land in the canal and throwing up great clouds of spray. He went back inside and moments later a shell landed ten metres away, shredding the bags of coke and a motorcycle parked against the wall. The explosion also shifted the bridge (drawbridge type) off its mountings and it lifted up, making it impossible to cross the canal by that route. Masters volunteered to carry out a dangerous reconnaissance under heavy shellfire to find a way over the canal. He set off and grabbed a bicycle to speed his progress. He found a pontoon bridge but it was too narrow for the ambulances and continued until he found one that was just wide enough. However, it required some skilful manoeuvring to get onto from the narrow towpath without the vehicle ending up in the canal.

Returning to the brewery he told the MO that he had found a workable route. By then the cellars were full of wounded and Masters made many hazardous runs to collect casualties under fire and take them to Fouquières. On one journey he went to the Tuning Fork, where a German aircraft strafed the road. In front of his ambulance was a water cart, pulled by two horses, and manned by a driver and orderly. In what appeared to be a very practised move, the driver lay on the pole between the two horses and the orderly swung smartly under the cart. Neither was hit, nor was Masters' ambulance damaged. After twenty-fours hours with almost no rest, Masters had cleared the dressing station at Gorre of all but three gas casualties.

By the end of 9th April, XI and XV Corps had established a continuous line around a sixteen by eight kilometres pocket, caused mainly by the collapse of the Portuguese in the centre. Much of the new line was behind the Lawe and Lys rivers. 55th Division's front had increased to ten kilometres from the La Bassée Canal to the Lawe Canal but it had proved what properly trained troops, with time to develop their defences, could achieve against even the most formidable onslaught. Despite the inroads made by the enemy, not a single gun or trench mortar was lost, a remarkable achievement in view of the strength of the German attack. It is also to the credit of the other divisions that, after ten days of hard fighting on the Somme, they responded so quickly and positively to the new challenge.

Haig again requested the French to take over more of the front in order to release reserves, as this second offensive proved that the Germans intended to destroy the British first. Foch refused to send any French divisions, pointing out that twenty-five unused German divisions poised south of the Somme were threatening Amiens and Paris. Haig had to thin out two divisions from Ypres to send south but the BEF could not withstand the pressure being exerted against it indefinitely. Unless it could form an adequate reserve it faced a decisive defeat.

350 Pte Arthur Poulter, 1/4th Duke of Wellington's (147th Brigade, 49th Division), Erquinghem-Lys, France

10th April 1918

On 10th April the Germans continued to attack First Army and extended the offensive into Second Army's area between Warneton on the Lys and the Ypres – Comines Canal. In XI Corps (First Army) the enemy made little progress against 55th Division but in 51st Division's area they crossed the Lawe before daylight. In the evening the Fosse bridgehead was lost but a new line was established 1,600m behind the river from Vieille Chapelle to Lestrum.

XV Corps was also in a precarious position. The withdrawal of the Portuguese on the 9th resulted in the front of five kilometres being increased to eighteen. There was enormous confusion. Unaware that 40th Division had been ordered to counterattack at Bac St Maur, where the Germans gained a bridgehead over the Lys, 74th Brigade (25th Division) advanced at 9 a.m. It was forced back and by 3.30 p.m. the enemy had encircled Steenwerck. However, by 5 p.m. a line had been established north of Steenwerck.

After midday, 40th Division in the Steenwerck switch came under attack from the south and later the north, as the enemy, who had crossed at Bac St Maur, advanced westwards. With its flanks threatened, the Division fell back 1,400m but as soon as the withdrawal was completed a general counterattack was launched to recover the switch. An average advance of 450m was made and the line had stabilised by nightfall. Touch was made with 50th Division on the right but not with 88th Brigade (29th Division) on the left until the early hours of the 11th.

In the Armentières salient it was clear that the Germans would renew their efforts against 34th Division's right flank between Fleurbaix and Bois Grenier. Soon after 7 a.m. 101st Brigade was attacked. The situation became more precarious as the flanking divisions fell back and abandonment of the salient and retirement behind the Lys was ordered. HQ 34th Division issued instructions at 10 a.m. for the withdrawal to commence at 3 p.m. Some Australian tunnellers and a gas company were sent to assist but gradually the line was pushed back onto the River Lys.

147th Brigade was to relieve 146th Brigade in the Polderhoek subsector near Ypres on the night of 9th/10th April but instead was ordered to move to the Reninghelst area. The move took place on 9th April, following the presentation of medal ribbons by General Plumer, GOC Second Army. The stay was short lived. At 10 p.m. orders were received to move. The Battalions embussed between 1.30 a.m. and 4 a.m. on the 10th and debussed at De Seule. They marched to L'Epinette, dumping packs en route. Orders were received to reinforce 101st Brigade with one battalion south of the Lys at Erquinghem.

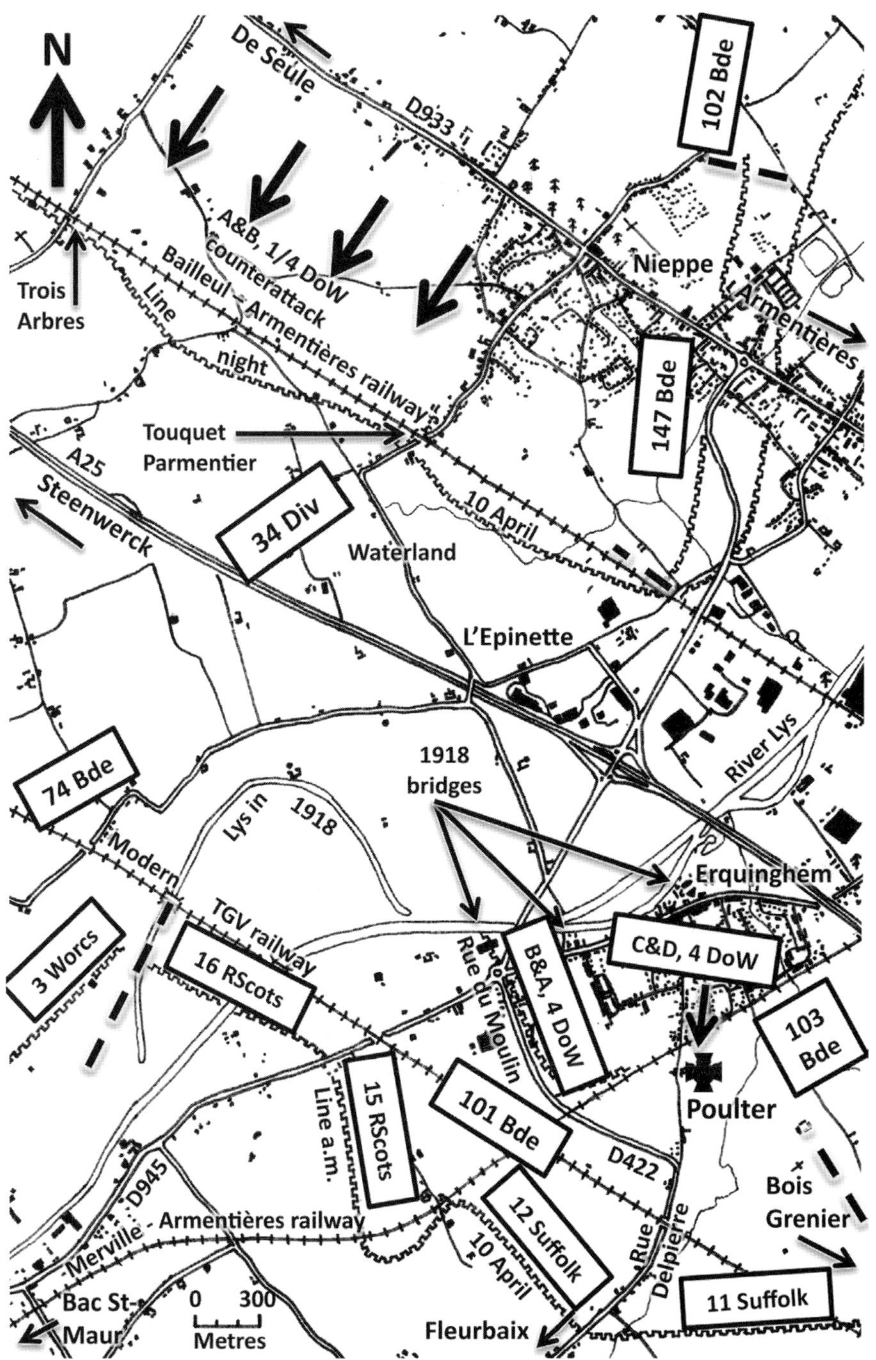

Enter Erquinghem from the west along the D945. In the centre, just before a central square in front of the church on the left, turn right into Rue Delpierre. Follow it southwards for 650m and park at the railway crossing which, although not busy, is still active. The Poulter memorial is on the far side on the right.

1/4th Duke of Wellington's (147th Brigade, 49th Division) was selected to reinforce 101st Brigade at 10 a.m. It crossed the Lys without difficulty, meeting large numbers of troops coming the other way and falling back north of the river. The other two battalions of the Brigade occupied the Nieppe system astride the Armentières – Bailleul railway and road.

101st Brigade held a line forward of the Lys. 11th Suffolk was on the left, two companies of 12th Suffolk (121st Brigade, 40th Division) were left centre, two companies of 15th Royal Scots were right centre and 16th Royal Scots was on the right. C Company, 18th Northumberland Fusiliers (Pioneers) acted as a rearguard in Erquinghem. The enemy had penetrated the forward battalions and the situation had to be restored. 1/4th Duke of Wellington's split into two. On the left, C Company, supported by D Company, moved along Rue Delpierre to close the gap in the front line, while B Company on the right, supported by A Company, assisted 16th Royal Scots near Rue du Moulin. By this time the main bridge had been destroyed and the Lys was crossed by means of a wooden bridge nearby and another near the church.

B and A Companies found the enemy just outside the western end of Erquinghem and took up positions to cover the approaches from the west and along the Rue du Moulin. They held under heavy fire, beating off two attacks, until ordered to retire about five hours later. An A Company platoon, sent to fill a gap for a detachment of 12th Suffolk near Rue du Moulin, was overrun and the survivors were taken prisoner.

The retirement of 34th Division to the north bank of the Lys commenced at 3 p.m. On the left, to the east of Armentières, 102nd Brigade got away without difficulty and, by 7 p.m., had crossed to the north bank and destroyed the bridges in its area. It took up positions with the left flank turned back to make contact with the right of IX Corps (Second Army). 103rd Brigade and elements of 101st Brigade had a more difficult time in the apex of the salient. Some units received the order to retire late and suffered heavy casualties retiring to and through Armentières. 11th Suffolk was asked to hold for two more hours to cover the flank, while three other battalions got away. However, the Germans observed preparations for the withdrawal and attacked. Two battalions in the apex managed to slip away, covered by rear and flank guards. Discovering that the Armentières railway and foot bridges over the Lys were down, the majority headed for the road bridge to the north, where they surprised the Germans and made the crossing there.

Meanwhile C Company, 1/4th Duke of Wellington's assembled near the top of Rue Delpierre in Erquinghem. The company commander, another officer, the CSM and two NCOs went forward on reconnaissance. They assumed that the original objective south of the Merville – Armentières railway could not be reached, as they had to crawl under machine gun fire even to reach where the road crossed the railway. It was decided to hold the line of the railway and they returned to arrange the change of plan. Men were already being hit as they waited. The right of the

The northern end of Rue Delpierre, with Erquinghem church in the background. This is where C Company assembled before advancing south to the railway line.

Looking south along Rue Delpierre from the assembly point towards the railway, which is out of sight around a slight right bend. Having held the German advance for some hours, C Company fell back along this road to the bridge behind the church.

Company was turned back to face southwest but enfilade fire from Rue du Moulin made this a poor position. Losses mounted and stretcher-bearers were hard pressed to keep up with the casualties. No.9 Platoon was sent over the railway line to a safer position, where, although sniped at, it was protected from other fire. The rest of the Company continued to sustain heavy casualties. The stretcher-bearers were

A 180° panorama taking in the area south of the railway where C Company, 1/4th Duke of Wellington's held the line. This is also where Arthur Poulter rescued many wounded men and carried them back along Rue Delpierre to safety and for medical attention.

also being hit but just managed to cope with the casualties. One stretcher-bearer, **Private Arthur Poulter,** carried ten men to safety despite the heavy barrage and machine gun fire. Two men were actually hit for a second time while he was carrying them.

At about 1 p.m. the Germans brought up a field gun into an enfilade position within a few hundred metres of C Company's position. After half an hour only twenty men remained unwounded and the position was untenable. Those who could crossed the railway to the south, where the fire was less intense. At about the same time D Company moved to support 11th Suffolk on the left, while 16th Royal Scots fell back in some disorder as the enemy had already crossed the Lys in that area. With the whole position in danger of being turned on the right, 11th Suffolk was ordered to retire. 1/4th Duke of Wellington's did not receive the order, as the runners did not get through. The Battalion held on until, at about 2.30 p.m., the enemy was seen advancing rapidly from south and west simultaneously and the position could no longer be maintained. No.9 Platoon was overrun and almost everyone was captured. Only twelve men of C Company got back over the railway. Once in cover each man helped a wounded man back into Erquinghem. Survivors made a last minute run for it but some were captured. Poulter recovered many of the wounded. His own account mentions going out in the face of enemy rifle and machine gun fire from as close as fifty metres. Each time he took a wounded man back 400–500m across a bridge to the medics. As well as rescuing the wounded, he also bandaged about forty men under heavy fire. During the final withdrawal he went back over the river to rescue another man. Poulter was eventually wounded severely but was able to walk to the field ambulance. A bullet had entered behind his ear and exited against his eye. Although blinded temporarily, he recovered his sight, but could not chew for a while.

The survivors of 101st Brigade, and other troops holding the bridgehead south of the Lys, pulled back over the emergency footbridges and formed up on the north bank. The Germans were quick to follow up and the bridges had to be destroyed before everyone was across. Many fell into German hands. 1/4th Duke of Wellington's fell back over the Lys and went into reserve at Nieppe. In the afternoon

147th Brigade extended its front and made contact with 102nd Brigade. It became apparent that a gap of about 1,600m existed between Waterland and Trois Arbres. By 6 p.m. the Germans were on the line of the Bailleul – Armentières railway. The Brigade commander sent A and B Companies, 1/4th Duke of Wellington's, and a company of stragglers to counterattack. This re-established the line of the railway from Trois Arbres to Touquet Parmentier and posts were established to the southwest. The Germans pulled back without coming into close contact, leaving some dead behind. 1/4th Duke of Wellington's suffered more losses in the attack, in particular in A Company. That night the Battalion was relieved by 103rd Brigade and moved back to Nieppe.

Elsewhere 50th Division fell back to a previously prepared line 1,100m from the river. The situation was unclear at HQ XV Corps and, at 5 p.m., 29th Division advanced to drive back any enemy found and to fill gaps in the line. 88th Brigade advanced to within 1,100m of Steenwerck, where it joined the survivors of 74th Brigade in its new line. Touch was established with 40th and 34th Divisions on the flanks.

At 10.25 p.m., 103rd and 101st Brigades (34th Division) formed up behind the Bailleul – Armentières railway, between 88th and 102nd Brigades, to complete the defence line around the Bac St Maur bridgehead. Although 34th Division had escaped from Armentières, it was still in a dangerously narrow salient in which were crowded the troops of eight brigades.

Battle of Messines

351 Capt Eric Dougall, A/88th Brigade, Royal Field Artillery (19th Division), Messines, Belgium

10th April 1918

The fighting north of Armentières (Battle of Messines) on 10th April affected IX Corps, whose front was held by 25th, 19th and 9th Divisions. All of these divisions were at half strength as a result of the March battles. In addition, 25th Division had lost its 74th Brigade to assist 34th Division in First Army. 19th Division had 57th and 58th Brigades in the line, right and left respectively, with 56th Brigade in Corps reserve. Ironically 19th Division had been sent to this quiet area to recuperate after being in action from 21st to 28th March on the Somme front. The forward positions consisted of two lines of posts, front and support. Behind them a third, reserve, line ran along the forward slopes of Messines Ridge. This was intended to be continuous but the work had not been completed. Further back was the Corps Reserve Line on the reverse slope of Messines Ridge and behind that was the Army Line (Green Line). Enemy preparations were so obvious that many believed them to be a diversion to tie down reserves.

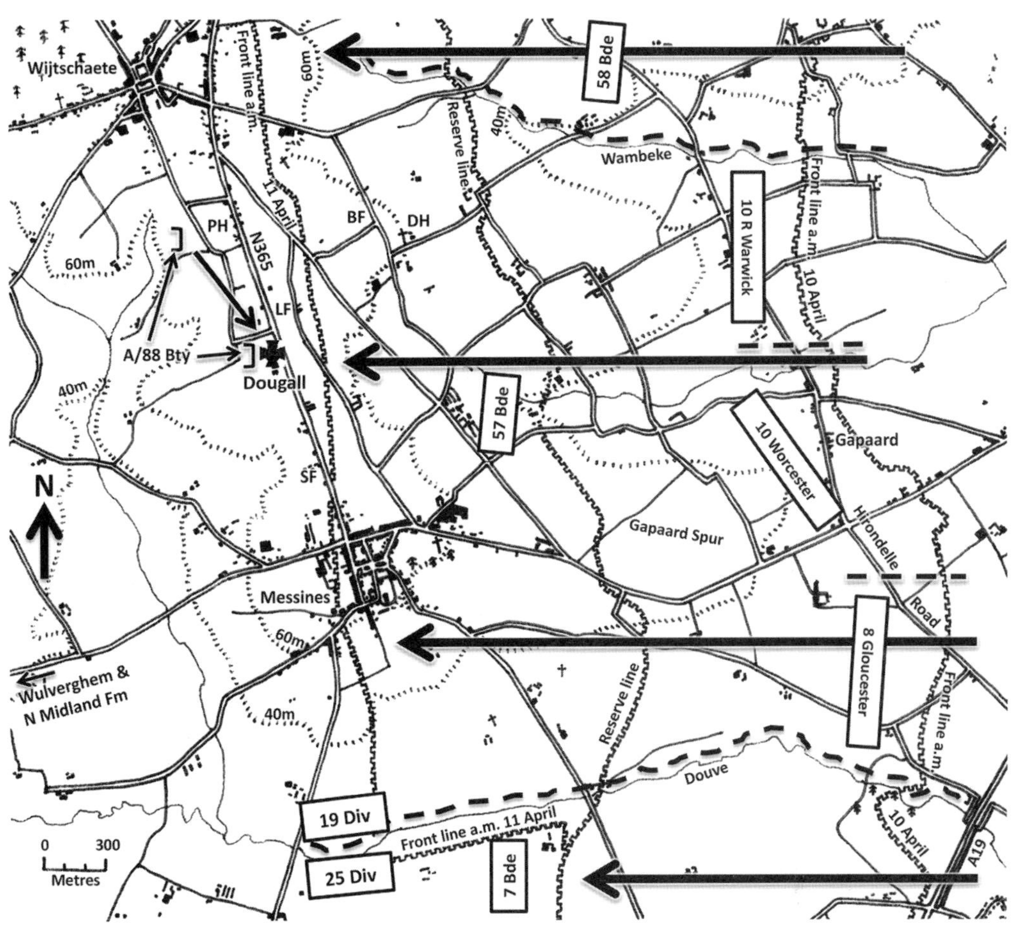

Drive north along Messines Ridge from Messines (Mesen) towards Wytschaete on the N365. About 1,500m after passing Messines church turn left into Schoolstraat. After 200m stop at the right hand bend. Dougall's second gun position was in the field to the left. Continue round the bend. After 500m the road swings left then right. Go on for another one hundred metres towards Wytschaete and stop. The guns were originally in the field on the left at this point before being run up to the second position. When visited in July 2018 there were heaps of roadstone and other material on the west side of the N365, north of the turning into Schoolstraat. Some of the photographs were taken from the top of these heaps, giving far more extensive views over the whole frontage of 57th Brigade than can be had from surface level. A number of abbreviations are used on the map – BF = Bay Farm, DH = Derry House, LF = Lumm Farm, PH = Pick House and SF = Swayne's Farm.

57th Brigade held a frontage of 3,100m east of Messines and Wytschaete, between the Wambeke in the north and the Douve in the south. 8th Gloucestershire was on the right, 10th Worcestershire was in the centre and 10th Royal Warwickshire was on the left. The Brigade was in contact with 58th Brigade on its left and 7th Brigade (25th Division) on the right. 57th Brigade had been in the line for eight days but, due to the German offensive, the planned relief on 10th/11th April had to be cancelled.

Until 4 a.m. on the 10th the situation on the front of 19th Division was normal and a thick mist formed as dawn approached. Heavy enemy shelling commenced at 5.30 a.m., mainly south of the Wambeke, and the attack commenced at 6 a.m. Thirteen battalions came on against 57th Brigade's weak lines of posts. By 6.30 a.m. the left of 25th Division had been driven back and the forward posts on the right and centre of 57th Brigade had either been overrun or bypassed. In the centre of 57th Brigade the enemy advanced against Gapaard Spur along Hirondelle road. By 6.40 a.m. they were attacking the reserve line. The left also launched SOS signals. 81st Field Company RE and B Company, 5th South Wales Borderers (Pioneers) were sent to occupy posts in the Corps Reserve Line. By 7.30 a.m. most of 57th Brigade had been pushed back to the support posts and Reserve Line. Two companies of 8th North Staffordshire (56th Brigade) were released from Corps reserve to advance from Wulverghem and occupy the Corps Reserve Line. However, the situation worsened and at 8.30 a.m. they were ordered to counterattack and retake Messines instead. The other two 8th North Staffordshire companies extended the Corps Reserve Line 200m east of North Midland Farm.

On the left of 57th Brigade the situation was obscure. HQ 58th Brigade to the north reported that 10th Royal Warwickshire had fallen back to Pick House and the Brigade had conformed by throwing back a defensive flank facing south. Meanwhile the sappers and pioneers in the Corps Reserve Line put up a good fight. Elements of 10th Royal Warwickshire linked up with 5th South Wales Borderers (Pioneers) at 11.15 a.m. The 8th North Staffordshire counterattack made good progress and reached the west of Messines around 11.35 a.m., where a few machine guns were taken. CO 8th Gloucestershire, with 700 new draftees for 57th Brigade, pushed forward to the north of Messines in the afternoon and recaptured Swayne's Farm on the Wytschaete road. Touch was gained on the right with 8th North Staffordshire. The other two companies prolonged the left flank to join up with 10th Royal Warwickshire at Pick House and, as a result, a continuous line was re-established. Eight machine guns were set up astride the Wulverghem – Messines road and another four were held in reserve with HQ 57th Brigade close to North Midland Farm.

At 12.25 p.m. the weak South African Brigade (9th Division) was placed at 57th Brigade's disposal for a counterattack, which was launched at dusk. On the left it succeeded in gaining the east side of the Messines – Wytschaete road at Bay Farm, Derry House and Lumm Farm. However, on the right it came up against heavy machine gun fire and did little more than reinforce 8th North Staffordshire's line. Fighting on 57th Brigade's front then came to an end for the day.

The Germans on average advanced 1,800m, although in one place they penetrated 3,650m. British losses were very heavy but, as the mist lifted, short-range firefights had prevented the Germans from making further substantial progress. In many cases the gunners remained in action until the infantry had fallen back in line with the guns. It was due to such determination that **Captain Eric Dougall**, commanding

Looking along Schoolstraat back towards the N365. The second position occupied by A Battery, 88th Brigade RFA was in the maize field to the right of Schoolstraat.

A Battery, 88th Brigade RFA, was awarded the VC. His diary for 10th April simply says, *Hun attacked. Fought guns all day till 7 p.m. and then got them all out to behind Wytschaete. Moved to Klein Vierstraat.*

A Battery, 88th Brigade RFA was in action throughout the day supporting 57th Brigade. Finding that his guns could not clear the ridge, Dougall ran them forward

The first position occupied by A Battery, 88th Brigade RFA was in the field on the right. Looking south towards the second position, which was between the house on the far right and the large barn beneath Messines church tower.

Panoramic view of the front held by 57th Brigade on 10th April 1918. On the extreme left, the first gun position of A/88th Brigade RFA was in the light coloured field. In the left background is Wytscaete. The N365 runs left to right towards Messines in the right distance. The second gun position was to the left of the house on the extreme right of the picture.

650m to the top to fire over open sights. As fifty survivors of 10th Worcestershire fell back, Dougall held his ground. He organised the infantry to continue the defence by establishing a line of resistance and supplying them with his Battery's Lewis guns and some rifles. Any spare gunners were sent to reinforce the infantry. One gun was turned over by a direct hit but Dougall organised its recovery and brought it back into action. He inspired all around him by calmly strolling about and promising the infantry that, as long as they stayed, he would not move the guns. His dogged resistance delayed the enemy entry into Messines for over twelve hours and allowed a new line to be established to the rear. When all ammunition had been expended, Dougall resolved to bring his guns out of action intact. This was achieved initially by manhandling them over 750m of shell torn ground that was also swept by machine gun fire.

To the north, 58th Brigade, which came under command of HQ 9th Division at 4 p.m., and 27th Brigade (9th Division) were not attacked until 2 p.m. Many posts were overrun but the enemy was halted in front of the support line. However, some troops did not receive the order to retire to this line and the Germans got around the flanks whilst the retirement was in progress. They broke up two battalions, leaving 58th Brigade in some disarray when darkness fell. Reinforcements from 26th Brigade were sent to restore the situation in Wytschaete. 62nd Brigade (21st Division), in reserve south of Ypres, was sent to recapture Wytschaete and fill the gap. By 5 a.m. on the 11th the village was secure. Having achieved that, IX Corps was able to form a continuous line of resistance in touch with XV Corps on the right and joining the old front line a few kilometres short of Gheluvelt on the left.

Due to the critical shortage of reserves throughout the BEF, Haig was forced to transfer a number of divisions from the south to counter the new threat in the north. That night he met Foch, who finally acknowledged that the German aim was to destroy the British. As a result he agreed to send French troops to intervene if necessary on the Arras front.

Battle of Hazebrouck

352 Lt Col James Forbes-Robertson, 1st Border (87th Brigade, 29th Division) near Vieux Berquin, France
353 Capt Thomas Pryce, 4th Grenadier Guards (4th Guards Brigade, 31st Division) near Vieux Berquin, France

11th April 1918

87th Brigade was relieved in the Passchendaele sector, near Ypres, on the night of 8th/9th April. It arrived by bus at its billets in Neuf Berquin at 8 a.m. on 10th April. At 9 a.m., 1st Border was placed at the disposal of HQ 50th Division and at 10 a.m. it was ordered to take up a position astride the Estaires – Neuf Berquin road. Although there was fierce fighting to the front, the positions occupied by 86th and 87th Brigades were not yet affected. At 3.35 p.m., 87th Brigade was ordered to advance, in conjunction with 86th Brigade, to clear up the situation in front. 87th Brigade was to advance with two battalions forward, with its left on le Petit Mortier and its right on Sailly-sur-la-Lys. 86th Brigade was to advance echeloned 2,700m to the left rear. The advance was to take them forward into a reserve position behind 40th and 50th Divisions. If they met the enemy in strength they were not to become engaged in a major battle.

1st Border was relieved by XV Corps Troops (Pioneers) and became the support battalion for 87th Brigade's advance, which was led by 1st King's Own Scottish Borderers on the right and 2nd South Wales Borderers on the left. The advance commenced at 5 p.m. The line held in front by 150th Brigade (50th Division) was ascertained and the commander of 87th Brigade anticipated that the Germans would attack in strength early the next day. Accordingly he established his HQ with that of HQ 86th Brigade, in order to ensure close cooperation.

German attacks recommenced at 4.30 a.m. on 11th April. On the extreme right in XI Corps, 55th Division drove off all attacks and took over some of 51st Division's

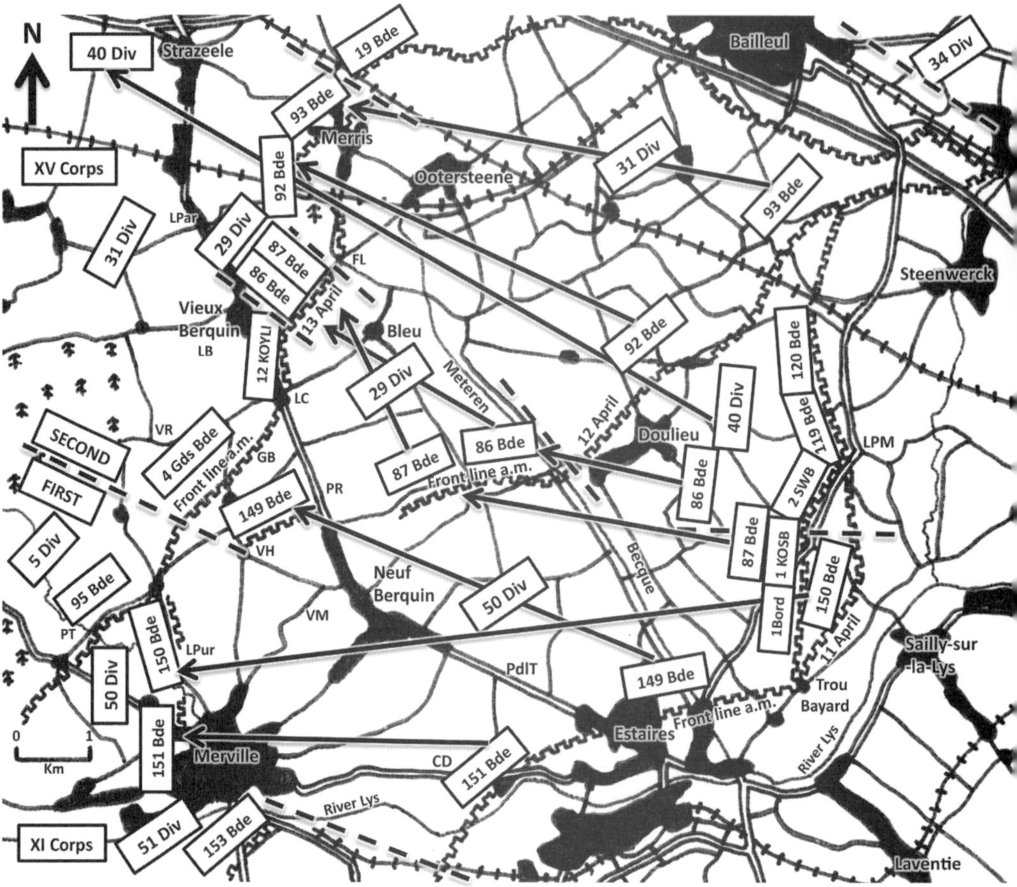

Positions of the main formations on 11th, 12th and 13th April 1918. A number of abbreviations are used – CD = Chapelle Duvelle, FL = Ferme Labis, GB = Gars Brugghe, LB = La Becque, LC = La Couronne, LPar = le Paradis, LPM = le Petit Mortier, LPur = les Puresbecques, PdlT = Pont de la Trompe, PR = Pont Rondin, PT – Pont Tournant and VR = Verte Rue.

frontage. Despite this, 51st Division was hard pressed to hold. There was no continuous line and the troops fell back fighting over the marshy ground. Disaster was averted by the arrival of 61st Division, along the River Clarence between Robecq and Merville, and 3rd Division concentrating behind 55th and 51st Divisions.

The attacks caused XI Corps to pivot back on its right, while XV Corps to the north pivoted on its left, effectively opening a double swing door. The main pressure was exerted on XV Corps, where the line had many gaps. 50th and 40th Divisions were in the line, with 87th and 86th Brigades (29th Division) in reserve behind 50th Division. Five kilometres behind was the newly arrived 31st Division (4th Guards, 92nd and 93rd Brigades).

By 7 a.m. the Germans had gained a lodgement in Trou Bayard at the junction of 149th and 150th Brigades (50th Division). Around 9 a.m. the left and centre of 150th Brigade was forced to retire 900m towards 87th Brigade. The right held on, assisted by 149th Brigade and patrols from 87th Brigade. Local counterattacks failed and soon after 87th Brigade found itself in the front line. 151st Brigade on the right was forced to retire and at 9.30 a.m. the junction of 151st and 149th Brigades, astride the Estaires – Neuf Berquin road, was attacked. The troops fell back slowly towards Merville and 150th Brigade concentrated southwest of Doulieu behind 87th Brigade.

87th Brigade was reinforced by 86th Brigade; on the right by 1st Lancashire Fusiliers, in the centre by a company of 2nd Royal Fusiliers and on the left by 1st Royal Guernsey Light Infantry. 87th Brigade also moved 1st Border to the right of 1st King's Own Scottish Borderers to prolong the line to the Meteren Becque. This force managed to hold the enemy but suffered severe casualties. The right was relatively secure but, on the left, the remnants of 40th Division, which amounted to only two battalion-sized brigades, fell back on Doulieu. On the extreme right, 151st Brigade fought a rearguard action to a line near Chapelle Duvelle (Duvette on modern maps) running towards Pont de la Trompe. At 11.35 a.m., 86th and 87th Brigades were ordered to take over the front line between Meteren Becque and le Petit Mortier. The left flank was to be protected and any gaps were to be filled. As soon as the line was held, the commander of 87th Brigade was to report on the possibility of recapturing Trou Bayard by counterattack.

During the afternoon the flanks of the 86th and 87th Brigade line were exposed. On the left the Germans managed to get into the rear and they also brought up field guns to drive out the posts at Pont de la Trompe. Orders were issued for 29th Division to fall back to a new line to be held by four battalions, leaving the other two in reserve. The new line was to gain touch with the newly arrived 4th Guards Brigade (31st Division) west of Neuf Berquin. However, 151st Brigade was pushed back westwards towards Merville, while 149th and 87th Brigades were driven northwards. 87th Brigade established a new line with 86th Brigade on its left. However, all troops were involved, there were no reserves and every machine gun was in action, including any that could be collected from 150th Brigade. At 8.10 p.m., HQ 87th Brigade was informed that the Germans were in Neuf Berquin and it was ordered to fall back. However, there were no troops available to achieve this.

At 8.45 p.m. **Lieutenant Colonel James Forbes-Robertson**, commanding 1st Border, made a personal reconnaissance and reported to HQ 87th Brigade that a 1,800m wide gap had opened east of Neuf Berquin. He was also able to report the positions of the various units in the line. It was clear that a major readjustment was necessary. Further north at 7 p.m., 92nd and 93rd Brigades counterattacked to recover the ground lost by 40th Division and then relieved it.

1st Border (87th Brigade) had been in action throughout 11th April. In the morning the Battalion was grouped around a number of farms, where the terrain was very confusing, with numerous overgrown hedges and small dense copses. Thick fog allowed the Germans to close unseen. D Company was in danger of being

1st Border's movements 10th–12th April. To visit the site of A Company's counterattack, approach Doulieu from the north on the D18. At the staggered crossroads in the centre of the village (there is a café and bread shop at this junction) go straight on (southeast). Continue for 1,200m to the t-junction and turn right. Just after the corner there is space to park on the right. The attack passed through the field on the right side of the road towards the buildings surrounded by trees to the south.

outflanked and pulled back but two platoons were surrounded by the advancing Germans. When the situation in 40th and 50th Divisions deteriorated, Forbes-Robertson made a quick horseback reconnaissance under heavy fire and organised a counterattack by A Company. He led the attack mounted until the horse was shot under him and he continued on foot. The Battalion held the enemy for two hours, until trench mortars and machine guns mounted on lorries subjected each farm to intense close range fire. The positions of A and B Companies became untenable and Forbes-Robertson set off alone on a borrowed horse (he considered it too dangerous to risk his own) to organise the defence of each farm. He discovered that the battalion on the left had been forced back and steadied his own men before organising a withdrawal. During this period his horse was wounded three times

The counterattack by A Company, led by James Forbes-Robertson, crossed this field from right to left.

and he was thrown on five occasions. About 5 p.m. Forbes-Robertson pulled the Battalion back to a new line and held off two determined attacks. He then organised a slow fighting withdrawal.

Elsewhere 34th Division was forced out of a dangerous salient around Nieppe and strong attacks were launched against IX Corps, which retired to comply with 34th Division to the south. By nightfall, IX Corps had fallen back 1,800–2,750m, mainly in 25th Division's area. North of the Douve, 19th and 9th Divisions held their ground until being forced to withdraw in order to keep touch with the divisions to the south.

12th April 1918

In the early hours of 12th April, 86th, 87th and 149th Brigades withdrew 2,400m, pivoting on 92nd Brigade behind Doulieu. The operation commenced at 2 a.m. under Commander 87th Brigade, as the senior brigade commander, and was completed by 7 a.m. without enemy interference. 1st Border and 1st Lancashire Fusiliers (86th Brigade) were in a supporting position about 800m behind. Casualties during the previous day had been heavy and both forward battalions, 1st King's Own Scottish Borderers on the right and 2nd South Wales Borderers on the left, were commanded by subalterns.

At 7 a.m. on the 12th, the Germans attacked along the whole front. On the right of 87th Brigade the gap between it and 149th Brigade began to increase. At 11 a.m. the right of 86th Brigade and the left of 92nd Brigade began to give way. About 1.30 p.m., 92nd Brigade began to pull back. 4th Guards Brigade moved up to the west of the Neuf Berquin – Vieux Berquin road, behind 149th Brigade. 86th and 87th Brigades were ordered to conform to the movements on their flanks. 1st Border was to maintain contact with 4th Guards Brigade on its right. At 4.30 p.m. news was received that the Germans had broken through 93rd Brigade, seized Outtersteene and were advancing on Merris. As a result, 86th and 87th Brigades had to fall back to a line from Vieux Berquin to Ferme Labis. 87th Brigade's right flank was thrown forward to join with 12th King's Own Yorkshire Light Infantry

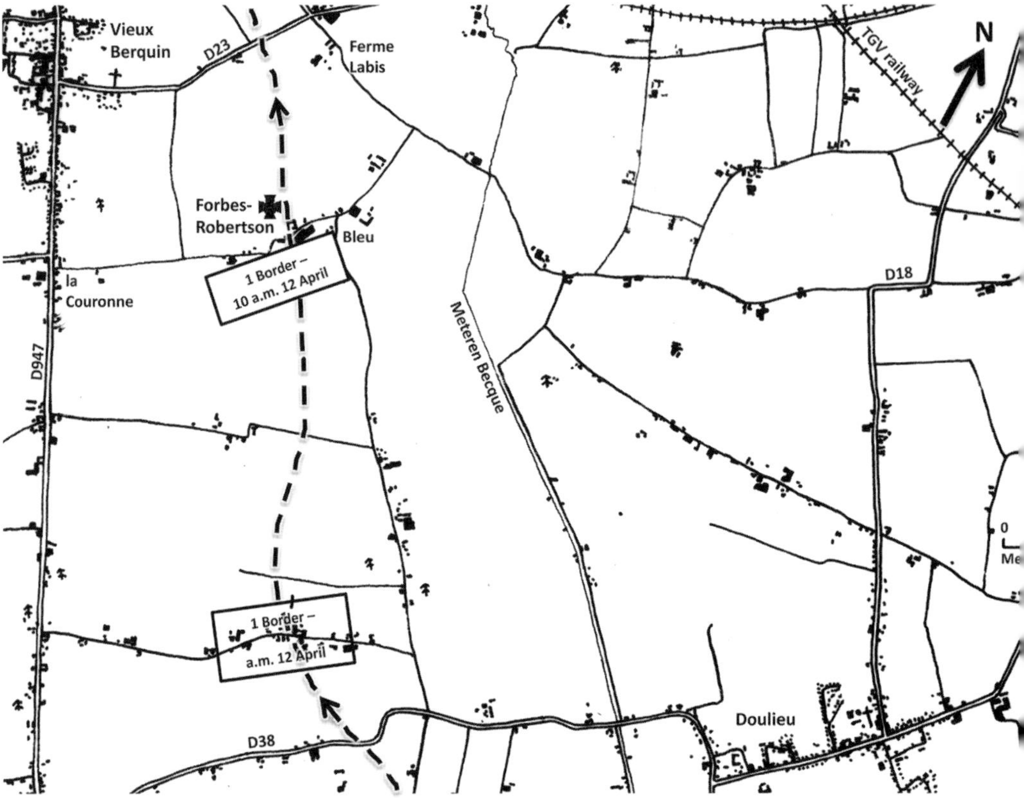

1st Border on 12th April. Drive north through the centre of Vieux-Berquin on the D947. Turn right onto the D23 and follow it for 600m to a left bend, where there is a track on the right. Park here and look southeast towards the buildings at Bleu about 900m away. This is where Forbes-Robertson made a stand with the remnants of the Battalion, having withdrawn to this position at 10 a.m.

From the D23 looking southeast over the line held by 1st Border after 10 a.m. on 12th April. The Battalion was positioned amongst these buildings.

(Pioneers) at la Couronne and 4th Guards Brigade. Meanwhile other troops were digging a support line behind at le Paradis and east of Strazeele. The night passed fairly quietly, which allowed time to resupply and consolidate. Although the troops remained confident, 87th Brigade had been reduced to a mere shadow. At dawn on 13th April it numbered just 351 men and 195 of these were in 1st Border.

During 12th April, 1st Border was under close range fire. There was little cover but Forbes-Robertson rode around his positions encouraging and directing small parties in the various farm buildings. Between Bleu and Vieux Berquin a second horse was shot from under him, but he returned undeterred with the good news that a 2nd Irish Guards company (4th Guards Brigade) was holding Vieux Berquin. The Battalion was forced to withdraw again at 10 a.m., with Forbes-Robertson personally guiding his men to the new line in and around Bleu. There, A Company was in touch with 12th King's Own Yorkshire Light Infantry (31st Division) and the other companies held a line south of Bleu. Later two platoons of C Company went to fill a gap for 1st Lancashire Fusiliers and 2nd Royal Fusiliers.

By mid afternoon the enemy was forcing back the line to the northwest. At 5 p.m., fifty survivors of 1st Lancashire Fusiliers and 2nd Royal Fusiliers, and an officer and three men remaining from the two C Company platoons, arrived at Battalion HQ. They reported that the brigade on the left had retired. 1st Border was forced to pull back to the railway in front of Mont de Merris. As it moved it came under heavy close range machine gun and artillery fire from north of Bleu and suffered many casualties. Forbes-Robertson once again guided his men back with great skill. A Company occupied a trench forward of the railway and the other companies held the cutting. This line was held while the Australians established a new line (Fôret de Nieppe to Meteren) to relieve the battered British formations late on 13th April.

In the face of overwhelming enemy pressure over three days and nights, Forbes-Robertson had conceded only 5,500m of ground and brought the advance to a standstill. He was always at the critical place at the right time, maintained control throughout and was ever cheerful and optimistic. His brigade commander

commented that he had been dull and morose until the action started, but as the situation worsened the brighter he became.

At the end of 12th April the British faced the prospect of a German breakthrough towards Hazebrouck, which threatened to separate First Army from Second Army and cut off the latter. Haig issued his famous *Backs to the Wall* order, which brought home the seriousness of the situation and had a positive effect in stiffening resistance.

12th-13th April 1918

On 12th April, while the situation in the British area hung in the balance, the Germans still had fifteen fresh divisions. The remnants of British units were led by junior officers and senior commanders rarely had a clear picture of the situation. Attacks against the flanks were not particularly strong, but were enough to cause a retirement. The troops pulled back slowly, while expecting the arrival of reinforcements on the right from 5th Division.

4th Guards Brigade (31st Division) arrived at Strazeele by bus late on 11th April. Just before dawn on the 12th it was in position west of the Vieux Berquin – Estaires road, south of la Couronne. It held a front of almost three kilometres, with 4th Grenadier Guards on the left and 3rd Coldstream Guards on the right. 2nd Irish Guards was in reserve at Verte Rue. As soon as it was light the enemy opened heavy fire along the whole front but an attack at 8 a.m. was driven back by small arms fire.

4th Guards Brigade was ordered to secure the line from Vieux Moulin (Hutton Mill on some contemporary British maps) to the college north of Merville, in order to deny the enemy the Neuf Berquin – Merville road. The leading battalions, 3rd Coldstream Guards on the right and 4th Grenadiers Guards on the left, were preceded by patrols along three roads leading to the southeast. It was expected that contact would be made with elements of 50th Division at les Puresbecques and Vierhouck. Two companies of 2nd Irish Guards were to advance in echelon behind the right flank.

They set off at 11 a.m. 3rd Coldstream Guards managed to advance 350m under heavy machine gun fire from the cottages at les Puresbecques and the orchard southwest of Vierhouck. The right of 4th Grenadier Guards was unable to make headway in the face of intense artillery and machine gun fire. However, on the left, No.2 Company, commanded by **Captain Thomas Pryce**, headed for Pont Rondin under close range fire, including a field battery firing over open sights from only 300m south of the village. Several houses were seized in fierce hand-to-hand fighting and two machine guns and two prisoners were captured. Thirty Germans were killed and Pryce accounted for seven of them. However, the left flank was in the air.

Around 3.30 p.m. the Germans attempted to outflank the right of 3rd Coldstream Guards, where no trace of 50th Division had been found. They penetrated between the right and centre companies. The right company repulsed the attack but was

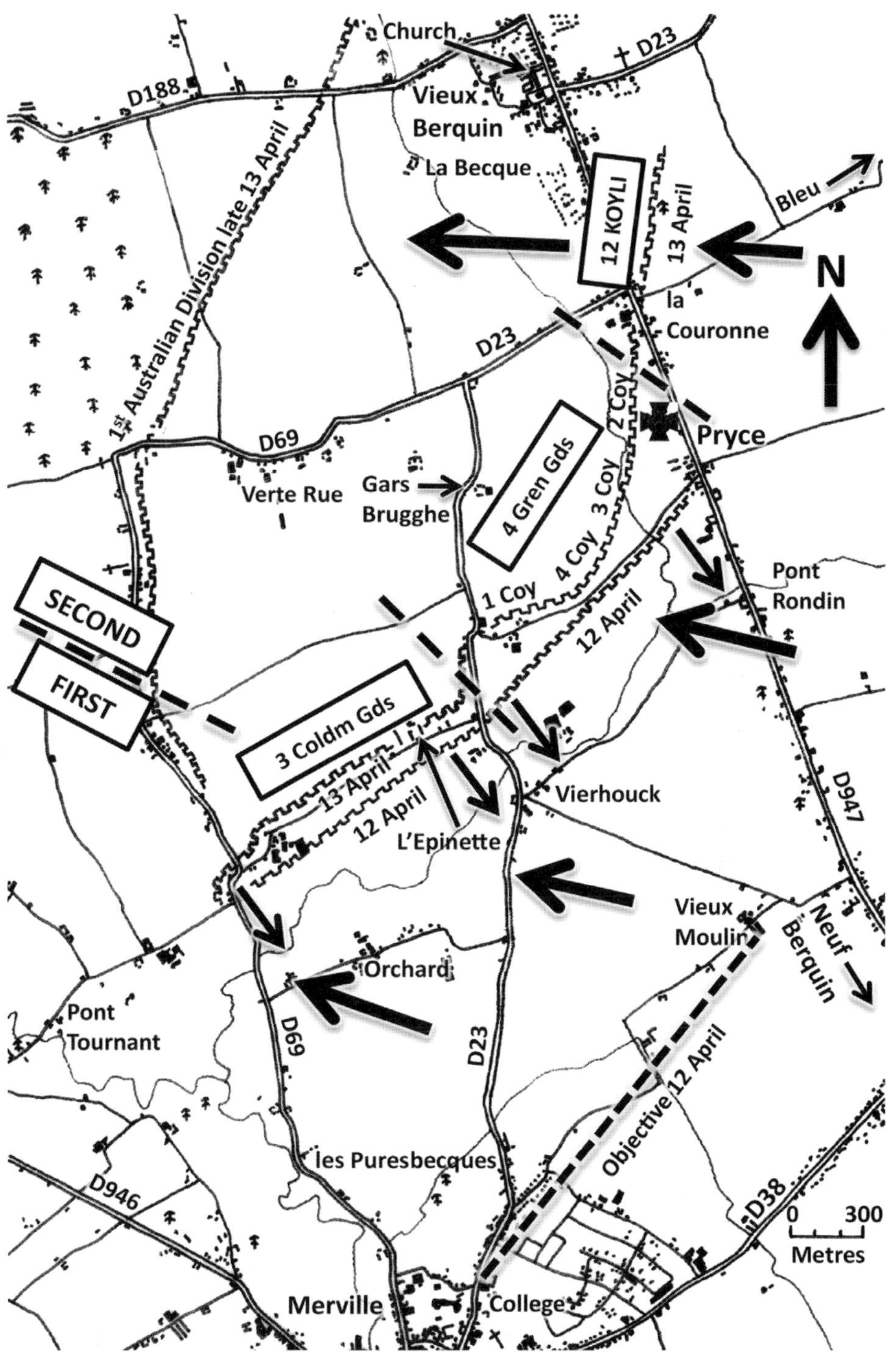

Approach Vieux-Berquin from the south on the D947. About 650m south of the village, at la Couronne, turn left onto the D23 (Rue de Merville). After 300m and just before the bridge over la Plate Becque pull in on the left, where there is an information board.

Thomas Pryce led No.2 Company in the attack on 12th April down this road (D947) into the buildings at Pont Rondin.

down to only forty men under a sergeant. It was forced to retire to Pont Tournant. The situation on the right of the centre company was restored by a counterattack by a company of 2nd Irish Guards and part of No.2 Company, 3rd Coldstream Guards.

An enveloping movement on the left remained a grave danger. Pryce reported the enemy was 900m in his rear, where the 200 survivors of 149th Brigade (50th Division) had been pushed back to the line in front of Vieux Berquin. This was held by 12th King's Own Yorkshire Light Infantry, which was also pushed back a little. Two companies of 2nd Irish Guards were sent forward, one each to reinforce 3rd Coldstream Guards and 4th Grenadier Guards. 4th Guards Brigade held against all attacks.

Pryce was ordered to withdraw to the road junction east of Gars Brugghe, where his left was still out of contact with flanking troops. At 4.20 p.m., following an intense bombardment, an attack on the centre of 3rd Coldstream Guards and the right and centre of 4th Grenadier Guards was driven off by small arms fire. In the afternoon 12th King's Own Yorkshire Light Infantry came under command of 4th Guards Brigade. A company of 2nd Irish Guards was allocated to 4th Grenadiers Guards to join its left with the right of 12th King's Own Yorkshire Light Infantry.

The Germans attacked 29th Division at Bleu at 6 p.m. As a result 12th King's Own Yorkshire Light Infantry was forced to form a defensive flank to the north, but 4th Guards Brigade continued to hold firm. Casualties had been heavy, with 4th

Grenadier Guards alone losing almost 260 men. The Battalion fired 70,000 rounds and all of its rifle grenades during the day's fighting.

In view of the situation on both flanks, after dark 4th Guards Brigade withdrew to a new line. It extended its line to cover the front of 150th and 149th Brigades, a total of 4,100m from Pont Tournant to la Couronne, about half of which overlapped into First Army's area. All three battalions were in the line, in addition to 12th King's Own Yorkshire Light Infantry on the left. It was arranged for 5th Division to take over 1,800m on the right to L'Epinette, thus relieving 2nd Irish Guards to reform a reserve. However, at daylight on the 13th the right of 4th Guards Brigade was still 900m south of the Army boundary. A thick fog formed overnight, allowing the Germans to bring machine guns close up to the Guards' line. An extended front, the need to dig in the new line and a shortage of men due to the heavy casualties the previous day, meant that 4th Guards Brigade was unable to patrol in any strength to ascertain what was happening in front.

On 13th April, German attacks continued either side of Bailleul but at a terrible cost. XV Corps's front was held by a number of weakened formations, when it was attacked at 6.30 a.m. From the south these were 95th Brigade (5th Division), 4th Guards Brigade (31st Division), survivors of 86th and 87th Brigades (29th Division) and 92nd Brigade, reinforced with elements of 93rd Brigade (both 31st Division).

4th Guards Brigade was weak and its defences amounted to scraps of trench and farmhouses. The Brigade line, from right to left, was held by 3rd Coldstream Guards, 4th Grenadier Guards and 12th King's Own Yorkshire Light Infantry, with 2nd Irish Guards and 210th Field Company RE in support. 4th Grenadier Guards had fewer than 200 men to cover 1,650m of front.

The attack against 4th Guards Brigade mainly hit 3rd Coldstream Guards. A German armoured car drove to within ten metres of one post and engaged it at point blank range with its machine gun. The right of the Battalion repulsed the attack but the Germans infiltrated between the left and centre companies. The left company refused its flank to remain in contact with 4th Grenadier Guards about Gars Brugghe. The breakthrough was halted by a company of 2nd Irish Guards and the support company of 3rd Coldstream Guards, resulting in only a slight indentation of the front.

At 9.15 a.m. more German attacks developed but were also repulsed, albeit with heavy casualties to the defenders. The Germans tried to work around the left of 4th Grenadier Guards into Vieux Berquin. Two enemy battalions advanced from Bleu and two attacks developed against the left company of the Battalion. Both were repulsed with heavy losses. The Germans then brought up two field guns to flatten the Grenadier's trenches.

12th King's Own Yorkshire Light Infantry repulsed four attacks but, at 12.20 p.m., reported that it had been blown out of its trenches at la Couronne and its right had fallen back 450m. Its left continued to pour fire into the flank of the Germans advancing north of the village and at 2.30 p.m. the Battalion pushed the Germans back to the church.

The line held by No.2 Company on 13th April extended from la Couronne, the buildings at the end of the road (D23) on the left, across the field in the centre to the bank of the la Plate Becque stream in the right distance.

The retirement of the right of 12th King's Own Yorkshire Light Infantry exposed the left flank of 4th Grenadier Guards, held by Pryce's No.2 Company. At 3 p.m. a message from him reported that he was under attack from both sides and his men were firing both ways back to back. A company of 2nd Irish Guards was ordered to restore the situation and form a defensive flank about Verte Rue but, as it moved along the la Couronne road, it was attacked from La Becque and the southwest. It also came under heavy machine gun fire from Vieux Berquin. Although the company delayed the German advance, it was surrounded and only seven men rejoined the Battalion that night.

The enemy tried to penetrate gaps in 4th Guards Brigade front. All three battalions were fragmented but clung to their ground tenaciously. By 6 p.m. the left had been forced back onto an Australian outpost line 1,600m in the rear. Pryce threw back four attacks during the day, despite the Germans bringing up field guns to within 275m. At 6.15 p.m., with the Germans only fifty metres away, Pryce realised the situation was hopeless. He led his men in a desperate bayonet charge. Fortunately the Germans were unable to open fire as many of their own men were behind Pryce's party. As a result the charge drove the Germans back one hundred metres and Pryce brought his men back to their positions. Half an hour later the Germans closed in again. Pryce had only seventeen men and no ammunition but led them in a final bayonet charge. Only one man escaped. Pryce was last seen in a desperate hand-to-hand struggle. His original party of forty men had resisted the advance of a German battalion for a complete day.

The centre and right companies of 4th Grenadier Guards were down to just twenty-six unwounded men between them and no officers. The Germans were on two sides. A few men managed to make their way back to the line established by the Australians that night. The centre and right of 3rd Coldstream Guards fell back in good order, fighting all the way but very few men got through.

The action fought by 4th Guards Brigade and the remnants of 29th and 31st Divisions saved Hazebrouck and allowed 1st Australian Division time to occupy a new line. However, it came at a cost. At the end of the day 4th Guards Brigade numbered only 250 men and 4th Grenadier Guards had lost ninety percent of its fighting strength. The Brigade's casualties for the period 12th-14th April amounted to 1,277–ninety-three killed or died of wounds, 371 wounded and 813 missing.

Overall, despite the losses, First Army had a successful day, with the enemy struggling to gain a 1,600m deep strip of land over a front of eight kilometres. Further north, Second Army began to withdraw to the line Kemmel – Pilkem, in order to shorten the front. The salient between Bailleul and Neuve Eglise was lost and the Germans advanced four kilometres between Bailleul and Neuve Chapelle. However, despite the measures taken, the length of British front actually increased and the men were even more tired and under-strength. Although some French reinforcements began to arrive (133rd Division at Kemmel), there was no immediate prospect of more reinforcements.

Battle of Bailleul

354 2Lt John Crowe, 2nd Worcestershire (100th Brigade, 33rd Division), Neuve Eglise, Belgium

14th April 1918

On 14th April the Germans realised that they were not going to shift the British in the south while they held Givenchy. In the meantime the offensive continued, with the Germans gaining little for the loss of thousands of men. In the north, on the right of Second Army, XV Corps was attacked in force throughout the day but only lost a few posts. There was little activity in First Army's area and I Corps took the opportunity to pinch out the salient at Robecq. XI Corps fought hard all day, but the line held. On the right, 19th Brigade (33rd Division) was involved in fierce fighting and lost some ground but Meteren was held. The centre of the Corps also held and a number of small losses were recovered by counterattacks.

On 11th April 100th Brigade was detached from 33rd Division to the command of 25th Division. It was allotted a frontage of about 2,700m in the partly completed Army Line behind 75th Brigade, southeast of Neuve Eglise (Nieuwkerke). 2nd Worcestershire was on the left and 16th King's Royal Rifle Corps was on the right, with 1/9th Highland Light Infantry in reserve on the high ground southwest of Neuve Eglise. A company of 33rd Machine Gun Battalion was allocated, with three of the four sections deployed in depth east and west of the Neuve Eglise – De Seule road. The fourth section was held in reserve well to the rear. The Brigade was in contact with 4th King's Own Yorkshire Light Infantry (148th Brigade) on the left and elements of 75th Brigade on the right.

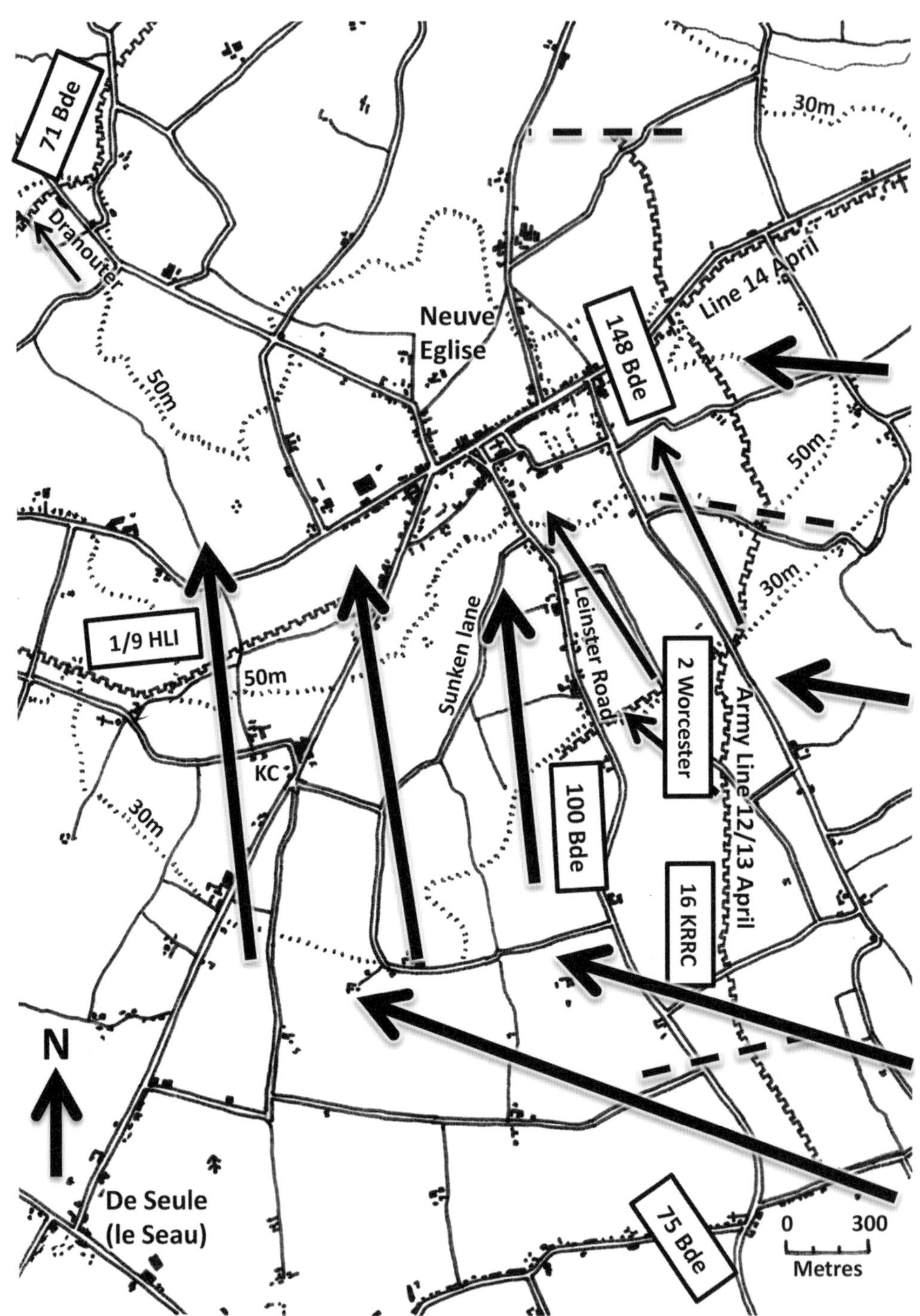

2nd Worcestershire's start positions on 11th April. KC = Kortepyp Cabaret.

The following day was quiet until 3 p.m. when the enemy shelled the Army Line heavily. At about 4 p.m. the 75th Brigade troops to the right of 16th King's Royal Rifle Corps fell back. Two of its support platoons were moved to cover the open right flank. At 6.15 p.m. a company of 1/9th Highland Light Infantry was ordered to move south to clear up the situation on the right of 16th King's Royal Rifle Corps. It discovered a considerable gap beyond 16th King's Royal Rifle Corps' right flank and the minimum reserves of both forward battalions were sent forward. However, by 1.30 a.m. on 13th April, 16th King's Royal Rifle Corps was reporting that the troops to its right had again fallen back. Part of 1/9th Highland Light Infantry was moved forward at 4.30 a.m. and elements of 88th Brigade, 75th Brigade and 2nd Worcestershire's battle reserve, under Major Donaldson, also moved to fill the gap. Despite this, the right of 16th King's Royal Rifle Corps remained fragile. In a subsequent fighting withdrawal most of Donaldson's party became casualties and the remainder was wiped out defending a railway embankment. However, the delay that they imposed allowed time for a new line to be organised behind and, as a result, the enemy advance was checked. Elsewhere the line was relatively quiet but planning and preparations were underway to fall back to other positions if this became necessary.

At 8.25 a.m. 2nd Worcestershire reported that it was still in contact on its left but there was no sign of 16th King's Royal Rifle Corps on its right. The Germans had broken through and were heading north towards Neuve Eglise in large numbers. By 9 a.m. they were in the town behind 2nd Worcestershire, which counterattacked with C Company from the east into the rear of the Germans in Leinster Road. At the same time every available man was moved to the crossroads west of the church, from where they also engaged the Germans in the Leinster Road area. They were reinforced by a few platoons of 1/4th York & Lancaster (148th Brigade). About sixty Germans were killed in the sunken Leinster Road and twenty surrendered as they were caught between the counterattack and 1/4th York & Lancaster. Six enemy light machine guns were recovered and destroyed. 1/9th Highland Light Infantry was also ordered to restore the town by immediate counterattack. This was carried out successfully, albeit with the enemy still in considerable numbers in the south of the town. About midday 2nd Worcestershire reported that it was in contact with the left of 16th King's Royal Rifle Corps, although this amounted to just three officers and forty men. B Company, 2nd Worcestershire wheeled back its right to join with the remnants of 16th King's Royal Rifle Corps. A portion of C Company in reserve was in contact with two platoons of 1/9th Highland Light Infantry at the crossroads west of the church. However, enemy parties were in Leinster Road behind 2nd Worcestershire and Battalion HQ was almost surrounded in the brewery, south of the church.

No further news of 16th King's Royal Rifle Corps was received. It was known that the CO and Adjutant were casualties and the remainder of the Battalion HQ was understood to have been captured. South of the village confused and desperate fighting continued all afternoon, with small parties from a number of battalions holding off strong German attacks. At 4.30 p.m. a patrol of 1/9th Highland Light Infantry found Neuve Eglise clear of the enemy. 2nd Worcestershire was ordered to throw back its right flank to cover all approaches into Neuve Eglise from the south and southeast but, before this could be carried out, the Germans attacked again and entered the town. At the same time another strong attack thrust northwards from Kortepyp Cabaret and pushed back 1/9th Highland Light Infantry. This thrust penetrated as far north as one kilometre directly west of Neuve Eglise, effectively separating 1/9th Highland Light Infantry from 2nd Worcestershire. The Germans there formed a line facing Neuve Eglise from the west but they did not attempt to enter the town during the night from that direction.

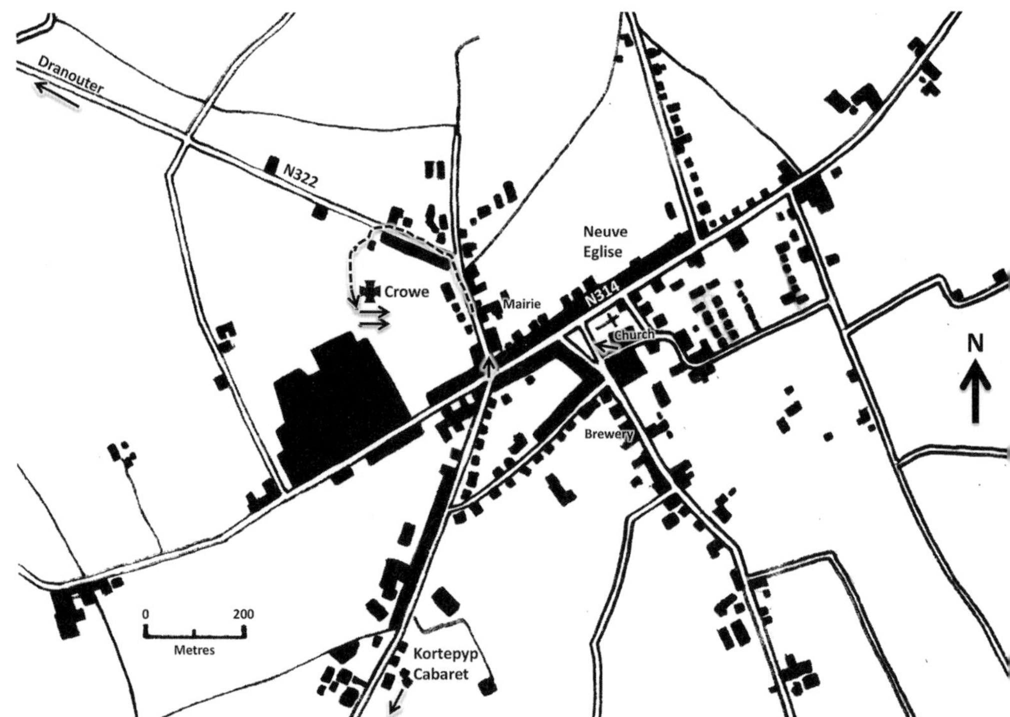

In the centre of Neuve Eglise (Nieuwkerke) turn off the main N314 road onto the N322 Dranouter road. Pass the Mairie on the right and park on the right just after the left hand bend. There is a large information board on the wall of the Mairie. Crowe came out of this building and made his way towards Dranouter around the left hand bend. About where the row of cottages ends on the left (they were not there in 1918), he turned left (south) with his small party into what was then fields to attack the machine gun posts. It is all now private land and not possible to progress further from this direction. Return to the Mairie. Opposite is the fire station (Brandweer), to the right of which is a public footpath. Follow it for 100m until there is a discrete left turn under the hazel trees and down a few steps onto a pathway leading towards the town. Follow it for a few metres and then look back. From here you can see the town church, Mairie and the high ground where the machine guns were sited. The whole area that was fields and hedgerows in 1918 is entirely overgrown now. Small arrows on the map indicate German machine gun positions.

2nd Worcestershire's companies gradually fell back on the village. C Company replaced B Company and the latter went into Battalion reserve on the north side of the town. Two of its platoons joined Battalion HQ, which had been forced to move to the Mairie (contemporary accounts refer to it thus but locally it was the hospice) on the Dranouter road. The other two platoons went to assist A and D Companies to withdraw. D Company on the left flank, under Lieutenant Charles Sargeant Jagger, gathered stragglers from other units as it fought its way back. Jagger was severely wounded and was awarded the MC for his part in this action. He became famous post-war as a sculptor, producing many war memorials, including for the Royal Artillery at Hyde Park Corner in London, as well as many other works.

The situation was critical, as the withdrawal of units on the right had left the Battalion's flank wide open. However, Battalion HQ had little knowledge of what had become of its own companies, except for B Company. Runners sent out at night to locate them did not return. A half platoon of B Company was based in a house thirty-five metres south of the Mairie to break up attacks from that direction. The remainder defended the Mairie itself. It was a very dark and active night, with the Germans on three sides of Battalion HQ.

1/9th Highland Light Infantry prepared to counterattack eastwards in order to regain contact with 2nd Worcestershire. However, at 4.50 a.m. it was ordered back to HQ 100th Brigade, which by then was at Hille, 4,400m west-northwest of Neuve Eglise.

Overnight in the town a party of about twelve Germans crawling towards HQ 2nd Worcestershire was detected in the light of a flare and driven off by a machine gun. Shortly afterwards it was knocked out by the fire of several enemy machine guns. A German machine gun at the crossroads was forced back by rifle grenades fired by the defenders from the Mairie gardens. About 1 a.m. a party of Germans was detected in the road outside trying to get to the rear of the building. They were engaged by the sentries and fled, leaving a seriously wounded sergeant major, who was taken to the aid post and interrogated there. The half platoon in the other house also endured a lively night and had to make a run for the Mairie once its ammunition was expended.

At 1.15 a.m. on 14th April news was received by HQ 100th Brigade that 71st Brigade had taken up a position astride the Neuve Eglise – Dranouter road, about 1,700m northwest of Neuve Eglise. HQ 71st Brigade reported that 2nd Worcestershire was still holding out in the town and sent two platoons of 1st Leicestershire to try to extract the survivors. HQ 100th Brigade also made arrangements to send two companies of 1/9th Highland Light Infantry to assist 2nd Worcestershire. Before this could happen an officer from HQ 2nd Worcestershire arrived at HQ 100th Brigade to report that the remnants of the Battalion HQ had managed to get away from Neuve Eglise, which was then entirely in enemy hands. He was also able to relate what had happened in the town.

Looking south along the Dranouter road, with the Mairie on the left, towards the crossroads where one of the German machine guns was sited.

Early on the 14th, with the Mairie completely surrounded, the Germans brought up trench mortars to reduce 2nd Worcestershire defences. Several direct hits on the roof caused a number of casualties, while machine gun fire poured in from the church, the crossroads to the south and the high ground to the west. A Lewis gun and snipers managed to keep the enemy at bay for a while but there was no let up in the enemy fire. By 8 a.m. drastic action was required. Second Lieutenant Anthony

Crowe left the Mairie building and charged over this road before crawling along it away from the camera. The fire station is just out of shot on the left.

Johnson MC volunteered to get to Brigade HQ but he was not seen alive again (Kandahar Farm Cemetery, south of Ypres – II J 12). Although a vigorous defence continued to check the Germans, it was clear that the Mairie could not resist forever.

About 11 a.m. **Second Lieutenant John Crowe**, the acting Adjutant, volunteered to clear the enemy. 235358 CQMS Albert Trotman (DCM for this action) joined him, together with a small party of about ten men. Crowe decided to clear the high ground to the west. First he had to secure the rear of the Mairie to maintain a cleared way for a withdrawal when that became necessary. He rushed out, captured a nearby cowshed and then led ten men in a charge over the road, with the intention of rushing the high ground directly. This proved impossible and so he left two NCOs and five men as a covering party and, with two others, crawled along the side of the Dranouter road. Having turned the corner, where they could not be seen, they turned inwards and advanced towards the machine guns. They surprised a party of enemy along a hedgerow and opened rapid fire on them from about ninety metres away, supported by the fire of the men on the roadside under Second Lieutenant Arnold Cecil Pointon and from the Mairie. Crowe counted twenty-three dead or wounded when he passed the position. The German machine gunners were not aware of this encounter as they were just beyond a slight rise. Crowe decided not to delay and charged, firing as he ran. He killed both machine gunners and his boldness unsettled the rest of the enemy, who, although they outnumbered the attackers, fired a few shots and fled. One of Crowe's companions was badly wounded and he was left in a shell hole during the charge. Crowe then recovered a Lewis gun being used by the Germans and began to return to the Mairie, when his other man was badly hit. Crowe was under fire from his right and could do nothing for his companion (he never knew the names of the two men with him). He dropped down for a few minutes and then ran back to the party along the roadside. A line of defence was then established on the high ground, together with a post on the road to maintain communication with Battalion HQ. Crowe reported to the CO, Major

Crowe and his companions continued to crawl along the side of the road here on the left. The houses were not there in 1918.

At this point they left the road and headed south towards the slightly higher ground, now covered in trees.

Looking north with the town church and Mairie on the right. Crowe's VC action was amongst the trees on the high ground in the centre.

Gerald Johnstone Lipyeatt Stoney, with the Lewis gun and made it clear that if they were going to get away it had to be soon.

For a short time the Germans pulled back and the opportunity was taken to try to regain contact with flanking units. The unit on the left said it would try to assist in a counterattack to regain the town but there was no reply from the right. An officer from VIII Corps School, who had been sent to reconnoitre the situation, arrived about 11 a.m. CO 2nd Worcestershire told him that if a battalion was sent immediately he would direct it to where it was most urgently needed. It was hoped that a counterattack by 71st Brigade could be arranged but the enemy continued to

Taken from a similar position to the last view in about 2000, before the trees grew up, looking over the fire station roof to the Mairie.

flood into the town, the rate of enemy fire increased and ammunition ran short. At 1.30 p.m. the CO accepted that reinforcements were not coming and he could hold on no longer. He ordered the Mairie to be evacuated fifteen minutes later. 22956 Private Francis Reginald Bough (DCM for this action) continued to resist from the Mairie with his Lewis gun, while the rest took as many wounded as possible and pulled back along the Dranouter road. They were covered by Crowe's party on the high ground and he was the last to leave. Although three seriously wounded men had to be left in the cellars, there were no further casualties in the withdrawal. The Germans made no attempt to pursue and that evening the remnants of the other companies were reunited with the Battalion near Hille, having fought their way back separately. The Battalion went into Brigade reserve and survivors continued to trickle in for the next day.

Meanwhile, as a result of action in 25th Division's area, 19th Division withdrew its right flank near Neuve Eglise and made contact with 71st Brigade. This closed a 1,800m gap that had existed in the morning. Plans were also put into effect to form a second line of defence, the Meteren – Kemmel Line, and by early morning on 15th April a continuous front had been re-established.

Although the British were weak, and the Germans had a considerable number of fresh divisions that could still tip the balance, the situation was improving slowly. However, when Haig appealed to Foch for assistance, he refused again. With hindsight this was probably the correct decision, as it retained the fighting power of the French for use later. In the short term, it led to numerous British casualties. A withdrawal of British troops east of Ypres, in order to reduce the length of the Salient, was to be completed by dawn on 16th April.

Chapter Three

Stemming the Tide

Second Battle of Villers-Bretonneux

357 Lt Clifford Sadlier, 51st Battalion, AIF (13th Australian Brigade, 4th Australian Division), Villers-Bretonneux, France

24th-25th April 1918

On the Somme front the German March offensive ground to a halt on 5th April. They still hoped to seize Amiens but plans to attack south of the Somme were gradually reduced in scope and were postponed a number of times. The aim was to round off the salient facing Amiens by capturing Villers-Bretonneux and diverting attention away from their attacks near Kemmel to the north. The British began to learn of the attack as early as 16th April. Early on the 17th the Germans fired gas into Villers-Bretonneux, Bois d'Aquenne and Cachy for three hours and again in the early evening. This was repeated a number of times over the following days and widened to include Bois l'Abbé, resulting in a total of 1.074 casualties. German gun registration increased and there was a great deal of air activity. In one engagement, Manfred von Richthofen, the Red Baron, was shot down by ground fire. The British were not idle in the face of these preparations and bombed railway centres in the German rear areas.

An expected attack on the 23rd did not materialise. However, prisoners taken by the British and French confirmed that the line holding divisions had been relieved by storm divisions. They revealed that the bombardment would commence early on the 24th and last for two and a quarter hours, followed by the infantry attack. The attack would include fifteen new German A7V tanks. A British airman spotted the Germans massing around Bois de Hangard and, as a result, the Allied guns fired all night into likely concentration areas and routes to the front. Aircraft bombed German billeting areas, railways and dumps with some success.

The defending British troops were tired after the exertions of the previous month. Many of the replacements were untried young reinforcements. Some work has taken place on the defences but four rear lines between the Avre and the Somme were shallow, with poor belts of wire in front, and few communications trenches and shelters. Between the rivers was a flat plateau with no obstacles, very little battle damage and good going for tanks. However, beyond the Villers-Bretonneux – Cachy Line was a series of almost continuous woods and the ground was broken by minor valleys.

Fourth Army's front was held by III and Australian Corps, right and left respectively. III Corps consisted of 58th, 8th and 18th Divisions and the Australian Corps of 2nd, 3rd, 4th and 5th Australians Divisions. One brigade each from 18th and 4th Australian Divisions were in Fourth Army reserve. To the right of III Corps was the French XXXI Corps (French First Army). The Australians had fought a key action at Villers-Bretonneux earlier in April to stem the Germans advance, before being regrouped to the north of the Somme.

The German bombardment commenced at 3.45 a.m. on 24th April and the day dawned foggy. The attack fell from Hangard to 1,350m north of the Villers-Bretonneux – Amiens road. Initially only a company on the right of 5th Australian Division was involved. There were a few diversions in the French area and north of the Somme but the main attack hit the left of the French 131st Division and 58th and 8th Divisions in III Corps. The two British divisions had just reconstituted after the March fighting, in which they had suffered between them 7,234 casualties. Up to 60% of the fighting strength of the battalions in these divisions was made up of untried youngsters who had never been in battle before.

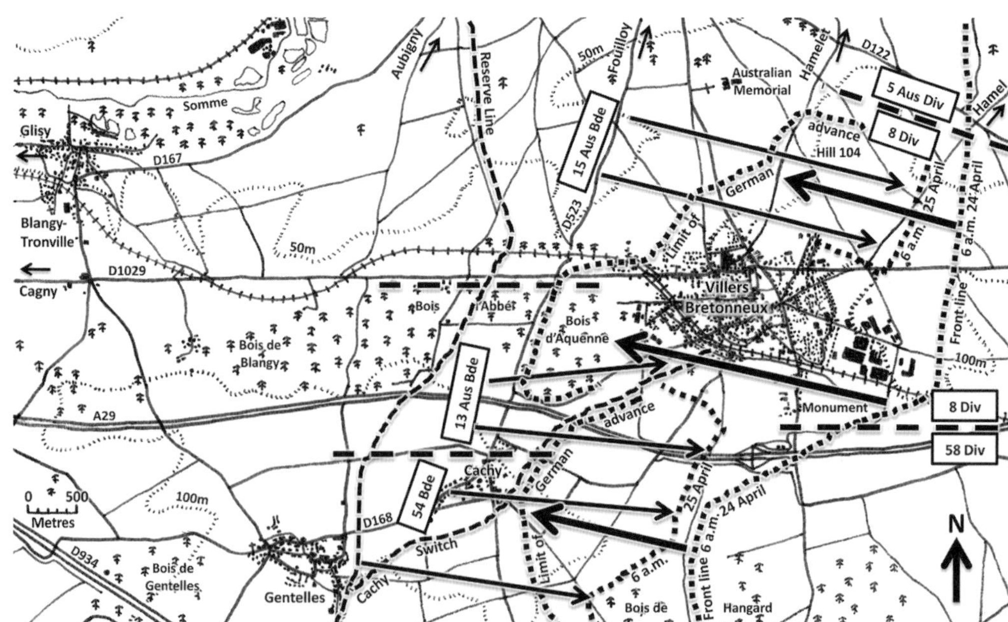

The area of the German attack on 24th April and the subsequent counterattacks.

58th Division had 173rd Brigade in the front line, with all three battalions forward – 3rd, 2/2nd and 2/4th London. 175th Brigade had 9th and 12th London in the reserve line and 2/10th London was the counterattack force for 173rd Brigade. 174th Brigade was in reserve at Cagny, 9,600m west of Cachy.

8th Division held the line with 23rd Brigade on the right and 25th Brigade on the left. The former was commanded by Brigadier-General GWStG Grogan, who was awarded the VC a few weeks later, and the latter by Brigadier-General C Coffin, who was awarded the VC for his actions at Westhoek, near Ypres, on 31st July 1917. 23rd Brigade had 2nd West Yorkshire on the right and 2nd Middlesex on the left in the front line covering Villers-Bretonneux, with 2nd Devonshire, the counterattack battalion, south of the town. 25th Brigade had 2nd Rifle Brigade in the front line, 2nd Royal Berkshire was the counterattack battalion north of the town and 2nd East Lancashire, in trenches around Villers-Bretonneux for its close defence, was under the direct command of HQ 8th Division. 24th Brigade was the Divisional reserve. 2nd Northamptonshire and 1st Worcestershire (minus two companies) were in the reserve line. The other two 1st Worcestershire companies and two companies of 6th Northamptonshire (54th Brigade) were in the Cachy Switch. 1st Sherwood Foresters was in the Blangy Tronville Line.

53rd and 54th Brigades (18th Division) were in Corps reserve south and southeast of Amiens. III Corps was therefore well deployed in depth. It had nine heavy and seven light Whippet tanks in a wood south of Blagny Tronville and four heavy tanks under 8th Division at Bois l'Abbé.

Early on the 24th fog limited visibility to thirty metres, gradually lifting to one hundred metres by 8 a.m. However, very little air work was possible. The German tanks were organised in three groups of three, six and four tanks respectively. Group 1 was to advance north of the railway on Villers-Bretonneux, Group 2 south of the railway between Villers-Bretonneux and Cachy and Group 3 against Cachy. Behind them four divisions were to advance against the fronts of 58th and 8th Divisions.

The attack started at 6 a.m. and the approach of the tanks and infantry was covered by the fog and the noise of the bombardment. They arrived at the British lines almost unnoticed. The tanks were decisive. Wherever they arrived the line broke, as there were no anti-tank weapons. The Germans reached Cachy Switch but the reserve line held. The tanks assisted a break-in in the centre, which forced the flanks to conform. The left flank of 173rd and 23rd and 25th Brigades were forced back into a pocket 6,400m wide. Villers-Bretonneux was lost.

173rd Brigade's left repulsed the attack initially but the tanks forced it back to Cachy Switch by 10 a.m. The centre conformed by swinging back. However, the right repulsed all attacks and held on all day, until the loss of Hangard by the French in the evening forced it to make a short withdrawal. The counterattack battalion (2/10th London) was stopped by machine gun fire from Bois de Hangard but filled a gap between the centre and left battalions. Machine gun fire held up the German advance here and they were halted short of Cachy.

23rd Brigade, covering Villers-Bretonneux, was attacked by tank Groups 1 and 2 and also by troops armed with flamethrowers. The front line was overwhelmed but the support line held for a while. 2nd West Yorkshire was down to just 140 men but held the railway station until 9 a.m., when the survivors had to pull back to the reserve line. 2nd Middlesex also fell back along the railway by stages to the reserve line.

In 25th Brigade, 2nd Rifle Brigade held its line initially as there were no tanks and the German artillery in this area shelled its own troops. Later tanks attacked from the rear and, with heavy attacking forces also to the front, the Battalion was overwhelmed. The left company remained until 8.30 a.m., when it formed a defensive flank. 2nd East Lancashire was badly gassed and held the eastern edge of Villers-Bretonneux until attacked by tanks and was outflanked from the south. It retired but, with the assistance of a few Australians, it remained in the northwest of the town for the rest of the day. 2nd Devonshire, the counterattack battalion, received no information before the enemy tanks hit two of its companies, scattering them and opening up a route for the following infantry to continue the advance towards Bois d'Aquenne. Fire from the two companies on the right, and those of 1st Worcestershire in the switch line, prevented the enemy from debouching southwards from the wood. The Germans brought forward machine guns along the edge of the wood and continued to advance westwards.

North of Villers-Bretonneux the counterattack battalion, 2nd Royal Berkshire, in contact with 14th Australian Brigade on its left, bent back to form a thin line facing southeast to block any attempt by the Germans to advance north from the town. A gap of 1,300m opened between the left of 2nd Devonshire in Cachy Switch and 2nd East Lancashire, northwest of Villers-Bretonneux. The Germans passed through to reach Bois d'Aquenne. Six guns of 290th Brigade RFA and all those of 291st Siege Battery RGA were lost west and northwest of Villers-Bretonneux but were recovered in a later counterattack.

As early as 4 a.m., 174th Brigade (less 6th London, which had been gassed in Villers-Bretonneux a few days before), in reserve to 58th Division, moved forward from Cagny to Bois de Gentelles. 7th and 8th London relieved 9th and 12th London of 175th Brigade so that they could reinforce 173rd Brigade. At 4 a.m., 1st Sherwood Foresters (24th Brigade) moved up to Bois de Blagny. At 4.15 a.m., 8th Division's pioneer battalion, 22nd Durham Light Infantry, moved to the reserve line north of Bois l'Abbé. At 4.30 a.m., HQ III Corps sent 53rd Brigade (18th Division) to a position between Glisy and Blagny Tronville. 13th and 15th Australian Brigades, either side of the Somme, were also stood to.

54th Brigade (18th Division) was allocated to 58th Division to replace 174th Brigade, which was in Divisional reserve. 11th Royal Fusiliers went forward to Bois de Gentelles, whilst 7th Bedfordshire, south of Cachy, and two companies of 6th Northamptonshire reinforced the rest of the Battalion in Cachy Switch.

8th Division had three Mk IV tanks of No.1 Section, A Company, 1st Tank Battalion hidden in Bois l'Abbé. They were intended to assist in mopping up Villers-Bretonneux but instead were allocated to 23rd Brigade to help with the defence of Cachy Switch. Brigadier General C Coffin VC briefed the tank section commander, Captain JC Brown; the tanks were to prevent the Germans from reaching the reserve line. At 9.30 a.m., led by Lieutenant Frank Mitchell (MC for this action), they set off over open ground through a barrage of German artillery fire and reached the Cachy line, where an infantryman warned, *Look out! Jerry tanks about*. About 300m in front a German A7V tank, named *Nixe*, commanded by Second Lieutenant Wilhelm Biltz, came into view, with two more tanks to left and right. Fire from the German tanks damaged the two female Mk IVs and, with no means of responding, they pulled back. Mitchell's male tank was also hit but he twisted and turned to give his left 6 Pounder gunner a clear shot. Firing on the move was inherently inaccurate and, after a few misses, Mitchell took a risk and halted. The gunner hit the leading German tank three times. It halted and the surviving crew scrambled out into a hail of machine gun fire, which killed five of them. Mitchell then turned his fire on the other German tanks. The crew of one abandoned it and the other was subjected to the fire of six guns of 58th Machine Gun Battalion. The concentrated bullet splash put it out of action and the crew surrendered. Mitchell later wrote, *....we had met our rivals at last! For the first time in history tank was encountering tank!* Biltz survived the war and became a prominent chemist and scientific editor. Another

Memorial to the first tank-on-tank action beside the D168, with Bois d'Aquenne in the background.

tank in Biltz's group, *Mephisto*, is in the Queensland Museum, Brisbane, Australia; it is the only surviving A7V.

At 8.40 a.m. two more tanks of 1st Tank Battalion were allocated to 8th Division. At 9.30 a.m. they advanced north of the railway in support of a counterattack by 1st Sherwood Foresters. By 12.30 p.m. this Battalion had reached the Cachy – Fouilloy road between Bois l'Abbé and Bois d'Aquenne, where it stopped any further German advance. This was the closest that the Germans got to Amiens, less than thirteen kilometres away. The male tank was knocked out by a shell but the female continued and cleared some Germans out of a copse north of Villers-Bretonneux, which enabled 2nd East Lancashire to improve its position.

At 10.20 a.m. seven Whippet tanks of E & F Sections, X Company, 3rd Tank Battalion, under Captain Tommy Price, in a wood south of Blagny Tronville, came under 58th Division. They were ordered to clear up the situation in front of Cachy. Two German battalions, forming up in a hollow in front of Cachy, were caught unawares. The Whippets charged southwards in line through the enemy, spitting fire as they went, and then returned, firing all the time. As a result of this shock action the Germans suffered at least 400 casualties and the survivors were dispersed. One tank was put out of action by a shell and three others were disabled.

15th Australian Brigade was in reserve to 5th Australian Division near Aubigny, less than five kilometres from Villers-Bretonneux. The Brigade commander sent patrols to check what was happening. They discovered British troops pulling back but some were standing, including a single gun of B/83rd Brigade RFA where the railway emerged from the cutting, which knocked out a German tank. These patrols established a line at right angles to the railway about 135m in front of the Aubigny Line where some men of 2nd East Lancashire and 2nd West Yorkshire were digging in. The Australian line was very exposed and was forced to pull back to join 2nd East Lancashire. The right flank of this line was pulled back along the railway to face the Germans advancing parallel with it to the south. Another Australian patrol about 450m to the north held on with a platoon and a half of 2nd Royal Berkshire. In the meantime 15th Australian Brigade moved to pre-arranged positions in readiness for a counterattack if required.

On the right of 14th Australian Brigade, 54th Battalion's right hand company poured fire into the advancing Germans to the south whenever they came into view. British survivors and elements of 14th Australian Brigade's 54th and 56th Battalions, together with all sixteen guns of 14th Australian Machine Gun Company, formed a flank facing south around Hill 104. There was no danger of the enemy making further progress there.

An offer of assistance by 5th Australian Division was initially turned down by HQ III Corps, as it was believed that 8th Division was capable of dealing with the situation. However, as soon as General Rawlinson at HQ Fourth Army heard of the loss of Villers-Bretonneux, he ordered 13th Australian Brigade (4th Australian Division), in reserve to the Australian Corps, to move to assist III Corps in the recapture of the town. The Brigade had been warned as early as 5.30 a.m. to be prepared to move. By 4 p.m. 13th Australian Brigade had concentrated about Bois de Blagny. 49th Battalion was sent to reinforce the reserve line north of Bois l'Abbé and replace 22nd Durham Light Infantry, which had been ordered to support 13th Australian Brigade in the forthcoming counterattack. 55th Brigade (18th Division), in Fourth Army reserve west of Amiens, was also placed at the disposal of III Corps.

Rawlinson insisted that Villers-Bretonneux be recaptured as soon as possible in order to protect Amiens. An attack by 23rd Brigade at 11 a.m. was cancelled because of the weight of enemy machine gun fire. Rawlinson suggested a simultaneous attack from north and south, commanded by 8th Division, in conjunction with 5th Australian Division to the north. Originally intended to be launched at 2 p.m., it was realised that it could not succeed in daylight across the open plain, which provided a perfect field of fire for the enemy machine guns. A moonlit attack was arranged for that night instead. However, this was not without complications, as the assault troops would be attacking over unfamiliar ground, without prior reconnaissance. A brigade was to attack either side of Villers-Bretonneux to pinch it out. At 12.30 p.m. Field Marshal Haig arrived at HQ Fourth Army and contacted General Foch to urge the cooperation of French troops to the south of the attack. He also urged Foch to move reserves north of the Somme to support the Australian Corps in place of the two Australian reserve brigades that had been sent to support III Corps's counterattack. He also asked the French to relieve III Corps as soon as possible.

At 3.10 p.m., 5th Australian Division was transferred temporarily to III Corps and HQ 8th Division issued orders for the attack at 5.30 p.m. It involved three brigades, each from different divisions, making communications difficult. 15th Australian Brigade was to assemble on the Cachy – Fouilloy road, north of the railway. It was to advance southeast past the north of Villers-Bretonneux. 2nd Northamptonshire was attached to mop up the town. 13th Australian Brigade was to assemble north of Cachy and attack eastwards south of Villers-Bretonneux to meet 15th Australian Brigade at the abandoned British front line, 550m north of the railway. 22nd Durham Light Infantry was attached to mop up. 54th Brigade was to assemble east of Cachy, to the south of 13th Australian Brigade and advance eastwards. The headquarters of 13th and 15th Australian Brigades were co-located at Tronville Chateau.

Zero hour was set for 10 p.m., with no preparatory bombardment. There was insufficient time to arrange a creeping barrage and so a standing barrage was laid on instead on well-defined targets. At 11 p.m. it would lift onto a protective barrage line, the heavies 450m beyond the objective and the field artillery 275m beyond that. There was a full moon but it was constantly obscured by cloud. Some assault troops had great difficulty moving to their start positions on time.

At zero hour, 54th Brigade (7th Bedfordshire, 9th London, attached from 175th Brigade, and 7th Royal West Kent, attached from 53rd Brigade) set off just as the moon clouded over. Contact between battalions was lost. Some of 9th London

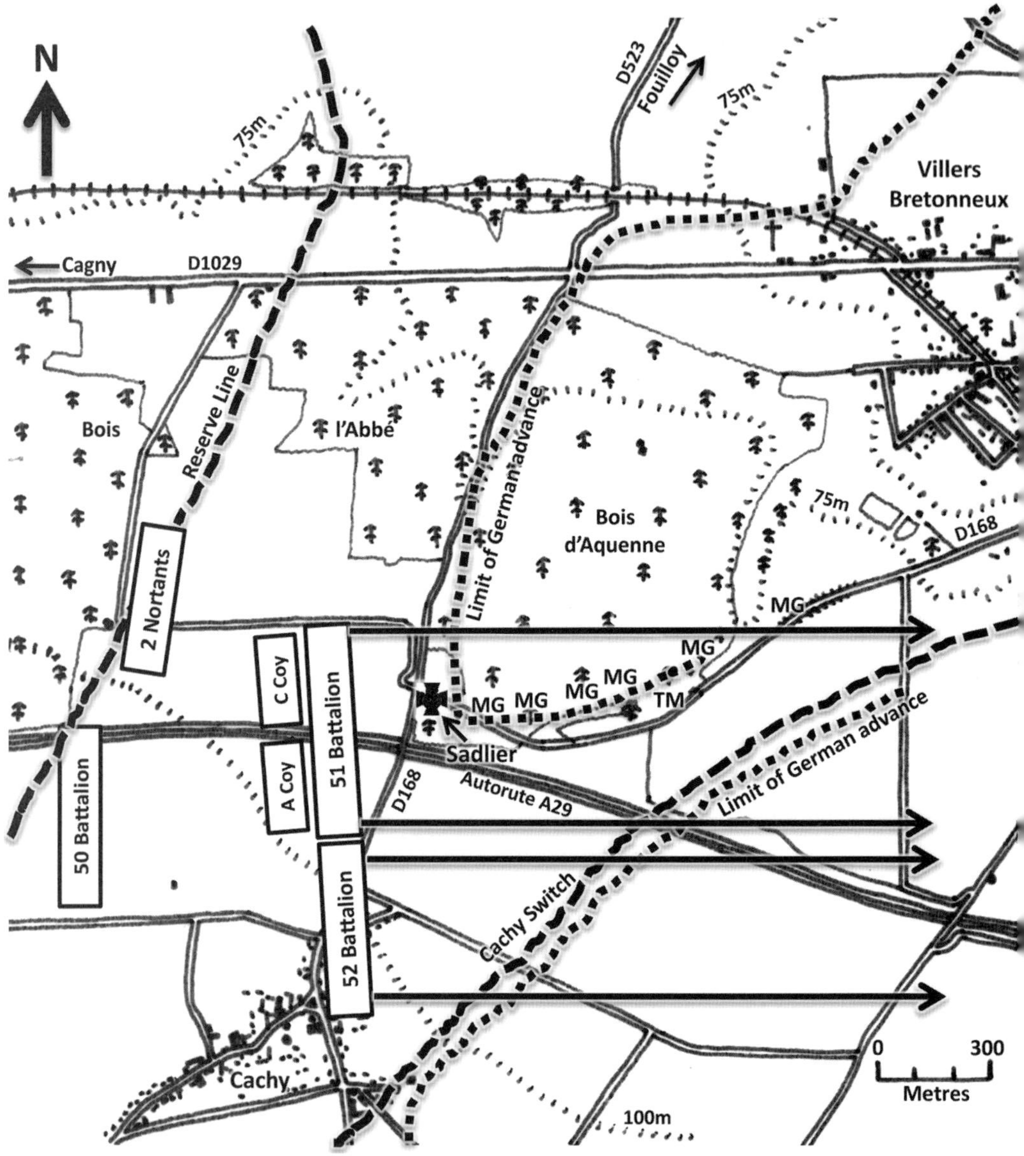

Pass through Cachy northwards on the D168 towards Fouilloy. Cross over the autoroute and after 150m park at the road junction. The road was crossed from left to right by 51st Battalion in the attack. The line of machine gun posts extended to the east along the edge of Bois d'Aquenne for just over a kilometre. The line of the new D168 road to Villers-Bretonneux runs parallel with and about 100m south of where the southern edge of Bois d'Aquenne was in 1918. Follow the road towards Villers-Bretonneux. After 1,200m turn right onto a track and follow it for 650m to a t-junction just before the autoroute. Turn right and continue for 300m, where there is a hedge line to the right leading back to the D168 road that you have just left. From here there is a view over the whole of the southern edge of Bois d'Aquenne along which Sadlier and his men fought to overcome the resistance of the various machine gun posts. The VC action was in the same place as the first tank on tank battle earlier on 24th April. TM = tank memorial and MG = machine gun post.

reached Bois de Hangard but were unable to hold it and fell back to the start line. 7th Royal West Kent met heavy machine gun fire and dug in half way to the objective. 7th Bedfordshire covered about 900m from the start line with little opposition. It crossed the Villers-Bretonneux – Hangard Wood road south of the town and then came under heavy artillery fire. It was forced to pull back 450m. There it found Germans manning shell holes, who called on them to surrender. However, the Battalion was in contact with 13th Australian Brigade on the left and hung on.

13th Australian Brigade's briefing for COs ended at 7.05 p.m., which allowed just sufficient time to return to their units, give their own orders and move to the start positions. Meanwhile taping parties were fired on from Bois d'Aquenne and had to pull the start line back 275m. They had been told that part of the wood was held by British troops but this was not the case. A small party of 1st Worcestershire and a few Australian scouts managed to drive the Germans back a little and suppressed their fire. The advance commenced ten minutes late, at 10.10 p.m., in order to allow 51st Battalion a little more time to get into position. 52nd Battalion was on the right in contact with 7th Bedfordshire (54th Brigade), 51st Battalion was on the left and 50th Battalion was in support. 49th Battalion remained in the reserve line. Wire in front of Cachy Switch caused delays and led to casualties. Once over it, 52nd Battalion came across some posts of 2nd Devonshire (23rd Brigade) and 1st Worcestershire (24th Brigade), which were holding out. The Australians charged, as German flares went up calling for artillery support. Resistance was overcome after some sharp bayonet fighting and the objective about Monument Wood was reached. However, 52nd Battalion found both its flanks were exposed and had to pull back in line with 7th Bedfordshire on the right.

51st Battalion's assault was led by A Company on the right, and C Company on the left, with B Company in support and D Company in reserve. The left was enfiladed by machine gun fire from the south of Bois d'Aquenne as soon as it set off. Before the advance commenced, the left platoon commander, **Lieutenant Clifford Sadlier**, had told his men not to worry about noise from the wood, as it would be British troops clearing up there. In reality the wood was strongly held by the enemy who sent up flares as soon as the advance commenced and opened fire. The company on the right was out of sight and continued but on the left the advance became difficult and expensive in casualties.

Precise details of what happened and where are conflicting. 51st Battalion's post-action report states that the advance on the left had covered 725m before it came into contact with the enemy machine guns. The Australian Official History map of the action in this area shows six German machine gun posts lining the southern edge of Bois d'Aquenne facing south. This is in the middle of 51st Battalion's frontage but Sadlier's platoon was on the extreme left flank. It is also unclear who took the initiative in clearing these posts. In one version the initiative came from Sadlier. In another, Sergeant Charlie Stokes, in the platoon next to Sadlier's, crawled over and asked what he intended doing. Initially Sadlier was going to press on to the

51st Battalion's assault started to the left of this road and headed east (right). Bois d'Aquenne is to the right of the road and to the left in the distance is Bois l'Abbé. The right turn is the D168 towards Villers-Bretonneux.

objective but Stokes pointed out that they would all be killed. Instead he suggested that Sadlier collect his bombers and clear the machine guns. Sadlier tried to inform his company commander what he intended but could not find him. He therefore asked the support company to fill the gap left by his platoon.

Having sited a Lewis gun to engage the nearest enemy machine gun, he passed word for his men to throw grenades into the wood and then to rush it. The Germans were not expecting such a bold move and the Australians were upon them before they knew it. Sadlier and Stokes led, the latter having secured a bag of bombs. They fired rifle grenades over the trees against the first machine gun post. The gun stopped and they rushed in. One German continued to fire the gun with one hand, while apparently holding up the other in surrender. Sadlier was hit in the thigh but he shot the German with his revolver. They cleared two more machine gun posts, the third by Sadlier alone. He was hit again and had to go to the rear.

From the north side of the autoroute looking north, with Villers Bretonneux on the right. The attack by 51st Battalion came in from the left. Clifford Sadlier and his men cleared the six machine gun posts along the southern edge of Bois d'Aquenne, which runs across the middle of the picture.

Some German machine guns were firing tracer, which added to the tension in the darkness, and none seemed ready to surrender. Stokes continued the attack from one gun to another. His party of six was reduced to two and he ran out of bombs. However, he met Corporal West, who found some German stick grenades and Stokes blew up another post with them. He went on to deal with another two posts. Corporal Browne with a Lewis gun also worked his way into the wood and shot down a party of Germans. The left flank of 50th Battalion following behind, became involved in the fight for the edge of the wood, as did the flank of 2nd Northamptonshire as it moved forward to mop up Villers-Bretonneux. All six machine guns were overcome and the danger to the flank of the main attack was removed. Both Sadlier and Stokes were recommended for the VC but only Sadlier received it in recognition of the action of the whole party. Stokes received the DCM. Having done more than anyone to destroy the German machine gun posts, one wonders how he felt about this apparent inequity.

The main advance by 51st Battalion continued in spite of the flanking fire. As the Battalion scrambled through the wire of Cachy Switch, it was again enfiladed by machine guns, this time from the Cachy – Villers-Bretonneux road, and suffered heavy losses. One gun was captured but the support company was unable to reach the others. Two Vickers were brought up to suppress it and the advance continued again. Not expecting the Australians to brush past these machine guns, there was panic in the German lines. 51st Battalion reached the Bois de Hangard – Villers-Bretonneux road. Opposition stiffened on the left, around the Monument and from the railway embankment on the southern edge of Villers-Bretonneux. The Battalion was attacked in the flank from the town and a company of 50th Battalion came up and drove the Germans back. Parties of 51st Battalion pushed forward between the Monument and Villers-Bretonneux but at 1 a.m. next morning it was ordered to fall back and align with 52nd Battalion. Flanking fire was still being received from the north. Seventy-four unwounded and twelve wounded prisoners were taken, as well as twenty machine guns and two heavy trench mortars. 13th Australian Brigade

suffered 1,009 casualties before being relieved on 27th April, including 398 in 51st Battalion.

Although 13th Australian Brigade was not on its objective, it was in a good position to pinch out Villers-Bretonneux, provided that 15th Australian Brigade was successful. 2nd Northamptonshire, following 13th Australian Brigade, suffered heavily crossing the wire of the Cachy Switch. From there it should have moved northeast but the Germans were alert and in strength along the railway and eastern edge of Bois d'Aquenne. After two attempts failed with 285 casualties, including the CO and Adjutant, touch was gained with 13th Australian Brigade and the Battalion lengthened the defensive flank on the left facing north.

15th Australian Brigade was almost two hours late starting as the assault battalion COs rushed back from the final conference. They were further delayed by detours in the darkness to avoid gas. It was nearly midnight before the Brigade advanced. 59th and 60th Battalions led on the right and left respectively, with two companies of 60th Battalion and all of 57th Battalion in support. Two companies of 57th Battalion were to extend the flank on the right on the final objective. The first objective on the Villers-Bretonneux – Hamelet road was reached without problems. Beyond it the Germans came to life and the Brigade rushed forward in a wild bayonet charge, guided by the light of burning houses and German flares calling for artillery support. There was little resistance on the left and they brushed past wild machine gun fire from the north of Villers-Bretonneux to reach the Hamel road at 1.30 a.m., having lost only 150 men. However, there was confusion as to the final objective. Commander 15th Australian Brigade in his earlier instructions had specified the road but at the final conference said correctly that it was the old front line. The two flank companies pushed to the right but found no sign of 13th Australian Brigade, which was 1,600m to the rear. These companies were completely exposed and came back. A flank was bent around to face the town but there was also no contact with 14th Australian Brigade to the north and this gap remained until the 27th. 22nd Durham Light Infantry, following behind to mop up, approached Villers-Bretonneux from the west, north of the Roman road. The Germans still held this area in strength and both attempts to get into the town were unsuccessful.

Although the counterattack was disjointed and failed to secure its objectives, it was far enough advanced to threaten the Germans in Villers-Bretonneux. In view of the circumstances in which it was launched, at short notice at night over unfamiliar ground with no artillery preparation, it was a considerable success. The Germans began escaping through the 1,350m gap between 13th and 15th Australian Brigades and at 6 a.m. all heavy guns were turned on it.

Meanwhile at 4 a.m. the remnants of 23rd Brigade, only 440 strong, collected in Bois l'Abbé and advanced on Bois d'Aquenne. Touch was gained with 22nd Durham Light Infantry on the left and 2nd West Yorkshire cleared the wood after ninety minutes, including the machine gun post on the Cachy – Villers-Bretonneux road, assisted by three tanks of 1st Tank Battalion. Seventy unwounded prisoners were taken, together with twenty-five machine guns and some heavy trench mortars. As the survivors fell back, they were engaged by 2nd Northamptonshire and 13th Australian Brigade. 23rd Brigade dug in east of Bois d'Aquenne and 2nd Northamptonshire then rushed the town to secure the station and cut off escape. 22nd Durham Light Infantry, 2nd Royal Berkshire (25th Brigade) and two companies of 57th Battalion resumed mopping up Villers-Bretonneux from the north. They met in the centre, having collectively captured 472 prisoners and sixty machine guns. As soon as the town was cleared, 15th Australian Brigade extended southwards and secured a line on the Villers-Bretonneux – Hamel road. It remained for 13th Australian Brigade to join it but movement in that area in daylight was very difficult. In the afternoon some Germans holding on west of Bois de Hangard were shot up by three Whippet tanks of 3rd Tank Battalion. The survivors were driven back and the gap was filled by 9th London and 7th Royal West Kent. The Germans also retained a section in front of Cachy, although this was not known to higher commanders. By 3.45 a.m. on the 26th the gap between 13th and 15th Australian Brigades had been filled.

Fourth Army had no reserves left and Foch ordered French forces to cooperate more closely. It was decided that the Moroccan Division would attack and establish a line from Bois de Hangard to the Monument. 58th Division would cooperate by attacking Bois de Hangard and 8th Division, with 13th Australian Brigade still under command, would join the left of the Moroccans. It was also arranged for the Australian Corps to take over III Corps' line as far south as the Monument. The Moroccan Division was to relieve the rest of III Corps on the night of 26th/27th April.

The attack, at 5.15 a.m. on 26th April, failed except for the British retaking Bois de Hangard. Early on the 27th the gap between 14th and 15th Australian Brigades was finally closed. Losses in the fighting from 24th April onwards are difficult to ascertain for the British formations. Collectively 8th, 18th and 58th Divisions lost 9,529 men in the period 5th-27th April. Australian casualties amounted to 2,473. German losses are estimated at 8,000–10,000.

Local Operations Spring 1918

355 Pte Jack Counter, 1st King's (Liverpool) (6th Brigade, 2nd Division) near Boisleux-St-Marc, France

16th April 1918

While the German offensives ground on, areas not directly affected were far from quiet. Raids and counter-raids were made to identify formations and also to keep the enemy guessing where the next moves would take place. One such raid was launched by the Germans near Boisleux-St-Marc on 16th April.

Driving northwards on the D917 through Boyelles, take the left turn onto the unclassified road to Boisleux-St- Marc. After 500m park at the water tower on the left and look northeast over the sunken road to the area where Jack Counter was in action on 16th April.

The open ground between the support and front lines criss-crossed by Jack Counter.

6th Brigade was holding the left sub-sector of 2nd Division's front, having completed the relief of 3rd Guards Brigade at 12.30 a.m. on 15th April. 2nd South Staffordshire was on the right and 1st King's was on the left, with 17th Royal Fusiliers in reserve at Blairville, eight kilometres to the rear. The Brigade was flanked on the right by 5th Brigade and on the left by 4th Canadian Brigade. HQ 6th Brigade noted that, although the front line trench was deeply dug and well wired, unusually there were no communications trenches. Later that day the 1st King's support and reserve lines were shelled and one man was killed and seven others were wounded.

At 9 a.m. on the 16th, the front line was hit by a heavy barrage for half an hour before it lifted onto the support and reserve lines and the railway embankment. Casualties in the front line were heavy and included the two forward company commanders. At 9.30 a.m. German infantry advanced rapidly along the sunken road leading from Boyelles to Boisleux-St-Marc. They also used a dummy communications trench leading to an unoccupied trench running parallel with the British front line. The line was breached in four places and the raiders bombed outwards from the entry points. The troops of 1st King's who were displaced fell back over the open to the support line. In doing so they suffered heavily from two enemy machine guns that had been brought forward by the raiders.

The British artillery inflicted heavy casualties on the enemy reserves as they hurried over no man's land but despite this, by 10 a.m., the raiders held 350–450m of the front line. Bombing blocks were established on 1st King's flanks and the process of regaining the lost section of trench commenced.

At 11 a.m. another attack up the sunken road was broken up by small arms fire from the support line astride the road. At some time during the day several low flying British aircraft also inflicted casualties on the enemy in the sunken road. On the right, the Germans who had gained the front line were driven back by B Company to within twenty-five metres of the road and a block was established by 1st King's in cooperation with 2nd South Staffordshire. The 1st King's bombing party on the left was very weak but also established a block with the Canadians. Before it was completed the party was reinforced by eighteen men and continued to press

forward. At 11.30 a.m. this party was relieved by another from D Company but the Germans were by no means finished. At 1.30 p.m. they attacked again, driving the left flank back 200m.

Battalion HQ had no precise knowledge of what was happening in the front line. All communications were cut and the absence of communication trenches in this area compounded the problem. The only route ran from the support line along the sunken road and then down the forward slope for 225m, in full view of the enemy. A party attempting to get through was halted by machine gun fire and five runners who attempted it were killed. Then **Private Jack Counter** volunteered to try. Miraculously he avoided a hail of fire and returned with vital information on the strength of the enemy, the position of the flanks and the strength of the defending troops. Counter later took another five messages to Company HQ under artillery fire. His performance was an inspiration to the many young and untried soldiers who had joined the Battalion only a few weeks previously.

Armed with the information provided by Counter, the CO was able to make an informed plan of action. At 2 p.m., 19th Canadian Battalion allocated two platoons and these were placed in reserve to 1st King's. Twenty minutes later HQ 6th Brigade sent two platoons of 2nd South Staffordshire to assist 1st King's. At 2.30 p.m. a counterattack was made by a platoon each from C Company, A Company and 2nd South Staffordshire. Two officers and twenty men arrived to reinforce the attackers at 3.15 p.m. and 19th Canadian Battalion's half company held the reserve line, as 1st King's had only one platoon uncommitted.

A counterattack over the open covered by smoke was arranged for 5 p.m. but was rendered unnecessary as marked progress was already being made by the platoons on the flanks. On the left the Canadians assisted in recovering 200m of the front line. Only three fire bays remained in German hands. The pressure built and the Germans began to pull back to their lines, losing heavily on the way. By 6.30 p.m. the front had been restored and a wounded officer and sergeant of 1st King's, who had been taken prisoner earlier, were released. Four wounded raiders were captured and eight dead were collected in the trenches, together with two abandoned machine guns. However, many more raiders were killed elsewhere and the majority of their wounded were evacuated as the Germans withdrew. 1st King's also suffered heavily, losing twenty-two killed or died of wounds, sixty-three wounded and twenty missing. That night the Battalion was relieved by 17th Royal Fusiliers and moved into reserve at Blaireville, less one company in the Purple Line.

356 LSgt Joseph Woodall, 1st Rifle Brigade (11th Brigade, 4th Division), La Pannerie, France

22nd April 1918

On 15th April, Ravelsberg Ridge and Bailleul were lost to the Germans and on the 16th so too were Meteren, Spanbroekmolen and Wytschaete. However, on the 17th and 18th they made no progress. Failure to break through at Ypres had a profound effect upon the Germans and, although the offensive continued, it began to waver. Attacks around Mount Kemmel also failed to make any impression. At 6 a.m. on 19th April, command of the Kemmel sector passed to the French, giving the British much needed respite. The period 19th-24th April saw a pause in the fighting in Flanders, although the indications were that fighting would recommence there and in Picardy.

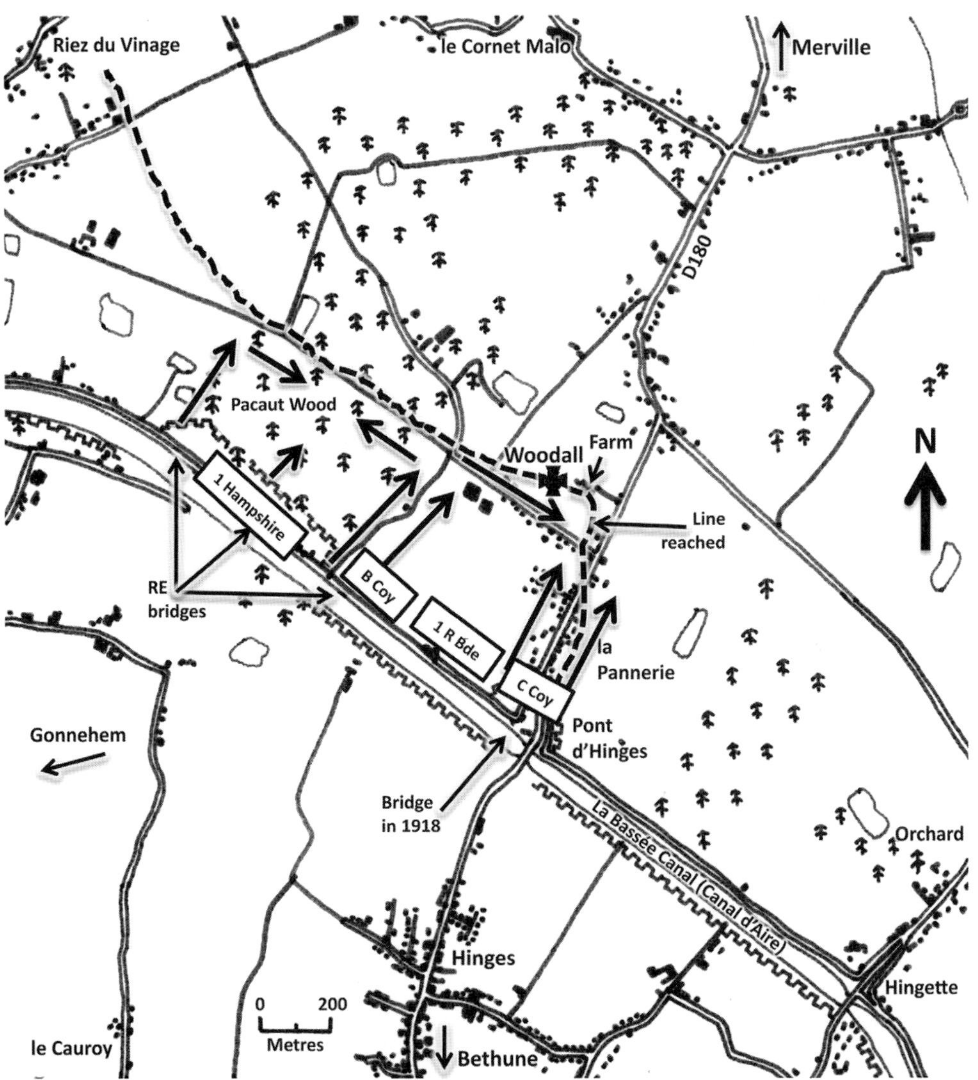

Leave Hinges on the D180 northwards towards Merville. At the bottom of the hill park on the left, where there is a large area of hard standing to overlook the bridge and canal. Continue over the bridge, drive on for just over 600m and turn left into Rue du Rietz. There is a demarcation stone on the right. Continue for 550m to the edge of Pacaut Wood, where there is space to park. Look left along the edge of the Wood towards the canal. Woodall advanced towards you initially before swinging southeast along the line of the road you just drove along. The farm he attacked is to the north of Rue du Rietz.

From the Hinges–Merville road looking north, with the realigned road and bridge over the canal on the right. The canal runs across the middle of the picture, marked by a line of small trees. Pacaut Wood is in the left background.

11th Brigade held the right sector of 4th Division's front from Hingette Bridge, east of Hinges, for 1,350m to the northwest along the La Bassée Canal. 1st Hampshire was on the left and 1st Rifle Brigade was on the right, with 1st Somerset Light Infantry in support. The following night the line was advanced a little north of the canal in the vicinity of Pacaut (Pacault on modern maps) Wood. On the right 76th Brigade took over part of 11th Brigade's frontage, allowing it to slip to the left. On 20th April a 1st Rifle Brigade patrol met with strong opposition at the orchard northeast of Hingette and was forced to withdraw.

That night some adjustments were made to the dispositions in preparation for a small attack on 22nd April north of the La Bassée Canal. 1st Somerset Light Infantry relieved the support company of 1st Hampshire in le Cauroy, the right forward company of 1st Hampshire and the left forward company of 1st Rifle Brigade. Two companies of 1st Somerset Light Infantry on the canal bank came under command of 1st Rifle Brigade. C Company, 1st Rifle Brigade crossed the canal over the partially destroyed bridge at Pont d'Hinges, where the sappers had improvised duckboards into a single file crossing. It took up positions in houses just

Opposite view to the previous picture, with the canal bridge on the extreme left. Pacaut Wood is on the right. Woodall advanced towards the camera position from the canal, parallel with the edge of Pacaut Wood.

The southeast–northwest road running though Pacaut Wood. The attack by 1st Hampshire was from left to right. The line held at the end of the attack was just north (right) of the road.

to the north of the bridge. Two platoons of B Company came under command of 1st Hampshire.

The attack was launched at 5.15 a.m. on 22nd April. 1st Hampshire on the left attacked with three companies and 1st Rifle Brigade on the right with one and a half companies. Following 1st Hampshire were two Stokes mortar teams and four machine guns to assist in holding the new line. A single machine gun accompanied 1st Rifle Brigade. There was a short but comprehensive fire support plan, with Stokes and 6″ Mortars engaging the southern face of the Wood, while the 18 Pounders fired an intense creeping barrage, commencing 200m beyond the tree

line. Three batteries of 6″ Howitzers fired along the la Pannerie (la Cobarderie on modern maps) – Riez du Vinage road, while another battery fired on la Pannerie. This barrage was preceded by one of 60 Pounders. Other mortars and howitzers were used against selected targets in depth, such as groups of houses.

At zero plus three minutes the barrage lifted and 1st Hampshire crossed the canal on three bridges erected by the Royal Engineers, before deploying into platoon columns for the advance. La Pannerie and objectives east and west of Pacaut Wood were captured quickly but machine gun fire from the Wood held up the centre company of 1st Hampshire. The flanking companies turned inwards and the objective fell about 2 p.m.

C Company, 1st Rifle Brigade attacked from the north bank of the canal at Pont d'Hinges. It advanced 450m astride the Hinges – la Pannerie road and captured a row of houses, but heavy shelling forced it out of the buildings. The Company dug in facing east and northeast amongst the hedges to form a defensive flank for the rest of the attacking force running back to the Canal.

B Company followed behind the right of 1st Hampshire and worked its way northwards along the eastern side of Pacaut Wood. **Lance Sergeant Joseph Woodall**, commanding one of the platoons, was held up by a machine gun, which he rushed single-handed and captured the eight-man crew. When the advance reached the Riez du Vinage – la Pannerie road, B Company turned right (east) and established a series of posts along and in front (north) of the road, linking up with C Company on the right. A great deal of fire was received from a farmhouse 200m in front. Woodall collected ten men and, with great gallantry, charged the position. Thirty prisoners were taken and an advanced post was established, with a Lewis gun in the farmhouse. Shortly after this incident the officer commanding was killed

Taken from the southeastern edge of Pacaut Wood looking southeast along the axis of advance for B Company, 1st Rifle Brigade, once it had made the right turn after the initial assault. The farm attacked by Woodall and his men is on the left in front of the prominent copse of poplars. The road running from the bottom right through the centre of the picture is Rue du Rietz.

Close up view of the farm attacked by Woodall on 22nd April.

and Woodall took command of both platoons, reorganising them and ensuring they were disposed correctly. For the rest of the day he moved about constantly, apparently oblivious to the danger, encouraging the men and sending back valuable information. 1st Rifle Brigade suffered seventy-seven casualties up until noon on 23rd April (twenty-five killed, forty-nine wounded, and three missing).

The Germans shelled the new line and the canal bank from 11 a.m., intensifying from 2 p.m. until it began to subside at 4 p.m. and ceased about thirty minutes later. Several machine guns and seventy-five prisoners were taken. Throughout the rest

of the tour in the line the shelling was intense, particularly along the canal bank, where many casualties were suffered by 1st Somerset Light Infantry. On 26th April, 1st Rifle Brigade was relieved and moved into reserve at Gonnehem, having suffered 160 casualties (forty-three killed, 113 wounded and four missing), including those during the attack on 22nd April.

358 LCpl James Hewitson, 1/4th King's Own (Royal Lancaster) (164th Brigade, 55th Division) near Givenchy, France

26th April 1918

A period of relative calm commenced in Flanders on 19th April, while the Germans made preparations to take Mount Kemmel. By the morning of the 21st the French had relieved the British of ten kilometres of front between Meteren and Spanbroekmolen, allowing some exhausted troops to rest. Most activity was confined to local actions, the exception being the amphibious operations against Ostend and Zeebrugge on 23rd April. Intelligence pointed towards a renewal of attacks against Kemmel but the first blow fell at Villers-Bretonneux on the 24th as the Germans drove towards Amiens.

In the Givenchy area a series of small-scale operations followed the heavy fighting earlier in the month. On the 20th the British retook Route A Keep but the Germans captured the craters area on the same day and recovered the Keep on the 22nd. By 24th April, 55th Division was back in the line, having relieved 1st Division, and 1/10th King's (166th Brigade) regained the Keep once again.

On 25th April the Germans renewed their offensive in the Bailleul – Ypres area and wrested Mount Kemmel from the French. Fighting continued the following day and during the night Second Army pulled back to the ramparts of Ypres in order to shorten its line. An outpost line was maintained along the previous front.

The other action on this day was an attempt by 55th Division to recover the old British front line, east and northeast of Givenchy, which was by then the German front line. 1/4th Royal Lancaster had moved into the front line north of the La Bassée Canal on 23rd April, relieving 1st Loyal North Lancashire. A Company was on the right, B Company was in the centre and C Company was on the left, with D Company in support. Just after dark, at 8.45 p.m., on 25th April, two fighting patrols moved out to occupy the front line between the junctions with Orchard Road and Finchley Road. The enemy was holding this section of the line in force and was in no mood to give it up; the patrols were driven back. At 11.20 p.m. a barrage was put down to enable a third party to rush the German held line but the range was too long and the shells came down behind the objective. Without artillery support it was impossible to advance against the enemy machine guns. At 4 a.m. next morning two platoons of A and D Companies rushed the enemy position and engaged in hand-to-hand fighting before being forced to withdraw.

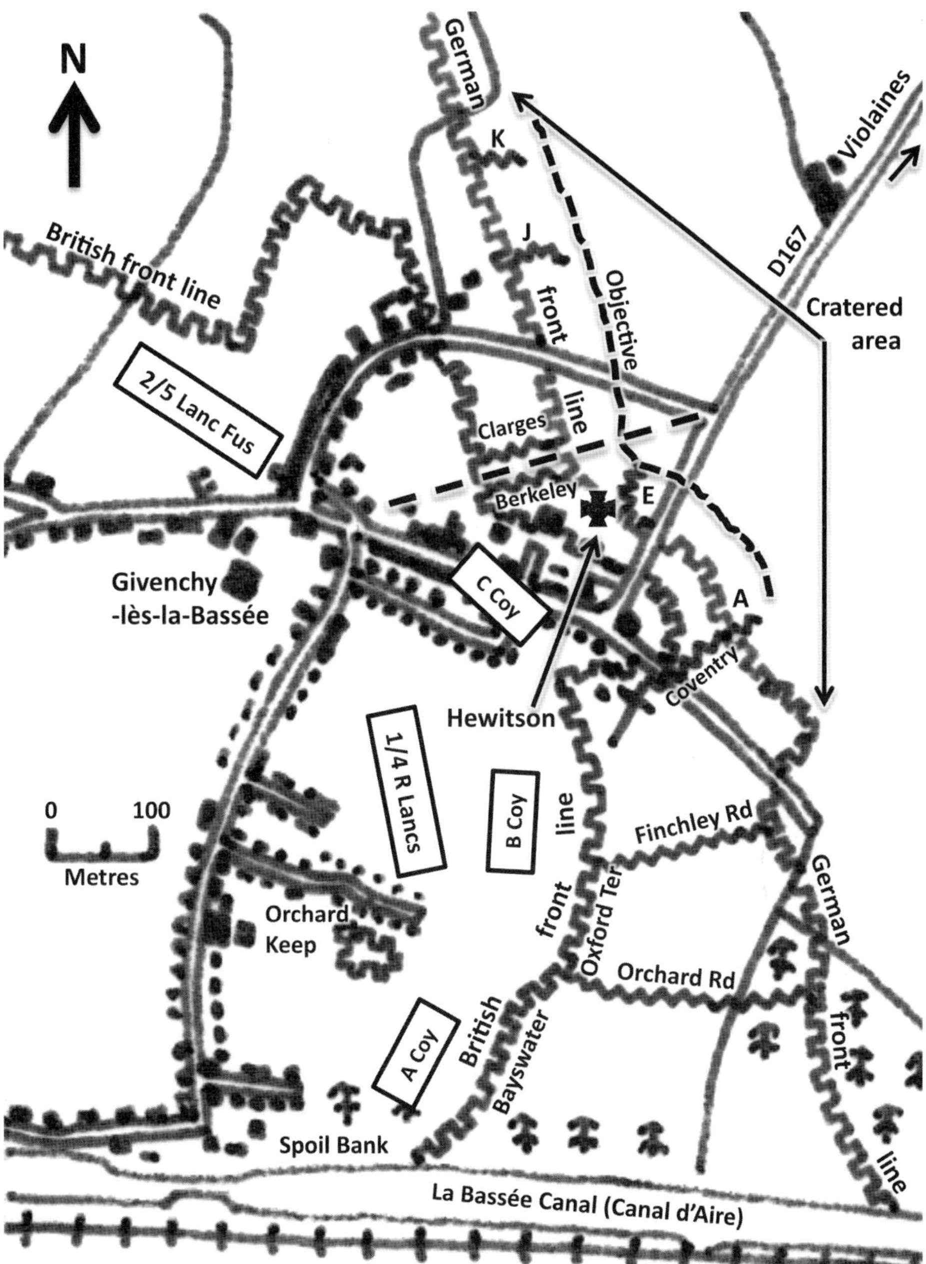

Leave Givenchy in a northeasterly direction on the D167 towards Violaines. Pass the 55th Division Memorial on the right and after just over 300m turn left into Rue du Calvaire and park on the open area on the right. Look back towards Givenchy. James Hewitson's VC action was somewhere between the village and Rue du Calvaire.

From the junction of the D167 with Rue du Calvaire, behind the German front line looking towards the British lines. The attack by 1/4th King's Own (Royal Lancaster) was made between Berkeley Street and Coventry Sap towards the camera position.

At 2.20 p.m., covered by artillery and machine guns, two platoons of C and D Companies attempted to retake the crater saps on the Battalion's left flank, in conjunction with a company of 2/5th Lancashire Fusiliers on the left. The barrage failed to materialise on K and J Saps and 2/5th Lancashire Fusiliers was unable to reach these objectives. 1/4th Royal Lancaster was more fortunate and reached its objectives after fierce fighting. Forty prisoners were taken. Parties of C Company on the left cleared Berkeley Street, E Sap and the front line. At the same time parties of D Company on the right rushed from Coventry Sap to take A Sap and gained contact with C Company. Contact was also made with 2/5th Lancashire Fusiliers.

In the assault **Lance Corporal James Hewitson** led a small party with great determination. In one dugout he killed six Germans who refused to surrender and, on reaching the objective, he noticed an enemy machine gun about to come into action. He worked his way around the edge of the crater and attacked, killing five

This photograph was taken in 1916 in almost the opposite direction to the previous picture.

of the gun team and capturing the sixth. Shortly afterwards he engaged a bombing party advancing towards a Lewis gun post and drove it away, leaving six dead.

Despite this success the 1/4th Royal Lancaster posts were surrounded on three sides and at 6 p.m. the Germans counterattacked. There was bitter fighting and heavy losses were inflicted on the enemy before the British were forced to withdraw. By 8 p.m. they were back in the British lines. Despite the intensity of the fighting, relatively few casualties were reported in 164th Brigade's war diary, just seventy-five killed, wounded and missing over the two days. However, CWGC records indicate that 1/4th Royal Lancaster lost thirteen killed and 2/5th Lancashire Fusiliers twenty-nine killed alone. Many of these men have no known grave and are commemorated on the Loos Memorial. The following morning, commencing at 4 a.m., the Germans bombarded Orchard Keep, Bayswater, Oxford Terrace and Spoil Bank for two hours but no infantry action followed. 1/4th Royal Lancaster reorganised on the 27th and was relieved on the 28th, going into support in the Village Line.

In the north fighting south of Ypres continued until 30th April, when this phase of the German offensive ended. Ludendorff decided to call a temporary halt to rest his troops and reorganise before recommencing operations.

359 Lt George McKean, 14th Battalion (Royal Montreal) (3rd Canadian Brigade, 1st Canadian Division) CEF, Near Gavrelle, France

28th April 1918

The Canadian Corps was not directly involved in the German March offensive. Instead it held an extended front of sixteen kilometres in the Gavrelle area. During the Battle of the Lys in April it found itself in a deepening salient. In order to disguise its weakness, a very aggressive attitude was maintained. A vigorous programme of harassing fire by the artillery, including gas shells, was adopted, whilst numerous raids and patrols were also launched. A shortage of infantry was offset by the

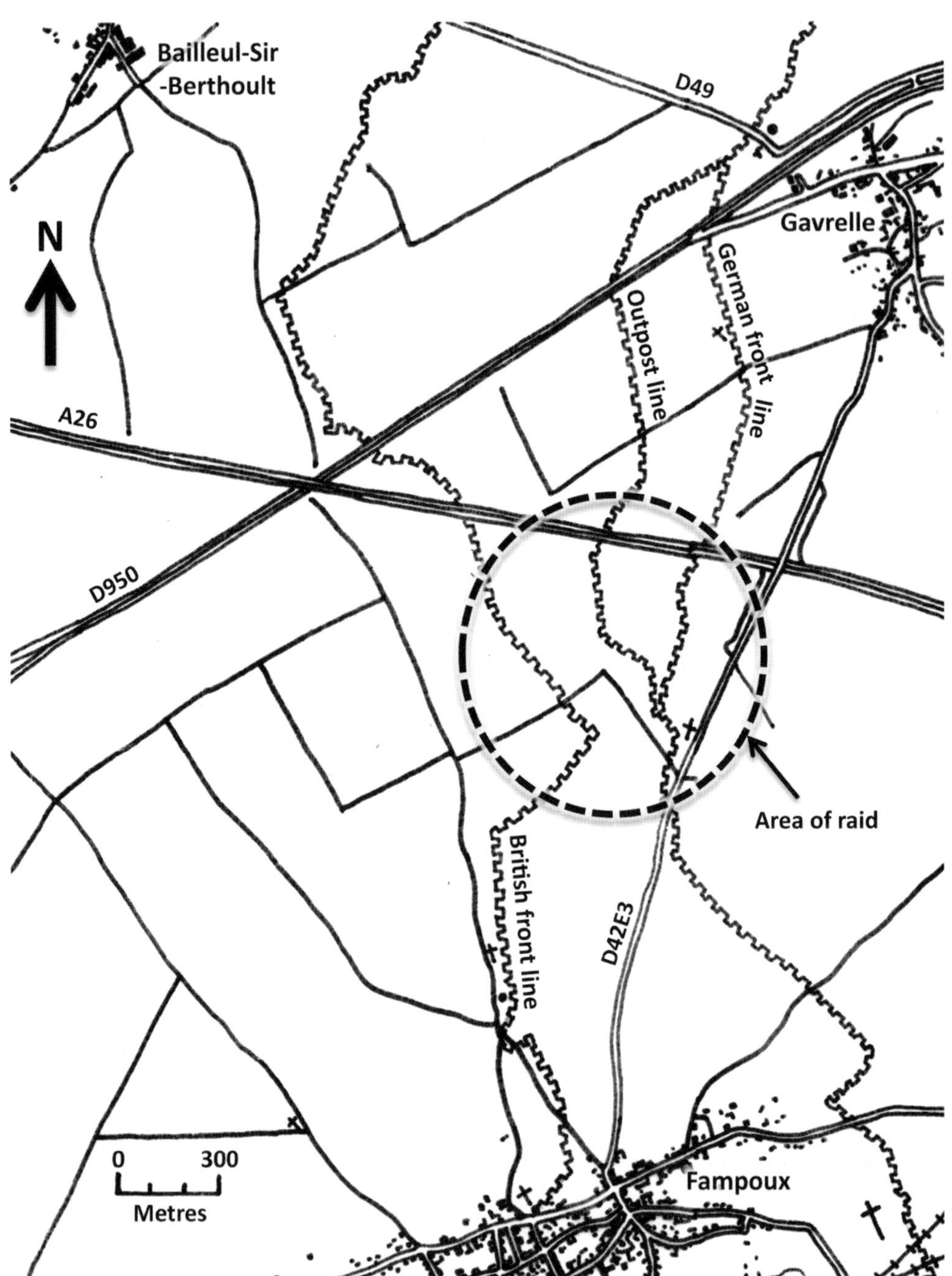

The general area of the raid by 3rd Canadian Brigade on the night of 27th–28th April.

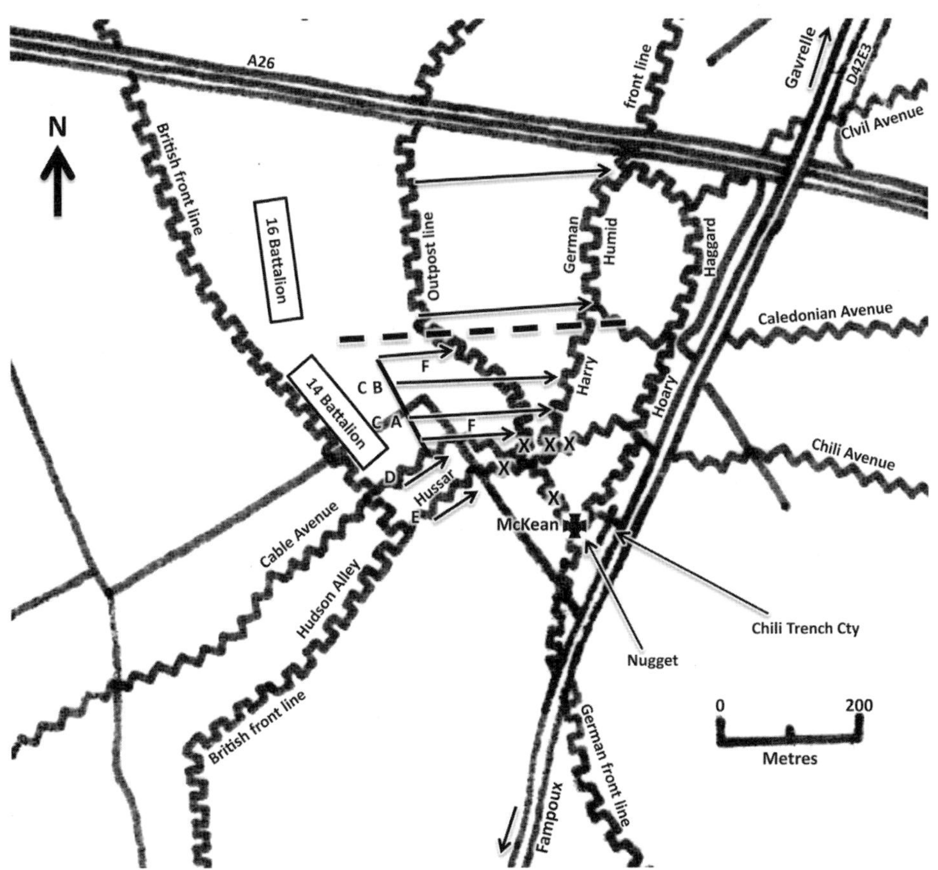

Despite its proximity to the raid, there are no casualties from it in Chili Trench Cemetery. However, the site of Nugget, where part of McKean's VC action took place, is only a few metres behind it and the Cemetery is a convenient place to park. X = block.

formation of two provisional brigades, totalling 8,900 all ranks. The manpower came from the four Divisional Wings of the Canadian Corps Reinforcement Camp, 1st Canadian Tunnelling Company, field companies of 5th Canadian Division and a number of other Canadian and attached British engineer units.

A large raid was launched on the night of 27th-28th April by 3rd Canadian Brigade's 14th and 16th Battalions. The latter was commanded by Lieutenant Colonel Cyrus Peck, who was destined to win the VC in September 1918. The aim was to gain identification, take prisoners, destroy dugouts and trenches and inflict casualties. Very detailed reconnaissance was carried out, as a result of which changes were made to the plan until the day of the launch. There were two objectives. In the original plan these were the front line in Harry and Humid Trenches and the support line in Hoary and Haggard Trenches. However, the discovery of a newly created outpost line meant the objectives were changed to the outpost line and front line respectively.

The raid area from Chili Trench Cemetery. Only the German support line and Nugget are shown. The junction between Nugget and Hoary is where George McKean overcame the strongpoint. The general thrust of the attack was towards the camera position.

14th Battalion's raiding party was commanded by Lieutenant J Patterson DCM. He had six groups:

A Group – Lieutenant Bey Ambrose Neville (MC for this action) with twenty-five men including a Lewis gun section.

B Group – Lieutenant HE Beckett with twenty-five men including a Lewis gun section.

C Group – Lieutenant G Beattie with twenty men.

D Group – Lieutenant RJ Allan with ten men.

E Group – Lieutenant GB McKean with fifteen men, including a Lewis gun section.

F Group – Lieutenant SJ McEwan with twenty-five men, including a Lewis gun section.

In addition, each group had a battalion scout and a stretcher-bearer and there were two small groups of battalion rifle bombers on the flanks. Lieutenant Jackson commanded a covering party to hold the assembly area in no man's land until zero minus fifteen minutes. Assembly was to be completed thirty minutes before zero, which was at 1 a.m. Gaps were pre-cut in the Canadian wire.

The operation was planned similarly in both battalions. In 14th Battalion F Group was to seize the new outpost trench and remain there to be used tactically at the discretion of the commander. A and B Groups were to cross no man's land as quickly as possible behind the barrage, pass through F Group and enter the front line, where dugouts etc were to be destroyed. When the front line was clear A Group was to push its Lewis gun southwards to form a block with three bombers. C Group was split into two parts behind A and B Groups. It was to follow behind and remain outside the enemy parapet to assist any group that had difficulty. If no

problems arose, C Group was to escort prisoners back and assist in evacuating the wounded. D Group was to advance along Cable Avenue, seize an enemy block and post three bombers in another block, in order to prevent the enemy withdrawing from the new outpost trench and a suspected post nearby. It was to clear Cable Avenue to the junction with the front line. E Group was to push along Hussar to seize an enemy block and set up a block to prevent the Germans reinforcing the front line from the support line. Twelve stretcher-bearers were positioned at the junction of Cable Avenue with the Canadian front line to carry casualties to the RAP. Another party waited in the front line to receive prisoners and take them to Battalion HQ. The raid HQ was to be established at the block in Cable Avenue and was connected to Battalion HQ by telephone. The raid groups were to report progress to Patterson by runner.

Fire support was comprehensive. The artillery was to fire on the enemy front line for ten minutes after zero. At zero plus twenty minutes it would lift into a box barrage on Hoary and Haggard Trenches. Chili, Caledonian and Civil communications trenches leading to the support line were to be bombarded by 4.5″ Howitzers. In addition two 4.5″ and one 6″ Howitzers were to bombard Nugget for the first fifteen minutes. Trench mortars and machine guns also had specific targets.

The raiders carried only basic equipment and carried no identification. Each Lewis gun had twelve magazines and riflemen carried six grenades and fifty rounds of ammunition in a bandolier around the waist. Bayonets, hands and faces were blackened. D and E Groups each carried three ammonal tubes to destroy wire in front of enemy blocks. A, B and F Groups carried mobile charges.

The withdrawal signal would be six red flares fired at zero plus forty minutes. The furthest posts would withdraw first. A and B Groups would be covered by C Group. D and E Groups would fall back via Hudson Alley and Lemon Trench. F Group would be the last to withdraw, covering the rest. Dead and wounded were to be brought back and all were to reassemble in Missouri Trench for a roll call.

Assembly went ahead without a hitch, although the presence of 16th Battalion was detected and the raiders were fired upon by the enemy for one minute before zero. The covering party withdrew at 12.55 a.m. and the barrage opened on time. During it F, A and B Groups improved their positions by edging forward stealthily.

The barrage was so good that one soldier said *we were all leaning on it*. The enemy wire was cut by Stokes mortars and by hand. There were three layers but no problems were experienced getting through. The raiders fired a volley of No.23 Rifle Grenades and tear gas grenades before rushing the first objective.

The enemy threw a volley of grenades at F Group as it crossed the wire but they were undeterred and rushed the outpost line. McEwan shot an enemy NCO and two other Germans were bayoneted. The remainder surrendered. McEwan's men pushed on and killed two other enemy and captured a grenade launcher.

A Group met considerable opposition in the front line trench due to a German officer rallying his men. However, when he was shot in the head resistance withered away. Three prisoners were taken from dugouts in Harry. Others hesitated below and mobile charges were thrown in. The Lewis gun section encountered five enemy, of whom two were killed and three others fled into the barrage and were destroyed. A full dugout at this point was blown up and the debris created helped to block the trench. An enemy section tried to rush this block along the trench and was allowed to get close before being engaged by bombs. The survivors were finished by bayonet and two prisoners were taken.

B Group overcame opposition in the first trench with the bayonet. A machine gun crew was scattered by rifle grenades and the survivors were shot or bayoneted. A dugout was destroyed and a water tank. C Group's support was not required but it joined enthusiastically in the mêlée anyway. D Group encountered opposition at both blocks. Lieutenant Allan shot the Germans at the first block and rifle grenades dispersed the enemy at the second. Several prisoners were taken.

E Group had the most difficult task. The German garrison in Hussar was hemmed in by the barrage and had the choice of surrendering or fighting it out. They decided to fight. **Lieutenant George McKean** had to send for more bombs from the front line three times. Wire in front of the block seemed impassable until McKean made a flying dive over it. He struck a German in the stomach with his head before shooting him with his revolver. The rest of the Group then tumbled over and the block was overcome. The second block resisted for a few minutes but, when rushed, the garrison ran for a dugout. 1054039 Sergeant David Jones threw in a mobile charge, which exploded almost immediately and he was killed (Canadian National Vimy Memorial). A strong point at Nugget put up fierce resistance and was only taken in the last few minutes of the raid due to McKean's determination and resourcefulness. If not taken this post would have caused great losses in the withdrawal. McKean personally accounted for eight Germans.

The withdrawal was carried out coolly and effectively by individual officers. E Group was the last to report in at 1.50 a.m. and at 1.57 a.m. the raid HQ was closed down. Material recovered by the raiders identified 188th Infantry Regiment of 187th Division, 122nd Wireless Detachment and 231st Field Artillery Regiment. Ten dugouts were blown up, five by each battalion, sometimes with the occupants in them. Overall the Germans fought well until their leaders were killed and then seemed to lose heart. 14th Battalion captured twenty-six Germans, including two wounded and two others who died. Two machine guns and a light trench mortar were also recovered in addition to other equipment destroyed and abandoned. 16th Battalion captured twenty-eight prisoners and three machine guns. Total German casualties may have been as high as 200. 14th Battalion counted thirty-two in the captured trenches and an unknown number of defenders were blown up in their dugouts. Canadian casualties were comparatively light. 14th Battalion had two killed (CWGC records four deaths on 28th April) and eleven wounded out of the 138 taking part. 16th Battalion lost five killed (CWGC records six deaths on 28th April) and fifteen wounded out of the 151 participants. Seven of the dead of the two battalions are buried in Roclincourt Military Cemetery. Three have no known grave and are commemorated on the Canadian National Vimy Memorial, including Sergeant Jones.

South of Fampoux 16th Battalion also attacked two posts 3,300m south of the main raid. This resulted in one machine gun and three prisoners being taken, but the results did not justify the casualties suffered. Later on 28th April, 14th Battalion was relieved by 13th Battalion.

360 Sgt William Gregg, 13th Rifle Brigade (111th Brigade, 37th Division), Bucquoy, France
361 Rfn William Beesley, 13th Rifle Brigade (111th Brigade, 37th Division), Bucquoy, France

8th May 1918

A new phase on the Western Front commenced at the beginning of May 1918, when the Germans switched attention to the French sector. They intended drawing Allied reserves from the north in order to strike a decisive blow against the British later. The battles in March and April had resulted in 240,000 British casualties, for which only 133,000 replacements had been received. The BEF needed time to rest, reinforce and re-equip its under-strength divisions, eight of which were reduced to cadre until manpower was received to bring them back to establishment. Five other divisions were replaced by the French and sent to quiet areas under French command. On 1st May the BEF could call on only thirty-seven of its fifty British divisions, plus ten more from the Dominion nations.

The Americans were arriving in strength; on 1st May there were 430,000 US troops in France and by the end of the month this had risen to 651,000. However, numbers alone do not tell the full story, as many US divisions were not combat ready. There was also fierce debate amongst the Allied high command on how they should be used. Understandably, the Americans wanted to fight under American command and were against proposals to fill gaps in the line as advocated by the British and French.

Bucquoy cemetery is on Rue du Bois Logeast on the eastern edge of the town. There is a parking place in front of the cemetery gates. Continue along Rue du Bois Logeast to the crucifix road junction. The crucifix is often difficult to see amongst the vegetation. Drive another 250m along Rue du Bois Logeast and stop to look back over the cemetery, crucifix and general area of the attack by 13th Rifle Brigade. DH = Doll's House and RP = Right Party,

Fortunately the Germans also needed time to rest. About 140 divisions had been used in the March and April offensives. Of these at least sixty were in need of reconstitution. The question was, would the Germans recover in time to make a decisive strike before the Americans began to make a significant impact? To ensure that the Germans could not move troops around with impunity, a number of small

Bucquoy cemetery looking northeast. Parties 2 and 3 attacked towards the camera position on 8th May.

operations were undertaken by the BEF to tie down reserves and ensure that they held their front.

One such operation was launched to the east of Bucquoy by 13th Rifle Brigade on 8th May. The aim was to bring the enemy lines in the valley east of the village under closer observation and to obtain prisoners and identification. The previous day reconnaissance patrols had thoroughly checked the enemy defences and located their posts. However, they had been unable to penetrate the defences in the Doll's House area. The night before the attack, parties of C Company cut gaps in the wire and marked them. Zero hour was set for 2 p.m. in the hope that an attack would not be expected in broad daylight.

13th Rifle Brigade's CO was given discretion to withdraw from the new line if he considered that no advantage was to be gained by remaining there. A and D Companies, right and left respectively, were to lead the attack, supported by C and B Companies. A Company was divided into five parties and its objectives centred on the cemetery and crucifix. D Company was also divided into five parties and was to prolong the line to the north. The attack was to be silent,

Some of the older gravestones still show signs of the battle in the cemetery in May 1918.

Looking south along the track that leads to the crucifix in the distance. No.4 Party attacked from right to left across the track in the direction of the small copse on the left. The cemetery is behind the tall trees in the centre, just to the right of the track. William Beesley's VC action was in the field to the left of the track.

with the artillery on call until required, in order not to alert the enemy. The field guns were stood by to fire a protective barrage and the heavy artillery was prepared to carry out counter-battery work. The trench mortars would fire on the area southeast of Doll's House in order to protect the right flank.

The signal for the attack to commence at 2 p.m. was the Brigade Trench Mortar Battery firing on the cemetery. The Germans were taken completely by surprise, except on the right flank, where they were very alert. The Right Party seized Doll's House but it could not be held against a determined counterattack and, at 3.45 p.m., the Party was driven out to houses twenty metres to the northwest. It was reinforced by a Lewis gun team at 4 p.m. and held on until ordered to withdraw at 5.40 p.m., having suffered sixty percent casualties. No.1 Party reached its objective at the crossroads but came under enfilade machine gun fire from the crucifix. It lost half its strength. A counterattack at 2.15 p.m. pushed the Party back fifty metres but it was reinforced by a section of the support company and, despite being almost surrounded, held on until ordered to withdraw at 5.40 p.m.

Machine gun fire from the cemetery caused many casualties to Nos.2 & 3 Parties. They rushed it and thirty enemy were encountered; eleven surrendered and the remainder, including the machine gun team, were killed. When his platoon commander, Second Lieutenant GD Fraser, was wounded in the fight for the

The crucifix is hidden amongst the clump of trees in the centre, with the cemetery in the left distance. The track to the right of the crucifix is the one seen in the previous view from the opposite direction.

cemetery, **Sergeant William Gregg** took over and pushed on to the crucifix. He rushed a machine gun post and killed the entire crew, before taking four men prisoner from a nearby dugout. He rushed another post, where he killed two more and captured another. As a result of his decisive action, the objective, and some posts to the north, were taken. Consolidation began immediately under Gregg's direction.

A counterattack turned the right flank and forced Gregg back to the cemetery but, when a reinforcement section from the support company arrived, he led his men forward and recovered the lost ground. In this attack Gregg captured another machine gun post and killed the crew. He was driven back by another counterattack but once again recovered the lost ground. Gregg held the position under heavy fire for several hours, during which he was fully exposed to fire but displayed the utmost coolness and determination. He was ordered to withdraw at 5.40 p.m., by when half of his men had been killed or injured.

No.4 Party reached its objective and then came under heavy enfilade machine gun fire from the right. The platoon sergeant and three section commanders were killed or wounded. **Rifleman William Beesley** took command and continued the advance. At the objective he rushed a machine gun alone and killed two of the crew with his revolver (Lewis gun in some accounts). When a German officer tried to reach the gun from a dugout on the right, Beesley shot him dead. Four other officers appeared from the dugout and he called on them to surrender. As one tried to dispose of a map, Beesley shot him in the hand. The map was recovered and proved invaluable in showing the enemy's dispositions. The four officers were captured and sent to the rear. Beesley then rushed the post to the left, where the machine gun was located and discovered one dead crewman. Two others he took prisoner and also sent them to the rear.

Having gained touch with the section on the left, Beesley returned to the machine gun position, where his No.2 arrived with the Lewis gun. They were the only survivors in the Party but set up the Lewis gun in the German machine gun position and engaged the enemy as they tried to withdraw to the support line. They remained in this position for the next few hours, firing 600–800 rounds and inflicting serious casualties on the enemy, particularly during their counterattack on the cemetery. At 7 p.m. the Germans counterattacked and the No.2 was wounded. Beesley carried on alone, maintaining the position even when the posts to left and right fell back. By continuing to resist, the remnants of A Company were able to pull back unmolested. After dark Beesley brought back his wounded comrade and the Lewis gun, arriving in the original line at 10 p.m. He set up the Lewis gun again and remained in action until the situation stabilised.

In D Company, No.5 Party was partly in dead ground during the advance, except from the crucifix, from where it was engaged. When ten metres from the objective, six of the Party threw in grenades and four or five enemy surrendered immediately. A German sergeant major threw a grenade back and wounded the sergeant.

Lieutenant Edgerton was wounded by a machine gun bullet at the same time. Nevertheless the Party got into the German position and took eleven prisoners, including the sergeant major. Second Lieutenant George in the support company rushed forward to take command and got the Lewis gun into action to cover the Parties advancing on the right. Second Lieutenant Mitchell subsequently arrived to take over and reorganise the party. The Party came under very heavy machine gun fire and had to keep well down. The Lewis gun was damaged by enemy fire and was sent back for a replacement under heavy fire. Contact was made with the Party on the right but, about 6.45 p.m., it was learned that A Company on the right had withdrawn. At the same time enemy fire was opened from the crucifix and large numbers of Germans began to advance. With no support on the right, the position was untenable and at 7 p.m. the Party withdrew.

No.6 Party consisted of just one lance corporal and six men. It came under heavy fire and they dropped into a shell hole. B/200841 Lance Corporal J Smith and one man got over the German wire and were only a few metres from the enemy positions, when both were hit, Smith fatally (Gommecourt British Cemetery No.2–V H 6). The rest of the men did not reach the objective but were within bombing distance and held on there until dark, when they fell back to the start positions.

Nos.7, 8 & 9 Parties reached a position twenty to thirty metres in front of the German wire without casualties. From there they had good observation over the enemy rear positions. Half the men dug in while the other half kept a nearby enemy post under fire. From 4 p.m. to 6 p.m. enemy troops massing in the valley to the east were engaged. At 6 p.m. the Germans fired a smoke barrage to the northeast. A red Very light was fired to bring down the protective barrage and again at 6.30 p.m. There was no response from the British artillery small red flares are difficult to see in daylight at a distance. At 7 p.m. the Germans opened a heavy machine gun crossfire behind the British posts. At the same time they advanced from both flanks. The position was hopeless and the three parties withdrew.

Numerous enemy casualties were inflicted and a total of thirty German prisoners were taken, including two officers. Two machine guns were brought back and

From the Little Caterpillar, looking in the direction of the attack by D Company on 19th May 1918. Morlancourt is in the distance on the right and the thick hedge on the left marks the Little Caterpillar. The open nature of the ground is evident. The line of low bushes on the far side of this field is Big Caterpillar. Ville is out of sight in the valley to the left.

two others were destroyed. A number of weaknesses in the planning of the attack were identified. The main one was the weakness of the right flank and failure to recognise its vulnerability, despite 1st Essex (112th Brigade) seizing a post on that flank in support of the main attack by 13th Rifle Brigade. In addition, no orders were issued for the consolidation period. The Battalion lost thirty-six men killed or died of wounds in the attack. Twenty-nine of them have no known grave and are commemorated on the Pozieres Memorial.

362 Sgt William Ruthven, 22nd Battalion, AIF (6th Australian Brigade, 2nd Australian Division), Ville sur Ancre, France

19th May 1918

The Australian Corps aimed to push forward a portion of its line every night in a series of small-scale operations, known as 'peaceful penetration'. They were generally launched without prior artillery preparation. One of these attacks, planned at Ville-sur-Ancre, had a number of aims – to shorten the line, deal the enemy a blow, weaken his position in the Morlancourt basin, thereby denying him a covered approach to Ville and to hamper plans for the next German offensive. At the time the next phase of the great German spring offensive was expected to fall north of the Australian Corps, between Albert and Arras.

6th Australian Brigade, under Brigadier General John Paton CB CMG, holding the Ancre valley, had been preparing the attack since 10th May. He envisaged attacking either side of Ville after the moon set but before dawn. It was clear that the village could not be held unless the wide cross spur, rising above it to the south, was also captured. That task fell to 22nd Battalion. It involved capturing two sunken roads, the Little and Big Caterpillars, about 400m apart, which ran parallel with and along the western and eastern sides of the spur. These roads were also the German front and main lines of defence. To the south, 18th Battalion (5th Australian Brigade) would also push forward on top of the plateau. On the left flank, 54th Brigade cooperated with a raid and Chinese attacks. 27th and 28th Battalions (7th Australian Brigade) also came under command of 6th Australian Brigade.

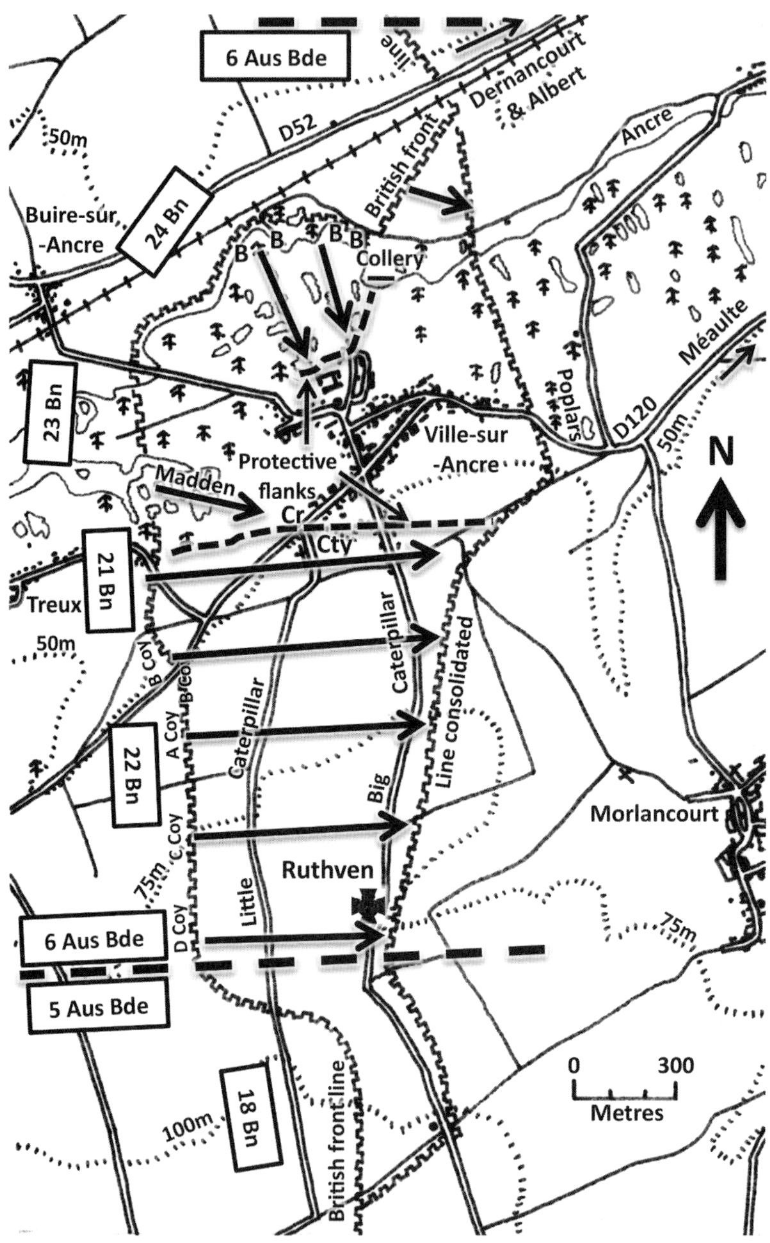

Drive through Ville-sur-Ancre on the D120 to the southwest. Just before the cemetery, turn left and follow the road (Little Caterpillar) uphill for 1,200m to where it levels out. This is the right flank of 22nd Battalion. Look left (east) through gaps in the thick hedgerow towards Morlancourt. The line of Big Caterpillar can be seen about 350m away. Continue uphill to the t-junction and turn left. After 450m turn left at the water reservoir into Big Caterpillar. After 500m round a right hand bend into the stretch of sunken road where Ruthven won his VC. Continue down the hill to re-enter Ville-sur-Ancre. B = bridge, Cr = crucifix, Cty = cemetery.

To the north, two companies of 21st Battalion would establish a line of posts along the flats to protect 22nd Battalion's left flank by masking the southern edge of the village. At 4.15 a.m., when the protective artillery barrage was timed to ceased, patrols would go on and hopefully seize another 200–300m of the Morlancourt spur. There was no intention to attack Ville directly. Instead it would be kept under artillery fire for several hours after the attack. Patrols would then move in after 6.30 a.m. If they found that taking the village in daylight would incur heavy casualties, they would halt and await a night attack, possibly supported by tanks. In order to isolate the village, an outpost line would be established to the east by 24th Battalion swinging forward posts on the north side and 21st Battalion from the south. They were to meet beyond the village but when this was to happen was left to Paton's discretion.

North of Ville the attack would be made by two companies of 24th Battalion. The river was to be spanned by four light manportable bridges, each about nine metres long. One platoon was to cross over each one. The two westernmost bridges would be pre-positioned by 6th Field Company and 23rd Battalion. However, the sites chosen for the other two were close to enemy posts on the south bank and were to be thrown across just before the attack commenced.

Artillery support was provided by seven field brigades, three of which were British. The Caterpillars, crucifix and cemetery, south of the village, and other defences were shelled frequently by heavy artillery and Newton mortars. The attack would be preceded by a five-minute barrage and gas was fired into the area on the previous day. It was hoped that the Germans would regard the five-minute bombardment before the attack as just another artillery fire mission and not the signal for an immediate attack. The creeping barrage would move forward ninety metres every three minutes. When the objective was reached, smoke was to be fired to mask the attackers while they dug in. Rear areas were subjected to the fire of twenty-nine machine guns, each gun firing almost 12,000 rounds. Four other machine guns and some Stokes trench mortars accompanied the assault troops. The Little Caterpillar, crucifix and cemetery were to be engaged by Stokes trench mortars for six minutes after zero hour. Other mortars were to engage known machine gun posts until zero plus thirty minutes.

On the night of 14th/15th May, 22nd and 24th Battalions were relieved in the front line by 21st and 23rd Battalions. The first two bridges were about to be laid when word came that the attack was postponed. They were taken back and covered in leaves and grass. On the night of 17th/18th May the bridges were laid without incident and covering posts were established one hundred metres on the far side. 18th May was very hot and a violent thunderstorm at 4 p.m. flooded the trenches. Although this made the ground difficult, assembly was completed on time and without incident. Zero hour was set for 2 a.m. on 19th May. Moonset was at 2.10 a.m. and dawn was at 4 a.m. Last minute changes to the position of the two easternmost bridges meant that a Lewis gun team, sent to suppress enemy fire, did not know where the bridges were to be set up. Covering parties were also late in being tasked. As a result there was some confusion and delay and a few skirmishes with German patrols, but the bridges were positioned.

Before zero hour, 24th Battalion's left company, north of the Ancre, swung forward and was signalling success by 2.35 a.m. The company on the right was to cross the river by the four bridges. The easternmost platoon had not heard that the engineers had had to change the bridge location at the last minute. The bridge could not be found and machine guns on the south bank raked the platoon. The commander, Lieutenant George Edward Buchanan Munro, was mortally wounded (died 22nd May, buried in Vignacourt British Cemetery – II C 7). 4388 Sergeant James Michael Collery (awarded the MM later) distributed the men on the north bank in three posts, in accordance with the alternative plan, and used the Lewis guns to suppress the German fire. From daybreak the snipers also kept the Germans under deadly fire. The next platoon to the west crossed its bridge and advanced in two parties in the dark. Visibility was ten metres at the most. The right party ran into an enemy machine gun post, which was charged and overcome. The party to the left was only fifty metres from village when it was challenged. Two grenades were thrown in response and the Germans replied with six stick grenades, which wounded four men. Despite this the Germans withdrew. The platoon pulled back twenty metres to avoid a small lake and took up positions facing the village. The platoon commander, Lieutenant EHD Edgerton DSO MM, realised that he was not as far east as he should be and took his runner on a reconnaissance along the river bank. They came upon a German machine gun post firing across the river at Collery's platoon. Both threw in a grenade, one crewman was shot by Edgerton and the rest surrendered. He sent them back with the runner and, with his left party, pushed on to overcome another enemy post. They were eventually halted by the marsh and pulled back a little to set up a post on the riverbank. The two platoons to the west crossed by their bridges, split into five parties and advanced fan-wise

Looking down the Big Caterpillar on the right from the south. D Company attacked from left to right. The line of Little Caterpillar is marked by the thin line of bushes on the left skyline.

southeastwards. A machine gun post was overcome and a screen was set up facing the village.

22nd Battalion assembled on tapes laid by 6th Field Company on the western slope of the spur. Because resistance was expected at the crucifix and cemetery on the left, a patrol under Lieutenant Norman John Madden was detached to advance ahead of 21st Battalion on the left and attack them from the north. 22nd Battalion advanced with all four companies in line (from the left B, A, C and D) in two waves on a frontage of 1,150m. The men were spread thinly, on average one every ten metres.

The barrage fell on time as one gun and flares shot up along the whole German front. When the flares died away, the way ahead was well silhouetted by shell bursts. Around the crucifix and cemetery the German posts resisted strongly but, when the Australians crept forward through the cemetery hedge, they fell back, carrying their machine gun, probably as a result of Madden's patrol appearing behind them. 21st Battalion met heavy fire from the crucifix when only ten metres away and two platoon commanders were wounded. The NCOs took over and got the men digging in to form the flank defence against the village.

On the right the commander of D Company, 22nd Battalion, Captain WR Hunter, was hit, Lieutenant Charles Maxwell Bowden was killed (Dive Copse British Cemetery, Sailly-le-Sec – III B 18) and Lieutenant Southwell was wounded. As a result some confusion occurred. **Sergeant William Ruthven**, the acting

The sunken road looking south. This is where William Ruthven captured thirty-two Germans in the second part of his VC action.

company sergeant major, grasped the situation, sorted the men out and took control of the Company. As they reached the Big Caterpillar a machine gun opened fire from about thirty-five metres ahead. The advance stopped and Ruthven realised the seriousness of the situation. He moved into grenade range, threw a bomb, which burst near the machine gun and then he rushed in, bayoneting one crewman and capturing the remainder. Other Germans then emerged from dugouts in the sunken road. Ruthven shot and wounded two and captured six others, together with two machine guns. At 3 a.m. D Company sent up its success signal. Lieutenant Ernest Ellerman Paterson took command of the Company and, with Ruthven, reorganised it and established a post forward of the sunken road. While digging in, the men came under sniper fire from their rear. Ruthven observed some enemy in the sunken road about 135m distant who had been overlooked by the moppers-up. Without hesitation, and armed only with a revolver, he crossed the open ground alone and rushed the position. He shot two Germans who refused to come out of a dugout and single-handedly mopped up, capturing the garrison of thirty-two and holding them until assistance arrived to escort them to the rear. For the remainder of the day Ruthven set a splendid example of leadership, moving around the position under fire, while supervising consolidation and encouraging the men.

C Company suffered casualties on the start line and the commander, Major JS Dooley MC, was wounded early on in the attack. Two Lewis gun teams were lost to heavy machine gun fire from the first objective. This post was cleared by Corporal Lawrence Thomas Binns firing his Lewis gun from the hip. Small arms fire from the Big Caterpillar was overcome quickly and isolated parties of the enemy were mopped up. The Company then dug in on the objective.

A Company also encountered machine gun fire on the start line coming from the first objective, but this was overcome quickly with only a few casualties. Opposition in the Little Caterpillar was cleared by a Lewis gunner. Another machine gun held up the advance from the top of the road bank of Big Caterpillar. Lieutenant PJ Abercrombie MC threw a grenade, hitting the gunner on the side of the head, killing him and also damaging the gun. The road was then rushed and another machine gun was dealt with by a Lewis gunner. Many Germans sheltering under British waterproof sheets surrendered and were sent to the rear.

B Company on the left flank sent Lieutenant Madden's patrol to clear the cemetery and crucifix. This was achieved successfully and two machine guns were seized. More machine gun fire was received from the Little Caterpillar and a Lewis gun team was knocked out. The commanders of the two platoons on the right, and the NCOs who took over, all became casualties early on in the attack. However, there was less opposition than expected from the Big Caterpillar and the Company advanced to its objective.

Meanwhile 21st Battalion reached the bottom of Little Caterpillar. Its right platoon under Lieutenant Bennie had to deal with the sunken section of the Méaulte road to the junction with Big Caterpillar. As they surged ahead, Germans came out of their shelters and surrendered. This platoon reached the farthest point in the attack, a road crossing 225m beyond Big Caterpillar. Bennie established two posts to form the easternmost section of the flank guard.

The company commanders of 22nd Battalion established posts to the east of Big Caterpillar in an attempt to avoid the inevitable German retaliatory fire. It was about 2.35 a.m. Two machine guns of 6th Australian Machine Gun Company and two Stokes mortars arrived at the northern end of Big Caterpillar. Another two machine guns were positioned further south, up the hill overlooking the Morlancourt basin. The forward half of the line held by 21st Battalion was heavily shelled, as was the left of 22nd Battalion. The fire was coming from the protective barrage falling short. Bennie's post was pulled back 135m and B Company on the left of 22nd Battalion had to retire about 250m.

Thus far the German artillery response had been feeble, indicating that the enemy commanders were unclear how far the attack had gone. An airman of 3rd Squadron AFC flew over at 4.20 a.m. and from the information he received from ground signals, was able to drop an accurate position map at Divisional HQ. Prior to this, reports reaching Paton indicated that enemy morale was poor. At 3.47 a.m. he decided to proceed immediately to seize Ville. The supporting artillery and machine guns were to cease at 4.15 a.m. and lift into a protective barrage to the east of the village until 5.15 a.m. 21st Battalion from the south and 23rd and 24th Battalions from the west and north, were then to mop up the village. Orders to the assaulting companies arrived promptly, except for the right company of 21st Battalion, which did not receive the message until 5.10 a.m.

A group of 23rd Battalion (two officers and twenty-two men), organised into three parties, was ready to go on the edge of the village. Within three minutes of the artillery lifting they had seized three machine guns defending the northwest edge of the village and continued against the outpost trenches that had fired on 21st Battalion earlier. 24th Battalion also carried out its share of the mopping-up quickly. 21st Battalion's left company attacked at the same time in sectional rushes. A party of up to thirty Germans flushed out by 23rd Battalion ran back to the trenches and nearest buildings of the village. At 4.40 a.m. the Germans in the trenches gave in and a post surrendered to 23rd Battalion on the left. 21st Battalion continued along the streets of the village, clearing houses and cellars as they went. Some resistance was encountered and many enemy were killed in short and sharp skirmishes. One hundred prisoners were sent back and many machine guns and a few trench mortars were captured. By 5.15 a.m. a line of poplars 180m beyond the village had been reached, well beyond the final objective. Other Germans continued to resist north of the church but were overcome by a combined attack by a number of small groups. Some prisoners were shot as the Germans here had twice pretended to surrender before reopening fire. Resistance in the village ended but many Germans, hiding in cellars and elsewhere, were winkled out later. The village was not considered to be clear until 7.30 a.m. Meanwhile the right company of 21st Battalion moved up to hold the line between the left flank of 22nd Battalion and the crucifix.

The line held by 21st Battalion east of the village was dangerously exposed to German machine gun fire and could be attacked by surprise at any time. It was decided to pull back to the village, out of sight of the hills from where the fire was coming, and to go forward again that night. A post was established on a solitary dry spot northeast of the village. The left of 21st Battalion pulled back, as it was suffering casualties, and the flank was covered by Sergeant Collery's party north of the river. Two platoons of 28th Battalion came forward to allow two platoons of 21st Battalion to take up positions on the outskirts of Ville. Five Lewis gun teams were established in shell holes to the southeast.

21st Battalion south of the village moved into the Méaulte road cutting on the left of 22nd Battalion. German artillery fire in enfilade on the extension of the Big Caterpillar killed five men and wounded eight. Machine guns and trench mortars at the northern end of the Big Caterpillar pulled back before being hit. Three Lewis gun posts were established northeast of the junction of Big Caterpillar and the Méaulte road. At 10 a.m. two machine guns joined them.

To the south, 5th Australian Brigade's attack on the plateau was carried out by two companies of 18th Battalion on a frontage of 450m. They were in contact with the right of 22nd Battalion. A third company to the right sent out a platoon to form a strongpoint to protect that flank. A fourth company on the right bent its left forward to keep in line. The attackers followed the barrage closely and were in the enemy posts quickly, some of which fought bravely until hit by grenades. By 3.25 a.m. 5th Australian Brigade was on its objective. However, the assault line had been too thin and a German post 180m behind the new line held out. Some Germans who had surrendered while going back joined this post. A party of 19th Battalion and 5th Field Company, digging a communication trench to join the new line, was fired on. It launched an attack, killing five Germans and taking two machine guns. A dangerously exposed post was pulled back. Isolated Germans continued harassing fire and were gradually overcome by artillery, rifle grenades and Lewis guns.

Airmen detected enemy formations moving forward east of Morlancourt and south of Dernancourt in the Ancre valley. Both were hit by artillery fire and no attempt was made to counterattack 6th Australian Brigade's position. Nine pairs of snipers were sent out and had considerable success, claiming fifty-seven hits. The early afternoon was very quiet but, at 5.45 p.m., German artillery fire increased on Ville and Big Caterpillar. During the night 21st Battalion pushed forward a line of posts to the east of Ville and 22nd Battalion's left company moved forward to its original objective. The forward posts were improved with the help of two companies of 28th Battalion. During the night 22nd Battalion's line was linked by a new communication trench, dug by 2nd Australian Pioneers. By dawn on the 20th, the new line was dug in and strongly held.

Total Australian casualties were 418, of which 316 were in 6th Australian Brigade. 22nd Battalion's share was 191. Three hundred and thirty enemy prisoners and forty-five machine guns were taken, in addition to many other Germans killed and wounded. German losses are likely to have totaled 800. In addition to Ruthven's VC, 22nd Battalion received another twenty-seven decorations for the attack on Ville sur Ancre:

DSO – Major Leslie William Matthews.

MC – Lieutenants Percy John Abercrombie, Charles William Hutton, Norman John Madden and Ernest Ellerman Paterson.

DCM – 1634 CSM Roland Charles Werrett and 3914 Sergeant George Francis Robinson.

MM Bar – 2493 Sergeant Robert Elliot Batton, 117 Corporal Lawrence Thomas Binns and R160 Private Timothy Gorman.

MM – Sergeants 5017 Arthur William Gould, 690 William George Speechley and 2396 Henry Percy Swift, 6616 Lance Sergeant Normoyle Francis Woolston, Corporals 1915 Martin Darrell Jinks, 4478 John Lambert and 5811 John Marsh, Lance Corporals 761 Stanley Wilfred Beckwith, 6401 James Paterson McCall, 681 Leslie Russell and 5686 Lewis Strawhorn and Privates 5342 James Taylor Douglas, 4699 Joseph Ellison, 4774A Percival Edward Smith (later POW, died 10th November 1918–Villers-Bretonneux Memorial, France), 4542 Victor Edwin Splatt, 6171 Colin Campbell Wilson and 6109 Edward Konza.

Battle of the Aisne 1918

363 Brig Gen George Grogan, Worcestershire Regiment commanding 23rd Brigade (8th Division), Treslon and Bouleuse Ridges, France

364 LCpl Joel Halliwell, 11th Lancashire Fusiliers (74th Brigade, 25th Division), Muscourt, France

27th-29th May 1918

By early May 1918 the British were desperate to rest and reconstitute their shattered divisions following the German spring offensives before they were thrown back into the fighting. As an example, during the March and April battles, 8th Division had suffered 8,515 casualties. Although it had almost been brought back up to strength with 7,896 replacements, they were inexperienced and a period of relative calm was

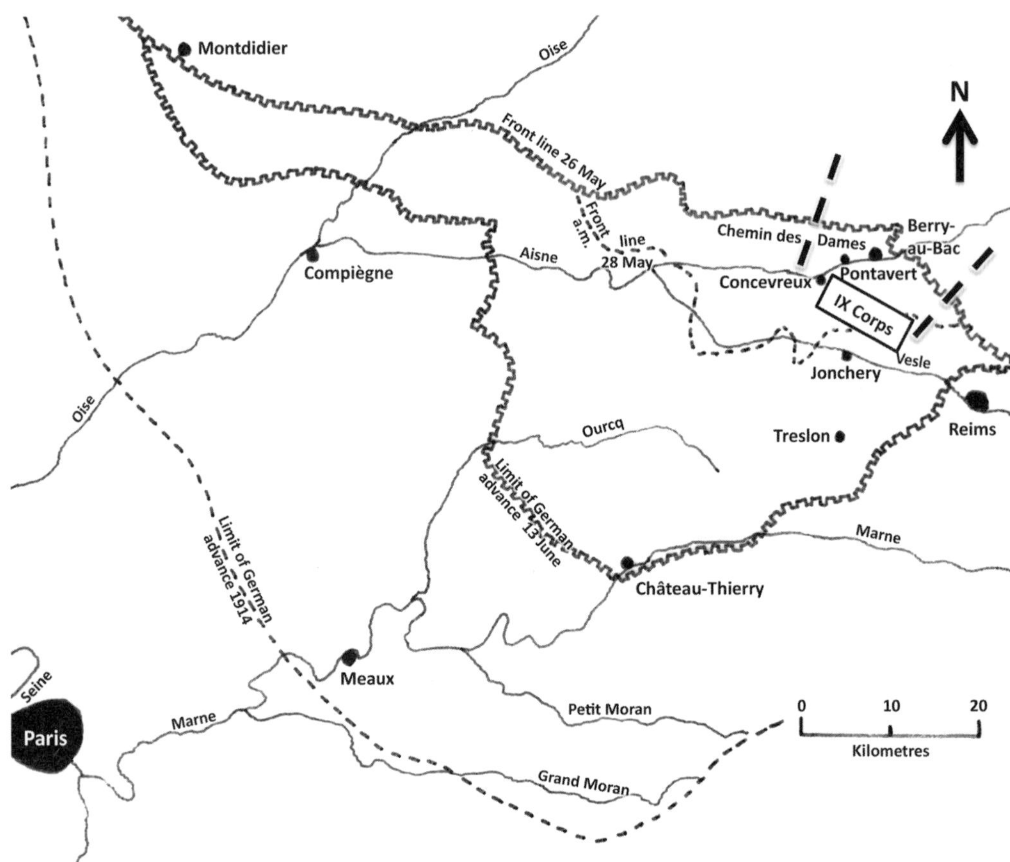

The area affected by the German offensive on the Chemin des Dames area in May and June 1918. The German onslaught fell well short of their advance in 1914.

required in which to assimilate these new men, reorganise, retrain and prepare for future operations. In addition, General Foch needed to create a General Reserve to meet the next onslaught. To satisfy both requirements, French divisions from the quiet Chemin des Dames sector were relieved by five exhausted British divisions.

The Allies had conflicting intelligence on where the Germans would strike next. The British were concerned about another offensive in the north, as there was little room for manoeuvre without threatening their rear areas. German preparations were detected opposite almost every sector of the British front. The French agreed that the blow would fall north of the Oise but it was the Americans who correctly identified the Chemin des Dames in the French sector.

By 19th May, the five British divisions of IX Corps had moved to the Chemin des Dames, an area held lightly by the French Sixth Army. A number of French artillery and machine gun units were attached. Despite the deceptive peace, the

Germans were using the terrain to conceal their preparations for the next offensive. The assault divisions were concentrated behind the ridge and in thick woods, just a day's march to the north. Three British divisions (from right to left 21st, 8th and 50th) were in the line, holding frontages of 7,300–9,100m. 25th Division was in reserve and 19th Division was training in the rear. The divisions in the line had to use all three of their brigades to cover their frontages. Two battalions in each brigade were in the Forward and Battle Zones, with the third in reserve. With such extended frontages, the divisions were unable to keep many units out of the line for training purposes. In addition the forward areas were a mass of used and disused trenches, some blocked by wire and others not even mapped properly, providing an attacker with numerous covered approaches.

The French Army commander insisted on fighting the main battle in the forward positions, although it was clear that a determined attack would capture the crest of the ridge quickly. A better option would have been to fight the main battle along the Aisne. Commander IX Corps protested but to no avail. With their experience of the spring offensives, the British noted telltale signs of an impending attack. Being forced to fight the main battle further forward than was wise, the British artillery was deployed mainly north of the Aisne, which would have major repercussions once the fighting started.

Units were ordered to man battle positions by 7 p.m. on the 26th. From midnight onwards counter-preparation and harassing fire was carried out by the artillery and machine guns. The German barrage opened at 1.00 a.m. the following morning along a frontage of thirty-eight kilometres, stretching back nineteen kilometres. The British faced forty enemy batteries for every 1,600m of front. Every road and rail junction, village, gun battery, communication centre and bridge was shelled systematically with gas and high explosives. The forward defences in the Outpost Zone were simply wiped out and by 6.00 a.m. many of the gun batteries north of the Aisne were out of action. The attack began in darkness at 3.40 a.m., covered by a creeping barrage, which included gas shells. The morning was also foggy, with visibility initially restricted to about forty metres, which severely handicapped the defence. The Germans achieved superiority of at least three to one along the whole front. At the focal point of the offensive, held by the French 22nd Division on the left of the British, the Germans achieved an advantage of five to one. 22nd Division lost the Chemin des Dames within an hour and by midday three bridges over the Aisne had been seized by the advancing Germans. The French 21st Division, to the west, was also pushed back over the Aisne but beyond it a defensive flank was formed.

The British 50th Division, on the right of the French, resisted fiercely. The Aisne was held at Cuiry until Germans from the French sector swept in from the rear. By midday, 5th Northumberland Fusiliers (149th Brigade) was the only formed battalion remaining in the Division and the artillery had been destroyed or overrun.

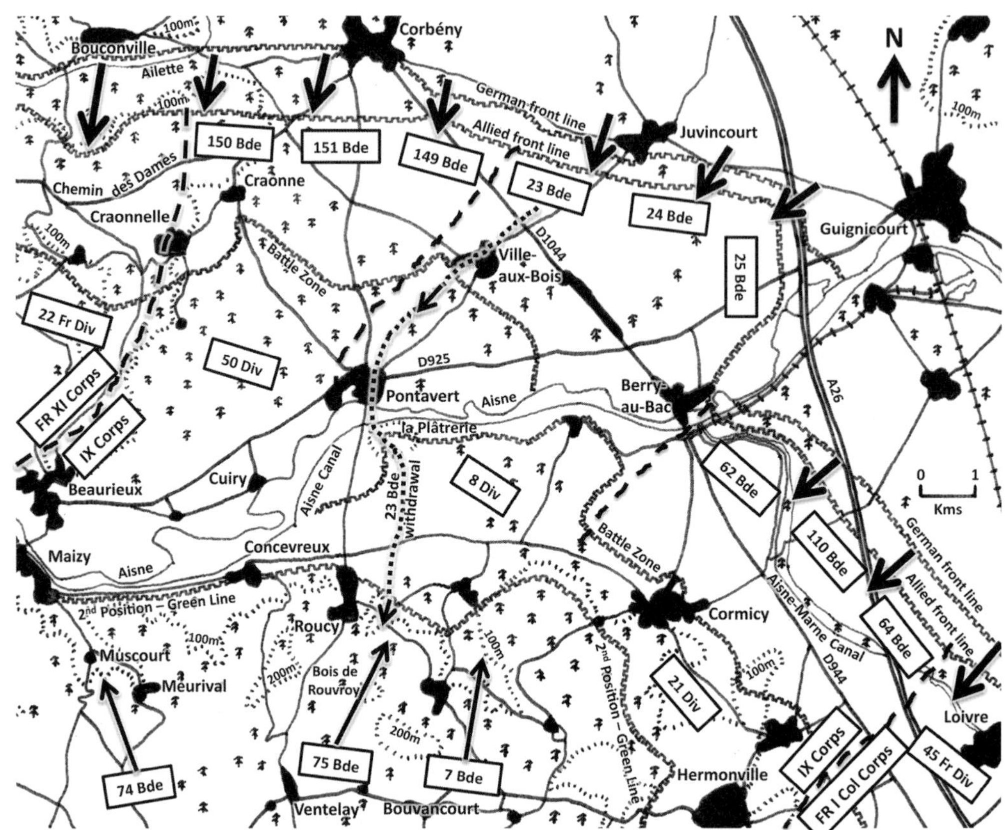

The retirement of 23rd Brigade on 26th May, together with its flanking formations.

8th Division, in the centre of IX Corps, had all three brigades in the line, with 23rd Brigade, commanded by **Brigadier General George Grogan,** on the left. 2nd West Yorkshire in the Forward Zone held for a while before being overwhelmed, as was 2nd Middlesex holding the Battle Zone. However, the 2nd Middlesex reserve company and 2nd Devonshire, in tunnels in the Bois des Buttes, survived the bombardment and manned trenches on the northern edge of the Wood. By 5.15 a.m. the German infantry were upon them with the support of some tanks. They held out for three hours against overwhelming odds, suffering 581 casualties. The Germans turned the left flank from 50th Division's area and only fifty men from 2nd Devonshire got back over the Aisne. However, they had bought time for Grogan to organise a new line south of Pontavert on the high ground of la Plâtrerie. The French awarded the Croix de Guerre to 2nd Devonshire for its magnificent stand. The Germans came across the Aisne in large numbers and the la Plâtrerie position was outflanked at 8.30 a.m. Grogan was forced to pull back again to the base of the hills around Roucy. Elsewhere 8th Division survivors fell back across the Aisne, where the divisional reserve and a French territorial battalion delayed the enemy until 1 p.m. The engineers in 8th and 50th Divisions performed extremely well, destroying thirty-six of the forty-one possible crossings over the river.

Elements of 25th Division started to arrive at Roucy and the remnants of 23rd, 24th and 25th Brigades assisted in garrisoning a system of trenches on the high ground around Roucy. During the morning about 650 Lewis gunners, who were attending a course at the 8th Division School, and others from the three 8th Division brigades, arrived and were used to cover the approaches to the east and west of the Roucy – Ventelay road around Bois de Rouvroy. Units of 8th and 25th Divisions became very mixed. During the afternoon the Germans pressed the mixed force back on the left, where contact with 50th Division had been lost. By evening the line had been forced back down the ridge above Ventelay and the enemy was more advanced on both flanks, making the position precarious.

On the right of IX Corps, 21st Division held eight kilometres of front, where the Aisne-Marne Canal separated the Forward and Battle Zones. Troops forward of the Canal were overwhelmed but on the right some held out until 11 a.m. Resistance in the Battle Zone was more effective than elsewhere but, when the enemy crossed the Aisne on the left, the Division faced being cut off and a withdrawal became necessary. Further to the right, the French 45th Division fell back behind the Aisne-Marne Canal but managed to form a defensive flank where the British had been forced back.

French reserves covered the rear of the French divisions and IX Corps sent a brigade of 25th Division over the Aisne to support 8th and 50th Divisions. However, in general at this time the senior commanders were unaware of the true seriousness of the situation. The next phase was the defence of the Second Position (Green Line), which for the British was to have been conducted by 25th Division. However, at 2.15 p.m. its brigades were placed under command of the forward divisions; 74th on the left to 50th Division, 75th in the centre to 8th Division and 7th on the right to 21st Division. In the centre, Grogan's 23rd Brigade was relieved by 75th Brigade and moved to organise the defence of the Vesle at Jonchery.

Following a lull, the Germans crossed the Aisne, the Second Position was breached and a 3,200m wide gap opened between the French and British. This allowed the Germans to reach the Vesle by 8 p.m. Both Allies pulled back to form defensive flanks and the gap between them had widened by nightfall.

50th Division's left, held by 74th Brigade (25th Division), was closest to the widening gap. The previous evening the Brigade, with B Company, 25th Division Machine Gun Battalion attached, had been ordered to be ready to move at 8.00 p.m. An hour later it was ordered to move to the Muscourt area and arrived there at 3 a.m. on 27th May. Meanwhile orders had been received from HQ 25th Division for the Brigade to occupy the Second Position from the Ventelay – Concevreux road to the Meurival – Maizy road. The frontage was divided between the battalions. 11th Lancashire Fusiliers on the right was allocated from the Ventelay – Concevreux road to the junction of a track with the Maizy – Concevreux road. 3rd Worcestershire

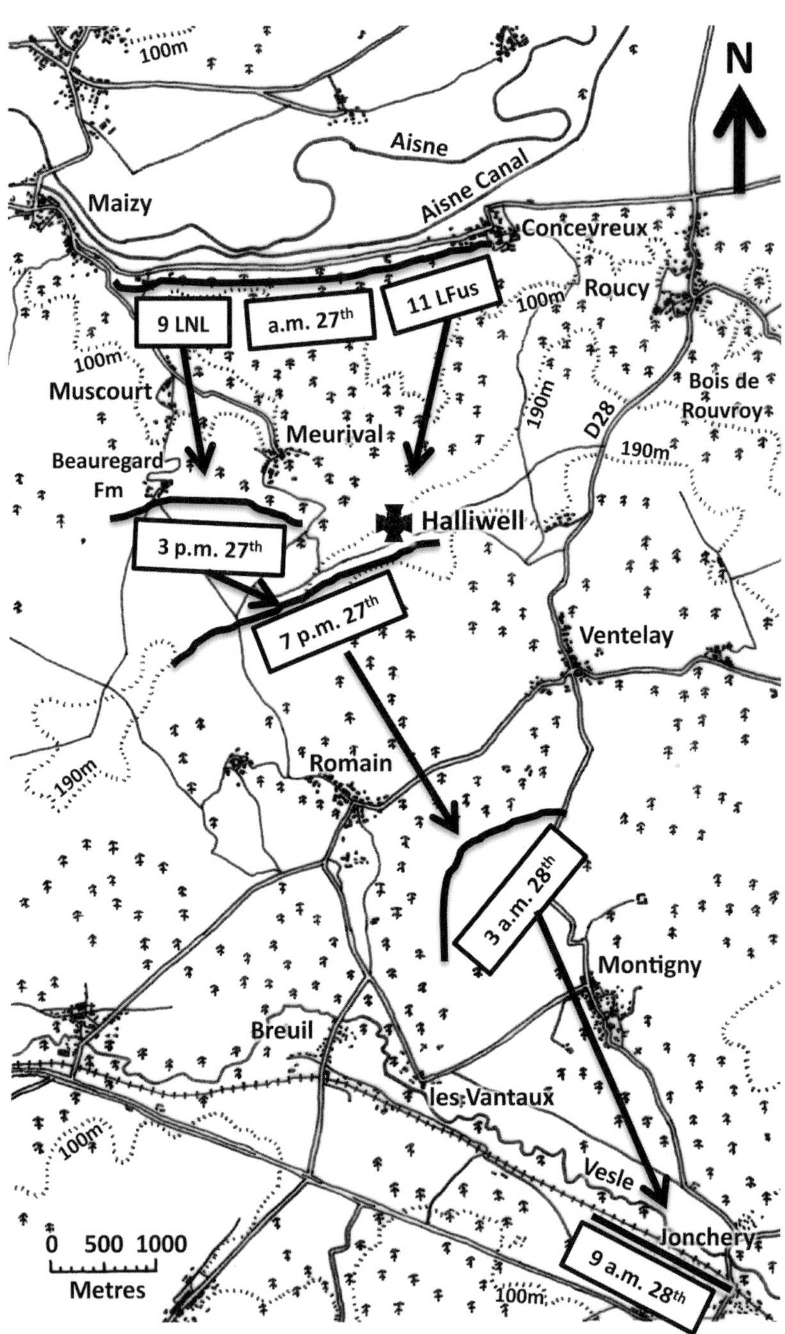

Leave Ventelay on the D28 northwards towards Roucy. The road climbs for 2,200m. At the crest turn left onto a track running along the ridge top. It is passable in a car with care. Follow for just over two kilometres to approximately where Halliwell won his VC. Continue to a track crossroads and turn right through a farm to join a tarmac road into Meurival.

was in the centre and 9th Loyal North Lancashire was on the left. Battalion reconnaissance parties set off immediately. However, in view of the deteriorating situation, at 6.15 a.m., HQ 25th Division ordered one platoon per company and eight machine guns to take up positions at once. At 8.30 a.m. 3rd Worcestershire was placed at the disposal of HQ 50th Division for attachment to 149th Brigade. It crossed the river to cover the bridgehead at Concevreux. At 9.10 a.m. the other two battalions were ordered to take up their positions. 11th Lancashire Fusiliers on the right and 9th Loyal North Lancashire on the left had to extend their lines in the centre to compensate for the loss of 3rd Worcestershire. They held the line of the railway (long since taken up) overlooking the canal. The advancing Germans appeared on the other side at 10.50 a.m.

On the left 9th Loyal North Lancashire was soon fully engaged. The Germans were held until they advanced through the unmanned French sector to the west. At 1.30 p.m. they crossed the bridge at Maizy and rushed towards Muscourt. 9th Loyal North Lancashire formed a defensive left flank, with a reserve section of machine guns and 74th Trench Mortar Battery. The CO was killed and Major J Lloyd, 130th Field Company RE, took over. About 5.30 p.m. small bodies of French troops began moving up on the left flank. By 6.20 p.m. the Battalion had been forced back to the area of Beauregard Farm, 650m south of Muscourt.

3rd Worcestershire was forced to fall back over the river at Concevreux when the Germans broke through on the right flank and got behind the three forward companies. 3rd Worcestershire took up a new position on the high ground south of Concevreux, only 120 strong.

11th Lancashire Fusiliers initially stopped the enemy advancing along the road leading south from Concevreux. However, when the Germans entered Muscourt, they threatened the left flank. 11th Lancashire Fusiliers then withdrew along the ridge near Meurival. It was shelled out of this location and forced back to another position 450m south of the ridge. In the new position the Battalion repulsed three attacks between 7.00 p.m. and 8.00 p.m. By then it had been reduced to only nine officers and one hundred men. By 9.00 p.m. it was holding a line about 400m long astride the Meurival – Ventelay road. It held there for an hour before pulling back at 10.00 p.m. with the rest of the Brigade to the high ground north of Romain, taking up a position on the left of the Brigade's line. The situation was so precarious that, on occasions, **Lance Corporal Joel Halliwell**'s account states that they were surrounded.

Throughout this tense day Halliwell rescued the wounded as the Battalion fell back. In his account Halliwell says that they had run out of stretchers and the CO asked if he could recover some of the wounded using his horse, which was German and had been found wandering about the battlefield. He galloped forward on the horse and, despite heavy machine gun and shell fire, brought back singly and unaided an officer and nine soldiers who were severely wounded. He ensured that they were evacuated, then made three attempts to bring in an eleventh man but was forced to give up when the Germans advanced again.

On the right of 74th Brigade the enemy had been stalled by the destruction of the Aisne bridges. Here the defence held, although it was threatened by crossings at Pontavert. However, at 3.15 p.m. the Germans outflanked the Brigade from the west and also broke through 75th Brigade to the east of Concevreux. Roucy was lost and withdrawal became vital. The right of 75th Brigade was forced back to the Bois de Rouvroy and later 74th and 75th Brigades were forced to withdraw in some confusion. However, they were established in contact with each other on the ridge north of Montigny by daybreak on the 28th. At 6.30 a.m. on 28th May the strength of 74th Brigade was estimated to be just 350.

7th Brigade held an enormous frontage and the Germans found gaps between it and 75th Brigade on the left. By 8.00 p.m. it was at Bouvancourt, three kilometres behind the Green Line. Stragglers from 8th and 50th Divisions swelled the numbers and 600 Corps troops came up from the rear. 7th and 62nd Brigades withdrew during the night but 110th and 64th Brigades hung on in the Battle Zone, with the French 45th Division on the right. They were ordered back to the Second Position at 7.00 p.m.

Dawn on the 28th found the British holding a disjointed and weak line. From the junction with the French on the right, 21st Division held from Hermonville to south of Bouvancourt. There was a gap before 25th Division carried on the line along the Montigny Ridge. By then brigades were little more than battalion strength and there was almost no artillery support, as it has been destroyed or cut off north of the Aisne. The original front line divisions, both French and British, had practically ceased to exist. Divisions on the flanks were in slightly better condition but the reserves (French 39th and 157th and British 25th Divisions) had already been badly battered. The Germans had punched a hole, forty kilometres wide at its base and nineteen kilometres at its deepest point, into the Allied line. The salient was held but with numerous gaps and the arrival of French reinforcements was vital. The British 19th Division also began to move forward from Châlons.

The top of the ridge south of Meurival held by 11th Lancashire Fusiliers on 26th May, looking north. The line held was essentially along the track in the foreground. Joel Halliwell was active in this area rescuing the wounded.

Attacks commenced against 74th and 75th Brigades at 5.00 a.m. At 7.00 a.m. 74th Brigade was ordered to fall back across the les Vantaux – Montigny road, while maintaining contact with 8th Division on the right and the French on the left. If forced to fall back across the Vesle, the Brigade was to hold the high ground north of Vandeuil. Straggler posts were established at bridgeheads over the Vesle with instructions to hold them at all costs. 11th Lancashire Fusiliers covered the withdrawal of the other two battalions from the position held overnight to the northwest of Montigny. There was hard fighting in the withdrawal. The remnants of 3rd Worcestershire and 9th Loyal North Lancashire managed to cross the Vesle to the south bank but 11th Lancashire Fusiliers was all but destroyed. Halliwell had spent the day carrying messages until the remnants of the Battalion was surrounded. The CO told him to get away and he escaped on his horse.

At 7.45 a.m., Brigadier General Grogan, commanding 23rd Brigade (8th Division), having handed over to 75th Brigade, was given command of all troops 1,600m either side of Jonchery for the defence of the line of the Vesle. The line was extended on the right by 75th Brigade. Grogan collected stragglers from 8th, 25th and 50th Divisions and established a line along the railway embankment, parallel with the river. The bridgehead at Jonchery was also held strongly. The Germans attacked just after 10.00 a.m. but Grogan held them, despite extreme pressure. However, by 1.00 p.m. the Germans had crossed at Breuil, three kilometres to the west of Jonchery and were pressing on in the direction of Vandeuil. The troops on the right had also been forced back, leaving Grogan no other option than to pull back slowly to form a defensive left flank between Branscourt and Vandeuil. The Jonchery bridge was not destroyed due to the explosives wagon being blown up en route. The Germans swarmed over it to remain in contact with Grogan's men as they fell back.

Grogan occupied the high ground, between the Vesle and the Ardre, astride the Savigny – Jonchery road, north of Montazin Farm. His right was relatively strong, as a French regiment had reinforced 75th Brigade and subsequently relieved it. However, the left was open and there was no contact with any Allied troops. At 8.00 p.m. the Germans came on against the left and drove the positions west of the road back to some old practice trenches. They dominated the area by holding the

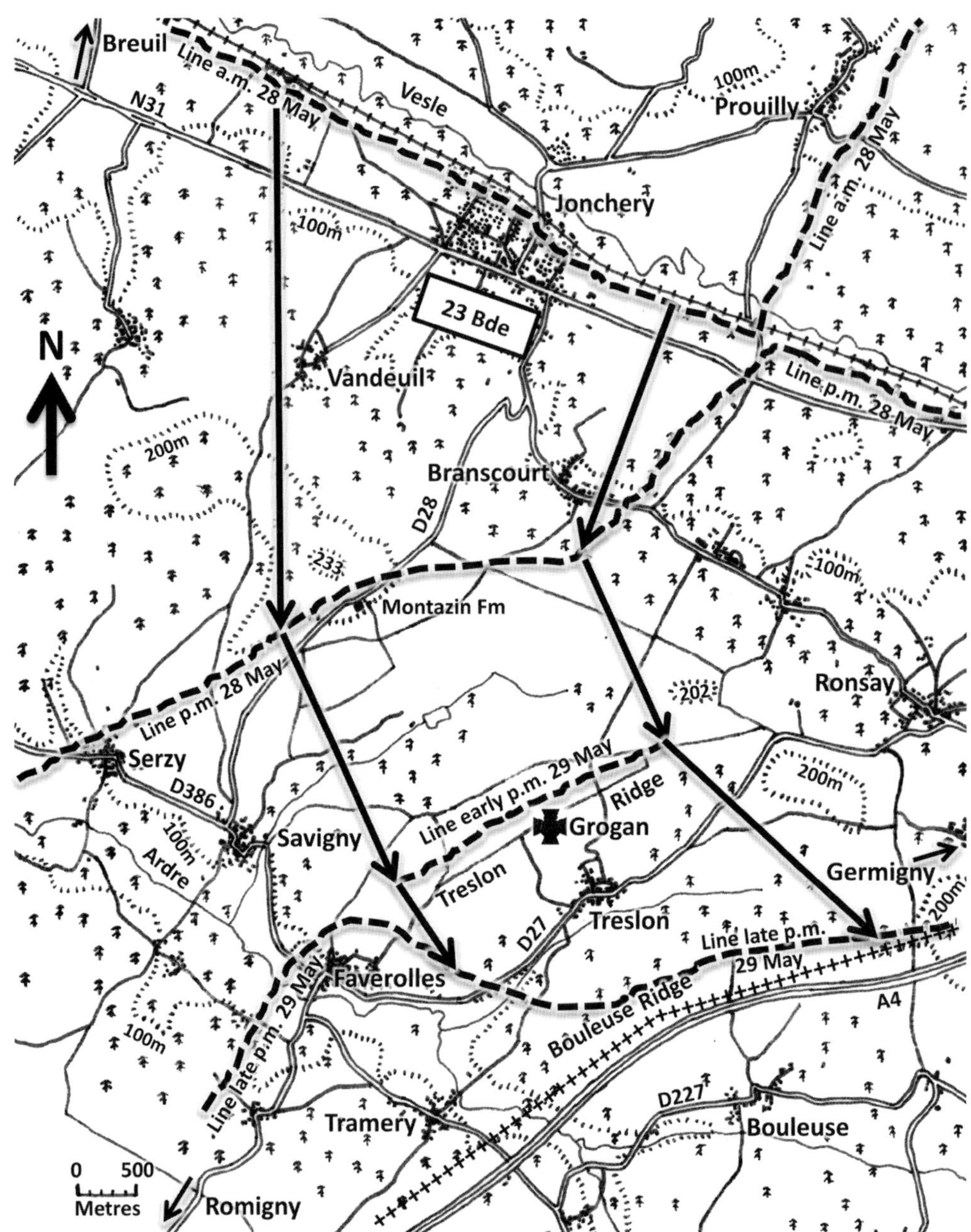

To reach the final position held by George Grogan on Bouleuse Ridge, approach Bouleuse from the west on the D227. In the centre of the village pass the church on the right. The road swings left, then right. At this right turn go straight on up the hill but beware traffic from the right, which has priority. After 250m take the left fork and follow the track over the autoroute and TGV railway line. There is a large area of hard standing on the right on which to park. From here look left and right along Bouleuse ridge parallel with the railway. In front, about two kilometres to the north, is Treslon Ridge. Half left the highest point is Hill 233, with Montazin Farm just this side of it. To visit Treslon Ridge approach the village from the southwest on the D27. Just before the church turn left uphill into Rue de la Planchette. After 250m the road swings sharp right. Beware, just after this corner there is a very deep storm drain across the road, which should be crossed at low speed. Follow this road as it zigzags through vineyards for 1,100m until the tarmac runs out. Continue cautiously on the rough track for another 200m to the crest of Treslon Ridge. Half left is Hill 233 and Montazin Farm. Look behind to Bouleuse Ridge. Continue 100m to a track crossroads, where you can turn around to return.

highest point (Hill 233). Grogan decided that it must be recaptured or he risked losing the whole position. One hundred and twenty men, mainly 2nd Devonshire who had been at the transport lines when the rest of the Battalion was lost, and a few from 1st Worcestershire, counterattacked. They seized the knoll and held back a determined German attack at 3.00 a.m. next morning. At nightfall the left was reinforced by a French regiment advancing from Savigny, so that both of Grogan's flanks were securely held by the French.

On the 29th, the French concentrated on the wings of the German break-in but without success. In the centre, the Germans pushed forward to a few kilometres short of the Marne. On the British left, the French lost Serzy, leaving British and French troops on the Branscourt – Montazin line exposed.

Grogan's orders were to hold for as long as possible but also to conform to the movements of the French on the left, who intended falling back to the heights above Treslon and Savigny. The line was held without difficulty until 11.00 a.m., when the French began to pull back. Grogan also fell back slowly for 1,800m to the plateau north of Treslon and took up a slightly reverse slope position. He was in contact with the French on the left and with elements of 21st Division and French troops on the right on Hill 202. Many casualties were caused by German machine gunners during the withdrawal but the troops were rallied by Grogan on the new line. Shortly afterwards the Germans surged over the ridge but were stopped by concentrated small arms fire. They then put up balloons and sent over reconnaissance aircraft to ascertain the new British line. In the distance a stream of German transport was seen moving along the Jonchery – Savigny road to Montazin Farm, recently vacated by Grogan's men. These proved to be medium trench mortars moving into position with which the Germans then pounded the British position. Many casualties were caused as the men had not been able to dig in properly in the time available. The pressure continued and, around 3.00 p.m., it looked as if some of the British were going to retire. Grogan rode up and down the line, encouraging the men to hold for almost three hours, which they did with a steadily increasing casualty list. Grogan's borrowed steed was wounded but a groom arrived with his pet pony, Sandy, and he resumed his ride along the weak line.

Then, at 5.45 p.m., there was no holding the Germans. A very strong attack was delivered with great determination, supported by numerous machine guns, trench mortars and artillery. The British and French were driven off the ridge. The few Allied guns left in the area added to the hopeless situation by shelling the British by mistake. Grogan had previously sent an advanced party back to establish a new line on Bouleuse Ridge and bring up reinforcements. Falling back across the Treslon valley for about three kilometres, Grogan organised rearguards until the survivors arrived on Bouleuse Ridge, where they found 2nd Wiltshire (58th Brigade, 19th Division) already dug in. The exhausted survivors, led by Grogan, strengthened this line and he took command of all troops on the Ridge. The Germans were quick to follow on and actually gained a footing on the crest in one place. Grogan hastily gathered a small party of about a dozen from 2nd East Lancashire and led them in

The line held on Treslon Ridge on 28th May, looking north towards the advancing enemy. Just left of centre in the distance is Hill 233, which was lost earlier in the day and retaken in a counterattack. The Jonchery–Savigny road runs along its base and Montazin Farm is marked by two prominent poplar trees.

a charge into a wood where the Germans were established. Surprise was complete and the enemy was driven back down the slope. During this sortie a German fired at Grogan from only twenty metres away but missed and hit Sandy in the nose. While others dealt with the German, Grogan dismounted and bandaged Sandy's nose with his handkerchief. Fortunately it was a clean wound through the fleshy part of the nose and the animal was not inconvenienced. Grogan was later reinforced by a composite battalion of 8th Division troops and seven machine guns.

On the British left, two brigades of the newly arrived 19th Division moved behind the gap with the French. The Germans advanced behind the left flank of 19th Division and an ad hoc collection of units from a number of formations re-established a line and made contact with the French over three kilometres away near Romigny.

The reverse view from Treslon Ridge looking south over Bouleuse Ridge in the middle distance, showing how exposed the Bouleuse Ridge position was from Treslon Ridge.

The British left was temporarily secure but on the right the situation on Bouleuse Ridge was critical. The position was on an exposed forward slope and woods to the front provided the enemy with covered approaches. From Treslon Ridge the enemy had unimpeded observation of the whole of Bouleuse Ridge. A party of enemy got onto the Ridge and the right almost gave way twice but they were driven back. Grogan again rode about the position, cheering the men and encouraging all by his calmness under fire. His recklessness paid off and the men were steadied sufficiently to hold the Ridge against continuous attacks. The right flank was open and, at Grogan's suggestion, two battalions of the reserve brigade (56th) of 19th Division arrived in the evening to extend it and make contact with the French 45th Division. Fighting died down at 9.00 p.m. and the Bouleuse position was held overnight by an ad hoc collection of troops from all three brigades of 8th Division, plus elements of 19th, 21st, 25th and 50th Divisions. Grogan's battered force was utterly exhausted. Men even fell asleep while under heavy bombardment. HQ 56th Brigade (19th Division) relieved the exhausted remnants of HQ 23rd Brigade at 3 a.m. on the 30th, although many of the survivors of the Brigade's units remained in the line for some time afterwards.

From Grogan's final position on Bouleuse Ridge on 29th May, looking north to Treslon Ridge. In the distance on the left is Hill 233.

On the extreme right, 21st Division conformed to events around Treslon and Bouleuse. During the night the French 45th Division relieved 21st Division in the front line and re-established contact with the British south of Germigny. A more or less continuous line of resistance was re-established. In these operations, 8th Division suffered 7,496 casualties to add to the 8,515 from the March and April battles. In just over two months the Division had sustained 16,011 casualties, almost its entire established strength.

Local Operations Summer 1918

365 Cpl Joseph Kaeble, 22nd Battalion (French Canadian) CEF (5th Canadian Brigade, 2nd Canadian Division), Neuville-Vitasse, France

8th June 1918

5th Canadian Brigade took over the left sector of 2nd Canadian Division's front on the night of 3rd/4th June. 22nd Battalion was in the front line on the left and 24th Battalion was on the right. The artillery on both sides was very active but otherwise it was quiet, just the normal routine of line holding, including patrolling at night. As was usual by this time, the front line was held lightly, relying mainly on the firepower of mutually supporting Lewis guns.

At 4.15 p.m. on 8th June a heavy bombardment was fired against the Canadian battery positions. At 9.45 p.m. the Germans fired a heavy barrage of all calibres, including trench mortars, against the front and support lines northwest of Neuville-Vitasse. The Beaurains – Neuville-Vitasse and Mercatel – Beaurains roads were also subjected to harassing fire. The barrage lifted from the front line and joined

that on the supports at 9.50 p.m. and the Germans launched three raiding parties against 22nd Battalion's front line. Each party was about fifty strong.

The northern raiding party was met with very effective Lewis gun fire and a barrage of bombs. It was repulsed completely before it reached the front line trench. Some Canadians then rushed out and captured a soldier from the 65th Infantry Regiment. Facing the southern raiding party, the Canadians suffered a number of casualties from trench mortar fire. Nevertheless the raiders were repulsed with bombs and Lewis gun fire.

A few Germans in the centre raiding party reached the parapet but did not get into the trench. **Corporal Joseph Kaeble** was commanding a Lewis gun section in the front line at this point. During the bombardment he remained at the parapet with his Lewis gun shouldered ready to fire, as the field of fire was very limited. By the time that the barrage lifted only one other man in his section had not been wounded. Kaeble jumped over the parapet and swept the attackers with his Lewis gun, firing from the hip, thereby stopping the advance of the raiders against his post. Although wounded several times by fragments of shells and bombs, he continued to fire as the raiders withdrew, until he collapsed exhausted into the trench with compound fractures of both legs. While lying in the trench, and before losing consciousness, he shouted encouragement to the wounded about him, *Keep it up boys; do not let them get through. We must stop them.* The repulse of the enemy at this point was due to his remarkable personal bravery and self-sacrifice. He died of his wounds shortly afterwards. There was also fierce bayonet fighting in this area as the Canadians rushed out of their trenches to meet the attackers.

The Canadian artillery response was swift and very effective. As soon as the raiders had been repulsed, patrols were sent out and discovered a number of German dead but the precise number of German casualties could not be ascertained with any certainty. However, the shouts and screams of the wounded could be heard as they tried to attract the attention of their stretcher-bearers. A second captured German

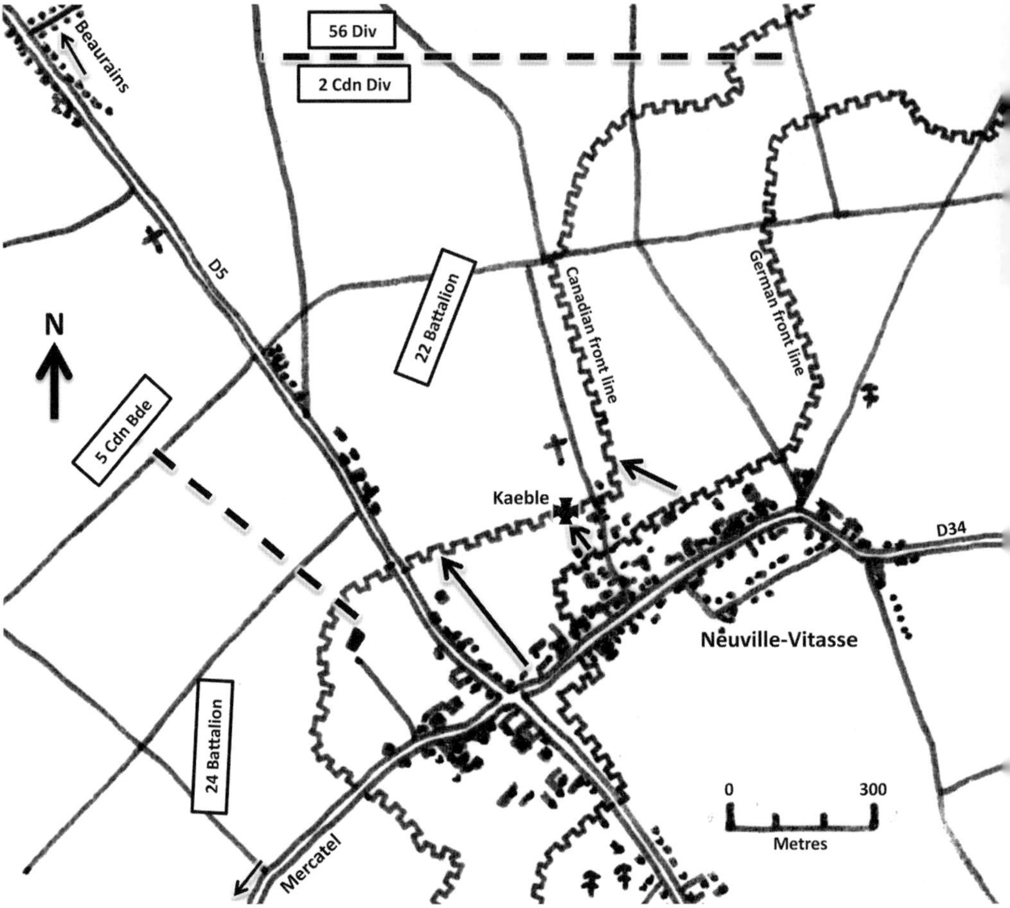

Turn into Neuville-Vitasse from the D5 along the D34 towards Wancourt. In the centre of the village, opposite the church, turn left into Rue du Bois de la Vigne, follow it for just over 300m and park at the village cemetery. Walk back uphill towards the village to No.13 on the right. This is where the front line crossed the road. Kaeble's VC action was in the back garden of this house. When visited in July 2018 there was a vacant plot to the right of No.13, allowing uninterrupted views over the VC action site, but it seems unlikely that the plot will remain vacant for long.

died. Amongst the items recovered from the Germans was what appeared to be a new type of grenade.

22nd Battalion had one officer, Lieutenant Langelier, slightly wounded and another, Lieutenant GH Murphy, was temporarily deafened by concussion. Four men were killed and thirty-eight were wounded. One man was missing but was not believed to have been captured as nowhere did the raiders enter the front line trench. After the action he must have been accounted for as no members of the Battalion are recorded as missing. The CWGC records seven members of the Battalion were killed or died of wounds on 8th and 9th June. Private Peter Paul Desjardins

Looking south into the centre of the village along Rue du Bois de la Vigne. The cemetery is behind the camera position. No.13 is in the centre, where the front line crossed the road at right angles. Kaeble's VC action took place in the back garden on the far right.

is buried alongside Kaeble in Wanquetin Communal Cemetery Extension. Private Zenon Diotte is buried in Dainville British Cemetery, Private Adelard Lafrance is buried in London Cemetery at Neuville-Vitasse and Privates Henri Pouliot, Andre Joncas and Francois Langlois are all interred in Wailly Orchard Cemetery.

366 Cpl Philip Davey, 10th Battalion AIF (3rd Australian Brigade, 1st Australian Division), Merris, France

28th June 1918

When the focus of the German offensives shifted to the French sector in the south, the northern sectors of the Western Front were far from peaceful. Numerous artillery bombardments were carried out, including counter-battery missions, and there were also a number of small operations and raids. On the night of 2nd/3rd June, 11th Battalion AIF (3rd Australian Brigade, 1st Australian Division), with the cooperation of 86th Brigade, captured Mont de Merris, eight kilometres east of Hazebrouck. Although the Brigade suffered about one hundred casualties, the attack resulted in 258 prisoners being taken, with twenty-seven machine guns and seventeen trench mortars. The line captured was improved in another attack on the night of 12th/13th June by 7th Battalion. Other minor operations were launched to seize a post here and there.

Much needed reinforcements for the BEF began to bring units back to strength. The artillery had more guns than ever before, although some were worn, and plenty of ammunition. The time to go over to the offensive had not yet arrived, there being far too many German reserves remaining. However, Haig was confident enough to begin launching larger operations in order to improve the line and prepare the way for future larger scale operations.

The first of these operations was carried out east of Nieppe Forest with the intention to provide space for an outpost zone clear of the forest, which was constantly deluged with gas shells. This required an advance of up to 1,500m on a frontage of five and a half kilometres. 5th Division, recently returned from Italy and still with thirteen battalions, and 31st Division (XV Corps) were tasked with carrying out the attack under XI Corps. It was to be launched exactly one year to the day after the two divisions had carried out a successful attack near Oppy. Artillery support was massive. Forty batteries of field artillery were available, in addition to the trench mortars of 5th Division, a 6″ battery from 61st Division and the heavy guns of XI and XV Corps. Barrages were fired early every morning in the days before the attack in an attempt to deceive the enemy. Nieppe Forest was almost intact and provided cover for the concentration of the assault troops immediately behind the attack frontage.

On the night of 26th/27th June, 13th York & Lancaster (93rd Brigade, 31st Division) secured Ankle Farm, just north of the main attack area. The attack was to be launched over firm dry ground, intersected by a number of hedges, ditches and waist high crops in places. From dawn on 28th June the skies above the battle area were dominated by the RAF and no German aircraft was able to fly over. Zero hour was at 6.00 a.m., with no preparatory bombardment, although there was some counter-battery fire. The assault was preceded by a creeping barrage of artillery and machine guns. Four brigades were employed; from the right these were 13th and 95th Brigades in 5th Division and 92nd and 93rd Brigades in 31st Division.

5th Division's troops followed the creeping barrage so closely that they were in the German trench before the barrage lifted. All objectives were reached and consolidated. Despite the relative ease with which the objectives were taken, the two assault divisions suffered 1,935 casualties, although the vast majority were wounded. One cheeky subaltern telephoned back that all objectives had been captured but a bottle of whisky would help to hold on to them. It was duly sent forward. The two divisions captured 439 prisoners, four field guns (with some mustard gas shells that were sent back to the previous owners next day), fourteen trench mortars and seventy-seven machine guns. In 92nd Brigade's area alone, 135 Germans were buried after the operation, indicating a large loss of life elsewhere. There was no noticeable counterattack.

To support the attack by 5th and 31st Divisions to the south, 1st Australian Division, on the left flank, fired an artillery and machine gun barrage, created a smoke screen and blew horns and fired signal flares as a diversion. 3rd Australian Brigade had taken over the right sub-sector from 2nd Australian Brigade on the nights of 16th/17th and 17th/18th June. 10th Battalion was initially in reserve but on the night of 25th/26th June it took over the left of the Brigade front from 11th Battalion. The Battalion was tasked with firing liberally with Stokes mortars, Lewis guns and rifle grenades against two known enemy posts and the line of a hedge. Two strombo horns in the front line were to blow a series of short blasts at zero plus five minutes and at zero plus fifty-five minutes. At the latter time special rifle grenade lights would also be fired. All these activities were to simulate an imminent attack

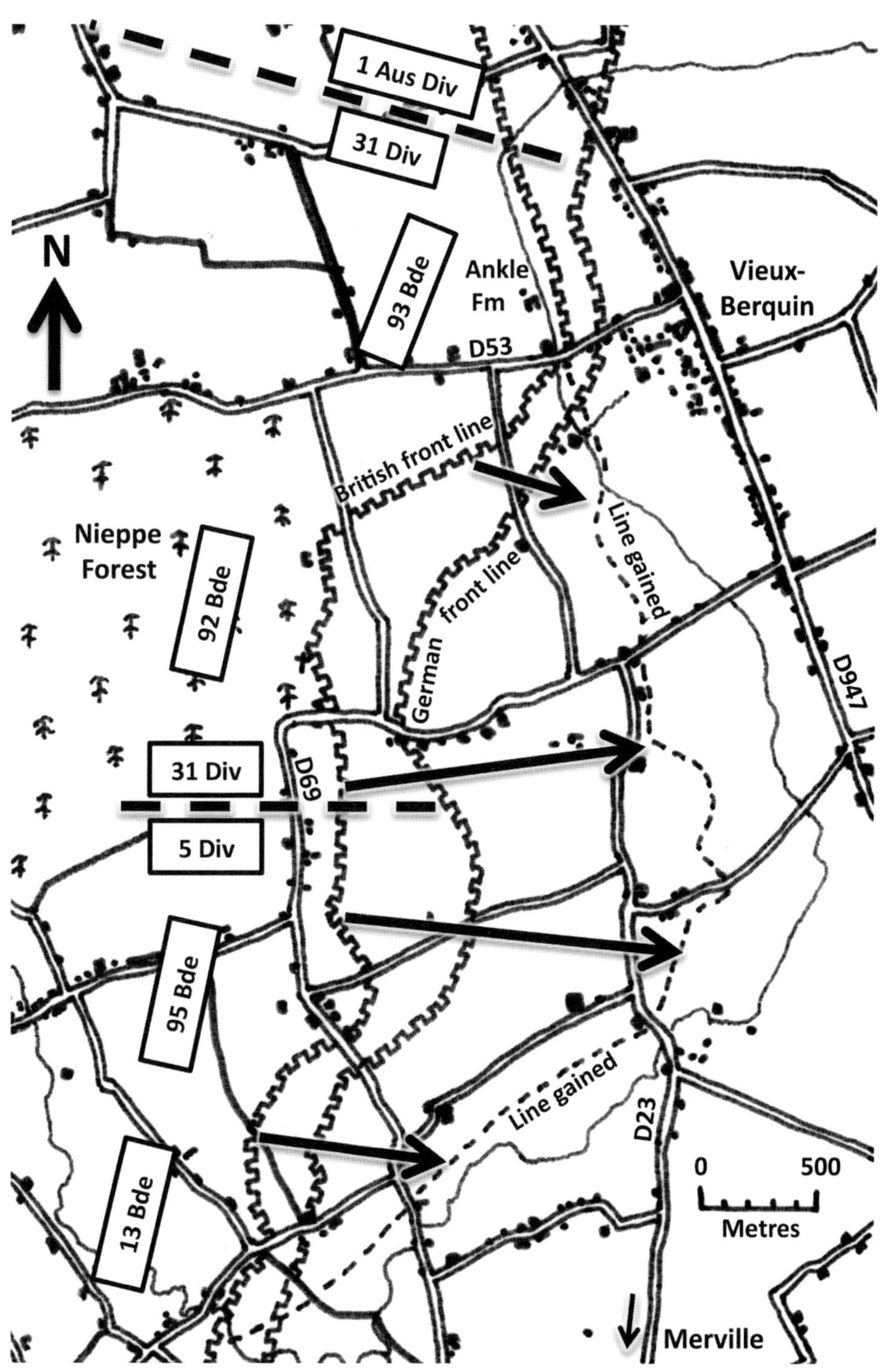

The main attack by 5th and 31st Divisions on 28th June.

on Merris and draw fire away from the main attack. 10th Battalion was commanded by an adventurous, restless and sometimes reckless Englishman, Lieutenant Colonel Maurice Wilder-Neligan CMG DSO DCM. He was not going to miss any opportunity to exploit the situation. Accordingly the front line companies had fighting patrols ready to make raids.

On the right was C Company under Major Clarence Rumball MC. When the barrage came down Sergeant Thomas Curson Leathley MM and four men crept out from the centre of the Company's line. They moved cautiously through the crops to within twenty metres of a German post at the corner of a hedge. They waited until a barrage of rifle grenades and Stokes mortars lifted at 6.05 a.m. Then three of them rushed in covered by a Lewis gun. Two Germans were shot running away and a third was captured. The party returned to report that an attack on a larger scale was likely to succeed. As soon as news reached Rumball, he sent Lieutenant William Stanley Bennett DSO MC and his platoon to clear the hedge, which it did, seizing several prisoners and establishing a post at the eastern end. To the south Lieutenant Howard Wilson Scudds MC and one man crawled forward to the edge of an adjoining field and took five prisoners and a machine gun. As a result, 11 Platoon of C Company was sent forward to establish a post there.

At 8.30 a.m. a platoon of A Company, in support, was sent forward to assist C Company. Under a light trench mortar and rifle grenade barrage and local smoke screen it worked forward using phosphorus grenades and ground flares to establish itself north of the hedge.

German artillery fire had cut the telephone cables but, at 7.00 a.m., a runner from Rumball brought news to Wilder-Neligan that he intended to advance his posts. Wilder-Neligan directed D Company on the left, under Lieutenant William Roy Jenkins, to advance in conformity. Jenkins was initially driven back by heavy machine gun fire but Wilder-Neligan was determined to succeed and sent an order to make the advance. Rumball was placed in command of both companies and two platoons of A Company, in support, were sent up to assist. The reserve company was also brought forward into the support position.

D Company advanced at 8.00 a.m. behind a smoke screen and Stokes mortar and rifle grenade barrage. There were no casualties. The left platoon of Rumball's company, under Lieutenant John Morris McInerney, advanced about the same time and reached the hedge without loss. While digging in, the platoon came under machine gun fire from close range and McInerney was killed (La Kreule Military Cemetery, Hazebrouck, France – I F 21). The survivors took cover in a ditch and resolved to dash back to the Australian lines. A few were captured by Germans who had reached the hedge behind them but Corporal Sydney Herbert Russell held on.

Another platoon digging in nearby was also fired on by a machine gun that had been brought up quietly nearby and suffered a number of casualties. **Corporal Philip Davey** crept out alone and threw some bombs into the hedge, putting half the German gun crew out of action. He crawled back across the lane (Lynde

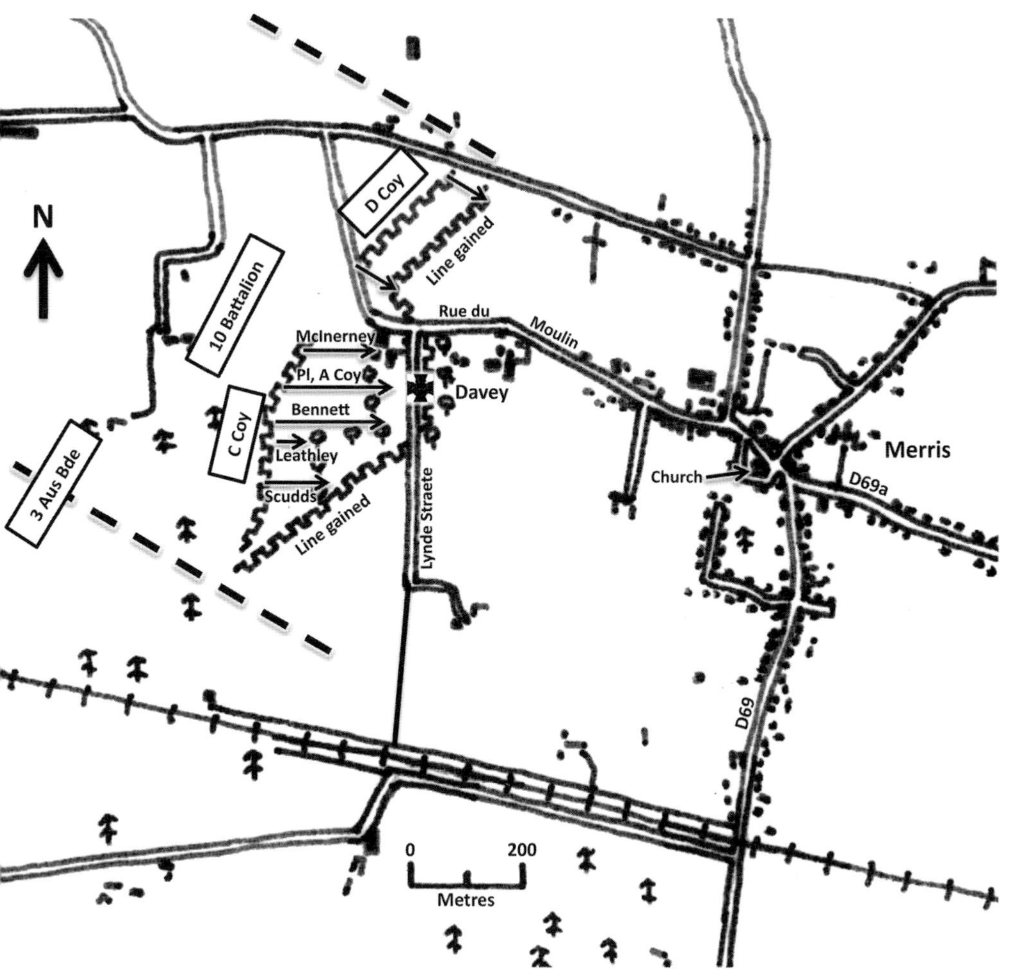

Drive through Merris on the D69 northwestwards. Pass the church on the left and seventy-five metres later turn left into Rue du Moulin. Follow it for 750m until there is a right hand bend with a farm on the left. Park straight in front in the entrance to what appears to be the village dumping ground for anything and everything. Climb on top of one of the heaps for a view of the action by D Company to the northeast. Return the way you came and after fifty metres turn right after the farm into Lynde Straete. The road drops down the hill for 300m to a rough track junction on the right. On the left side of the road here is an information board about Davey's VC action. However, the view from here is restricted, so continue another 150m to the entrance gate into No.530 on the left and park on the right. Look back over the various hedges and field boundaries, which remarkably are just as they were in June 1918.

Straete) for more bombs and then disposed of the rest of the gun team. At noon Rumball personally led the remnant of McInerney's platoon and a reserve platoon to re-establish the post.

A German counterattack about noon under heavy artillery fire failed to regain any of the losses. Davey used the captured German machine gun to assist in

From the rubbish dump behind the farm at the bend on Rue du Moulin. The D Company attack was in the field to the left. C Company attacked on the right through the scrub and rubbish.

repelling the attack and was wounded in the encounter. When the first phase of this operation ended at about 1.30 p.m., the Battalion had lost three killed and eleven wounded. It was realised that the new outpost line was being dug close to a number of German posts. Wilder-Neligan resolved to capture these as well. Another attack was arranged for 6 p.m. under cover of smoke fired by the Stokes mortars and the rifle grenadiers. The artillery also provided support. The barrage was perfect and the two companies advanced quickly behind it. The defenders ran and the Lewis guns were quickly in action firing at them as they retreated. The mortars kept flanking machine guns from firing and smoke protected the attackers as they dug in. German retaliatory artillery fire fell mainly between the front and support lines. By 7 p.m. the new line was being consolidated.

The result was the capture of 450m of enemy front line together with thirty-five prisoners, nine machine guns and two trench mortars. Many other enemy soldiers were killed and wounded. The Battalion suffered forty-four casualties (seven killed

From the south, with the various lines of attack on the left. Davey's VC action was just to the right of Lynde Straete, which runs up the middle of the picture.

and thirty-seven wounded), some in the rear areas to enemy shellfire and a few to short shooting by the Australian artillery. The support and reserve companies took over the new line. A German counterattack was thrown back, leaving some dead and another machine gun.

372 Sgt Richard Travis, 2nd Otago (2nd New Zealand Infantry Brigade, New Zealand Division), Rossignol Wood, France

24th July 1918

On 9th July, 2nd New Zealand Brigade took over the left sub-sector of the New Zealand Division's front. It was opposite Bucquoy in the north and near Hébuterne in the south. On the night of 12th/13th July, 1st Canterbury raided enemy posts in front of Rossignol Wood, captured a prisoner and secured a suitable start line for a future attack. On 15th July a minor operation was carried out, resulting in the line being advanced a short distance in front of Hébuterne and Rossignol Wood. This was followed by considerable activity on both sides and the situation was unsettled

Looking south along Lynde Straete to where Philip Davey crossed to attack the machine gun post on the left side.

for some time. The Germans concluded that Rossignol Wood could not be retained and, about midnight on the 19th, they blew up their pillboxes and evacuated the position. Early on the 20th a number of reconnaissance patrols were sent out, including one led by **Sergeant Richard Travis**. These established that the enemy had evacuated the Wood entirely. All posts were advanced and preparations were made to regain touch with the enemy.

2nd Otago established posts on the south-western edge of the Wood and patrols were pushed towards Owl Trench. Trenches east of the Wood were found to be filled with wire, which forced patrols into the open and hindered their progress. The enemy was holding Moa and Shag Trenches in strength and offered considerable resistance to any advance. There were several bombing fights at close range and German minenwerfer fire was used to dislodge patrols. In addition the sunken road running at right angles to the head of Railway Trench was also strongly held. The line established at the end of the day was in advance of Rossignol Wood on the southern and eastern sides. During the night a new trench was dug by 1st Otago to give access to the new line without having to pass through Rossignol Wood. There was an increase in artillery fire over the Wood and machine gun fire from Fork Wood and the high ground nearby.

When news was received of the evacuation of Rossignol Wood, HQ 1st New Zealand Brigade, in the right sub-sector, ordered its two forward battalions to move

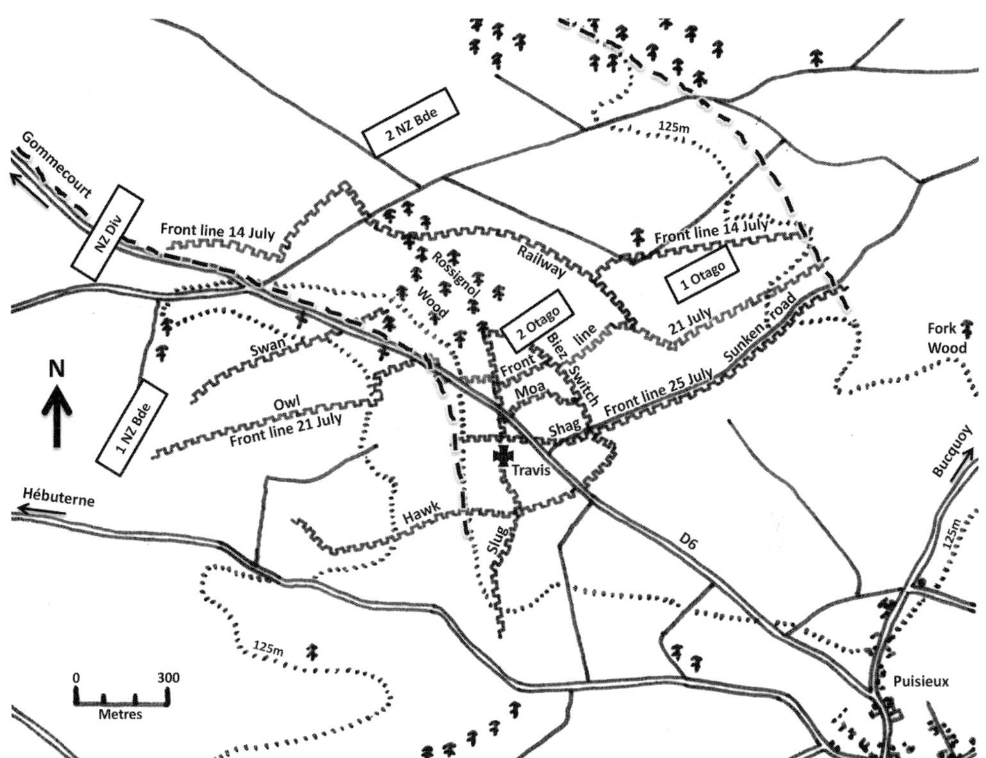

Pass Rossignol Wood on the left on the D6 Gommecourt–Puisieux road. As you crest the top of the rise find somewhere to pull off the road on the right side. There are usually a few places to park safely in this area. Slug Trench ran north-south through this point.

forward. Some progress was also made on the 21st and that night a strong German attack was repulsed.

On the 21st both Otago Battalions carried out inter-company reliefs. On the 22nd slight improvements were made to the general line and patrols were active in front. However, it was highly desirable that the line be advanced further, in order to secure higher ground, improve observation and fields of fire and more effectively clear Rossignol Wood. A minor operation to achieve this was planned for 5.00 p.m. on 23rd July. However, storms flooded the trenches and approaches and forced a postponement for twenty-four hours.

Saps running to the enemy trenches had been filled with entangled barbed wire by the withdrawing Germans. One in particular, in front of 2nd Otago, was impassable due to a thick block. Shortly before the attack, Travis crawled out with two Stokes mortar bombs, disregarded the enemy posts close by and reached the block. There he waited until just before zero hour and then blew up the wire entanglement and cleared a passage for the attack. At 5.00 p.m. on the 24th, 10th Company of 1st Otago on the left and 10th Company of 2nd Otago on the right, advanced behind a one minute light trench mortar bombardment, which then stepped back. Moa Trench was the target until zero plus three minutes and then Shag Trench until zero plus thirteen minutes. Although not involved in covering the advance, the artillery was in support. As the attack went in, 1st and 3rd New Zealand Brigades RFA opened fire on other enemy positions in the area. 37th Division's artillery fired a diversionary bombardment against Bucquoy, in addition to a smoke barrage, which blew over the German rear defences.

The enemy was taken by surprise and resistance was weak. Posts were rushed or bombed in quick succession. On the left, the first post captured by 1st Otago resulted in two prisoners and a machine gun being taken. At the junction of a communication trench with Shag Trench another post was bombed and the enemy was driven out, leaving one dead. The left platoon was checked by a machine gun position in Shag Trench until parties worked round the right flank and the enemy abandoned the machine gun as they pulled back. A block was established in Railway Trench and the platoon worked across the open to the sunken road and rushed a position, where a block was established at the junction of the sunken road and Railway Trench. A number of the enemy were killed and three prisoners, two machine guns and a quantity of other equipment were captured.

On the right, 2nd Otago also surprised the Germans but some resistance was encountered working along Biez Switch. Several enemy were killed and a number escaped down the communication trenches, which they tried unsuccessfully to hold by bombing. Moa Trench was rushed overland from Owl Trench. A strong patrol with a Lewis gun pushed along Slug Street to the junction with Hawk Trench, fighting for it all the way. During this action Travis' bombing party was held up by two machine guns, which threatened the success of the whole operation. Travis had lit a cigarette and was watching the left of the attack when he heard the German machine guns. Disregarding the danger, he rushed the position with a revolver in each hand, killed the seven men crewing the machine guns and captured the guns. An enemy officer and three men rushed at him from a bend in the trench but he killed all four.

The bombing party was able to advance once more. It completed clearing Slug Trench to the junction with Hawk Trench, a total distance of about 225m. Two minenwerfers were seen at the junction but could not be removed. The party ran short of bombs and enemy resistance stiffened. A temporary block was constructed and the enemy was held until a permanent barrier could be established behind. An attempt to cut the party off from the left of Hawk Trench was beaten off using German grenades. Having withdrawn to the new block, a Lewis gun post was established there.

About fifty enemy were killed in this operation and four prisoners were taken from 73rd Fusilier Regiment, 111th Division, in addition to six machine guns and two trench mortars. The trenches in the new position were in good condition, with dugouts and shelters, and they allowed direct observation into Puisieux. New

Slug Trench ran from this position towards the middle of the right face of Rossignol Wood. The car is on the D6. Travis' VC action was in the foreground.

Zealander casualties were light initially but increased later due to enemy artillery fire, which commenced fourteen minutes after zero. This fire continued throughout the night, with most shells falling in rear of the new line. However, it had some effect. 2nd Otago lost only one man killed and another wounded in the assault but nine men were killed and twenty-one were wounded in this bombardment.

On the right flank, 1st New Zealand Brigade pushed forward simultaneously with 2nd New Zealand Brigade's attack. The advance pressed on for over 450m until stopped by a strong block. Contact was established with 2nd Otago. As a result of the four days of operations, the New Zealand Division's front was advanced by up to 1,400m and more advantageous positions were gained.

Three times during 25th July the enemy bombarded the sector, with heavy machine gun fire being added at 7 p.m. The Germans were observed massing in the valley to the south of Rossignol Wood and the SOS signal was sent up. The attack struck the front of both Otago Battalions. Two parties attacked 1st Otago. The left, at the junction of the sunken road and Railway Trench, was met by Lewis gun and rifle fire and was beaten off with a number killed. The right party worked along old communication trenches and threw stick grenades before launching the assault. It too was driven back by Lewis gun fire and bombs. The New Zealand artillery added to the destruction.

2nd Otago was attacked in greater strength, the attackers taking advantage of disused saps to move forward. When the barrage lifted they attacked over the open in three parties, each of about forty men. The right party overwhelmed a post and penetrated the line but, at the other points, they were halted and many casualties were inflicted. Platoons in readiness in Moa Trench counterattacked from two directions simultaneously. All of the enemy who penetrated the trenches were killed or wounded and the line was re-established. About thirty prisoners, mostly wounded, were taken and along the front of 2nd Otago about sixty enemy dead were counted. Later an enemy concentration at Fork Wood was dealt with by the artillery. A few hours later 2nd Otago was relieved as planned by 3rd New Zealand Brigade, albeit slightly delayed by the German attack.

One of the casualties of the morning bombardments was Travis, whose loss was felt throughout the Battalion and beyond. His body was brought out of the line and was buried in falling rain on the late afternoon of 26th July in the cemetery above Couin. A large number of men attended, including the brigade commander.

Chapter Four

Return to the Offensive

Capture of Hamel and Subsequent Operations

367 LCpl Thomas Axford, 16th Battalion AIF (4th Australian Brigade, 4th Australian Division), Hamel Wood, France
368 Dvr Henry Dalziel, 15th Battalion AIF (4th Australian Brigade, 4th Australian Division), Hamel Wood, France

4th July 1918

An operation to seize the ridge running northwards from the Villers Bretonneux plateau, on which were situated Vaire and Hamel Woods and Hamel village, had been mooted in April 1918. However, at that time, Australian formations were understrength as the flow of volunteers had slowed and there were insufficient reserves to carry it out safely. By late June the Australian infantry in France was 8,255 understrength. Replacements in England and France amounted to only 5,221 and they could not all be deployed immediately. As a result the establishment of infantry battalions was reduced from 966 NCOs and men to 900, which conformed to the British model.

The situation changed when 13th Tank Battalion (5th Tank Brigade) arrived to replace 1st Tank Battalion. The latter was equipped with older tanks with which the Australians had had a disastrous experience at Bullecourt the previous year. 13th Tank Battalion had the latest Mark V model. When demonstrated to senior Australian commanders they were most impressed with its performance.

General Sir Henry Rawlinson, commanding Fourth Army, directed that a plan be put together using sufficient tanks to secure success, with the minimum casualties to the Australian Corps. The Australians had not been at Cambrai in November 1917 and had no experience of what tanks could achieve. Tactics had developed considerably since Bullecourt. The tanks advanced in three groups. The first moved ahead of the infantry to cut lanes through the enemy wire, get behind the key enemy positions to cut them off and also to block reinforcements coming forward. The second group was in close support of the infantry to overcome strongpoints. A third group in the rear was to replace losses and deal with any strongpoints overlooked. The tank commanders wanted to advance without a creeping barrage in order to preserve visibility. However, this was firmly quashed by the Australian infantry commanders, who regarded the barrage as essential to success. Given their experiences at Bullecourt, they were not prepared to rely on tanks alone. As a result of this change, the first group of tanks was subsumed into the second.

Exercises were held well behind the lines and helped to dispel the Australian objections to cooperating with tanks. The Mark I used at Bullecourt was slow, required three men to drive it and was vulnerable to armour piercing bullets. In contrast, the new Mark Vs were operated by a single driver, were as fast as a doubling infantryman and their armour would resist steel bullets. In between phases of these exercises the infantry were allowed to crawl all over the tanks, even drive them, and the commanders discussed all aspects of operations with their infantry counterparts.

Some of the newly arrived American divisions in France were attached to a British division behind the lines, where they trained for a month with British advice. Then each battalion was attached to a British brigade in the line, with its British advisers. American regiments would then reform and serve as a brigade in a British division. After that the divisions would reform for service wherever required. Americans were to be included in the operation at Hamel to give them experience of a set-piece attack, launched by highly experience Australian troops. It would also swell the ranks of the attacking force. Rawlinson deliberately chose the date of the attack, 4th July, American Independence Day, as it would be the first time in France that the Americans fought alongside Empire forces.

The attack frontage was 5,500m long and the maximum advance required was 2,300m. By seizing this ridge, Fourth Army would improve its position by creating more depth and thereby strengthen the defence of Amiens. It would also provide observation over the Somme valley, deprive observation to the enemy, test German morale, which was believed to be deteriorating, and trial attack methods for larger operations later. The ground was particularly suitable for tanks.

Although the defences of the two woods and Hamel village were strong, in other places the trenches were shallow, non-continuous and were often no more than shell holes. There was little wire, no communications trenches and no shelters in the forward trenches.

4th Australian Division was to make the attack, with 11th Australian Brigade (3rd Australian Division) attached, and supported by 5th Tank Brigade and Nos.8 and 9 Squadrons RAF and No.3 Squadron Australian Flying Corps (AFC). The right flank was to be guarded by two battalions of 6th Australian Brigade. There was little natural cover behind the Australian front and every possible measure was taken to maintain secrecy in order to achieve surprise. While planning proceeded in the early stages, little was written down. The final conference was held just three days before the attack was launched. Units involved were withdrawn from the line before receiving their orders.

Formations on the flanks of the attack were to extend the barrage and neutralise enemy artillery groups. To the north of the Somme, 5th Australian Division was

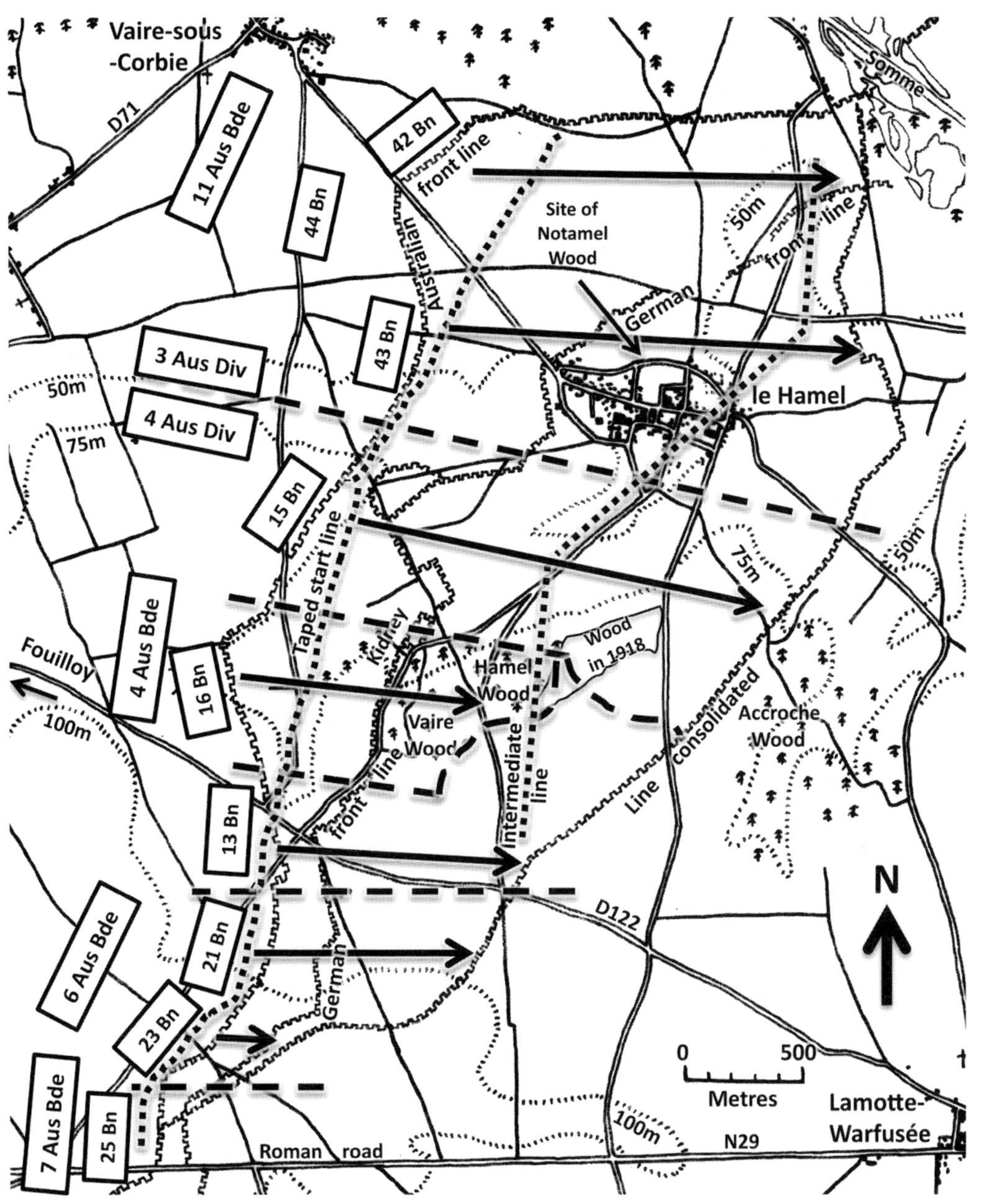

Overview of the whole operation to seize Hamel and Vaire and Hamel Woods on 4th July 1918.

to carry out a minor operation on a frontage of 1,100m. All these measures were to confuse the enemy as to the real objectives. On the attack frontage ten per cent of field artillery shells were to be smoke to help cover the infantry advance. This would also suggest to the enemy that gas was being used and thereby reduce their effectiveness as they donned gas masks. No.1 Special Company RE was to form several smoke screens. However, on the day of the attack the ground was hard and dry. Artillery fire and the movement of tanks created copious amounts of dust and rendered the smoke unnecessary. Indeed there was so much smoke and dust that the progress of the tanks was hampered in places. Harassing fire over the preceding days, including gas and smoke, was to divert attention from the real barrage when it opened.

The noise of the tanks moving forward was covered by aircraft flying up and down the entire frontage of Fourth Army. The tanks were to lead behind the creeping barrage with the infantry following. Special detachments were formed to deal with the two woods and Hamel village, while the troops who were to advance to the final objective passed around these strongpoints. A pause would be made on an intermediate objective before the final advance.

Fourth Army allocated extra field and heavy artillery, resulting in the Australian Corps having 326 field guns and howitzers and 302 heavy guns for the operation. There were also 111 machine guns from 2nd, 3rd, 4th and 5th Australian Machine Gun Battalions. Another thirty-six machine gun teams accompanied the advancing infantry. There was no wire cutting prior to the operation in order to preserve security. In any case the wire defences were weak and the passage of the tanks was expected to be sufficient.

The night before the attack No.1 Squadron RAF dropped 350 bombs on enemy billeting areas in the rear areas. No.8 Squadron RAF and No.3 Squadron AFC were to cooperate with the assault troops. The former had trained to support tanks in the advance by bombing and machine gunning anti-tank gun positions. No.205 Squadron RAF was to bomb enemy dumps and bivouac areas at zero plus thirty minutes and No.9 Squadron RAF was to drop ammunition at pre-arranged points or on seeing ground signals.

Numerous signals were to be used between infantry, tanks, artillery and aircraft. Aircraft observing enemy preparations for counterattack were to drop parachute flares above the enemy formations. These would burn for fifteen minutes. Numbered calico sheets would indicate the location of battalion HQs to aircraft. The infantry would carry white smoke rifle grenades (No.27) to direct the attention of the tanks onto targets.

On 2nd July about 200 representatives of each assault brigade assembled in woods near their camps to be visited by the Australian Prime Minister, William Morris Hughes, who was in the area for a meeting of the Supreme War Council. Zero hour was set for 3.10 a.m. on 4th July, when there would be just sufficient light to see. During the preceding two nights, 4th and 11th Australian Brigades moved into position and relieved 13th and the right of 12th Australian Brigades.

Five American companies were attached to each assault brigade initially. However, on 3rd July the Americans removed six of the ten companies, which required a great deal of last minute reorganisation and movement. The reason given by General

John 'Black Jack' Pershing was that the troops were insufficiently trained. Pershing later decided not to allow the other four companies to take part. There were frantic telephone calls and discussions involving Monash, Rawlinson and Haig. However, the decision came too late to remove the last four companies and the attack went ahead with them. The four companies came from 131st and 132nd Regiments, 33rd Division and were incorporated by platoons within the Australian assault battalions.

On the night of 2nd/3rd July, sixty fighting and twelve supply tanks of 5th Tank Brigade (8th and two companies of 13th Tank Battalions) moved up to 1,600m behind the front line, where they were carefully hidden in orchards and amongst ruined buildings around Aubigny. Six tanks were allocated to 6th Australian Brigade for the flank guard. 4th Australian Brigade had twelve tanks, half to protect the infantry passing north and south of the two woods, while the other half assisted in clearing the woods. 11th Australian Brigade had eighteen tanks, six to assist in clearing Hamel and the rest to cooperate in the advance. Another twelve tanks were to form a link between the two brigades, three tanks being allocated to capture Pear Trench, a strongpoint in the centre of the attack frontage. Another company of twelve tanks, divided between the two brigades, was to remain in the rear until the intermediate objective. From there it would move forward with the others to the final objective and assist the infantry during consolidation. Every tank carried some ammunition boxes, Lewis gun drums and water for the infantry, in addition to the supply tanks, which also had engineer stores aboard. A typical load for a supply tank was 120 coils of barbed wire, 360 screw pickets, fifty sheets of corrugated iron, fifty tins of water, 150 trench mortar bombs and ten boxes of small arms ammunition.

The tanks began moving forward with throttled down engines at 10.30 p.m. on 3rd July. The last was in its start position 900m behind the infantry by 1.15 a.m. on the 4th. The night was quiet as the infantry filed out of their trenches onto their start tapes. All were in position by 2.30 a.m. and many fell asleep there. Within 11th Australian Brigade some troops pulled back fifty metres to account for the supporting field artillery not being able to register accurately beforehand. Normal harassing fire was opened at 3.02 a.m. (zero minus eight minutes), at which time the tanks began moving forward at full speed. The noise was partly covered by the artillery and also by No.101 Squadron RAF dropping 350 twenty-five pound bombs on Hamel and the valley beyond it from 10 p.m. onwards. Every pilot made three flights and some four. Although some German officers in the forward areas suspected something was afoot, possibly a raid, and stood their men to, there was no general alarm and no suspicion that they were about to face a strong attack with tanks. The barrage opened at zero with every gun firing one smoke shell and remained on a line 200m in front of the infantry for four minutes. This was sufficient time for the tanks to join the infantry as they set off.

The infantry's three assault waves closed up to avoid the expected enemy barrage and kept as close as possible to the creeping barrage. The first wave was to overcome the main resistance in Hamel village, Pear Trench and Hamel and Vaire Woods. The second, twice the strength of the first, was to go through to the final objective, while the third acted as carriers, reserves and to mop up any centres of resistance missed in the advance. Some guns fell short in about six places, a tank was hit and a number of casualties were suffered amongst the infantry. At the junction of 4th and 11th Australian Brigades a section of Americans and a platoon of 43rd Battalion was hit. 15th Battalion lost forty-two men before the advance commenced. The experienced troops reacted to these problems in two ways. Some hung back, allowing the rogue guns plenty of space, whereas others kept as close to the barrage as possible, allowing the stray shells to fall behind them. In general the barrage was excellent and counter-battery fire ensured that there was little German response for a few hours. The Americans were keen not to be left behind by the Australians and, as a result, suffered most of their casualties by running into the barrage.

On the right flank, 23rd and 21st Battalions, right and left respectively, of 6th Australian Brigade, each with three tanks from C Company, 13th Tank Battalion in support, encountered only a little opposition in wheeling to form the flank. The smoke screens ahead and on the flank provided effective protection, allowing the attackers to be on top of the German positions before they could open fire. By 6.00 a.m. they were in contact with 13th Battalion on the left. On the extreme right, 25th Battalion (7th Australian Brigade) met more stubborn opposition astride the Roman road. A counterattack at the extreme southern point of the attack almost succeeded in retaking the lost strongpoint; but accurate artillery and machine gun fire, followed by a fierce bombing fight, restored the situation. The Battalion lost ninety-three men in the attack but took ninety-two prisoners in addition to many other enemy being killed and wounded.

4th Australian Brigade advanced with 13th Battalion on the right, 16th Battalion in the centre and 15th Battalion on the left. 14th Battalion was in reserve. Twenty-four tanks were attached from A and B Companies, 8th Tank Battalion – three to 13th Battalion, six to 16th Battalion, nine to 15th Battalion and six to 14th Battalion. Two trench mortars were attached to each forward battalion and three machine gun teams were attached to 13th and 15th Battalions. Three platoons (one each from 13th, 14th and 15th Battalions) were specially trained in the construction of strongpoints in the consolidation phase and each had two machine gun teams attached. These strongpoints would form the backbone of a new support line. Forming up on the start line tapes was carried out quietly and without problems. At zero hour the troops set off behind the barrage. It was more than five minutes before the enemy barrage fell, by then well behind the assault troops.

13th Battalion advanced on a narrow frontage of one company (360m) initially, in order to pass to the south of Vaire Wood, before opening up to the north at the double to cover the last 1,100m to the final objective. It met up successfully with 15th Battalion on the left as it came around the north of the Wood. Two tanks were to guard the Battalion as it passed around the south of the wood, while a third was to work along the Fouilloy – Warfusée road. The left company in the second line came

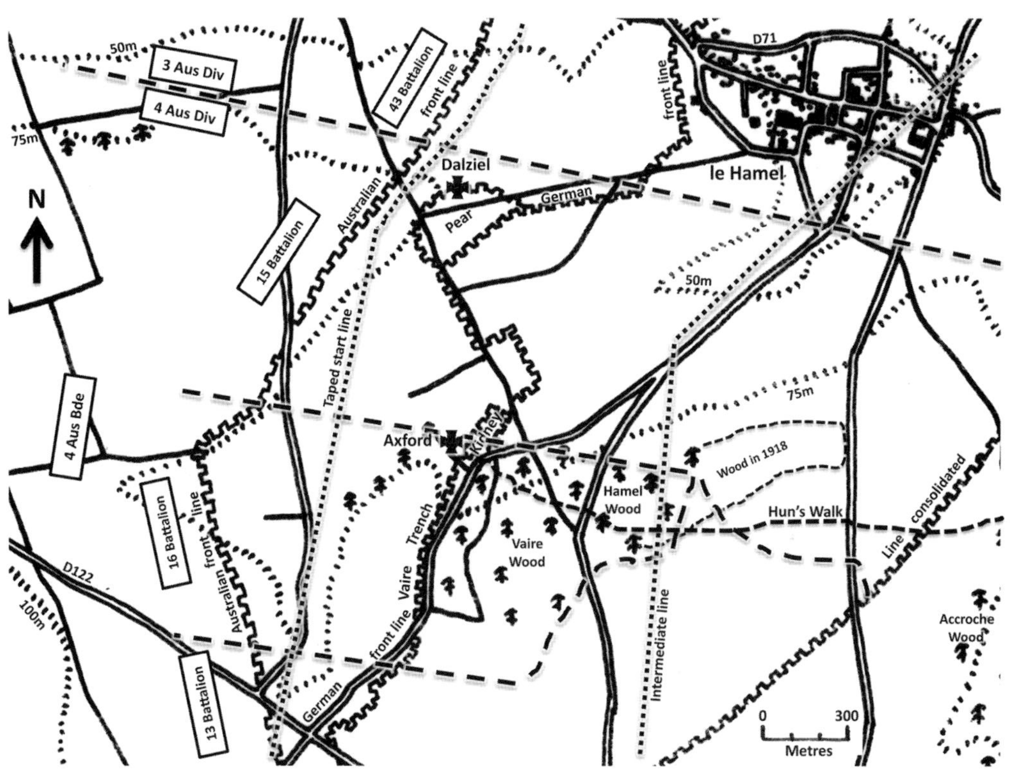

Leave le Hamel on the minor road to the southwest. Pass a sports pitch on the left and continue for 550m. Take the right fork and continue for 450m to where there is a track on the right running northwards, with Vaire Wood on the left. Park here. 4 x 4s will be able to continue but other vehicles should not attempt this section. Walk along the track for 450m then look back. Half right on the high ground is the site of the Kidney and Axford's VC action. Continue uphill along the track for another 250m, passing a clump of bushes on the left, to the top of the hill. This is the site of Pear Trench and the scene of Dalziel's VC action. Climb on top of the bank on the left of the track here for an excellent view of the whole attack frontage of 4th Australian Brigade.

under fire from a machine gun in Vaire Wood but it was overcome in a rush. More opposition was encountered as the left extended north beyond the Wood. This was overcome quickly when a tank crushed a machine gun post. Seeing this, another post nearby surrendered. The right company overcame a strongpoint halfway to the final objective, which was reached at 4.18 a.m. The tanks came forward to provide cover during consolidation and at 6.00 a.m. the fourth company arrived to fill gaps.

16th Battalion was to clear Vaire and Hamel Woods quickly to ensure that the flanking battalions were not held up by enfilade fire. The attack was launched at almost half the planned strength as the Battalion lost its two American companies the previous evening. The woods were divided into four sectors, each allocated to a company, from the right A, C, B and D. The six tanks with the Battalion operated

Alongside the track at Pear Trench is this unexploded shrapnel shell with the lead balls clearly visible. The fuse has either sheered off on impact or, as if often the case, it has been removed later for its scrap or antique value.

in pairs, one on each flank and the third in the centre. There was strong resistance on the edge of Vaire Wood. In the approach to Kidney Trench, **Lance Corporal Thomas Axford**'s platoon passed through the wire and reached the first enemy defences. However, the adjoining platoon was held up by uncut wire and the delay enabled the enemy to set up a machine gun and inflict a number of casualties. The company commander, Captain Frederick Frank Wood, and sergeant major, 1457 CSM Harold Goldie Binman, were mortally wounded (Daours Communal Cemetery Extension – III D 36 & 37) and a Lewis gun team was wiped out. Axford at once rushed to the flank, throwing bombs amongst the machine gun team and then jumped into the trench, where he killed ten Germans and captured another six. Having thrown the machine gun onto the parapet, he called the delayed platoon to come on before rejoining his own platoon. Axford had earlier been involved in laying out the start tapes and remaining to ensure that they were not interfered with. Another forty-seven prisoners were taken in the dugouts in the sunken road behind Kidney Trench. Many were wearing gas masks. Once inside the woods many strongpoints and machine gun posts had to be cleared. However, it was found that tanks could advance on the main ride. The advancing Australians forced the retiring Germans into the barrage. The woods were cleared in ninety minutes and 400 prisoners were taken. The Lewis gunners did good work, firing shoulder slung weapons from the hip. At 5.00 a.m. Battalion HQ heard that 13th and 15th Battalions were on the final objective. 16th Battalion had completed its mission and fell back into reserve, having suffered seventy-eight casualties.

15th Battalion went into the attack 636 strong, with 216 men of the American 132nd Regiment attached. All four companies were in the line, with D Company on the right, then C, B and A Companies. The Battalion encountered stiff resistance from the outset. On the left, short shooting by the supporting artillery meant that the assault troops had to hold back 180m. Twelve men were killed and thirty were wounded on the start tape. The Germans were thereby enabled to man the Pear Trench salient, which was not damaged by the barrage, before the left of the Battalion

From Pear Trench, scene of Dalziel's VC action, looking southeast, with Hamel and Vaire Woods in the background. The approach track runs away from the camera position on the left to the Hamel road, which runs along the forward edge of the woods. On the right the small copse is on the site of the Kidney, where Axford's VC action took place.

Also taken from Pear Trench, with Hamel on the left, the Kidney on the right and Hamel and Vaire Woods in the background. In 1918 Hamel Wood extended further to the left. The mutual support enjoyed by these positions is evident.

reached it. The tanks for this sector went astray in the smoke and the wire had to be cut by hand in places under fire. The Lewis gunners (each platoon had two by this stage of the war) sprayed enemy machine gun positions to subdue their fire. Two machine guns were silenced in this way and the men then rushed the positions. As they did so, another machine gun opened fire on the left. **Sergeant Henry Dalziel** slapped a fresh drum of ammunition onto the Lewis gun, manned by the only other unwounded man in his section, then drew his revolver and rushed the gun position. He shot two of the crew and captured the post. The end of Dalziel's trigger finger was shot away in this action and he was ordered to the rear. In his own account Dalziel said that he killed seven Germans with his two revolvers. One German wounded him in the hand but he forced him to the ground and stabbed him over the heart with his German dagger. The German's dying cry made Dalziel shiver.

The right flank, pressing on with three tanks, also suffered from enfilade fire from Pear Trench. In addition Vaire Trench offered considerable resistance until it was assaulted and taken. At least one machine gunner continued to fire until the assault reached him. Some Germans surrendered but others continued to throw bombs. In the heat of the action many of those attempting to surrender were killed. Only after a fierce bayonet fight was the garrison overcome. Having cleared the position, the assault swept on to catch up with the barrage. The intermediate line was then reached, although fire from strongpoints on the flanks continued until dealt with by the tanks. 15th Battalion's left flank had to call upon tank support in the final advance, having suffered further losses. The defenders made a stand there until they were driven off with the help of a tank. Fifty prisoners and twenty-seven light machine guns were taken.

The right of 16th Battalion and the left of 13th Battalion were to clear a communication trench, Hun's Walk, through Vaire Wood. A tank was allotted for

this operation. Many Germans escaped along this trench to Accroche Wood and a crossroads. Despite having been ordered to the rear earlier, Dalziel followed to the final objective with blood pouring from his wounded hand. He set up the Lewis gun and filled some sandbags to support it, then fired short bursts at Germans he could see running out of a broken trench about 300m away. He was again ordered to the aid post but instead brought up ammunition dropped by an aeroplane (a tank according to Dalziel) about 220m to the rear of his position. Reaching the ammunition dump under machine gun fire, he noticed that two spent bullets had lodged in his puttees. He put an ammunition box on his shoulder and started back. A whizz-bang (5.9″ shell) burst behind him and he landed in a shell hole full of water. Having crawled the rest of the way back to the Lewis gun position, he discovered that he was carrying a box of grenades rather than Lewis gun ammunition. He handed the grenades to the troops around him and set off back to recover ammunition for the Lewis gun. He returned as Germans were seen advancing about 450m away. He and those around him opened a terrific fire into the attacking ranks. A very young German in front was shouting for mercy and two Americans went for him with their bayonets. Dalziel yelled at them to stop and they took the youngster prisoner instead. Having fired off his last drum of ammunition, Dalziel went back over the hill for more. Passing a dressing station, he noticed a German, with his foot blown off, and the young German chatting with the two Americans. The older German thanked Dalziel for saving his son and shook his hand. Dalziel returned with another box of ammunition and filled several drums. German fire was slackening by then but snipers continued to be a menace. Suddenly he felt a pain in his head and blood streamed down the left side of his face. He had been shot through the head and very seriously wounded.

Due to a shortage of men, 13th and 15th Battalions had to leave gaps in the new line. 14th Battalion brought forward engineer stores and ammunition before digging a support line 275–450m behind. In the advance one company assisted in connecting 13th and 15th Battalions on the final objective. By 7.00 a.m. a reasonable line had been dug and consolidated. Fighting patrols with Lewis gun teams were pushed forward with tanks to drive away small parties of the enemy close in front. The Battalion suffered 240 casualties in the attack and consolidation, while the attached Americans had a further seventy-one.

11th Australian Brigade, with its American attachments, was to capture Hamel and beyond it was to consolidate the old French line. 43rd and 42nd Battalions led, the former supported by six tanks and the latter by three, provided by C Company, 8th Tank Battalion and two sections of C Company, 13th Tank Battalion. There was little opposition except near Pear Trench, where the right of 43rd Battalion became involved in heavy fighting and lost the barrage. The German line here ran to the northeast and this meant that no man's land in the centre of the Battalion was nearly 900m wide. To the north, a machine gun held up the flank platoon until it was overcome by an Australian Lewis gunner and an American corporal. The centre company of 43rd Battalion ran into strong resistance where the German defences bent around the western end of Hamel. The enemy in the front line fired for a short while and then withdrew. The Australians swept on but about one hundred metres from the village, there was resistance from a heap of mangelwurzels south of the road. The tanks had not yet arrived and a short sharp fight followed. Many of the grenades bowled by the attackers rolled back down the pile harmlessly. A platoon went forward along the road to outflank the enemy, followed by a rush on all sides, which resulted in fifteen Germans being killed and about forty being captured, most of whom were in a dugout behind the heap.

North of the village the line ran through Notamel Wood and was held in strength. The left company lost direction at first in the smoke, but corrected this when they saw the treetops of the Wood. A party gained the trench and worked its way northwards along it. Another crossed the trench and, while some men engaged the enemy from the front, others bombed them from the rear. A machine gun firing from the village was rubbed out by a tank. When the intermediate line was reached, all three companies were ready to enter the village to clear it. A few posts had to be dealt with on the outskirts of Hamel. As a disorientated tank came back, its fire scattered an Australian and an American platoon. It was a while before the officers could collect their men together again.

42nd Battalion's attack went according to plan. Some men had sneezing fits during the assembly, due to blue cross gas being used at the northern end of the line near the Somme. However, no man's land was wide at this point and the enemy did not hear them.

At the intermediate line, 44th Battalion passed through 43rd Battalion and resumed the advance with six supporting tanks. Half of the Battalion passed to the north and the other half to the south of Hamel. Both 44th and 42nd Battalions met some resistance. Behind Hamel village 44th Battalion encountered a strongly held knot of old trenches on the crest. Machine guns opened fire and the infantry called on the tanks for support. The knoll was rushed and from this position the river was overlooked. 44th and 42nd Battalions were on the final objective by 4.55 a.m.

The other six tanks helped 43rd Battalion in clearing the village, which was carried out quickly, as most of the garrison was caught in the deep dugouts. Three hundred surrendered, including a battalion HQ and staff. Two tanks were disabled on the edge of the village and another overturned within it. Once the village was cleared two companies formed a line behind it and 43rd Battalion went into reserve.

The diversionary attack by 15th Australian Brigade north of the Somme was also successful. The assault troops (four companies and a platoon) were consolidating by 5.00 a.m. There were 142 casualties and sixty-four prisoners were taken.

While the new line was being consolidated, a protective barrage and smoke screen was fired 360m ahead. Four carrier tanks delivered their loads of stores close behind the new line, a task that would normally have required 1,200 men to achieve. The fighting tanks also continued to provide valuable support until they were released and moved back to their musters. No.9 Squadron RAF came over and each aircraft dropped two parachute loads of ammunition from 300m or less. Most aircraft returned three times with other loads. Although not generally very accurate, all agreed that, with practice, this was the way ahead. When most of the British aircraft withdrew at 9.30 a.m., German aircraft dominated the skies above the battlefield, swooping down to drop bombs and machine gun the new positions. This was more annoying than effective but the aircraft were also used to direct the German guns, which was a more serious matter.

Corporal Thomas Ambrose Pope was awarded the Medal of Honor for his part in the attack on 4th July 1918. The Medal of Honor is the highest American award for gallantry and as such equates to the Victoria Cross.

Overall the German response was feeble and as a result the wounded could be withdrawn with ease. Any concentration of German troops was instantly pounced upon by the artillery and machine guns. At 10.00 p.m. the Germans launched a counterattack with about 300 infantry. They were ahead of the British barrage and hit 44th Battalion. The Stokes mortars of 11th Light Trench Mortar Battery were well supplied with bombs and engaged the Germans in 200m of trench between the centre and left companies. A bombing party was organised to attack northwards along the trench, while the left company attacked southwards. 43rd Battalion and some Americans also took part. The southern attack was more successful than the northern but the enemy was driven back down a communication trench. The lost trench was retaken and fifty-six Germans were taken prisoner as well as ten machine guns being seized. Eleven Australian prisoners were also released. An

American, Corporal Thomas Ambrose Pope, Company E, 131st Infantry Regiment, was awarded the British Distinguished Conduct Medal for his part in this action and also received the Medal of Honor. His company was halted by machine gun fire and he rushed the post alone, killing several of the crew with the bayonet and held off the others until reinforcements arrived to capture them. Pope was born in Chicago, Illinois on 15th December 1894 and died on 14th June 1989. He was also awarded the American Distinguished Service Cross. He is buried in Arlington National Cemetery, Virginia (Section 35, Site 3157).

The main attack resulted in 1,062 Australian and 176 American casualties. Five tanks were disabled but were recovered by the night of 6th/7th July. Five aircraft were lost for the loss of five German aircraft and a balloon. Over 1,600 prisoners were taken, in addition to two field guns, thirty-two trench mortars, 177 machine guns and two anti-tank rifles. The position on the Villers Bretonneux ridge had been strengthened and the German position was weakened. A great deal had been learned about how the forthcoming offensive would be carried out. It was a model of infantry – tank cooperation and restored Australian faith in the new weapon.

369 Cpl Walter Brown, 20th Battalion AIF (5th Australian Brigade, 2nd Australian Division), Villers-Bretonneux, France

6th July 1918

Immediately after the Battle of Hamel it became clear that the German outpost line was unusually disorganised. It consisted of small sections of old British and German trenches, generally without barbed wire in front. HQ 2nd Australian Division, having consulted the front line battalion COs of 6th and 7th Australian Brigades, resolved to advance the outposts in order to secure a better view. A number of advanced posts were established by simply moving forward along abandoned communication trenches. One party of 21st Battalion (6th Australian Brigade) penetrated a small trench system north of the Roman road until it came under fire from a German machine gun post. Lieutenant Richard Lewis Weir DCM (MC for this action) rushed the post after dark with his platoon (killed on 26th July and buried in Villers-Bretonneux Military Cemetery – XX C 3). 7th Australian Brigade made similar advances south of the Roman road.

6th Australian Brigade was to be relieved by 5th Australian Brigade in the left brigade sub-sector on 6th and 7th July. Despite the impending move into the line, a 6th Australian Brigade team played the French 5th Division at rugby and won 18–10. Some work was carried out on the effectiveness of buried 2″ Mortar bombs being used as anti-tank mines. There was some doubt about the sensitivity of the fuse. Commander 6th Australian Brigade was not in favour on the current front as offensive operations were envisaged in the near future. The sowing of mines would impede progress.

During the night of 5th/6th July, advance parties of the incoming battalions arrived at the front line. Battalion HQs sent an officer, two NCOs and five men and each company sent an officer, three NCOs and one man. Next morning **Corporal Walter Brown**, a member of 20th Battalion's advance party, was wandering around the trenches seized by Weir's party the previous day. A sergeant of the 21st told him that his men were being troubled by German snipers and indicated a vague location 'over there'. Brown waited for half an hour for the Germans to reveal their location by firing another shot but nothing happened. Brown then walked along the empty trench to see if he could get close enough to spot the snipers and 'have a pot at them' himself. He followed the trench in the direction indicated. It became shallow and about sixty metres was over open ground. Brown spotted a mound and soon after a shot was fired, apparently from there. He dropped his rifle and, with two Mills bombs, ran towards it. Another shot was fired but he was not sure whether he was the target or not. He threw a bomb at the mound but it fell short and he dropped into the cover of some broken ground to see what would happen next.

Several minutes passed without incident, so he got up and ran to the mound. He was looking down into one end of an empty kidney-shaped trench, with the entrance to a dugout at the far end and a machine gun on the parados in the middle. He jumped into the trench and ran to the dugout. As he reached it a German appeared

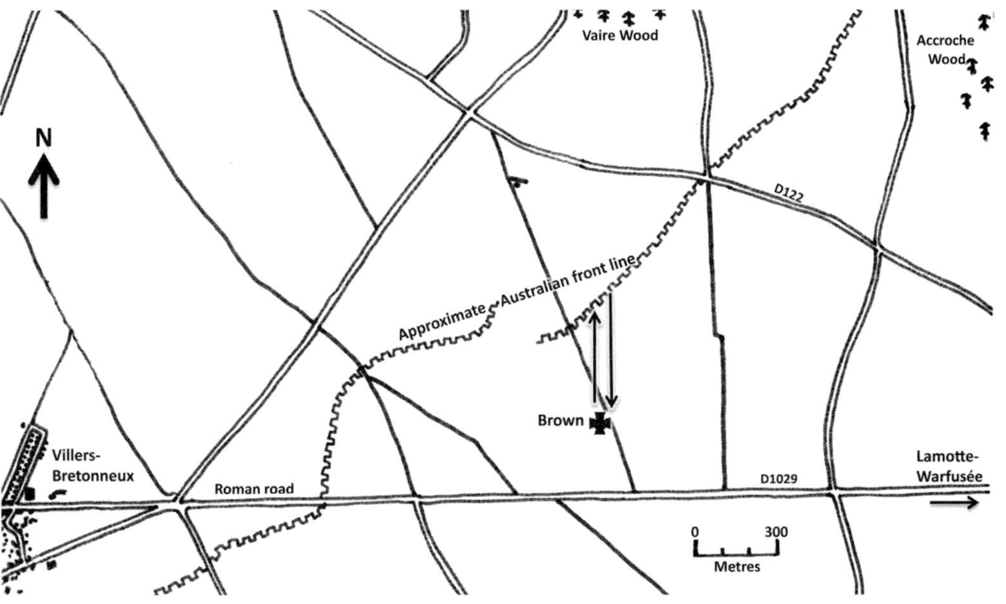

Brown's VC action took place in almost featureless terrain. Leave Villers-Bretonneux on the D1029 eastwards towards Lamotte-Warfusée. Go straight on at the roundabout and after 1,650m take the left turning onto a track. Follow it northwards for almost 300m. Brown's VC action was on the left side of the track in this general area. Continue for 350m to where the Australian front line crossed the track and look back towards the D1029 to overlook the whole length of trench that he captured.

Brown's VC action took place at this point, just to the right of the track. Cars can be seen on the D1029, which runs across the middle of the picture, heading towards Villers-Bretonneux, which is out of sight to the right. Beyond, two water jets attempt to irrigate the crops in the heatwave of July 2018. In the far distance above the track amongst the trees is the church spire in Marcelcave.

in the entrance and Brown thumped him on the jaw. The German cried *Kamerad* as he was knocked down the stairs. Brown backed off to the machine gun and held the remaining bomb ready to throw. Hearing movement behind him, he turned and saw at the other end of the trench, another dugout entrance, with Germans emerging from it. He could not throw the bomb, because without it he was unarmed and would have been overwhelmed. He held it threateningly and the Germans immediately put up their hands. He ordered them over the parapet, while he kept turning his head to keep an eye on both dugout entrances. Thirteen Germans emerged in total, including an officer, and trotted back to the Australian lines with Brown following. There was some German machine gun fire, followed by some shelling.

The prisoners, from 137th Infantry Regiment, had been holding the support line posts during the Battle of Hamel. Afterwards they found themselves in the front line. Having handed over the prisoners, Brown went back to his post, where he was far from popular with his comrades for having drawn the enemy artillery fire. Word of the incident spread rapidly. An officer of 21st Battalion confirmed with Brown that he was the man who had gone out. When his own battalion came into the line, his company commander, Lieutenant Claude Ewan Cameron (later MC & Bar), also asked him what he had been doing. The news spread to every part of the Corps. Even 1st Australian Division at Hazebrouck, well to the north, heard about it.

While Brown sat in his trench, probing of the German trenches continued elsewhere and that afternoon a small German post near Accroche Wood was rushed. Most of this Australian activity was by single men or small parties on local initiative, rather than part of a grand plan. By 3.30 a.m. on 7th July, 6th Australian Brigade had completed the relief of 7th Australian Brigade. There were no casualties. That night 6th Australian Brigade advanced the line again.

370 Lt Albert Borella, 26th Battalion AIF (7th Australian Brigade, 2nd Australian Division), Villers-Bretonneux, France

17th July 1918

By using the tactic of 'peaceful penetration' the Australians had just about secured the whole of the objective set in Lieutenant General Sir John Monash's plan for an Anglo-French offensive on the Villers-Bretonneux plateau. All that remained was the extension authorised by General Sir Henry Rawlinson on 11th July. However, this required the French to carry out their part of the plan but they had never formally agreed to it. On 15th July, GOC 2nd Australian Division, Major General Sir Charles Rosenthal, toured the newly captured front. The French 37th Division

Leave Villers-Bretonneux southwards on the D23 towards Demuin. Go over the railway and after 650m turn left into the Zone Industrialle at the roundabout with a supermarket on the left. Drive on round the left hand bend and just before a roadstone depot on the right turn right along a rough track for 200m. Stop here and look left to the Mound, with the railway running parallel with it beyond.

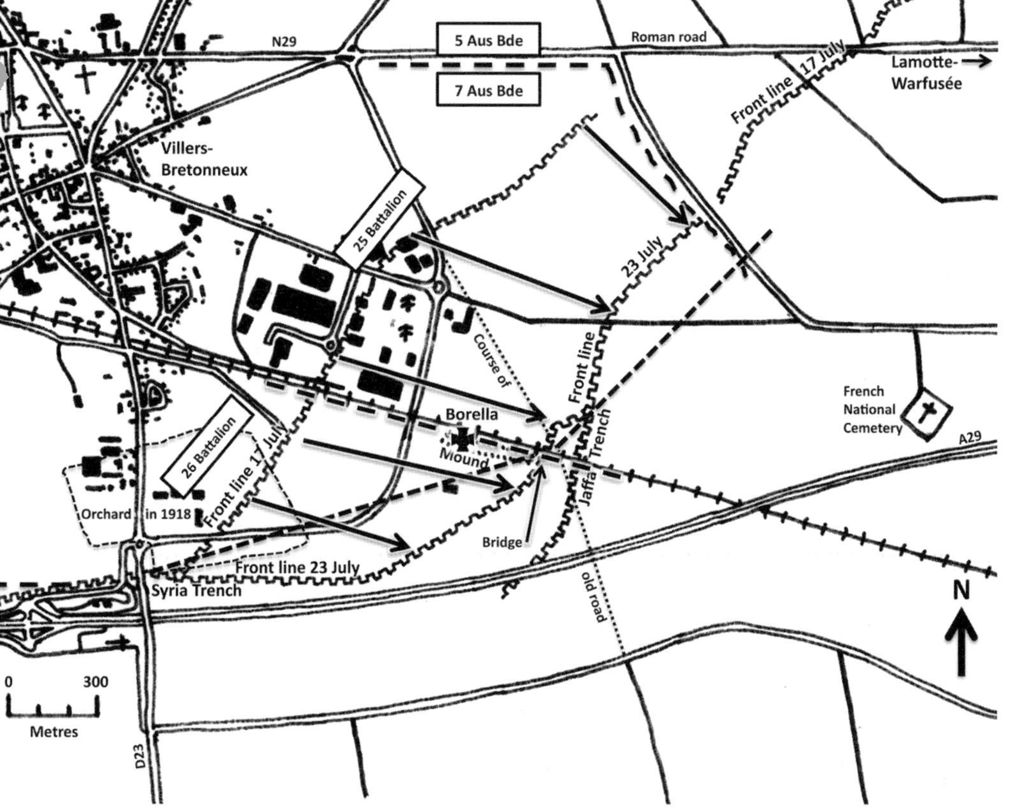

on the Australian right flank had watched the daring daylight Australian excursions into enemy territory with admiration. Rosenthal saw the opportunity to induce the French to undertake a substantial advance as he was on good terms with the local French commanders.

Rosenthal also wanted to seize a scrub-covered hummock of spoil beside the railway, known as the Mound. To achieve this would require an advance of about 900m astride the railway. He met with Rawlinson that evening and explained the position of the Mound and that the objective was slightly more than originally envisaged but less than that authorised on 11th July. He believed the whole could be achieved by penetration in a week. Due to the uncertainty of French cooperation, Rawlinson ordered that the advance must not be further than the Mound for the time being. He also authorised Rosenthal to liaise directly with local French regimental and divisional commanders to try to enlist their support.

The advance to the Mound by peaceful penetration began the same night, 15th-16th July. A party of 25th Battalion reached an old British trench dug after 4th April, about 550m north of the Mound. A post was first established along the road before the old trench was reached. While digging in, the party was attacked from the south by forty Germans with bombs. More than half of the Australian party were killed or wounded and the survivors were driven out.

On the same night 5th Australian Brigade was to advance the line of posts between the left of 25th Battalion and the Roman road. At the same time it was to seize a communication trench north of the road. 19th Battalion was to bomb down the trench, while 17th Battalion attacked frontally a strongpoint in a parallel trench one hundred metres west of it on the Roman road. Two platoons of 17th Battalion rushed the strongpoint and the garrison ran, leaving two dead behind. At dawn Lieutenant Albert Smethurst West and four men jumped into the next

The Mound from the south. 26th Battalion attacked from left to right.

trench, down which 19th Battalion was to bomb. However, the latter was still some distance away and West's party was killed or wounded except for one man (West is buried in Crouy British Cemetery – IV A 9, 6650 Private John Willoughby Ferrier Rhoades is buried in Adelaide Cemetery, Villers-Bretonneux – III P 19 and 3906, Private Francis Joseph Sullivan is buried in Villers-Bretonneux Military Cemetery – III A 2). The Germans were very accommodating to the Australian stretcher-bearers, pointing to where the wounded lay. 19th Battalion completed the task the following night. At 2.00 a.m. on 17th July parties of the Battalion worked round to the front and rear. The Germans, realising that they were about to be surrounded, ran back, leaving a number of dead. This thrust, although not known at the time, had disrupted preparations for a German counterattack.

Patrols of 7th Australian Brigade in the railway sector had been unable to gain ground. Indeed the Germans, for the first time in months, were actively digging and wiring a new line of defence behind their advanced posts. The Germans had clearly had enough of 'peaceful penetration'. Monash and Rosenthal realised that, in this situation, the best course of action was a formal assault. An attack was therefore arranged at short notice by the two forward battalions of 7th Australian Brigade. Zero hour was set for 9.45 p.m. on 17th July. 25th Battalion was north of the railway and 26th Battalion to the south. The barrage, provided by two Australian and two British field artillery brigades, was well laid but thin.

Three companies of 25th Battalion advanced through the wheat on a frontage of 900m. They quickly took the old trench, which patrols had failed to capture two nights before. Beyond it the German posts had to be captured individually by manoeuvre. This was achieved but the barrage was lost in the process. Every post offered some resistance and, in two cases, the garrisons came out to meet the advancing Australians in hand-to-hand fighting. The German machine gunners generally resisted to the end but riflemen fired a few shots and then fell back to the next post, where the fight began again. On the parapet of one post there were five machine guns. Having lost the barrage, and with few landmarks, it was difficult to work out when the objective had been reached. As soon as the general line of 7th Australian Brigade was known, posts of 5th Australian Brigade were also pushed forward. At dusk on 18th July the line was surveyed and linked up.

South of the railway, 26th Battalion had to cover 450m from its start line in an orchard to the first German trench. Because of this, the barrage remained there for six minutes. Here too the artillery support was noticeably thin. On the left, Captain Joseph Kevin Murphy's (MC for this action) company reached the western end of the Mound but a German machine gun there continued firing through the barrage at the advancing troops. It was seen by **Lieutenant Albert Borella**, who was leading his platoon in the first of the two attacking waves. He ran ahead of his men into the barrage, shot two gunners with his revolver and captured the machine gun. The attackers were fired upon by other machine guns but for the most part their fire was inaccurate.

The western end of the Mound, where Borella overcame the machine gun post, is now heavily overgrown. The railway is behind the trees on the left.

The objective for the left company was the road bridging the railway. The road has since been ploughed over but there is still a bridge over the railway. The company passed over the Mound near its eastern end but the road was so badly cut up by shellfire that Borella's party (two platoons) passed over without seeing it. Pressing forward, searching for the road, they suddenly came upon a trench full of Germans, who were obviously surprised by their appearance. Borella's men showered them with bombs and a Lewis gunner, firing from the hip, sprayed bullets into the trench. The defenders disappeared into dugouts and, after a few bombs had been thrown down the stairs, thirty of them surrendered. Borella had seized Jaffa Trench, about 175m beyond his objective. Just after the prisoners had come out, the two dugouts burst into flames and it was assumed that the fires had been started

The bridge over the railway at the eastern end of the Mound appears not to be the original but is on the same site. Today, due to changes to the road layout in the area and the building of the autoroute to the south, it leads nowhere.

deliberately by the Germans to burn papers and maps etc. The two platoons with Borella had by then been reduced to about twenty men with several Lewis guns. He could see 25th Battalion engaged in heavy fighting north of the railway but far behind him. With the flames from the burning dugouts illuminating his men and making them easy targets, he decided to withdraw to some shell holes just outside the area of illumination. For an hour German reinforcements continually came up and assembled in the light of the fires, offering well-silhouetted targets to Borella's men.

The southern company of 26th Battalion established a line of posts connecting Borella's position with the old line south of the orchard. The company only met with resistance in Syria Trench, where a few prisoners were taken. A strongpoint in that trench, that might have barred the right of the advance, had been surrounded and taken by three parties from another company earlier.

Carrying parties arrived, as did two Stokes trench mortars with their ammunition and four machine guns. The new line was quickly consolidated and the 26th Battalion signallers had telephone lines through to the objective within a few minutes of its capture.

As dawn approached, Borella watched about two companies of Germans filing into Jaffa Trench and one by one leap over an obstruction. They then passed what he believed to be bundles of stick grenades hand-to-hand. A counterattack was clearly about to be made. Borella moved his men a few metres back, out of bomb throwing range, and fired the SOS signal for artillery support. North of the railway 25th Battalion carried out similar action, when a party of about 250 Germans were seen moving towards the Mound, while others crept forward through the crops. The barrage came down upon the enemy and also on Borella's party, which was far ahead of its objective. Rifles and Lewis guns opened fire at short range. Although the Germans continued to drift forward for another ten minutes, there was no attack.

Throughout the day the German artillery shelled their old line and the Mound. Late in the afternoon the enemy was seen to be reinforcing his line and at 8.30 p.m. they began moving forward through the crops along their entire front. At 9.00 p.m., when 500 of them lay out ahead of the line, the German artillery opened fire. Through the smoke and dust Borella's party saw large numbers of the enemy advancing. Three machine guns concentrated on Borella's position, forcing his men to keep low but, the moment their fire eased, his party was up and shooting back. Borella fired the SOS, having this time previously moved his men back to the true line of his objective. With the protective artillery fire falling accurately, the Australian rifles and machine guns opened up at point-blank range in good light. Overhead a British airman strafed the enemy again and again with his machine gun. The counterattack melted away with heavy losses. The German formation involved in the counterattack admitted to losing nine officers and 285 men. Two officers and sixty-eight men were captured in addition to two anti-tank guns, four heavy and eleven light machine guns. 7th Australian Brigade's casualties in the attack were six officers and 123 men. In the shelling that followed over subsequent days, losses on both sides increased considerably.

2nd Australian Division was forbidden to move further until the French came up on the flank. On the 18th Rosenthal visited the Mound in the morning wearing his red staff cap instead of a helmet. This attracted the attention of a German sniper and Rosenthal was severely wounded. That day French patrols felt their way into Bertha and Krauss Trenches. On the night of the 21st, bombing parties of 23rd Battalion assisted the French by pushing down Stamboul and Craft Trenches, where they established themselves. However, the French were still about 1,600m behind the general line of the Australian front.

Overall the Australian achievement had been remarkable. Two brigades on a front of 4,100m had, mainly by 'peaceful penetration', advanced 900m. In two weeks these brigades had suffered 437 casualties, only sixteen more than the two neighbouring brigades holding the line near Hamel. An interesting comment in 7th Australian Brigade's war diary relates to salvage. During the month of July the Brigade returned to the railhead 719 lbs of paper, 647 lbs of cardboard, 516 lbs of solder and 2,332 lbs of dripping, with a total value of £1,236/6/8.

Battles of the Marne 1918–Battle of Tardenois

371 Sgt John Meikle, 1/4th Seaforth Highlanders (154th Brigade, 51st (Highland) Division), Marfaux, France

20th July 1918

The German offensive commencing on the Chemin des Dames on 27th May 1918 was brought to a halt on the Marne on 6th June. The fighting was so intense that some British divisions were reduced to battalion strength. They were gradually withdrawn and moved north, with 19th Division being the last to leave the area on 30th June. The Battle of the Aisne 1918 resulted in 28,700 British casualties; it had proved to be far from an ideal rest area. The BEF received 70,000 much needed reinforcements, mostly B grade men, following which there was frantic activity as the drafts were absorbed, units were reconstituted and divisions were brought to France from other theatres.

The Allies had a dilemma. A German breakthrough on the Marne would threaten Paris, creating panic and a major political crisis. Conversely if reserves were withdrawn from the north, where the Germans threatened the British front with a reserve of thirty divisions, the Allies risked being split by a renewed German thrust towards the sea. To be able to react to either eventuality the British positioned three divisions west of Amiens.

There were indications of an impending German offensive between Château-Thierry and Mondidier, which could decide the outcome of the war. If it occurred, the British were to be prepared to take a major part in the battle. The French pressed for up to nine British reserve divisions but almost every one had been involved in at least one of the spring offensives and all were understrength. Haig was in a difficult position; he had to obey Foch but could not take any action that threatened the BEF. Following intervention by the British government, it was agreed that Foch's instruction must be obeyed but French forces were also warned to move to support the BEF if the blow fell in the north.

The Germans attacked the French between Montdidier and Noyon on 9th June. Some ground was lost but there was no breakthrough and the fighting fizzled out on the 15th. A period of relative calm followed, while both sides reconstituted their

The eastern part of the Château-Thierry salient showing the front line on various dates between 17th July and 7th August.

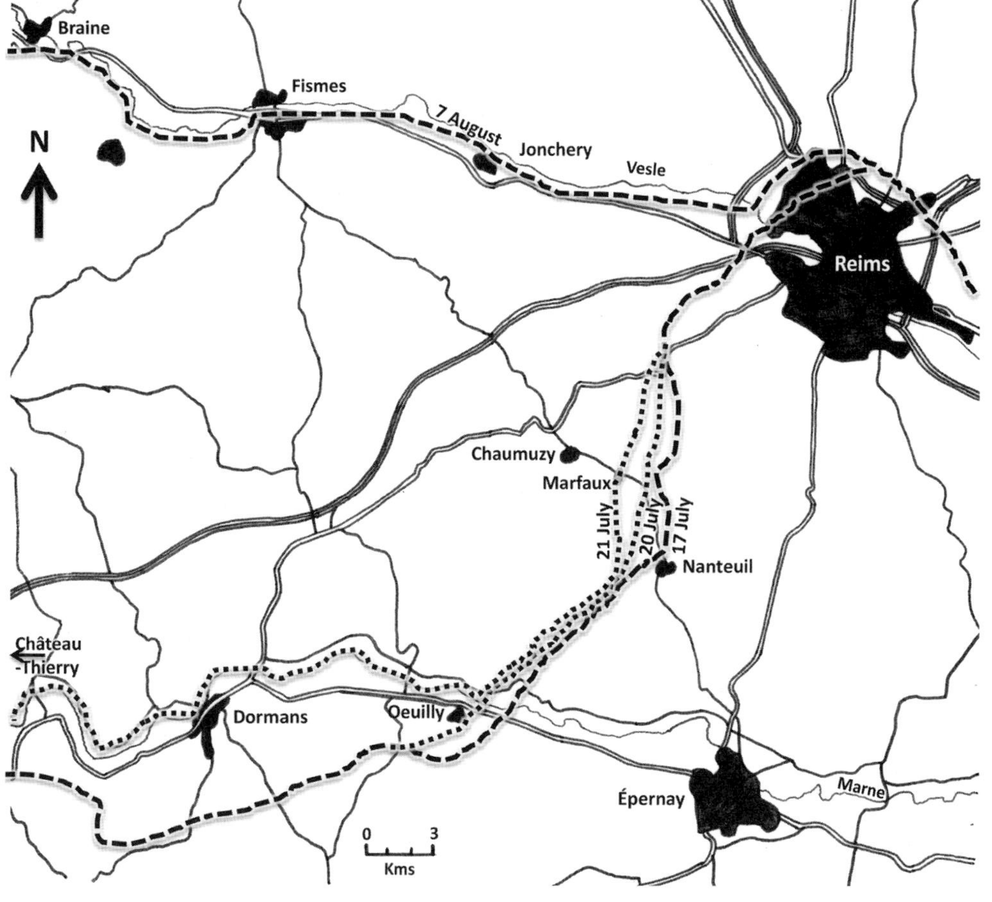

strength. In the intervening period the British had some successes in minor local operations to improve their positions and disrupt enemy preparations.

Allied thoughts were not limited to defence, as cracks were beginning to appear in the cohesion of the German Army. Repeated offensives, which failed to achieve decisive breakthroughs, eroded morale and influenza also took a heavy toll. In this situation, and given the build up of American forces, Allied leaders began to consider the prospects for offensive operations within two months.

Foch reasoned that the Germans could only achieve a major success by driving to the sea at Abbeville and splitting the French from the British, or by threatening Paris. Attacks elsewhere had no hope of achieving such spectacular results. He directed the Allies to concentrate upon repelling offensives in these areas. Reserves created behind the British and French fronts would be available anywhere in case of attack. Haig positioned XXII Corps, with three divisions and an armoured machine gun battalion, astride the Somme. He also had the Canadian Corps, Cavalry Corps and three more infantry divisions in general reserve for use wherever required.

On 15th July, the Germans attacked the French on a 130 kilometres front either side of Reims. It would be their last offensive. They failed to breakthrough and on 18th July the French launched a counter offensive against the flanks of the Château-Thierry salient. The initial attack was successful and it was imperative to maintain momentum in order not to allow the Germans to recover. The French advance continued on the 19th modestly, allowing the Germans time to evacuate most of their personnel and stores over the Marne, which was reached by the French on the 20th.

By 18th July, XXII Corps had moved to the French area behind the Château-Thierry salient. 51st and 62nd Divisions were ordered to attack on the morning of the 20th. French orders for the attack did not reach the British until late afternoon and there was very little time for reconnaissance. The British also had an exhausting approach march in order to be in position in time. The wooded and hilly terrain was a new experience to the troops from Flanders and, although the ground was the same as that operated over by IX Corps a few weeks earlier, it was unknown to XXII Corps.

The attack by the French Fifth Army (four French and two British divisions) was to commence at 8.00 a.m. The British were flanked by the French 2nd Colonial Division on the right and 9th Division on the left. The Germans were expected to fight a rearguard action but in the event clung to their positions and fought for every inch of ground.

The boundary between the British divisions was the Ardre river, with 51st Division on the left and 62nd Division on the right. The terrain favoured the defence with almost impenetrable woods, dominating ridges and spurs and sunken roads providing ideal defensive lines. The Germans sited their defences well and made maximum use of standing crops for cover. Because of the rush to launch the operation, the forward line of the French troops was not known precisely and the

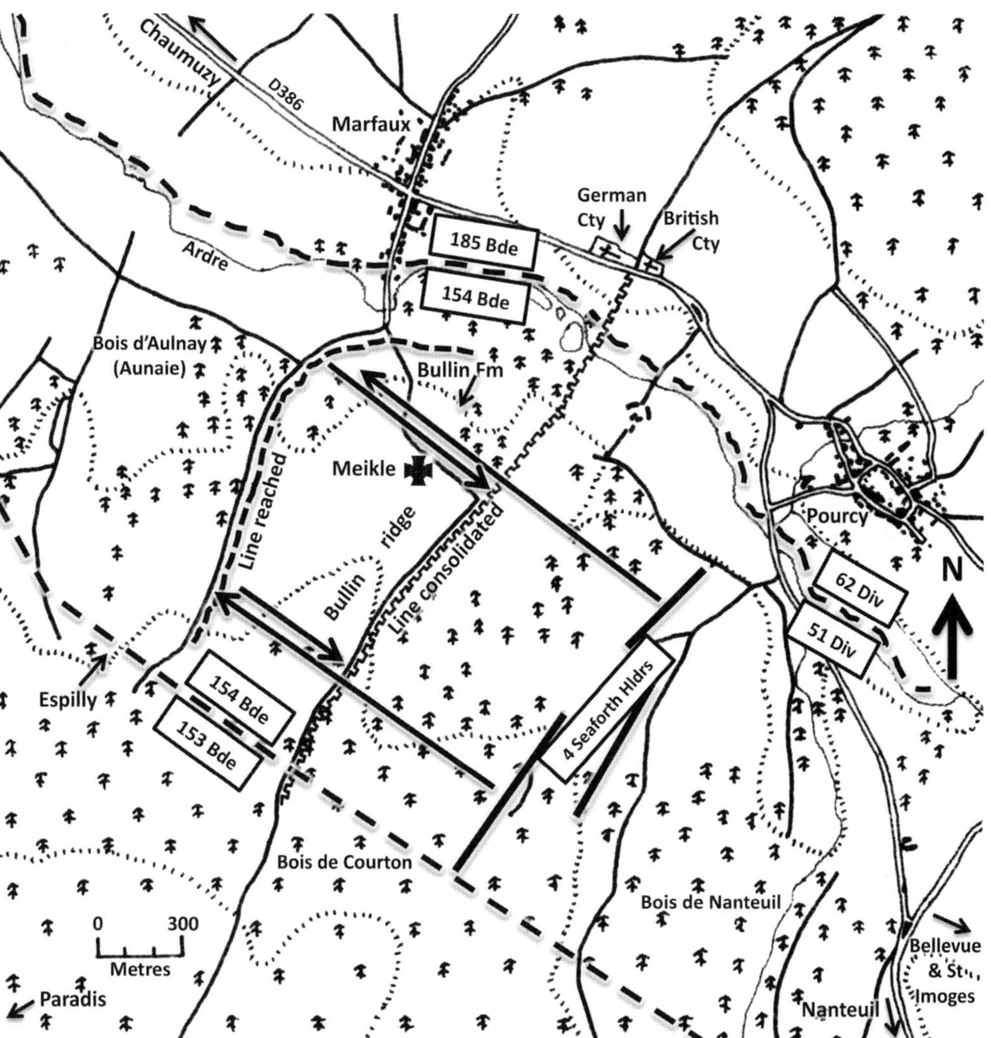

Approach Marfaux from the southeast along the D386. Visit the CWGC cemetery on the right about one kilometre before the village, where John Meikle is buried. The track running between the British and German cemeteries is on the line consolidated by 1/4th Seaforth Highlanders. Continue into the village and turn left at the crossroads, passing the church after 100m. Follow this road to the south over the Ardre for another 400m and take the right fork. The track is a little rough in places but passable in a car with care. Continue uphill along the track, which was the line reached in the attack, for 1,600m to where it levels out. Turn round here and look back towards Marfaux. The cemeteries are clearly visible from here, as is the Bullin ridge, where Meikle is likely to have performed the deeds for which he was awarded the VC. Return to the fork in the track and turn right. This section is a little rougher than the other and you may prefer to walk but it can be driven. Follow it for 750m until it turns sharp right. Ignore an earlier right turn into a small but deep re-entrant. Where you stop, the continuation of the track to the southwest is the line that the Battalion retired to later in the day. Park here and walk into the field to the southwest on the Bullin spur. This is approximately where Meikle's VC action took place.

barrage fell too far forward. As a consequence many enemy positions were missed, the barrage moved on and left the infantry unsupported.

51st Division on the left faced the Bois de Courton, straddling a flat-topped ridge, with the right flank falling away into the Ardre valley. Each of the forward brigades (154th right and 153rd left) advanced with one battalion leading. In the days before the attack, 154th Brigade had endured a twenty-nine hours railway journey, followed by eighty-five kilometres by lorry and some long marches. On arrival in the area on 17th July, it was bivouaced south of the Marne in woods around Chouilly. Routes through the woods were recced in case the Brigade was ordered forward. That night there was a very severe thunderstorm. Maximum opportunity was taken to rest the following day, until 4 p.m. when a warning order was received to move forward. The Brigade moved off at 6.00 a.m. on 19th July to a point 1,600m north of Bellevue. The march was complicated by two brigades of 62nd Division crossing the route, which caused long delays and the Brigade did not arrive until noon. At 2.30 p.m. there was a conference at HQ 51st Division at which instructions for an attack in the Ardre valley next day were issued.

The French 14th Division was still fighting on the front to be taken over and it was not possible to fix a definitive start line. Following the conference the commander of 154th Brigade went to HQ 14th Division, where he had to wait for some time before receiving details of guides etc. At 5.30 p.m. he returned to Brigade HQ where battalion COs received verbal instructions and received a map marked with objectives and boundaries. A warning order was issued to the units at 7.45 p.m. and at 8.00 p.m. the Brigade began moving forward to the northern edge of Bois de Nanteuil. The roads were congested but French guides led the battalions into position for the attack under scattered enemy shelling. At 2.00 a.m. next morning Brigade HQ was shelled out of a hut on the northern edge of Bois de Nanteuil and had to move deeper into the wood.

4th Seaforth Highlanders was assembled in woods between Bellevue and St Imoges when, about 6.00 p.m., it received verbal orders for the attack next day. Maps

4th Seaforth Highlanders advanced from the right onto Bullin ridge from where this picture was taken. The line of trees on the edge of this field mark the sunken lane that was eventually consolidated when the Battalion was forced to withdraw from the furthest extent of its advance. Marfaux is on the left.

showing objectives etc arrived later. The Battalion was to take the first objective, known as the intermediate line, following which the other two battalions in 154th Brigade would move on to secure the first and second objectives.

The Battalion was to move forward to just behind the front line troops of 14th Division by midnight. The time between then and zero at 8.00 a.m. was to be used for reconnaissance and observation of the ground over which the attack would be made. It came under heavy shellfire and did not reach its assembly position until 4 a.m. by when it was light. This was due to a number of circumstances but mainly because the routes were congested and the French guides had arrived in the area only the day before and were unsure of their whereabouts. Indeed, the HQ of the French 44th Regiment had not been informed about the forthcoming attack. However, it sprang into action immediately and provided whatever assistance it could, including suggesting assembly positions and providing guides, but the Regiment was itself largely unfamiliar with the ground. For example the locations of its forward posts were unclear. The line taken up by 4th Seaforth Highlanders did not correspond with the barrage line. As a result one platoon of the right company was in front of it and the left company was up to 700m behind and gained no advantage when it fell.

At 8 a.m. the attack commenced. 62nd Division only managed to advance 800m and the village of Marfaux on the left flank was not taken. The French 2nd Colonial Division on its right made no progress at all.

4th Seaforth Highlanders led the 154th Brigade advance, with 153rd Brigade on the left and 185th Brigade (62nd Division) on the right beyond the Ardre. The Battalion had No.1 Company on the right, No.2 Company in the centre and No.4 Company on the left, with No.3 Company in support. The barrage was assisted by French artillery. The right was in contact with the flanking troops but not on the left. A trench held by French troops was crossed and good progress was made at first through the wood, although it was difficult to maintain direction in the thick undergrowth. The German barrage came down on the northern edge of Bois de Courton at 8.10 a.m. and other enemy concentrations were fired in depth, resulting in casualties to the other battalions. 185th Brigade on the right did not keep up.

The advance continued on the right and centre until the crest of the ridge running southwest from Bullin Farm was reached. When the Battalion emerged from the

wood it encountered strong resistance from Bullin Farm, Espilly and Bois d'Aulnay (Aunaie on modern maps), in addition to enfilade fire from across the Ardre. The barrage was too weak to silence the enemy machine guns. At 9 a.m., No.1 Company on the right was about one hundred metres northwest of Bullin Farm. However, No.2 Company in the centre mistook Marfaux in 62nd Division's area for the final objective at Chaumuzy and went too far to the right, where it became mixed up with No.1 Company. This resulted in a gap between the centre and left. During the advance No.2 Company was pinned down by a post containing two machine guns. **Sergeant John Meikle** advanced alone over 135m of open ground and rushed the position. He emptied his revolver into the gun crews and put the rest out of action with a heavy stick, before waving the Company on. A few minutes later another machine gun halted the Company. Most of Meikle's platoon were already casualties. Seizing a rifle from a dead comrade, he charged the post but was killed just before he reached it. However, his courageous attempt distracted the German gunners sufficiently to allow two men, who had followed Meikle, to put the gun out of action.

A few men of No.1 Company on the right penetrated into Marfaux and, about 10.00 a.m., four Lewis guns were sent to reinforce the right flank. Around noon a partial withdrawal was made to the sunken road south of Bullin Farm due to enfilade fire from Marfaux. A platoon was left on the right to form a defensive flank to the right of Bullin Farm facing the river and Marfaux, where 62nd Division had been unable to keep up.

No.4 Company on the left lost touch with the rest of the Battalion and also had no contact with 153rd Brigade. It pushed down the forward slope to reach the crossroads 450m east of Espilly, where it was subjected to heavy machine gun fire from Espilly. Part of the Company tried to work around the left but without success. The Company therefore withdrew to French trenches inside the northern edge of Bois de Courton, about 350m in front of its start point.

No.3 Company in support was split, with one half supporting No.4 Company and the other filling the gap between it and No.1 Company. Two Brigade machine guns

The track on the right marks the limit of the advance by 4th Seaforth Highlanders. Bullin ridge is in the centre and Meikle's VC action probably took place at the left end, where it falls away into the Ardre valley. A few buildings on the edge of Marfaux can be seen on the left.

View from within the German lines on the D386 northwest of Marfaux, looking southeast. Bullin Ridge is the light coloured field running from the right into the centre, down into the Ardre valley.

set up in the sunken road behind the ridge. Part of No.2 Company in the centre and a platoon of No.3 Company advanced down the slope towards Bois d'Aulnay and nearly reached the bottom. In the face of heavy fire they were forced to withdraw back up the ridge. They held their position until 4.00 p.m., when shellfire forced them back to just beyond the ridge. By then there was only one officer and ten men remaining. Another platoon of the support company worked forward under machine gun fire across the front of Bois d'Aulnay towards the right company. The centre company also had to fall back under fire to the sunken road.

There was no touch with 6th Black Watch (153rd Brigade) on the left and elements of 4th Gordon Highlanders moved into the gap, immediately becoming embroiled in the fighting. This Battalion seized the road running south from Marfaux to Espilly but suffered heavy casualties in doing so.

At 10.15 a.m., 7th Argyll & Sutherland Highlanders advanced from the edge of the wood northeast of Nanteuil. About 11.15 a.m. the Germans counterattacked against 185th Brigade from Marfaux. Communications were very difficult and it was not until midday that HQ 154th Brigade began to gain clear information about progress. At that time it was revealed that several observers had mistaken Marfaux for Chaumuzy. At 1 p.m., 7th Argyll & Sutherland Highlanders arrived and was soon in action alongside 4th Seaforth Highlanders. However, it too was unable to get forward and the attempt was eventually abandoned. 7th Argyll & Sutherland Highlanders went into the line on the right and 4th Seaforth Highlanders slipped to the left. A small party of 4th Seaforth Highlanders in the centre fell back off the ridge they had clung to determinedly all day but re-established their position there later. Scattered parties of 4th Gordon Highlanders were also involved in holding the line. Later in the day the battalions were reorganised, with 4th Seaforth Highlanders on the right, 7th Argyll & Sutherland Highlanders in the centre and 4th Gordon Highlanders on the left.

153rd Brigade on the left broke through in one place but the gain was wiped out by a counterattack. Despite great efforts, the French 9th Division on the far left failed to take Paradis and this exposed the left flank of 51st Division, which had to be pulled back. At the end of the day 51st Division was at best 1,600m ahead of its start positions. However, it was well enough established to drive off three determined attempts to retake the high ground on the left of 7th Argyll & Sutherland Highlanders during the evening.

By the end of the month 154th Brigade had suffered 1,032 casualties, including 395 in 4th Seaforth Highlanders. The Battalion took seventy-eight prisoners, thirty machine guns, four trench mortars and three batteries of field guns.

The British had done little more than drive in the German outposts at considerable cost. However, the Allied effort convinced the Germans that they could not hold the Château-Thierry salient. That night an orderly withdrawal commenced. More significantly, reserves from the north, earmarked for a renewed offensive against the British, had been used in the offensive. The Germans concluded that the British were well prepared to receive an offensive around Ypres and had observed preparations for a counter-stroke at Arras. A German offensive in the north had limited chance of success and was not pursued. Although not known at the time, the turning point in the whole war had been reached.

Biographies

LIEUTENANT COLONEL WILLIAM HERBERT ANDERSON
12th Battalion, The Highland Light Infantry

William Anderson was born on 29th December 1881 at 17 Woodlands Terrace, Glasgow, Lanarkshire, Scotland. He was known as Bertie. His father, William James Anderson, (30th November 1851–13th January 1922) was educated at Glasgow Academy before entering his father's firm for training as an accountant. He became a member of the Glasgow Stock Exchange Association in 1875 and a year later was admitted to the Institute of Accountants and Actuaries in Glasgow. William went into partnership with his father, specialising in the management of estates and trusts as a chartered accounttant and sharebroker with Messrs Kerr, Anderson & Macleod at 149 West George Street, Glasgow. He was on the Committee of Management of the Stock Exchange for several terms between 1884 and 1906 and was elected Chairman in 1896. He resigned from the Association in 1906. William was a noted cricketer and golfer. He married Eleanora 'Nora' née Kay (22nd September 1859–23rd August 1939) on 30th March 1881 at Cornhill, Coulter, Lanarkshire. They lived at 17 Woodlands Terrace, Glasgow. By 1887 they were at 9 St James Terrace, Hillhead, Glasgow, later at 18 Woodside Terrace and at 22 Woodside Place, Glasgow in the early part the Great War. William was appointed CBE for his work as Honorary Treasurer of the Scottish Branch, British Red Cross Society (LG 7th January 1918). From September 1914 Nora and Mrs Isabella Lilburn ran a depot collecting comforts for 1st and 10th Highland Light Infantry in the Grand Hotel, Glasgow. William was also a Justice of the Peace for Lanarkshire and treasurer of Park parish, Glasgow. Later they lived at 9 Lynedoch Crescent, Glasgow. He was living at Strathairly, Largo, Fife at the time of his death there. She was living at Priory Acres, St Andrews, Fife at the time of her death there. Bertie had four brothers:

- Alexander Ronald 'Ronnie' Anderson (11th February 1884–8th October 1915) was educated at Fettes College, Edinburgh, Midlothian 1898–1901. He served

Woodlands Terrace, Glasgow, where Bertie was born in 1881.

The Glasgow Stock Exchange was founded in 1844. The current building, completed in 1877, on the corner of St George's Place (Nelson Mandela Place from 1986) and Buchanan Street, was designed by John Burnet in the Venetian Gothic style. Burnet was responsible for a number of other Glasgow public buildings, It was extended in 1906, entirely remodelled in 1969–71 and merged with the London Stock Exchange in 1973.

in the Lanarkshire Artillery 1904–05 before farming on an estate in Southern Rhodesia. He returned to enlist in 2nd Lovat Scouts on 28th August 1914 (5732 later 2636) and was embodied the same day. Ronnie transferred to 1st Lovat Scouts on 8th January 1915 and was commissioned in 13th Highland Light Infantry on 27th January. He went to France in May and died of wounds at 8th Field Ambulance on 8th October, while serving with 1st Highland Light Infantry. He was buried at Vielle Chapelle but after the war his remains were transferred to Caberet-Rouge British Cemetery, Souchez, France (XVII C 30).

- Harry Anderson (28th February–7th March 1887).
- Charles Hamilton Anderson (18th August 1888–19th December 1914) was educated at Fettes College 1902–06 and at West Wratting Park, Cambridge from January 1907. He was commissioned in 1st Highland Light Infantry on 14th October 1908 and was posted to Lucknow, India. He was known as 'The Babe'. Charles went to France on 12th December 1914 as a captain and was

Alexander Anderson's grave in Caberet-Rouge British Cemetery, Souchez. In the far background, behind the tree trunk, is the spectacular French cemetery at Notre Dame de Lorette. Co-located with it is the very moving Ring of Remembrance inaugurated in 2014.

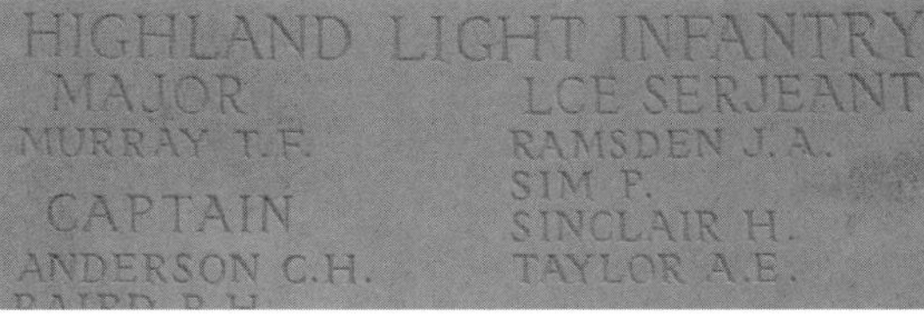

Charles Hamilton Anderson's name on the Le Touret Memorial.

killed in action on 19th December (Le Touret Memorial – Panel 37–38). His CO, Lieutenant Colonel Ronaldson, stated that Charles had taken two trenches and shouted that he was going to attack the village of Chapelle de Bois. He was not seen again and his whole platoon disappeared. Later Sergeant W Wolstencroft wrote from a prison camp that he had stepped over Charles' body when he was captured. Conflicting information about his fate continued until the War Office accepted the evidence that he had been killed as his name had not appeared on any list of prisoners by October 1915. His father was executor to his will, valued at £108/7/6.

• Edward 'Teddie' Kerr Anderson (11th July 1896–16th March 1918) was also educated at Fettes College 1910–13, where he was a member of the OTC. He was commissioned in 5th Highland Light Infantry on 19th October 1914. Teddie was attached to the Royal Flying Corps and his commission was antedated to 19th July 1915. He was posted to 9 Squadron RFC. He was granted leave to Britain, departing Boulogne on 24th August and returning on 1st September 1916. On 17th March 1917 he was posted as a flight commander to the Artillery Cooperation Squadron at Netheravon, Wiltshire. On 27th July 1917 he was instructing new observers in artillery observation at Lydd, Kent, when a fuse, timed for ten seconds, exploded instantaneously before he could throw it. He was admitted to Manor House, Folkestone with superficial burns to

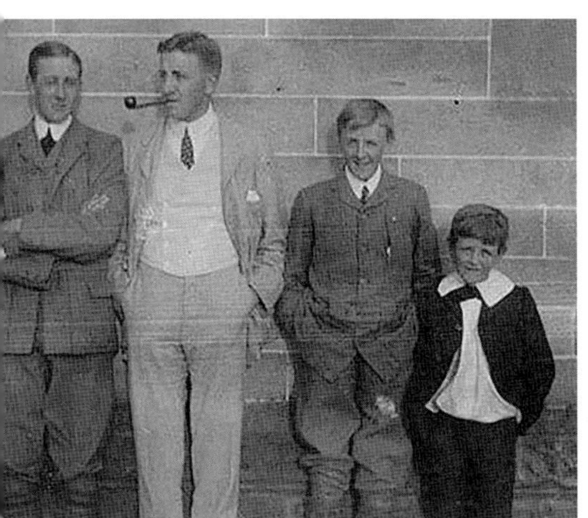
The four Anderson brothers, all of whom died during the Great War. From the left – Bertie, Ronnie, Charlie and Teddie.

Teddie Anderson.

his arms and face. He was passed fit for General Service on 7th August and was ordered to report to Netheravon. Teddie was killed in a flying accident at Winchester, Hampshire and is buried in New Kilpatrick Parish Churchyard, Dunbartonshire (New Ground Grave 83). His father was executor to his will, valued at £6786/8/0.

Bertie's paternal grandfather, William Anderson (1817–13th November 1889) was educated at Irvine Academy. On leaving school in 1831 he became a clerk in the office of Irvine Town Council. Two years later he moved to Glasgow to start an accounting apprenticeship. In 1840 he founded a public accountancy practice in Glasgow and two years later was appointed a burgess of the city. At that time he entered into a partnership with the accountants James & Henry Kerr, as Kerr & Anderson, which was well known for accountancy services to the growing railway industry. William married Janet Wilson née Dick (30th January 1822–31st May 1899) on 21st June 1842 at Barony, Glasgow. In 1844 William was a founding member of the Glasgow Stock Exchange Association. His practice in Renfield Street in Glasgow's commercial centre provided arbitration and liquidation services and was an arbiter for Glasgow Corporation in 1856 during the acquisition of the Glasgow Water Company and the Glasgow Gas Company. In 1853 he was one of the senior practitioners involved in the formation of the Institute of Accountants and Actuaries in Glasgow and was a founding Council member until 1866. He served further terms on Council and was President in 1871 and 1874. William was also auditor of the IAAG 1867–71. He was a member of the Bankruptcy Committee and a petitioner for the royal charter in 1854. In 1878 he was appointed to examine the affairs of the City of Glasgow Bank and subsequently became a liquidator, having held a similar position during the failure of the Western Bank in 1857. William was also a director of the Merchants' House of Glasgow and the Andersonian University in Glasgow, auditor of the Glasgow City Trust, trusteeship of the Ferguson Bequest Fund and a Justice of the Peace for Lanarkshire and Dunbartonshire. He was a devoted Christian, a member of the United Presbyterian Church of Scotland and a regular financial contributor to the West of Scotland Bible Society. He wrote a book, *Self-Made Men*, in 1861. William died at 20 Newton Place, Glasgow. Janet was living with her son Thomas and daughter Jane at 2 Newton Place, Kelvin, Glasgow in 1891 and she subsequently died there. In addition to William they had ten other children:

Renfield Street in Glasgow was well known for its shops, office-based businesses and music halls, theatres and cinemas.

- Margaret Russell Anderson (4th May 1843–8th August 1888) married Hugh Beckett (24th February 1824–19th March

1905), a merchant and later a calico printer, on 29th May 1862 at Ledcameroch, New Kilpatrick, Dunbartonshire. He was living at 9 Hamilton Drive, Glasgow at the time of his marriage. They were living at 3 Windsor Terrace, Glasgow in 1881. She died at 3 South Crescent, Ardrossan, Ayrshire and he at 7 Windsor Terrace, Glasgow. They had seven children – Elizabeth Crawford Beckett 1863, Janet Dick Beckett 1864, Hugh Beckett 1865, Margaret Anderson Beckett 1866, William Anderson Beckett 1868, Robert Harold Beckett 1878 and Jane Hilda Beckett 1879.

- James Anderson (born 15th September 1844).
- Jane Anderson (27th July 1846–25th May 1913) married Thomas Brownlie (17th January 1844–20th February 1902), a coalmaster, on 21st November 1873 at Ledcameroch, New Kilpatrick, Dunbartonshire. They were living at 1 Beauly Terrace, Maryhill, Lanark in 1881. He died at 7 Queen Margaret Crescent, Glasgow and she at 5 Queen Margaret Crescent. They had two children – Thomas Graeme Brownlie 1873 and Janet Ida Brownlie 1876.
- Janet 'Jessie' Dick Anderson (18th February 1848–25th September 1932) married William Hector (born c.1843), a merchant of Rio de Janeiro, Brazil, on 27th November 1874, at Ledcameroch. He was living at Shawlands, Eastwood, Renfrewshire at the time. She was living at 8 Burnbank Terrace, Barony, Glasgow in 1881 and at 6 Salton Gardens, Glasgow in 1911. William predeceased Janet. She died at 8 Loudon Terrace, Glasgow. They had a son, William Cunningham Hector, born in 1875 in Brazil.
- Elizabeth Anderson (23rd May 1850–27th January 1926) married John Cross Aitken (c.1844–18th October 1928), a shipowner, on 25th July 1871 at Ledcameroch. They both died at 53 Hamilton Drive, Glasgow. They had two children – James Ewart Aitken 1872 and Janet Eleanor Aitken 1878.
- Henry Kerr Anderson (17th January 1854–3rd June 1911) was educated at Glasgow Academy and in 1869 was apprenticed in his father's firm. In 1875 he joined the Glasgow Stock Exchange Association, became an IAAG member and joined his father's firm as a partner. He specialised in bankruptcy, including the City of Glasgow Bank in 1878. He later concentrated on estate management services. He was an active cricketer and golfer and was residing at a gentleman's club in Renfield Street, Glasgow in 1881. Henry married Jessie Mitchell Stewart (23rd April 1857–12th January 1951) on 9th June 1881 at 18 India Street, Glasgow and they lived at Torlea, Regent Park, Prestwick. In 1891 they were living at 2 Bruce Street, Partick. They separated and Henry was a boarder at Mansewell Road, Ravenscrag, Prestwick in 1901 and was living at Torrlea, Regent Park, Prestwick in 1911. He died at Prestwick Golf Links while organising the Scottish amateur golf championship. Jessie was living at The Royal Hotel, Bridge of Allan, Stirlingshire at the time of her death.
- Helen Isabella Anderson (18th September 1855–15th August 1949) married Campbell Martin (1858–13th February 1948), a shareholder and later a hardware

merchant, on 11th December 1883 at 2 Newton Place, Glasgow. He was living at Auchendrennan, Alexandria, Dunbartonshire at the time. He died at Drumhead, Cardross and she at Lylestone, Cardross. They had a daughter, Janet Winifred Campbell Martin in 1885.
- Hugh Andrew Anderson (born 19th March 1858) was a single farmer living with his parents in 1881.
- Charles Brunton Anderson (born 7th January 1860) was a general clerk in 1881, living with his sister Jessie.
- Thomas Anderson (born 17th May 1863) was a chartered accountant's clerk in 1891. He was living at 4 Cleveden Crescent, Glasgow in 1932.

His maternal grandfather, Alexander Kay JP (20th February 1811–20th April 1899) was a cotton farm merchant and a partner in the cotton merchant and manufacturing firm of James Finlay & Co. He married Jane Brock née Miller (c.1815–3rd June 1896) on 13th September 1840 at Barony, Glasgow. They lived at Laurel Bank, Wilson Street, Govan, Glasgow and by 1881 at Cornhill, Coulter, Biggar, Lanarkshire, when he was an East India merchant. They both died there. In addition to Nora they had nine other children:

- Margaret Morrison Kay (30th June 1841–28th August 1929) married John (later Sir John) Muir (8th December 1828–August 1903) on 26th July 1860 in Glasgow. John was educated at Glasgow High School and Glasgow University. He joined James Finlay & Co in 1849 and assumed control of the company in 1873. He was elected a Bailie of Glasgow Town Council in 1886 and was Lord Provost of Glasgow 1889–92, receiving a baronetcy at the end of his term. He held a number of other appointments – Honorary Colonel 4th Volunteer Battalion Cameronians (Scottish Rifles), Justice of the Peace Lower Ward of Lanarkshire, Deputy Lieutenant of Ayr and Lanark, elder of St George's United Free Church in Glasgow and of Bridge of Teith United Presbyterian Church. John took over Deanston House, Deanston, Kilmadock, Perthshire in 1873 following the death of John Finlay. By the time of his death John had amassed a fortune totalling £998,644 (£59.7M in 2018). They had ten children – Jane Miller Muir 1861, Elizabeth Brown Muir 1863, Margaret Anne Muir 1865, Agnes Bunton Muir 1866, Alexander Kay Muir 1868, James Finlay Muir 1870, Edith Mary Kay Muir 1872, Catherine Hetherington Muir 1874, John Buchanan Muir 1876 and Matthew William Muir 1878.
- Jane Kay (born 6th July 1843) married John Buttery (born c.1832), an East India merchant, in 1866.
- Janet 'Jessie' Kay (born 13th October 1844).
- Alexander Kay (born 11th September 1846) probably died in infancy.
- Robert Kay (born 18th December 1847) probably died in infancy.
- Mary Kay (born 12th July 1849).

- Emily Agnes Kay (22nd March 1851–23rd December 1915) married Anthony Scott Hannay (c.1847–9th February 1925), a cotton broker, on 17th April 1872 at Cornhill, Coulter, Lanarkshire. He was born in Glasgow but lived later at St Michael's Hamlet, Liverpool, Lancashire. They were living at 6 Grosvenor Terrace, Toxteth Park, Liverpool in 1881. By 1901 they were living at 2 Mossley Hill Drive, Liverpool and they both subsequently died there. She left effects valued at £456/19/6 to her husband. He left effects valued at £74,215/9/4 with probate being granted to his children Alexander, Emily and Dorothy and Charles Maxwell Kinnear. They had eight children – Marion Scott Hannay 1873, Jane Kay Hannay 1874, Percival Kay Hannay 1876, Norman Kay Hannay 1879, unnamed male (born and died 1880), Alexander Kay Hannay 1881, Emily Gladys Hannay 1887 and Dorothy Kay Hannay 1890.
- Eliza Ann Kay (4th December 1852–28th May 1925) married John Colin Mitchell (c.1841–11th June 1918), a writer, on 2nd August 1876 in Glasgow. They were living at 160 West George Street, Glasgow at the time of his death there on 11th June 1918, probate granted to Robert Harold Beckett, stockbroker, Robert Valentine Reid, Maltster and John Robertson Johnston. She died at Borrowfield, Cardross, usual residence 13 Windsor Terrace, West Kelvinside, Glasgow at the time of her death. Probate was granted to Douglas Kay Mitchell, writer, and Robert Harold Beckett, stockbroker. They had at least a son, Douglas Kay Mitchell 1882. John McMorland Mitchell (1880–1953) may also be their son. He was commissioned in 4th Volunteer Battalion, The Cameronians (Scottish Rifles) on 31st January 1900 and was promoted lieutenant 16th March 1901, captain 9th November 1906 and last appears in the Army List in January 1908. John was appointed captain in 17th Highland Light Infantry on 10th September 1914 and major on 30th July 1916. He last appears in the Army List in June 1920. He was a coalmaster in 1928.
- Alice Kay (28th October 1854–10th December 1932) married William James Finlayson (c.1848–31st March 1925), a thread manufacturer, on 10th July 1878 at Cornhill, Coulter. In 1891 they were living at The Oaks, Johnstone, Renfrewshire. He died there and she at Westercroft, Dundonald, Ayrshire, usual residence 17 Ewenfield Road, Ayr. They had two children – Charles Kay Finlayson 1879 and Mary Kay Finlayson 1882.

Bertie was educated at:

Cargilfield Preparatory School, Cramond Bridge, Edinburgh, Midlothian.
Glasgow Academy.
Fettes College, Edinburgh, where he was a member of Moredun House 1895–1900.
Tours, France, where he studied French language and literature.

Glasgow Academy was founded in 1845 and is the oldest continuously fully independent school in Glasgow. In 1991 it merged with Westbourne School for Girls and has about 1,350 pupils spread over four sites. Famous alumni include:

JM Barrie author of Peter Pan.
Donald Dewar, Labour MP and the first First Minister of Scotland.
George MacDonald Fraser, author of the Flashman novels.
John Reith, 1st Baron Reith, founder of the BBC.

Sir William Fettes (1750–1836) founded the school in memory of his only son, William, but it was not built until 1870. It was a boy's school until 1970 and became fully co-educational in 1983. Ian Fleming's character, James Bond, attended Fettes College. Coincidentally a real James Bond did attend Fettes and was a frogman with the Special Boat Service. In addition to William Herbert Anderson, three other members of the school have been awarded the VC – Donald Mackintosh, Hector Lachlan Stewart MacLean and Matthew Fontaine Maury Meiklejohn. Another old boy is Tony Blair, Prime Minister of the United Kingdom 1997–2007.

He was a partner in his father's firm of Messrs Kerr, Anderson and McLeod at 149 West George Street, Glasgow and in 1907 became a member of the IAAG. He was also President of the Junior Imperial Unionist Association. On 4th July 1909 Bertie married Gertrude Campbell Gilmour (30th September 1884–1953) at the Parish Church (St Andrew's), Alexandria, Dunbartonshire. They had two sons:

Alexandria Parish Church (St Andrew's) was completed in 1840. The burial ground at the church was the only one in Alexandria for forty years. After the Disruption of 1843 the Church was reduced to the status of a chapel and the minister lost his seat on the Presbytery. Most of the congregation transferred to a new Free Church in Alexandria. It was not until 1866 that the Church regained its status and it was extended in 1906. Recently it has been a children's soft play and dance school.

- William Allen Campbell Anderson (4th May 1911–12th April 1972) was born at Brookfield, Skelmorlie, Ayrshire. He was commissioned in 17th/21st Lancers on 27th August 1931. William was promoted lieutenant 27th August 1934, captain 27th August 1937, acting major 9th November 1940–8th February 1941, temporary major 9th February 1941–5th March 1944, acting lieutenant colonel 6th December 1943–5th March 1944, war substantive major 6th March 1944, temporary lieutenant colonel 6th March 1944–2nd May 1946, major 1st July 1946, temporary lieutenant colonel 12th November 1947–18th July 1952, lieutenant colonel 18th July 1952, temporary colonel 3rd December 1955–28th October 1956, colonel 7th February 1957, temporary brigadier 29th October 1956–13th February 1961 and brigadier 14th February 1961. William's appointments included – brigade major armoured brigade 3rd May 1946–11th November 1947, GSO1 armoured division TA 19th October 1955–6th November 1955, GSO1 War Office 3rd December 1955–27th October 1956, Commander 22nd Armoured Brigade TA 29th October 1956–5th October 1958, Commander Royal Armoured Corps HQ I British Corps 30th December 1958 and ADC to the Queen 29th October 1959. He retired on 11th May 1962. He was awarded the DSO for Normandy (LG 31st August 1944), was Mentioned in Despatches (LG 7th January 1949) and awarded the CBE (LG 2nd June 1962). William married Edith Isabella Scobell (1912–83) in 1938 at Westminster. He died at the Northern Infirmary, Inverness, usual residence The Manse, Roschall, Sutherland. Edith died at Crieff.
- Charles Patrick Anderson (4th August 1913–12th November 1998) was born at Tighcruachan, Cardross, Dunbartonshire. He was commissioned from the Supplementary Reserve of Officers, Argyll & Sutherland Highlanders on 30th August 1935. He was promoted lieutenant 30th August 1938, acting captain 26th July–22nd September 1940 and 28th September–29th October 1940, temporary captain 30th October 1940–31st January 1942, acting major 1st November 1941–31st January 1942, war substantive captain 1st February 1942, temporary major 1st February 1942–13th March 1944, captain 30th August 1943, acting lieutenant colonel 14th December 1943–13th March 1944, war substantive major 14th March 1944, temporary lieutenant colonel 14th March–29th July 1944, temporary lieutenant colonel 16th June–22nd July 1945, major 30th August 1948, temporary lieutenant colonel 1st – 11th March 1957 and lieutenant colonel 12th March 1957. He served on the North West Frontier 1936–37 (MID LG 16th August 1938). His appointments included Instructor Middle East Junior Staff School 20th May–29th November 1943, GSO1 Military Warfare Training Centre 30th November 1943–1st April 1944, GSO1 HQ 46th Division 2nd April–29th July 1944 and Brigade Major 27th Infantry Brigade 11th May 1951–22nd May 1953. Charles married Christina Maule J Jardine (born 1916) on 15th October 1940 at St Giles Cathedral, Edinburgh. Christina was serving as a 3rd officer with the Women's Royal Naval Service at the time, stationed at Craiggowan, Lockerbie, Dumfriesshire. She was the daughter of Sir Alexander Jardine, landed proprietor,

and Winifred Young. Charles retired on 21st December 1959. He died at the Dunara and Salen Sick Bay, Aros, Island of Mull, Argyll, usual residence Benvue, Ulva Ferry, Mull. Christina and Charles had a daughter, Andrena Christian Anderson, in 1943. She married Lieutenant Colonel Alastair William Scott-Elliot, son of Major General James Scott-Elliot, in 1969 at Salen, Isle of Mull. They had two children – Robin James Scott-Elliott 1970 and Simon Charles Scott-Elliott 1972.

Gertrude's father, William Ewing Gilmour (21st May 1854–31st January 1924) was born at Torquay, Devon. His father, Allan Gilmour, was born on 4th May 1820 at New Brunswick, Canada. William was educated at Edinburgh Academy and University where he was prominent in athletics. In 1874 he joined his uncle's firm, John Orr Ewing & Co, Turkey Red Dyers, in the Vale of Leven and later became managing director of the United Turkey Red Co Ltd. William married Jessie Gertrude née Campbell (12th January 1856–25th February 1923) on 20th July 1882 at Tulliechewan Castle, Alexandria, Dunbartonshire. His usual residence was Croftangea, Bonhill but the family also resided at Woodbank, Alexandria, Dunbartonshire and at Glencassley Castle, Sutherland. In 1891 they were living at Oykel Bridge Inn, Kincardine,

Turkey red dye, widely used in the 18th and 19th centuries, was made using the root of the rubia plant, involving a long and laborious process. It originated in Turkey and India. John Orr Ewing (born 1809) worked as a clerk and a sales agent. He came into contact with Turkey red products of the Croftengea Works in the Vale of Leven and with Robert Alexander acquired Croftengea in 1835. It was soon one of the major producers of Turkey red. By 1839 it was employing 192 men, 142 women and 104 children, with an annual output of almost three million yards of printed goods. By 1845 John Orr Ewing had made a fortune and left the business in the sole ownership of his partner. The firm faltered and John Orr Ewing resumed an active role in 1860. By the 1870s the workforce had risen to 1,600 and was the largest such firm in Britain.

Tullichewan Castle was built on an estate in the Vale of Leven, near Loch Lomond in 1792. During the Second World War Tullichewan Castle Estate was requisitioned by the Royal Navy. After the war the upkeep became too much for the owner and the castle was abandoned until it was demolished in 1954. Most of the estate has since been covered by housing and the Vale of Leven Hospital.

Ross & Cromarty. Gertrude was living at Woodbank House, Bonhill, as head of household at the time of the 1901 Census, with her daughters Margaret and Isobel. They were noted philanthropists. William built the Ewing-Gilmour Men's Institute in Alexandria and Gertrude built the Women's Institute there and the Jessamine Holiday Home at Drymen. He became chairman of Bonhill School Board and was a staunch Conservative, representing Alexandria East Division as a member of the County Council of Dumbarton. William was also a Justice of the Peace in Dunbartonshire, Sutherland and Ross-shire and was chairman of the Glasgow and the Dunbartonshire Agricultural Societies. His estates in Ross, Sutherland and Shetland are reputed to have totalled more than 300,000 acres. Their address in February 1915, given by son Allan, was Rosehall, Sutherland. Gertrude died in London and William in a Glasgow nursing home, leaving an estate valued at £238,421/19/5 (£13.7M in 2018). In addition to Gertrude they had four other children:

- Jessie Campbell Gilmour (11th May 1883–1st July 1895) was born at Tulliechewan Castle, Bonhill, Dunbartonshire and died at Woodbank House, Bonhill.
- Margaret Campbell Gilmour (born 29th May 1886) was born at Woodbank House, Bonhill as were her younger siblings.
- Allan Gilmour (26th August 1889–16th December 1917) was a boarder at Jeffrey House, Kinnear Road, Edinburgh in 1901, whilst attending Edinburgh Academy 1900–08, where he was in the Football (Rugby) XV. He went up to Trinity College, Oxford until 1911 and captained the College Rugby XV at one stage and was also in the Rowing VIII. He was in the Oxford University OTC Cavalry unit 20th October 1908–20th January 1911 and passed Certificates A and B on 1st September 1910 and 1st December 1910 respectively. On 21st January 1911 he was commissioned in the Lovat Scouts TF and undertook some courses at the Irish Cavalry Depot 28th April–12th May 1913. Allan played for Edinburgh Academical Football Club. He was in E Squadron, 2nd Lovat Scouts when he was embodied on 5th August 1914. Promotion to lieutenant was backdated to 1st August 1914. He married Mary Henderson Mackenzie Macdonald (born 1883), of Viewfield, Portree, Isle of Skye on 18th August 1915 at St Stephens Church, Inverness. Mary's address in February 1915 was Viewfield, Portree, Skye. Her address was Woodbank, Alexandria, Dunbartonshire in December 1917. Allan passed as a 1st class instructor at Bisley and qualified to instruct on the Barr & Stroud Rangefinder 12th-30th July 1915. He embarked at Devonport on 7th September 1915 and disembarked at Suvla Bay, Gallipoli on 26th September. He was admitted to the Scottish Horse Field Ambulance with dysentery on 11th October and transferred to No.14 Casualty Clearing Station and HS *Neuralia*, arriving at 19th General Hospital, Alexandria, Egypt on 16th October. He was discharged on 27th December and rejoined his unit next day in Alexandria. Allan was appointed temporary captain on 12th May 1916, whilst commanding

a squadron. He transferred to 10th Cameron Highlanders, formed from two dismounted squadrons of 1/1st and 1/2nd Lovat Scouts, on 27th September 1916 and embarked with the Battalion at Alexandria on 17th October 1916, disembarking at Salonica on 20th October. He was granted leave to Britain 22nd December 1916–8th February 1917, including travel there and back. Promotion to captain on 17th June 1917 was backdated to 12th September 1916 and later to 1st June 1916. He attended a Lewis gun course at the Base on 1st October 1917. On 25th October he received gunshot wounds to the right arm and left knee and was admitted to 82nd Field Ambulance and 18th Stationary Hospital at Lahana, where the left leg was amputated. He died of bronchopneumonia on 16th December 1917 and is buried in Lahana Military Cemetery, Greece (III B 16). Grantees to his estate, valued at £8,644/4/2, were John Fulton Christie, Director of United Turkey Red Co Ltd of 46 West George Street, Glasgow, and David Bruce Warren, writer of Messrs Moncrieff, Warren, Patterson & Co of 45 West George Street, Glasgow. Allan and Mary had twins:

- Flora Macdonald Gilmour (23rd November 1916 -1980) was fifteen minutes older than her brother. She married 47680 Captain Kilner Swettenham (1st August 1910–4th September 1944) Highland Light Infantry at Westminster in 1944. He was commissioned on 28th August 1930 and was promoted lieutenant on 28th August 1933, captain 28th August 1938, acting major 17th March 1942 and temporary major 17th June 1942. He served in Palestine 1936–39. Kilner was Mentioned in Despatches (LG 30th December 1941). He died on active service and is buried in Bruyelle War Cemetery, Hainaut, Belgium (II D 2). Flora married Major Duncan Marshall Geddes MBE MC psc (8th July 1913–1963) Cameron Highlanders on 22nd July 1946 at the Church of Scotland, Rosehall, Sutherlandshire. She was living at Invernauld, Rosehall, Sutherlandshire at the time. Duncan was commissioned on 1st February 1934 and was promoted lieutenant on 1st February 1937, acting captain 1st September 1939, temporary captain 1st December 1939, acting major 1st February 1941, war substantive captain 1st May 1941, temporary major 1st May 1941–26th January 1942 & 13th August 1942–31st March 1945, captain 1st February 1942, war substantive major 1st April 1945, acting lieutenant colonel 1st January 1945, temporary lieutenant colonel 1st April 1945–12th August 1946, major 1st February 1947, local lieutenant colonel 11th – 18th August 1953 and temporary lieutenant colonel 19th August 1953. He served in Palestine 1936–39 and was employed with the King's African Rifles 11th November 1938–31st August 1939. He was awarded the MC (LG 11th May 1937) serving with 2nd Cameron Highlanders, MC Bar (LG 30th December 1941) serving with 1st East African Armoured Car Regiment in East Africa and Madagascar, MID (LG 10th January 1946) and MBE (LG 6th June 1946). Retired as honorary lieutenant colonel 10th September 1955.

Kilner Swettenham's grave in Bruyelle War Cemetery. His is the only burial there from September 1944. The other 146 graves result from the fighting in May 1940.

° Allan 'Bun' Macdonald Gilmour (23rd November 1916–22nd November 2003) was commissioned in the Seaforth Highlanders on 28th January 1939 from the TA. Promoted war substantive lieutenant 2nd October 1940, lieutenant 1st January 1941, acting captain 2nd July 1940, temporary captain 2nd October 1940, war substantive captain 26th April 1942, acting major 26th January 1942, temporary major 26th April 1942–27th January 1952, captain 1st July 1946 and major 28th January 1952. He was awarded the MC for his actions on 24th October 1942. On 6th April 1943 he was in action at Wadi Akarit, east of the Roumana feature, Tunisia under Lieutenant Colonel Lorne Maclaine Campbell, who was awarded the VC. Allan was awarded a Bar to his MC. He was also awarded the US Distinguished Service Cross for gallantry at Deune Canal, Netherlands in 1945 and was Mentioned in Despatches. Allan transferred to the Queen's Own Highlanders when the Seaforth and Cameron Highlanders amalgamated on 7th February 1961. Promoted local lieutenant colonel 19th June 1952–25th April 1954, temporary lieutenant colonel 10th June 1959–20th October 1960, lieutenant colonel 21st October 1960 and acting colonel 10th April 1964. Supernumerary 21st October 1963. He had numerous appointments – GSO2 Stirling Sub District 2nd July 1946, GSO2 Scottish Infantry Division 1st January 1947, DAMS HQ BAOR 15th May 1947, DAA&QMG 21st March 1949, GSO2 Staff College Quetta 19th June 1952, GSO2 RAC Centre 17th June 1957, Chief of Staff to the Ghanaian Armed Forces at Accra (during which he played polo for Ghana against Nigeria) (OBE), GSO1 HQ West Midland Division TA and Chief Recruiting Liaison Staff, Edinburgh. He retired on 11th May 1967. Allan was a captain when he married Phyliss (sic) Jean Olive Wood (8th May 1921–31st January 2015), a mobile canteen worker, on 27th December 1941 at St Columba's Episcopal Church, Nairn. They had four children including – David Allen Gilmour 1943, Colin Edward Gilmour 1946 and Patrick Nigel Gilmour 1950. Allan was on Sutherland County Council (Chairman 1974–78) and was Lord Lieutenant of Sutherland 1972–91. He was a member of the Highlands and Islands Development Consultative Council 1975–87, Chairman of the Highland Health Board 1981–83,

President of the Highland Territorial Army Volunteer Reserves Association 1989–91 (KCVO 1990) and Chairman of the Highland River Purification Board 1994–96.

- Isobel Buchanan Gilmour (27th January 1892–1976) married William Denny in 1945 at Lochwinnoch, Renfrewshire. Isobel died at Bonar and Kincardine, Highland.

Bertie enlisted in 1st Lanarkshire Volunteer Rifle Corps, The Cameronians (Scottish Rifles) in 1900 and was commissioned on 20th December 1902. He was promoted lieutenant on 3rd May 1905 and the unit was redesignated 5th Battalion, The Cameronians (Scottish Rifles) on 1st April 1908 on the formation of the Territorial Force. Bertie resigned his commission on 31st December 1909. He applied for a commission in 3rd Highland Light Infantry at Gailes Camp, Irvine on 21st September 1914, giving his work address at 149 West George Street, Glasgow. Passed fit for service at 3rd Scottish General Hospital the same day and on 10th September was commissioned as a temporary captain in 17th (3rd Glasgow) Highland Light Infantry. He was heavily involved in training the Battalion at Troon, Ayrshire and Codford, Wiltshire. On 1st November 1915 he was appointed temporary major and second-in-command of 19th (Reserve) Battalion, Highland Light Infantry, part of 18th Reserve Brigade at Ripon, Yorkshire. It moved to Montrose, Angus in March 1916, where it became 78th Training Reserve Battalion on 1st September.

Bertie went to France on 15th October 1916 and was attached to 9th East Surrey Regiment as second-in-command on 31st October. He was admitted to 72nd Field Ambulance and No.23 Casualty Clearing Station with pyrexia on 24th February 1917 and was invalided home from 20th General Hospital at Camiers on HS *Stad Antwerpen*, returning to France in June. On 1st July he was appointed second-in-command of 12th Highland Light Infantry and was promoted captain on 1st November, remaining as temporary major. He was appointed acting lieutenant colonel and CO 12th Battalion on 12th March 1918. **Awarded the VC for his actions at Maricourt, France on 25th March 1918, LG 3rd May 1918 with location and deeds published on 31st March 1919.**

William Anderson's grave in Péronne Road Cemetery on the western outskirts of Maricourt.

Bertie was killed during his VC action. The Germans removed his identity disk and sent it to the International Red Cross in Geneva, Switzerland. He is buried in

The Orthopaedic Hospital, Beckett Park was constructed in 1912 as a teacher training college. It was used as a military hospital in both world wars, treating 57,200 soldiers in 1914–18 alone. Today it is the James Graham Building, part of Leeds Beckett University.

Péronne Road War Cemetery, Maricourt, France (II G 36). Bertie was the last of the five brothers to die, four of them during the Great War, leaving his parents childless. Grantees to his estate, valued at £9,582/3/5, were his widow, his father, Andrew James Macharg a chartered accountant in Glasgow and Andrew McNair a writer in Glasgow. The story of the Anderson brothers is the basis of the novel, *The Way Home*, by Bertie's great-grandson, Robin Scott-Elliot, published in 2007. The VC was presented to his widow by the King at the Orthopaedic Hospital, Beckett Park, Leeds on 31st May 1918. Gertrude was living at 23 Abingdon Court, Kensington, London at the time and at 14 Hope Street, Edinburgh in July 1919. Bertie's identity disc was returned to her in May 1919 having been sent through diplomatic channels from Germany with a number of others. She died at Buckrose, Yorkshire in 1953 and is buried at Invershin, Sutherland. Bertie's wooden grave marker was sent to her when the Imperial War Graves Commission replaced it with a headstone. The marker was subsequently placed on her grave at Invershin, Sutherland. Bertie is commemorated in a number of other places:

The Anderson family grave in New Kilpatrick Churchyard also commemorates Charles, Alexander and Bertie who are buried in various places in France.

- On the family grave at New Kilpatrick Churchyard, Manse Road, Bearsden, Glasgow, Lanarkshire.

Cardross War Memorial.

Fettes College War Memorial.

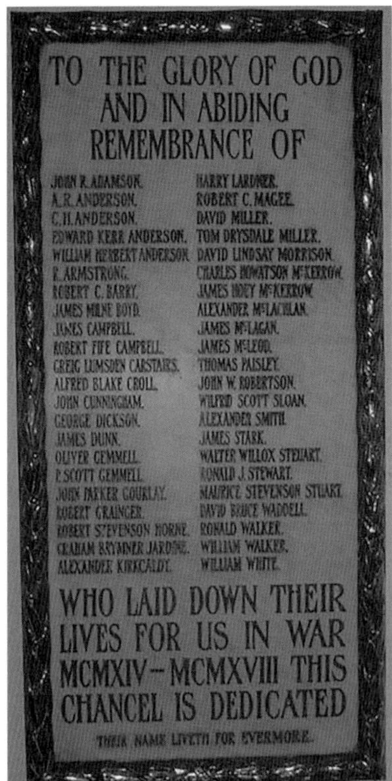

Sandyford Henderson Memorial Church War Memorial.

The Victory Medal (or Inter-Allied Victory Medal) was first proposed by French Marshal Ferdinand Foch as a common award for all the nations allied against the Central Powers. Regardless of nationality, each medal is 36mm in diameter, the ribbon is a double rainbow and the obverse shows winged victory (except Japan and Siam where winged victory has no relevance). For British Empire forces the medal was issued to all who received the 1914 or 1914–15 Star and to almost all who received the British War Medal. The British alone struck 6,335,000 Victory medals. These three medals were known as Pip, Squeak and Wilfred after a popular newspaper comic strip. To qualify for the Victory Medal recipients had to be mobilised for war service and have entered a theatre of war between 5th August 1914 and 11th November 1918, plus Russia 1919–20 and mine clearance in the North Sea until 30th November 1919. Those Mentioned in Despatches wore an oakleaf on the Victory Medal ribbon as shown here.

- Plaque in Glasgow Cathedral, dedicated to the four Anderson brothers.
- Roll of Honour, Scottish National War Memorial, Edinburgh Castle.
- A Department for Communities and Local Government commemorative VC paving stone was dedicated at People's Place, Glasgow Green on 25th March 2018 to mark the centenary of his award.
- War Memorials at:
  - Main Road, Cardross, Argyll and Bute.
  - Largo and Newburn Parish Church, Church Place, Kirkton of Largo, Lundin Links, Fife.
  - Fettes College, Carrington Road, Edinburgh.
  - Glasgow Academy Great Western Road, Glasgow.
  - Sandyford Henderson Memorial Church, Kelvinhaugh Street, Glasgow.
  - Western Club, 33 Royal Exchange Square, Glasgow.

In addition to the VC he was awarded the British War Medal 1914–20 and Victory Medal 1914–19. The VC group was acquired by Lord Ashcroft on 8th November 2016 and is held by the Michael Ashcroft Trust, the holding institution for the Lord Ashcroft Victoria Cross Collection. It is displayed in the Imperial War Museum's Lord Ashcroft Gallery.

3399 LANCE CORPORAL THOMAS LESLIE AXFORD
16th Australian Infantry Battalion AIF

Thomas Axford was born on 18th June 1894 at Carrieton, South Australia. He was known as Jack. His father, Walter Richard Axford (4th August 1853–26th August 1918), was born at Bothwell, Tasmania. He moved with his parents and siblings to Ballarat, Victoria, where he worked for the Ballarat Hardware Co for twenty years and was a member of the Ballarat City Fire Brigade. The family moved to Carrieton, South Australia, where he took up farming and served as a sergeant in I Company, Carrieton Mounted Rifles, Volunteer Force. He was commissioned as a lieutenant on 26th April 1888. He married Margaret 'Maud' Anne Helena née McQuillan (4th June 1868–15th January 1939), of Irish extraction, on 25th November 1890 at Archbishops Court, Adelaide, South Australia. She was educated at Cabra Dominican College, Adelaide, South Australia. When Walter's father's health failed, they sold the farm and he worked as an auctioneer and commission agent at Carrieton and was appointed the Town Clerk and a JP. The family moved to Coolgardie, Western Australia in 1896. Later they lived at 113 Bourke Street,

Piccadilly, Kalgoorlie. Walter died at his home at 29 Bourke Street, Kalgoorlie a few days after the announcement of his son's VC. Jack had nine siblings:

Jack's father was a member of the Ballarat City Fire Brigade.

- Lucy Slade Axford (12th December 1891–12th May 1941) married William Harold Thomas Rosewarne (28th August 1890–9th October 1970), a grocer, in 1913 in East Coolgardie, Western Australia. He was known as Harold and they lived at Terrace Road, Guildford. Western Australia. He enlisted in 16th Battalion AIF on 9th May 1917 at Perth (7814), described as 5′ 7″ tall, weighing 130 lbs, with fresh complexion, grey eyes, brown hair and his religious denomination was Church of England. He embarked at Sydney, New South Wales aboard HMAT A7 *Medic* on 1st August with 26th Reinforcements, transferring to SS *Orita* on 21st September via Halifax, Nova Scotia for Liverpool, Lancashire, arriving on 3rd October. He was posted to 13th Training Battalion, Codford, Wiltshire on 16th January 1918. He went to France and was wounded in the right buttock and had a compound fracture of the femur on 2nd May. He was admitted to 12th Australian Field Ambulance the following day, transferred to 26th General Hospital, Étaples and 1st Canadian General Hospital on 7th May. He was evacuated to 1st Southern General Hospital, Edgbaston, Warwickshire on 3rd June and transferred to 1st Auxiliary Hospital, Harefield, Middlesex on 14th September. He was discharged to No.2 Convalescent Depot, Weymouth, Dorset on 17th September. He was absent without leave from 3 p.m. on 23rd October until 9.11 p.m. on 24th October, but was admonished, although he forfeited two days' pay. William returned to Australia aboard HT *Nestor* on account of his wounds on 12th December 1918. He was discharged at 5th Military District, Perth on 20th October 1920, giving his address as 29 Bourke Street, Kalgoorlie. Lucy and Harold had a son, Leonard Clarence Rosewarne (1913–21st November 1991), who married Juanita Daphne Martin (c.1914–6th November 1986).
- Henry 'Harry' Arnold Axford (19th January 1893–13th August 1947) was an electrician when he enlisted on 11th January 1915 in 16th Battalion AIF (1581). He was described as 5′ 9¼″ tall, weighing 148 lbs, with dark complexion, blue eyes, black hair and his religious denomination was Roman Catholic. He embarked on HMAT A54 *Runic* at Melbourne on 25th February and was taken on strength 16th Battalion at Gallipoli on 7th May. Having been admitted to No.16 and No.25 Casualty Clearing Stations at Anzac on 31st August with a hernia, he was

transferred to the Base on 2nd September with rheumatism and was admitted to No.1 Australian Stationary Hospital, Mudros, on 5th September with hydrocele and diarrhoea. He returned to the Base on 15th September, embarked on RMS *Aquitania* on 18th September and was admitted to 5th Southern General Hospital, Portsmouth on 26th September. He departed Monte Video Camp, Weymouth on 21st February 1916, embarked at Devonport, arrived at Alexandria, Egypt on 5th March and rejoined his unit at Tel-el-Kebir on 9th March. Harry embarked on HMT *Canada* at Alexandria on 1st June. On 4th June he was absent from the 2.30 p.m. parade, for which he was confined to barracks for a day and forfeited a day's pay. He disembarked at Marseille, France on 9th June and was appointed lance corporal on 16th July and promoted corporal on 31st July. He received a gunshot or shrapnel wound to the back on 7th August, was admitted to 12th General Hospital on 10th August, transferred by ambulance train at Rouen on 14th August and embarked at Le Havre on HMHS *Asturias* for evacuation to England next day. He was admitted to Lord Derby War Hospital, Warrington on 16th August, transferred to 1st Anzac Rest Station on 17th August and was discharged to No.2 Convalescent Depot, Perham Down on 12th October. He transferred to Wareham on 3rd November and to Weymouth on 8th November. On 14th December he embarked on *Princess Henrietta* at Folkestone for 4th Australian Division Base Depot, Étaples and rejoined his unit on 19th December. Harry was promoted sergeant on 13th February 1917 and was taken sick on 8th April. He moved by ambulance train next day and was admitted to 4th Australian Field Ambulance and 5th General Hospital, Rouen on 11th April. He transferred to No.2 Convalescent Depot, Rouen on 14th April, the Base Depot next day and returned to his unit on 6th May. He was taken sick and admitted to hospital from 13th Training Battalion at Codford, Wiltshire on 17th July and rejoined his unit two days later. He received gunshot wounds to the head, left leg and right thigh at Messines on 10th August and was admitted to 4th Australian Field Ambulance. The head wound caused deafness in his right ear. He was treated at 3rd Australian General Hospital, Abbeville on 11th August, transferred by ambulance train on 15th August and was evacuated to Britain aboard HMHS *St Patrick*, where he was admitted to the Royal Victoria Hospital, Netley, Hampshire on 16th August. He transferred to the Red Cross Hospital, Netley and later to 3rd Australian Auxiliary Hospital, Dartford on 25th September. A medical board there on 24th October found him permanently unfit for service and he was discharged on 25th October for leave until 8th November, then to the Depot at Weymouth. He was charged with neglect of duty whilst in charge of Hut 17, Monte Video Camp and was admonished. He embarked on HT *Port Darwin* on 12th January 1918 and disembarked on 28th February at Fremantle for 8th Australian General Hospital. A medical board there on 1st March recommended discharge. He was discharged from 5th Military District on 15th March with a pension of 11/6 fortnightly. Harry was President of the Kalgoorlie Branch of the RSL and ran an electrician's business from 113 Bourke Street, where he lived with his parents. He married Hilda Elsie Buckham (1901–11th January 1980) at East Coolgardie on 18th June 1921. She was born as Elsie Hilda Buckham. Harry re-enlisted on 17th September 1941 at Fort Swanbourne, Perth, Western Australia and was promoted sergeant (W4446). He was posted to 39 Works Section until his discharge on 5th October 1945. Elsie was living at 50 Anstey Street, Swan, Western Australia in 1949. They had three children:

  - Elsie Gertrude Axford (1922–2006) was a nun living at Community House, Higginbotham, Victoria in 1967.
  - Ronald Arnold Axford (1926–30th July 1984) married Vera Joan before 1949, by when he was a clerk and they were living with his mother. He was a secretary in 1958 and they were living at 28 Crawshaw Crescent, Manning, Western Australia. By 1977 he was an accountant and they were living at 174 Attunga Road, Miranda, New South Wales. He died at Yowie Bay, Sydney. They had at least three children – Geoffrey Alan Axford, Laurie John Axford and Stacey Jan Axford.
  - Betty Dorothy Axford (10th October 1930–6th April 2013) married Lyall George Youd (5th May 1927–7th May 1994), a salesman. They had a son.

- Harold Don Axford (9th September 1895–2nd October 1946), a brewer, married Jessie Evelyn Clayton (1899–12th June 1974) on 10th April 1919 and they lived at 22 Forest Street, Kalgoorlie, Western Australia. They had two sons and three daughters including:
  - Stanley Don Axford (5th February 1920–8th December 1942) enlisted in the Australian Army on 26th July 1940 at Torrens Hall, Adelaide, South Australia (S29037). He served with 7 Supply Personnel Company before transferring to the Royal Australian Naval Reserve (PA 2618) on 21st April 1942. He was serving aboard HMAS *Armidale* when she was sunk (Plymouth Naval Memorial, Devon, England – Panel 75, Column 3).
  - Keith Noel Axford (30th May 1931–7th September 2000) married on 23rd October 1964 and had three daughters.
- Laurence Walter Axford (15th October 1896–11th January 1898).
- Gertrude Axford (c.1898–4th December 1984) married Bernard Ford (c.1897–27th June 1978) in 1926. They had four children, including Keith Ford in 1929.
- Aileen Florence Axford (1900–14th June 1955) married Kenneth Hugh McLeod (14th May 1902–13th May 1951) at Plantagenet in 1931. He had married Emily Gilbert Edwards (1904–27) in 1924 and had two children – Kenneth Thomas McLeod 1925 and June Dawn McLeod 1927.
- Elsie Leonora 'Nora' Axford (1906–89) married Thomas Stanley Buckham (born 1908), a salesman, in 1930. They were living at 50 Auckland Street, North Perth in 1954. They had a daughter, Dallas Veronica Buckham, in 1931.
- Walter Leonard Axford (10th September 1908–24th November 1955) enlisted on 7th November 1939 at Kelmscott, Subiaco, Western Australia and served in

HMAS *Armidale* (680 tons), named after Armidale, New South Wales, was one of sixty vessels popularly known as corvettes that were approved in September 1939 to fill a requirement for locally built all-purpose vessels. They were the *Bathurst* class and were initially referred to as 'Australian minesweepers' to disguise their anti-submarine capability. They were capable of 15.5 knots, with a range of 2,850 nautical miles and were equipped with ASDIC, a 4″ gun, 20mm Oerlikons and could be fitted with either depth charges or minesweeping equipment. *Armidale* was laid down in Sydney on 1st September 1941 in a dry dock and was floated on 24th January 1942. Following commissioning on 11th June, she escorted convoys until October when she was assigned to the 24th Minesweeping Flotilla at Darwin. In late November, the RAN was called upon to evacuate 2/2nd Independent Company, following a failed attempt in September. *Armidale*, her sister-ship *Castlemaine* and the patrol boat *Kuru* were tasked. *Kuru* was to reach Betano Bay early on the night of 30th November, offload supplies and evacuate civilians. The two corvettes were to arrive two hours later, when *Kuru* would deliver her passengers to *Castlemaine*, which was to head for Darwin. *Kuru* was then to shuttle relief troops aboard *Armidale* to shore and evacuate the soldiers there on the return trips. At 9.00 a.m. on 30th November, the two ships were spotted by a Japanese reconnaissance aircraft. They radioed Darwin, suggesting that the mission be aborted but were instructed to continue. *Armidale* and *Castlemaine* were attacked at midday by fourteen Japanese bombers, but they were driven off by Beaufighters. Another attack at 2.00 p.m. resulted in no damage. Delayed by taking an evasive course and the two air attacks, the corvettes did not reach Betano Bay until 2.30 a.m. on 1st December. *Kuru* was sighted at dawn. It had assumed that the corvettes were not coming and turned for Darwin with the civilians. They were transferred to *Castlemaine* and *Armidale* and *Kuru* were ordered to take separate routes and attempt the operation again that night. At 1.00 p.m. *Armidale* was attacked by five Japanese dive-bombers. Two aircraft were damaged by the corvette's guns and the rest missed their target. A second air attack occurred an hour later. Five Zero fighters distracted the corvette while nine torpedo bombers made attack runs. At 3.10 p.m. she was hit on the port side by two torpedoes. As the soldiers and sailors took to the water, the Zeroes strafed the wreck. Ordinary Seaman Edward 'Teddy' Sheean was hit by two bullets in the chest and back. He strapped himself into the aft 20mm Oerlikon and began shooting at the fighters to protect those in the sea. Sheean shot down one Japanese aircraft and damaged two more. He carried on firing even as he disappeared beneath the surface. *Armidale* was the only *Bathurst* class corvette to be lost to enemy action. Sheean was one of one hundred of the 149 people on board who were killed during the sinking and its aftermath, as was Jack Axford's nephew, Stanley Don Axford. Sheean was posthumously mentioned in despatches but many felt that his gallantry, devotion to duty and self-sacrifice were worthy of the VC. On 1st May 1999 the submarine HMAS *Sheean* was launched by his sister, Ivy Hayes. In 2003, the training ship NTS *Sheean* was established for Australian Navy Cadets. In 2011 the Valour Inquiry was set up to look into thirteen cases of unresolved recognition for past acts of gallantry, including Sheean. It reported its findings in January 2013. In Sheean's case there was no new evidence to support awarding the VC. If he had lived, he might have been recommended for the CGM or DSM but neither could be awarded posthumously in 1942.

2/11th Battalion (WX308) until his discharge on 18th August 1945. He married Reta Jane Davies (born 1st November 1918) and they had four children. She was born at North Sydney, New South Wales and enlisted in the Australian Army on 7th October 1942 at West Marrickville, New South Wales (NX117468 (N391853)). She was discharged as a lance sergeant on 19th June 1945 from 12 Australian Camp Hospital.
- Robert Decimus Axford (10th November 1910–15th October 1995) enlisted in the Australian Army on 20th May 1940 at Coolgardie (WX2904). He was discharged as a private on 20th October 1945 from HQ 19th Australian Infantry Brigade. He married Mary Bernadette Moloney (17th August 1915–15th February 1976). She enlisted in the Australian Army on 27th September 1942 at Claremont, Western Australia (W96800) and was discharged as a private on 5th April 1946 from the Australian Army Canteen Service, NG Detachment. He was a shop assistant and they were living at 50 Kalgoorlie Street, Stirling, Western Australia in 1958.

Thomas' paternal grandfather, Thomas Axford (24th October 1826–21st September 1899), was born in Van Diemen's Land (Tasmania), Australia, son of Thomas Axford (1788–1855) and Martha Slade (1798–1879). Thomas senior was born at Abingdon, Berkshire, England, moved to Australia in 1822 and built the first water/flour mill in Tasmania. Martha was also born in Berkshire. Their daughter, Rose, married Edward Bisdee, brother of John Hutton Bisdee VC's paternal grandfather, on 23rd October 1844 and they lived at Lovely Banks, Bothwell, Tasmania. Thomas senior was the first person to be murdered by a bushranger (Rocky Whelan) in May 1855 on Constitution Hill, Thorpe, Tasmania. Jack's grandfather, Thomas, married Mary Ann Jane née Allwright (2nd March 1828–3rd October 1874), born in Tasmania, on 8th January 1850 at St Augustine's Church, Broadmarsh, Tasmania. They moved to Ballarat, Victoria and remained there for about twenty years before moving to Carrieton, South Australia, where he became a farmer. When his health began to fail, he sold the farm and moved to Adelaide, where he died at Tarrawatta, Angaston. In addition to Walter they had seven other children:

- Francis 'Frank' Richard Axford (25th November–28th December 1850.
- Thomas Axford (29th January 1852–14th November 1889) married Martha Ann Foster (6th August 1863–18th May 1936). He died at Thargomindah, Queensland. Thomas and Martha had four children:
    - Leonard Frank Axford (1884–1939) married Alice Miell in 1906 at Norwood, South Australia.
    - Edith Alice Martha Axford (8th-19th December 1885).
    - Walter John Axford (31st October 1887–1933) married Elizabeth Walton (1882–1960) and they had four children – Beryl, Len, Harold and Alice.
    - Arthur William Axford (born 24th October 1889).

  Martha married Thomas Reed (c.1857–30th June 1939) in 1898. They had three children, including Ralph Reed in 1899 and Mona Reed.

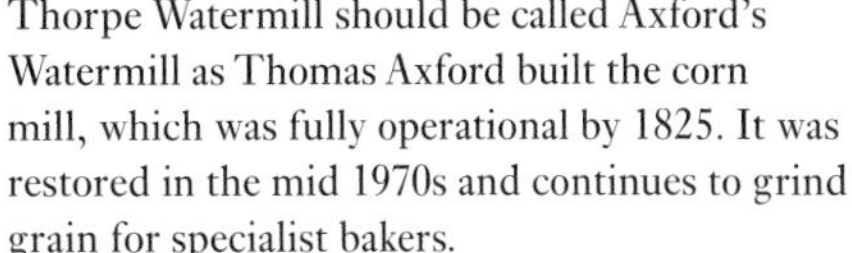

Thorpe Watermill should be called Axford's Watermill as Thomas Axford built the corn mill, which was fully operational by 1825. It was restored in the mid 1970s and continues to grind grain for specialist bakers.

Jack's paternal grandparents married at St Augustine's Anglican Church, Broadmarsh in January 1850. It opened on 27th May 1847 and is now owned privately.

- Francis Thomas Axford (15th May 1855–30th November 1906) married Emma Elizabeth Farr (born 1856), in Victoria on 21st August 1879. She was born at Ballarat. They had four children – Irene Violet Axford 1880, Hazel Thorpe Axford 1883, Edith Millicent Axford 1888 and Meryl Lucille Axford 1891.

John Whelan, born in England, stood 6′ 1″ tall and was of heavy build. He gained the name Rocky due to the crags and deep pockmarks on his face. He was sentenced to seven years by Chester Quarter Sessions on 31st July 1827 and was transported to Sydney on the *Marquis of Hastings*. He escaped from custody and took to highway robbery. He was arrested, tried in Sydney and transported to Norfolk Island, where he was involved in the unsuccessful taking of the brig *Governor Phillip*. He spent eighteen years there until 1854 when the penal colony closed and the convicts were relocated. Whelan was sent to Hobart and was assigned to the public works gang. After two days he absconded into the rugged bush land of Mount Wellington, above Hobart. He and Peter Connolly, who was also on Norfolk Island, became highway robbers, targeting isolated homesteads and ambushing lone travelers. An argument one night in Hobart caused the two to separate. Whelan was captured by a constable, with the help of a civilian, on 19th May 1855 in Hobart outside a bootmakers shop. Whelan's boots had been taken off Magistrate Dunn and had 'Dunn' branded on them. Dunn's body was found three days later. Whelan confessed to the murders of at least five men, including Dunn and a man believed to be Thomas Axford. He was convicted of 112 offences. Whelan and three others, including Connolly, were hanged at Hobart Gaol later in 1855. It is understood that this cave on Mount Wellington was his hideout.

- Charles Edward Axford (12th February 1857–20th November 1933) married Annie Caroline Pawlson (1871–24th November 1955) in 1902 at Malcolm, Western Australia. They had two children:
  - Maisie Clarice Axford (1903–14th September 1979) married Norman W Burnell in 1924.
  - Dorothy Caroline Axford (1905–20th January 1999) married Robert P Saunier (died 1937) in 1926.
- Mary Jane Axford (4th January 1859–29th October 1921).
- Laura Martha Axford (25th September 1860–16th April 1928) married Robert Martin Osborne (1861–22nd September 1931) on 26th January 1887. They travelled to England with their daughter, Dorothy, aboard the *Saxonia*, arriving in London on 13th August 1919. Laura died in Hobart and he was living at 12 North Bank Road, Trevallyn, Launceston, Tasmania when he died at Sydney, New South Wales. They had three children:
  - Laura Floris Osborne (born 19th January 1888) married as Sutherland and they had three children, including Ian and Robert.
  - Robert Keith Osborne (27th March–14th June 1889).
  - Dorothy Osborne (born 1895) married Vernon Statton.
- Melville Leonard Axford (30th June 1862–1st February 1929) married Hannah Thorn (24th July 1866–21st May 1901) on 31st January 1894 at the Presbyterian Church, Spalding, South Australia. They had two children – Dorothy Hannah Axford (born 15th December 1894) and Laurence Melville Axford (25th February 1896–6th August 1976). Melville married Amy Lavinia Watts (1866–20th October 1932) on 19th February 1902. He was a gardener when he enlisted in No.3 Squadron, 1st Remount Unit AIF on 22th September 1915 at Adelaide (659), having previously served in the South Australian Volunteer Force. He was described as 5′ 10 ¼″ tall, weighing 152 lbs, with fair complexion, blue eyes, dark brown hair and his religious denomination was Church of England. He sailed for the Middle East and was admitted to No.2 Australian General Hospital, Gezira, Egypt with diarrhoea on 27th December and transferred to Ras-el-Tin Convalescent Hospital, Alexandria on 6th January 1916. He returned to duty on 19th January and was posted to Moascar Garrison, Heliopolis on 9th October. Melville embarked for Australia aboard HT *Vestalia* on 18th October, arriving at Melbourne, Victoria on 21st November and was discharged on 6th December at Adelaide on account of the disbandment of his unit. They had a daughter, Laura Phyllis Axford (21st March 1903–4th July 1983), who married Brian Lee Paltridge in Adelaide in 1927.

His maternal grandparents were Patrick McQuillan (c.1848–1905) and Ann Theresa née O'Neill (1845–3rd August 1930), were both born in Ireland and emigrated to Adelaide, South Australia. They married in 1867. He died at Glanville and she at Norwood, South Australia. In addition to Margaret they had three other children:

- May 'Minnie' Theresa Clare McQuillan (born 1871).
- Abi Jane McQuillan (born 1873).
- Agnes 'Cissie' Lucy McQuillan (1875–98).

As a child, Jack worked on a farm and was educated at Coolgardie State School, Western Australia. He was caught stealing apples and appeared in court in January 1909, where he was cautioned and paid 13/- costs. He was employed at Boulder Brewery, Kalgoorlie, Western Australia from 1910 and also served in 84th Infantry (Militia) Goldfields Regiment of the Citizen Military Forces 1912–15. He enlisted in the AIF at Kalgoorlie on 19th July 1915, described as a labourer, 5′ 7¼″ tall, weighing 137 lbs, with dark complexion, grey eyes, black hair and his religious denomination was Roman Catholic. He joined 21st Depot Company at the training camp at Blackboy Hill, Northam, Western Australia on 8th August and transferred to 1st Depot Battalion on 23rd August. While at Blackboy Hill an officer jokingly pinned a tin VC replica on his chest because he looked like the type who would win one. Jack was allotted to the 11th Reinforcements for 16th Battalion AIF on 27th September. He embarked on HMAT A24 *Benalla* for the Middle East from Fremantle, Western Australia on 1st November and was taken on strength by 16th Battalion at Tel-el-Kebir, Egypt on 7th March 1916. He embarked on HMT *Canada* at Alexandria on 1st June and disembarked at Marseille, France on 9th June.

Jack suffered from shell shock on 11th August near Mouquet Farm on the Somme but rejoined the Battalion two days later. He was charged for being absent without leave from night operations from 7.00 p.m. until 9.00 p.m. on 6th November and received seven days Field Punishment No.2. On 10th August 1917 he received a gunshot wound to his left knee near Ypres and was admitted to 4th Australian Field Ambulance and No.2 Australian Casualty Clearing Station the same day. He transferred to 3rd Australian General Hospital next day and was moved by ambulance train on 15th August. Next day he embarked on HMHS

Coolgardie State School, now Coolgardie Primary School, opened in 1894. It was built during the gold rush on a rise overlooking the town and gold mines. The external view shows the temporary structure on the day it opened.

Boulder Brewery, where Jack worked from 1910. In 1895 Tom Elliott built a cordial factory near the Kalgoorlie rail line and the Federal Brewery for FW Whitfield. In 1898 he built his own brewery at the Boulder Block and named it the Boulder Brewery. The structure had a frontage of only twelve feet and a depth of seventy-five feet. It was wedged within a group of six hotels in an area known as the 'Dirty Acre'. Within a few years Boulder had thirty-six hotels open twenty-four hours a day to cater for the shift workers at the mines. The total output of Boulder Brewery was delivered to hotels close by and no transport was needed. Kegs were simply rolled down the street to wherever they were needed.

TSS *Benalla* (11,118 tons) was a passenger/cargo steamship built at Greenock in 1913 for the Pacific & Orient Steam Navigation Co for its Britain – Australia emigrant service via the Cape. In November 1914 she was part of the first convoy from King George's Sound, Albany, Western Australia, carrying the First Detachment of the Australian and New Zealand Imperial Expeditionary Forces. In January 1915 she was returned to her owners and on 19th July caught fire three days out of Cape Town bound for Sydney with 800 emigrants on board. She reached Durban under her own power, where the fire was extinguished by the local fire brigade. In October she was refitted at Sydney as a troopship and resumed military service, making four round trips from Australia in total. On 3rd December in the Mediterranean she was carrying 2,500 troops when she intervened in a duel between the British India steamer *Torilla* and a U-boat, which she drove off with her 4.7″ gun. On 6th June 1917 *Benalla* was taken over under the Liner Requisition Scheme for the transatlantic munitions and supplies service. She returned to P&O service in 1921. On 13th May 1921 she was struck by the tanker *Patella* in thick fog off Eastbourne and beached in Pevensey Bay. She was pumped out and repaired at Royal Albert Dock in London. In 1927 she carried the first consignment of steel from the northeast of England for the construction of Sydney Harbour Bridge. *Benalla* was scrapped in 1930.

St Patrick and was evacuated to the Royal Victoria Hospital, Netley, Hampshire. While there he was transferred to the Red Cross Hospital, Netley and to 3rd Australian Auxiliary Hospital, Dartford, Kent on 25th September. He was granted leave 25th October–8th November and then reported to No.2 Command Depot, Weymouth. He transferred to No.3 Command Depot, Hurdcott on 12th December and to No.4 Command Depot there on 18th December. On 5th January 1918 he transferred to the Overseas Training Brigade, Longbridge Deverill and on 17th January embarked at Southampton for the Australian Infantry Base Depot, Le Havre, arriving next day. He rejoined 16th Battalion on 26th January and was promoted lance corporal on 14th February.

Awarded the Military Medal for devotion to duty as a stretcher-bearer, probably for operations at Hébuterne, France in April 1918. The award was published in 4th Australian Division Routine Order 490 on 25th May

SS *Canada* was a Dominion Line ship operated under the White Star-Dominion Line, which did not actually exist but was a passenger service operated jointly by White Star Line and Dominion Line. *Canada* was built by Harland & Wolff, Belfast and launched in 1896. Her maiden voyage was Liverpool–Québec–Montréal, commencing on 1st October 1896. During the Second Boer War she was a troop transport. Her normal routine was to operate the Canada route in summer and Boston, USA in winter. In April 1912 *Canada* was in the same ice field as RMS *Titanic*. At the investigation in June 1912, Canada's captain, RO Jones, confirmed that he had received ice warning wireless messages but … *kept the* Canada *going at full speed as he always had done for twenty years*. In August 1914, she was in Canada and was taken over to transport troops to England. On arrival she was used to accommodate German prisoners for the rest of the year. In 1915 she became a transport ship and was used as such until the end of the war. She returned to civilian traffic in November 1918. She transferred to the Leyland Line in 1921 and remained in service until August 1926. She was scrapped in Italy.

1918, LG 13th September 1918. He was detached to the Corps Gas School for training 19th-26th May 1918. **Awarded the VC for his actions at le Hamel, France on 4th July 1918, LG 17th August 1918.** The initial recommendation came from Lieutenant James Basil Minchin, with whom Jack developed a great

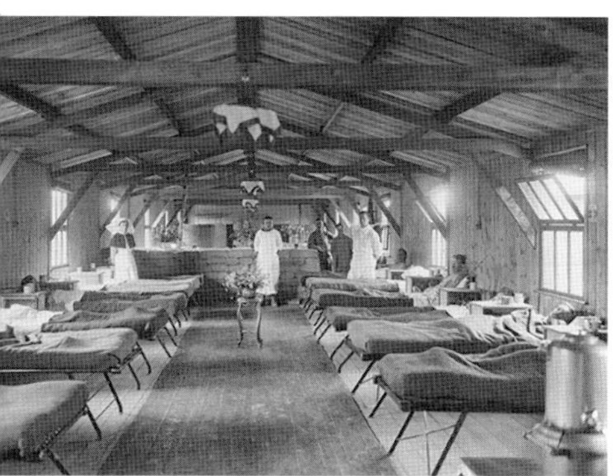

A ward of 3rd Australian General Hospital in France. It was established on Lemnos, in the Aegean Sea, near Gallipoli in August 1915. After the evacuation of Gallipoli the Hospital moved to Egypt in January 1916 and later to Brighton, England and then Abbeville, France. It remained there until 1919 (Australian War Memorial).

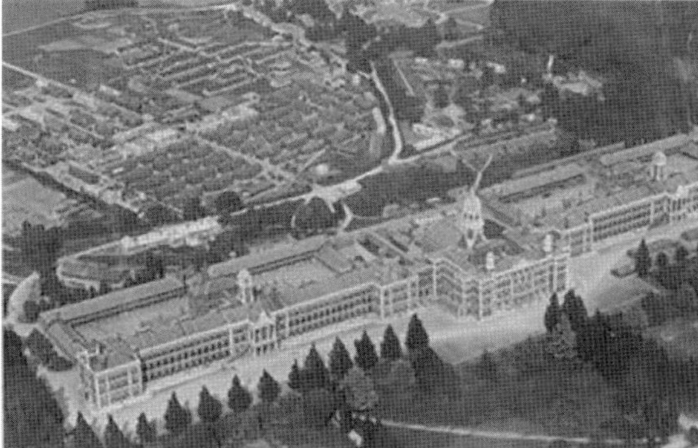

The Royal Victoria Hospital, Netley during the Great War, with the hutted Red Cross Hospital top left.

St Patrick was one of the first five ships to be requisitioned at the outbreak of the Great War. She was one of three ships that started the Fishguard–Rosslare service in 1906. She was converted into a hospital ship and remained in service until January 1919. In April 1929 she caught fire while moored at Fishguard and was sold for scrap the following year after her engines had been transferred to *St Andrew*.

3rd Australian Army Auxiliary Hospital was established at the Orchard Hospital in Dartford on 9th October 1916. It eventually had a capacity of 1,200 patients. Orchard Hospital opened in 1902 as a temporary hospital for smallpox patients. In 1910, with the decline of smallpox, it became a fever hospital but spent much of its time closed, being opened only for epidemics of scarlet fever and diphtheria. It was empty at the outbreak of war and became the Orchard Military Hospital until transferred for Australian use. A total of 56,441 patients were treated there. Many soldiers married local women. The Australian government presented the town with a German gun captured by the Australians in appreciation of its hospitality during the war. The gun was scrapped during the Second World War (Australian War Memorial).

friendship. James died on 1st November 1936 and Thomas was one of the pallbearers at his funeral. Thomas was promoted corporal on 14th July and trained at the Australian Corps School 24th August–18th September. However, four days before the end of this period he was transferred to AIF HQ in London. The VC was presented by the King in the quadrangle at Buckingham Palace on 26th September 1918. Jack embarked on HMAT D24 *Sardinia* on 19th October, along with Lance Corporal Philip Davey VC MM, and returned to Australia on leave, arriving at Albany, Western Australia on 17th December. He was there for seven days and arrived at Kalgoorlie railway station on 24th December to a rousing welcome, which he did not enjoy. Thomas was discharged at Perth on 6th February 1919. That month he was welcomed home by the Kalgoorlie Lodge of the United Ancient Order of Druids.

Jack returned to work on a farm for the HV McKay Sunshine Harvester Co

During the Crimean War, Queen Victoria ordered a military hospital to be built in order to train army nurses and doctors and to treat military patients. The foundation stone was laid by Queen Victoria on 19th May 1856. She arrived by Royal Yacht and the pier that had been built for her visit. One of the guns firing the Royal Salute was discharged early and two sailors were killed but the foundation stone ceremony went ahead. Beneath the stone a copper casket was laid containing the plans of the hospital, the first Victoria Cross, a Crimean Medal with all four campaign bars and coins of the realm. Netley was the largest military hospital in its day, with 138 wards and about 1,000 beds. The building was 400m long and had three floors. Florence Nightingale helped to write the military nursing regulations. The first patients were admitted on 19th May 1863 from the 170m long pier. However, the pier was little used, as it did not reach deep water and most hospital ships had to discharge in Southampton. It was demolished in 1955. Queen Victoria made regular visits, during which she awarded medals, including three Victoria Crosses to Private Frederick Hitch, 24th Regiment (Rorke's Drift), Piper George Findlater, Gordon Highlanders and Private Samuel Vickery, Dorset Regiment. A railway branch line from Netley station, linked the Hospital with the main line and Southampton Central Station. A steam train was driven to the site and for the next seven years was used to drive giant cement mixers, whilst the building was being constructed. The Army Medical School moved to Netley in 1863 from Chatham and remained until it moved to London in 1902. During the Great War about 50,000 patients were treated at Netley. The capacity was doubled to 2,000 beds with the building of the Red Cross Hospital in huts behind the main building. The poet Wilfred Owen was treated for shell shock there before being transferred to Craiglockhart War Hospital, Edinburgh. The Hospital was the mobilisation centre for the Queen Alexandra's Imperial Military Nursing Service Reserve and the Territorial Army Nursing Service in 1939. It was also the muster point for 4th British General Hospital before it moved to France and also for 11th General Hospital. In September and October 1943 the Hospital admitted the first exchange of prisoners with Germany for examination and treatment before the British troops went on leave. Netley was handed over to the US military in 1944 and over 68,000 patients were treated before the end of the war, included wounded from Normandy and German prisoners. It is said that the Americans found the 400m long corridor too long to walk and drove Jeeps along the ground floor. In July 1945 the Hospital was handed back to the British Army. A psychiatric asylum was established in D Block, Victoria House, in 1870. It treated over 15,000 patients during the Great War. Adolf Hitler's deputy, Rudolf Hess, was also treated there after his flight from Germany and capture. In 1950 E Block was added and the army psychiatric facility was renamed Albert House. From 1960 Royal Navy personnel was also treated there. The main part of the Royal Victoria Military Hospital closed in 1958. It was unused for several years and was badly damaged in a fire in June 1963. Further damage was caused by pipes bursting in the bitter winter of 1963. The main hospital building was demolished in 1966. The psychiatric hospital remained until 1978. The grounds and buildings were purchased by Hampshire County Council in 1979 and were developed into Royal Victoria Country Park. Only the Royal Chapel and officers' mess building remain. The Chapel is now a museum and the mess was converted into luxury apartments. Netley Military Cemetery has over 700 graves from the Great War and thirty-seven from the Second World War.

in Western Australia. By coincidence Walter Peeler VC BEM and Lawrence McCarthy VC worked for the same company at Sunshine, Victoria. Later, prior to 1936, Jack was a civil servant with the Mines Department in Perth until retirement.

Hurdcott Camp on what is now the A30 Salibury – Shaftesbury road. Other camps existed nearby at Fovant and Sutton Mandeville. 31st Division units, including the Sheffield City Battalion, were there in late 1915 prior to embarking for Egypt. Some Australian battalions were there from 1916 and on 12th March 1917 Hurdcott was officially taken over by the AIF as a Command Depot, where soldiers discharged from hospitals recuperated and regained fitness. There were four Command Depots in Wiltshire and Dorset:

No.1 – Perham Down, Salisbury Plain moved to Sutton Veny in October 1917.

No.2 – Monte Video Camp, Weymouth from June 1915 expanded to include Westham and Littlemoor Camps.

No.3 – Bovington Camp, Dorset received the overflow from Perham Down and moved to Hurdcott in March 1917.

No. 4 – Wareham, Dorset moved to Codford, Salisbury Plain in June 1917 and to Hurdcott in November 1917.

(Australian War Memorial)

Early in 1920 Jack was admitted to the Base Hospital in Fremantle for treatment. In March he travelled to Melbourne for the St Patrick's Day procession in which 10,000 returned soldiers and sailors took part. Archbishop Mannix led the procession in his car, surrounded on horseback by a guard of honour of fourteen Catholic VCs, including Jack. In July, Jack was introduced to the Prince of Wales during his visit to Kalgoorlie.

On 19th June 1921 a crowd of 3,000 went to the Esplanade Hotel in Perth. A deputation went inside and the 'Red Flag' and 'Solidarity' were sung. When the police went to move them on, Jack yelled and hooted at them. He refused to move and was arrested. In court on 24th June 1921 he was charged with behaving in a disorderly manner and was cautioned as to his future behaviour. He appeared in the Bruce Rock Police Court, Western Australia on 2nd March 1922, accused with William Luke Cusack of assaulting Charles William Watt, an Agricultural Bank inspector. On 24th February Watt had inspected work carried out by them, declared it unsatisfactory and refused to pay them. Jack Axford struck him repeatedly and William Cusack threw him to the ground. They were fined £2 and £1 respectively and ordered to pay court costs of £10/11/-.

Jack Axford married Lily Maud Foster (1904–25th July 1983), born at Mount Margaret, Western Australia, on 26th November 1926 at St Mary's Catholic Cathedral, Perth, Western Australia. Lily's parents were William John Foster and Lily Maud née Stephens. Thomas and Lily lived at 12 Harrow Street, Mount Hawthorn, Perth. They had five children:

- Jack Thomas Richard Axford (21st May 1927–4th September 2013) served in the Australian Army. He married Brenda Morris and they had six children – Marilyn Axford, Robert Axford, John Axford, Christina Axford, Donald Axford and Angelia Axford.
- Aileen Maud Axford (born 3rd February 1929) married Norman Lloyd Carvell and they had four children – Desmond Lloyd Carvell, Susan Patricia Carvell, Debbie Lorraine Carvell and Dianne Michelle Carvell.
- Norman Edward Axford (born 28th July 1930), a fireman on the railways, married Alma Waite and they had a son, Wayne Axford.
- Doreen May Axford (born 2nd May 1932) married Sydney James Carvell (died 13th October 2010) and they had two children – Terrase Carvell and Darlene Carvell.
- Phyllis Shirley Axford (born 1st August 1933), known as Shirley, married Peter Lang and they had two children – Kyme Lang and Stephen Lang.

The Esplanade Hotel on the northern side of the Esplanade Reserve, Perth opposite the Perth Bowling Club. Its demolition in 1972 was controversial because of the building's beauty and popularity.

Jack was one of twenty-three VCs who attended an Anzac Dinner on 23rd April 1927, hosted by Lieutenant General Sir John Monash GCMG KCB VD. For an unknown

12 Harrow Street, Mount Hawthorn, Perth, where Jack and his family lived.

reason The Duke of York (future King George VI) was not invited. Jack took part in the Anzac Commemoration Service on 25th April 1927 at the Exhibition Building, Melbourne, Victoria in the presence of The Duke of York. In the march past the VCs conceded pride of place to blinded soldiers who insisted on marching. In October 1928 the police raided three tobacconist shops and charged them with keeping a common betting shop. Jack was unlucky enough to be caught and was fined £5 plus £2/2/- costs. Four months later he was found guilty of the same offence and was fined £20.

On 25th June 1941 Jack enlisted in the Australian Military Forces at Mount Hawthorn, Perth and served with the Western Australia Echelon and District Regional Records Office as a corporal (W18283). He was promoted sergeant on 22nd February 1943. On 11th September 1944 he was charged with being improperly dressed and was admonished by the CO. On 10th March 1947 he transferred to HQ Western Command and was discharged on 14th April.

In 1954 Jack was invited by the RSL to be presented to the Queen in Perth. He declined because his wife was not allowed to sit with him but had to sit in the gallery, although politicians' wives could sit with their husbands. He also declined to take part in any future Anzac Day parades.

St Mary's Cathedral, Perth (Cathedral of the Immaculate Conception of the Blessed Virgin Mary), is the cathedral church of the Roman Catholic Archdiocese of Perth. It was constructed in three main phases, the first being completed in 1865. However, the current structure was not completed until December 2009. Alterations between 1897 and 1910 included the addition of a spire to the bell tower seen here. The latest additions include a second spire, although it is not identical to the original spire.

Jack attended three VC Reunions, commencing with the VC Centenary Celebrations at Hyde Park, London on 26th June 1956, travelling on SS *Orcades* with other Australian VCs who were part of the 301 Victoria Cross recipients from across the Commonwealth. He also attended the 12th VC & GC Association Reunion at the Savoy Hotel, London on 18th May 1981.

Following the death of his wife in July 1983, Jack used his entitlement for two first class air tickets to attend the 13th VC & GC Association Reunion at the Café Royal, London on 6th October 1983. He exchanged one ticket for two economy class tickets and his sons Jack and Norm accompanied him. On the return flight he died between Dubai and Hong Kong on 11th October. At Keith Payne VC's suggestion, the body was placed upright in the lavatory for easier removal after rigor mortis set in. After a State Funeral at the Roman Catholic Chapel, Campbell Barracks, Perth, attended by fellow VCs James Gordon and Keith Payne, he was cremated at Karrakatta Crematorium Chapel on 21st October 1983. His ashes, and those of his wife, are in Ground Niche MCA 0079 at Karrakatta Crematorium. He is commemorated in a number of other places:

The memorial plaque in King's Park, Perth.

- Western Australia
  - The nineteen wards at Hollywood Private Hospital, Perth, Western Australia were named after VCs and GCs, including one after Thomas Axford.
  - Axford Park, on the corner of Hobart Street and Scarborough Beach Road, Mount Hawthorn, Western Australia was dedicated on 25th April 2001. There is a memorial plaque in the Park.
  - Axford Road, Alexander Heights, Perth, Western Australia.
  - Plaque on Wall 19, Row A, Western Australian Garden of Remembrance, Smyth Road, Nedlands.
  - Plaque unveiled on Kalgoorlie-Boulder's Walk of Fame, Hannan Street, Kalgoorlie on 25th April 2018.
  - Memorial plaque at the State War Memorial, King's Park, Perth, Western Australia, dedicated on 26th January 1996.
- New South Wales
  - Victoria Cross Memorial, Queen Victoria Building, George Street, Sydney, New South Wales dedicated on 23rd February 1992 to commemorate the visit of Queen Elizabeth II and Prince Phillip on the occasion of the Sesquicentenary of the City of Sydney. Sir Roden Cutler VC AK KCMG, Edward Kenna VC and Keith Payne VC were in attendance.
  - Victoria Cross Recipients Wall, North Bondi War Memorial, New South Wales donated to the community of Waverley on 27th November 2011 by The Returned & Services League of Australia.

- Australian Capital Territory
  - Australian Victoria Cross Recipients plaque on the Victoria Cross Memorial, Campbell, dedicated on 24th July 2000.
  - Named on one of eleven plaques honouring 175 men from overseas awarded the VC for the Great War. The plaques were unveiled by the Senior Minister of State at the Foreign & Commonwealth Office and Minister for Faith and Communities, Baroness Warsi, at a reception at Lancaster House, London on 26th June 2014 attended by The Duke of Kent and relatives of the VC recipients. The Australian plaque is at the Australian War Memorial.
  - Display in the Hall of Valour, Australian War Memorial.
- Axford Boulevard, Wodonga, Victoria on White Box Rise estate built on land formerly part of Bandiana Army Camp.
- Communities and Local Government commemorative paving stones for the 145 VCs born in Australia, Belgium, Canada, China, Denmark, Egypt, France, Germany, India, Iraq, Japan, Nepal, Netherlands, Newfoundland, New Zealand, Pakistan, South Africa, Sri Lanka, Ukraine and United States of America were unveiled at the National Memorial Arboretum, Alrewas, Staffordshire by Prime Minister David Cameron MP and Sergeant Johnson Beharry VC on 5th March 2015.

Jack's Communities and Local Government commemorative paving stone at the National Memorial Arboretum (Memorials to Valour).

In addition to the VC and MM he was awarded the 1914–15 Star, British War Medal 1914–20, Victory Medal 1914–19, War Medal 1939–45, Australian Service Medal 1939–45, George VI Coronation Medal 1937, Elizabeth II Coronation Medal 1953 and Elizabeth II Silver Jubilee Medal 1977. Jack made it known that he wanted his

The Queen Elizabeth II Silver Jubilee Medal was created in 1977 to mark the 25th anniversary of the Queen's accession in the United Kingdom, Canada, Australia and New Zealand. Until 1977 the United Kingdom authorities decided on a total number for coronation and jubilee medals, which were then allocated to Empire, Dominion and Commonwealth countries. From 1977 the award was at the discretion of each national government – 30,000 in Britain, 1,507 in New Zealand, 6,870 in Australia and 30,000 in Canada.

medals to be retained by his family and not to be sold after his death. The Public Trustee of Axford's medals held a ballot within the family. As a result Shirley Lang received the VC and Aileen Carvell the MM. Shirley and Aileen agreed that the two gallantry awards should be presented to the Australian War Memorial and this took place at a ceremony on 27th September 1985. The other medals are still with members of the family. The VC is held in the Hall of Valour, Australian War Memorial, Treloar Crescent, Campbell, Australian Capital Territory.

B/203174 PRIVATE WILLIAM BEESLEY
13th Battalion, The Rifle Brigade (The Prince Consort's Own)

William 'Bill' Beesley was born on 5th October 1895 at 74 Top Colliery Rows, Gresley, Burton-upon-Trent, Staffordshire. His father, John Beesley (1869–1901), was born at Stratford-upon-Avon, Warwickshire. He married Emma Marriott late Hinds née Hill (1868–1936), born at Ashby de la Zouch, Leicestershire in 1895 at Burton-upon-Trent. She had married Edward Henry Hinds (1868–94) in 1888 and they had two children:

- George Henry A Hinds (1889–1924) was a miner in 1911 living with his grandparents, Henry and May Hill. He married Edith Annie Foster (born 1893) in 1914. They had four children:
    - May Hinds (born 1915) married Samuel Edwards in 1936.
    - Edward Hinds (1918–25th June 1940) married Gertrude Kirk (4th October 1918–June 2004) in 1940 at Repton, Derbyshire. He enlisted as an ordinary seaman in the Royal Navy (D/JX 179349) and was serving aboard HMCS *Fraser* when she sank after colliding with HMS *Calcutta* in the Gironde estuary, France (Plymouth Naval Memorial – Panel 39). Gertrude married David Y Gourlay (c.1917–45) in 1942 at Repton. They had a daughter, Margaret A Gourlay, in 1943. Gertrude married Reginald A Fairbrother in 1949.
    - George Hinds (born 1920).
    - William Hinds (born 1922).
- Mary Alice Hinds (born 1891) was a dressmaker in 1911, living with her grandparents, Henry and May Hill.

John and Emma had a daughter:

- Emma Beesley (5th May 1898–1954), born at Tunnell Cottages, Atherstone, Warwickshire, married James Wilson (29th April 1903–9th April 1962) in 1928 at

Nuneaton, Warwickshire. He was a colliery pan man in 1939 and they were living at 31 Norman Avenue, Nuneaton. They had two children:
   - Joyce Ellen Wilson (15th April 1929–8th December 2008) married Howard Edwin C Pugh (1928–November 1995) in 1949. They are believed to have had a son, Leroy J Pugh, in 1964.
   - Kenneth John Wilson (7th May 1935–4th March 1997) is understood to have married Betty M Robottom (born 1948) in 1967. They had two children – Paula Rosemary Wilson 1968 and Kenneth John Wilson 1973.

  James married Dora Heathcote in 1955 (22nd February 1901–1st February 1993) at Nuneaton. She was born at Leicester. They were living at 31 Norman Avenue, Nuneaton at the time of his death there. She died at Butts Croft House (a care home), Tamworth Road, Corley, Coventry, Warwickshire.

Emma was living with her children, William and Emma, at 18 Tunnel Cottages, Nuneaton in 1901. James Ealing, her future husband, was boarding with the family at that time. Emma married James Ealing (1871–1937) in 1902. He was in the Atherstone Union Workhouse with his mother and siblings in 1881. By 1911 James was a miner holer and she was a domestic servant, living at Emery's Cottages, Ansley, near Nuneaton. Emma and James had two children:

- Violet Ethel Ealing (born 25th January 1906–November 1985) married Benjamin Wilkins (30th September 1904–1983) in 1928. They had eight children:
   - Violet A Wilkins (born 1929) married Hans Kremer in 1948. They had three children – Otto J Kremer 1949, Heidi R Kremer 1959 and Tania K Kremer 1961.
   - Ivy M Wilkins (1933–34).
   - Benjamin Wilkins (born 1935).
   - Rose N Wilkins (born 1937).
   - Barrie/Barry J Wilkins (born 1939) married Annie M Oldfield in 1963.
   - Raymond B Wilkins (born 1942) married Christine R Batts (born 1944) in 1963. They had two children – Andrew Wilkins 1963 and Amanda Wilkins 1965.
   - Frank Wilkins (born 1945).
   - Mary Wilkins (born 1948) is believed to have died at or soon after birth.
- Percy Claude Ealing (20th March 1909–29th June 1981) was a colliery clip man in 1939, living with his half-sister, Emma Wilson and her family, at 31 Norman Avenue, Nuneaton.

Bill's paternal grandfather, Andrew Beesley (1840–83), was born at Clifford Chambers, near Stratford-upon-Avon, Warwickshire. He married Mary Anne née Hortin (1840–95), born at Snitterfield, near Stratford-upon-Avon, on 30th December 1858 at Alveston, Warwickshire. She was a milliner and he was a brewer

Clifford Chambers, where Bill's paternal grandfather was born, is about three kilometres south of Stratford-upon-Avon and in 2011 had a population of just 432. The moated manor house was visited by William Shakespeare. The manor was remodelled by Edwin Lutyens in 1918 and the gardens were designed by him and Gertrude Jekyll. Since 1996 Clifford Chambers village has been the headquarters of the Hosking Houses Trust, a charity for female writers. The actor Sir Ben Kingsley lived there at one time.

Snitterfield is a small village about seven kilometres from Stratford-upon-Avon, with a population of 1,226 in 2011. Bill's paternal grandmother was born there. Richard Shakespeare, grandfather of William, the playwright, is mentioned in the manorial records 1535–60. William Shakespeare's father, John, was born there and moved to Stratford-upon-Avon, having married Mary Arden. John Grant, born in Snitterfield, was involved in the Gunpowder Plot. After the failure of the Plot some of the conspirators made a last stand at Holbeche House in Staffordshire. Grant was blinded when a spark ignited the gunpowder they were trying to dry. He was captured and executed outside St Paul's Cathedral in London, refusing to confess his treason to the end.

in 1861, living in a cottage in Stratford-upon-Avon. By 1871 they had moved to Bridgetown, Stratford-upon-Avon and to 36 Henley Street, Stratford-upon-Avon by 1881. In addition to John they had three other children:

- Andrew Beesley (1864–1902), birth registered as Beeslee, was a brewer in 1881 living with his parents. He married Sarah Edge (1864–1925) in 1883. They were

Alveston is about five kilometres from Stratford-upon-Avon. Bill's paternal grandparents were married there. The playwright JB Priestley lived at Kissing Tree House in the village.

William Shakespeare's birthplace on Henley Street in Stratford-upon-Avon is only a few metres away from where Andrew and Mary Beesley were living in 1881.

living at 28 Greenhill Street, Stratford-upon-Avon in 1891 and 1901. They had three children:
    - Gertrude Nellie Beesley (1883–1958) married Arthur John Wearing (1888–1955) in 1910. They had three children – Kathleen A Wearing 1913, Dorothy M Wearing 1921 and Jack Wearing 1926.
    - Elsie May Beesley (1885–1908).
    - Alice Beatrice E Beesley (21st October 1887–1976) married Richard Henry Hancox (1891–1956) in 1915. They had two children – Katharine B Hancox 1916 and Beatrice N Hancox 1921.
- Edwin Charles Beesley (1871–1942), known as Charles.
- Lucy Ann Esther Beesley (1873–10th May 1929) had a son, Henry Beesley (9th June 1891–1971). He married Ethel Edwards (8th November 1891–1981) in 1915 and they had two daughters – Olive Beesley 1918 and Winifred A Beesley 1919. Lucy married Charles Henry Beckett (born 1871) on 28th January 1892 at Holy Trinity, Stratford-upon-Avon. He was a miller's carter in 1901 and a railway carter in 1911 and they were living at 6 Waterside, Stratford-upon-Avon at the time of both censuses. They emigrated to Canada, arriving at Quebec in 1913, and were living at Rosedale, Neepawa, Manitoba in 1916. Lucy died at Winnipeg, Manitoba. They had six children:
    - Thomas Andrew Beckett (born 1892).
    - William Francis Beckett (13th December 1894–1979) married Lucy Mitchell on 20th November 1915.
    - Archibald Ernest Beckett (1896–19th December 1975).
    - Violet Lucy Beckett (30th December 1898–5th January 1980) married Hugh McKay on 21st August 1918.
    - Denis Baden Beckett (1900–7th February 1990) married Elizabeth Daly on 21st February 1934.
    - Roland Beckett (1902–21st October 1925).

His maternal grandfather, Henry Hill (1844–1913), born at Ticknall, Derbyshire, was a coal miner. He married Mary Draper née Marriott (1848–1926), also born at Ticknall, in 1866 at Derby. They were living at 6 Dog Kennel Buildings, Gresley, Staffordshire in 1881. By 1891 they had moved to Linton Heath, Burton-upon-Trent and to New Road, Castle Gresley, Derbyshire by 1901. In 1911 they were living at 32 Linton Heath, Burton-upon-Trent. In addition to Emma they had three other children including:

- George Hill (born 1866).
- Alice Hill (1871–1945) was a dressmaker in 1891. She married John Roland Fairbrother (1870–1949), a coal miner hewer, in 1892 at Burton-upon-Trent. His birth was registered as Roland Fairbrother at Ashby de la Zouch. He was living as a lodger, as Rowland Fairbrother, with his future parents-in-law at the time of the

1891 Census. Alice and Roland were living at New Road, Castle Gresley in 1901. They had four children:

- John Wilfred Fairbrother (6th January 1894–1970).
- Arthur Fairbrother (born and died 1896).
- Alice Evelyn Fairbrother (born 1907) married Arthur E Holmes in 1928. They had at least two children – Philip J Holmes 1933 and John B Holmes 1935.
- Joseph Fairbrother (born March 1911).

Bill was educated at Ansley Village School, near Nuneaton. He worked as a miner at Haunchwood (Tunnel) Colliery, Nuneaton. In 1911 he was living with his mother and her third husband, James Ealing, and was described as a point lad on a pit bank. He enlisted in the King's Royal Rifle Corps (A/2545) at Nuneaton Police Station on 27th August 1914 but was rejected at the first attempt on account of his age. He joined the back of the queue, gave his age as twenty and was successful at the second attempt. He went to France on 21st May 1915 with 9th Battalion. On 30th July he was wounded by a splinter in the shoulder at Hooge, Belgium. This occurred during the counterattack following the first use of flamethrowers by the Germans against the British. Second Lieutenant Sydney Woodroffe, 8th Rifle Brigade, was awarded the VC for the same action. Bill was wounded again on 25th November in the legs whilst taking supplies up the St Julien road. He was evacuated to Britain on 8th December.

Bill transferred to the Rifle Brigade in early 1916 and returned to France in time for the Somme

Haunchwood (Old or Nowells) Colliery dated back to the 1730s, although mining at Haunchwood went back as far as the 14th century. The original shaft was sunk next to Haunchwood Brick and Tile Company, which was owned by the Knox family, whose son, Cecil Leonard Knox was also awarded the VC in the Great War. Two more shafts were sunk in 1891–92 at Galley Common and were known as the Tunnel Pit because they were close to the railway tunnel. Full extraction began in 1894, by when 817 men worked underground. On 23rd December 1911 a fire broke out underground that could not be contained and Tunnel Pit was closed, with the loss of 1,012 jobs, a disaster for the local community. The mine was gradually cleared and repaired and it eventually reopened. Tunnel Pit remained open until the 1970s, when it closed and was demolished. The site is now a park and a housing estate.

Ansley Common, where Bill lived and went to school.

Cecil Leonard Knox VC receiving the Freedom of Nuneaton on 17th July 1918. Bill Beesley VC, who was granted the Freedom on the same day, is seated on the right.

Nuneaton Police Station, where Bill enlisted on 27th August 1914.

The investiture at HQ Third Army, Frohen-le-Grand, on 9th August 1918. In the background is Mary Elizabeth Hardy, daughter of the Reverend Theodore Bayley Hardy, who was also presented with the VC at the same investiture. Elizabeth, as she was known, was a nurse at a Red Cross Hospital in Dunkirk, France.

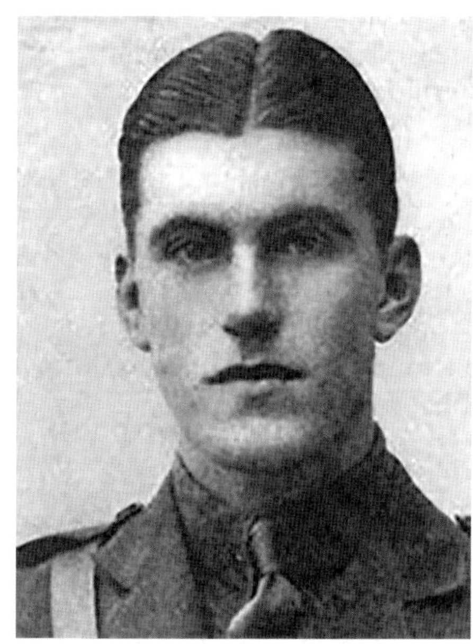

Second Lieutenant Sydney Woodroffe, 8th Rifle Brigade, was awarded the VC for his actions on 30th July 1915 during the fighting at Hooge in which the Germans made the first use of flamethrowers against the British. Bill was wounded in the same action.

offensive with 13th Rifle Brigade. He was wounded a third time on 3rd May 1917. **Awarded the VC for his actions at Bucquoy, France on 8th May 1918, LG 28th June 1918.** He was promoted corporal on 28th June, the same day that his VC appeared in the London Gazette. He was invited to tea in the trenches with his CO and the Divisional GOC invited him to lunch and gave him a box of chocolates. Bill

Following riots in Stockingford over reduced wages, the Church of St Nicholas in Nuneaton decided to build a chapel of ease to help quell the violence. Work began in 1822 and two years later St Paul's Church was consecrated. It has been added to several times since, the latest additions being made in 2008. The pipe organ, installed in 1909, was removed and reassembled in a church in Dijon, France. It was replaced with a digital organ. The church and its clergy appear in George Eliot's book, *Scenes of Clerical Life*, with different names.

Bill and Ada on their wedding day (Mike Shaw).

was granted the Freedom of the Borough of Nuneaton at a ceremony in Riversley Park on 17th July 1918 at the same time as Cecil Leonard Knox VC. Bill was also presented with £700 in War Bonds and a marble clock by the town. The VC was presented by the King at HQ Third Army at the chateau at Frohen-le-Grand on 9th August 1918. **Awarded the French Médaille Militaire by the President of**

Family wedding photograph. Bill's mother, Emma, is to his right (Mike Shaw).

The Royal Oak in Hartshill, where the reception took place, is still a thriving inn.

the French Republic, LG 14th July 1919. It was presented by GOC First French Army on 8th September 1918, ten months before the award was published in the London Gazette. Bill was demobilised to the Class Z Reserve in 1919.

William Beesley married Ada Mary Wilson (3rd April 1893–1971) on 4th April 1920 at St Paul's Church, Stockingford, Nuneaton. The four bridesmaids wore miniature VCs. The reception was held at the Royal Oak pub in Hartshill and they settled in Coventry. They were living at 88 St Pauls Road, Nuneaton at the time of the 1939 Census. They had four children:

- Rosemary Beesley (8th March 1921–13th October 2000) was a trimmer in a hat factory in 1939, living with her parents. She married John Hillary Barnett (19th February 1920–10th August 1994) on 19th December 1940 at Chilvers Coton Parish Church, Nuneaton. He was living at 6 Greenhill Road, Stoke Golding, Leicestershire at the time of his death there. Rosemary also died at Stoke Golding. They had three children:
    - John Clifford Barnett (born 1942) married Ann T McLeod in 1972.
    - Anthony L Barnett (born 1947).
    - Hilary A Barnett (born 1949).
- John Clifford Beesley (10th September 1922–11th January 1979) was a garden boy in 1939, living with his parents. He was living at 23 Caldwell Caravan Site, Caldwell, Nuneaton at the time of his death there.
- Kenneth George Beesley (3rd July 1924–28th November 2010) married Lilian Davies in 1954. They had a son, Keith Gerd Beesley, in 1967.
- William Beesley (19th December 1925–19th January 2010).

Ada's father, John Wilson (c.1853–16th November 1936), a coal miner, was born at Chapel End, Nuneaton. He married Mary Jane Taylor (1863–13th June 1941), born at Bentley, Warwickshire, on 19th January 1891 at St Paul's Church, Stockingford. They were living at Galley Common, near Nuneaton in 1901 and 1911. Mary had a daughter, Ellen Taylor, in 1888. At the time of the 1901 Census a William Wilson (born c.1878), a coal miner described as a son, was also living with them. In addition to Ada they had nine other children, one of whom died in infancy:

Chapel End, Nuneaton where Ada's father was born.

- Albert Henry Wilson (1891–19th October 1954) married Caroline Mears (1891–6th October 1957) in 1916. She was born at Fenny Drayton, Leicestershire and was a domestic servant at Priesthills House, Hinckley, Leicestershire in 1911. They had nine children – Joseph A Wilson (1916–90), Rosalie Wilson (1918–2012), Vera Lillian Wilson (1920–2010), Barbara Joan Wilson (1922–1936), Thomas J Wilson (1923), Bernard Wilson (1925), Margaret Wilson (1927), Stanley Wilson (1930) and John Wilson (1934).

- Joseph Clifford Wilson (12th October 1894–1970).
- Frederick Wilson (born 1896).
- David Wilson (17th December 1898–1972). He is believed to have married Florence Victoria Hall (4th February 1898–1978) in 1923. They had a daughter, Joan M Wilson, in 1924.
- Ernest Wilson (born 1900).
- Rose Annie Wilson (1st December 1901–August 1989) married Thomas Henry Piper (12th May 1902–June 1983) in 1929 at Atherstone. They had four children – John H Piper 1929, Margaret Piper 1931, Kenneth Piper 1933 and Peter Piper 1936.
- Sidney James Wilson (7th March 1904–1976) married Ann Fairfield (born 1908) in 1930.
- George Herbert Wilson (20th January 1906–11th March 1986) was living at 2 Berrington Road, Nuneaton at the time of his death there.

Bill during the Second World War, serving in the Royal Artillery.

An advertisement for Wickman's in the early 1950s.

Bill returned to coalmining at Haunchwood for a time after the war, where one of the directors was Cecil Knox VC. Bill was later employed at Wickman's, a Coventry machine tools manufacturer. He was a lavatory attendant with the Borough Council in 1939. He rejoined the Army as a sergeant at the outbreak of the Second World War and served in the Royal Artillery, instructing recruits at Aintree Racecourse, Liverpool. Later he transferred to other duties at Meriden, Warwickshire and was discharged in 1941. His marriage to Ada failed about the start of the Second World War and the couple never reunited after he rejoined the Army.

Bill lived with Elizabeth 'Bessie' May Shore née Shaw (10th October 1896–1975). She was born at Abergavenny, Monmouthshire and had married Herbert Shore (1876–1954) in 1918 at Coventry. Herbert had married previously Sarah Ann Collins (1881–1916) in 1904 at Dartford, Kent. She was born at Cambridge. Herbert was a tinsmith's labourer in 1911 and they were living at 14 St Agnes Lane, Coventry. Herbert and Sarah had four children – Elsie Violet Shore 1906, Herbert Shore 1908, Percy W Shore 1913 and Arthur W Shore 1915. Herbert and Bessie had five children:

- Elizabeth M Shore (born and died 1918).
- Irene Doris Shore (March 1920–7th May 1980) married John Quinn in 1938. They had two children – John T Quinn 1940 and Robert Quinn 1942. Irene married Edward William Gaylor (10th March 1917–28th July 1980) in 1960. He had previously married Iris L Catchpole (born 1919) in 1941 and they had two children – Edward A Gaylor 1943 and Yvonne I Gaylor 1944. Irene was living at 24 Brooklyn Road, Coventry at the time of her death there. Edward was living at 21 Hunter Street, Rugby, Warwickshire at the time of his death there.
- Bessie Ethel Shore (11th July 1922–17th October 2007) married Arthur K Houghton in 1945. It is understood that the marriage ended in divorce. Bessie married Richard Martin (1925–2013) in 1971. Arthur married Joan G Povey also in 1971.
- Joseph H Shore (1925–47).
- June R Shore (born 1935).

24 Brooklyn Road, Foleshill, where Bill and Bessie lived.

No trace of a marriage between William and Bessie has been found. Bill moved to 24 Brooklyn Road, Foleshill, Coventry in 1947 and joined the Coventry Gauge & Tool Co as a commissionaire and later as a progress chaser until he retired in 1960. He and Bessie were living at 24 Brooklyn Road in 1954. Bessie's death was registered as Elizabeth May Beesley and she was buried with

Bill, recorded as his wife on the gravestone. Bessie's father, Joseph Shaw (1st July 1870–1943), was born at St Phillips Marsh, Bristol, Gloucestershire. He was living with his mother, Elizabeth, and grandfather, Thomas Shaw, at 9 Mill Street, Abergavenny, Monmouthshire in 1881. Joseph joined the Army and served during the Second Boer War in South Africa. He married Mary née Jones (1878–1947), born at Crickhowell, Monmouthshire, on 1st December 1895 at Crickhowell. They lived at 6 Lion Street, Abergavenny. In addition to Bessie they had nine other children, including:

- Rose Shaw (born and died 1898).
- William Joseph Shaw (1906–4th December 1968) married Florrie 'Dolly' Rice (7th July 1906–11th December 1967) on 31st January 1928 at St Faith's Church, Llanfoist, Abergavenny, where she was born. They had twins, born on 7th September 1930– Neville E Shaw (stillborn) and William Joseph Shaw (died 4th February 1990).
- Reginald John Shaw (born and died 1909).
- Thomas Edwin Shaw (16th December 1914–January 2002) married Gladys Edith Phillips (17th September 1918–June 2002) in 1939. They are understood to have had four children – Michael J Shaw 1944, Peter E Shaw 1949, Jeanette MM Shaw 1951 and Richard S Shaw 1953.

Bill attended a number of VC Reunions – the VC Garden Party at Buckingham Palace on 26th June 1920, the VC Dinner at the Royal Gallery of the House of Lords, London on 9th November 1929, the Victory Day Celebration Dinner & Reception at The Dorchester, London on 8th June 1946 and the VC Centenary Celebrations at Hyde Park, London on 26th June 1956. He attended the

Coventry Gauge & Tool Co was started in 1913 by Walter Tatlow at Earlsdon House, making tools and gauges for the engineering industry. He was bought out by his brother-In-law, Harry H Harley (later Sir Harry CBE), who changed the company name to Coventry Gauge and Small Tool Co Ltd. In 1936 a new factory was built in Coventry and in 1939 a factory was established at Brechin, Scotland. The company later changed its name to Matrix and continues in various forms but no longer produces high quality tools.

Bessie's father, Joseph (top centre), while serving in the Army.

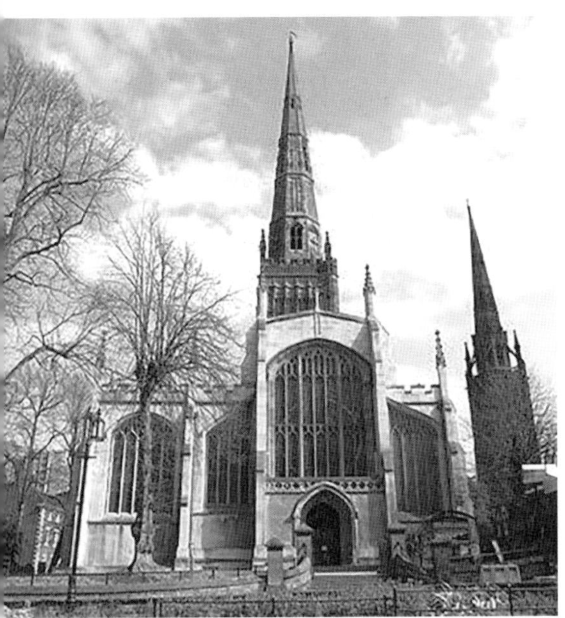

Holy Trinity Church dates from the 12th century and is the only complete medieval church in Coventry. Its spire, at seventy-two metres high, is one of the tallest non-cathedral spires in the country. Various repairs and additions were made, particlarly in 1665–68, 1786, 1826, 1843 and 1854. The 'doom painting', created above the tower arch in the 1430s, was discovered in 1831 covered in lime wash, and was restored. It required complete restoration again in 1995 and the conservation work was completed in 2004.

Bill's grave in St Paul's Cemetery, Harbrook Lane, Coventry (Memorials to Valour).

Nevill Hall was built in the 1860s for James Charles Hill of Blaenafon Iron Works. Originally known as The Brooks, it was purchased in 1890 by the Marquess of Abergavenny and renamed Nevill Court. He died in 1915 and the house was sold as Nevill Hall. In 1920 it became a hospital and Bill Beesley died there in September 1966. When the modern Nevill Hall Hospital was built in the 1970s, the old house became a conference and training centre for the health authority.

Dedication of the memorial to Arthur Hutt VC in War Memorial Park, Coventry on 17th April 1955. On the left is the Reverend Arthur Proctor VC. To the left of the memorial is Henry Tandey VC DCM MM and to the right is William Beesley VC. Henry Tandey attended Bill's funeral in 1966.

funeral of Arthur Hutt VC on 20th April 1954, at Canley Crematorium, Coventry, with fellow VCs Henry Tandey and the Reverend Arthur Procter. A year later, on 17th April 1955, Bill was present with Henry Tandey VC at the dedication ceremony

Memorial in the Memorial Park (Memorials to Valour).

Bill's commemorative paving stone in War Memorial Grounds, High Cross Bank, Castle Gresley (Memorials to Valour).

The Defence Medal was instituted in May 1945 for non-operational military and certain types of civilian war service (Home Guard, Civil Defence, Royal Observer Corps, Fire Service and other approved civilian services) from 3rd September 1939 to 8th May 1945 and for the Pacific Theatre until 2nd September 1945. In the United Kingdom military personnel in headquarters, training units and airfields were eligible for the award. Qualifying service varied. In the United Kingdom the requirement was three years or three months in a Mine and Bomb Disposal Unit. In a non-operational area, not subjected to air attack and not closely threatened, the requirement was one year's service overseas outside the individual's country of residence. In a non-operational area subjected to air attack or closely threatened, the requirement was six months.

of a memorial to Arthur Hutt VC in Coventry's War Memorial Park. The ceremony was performed by the Reverend Arthur Procter VC and the memorial was unveiled by the Lord Mayor, Alderman J Fennell.

Bill was on holiday with his wife at Abergavenny, when he was taken ill on 23rd September 1966 and died at Nevill Hall Hospital, Abergavenny. His funeral was held at Holy Trinity Church, Coventry on 29th September and was attended by Henry Tandey VC DCM MM. Bill is buried in St Paul's Cemetery, Harbrook Lane, Coventry. The gravestone was vandalised in April 2007 and was later refurbished and an additional plaque was added. He is commemorated in a number of other places:

- William Beesley Crescent, Gamecock Barracks, Bramcote, Nuneaton.
- Rifle Brigade Memorial, Winchester Cathedral, Hampshire.
- Memorial plaque on the War Memorial, Coventry.
- A Department for Communities and Local Government commemorative paving stone was dedicated at War Memorial Grounds, High Cross Bank, Castle Gresley, Swadlincote, Staffordshire on 8th May 2018 to mark the centenary of his award.

In addition to the VC he was awarded the 1914–15 Star, British War Medal 1914–20, Victory Medal 1914–19, Defence Medal, War Medal 1939–45, George VI Coronation Medal 1937, Elizabeth II Coronation Medal 1953 and the French Médaille Militaire. Bill used to keep his medals in a brown paper bag in a drawer. They are held by the Royal Green Jackets (Rifles) Museum (incorporating The Rifle Brigade (Prince Consort's Own) and Oxfordshire & Buckinghamshire Light Infantry King's Royal Rifle Corps), Peninsula Barracks, Romsey Road, Winchester, Hampshire.

LIEUTENANT ALBERT CHALMERS BORELLA
26th Australian Infantry Battalion AIF

Albert Borella was born on 7th August 1881 at Borung, near Mysia, Victoria, Australia. His father, Louis Borella (c.1853–16th February 1922), a farmer, married Annie Fair Black née Chalmers (21st October 1853–10th January 1885) in 1880. He married Catherine 'Kate' Baines (1862–1941) in 1889. They moved to the Southern Riverina in 1902, where his brother-in-law, Archie Chalmers, had set up at *Rangemore*, west of Deniliquin in 1895. The Borella farm was named *Deepdene* at Thyra Road, Moama, part of the Perricoota Station. The property was farmed by the Borella family for almost a century. Louis and Kate drove to Echuca on 16th February 1922 and were sitting outside the American Hotel when he fell off his chair. He was pronounced dead when medical assistance arrived. Albert had eight siblings from his father's two marriages:

Albert's father, Louis Borella.

- Beatrice Elizabeth Alfreda Borella (1880–1955), born at Mount Korong, Victoria (registered as Elizabeth Borella), married Alfred Henry Kirkland (1876–1954) on 14th March 1914 at Thyra, Moama, Victoria. She is understood to have been known as Lily.
- Annie Aurora Borella (1884–1927) married Donald Brown in 1910. He was a police constable in 1914 and they were living at Howitt Street, Ballarat North. By 1925 he was a hotelkeeper and they were living at 138 Peel Street, Ballarat North. They had two children:
    - Douglas McGregor Brown (29th August 1911–5th May 1976) married Irene Gladys Nelson (born 9th December 1915) in 1935 and they were living at 46 Tress Street, Ballarat in 1937. He was a foreman in 1963, living at Lot 89, Highlands Road, Thomastown, Victoria and a painter in 1967 living at 156 Sackville Street, Collingwood North, Victoria and was still there in 1972. They had a daughter, Irene Aurora Brown (20th August 1935–27th

December 2016). It is assumed that the marriage broke down. Irene married William Charles Tasman Fazackerley (6th June 1922–11th August 2000), born at Hobart, Tasmania, in 1946. He was a machinist in 1949 and they were living at 131 Bathurst Street, Denison, Hobart. They moved to Victoria in August 1950 after he joined the Royal Australian Air Force Air Training Corps as a pilot officer. Irene was a saleswoman and they were living at 8 Craigavad Street, Henty, Carnegie, Victoria.

  - Dorothy Nicholson Brown (20th November 1916–1991) married Percival Phillip Chalmers (14th September 1906–5th July 1969) on 20th December 1945. He was born at Moama, New South Wales, son of Archibald Gordon Chalmers, son of the VC's cousin. He enlisted in 2/8th Australian Infantry Battalion at Caulfield, Victoria (VX43805) on 8th July 1940 and reached the rank of sergeant before being discharged on 12th December 1945. He was a farm labourer and they were living at Springdale, Rangemore, New South Wales in 1958.
- Margaret Olive Borella (18th February 1890–2nd December 1979), born at Korong Vale, Victoria, married William John Swan (13th May 1891–26th August 1971) on 27th September 1915. They had two children:
  - James Borella Swan (23rd November 1918–3rd March 1969) won certificates for his writing and art contributions in the *Sunbeams* supplement to *The Sunday Sun* newspaper. He studied art at East Sydney Technical College, Darlinghurst and an exhibition of his work was published in *The Sydney Morning Herald* in 1938. He had a cartoon published in *The Australian Women's Weekly* in 1936 and *Smith's Weekly* in May 1940, before regularly contributing cartoons to *The Bulletin*. James enlisted in the Australian Army at Kyogle, New South Wales on 1st September 1942 (NX141757 (N99868)). He was discharged as a sergeant from 2 Australian Field Survey Company on 9th November 1945. He married Dorothy Margaret Doyle, a nurse from Queensland, in September 1945. His work appeared regularly in *The Australian Women's Mirror* 1946–51 and he also contributed one-page humorous features for KG Murray comics, including *The Adventures of Billy Binghi*, *Splinter*, *Herb's Helicopter*, *Michael and his Midget Racer* and *Atomical Tom the Boy Inventor*. He was a salesman and they were living at 4 South Street, East Toowoomba, Queensland in 1954. They had several children, including William Doyle Swan.
  - Lawson John Swan (26th April 1923–26 February 1995) married Melva Ruth and they had two daughters. He was a manager in 1977 and they were living at 20 Dalton Road, St Ives, New South Wales.
- Percy Louis Borella, born and died 1891.
- Charles Borella (1893–28th October 1960) was a labourer when he enlisted in 7th Battalion AIF on 3rd November 1915 at Melbourne, Victoria (6224). He was described as 5′ 6″ tall, weighing 131 lbs, with fresh complexion, hazel eyes,

auburn hair and his religious denomination was Methodist. He embarked at Melbourne aboard HMAT A14 *Euripides* on 11th September 1916, arriving at Plymouth, Devon on 26th October. He went to France aboard HMS *Golden Eagle* from Folkestone, Kent, arriving at Étaples on 18th December. Charles received a gunshot wound to his right leg on 25th February 1917 and was admitted to 2nd Australian General Hospital. He was evacuated to England, where he was admitted to the County of Middlesex Red Cross Hospital, Fulham on 4th March. He transferred to 3rd Auxiliary Hospital on 23rd March and to Windmill Hill Camp, Perham Down, Wiltshire for convalescence on 26th March. He transferred to 66th Battalion on 28th April and was appointed temporary driver 26th May–24th September. He sailed for France from Southampton, Hampshire on 1st January 1918. Charles received a gunshot wound to the chest on 14th April and was treated at 2nd Australian Field Ambulance before being transferred to No.15 Casualty Clearing Station on the same day. He was transferred to 25th General Hospital, Étaples the following day and was evacuated to England, where he was admitted to 1st Southern General Hospital, Birmingham on 20th April. He was transferred to 1st Auxiliary Hospital, Harefield on 31st May and embarked for return to Australia for discharge on 30th June. He married Eva Florence Cowell (18th February 1894–8th September 1977) in 1922. Charles was a farmer in 1935 and they were living at *Deepdene*, Thyra Road, Moama.

- James Borella (1895–19th August 1919), born at Boort, Victoria, enlisted in 7th Battalion AIF on 24th May 1916 at Melbourne (6226). He was described as 5′ 7¼″ tall, weighing 136 lbs, with fresh complexion, blue eyes, brown hair and his religious denomination was Church of England. He embarked at Melbourne aboard HMAT A14 *Euripides* with his brother Charles on 11th September 1916, arriving at Plymouth on 26th October. He went to France aboard HMS *Golden Eagle* from Folkestone, Kent, arriving at Étaples on 18th December. James was evacuated to England aboard HMHS *Dunluce Castle* with influenza on 29th December and was admitted to Norfolk War Hospital, Norwich. He convalesced at Windmill Hill Camp, Perham Down. On 15th February 1917 he transferred to No.4 Command Depot, Wareham, Dorset. He was charged with the theft of a pair of infantry breeches from a comrade on 16th March and forfeited two days' pay. James was taken on strength of 65th Battalion on 23rd March and returned to 7th Battalion on 19th September. He received a gunshot wound to the left thigh on 9th August 1918 and was evacuated to England, where he was admitted to the Royal Victoria Hospital, Folkestone, Kent on 13th August. He was transferred to the Military Hospital, Shorncliffe, Kent on 9th September and to No.3 Australian Auxiliary Hospital, Dartford, Kent 13th September–20th September. James was attached to 177th Tunnelling Company RE on 13th December. He embarked on HMAT A40 *Ceramic* on 25th January 1919 and was discharged from 3rd Military District, Melbourne on 30th April. James died at Echuca, Victoria.

- Rex Thomas Borella (1897–16th August 1954), born at Wychitella, near Boort, enlisted in 8th Light Horse Regiment AIF on 2nd August 1915 at Melbourne (1949). He was described as 5′ 7¾″ tall, weighing 126 lbs, with fair complexion, blue eyes, light brown hair and his religious denomination was Presbyterian. He sailed aboard HMAT A1 *Hymettus* on 27th January 1916 and was taken on strength of 3rd Reserve Regiment at Heliopolis, Egypt on 6th March. He joined the Australian Camel Training Unit at Port Said on 2nd November and attended 17th Signals Course at the Imperial School of Instruction, qualifying on 9th December. Rex was posted to No.4 Anzac Battalion, Imperial Camel Brigade on 12th February 1917 and transferred to the Reserve Depot Company (Imperial Camel Corps) the following day. He was admitted to the Government Hospital, Suez with mumps on 17th March. Admitted to 24th Stationary Hospital with cystitis 2nd-4th August, then transferred to No.14 Australian General Hospital, Abbassia, Cairo with debility. He transferred to the British Red Cross Convalescent Hospital, Montaza on 31st October and forfeited three days' pay for being in town without a pass on 9th November. He returned to duty next day, was taken on strength at HQ Abbassia on 13th December and was detached to Port Said Rest Camp on 22nd May 1918. He rejoined 4th Anzac Battalion on 2nd June and 8th Light Horse Regiment on 31st July. Rex returned to Australia aboard HT D17 *Malta* on 3rd July 1919. He married Ruby Elizabeth Clemo (1894–1958) in 1922. In 1920 he was a noxious weed inspector and they were living at Chanter Street, Moama. By 1935 they had moved to Livingstone Street, Mathoura. Rex had taken up farming at Macorna, Victoria by 1949. They had at least one son:
    - Louis Maxwell Borella (1st April 1924–1986) enlisted in the Royal Australian Air Force on 19th May 1942 (56125) and joined No.4 School of Technical Training, Adelaide, South Australia on 7th June. Appointed mess steward at No.2 Air Navigation School, Nhill, Victoria on 26th August and joined No.31 Squadron, Wagga Wagga, New South Wales on 25th September. Promoted leading aircraftsman on 20th November. The Squadron moved to Batchelor, Northern Territory on 17th October and Coomalie Creek on 12th November. He was posted to No.55 Operational Base Unit, Birdum on 23rd August 1943 and reverted to aircraftsman class II on re-muster on 9th October. Posted to No.1 Initial Training School, Somers, Victoria for aircrew training 9th October–30th December. Promoted leading aircraftsman at No.2 Embarkation Depot, Sydney on 3rd January 1944. Moved to No.1 Embarkation Depot, Ascot Vale, Victoria on 13th January and sailed to Canada from Melbourne 17th January–8th February. Joined No.2 Manning Depot RCAF, Brandon, Manitoba for Wireless Operators' Course, Winnipeg 26th February–6th October. Attended a Wireless Operator (Air Gunner) and Air Gunners' Course at No.2 Bombing and Gunnery School, Mossbank, Saskatchewan 23rd October–1st December 1944. Promoted sergeant 1st December and returned to Australia, arriving

at Brisbane, Queensland on 16th January 1945, where he was posted to No.3 Personnel Depot. Transferred to No.1 Personnel Depot, Melbourne on 18th February and to No.1 Wireless Air Gunners' School, Ballarat, Victoria on 1st March. Appointed temporary flight sergeant 1st June. Returned to No.1 Personnel Depot, Melbourne on 20th August and transferred to the Reserve on 29th August 1945. Demobilised on 25th July 1947. Louis assisted his father on the family farm at Macorna, Victoria. He married Alice Kathleen Robinson (4th November 1927–25th July 1986) on 23rd May 1959. They were farming at Macorna in 1977 and at Murrabit, near Kerang, Victoria in 1980. They had a son and two daughters.

- Louis Borella (1899–1966), born at Korong Vale, married Olive Mary Raggart in 1944 at Lake Cargelligo, New South Wales. He was a grazier and they were living at Bogia Tank, Cargelligo in 1963.

Albert's paternal grandfather, Pietro 'Peter' Borella (c.1819–22nd November 1891), was born in Florence, Tuscany, Italy, son of Pietro Borella and Maria Biseti. He moved to Britain on 1st May 1839 and teamed up with a Frenchman, known as William Quinton, to defraud Thomas Barton Rutley of the Ship Hotel, Dover, of 500 Francs. They used a forged promissory note from GJ Mauduit of 41 Regent Circus, London. Rutley had occasionally acted as an agent for Mauduit and assumed that the note from Quinton was genuine. He handed over the money but subsequently contacted Mauduit and learned that no such promissory note had been issued. Borella (also known as Luigi Baldassi) was apprehended at Commercial Quay public house on 2nd December 1839. Quinton was located from a letter found in Borella's possession and was also apprehended. The two men appeared before Lord Abinger at the Crown Court Spring Assizes at Maidstone, Kent and were convicted on 9th March 1840. They were sentenced to fourteen years penal servitude in Van Dieman's Land (Tasmania) and sailed on 25th April 1840 on SV *Asia*. Pietro married Alfreda née

Albert's paternal grandfather, Pietro Borella was born in Florence, Italy.

The Ship Hotel in Dover, where Pietro Borella and William Quinton defrauded Thomas Barton Rutley of 500 Francs, using a forged promissory note. They were convicted on 9th March 1840 and sentenced to penal servitude in Van Dieman's Land. Pietro was eventually freed there and lived the rest of his life in Australia.

Kidner (20th August 1831–25th May 1867), born at Sorell, Tasmania, on 15th May 1849 at Port Sorell, Hobart, Tasmania. Pietro made a number of journeys from Launceston to Melbourne on a conditional pardon on 21st February 1852, 20th May 1853 and 20th December 1853, the first aboard the *Gem* and the others on the *Yarra Yarra*. On 29th August 1854 he made the same journey as a free man on the *Lady Bird*. He died in Talbot Hospital, Victoria. In addition to Louis they had six other children:

- Louisa Borella born on 6th August 1849 at Spring Bay, Tasmania.
- Albert Borella (26th September 1853–1st March 1906), born at Hobart, Tasmania, married Annie Kershaw (2nd September 1861–2nd August 1942) in 1885 at Baulkamaugh, near Creswick, Victoria. He died in Queensland. They had a daughter prior to their marriage, Annie Borella Kershaw, in 1883. Annie senior married John Scott (c.1857–25th December 1939).
- Michael Angelo Borella (1860–61), born at Baulkamaugh, Victoria.
- Angelo Borella (1861–77), born and died at Talbot, Victoria.
- Ellen Borella (1863–1902) married Robert Hill (5th April 1859–1925), born at Warrnambool, Victoria, on 18th March 1883 at Talbot. He was a carter in 1914 living at Talbot Flat, Victoria. They had eight children – Albert Louis Hill 1883, Robert Angelo Hill 1884, Albert Robert Hill 1885, Florence Alfreda Hill 1886, Harry Hill 1889, Albert Louis Hill 1892, Leonard Hill 1893 and Helen Hill 1899. Ellen's death was recorded as Helen.
- Pietro Borella (1865–67).

His maternal grandfather, Archibald Chalmers (31st January 1826–16th November 1909), a joiner, was born at Airdrie, Lanarkshire, Scotland. He married Beatrice (or Beatrix) née Main (3rd March 1825–4th January 1906), also born at Airdrie, Lanarkshire, on 9th August 1846 at Airdrie. She died at Fell Brae Farm, Ballarat, Victoria and he died at 51 Gower Street, Kensington, Victoria. In addition to Annie they had nine other children:

Both of Albert's maternal grandparents came from Airdrie, Lanarkshire, Scotland.

- Janet Chalmers (born 1st November 1848), born at Airdrie.
- Jessie Forsyth Main Chalmers (1849–23rd March 1919), born at Airdrie, married George Bedford Leech (1850–1928) in 1877 in Victoria, Australia. They lived at 38 Park Street, St Kilda, Victoria. They had six children – Beatrice Annetta Leech 1878, Katie Annie Aurora Phyllis Leech 1879, Jessica Grazilda D'Auvert Leech 1881, George Hugo Henry John Chalmers Leech 1883, Archie Royal Percy Gordon Leech 1888 and Grace Leech.

- John Banks Chalmers (1851–1925), born in Geelong, Victoria, married Annie Bird (1858–1931) in 1884. He died at Mysia, Victoria and she at Boort, Victoria. They had five children – John Chalmers 1885, Annie Chalmers 1886, Archibald Thompson Chalmers 1887, Arthur Gordon Chalmers 1890 and Roderick Thomas Chalmers 1895. The first three children did not survive infancy.
- David Forsyth Main Chalmers (5th April 1856–23rd June 1932), born at Ballarat, Victoria, married Amelia Chesterman (12th August 1858–4th July 1916) on 9th July 1877 at Wedderburn, Victoria. He was a farmer living at Canary Island, Pyramid Hill, Victoria in 1931. They both died at Bendigo, Victoria. They had sixteen children – Beatrice Hannabel Chalmers 1877, John White Chalmers 1879, James Chesterman Chalmers 1881, Amelia Elizabeth Chalmers 1882, Annie Isabella Chalmers 1884, Rose Chalmers 1886, David Forsyth Main Chalmers 1888, Archibald Chesterman Chalmers 1889, Grace Gordon Chalmers 1891, Jessie Charlotte Chalmers 1892, Gertrude Jean Chalmers 1895, Wallace Hugh Chalmers 1897, Ninnie Mildred Chalmers 1897, Gordon Mark Grafton Chalmers 1898, Mildren Winfred Chalmers 1902 and Dorothy Chalmers 1906.
- Thomas Main Gordon Chalmers (6th August 1859–21st February 1939) married Elizabeth Chalmers (1858–23rd December 1941) in 1878. He was one of the largest landowners in the Edward River district of New South Wales and was elected to the Korong Shire Council until his retirement in 1929. They both died at Mysia, Victoria. They had nine children – Archibald Gordon Chalmers 1878, Elizabeth Beatrice Chalmers 1881, Jessie Victoria Chalmers 1884, Thomas Main Chalmers 1887, John Bird Chalmers 1889, David Alexander Chalmers 1891, Peter Chalmers 1893, George Hugh Chalmers 1895 and Annie Isabel Chalmers 1900. David Alexander Chalmers served as a private in 7th Battalion AIF (2598A) and was killed in action on 20th August 1916 (Villers-Bretonneux Memorial, France). Peter Chalmers served as a private in 38th Battalion AIF (1815) and was killed in action on 13th October 1917 (Ypres (Menin Gate Memorial, Belgium).
- Isabelle Aurora Chalmers (25th January 1860–16th November 1945) married Roderick Falconer Munro (1858–4th July 1924) in 1893 at Mount Rowan, Ballarat. He died at Clifton Hill, Victoria and she at Surrey Hills, Victoria. They had two children – Erle Falconer Munro 1895 and Aurora Rhoda Alfreda Munro 1901.
- Elizabeth Beatrice Chalmers (1863–28th June 1934) married Henry George Frederick Chick (1866–1936) on 22nd January 1895 at Pancras, London, England. His birth was registered at St Luke, London. He was a musician and a seaman. His death was registered at London City. Elizabeth died at Bondi, New South Wales. They had four children – Beatrice Marguerite Chick 1895, Edward Archibald Chick 1897, George Frederick Walter Chick (28th July 1899–24th June 1954) and Francis Kelsall Chick (1904–77).
- Grace Gordon Chalmers (1866–1939) married Alex Constantine Horne (1872–1913) in 1900 at Melbourne, Victoria. He was born in Russia, son of Ulevos Andreaff and Nadeshda Nicoliva, and emigrated to Australia, where he changed his name to

Horne. Alex was a cycle agent in 1905 and they were living at Laanecoorie, Victoria before moving to Dawson Street, Ararat, Victoria c.1909. Grace moved in with her son, Gordon, at Banfield Street, Ararat in 1925. They had a son, Gordon Chalmers Horne (1901–28), who was a gas fitter.

- Archibald Hugh Chalmers (19th December 1869–20th July 1957) married Cecilia Elizabeth Brewster (4th May 1868–1958) in 1899 at Learmonth, Victoria. They were living at Rangemore, Deniliquin, New South Wales in 1936 and at 90 Harfleur Street, Deniliquin in 1954. They had six children – John Chalmers 1900, Neimur Grace Chalmers 1903, Cecilia E Chalmers 1904, Archibald Alexander Chalmers 1907, Ernest J Chalmers 1909 and Marion Agnes Chalmers 1912.

After his mother's death, Albert lived with his maternal grandparents for four years at Mount Rowan, returning to live with his father when he remarried in 1889. Albert was educated at Borung State School and Wychitella State School, both in Victoria. He worked with his father as a farmer in the Borung and Echuca district. In 1903, while out hunting game, he was bitten on the finger by a venomous tiger snake. Being fifty kilometres from medical aid he put the finger over the muzzle of his rifle and blew off the affected part. He was a member of Thyra Rifle Club, which was affiliated to the Victorian Rangers. Albert served for eighteen months with a volunteer infantry company of the Victoria Rangers around 1909. He moved to Melbourne in April 1910 and joined the Metropolitan Fire Brigade, serving until he resigned on 17th January 1913, with two work colleagues, Ronald Parker and Albert Lewis.

Wychitella State School, where Albert was educated.

Albert worked for three years on the Melbourne Metropolitan Fire Brigade between 1910 and 1913. A volunteer Melbourne Fire Prevention Society was established in 1845 and later a number of volunteer brigades were formed by insurance companies, municipalities and other institutions. By 1890 there were fifty-six volunteer brigades in Melbourne. After several serious fires that year resulted in the loss of life of six firefighters, the *Fire Brigades Act 1890* was passed to unite the rival fire brigades. The fifty-six existing brigades were disbanded and firefighters were invited to join the new organization. On 1st May 1891 the Metropolitan Fire Brigade formed with a strength as fifty-nine permanent firefighters, 229 auxiliary firefighters, four steam fire engines, twenty-five horse drawn hose carts and fifty-eight hose reels, thirty-three horses and forty-eight stations. In 1950, volunteer and partly-paid firefighters were discontinued and in September 1988 female firefighters were permitted to join for the first time.

He travelled with them to Darwin, Northern Territory to return to farming, arriving on SS *St Albans* on 24th February. When they arrived, the blocks of farming land had not yet been allotted, so they worked for two months at the Batchelor experimental farm and one month in Darwin. In April 1913 they gained Section 2 or 3, Hundred of Berinka, County of Malmesbury, west of Hermit Hill on the Daly River. It was described as, *about 100 acres of jungle with good dark soil, 30 acres of swamp. Dry about six months of the year; remainder open with few bushes and trees, and well grassed. Good soil.* They found farming there very different to Australia's south, so they applied to the Land Board in May for a block on the other side of the Daly River. The Land Board agreed and they made a direct swap to Section 9 in the Hundred of Hawkshaw of 566 acres. During the dry season they spent another five months working on the experimental farm to gain experience and earn some money. In November 1913 Parker withdrew from the lease and Albert decided to go on alone. In January 1914 he applied to the Board for land on higher ground for the wet season. An additional fifty acres was allocated in Section 10. With the assistance of Aboriginal workers, and a loan at four percent from the Land Board, he purchased building materials and set to work on a house. While it was being built, he was not earning and had to feed himself and his workers. The house was described by the Land Board as *one of the best houses on the Daly*. He cleared ground for cultivation, ring-barked the trees and sunk a timber lined well ten metres deep. With his Aboriginal workers he erected about three kilometres of fencing. The government had agreed to supply farming equipment and livestock but after five months he received a single horse and eventually harness and a dray, but no plough. In May 1914 he signed an unregistered Memorandum of Mortgage with the Board to cover the £125 that had been advanced and a further loan of £190, using his house, horse and fencing wire as security. In October he travelled to Darwin to meet with officials and resolve his financial commitments. He then intended to join the Army. However, the government would not enlist volunteers from the Territory. On the strength of the capital improvements he had made, he was advanced £67 but did not have an income and could not look for work elsewhere because he was tied to the block. An old friend, an assistant surveyor heading to Tennant Creek on a survey party, offered him a job as the cook. In October 1914 Albert set off with the survey party but did not like the work. He remained until January 1915, by when he had saved enough money to pay back the loan.

Albert left the survey party and set off on foot with an Aboriginal named Charlie. They walked along the Overland Telegraph track and crossed flooded rivers to reach Renner Springs, where he borrowed a horse from the mailman at Powell Creek. He rode the 400 kms to Katherine and hitched a ride on a horse drawn mail buggy. At Pine Creek he took a train to Darwin, arriving towards the end of February. The 1,000 kms journey had taken six weeks. It was re-enacted in 2015 as the Borella Ride. However, he could not enlist at Darwin and had to get to Townsville, Queensland, 2,000 kms away. He did not have any money but was helped by Walter Bell, a keen supporter of the war effort, who arranged Albert's move on SS *Aldenham*, embarking on 8th March.

He enlisted in 26th Battalion AIF at Townsville, Queensland on 15th March 1915 and was assigned to B Company at Enoggera, Brisbane on 24th May (275). He embarked the following day from Brisbane aboard HMAT A11 *Ascanius* and disembarked at Suez, Egypt, then proceeded to the camp at Heliopolis. He proceeded on operational service with the Battalion from Alexandria to Gallipoli on 4th September and was promoted corporal on 8th September. On 19th November he reported sick with jaundice and was transferred successively to 5th Field Ambulance, 7th Field Ambulance, No.13 Casualty Clearing Station and then to Mudros. He was evacuated on 20th November on HMHS *Delta* to Heliopolis, Egypt, where he was admitted to No.3 Auxiliary Hospital on 26th November. On 10th December he transferred to the Australian Overseas Base, Cairo and to the training camp at Zeitoun, Cairo on 28th January 1916. He rejoined the Battalion at Tel-el-Kebir on 5th February.

Albert embarked with the Battalion at Alexandria on 15th March to join the British Expeditionary Force, arriving at Marseille, France on 21st March. He suffered from mumps and parotitis and was transferred successively to 6th Field Ambulance, 1st Canadian Casualty Clearing Station and 7th General Hospital on 8th May. Promoted lance sergeant the same day. He was discharged from hospital on 30th May and returned to the Battalion on 2nd June. He received a gunshot wound to the right arm near Fleurbaix on 29th July and was evacuated to No.4 Casualty Clearing Station next day. He was transferred by ambulance

Enoggera Camp in 1915.

HMAT A11 *Ascanius* leaving Melbourne in November 1915. SS *Ascanius* (10,048 tons) was built in 1910 at Liverpool for the Ocean Steamship Co, known as the Blue Funnel Line because of the distinctive funnels. She was requisitioned by the Commonweath of Australia in 1914 as a troopship and was one of the fleet of twenty-eight Australian and ten New Zealand transports that left Albany, Western Australia on 1st November 1914 carrying the First Detachment of the Australian and New Zealand Imperial Expeditionary Forces. *Ascanius* was returned to her owner in 1920. In 1940 she was requisitioned by the Admiralty as a troopship. On 30th July 1944, U-621 attacked convoy EBC-54 in the English Channel and claimed a ship sunk. This was *Ascanius* but she was only damaged and was towed to Normandy and later to Liverpool, where she was repaired by Cammell Laird. She had been en route to the Normandy beaches for use as a depot ship. After the war, *Ascanius* carried Jewish emigrants from Marseille to Haifa and in 1949 was sold and renamed *San Giovannino* for Cia de Nav Florencia, Genoa. She was broken up at La Spezia in July 1952.

train to 3rd Canadian General Hospital, Boulogne the same day. On 3rd August he was evacuated to England aboard HMHS *Jan Breydal* and was admitted to 3rd Northern General Hospital, Sheffield. He was discharged to Tidworth, Wiltshire on 12th September and to No.1 Command Depot, Perham Down next day. He was on convalescent leave 14th September–1st November and returned to France on *Princess Henrietta* on 2nd November. Next day he joined 2nd Australian Division Base Depot at Étaples and returned to the Battalion on 20th November.

Marseille was the main port of disembarkation for troops moving from Egypt to the Western Front.

Albert was promoted sergeant on 6th January 1917. He suffered from influenza and was transferred successively to 5th Australian Field Ambulance followed by the ANZAC CR Station on 14th January. He rejoined the Battalion on 22nd January. **Awarded the MM for his actions at Malt Trench, north of Warlencourt, on 1st-2nd March. He displayed conspicuous bravery and assisted Lieutenant Ward in reorganising the men and consolidating the line, LG 11th May 1917. Mentioned in Sir Douglas Haig's Despatch dated 9th April 1917 in recognition of his devotion to duty and general good work in the trenches since the Battalion has been in Gallipoli and France, LG 1st June 1917.**

During his leave in England in June 1917, Albert met up with his half-brothers, Jim (left) and Charlie, in London.

On 7th April 1917 Albert was commissioned and was granted leave to England on 2nd June, returning to the Battalion on 13th June. He was posted to England on 9th August to attend an officers' training course with 7th Training Battalion at Rollestone Camp, commencing on 12th August. He was promoted lieutenant on 28th August and, having passed the course, transferred to 5th Training Battalion, Overseas Training Brigade at Longbridge Deverill, Wiltshire on 8th November. He returned to Belgium from Folkestone on 27th November and rejoined the Battalion two days later. Albert was detached to the 7th Australian Brigade Raiding Party 2nd-31st December. He was granted leave in England on 28th January 1918. On 7th

March he was detached to the Australian Corps School and rejoined the Battalion on 28th March.

Awarded the VC for his actions at Villers-Bretonneux, France on 17th/18th July 1918, LG 16th September 1918. He was recommended initially for the DSO by Brigadier General Evan Alexander Wisdom, Commander 7th Australian Infantry Brigade, and Major General Sir Charles Rosenthal, GOC 2nd Australian Division, on 25th July 1918, but it was upgraded to a VC by higher authority. He was granted leave to Paris on 4th August and returned to the Battalion on 18th August. On 1st September he was granted leave to England. When it ended on 16th September, he was detached to AIF Headquarters, London pending special furlough to Australia. The VC was presented by the King at York Cottage, Sandringham, Norfolk on 7th October. He returned to Australia on HT D27 *Marathon*, embarking on 6th November and disembarking at Melbourne on 1st January 1919. He was discharged on 23rd February 1919.

Albert returned to farming on a soldier-settlement block near Hamilton, Victoria 1920–39. He was narrowly defeated as the National Party candidate for Dundas in the 1924 Legislative Assembly election. Albert married Elsie Jane Love (1895–10th August 1974), born at Hamilton, at the Wesley Church, Hamilton, Victoria on 16th August 1928. They lived at 958 Sylvania Avenue, North Albury, New South Wales. Albert changed his name by deed poll in September 1939, from when he and his family used the surname Chalmers-Borella. They had four children:

The Aberdeen Line ship, *Marathon* (6,793 tons), was built by Alexander Stephen & Sons, Glasgow in 1903. She, and her sister ship *Miltiades*, were the last two ships of any size to be built with a clipper stem and figurehead. *Marathon* commenced her maiden voyage from London for Cape Town, Melbourne and Sydney on 27th January 1904. In 1912 she was lengthened by fifteen metres to 153.57m and a second, dummy, funnel was added. In 1915 she became a troop transport as HMAT A74 *Marathon*. On 21st October 1920 she started her only post war commercial sailing from London for Cape Town, Sydney and Brisbane. In 1921 she was sold to Pacific Steam Navigation Co and was renamed *Oruba*. However, she only completed a few trips between Liverpool, Rio de Janeiro, Montevideo, Valparaiso and Panama Canal and was then laid up at Liverpool. In 1924 she was scrapped in Germany. The second picture shows troops disembarking from her at Port Melbourne in 1919.

- Mervyn Chalmers Borella (1930–16th August 1954) was a weaver.
- Maxwell Borella (1st March 1932–January 1999) was a timber worker in 1954, living with his parents. He married Mary Hilliar née Morrison (20th October 1916–23rd May 2005), born at Kyneton, Victoria, on 12th June 1963 at Alice Springs, Northern Territory. They had a son, Neville Chalmers-Borella. Mary had married Robert Thomas Hilliar (1907–94) in 1947 at Concord, New South Wales and had two children – Thomas Hilliar and Judith Hilliar. They divorced c.1960. Max died at Warrak, near Ararat and Mary at Ballarat, Victoria.
- Neville Chalmers Borella (c.1933–4th December 1960) drowned accidentally at Benning Waterhole on the Daly River, near Pine Creek, Northern Territory.
- Rowan Borella (born 1934) married Mary Helen Britt in 1959 and they lived at Lavington, Albury, New South Wales. He inherited his father's medals. They had a son, Richard Borella.

Elsie's father, George Frederick Love (1863–26th January 1924), married Alice née Thompson (1867–1961) on 31st March 1891.

Albert was transferred to the Reserve of Officers in 1934, from which he was appointed to serve as a lieutenant in 12th Australian Garrison Battalion on 15th October 1939. He transferred to the Prisoner-of-War Group, Rushworth, Victoria in July 1941 and was promoted captain on 2nd January 1942. He transferred to 51st Garrison Company, Myrtleford, Victoria on 16th March 1943 and served with it until 1945. After the war he became an Inspector of Dangerous Cargoes for the Commonwealth Department of Supply & Shipping until his retirement in 1956. He also ran a store in Albury with his wife.

He was one of twenty-three VCs who attended an Anzac Dinner on 23rd April 1927, hosted by Lieutenant General Sir John Monash GCMG KCB VD. For an unknown reason The Duke of York (future King George VI) was not invited. Albert took part in the Anzac Commemoration Service on 25th April at the Exhibition Building, Melbourne, Victoria in the presence of The Duke of York. In the march past the VCs conceded pride of place to blinded soldiers who insisted on marching. On 13th February 1954 Albert was presented to Queen Elizabeth II at Wagga Wagga, New South Wales during her Royal Tour of Australia. He was invited to attend the VC Centenary Celebrations at Hyde Park, London on 26th June 1956, travelling on SS *Orcades* along with other Australian VCs who were part of the 301

Albert meets Queen Elizabeth II and Prince Philip at Wagga Wagga in February 1954.

Albert's grave marker.

St David's Presbyterian Church, Albury was built in 1905 and is now a Uniting Church. Albert's funeral was held there in 1968.

Victoria Cross recipients from across the Commonwealth to attend. In 1964 he attended the opening of VC Corner at the Australian War Memorial by Governor General, Lord De L'Isle VC, along with seventeen other Australian VC's.

Albert died at his home at 958 Sylvania Avenue, North Albury, New South Wales on 7th February 1968. The funeral service at St David's Presbyterian Church, Olive Street, Albury was followed by burial in Pioneer Cemetery (Plan 11, Section PRES, Row B, Lot 12, Burial No.33605) on 9th February. He is commemorated in a number of other places:

- Australian Capital Territory
  - Australian Victoria Cross Recipients plaque on the Victoria Cross Memorial, Campbell, dedicated on 24th July 2000.
  - Named on one of eleven plaques honouring 175 men from overseas awarded the VC for the Great War. The plaques were unveiled by the Senior Minister of State at the Foreign & Commonwealth Office and Minister for Faith and Communities, Baroness Warsi, at a reception at Lancaster House, London on 26th June 2014 attended by The Duke of Kent and relatives of the VC recipients. The Australian plaque is at the Australian War Memorial.
  - Display in the Hall of Valour, Australian War Memorial.
  - Borella Street, Canberra.
- Northern Territory
  - Borella Park and Borella Circuit, Jingili, Darwin. A plaque was dedicated on 30th September 1980.
- Victoria
  - Borella VC Club, Bandiana, Albury Wodonga Military District.
  - Borella House, Bandiana Primary School, 44 Leumeah Road, Bandiana.
  - Borella Park, Korong Vale.

    - Named on the Victoria Cross Memorial at Springvale Botanical Cemetery, Melbourne unveiled on 10th November 2013.
    - Named on the War Memorial, Civic Gardens, Echuca.
- New South Wales
    - Victoria Cross Memorial, Queen Victoria Building, George Street, Sydney dedicated on 23rd February 1992 to commemorate the visit of Queen Elizabeth II and Prince Phillip on the occasion of the Sesquicentenary of the City of Sydney. Sir Roden Cutler VC AK KCMG, Edward Kenna VC and Keith Payne VC were in attendance.
    - Borella Road, Milperra, Sydney.
    - Victoria Cross Recipients Wall, North Bondi War Memorial donated to the community of Waverley on 27th November 2011 by The Returned & Services League of Australia.
    - Borella Cup contested quarterly at Deniliquin Golf Club.
    - Albury
        - Borella Road and a life sized bronze statue at Peards Complex.
        - Cafe Borellas, where a commemorative display was unveiled by Keith Payne VC on 7th June 2011.
        - Borella House Hostel, 331 Borella Road.
    - Roll of Honour, Sports Centre, Moama.
    - Roll of Honour, Womboota Hall.
- Communities and Local Government commemorative paving stones for the 145 VCs born in Australia, Belgium, Canada, China, Denmark, Egypt, France, Germany, India, Iraq, Japan, Nepal, Netherlands, Newfoundland, New Zealand, Pakistan, South Africa, Sri Lanka, Ukraine and United States

Echuca War Memorial was originally erected in High Street in 1927, as seen here. It has since been moved to the Civic Centre Gardens on Hare Street. The honour roll for the Second World War Two and later conflicts was unveiled on 30th January 1989.

Albert Borella's statue at Peards Complex, Albury.

of America were unveiled at the National Memorial Arboretum, Alrewas, Staffordshire by Prime Minister David Cameron MP and Sergeant Johnson Beharry VC on 5th March 2015.

In addition to the VC and MM he was awarded the 1914–15 Star, British War Medal 1914–20, Victory Medal 1914–19 with MID Oakleaf, War Medal 1939–45, Australia Service Medal 1939–45, George VI Coronation Medal 1937 and Elizabeth II Coronation Medal 1953. The VC is held by the Australian War Memorial, Treloar Crescent, Campbell, Australian Capital Territory.

1689A CORPORAL WALTER ERNEST BROWN
20th Australian Infantry Battalion AIF

Walter Brown was born on 3rd July 1885 at New Norfolk, Tasmania. He was known as Wally. His father, Sidney Francis Brown (8th June 1852–29th July 1930), of 48 Bathurst Street, Hobart, was a miller. He married Agnes Mary née Kearney (1852–94) on 6th July 1876 in Hobart. A number of variations of her surname have been seen. Walter had seven siblings:

- Agnes Mary Brown (1878–1949).
- Cecil Francis Michael Brown (born 27th May 1880) in Hobart.
- Sidney Thomas Brown (born 13th April 1882) emigrated to the USA and married Ann Parnel Hallett (born 1884) on 27th October 1913 at San Francisco.
- Charles James Emerald Brown (29th December 1883–1955), born at New Norfolk, served as a captain in the Mercantile Marine. He was Master of the schooner *Relic* (100 tons), which sailed from Adventure Bay, Tasmania for Adelaide, South Australia with a cargo of timber on 29th March 1910. The weather turned stormy at the Bay of Fires so Brown turned the ship towards Eddystone Point off the northeast coast of Tasmania, to seek shelter but was blown onto rocks there on 2nd April. A Court of Enquiry ruled that Brown's decision to seek shelter at

Petersham, New South Wales, to where the Browns moved from Tasmania. Now a suberb of Sydney, it began when Major Francis Grose had the bush cleared in 1793 to plant corn and wheat. He named the area after his native village in Surrey.

New Norfolk, Tasmania was established by 163 pioneers when the first Norfolk Island settlement closed, arriving between November 1807 and October 1808. They were mainly farmers, who were offered land in Tasmania in compensation. In 1825 the original name of Elizabeth Town was changed to New Norfolk. Many of the founders were *First Fleeters*, transferred from Sydney to Norfolk Island when it was settled a few weeks after Sydney. Ten of them are buried in the Methodist Chapel at Lawitta, New Norfolk. Amongst them is Betty King née Thackery, a first fleet convict who married at New Norfolk on 28th January 1810, *the first white woman to set foot in Australia*. Her husband, Marine Samuel King, arrived on HMS *Sirius*. The pioneers were successful farmers and hops were introduced in 1846. The settlement was connected to Hobart by road in 1818 and by rail in 1887.

Eddystone Point was reckless given the size of the vessel and he was suspended from holding a Master's Certificate for three months and reclassified as Mate. There was no financial penalty as he had suffered sufficient punishment by losing his ship and cargo. Charles married Edith Augusta Wilson (3rd October 1886–28th September 1956) in 1918 in Queensland. They were living as 39 Canning Street, Fremantle, Western Australia 1925–26.
- Hilda Brown (born 21st May 1887).
- Ruby Maud Brown (10th June 1889–2nd January 1890) in Hobart.
- Norman Cyril Brown (11th December 1890).

Walter's paternal grandparents were Thomas Brown and Mary Maria Bullock. His maternal grandparents are not known. Walter was a grain merchant in Hobart until 1911 and then moved to Petersham, New South Wales.

Walter enlisted in the Australian Imperial Force at Sydney, New South Wales on 11th July 1915. He was described as 5′ 7″ tall, weighing 146 lbs, with fair complexion, blue eyes, fair hair and his religious denomination was Church of England. His next of kin was his father, c/o Mrs Hill, 48 Bathurst Street, Hobart, Tasmania. Although keen to serve in the infantry, his desire to get to the front led to his transfer to the Light Horse. He embarked on SS *Hawkes Bay* at Sydney on 4th October as part of the 11th Reinforcement Group for 1st Light Horse Regiment. He disembarked

SS *Hawkes Bay* (4,583 tons), built at Sunderland in 1891 for the Tyser Line, was its first steam ship and operated on the Australian route. In 1912 she was sold to Chasehill Steamship Co, London, later Essex Chase Steamship Co and subsequently Chasehill. On 22nd February 1915 she was captured by the German Auxilliary Cruiser *Kronprinz Wilhelm* but was released on 9th May, carrying the prisoners taken by the cruiser and who could no longer be fed. On 18th January 1916 *Hawkes Bay* foundered on a voyage from New York to Le Havre.

at Alexandria, Egypt and proceeded to the training camp at Heliopolis. On 24th November he was admitted to 1st Australian General Hospital, Heliopolis, suffering from otitis media (middle ear infection). He transferred to 2nd Auxiliary Hospital on 16th December and was discharged on 30th December. On 14th January 1916 he transferred to the Western Frontier Force. On 4th May he again suffered with otitis media and was treated at 4th Dismounted Brigade Field Ambulance at Minya and then No.3 Australian General Hospital at Abbassia. He transferred to Ras el Tin Convalescent Depot on 20th May, was discharged on 29th May and returned to 1st Light Horse Training Regiment at Tel el Kebir on 30th May. Walter transferred to 20th Battalion AIF on 5th July and embarked with the Battalion at Alexandria for England on 8th August. He underwent infantry training with 5th Training Battalion from 21st August and moved to France on 29th September, arriving at 2nd Australian Division Base Depot, Étaples on 2nd October. His group of reinforcements was taken on the strength of 55th Battalion on 15th October.

Ras el Tin Convalescent Depot during a celebration.

Walter transferred to 1st Australian Field Butchery on 12th November. He was granted leave in England 14th-24th April 1917 and rejoined his unit on 30th April. He transferred to 2nd Australian Field Butchery at Calais on 4th May. Walter requested a transfer to 20th Battalion on 22nd July and joined 2nd Australian Division Base Depot, Calais the following day. He joined 20th Battalion on 5th August and was officially taken on strength on 8th August. **Awarded the DCM for his actions at Passchendaele, Belgium 5th-10th October 1917. During an attack he displayed self-sacrificing devotion to duty, attending to the wounded of his company under very heavy shellfire. Later on he took charge of his section, after its sergeant had become a casualty, and showed a fine example of courage and leadership to the men, LG 3rd June 1918, with citation published 21st October 1918.**

The memorial constructed by Walter and his comrades over Claude Hughes' grave. It was lost in subsequent fighting and Claude is commemorated on the Ypres (Menin Gate) Memorial.

Walter was promoted lance corporal on 19th October and was wounded by a slight gunshot to the head on 3rd November. He was treated at 134th Field Ambulance and the following day at No.11 Casualty Clearing Station before rejoining the Battalion on 8th November. He was due leave in January 1918 but instead sought permission, with others, to search for the body of a comrade, 9712A (97122 in CWGC records) Private Claude Clark Hughes. This was granted and they found the body and buried him properly, leaving a cross over the grave. However, post-war the grave could not be identified and Hughes is commemorated on the Ypres (Menin Gate) Memorial (Panel 59). Walter was granted leave to Calais 3rd-14th February and was promoted corporal on 7th April.

Awarded the VC for his actions at Villers-Bretonneux on 6th July 1918, LG 17th August 1918. He was wounded by a gunshot to the left knee on 11th August and was treated at 15th Australian Field Ambulance, No.53 Casualty Clearing Station and 12th American General Hospital, Rouen. He transferred to 2nd Convalescent Depot on 16th August, the Australian Infantry Base Depot on 20th August and rejoined his unit on 26th August. He was granted leave to Calais 3rd-13th September and was promoted sergeant on the latter date. On 22nd September he arrived at Folkestone, Kent and reported to HQ AIF, London. The VC was presented by the King at York Cottage, Sandringham, Norfolk on 7th October. Walter transferred to No.2 Command Depot, Weymouth on 15th October. He embarked at Devonport on 20th October, but requested to return to his unit on 28th October and disembarked as a result of a wire from HQ AIF, London on 5th November. He returned to France on 11th November and rejoined his unit on 18th November. On 8th January 1919, at his request, his VC and DCM were sent to Mr G Jolly, 13 Warwick Street, Stanmore, New South Wales for safe keeping. He embarked at Le Havre on 18th April and disembarked at Southampton next day

The surgical ward of Base Hospital No.12, which was organized in July 1916 at the Northwestern University Medical Department, Chicago, Illinois, with personnel from Mercy, Wesley, Cook County and Evanston Hospitals and Northwestern University. Mobilised on 1st May 1917, it boarded the *Mongolia* at New York and sailed on 19th May for Europe. However, during target practice two nurses were killed accidentally and the ship returned to New York. *Mongolia* sailed again on 24th May and docked at Falmouth on 2nd June. The unit moved by rail to London, then to Folkstone and Boulogne, France. At Dannes-Camiers it took over the British 18th General Hospital in huts and tents, with a capacity of 2,000 beds. During its active service the Hospital treated 27,438 British and 2,229 American patients. On 8th March 1919 it entrained for Brest and sailed on the 26th on the *Leviathan*. It arrived in New York on 2nd April and demobilised at Camp Grant, Illinois shortly afterwards.

Parkhouse Camp, Salisbury Plain.

Horseferry Road, London. HQ AIF was in the buildings on the right.

York Cottage, Sandringham, Norfolk where Walter Brown received his VC from the King.

HMAT A71 *Nestor* (14,501 tons) was owned by the Ocean Steamship Co Ltd, Liverpool and was leased by the Commonwealth of Australia until 26th June 1917. When she arrived at Port Melbourne in June 1913 she was the largest merchant ship then to visit Australia.

to report to the Australian Army Service Corps Training Depot, Parkhouse Camp, Salisbury Plain.

Walter was assigned to non-military duties as a trainee cinema manager and bioscope operator at the Victoria Cinema, 36 Rathbone Place, Oxford Street, London and the Imperial Film Co Ltd, 167 Wardour Street, London from 24th April to 24th June 1919, later extended to 19th August. He embarked at Folkestone on 21st August to return to 20th Battalion. He embarked for return to Australia aboard HMT *Nestor* on 1st November and disembarked in 3rd Military District on 15th December. He was discharged from 2nd Military District on 15th February 1920.

Walter worked as a brass-finisher in Sydney, New South Wales 1920–30 and as a water bailiff at Leeton with the New South Wales Water Conservation and Irrigation Commission 1931–40. He

Sydney Town Hall, where the first AIF Reunion Dinner was held on 8th August 1928. It was built in the 1870s-80s. The architecture was inspired by the French Second Empire. In addition to the Sydney City Council Chamber, there are reception rooms, the Centennial Hall and offices for the Lord Mayor and councillors. The Centennial Hall contains the world's largest pipe organ, built beyween 1886 and 1889 and installed by the English firm of William Hill & Son. Before the opening of Sydney Opera House, the Town Hall was Sydney's main concert hall.

Maude and her two children.

The opening of the railway in 1884 and the increase in population led to a number of churches being established. Christ Church (St George's) was built 1886–87, with the foundation stone being laid by the Archbishop of Sydney. A patron was Henry Kinsela, a wealthy landowner in the 19th century. The church was extended in 1930 when a single central aisle replaced the original side aisles.

attended the first AIF Reunion Dinner at Sydney Town Hall on 8th August 1928 to celebrate the tenth anniversary of the commencement of 'The Big Push', together with fellow VCs Bede Kenny, George Cartwright, Snowy Howell, Percy Storkey, John Whittle, William Currey and Blair Wark.

Walter was one of twenty-three VCs who attended an Anzac Dinner on 23rd April 1927, hosted by Lieutenant General Sir John Monash GCMG KCB VD. For an unknown reason The Duke of York (future King George VI) was not invited. Jack took part in the Anzac Commemoration Service on 25th April 1927 at the Exhibition Building, Melbourne, Victoria in the presence of The Duke of York. In the march past the VCs conceded pride of place to blinded soldiers who insisted on marching. Walter was a Freemason, being Initiated into the Gogeldrie Lodge (No.558), United Grand Lodge of New South Wales on 7th April 1931. He was Passed on 7th July and Raised on 3rd November.

Walter Brown married Maude 'Meg' Dillon (17th August 1906–23rd May 1980), born at Kilrainy, Co Kildare, Ireland, at Christ Church, Bexley, New South Wales on 4th June 1932. A surprise guard of honour of eight VCs was in attendance, including Blair Wark, John Hamilton, George Cartwright, Snowy Howell, William Currey, Thomas Kenny and Arthur Sullivan. Walter and Maude lived initially at Commission Reserve, Wamoon, via Leeton, New South Wales, before moving to 38 Arthur Street, Carlton, New South Wales. They had two children:

- Walter Ernest Brown (1936–5th June 1943) died of meningitis and is buried at Woronora Memorial Park, Sutherland, New South Wales.
- Pamela Brown, who married as Gould, and moved to Washington DC, USA in 1956.

Maude's father, George Henry Dillon (1857–25th September 1921), born in Co Kildare, Ireland, married Charlotte Louisa née Stronge (2nd March 1865–1918), born at Kilmeage, Co Kildare, on 6th September 1892. They were living at Derryart, Kilrainy on 2nd April 1911. In addition to Maude they had six other children:

- James Henry Dillon (25th June 1893–14th July 1962) was born at Moyvalley, Co Kildare and died at Regina, Saskatchewan, Canada.
- Samuel George Dillon (5th May 1896–29th June 1976) born at Kilrainy, Co Kildare and died at Mount Mellick, Ireland.
- George Sydney Dillon (21st January 1898–13th May 1961) died at Carbury, Co Kildare.
- Mathilda Olive Dillon (11th September 1899–23rd December 1925) died unmarried at Hendon, Middlesex.
- Violet Charlotte Dillon (27th December 1903–1978).
- Edith Elizabeth Dillon (12th April 1907–6th February 1987) emigrated to Australia and married James Sylvester in 1941 at Sydney, New South Wales. They had a son and a daughter.

Walter enlisted in the Second Australian Imperial Force at Wagga Wagga, New South Wales on 21st June 1940 (NX35492), giving his occupation as labourer and date of birth falsely as 3rd July 1900. He marched out of Redbank Recruitment Depot, near Ipswich, Queensland to 8th Battalion and was promoted temporary corporal on 21st June. His correct age was discovered and he was promoted lance sergeant on 1st July. Walter was posted to 13th Infantry Training Battalion on 2nd September and transferred to Eastern Command Signals Training Depot, Tamworth, New South Wales on 29th October. He was posted to 2/15th Field Regiment, Royal Australian Artillery on 27th November and reverted to gunner at his own request on 24th April 1941 when posted to Holsworthy, New South Wales. He embarked at Sydney, New South Wales on 29th July, transferred at Fremantle and disembarked in Singapore on 15th August.

On the last day of the Battle of Singapore, 15th February 1942, Walter went missing in action and no trace has ever been found of him. His wife was told by two of her husband's comrades that they were being evacuated by truck when a young soldier ran behind in an attempt to climb aboard. Walter ordered the driver to stop and gave up his position to the young soldier. He was last seen with two hand grenades moving off in the direction of the enemy saying, *No surrender for me*. In another version, his position was about to be overrun, when he picked up the two hand grenades and headed towards the enemy, never to be seen again. Another version states that they had reached a beach and were escaping into the water, many being shot as they ran. Walter was in one of the few small boats and attempts to get to sea were hampered by a terrified soldier clinging to the side. Walter gave up his seat to the young soldier and waded ashore toward the advancing enemy. A soldier in another boat witnessed Walter being captured and executed. He was listed as missing from 16th February. On 22nd May 1946 he was officially presumed dead on 28th February 1942. Walter is commemorated on Column 115 of the Singapore War Memorial, Kranji.

Maude's ashes are in Oak Hill Cemetery, Georgetown, Washington DC, founded in 1848. Amongst those buried there is Dean Gooderham Acheson (1893–1971), Secretary of State in President Harry S Truman's administration 1949–53. He played a central role in defining American foreign policy during the Cold War, helped design the Marshall Plan and Truman Doctrine and create NATO. Also buried there is Katharine Meyer Graham (1917–2001), the first female publisher of a major American newspaper, *The Washington Post*, including during the events that lead up to the resignation of President Richard Nixon (Tim Evanson).

His wife was in receipt of an allowance from the New South Wales Water and Conservation Commission, making up the difference between her husband's military pay and his civilian salary. This allowance was terminated in August 1942, under a government ruling that it be paid for six months in the case of a married man reported missing in action. This caused uproar amongst the community as he had not been officially reported missing until April 1942 and his wife was therefore entitled to the allowance for a further two months. His wife's parting shot to the authorities was, ... *little gratitude to a man who has offered his life to his country – a second time.*

Maude followed her daughter, Pamela, to Washington DC, USA in 1958. She eventually died at Alexandria, Virginia and her ashes are in Oak Hill Cemetery, Washington DC. Walter is commemorated in a number of places:

- Australian Capital Territory
  - Australian Victoria Cross Recipients plaque on the Victoria Cross Memorial, Campbell, dedicated on 24th July 2000.
  - Roll of Honour at the Australian War Memorial, Canberra, Australian Capital Territory.
  - Named on one of eleven plaques honouring 175 men from overseas awarded the VC for the Great War. The plaques were unveiled by the Senior Minister of State at the Foreign & Commonwealth Office and Minister for Faith and Communities, Baroness Warsi, at a reception at Lancaster House, London on 26th June 2014 attended by The Duke of Kent and relatives of the VC recipients. The Australian plaque is at the Australian War Memorial.
  - Display in the Hall of Valour, Australian War Memorial.
  - Brown Street, Canberra.
- New South Wales
  - Victoria Cross Memorial, Queen Victoria Building, George Street, Sydney dedicated on 23rd February 1992 to commemorate the visit of Queen Elizabeth II and Prince Phillip on the occasion of the Sesquicentenary of the City of Sydney. Sir Roden Cutler VC AK KCMG, Edward Kenna VC and Keith Payne VC were in attendance.
  - Victoria Cross Recipients Wall, North Bondi War Memorial donated to the community of Waverley on 27th November 2011 by The Returned & Services League of Australia.
  - Named on the family grave at Woronora Memorial Park, Sutherland, New South Wales.
  - The Shrine of Remembrance at Leeton Soldiers Club, Leeton, New South Wales.

The grave of Maude's and Walter's son, Walter, who died in 1943, with a memorial to Walter VC at the bottom.

- Tasmania
  - Memorial plaque at New Norfolk Primary School.
  - Victoria Cross Memorial, Hobart Cenotaph dedicated on 11 May 2003.
- Communities and Local Government commemorative paving stones for the 145 VCs born in Australia, Belgium, Canada, China, Denmark, Egypt, France, Germany, India, Iraq, Japan, Nepal, Netherlands, Newfoundland, New Zealand, Pakistan, South Africa, Sri Lanka, Ukraine and United States of America were unveiled at the National Memorial Arboretum, Alrewas, Staffordshire by Prime Minister David Cameron MP and Sergeant Johnson Beharry VC on 5th March 2015.
- Named on a plaque at Ashworth Barracks Museum, Doncaster, South Yorkshire, unveiled by Lord Lieutenant Andrew Coombe on 22nd June 2015.
- He was featured in Issue No. 462 of the Victor Comic entitled *Never Surrender* dated 17th December 1969.

The Victoria Cross Memorial either side of Hobart Cenotaph, Tasmania. The walls contain soil from the birthplace of all thirteen Tasmanian VCs and soil from the battlefields where their VCs were earned. Two of the thirteen were won during the Boer War and eleven during the Great War. The Tasmanian awards include the first two VCs awarded to Australians serving in Australian forces.

In addition to the VC and DCM he was awarded the 1914–15 Star, British War Medal 1914–20, Victory Medal 1914–19, 1939–45 Star, Pacific Star, War Medal 1939–45, Australia Service Medal 1939–45 and George VI Coronation Medal 1937. The medals are held in the Hall of Valour, Australian War Memorial, Treloar Crescent, Campbell, Australian Capital Territory.

SECOND LIEUTENANT BERNARD MATTHEW CASSIDY
2nd Battalion, The Lancashire Fusiliers

Bernard Cassidy was born on 17th August 1892 at Fulham, London. His father, also Bernard Cassidy (c.1866–1917), was born at Castlereagh, Co Roscommon, Ireland. He married Julia née Butler (c.1872–1929) in December 1889 at Manchester, Lancashire. She was born at Cashel, Co Tipperary, Ireland. Bernard senior was a carpet dealer in 1891 and the family was living at 11 Murray Street, St Pancras, London. By 1901 they had moved to 134 Dartmouth Park Hill, Islington, London and to 29 Watford

Road, Victoria Docks, Canning Town, Essex by 1911. His son, Bernard, described him as a traveller (drapery) when he applied for a commission in February 1917. Bernard junior had six siblings:

Fulham at about the time that Bernard was born there.

- John Cassidy (born 29th November 1890) was a warehouseman in the cycle trade in 1911 and later a traveller in the drapery trade. He enlisted in the Irish Guards on 25th May 1916 (11300), was promoted lance corporal and served with his brother Bernard. He applied for a commission on 5th February 1917, described as 5′ 10½″ tall, weighing 139 lbs and was posted to No.7 Officer Training Battalion at Fermoy, Co Cork, Ireland on 5th May 1917 with his brother, Bernard. John was commissioned in the Lancashire Fusiliers on 29th August and later served with 1st Royal Dublin Fusiliers. He was awarded the MC, LG 4th February 1918. Promoted lieutenant on 1st March 1919 and was released from No.1 Dispersal Unit, Crystal Palace on 10th April 1919, giving his address as 7 Rochester Row, London. He relinquished his commission on 1st September 1921, retaining the rank of lieutenant.
- Martin Cassidy (1894–1967) was a packer in the stationary trade in 1911. He served during the Great War.
- Joseph Cassidy (17th June 1896–22nd January 1969) was a press messenger in 1911. He was a labourer living at 29 Watford Road, Canning Town, London at the time of his enlistment in the Irish Guards on 10th December 1915 at Stratford, London (11994). He was described as 5′ 8″ tall, weighing 110 lbs and his religious denomination was Roman Catholic. He was transferred to the Army Reserve next day and recalled on 29th March 1917 to Caterham, Surrey for training. Joseph was admitted to hospital at Caterham with an abscess on his back 10th-29th May. He was appointed unpaid lance corporal on 19th October and joined the 1st Battalion in France on 13th November. He was admitted to hospital with arthritis of the right knee on 26th November and was evacuated to Britain from Rouen on 3rd December, where he was treated at Dublin University Voluntary Aid Detachment Hospital at 19 Mountjoy Square, Dublin 5th-22nd December. Joseph was awarded the 2nd Class Certificate of Education on 1st February 1918 and embarked for France from Southampton on 21st March. On 28th May he was wounded, resulting in a rupture of the tympanic membrane, and was admitted to No.19 Casualty Clearing Station. Having been transferred to various medical facilities in the field and at Étaples, he was sent to 13th Convalescent Depot, Trouville on 20th June. Two days later he was promoted lance corporal. Joseph was granted leave to Britain 11th-25th February 1919 and transferred to the Class

The Dublin University Voluntary Aid Detachment Hospital was established at 19 Mountjoy Square, Dublin. Mountjoy was one of five Georgian squares in Dublin. It was planned and developed in the late 18th century by Luke Gardiner, 1st Viscount Mountjoy. All four sides, each 140m long, were terraced, red-brick Georgian houses. Construction began in the early 1790s and was completed in 1818. The square has been home to many prominent people, including the brewer Arthur Guinness and the writer James Joyce. Sean O'Casey, playwright and founder member of the Irish Citizen Army, lived there during the Irish War of Independence. Some of the planning for the Easter Rising took place in the Square as did some of the earliest meetings of the Dáil, when it was suppressed by the British authorities in September 1919. An infamous brothel, The Kasbah Health Studio, frequented by senior businessmen, politicians and churchmen, was in the basement of No.60 from the late 1970s until the early 1990s. The film *Once*, filmed in an apartment on Mountjoy Square East, won the Academy Award in 2007 for best original song. The pop band U2 rehearsed in a squat in the Square in the late 1970s.

Z Reserve on demobilisation on 22nd April. He married Alice May Crouch (21st March 1893–5th March 1990) in 1924 at West Ham, London. She was born at Bishampton, Worcestershire and was a needle worker in embroidery in 1911, living with a relative at 53 Clarence Road, Canning Town, London. They were living at 15 Wilsman Road, South Ockendon, Essex at the time of his death there. She was still living there at the time of her death at Orsett Hospital, Essex. They had three children:

- Kathleen Margaret Cassidy (11th March 1925–1974) married Bernard AJ Benson (born 1924) in 1948.
- Joseph P Cassidy (born 1927) married Bina A Patton (believed to have been born in Glenamaddy, Co Galway, Ireland in 1926) in 1951. They had four children – Michael G Cassidy 1955, John P Cassidy 1958, Patrick J Cassidy 1961 and Mary F Cassidy 1962.
- Maureen A Cassidy (born 1929) married Stanley Groves in 1963. They had a son, Paul Gerard Groves, in 1966.

- James Cassidy (born 1898) enlisted in the Irish Guards (11780) on 8th January 1917 at Stratford, London and joined at Caterham the same day, giving his employment as a delivery checker. He was described as 5′ 7½″ tall, weighing 126 lbs, with an overlapping fifth left toe and his religious denomination was Roman Catholic. At 4th London General Hospital on 13th April he was found to have a high myopic astigmatism and his vision was not improved by glasses. He went to France on 1st April 1918, embarking at Folkestone and disembarking at Calais, and joined the 1st Battalion on 6th April. James was granted leave in Britain 15th February–1st March 1919 and joined the 1st Battalion at Warley afterwards. He

was demobilised to the Class Z Reserve on 24th April 1919.
- Albert Cassidy (1900–05).
- Kathleen Cassidy (born 1902).

Warley was used as a military camp for some decades before a permanent barracks was constructed. Its location was ideal, less than a day's march to Tilbury, where troops could embark for foreign service. Warley Barracks was made permanent in 1804. In 1842 the East India Company's barracks at Chatham became inadequate and Warley was purchased for its troops. New accommodation was created, including married quarters. In 1856 further building was carried out. In 1861 the barracks was bought by the War Office and became the depot of the Brigade of Guards. In 1873 it became the depot of the 44th (East Essex) and 56th (West Essex) Regiments of Foot. In 1881 they amalgamated to form the Essex Regiment. The barracks were sold to Ford Motor Co in 1958. The Essex Regiment Chapel built in 1857, originally for the East India Company, remains, as does the officers' mess (now a nursing home) and one of the gyms (Keys Hall).

Nothing is known about Bernard's paternal grandparents beyond his grandfather's name, John Cassidy. His maternal grandfather, Matthew Butler (c.1831–95), born in Ireland, served in the Army. He married Mary née Walsh (born c.1831), also born in Ireland. He was retired and they were living at 11 Buxton Street, Manchester, Lancashire in 1891. In addition to Julia they had three other children:

- Margaret Butler (born c.1861 in India) was a machinist in 1891.
- John Butler (born c.1863 in India) was a spreader in 1891.
- Ellen Butler (born 1866 at Colchester, Essex) was a machinist in 1891.

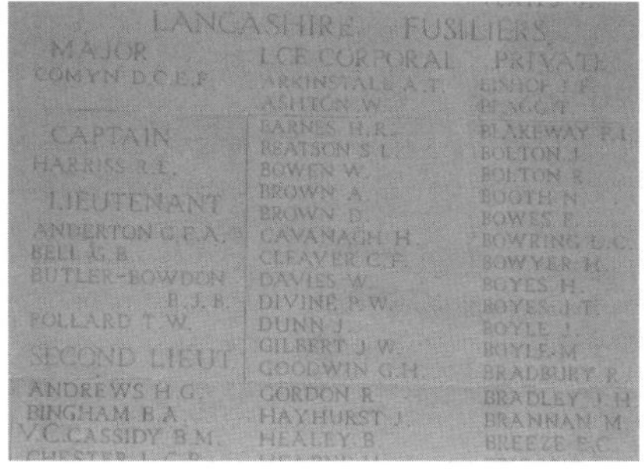

Bernard Cassidy's name (bottom left) on the Lancashire Fusiliers panel of the Arras Memorial.

Bernard was educated at St Margaret's School, Barking Road, London. In 1911 he was an insurance clerk and was later employed as manager of the counting house for Glyn & Son, hat manufacturers of Chiswell Street, London. He enlisted in the Irish Guards on 16th May 1916 (11276) and was promoted lance corporal whilst serving with No.1 Company, 3rd (Reserve) Battalion at Warley Barracks, near Brentwood, Essex. He applied for a commission and was posted to No.7 Officer Cadet Battalion at Fermoy, Co Cork, Ireland with his brother, John, on 5th May 1917. Bernard was commissioned in the Lancashire Fusiliers on 29th August and went to France on 28th October. **Awarded the VC for his actions southwest of Gavrelle, France on 28th March, LG 3rd May 1918.** As he never married the VC was presented to his mother by the King at Buckingham Palace on 26th June

1918. Bernard was killed during his VC action and is commemorated on Bay 5 of the Arras Memorial, France. Bernard is commemorated in a number of other places:

- Cassidy Street, Canning Town, East London was named after him.
- A Department for Communities and Local Government commemorative VC paving stone was dedicated at The Cenotaph, Central Park, High Street South, East Ham on 28th March 2018 to mark the centenary of his award.

In addition to the VC he was awarded the British War Medal 1914–20 and Victory Medal 1914–19. The VC was purchased privately by Lord Ashcroft in 2002. It is held by the Michael Ashcroft Trust, the holding institution for the Lord Ashcroft Victoria Cross Collection, and is displayed in the Lord Ashcroft Gallery, Imperial War Museum, London.

The street named after Bernard in Canning Town (Memorials to Valour).

SECOND LIEUTENANT JOSEPH HENRY COLLIN
1/4th Battalion, The King's Own (Royal Lancaster Regiment)

Joseph Collin was born on 11th April 1893 at Jarrow, Co Durham. His father, Joseph Collin (1853–12th January 1931), an engine fitter, was living with his maternal grandparents, Joseph and Margaret Taylor, in 1861 at Bridge and Yanwath, Westmorland. He married Fanny Eliza née Mursell (1846–15th February 1885) on 26th August 1876 at the Church of St John the Baptist, Northwood, Isle of Wight, Hampshire. Fanny was a general servant in 1861, living with her parents at 5 Back Court, Northwood, West Cowes, Isle of Wight. By 1871 she was a general servant at the home of Richard Barrow at Birmingham Road, West Cowes. Joseph and Fanny were living at 4 Orchard Street, Botchergate, Carlisle, Cumberland in 1881, together with four lodgers. She died at 8 Millholme

Botchergate, Carlisle.

The Church of St John the Baptist, Northwood, where Joseph's father married for the first time in August 1876, was built in the early 12th century. It has undergone many changes since, particularly by the Victorians.

Terrace, West Cuthbert, Carlisle. Joseph lived at 8 Petteril Terrace, Harraby, Carlisle. He married Mary née McDermond (1864–24th December 1925) (also seen as McDermott and McDermont) in 1887. They were living at 72 Union Street, Carlisle by 1891, at 52 Thomson Street, Botchergate, Carlisle by 1901 and back to 8 Petteril Terrace by 1911. Joseph junior had eight siblings from his father's two marriages, all born at Carlisle, except for George:

- George Thomas Collin (21st April 1877–1947), born on the Isle of Wight, was a railway engine fitter, living with his paternal grandparents at 2 Dresden Terrace, Botchergate, Carlisle, Cumberland in 1901. He married Jane Ann Dobson (1881–1919) in 1908. They were living at 8 Adelphi Terrace, Carlisle in 1911. George married Sarah Taylor (c.1874–1965) in 1924. He had three children from his first marriage:
    - George Dobson Collin (1909–17th December 1961) married Alice Thompson (24th December 1904–1973) in 1930. They were living at 14 Wellbank Place, Carlisle at the time of his death at The Cumberland Infirmary, Carlisle. They had two children – Joyce Collin 1931 and George E Collin 1934.
    - Leonard Collin (born 1911).
    - Frances E Collin (1914–1919).
- William James Collin (1890–1964) was a cabinet maker in 1911. He married Sarah Agnes Threlfall (8th October 1893–1975) in 1919. They had a son,

8 Petteril Terrace, Harraby, Carlisle where Joseph's family lived. The house now carries a Heritage Blue Plaque (Richard Tinker).

James Collin (1933–65), who married Vera Wilkinson (1935–65) in 1956. They were living at 46 Myrtle Avenue, Selby, Yorkshire at the time of their deaths on 17th September 1965 at Marley Head, South Brent, Totnes, Devon.

- Sarah Ann Collin (born 1891) was a tailoress in 1911.
- Tom Collin (27th August 1897–1971).
- Christopher Collin (1st September 1899–1972) married Harriet Stuart (1893–1967) in 1923. They had a son, William J Collin (born 16th October 1924), who married Rosalind Cavaghan (born 13th June 1928) in 1948 and they had three children – Michael Collin 1949, Christopher Collin 1954 and Sheila Collin 1957. It is understood that Christopher and Harriet divorced. She married John Brown in 1970 and he married Mary J White in 1972.
- John McDermont Collin (born 1901) married Annie Hornsby in 1924.
- Margaret Hannah Collin (born 1903) married Albert Deacon (15th October 1902–1978) in 1931. They had a son, Joseph C Deacon, in 1934, who married Marjorie V Maddison in 1962.
- Vincent Collin (2nd January 1906–1977) married Mary Emma B Boothman (14th February 1908–22nd August 1984) in 1936. Mary was living at 16 Graham Street, Carlisle at the time of her death at Thanet, Kent. They had two children:
    - William G Collin (born 1938) married Enid M Williams (born 1936) in 1957 at Carmarthen, Carmarthenshire. They had twins, Richard W and Robert W Collin, in 1958.
    - Margaret M Collin (born 1940) married George J Noble in 1962. They had two children – Angela Noble 1964 and David George Noble 1967.

Joseph's paternal grandfather, George Collin (c.1831–18th February 1905), born at Clifton, Westmorland, was a railway engine driver. He married Hannah née Taylor (c.1832–2nd April 1910) on 21st February 1852 at St Cuthbert, Carlisle, Cumberland. In 1871 they were living at 12 Hasell Street, Upperby, Carlisle. By 1881 they had moved to Botcherby, Carlisle. George was a grocer by 1901 and they were living at 2 Dresden Terrace, Botchergate, Carlisle. In addition to Joseph they had four other children:

Joseph's paternal grandparents married at St Cuthbert, Carlisle in February 1852. There has been a church on the site dedicated to St Cuthbert since 685. It was rebuilt in 870, 1095 and 1778, when it took on its current Georgian style. An unusual feature is the pulpit, which moves on rails and is very tall so that the vicar could preach to the gallery.

- Tom Collin (1858–27th November 1931) was an engine fitter in 1881. He married Eleanor Wilkinson (1861–1939) in 1882. By 1911 he was a steam-shed foreman and they were living at 1 Hill Place, Oxenholme, Westmorland. They were living at Bolefoot, Oxenholme at the time of his death at the County Mental Institution, Garlands, Carlisle. They had seven children – Hannah Collin 1883, John George Collin 1885, Mary Elizabeth Collin 1888, Joseph Collin 1890, Fanny Collin 1892, Tom Collin 1898 and Gilbert Collin 1899.

- George Collin (1860–5th August 1940) was an engine fitter in 1881. He married Elizabeth Jane Nixon (1868–16th January 1929) in 1890. They were living at 27 Aglionby Street, Carlisle in 1911 and at 8 Chertsey Mount, Carlisle by the time she died there, leaving effects valued at £1,814. He was still living there when he died, leaving effects valued at £2,835/2/11. They had four children – John Maxwell Collin 1891, Rhoda Hannah Collin 1892, Hilda Catherine Collin 1893 and Eva Margaret Collin 1895.
- Margaret Ann Collin (1862–99) was a dressmaker in 1881. She married Joseph Graham (born c.1863), an innkeeper, in 1888. He was born in Scotland. They were living at 3H Willow Holme, Caldewgate, Carlisle, Cumberland in 1891. They had a daughter, Jane Graham, in 1889. Joseph and Jane were living with his parents-in-law in 1901.
- William John Collin (1864–1939) was a hosiery apprentice in 1881. He married Margaret Thompson (1868–6th May 1943) in 1898. By 1901 he was a railway engine driver and they were living at 52 Edward Street, Botchergate, Carlisle. They were living with her sister, Mary Thompson and siblings Elizabeth, William R and Sarah Thompson, at 56 London Road, Carlisle in 1911. She was living at 56 London Road, Carlisle at the time of her death at City General Hospital, Carlisle. They had two children, one of whom died in infancy, and Margaret Thompson Collin, in 1899.

His maternal grandfather, James McDermon (1841–31st October 1915), was born in Co Tyrone, Ireland. His surname has also been seen as McDermont, McDermitt, McDermot, McDermet and McDermott. He married Margaret née Cairns (1841–1909), born at Carlisle, Cumberland, in 1860 at Carlisle. James was a street paviour's labourer and Margaret was a cotton steam loom weaver in 1861, when they were living at Armstrong's Lane, Rickergate, Carlisle. By 1871 he was a street paviour and they had moved to 2 James Place, St Mary, Rickergate. They had moved to East Tower, St James Place, Rickergate by 1881 and he was a master paviour. The firm he worked for laid the cobblestones outside Carlisle Citadel railway station. In 1911 James was living with his daughter, Alice, and her family. He died at 32 Linton Street, Carlisle. In addition to Mary they had seven other children:

- James McDermond (born 1860).
- Sarah Ann McDermond (1862–1935) was a farm servant in 1881 at Rickergate, Carlisle. By 1901 she was a cook at Burgh by Sands, Cumberland. She died unmarried.
- Henry McDermond (1866–1941) was a paviour, boarding at 14 Solway Street, Holme Low, Cumberland in 1891. He married Margaret McGrath (c.1867–1950)

in 1899. They were living at 15 Southview Terrace, Botchergate, Carlisle in 1901 and at 6 Grace Street, Carlisle in 1911. They had three children – James McDermott 1901, Francis McDermott 1908 and Jane Anne McDermott 1908.
- Thomas McDermond (born 1868) was a paviour. He married Ellen Ann 'Elena' Loughran (1871–1952) in 1892. They were living at Hodgsons Court, Scotch Street, Carlisle in 1911. They had ten children – Henry Loughran McDermott 1893, Theresa McDermott 1894, James McDermott 1897, Thomas McDermott 1898, Henry Loughran M McDermott 1900, Ellen Ann McDermott 1902, John McDermott 1907, Margaret McDermott 1909, Mary McDermott 1910 and Francis McDermott 1913.
- John McDermond (1871–1908).
- Alice McDermond (1873–1932) married George Scott (1871–1936), who was a railway engine driver, in 1892. They were living at 6 Hasell Street, Botchergate in 1901 and 4 Margery Street, Carlisle in 1911. They had two daughters – Mary Ellen Scott 1893 and Margaret Alice Scott 1898.
- William Joseph McDermond (1876–1952) married Mary Elizabeth Curran (1877–1913) in 1898. She had a daughter, Elizabeth Curran, in 1895. In 1911 he was a paviour for the City of Carlisle Electric Tramways Co Ltd, run by Balfour Beatty, and they were living at 88 Union Street, Botchergate. They had eleven children – Alice McDermott 1898, Margaret McDermott 1900, Joseph McDermott 1902, Nora McDermott 1905 James McDermott 1906, Ida McDermott 1909, George McDermott 1911, Henry McDermott 1914, Kathleen McDermott 1916, Thomas J McDermott 1920 and Elizabeth McDermott 1929.

Joseph was educated at St Patrick's School, Carlisle. He was employed by clothier Messrs Joseph Hepworth & Son of Leeds, Yorkshire. Joseph enlisted in 8th Argyll and Sutherland Highlanders at Dunoon on 7th January 1915 (2692). He was appointed acting lance corporal on 18th November 1915 and acting corporal on 2nd February 1916 but reverted to private when he embarked for France on 1st August 1916 to join 19th Infantry Base Depot. He joined 1/6th Argyll & Sutherland Highlanders (Pioneers) on 27th August (7468 later 253892), serving in 16 Platoon, D Company and was granted three pence per day proficiency pay from 7th January 1917. He was an acting sergeant when he applied for a commission on 30th January 1917 and returned to Britain on 21st February to attend officer training at 9th or 10th Officer Cadet Battalion, Gailes, Ayrshire. Joseph was commissioned in 1/4th King's Own on 29th August and was described as 5′ 8″ tall, with medium complexion, blue eyes, dark brown hair and his religious denomination was Roman Catholic. He joined the Battalion in France in October.

Awarded the VC for his actions at Orchard Keep, Givenchy-lès-la-Bassée, France on 9th April 1918, LG 28 June 1918. He was killed during his VC action and was originally buried in King's Liverpool Graveyard at Cuinchy. After the war his remains were reinterred in Vielle-Chapelle New Military Cemetery,

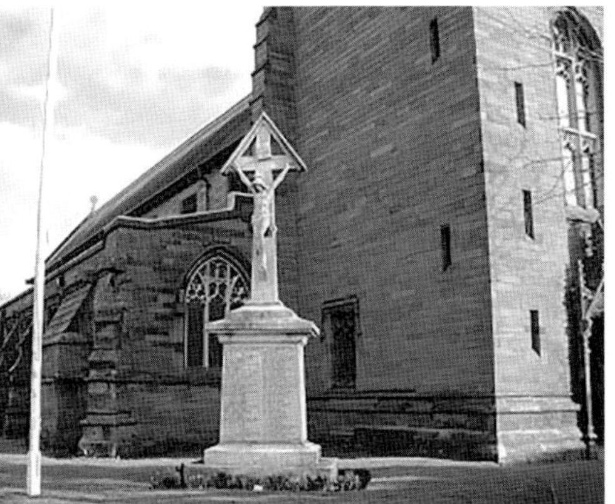

Joseph is commemorated on the war memorial outside Our Lady & St Joseph's Roman Catholic Church in Carlisle.

Joseph's grave in Vielle-Chapelle New Military Cemetery, Lacouture.

Lacouture, France (III A 11). The VC was presented to his parents by the King in the quadrangle at Buckingham Palace on 25th July 1918. Joseph left £156/7/2 to his mother in a soldier's will dated 5th November 1917. He is commemorated in a number of other places:

- The Collin VC Memorial Shield, donated by his family in 1919, was awarded at the Carlisle Schools annual sports event to the winner of the 100 yards handicap open to boys aged seven to sixteen. It was last awarded in 1988 and is owned by the Cumberland & Westmorland Wrestling Association. It was loaned to the Royal British Legion's Carlisle Branch on 9th November 2011.
- Collin Place, off Harrogate Road, Carlisle.
- Named on the family headstone in Carlisle Cemetery, Richardson Street, Carlisle.
- Named on the war memorial at Our Lady & St Joseph's Roman Catholic Church, Warwick Road, Carlisle.
- Plaque attached to Harraby War Memorial, Carlisle.
- Heritage Blue Plaque at Petteril Terrace, Harraby, Carlisle.
- Plaque in the Regimental Chapel, The Priory, Lancaster, Lancashire.
- Plaque at Palmer Community Hospital, Jarrow, Tyne & Wear.
- Department for Communities and Local Government commemorative VC paving stones were dedicated at Joseph Collin House, North Street, Jarrow on 9th April 2018 and at Carlisle War Memorial, Green Market on 23rd June 2018 to mark the centenary of his award.

In addition to the VC he was awarded the British War Medal 1914–20 and Victory Medal 1914–19. The VC only was presented to the Regiment in 1956. It is held by the King's Own (Royal Lancaster) Regiment Museum, City Museum, Market

Square, Lancaster, Lancashire. Joseph's memorial plaque was auctioned in Carlisle on 11th August 2006. It was purchased by the Museum for £2,500, assisted by public donations, and is displayed alongside his VC.

LIEUTENANT COLONEL JOHN STANHOPE COLLINGS-WELLS
4th Battalion, The Bedfordshire Regiment

(Rosemary Beharrell)

John Collings Wells was born on 19th July 1880 at 3 Albert Place, Dickenson Road, Rusholme, Manchester, Lancashire. His birth was registered as Joseph Frederick but he was christened John Stanhope. His father, Arthur Collings Wells (1857–11th May 1922), an engineer, married Caroline Mary née Eisdell (1855–3rd December 1929) on 21st May 1879 at Reading, Berkshire. In 1881 they were living at 3 Albert Place, Rusholme and by 1891 had moved to Arrandene, Hendon, Middlesex. By 1901 they had moved to Caddington Hall, Markyate, Hertfordshire. The family later resided at Brand's House, Hughenden, High Wycombe, Buckinghamshire. Arthur was a partner in Frank Pearn, Wells & Co and founded AC Wells & Co. The latter company was based at 102–105 Midland Road, St Pancras, London. He was also a director of Chelmsford Brewery and the Unbreakable Pulley & Mill Gearing Co. He was appointed JP Hertfordshire and was a

John was born at Albert Place, Rusholme, just off Dickenson Road, which became home to the first BBC television studio outside London in 1954. The Dickenson Road Studios were in this converted church. *Top of the Pops* was first broadcast from there on New Year's Day 1964, hosted by Jimmy Savile and Alan Freeman. The Beatles *I want to hold your hand* was No.1. In 1975 the BBC moved to New Broadcasting House, Oxford Road, in the centre of Manchester.

The Collings Wells family was living at Caddington Hall at Markyate in Hertfordshire in 1901. It was built in the early 1800s. It subsequently became a nursing home and was demolished in 1975, making way for a new home on the site.

Hertfordshire County Councillor. In 1920 he changed his surname to the hyphenated form of Collings-Wells by deed poll. Arthur died at Brands, leaving effects valued at £82,327/16/4 (£3.8M in 2018). Caroline died at Glebe House, Dinton, Buckinghamshire, leaving effects valued at £14,917/4/7. John had four siblings:

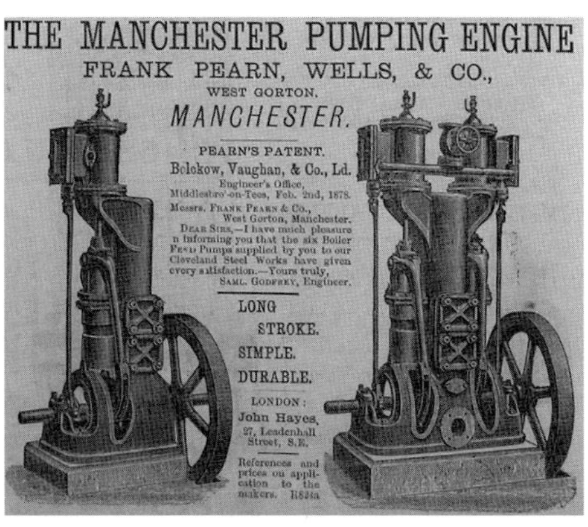

An advertisement for Frank Pearn, Wells & Co.

An advertisement for AC Wells & Co from 1905.

- Russell Primrose Collings Wells (11th November 1882–22nd November 1954) was educated at Harrow and the Royal Military College, Sandhurst. He was commissioned in 15th (The King's) Hussars on 22nd October 1902, was promoted lieutenant on 25th October 1905 and served in India. In the 1911 Census he was based with his Regiment at Potchefstroom, Transvaal, South Africa and his surname was given simply as Wells. He was promoted captain on 5th August 1914 and embarked at Southampton on 16th August. At Mons, Belgium on 23rd August he was wounded severely by a shrapnel ball. It entered the lower right leg, passed through the calf muscles, exited behind the knee, re-entered the thigh and lodged in the back of it. Having been evacuated to Britain on 31st August, a medical board at Queen Alexandra Military Hospital, Millbank, London on 5th September found him unfit for service for four months and granted leave to 4th January 1915. That day a medical board at Bedford found him unfit for service for one month and he joined 14th Reserve Regiment of Cavalry on 11th January for attachment to 2/1st Ayrshire Yeomanry at Hawick for instructional purposes. Medical boards at Cambridge Military Hospital, Aldershot on 11th February and 10th March found him unfit for General Service for one month but fit for Home Service. Further medical boards on 13th April, 13th May and 15th June found him unfit for General and Home Service for periods of one to two months but fit for light duty. He transferred from 2/1st Ayrshire Yeomanry to 2/1st East

Kent Yeomanry at Maresfield Park Camp, Uckfield for instructional purposes, arriving on 1st July. On 15th July he was found fit for service and received a wound gratuity of £229/3/4. He embarked on 30th July and landed at Boulogne next day. He embarked at Marseille on 8th January 1916 and disembarked at Alexandria on 13th January. He joined the Light Armoured Car Batteries (Duke of Westminster's) on 21st September, as he could not ride because of his wound. Russell was granted five weeks leave and embarked on SS *Malwa* from Port Said to Marseille on 26th August and returned to Egypt on 18th October. He embarked for Matruh from Alexandria on 16th December and took part in the campaign against the Senussi in February 1917 (DSO, LG 3rd March 1917 and Mentioned in General Sir Archibald Murray's Despatch of 1st March 1917), during which he was slightly wounded and admitted to hospital 3rd-9th February. He returned to Alexandria on 8th April and joined the Dorset Yeomanry as second-in-command on 13th April as acting major until 7th May. He was admitted to No.54 Casualty Clearing Station with myalgia on 4th May and transferred to 24th Stationary Hospital, Moascar on 9th May but had recovered in time to attended Mena Staff College, Cairo 22nd May–16th June. Next day he was appointed Commandant of Change of Air Camp, El Arish. Russell was an acting major MGC 13th July–20th August, while commanding No.1 Battery, Light Armoured Car Batteries (Duke of Westminster's). He was a temporary major while Chief Instructor, Australian and New Zealand Training Centre, Moascar from 21st September and was appointed unpaid local lieutenant colonel for seventeen months (OBE, LG 1st January 1919 and MID, LG 22nd January 1919). On 17th February 1919 he was admitted to 88th General Hospital and was invalided home, embarking on HT *Norman* at Port Said on 13th March. An operation on his leg was carried out on 16th May for neuritis, resulting from the wound in August 1914. A medical board at Prince of Wales's Hospital, London on 4th June found him unfit for 'A' (active service) and 'B' (lines of communications and garrisons) service for six months and he was sent on leave until 3rd August. He changed his surname to Collings-Wells by Deed Poll dated 26th June 1919. Medical boards at Bedford Military Hospital on 25th August and 31st October found him unfit for 'A' and 'B' service for four months and he was sent on leave until 24th October and 30th December respectively. He retired from the Army on 1st November 1919, retaining the rank of major. He applied for the rank of lieutenant colonel but he had served less than twenty years and was not entitled. In March 1923 he commuted £30 of his annual pension of £180 to realise £372/7/9. Russell ceased to belong to the Regular Reserve of Officers on 11th November 1932, having attained the age limit. His marriage to the Hon Olive Mary Kitson, daughter of Lord and Lady Airedale of Stoner House, Petersfield, Hampshire, was announced in The Times on 29th August 1919. The marriage did not take place and a notice to that effect appeared in The Times on 27th September 1919. Russell married Victoria Oliver-Hutchinson, daughter of Colonel Edward Oliver Hutchinson, on 27th August 1921 at Johannesburg, South

Africa. They lived at Greenfields, Gorse Hill Road, Virginia Water, Surrey. He was fined 30/- for causing an obstruction with a motorcar at Hertford Street, London on 19th November 1937. His address was given as 10 Norfolk Crescent, London. He was fined 10/- for failing to conform to an automatic traffic signal at the junction of Fulham Palace Road and Lillie Road in London on 11th October 1938. Russell was a deputy regional controller for the Board of Trade 1940–44. They had two children:

  - Rosemary Joy Collings-Wells (born 10th October 1922) married John Michael Beharrell on 12th June 1948 at Christ Church, Virginia Water, Surrey. They had three children – Jonathan N Beharrel 1950, Russell C Beharrel 1955 and Andrew M Beharrel 1959.
  - Anthony Arthur Collings-Wells (born 31st December 1928), a coffee merchant, married Juliet Philippa C Coldstream (born 1932) at St James's, Spanish Place, Marylebone, London on 19th April 1956. Her birth was registered as Philippa Juliet C Coldstream, daughter of Professor William Menzies Coldstream (later Sir William CBE) (1908–87). Anthony was a bank official in 1961.

- Mabel Bertha Collings Wells (1884–21st November 1961) married the Reverend Francis Reginald Pemberton (August 1863–8th November 1942) on 8th December 1927 at Aylesbury, Buckinghamshire. Francis was later Rector of Little Hallingbury, Essex. He had married Lilian Reynolds Davies (1869–26th June 1926) on 17th April 1895 at Christ Church, Adlington, Lancashire and they had two daughters – Marjorie Lilian Pemberton 1898 and Sybil Frances Pemberton 1900. They were living at Church House, Sissinghurst, Cranbrook, Kent at the time of his death at 12 Clarence House, Windsor, Berkshire. Mabel was living at 2 Ash Court, Bilton, Rugby, Warwickshire at the time of her death at The Hospital of St Cross, Rugby.
- Alice Madeline Collings Wells (1885–7th January 1952) married Lieutenant (later Colonel) Francis William Watson CB MC TD DL JP RFA (1893–10th June 1966) on 12th September 1916 at St John's Church, Markyate, Hertfordshire. Francis was commissioned in the Royal Field Artillery and was promoted lieutenant on 1st June 1916 (MC, LG 26th September 1917). He was a member of 99th (Bucks & Berks Yeomanry) Field Brigade RFA) and later Chairman of the County of Buckingham Territorial and Auxiliary Forces Association. On 24th August 1939 he was promoted lieutenant colonel with seniority from 5th May 1939 and was appointed temporary colonel on 1st December 1941. He was made honorary colonel on 28th April 1945. Francis was appointed Deputy Lieutenant Buckinghamshire, Sheriff for Buckinghamshire (LG 17th November 1944) and High Sheriff 1947. Awarded the CB, LG 1st January 1955. They lived at The Glebe House, Dinton, Buckinghamshire and had a son:

  - Richard Charles Chalinor Watson MA (16th February 1923–1st March 1998) was educated at Rugby School, New College Oxford and Westcott

House at Cambridge. He was commissioned in the Royal Artillery on 13th December 1942 and served in the Indian Artillery during the Second World War in South East Asia 1942–45. He held a number of appointments: curate at Stratford, East London 1952–53; tutor and chaplain at Wycliffe Hall, Oxford 1954–57; chaplain of Wadham College and Oxford Pastorate 1957–61; Vicar of Hornchurch, Essex 1962–70; Examining Chaplain to the Bishop of Rochester 1956–61; Examining Chaplain to the Bishop of Chelmsford 1962–70; Assistant Rural Dean to Havering 1967–70; Rector of Burnley, Lancashire 1970–77; and Bishop Suffragan of Burnley 1970–87. Richard married Anna Chavasse (born 1927) in 1955, daughter of the Right Reverend Christopher Maude Chavasse OBE MC MA DD, Bishop of Rochester, twin brother of Noel Geoffrey Chavasse VC & Bar MC. They had two children – David Watson 1956 and Rachel B Watson 1959.

Francis married Gladys Joan Macbeth in 1958 at Oxford. They were living at St Osyths Cottage, Parsons Fee, Aylesbury at the time of his death.

- Leonard Collings Collings Wells (5th April 1889–14th February 1977) was educated at Winchester and Trinity Hall, Cambridge (MA 1919). He was commissioned in 4th Bedfordshire on 6th March 1907 and promoted lieutenant on 24th May 1909. He served in 1st King's African Rifles and was severely wounded by a gunshot to the right elbow at M'buyuni on 14th July 1915. He embarked on SS *Galway Castle* at Mombasa on 6th September and disembarked in London on 2nd October. Medical boards on 7th October 1915, 15th February 1916 and 22nd May found him unfit for General Service for periods of three to five months. A medical board on 15th August found him unfit for General Service for six weeks but fit for light duty at the Depot at Nairobi. His leave was extended to 22nd October and he embarked at Marseille on 9th November, disembarking at Mombasa on 3rd November. A medical board at the British General Hospital, Nairobi on 12th December found he had only partial use of the right hand due to damage to the ulnar and median nerves, which was permanent. Other medical boards followed, all agreeing that he was permanently unfit for service. A medical board at Nairobi on 27th November found him unfit for General Service permanently. Leonard was a member of the Legislative Council, Kenya Colony 1920–23. He married his cousin, Phyllis Cooper (1893–15th May 1963), on 2nd June 1921 at Wycombe, Buckinghamshire. They were living at Herepath, Crow Hill, Ringwood, Hampshire in 1954. Phyllis died on 15th May 1963 at Salisbury Infirmary, Wiltshire. They had at least one son:
    - Peter Darroll Collings-Wells (24th April 1928–2000) married Anne Holt Wilson (born 1927) in 1955 registered at Surrey North Eastern. She was the younger daughter of Captain Edward Rowland Wilson, late Royal Irish Fusiliers, of 14 Lauriston Road, Wimbledon, Surrey. Peter left an estate valued at £1,615,450. They had two sons – Jonathan Collings-Wells 1956 and Peter H Collings-Wells 1959. Edward Rowland Wilson (1886–1960) was commissioned on 20th April 1910 and rose to captain on 28th November

1915. He served in France 19th December 1914–13th February 1915 and 5th May–1st July 1916 and was wounded twice. He was appointed Staff Captain, Military Secretary, War Office 8th February–14th September 1919 and retired on Half Pay on 1st April 1921.

Leonard married Lilla Mary Butler (14th January 1898–31st August 1985) on 2nd May 1964 at Rugby, Warwickshire. They were living at Smith's Corner, Upper Basildon, Reading, Berkshire at the time of their deaths.

John's paternal grandfather, Joseph Wells (c.1818–24th January 1892), born at Braintree, Essex, married Maria Primrose née Primrose (c.1819–6th May 1906), born at Wrentham, Suffolk, in 1841 at Blything, Suffolk. At the time of the 1851 Census she was living with her parents and daughter Jessie at St Mary's Green, Ipswich, Suffolk. Joseph was a farmer of 330 acres, living at Wood House, Little Waltham, Essex with his daughter Catherine and his sister Eliza Wells. By 1861 his farm had increased to 476 acres and he employed twenty-six men and five boys. By 1881 he was a brewer and a farmer. He left effects valued at £101,309/7/6 (£11.8M in 2017). In addition to Arthur they had eleven other children:

- Sarah Agnes Wells (1842–9th April 1911) married William Vacy Lyle (1838–1st December 1888), a general medical practitioner, in 1866. They were living at 21 Westbourne Villas, Paddington, London in 1871 and at 19 Westbourne Square, Paddington in 1881. He died there, leaving effects valued at £11,142/8/-. She was living at 21 Enis Road, Eastbourne, Sussex at the time of her death at 73 Royal Parade there. They had seven children – Agnes Kingsford Lyle 1867, Joseph Vacy Lyle 1868, John Primrose Lyle 1869, William Percival Lyle 1873, Catherine Maria Lyle 1876, Mary Isabel Lyle 1878 and Eva Primrose Lyle 1880.
- Catherine Maria Wells (1843–13th August 1932) married James Richard Field (c.1822–26th March 1907), a warehouseman, in 1866. He was an annuitant in 1881 and they were living at Albion House, St Peter's, Broadstairs, Kent. She was living at Wellesley, Broadstairs in 1911. James had married Harriet Golding (c.1827–64) in 1847 at Islington, London. They were living at 114 Fore Street, Cripplegate, London in 1851. James died without issue, leaving effects valued at £2,238/19/5. Catherine was living at Wellesley, Gladstone Road, Broadstairs in 1911 and died there in 1932.
- Jessie Wells (born 1844) was at boarding school in 1861 at 6 Effingham Street, Dover St Mary, Kent. She was single and living with her parents in 1881.
- William Woodcock Wells (1846–18th October 1904), a merchant, married Mary Alice May (1845–10th October 1929) in 1869 at Maldon, Essex. Mary was living at Crowley House, Bury Cross, Alverstoke, Hampshire in 1911 and died there in 1929, leaving effects valued at £8,446/7/9. They had three children – Ethel May Wells 1869, and twins Edith Primrose Wells and Mabel Parker Wells 1870.

- Joseph Fleetwood Wells (1850–20th June 1925) married Jessie Matilda Campbell (died 14th May 1922). They had three children – Louisa Frances Primrose Wells 1881, Lucy Josephine Wells 1882 and Constance McIver Wells 1884.
- Eugene Wells (1852–21st June 1925) was studying farming in 1871 and was a merchant and farmer by 1881, living with his wife Gertrude Rose (born c.1853) at Baylham House, Coddenham, Suffolk. She was born at Niagara, Canada. By 1901 he was a maltster and they were living at Buxhall Vale, Suffolk. They had no children.
- Charles Henry Wells (1853–1938) was a student of medicine in 1871.
- Albert Primrose Wells (13th October 1854–5th December 1948) married Grace Woosnam (born 20th October 1857) on 10th January 1883 at Weston-super-Mare, Somerset. She was born at Bombay, India, the youngest daughter of Colonel James Bowen Woosnam, Royal Artillery (1812–77) who retired as honorary major general on 13th July 1863. Albert was a general practitioner in 1891 and they were living at 7 Georges Road, Beckenham, Kent. By 1911 he was also an electrical specialist and they were living at Pinner Wood, Harrow, Middlesex. Grace was his assistant. In 1918 they were living at Picton House, 38 Lee Terrace, Blackheath and later at 19 Lawn Terrace, Blackheath. In November 1914 they were living at Burnside Road, Victoria, British Columbia and in October 1916 at 'Casa Loma', Banbury, Oxfordshire, England. They emigrated to Canada and lived at Pinner Wood, near Duncan, Vancouver Island. He died at Quamichan Lake, Vancouver Island, leaving effects valued at £7,840/2/6. They had six children:
    - Joseph Hamilton Primrose Wells (1884–9th October 1967) was a clerk in a shipping office in 1911 and later served as a lieutenant in the Sind Volunteer Rifles, Indian Army. He married Joan Fortescue Wilson (25th May 1919–18th June 1977) on 16th January 1946 at Swanage, Dorset. She was the daughter of Colonel Cyril Wilson CMG CBE DSO. They were living at 9 Newton Road, Swanage at the time of his death. She was living at 7 Peveril Heights, Swanage at the time of her death.
    - Helen Phyllis Primrose Wells (born c.1886).
    - Ursula Primrose Wells (born c.1887).
    - James Bowen Primrose Wells (18th October 1887–4th April 1918) was educated at Abbey School, Beckenham, Epsom College and University College, London. He served in the Epsom College Cadet Corps as a bugler and the Honourable Artillery Company as a driver 1908–09, while working for HM Board of Trade, Whitehall in the Labour Exchange Department for two years. He moved to Canada with his family, living at Burnside Road, Victoria, British Columbia. He was an accountant when war broke out and enlisted in 30th Battalion CEF (77820) on 18th November 1914, described as 5′ 5″ tall, with dark complexion, blue eyes, dark brown hair and his religious denomination was Christian Scientist. He was serving at Napier Barracks, Shorncliffe, Kent when he applied for a commission on 18th April 1915. He was commissioned in the Special Reserve of Officers to serve in 4th Bedfordshire on 22nd May

1915. He went to France on 19th May 1916 and joined 2nd Bedfordshire on 13th June. He left the unit on 5th September for a Lewis gun course at Le Touquet but on 8th September was admitted to hospital with enteritis. The problem started on 10th August at Béthune with a fever and diarrhoea. He embarked on HMHS *Brighton* (carried the King, PM David Lloyd George and President Woodrow Wilson across the Channel at various times during and shortly after the war) at Calais for Dover on 18th September and was treated for enteritis and influenza at the Royal Free Hospital, London next day and later at Lady Ashton-Smith's Convalescent Home for Officers, The Hoo, Willingdon, near Eastbourne. A medical board at Eastbourne on 23rd October found him unfit for General Service for three months and leave was granted until 22nd November. His address was 38 Orsett Terrace, Porchester Square, London. A medical board on 4th December found him unfit for General Service for two months but fit for light duties and he joined the 3rd Battalion next day. A medical board on 6th January 1917 found him unfit for General Service for one month and a board at Tunbridge Wells on 14th February found him fit. He was posted to 4th Battalion and was wounded in the left thigh in the attack on Gavrelle on 23rd April 1917 and was admitted to 14th General Hospital, Boulogne next day. He embarked on HMHS *St Andrew* at Boulogne on 25th April, arriving at Dover next day. Medical boards at Caxton Hall on 25th May and 2nd July found him unfit for General Service for two and three months respectively. He was granted leave 25th April–23rd July and then joined 3rd Bedfordshire. On 1st July he was promoted lieutenant. A medical board at Felixstowe on 3rd September found him unfit for General Service for one month but he was declared fit on 4th October and rejoined the Battalion on 15th November. He was wounded during the same action in which his cousin, John Collings-Wells, was awarded the VC, on 27th March 1918 and was posted missing. James died in captivity on 4th April 1918 from a spinal wound and was buried in Bécourt German Military Cemetery (referred to as Little Chateau Cemetery in British correspondence). However, his grave was one of five subsequently lost and he is commemorated in Blighty Valley Cemetery (Bécourt German Cemetery Memorial 1)), He died intestate and left £177/13/-.

James Bowen Primrose Wells' memorial in Blighty Valley Cemetery.

- Eric Woosnam Primrose Wells (19th October 1889–1954) attested in 190th Overseas Battalion CEF (892478) on 6th October 1916 at Winnipeg, Manitoba, Canada, described as

Frank Irving Pascoe Wells' grave in St Vaast Post Military Cemetery.

5′ 8″ tall, with fair complexion, light blue eyes, fair hair and his religious denomination was Church of England. He was living at 403 Bedford Street, St James, Manitoba and was a bookkeeper. He declared four years previous service in the Royal North West Mounted Police. Eric married Edna G Underhill in 1940.
    - Cathleen Mona Primrose Wells (born 1892).
- Emilie Beatrice Wells (27th June 1859–17th January 1952) married Charles Henry Downes (25th September 1857–12th May 1934), as Emily Beatrice Wells, in 1882. He was a solicitor, born at Palgrave, Suffolk. They were living at 1 Wolsey Terrace, Walton, Suffolk in 1891. They were living at 25 Avenue Crescent, Acton, Middlesex at the time of his death there. Emilie was living at Baylham Cottage, Fairwarp, Sussex at the time of her death there. They had four children – Gwendoline Beatrice Downes 1884, Olive Primrose Downes 1885, Eugene Charles Alistair Downes 1889 and Joan Calthrop Downes 1893.
- Alexander Wells (1861–10th October 1938) married Blanche Ada Gassner (20th May 1865–29th August 1946) on 11th June 1896 at Christ Church, Lancaster Gate, London. She was born at sea, the daughter of Giovanni Gassner (c.1828–1893), Bandmaster of the 50th Regiment, who served from 19th August 1865 until 22nd July 1884. They were living at Willingdon, Sussex in 1911 and, at the time of his death, at The Five Gables, Wish Hill, Willingdon, Sussex. He left effects valued at £23,065/19/9. She was also living there when she died at Princess Alice Memorial Hospital, Eastbourne, leaving effects valued at £2,878/1/-.
- Frank Edward Wells (1864–30th May 1948) married Emmy Pascoe Morgan (1871–19th January 1959) in 1892 at Kensington, London. He was a dairy farmer living with his family at Uphill House, Hawkinge, Kent in 1911. They were living at Glenleigh, Linden Gardens, Tunbridge Wells, Kent in 1915. They were living at 55 Madeira Park, Tunbridge Wells, Kent at the time of his death there. She died at The Gables Nursing Home, Aldwick Road, Bognor Regis, Sussex. They had three children:
    - Frank Irving Pascoe Wells (1893–9th May 1915) was serving as a lieutenant in 2nd Welsh when he was killed in action. He is buried in St Vaast Post Military Cemetery, Richebourg-L'Avoué, France (I B 1).
    - Jack Pascoe Wells (1894–6th April 1976) was educated at Haileybury College and Pembroke College, Cambridge (BA), where he was attached to the UOTC medical unit. He received a TF commission (unattached) in November 1914 and applied for a regular commission on 5th May 1918,

while a senior house surgeon at St Bartholomew's Hospital, London (MRCS, LRCP). He was described as 5′ 9″ tall and weighed 144 lbs. His address was Bella Vista, Southborough, Kent. He was ordered to report to the RAMC Training Centre, Art Gallery, Blackpool on a Special Reserve commission on 1st August 1918. However, in the meantime he was commissioned as a lieutenant in the RAF on 24th July 1918 and was promoted flight lieutenant on 13th July 1922, with seniority later from 13th July 1919. He was appointed to the Medical Branch, Marine and Armament Experimental Establishment, Isle of Grain, Kent on 2nd April 1922 and last appears in the Air Force List in July 1922. Jack married Joyce Beaumont (1902–46) in 1927 at Chelmsford and they had two children – Daphne M Wells 1928 and Peter CP Wells 1929. He married Brenda M Parsfield in 1947 at Chelmsford. Jack was living at Stuarts Hopping, Jacks Lane, Danbury, Essex at the time of his death there.

- Mary Elinor Wells (4th August 1896–November 1995).

His maternal grandfather, Arthur Russell Eisdell (c.1830–27th June 1890), was the son of Joseph Carter Eisdell (1787–1854), Town Commissioner and Borough Magistrate for Colchester. Arthur was living with his parents at East Hill, St James, Colchester in 1841. He was a tanner in 1851, living with his father and siblings at East Bay, Colchester. He married Eliza Crisp née Buck (c.1831–26th August 1914) on 23rd March 1854 at Ipswich, Suffolk. By 1861 he was a miller, employing five men and a boy, and they were living at Abbey Mill, Reading, Berkshire. They had moved to 1 Craven Road, St Giles, Berkshire by 1871 and to Brooklyn, 1 Kendrick Road, St Giles by 1881, by when he was a master miller employing twenty-four men. He left effects valued at £27,206/9/6 (£3.3M in 2016). Eliza was living with her daughters, Ellen and Emily, at 5 Southern Hill, Reading, Berkshire in 1911. In addition to Caroline they had seven other children:

John's maternal grandfather, Arthur Russell Eisdell, ran Abbey Mill in Reading, which was built by the monks of Reading Abbey in the late 12th century. They created the Holy Brook, seen here running through one of the few remains of the Mill, to supply this and other mills. The Mill was still grinding corn in the 1950s, over 400 years after the demise of the Abbey. The Holy Brook was narrowed before the Mill to speed the water flow, which turned the undershot wheel. Today all that remains is a section of wall with three arches behind Reading's Central Library in King's Road.

- Eliza Lilian Eisdell (23rd December 1856–1900) never married.
- Ellen Jessie Eisdell (1858–12th February 1940) died unmarried at 5 Southern Hill, Reading.

- Agnes Maud Eisdell (1860–6th June 1935) married William Griffith Milsom (1850–2nd March 1923) in 1883. He was a coal and building goods merchant in 1881, living with his parents at 100 King's Road, St Giles, Reading. They were living at 24 Bath Road, Reading in 1911 and at 3 Upper Redlands Road, Reading at the time of his death. She was living at 5 Southern Hill, Reading at the time of her death there. They had four children – Hilda Maud Milsom 1884, Greta Mary Milsom 1885, Agnes Monica Milsom 1889 and Brands Milsom 1890.
- Nora/Norah Margaret Eisdell (1861–20th April 1920) married Arthur Leslie Cooper (1853–16th December 1913) in 1883. He was a quantity surveyor in 1891 and they were living at Elm Side, Coley Avenue, St Mary, Berkshire. By 1901 they had moved to 5 Addington Road, St Giles, Reading. They were living at 6 Southern Hill, Reading at the time of his death at Manor House, Drayton, Daventry, Northamptonshire. She died at 6 Southern Hill, Reading. They had eight children – Carey Cooper 1884, Godfrey Cooper 1886, Eisdell Cooper 1887, Dorothy Cooper 1889, Alice Margery Cooper 1892, Phyllis Cooper 1893, Basil Cooper 1895 and Muriel Cooper 1898. Basil Cooper was educated at Reading School and became a quantity surveyor. He enlisted in 20th Royal Fusiliers (4681 & 47330) on 2nd September 1914 at Reading and joined at Epsom on 16th September, described as 5′ 10¼″ tall, weighing 143 lbs, with fresh complexion, grey eyes, black hair and his religious denomination was Baptist or Congregationalist. He was appointed unpaid lance corporal on 27th September 1915 and went to France with the Battalion on 14th November. He was appointed acting sergeant on 22nd March 1916 and was wounded in the neck on 16th July. Having been treated at a general hospital in Rouen, he was evacuated on 23rd July for treatment at the Red Cross Hospital, Bellahouston, Glasgow from 24th July. The shrapnel remained in his neck. He was granted leave 28th August–7th September and was posted to 6th Battalion on 12th September. While attached to A Company, 22nd Training Reserve Battalion at St Albans, he applied for a commission on 19th October, described as 6′ tall, weighing 160 lbs, He trained at No.2 Officer Cadet Battalion, Pembroke College, Cambridge as a corporal from 1st December 1916. On 23rd February he was admitted to 1st Eastern General Hospital, Cambridge for an operation to remove shrapnel from the jugular vein, following which he was medically graded 'C2' on 28th June. He was commissioned on 22nd July in the Labour Corps and was serving at Eastern Command Labour Centre, Sutton, Surrey in November. Medical boards on 25th February and 14th June 1918 and 11th August 1919 found him unfit for 'A' and 'B' service permanently. He relinquished his commission on account of ill health on 25th September 1919, retaining the rank of lieutenant. Basil married Mary Irene Atkinson in 1921 at Edmonton, Middlesex. They were living at 82 Elmhurst Road, Reading at the time of his death on 10th December 1951 at 344 Oxford Road, Reading. She was living at 14 Burnham Rise, Emmer Green, Reading at the time of her death there on 1st July 1964. They had three children – Basil Keith Cooper 1922, Jean Mary Cooper 1926 and Ellen V Cooper 1930.

- Alice Bridget Eisdell (1863–80) never married.
- Joseph Carter Eisdell (1869–25th June 1930) was a solicitor in 1911. He was living at Down House, Hurstpierpoint, Sussex at the time of his death there.
- Emily Carter Eisdell (1870–22nd December 1945) died unmarried at Cowlas, Burrington, Umberleigh, Devonshire.

John was educated at Aldeburgh Lodge School, Aldeburgh, Suffolk and Uppingham School, Rutland in Fircroft House 1895–1900. He was tutored at Christ Church, Oxford but did not graduate. Whilst there he became a Freemason, being Initiated into the Apollo University Lodge (No.357). At least two other members of that Lodge received the VC – John Norwood and Eric McNair. John was employed in his father's engineering business until 1906, when he went to live with his great uncle and aunt, Will and Flora Buck, at Field House, Staines Road, Marple, near Stockport, Lancashire, in order to run his father's business at 3 Carnarvon Street, Cheetham, Manchester.

John joined the Hertfordshire Militia in 1903. He was commissioned in 4th Bedfordshire (Hertfordshire Militia) on 14th March 1904 and was promoted lieutenant on 17th September 1904 and captain on 3rd January 1907. He sailed to France on 22nd August 1914 and may have served with 1st Battalion. Later he joined the 2nd Battalion there. It arrived at Southampton from South Africa on 19th September and landed at Zeebrugge on 6th October. John was wounded by a gunshot to the right thigh at Fleurbaix on 12th January 1915 and was treated at 4th General Hospital, Versailles from 14th January until invalided to Britain, departing Le Havre on HMHS *Asturias* on 20th January, arriving at Southampton next day. He was treated at a hospital at 8 Chesterfield Gardens, London. A medical board at Caxton Hall on 27th January found him unfit for one month and leave was granted to 26th February. Medical

Uppingham School, founded in 1584, remained small until expanding in the 19th Century. By the 1960s it had 600 pupils. The first girl attended in 1973. In addition to John Collings Wells, four other Old Uppinghamians have been awarded the VC – Arthur Lascelles, George Maling, Thomas Maufe, and Willward Sandys-Clarke. Famous alumni include:

Jonathan Agnew, the BBC's Chief Cricket Correspondent.
Rowan Atkinson, actor and comedian.
Edward Brittain, brother of Vera Brittain, who wrote *Testament of Youth*.
Sir Malcolm Campbell and Donald Campbell, world land and water speed record holders.
Stephen Fry, actor, comedian and writer.
Lieutenant General Sir Brian Horrocks, commander of XXX Corps in the Second World War.
CRW Nevinson, official war artist in both World Wars.
William Henry Pratt, film actor using the stage name Boris Karloff.
John Schlesinger, film director.
Rick Stein, chef, restaurateur and television broadcaster.

boards at Bedford on 5th March and 12th October found him fit for General Service. He reported to 4th Battalion on 8th March.

John's grave in Bouzincourt Ridge Cemetery near Albert. In the background beyond the cemetery wall is the Basilique in Albert.

John never married but his engagement to Miss Marjory Holt of Woodthorpe, Prestwich and Blackwell, Windermere was announced in *The Times* on 22nd June 1915. He returned to France on 25th July 1916, when 4th Battalion deployed abroad, having been converted from Extra Reserve to a service battalion. John was commanding a company as a major. Later he was appointed second in command. On 20th October 1916 John was promoted acting lieutenant colonel to command 4th Battalion. **Awarded the DSO for his actions at Gavrelle on 23rd-29th April 1917, when he led his Battalion straight through the village, gained his objective, consolidated on the northern outskirts and, although heavily shelled and counterattacked, he drove the enemy off. Later he commanded a composite battalion of 7th Royal Fusiliers and 4th Bedfordshire in the attack on the Oppy trench system from the railway to 450m north of it on the left. He formed up his command on strange ground in the dark and under heavy shellfire. He achieved his objective but was driven out by a determined enemy counterattack. He attacked again and retook the trench. Although heavily shelled for the rest of the day he held on until relieved, LG 18th July 1917.** John commanded 190th Brigade temporarily 4th-9th and 18th-19th June 1917. The DSO was presented by the King at Buckingham Palace on 5th December 1917.

Awarded the VC for his actions at Marcoing to Albert, France 22nd -27th March 1918, LG 24th April 1918. The VC was presented to his parents by the King at Buckingham Palace on 1st June 1918. John was also Mentioned in Sir Douglas Haig's Despatch dated 7th November 1917, LG 18th December 1917. He was killed during his VC action west of Albert, France on 27th March 1918. The location of his grave was unknown at first. However, the IWGC sent a battered map case found with an unidentified dead officer back to its owner, Lieutenant G Martin of 4th Bedfordshire. Martin identified the map case as the one he had given to John when he left the Battalion in 1916. As a result John's grave was identified in Bouzincourt Ridge Cemetery, Albert, France (III E 12). However, inexplicably the *Concentration of Graves (Exhumation and Reburials)* form dated 14th June 1923 shows that his body was recovered from map reference 57dQ17a95. This is south of Beaumont-Hamel and east of Newfoundland Memorial Park, some eight kilometres from where he was killed. He left effects valued at £7,406/5/2. John is commemorated in a number of other places:

Markyate war memorial was dedicated on Armistice Day 1921.

The Collings-Wells family grave in the churchyard of St Michael & All Angels, Hughenden, Buckinghamshire. A church has existed on this site since the 12th century. The Earl of Beaconsfield, Benjamin Disraeli, Prime Minister in 1868 and 1874–80, is buried in the family vault on the west wall of the church. Queen Victoria visited the tomb a few days after the funeral.

- Collings-Wells VC Memorial Hall, Caddington, Hertfordshire was opened by his brother, Lieutenant Colonel Russell Primrose Collings-Wells DSO OBE, on 26th January 1935.
- Collings-Wells Close, Caddington, Hertfordshire.
- Caddington War Memorial, Hertfordshire in All Saint's Churchyard.
- Marble plaque erected by his parents near the altar of All Saints Church, Luton Road, Caddington.
- Named on the family gravestone at Hughenden Manor Church (St Michael & All Angels), Buckinghamshire.
- Memorial to him and the men of 4th Bedfordshire at St Ethelreda's Church, Hatfield, Hertfordshire.
- War Memorial, High Street, Markyate, Hertfordshire.
- St John the Baptist Church, Markyate – stained glass window, plaque and War Memorial.
- Aldeburgh Lodge School War Memorial, St Peter & St Paul Church, Victoria Road, Aldeburgh, Suffolk.
- Three memorials at Uppingham School, Rutland – in the chapel, in Fircroft dining room and on the Victoria Cross Memorial.
- Uppingham School memorial plaque in St George's Memorial Church, Elverdingsestraat 1, Ieper, Belgium.
- Memorial at Christ Church College, Oxford.
- All Saints War Memorial, Marple, near Stockport, Lancashire.
- Memorial paving stone unveiled outside Freemason's Hall, Covent Garden, London on 25th April 2017 by The Duke of Kent KG. John is also named on the Masonic Roll of Honour Scroll, First Vestibule, Freemasons' Hall, Great Queen Street, London.

St John the Baptist Church, Markyate dates from 1734 and was extended in 1811 and 1892. John Collings Wells is commemorated on its War Memorial, in a stained glass window and on this plaque.

The 1914 Star was authorised for the Army in 1917 and for the Royal Navy in 1918. It was awarded to officers and men who served in France and Belgium between 5th August and midnight on 22nd-23rd November 1914. The closing date was the formal end of the First Battle of Ypres. The recipient's number, rank, name and unit are stamped on the reverse. In October 1919 a clasp was authorised, '5th Aug – 22nd Nov. 1914', for those who had been under fire or within range of enemy artillery during the period. A total of 365,622 medals were awarded. Approximately 145,000 clasps were awarded but the precise number is unknown as it had to be claimed personally and many of those eligible died before 1919 or simply failed to apply. Some Royal Navy personnel qualified by landing at Antwerp. A few women also qualified, serving as nurses or auxiliaries. However, the majority of recipients were members of the pre-war regular British Army and its reservists, the Old Contemptibles, and the medal became known as the 'Mons Star'. A small number were awarded to Canadians, mainly members of 2nd Canadian Stationary Hospital, which served with the BEF from 6th November 1914. The 1914 Star was always awarded with the British War Medal and Victory Medal. Anyone awarded the 1914 Star did not also qualify for the 1914–15 Star.

- Department for Communities and Local Government commemorative paving stones for John were dedicated at Markyate War Memorial, Park View Drive, Markyate and at the junction of Luton Road and Dunstable Road, Caddington, Hertfordshire on 27th March 2018 to mark the centenary of his award. A copy stone was also dedicated at Manchester Cenotaph in St Peter's Square.

In addition to the VC and DSO he was awarded the 1914 Star with 'Mons' clasp, British War Medal 1914–20 and Victory Medal 1914–19 with Mentioned-in-

Despatches Oakleaf. His father left the medals to his son, Russell Primrose Wells, in 1922. The VC is held by the Bedfordshire & Hertfordshire Regimental Museum Collection, Wardown Park Museum, Wardown Park, Luton, Bedfordshire.

94081 PRIVATE JACK THOMAS COUNTER
1st Battalion, The King's (Liverpool Regiment)

(FA Swaine)

Jack Counter was born on 3rd November 1898 at 11 Damory Street, Blandford Forum, Dorset. His father, Frank Counter (16th July 1871–28th May 1945), born at Salisbury Street, Blandford Forum, was a cabinet maker. He married Rosina 'Rose' née Edmunds (1871–1903), a domestic servant, also born at Blandford Forum, on 18th July 1893 at the Independent Chapel there. They were living at Herston Villa, Blandford Forum in 1898. By 1901 they had moved to Queen's Road. Frank married Minnie Sophia Thyer (1880–1942), born at Langport, Somerset, in 1908 at Blandford Forum. They were living at Damory Street, Blandford Forum in 1911, moving to Dorset House, Dorset Street, Blandford Forum by 1919. Jack had four siblings from his father's two marriages:

- Percy William Counter (1894–12th December 1942) was an apprentice agricultural engineer in 1911. He lost his leg while serving as a corporal in the Dorsetshire Regiment (10901) during the Great War. He married Edith Ferris (22nd September 1891–19th September 1976) in 1919. She was born at Goonpiper, St Feock, Cornwall. They were living at Dorset House, Blandford Forum at the time of

Jack was born on Damory Street, Blandford Forum, in 1989 (Andrew Auger).

Salisbury Street, Blandford Forum, where Frank Counter was born in 1871.

his death. She was living at Three Pines, 146 Richmond Park Road, Bournemouth at the time of her death. They had a son, Herbert Frank Counter (1922–29th April 2015), who married Barbara B Spreadbury (born 1924) in 1948 at Bournemouth, Dorset. She was born at Shaftesbury, Dorset. They had a daughter, Jacqueline A Counter, in 1954.

Dorset House on Dorset Street, Blandford Forum, where the Counter family was living by 1919. Jack died there on a visit in 1970. To the right of the front door is a Blue Plaque.

- Gertrude Lily Counter (23rd September 1896–4th February 1977) was a tailor's apprentice in 1911, living with her uncle, Arthur Joseph Counter, at 27 Maidstone Street, Victoria Park, Bedminster, Bristol. She married George Herbert Weeks (24th February 1894–23rd February 1969), a railway ticket collector, on 4th June 1932 at the Baptist Chapel, East Street, Bedminster, Bristol. They lived at 27 Maidstone Street, Victoria Park, Bedminster. George died at Southmead Hospital, Bristol. Gertrude died at the General Hospital, Redcliffe, Bristol.
- Alfred Frank T Counter (1909–31).
- Herbert FJ Counter (1913–14).

Jack's paternal grandfather, George Counter (c.1828–95), a shoemaker, married Mary Pearce née Riggs (c.1833–96) on 9th September 1852 at Blandford Forum parish church (St Peter & St Paul). In 1861 they were living at New Buildings, Blandford. By 1871 they were living at Salisbury Street and by 1881 at The Rookery. In addition to Frank they had nine other children:

Blandford market place with the parish church in the background. The town suffered a devastating fire in 1731, which destroyed the whole town, including the medieval church. Rising from the ashes was a new Georgian town, one of the finest in Britain. Most of the work fell to local architects and builders, John and William Bastard. The largest new building was the parish church of St Peter & St Paul, just off the market square, built between 1733 and 1739, arguably the finest example of Georgian church architecture outside London. The structure is in poor condition and much repair work has been carried out in recent years with the assistance of the Heritage Lottery Fund. Jack's grandparents married there in 1852.

- Frederick Counter (born 1853), a twin with Alfred, was a general servant in 1871.
- Alfred Counter (born 1853), a twin with Frederick, was a tailor in 1871.
- Edward Counter (1855–96) married Mary Susan Burbridge (1856–94) in 1885 at Marylebone, London. She was born at Leamington Spa, Warwickshire, registered as Burbidge. In 1891 he was a coachman/domestic servant and they were living at 2 Kendrick Mews, Kensington, London. They both died in Chelsea, London. They had three children:
    - Edward Cyril Counter 1886–94.
    - Percival George Counter 1888.
    - Albert Walter F Counter 1892.
- Louisa Jane Counter (1856–1917) was a domestic servant in 1871 and a dressmaker in 1891.
- Augustine Henry Counter (1858–1926) was a servant in 1871. He married Alice Johnson (1864–1943) in 1894 at Lambeth, London. She was born at North Chapel, Sussex. He was a domestic coachman in 1901 and they were living at Moorclose, Binfield, Berkshire.
- James John Counter (30th October 1860–1933) was a bricklayer in 1881. He married Anne Pauley (1867–1925) in 1885 at Wincanton, Somerset. She was born at Sherborne, Dorset. James was a postman by 1891 and they were living at Butts Pond, Sturminster, Dorset and at Templecombe, Somerset by 1911. They had seven children including:
    - Florence Lily Counter (21st February 1888–1975) married Albert George Spearing (8th June 1883–1970) in 1910 at Wincanton. They had at least two children – Phyllis FA Spearing 1912 and Lily EM Spearing 1916.
    - George Counter (1890–4th November 1957) married Daisy Leadbetter (22nd March 1893–1978) at Basingstoke in 1917 and they had a daughter, Phyllis M Counter, in 1920. They were living at 228 Market Street, Eastleigh, Hampshire when he died.
    - William Counter 1894.
    - Elder Mary Counter 1898.
    - Winifred Counter 1900.
    - Edith Annie Counter (30th November 1902–1975) married Edwin Cross at Wincanton in 1923.
- Charles Counter (1863–1905) was a groom, living with his parents in 1881 and at 8 Farm Street, St George Hanover Square, London in 1891. He died at Melton Mowbray, Leicestershire.
- William George Counter (1865–81) was a bookbinder.
- Arthur Joseph Counter (c.1869–1941) was an errand boy in 1881. He married Eliza Amelia Hillman (1870–1958) in 1894 at Bedminster, Somerset. She was born at Wheatenhurst, Gloucestershire. By 1911 he was a tailor maker and they were living at 27 Maidstone Street, Bedminster, Bristol.

His maternal grandfather, Edwin Edmunds (c.1836–1915/17), born at Child Okeford, Dorset, was an agricultural labourer. He married Emily née Windsor (1843–1911) at Blandford Forum parish church on 2nd October 1864. In 1871 they were living at Salisbury Street, Blandford Forum, at Pimperne, Dorset by 1881, at 2 Fishers Row, Victoria Road, Blandford Forum by 1891 and at 1 Albert Place, Blandford Forum by 1901, by when he was an under gardener (domestic). In 1911 he was living with his son, Charles and family, at 1 Stanley Street, Bournemouth, Hampshire. In addition to Rosina they had four other children:

Child Okeford, where Jack's maternal grandfather was born, has an Iron Age hillfort on nearby Hambledon Hill, which was the site of an English Civil War battle in 1645. In the following century General James Wolfe trained his troops on the Hill's steep slopes before deploying to Canada.

- Charles Edmunds (1866–1933) was an agricultural labourer in 1881. Thereafter his surname appears as Edmonds. He married Amelia Jane White (1863–1959) in 1889 at Christchurch, Hampshire. She was born at Clarendon, Alderbury, Wiltshire. He was a foreman for a builder's merchant in 1911 and they were living at 1 Stanley Street, Bournemouth. They had a son, George Edwin Edmonds (1890–1981).
- Fanny Eliza Edmunds (1868–72).
- Ellen Frances Edmunds (1874–1952) married Walter Puckett (1871–24th June 1906) in 1896. He was born at Puddletown, Dorset. In 1901 he was a machine minder in pottery and they were living at May Cottage, Westons Lower, Poole St James, Dorset. She was still there in 1911. They had two children:
    - Elsie May Puckett (1897–8th July 1963) married George HJ Puckett (1894–1948) in 1925.
    - Leslie Harold Puckett (born 1901).
- William James Edmunds (1876–August 1957) married Emma Jane Bush (1876–1963) in 1897 at Christchurch. He was a storeman for a builder's merchant in 1911 and they were living at 47 Church Road, Guildford, Surrey. Living with them was Emma's sister, Maude Rosina Bush. They were living at Longfield Drive, West Parley, Hampshire at the time of his death there. They had a son, Sidney William Edmonds, in 1903.

Jack was educated at Blandford National School and was serving an apprenticeship with the International Stores there when war broke out. He enlisted in February 1917. **Awarded the VC for his actions at Boisleux-St-Marc, France on 16th April 1918, LG 22nd May 1918.** The VC was presented by the King in the

Ada Vauvert was born in St Peter, Jersey (J Bridle).

The reception outside the Corn Exchange in the Market Place in Blandford at which Jack Counter received the Freedom of the Borough.

Jersey and the other Channel Islands were occupied by German forces for almost five years during the Second World War.

quadrangle at Buckingham Palace on 22nd June 1918. After the investiture he returned to Blandford, where he was presented with £100 in War Savings Certificates and a gold watch from the International Stores. He was also appointed the first Freeman of the Borough on 19th June 1918. Jack was later promoted corporal, admitting to a comrade, W Jotham, a bandsman with the Regiment, that he only took the stripes to get out of potato peeling. Jack was posted to Jersey in 1919 and was demobilised in 1922.

Jack received the Imperial Service Medal for his long service as a postman. The medal was established on 8th August 1902 for presentation to selected civil servants for at least twenty-five years service on retirement.

GD Laurens' store in St Helier.

Jack Counter married Ada Louise Marie Vauvert (29th January 1899–28th June 1970) in 1921 at West Derby, Lancashire. She was born at St Peter, Jersey. They lived in Jersey, where Jack worked for the Post Office in St Ouen as an auxiliary postman. He transferred to Sunbury Common, Middlesex, London in 1925, in order to become an established postman, and lived at 46 Cavendish Road, Sunbury. They returned to Jersey on 24th November 1929 and lived at Como, Valley des Vaux, St Helier and later at Conamur, Hansford Lane, First Tower, St Helier. Jack became a postman in St Helier and remained there throughout the German occupation 1940–45. He retired from the postal service on 11th April 1959. **Awarded the Imperial Service Medal for long service as a postman, LG 19th May 1959.** He then worked for GD Laurens on Queen Street and Bath Street, St Helier, dealing in ships' chandlery and general goods. Later he worked for R Le Bail & Co of Grenville Street, dealing in groceries and frozen foods. They had a daughter, Pearl Winnie Jacqueline Counter (25th November 1923–16th September 1963), who married as Harman. Ada is buried with her daughter at St Saviour's Church Cemetery, Jersey.

Ada's father, Jules Vauvert (born c.1869), born in France, was a farmer. He married Mathurine Vauvert (born c.1874), also born in France, about 1895. They were living near St Anastase, Coin Varin, Jersey in 1911. In addition to Ada they had another daughter, Angel M Vauvert, born c.1897 at St Peter, Jersey.

Jack was an active member of the local branch of the British Legion from 1930 and was usually the bearer of the King's and Queen's Standard on Legion parades. He attended a number of VC Reunions – the VC Garden Party at Buckingham Palace on 26th June 1920, the VC Dinner at the Royal Gallery of the House of Lords, London on 9th November 1929, the Victory Day Celebration Dinner & Reception at The Dorchester, London on 8th June 1946, the VC Centenary Celebrations at Hyde Park, London on 26th June 1956 and the 3rd VC & GC Association Reunion at the Café Royal, London on 18th July 1962.

Jack Counter was visiting his sister-in-law, Edith Counter, at Dorset House, Dorset Street, Blandford Forum, when he collapsed and died whilst drinking a cup of tea on 17th September 1970. He was cremated at Bournemouth Crematorium on 24th September 1970 and his ashes were buried in his daughter's and wife's grave at St Saviour's Church Cemetery, Jersey. Jack is commemorated in a number of other places:

Jack Counter's name is the first on the Freemen Roll of Honour in the Town Hall, Blandford Forum.

Jack's ashes were buried in his daughter's and wife's grave at St Saviour's Church Cemetery, Jersey. Lily Langtry, the actress and mistress of Edward VII, is also buried in the Cemetery. The author was a choirboy for a few months at St Saviour's around 1970.

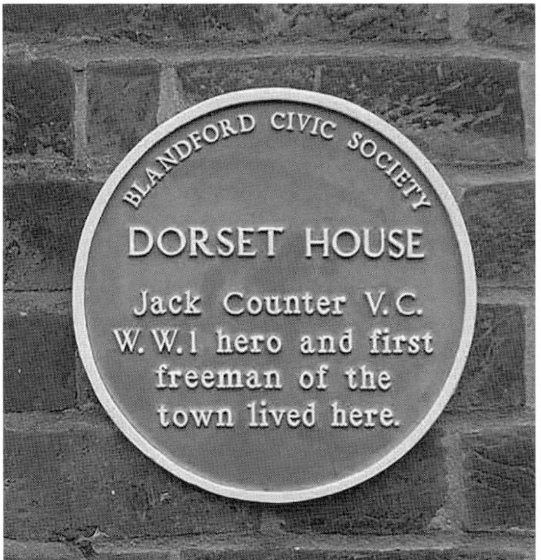

The Blue Plaque on Jack's former home at Dorset House, Dorset Street, Blandford. It fails to mention that he also died there on a visit in 1970.

Jack's Department for Communities and Local Government commemorative paving stone is on the pavement just to the right of the Town Pump in the Market Place, Blandford Forum. The Pump is a memorial to the Blandford Fire in 1731, erected by John Bastard in 1760.

- Jack Counter Close, First Tower, St Helier, Jersey.
- Counter House, St Saviour's, Jersey.
- Honorary Freemen Roll of Honour, Town Hall, Blandford Forum, Dorset.

- Memorial in St Andrew's Church, First Tower, St Helier, Jersey dedicated on 20th August 1972 by the Jersey Branch of the Royal British Legion.
- Book of Remembrance of the Manchester and King's Regiments in Manchester Cathedral.
- Heritage Blue Plaque on his former home at Dorset House, Dorset Street, Blandford Forum.
- A Department for Communities and Local Government commemorative paving stone was dedicated at the Town Pump, Market Place, Blandford Forum on 9th November 2014. Pavers are usually laid to commemorate the centenary of the award but this ceremony was brought forward to allow Jack's nephew, Herbert Frank Counter, to attend, who was aged ninety-three and in failing health.
- Information board at the Town Pump, Blandford Forum unveiled in April 2018.
- A set of four commemorative stamps were issued by Jersey Post on 15th July 1971 to mark the 50th anniversary of the British Legion. Jack Counter's portrait was on the 7½p stamp.

In addition to the VC he was awarded the British War Medal 1914–20, Victory Medal 1914–19, Imperial Service Medal, George VI Coronation Medal 1937 and Elizabeth II Coronation Medal 1953.

The medals were sold to a Canadian buyer in the 1970s but were bought by the Société Jersiaise on 2nd March 1989 at a Glendining's auction for £12,000. The VC is held by the Jersey Museum, The Weighbridge, St Helier, Jersey, Channel Islands.

The Jersey Post stamp 7½P stamp with Jack's portrait.

62990 LANCE CORPORAL ARTHUR HENRY CROSS
40th Battalion Machine Gun Corps

Arthur Cross was born on 13th December 1884 at Shipdham, near Dereham, Norfolk. He was known as 'Henry' or 'Crossy'. His father, William Cross (7th April 1835–1911), a wheelwright and carpenter, was lodging at White House Street in 1871 when he was recorded as a blacksmith in the Census. He married Susan Hall (1844–77) later in 1871. William married Emma Maria née Spelman (5th February 1854–1943) in 1877. Her maiden name has also been seen as Spilman. She was a servant in 1871 in the home of Edward and Mary Ann Sharman at 13 Badley Moor, Mattishall, Norfolk. Emma had two sons:

- Alfred Spelman (1875–1957) was an agricultural labourer in 1891. His surname often appears as Spilman.
- William Spelman (1877–87), whose birth was registered as Spilman. His first name has also been seen as Miller, a corruption of the spelling of William.

High Street, Shipdham, where the Cross family was living in the 1890s.

The family was living at Daffy Green, Scarning, Norfolk in 1881, at 11 High Street, Shipdham in 1891, when Emma was recorded as Anna, near the Methodist Church, Shipdham in 1901 and back to the High Street, Shipdham in 1911, by when William was an invalid. In that Census, Emma was described as a farm worker.

Henry had seven siblings from his father's two marriages:

- Anna Elizabeth Cross (born 5th November 1872–1949) was a domestic servant in 1890. She had two children with an unknown father:
    - Edith Cross (born 2nd March 1890) was a servant in the home of Nathaniel Mardall, a wheelwright, at High Street, Homerton, London in 1911.
    - Ernest Henry Cross (3rd January 1892–27th July 1960) was a cycle mechanic in 1911. He enlisted in the Army Service Corps (M2/047522) on 1st February 1915 at Colchester, Essex and joined next day at Grove Park. He was described as 5′ 8¼″ tall and was a motor mechanic, living with his mother and stepfather at Moor Lane, Cranworth, Norfolk. He went to France on 21st March 1915, embarking on SS *Balmoral* at Southampton and disembarking at Rouen next day. Granted leave 23rd-29th September 1915 and 24th February–23rd March 1916. Posted to 2nd Division Supply Column on 7th April. Awarded the Good Conduct Badge 1st February 1917. On 16th June, while serving with 61st Company ASC, he was admitted to 5th Field Ambulance and No.42 Casualty Clearing Station after a piece of metal he was grinding struck him in the cornea. He returned to duty two days later. Granted leave 25th July–7th August. Posted to 2nd Division Motor Transport Company on 13th March 1918. Granted leave 10th-24th September. Posted to 3rd Auxiliary Petroleum Company as acting corporal 30th October and was promoted corporal next day. Ernest returned to Britain on 28th February 1919 and transferred to the Class Z Army Reserve at

Woolwich, London on 30th March. He married Elsie Maud Godfrey (born 1901) in 1927 and they had a son, Jack G Cross, in 1929. Ernest was living at 54 High Street, Watton, Norfolk at the time of his death at West Norwich Hospital, Norwich, Norfolk. He left effects valued at £11,671/15/-.

Anna married James Rose (c.1836–1926) in 1894 and they were living at 10 Moor Lane, Cranworth, Norfolk in 1901 and 1911. James was a teamster on a farm.

- Robert Cross (11th December 1873–1884).
- Walter Cross (4th March 1876–1884).
- Diana 'Dinah' Elizabeth Cross (1879–1967) married Henry 'Harry' Lowther Halford (1880–1957) on 6th August 1907 at the parish church Shipdham. They were living at 45 Waldeck Road, Norwich in 1911. She believed that her brother, Henry, had been killed on 10th May 1941 when his flat was hit by a bomb. She realised that he was still alive when she read an article in *The Weekly News* on 31st July 1954 about him loaning his VC for the making of a film. They were reunited shortly afterwards in Norfolk. Dinah and Harry had five children:
    - Henry Lowther Halford (11th June 1908–1995) married Ethel May Huggins (25th March 1914–18th November 1998) in 1936. They had a son, Barry L Halford, in 1939.
    - Diana Grace Halford (born 1910) married Albert E Clark in 1937. They had a son, Roger E Clark, in 1940.
    - Eric Russell Halford (22nd February 1915–2003) married Irene G Hales (born 1920–) in 1941. They had three children – Keith B Halford 1943, Richard E Halford 1947 and Peter J Halford 1952.
    - William F Halford (born 1917) married Elsie M Wodehouse (born 1920) in 1940. They had a daughter, Susan J Halford, in 1951.
    - Sidney Ernest Halford (14th October 1918–June 1998) married Gladys E Thrower (born 1914) in 1946. They had a son, David N Halford, in 1953.
- Edward Cross (1881–1948), an agricultural labourer, married Fanny Frances Dalton (2nd April 1885–1980) in 1909. Fanny had a daughter, Frances Gertrude Dalton, in 1906. They were living near the church, East Bradenham, Norfolk in 1911. They had five children:
    - Percy Edward Cross (born 1910) married Beryl Rose Mann (21st June 1915–2nd March 1978) in 1935. They had two children, Graham N Cross 1939 and Victoria Cross 1942. She was living at 98 Earlham Road, Norwich at the time of her death.
    - William J Cross (born 1912).
    - Olive M Cross (born 1914) married Robert A Tolva in 1944 and they had a daughter, Jacqueline A Tolva in 1947. Olive married Herbert J Browning in 1954.
    - Edith Dora Cross (born 21st February 1916) married Walter Jermy (born 1912) in 1935. They had thirteen children – Mary E Jermy 1936, Michael W Jermy 1937, Maurice E Jermy 1938, Malcolm D Jermy 1940, Maureen F

Jermy 1942, Ronnie Jermy 1944, Keith Jermy 1946, Anthony J Jermy 1947, Angela A Jermy 1950, twins Dennis C and Lynne C Jermy 1951, Yvonne E Jermy 1953 and Trevor F Jermy 1957.
    - Margaret P Cross (1923–28).
- Alice Elizabeth Cross (15th April 1888–22nd April 1976) married Belford Simpson (January 1878–1938) in 1911. They were living at Greens Row, Bedale when he enlisted in 3/4th Yorkshire (4127) at Richmond, Yorkshire on 3rd June 1915. He was 5′ 7″ tall and declared previous service with the Yorkshire Regiment Volunteers. He was discharged on 23rd September 1916 and on 17th October was awarded a pension of 10/- per week. Alice and Belford had eleven children:
    - Alice Maud Simpson (25th August 1911–February 1995) married Alexander S Noble at Westminster in 1939. They had a daughter, Sheila S Noble, that year and a son, Clifford Simpson in 1946. Alice and Alexander are believed to have divorced. She had a daughter, Heather E, registered as Beckett and Noble, in 1951 and married George Beckett in 1955. Alexander is understood to have married Evelyn M Bugg at Eton, Buckinghamshire in 1946.
    - Emma Elizabeth Simpson (11th December 1912–1974) married Randolph James Ronald Lancaster (12th September 1913–30th November 1992) in 1934. He was living at 32 Fisher Gardens, Knaresborough, Yorkshire at the time of his death. They had three sons – Kenneth R Lancaster 1936, James William Lancaster 1937 and Michael R Simpson 1944.
    - Belford William Simpson (19th March 1914–1983).
    - Nellie Simpson (9th April 1915–19th November 1998) married Frederick Kirkbride (born 23rd December 1914) in 1955. They had a daughter, Linda Kirkbride, in 1955.
    - Mary Simpson (8th August 1917–27 September 2003) married John Verity (2nd December 1913–9th March 1980) on 31st May 1936. They had two daughters – Mary Eleanor Verity 1936 and Jean Verity 1945.
    - Nancy Fleatra Simpson (1919–2007) married John Hope in 1938. They had four children – Charles B Hope 1939, John R Hope 1940, Arthur H Hope 1942 and Audrey Hope 1945. She married Ronald Ernest J Haycraft (registered as Haycroft) (20th June 1923–2003) in 1949. They had three children – twins Ann and Gillian Hope/Haycraft 1947 and Sheila ME Haycraft 1955.
    - Percy Clifford Simpson (3rd May 1921–6th July 1979) married Jean Hilda E Gillingham (13th March 1922–October 1992) in 1941. They had five children – Jack C Simpson 1943, David A Simpson 1946, Jean B Simpson 1949, Keith P Simpson 1959 and Philip Belford Simpson 1967.
    - Unnamed female (born and died 1923).
    - Sheila Simpson (born 1924).
    - Kenneth Simpson (25th May 1926–February 1994).

  - John Simpson (10th October 1928 -13th March 1981) married Mary A McKay in 1949 at Portsmouth, Hampshire. They had four children – John Henry Simpson 1950, Colin B Simpson 1953, Kevin J Simpson 1954 and Ann E Simpson 1960.
- Percy Charles Cross (4th April 1891–16th November 1918) was a farm servant in 1911, working for Mr Gibson at Brecks Farm, Colton, Tadcaster, Yorkshire. He enlisted in the Yorkshire Regiment (20722) and transferred to 38th Battalion Machine Gun Corps (11131). He was promoted sergeant and was awarded the MM (LG 11th February 1919). Percy died on 16th November 1918 and is buried in St Sever Cemetery Extension, Rouen, France (S III F 1). He is named on the Shipdham War Memorial, Norfolk.

Henry's paternal grandfather, Edward Cross (c.1799–1888), a bricklayer, lived in Shipdham all his life. He married Dinah née Atkin (c.1806–49) on 17th November 1829. They were living at Cootes Yard in 1841 and 1851. By 1881 he was living on the High Street, with his daughter Maria Sadd as his housekeeper. In addition to William they had seven other children:

- Diana Cross (c.1831–54).
- Edward J Cross (c.1834–1903) was an agricultural labourer in 1851.
- Henry Cross (1838–5th December 1917), an agricultural worker, married Hannah Bowman (1840–1914) in 1868. They were living at Old Post Office Street, Shipdham in 1871. Henry was the publican of the *Old George* at Shipdham 1877–83. In 1891 he was an agricultural labourer and they were living at 18 Watton Road, Shipdham.
- James Cross (1840–99) was a bricklayer's labourer in 1861.
- Maria Cross (born 1842–1929) was a housekeeper in 1861. She married Alfred Sadd (1843–83) in 1872. They had three children – Harriet Sadd 1875, Rosa May Sadd 1876 and Tom Sadd 1881. She married Robert Baldwin (1853–1927) in 1885. Robert had married Emily Mann (1844–83) in 1874 and they had three children – Harriet Emma Baldwin 1875, Alice Jane Baldwin 1877 and Thomas Frederick Baldwin 1880.
- John W Cross (1845–64) was a bricklayer's labourer in 1861.
- Thomas Cross (1848–74).

His maternal grandfather, Richard Spelman (c.1826–24th August 1904), an agricultural labourer, married Sarah née Betts (c.1830–1916) in 1850. They were living with his parents at Street, Swanton Morley in 1851. By 1861 they had moved to 2 Church Street, by 1871 to 19 Greengate and by 1881 to 'cottage near Hoe Hall', all in Swanton Morley. In addition to Emma they had eight other children:

- Richard Spelman (1850–1932) was a farm lad in 1861 and later a farm labourer. He married Amelia Alcock (1851–1933) in 1872. They had three children – Amelia Elizabeth Spelman 1874, George Spelman 1876 and Alice Lydia Spelman 1880.
- William Spelman (born 1852) was a farm lad in 1861.
- Elizabeth Alice Spelman (born 1858).
- Mary Ann Spelman (1861–1947) had a son, Ivory John Spelman, in 1884. She married Benjamin Chapman (1865–1937), a shepherd, in 1889. They were living at Blackdyke Hock, Hockwold cum Wilton in 1901. They had a son, Sidney Benjamin Chapman, in 1900.
- Robert Charles Spelman (24th February 1864–15th September 1950), a milkman, married Evora Butters (1863–1920) in 1889. Her birth was registered as Batters. They were living at 167 King Road, East Dereham, Norfolk in 1911. There were no children. Robert married Anna Elizabeth Bruce (12th December 1874–20th March 1960) in 1921.
- Edward Spelman (1866–1949), a farmer, married Emily Elizabeth Betts née Coppin (1871–1936) in 1905. Emily had married Arthur Betts (1871–1901), a brewer's labourer, in 1895. They were living at 116 Southend, East Dereham in 1901. Edward and Emily were living at Dale Farm, East Dereham in 1911. They had a son, Edward Spelman, in 1907.
- Henry Spelman (1870–1958).
- Martha Ann Spelman (1872–1961) married Thomas Dent Backlog (1872–1954), a carter, in 1895. They were living at 26 Melrose Road, Norwich in 1911. They had three children – Hilda May G Backlog 1896, Harry Thomas Backlog 1898 and Edith Maud Backlog 1904. Harry Thomas Backlog enlisted as a gunner in 1st East Anglian Brigade RFA(T) (1766 later 875643) at Norwich on 18th February 1915 and was posted to 2/1st Battery. He was 5′ 6½″ tall and his religious denomination was Church of England. He served in France from 15th November 1915 and with the Mediterranean Expeditionary Force from 3rd February 1916 in A Battery, 270th Brigade RFA. He returned to Britain on 18th August and mustered on 26th August as a driver. He was appointed acting bombardier on 31st January 1917. On 16th October he reverted to driver and on 23rd May 1918 was posted to 4th 'A' Reserve Brigade RFA. He went to France on 17th June and was posted to 18th Division Ammunition Column on 23rd July. He was appointed paid acting bombardier on 8th May 1919, returned to Britain on 27th May and was disembodied on 8th July. He was demobilised on 31st March 1920.

Henry was probably educated at Shipdham village school. He left home aged seventeen and was employed by a local butcher. About 1902 he moved to Camberwell, London, where he was employed on the Great Eastern Railway and later at Woolwich Dockyard. When he married, he was described as a painter and was a porter in 1911. Arthur Henry Cross married Theresa Frances Grace Coxhead (5th February 1882–24th October 1931) on 31st May 1903 at Southwark, London.

Woolwich Dockyard dates back to 1512, when Henry VIII's flagship *Henri Grace à Dieu*, the largest ship of its day, was laid down there. The Dockyard moved in the 1540s to its permanent site and two dry docks were constructed. In the early 18th century the Dockyard doubled in size and more ships were launched there than from any other English yard. Expansion westwards in the 1780s again almost doubled its size, reflecting the increasing size of the Royal Navy's ships. In the early 19th century silting became a problem in the Thames as ships grew ever bigger and the riverside dockyards began to wind down in favour of Portsmouth and Devonport. From 1831 Woolwich specialised in steam engineering but the same facilities were constructed at Portsmouth in 1848 and Devonport in 1853. In addition Woolwich's basins were too small for the modern ships and the Dockyard closed in 1869. The War Office took over much of the land as storage for the Ordnance Stores Department at the nearby Royal Arsenal. Warehouses were built and existing buildings were converted. A narrow-gauge railway was linked by tunnel under Woolwich Church Street to the North Kent Line. In 1905 an Army Service Corps depot was established and during the Great War the country's largest Army Pay Office was set up alongside the ordnance depot. Reduction of the site commenced in 1926 when the western part was sold to the Royal Arsenal Cooperative Society. The remainder of the site was used for storage, workshops and offices until the Royal Arsenal closed in the 1960s. The Dockyard has become a housing estate. Amongst the many famous ships built at Woolwich were:

Vanguard 1586, the first of many ships of that name in the Royal Navy.
HMS *Dolphin* 1751, circumnavigated the world twice.
HMS *Royal George* 1756, sank in 1782, resulting in one of the worst disasters in Royal Navy history, with 800 lives lost.
HMS *Beagle* 1820, used by Charles Darwin on his famous voyage of discovery.
HMS *Agamemnon* 1852, the first British battleship designed and built with steam power.
HMS *Repulse* 1868, the Royal Navy's last wooden battleship.

They lived at 10D Pasley Road, Walworth and, after 1911, at 15 Trinity Buildings, Mermaid Court, Southwark. The two youngest children were not with the family at the time of the 1911 Census, probably due to lack of space as the dwelling comprised a single room only. They had seven children:

- Henry 'Harry' Arthur Cross (25th September 1903–3rd January 1994) was born at 2 Doctor Street, Walworth, London. He was employed in the delivery department of Whitbread's Brewery. He married Elsie Florence Reed (born 31st July 1917) in 1939. They had a son, Michael H Cross, in 1943.
- Frances Grace Cross (30th December 1905–1917).
- Rose Emily Cross (30th June 1908–1984) married Richard William Allen (4th June 1907–1982) in 1929. They had ten children – Richard Arthur Allen 1931, Walter Henry Allen 1932, Roy Kenneth Allen 1933, Alec George Allen 1935, twins Dorothy Rose and Betty Christine Allen 1937, Frederick John Allen 1939, David Allen 1941, Kathleen Margaret Allen 1944 and Peter Edward Allen 1948.
- Mabel Lillian Dinah Cross (22nd July 1910–1914).

- William Albert Cross (30th September 1912–1914).
- Percy William Cross (12th August 1915–1916).
- Victor George Cross (19th August 1918–5th September 2005) was born six hours after his father returned home on leave. He married Elizabeth M James in 1947 and they had two children – Lynda A Cross 1951 and Clive E Cross 1954.

Theresa's father, Joseph Albert Coxhead (31st March 1839–26th December 1905), a printer, married Matilda née Weller (10th February 1838–19th March 1906) in 1858. They were living at 1 Albion Place, Clerkenwell, London in 1861. By 1871 they had moved to 3 Garden Row, Scholars Lane, Stratford-upon-Avon, Warwickshire. They returned to London by 1881 and were living at 3 Hunter Place, Southwark. By 1891 they were at 7 Drummond House, John Street, Southwark, by when he was a railway porter. At some time he was also employed at Whitbread's Brewery. Matilda was living at 148 Rolls Road, Bermondsey at the time of her death there. In addition to Theresa they had nine other children:

- Joseph Henry Coxhead (born and died 1860).
- John Albert Coxhead (1861–1924) married Hannah Parkin (c.1861–1914) in April 1892 at All Saints, Newington, Surrey. She had a son, John Charles Parkin, in 1890. John senior was a labourer in 1901 and they were living at Camberwell. They had three children – Henry Coxhead c.1892, Rose Elizabeth Coxhead 1894 and Nellie Coxhead 1896.
- Sarah Jane Coxhead (1863–64).
- Matilda Maria Emma Coxhead (1865–66).
- Susannah Jane Coxhead (14th October 1867–1950) was a servant in 1881. She married James William Cooper (c.1866–1939) on 24th January 1886. He was a dock labourer in 1891 and they were living at 3 Page's Walk, Bermondsey. By 1901 he was a general labourer and they were living at 9 Thetford Place, Neptune Street, Rotherhithe, London. He was a crane driver at the wharf in 1911. They had ten children, including – Joseph Cooper 1887, James William G Cooper 1890, Alfred John Cooper 1893, Robert Cooper 1895, Matilda Jane Cooper 1901 and George Cooper 1905.
- Henry Ebenezer Coxhead (15th August 1870–23rd June 1943) was a miller's labourer in 1891. He married Emma Butler (born c.1872) on 28th March 1892. He was a carman in 1901 and they were living at 31 King James Street, Southwark. By 1911 he was a cooper's labourer and they were living at Walworth, London. They had eight children, including – Emma E Coxhead 1893, Henry Ebeneza Coxhead 1897, Mary Ann Matilda Coxhead 1898, Thomas Joseph Coxhead 1899, Frances Martha Coxhead 1901 and William Charles Coxhead 1902. Henry married Ellice Emma Grant (1894–1940) on 8th April 1930.
- William Walter Coxhead (30th January 1873–12th June 1955) was a clerk in 1891 and a grocer's warehouseman in 1901. He married Edith Agnes Tansley (1876–

1908) in July 1907 at All Saints, Rotherhithe. By 1911 he was a life assurance agent living at 19 Stork's Road, Bermondsey. William enlisted in the Royal Air Force on 20th September 1918 (297238) and was described as 5′ 8″ tall, with dark brown hair, grey/blue eyes and fresh complexion. He gave his civilian occupation as clerk and his religious denomination was Church of England. He was posted to the Dispersal Unit, Crystal Palace on 2nd February 1919, transferred to the Reserve on 3rd March and was deemed to have been discharged on 30th April 1920.

- Charles Thomas Hammond Coxhead (1875–1949) was a tea packer grocer in 1891. He married Emma Flower Whitmarsh (1880–1932) in March 1900 at St Peter's, Walworth. He was a railway guard in 1911 and they were living at 48 Strathleven Road, Brixton, London. They had four children – Charles Thomas H Coxhead 1900, Edith Emily M Coxhead 1903, Hilda Maud Coxhead 1905 and Albert Victor Coxhead 1906.
- James Edward Coxhead (1878–1937) was a printer's porter in 1901. He married Ada Lockyer (1880–1939) in 1901. By 1911 he was a printer's clerk and they were living at Clarence Road, Walthamstow. They had three children – Reginald Arthur Coxhead 1901, Florence Ada Coxhead 1907 and Vera May Coxhead 1917.

Henry's first attempt to enlist was rejected on medical grounds. He enlisted under the Derby Scheme at Camberwell in 21st London (First Surrey Rifles) on 30th May 1916. He went to France towards the end of 1916 and transferred to 121st Company, 40th Battalion, Machine Gun Corps in 1917. **Awarded the VC for his actions at Ervillers, France on 25th March 1918, LG 4th June 1918. Awarded the MM for holding a bridge against a German attack at Bullecourt on 18th May 1918, LG 29th August 1918.**

Henry was granted leave to attend the investiture. The VC was presented by the King at Buckingham Palace on 4th September 1918. He was presented with £130 of War Savings Certificates at Woolwich Dockyard and, on 16th September, was presented with a gold watch by the vicar on the village green at Shipdham inscribed, *Presented by the people of Shipdham to Lance Corporal A.H. Cross VC, September 1918*. On 20th September he was charged with being absent without leave at Dereham, Norfolk. He claimed he had been granted extra leave to visit his mother in Shipdham and was also to receive a presentation at Southwark the following week. The Court concluded that a mistake had been made and adjourned the case for enquiries. He appeared before the magistrate at Dereham again on 28th September. The police superintendent had ascertained from the military that Henry had been granted leave 31st August–7th September. Henry maintained that he was also granted leave to see his mother and his officer had provided an Army form to travel half-fare. However, he had no documentary proof and the magistrate handed him over to the military authorities. Henry was discharged as a corporal on 31st March 1919. He was awarded a disability pension of £2/5/- per week.

Henry was often unemployed after the war and found it difficult to support his family on his disability pension. He suffered from gastritis and was only fit enough for light work. He was offered a job as a council scavenger at £3/17/- per week but this was too heavy for him. Later he was offered a job in the carriage department of the Great Eastern Railway at Stratford. In April 1923 he was charged with loitering for the purposes of passing betting slips with an accomplice in public houses. His accomplice was fined £3. In 1925 Henry was working for the Post Office when he was bound over for stealing a postal order. On 10th May that year he attended the dedication of the Machine Gun Corps Memorial by HRH The Duke of Connaught at Hyde Park Corner, together with fellow Machine Gun Corps VCs – AE Ker, JRN Graham and WA White. Henry was a member of the Marylebone British Legion and was vice president.

The Machine Gun Corps Memorial (*The Boy David*) is located on the traffic island at Hyde Park Corner. A number of other memorials are close by – Wellington Arch, an equestrian statue of Wellington, the Royal Artillery Memorial, New Zealand War Memorial and Australian War Memorial. The MGC Memorial is surmounted by a bronze statue of David by Francis Derwent Wood, who served in France with the RAMC and designed masks for soldiers with facial disfigurements. The Memorial bears a Biblical quotation, *Saul has slain his thousands but David his tens of thousands*. The Machine Gun Corps formed in October 1915 and disbanded in 1922. During that time 11,500 officers and 159,000 other ranks served in the Corps. The memorial was originally erected next to Grosvenor Place, near Hyde Park Corner. It had to be dismantled due to road works in 1945 and was rededicated in its present location in 1963.

Henry married Minnie Rosina Harrison (1905–10th May 1941) on 11th August 1934. They had two children – Terence Edward Cross (born 29th July 1935) and Mary Rose Cross (born 6th January 1938). The last major raid of the Blitz occurred on the night of 10th/11th May 1941. Minnie took Terence and Mary to the shelter at their home at Douglas Buildings, Marshalsea Road, Southwark. A direct hit on the shelter killed all three and they are buried in Streatham Vale Cemetery, Lambeth. Henry refused to leave the flat and survived.

Minnie's father, James Andrew Harrison (c.1878–1937), married Ellen Florence née Gear (1882–1955) in 1904. He was a timber porter in 1911 and they were living at 39 Bitton Street, Southwark. In addition to Minnie they had two other children – Florence Amelia Harrison 1909 and James A Harrison 1919.

During the Second World War Henry was a Civil Defence Service volunteer as a fire-spotter. He subsequently became a city messenger with Stewarts and Lloyd of Kennington Lane. Henry attended a number of VC reunions:

Henry with David Niven during the filming of *Carrington VC* (Heather & Raymond Allen).

Douglas Buildings, Marshalsea Road, Southwark, where Henry lived for thirty years. The Luftwaffe launched 505 bombers against London on the night of 10th/11th May, which proved to be the last major raid of the Blitz. Bombs fell from 11 p.m. until 5.50 a.m. Thirty-three aircraft were brought down by flak and night-fighters but it proved to be one of the most destructive raids of the war, including the House of Commons. The highest number of casualties of any raid on London was suffered, with 1,436 people killed (including Henry's wife and two children) and over 2,000 seriously injured.

- VC Garden Party at Buckingham Palace on 26th June 1920. Theresa was also invited but refused initially as she did not have suitable footwear for the occasion. Her story appeared in *The Daily News* and a reader donated a sum of money through the newspaper to allow her to purchase a new pair of boots. As a result she did accompany her husband.
- VC Dinner at the Royal Gallery of the House of Lords, London on 9th November 1929.
- Victory Day Celebration Dinner & Reception at The Dorchester, London on 8th June 1946.
- VC Centenary Celebrations at Hyde Park, London on 26th June 1956.
- First four VC & GC Association Reunions at the Café Royal, London on 24th July 1958, 7th July 1960, 18th July 1962 and 16th July 1964.

In 1954 he loaned his VC to actor David Niven during the filming of *Carrington VC*, as a result of an appeal by the studio for a genuine VC for the courtroom scenes. Henry died in an armchair in his flat at 50 Douglas Buildings, Marshalsea Road, Southwark, London, his home of thirty years, on 23rd November 1965. He was discovered the following day by his daughter. He is buried with his second wife

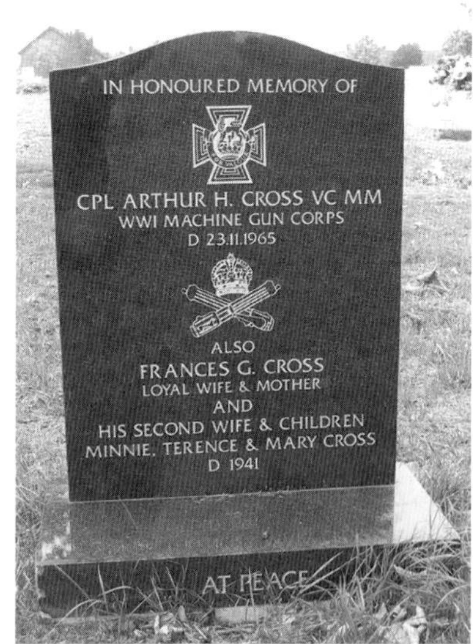

Arthur Henry Cross is buried with his second wife and two children in Streatham Vale Cemetery, Lambeth (Findagrave).

and children in Streatham Vale Cemetery, Lambeth, London (Plot E, Square 27, Grave 43885). The grave was unmarked until a headstone was dedicated from funds raised by the Machine Gun Corps Old Comrades' Association on 27th September 2001. Henry is commemorated in a number of other places:

- Henry Cross Close, Shipdham, Norfolk, named in 1969.
- Blue Plaque on his home at 50 Douglas Buildings, Marshalsea Road, Southwark, London.
- Portrait in the village museum at Shipdham, Norfolk.
- A compact disc, entitled *Forever*, released by Decca Records on 14th July 2014 to commemorate the centenary of the Great War, features seven VC recipients, with contributions from descendants. The seven VCs are – Eugene Paul Bennett, Henry Arthur Cross, Albert Edward McKenzie, Cecil Harold Sewell, William John Symons, Thomas Turrall and William Young.
- A Department for Communities and Local Government commemorative VC paving stone was dedicated at Shipdham War memorial, All Saint's Church, Church Close on 25th March 2018 to mark the centenary of his award.

In addition to the VC and MM he was awarded the British War Medal 1914–20, Victory Medal 1914–19, George VI Coronation Medal 1937 and Elizabeth II Coronation Medal 1953. His medals were sold at a Spink auction at 69 Southampton Row, Bloomsbury, London on 19th April 2012 for £220,000 to an unidentified bidder. The current location of the VC is unknown.

SECOND LIEUTENANT JOHN JAMES CROWE
2nd Battalion, The Worcestershire Regiment

John Crowe was born on 28th December 1876 at the Female Garrison Hospital, Devonport, Devon. His birth was registered as Crow at Stoke Damerel. His father, also John James Crow (16th May 1844–22nd December 1930), was born at March, Cambridgeshire. He enlisted in the Royal South Lincolnshire Militia on 6th February 1861. On 21st May 1863 he enlisted in the 104th Regiment (3255) at Westminster Police Court and was described as 5′ 7″ tall, with grey eyes and brown hair. He joined at Parkhurst, Isle of Wight. Having not declared his ongoing service in the Militia, he forfeited pay and seniority. He embarked for India on 6th July 1864 and arrived at Calcutta on 15th October. The Regiment went to Jhansi and over the next

Stoke Damerel Military Hospital, completed in 1797 for the Army, is on the north side of Stonehouse Creek opposite the Royal Naval Hospital. The workforce was mainly French prisoners of war. The hospital remained in use until the end of the Second World War, when Devonport High School returned from evacuation and took it over. Part of the building was already Tamar High School, which closed in 1989 and was absorbed by Devonport High School.

eleven years he served at Sippiee, Morar, Dugshaie, Peshawar, Cholera Camp, Khyber Pass, Jalalabad, Kabul, Nowshera, Fort Attack and Allahabad. He was granted Good Conduct Pay of 1d per day in February 1869, which increased steadily to the maximum of 5d per day in May 1881. On 17th April 1871 he extended his service to complete twenty-one years. He transferred to the 36th Regiment (1918) in August 1871 and moved to Rawalpindi that November, where he remained until March 1873. He was also at Meen Mere, Dugshaie and Solace. The Regiment moved to Raglan Barracks, Devonport, Devon in November 1875. John married Caroline Elizabeth née Turpin (4th March 1855–1935) at Stoke Damerel Registry Office on 20th October 1876. She was born at 12 Cherry Garden Street, Stoke Damerel. They lived at 2 Market Lane, Stoke Dameral initially. The Regiment moved to Pembroke Dock in November 1877 and to Fleetwood, Lancashire in March 1878. John transferred to the 48th Regiment in February 1880 and served briefly in India again but, by the end of the year, was in Tralee, Ireland, moving to Tipperary in 1881. He transferred to 1st Northamptonshire on 1st July 1881 and served at Curragh Camp, near Dublin until he was discharged in June 1884, having been awarded the Long Service and Good Conduct Medal. He was an excellent shot and was approached by Colonel Robert Joseph Pratt Saunders CB JP DL, commanding the Mid-Ulster Artillery (Militia), to help him run his estate at Woodrange, Baltinglass (previously Baltinglas), Co Wicklow, as a gamekeeper, which he did for twenty years.

John's father was born at March, which before the fens were drained was effectively an island. It stands on a ford on the River Nene. In earlier days it was a minor port. It was the county town of the Isle of Ely when it was a separate administrative county from 1889 to 1965.

Baltinglas is a small town rich in historical sites from the Stone Age onwards, including the ruins of a monastery. John's father helped to run an estate there for many years.

John's father died at the Royal Hospital, Chelsea. It was founded by Charles II in 1682 as a retreat for veterans in an incomplete building, Chelsey College, founded by James I in 1609. Many of the buildings added were designed by Sir Christopher Wren. The Royal Hospital Founder's Day is officially 29th May, the birthday of Charles II and the date of his restoration in 1660, known as Oak Apple Day to commemorate his escape after the Battle of Worcester in 1651 by hiding in the Royal Oak from Parliamentary forces. The Royal Hospital continues as a retirement and nursing home for 300 Army veterans. Anyone over the age of sixty-five who served as a regular soldier may apply to become a Chelsea Pensioner, if they find themselves in need and are of good character.

The family was living on the estate at Saunders Grove and appear there in the 1901 Census of Ireland. They lived in a few rooms in the main house and also in Grove Cottage at various times. While at Baltinglass he added an 'e' to the end of his surname. John and Caroline eventually returned to England around 1905 and were living at 28 Dorset Street, Reading, Berkshire by 1911. He died at the Royal Hospital, Chelsea, London. John junior had eleven siblings:

- William James Turpin (born 3rd March 1871), born to Caroline, father unknown, at Stoke Damerel Workhouse.
- Jessie Kate Turpin (7th February 1874–1888), born to Caroline, father unknown, at Stoke Damerel. She was living with her grandparents, George and Caroline Turpin, in 1881.
- Charles Fredrick Crowe (22nd May 1883–1919), known as Frederick, married Janey Keily (c.1880–1954) on 15th April 1906 at Sunninghill, Berkshire. He was living at 197 Church Street, Paddington Green and she was living at Sunninghill at the time. She was born in Co Limerick, Ireland. Fredrick was a cowman in 1911 and they were living at Penneys Lane, Henley-on-Thames, Berkshire. They had a son:
    - John Fredrick Crowe (1907–April 1991) married Dora Evelyn Smith (20th July 1908–1982) in 1929. She was born at Twyford, Berkshire. They had a daughter, Barbara P Smith, registered as Smith in the 2nd quarter of 1928 at Wokingham and again as Crowe in the 4th quarter of 1929.

Janey married Robert Harrison in 1921 at Reading, Berkshire and they had a daughter, Mavis M Harrison, in 1930.

- Robert Henry 'Harry' Crowe (14th May 1885–3rd November 1945) married Ellen 'Nelly' Langron (10th July 1892–25th January 1946) on 26th July 1913 at the Register Office, Lewisham, London. She was born at Gorman's Yard, Golden Bridge, Palmerston, South Dublin, Ireland and was the sister of Margaret Ellen Langron, who married John James Crowe VC. Harry served in the Royal Berkshire Regiment during the Great War. He worked as a shot blaster at the anhydrite mine at Billingham, Co Durham. They were living at 35 Mill Lane, Billingham at the time of their deaths there. They had seven children:
  - John Hugh 'Robin' Crowe (18th October 1915–29th January 2000) was born at 24 Hawthorne Terrace, Church Road, Inchicore, Ireland. He married Amelia Violet Menzies (24th June 1914–6th December 1981) in April 1952. She was born at Durham. They had a daughter, Anne LM Crowe, in 1959. The marriage ended in divorce. Amelia did not remarry. John married Elizabeth Marshall.
  - Albert Henry Crowe (15th December 1916–1st December 1979), born in Ireland, worked for Imperial Chemical Industries. He married Dorothy Newbould (born 1920) in 1940 at Durham South East. She was born at Stockton-on-Tees, Co Durham. They had two sons, Terence Michael Crowe 1940 and Brian W Crowe 1944.
  - Frederick Sydney Joseph Crowe (21st April 1919–31st July 2009), born in Scotland, was a laboratory assistant in 1945. He married Edna Horner (24th February 1921–June 1988) in October 1941 at Bulmer, Yorkshire. They had a daughter, Michele L Crowe, in 1956. He died at Northallerton, Yorkshire.
  - Francis Aldhelm Crowe (1921–9th June 2018), born at Middlesbrough, Yorkshire, married Hilda May Slack (14th May 1921–20th June 2007) in 1944 at Durham Eastern. She was born at Easington. They had a son, Barry A Crowe, in 1949. Hilda died at Northallerton.
  - William Martin Crowe (1st November 1922–22nd December 1998), born at Eston, Cleveland, was a progress chaser with Imperial Chemical Industries. He married Hazel Elizabeth Hall (25th April 1926–25th January 2005) on 31st March 1945 at Norton-on-Tees. She was born at Hartlepool, Co Durham. They had two daughters – Christine M Crowe 1949 and Elizabeth A Crowe 1953. William and Hazel both died at Stockton-on-Tees.
  - Hazel Doreen Crowe (1st October 1924–1993), born at Middlesbrough, married Mordecai Davies (1st January 1922–1st November 2006) in 1945 at Durham South Eastern. He was born at Pontypridd, Glamorgan and was known as David. They emigrated to Canada and he may have served in the Royal Canadian Air Force. They had three children, including Robert Stephen Davies 1948 and Linda Davies 1952.
  - Annie P Crowe (born 1927), born at Middlesbrough.

- William George Crowe (21st November 1887–27th April 1971), born at Co Wicklow, Ireland and known as George, married Louisa Maud Pocock (1882–14th July 1961) in 1915 at Reading. She was a housemaid in 1911, working for Mrs Carter at Head's Farm, Chaddleworth, near Wantage, Berkshire. They were living at 120 Upper Lewes Road, Brighton soon after the outbreak of the Great War. He served in 12th Divisional Cyclist Company. They were living at The Maisonette, High Street, Ticehurst, Sussex at the time of her death there. He was living at 84 Kings Avenue, Rye, Sussex at the time of his death there. His year of birth was recorded as 1888. They had a son, Frederick George Crowe, in 1920, registered at Watford. He married Dorothy 'Dolly' Fuller in 1946 at Battle, Sussex.
- Minnie Crowe (19th January 1890–1975) married Henry 'Harry' Crawford More (16th April 1891–1965) in 1922 at Maryhill, Glasgow, Scotland and they had a child, possibly Mary More, in 1927 at Maryhill.
- William 'Bill' Crowe (12th May 1892–1980) served in the Worcestershire Regiment from July 1911, initially with 2nd Battalion. He was serving with 4th Battalion, which returned from Burma on 1st February 1915, disembarked at Avonmouth and spent a month at Banbury before marching to Leamington to join 88th Brigade, 29th Division. Departed Avonmouth 22nd March and disembarked at Alexandria, Egypt on 6th April. Embarked on SS *Aragon* on 8th April and sailed on 11th April for Lemnos, arriving on 13th April. The Battalion landed on W Beach on 25th April at Gallipoli. He was wounded during the campaign and was evacuated to Egypt. He rejoined the Battalion and embarked on 15th March 1916 on the *Transylvania* for Marseille, France. He was granted leave in August 1916, during which he married. He was wounded again in the autumn of 1918 by a gunshot to the wrist and was treated at Reading War Hospital. He was discharged from the Army on 25th October 1918 (Silver War Badge). Bill married Daisy Elizabeth Chidgey (1894–1963) in 1916 at Reading, where she was born. She was a servant in 1911 at 13 St Luke's Road, Maidenhead, Berkshire. She died at Reading and he died at Ticehurst, East Sussex. They had three children:
  - Albert William Crowe (4th July 1918–1977) married Lilian Day (born 1921) in 1937 and they had two children – Marian Crowe 1940 and William EF Crowe 1944.
  - Frederick C Crowe (born 1921).
  - Ernest D Crowe (born 1927) married Barbara E Frost (born 1935) in 1955 at Wokingham. They had two sons – Robert K Crowe 1959 and Martin D Crowe 1962.
- Albert Edgar Crowe (13th April 1894–16th September 1916) was a box maker in a tin works in 1911, living with his parents. He was killed in action in France serving as a guardsman in 2nd Grenadier Guards

John's brother, Albert, is commemorated on the Thiepval Memorial under the Grenadier Guards.

(21726). He is commemorated on the Thiepval Memorial (Pier and Face 8D) as Albert Edward Crow.
- Florence Crowe (born 16th December 1895), a twin to Annie.
- Annie Crowe (born 16th December 1895), a twin to Florence, married Henry King.
- Charles Crowe (11th December 1899–2nd September 1955) enlisted as a mechanic in the Royal Naval Air Service on 26th February 1918 at Tregantle, Plymouth, Devon. He was described as a turner, 5′ 10½″ tall, with dark brown hair, brown eyes and fresh complexion. He was on the strength of HMS *President II* when he transferred to the Royal Air Force on 1st April 1918. He married Adelaide 'Peggy' May Savage (8th June 1899–23rd March 1976) in 1919 at Reading, where she was born. They were living at 24 Chapel Hill, Tilehurst, Reading at the time of their deaths there. They had five children:
    - Anthony PM Crowe (born 1922).
    - Ronald Crowe (born 1925).
    - Kenneth James Crowe (1928–88) died at Port Moody, British Columbia, Canada.
    - Patricia Crowe (born 1929) married John W Charles in 1953 at Reading and they are understood to have had four children – Julie Charles 1956, John W Charles 1958, Billie Charles 1968 and Amy Charles 1972.
    - James D Crowe (born 1937) married Penelope A Cooke (born 1944) in 1967 at Wokingham, Berkshire. She was born at Reading.

John's paternal grandfather, James Crow (1820–20th June 1895), was born at Hail Weston, Huntingdonshire. He married Sarah née Goodwin (c.1824–99) in 1842 at Whittlesey, Cambridgeshire, where she was born. He was a vermin destroyer in 1851 and they were living at Inham's End, Whittlesey. They had moved to Boston East or Parochial Allotment, Lincolnshire in 1853, by when he was a farm labourer. They returned to Whittlesey by 1871, living at Horsegate, by when he had reverted to working as a vermin destroyer. He died at Whittlesey and she died at Peterborough, Northamptonshire. In addition to John they had ten other children:

- Harriet Crow (born 10th February 1843) was born at Whittlesey.
- Susan Crow (born c.1848) was born at March, Cambridgeshire.
- James Crow (10th July 1849–1909), born at Whittlesey, was an agricultural labourer by 1871, living with his parents. He married Mary Speechley (1853–28th January 1938) in 1875. They were living at Horsegate, Whittlesey in 1891. They had five daughters – Mary Jane Crow 1876, Lucy Crow 1878, Alice Ann Crow 1885, Maud Crow 1887 and Sarah Crow 1889.
- Mary Jane Crow (born 1851).
- William Crow (born 1854), born at Boston, Lincolnshire, was an agricultural labourer by 1871, living with his parents.

- Robert Crow (1856–1937) married Clara Smith (c.1844–1905) in 1878. She was born at Hitchin, Hertfordshire and had a son prior to their marriage, William Henry Smith, in 1877, whose name had been changed to Crow by 1881. Robert was an agricultural labourer in 1881 and they were living at Stonald Field, Whittlesey. By 1891 he was a gas stoker and they were living at 245 Mount Street, Bradford, Yorkshire and at 5 Malvern Street by 1901. Robert and Clara had two daughters – Ellen Crow 1880 and Harriet Crow 1882. He was living with his daughter, Harriet Broadbent and her husband Harry, a labourer in an iron foundry, with their two children, Clara aged three and Harriet aged one, at 50 Daniel Street, Killinghall Road, Bradford in 1911.
- Sarah Ann Crow (23rd April 1859–1892) had a daughter, Annie, c.1877 at Grimsby, Lincolnshire. She married James Bellamy (13th May 1840–2nd April 1914), a brickmaker, on 27th September 1879 at St Andrews, Whittlesey. He was born at Stanground, Huntingdonshire. Sarah and James had three sons – James Bellamy 1880, John Bellamy 1885 and Charles William Bellamy 1890. They were living at 79 Kenninghall Street, Brightside Bierlow, Yorkshire in 1881 and 1891. He was boarding with his sons, John and Charles, at Town Road, Whittlesey in 1901 and with his son, Charles, at 19 Inham's Road, Whittlesey in 1911. He died of acute pneumonia at Inham's Road.
- Henry Crow (1862–1927) married Sarah Wilson (c.1861–1904) in 1884 at Sheffield, Yorkshire. They had three children – Harry Crow 1888, Ruth Crow 1891 and Robert Crow 1894. He was a foreman (construction) in a steel works in 1901 and they were living at 64 Carwood Terrace, Petre Street, Brightside Bierlow. He was still living there with his children, Ruth and Robert, in 1911. Robert served in the York & Lancaster Regiment (1484) and died of wounds on 30th December 1915. He is buried in Sheffield (Burngreave) Cemetery (X3 C 51).
- Matilda Crow (born c.1865), born at Whittlesey, married John Thomas Smith (1862–1932), born at Worksop, Nottinghamshire, in 1883 at Sheffield. He was a mineral water vanman in 1891 and they were living at Dorking Street, Brightside Bierlow. They had moved to 21 Newark Street, Attercliffe, Sheffield by 1901. By 1911 he was a church caretaker and they were living at 27 Newark Street. They had seven children including – John Henry Smith 1883, Nellie Smith 1885, Florence Smith 1889, Matilda 'Tilly' Smith 1893, James Leonard Smith 1895 and Sidney Thomas Smith 1897.
- Charles Crow (26th February 1867–1898) was an agricultural labourer by 1881, living with his parents. He was a general labourer in 1891 boarding with his sister, Matilda and her family, at Dorking Street, Brightside Bierlow.

His maternal grandfather, George Henry Turpin (c.1826–1916), was born at Devonport, Devon. He married Caroline Elizabeth née Stevens (c.1822–1902) in 1844 at Stoke Damerel, Devon. George was a currier in 1851 and they were living at 12 Cherry Garden Street, Stoke Damerel. They had moved to 11 Cherry Garden by 1861, to 2 Market Lane by 1881 and to 2 Sydney Street by 1891. In addition to Caroline they had five other children:

- Henry James Turpin (1850–52).
- George James Turpin (1852–1928) was a naval apprentice in 1871. He married Eliza Cloke (1857–1937) on 18th December 1884 at Plymouth, Devon. They had a son, George James Fernley Turpin (1888–1959). She died at Newton Abbot, Devon.
- Maria Louisa Turpin (1861–1935) was a domestic servant in 1881. She married Frederick John Ball (1859–1936), a shipwright, in 1885 at Stoke Damerel. They were living at 10 Portland Road, Stoke Damerel in 1911. They had four children including:
    - Lilian Maud Ball (born 1886).
    - Frederick George Ball (1887–1945).
    - Florence Georgina Ball (1892–1925) married Cecil F Netherton (1890–1952) in 1917 and they had a son, Geoffrey C Netherton, in 1924.
- Emma Jane Turpin (1865–1916) married Henry Thomas Andrews (1854–1914) in 1885 at Stoke Damerel. They had four children including:
    - Frederick Henry Andrews (born 1886).
    - Florence Emma Andrews (1891–1964) married Albert Victor Coldridge (1889–1954) in 1917 at Devonport and they moved to Pontypool, Wales. They had two sons – Arthur VG Coldridge 1923 and Kenneth F Coldridge 1925.
    - Mabel Louise Andrews (born 1898) married George William Gorrill (1894–1935) in 1918 at Devonport and they had a son, Frederick G Gorrill, in 1919. Mabel married Charles Anthony Livingstone (3rd December 1903–1970) in 1938.
- William Henry Turpin (born 1868) was an unmarried dockyard labourer in 1911, boarding at 64 Albert Road, Devonport.

John was educated at Baltinglass, Co Wicklow, Ireland and then worked as a footman in Dublin. He enlisted in the Worcestershire Regiment (4950) in Dublin, Ireland on 1st July 1897 (Queen Victoria's Diamond Jubilee) and was posted initially to Norton Barracks, Worcester. He was described as 5′ 6″ tall, weighing 123 lbs, with fresh complexion, grey eyes and brown hair. He was promoted lance corporal on 4th August 1897, which he relinquished on joining 1st Battalion but was promoted again on 8th September 1898. Posted to 4th Battalion on 23rd February 1900 and was promoted to corporal, lance sergeant 1901 and sergeant four months later. He married Margaret Ellen Langron (20th August 1874–22nd September 1953) at the Catholic Chapel of St James in Dublin on 3rd February 1902. They met in Dublin before he joined the Army. She was living at 20 Woodfield Terrace, Inchore Road, Dublin at the time, where she had been born, although she had moved several times between. They were living at 124 Clarendon Place, Dover, Kent in 1911 before moving to married quarters at Tidworth. She moved to 120 Upper Lewes Road, Brighton, Sussex, the home of George and Louise Crowe, and later to 2 Dudley Road, Brighton. They lived apart from 1923 and in November 1925 she sued him for desertion and numerous cases of cruelty. Margaret was still living at 2 Dudley Road, Brighton when she died, having never divorced John. She left effects valued at £976/11/4, probate granted to Eric Sidney Diplock, solicitor. They had four children:

- Anne Margaret Crowe (30th April 1904–2nd January 1976) was born in Barbados, West Indies. She married Alexander Murray (1900–68) and lived at Rottingdean, East Sussex. He was reportedly taken prisoner during the Second World War and was a retired company director in 1965. She was living at 18 Park Manor, London Road, Brighton, Sussex at the time of her death there. They had two children:
    - Doreen A Murray (born 1933) married Robin James Pannett (18th February 1931–27th November 2004) in 1958 and they had a son, Murray J Pannett, in 1961. They lived at Grittleton, near Chippenham.
    - Andrea J Murray (born 1937) married Colin AC Tingey (born 1935) in 1962. They had two children – Paul Murray Tingey 1967 and Joanne Grace Tingey 1973.
- Mary Josephine Crowe (14th May 1906–24th February 1990) was born at Worcester, Worcestershire. She married as Gillot and lived in London. She died at Sunbury Nursing Home, Sunbury-on-Thames, Middlesex.
- John 'Jack' Crowe (born 10th October 1907) was born at Dublin St Stephen, Ireland. In Brighton he looked after the family goat, a task he did not enjoy, and worked in the family garden. He was a cinema manager in 1939 living with his future wife, Mrs Evelyn Peake, and his sister, Christina, at 5 Murray Avenue, Heston and Isleworth, Middlesex. He married Evelyn Stella Peake née Reid (born 7th March 1908) in 1947 at Brentford,

John was serving in Barbados, West Indies when his first child, Anne Margaret Crowe, was born on 1st May 1904. This picture in Bridgetown, the capital, is from about that time. The island is thirty-four kilometres long and up to twenty-three kilometres wide. It was inhabited by a variety of Amerindian peoples, including the Kalingo from the 13th century. The Spanish claimed it in the late 15th century. The English arrived in 1625 and took possession in the name of James I. The first permanent settlers arrived two years later. Sugar was the main economy, using African slaves until the trade became illegal in 1807. Barbados became independent on 30th November 1966, with the British monarch as hereditary head of state. One of its famous sons, Sir Garfield Sobers (born 1936), played cricket for the West Indies 1954–74 and was arguably the best all-rounder of the 20th century (J Murray Jordan).

Middlesex. Evelyn had married George Maurice T Peake (6th May 1907–1973) in 1934. He was born in Bristol. The marriage ended in divorce and George married Florence A Larkin/Yearly in 1954 at Worthing, Sussex. John and Evelyn emigrated to Adelaide, South Australia, where they are understood to have had three daughters.

- Christina Ellen Crowe (31st December 1913–1970), birth registered at Amesbury, Wiltshire, was a telephonist in 1939 living with her brother, John. She married Arthur William Harold Pullen (born 1st September 1915) in 1940 at Brighton, Sussex. He was born at Chelsea, London. They lived at Canvey Island, Essex. Her death was registered at Kingston upon Thames, Surrey.

Margaret's father, Hugh Langron (7th February 1846–September 1916), an engine fitter, was born at Liverpool, Lancashire. He married Anne Josephine née Tyrrell (1853–1903) at St Mary's, Haddington Road, Dublin, Ireland on 5th November 1871. In addition to Margaret they had nine other children, all born at Dublin:

- Mary Josephine Langron (18th August 1872–September 1938) married Martin Clinton (born 1856) on 11th January 1909 at Aughrim, Dublin. He was born at Calry, Co Sligo.
- Christina Alice Langron (29th December 1876–1941), a twin with Joseph, married James O'Neill (c.1875–9th October 1917) in 1907 and they had two children, Alice O'Neill and Thomas O'Neill. They lived at 3 Maxwell Street, Dublin. James enlisted in 1st Irish Guards (7898) and was killed in action at Passchendaele, Belgium (Tyne Cot Memorial, Belgium -Panel 10–11). Christina married Edward O'Neill (born c.1879) in 1921 at Dublin South. He was a labourer at St Catherine's, Dublin and served in No.2 Company, Dublin City Artillery Militia (175) before enlisting in the Royal Artillery on 10th December 1897 at Dublin (24654). He was described as 5′ 6⅛″ tall, weighing 124 lbs, with fresh complexion, grey eyes, light brown hair and his religious denomination was Roman Catholic. He joined at Seaforth, Scotland on 14th December 1897 and was posted to 41st Company on 5 February 1898. Awarded the 3rd Class Certificate of Army Education on 24th October. He was appointed acting bombardier in 15th Company (92nd Company on reorganisation on 1st July 1901) on 21st September 1899 and went to South Africa on 9th November. Granted Good Conduct Pay of 1d per day from 10th December. He was promoted bombardier on 21st January 1901. Transferred to the Royal Garrison Artillery on 1st January 1902 and was posted to Malta on 22nd September. Awarded the 2nd Class Certificate of Army Education on 22nd January 1903. He was promoted corporal on 27th May and was granted Class I Service Pay on 1st April 1904. Extended his service to complete twelve years on 10th April and was sent on a short course on gunnery on 12th October. Posted to 1st Company (46th Company on reorganisation on 1st April 1906) in Britain on 12th November and on 15th March 1906 he was posted to Dover Defences, Kent.

He suffered synovitis on 10th March 1907. He attended a number of courses – Signallers 28th November 1908, Gunnery Staff 7th December and Range Finding 1st March 1909. Extended his service to complete twenty-one years on 29th March. Service Pay ceased on 10th December. Posted to Gibraltar on 9th September 1910 to join 54th Company and was promoted sergeant on 4th April 1911. Posted to 52nd Company in India on 18th December. Appointed company sergeant major on the Indian Unattached List while serving with the Rangoon Port Defence Volunteers, Rangoon, Burma on 23rd March 1914. He reverted to sergeant on 10th January 1915, rejoined 52nd Company and returned to B Depot Siege Artillery, Bexhill on 12th October. Posted to 139th Heavy Battery RGA and was appointed battery quartermaster sergeant, on 30th October. Promoted warrant officer class II, and appointed battery sergeant major on 13th March 1916. Posted to 119th Siege Battery RGA on 24th March and went to France via Southampton on 2nd July. To hospital 1st October with a cartilage problem and transferred to 5th General Hospital on 5th October. He was evacuated to Britain aboard HMHS *Asturia* on 1st November and was on the strength of No.2 Depot RGA, Gosport from the following day. Awarded the Army Long Service and Good Conduct Medal in 1916. Joined Western Forts on 30th December, the Signalling Depot on 20th January 1917 and 302nd Siege Battery on 3rd March. He embarked at Southampton on 12th April and disembarked at Le Havre next day. On 14th April he was posted to Italy but appears to have left again on the 16th (Italian Bronze Medal for Military Valour 4th January 1918). To hospital sick on 19th February 1918 and was invalided to Britain from 57th General Hospital aboard SS *Panama* on 16th April. Posted to the Royal Artillery Command Depot, Ripon on 24th August. Posted to 3rd Battery, 1st Siege Artillery Reserve Brigade, Shoreham-by-Sea on 22nd November. He extended his service for twelve months on 25th February 1919. Posted to 1st Battery, 1st Siege Artillery Reserve Brigade on 6th March and returned to 3rd Battery on 14th April. He was attached to No.3 Depot RGA on 30th March 1920 and was discharged on 3rd May.

- Joseph Christopher Langron (29th December 1876–4th October 1968), a twin with Christina), emigrated to Halifax, Nova Scotia and became a boat builder and steam engineer. He was a boilermaker at the time of his enlistment in 197th Overseas Battalion CEF (913706) on 12th September 1916 at Winnipeg, Manitoba. He gave his date of birth as 29th September 1875 and was living with Mrs GW Thomas at Coghlan Road, Coghlan, British Columbia. He was described as 5′ 4″ tall with dark complexion, brown eyes, dark hair and his religious denomination was Church of England. He was gassed in France. Joseph retired in 1935 and was living at 8650 South West Marine Drive, Vancouver, British Columbia when he died at Shaunessy Hospital there.
- Hugh Langron (4th January 1879–1885).
- William Langron (c.1880–1905).

John Langron was killed in the initial landings on V Beach, Gallipoli from SS *River Clyde*. He rests in V Beach Cemetery in the centre.

- Annie Langron (15th March 1881–15th September 1957) married Thomas William Robinson (1881–23rd October 1956) on 5th July 1944 at St Martin's, Kirkleavington, Yorkshire. They both died at 1 The Cottages, Kirkleavington.
- Richard Langron (born 2nd September 1884) married Ellen Murray in 1911 at West Derby, Lancashire. They had at least two sons in Britain – John M Langron 1913 and Hugh Langron 1920. Richard served as a fireman in the Mercantile Marine Reserve (807339) during the Great War. He qualified for the Great War medal trio and the Mercentile Marine War Medal, a combination unavailable to members of the Merchant Navy, but was awarded to some Royal Navy personnel who served on Merchant Navy ships as gunners etc. They subsequently emigrated to Chicago, Illinois, USA. He died on 25th March 1950 at Eloise, Wayne, Michigan. It is believed that they may have had a total of four sons and three daughters.
- John 'Jack' Langron (1888–25th April 1915) was serving in 2nd Royal Dublin Fusiliers (10417), when he was convicted of desertion by a court martial at Aldershot on 22nd December 1909 and sentenced to fifty days detention. He was killed in action serving with 1st Battalion at Gallipoli, Turkey and is commemorated on Special Memorial B18 in V Beach Cemetery.
- Ellen Langron (born 10th July 1890) married the brother of John Crowe VC, Robert Henry Crowe (see above).

4th Battalion sailed aboard HMS *Harlech Castle* for Bermuda, arriving on 4th March 1902. Detachments were sent to Jamaica, St Lucia and Barbados in the West Indies in 1903. He was in the detachment on Barbados and sailed there on the *Dunera*. He was promoted colour sergeant in 1904 and was posted to the Depot at Norton Barracks, Worcester on 4th January 1906. A month later he was appointed Colour Sergeant Instructor of Musketry. On 1st November 1907 he was posted to 3rd Battalion at Mandora Barracks, Aldershot, at the time regarded as the best shooting battalion in Britain, having won the Whitehead Cup in 1903 and the Queen Victoria Cup 1903–05. 3rd Battalion moved to South Africa on 27th November, arriving at Cape Town three weeks later, and was based at Wynberg. The Battalion returned to Dover in early October 1908. John was awarded the 1st Class Certificate of Education in March 1911. 3rd Battalion moved to Tidworth in 1912 and he was appointed company sergeant major on 1st October 1913.

John was taught to shoot with a rifle by his father on the estate at Baltinglass. They spent time shooting rabbits and catching fish there. During his service life he became a champion shot, winning many prizes at Bisley, the premier British

John Crowe in 1908 or later, holding the Short Magazine Lee-Enfield rifle with which he won so many shooting prizes.

Field Marshal Lord Frederick Roberts VC KG KP GCB OM GCSI GCIE KStJ VD PC (1832–1914), known as 'Bobs', was one of the most successful commanders of the 19th century, serving during the Indian Mutiny (awarded the VC), Expedition to Abyssinia, Second Afghan War and Second Boer War. He was the last Commander-in-Chief before the post was abolished in 1904.

Army shooting competition. He was a member of the teams that gained the Inter-Colonial Rifle Cup in 1904 and 1905, the Inter-Colonial Challenge Cup in the Naval and Military Rifle Meeting in 1903 and 1909, the Henry Whitehead Cup in 1909 and 1913 and was one of three winners of the Colonial Cup (receiving the trophy on the very last occasion it was presented by Field Marshal Lord Roberts of Kandahar & Waterford VC at Bisley in 1913). On that occasion John also received a walking stick from Lord Roberts. He also won the Shooting Cup at Dover 1910–12 and several trophies in the Salisbury District Rifle Meeting in 1913, including the Inter-Regimental Cup and Sergeants Cup. In 1910 he participated in the Queen's Cup, organised by the Society of Miniature Rifle Clubs. John was also noted as an all-round athlete and held numerous prizes for hockey, running and obstacle competitions, including the 3rd Battalion Athletic Cup in 1912. John was a member of the Army Temperance Society and was a keen fisherman and gardener.

John was appointed regimental quartermaster sergeant on 5th August 1914 and left for France next day, where he was based at 29th Infantry Base Depot, Rouen for three years. 3rd Worcestershire left Tidworth for France on 12th August 1914, arriving at Rouen on SS *Bosnian* via Southampton on 16th August. John was promoted warrant officer class II on 15th January 1915. He was awarded the Long Service and Good Conduct Medal in April 1917. There was a great demand for fresh vegetables during the war and John transformed the ground around his quarters in Rouen into a four-acre garden. These efforts were recognised by the French Government, awarding him a Diplôme d'Honneur de l'Encouragement in October 1917.

On 6th September 1917 he was posted to 3rd Battalion as regimental sergeant major. **Mentioned in Field Marshal Sir Douglas Haig's Despatch of 7th April 1918 for his service in the period 25th September 1917–24th February 1918, 23rd May 1918.** Having served in the ranks for a total of seventeen years and 211 days and as a warrant officer for a further three years and sixty-three days, he was commissioned on 1st April 1918 and transferred to the 2nd Battalion as acting adjutant. **Awarded the VC for his actions at Neuve Église, Belgium on 14th April 1918, LG 28th June 1918.** The VC was presented by the King at HQ Second Army, Blendecques, France on 6th August 1918. **Awarded the French Croix de Guerre 1914–18 with Bronze Palm, LG 17th August 1918.**

John was appointed acting captain 26th May 1918–3rd June 1919. He was granted leave to Britain on 10th June 1918 and returned there on 14th November for posting to 4th Reserve Battalion, Northamptonshire Regiment at St Leonard's on 30th November. He was appointed Adjutant, Shorncliffe Disembarkation Camp, Folkestone on 24th February 1919 and was later posted to Ireland. He was one of three VCs guarding a temporary cenotaph in Worcester Cathedral grounds during a Victory Parade on 23rd August 1919. He was promoted lieutenant on 1st October 1919 and retired from the Army on 22nd November 1920.

John Crowe receives the VC from the King on 6th August 1918.

John was employed as the School Attendance Officer for Brighton Education Committee in 1921. He retired in 1946 as the Children's Care Enquiry Officer for Brighton Education Committee, having served on beyond retirement age, which he reached in 1941. He was a member of the Education Committee cricket team. He and his wife, Margaret, also ran a boarding house in Brighton. On 2nd January 1929 he was fined £5 by Brighton Magistrates for causing diversion of electric current at his house and stealing electricity belonging to the Corporation. The defence

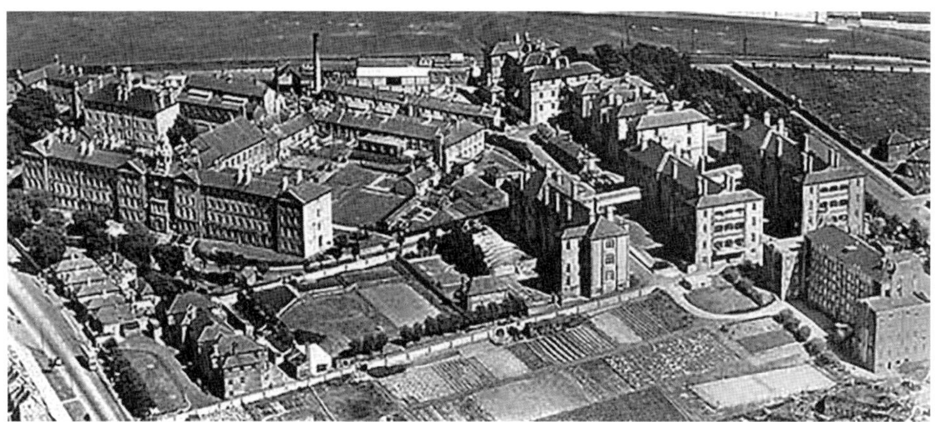

Brighton General Hospital, where John died on 27th February 1965.

persuaded the Bench to delete any reference to stealing. John attended a number of VC Reunions – the VC Garden Party at Buckingham Palace on 26th June 1920, the VC Dinner at the Royal Gallery of the House of Lords, London on 9th November 1929, the VC Centenary Celebrations at Hyde Park, London on 26th June 1956 and the 2nd VC Association Reunion at the Café Royal, London on 7th July 1960. At the Garden Party in 1920 there was a downpour and his daughter Annie dashed into a tent for shelter to find it was the Royal Tent. Much embarrassed, she was put at ease by Queen Mary, who allowed her to stay until the rain stopped. John was a member of the Woodingdean Happy Circle Club for the over-60s for sixteen years and the Woodingdean Horticultural Society. He was also a prominent member of the British Legion and sold poppies each year, his favourite patch being London's Victoria Station.

John Crowe was living at 16 McWilliam Road, Woodingdean, Brighton when he died at Brighton General Hospital, Sussex on 27th February 1965, leaving effects valued at £353. His funeral was to be held on 4th March 1965 at the Church of the Holy Cross, Woodingdean, Brighton, conducted by the Reverend EV Tanner, who was the chaplain at Neuve Eglise on 14th April 1918. However, many mourners were prevented from attending due to heavy snow and the venue was switched to the Downs Crematorium, Bear Road, Brighton, starting forty minutes late. His ashes were scattered in Section L of the Garden of Remembrance. He is commemorated in a number of other places:

- A seat at Woodingdean Community Centre, Brighton, Sussex.
- Plaque on the wall of the former hospice (Mairie) in Neuve Eglise, dedicated by the Ramsgate 1957 and Dover 1900 Rifle Club on 16th April 2011. About thirty members of John's family attended, including grand daughters Doreen Pannett and Andrea Tingey, as did representatives of the Regiment and the Worcestershire Western Front Association.

- A Department for Communities and Local Government commemorative paving stone was dedicated at the War Memorial, Plymouth Hoe, Plymouth, Devon on 13th April 2018 to mark the centenary of his award.
- The JJ Crowe VC Memorial Shoot – a prone rifle shooting match fired annually from twenty-five yards and organised by the Ramsgate & Dover Rifle Club, Kent.

In addition to the VC he was awarded the 1914 Star with 'Mons' clasp, British War Medal 1914–20, Victory Medal 1914–19 with Mentioned-in-Despatches Oakleaf, George VI Coronation Medal 1937, Elizabeth II Coronation Medal 1953, Army Long Service & Good Conduct Medal and French Croix de Guerre 1914–18. His VC group was presented to the Regiment in 1971 and are held by the Museum of the Worcestershire Soldier, City Museum & Art Gallery, Foregate Street, Worcester.

1936 DRIVER HENRY DALZIEL
15th Battalion AIF

Henry Dalziel was born on 18th February 1893 at Ragged Camp, near Irvinebank, North Queensland, Australia. He was known as Dal or Harry in the family. His father, James Dalziel (22nd February 1866–26th December 1930), born at Costerfield, Victoria, married Eliza Mary 'Maggie' née McMillan (11th January 1866–7th August 1952), born at Dalby, Queensland, on 14th August 1889 at Northgate (later Garbut), Queensland. They were living at Smith's Creek, Queensland in 1903, when his sons Henry and Victor discovered tin samples which led to the opening of Boulder Mine near Emuford. The mine became one of the lrgest in the area and remained in production until the 1960s. Henry founded Dalziel Tin Mine Ltd and later purchased Carmel Bank Farm of 160 acres. They were living at California Creek in 1905 and moved to Atherton, Queensland shortly afterwards. Henry donated some of the proceeds of the tin mine towards the building of Atherton Hospital. Harry had ten siblings:

Harry Dalziel shortly after his investiture. The bandages on his head wound can still be seen.

- Emma Muriel Dalziel (6th June 1890–4th December 1960), born at Herberton, Queensland, was a nurse. She married Dermott Parnell Dillon Cusack (4th June 1882–10th June 1963), born at Charters Towers, Queensland, on 8th September 1915 at Atherton, Queensland. They had a son, Roderick Douglas Clive Cusack

Harry was born near Irvinebank, North Queensland.

Carmelbank.

(15th April 1921–3rd August 1986). Roderick was a bank clerk and served for one year in 51st Battalion Militia. He was a cadet lieutenant from 7th November 1938 until he resigned on 27th March 1941. He enlisted on 24th June 1940 (Q302617) and was promoted sergeant on the same day. Posted to Miowera, New South Wales on 24th June, to the Anti Tank Training Depot on 1st November, a physical training course at Frankston 23rd November–21st December and another course at the Gabba, Queensland on 13th January 1941. Promoted WO2 on 31st January. Detached to duty at Hughenden, Queensland on 12th June and to the Australian Army Service Corps (AASC) on 19th July. Posted to AASC Cairns, North Queensland on 2nd August and to HQ AIF Training Depot on 14th January 1942. Appointed temporary WO1 on 16th January. He applied to join special forces on 10th June. Detached to duty at Goondiwindi, Queensland 30th July–6th August. Change of number to QX35742. Attended a course at the Physical & Recreational Training School, Frankston 20th September–18th October. Detached to duty at Goondiwindi 9th November–24th December. Transferred to Z Special Unit on 21st October 1943. He married Ann Caroline Henrietta Shaw (26th July 1918–18th March 1988) on 16th January 1943. She was living at 50 Albion Rd, Albion, Brisbane in December 1943, had moved to Stratford, Cairns by July 1944 and later c/o Mrs Nichol, Berry St, Sherwood, Brisbane. He attended a course at 1st Australian Parachute Training Centre 24th November 1944–8th January 1945 and qualified as a parachutist. Promoted WO1 on 10th January. He departed for service outside Australia on 15th March.

The Dalziels lived in Atherton for many years.

Z Special Unit was formed during the Second World War to operate behind Japanese lines. Although mainly an Australian special forces unit, it included British, Dutch, New Zealand, Timorese and Indonesian personnel. It operated mainly in Borneo and the former Dutch East Indies and carried out eighty-one covert operations, including raids on Japanese shipping in Singapore harbour. The unit was modelled on the Special Operations Executive. There is a memorial to Z Special Unit on the esplanade in Cairns, Queensland.

101 Squadron RFC formed at Farnborough in July 1917. It moved to France as a night bomber squadron and returned to Britain in March 1919. It disbanded on 31st December 1919. The Squadron was reformed in March 1928 with day bombers. In 1941 it changed to medium bombers with the Vickers Wellington and the following year to heavy bombers with the Avro Lancaster. In October 1943 it was equipped with radio jammers, codenamed *Airborne Cigar*, operated by an eighth crew member, to disrupt German fighter controller's broadcasts. The aircraft were distinctive, with two large vertical antennae in the middle of the fuselage. Because they broke radio silence to conduct their operations, they were much more vulnerable to being tracked. As a result 101 Squadron had the highest casualty rate of any RAF squadron. On 25th May 1950, the Squadron became the RAF's first jet bomber unit with the English Electric Canberra B2. It operated in Malaya, where it dropped the first operational bomb from an RAF jet bomber. It also operated during the 1956 Suez crisis. In 1957, 101 Squadron became part of the V Bomber force with the Avro Vulcan B1 at RAF Finningley and later at Waddington. The Squadron operated during the Falklands War and was disbanded on 4th August 1982. It reformed at RAF Brize Norton on 1st May 1984 to operate the Vickers VC10 K2 aerial refuelling tanker and took part in operations in the Gulf, Kosovo, Afghanistan, Iraq and Libya. The VC10 was retired in September 2013 and was replaced by the Airbus Voyager.

Attached to 1st Australian Parachute Training Centre 25th November. Returned to Brisbane 30th November and was on the held strength of Z Special Unit 14th December. MID. Discharged 27th December 1945, by when he had two children. He was described as 6′ 2″ tall, with green eyes, dark complexion and dark hair. War Badge issued (A227377). His service record shows he was on operational overseas service 8th-11th August 1944 and 30th January–26th March 1945. He also served in Northern Territory 16th April–23rd August 1944.

- James Dalziel (6th October 1891–5th April 1967), born at Orient Camp, Irvinebank, married Georgina Leavis (c.1897–12th February 1989), born at Gladstone, Queensland, on 20th August 1919. They had three children:
    - James Samuel Kevin Dalziel (25th March 1921–4th September 1943) was a woodworking machinist when he enlisted in the Royal Australian Air Force on 13th September 1941 (414339). He was described as 5′ 6½″ tall, weighing 133 lbs, with fair complexion, blue eyes, auburn hair and his religious denomination was Roman Catholic. Promoted leading aircraftsman 6th December and was posted to 12th Elementary Flying Training School, Bundaberg, Queensland on 10th December 1941. Moved to Winnipeg, Canada on 6th June 1942. He qualified as an air navigator and was appointed temporary sergeant on 25th September 1942. Arrived at RAF Bournemouth, Hampshire on 5th November 1942. Posted to 27th Operational Training Unit on 19th January 1943. Appointed temporary flight sergeant on 25th March and was posted to 101 Squadron on 19th May at Holme-on-Spalding Moor, Yorkshire moving to Ludford Magna, Lincolnshire with the Squadron next month. He was commissioned as a pilot officer on 21st August 1943. His Lancaster was reported missing on a raid on Berlin (Berlin War Cemetery, Germany – 4 F 17).
    - Mary Joy Dalziel (born and died 11th March 1924).
    - Gordon Philip Dalziel (1928–23rd July 2001), married Marie Joan Baxter.
- Eliza Maggie Dalziel (c.1894–6th October 1939), born at East Ballarat, Victoria, married Archibald Thomas Foley (born 3rd January 1894), a miner born at Croydon, Queensland, on 12th January 1917. He enlisted in 15th Battalion AIF at Townsville, Queensland on 17th September 1914 (10), described as 5′ 5½″ tall, weighing 125 lbs, with medium complexion, dark grey eyes, brown hair and his religious denomination was Protestant. His next of kin was a farmer, Stephen Henry Foley, of Stone River, Ingham, Queensland. He served in the cadets at Toowoomba, Queensland and 27th Army Rail Head, Ingham. Assigned to the Battalion Transport Section as a driver and departed Australia on 22nd December. He embarked at Suez, Egypt on 10th June 1915 on HMAT A55 *Kyarra*, arriving at Melbourne, Victoria on 17th July. He was discharged as medically unfit with epilepsy from 1st Military District on 15th December 1915. A pension of £2/6/6 per fortnight was reduced to £1/11/- on 11th April 1918. His wife's pension of £1/3/3 per fortnight was also reduced to £-/15/6. Eliza married Julius Suhle (25th May 1898–13th July 1984) on 4th May 1935. He was living at 132 Powlett Street, Melbourne in 1945, c/o John Clark. Julius married Cecilia Margaret Hughes (1893–1989) in 1940 in Queensland. Cecilia had married Christopher Rutherford (born 1884) in 1914 in Queensland.
- Mary Cecilia Dalziel (15th May 1896–27th August 1923), born at Steiglitz, Victoria, married Thomas Patrick 'Bunnie' Harrison (12th April 1895–3rd July 1938), born at Cairns, Queensland, on 3rd November 1917. They had two

daughters – Margaret Harrison and Cecilia Harrison. He enlisted at Cairns on 27th April 1916, described as a locomotive driver, 5′ 10″ tall, weighing 136 lbs, with fair complexion, blue eyes, black hair and his religious denomination was Roman Catholic. He was posted to No.11 Depot Battalion on 6th May and was diagnosed with lumbago caused by a railway accident three years before. A medical board at Enoggera on 8th May recommended discharge, which was carried out on 16th May.

- Victor Dalziel (10th July 1898–1973) was a farmer. He enlisted in the AIF (58085) at Cairns, Queensland on 8th June 1918, described as 5′ 7″ tall, weighing 136 lbs, with fair complexion, hazel eyes, light brown hair and his religious denomination was Church of England. Posted to Reserve Unit on 13th July and 6th Reinforcements on 16th July. He embarked at Sydney on HMAT A41 *Bakara* on 4th September, arrived in London, England and was allotted to 5th Training Battalion, Fovant, Wiltshire on 14th November. He was allocated to 9th Battalion and moved to France from Southampton on 22nd January 1919. Arrived at the Australian Staging Camp, Abaucourt and the Australian Infantry Base Depot on 25th January. He joined 9th Battalion on 28th January and returned to England on 28th May. He returned to the 3rd Military District, Melbourne aboard HMT *Takada* on 18th July and during the voyage was admitted to the ship's hospital 21st-31st July. He was granted home leave 19th July–8th August and was discharged from 1st Military District in Queensland on 24th September 1919.
- Mabel Hartley Dalziel (18th March 1900–19th July 1968), born at Norseman, Western Australia, married James Malcolm McMillan (2nd May 1893–18th September 1969), born at Glasgow, Lanarkshire, Scotland, on 13th July 1923 at Atherton. He enlisted at Rockhampton (290) on 17th March 1916. His next of kin was his father, Alexander, of Moscow Station, Longreach Road, via Winton. He was described as a labourer, 5′ 8″ tall, weighing 147 lbs, with fresh complexion, blue eyes, brown hair and his religious denomination was Presbyterian. Posted to No.11 Depot Battalion on 20th March and joined 3/3rd Machine Gun Company on 26th April. He embarked on HMAT A46 *Clan McGillivray* at Brisbane on 1st May and on HMT *Arcadia* at Alexandria, Egypt on 29th July. On 21st August he transferred to Grantham from the Machine Gun Training Depot. He overstayed his leave at Belton Park from 2.00 a.m. on 28th October to 8.00 a.m. on 29th October and was confined to barracks for eight days and forfeited two day's pay. He embarked for France at Folkestone on SS *Princess Henrietta* on 14th November, landing at Boulogne next day. He was absent from roll call at 9.30 p.m. on 4th January 1917 until apprehended by the military police at 10.30 p.m., for which he was confined to barracks for seven days. Taken on strength of 7th Machine Gun Company on 21st January. He received a gunshot wound to the abdomen on 20th September and was admitted to 33rd Field Ambulance and No.3 Canadian Casualty Clearing Station. On 23rd September he was admitted to 2nd Australian General Hospital, Wimereux and was evacuated to Britain on HMHS *St Stephen*,

where he was admitted to Bradford War Hospital on 26th September. Transferred to 1st Auxiliary Hospital, Harefield on 23rd October and was granted leave 27th October–10th November, then reported to No.2 Command Depot, Weymouth. Transferred to No.1 Command Depot, Sutton Veny on 16th November and the Overseas Training Brigade, Longbridge Deverill on 11th December. Posted to the Machine Gun Depot, Grantham on 18th January 1918 and embarked at Folkestone on 8th February for the Machine Gun Corps Base Depot, Camiers, France. He rejoined his unit on 14th February and his number was amended to 290A on the formation of 2nd Australian Machine Gun Battalion. Granted leave in Britain 12th December 1918–4th January 1919. He departed Le Havre for Britain on 18th April and joined No.2 Group at Sutton Veny next day. He embarked on HT *Mahia* on 4th June and disembarked in 2nd Military District in Australia on 20th July. He was discharged from 1st Military District, Brisbane on 4th September 1919. They were living at Braeside, Ravenshoe, via Cairns, North Queensland in July 1930 and had moved to 22 Patrick Street, Rockhampton, Queensland by November. He served again in the Second World War (Q302723) but the details are not known. They had six children:

- Mershal Henry McMillan (born 21st August 1923) was a cabinet maker when he enlisted in the Australian Army on 31st Jul 1943 at Woolloongabba, Queensland (QX55867 later Q268935). He had been promoted corporal by the time of his discharge from 51st Field Park Company on 27th September 1948. He married Betty May Perigo (c.1924–2nd April 1995), a process worker, on 29th March 1947 at All Souls Church, Leichhardt, New South Wales. They were living at 243 Elswick Street, Leichhardt in 1949 and 26 Kalgoorlie Street, Leichhardt in 1980.
- Donald James McMillan (20th January 1925–23rd February 1992) was a postal clerk and enlisted in the Australian Army on 12th October 1942 at Tully, Queensland (Q156364). He was a signalman at the time of his discharge from 1 Lines of Communication Signals on 17th January 1945. He married Esther Adelaide (surname unknown) (died 17th December 2013) and they were living at Butler Street, Tully in 1954 and at Cook and Henry Streets, Tully in 1958.
- Gladys McMillan (24th June 1926–17th February 2011) married James Alexander Cockburn (born 14th May 1910) in 1956. He enlisted in the Australian Army on 20th May 1940 at Paddington, New South Wales (NX15769). He was a bombardier by the time of his discharge from New South Wales Lines of Communication Car Company on 24th November 1943. James was the proprietor of a delicatessen in 1963 and they were living at 507 High Street, Penrith, New South Wales.
- John Alexander McMillan (born and died 1928).
- William Roland McMillan (born and died 13th June 1928).
- Robin McMillan (20th February 1935–16th December 1966).

- Helen Sarah Dalziel (31st July 1903–4th July 2002) married David Burt in 1936 and died at Ipswich, Queensland.
- Doris Kathleen Dalziel (15th May 1905–14th March 1948) married Andrew Joseph Long (6th June 1898–15th October 1977) on 20th September 1924.
- Jessie Gladys Dalziel (27th May 1907–28th August 1983) married Cecil Ralph Newman Morris (26th June 1906–7th June 1971) on 5th January 1933. They have a daughter, Nola Morris.
- William McGregor Dalziel (21st June 1910–3rd May 1987) was a civil servant in 1936 living with his mother in Poole Street, Bowen, Queensland. He married Ruby May Stephensen (6th January 1909–21st May 2001) on 18th March 1938 and they had two children – Maxine Dalziel and Stephen Dalziel. By 1954 he was a clerk and they were living at 109 Pashen Street, Morningside, Queensland.

Harry's paternal grandfather, James, came from Durisdeer in Scotland.

Harry's paternal grandfather, James Dalziel (25th October 1834–13th September 1905), born at Durisdeer, Dumfriesshire, Scotland, emigrated to Australia and settled in Queensland. He married Mary Ann née Cook (22nd September 1840–9th October 1910), born at Woolwich, London, England, on 12th August 1858. He died at the Goodna Asylum for the Insane, Queensland and she died at 36 Nicholson Street, Collingwood, Victoria. In addition to James they had nine other children:

- William George Dalziel (c.1859–7th January 1860).
- Margaret Harkness Dalziel (17th June 1860–25th January 1901) married Robert William James in 1878. They had two children – Sarah Ann Dalziel James 1879 and George Doran James 1881.
- Sarah Ann Dalziel (14th February 1862–12th August 1915) married Edward O'Brien in 1880. They had a daughter, Maud O'Brien, in 1888.
- William James Dalziel (c.1864–18th September 1905) married Kate Florence Dent (born 1862) in 1886.
- Mary Dalziel (27th May 1868–20th July 1943).
- John Dalziel (1870–13th April 1871).
- Samuel John Dalziel (c.1872–1916) died at Beechworth Asylum, Victoria.
- George Robert Dalziel (1873–8th February 1875).
- Emma Pennell Dalziel (24th December 1875–26th November 1959) had a son, James Samuel Wood Dalziel (born 22nd July 1893). She married Robert Reed (1871–16th November 1901) in 1895 at Free Presbyterian Church of Victoria, 23 Mair Street, Ballarat, Victoria. Robert and Emma had five children – William John

Reed (21st March 1896–21st March 1899), Robert Leslie Reed (30th July 1897–21st March 1899), Ernest Arthur Reed (1898–98), Francis John Reed (born 2nd October 1899) and Robert George Reed (9th June 1901–26th May 1902). Emma married James Edward Rae (1874–3rd April 1956) in 1903 at the Presbyterian Manse, East Ballarat. James and Emma had six children – Margaret Mary Rae (18th April 1903–23rd July 1986), Emma May Rae (19th May 1904–1967), James Joseph Rae (22nd October 1905–23rd November 1956), Lilian Maud Rae (5th May 1907–2nd August 1989), Eileen Veronica Rae (28th September 1912–12th March 1976) and Nellie Florence Alphreda Rae (28th September 1915–14th February 1993).

His maternal grandfather, John McMillan (25th January 1839–13th March 1885), born at Girvan, Ayrshire, emigrated to Queensland and settled at Ravenhoe. He married Mary Ann née Seckington (30th September 1851–31st July 1922), born at Lambeth, London, England, on 2nd March 1865 at Jondaryan, Queensland. In addition to Eliza they had six other children:

- Henry Carpenter McMillan (25th December 1867–30th August 1930) married Margaret Eliza Julia Gooch (18th March 1874–23rd April 1957), born at Melbourne, Victoria, on 13th November 1893. He died at Cairns, Queensland and she at Ballarat, Victoria. They had six children – Violet Marion McMillan 1894, Harry John McMillan 1896, Percy Carpenter McMillan 1897, Cecil Vivian McMillan 1899, Myrtle Mildura McMillan 1901 and Thomas Henry McMillan 1904.
- Anne Gillespie McMillan (18th May 1870–12th May 1874).
- John 'Jack' McMillan (6th September 1872–3rd December 1951).
- Isabel Gillespie McMillan (14th August 1875–23rd December 1930).
- Mary Ann McMillan (9th December 1877–28th August 1957) was a nurse who emigrated to Canada, arriving at Vancouver, British Columbia in October 1907. She married George Storey Boulton (25th April 1879–8th April 1942), an engineer born at Ulverston, Lancashire, on 4th June 1910 at Christ Church Cathedral, Vancouver. They had two children – Nancy Seckington Boulton 1911 and Mary Storey Boulton 1912.
- Helen 'Nell' Elderslie McMillan (1st April 1880–21st May 1952).

Harry was educated at Mount Garnet School 1902, Irvinebank and Atherton State School, all in Queensland. He worked as a fireman on the Queensland Government Railways on the line between Millaa Millaa and Malanda. He was a talented athlete and horseman and won the North Queensland High Jump Championship.

Harry enlisted in the AIF at Cairns on 16th January 1915 (1936), described as 5′ 7″, weighing 136 lbs, with fair complexion, grey eyes, dark brown hair and his religious denomination was Church of England. He had an irregular scar on the roof of his

King George's Hospital, Stamford Street, Waterloo, London. In 1914, it was a newly built warehouse for HM Stationery Office and was commandeered to be converted into a hospital, reputedly the largest in the country. The King opened it at the end of May 1915, the project having suffered from labour disputes and strikes. Convoys of wounded were brought by train to Waterloo Station nearby and transferred by tunnels to the hospital. The flat roof was converted into a roof garden with flowerbeds and shrubs, where patients could exercise. On Christmas Day 1916 the King, the Queen or one their children visited every ward. The Hospital closed on 15th June 1919 having treated 71,000 patients. Today, it is the Franklin-Wilkins Building of King's College London.

The *Kyarra* (6,953 tons) was built in Scotland in 1903 for the Australian United Steam Navigation Co. She operated on the Fremantle and Sydney routes until 6th November 1914, when she was requisitioned in Brisbane and converted to transport Australian medical units to Egypt. In March 1915 she was converted into a troop transport and operated as such until 4th January 1918. On 26th May 1918, *Kyarra* was sailing from Tilbury to Devonport, when she was sunk by UB-57 a mile off Anvil Point, near Swanage, with the loss of six lives. UB-57 is believed to have hit a mine and was destroyed in the area of the Sandiette Bank, east of the Straits of Dover, in August 1918. The wreck of the *Kyarra* was discovered in the late 1960s and is popular with divers.

Rollestone Camp on Salisbury Plain in Wiltshire.

In August 1914, the Royal Victoria Patriotic School in Wandsworth became the 3rd London General Hospital, one of four Territorial General Hospitals in London. It was built in 1859 as the Royal Victoria Patriotic Asylum, an orphanage for the daughters of soldiers, sailors and marines who had fought in the Crimean War. In 1914, a temporary railway station was built to enable wounded to be brought easily from the south coast. Hutted wards were added in the grounds, bringing capacity to 2,000 beds by May 1917. The Hospital closed in August 1920, having treated 62,708 patients. The building now contains twenty-nine apartments, several studios and workshops, a drama school and a restaurant.

nose. He embarked on HMAT A55 *Kyarra* at Brisbane on 16th April 1915 with the 5th Reinforcements for 15th Battalion and disembarked at Alexandria, Egypt in July. Moved to Camp Heliopolis and was promoted lance corporal but reverted to the ranks on 13th July. He served at Gallipoli with 15th Battalion from 13th July and reported sick with rheumatism on 28th August. He passed through 40th Field Ambulance before being evacuated to Mudros, from where he was moved to Malta aboard HMHS *Devanha* on 29th August. Evacuated from there to England, where he was treated at King George Hospital, Stamford and later in September at 3rd London General Hospital, Wandsworth, London. He was charged with breaking bounds, absence without leave 15th-16th December and insolence, for which he was awarded seven day's detention and forfeited seven day's pay. He was posted to Weymouth, Dorset in January 1916 and returned to Egypt on 28th March. He went to France on 14th August from 4th Training Battalion, Rollestone Camp, Wiltshire. He was at 4th Australian Division Base Depot, Étaples 16th-31st August and rejoined 15th Battalion on 4th September. Harry was appointed driver on 9th September and attended a course at the School of Farriery on 1st April 1917. He was absent without leave from 3.45 p.m. on 7th May until apprehended by the military police at 4.20 p.m., for which he was awarded seven day's detention.

Harry reverted to private at his own request on 31st July. On 16th October he was wounded by shrapnel in his arm at Polygon Wood near Ypres. He was admitted to 3rd Australian Field Ambulance and No.10 Casualty Clearing Station on 17th October and to 11th General Hospital, Dannes-Camiers on 18th October. On 29th October he was evacuated to England and was admitted to Colchester War Hospital, Essex next day. He transferred to 3rd Australian Auxiliary Hospital, Dartford on 16th November and was discharged to No.3 Command Depot, Hurdcott on 5th December. Harry was posted to the Overseas Training Brigade, Longbridge Deverill on 30th January 1918, transferred to No.1 Command Depot, Sutton Veny on 28th March, the Overseas Training Brigade, Longbridge Deverill 2nd May and returned to France from Folkestone on 30th May. He joined the Australian Infantry Base Depot on 1st June and rejoined 15th Battalion on 7th June 1918. **Awarded the VC for his actions at le Hamel, France on 4th July 1918, LG 17th August 1918.** He gained the nicknamed *Two Gun Harry*.

The wound to his head, received during his VC action, smashed his skull and exposed his brain. Many thought he would die within the hour but skilful medical treatment eventually returned him to moderate health, although he never fully recovered. He was admitted to 4th Australian Field Ambulance and No.47 Casualty Clearing Station on 4th July and transferred to 12th General Hospital, Rouen on 6th July, where he was treated by American doctors. On 19th September he was evacuated to England aboard HMHS *Panama*, where he was treated at 4th London General Hospital, Denmark Hill, before being moved to 3rd Scottish General Hospital, Stobhill, Glasgow on 29th October for psychiatric assessment. He moved to 1st Australian Auxiliary Hospital, Harefield, Middlesex on 27th November.

TSS *Kanowna* (6,993 tons) was constructed in 1902 in Scotland for the Australian United Steam Navigation Co. Soon after war broke out she was requisitioned as an Australian military transport. She carried 1,000 troops to German New Guinea as part of the Australian Naval and Military Expeditionary Force, sailing from Townsville on 8th August but did not arrive at Port Moresby until 6th September. The Expeditionary Force sailed next day for Rabaul but *Kanowna* fell behind. The boiler stokers and firemen stopped work because of a shortage of water to remain hydrated in the boilerrooms and to wash off the coal dust. *Kanowna* was ordered back to Townsville with volunteer soldiers keeping the ship running. *Kanowna* was returned to her owners on 21st September, but was requisitioned again on 1st June 1915 to transport troops and supplies to Egypt. She moved to England to be converted into a hospital ship, with a capacity of 452 wounded in cots. She was used mainly in the Mediterranean. In October 1918 *Kanowna* collected 900 British and Commonwealth prisoners from Turkey. She was returned to her owners in July 1920 and resumed normal passenger and cargo services. On 18th February 1929, *Kanowna* ran into rocks on a voyage between Sydney and Melbourne. All the passengers and crew were taken off and she sank the following morning.

In November 1914 Mr and Mrs Charles Billyard-Leake, Australians living in Britain, offered their home, Harefield Park House, to the Minister of Defence in Melbourne as a convalescent facility for the AIF. It became No.1 Australian Auxiliary Hospital in December 1914, the only solely Australian hospital in Britain. Hutted wards were built on the lawn and by May 1915 eighty beds were ready. The first patients arrived on 2nd June and by the end of that month the Hospital had 170 patients and more huts were built. In August the King and Queen visited, by when there were 362 patients. Growth continued with an artificial limb and an eye ward. By March 1916 the Hospital had 803 beds and that October had 960 patients. In November the facility also became a general hospital, complete with operating theatres and X-ray department. An Australian Red Cross store opened in December and a magazine was produced by the patients, the *Harefield Park Boomerang*. At its height the Hospital could accommodate over 1,000 patients. It gradually closed during January 1919 and in 1920 was sold to Middlesex County Council for a tuberculosis sanatorium. Today it is Harefield Hospital.

The VC was presented by the King in the ballroom at Buckingham Palace on 13th December. Harry embarked for Australia on 5th January 1919 aboard HMHS *Kanowna*, arriving at Melbourne, Victoria on 7th March. He travelled to Queensland on the steamer *Kuranda*, where he was admitted to 1st Military Hospital and later 17th Australian General Hospital. He was discharged in Brisbane as medically unfit on 16th June 1919.

Harry was given a civic reception in Brisbane, with fellow VC Bernard Sidney Gordon, attended by the Governor, Sir Hamilton Goold-Adams, Acting Premier Mr Theodore, Mayor Alderman Buchanan and about 5,000 spectators. He received a hero's welcome at every station between Townsville and Atherton, Queensland, where he was guest of honour at a dinner given by the Atherton Sub-Branch of the Sailors' and Soldiers' Imperial League of Australia at Markham's Barron Valley Hotel.

Harry and Ida (Dalziel family).

Harry Dalziel married Ida Maude Ramsay (23rd December 1890–14th January 1986), a nurse he met whilst a patient at 17th Australian General Hospital, at the Congregational Manse, Fortitude Valley, South Brisbane on 8th April 1920. They lived at Zenith, Atherton, Queensland. The marriage failed and they had separated by 1933. He then lived with a Mr Napier at 37 Railway Terrace, Milton, Brisbane. Ida remained at Atherton and died there. There were no children.

Ida's father, Richard John Ramsay (21st February 1851–2nd January 1918), born at Newcastle upon Tyne, Northumberland, England, married Rhoda Fanny White (2nd May 1851–26th August 1925), born in Queensland, on 20th March 1872. He died at Maryborough, Queensland and she at Brisbane. In addition to Ida they had seven other children:

- Allison Annie Ramsay (20th October 1872–2nd February 1939) married Robert Hamilton on 14th February 1894. She married Thomas Blondell Blondell (2nd June 1878–3rd September 1953) on 28th May 1924. Thomas married Sarah Jean Clarkson on 23rd May 1940.
- William Richard Ramsay (17th August 1874–21st September 1954) married Maggie Donnelly on 7th February 1899. They had at least a son, also William Richard Ramsay, on 10th July 1914.
- Mary Ann Jane Ramsay (born 27th June 1876).
- Frederick John Ramsay (11th May 1879–21st June 1949) married Elizabeth Mary Shelly (died 2nd May 1973), born at Townsville, Queensland.
- Martha May Ramsay (20th August 1881–30th June 1925) married David Mackintosh on 7th September 1910.
- Ethel Cecilia or Zetelia Ramsay (1884–3rd June 1942) married Henry 'Harry' Ross Walsh (born 8th July 1872) on 26th March 1902 in Queensland. She married Frederick William Britton (1894–11th August 1949) on 19th July 1926.
- Alfred Robert Ramsay (13th September 1886–8th June 1972) married Maud Helena Nargar (2nd August 1891–14th December 1967), born at Maryborough, Queensland, on 16th November 1908. They had four children – Alfred John

Ramsay (25th September 1909–30th September 1953), Edward Charles Ramsay (1910–16th September 1912), Ethel Maud Ramsay (1911–19) and Desmond Dalziel Ramsay (1914–31st October 1955).

Harry returned to his old job on the railways but was unable to cope and tended a small orchard near the railway station. He and Ida acquired a soldier settlement block of land, which they named 'Zenith' on the Tolga railway line. Running the small mixed farm also proved too much for him and Ida had to run it while he travelled in search of employment during the depression. He worked in a Sydney factory in the late 1920s and also tried gold prospecting at Bathurst, New South Wales with his brother Victor. He returned to Queensland when his wife was seriously ill. He settled in Brisbane, Queensland for a time in 1933 but remained unemployed. He qualified for a war pension and wrote some songs, some of which were published in Britain and USA, including *A Song of the Tableland*, *Love Time*, *Merry Love Time*, *Boys of the New Brigade Swing Along*, *Oh! Girlie just be careful of the Royal Marines* and *Don't forget we have a Navee*, the last three were copyrighted with Muriel King. He also tried drawing, pottery and poetry, including *Only a Golden Memory*.

One of the songs that Harry composed.

Due to complications with his first marriage, Harry entered into a de facto relationship with Elsie 'Dallo' Kanowski (4th March 1907–5th September 1999), born at Glencoe, New South Wales, on 15th December 1935. Elsie was brought up on family farms at Glencoe and Kingsthorpe, near Toowoomba, Queensland and could only speak German when she started school. When Harry enlisted in 1940 he still recorded Ida as next of kin. Elsie spent more than ten years working for Meals On Wheels in Brisbane and was a member of Legacy and War Widows. They lived at various addresses in Queensland, including:

Harry and Elsie with their three children at Oxley (Dalziel family).

221 Campbell Street, Toowoomba.
56 Kennigo Street, Valley, Brisbane.
262 St Paul's Terrace, Valley, Brisbane.
157 Ardoyne Road, Oxley.

Harry and Elsie had three children:

- David Henry Alexander Dalziel (born 1942) married Sandra Ruth Hunter in 1965 and they had four children – Lisa Wendy Dalziel, David John Dalziel, Nicholas 'Nick' John Dalziel and John Hunter Dalziel.
- Ann Elizabeth Dalziel (born 31st January 1944) married William John Salisbury on 5th April 1969 and lived in Cunnamulla and Toowoomba. They had five children – Aaron John Salisbury, Stuart Dalziel Salisbury, Iain Andrew Salisbury, Nathan Peter Salisbury and Megan Louise Salisbury.
- Francis 'Frank' James Archibald Dalziel (born 31st July 1946) married Diana Georgina Politios in 1973 and they lived at Brisbane and Goondiwindi. They had three children – Daniel James Lawrence Dalziel, Jacqueline Ann Dalziel and Elizabeth Ann Dalziel.

Elsie's parents are understood to have been Charles Voll and Christiana Maria Kanowski (born 18th August 1887), born at Glencoe, Queensland of German origin, daughter of Carl Kanowski (1860–1934) and Maria Kajewski (1867–1917).

Harry was appointed to a temporary position in the Australian Air Corps 17th May–14th June 1920 (109 later Q302305). He was one of twenty-three VCs who attended an Anzac Dinner on 23rd April 1927, hosted by Lieutenant General Sir John Monash GCMG KCB VD. For an unknown reason The Duke of York (future King George VI) was not invited. Jack took part in the Anzac Commemoration Service on 25th April 1927 at the Exhibition Building, Melbourne, Victoria in the presence of The Duke of York. In the march past the VCs conceded pride of place to blinded soldiers who insisted on marching.

On 6th July 1933, Harry joined the Citizen Military Forces in 9th/15th Battalion (411333) at Brisbane for three years initially and was promoted lance sergeant immediately. He was described as 5′ 7½″ tall and weighed 158 lbs. He became the first holder of the VC to be a member of the Guard of Honour at the opening of the Queensland Parliament, when he was part of the King's Colour escort. He transferred to 9th/49th Battalion on 1st October 1934 and was discharged on 19th May 1939. On 14th June 1940 he re-enlisted in the Australian Military Forces in Brisbane and was appointed pioneer sergeant. He was posted to Caloundra Infantry Training Depot, Queensland to assist in training recruits. His duties also consisted of speaking on recruiting drives and fund raising appeals. He visited many training camps advising and talking to the troops. He reported sick with a septic leg at Warwick and was treated at 8th Australian General Hospital, Kangaroo Point,

Queensland 27th January–26th February 1943, whilst serving with 11th Australian Infantry Training Battalion. He was discharged at Brisbane on 24th December 1943, described as 5′ 6½″ tall, with blue eyes, dark complexion and black hair.

Harry (right) with Lord De L'Isle. William Philip Sidney, 1st Viscount De 'Isle VC GCVO KG GCMG KStJ PC (1909–91), served as a British Army officer and politician. He was the fifteenth Governor-General of Australia 1961–65, the last non-Australian to hold the office and the last to wear the traditional viceregal uniform. He was educated at Eton College and Magdalene College, Cambridge before becoming a chartered accountant. He served in the TA and during the Second World in the Grenadier Guards in France and Italy. He was awarded the VC in 1944 for his actions at Anzio. He became a Conservative MP. When he succeeded his father as Baron De L'Isle and Dudley, he was elevated to the House of Lords. He was Secretary of State for Air 1951–55 in Winston Churchill's government.

Harry Dalziel was visiting the Jensens, related to his wife Elsie, when he met the family of Reinhard Mayer. They had migrated to Oxley, Queensland from Germany in 1928 and purchased a dairy farm. Mrs Mayer never really accepted Australia as her home and longed to return to Germany but her hopes were dashed with the outbreak of the Second World War. She was ostracized by some people as anti-German feelings fermented. Security officers from Brisbane searched the property following reports that the Mayers had secret documents from Berlin regarding sabotage activities and a radio to relay military secrets to Japanese submarines. Nothing of the sort was located but people of German origin were being interned and soon afterwards the police arrested Mrs Mayer. She was not allowed to say goodbye to her three children at school and was interned in Victoria for almost three years. Harry wrote to the Head of National Security in Canberra, requesting Mrs Mayers' release and accepting responsibility for her. The request was granted within a month and Mrs Mayer was returned to her family. His generous action, having been on the opposite side to the Mayers during the Great War, was not lost on them as he reached across the barriers of enmity and put his own status and integrity on the line for them.

Harry was a life member of the Sherwood Sub-Branch of the Returned Services League in Brisbane. He was also a Freemason in Duke of Connaught Lodge No.3358. He carried the 15th Battalion Colour on Anzac ceremonies in Brisbane and never missed an Anzac Day parade in all the years he lived in Queensland.

In 1956 Harry sailed on the P&O liner *Arcadia* with other Australian VCs who were part of the 301 Victoria Cross recipients from across the Commonwealth who attended the Victoria Cross Centenary Celebrations at Hyde Park, London on 26th

RMS *Orion* (23,371 tons) was built for the Orient Steam Navigation Co in 1934. During her career she carried about half a million passengers, mainly from Europe through the Pacific to Australia. Her construction was documented in the 1935 film *Shipyard*, by Paul Rotha. She was launched on 7th December 1934 in Barrow-in-Furness remotely by wireless by the Duke of Gloucester, who was in Brisbane, Australia. She alternated voyages to Australia with short cruises until the outbreak of war in 1939, when she was requisitioned by the British government as a troopship. *Orion*'s first voyage was to Egypt and New Zealand. On 15th September 1941 she was in a convoy carrying troops to Singapore, following the battleship HMS *Revenge* in the South Atlantic, when the warship's steering gear malfunctioned. *Orion* rammed *Revenge*, resulting in severe damage to *Orion*'s bow. She made Cape Town for temporary repairs and continued to Singapore for more permanent repairs. With the Japanese advancing on Singapore, *Orion* evacuated civilians to Australia. In late 1942 *Orion* took part in Operation Torch, making two voyages to North Africa, carrying over 5,000 troops each time. In 1943 her capacity was increased to 7,000. She was then used in the Pacific. She was released back to her owners in 1946, having carried over 175,000 personnel and steamed over 380,000 miles. She was refitted at Barrow and resumed the Australia service from Tilbury on 29th September 1947. After that she was used for cruises along the US west coast, in addition to voyages between Europe and Australia. In 1961 she became a single class ship carrying up to 1,691 passengers, mainly immigrants, but the demand for sea voyages to Australia was declining. *Orion* departed Sydney for the last time on 8th April 1963 and arrived at Tilbury on 15th May. She was used as a floating hotel for 1,150 guests during the International Horticultural Exhibition in Hamburg and in October left for Antwerp, where she was scrapped.

June 1956. While in Europe he visited Le Hamel on 4th July and laid a wreath but was unable to identify the spot where he won the VC thirty-eight years earlier. He returned to Australia on the *Orion* and after landing opened the YMCA Camp Warrawee at Joyner, Queensland, on the North Pine River. He was introduced to Queen Elizabeth, the Queen Mother during her visit to Australia in February and March 1958. In 1960 Harry met Lord de L'Isle VC at a Garden Party at Parliament House, in Brisbane to welcome the new Governor General. Harry was one of eighteen VCs present at the opening of the VC Corner at the Australian War Memorial in 1964 by Lord De L'Isle.

Harry suffered a stroke and was admitted to Greenslopes Repatriation Hospital, Brisbane, Queensland, where he died on 24th July 1965. A funeral with full military honours, conducted by Dean Baddeley at St John's Anglican Cathedral, Brisbane on 27th July, was followed by cremation at Mount Thompson Crematorium. His ashes are buried in Ground Niche 1, Plot M, Row C and there is a memorial plaque (Wall 12, Section 16, No.106). The authorities were unaware that he was no longer with his first wife, Ida. She was brought from Atherton for the funeral and sat with Harry's children from his second marriage in the second row, while his second wife, Elsie, was seated with Department of Veteron's Affairs personnel in the third row. Harry is commemorated in a number of other places:

Greenslopes Repatriation Hospital, where Harry Dalziel died, began as 112th Australian General Hospital during the Second World War, opening on 2nd February 1942. It then became Repatriation General Hospital Greenslopes operated by the Repatriation Commission (now Department of Veterans' Affairs) for war veterans. It 1970 it became a university teaching hospital with the University of Queensland and in 1974 the first members of the general public were admitted. Ramsay Health Care assumed responsibility for Greenslopes in January 1995 and it was renamed Greenslopes Private Hospital. By 2003 it had grown to become the largest private hospital in Australia.

The Brisbane Cathedral movement began in 1887 to celebrate Queen Victoria's Golden Jubilee. St John's was to be paid for by public subscription but there were insufficient funds to construct the cathedral in one. The building was therefore constructed in three phases between 1906 and 2009. The site was purchased in 1899 and on 22nd May 1901, the Duke of Cornwall and York (later King George V) laid the foundation stone. The first stage of construction began in 1906 and took four years to complete, being consecrated in October 1910. After the Second World War it was hoped to complete the cathedral as a war memorial and in 1947 Field Marshal Montgomery laid the foundation stone for the next stage. Construction ceased after the laying of foundations until 1965 and took a further four years to complete. The third stage commenced in 1989 and was completed in 2009. The Archbishop of Brisbane, Dr Phillip Aspinall, reconsecrated the completed cathedral on 29th October 2009, 108 years after the laying of the foundation stone.

- Australian Capital Territory
  - Australian Victoria Cross Recipients plaque on the Victoria Cross Memorial, Campbell, dedicated on 24th July 2000.
  - Named on one of eleven plaques honouring 175 men from overseas awarded the VC for the Great War. The plaques were unveiled by the Senior Minister of State at the Foreign & Commonwealth Office and Minister for Faith and Communities, Baroness Warsi, at a reception at Lancaster House, London on 26th June 2014 attended by The Duke of Kent and relatives of the VC recipients. The Australian plaque is at the Australian War Memorial.
  - Display in the Hall of Valour, Australian War Memorial.
  - Dalziel Street, Canberra, gazetted on 8th February 1978.

- New South Wales
  - Victoria Cross Memorial, Queen Victoria Building, George Street, Sydney dedicated on 23rd February 1992 to commemorate the visit of Queen Elizabeth II and Prince Phillip on the occasion of the Sesquicentenary of the City of Sydney. Sir Roden Cutler VC AK KCMG, Edward Kenna VC and Keith Payne VC were in attendance.
  - Victoria Cross Recipients Wall, North Bondi War Memorial donated to the community of Waverley on 27th November 2011 by The Returned & Services League of Australia.
  - A street in Singleton Barracks.

Harry's memorial at Mount Thompson Crematorium.

- Victoria
  - Dalziel Lane, Wodonga on White Box Rise estate, built on land formerly part of Bandiana Army Camp.
- Queensland
  - Harry Dalziel VC Centre, 2 Clewley Street, Corinda, opened on 15th October 2005 by Her Excellency Dame Quentin Bryce AD CVO, Governor of Queensland.
  - Dalziel Lodge, YMCA Camp Warrawee, Joyner named on 4th July 2016. Brisbane YMCA purchased the site in November 1949 on the North Pine River. Development commenced in 1951 and Harry opened it on 23rd September 1956.
  - Memorial at Corinda High School.
  - Memorial plaque on a granite boulder at EP Hole Gardens, Kennedy Highway & Cook Street, Atherton.
  - Henry Dalziel VC Club, Enoggera Barracks, where a street is also named after him.
  - Dalziel Street, Nundah, previously named Maud Street, renamed in 1948. The street sign coincidentally fell down during his funeral on 27th July 1965.
  - Henry Dalziel VC Dialysis Centre, Greenslopes Private Hospital, Brisbane, opened by Danna Vale MP, Minister for Veterans' Affairs, on 28th August 2003.
  - Harry Dalziel VC Memorial Bar, Atherton Returned Serviceman's Club was opened

Harry at the opening of YMCA Camp Warrawee on 23rd September 1956.

by Keith Payne VC. In the park nearby is a Great War artillery piece as a memorial to him.
- Communities and Local Government commemorative paving stones for the 145 VCs born in Australia, Belgium, Canada, China, Denmark, Egypt, France, Germany, India, Iraq, Japan, Nepal, Netherlands, Newfoundland, New Zealand, Pakistan, South Africa, Sri Lanka, Ukraine and United States of America were unveiled at the National Memorial Arboretum, Alrewas, Staffordshire by Prime Minister David Cameron MP and Sergeant Johnson Beharry VC on 5th March 2015.
- Named on a memorial paving stone unveiled outside Freemason's Hall, Covent Garden, London on 25th April 2017 by the Duke of Kent.

In addition to the VC he was awarded the 1914–15 Star, British War Medal 1914–20, Victory Medal 1914–19, War Medal 1939–45, Australia Service Medal 1939–45, George VI Coronation Medal 1937 and Elizabeth II Coronation Medal 1953. Harry was a staunch royalist and sent his VC to Princess Elizabeth just before the birth of her son, Prince Charles, in November 1948. The Princess thanked him personally in a letter on 5th January 1949 but politely declined, preferring that the VC remain with Dalziel and thanked him for the depth of his loyalty and affection. The VC was sold at auction at Noble Numismatics, Sydney, New South Wales on 25th November 2010 for A$612,000 (hammer price A$525,000). It was purchased by Kerry Stokes AO (born 1940), chairman of the Seven Network, one of the largest broadcasting corporations in Australia, who donated it to the Australian War Memorial. The VC is held in the Hall of Valour, Australian War Memorial, Treloar Crescent, Campbell, Australian Capital Territory.

1327 CORPORAL PHILLIP DAVEY
10th Australian Infantry Battalion, AIF

Phillip Davey was born on 10th October 1896 at Goodwood, near Unley, South Australia. His father, William George Davey (c.1865–1923), a carpenter, married Elizabeth née O'Neill (c.1876–1941), born at Kanmantoo, South Australia, on 1st May 1890 at Goodwood, South Australia. They lived at Harris Street, Exeter, South Australia before moving to 144 Barton Terrace, North Adelaide, South Australia. By 1917 they were at Kerry, Separation Street, Northcote, Victoria. She was living with her daughters, Thurza and Clara, at 400 Richardson Street, Melbourne Ports, Victoria in 1931 and at 23A Esplanade, St Kilda, Victoria in 1936. Phillip had seven siblings:

144 Barton Terrace, North Adelaide, where the Davey's lived.

- Arthur George Davey (born 9th January 1891) was a plumber when he enlisted in 23rd Battalion AIF on 29th June 1915 at Melbourne, Victoria (3813). He was described as 5′ 7″ tall, weighing 151 lbs, with fresh complexion, blue eyes, light brown hair and his religious denomination was Roman Catholic. He sailed for Egypt aboard HMAT A69 *Warilda*, arriving at Suez on 5th November. On 27th March 1916 he embarked for France aboard HT *Oriana*, disembarking at Marseille. Admitted to 26th General Hospital, Étaples with tonsillitis on 7th May and returned to duty on 15th May. He was charged with creating a disturbance in the lines on 29th May and was confined to camp for seven days. On 3rd August he was wounded in the right arm and admitted to No.44 Casualty Clearing Station. Next day he was diagnosed with synovitis of the left knee, admitted to 4th General Hospital, Camiers and was evacuated to England aboard HMHS *Newhaven* from Boulogne on 10 August. He was admitted to County Hospital, Guildford, Surrey on 12th August and rejoined his unit in France on 13th November. On 28th January 1917 he was charged with being drunk on parade and was awarded seven days Field Punishment No.2. He was charged with drunkenness on 10th March and awarded fourteen days Field Punishment No.2. On 24th March he was admitted to 6th Australian Field Ambulance with pyrexia of unknown origin and transferred to the Divisional Rest Station. The following day he was diagnosed with trench fever and admitted to 7th Australian Field Ambulance, transferred to a casualty clearing station on 30th March, to No.30 Ambulance Train on 3rd April and 3rd Canadian General Hospital, Boulogne next day. On 10th April he moved to No.7 Convalescent Depot and to 10th Convalescent Depot on 12th April. He was charged with drunkenness at Écault on 17th April and forfeited twenty-one day's pay. He rejoined his unit on 31st July. On 2nd October he was wounded in both legs, admitted to 3rd Australian Field Ambulance and was evacuated to Summerdown Camp Military Convalescent Hospital, Eastbourne, Sussex on 9th October. He transferred to No.3 Command Depot, Hurdcott, Wiltshire for convalescence on 30th January 1918 and to No.2 Command Depot, Weymouth, Dorset on 5th February. Arthur embarked for Australia via South Africa aboard the *Dunvegan Castle* on 13th March 1918, transferring to *Tofua* for the final leg of the journey, arriving on 14th June and was discharged at Keswick Barracks, Adelaide on 1st July as medically unfit. He married Alice Edith Emily, who was living at 16 Ashford Road, Keswick, South Australia at the time of his discharge. He served in the Royal Australian Air Force from 1943.

- Richard Davey (born 19th March 1894) was a stockman when he enlisted in 10th Battalion AIF on 12th April 1915 at Keswick Barracks (2587). He was described as 5′ 6½″ tall, weighing 146 lbs, with grey eyes, brown hair and his religious denomination was Roman Catholic. He sailed for Egypt on 24th June and was stationed at Zeitoun Camp when he went absent without leave 31st July–1st August, for which he forfeited two days pay. He sailed for Gallipoli aboard HT *Kingstonian* on 11th September and returned to Alexandria aboard HMAT A48 *Seang Bee* on 29th December. He was stationed at Tel-el-Kebir and went absent without leave from there 4th-13th January 1916, for which he underwent eighteen days detention and forfeited ten days pay. He went to France aboard HMT *Saxonia*, arriving at Marseille on 3rd April. He was charged with creating a disturbance in his billet on 4th May and was awarded five days Field Punishment No.1. On 23rd July he received a gunshot wound to the head and was admitted to a stationary hospital at Rouen three days later. He was evacuated to England aboard HMHS *Asturias* on 1st August and moved to No.1 Command Depot at Perham Down, Wiltshire on 14th August. He transferred to 1st Southern General Hospital, Birmingham, Warwickshire on 17th August and returned to duty in France on 29th September. On 22nd January 1917 he was promoted lance corporal. He was awarded the MM for his devotion to duty on 24th/25th February, when he was in a party of bombers ordered to dispose of an enemy machine gun near Le Barque. Shortly after the party moved off the officer was killed. Richard assumed command and succeeded in dislodging the enemy gun (LG 11th May 1917). He continued until wounded in the left wrist on 26th February and was admitted to 1st Field Ambulance. He rejoined his unit on 1st March and was wounded accidentally in the right foot when a bomb exploded on 15th March. He was admitted to 1st Field Ambulance and No.3 Casualty Clearing Station before being transferred to 9th General Hospital, Rouen on 9th April. He rejoined his unit on 22nd May. On 30th July he was posted to 3rd Training Battalion at the School of Instruction, Jellalabad Barracks, Tidworth and was appointed acting sergeant on 13th September. He transferred to Longbridge Deverill, Wiltshire on 7th November and reverted to corporal on returning to France on 8th February 1918. He was wounded in the shoulder and chest on 16th April and admitted to 1st Australian Field Ambulance and to No.15 Casualty Clearing Station. On 20th April he was transferred to 3rd Canadian General Hospital, Camiers and was evacuated to England aboard HMHS *Cambria* on 27th April, where he was admitted to the City of London Military Hospital, Clapton. He transferred to 3rd Auxiliary Hospital, Dartford, Kent on 20th May and to No.2 Command Depot, Weymouth for convalescence on 2nd July. Richard was invalided to Australia aboard HMAT D21 *Medic* on 24th August and was discharged in Adelaide on 25th November.
- Claude Davey (28th August 1895–6th May 1917) was a bricklayer when he enlisted in 10th Battalion AIF on 15th December 1914 at Oaklands, South Australia

(1456). He was described as 5′ 8½″ tall, weighing 140 lbs, with fair complexion, grey eyes, brown hair and his religious denomination was Roman Catholic. He embarked for Egypt from Melbourne aboard HMAT A54 *Runic* on 19th February 1915 and served at Gallipoli from 7th May. On 9th August he was charged with using obscene language to an NCO and was awarded three days Field Punishment No.2. On 12th December he used a boat belonging to officers of 11th Battalion at Sarpi Camp, Lemnos and was confined to barracks for fourteen days. He returned to Egypt and was stationed at Tel-el-Kebir. On 2nd January 1916 he was charged with breaking out of barracks and was awarded fourteen days detention and forfeited fifteen days pay. Claude went to France aboard HMT *Saxonia*, arriving at Marseille on 3rd April. On 23rd August he received a gunshot wound to the shoulder and was admitted to 7th Canadian General Hospital, Étaples from where he was evacuated to England aboard HMHS *Newhaven* from Calais on 27th August. He was admitted to Stoke-on-Trent War Hospital, Staffordshire on the following day and transferred to No.2 Command Depot, Weymouth on 8th September. Claude returned to France on 24th November and was promoted lance corporal on 16th January 1917. He was awarded the MM for his actions at Le Barque in February 1917 (LG 11th May 1917). This appears to be the same action in which his brother Richard was also awarded the MM. He was promoted corporal on 3rd March 1917 and was admitted to the New Zealand Stationary Hospital, Wisques with inflamed connective tissue of the toe on 28th March and transferred to 5th General Hospital, Rouen the same day. He returned to duty on 1st May and was killed in action at Bullecourt on 6th May (Villers-Bretonneux Memorial, France).

- Joseph William Davey (31st December 1898–21st May 1976) was a plumber when he enlisted in 10th Battalion AIF at Oaklands on 21st January 1915 (299). He was described as 5′ 7½″ tall, weighing 126 lbs, with fair complexion, grey eyes, fair hair and his religious denomination was Roman Catholic. He embarked for Alexandria aboard HT *Invernia* on 31st May. He served at Gallipoli from 22nd October and went to France aboard HT *Corsican*, arriving at Marseille on 5th April 1916. He was charged with drunkenness and absence from his billet on 26th April and was sentenced to five days Field Punishment No.2. He received a gunshot wound to the knee on 24th July and was admitted to 1st Field Ambulance. Despite this he

Claude Davey's name on the Villers-Bretonneux Memorial, bottom right.

transferred to 6th Machine Gun Corps next day. He was evacuated to England aboard HMHS *Jan Breydel* on 2nd August and was admitted to 3rd Northern General Hospital, Sheffield, Yorkshire on 20th October. He transferred to No.2 Command Depot, Weymouth on 6th November and was granted leave at Wareham, Dorset 14th-28th November. On 6th March 1917 he was posted to the Australian Machine Gun Training Depot, Grantham, Lincolnshire and returned to France on 10th March. He transferred back to the 10th Battalion on 24th July and was granted leave in Paris 25th-31st October. He attended the Brigade School 20th January–16th February 1918 and next day was granted leave in Britain. On 22nd February he was promoted lance corporal. He was charged with being absent without leave from 6.30 a.m. on 6th March until 10.00 p.m. on 7th March, for which he forfeited seven days pay. However, the finding was subsequently overturned. He was returned to Australia as underage on 12th May aboard HT D8 *Ruahine*. Joseph enlisted in 34th Australian Infantry Training Battalion at Royal Park, Canterbury, Victoria on 21st April 1941 (V13514) and reached the rank of lance sergeant. He was discharged on 24th January 1944 and enlisted in the Royal Australian Air Force at Royal Park, Canterbury on 18th April 1944 (148594). He was promoted leading aircraftman and was discharged at Headquarters, Point Cook, Victoria on 21st November 1945. Joseph married Mary Catherine Brown (born 1907), born at Bendigo, Victoria, on 17th February 1934 at St Peter's Church, Eaglehawk, Victoria. Mary had a daughter, Kathleen Theresa Brown (1933–31st October 1979) at Bendigo. Kathleen married Dominic Borin, a turner, and they were living at Lot 4, Joffre Street, Noble Park, Victoria in 1963. They had four children, possibly including Carmello Borin, Margaret Borin and Mary Borin. Joseph and Mary had five children including:

  - Joseph William Davey (1937–16th February 2014), a cutter, married Betty Norma Evans (born 20th April 1933) on 5th August 1955. They had three children – Wayne Davey, Kerryn Davey and Stephen Davey. Betty later married Brian O'Donnell Weldon (c.1927–24th May 1999).
  - Brian James Davey (born 1942), a driver, was living with his wife, Pauline Dorothy, at 14 Stott Street, Batman, Victoria in 1967.

- John Hallett Davey (22nd January 1902–5th August 1968) married Violet Savage (born 1900) at Port Adelaide in 1923. They had a daughter, Joyce Verna Davey, in 1925. He was a labourer and they were living at 404 High Street, Golden Square, Bendigo in 1931. By 1939 they had moved to 47 Amy Street, West Croydon, Hindmarsh, South Australia.
- Thurza Rose Herbert Davey (19th September 1903–1953) was a typist in 1931, living with her mother. She never married.
- Hilary Ernest Davey (7th July 1905–August 1926).
- Clara Dorothy Davey (25th February 1908–7th June 1944) was a clerk in 1931, living with her mother in 1936.

Phillip's paternal grandfather, George Davey (born c.1845), married Esther Hallett c.1864 in South Australia before moving to Melbourne, Victoria in 1866. In addition to William they had two daughters – Clara Davey, who was born in 1866 at sea, and Esther Davey, who was born and died in 1870 at Richmond, Victoria.

His maternal grandfather, Arthur Joseph O'Neill (1839–8th March 1902) was born in Ireland and died at Glenelg, South Australia. He married Esther 'Ettie' née Critchley (1841–7th May 1884), born at Avoca, Co Wicklow, Ireland, on 12th February 1861 at Mount Barker, South Australia. In addition to Elizabeth they had six other children:

- Mary Teresa O'Neill (13th April 1861–17th September 1891) married William John Borley (22nd October 1855–28th May 1918), born at Hobart, Tasmania, on 20th November 1880 at Adelaide. She died at Leichardt and he died at Clarendon, both in New South Wales. They had five children – Bridget Borley 1880, Esther Borley 1882, Emily Borley 1883, Margaret Borley 1885 and Nellie Beatrice Borley 1888.
- Anastasia O'Neill (4th September 1862–1910), born at Kanmantoo, South Australia, married Patrick Walsh on 22nd October 1873 at Mount Barker. They had a daughter, Anastasia Mary Walsh.
- Margaret Agnes O'Neill (16th March 1864–3rd May 1918) married Cornelius Donnes (c.1859–28th April 1933) in 1882 at Adelaide. They had nine children – Michael Donnes 1884, Esther Catherine Donnes 1886, Elizabeth Donnes 1887, Lucy May Donnes 1888, Irene Donnes 1889, twins Margaret and Julia Donnes 1889, Mary Ellen Donnes 1890 and Julia Donnes c.1899.
- Hanorah 'Norah' O'Neill (23rd February 1866–13th September 1950) married John Reardon (3rd May 1858–4th July 1940), born at Hobart, Tasmania, on 22nd August 1885 at Mount Barker. They had six children – Owen Reardon 1885, William Arthur Reardon 1888, John Joseph Reardon 1890, Olive May Reardon 1893, Veronica Frances Reardon 1896 and William Reardon 1902.
- Arthur O'Neill (born 18th November 1867).
- Esther O'Neill (29th February 1872–2nd December 1960) married George Seagrott (died 1927) in 1916 at East Murchison, Western Australia. He was a general storekeeper and cycle agent running G Seagrott and Co at Wiluna, Western Australia. They both died at Inverell, New South Wales.

Phillip was educated at Flinder's Street Model School and Goodwood Public School, both in Adelaide. He was a horse driver when he enlisted in the Australian Imperial Force at Morphettville, South Australia on 22nd December 1914, described as 5′ 10″ tall, weighing 158 lbs, with fair complexion, grey eyes, fair hair and his religious denomination was Roman Catholic. Because of his age his mother had to give her consent for him to enlist. Phillip embarked for the Middle East on 2nd February 1915 from Melbourne aboard HMAT A46 *Clan MacGillivray*

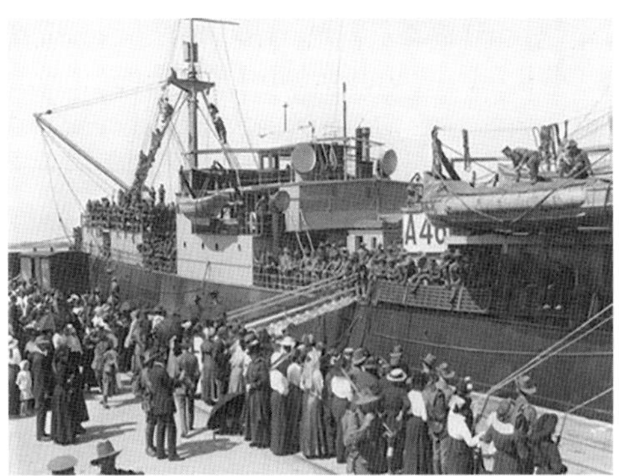

SS *Clan McGillivray* (6,447 tons) was built by Armstrong, Whitworth & Co Ltd at Wallsend and launched on 12th June 1911. She was owned by Clan Line Steamers Ltd (Cayser, Irvin and Co of Glasgow). She was sold to the Eastern Asia Navigation Co Ltd (Wheelock, Marden & Co of Hong Kong) in 1948 and her name was changed to *Maclock*. However, in 1949 she was boken up at Bruges, Belgium. Seen here at Brisbane in 1916.

SS *Hobart* (5,923 tons), owned by Deutsche-Australische Line of Hamburg, was captured early in the war and crewed by Australians. Her name was changed to HMAT A37 *Barambah* and she made four trooping journeys to war zones and three with cargo only. She transferred to the Commonwealth Government Line on 23rd May 1918. This picture was taken as she left Port Melbourne on 27th June 1916, with Phillip Davey aboard (Australian War Memorial).

Flinder's Street Model School, attended by Phillip Davey, was the first two-storey public school built in South Australia. It opened in October 1878, three years after the Education Act, which made primary education compulsory. The school could accommodate up to 800 pupils but average daily attendance was 593. Fees to attend were based on a means test. Boys and girls were segregated, which was normal at that time. In 1879 the school was renamed East Adelaide Model School and later to Flinders Street Public School. In 1969 it became Flinders Street Adult Education Centre and in 1978 was taken over by the Adelaide College of Further Education, School of Music. It is now the offices for the Australian Centre for Social Innovation and the Baha'i Council of South Australia.

19th General Hospital in Alexandria, Egypt.

with the 2nd Reinforcements for 10th Battalion. He disembarked at Alexandria, Egypt and moved to Camp Mena. On 10th April 1915 he embarked at Alexandria aboard SS *Ionian* for Lemnos, where he joined the 10th Battalion. He took part in operations on Gallipoli from 25th April and reported sick with enteric fever on 2nd

November. Phillip was evacuated to 19th General Hospital, Alexandria, Egypt and transferred to the Convalescent Camp, Port Said on 28th December. His illness was serious enough for him to be invalided home, embarking at Suez aboard HMT *Commonwealth* on 21st January 1916. Following treatment he was ready for duty on 6th April and embarked at Melbourne, Victoria with the 18th Reinforcements on 27th June aboard HMAT A37 *Barambah*. He disembarked at Plymouth, Devon and joined 10th Training Battalion on 25th August.

Phillip was charged with overstaying his leave from midnight on 7th September until 5.00 a.m. on 8th September, for which he forfeited one day's pay but the charge was reduced to admonishment. He embarked at Southampton for Le Havre, France on 22nd September and rejoined 10th Battalion on 3rd October. He reported sick with trench feet on 9th November and was hospitalised at Rouen until 2nd December. On 15th March 1917 he was wounded accidentally by a bomb near Lagnicourt and evacuated to a hospital at Rouen. He rejoined his unit on 7th April and was promoted lance corporal on 9th May. He reported sick and was treated at No.1 New Zealand Stationary Hospital, Hazebrouck 29th July–26th August. Joseph was gassed on 3rd October near Polygon Wood and was treated at No.17 Casualty Clearing Station before being admitted to 11th General Hospital on 4th October. He rejoined the unit on 1st November.

No.1 New Zealand Stationary Hospital arrived at Port Said, Egypt on 1st July 1915. It moved to France on 13th June 1916. It opened at Amiens in July, with the main part being in part of St Famille Convent, near the station, and the Lycee Girls' School. While there it was also used as a casuality clearing station. After ten months the Hospital moved to Hazebrouck, where this picture was taken. It had 1,040 beds and occupied two schools and a field of tents. However, when the town was heavily shelled, the hospital had to be evacuated. In February 1918 it moved to Wisques, three miles from St Omer, initially entirely tented until Nissen huts were erected.

Unlike many Great War camps, Tidworth existed before hostilities and was brick built. The original design was for eight barracks for one infantry and one cavalry brigade in purpose built accommodation. Lucknow and Mooltan Barracks were completed in 1905, Tidworth Military Hospital in 1907 and Aliwal, Assaye, Bhurtpore, Candahar, Delhi and Jellalabad Barracks were added a little later. A branch line of the Midland and South Western Junction Railway from Ludgershall opened in 1902. This was extended by the Tidworth Military Railway from Tidworth station. The branch line closed in 1963. The barracks are still in use, although extensively refurbished and redeveloped in 2006–14. This picture shows part of Aliwal Barracks.

Awarded the MM for his actions at Warneton, Belgium on the night of 3rd January 1918. One man in a patrol was badly wounded by machine gun fire, which he observed from a forward post and crawled out through the wire for fifty metres. With another NCO he brought in the wounded man in bright moonlight and under heavy enemy machine gun fire, LG 2nd April 1918. Phillip attended the Brigade Engineer School on 4th February and was promoted corporal on 24th April. He was posted to Longbridge Deverill, Wiltshire on 1st May and moved to Tidworth Camp, Wiltshire on 15th May. He rejoined the unit in France on 23rd June near Merris.

A sub-depot of No.2 Command Depot at Weymouth, Dorset. There is still a military training camp there, named Wyke Regis. A street alongside it is named Australia Road.

Awarded the VC for his actions at Merris, France on 28th June 1918, LG 17th August 1918, with a small correction on 15th October 1918. He was originally recommended for the DCM but it was changed to the VC on the same day and resubmitted with exactly the same wording. Phillip was admitted to 83rd General Hospital, Boulogne on 29th June and was evacuated to St John's Hospital, Weymouth, Dorset on 4th July. He was discharged to No.2 Command Depot, Weymouth on 20th August and was presented with the VC by the King at Buckingham Palace on 11th September. Phillip returned to Adelaide aboard HMAT D24 *Sardinia* in October. He was discharged in Adelaide on 24th February 1919. Corporal Jack Axford VC MM was also on board.

SS *Sardinia* was built by Barclay Curle & Co of Glasgow for the Peninsular and Oriental Steam Navigation Company. She was launched on 12th June 1902 and was immediately chartered by the British government to bring back troops from the Second Boer War. During the Great War she was torpedoed in the bow in the Mediterranean. Her passengers and most of the crew were transferred to a warship, while a few senior officers and crew remained aboard. To prevent a forward bulkhead from collapsing, she was steamed backwards for over sixty miles to Oran, where temporary repairs were made, and she was then moved for permanent repairs in Gibraltar. *Sardinia* was scrapped in Osaka, Japan in 1925.

Phillip worked as a labourer and linesman with the Signal and Telegraph Branch, South Australian Railways in three periods; 27th April 1926–4th October 1938, 6th March 1939–12th February 1942 and 17th December 1943–22nd February 1946. He married Eugene Agnes Tomlinson (24th August 1888–2nd January 1954), born at Norwood, South Australia, on 28th August 1928 at Adelaide, South Australia and they lived there at Brooklyn Park. They may have had a daughter.

Phillip Davey's headstone.

Phillip died at the Repatriation General Hospital (Repat), Springbank, Adelaide. It was one of a number of Repatriation General Hospitals set up in the Second World War to cater for returned serviceman. They were originally Army hospitals before becoming Repatriation General Hospitals administered by the Repatriation Commission (now the Department of Veterans' Affairs). In 1990 the Commonwealth Government divested itself of these hospitals and they are now either under State Government administration or privately run. The Adelaide Repat opened in February 1942 in tents and temporary huts. By late 1944 the buildings were completed. It closed in November 2017.

Eugene's father, Alfred James Tomlinson (c.1860–1944) married Margaret née O'Neill (c.1862–1st March 1914) on 26th November 1887 at Norwood, South Australia. They were living at 45 Kent Terrace, Kent Town, South Australia in 1902. He had retired by 1943 and was living at 7 Lysle Street, Hindmarsh, South Australia, where he died. In addition to Eugene they also had a son:

- Alfred James Tomlinson (born 4th May 1890), born at Parkside, Adelaide, was a tailor. He married Edith Amy Honey (4th November 1887–12th July 1980). They were living at 686 Seaview Road, Grange, South Australia in 1939 and 1943. Deaths of Alfred James Tomlinsons were registered in South Australia in 1944 and 1954.

Phillip suffered from emphysema and bronchitis and died from coronary occlusion at the Repatriation General Hospital, Springbank, Adelaide, South Australia on 21st December 1953. He was buried with full military honours in the Australian Imperial Force Cemetery, Garden of Memorial, West Terrace Cemetery, Adelaide. He is commemorated in a number of other places:

- Davey Walk, Wodonga, Victoria on White Box Rise estate built on land formerly part of Bandiana Army Camp.
- Named on the Victoria Cross Memorial at Springvale Botanical Cemetery, Melbourne, Victoria unveiled on 10th November 2013.
- Named on the Victoria Cross Memorial, North Terrace, Adelaide, South Australia.
- Victoria Cross Memorial, Queen Victoria Building, George Street, Sydney, New South Wales dedicated on 23rd February 1992 to commemorate the visit of Queen Elizabeth II and Prince Phillip on the occasion of the Sesquicentenary of the City of Sydney. Sir Roden Cutler VC AK KCMG, Edward Kenna VC and Keith Payne VC were in attendance.
- Victoria Cross Recipients Wall, North Bondi War Memorial, New South Wales donated to the community of Waverley on 27th November 2011 by The Returned & Services League of Australia.
- Australian Victoria Cross Recipients plaque on the Victoria Cross Memorial, Campbell, dedicated on 24th July 2000.
- Named on one of eleven plaques honouring 175 men from overseas awarded the VC for the Great War. The plaques were unveiled by the Senior Minister of State at the Foreign & Commonwealth Office and Minister for Faith and Communities, Baroness Warsi, at a reception at Lancaster House, London on 26th June 2014 attended by The Duke of Kent and relatives of the VC recipients. The Australian plaque is at the Australian War Memorial.
- Display in the Hall of Valour, Australian War Memorial.
- Communities and Local Government commemorative paving stones for the 145 VCs born in Australia, Belgium, Canada, China, Denmark, Egypt, France, Germany, India, Iraq, Japan, Nepal, Netherlands, Newfoundland, New Zealand, Pakistan, South Africa, Sri Lanka, Ukraine and United States of America were unveiled at the National Memorial Arboretum, Alrewas, Staffordshire by Prime Minister David Cameron MP and Sergeant Johnson Beharry VC on 5th March 2015.

The Victoria Cross Memorial at Springvale Botanical Cemetery, Melbourne, Victoria.

In addition to the VC and MM he was awarded the 1914–15 Star, British War Medal 1914–20, George VI Coronation Medal 1937 and Elizabeth II Coronation Medal 1953. He bequeathed his medals to his cousin, Mrs J Whisson, Seaton Park, South Australia, who presented them to the Australian War Memorial in 1967. The VC is held in the Hall of Valour, Australian War Memorial, Treloar Crescent, Campbell, Australian Capital Territory, Australia.

20765 CORPORAL JOHN THOMAS DAVIES
11th Battalion, The Prince of Wales's Volunteers (South Lancashire Regiment)

John Davies was born on 29th September 1895 at 19 Railway Road, Tranmere, Rock Ferry, Cheshire. He was baptised on 21st November and was known as Jack. His father, John Davies (c.1866–1942) was born at Birkenhead, Cheshire of Welsh origin. John married Margaret née Hughes (c.1862–1942), born at Mostyn, Flintshire, about 1886. He was a labourer before moving to St Helens, Lancashire c.1898, where he worked at Cannington & Shaw's glass bottle factory. They were living at 5 Sutton Heath Road, St Helens in 1901. By 1911 he was a platelayer's labourer at Ravenhead Brick & Pipe Works and they were living at 22 Essex Street, St Helens. The family later moved to Alma Street, Peasley Cross, where they lived until the 1920s. John junior had three siblings:

- Mary Davies (born 1889) was a labeller at a mineral water works in 1911, recorded as Margaret.
- Ellen Davies (born 1895) was a glass works split girl in 1911, recorded as Esther.
- Thomas Davies (20th April 1897–1993) married Maud Wheeler (24th June 1895–1979) in 1920. Maud had a daughter, Lily Wheeler (31st July 1919–2005) at Warrington, Lancashire. Lily married James Dean (14th May 1918–1999) in 1942 at St Helens. Thomas and Maud had seven children:
    - Thomas Davies (1921–22).
    - Edna May Davies (15th March 1923–1985) married Ralph Tootle (1904–59) in 1945. They had four children – Ralph Tootle 1946, Valerie J Tootle 1948, Margaret Tootle 1950 and Robert Tootle 1953.
    - Jean Davies (born 1930) married James Reid in 1955 and they had a daughter, Karen Reid.
    - Eric Davies (1932–33).
    - Ellen Davies (born 1933).
    - Margaret Davies (12th March 1937–14th February 2014) married James Swift (born 1937) on 30th August 1958 at the Church of St Mary, Lowe House, North Road, St Helens. They had four children – Pamela Swift 1959, Julie Margaret Swift 1962, Paul A Swift 1963 and Anthony John Swift 1971.
    - Brian Davies (1939–53).

John's paternal grandfather, Thomas Davies (1st March 1829–17th February 1897), a sawyer, was born at Llanfair, near Welshpool, Montgomeryshire. He married Margaret née Oversby (born c.1836), born at Priest Hutton, Lancashire, on 11th February 1860 at Holy Trinity, Birkenhead, Cheshire. She was a domestic servant at Burton in Kendal, Westmoreland in 1851. They were living at Oliver Place, Birkenhead, Cheshire in 1861, at 3 Arthur Street, Birkenhead in 1871 and at 2 Livingstone Street, Birkenhead in 1881. Thomas was a resident of the Guardians of the Birkenhead Union at the time of the 1891 Census. In addition to John they had two other sons:

Holy Trinity Church on Price Street, Birkenhead was founded in 1841 as a district church. The size of the parish was reduced in 1861, 1868 and 1914. The church closed in 1974 and was later demolished.

- George Davies (born 1860).
- Henry David Davies (25th November 1869–19th May 1924), known as David, was a coal carter with Wallasey Corporation. He married Clara Robinson (26th September 1874–27th October 1955) on 13th October 1895 at St Paul, Seacombe, Wallasey, Cheshire. They had ten children – Emily Davies 1895, Margaret Davies 1898, William Davies 1900, George Davies 1903, Clara Davies 1905, David Davies 1907, John Davies 1910, Elsie Davies 1913, Doris Davies 1915 and Gladys Davies 1917.

John's maternal grandparents are not known. He was educated at Arthur Street School, St Helens and was a brick worker at Ravenhead Sanitary Brick & Pipe Works. In 1911 he was a colliery screen labourer. John enlisted in September 1914 and joined 11th Battalion (St Helens Pals/St Helens Pioneers). He trained with the Battalion at Bangor, Grantham and Larkhill on Salisbury Plain before moving to France on 6th November 1915, arriving at Le Havre the following day. He was twice wounded in 1916 and was involved

Established around 1850 by W Edwards, David Horn and John William Kelly as Lavender and Co, the company name changed successively to Horn & Kelly, Ravenhead Sanitary Brick Co and in 1875 to the Ravenhead Sanitary Pipe and Brick Co Ltd. In 1960 the company was taken over by Roughdales and it closed a few years later.

in the capture of Montauban on 1st July. He also took part in the Battles of Messines and Third Ypres in 1917. **Awarded the VC for his actions near Eppeville, France on 24th March 1918, LG 22nd May 1918.** It is understand that this is the only instance of a posthumous award being made to a living recipient.

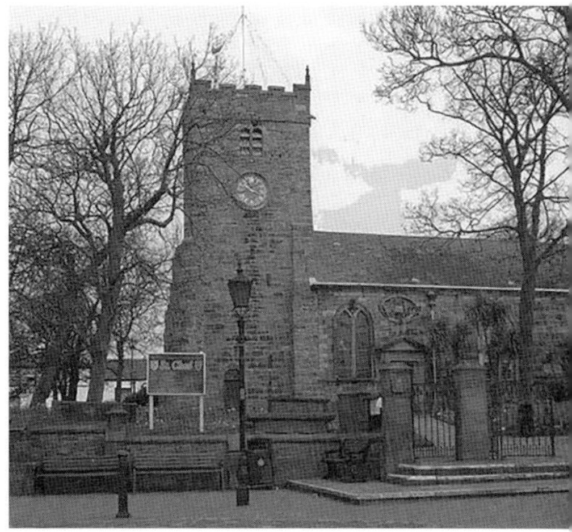

There has been a church on the site of St Chad's since at least 1094 but probably much earlier. In 1291 it was the third richest church in Lancashire. The tower was built in the 16th century and in 1751 the church was extensively renovated. By 1884 the churchyard was full and thereafter burials took place in a new cemetery in the town. Additions and renovations took place in 1868, 1881–83, 1908, 1955 and 2005 (Colin Eastwood).

John was taken prisoner although the British authorities did not know this for some time and listed him as 'missing presumed killed'. He was held at Sagan, Silesia until being repatriated to England, arriving at Dover, Kent on 7th January 1919. The VC was presented by the King at Buckingham Palace on 5th April 1919. The following day John was discharged from the Army. He returned to Alma Street, Peasley Cross, St Helens and was employed in the local glass and bottle factory. He was presented with £650 of War Bonds and an illuminated address by the people and Borough of St Helens.

John Davies married Beatrice Travers (31st March 1891–27th August 1976) on 31st March 1920 at St Chad's, Poulton-le-Fylde, Lancashire. They had three children:

- Eunice Davies (1921–10th May 2012) married Edwin Swift (16th September 1919–1973) a painter and decorator, in 1954 at the Wesleyan Methodist Chapel, Upper Aughton Road, Ormskirk, Lancashire.
- Alan Davies (1923–27th November 1943) died in an accident on the ice at Taylor Park Lake, St Helens.
- Sydney Davies (1932–6th June 1990) became a postman in St Helens in 1948. He was living at 228 West End Road, Haydock, St Helens at the time of his death.

John and Beatrice's son, Alan, died in an accident at Taylor Park Lake in November 1943. The park opened in 1893 on land formerly part of the grounds of Eccleston Hall.

Beatrice's father, Isaac Travers (1853–1909) married Margaret née Birchall (c.1859–16th January 1929) as Traverse in 1877 at Prescot,

Lancashire. Isaac was a butcher in 1871 and they were living with his parents at 43 Appleton Street, Sutton, Lancashire. By 1881 he was a provision dealer and the family was living at 58 St Mary's Road, Garston, Lancashire. By 1901 he was a grocer and they were living at 20 Essex Street, St Helens. In 1911 Margaret was living with her son Samuel. She was living at 4 Sherdley Road, Peasley Cross, St Helens in 1918. When she died in 1929 she left effects valued at £181/0/6. In addition to Beatrice they had nine other children:

St Mary's Road, Garston, where Beatrice's family lived in the 1880s.

- Emma Travers (born 1877) was working at a brickworks in 1901. She married Robert Brown (born 1871) on 27th June 1903 at Ravenhead, St Helens. She was living at 241 Burtonhead Road, St Helens in 1920.
- May Travers (born 1879) married John Davies (born c.1882), a fitter, on 31st July 1907 at Ravenhead. They were living with his father at Sutton, Lancashire. She was living at Blake House, St Helens in 1920. May and John had five children – Lawrence Davies 1910, Jessie Davies 1912, Harold Davies 1915, Eunice Davies 1921 and Alan Davies 1923.
- Samuel Travers (1882–1938) was a brick burner in 1911, when he was head of household at 20 Essex Street, St Helens living with his mother and siblings Frank, Caroline (appears as Emily in the Census), Jessie, Donald and Elsie. He was living at 4 Sherdley Road, St Helens in 1920 and was a miner in 1929.
- Francis Travers (1883–1953) was a bottle maker's apprentice in 1901 and a coal miner hewer in 1911. He married Margaret Davies in 1918 and they had two children – John F Travers 1919 and Samuel I Travers 1923. He was living at 10 Alma Street, Peasley Cross, St Helens in 1920.
- Camilla Travers (1885–1944), whose birth was registered as Traverse, was a sheet glass worker in 1901. She had a daughter, Adeline Travers, in 1910, who was recorded as Smith in the 1911 Census. Camilla married Charles Smith (born 1887), a glassmaker, on 11th June 1910 at Ravenhead. He was a furnace man stoker at Pilkington Brothers glassworks at the time of the 1911 Census and they were living at 239 Burtonhead Road, St Helens. Camilla and Charles had seven children – Bertha Smith 1912, Albert Smith 1914, Charles Smith 1918, Donald Smith 1920, George R Smith 1926, Leslie Smith 1928 and Adeline Smith 1932.
- Caroline Travers (1889–1947) was a brickmaker in 1911. She married Arthur Travers (sic) (21st November 1887–1950), a glass worker, on 20th April 1912 at the parish church Ravenhead, Lancashire. He joined the Royal Navy on 1st February 1907 at Devonport, Devon, giving his date of birth as 21st November 1888. He

was described as just under 5′ 4″ tall, with brown hair, blue eyes, fresh complexion and a tattooed heart and arrow on his left forearm. He was a stoker 2nd class on HMS *Vivid*. He was rated stoker 1st class and transferred to HMS *Doris* on 21st October 1909. Arthur also served aboard HMS *Excellent* and *Terrible*. He transferred to the Reserve on 29th January 1912 and was recalled on 5th August 1914. He served on HMS *Vivid II*, *Victory I*, *Otway*, *Teutonic* and *Foresight* and was demobilised on 13th June 1921.

- Jessie Travers (1894–1912) was a brickmaker in 1911. She never married.
- Donald Travers (1896–1918) was a shop assistant in 1911. He was a brick moulder when he enlisted in the South Lancashire Regiment (24931) on 10th December 1915, described as 5′ 2″ tall and weighing 103 lbs. He served in France and was granted leave to Britain 4th-18th November 1917. He received a gunshot wound to the neck on 23rd November and was treated at 136th Field Ambulance and No.3 Casualty Clearing Station. However, the wound cannot have been serious as he returned to duty on 28th November. He was posted to 13th Royal Welsh Fusiliers (45515) on 19th April 1918 and joined on 21st April. His service records shows he was posted to 19th Royal Welsh Fusiliers but it disbanded in February 1918. Donald was killed in action on 22nd April 1918 and is buried in Bouzincourt Ridge Cemetery, Albert, France (I B 6). Lieutenant Colonel John Stanhope Collings-Wells VC is also buried in the Cemetery.
- Elsie Travers (18th May 1900–1972).

Donald Travers' grave in Bouzincourt Ridge Cemetery.

John attended the VC Garden Party at Buckingham Palace on 26th June 1920, the VC Dinner at the Royal Gallery of the House of Lords, London on 9th November 1929 and the Victory Day Celebration Dinner & Reception at The Dorchester, London on 8th June 1946. On 19th July 1924 King George V and Queen Mary visited Liverpool for the consecration of the new Cathedral. During the afternoon the King reviewed 55th West Lancashire Territorial Division at Wavertree Playground. John Davies was one of nine VC holders presented to Their Majesties. The others included Cyril Gourley, William Heaton, Arthur Procter, Ronald Stuart, Arthur Richardson and John Molyneux. The latter was a lifelong friend and the two men attended functions together regularly. They were presented to the Prince of Wales in 1929. John may have served in the Territorial Army as a sergeant during the 1930s and was commissioned as a captain in 75th Battalion, West Lancashire Home Guard during the Second World War.

John Molyneux meeting the Prince of Wales (future King Edward VIII) at Victoria Park, St Helens in 1929. His close friend, John Davies VC, is next in line to meet the Prince.

Wavertree Playground, where King George V reviewed 55th West Lancashire Territorial Division on 19th July 1924 and was introduced to John Davies.

John Davies died of a heart attack at his home at 27 Leslie Road, Thatto Heath, St Helens, Lancashire on 28th October 1955. A funeral, with full military honours, was held at Ormskirk Road Congregational Church on 2nd November and he was buried in the Church of England Section (Area 59, Grave 426) of St Helens Borough Cemetery, Lancashire. He left effects valued at £2,797/5/2 to his widow. Beatrice died on 28th August 1976, leaving effects valued at £9,168. John is commemorated in a number of other places:

John Molyneux was awarded the VC for his actions near Poelcapelle, Belgium on 9th October 1917 during the Third Battle of Ypres.

John Davies' funeral was held at Ormskirk Road Congregational Church seen here right of the tram.

John Davies' grave in St Helens Borough Cemetery.

The 1914–15 Star was instituted in December 1918 for personnel who served in any theatre between 5th August 1914 and 31st December 1915. Those awarded the 1914 Star, Africa General Service Medal and Khedive's Sudan Medal 1910 were ineligible to receive it. The 1914–15 Star was awarded with the British War and Victory Medals, the trio known as *Pip, Squeak and Wilfred* after comic strip characters. 2,366,000 medals were awarded to members of the British, Dominion and Empire forces.

- Framed collage in the VC & GC Association Office, Horse Guards, London.
- Framed collage in the Heroes Gallery, Wirral Museum, Birkenhead Town Hall, Hamilton Street, Birkenhead, Cheshire.
- Department for Communities and Local Government commemorative paving stones were dedicated at St Helens Cenotaph, Victoria Square on 23rd March 2018 and at Birkenhead War Memorial, Hamilton Square Gardens on 11th November 2018 to mark the centenary of his award.

In addition to the VC he was awarded the 1914–15 Star, British War Medal 1914–20, Victory Medal 1914–19, George VI Coronation Medal 1937 and Elizabeth II Coronation Medal 1953. The VC is held by the Imperial War Museum, Lambeth Road, Kennington, London, where it is displayed in the Lord Ashcroft Gallery.

MAJOR ERIC STUART DOUGALL
A Battery, 88th Brigade Royal Field Artillery

Eric Dougall was born on 13th April 1886 at Brookside, Auckland Road, Tunbridge Wells, Kent. His father, Andrew Dougall (19th April 1857–26th March 1919) was born at 12 Glen Street, Paisley, Renfrewshire. He married Emily Elizabeth née Harker (26th January 1856–9th October 1936), born at Holy Trinity, Hull, East Riding of Yorkshire, on 31st August 1882 at Albion Congregational Church, Hull. Andrew was a gas engineer and later general manager of the Tunbridge Wells Gas Company. They lived at Brookside, Auckland Road, Tunbridge Wells before moving to 13 Mount Ephraim Road, Tunbridge Wells. He had retired through ill health by 1918. Emily lived at

Eric's parents married at Albion Congregational Church, Hull, seen here after its destruction in an air raid in 1941.

Eric's mother, Emily, later lived on Loudoun Road, St John's Wood, London.

16a Loudoun Road, St John's Wood, London and later at 18a Richmond Road, Bayswater, London. She was living at 53 Carlton Hill, St John's Wood at the time of her death. Eric had two sisters:

- Ellen Mary Dougall (1884–11th March 1953) was an art teacher in 1911. She died unmarried at Flat 3, Somerville Court, Tunbridge Wells.
- Kathleen Jerrett Dougall (1892–25th February 1969) was a nurse. She died unmarried at 5b Molyneux Park Road, Tunbridge Wells.

Eric's paternal grandfather, Andrew Dougall (10th December 1835–17th August 1905) was born at Paisley, Renfrewshire. In 1851 he was an apprentice tinsmith, living with his parents at 12 Glen Street, Paisley. He married Isabella née Jerrett (c.1836–4th October 1909), a millworker born at Rutherglen, Lanarkshire, on 6th March 1857 at 3 Hamilton Street, Paisley. She was living at 5 Carlile Place, Paisley at the time. Andrew was a gas engineer (fitter) and they were living at 25 Glen Street, Paisley in 1861. By 1871 they had moved to 12 Leswell Lane, Kidderminster, Worcestershire. By 1881 they had moved to the Gas Works Manager's House, Sculcoates, Hull and by 1901 to Claremont House, Sculcoates. Andrew was living at Argyle Lodge, Hessle, East Riding of Yorkshire at the time of his death there, leaving effects valued at £19,714 (£2.3M in 2018). Isabella was still living there at the time of her death. In addition to Andrew they had eight other children:

- Jonathan 'John' Stewart Dougall (13th December 1860–20th June 1928) married Alice Hamilton (c.1865–13th June 1905) in 1892 at Sculcoates. He was manager of the Boston Gas Company in Lincolnshire in 1911 and they were living at Fydell Lodge, Boston. Alice died at the Victoria Institute for Nursing, Wilberforce Street, Hull. He died at the Cottage Hospital, Boston. They had two children:
    - Flora Hamilton Dougall (born 1893).
    - Norman Stewart Dougall (born 8th January 1897) was commissioned in 6th Lincolnshire on 25th January 1915, transferred to 7th Battalion and was

attached to 8th Battalion. He was severely wounded at Armentières on 17th November 1915, embarked at Calais on 26th November, disembarked at Dover and was treated at Lady Bathurst's Hospital, 12 Belgrave Square, London. A medical board on 9th December found him unfit for General Service for three months and he was granted leave until 8th February 1916, then reported to 9th (Reserve) Lincolnshire at Litchfield. A medical board on 12th February found him unfit for General Service for a month and he was granted leave to 12th March, then reported to 9th (Reserve) Lincolnshire, by then at Brocton Camp, Cannock Chase. Medical boards on 13th March and 25th April found him unfit for General Service for a month but on 24th May found him fit. He joined 7th Lincolnshire in France on 1st September. He reported to 13 Squadron RFC on 29th November on probation and was appointed flying officer observer next day. Awarded the DFC and was developing into a promising observer but had an epileptic seizure. He was transferred to the home establishment General List on 19th January 1917 and was posted to the Training Brigade RFC, Mason's Yard, Duke Street, St James's, London. A medical board on 24th January found him permanently unfit for General Service but he was considered fit for Home Service as a recording officer or other ground duties. Posted to 41 Reserve Squadron RFC on 27th February as assistant adjutant. Lieutenant RAF Administrative Branch 1st April 1918 and flying officer later with effect from the same date. Appointed Assistant Adjutant Reserve Depot, Blandford 11th April. He was considered fit for overseas service by a medical board at Hampstead on 20th June and was ordered to report to Room 29, Air Ministry on 6th July for overseas duty. He served in the Middle East and retired on 10th January 1923.

- Mary Stewart Dougall (born 28th February 1863).
- Isabella Dougall (31st July 1865–1873).
- Martha Stewart Dougall (11th November 1867–9th February 1939) married Alfred Webster Tarbolton (c.1851–3rd May 1902), a shipping agent, in 1899. They lived at 14 Albany Street, Hull. He died at Sculcoates, leaving effects valued at £15,332/17/7 (£1.8M in 2018). She was living at Sevenoaks, Kent in 1911 and at 36 Highcroft Gardens, Golders Green, London at the time of her death there. They had two children – Violet Mary Tarbolton 1900 and Leslie Noel Tarbolton 1902.
- William Jerrett Dougall (26th July 1869–10th July 1913) was a gas engineer in 1911, living with his sister, Grace, at Glenbank, Otford Road, Sevenoaks.
- James Dougall (1871–2nd October 1930) was a gas engineering contractor. He married Eleanor Constance Toogood (1871–1948) in 1896 at Sculcoates. They were living at 9 Heath Close, Hampstead Way, Hendon in 1911. They were living at Hill End, Bridle Road, Pinner, Middlesex at the time of his death at the Pharmacy, Forest Row, East Grinstead, Sussex. Her death was registered at Rochford, Essex. They had two children – Lawrence Edson Dougall 1897 and Eleanor Janet Dougall 1902.

- Elizabeth Dougall (born 1873).
- Grace Dougall (born 1879) married to Roderick MacKenzie in 1917 at Sevenoaks.

His maternal grandfather, Portas Hewart Harker (c.1822–5th June 1888) was born at Hull. He married Ellen Mary née Tarbotton (c.1823–79), also born at Hull, in 1850 at Sculcoates. Portas was a seed merchant and they were living at 42 Spring Street, Hull in 1861. He had become a general merchant by 1871 and they were living at Springfield House, Spring Bank, Sculcoates. In addition to Emily they had seven other children:

- Frederick George Harker (born 1851).
- Walter Harker (21st November 1853–28th February 1855).
- Alfred Harker (19th February 1859–28th July 1939) was an undergraduate at St John's College, Cambridge in 1881 and also lived there later in his life. He died at Evelyn Nursing Home, Cambridge, leaving effects valued at £33,962/18/4 (£2.2M in 2018).
- Florence Harker (27th March 1861–1901) never married.
- Charles Harker (21st August 1863–22nd October 1938) was a mercantile clerk in 1881 and a warehouse keeper and general merchant in 1891, living as head of household with his three sisters at 3 Park Avenue, Cottingham, East Riding of

Eric attended Tonbridge School as a dayboy 1899–1905. The school dates back to 1553 and has a close association with the Worshipful Company of Skinners, one of the City livery companies. It expanded significantly, with many new buildings, in the early 19th century. The school lost 415 former pupils and three masters in the Great War and 301 in the Second World War. It remains an all boys establishment. In addition to Eric Dougall, Tonbridge School has one other VC – James Brindley Nicolson, the only Battle of Britain, indeed the only Fighter Command, VC in the Second World War. Harold Newgass GC was also a pupil at the School. Amongst its other many famous alumni are:

- Peter Fisher, the Queen's personal physician.
- Marshal of the Royal Air Force William Sholto Douglas, 1st Baron Douglas of Kirtleside GCB MC DFC (1893–1969), C-in-C Fighter Command after the Battle of Britain and later AOC-in-C Middle East.
- Field Marshal Edmund Ironside, 1st Baron Ironside GCB CMG DSO (1880–1959) was CIGS in the early part of the Second World War.
- Sir Tim Waterstone, founder of Waterstones bookshops.
- Novelists EM Forster and Frederick Forsyth.
- Sir Herbert Baker (1862–1946), an English architect dominant in South African architecture. He designed some of New Delhi's most notable government buildings and was one of the four principal architects appointed by the IWGC to design its cemeteries and monuments after the Great War. Amongst Baker's designs were those for Tyne Cot Cemetery and Memorial, Delville Wood Cemetery and Memorial and the Loos Memorial.
- Sir Colin Cowdrey, Baron Cowdrey of Tonbridge (1932–2000), Kent and England cricketer.

On Christmas Eve 1347, Edward III granted Marie de St Pol, Countess of Pembroke (1303–77), a licence to found a new establishment in the university at Cambridge. It was known as the Hall of Valence Mary, later renamed Pembroke Hall and became Pembroke College in 1856. It is the third-oldest college of Cambridge University. The first chapel designed by Sir Christopher Wren is at Pembroke. In addition to Eric Dougall, two other Great War VCs are associated with the College – Walter Stone and Sidney Woodroofe. Famous alumni include:

- William Pitt, Prime Minister 1783–1801 and 1804–06.
- Roger Bushell, organiser of the Great Escape.
- Writers, Clive James and Tom Sharpe.
- Comedians, Tim Brooke-Taylor, Peter Cook, Eric Idle and Bill Oddie.

The offices of the Bombay Port Trust on Ballard Pier. Bombay harbour has been used for centuries but the building of the present docks commenced in the 1870s. The Bombay Port Trust was established on 26th June 1873, under its founding chairman, Colonel JA Ballard. The port quickly developed into the gateway to India and led to Bombay (now Mumbai) becoming its commercial capital.

Yorkshire. He married Alice Beatrice Scott (1866–13th February 1958) in 1893 but no marriage record has been found. By 1901 he was a hay and straw merchant and they were living at 60 Mountain Villa, Hornsea, East Riding of Yorkshire. By 1911 they were living at Redroofs, Hornsea before moving to Wayside, Football Green, Hornsea, where he died. She was living at Stydd House, Lyndhurst, Hampshire at the time of her death. They had four children including – Hewart Scott Harker 1894, Gwyneth Mary Harker 1898 and Charles Geoffrey Harker 1906. The fourth child died before the 1911 Census. Hewart was commissioned in 18th (Home Service) Battalion, Essex Regiment and was promoted lieutenant on 27th July 1917. He was detached to the Huntingdonshire Cyclist Battalion on 27th April 1918. On 24th August 1939 he was recalled from the TA Reserve as a lieutenant Northamptonshire Regiment TA with seniority from 27th July 1917.

- Ellen Rose Harker (twin with Harriet) (4th September 1866–1946), born at 7 Minerva Terrace, Spring Bank, Hull, died unmarried.

- Harriet May Harker (twin with Ellen) (4th September 1866–24th February 1942) was living at Highfield, 33 Swanland Road, Hessle, East Riding of Yorkshire at the time of her death. She never married.

Royal Artillery at Topsham Barracks (later Wyvern Barracks), Exeter. Eric was posted there in March 1916.

Eric was educated at Grove House School Tunbridge Wells and at Tonbridge School, Tonbridge, Kent 1899–1905, where he won an exhibition in 1904. He was at Pembroke College, Cambridge 1905–08, graduating with a third class degree in the Mechanical Science Tripos. Whilst there he achieved a 'blue' in athletics and cross-country. Eric then worked for the Mersey Docks and Harbour Board and in the 1911 Census was described as a premium apprentice to a civil engineer. He worked as an engineer under AG Lyster until 1912 and was living at 17 Kimberley Street, Liverpool at that time. Whilst living there, he was a member of the Liverpool Pembroke Athletics Club and Liverpool Rugby Union Football Club. He then moved to India and worked for the Bombay Port Trust as an assistant engineer from March 1912.

In India Eric enlisted in the Bombay Light Horse on 8th July 1912 (also seen as April 1912) and he was promoted lance corporal. He was discharged in February 1916 and used his terminal leave to return to England, where he enlisted in B Reserve Brigade, Royal Horse Artillery (127027) at St John's Wood on 21st February, having already applied for a commission in the artillery, engineers and infantry on 14th February. He was described as 5′ 11″ tall and weighed 158 lbs. During his medical it was noted that he was suffering from slight hydrocele on the right side. He was posted to 3rd B Reserve Brigade, Royal Field Artillery at Topsham Barracks, Exeter, Devon on 1st March and applied again for a commission on 14th April, this time exclusively for the artillery. He underwent training at No.1 Officer Cadet School, St John's Wood, London and was commissioned in the Royal Field Artillery Special Reserve on 7th

Eric Dougall is buried in Westoutre British Cemetery but precisely where is not known. He is therefore commemorated on this special memorial in the Cemetery (Memorials to Valour).

Liverpool Cricket and Rugby Football Clubs War Memorial. Eric Dougall's name is fourth down on the second panel from the left (James O'Hanlon).

The Bombay Port Trust memorial in the Ballard Estate area of Mumbai.

July 1916. Later that month he went to France and joined 19th Divisional Ammunition Column on 28th July. He transferred to 88th Brigade RFA on 8th September and was granted leave to England 6th-15th December. On 11th May 1917 he was appointed acting captain and second in command of A Battery, 88th Brigade RFA.

Awarded the MC for his actions at Messines, Belgium on 7th June 1917 as group intelligence officer and forward observation officer – he took up a succession of observation posts in advanced and exposed positions from which he successfully maintained communication with headquarters. He was slightly wounded, but remained at duty, and frequently performed work requiring initiative under heavy fire with great coolness and gallantry, LG 25th August 1917. Eric was granted leave to England 10th-19th July and 22nd October–1st November. He attended a course at Shoeburyness 22nd-27th November. On 7th January 1918 he was promoted lieutenant and on 4th April was appointed acting major to command A Battery. **Awarded the VC for his actions at Messines, Belgium on 10th April 1918, LG 4th June 1918.** Eric was killed by a shell splinter to the left side of his neck near Mont Kemmel, Belgium on 14th April 1918. He is buried in Westoutre British Cemetery, Belgium (Special Memorial No.1), although the precise location of his grave is not known. The VC was presented to his sister, Ellen Mary Dougall, on behalf of her parents who were unable to attend, by the King at Buckingham Palace on 10th July 1918. Eric left effects valued at £1,337/11/8. When his father died on 26th March 1919, administration of the will passed to Eric's mother and sisters. Eric is commemorated in a number of other places:

The Royal Artillery VC memorial plaque is on the far wall of the Royal Artillery Tercentenary Chapel.

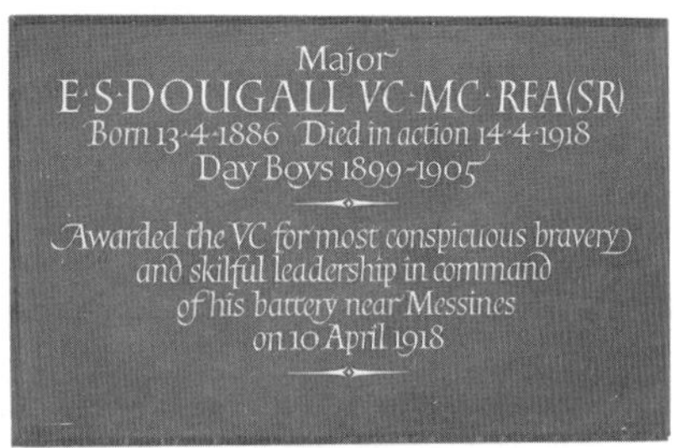
Major
E·S·DOUGALL VC·MC·RFA(SR)
Born 13·4·1886 Died in action 14·4·1918
Day Boys 1899-1905
Awarded the VC for most conspicuous bravery and skilful leadership in command of his battery near Messines on 10 April 1918

Eric Dougall's memorial at Tonbridge School.

Pembroke College War Memorial. Eric Dougall's name is on the second panel from the left under 1905.

- Dougall Close, High Brooms, Tunbridge Wells, Kent named on 26th April 2007. Dougall Close is on an estate where other roads are dedicated to local VCs, including Queripel Close, Addison Road, Temple Way and Lucas Close.
- Liverpool Cricket & Rugby Football Club War Memorial, Aigburth Road, Liverpool, where there is also a Dougall Lounge, named in 1986.
- Named on the family grave in Tunbridge Wells Cemetery, Kent.
- Named on the memorial to 4th Bombay Light Horse in St Thomas's Cathedral, Mumbai, India.
- Memorial to three members of the Bombay Port Trust, including Eric Dougall, at a road junction in the Ballard Estate area of Mumbai, India.
- Named on the Royal Artillery VC Memorial in the ruins of St George's Chapel, the former Garrison Church at Woolwich on Grand Depot Road, which was reduced to a roofless shell by a V1 in 1944.
- War Memorial and a slate memorial plaque at Tonbridge School, Kent (Memorials to Valour).
- War Memorial, High Street, Tunbridge Wells, Kent.
- Pembroke College War Memorial, Chapel Cloisters, Cambridge.
- Victoria Cross Grove, Dunorlan Park, Tunbridge Wells was dedicated on 8th May 1995, to honour the ten Borough of Tunbridge Wells VC holders – Charles Lucas, Matthew Dixon, William Temple, John Duncan Grant, Douglas Belcher,

William Addison, Eric Dougall, William Clarke-Kennedy, Lionel Queripel and John Brunt.
- A Victoria Cross memorial was dedicated by the Princess Royal at the Victoria Cross Grove on 13th October 2006, marking the 400th anniversary of Royal Tunbridge Wells and the 150th anniversary of the Victoria Cross.
- Memorial plaque to all Royal Artillery VCs on the wall of the Royal Artillery Tercentenary Chapel and Cloister, Larkhill, Wiltshire unveiled by Queen Elizabeth II on 26th May 2016.
- A Department for Communities and Local Government commemorative paving stone was dedicated at Tunbridge Wells War Memorial, Mount Pleasant Road, Tunbridge Wells, Kent on 14th April 2018 to mark the centenary of his award.

In addition to the VC and MC he was awarded the British War Medal 1914–20 and Victory Medal 1914–19. The VC was bequeathed to Pembroke College by his sister, Kathleen, when she died in 1969, together with his diaries and related documents. The VC is still held there. His other medals were sold at Glendining's for £3,000 in 1994, together with a copy of the VC. Other medals in the lot belonged to his sister, Kathleen, a former nurse. The MC group was sold again at a Spink's auction on 12th March 1996 for £2,900.

LIEUTENANT GORDON MURIEL FLOWERDEW
Lord Strathcona's Horse (Royal Canadians), Canadian Expeditionary Force

Gordon Flowerdew was born on 2nd January 1885 at Billingford Hall, Billingford, Scole, near Diss, Norfolk. He was baptised on 1st March 1885 at St Leonard's Church, Billingford. His father, Arthur John Blomfield Flowerdew (c.1834–16th July 1913) was educated at Framlingham College, Woodbridge, Suffolk and became a farmer of 441 acres, employing sixteen men and seven boys. He married Hannah née Symonds (5th May 1850–3rd December 1930) in 1869 at Stow, Suffolk. They lived at Billingford Hall, Scole, near Diss. He died there, leaving effects valued at £13,087/6/8. Hannah was living with her daughter, Eleanor, who was working at St Thomas's Hospital, London in September 1914, while retaining her family home at Billingford, Norfolk. Her address was also given as c/o Stanford Tillott, The Knoll, Yaxley, Eye, Suffolk. She died at Chilton, Sudbury, Suffolk, leaving effects valued at £654/16/7. Gordon had fifteen siblings:

- George Symonds Flowerdew (26th November 1869–1947) was educated at Framlingham College 1883–85. He emigrated to Canada on 16th April 1890, settling at Winnipeg, Manitoba and in British Columbia, before moving to Washington State and California, USA. He returned to Suffolk in 1895 before moving to Perth, Western Australia. He prospected for gold, which was unsuccessful, so he joined the mounted police force in 1898. He moved the following year to New Zealand where he met his wife, Hannah Elizabeth Moore (c.1871–1964). They married in 1902 in New Zealand. He eventually returned to Suffolk and ran one of his father's farms at Oak Lawn Farm, Eye, Suffolk. He was appointed to the local council and was Mayor of Eye on more than one occasion. George served during the Great War with the Suffolk RAMC (V) and was appointed quartermaster and temporary lieutenant on 1st June 1918. They had four children:
  - Audrey Ao-Tea-Roa Flowerdew (20th March 1903–5th February 1980) never married and was living at 12 Bartholomew Green, Southwold, Suffolk at the time of her death.
  - Arthur Kenneth George Flowerdew (7th December 1904–13th March 1979) married Patricia Hoggarth in 1935. He was living at Gardiners Farm, Cock Road, Eye, Suffolk at the time of his death.
  - Hannah Arete Flowerdew (8th September 1906–15th September 2000) married Oliver West (2nd September 1904–6th August 1981) in 1929. They had a son, Adrian West, in 1943. The marriage ended in divorce and Hannah did not remarry. Oliver married Doris Marie Pauline Rebbertoy née Eastoe (1917–80) in 1971 and Vilma Patricia Allen (born 1927) in 1981. Doris had married as Rebbertoy and had a daughter, Jane E Easto (sic) (1943–51). Oliver and Doris were living at The Hall, Brome, Eye, Suffolk at the time of her death. He also died there, leaving effects valued at £572,400.
  - Richard Allan Flowerdew (20th January 1909–2nd May 1993) married Rona Eva Brundell (1910–69) in 1932. They had three children – David Flowerdew 1934, Philip Flowerdew 1938 and Raymond Flowerdew 1943. Richard married Janis E Powell (born 1947). He was living at Chilton Meadows, Union Road, Onehouse, Stowmarket, Suffolk at the time of his death.

The 14th century St Leonard's Church at Billingford has a rather stunted tower, which may never have been completed. Some medieval wall paintings have survived (George Plunkett).

- John Lionel Flowerdew (7th March 1871–1937) was baptised on 7th May 1871. He was educated at Framlingham College 1883–85 and was a census enumerator at Billingford in 1891. He enlisted in 6th Dragoon Guards in March 1896 but his father purchased his discharge in September 1896 for £12. John re-enlisted in October 1899 and the £12 was refunded. He sailed for South Africa and took part in the Second Boer War, returning to England in 1901. He went to Bengal, India in 1903 and was promoted sergeant in 1905 at the Depot. He qualified as an assistant overseer in the Military Farms project at Allahabad 1905–10 and was appointed overseer at Bangalore. John was promoted conductor in the Indian Army on 18th February 1919 in the Military Farms Department while stationed at Ambala. He was promoted assistant commissary with the rank of lieutenant on 17th November 1919. He was promoted captain before retiring in 1924 and returning to England. John married Honoria Montgomery Lawrence (27th March 1890–1971) in 1910 at Bangalore, Karnataka, India. He died at Chilton House, Sudbury, Suffolk. They had three children:

- Unknown who died after 1910 at Ambala.
- John Bernard Flowerdew (1913–43) was educated at Framlingham College 1930–32. He served as a squadron leader (1st September 1941) in the Royal Air Force (37542) with 102 Squadron at RAF Pocklington, Yorkshire. He took part in a sortie aboard Halifax II HR667 DY-O on 5th May 1943, when it was shot down by a German night fighter (Leutnant Robert Denzel, IV/NJG1) over Voorweg, Westergeest, Friesland, Netherlands. He is commemorated on the Runnymede Memorial, near Windsor, Berkshire (Panel 118).
- Laurence Lionel Flowerdew (born 7th July 1920) was educated at Framlingham College 1933–35. He married Chrysanthe Nora Howard (5th July 1919–November 1993) on 2nd August 1945 at Hailsham, Sussex. They had a son, Nicholas Johnathan Flowerdew, in 1947.

The Air Forces Memorial, or Runnymede Memorial, near Egham, Surrey was dedicated in 1953 to commemorate 20,456 airmen and women who were lost on operations during the Second World War and have no known grave.

- Eleanor Mary 'Ella' Flowerdew (25th June 1872–13th July 1961) was baptised on 15th September 1872 and finished her education in Germany. She trained at St Thomas's Hospital, London, and was reportedly interviewed by Florence Nightingale, where she qualified as a nurse in 1906 and was later a sister. She left to look after her sister, Lorna, and later went to British Columbia but the climate affected her heart and she was forced to return home. When war broke out she resumed working at St Thomas's as an assistant matron. It is understood that Ella lived for many years with Thomas Brooke (1849–20th September 1923) but they never married because of a case of insanity in Thomas' family history. He died at East Rudham, Norfolk, leaving effects valued at £30,194/8/10. Ella nursed her mother at Chilton House, Sudbury, Suffolk until her death in 1930. She lived at Gissing, Norfolk, followed by The Cottage, Rickinghall, before living with her sister, Lorna, for five months. Ella opened a fete at Harleston, on the Norfolk-Suffolk border in July 1939, assisted by William Robert Fountaine Addison VC. She died unmarried at Scale Lodge Nursing Home, Scale, Norfolk, leaving effects valued at £8,520/6/-.
- Florence Hannah Flowerdew (17th December 1874–5th January 1963) was baptised on 22nd February 1874. She married Surgeon Captain Ernest Hudson (died 14th October 1916) on 19th July 1894 at Harleston, Norfolk. He was promoted captain in the Indian Medical Department on 1st April 1886 and was appointed Medical Officer with 15th Bengal (Cureton's Mooltani) Lancers on 21st March 1890. They lived in India, where Ernest worked with prisoners in various jails. He was a lieutenant colonel in the Indian Medical Service at the time of his death at Naini Tal, leaving effects valued at £2,442/18/-. After his death, Florence settled in South Africa and grew oranges at Rustenburg before moving to The Chalet, Camps Bay, Cape Town in 1947. She died at Monastery Nursing Home, Sea Point, Cape Town, leaving effects valued at £1,774/13/-. Florence and Ernest had a daughter, Eleanor Viola Hudson (c.1895–9th May 1973) born at Murree, India. She never married and was living at Chandos Lodge, Black Pond Lane, Farnham Common, Buckinghamshire at the time of her death, leaving effects valued at £33,757.
- Arthur Harold 'Harry' Flowerdew (22nd May 1875–15th November 1953) was baptised on 1st August 1875. He was educated at Framlingham College 1887–90 and was an apprentice machine maker in 1891. He joined the Royal Navy in 1895 and was a leading carpenter/crew aboard HMS *Pigmy*, a Yangtze River gunboat 2nd November 1899–7th September 1901, including during the Boxer Rebellion in China. Arthur studied mining engineer and went to Southern Rhodesia, where he worked as an accountant at a mine 1902–09. He returned to England and attended the Camborne School of Mines 1909–12, during which he met Nina Flora Clara Hoskins (1877–30th September 1950), who ran a school at Camborne. Arthur travelled to Nigeria, possibly to a mine at Joss. Nina followed him and they married in 1913 at Lagos, Nigeria. In February 1914 they went to Malaya

HMS *Pigmy* (755 tons), name ship of the *Pigmy* class of gunboats, was constructed at Sheerness in 1888. She carried six 4″ QF guns and had a crew of seventy-six. She was broken up at Falmouth in April 1905.

Harrietville, Victoria began as an alluvial goldmining settlement during the Victoria Gold Rush. Many of the early miners were Chinese. Later mining shifted to deep reefs. A large dredge, the 'Tronoh Monster' extracted alluvial gold from the Ovens River flats. It left three large and deep lakes when dredging operations ceased.

where he worked as a mine manager at Tronoh Mines, Perak. They moved to Kuala Lumpur in 1918, where he was a consultant engineer until 1938. They then moved to Tronoh Mines, Harrietville, Victoria, Australia, where he was appointed mine manager. They returned to England in 1945 but went back to Malaya to help with the rehabilitation of the country. They had a home at 450 Banbury Road, Oxford. Nina was living at 85 Comeragh Road, Fulham, London at the time of her death at Chartwell House Nursing Home, 12 Ladbrooke Terrace, Notting Hill, London, leaving effects valued at £5,901/19/10. Arthur married Florence Garrett Green née Bastard (23rd October 1888–28th January 1974) on 17th July 1951 at Oxford. Her father, Segar Bastard, was a solicitor who played football for Upton Park Football Club 1873–87 and once for England in 1880. He became an international football official, refereeing the 1878 FA Cup Final between Wanderers Football Club and Royal Engineers Football Club at The Oval and the international between England and Wales at the same venue on 18th January 1879. He also played cricket for Essex and Marylebone Cricket Club. Florence had married the Reverend Vincent Coke Boddington (1886–1917) on 6th November 1915 at St Mary Abchurch, Abchurch Lane, London City in 1915. Vincent was commissioned as a temporary chaplain 4th class in the Army Chaplains' Department on 22nd November 1914 and was attached to 35th General Hospital RAMC at Calais. He contracted tuberculosis and had to relinquish his commission on account of ill health on 1st December 1916. He was admitted to the London Open Air Sanatorium, Pinewood, Wokingham, Berkshire and died there on 13th

March 1917, leaving effects valued at £199/6/8 to his widow, who was living at 25 Victoria Road, Shoreham, Sussex. Florence married as Green but no record has been found. Harry and Florence lived at 11 Caledonia Road, Nairobi. He died at The Maia Carberry Nursing Home (later Kenya School of Law), Nairobi, leaving effects valued at £11,904/18/4. When Florence returned to England aboard SS *Warwick Castle* in 1954, her address was Foxhounds, Chigwell Row, Essex. She was living at 6 St Edmunds Court, Harwich Road, Colchester, Essex at the time of her death. Arthur and Nina had two daughters:

  - Gwendolen 'Wendy' Nina Flowerdew (20th October 1914–11th March 2007) married John Noel Mason Ashplant Nicholls (26th December 1907–24th June 1987), Chief Police Officer at Batu Pahat, Johor, Malaysia, on 15th January 1937 at St Mary's Church, Kuala Lumpur. When they travelled to England they lived at 85 Comeragh Road, Barons Court, London. They were living at Steward's House, North Green Road, Pulham St Mary, Diss, Norfolk at the time of his death. They had three daughters – Christian Esther Flowerdew Nicholls 1937, Nina Dilys Ashplant Nicholls 1944 and Finola Marianne Ashplant Nicholls 1947.
  - Nancy Mapleton Flowerdew (26th July 1917–1997) was educated in England and mainland Europe before becoming a secretary. She moved to Kuala Lumpur, Malaya to work for her father and then for another large British firm. She enlisted in the Australian Women's Army Service at Royal Park, Victoria, Australia (VF345015). By the end of the war she was a captain in the Intelligence Service. She married Thomas Quartus Gaffikin (1907–80), Malayan Police Service, in 1945. Thomas was interned by the Japanese in Singapore during the Second World War. They returned to Malaya in 1957 and in 1959 they retired to the Isle of Man. Nancy wrote short stories, newspaper articles and one-act plays, including *Mannin Line*, which won an international playwriting competition sponsored by the Ilkley Players. Other plays included *The Long Divorce* and *Master Carver*.

- Allan Blomfield Flowerdew (27th August 1876–23rd March 1901) was baptised on 5th November 1876 and was educated at Framlingham College 1890–92. He became a clerk with Barclay's Bank at Bury St Edmunds, Suffolk and won a carving set in a bicycle race at Botesdale, Suffolk. He enlisted in 43rd Company, 12th Imperial Yeomanry (6825) after his younger brother Edgar and served in the Second Boer War. He was captured with his best friend by the Boers and held at Zeerust. They both died of enteric fever on 23rd March 1901, just before they were due to be released. Allan is named on the Norfolk War Memorial, unveiled by Major General Arthur Singleton Wynne on 12th November 1904.
- Edgar Frank Flowerdew (13th September 1877–26th March 1952) was baptised on 25th November 1877 and was educated at Framlingham College 1891–93. He became a clerk with Barclay's Bank at Bury St Edmunds before enlisting in 12th Imperial Yeomanry on 6th January 1900 (6789) and took part in the Second Boer

War. He was in action at Frederikstad on 31st July 1900, when he was wounded in the left shoulder. He was commissioned as a lieutenant in November 1901. Edgar returned to South Africa between 1902 and 1910, where he was a secretary and mine accountant before returning to Suffolk. He was appointed manager of three of his father's farms. He was thrown from his horse during a hunt in 1912, when it was startled by a passing motorist, and underwent trepanning surgery on his skull to relieve pressure. He married Kate Ellen Spink (24th September 1887–4th January 1970) in 1914. Edgar later ran his own farm but in the Second World War it may have been confiscated due to poor management practices. They were living at 10 Upper Park Road, Brightlingsea, Essex at the time of his death at 14 Popes Lane, Colchester, Essex, leaving effects valued at £5 to his widow. She died at 10 Upper Park Road, on 4 January 1970, leaving effects valued at £4,104.

- Hermann Herbert Flowerdew (18th October 1878–15th September 1964) was baptised on 6th December 1878 and was educated at Framlingham College 1893. He went to London, where he worked as a brewer's clerk and met his future wife, Gladys Maud Farrar (1885–11th June 1961). He enlisted in the City of London branch of the Imperial Yeomanry and served with his brothers Allan and Edgar in the Second Boer War. He returned to his old job in 1901, before going to Bulawayo, Southern Rhodesia as a mine accountant and secretary of a gold mine. He returned to England on account of his health and went to Queen's Bay, Canada in 1903 with his brother Gordon to live with their aunt, Alice Mahood. Hermann's fiancée, Gladys, arrived at Quebec on 21st May 1909 and they married on 7th September 1909 at Nelson, British Columbia, where he was employed as an accountant for an estate agency. They were living at 17 Nelson Street, Vancouver, British Columbia in 1933. Gladys died in Vancouver, British Columbia and afterwards Hermann moved in with his son, Alan and wife Elizabeth. They had at least three sons, born at Vancouver, and possibly another with initials GM:
    - John 'Jack' Hermann Flowerdew (17th January 1911–12th June 2005) was born at Vancouver and worked on a cruise ship travelling between Boston, Bermuda and Havana. He was later a clerk at Spencer's Department Store, Vancouver, where he met his future wife, Alice Zella Marr (1st May 1915–26th July 2010), who was working in the advertising department. She was born at Chilliwack, British Columbia. They married in 1940. Zella was an avid supporter of the Vancouver Symphony and assisted as a volunteer in establishing the Vancouver Opera Association. John served in a Canadian Scottish regiment in Britain and Europe during the Second World War (6411350). He was promoted to sergeant and transferred to the Intelligence Corps (LG 29th November 1945). He returned to work at Spencer's before moving to T Eaton Co Ltd until retirement in 1975. They had a son, Roger Flowerdew.
    - Norman Eric Flowerdew (22nd March 1915–11th January 2001) married Olive 'Ollie' F Cummins (1918–2003), possibly born in Ireland. He was

a supervisor in 1958 and they were living at Lougheed Highway, Maple Ridge, British Columbia. He was a personnel manager in 1963 and they were living at Haney, Fraser Valley, British Columbia. It is understood that the marriage ended in divorce. They had two children – Pat Flowerdew 1950 and Julie Flowerdew. Norman married Elizabeth Lilian Anderson (14th September 1917–15th September 2009) in 1972. He died at Richmond, British Columbia. Elizabeth had married Jack Fraser (born 1915) and they had two sons. She died at Kelowna, British Columbia.
  - Alan Raymond Flowerdew (18th October 1916–30th March 2014) married Elizabeth Jane Hodgson (16th September 1926–1st July 2015). He was a manufacturing agent in 1963, living with his wife and his father at West 62nd Street, Vancouver.
- Louisa Mildred Flowerdew (born and died 1880) was baptised on 7th April 1880.
- Spencer Pelham Flowerdew (6th October 1881–21st March 1959) was baptised on 4th December 1881. He was an engineer working for the Indian State Railways in 1902. He married Angel Dorothy Knox (c.1884–10th September 1967) on 17th November 1908 at Allahabad, Uttar Pradesh, India. Spencer served in the United Provinces Light Horse as a trooper. He was commissioned on 1st June 1908 in 1/24th North-Western Railway Battalion and was appointed temporary captain on 1st April 1917. He was involved in various local skirmishes and did valuable work keeping communications open during the Amritsar Riots in 1919. On 1st January 1925 he was promoted major in 3rd Battalion attached 1st Battalion, East Indian Railway Regiment at Lillooah. By 1925 he was a divisional superintendent of a division of the Indian State Railways and later that year was appointed its Chief Engineer. Spencer was appointed Director of Civil Engineering (Railway Board) in 1929 and retired the following year. He was appointed Chief Engineer of the Northern Extension, Nyasaland Railways in 1930 (CBE, LG 1st January 1936) and built the Church of England church at Limbe. He retired to Rickinghall, Suffolk in 1935 and was Chairman of the Council of Thedwastre, Suffolk during the Second World War and was also a county councillor and a magistrate. During the war he was also a member of the Observer Corps and ran salvage and savings schemes. Spencer died at The Cottage, Rickinghall, leaving effects valued at £18,987/3/1. Angel was living at St Martins House, 50 Randall Road, Chandlers Ford, Hampshire at the time of her death, leaving effects valued at £12,382. They had four sons:
  - George Douglas Hugh Flowerdew (12th January 1910–24th January 1997) was a cadet at the Royal Military Academy, Woolwich and was commissioned in the Royal Artillery on 30th January 1930 (44858). Promoted lieutenant 30th January 1933 and served with the Territorial Army as Adjutant, 4th Survey Company 1st January 1937–31st August 1939. He was promoted captain on 1st August 1938, acting major 1st September 1939 and temporary major 1st December 1939–18th February 1941, 12th February 1942–18th

February 1944 and 1st February 1945–30th June 1946. MBE, LG 27th April 1944. George was an instructor at the School of Artillery 1st February–14th October 1945 and Chief Instructor 22nd November 1945–19th March 1946. He attended Staff College and was promoted major on 1st July 1946, following which he was appointed DAQMG GHQ MELF 5th April 1947–11th August 1948. Promoted temporary lieutenant colonel 12th August 1948–27th December 1949 and 27th December 1951–11th April 1952. He was appointed AA & QMG HQ Cyrenaica District 12th August 1948–23rd October 1949. George's final promotion was to lieutenant colonel on 12th April 1952. He was appointed AA & QMG 51st Infantry Division (TA) on 1st March 1955. He transferred to the Reserve of Officers on 19th September 1957 and retired having attained the age limit on 12th January 1965. George married Sheila Mary Bishop (20th September 1911–July 2005) on 4th September 1933. He attended Wycliffe Hall, Oxford in 1966, was ordained in 1967 and appointed curate of Chandler's Ford 1967–70. He was Rector of Baughurst with Ramsdale, Suffolk 1970–80 and was also Bishop's Ecumenical Officer for the Diocese of Winchester 1974–80. He died at John Radcliffe Hospital, Headington, Oxford. They had four children – June Flowerdew 1934 (born in Hong Kong), Anthony David John Flowerdew 1935, Barbara Penelope F Flowerdew 1946 and Robin Timothy Nicholas Flowerdew 1947.

◦ John 'Jack' Pelham Blomfield Flowerdew BA (4th August 1911–7th June 1960) was a cadet at the Royal Military Academy, Woolwich and was commissioned in the Royal Engineers on 27th August 1931. He was promoted lieutenant on 27th August 1934. John was placed on Half Pay on account of ill health on 8th November 1936. He was appointed lieutenant on 22nd January 1941 (52618) and was promoted acting captain 25th February 1941, when he was appointed adjutant until 21st September 1941. Appointed temporary captain 25th May 1941–9th November 1943 and was promoted captain on 25th February 1941, with pay from 10th November 1943, and major 1st July 1946. The same day he was appointed Applied Ballistics Officer, Ordnance Board, Ministry of Supply until 13th June 1948. He was appointed TSO2, Proof & Experimental Establishment, Ministry of Supply 14th June–31st August 1948 and was under Chief Superintendent of Ranges 1st September–10th October 1948. Jack was employed at the Armament Research Establishment 11th October 1948–30th September 1949 and was appointed temporary lieutenant colonel 1st October 1949–31st March 1956. He was appointed TSO1 Armament Research Establishment 1st October 1949–17th February 1952, at the Armament Development Establishment 18th February 1952–30th January 1955 and the Directorate of Guided Weapons 31st January 1955–5th May 1957. He was promoted lieutenant colonel on 1st April 1956 and was appointed TSO1 Ordnance

Board 24th June–30th December 1957. He last appears in the Army List in March 1958. He married Ella Frieda Catherine Christine Wiegand (15th June 1913–19th October 2003) in 1939 at Bury St Edmunds. She was born in Switzerland. They were living at Wiston Church Road, Crowborough, Sussex at the time of his death at Pembury Hospital, Kent, leaving effects valued at £6,563/0/3. They had three children – James A Flowerdew 1941, Diana Mary Flowerdew 1944 and Gordon J Flowerdew 1949.

  - Alan Flowerdew (9th April 1913–7th March 2003) was born at Gorakphur, India. He was commissioned as acting pilot officer in the Royal Air Force and was confirmed in the rank on 24th August 1935. Promoted flying officer 24th March 1937 and flight lieutenant 24th March 1939. He transferred to the Reserve (Administrative and Special Duties Branch), and returned to the active list on 24th August 1940 (34220). Appointed temporary squadron leader 1st March 1942 and resigned his commission on 22nd August 1946, retaining the rank of squadron leader. Alan married his cousin, Audrey Ruth Symonds Miller Higgs (17th December 1920–3rd October 2006), in 1938 at Henley, Oxfordshire. She was born at Victoria, British Columbia, Canada. They had three children – Michael JM Flowerdew 1939, Felicity A Flowerdew 1944 and Benjamin N Flowerdew 1946.
  - David Alexander Flowerdew (11th August 1916–26th May 1928) was born at Simla, India and died in Guernsey, Channel Islands.

- Charlotte Audrey Eunice Flowerdew (27th April 1883–21st February 1967) was baptised on 29th July 1883. She was educated at Mrs Taylor's School, Botesdale, Suffolk as a boarder and at Nottingham High School for Girls, gaining the Higher Certificate in 1901 and Matriculated in 1902. She is understood to have become a stenographer. She emigrated to British Columbia, Canada about 1910 and ran a hotel at Walhachin. She married William Miller Higgs (23rd May 1878–8th September 1958) on 20th February 1911 at Government House, Ashcroft, British Columbia. He was born at Kennington, London and was a contracting engineer before moving to Canada between 1909 and 1911. They lived at Sooke, British Columbia, where they cleared land, built a house and ran a poultry farm. They were living at 889 Transit Road, Oak Bay, Victoria, British Columbia at the time of his enlistment into the Canadian Expeditionary Force on 17th June 1918, described as 5′ 10¾″ tall, with medium complexion, blue eyes, grey hair and his religious denomination was Church of England. The marriage ended in divorce on 21st December 1921. Charlotte and William had a daughter:
  - Audrey Ruth Symonds Miller Higgs (17th December 1920–3rd October 2006) married her cousin, Alan Flowerdew (9th April 1913–7th March 2003), in 1938 at Henley, Oxfordshire. See above for details of their lives and his service in the RAF.

  Charlotte married Hector Maclean (1865–1946) on 2nd August 1929 at Vancouver, British Columbia. He was born at Aberdeen, Scotland. They had a market garden. William Higgs had married Edith Monica Brown (29th April 1883–23rd March 1954) on 8th July 1902 at Lambeth, London and they had two sons – William Oswald Barrett Higgs 1902 and Archibald Geikie Higgs 1906. They were divorced in December 1909. Edith married Sydney Leonardo Ruffo Hollis (born 1886), born at Muzaffarpur, India, in December 1909 at Westhampnett, Sussex. They had a son, Leonard Ruffo Denzil Hollis in 1910 in Argentina. That marriage also ended in divorce. Edith married Charles James Savage (1888–1957) in 1932 at Brighton, Sussex. Charles was a third class steward (victualling crew) on RMS *Titanic* and his brother-in-law, first class bedroom steward Sidney Conrad Siebert (1882–1912), was also aboard. When *Titanic* sank on 15th April 1912, Sidney leapt overboard and was dragged into a lifeboat, but he did not survive. Sidney's widow, Winifred Rose (Charles Savage's sister), gave birth to a daughter, Constance Winifred Siebert on 18th November 1912. Charles was rescued in Lifeboat 11. He served in the Merchant Service during the Great War. Edith and Charles emigrated to Canada in September 1946, settling at 1633 Davie Street, Victoria, where he worked as a janitor. They retired to Port Alberni, British Columbia. William Higgs married for the third time in 1926 to Evelyn Mary Locke at Victoria. He returned to England and was living at 24 Leyburne Road, Dover, Kent at the time of his death.

- Richard Edward Flowerdew (26th September 1886–9th December 1971) was baptised on 7th November 1886 and was educated at Framlingham College 1896–1903. He was commissioned as a lieutenant in the Indian Medical Service on 30th January 1909 and was promoted captain on 30th January 1912. He was appointed Medical Superintendent of Cellular and Female Jails at Port Blair, Andaman Islands on 19th March 1914. In October 1914 he was recalled and posted to Mesopotamia as MO of 76th Punjabis and was present at Shaiba, Karun River and Nasariyah. He was appointed MO with 135th Indian Field Ambulance in Egypt from 10th December 1914 and was mentioned in General John Nixon's Despatch for operations on the Euphrates 26th June–25th July 1915 (LG 5th April 1916). He was invalided to India and appointed Senior MO Delhi Cantonments in 1916 and travelled to the Persian Gulf aboard HMHS *Ellora* as part of his duties. He joined 2nd Battalion, 113th Infantry as MO at Dera Ismail Khan in 1917. On 1st August 1918 he was appointed temporary major and Deputy Assistant Director Medical Services (Sanitary) Frontier Brigades, Northern Command, and was on active duty in Waziristan, North West Frontier in 1919. He was appointed acting lieutenant colonel while commanding an Indian general hospital 11th September–11th October 1919 and 13th-15th October 1919 while commanding an Indian casualty clearing station. On 17th October 1919 he was appointed acting major and Deputy Assistant Director of Medical Services. In 1922 he was appointed to the Gaol Department of the Government of Burma and was Superintendent of Rangoon Gaol and was involved in the Rangoon Gaol riots on 24th June 1930. Promoted lieutenant colonel on 30th July 1928. He returned to

India and was posted to Calcutta 1931–36 (awarded CIE). In 1937 he was posted to the North West Province of Bannu to command Combined Military Hospitals and retired on 16th April 1939. Richard was recalled on 30th September 1940 and was posted to Meerut for hospital and station duties but was invalided to Britain in 1940 and does not appear in the Indian Army List thereafter. He was appointed MO of an internment camp on the Isle of Man and retired in 1944. Richard married Caroline Jane Mackworth (1881–12th October 1957) on 4th October 1912 at Bombay Cathedral, India. She was born at Noel House, Bucksburn, Aberdeenshire. She was living at Elmsdene, Constitution Hill, Woking, Surrey in June 1940. They travelled to Kenya to be with their son, Frank, in 1944. She died at Maia Carberry Nursing Home, Nairobi, Kenya, leaving effects valued at £2,991/11/9. He also died at Nairobi, leaving effects valued at £17,574. They had a son:

The Cellular Jail at Port Blair, completed in 1906, was made up entirely of individual cells for solitary confinement. The prison was used by the British Indian authorities to exile political prisoners. It originally had seven blocks radiating from a central tower. The Jail is now a National Memorial.

- ◦ Frank Digby Mackworth Flowerdew (1st October 1913–28th July 1987) was educated at Framlingham College 1928–31, where he was a lance corporal in the Junior Division, Officer Training Corps. He was commissioned in the Royal Army Medical Corps (TA) on 20th July 1939 and was mobilised on 24th August 1939. He was promoted war substantive captain on 20th July 1940 and served in France and with East African Command in Kenya, Abyssinia and Madagascar. He was promoted temporary major on 14th May 1944 and temporary lieutenant colonel later before relinquished his commission in April 1946 with the honorary rank of major. Frank married Margaret 'Margot' Stewart (11th March 1915–November 1999) on 10th January 1942 at St Andrew's Presbyterian Church, Bournemouth, Hampshire. Frank was a physician at St Thomas's Hospital, Westminster Bridge Road, London, at the Royal North Hospital, Holloway, London and the Royal Victoria Hospital, Boscombe, Bournemouth, Hampshire. He returned to East Africa to join a general practice in Nairobi, where he specialised as an anaesthetist. They returned to England and settled at Ferndown, Dorset in 1979.

- Lorna MacNaught Flowerdew (10th September 1888–29th December 1980) was educated at a boarding school. She married Stanford Tillott (29th May 1878–9th August 1969), a farmer, on 20th April 1910 at Billingford Hall. Lorna threatened him with a knife shortly after their marriage and she was admitted to Bethel Hospital for Lunatics, Bethel Street, Norwich by the time of the 1911 Census. He was living at White House Farm, Yaxley at the time. Stanford served in the Royal Fusiliers during the Great War (7443) and later in the Labour Corps (503403). Lorna was released into the care of her sister, Eleanor, and they moved to Eye, Suffolk in 1937, where she became an avid gardener. She threw herself into social work, including the Women's Institute in which she served as section president, chairwoman and treasurer of the county committee, and with the Hartismere Blind Association. She also worked with the Blind Canteen. Stanford was on the committee dealing with the confiscation of farms due to bad management practices during the Second World War. He may have been involved in the confiscation of Edgar Flowerdew's farm, his brother-in-law. They were living at 4 Castle Street, Eye at the time of his death, leaving effects valued at £23,576. She died at The Nunnery, Denmark Street, Diss, Norfolk, leaving effects valued at £8,109.

- Possibly an unnamed boy, born and died in 1893 at Bosmere, Suffolk.
- Eric Symonds Flowerdew (6th January 1896–29th April 1972) was baptised on 29th March 1896. He joined his brother, Gordon, at Walhachin, British Columbia in 1910. Enlisted in Lord Strathcona's Horse on 23rd September 1914 (2534) at Valcartier, described as a farmer/rancher, 5′ 9¾″ tall, weighing 155 lbs, with medium complexion, blue eyes, light brown hair and his religious denomination was Church of England. Eric served in France for two years and ten months, was wounded and was promoted corporal in 1917. He applied for a commission on 5th May 1917 and this was supported by the Commander Canadian Cavalry Brigade, Brigadier General JEB Seely. While on leave Eric's address was 36 Crozier Street, Lambeth, London. He was posted to 23rd Brigade RFA, Preston Barracks, Brighton on 5th February 1918 and trained at No.2 RFA Officer Cadet School, Exeter 2nd April–23rd September 1918. His final report indicates he performed fairly throughout and was fit for a commission but needed more training at home before deploying abroad. Commissioned in the RFA on 24th October 1918 and relinquished it on 28th March 1919. He was serving with 57th Battery Reserve at

Walhachin, south of the Thompson River in British Columbia, was established as a farming community for British settlers. An American entrepreneur, Charles Barnes, convinced the British Columbia Development Association, to create a horticultural colony there. The company claimed that Walhachin meant 'bountiful valley' and 200 came to settle the well-planned, tailor-made community that opened in 1910. Many of the residents were relatively affluent and employed Chinese and Indians as domestic servants. Tennis, cricket, golf, polo, shooting and amateur theatricals were popular activities. By 1914 the community had grown to nearly 300. Although the area has over 2,000 hours of sunshine annually, it is extremely arid. An elaborate irrigation system was necessary to bring water from higher lands but it struggled to provide sufficient. In the long term the community was economically unfeasible and the outbreak of war denuded it of much of its manpower. The community ended in 1922.

Larkhill at the time. His forwarding address was PO Victoria, British Columbia, Canada. Eric married Anne Dorency Gilbert Hall (born 1896) in 1919. They arrived at Halifax, Nova Scotia from Liverpool on 12th February 1919 and he was granted a Soldier's Settlement property near Vancouver before moving to Cognam in the Fraser Valley, where he became a poultry farmer. He was the first British Columbian poultry breeder to win an international egg-laying competition at Central Experimental Farm, Ottawa.

Gordon's paternal grandfather, John Symonds Flowerdew (3rd June 1802–1849), married Emily née Blomfield (c.1807–1st June 1875) on 25th September 1828 at Billingford with Thorpe Parva, Norfolk. They were living at Brome, Suffolk in 1841. She was living as a widow at the Halls, Hinderclay, Suffolk with her family in 1851, farming 624 acres and employing twenty-nine labourers and nine boys. She was still there in 1861, farming 625 acres and employing twenty-three men and fourteen boys. She was living at 12 Northgate, St James, Bury St Edmunds, Suffolk by 1871. She died at Bury St Edmunds. In addition to Arthur they had four other children:

- Edgar Henry Flowerdew (c.1837–10th November 1860) never married.
- Frederick Charles Flowerdew (1839–1900) married Catherine 'Kate' Ann Moore (born c.1846–20th June 1905) in 1863. He was a lodging housekeeper in 1881, living with his family at 44 South Parade, Portsea, Hampshire. She was living at 3 Carnoustie Villas, Crescent Road, Hunstanton, Norfolk at the time of her death, leaving effects valued at £95/4/9. They had four daughters – Alice R Flowerdew 1866, Maude Charlotte Flowerdew 1871, Irene Kate Flowerdew 1872 and Clara May Flowerdew 1875.
- Laura Emily Flowerdew (1842–21st March 1930) married Edward Henry Denton (1842–29th December 1915), a farmer, in 1867. They lived at Cattishall Farm, Great Barton, Suffolk, where they were farming 400 acres and employing fourteen men and four boys in 1881. They retired to Bury St Edmunds and were living there at 5 Orchard Street in 1911. She was living at 18 Crown Street, Bury St Edmunds at the time of her death, leaving effects valued at £807/9/-. They had eight children – Emily Sophia Denton 1868, Edith Kate Denton 1869, Helen Marian Denton 1872, Eva May Denton 1875, Henry Flowerdew Denton 1877, Agnes Laura Denton 1879, Mildred Louise Denton 1884 and George Edward Denton 1886.
- Ellen Kate Flowerdew (1845–25th June 1889) married Spencer Freeman (1840–1914) in 1865. He was a farmer of 440 acres and they were living at The Hall, Mendlesham, Suffolk in 1881. He was living with two of his children at The Limes, Washbrook, Suffolk in 1891. They had nine children – Algernon Freeman 1867, Hugh Flowerdew Freeman 1869, Frederick William Freeman 1870, Henry Norman Freeman 1871, Elinor Mary Freeman 1875, Lilian Christine Freeman 1878, Edwin Freeman 1880, Kathleen Freeman 1882 and Dorothy Freeman 1887.

His maternal grandfather, George Symonds (5th September 1819–22nd May 1888), married Hannah née Wright (6th July 1820–1888) in 1841. In 1851 he was farming 560 acres, employing twenty-seven men and boys, living with his family at Rickinghall Superior, Suffolk. In 1861 they were living at West Hall, Rickinghall Superior, Suffolk, and he was farming 1,150 acres, employing forty-eight labourers and twenty-nine boys. By 1871 they were living at 35 The Street, Botesdale, Suffolk, and he was farming 1,750 acres, employing seventy men and forty-seven boys. By 1881 he was farming 1,125 acres, employing forty-seven men and fifteen boys, and they were living at 31 The Street, Botesdale, Suffolk. He died at Badwell Ash, Bury St Edmunds leaving effects valued at £11,733/10/- (£1.5M in 2018), and she died at her home at Botesdale, Suffolk. In addition to Hannah they had nine other children:

- Edward Symonds (c.1848–1906) married Elizabeth Betts (1852–1947) in 1874. He was farming 360 acres and they were living at Church Farm, Brome, Suffolk in 1881 and at Charidos Farm, Thornham Parva, Suffolk in 1891. Elizabeth and her daughter Margery were living with her mother at Winfarthing in 1911. They had eight children – George Edward Symonds 1875, Thomas Wilfrid Symonds 1876, Edith Elizabeth Symonds 1877, Ernest Henry Symonds 1878, Walter Hugh Symonds 1880, Alexander Wolseley Symonds 1882, Nora Mary Symonds 1884 and Margery Wright Symonds 1885.
- Elizabeth Symonds (1852–26th June 1898) married William Stevens Grimwade (20th February 1850–31st December 1895) in 1879. He had married Clara Harriet Burt (1855–77) in 1876 and they had a son, Arthur William Burt Grimwade, in 1877. William and Elizabeth were living at Stonham Aspall, Suffolk in 1881 and at St Mary Stoke, Suffolk in 1891. She was living at Broughton House, Felixstowe, Suffolk in 1897. She died at Boscombe, Bournemouth. They had five children – Elizabeth Clara Grimwade 1880, George Symonds Grimwade 1881, Alice Roza Grimwade 1883, Emma Elsie Grimwade 1886 and Hannah Victoria M Grimwade 1887.
- George Symonds (1855–19th November 1935) married Elizabeth Alice Grimwade (9th July 1855–3rd October 1945) in 1878. She was the sister of William Stevens Grimwade, who married George's sister, Elizabeth. In 1881 they were living at Burgate, Suffolk and George was an auctioneer and farmer of 373 acres. In 1901 they were living at Ellesmere House, Wortham, Suffolk. They were living at 15 Jupiter Road, Ipswich at the time of his death at the Nursing Home, Foxhall Road, Ipswich, leaving effects valued at £11,991/15/6. She was living at 36 Britannia Road, Ipswich at the time of her death at Borough General Hospital, Ipswich, leaving effects valued at £9,381/18/6. They had a daughter, Alice Grace Symonds, in 1879.
- Harry Symonds (1856–29th August 1936) married Emma Hale (1857–1941) in 1876. He was an innkeeper and a farmer, living with his family at Shimpling,

Suffolk in 1881. They were living at Brettenham, Suffolk in 1891, at Tilney cum Islington, Cambridgeshire in 1901 and at Smeeth Station Inn, Emneth, Norfolk in 1911. They were living at Smeeth Road, Walsoken, Norfolk at the time of his death, leaving effects valued at £1,529/13/4. They had ten children – Charles Symonds 1877, Beatrice Symonds 1879, Clara I Symonds 1880, Amelia Symonds 1882, Rose Maud Symonds 1884, Frederick Symonds 1886, Robert Symonds 1888, Archibald Symonds 1890, Morris William Symonds 1895 and Ethel M Symonds 1900.

- Mary Symonds (17th March 1858–29th October 1915) emigrated to Canada and married the Reverend Stanley John Stocken (1864–16th January 1916), born at Wrexham, Denbighshire. He taught at the Indian school on the Blackfoot Reserve on weekdays and held church services on Sundays at various section houses from Langdon to Tilley. He also carried out his ministry at the Sarcee Reserve and other locations, including Priddis, Millarville, Pine Creek, Red Deer Lake and Glenmore. Stanley and Mary returned to Gleichen, Alberta around 1896, where he was appointed Principal of the Sun Anglican Mission School, Blackfoot (Siksika) Reserve and also incumbent of St. Andrews Church, Gleichen. He was appointed Bishop's Chaplain for Indian work and was Diocesan Secretary of Sunday Schools. Ill health forced his retirement in 1915. Mary died at Tsuu T'ina Nation Reserve, Calgary, Alberta.
- Alice Symonds (1859–60).
- Herbert Symonds (28th December 1860–24th May 1924) was educated at Framlingham College and emigrated to Canada in 1881. He attended Trinity College, Toronto 1886–87, took a postgraduate course in Theology at the University of Cambridge (MA) and was ordained deacon in 1885 and priest on 6th March 1887. He held a number of appointments: Fellow of Trinity College; Professor of Divinity 1890; Vicar of St Luke, Ashbunham 1892; Headmaster of Trinity College School, Port Hope 1901; Honorary Doctor of Divinity, Queen's College, Kingston 1901; Vicar of Christ Church Cathedral, Montreal 1903; President of the Protestant Board of School Commissioners of Montreal 1907–12; and Doctor of Law, McGill University, Montreal 1912. In 1918 he helped organise and acted as chairman of the Committee of Sixteen, which sought to combat organised prostitution in Montreal. He went to England to visit the Canadian Expeditionary Force in 1918. Herbert married Emma Blackhall Boyd (July 1856–22nd March 1924) on 27th May 1883 at Bobcaygeon, Ontario. He fell ill on 27th April 1921, while on a speaking tour in Ontario and died a month later at Montreal. They had eight children – Bertha Caroline Symonds 1884, Hannah Greta Lydia Symonds 1887, Hilda B Symonds 1888, George B Symonds 1890, Herbert Boyd Symonds 1893, Isobel Mary Symonds 1894, Spencer Rupert Symonds 1895 and Victor Kingsley Symonds 1897. Herbert Boyd Symonds served as a lieutenant in 14th Battalion, Canadian Infantry and died on 9th April 1917 in France (Nine Elms Military Cemetery – I A 29).

- Spencer Symonds (27 June 1862–2nd June 1938), a farmer, married Minnie Emmaretta Hatten (1866–30th June 1951) in 1891. They were living at Badwell Ash, Suffolk in 1901 and at Thackerland Hall, Badwell Ash in 1911. He died there, leaving effects valued at £22,140. She was living at White House, Walsham-le-Willows, Suffolk at the time of her death, leaving effects valued at £5,158/4/6. They had five children – George Raymond Hatten Symonds 1892, William Harry Symonds 1894, Spencer Leslie Hatten Symonds 1897, Herbert Eric Hatten Symonds 1899 and Margaret Evelyn Joy Symonds 1907.
- Alice Symonds (28th April 1864–14th January 1942) emigrated to Canada, where she married the Reverend John Samuel Mahood (1870–19th September 1936) in 1894. He was born at Foochow, China and emigrated to Canada in 1888. He was Vicar of Kokanee, British Columbia and they were living at Queen's Bay in 1915. In c.1916 he was appointed Vicar of Kootenay, British Columbia. They had four sons including, Douglas Symonds Mahood c.1895, Hubert John Mahood 1896 and Herbert Edward Mahood c.1898. Hubert was a rancher when he enlisted in 8th Battalion CEF (442927) on 16th May 1915, described as 5′ 8″ tall, with dark complexion, grey eyes, dark brown hair and his religious denomination was Church of England. He was killed in action on 28th April 1917 and is commemorated on the Canadian National Vimy Memorial, France.

Herbert Boyd Symonds' grave, on the right, in Nine Elms Military Cemetery.

Gordon's cousin, Hubert John Mahood, is commemorated on the Canadian National Vimy Memorial. Also commemorated there is Trooper Reginald George Longley, Gordon Flowerdew's trumpeter at Moreuil Wood.

Gordon was a sickly child and his parents feared the British climate would lead to pneumonia. He was educated at Framlingham College, Woodbridge, Suffolk 1894–99. In 1903 he and his brother, Hermann, were sent to join relatives in British Columbia, Canada. Gordon worked initially as a cowboy and became a farmer at Duck Lake, Saskatchewan. He settled at Kootenay Lake, Queen's Bay, near Nelson,

British Columbia about 1910, before becoming a butcher at Walhachin. He also ran the general store there and, as a temporary lawman, arrested two outlaws who had robbed a store and beaten its Chinese proprietor.

Gordon served in 31st Regiment, British Colombia Horse, a militia unit, from about May 1911. It was not mobilised in August 1914. On 4th September he

Framlingham College, originally Albert Memorial College, was founded in 1864 by public subscription as the Suffolk County Memorial to Prince Albert. Built to accommodate 300 boys, the College opened on 10th April 1865. During the invasion scare of 1940, the College was evacuated for a short time to Repton School, Derbyshire. The College has a prep school at Brandeston Hall, opened by Princess Alice in July 1949, purchased by The Society of Old Framlinghamians as a memorial to those who 'in two Great Wars gave their lives for the freedom of the world'. The College was expanded and modernised in the 1970s and admitted girls. The College has two other VCs – William Hewitt and Augustus Agar. Commander Henry Tupper was awarded the Albert Medal in 1918, which was later replaced by the George Cross. A former pupil was Group Captain Percy Charles Pickard DSO and two bars DFC. He featured in a wartime film, *Target for Tonight*. He led 51 Squadron in dropping the paratroopers who carried out the Bruneval Raid in February 1942. Charles Pickard was killed during the raid on Amiens Prison in 1944, later known as Operation Jericho.

A military training camp sprang up at Valcartier in August 1914 as part of the mobilisation of the Canadian Expeditionary Force. Its proximity to the port of Quebec resulted in it expanding to become the largest military camp in Canada, able to accommodate 32,000 men and 8,000 horses. Canadian Forces Base Valcartier is today home of the 5th Canadian Mechanized Brigade Group.

Pond Farm Camp was home to the Royal Canadian Dragoons and Lord Strathcona's Horse in the autumn and early winter of 1914, one of the wettest on record. Nothing remains of the farm today, which is in the middle of the Larkhill artillery range impact area.

A pre-war photograph of members of 31st Regiment, British Colombia Horse. Gordon is in the front row second from the right.

was medically examined and enlisted in the Canadian Expeditionary Force at Valcartier, Quebec on 24th September (2505). He was described as a rancher, 5′ 7″ tall, weighing 136 lbs, with medium complexion, brown eyes, brown hair and his religious denomination was Church of England. He transferred to 5th Battalion (Western Cavalry) CEF for a very short period before joining Lord Strathcona's Horse (Royal Canadians) with effect from 7th September and was promoted lance corporal on 22nd September. The Regiment embarked for England on 3rd October and he was promoted corporal on 29th October at Pond Farm Camp on Salisbury Plain. Gordon was promoted lance sergeant on 4th May 1915, the day he landed in France, and sergeant on 5th July. He was granted leave in England 8th-18th December.

Gordon's mother, two of his sisters and brother, Eric, who was an officer cadet, outside Buckingham Palace following the investiture.

On 26th March 1916 Gordon was commissioned and was granted leave to England 26th April–4th May. He attended the first General Course at the Divisional School 12th November–6th December 1916 and was granted leave 19th January–2nd February 1917. He was slightly wounded on 19th May and went on leave again 29th May–9th June. Further leave was granted 15th-25th August. Gordon was attached to HQ Canadian Cavalry Brigade 18th December 1917–22nd January 1918. Following fourteen days leave in England from 18th February, he returned to command C Squadron, Lord Strathcona's Horse, whose commander, Major Jackie Tatlow, was killed on 23rd March. **Awarded the VC for his actions at Moreuil Wood, France on 30th March 1918, LG 24th April 1918.** The VC was presented to his mother by the King in the quadrangle of Buckingham Palace on 29th June 1918.

Gordon Flowerdew's grave in Namps-au-Val British Cemetery, with the village church in the background.

The Framlingham College War Memorial in the Chapel.

The Canadian Cavalry Brigade Memorial, northeast of Moreuil Wood on the D23, close to Rifle Wood.

Gordon died of his wounds at No.41 Casualty Clearing Station on 31st March 1918 and is buried in Namps-au-Val British Cemetery, near Amiens, France (I H 1). He is commemorated in a number of other places:

- The Canadian Cavalry Brigade memorial to the actions at Moreuil and Rifle Woods, alongside the D23, south of the D934, two kilometres northeast of the former northeast corner of Moreuil Wood, France.
- Flowerdew Meadow, Scole, Diss, Suffolk.

The wooden cross that marked Gordon's grave until replaced by a CWGC headstone.

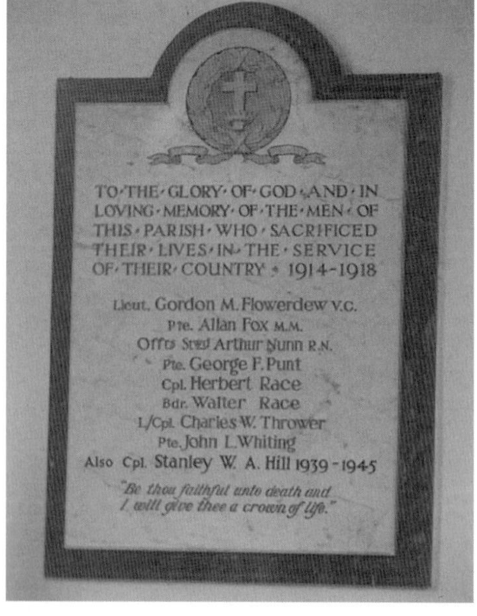

The war memorial in St Leonard's Church, Billingford.

- War Memorial at St Leonard's Church, Billingford, Scole, near Diss, Norfolk.
- War Memorial at Framlingham College, where there is also a copy of his VC citation, a replica VC and the original wooden cross from his grave.
- Memorial plaque at Duck Farm, Saskatchewan, Canada.
- Canadian Book of Remembrance held in the Peace Tower of the Canadian Parliament Buildings, Ottawa, Ontario records the members of the Canadian Forces and Canadian Merchant Navy killed on active service.
- The painting *The Flowerdew Charge* by Sir Alfred Munnings is held in the Canadian Houses of Parliament, Ottawa. A copy was presented to Framlingham College when the VC was handed over in 1991. A copy is also held at the Canadian War Museum, 1 Vimy Place, Ottawa.
- Named on one of eleven plaques honouring 175 men from overseas awarded the VC for the Great War. The plaques were unveiled by the Senior Minister of State at the Foreign & Commonwealth Office and Minister for Faith and Communities, Baroness Warsi, at a reception at Lancaster House, London on 26th June 2014 attended by The Duke of Kent and relatives of the VC recipients. The Canadian plaque was unveiled outside the British High Commission in Elgin Street, Ottawa on 10th November 2014 by The Princess Royal in the presence of British High Commissioner Howard Drake, Canadian Minister of Veterans Affairs Julian Fantino and Canadian Chief of the Defence Staff General Thomas J Lawson.
- Named on a Victoria Cross obelisk to all Canadian VCs at Military Heritage Park, Barrie, Ontario, dedicated by The Princess Royal on 22nd October 2013.

The Canadian VC memorial plaque (back right) outside the British High Commission in Ottawa (Memorials to Valour).

The Victoria Cross obelisk in Military Heritage Park, Barrie, Ontario.

- Plaque on the York Cemetery VC Memorial, West Don River Valley, Toronto, Ontario dedicated on 25th June 2017.
- Display in Lord Strathcona's Horse Museum, Canadian Forces Base Calgary, Alberta.
- The dress of Lord Strathcona's Horse was modified to honour the Victoria Cross winners of the Regiment. Two scarlet hose flashes are worn for Lieutenants Harvey and Flowerdew and one myrtle green flash for Sergeant Richardson.
- Commemorated in a play, *Mary's Wedding*, premiered in November 2011 by Pacific Opera Victoria, the story of a young couple caught up in the horror of the First World War.
- Two 49 cents postage stamps in honour of the ninety-four Canadian VC winners were issued by Canada Post on 21st October 2004 on the 150th Anniversary of the first Canadian VC's action, Alexander Roberts Dunn VC.
- A Department for Communities and Local Government commemorative VC paving stone was dedicated at St Leonard's Church, Northgate Lane, Billingford, Norfolk on 10th April 2018 to mark the centenary of his award.

The 49 Cent postage stamps issued by Canada Post on 21st October 2004.

The Memorial Cross is awarded to the next of kin of a member of the Canadian armed forces who lost their life on active service. It was created on 1st December 1919 by King George V.

In addition to the VC he was awarded the 1914–15 Star, British War Medal 1914–20 and Victory Medal 1914–19. As he died on operational duty, his next of kin is eligible for the Canadian Memorial Cross. The VC was presented to Framlingham College by his brother and sister in 1991. It was subsequently loaned to Lord Strathcona's Museum, Calgary, Alberta until it was returned at a ceremony at Framlingham College on 3rd February 2003. Guests included officials from the Canadian High Commission, Lord Strathcona, the great grandson of the founder of the Regiment, and members of the Flowerdew family. The VC was handed over by the CO and RSM (Lieutenant Colonel Jamieson Cade CD and Chief Warrant Officer David

Matthew Biener MMM CD) of Lord Strathcona's Horse. The two VCs owned by the College (Gordon Flowerdew and William Hewitt) were loaned to the Imperial War Museum on 23rd April 2004 and are displayed in the Lord Ashcroft VC Gallery. The whereabouts of Gordon's campaign medals is not known.

LIEUTENANT COLONEL JAMES FORBES-ROBERTSON
1st Battalion, The Border Regiment

James Forbes-Robertson was born on 7th July 1884 at Slead Hall, Hipperholme cum Brighouse, West Riding of Yorkshire. His father, Farquhar Forbes-Robertson (19th June 1838–12th November 1912), was born at Newhills, Aberdeen, Aberdeenshire, Scotland. He married Laura Ann née MacAulay (1850–14th December 1946) in 1872 at Halifax, Yorkshire. Her birth was registered unnamed at Halifax. Farquhar was a landowner in 1881 and they were living at Slead Hall, Hipperholme cum Brighouse. By 1901 they had moved to Langton Lodge, Cudnall Street, Cheltenham, Gloucestershire and to 2 Keynsham Bank, Cheltenham, Gloucestershire by 1911, where they both subsequently died. James had six siblings:

- Kenneth Forbes-Robertson (17th April 1882–7th November 1914) was commissioned in the Seaforth Highlanders and was killed in action serving with the 2nd Battalion (Ploegsteert Memorial, Belgium – Panel 9). He left effects valued at £12,795/15/5 (£1.4M in 2018).

James' mother came from Halifax in Yorkshire.

The Forbes-Robertson family was living at Langton Lodge, Cheltenham in 1901 (Zoopla).

- Elspeth Forbes-Robertson (12th May 1873–17th October 1948) married James Edgar Dennis (1870–11th July 1955) on 28th December 1901 at Cheltenham, Gloucestershire. His birth was registered at West Derby, Lancashire. James was a manufacturer of copper sulphate in 1911 and they were living at Greysfield, Great Barrow, Chester, Cheshire. They were living at Sishes End, Stevenage, Hertfordshire at the time of her death. He also died there, leaving effects valued at £93,869/15/2 (£2.5M in 2018). They had four children:

James' brother, Kenneth, is commemorated on the Ploegsteert Memorial.

    - Hilary Mary Dennis (born 1902) married George Andrew Crompton (1903–31st July 1966) at Chester in 1924. They had a son, John B Crompton, in 1926. The marriage ended in divorce. Hilary married Guy Lloyd Carter (1900–18th July 1944) in 1939 at Westminster. Guy, born at Carnarvon, Caernarvonshire, was commissioned as a second lieutenant in the RAF on 1st April 1918 and was captured by the Germans. He was specially mentioned in reports for valuable services whilst in captivity (LG 16th December 1919). He was granted a short service commission as a flying officer on 20th January 1920, later converted to a permanent commission with effect from the same day. He was promoted flight lieutenant on 1st July 1926 and was seconded to the Iraq Government 1st March 1931–1st March 1934 (Air Force Cross, LG 4th June 1934). Guy was promoted squadron leader 1st February 1936 (07009), wing commander 1st January 1939, temporary group captain 1st March 1941 and war substantive group captain on 2nd November 1943. He was Mentioned in Despatches (LG 1st January 1941) and was awarded the DSO while commanding the fighter force in the Western Desert (LG 19th February 1943). He was also awarded the US Legion of Merit. Guy was serving at HQ Balkan Air Force as an air commodore, when he was a passenger onboard a 267 Squadron Dakota 'KG 472' that stalled on overshoot near Bosnanski Dubica, Yugoslavia on 16th July 1944. Major Randolph Churchill was injured slightly and Guy seriously. Several attempts to fly him out were thwarted by bad weather until Dakota 'KG 466' flew him successfully to Foggia Main in Italy on 18th September, where he died later that day (Bari War Cemetery, Italy – VII C 9). Hilary served in the British Volunteer Ambulance Corps, Liverpool Road Hospital, Chester and was living at Brook House, Huxley, Cheshire at the time. Guy previously married Eileen Rosetta Galloway née Reed (born 1896) in 1924 at Kensington, London. They had two children – Rosemary Carter

1920 and Lavender Jane Lloyd Carter 1923 before the marriage ended in divorce. George Crompton married Violet Alison Crompton (sic) in 1961 at Penzance, Cornwall. They were living at Trehivin, Madron, Penzance at the time of his death at West Cornwall Hospital, Penzance.

- James Hawke Dennis (1904–4th May 1985) was commissioned in the Cheshire Yeomanry on 9th December 1922. He married Brenda Winifred Fox (1902–70) on 16th July 1925 at Eastham, Cheshire. She was the sister of Henry Fox, who married James' sister Marjorie. James was recalled from the Reserve on 24th August 1939, served in the Royal Signals and was promoted lieutenant colonel on 11th April 1945 (TD). They were living at Coles Hill House, Buntingford, Herefordshire in 1961. He was appointed Sheriff in the Queen's Bench Division of the High Court of Justice on 13th November 1962. Brenda was living at Flat 8, Carlton Lodge, 37/39 Lowndes Street, London at the time of her death. They had three children – Gerald JH Dennis 1926, Anthony FF Dennis 1929 and Caroline J Dennis 1933. James married Adria Margaret Acland (1904–2001) in 1971 at Westminster. She had married Arthur Francis Procter (1902–70) in 1935. Arthur and Adria had two children – Nigel H Procter 1937 and Susan Caroline Procter 1939. James was living at 37 Church Street, Henley-on-Thames at the time of his death.
- Marjorie Elspeth Dennis (1905–6th February 1986) married David E Williams in 1927 at Chester. She married Henry Arthur Fox (1903–63), her brother-in-law, in 1946 at Westminster. They were living at Inglewood, Ledsham, Cheshire at the time of his death, leaving effects valued at £337,548 (£6.8M in 2018). She was living at Chapel House, Puddington, South Wirral at the time of her death.
- Violet Alison Dennis (1914–2003) married Wilfred George Tear (1905–95) in 1937 at Biggleswade, Bedfordshire. He was born at Potton, Bedfordshire. They had four children – Jacqueline C Tear 1937, Robert M Tear 1938, Alan W Tear 1941 and Dennis G Tear 1948.

- Helen Forbes-Robertson (14th February 1876–22nd February 1960) married Henry Cotes Foster (6th October 1871–13th December 1953) on 19th June 1902 at Cheltenham, Gloucestershire. Henry was born at Ebley, Stroud, Gloucestershire. He was a rancher in Argentina in 1911 and their address in Britain was Elmhurst, Lypiatt Road, Cheltenham. Henry was commissioned in the Devonshire Volunteer Regiment, serving in 3rd Battalion until transferring to 4th Battalion on 1st April 1918. He resigned his commission on 6th January 1919 and was granted the honorary rank of lieutenant on 21st May 1919. He was living at Kilrenny, Bideford, Devon at the time of his death there. She was still living there at the time of her death at 39 Molyneux Park Road, Tunbridge Wells, Kent. They had five children:
  - Roderick Nelson Foster (22 July 1904–9th October 1964), born at Buenos Aires, Argentina, trained at the Royal Military Academy Woolwich and was

commissioned in the Royal Engineers on 26th August 1924 (30527). He was promoted lieutenant on 26th August 1926 and captain on 26th August 1935. Roderick served on the North West Frontier of India (Loe Agra and Mohmand) in 1935 (MID LG 7th February and 8th May 1936, MBE). Appointed adjutant 14th December 1936–31st January 1940. Appointed acting major 20th September 1940, temporary major 20th December 1940 and was promoted major 26th August 1941. Appointed acting lieutenant colonel 20th April 1942 and promoted lieutenant colonel 20th July 1942. Appointed Commander Army Group RE 3rd January–12th November 1945, war substantive lieutenant colonel 3rd July 1945, acting colonel 3rd January 1945, temporary colonel 3rd July 1945 and GSO1 13th November 1945–26th August 1947. Awarded the DSO (LG 21st June 1945) and OBE (LG 24th January 1946). Promoted lieutenant colonel 12th May 1949 and colonel 19th May 1949 (with seniority backdated to 3rd July 1948). Appointed Group Commander Western Command 19th May 1949–1 April 1951, Chief Engineer HQ London District 19th April 1951–22nd July 1953 and Chief Engineer HQ Northern Command 1st September 1953. Promoted brigadier 19th August 1953. Supernumerary 19th May 1955 and retired on 12th January 1957. He ceased to belong to the Reserve of Officers on 22nd July 1962. Roderick married Moira Alice Beatrix Orr (15th April 1908–13th April 1999) on 5th August 1936 in Fife, Scotland. They were living at Taira House, Gargrave, Skipton, Yorkshire at the time of his death at The Duke of Yorks Home, Bradford. She died at Princess Margaret's Hospital, Swindon, Wiltshire. They had two sons – Keith Nelson Foster 1938 and Alan Foster.

- Laura Innes Foster (1907–12th December 1982) married Denis Herbert Scott (1899–10th February 1958) in 1931 at Bideford, Devon. He was born at St Albans, Hertfordshire. Denis was promoted flying officer 1st September 1939, flight lieutenant 6th August 1940 and squadron leader Technical Branch (Signals) 18th February 1941. Appointed to the Directorate of Intelligence (Operations) at the Air Ministry as a wing commander on 19th September 1941. Temporary wing commander 1st January 1943 and last appears in the Air Force List in July 1945. He was appointed Deputy Chairman of the Public Works Loans Board and was awarded the CBE (LG 2nd January 1956). They were living at Farley Grange, Westerham, Kent at the time of his death, leaving effects valued at £96,224/17/11 (£2.2M in 2018). She died at Farmstone, Halwell, near Totnes, Devon. They had three daughters – Lorna L Scott 1934, Valerie Helen Scott 1936 and Carrol M Scott 1940.
- Keith Forbes Foster (10th May 1910–16th December 1936) trained at the Royal Military College Sandhurst and was commissioned in The King's Regiment on 28th August 1930. He transferred to the Seaforth Highlanders on 28th January 1931 and was promoted lieutenant on 28th August 1933. Keith died at Fort George, Inverness.

- Robert 'Bobby' Cotes Foster (30th January 1913–1980) married Iris Margaret Elmore (died 17 July 2005) in 1940 in Argentina and they had three children. He died there and she died at Woking, Surrey.
- Francis 'Pinto' Henry Foster (6th June 1916–23rd December 1974) served in the Royal Navy. He was promoted lieutenant on 1st June 1938 and served on HMS *Cornwall*, HMS *Cook* and at HMS *Mercury*. He was living at Penhein, Llanvair, Chepstow, Gwent at the time of his death at the Royal Naval Hospital, Stonehouse, Plymouth.

- Ann Forbes-Robertson (born 3rd July 1877) married Alexander Macdonald (1862–before September 1943) on 15th October 1907 at Holy Apostles Church, Charlton Kings, Cheltenham. He was born at Govan, Lanarkshire and married Ana Ruby Whitelegg (c.1883–October 1903) on 12th January 1902 at Tarapaca, Chile. She was born at Agna Santa, Chile. Ana died in Kensington, London. Alexander was an estancia administrator in Buenos Aires, Argentina, living at St Helen's Parish, North Kensington, London at the time of his marriage. Ann was living at 645 Avenidon de Mayo, Buenos Aires in September 1943, at Hurlingham, Buenos Aires in May 1944 and at Roslin, Midlothian by August 1944. They had four children:
  - Duncan Farquhar Macdonald (2nd November 1908–6th May 1944) was born at Buenos Aires, Argentina. He was commissioned as a pilot officer on probation in the RAFVR on 12th December 1942 (134739). He was promoted flying officer on probation (war substantive) on 12th June 1943. He was serving in 160 Squadron in the Far East when he was reported missing in action (Singapore Memorial – Column 432).
  - Margaret 'Peggy' Ann Macdonald (12th January 1913–1st May 1998), born at Buenos Aires, married Raymond Alexander Cameron (24th March 1905–31st August 1976), a farmer, c.1938, probably in Argentina. He was born at Tierra del Fuego, Chile. Raymond died at Buenos Aires. She died at Maori, Necochea, Argentina. They had two children.
  - Kenneth Forbes Macdonald (c.1914–11th September 1943) enlisted in the RAFVR (1377725) as a leading aircraftman. He was commissioned as a pilot officer on probation (100649) on 6th July 1941. He was promoted flying officer 6th July 1942, flight lieutenant 6th July 1943 and later squadron leader. He was serving with No.93 Squadron when he died on active service (Salerno War Cemetery, Italy – VI E 30).
  - Hugh Lamond Marshall Macdonald (c.1919–14th August 1944) served as a sergeant in the Royal Army Medical Corps (7359659) and died in service as a result of fractured ribs and laceration of the ears (Bari War Cemetery, Italy – VII D 1). His surname is recorded as McDonald by the CWGC.
- Innes Forbes-Robertson (8th June 1879–16th August 1958) married Charles Copley Singleton (1876–26th February 1962) in 1905 at Cheltenham. He was born at Hardingstone, Northamptonshire. Charles was a solicitor and they were living at Ley Hey Road, Marple, Stockport, Cheshire in 1911. They were living at 32 Pembroke Avenue, Worthing, Sussex at the time of her death there. He was still

living there at the time of his death at Seabrook Nursing Home, Shelley Road, Worthing. They had at least three children:

  - Eileen Margaret Singleton (1906–65) died unmarried at Bristol, Gloucestershire.
  - Marcella Singleton (16th January 1908–28th July 1993) died unmarried at Sussex Nursing Home, 12 Queen's Road, Worthing. Her birth was also registered in 1915.
  - Helen Singleton (born 1910).
- Mary Forbes-Robertson (13th November 1880–15th May 1957) never married and died at Clanmere Nursing Home, Malvern, Worcestershire.

James' paternal grandfather, William Forbes-Robertson (September 1791–21st March 1840) married Helen née Hadden (1796–post-1860) on 4th October 1824. She was born at St Nicholas, Aberdeen. He died at Hazelhead, Aberdeen, Aberdeenshire. In addition to Farquhar they had six other children:

- William Forbes-Robertson (born 7th January 1826) baptised on 4th March 1826 at Peterculter, Countesswells, Aberdeenshire.
- James Forbes-Robertson (20th July 1827–26th March 1897), born at Hazelhead, Aberdeenshire, served as a colonel in the Bombay Staff Corps. He married Fanny Cobb (1837–22nd February 1911) in 1862 at Romney Marsh, Kent. They were living at York Lodge, Cheltenham, Gloucestershire in 1881 and at Lewisland, Cheltenham in 1891. James changed his surname to plain Forbes before his death at Watertoune, Lee Park, Blackheath, London. Fanny also died there. They had six children – Gordon Forbes-Robertson 1863, Amy Violet Forbes-Robertson (died 1866), Charles Forbes-Robertson 1866, twins Mabel Forbes-Robertson and Lily Forbes-Robertson 1870 and Violet Forbes-Robertson 1876.
- Alexander Forbes-Robertson (born 4th June 1830).
- Thomas Forbes-Robertson (born 1st April 1832).
- Arthur Forbes-Robertson (born 20th May 1834) was commissioned in 67th Foot as an ensign on 20th October 1854 and was promoted lieutenant on 30th November 1855 and captain on 22nd July 1861. He served in the East Indies 16th October 1858–15th October 1859 and then in China.
- George Forbes-Robertson (born 10th September 1836).

James' grandmother, Anne Armitage, came from Rastrick, Yorkshire.

His maternal grandfather, Dr Charles Harold Macaulay (c.1809–11th February 1869), was born at Birkby, West Riding of Yorkshire and was a retired surgeon in 1861. He married Anne late Atherton, née Armitage (c.1812–2nd November 1883),

Cheltenham College was founded in 1841 to educate the sons of gentlemen, both boarding and dayboys, and was originally divided into Classical and Military sides. The first girls were admitted in 1969 but it was not until 1998 that the College became fully coeducational. The College lost 675 Old Cheltonians in the Great War and 363 in the Second World War. In recognition of its military contribution, Cheltenham is one of only three schools in England to have its own colours, the others being Eton College and the Duke of York's Royal Military School. James Forbes-Robertson is one of fourteen VCs and one GC awarded to Old Cheltonians. The College was the main location used in the 1968 film *If....* . Amongst its many famous alumni are:

- Arthur Nigel Davenport (1928–2013) stage, television and film actor.
- Lieutenant General Sir John Bagot Glubb KCB CMG DSO OBE MC KStJ KPM (1897–1986), Glubb Pasha, who led the Transjordan Arab Legion 1939–56.
- Major General Sir Colin McVean Gubbins KCMG DSO MC (1896–1976) set up the secret Auxiliary Units to operate behind German forces if Britain was invaded. He also played a major part in founding the Special Operations Executive.
- Michael John Lithgow OBE (1920–63), chief test pilot for Vickers Supermarine and holder of the World Absolute Air Speed Record in 1953.

The barracks at Wellington, Tamil Nadu, India, where 1st Border was based in 1908. Renamed Shrinagesh Barracks in 1947, it became the Madras Regimental Centre, the Indian Army's oldest regiment, formed in the 18th century. Wellington is also the home of the Defence Services Staff College.

Mudros harbour, on the island of Imbros, was the main support base for the Gallipoli campaign.

born at Rastrick, Yorkshire, at Halifax, Yorkshire in 1849. She had married Captain John Atherton (died 1845), 6th Regiment of Foot, in 1842 at Halifax. John and Anne had two children:

- John Armitage Atherton (1845–1906) married Emily Jessop Barber (1850–78) on 17th August 1871 at Southowram Church, Halifax.
- William Armitage Atherton (1846–74).

Charles and Anne had no other children other than Laura Ann Macaulay in 1850. They were living at Woodhouse, Rastrick, Yorkshire in 1861, where they both subsequently died.

James was educated at Cheltenham College, Gloucestershire 1897–1902, where he was a member of the Rifle Corps. He was commissioned in the Border Regiment on 2nd March 1904 and joined the 1st Battalion at Plymouth on 9th April. He was posted to Gibraltar on 30th August 1906 and was promoted lieutenant on 31st August. On 4th October 1908 he was posted to Wellington, India and to Burma in October 1910. On 30th October 1914 he was appointed temporary captain and was promoted captain on 3rd November. The Battalion left Burma, arrived in England on 9th January 1915 and sailed for Egypt on 17th March aboard SS *City of Edinburgh*. It landed at Alexandria on 30th March, embarked again on 10th April and arrived at Mudros on 12th April. The Battalion landed at Gallipoli on 25th April 1915, where James was the transport officer initially. He was appointed adjutant and second in command on 2nd May and received a gunshot wound on 8th May, which required him to be evacuated to Cairo, Egypt. James returned to the Battalion and assumed command of B Company on 12th June but was again appointed adjutant and second in command in August. On 28th November he became a staff officer at HQ 32nd Brigade. The appointment lasted officially until 7th May 1916, although he relinquished the post on 29th March. James was evacuated from Suvla to Imbros on 20th December 1915 and moved to Alexandria on 3rd February 1916. On 29th February he went to hospital sick. He was then posted to 3rd Border at Conway on 8th May and rejoined 1st Battalion in France on 12th June. The Battalion had moved there from Egypt in March.

James was appointed temporary major and second in command of 1st Newfoundland Regiment 15th June–10th December 1916. The Battalion took part in a disastrous attack at Beaumont Hamel on the Somme on 1st July 1916. Of the twenty-two officers and 758 other ranks who took part in the action, only 110 did not become casualties. James was left out of battle with ten percent of the Battalion's strength, otherwise he would almost certainly have been killed or seriously wounded. He was appointed temporary lieutenant colonel and CO 1st Newfoundland on 26th November and was appointed acting lieutenant colonel on 11th December. **Awarded the MC for gallantry while serving with 1st Newfoundland (LG 1st January 1917).** The Battalion took part in the First and Second Battles of the Scarpe. **Awarded the DSO for his actions at Monchy-le-Preux on**

The Newfoundland Regiment memorial at Monchy-le-Preux is one of six identical memorials erected by the Government of Newfoundland after the Great War. Five are in France and Belgium and the sixth is at Bowring Park, St John's, Newfoundland.

Nine of the ten men who halted the German counterattack at Monchy-le-Preux on 14th April 1918. Missing is Private VM Parsons, 1st Essex. Ranks below in brackets were granted after the action.
Front Row – Private Frederick Curran, signaller; Corporal John H Hillier, Orderly Room Corporal, who was knocked out during the rush forward and crawled in ninety minutes later; Private Japheth Hounsell, signaller.
Back Row – Corporal Albert S Rose, runner; Lance Corporal (Sergeant) Walter Pitcher, provost; Lieutenant Colonel James Forbes-Robertson, CO; Lieutenant Kevin J Keegan, Signalling Officer; Corporal (Sergeant) Charles Parsons, signaller; Sergeant J Ross Waterfield, Provost Sergeant (Kenneth Forbes-Robertson).

James Forbes-Robertson, on the left, chatting with Henry Murray at the huge Hyde Park investiture on 2nd June 1917, at which the former received the DSO and MC and the latter the VC and DSO & Bar.

14th April 1917 after the Battalion had attacked Infantry Hill, it was subjected to a strong German counterattack, which surrounded most of 1st Newfoundland and 1st Essex, and reached the edge of the village. He collected all the men he could find of his HQ staff and took up a position on the outskirts of the village, from where he brought the enemy advance to a halt by his fire, thus saving a very critical situation. He held the position for eleven hours before being relieved, LG 18th June

1917. James relinquished command of 1st Newfoundland on 5th May 1917 and reverted to acting major. He was presented with the DSO and MC by the King at Hyde Park, London on 2nd June 1917.

On 14th August 1917 he was appointed CO 16th Middlesex and on 29th August was appointed acting lieutenant colonel, while also being a substantive major in the Newfoundland Regiment and a substantive captain in the Border Regiment. He was appointed temporary lieutenant colonel on 27th October 1917. **Awarded a Bar to the DSO during the Battle of Cambrai at Masnieres on 30th November 1917, when he led the Battalion with great dash and determination in a successful attack. Later, in the defence of Masnieres, during continual enemy attacks, although wounded in the eye by shellfire and unable to see, he was led about by an orderly amongst his men in the front line encouraging and inspiring them with his magnificent example, LG 26th March and 24th August 1918.** He was presented with a silver (hallmarked Birmingham 1917) and enamel cigarette case by the officers and men of 16th Middlesex who served under him at Cambrai. The cigarette case was sold at auction by Britannia Military Antiques & Collectables in December 2010 for £695.

On 21st February 1918 James was appointed CO of 1st Border. **Awarded the VC for his actions near Vieux Berquin on 11th-12th April 1918, LG 22nd May 1918.** He was temporary Commander of 87th Brigade from 7th June 1918 and relinquished command of 1st Border on 18th June. He was appointed Commander of 155th Brigade on 19th June as temporary brigadier. The VC was presented by the King at HQ First Army, Ranchicourt, France on 8th August 1918. He relinquished command of 155th Brigade on 23rd September, the same day as his next superior officer, GOC 52nd Division, Major General J Hill. On 26th September he assumed command of 13th London and was appointed acting lieutenant colonel until 31st December 1918. On 23rd October he again assumed command of 1st Border and moved with the Battalion to Germany on 4th December. **He was mentioned in Field Marshal Sir Douglas Haig's Despatches dated 9th April 1917, 7th November 1917 and 7th April 1918 (LG respectively 22nd May 1917, 18th December 1917 and 24th May 1918.**

James assumed command of 1/5th Border on 1st January 1919 at Ivoir on the Meuse, Belgium and at Bonn, Germany from February onwards. He was recalled to Britain on 14th August and joined 2nd Border as second on command next day. He reverted to his substantive rank of captain on 31st December 1919. James served in Ireland 1919–20. He was promoted major on 16th October 1921 and brevet lieutenant colonel the following day. He assumed command of the Depot on 25th September 1922. On 20th December 1926 he was promoted lieutenant colonel and CO 2nd Gordon Highlanders until 1930.

On 6th August 1927 James Forbes-Robertson married Hilda Forster (4th February 1893–28th June 1976) at Christ Church, Sutton, Surrey. She was born at Bromley, Kent. Hilda was awarded the Royal Red Cross 2nd Class while

James and Hilda were married at Christ Church, Sutton in August 1927. In 1876 a temporary iron church was erected to cater for the growing population in the area. The permanent building was dedicated in May 1888 and became a parish in its own right. In 1902 a chapel was added, donated by the Forster family, Hilda's parents, after the loss of two of their children. Officially it is the *Chapel of the Holy Child*, usually referred to as the *Forster Chapel*. Various changes and additions have been made to the church over the years and in 2012 major repairs were undertaken with the assistance of an English Heritage Grant.

Hilda was born at Bromley, Kent. This is the Market Square and Town Hall.

James and Hilda leaving the church after the marriage ceremony.

Commandant and Matron of Stanwell House, Sutton, Surrey (LG 9th April 1919). She was living at 1318 Minster House, Buckingham Gate, London at the time of her death. They had three children:

- Ann Forbes-Robertson (born 15th January 1929) born at Epsom, Surrey, married Captain John Douglas Watson MBE BA AMBIM RE ptsc (born 1st May 1922) at Bourton-on-the-Water, Gloucestershire in 1951. John was granted an Emergency Commission on 12th October 1941 (210874) and was promoted war substantive lieutenant on 1st October 1942 and lieutenant on 1st November 1944. Appointed acting captain 3rd February 1945, temporary captain 3rd May 1945 and was promoted captain on 1st May 1949. Appointed temporary major 21st February 1955 and was promoted major 1st May 1956, lieutenant colonel 31st December 1966 and colonel 31st

December 1966. He retired on 28th May 1976. He was awarded the MBE (LG 13th December 1945). They had two children – Sally Watson 1952 and James D Watson 1955.

The Royal Red Cross was established by Queen Victoria on 27th April 1883. The first award was to Florence Nightingale. A second class, Associate, was added in 1917. It is awarded to nurses, military or civilian, who have shown exceptional devotion and competence in the performance of their duties over a continuous and long period, or for an exceptional act of bravery and devotion duty. It was awarded exclusively to women until 1976.

- Jean Forbes-Robertson (born 26th September 1930) married Peter Brian Godley (4th October 1933–14th April 2014) in 1960 at Westminster, London. He was born at Chesterfield, Derbyshire, son of Brigadier Brian Richard Godley (1899–1954) and Margaret Valiant Livingstone-Learmonth. Peter was educated at Cheltenham College and the Royal Naval College, Dartmouth, Devon. Appointed acting sub lieutenant 1st January 1954, later substantive on the same date and was promoted lieutenant on 1st July 1956. He served on HMS *Alcide* and HMS *Tiptoe*. Appointed First Lieutenant of HMS *Talent* 8th May 1961 and captain of HMS *Upton* on 11th November 1963. Promoted lieutenant commander 1st July 1964 and served at HMS *President* and on HMS *Minerva* from 6th February 1967. He was appointed Special Assistant to Chief of Allied Staff, Vice Admiral Peter William Beckwith Ashmore CB MVO DSC, at HQ Naval Command South on 4th November 1968. He last appears in the Navy List in Spring 1973. He was later managing director of Charterhouse Pensions Ltd 1978–83. They had three children – Sarah Jean Godley 1960, John Peter Godley 1962 and Joanna Godley 1968.
- Kenneth Hugh Forbes-Robertson (12th September 1933–10th May 2018) served in the Royal Navy. He was a cadet on 1st January 1952 and was appointed acting sub lieutenant on 1st January 1954 (later substantive on the same date). He was promoted lieutenant on 16th February 1956 and served on HMS *Trump*. Appointed First Lieutenant of HMS *Thermopylae* on 28th February 1959 and First Lieutenant of HMS *Sea Lion* on 25th July 1961. He was appointed to command HMS *Yarnton* on 7th October 1963. Promoted lieutenant commander on 16th February 1964 and served at HMS *Ganges*, RN Junior Training Establishment, Shotley Gate, Ipswich, Suffolk. He was appointed First Lieutenant of HMS *Aurora* on 22nd May 1967 and was promoted commander on 30th June 1972. Appointed to command HMS *Londonderry* on 16th October 1972. He served on the Defence Intelligence Staff and was appointed to command HMS *Kent* on 2nd June 1980. He attended the National Defence College, Latimer and retired in 1983. Kenneth married Elspeth JM Puttock (born 1936) in 1959 at Westminster. They

had three children – Fiona D Forbes-Robertson 1960. Kirsten Forbes-Robertson 1962 and Grania Helen Forbes-Robertson 1966.

Hugh Forster's grave in Noeux-les-Mines Communal Cemetery.

Hilda's father, Sir Ralph Collingwood Forster DL JP (18th January 1850–17th April 1930) was born at Chillingham, Northumberland. He was an import and export merchant, governing director of Bessler Waechter & Co, Chairman of the Merchants Marine Insurance Co and a director of the Bank of Tarapaca and Argentina Ltd. He was also a great philanthropist. In 1902 he donated land in Hill Road, Epsom, Surrey for a hospital and became chairman of its board of governors. The same year he was a major benefactor of Christ Church, paying for the Chapel of the Holy Child. A chancel screen and choir stalls were added in 1907 in memory of his wife and a church hall followed in 1920. After the Great War he donated £5,000 towards a memorial hospital but there were insufficient funds and part of the donation was used for a war memorial, which he unveiled in 1921. He also donated a pavilion to the Cheam Road cricket ground. Ralph married Catherine 'Kate' McKechnie (died 1877) in 1874 at Darlington, Co Durham. Ralph married Elizabeth née Burnip (1859–29th July 1906) on 15th April 1880 at Gateshead, Co Durham. She was born at Newcastle upon Tyne, Northumberland. They lived at The Grange, Sutton, Surrey from about 1886 and also had a residence at Salisbury House, Finsbury Circus, London. He was appointed High Sheriff of Surrey in 1906 and was created a baronet on 2nd February 1912. Ralph and Elizabeth both died at Epsom, Surrey. He left effects valued at £925,191/7/11 (£55.9M in 2018). In addition to Hilda they had five other children:

- Stanley Collingwood Forster (1881–93).
- Hugh Murray Forster (8th September 1883–26th September 1915) served in the Surrey Yeomanry 1907–10 and was commissioned on 1st February 1909. He tried to enlist in the cavalry in 'Kitchener's Army' on 24th August 1914 and was told he was ineligible. He applied for a commission on 27th September 1914 and served as a major in 8th King's Own Scottish Borderers. He died of wounds at 6th London Field Ambulance (Noeux-les-Mines Communal Cemetery, France – I K 5).
- Mary Forster (born 1886) was not with her parents in 1901.
- Eva Forster (born 18th March 1889) married Major Francis Rowley Hill (1872–12th December 1939), of Lindon Court, Epsom Downs, Surrey, on 23rd June 1917. He was born at Clifton, Gloucestershire, son of Colonel PE Hill CB. Francis was educated at Marlborough College and was apprenticed for four years to the Bank of Scotland at Kelso and Edinburgh. Francis served in the Public Schools

Battalion, Middlesex Regiment (1114), enlisting at 24 St James's Street, London on 4th September 1914, described as a director of public companies, 5′ 6″ tall, weighing 140 lbs, with dark complexion, brown eyes, dark brown hair and his religious denomination was Church of England. He had worked in India and Straits Settlement and had served previously in 1st Roxburgh & Selkirk Rifle Volunteers for two years, Queen's Rifle Volunteers for a year and the Bombay Light Horse for fourteen years. He was commissioned on 15th September 1914. He received a gunshot wound to the right arm and hand (no nerve or bone damage) at Beaumont Hamel, France on 1st July 1916, serving with 16th Middlesex. He was evacuated to Rouen, embarked on SS *Lanfranc* at Le Havre on 4th July and was on the held strength of 24th (Reserve) Battalion at Aldershot. A medical board at 3rd London General Hospital, Wandsworth on 7th July found him unfit for any service for five weeks and granted leave until 10th August. A medical board at Reading War Hospital on 12th August found him fit. He joined 20th Battalion on 9th March 1918. On 9th April a raid was to be mounted on the enemy lines by two platoons of B Company. They were lying in front of the enemy wire, when at 4.15 a.m. a massive German bombardment came down. The British guns abandoned the raid programme to switch onto the German lines. Some casualties were inflicted on the raiders and they were withdrawn. The battalion on the right was overwhelmed and Francis and some men at Battalion HQ formed a defensive flank. B and D Companies had also been overwhelmed. He pulled the flank back to the road leading to Battalion HQ at Wye Farm, Bois Grenier and poured fire into the advancing Germans. Eventually he had only a few men left and the enemy were 450m behind them. At 10.30 a.m. the CO could not be found and Francis assumed command. He contacted brigade HQ at 11.14 a.m. and asked for the British artillery to be lifted as it was falling on their positions. Shelling continued until 12.30 p.m., causing more casualties. The brigade commander ordered up reinforcements but by 1.15 p.m. all telephone lines had been cut and they were surrounded. Francis ordered all instruments and papers to be destroyed and prepared to fight their way out to the north. Before they could attempt to get away the Germans closed in and Francis decided to surrender, having sent off a final message by pigeon. He did not appear on a list of prisoners until 30th August. He was mentioned in Sir Douglas Haig's despatch of 8th November 1918 (LG 8th December 1918) and was awarded the DSO (LG 16th September 1918) and Bar (LG 3rd June 1918 [sic]). He was repatriated to Leith on 17th December 1918 and was demobilised on 19th March 1919 from the Officers' Dispersal Centre, London.

James' and Hilda's headstone in Cheltenham Borough Cemetery is largely unreadable (Memorials to Valour).

Detail of the base of the candlestick.

The commemorative candlestick in St Lawrence's Church, Bourton-on-the-Water.

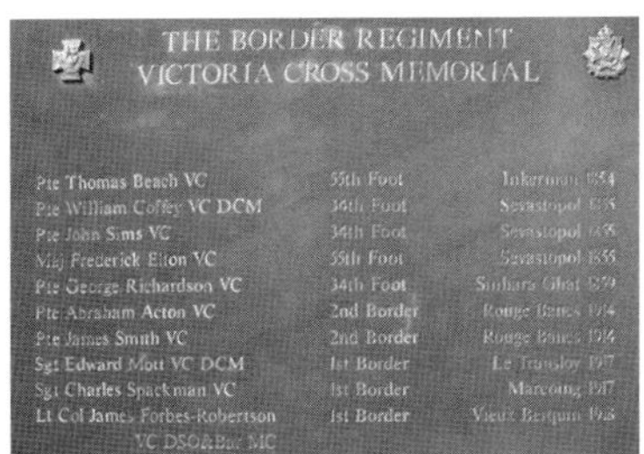

The Border Regiment Victoria Cross Memorial in Carlisle Cathedral.

He became a banker and spent fourteen years working in Scotland and India and four years as a rubber planter in Malaya. They were living at Holt Hatch, Alton, Hampshire at the time of his death.

- Ruth Forster (7th May 1891–17th January 1976) married Captain Andreas J Floor (c.1885–1950) on 27th May 1920 at Epsom, Surrey. She was living at Tamarisk House, Marine Drive, Goring-by-Sea, Sussex at the time of her death there. They had four children – Margaret E Floor 1921, Audrey R Floor 1923, Constance M Floor 1924 and Hannah R Floor 1929.

James was promoted colonel and placed on half pay on 20th December 1930 with seniority from 17th October 1925. He was appointed Commander of 152nd (Seaforth and Cameron) Infantry Brigade TA on full pay on 20th October 1932 and retired on 15th August 1934. He and Hilda lived on a rented estate in Ross & Cromarty, Scotland before moving to Chardwar, Bourton-on-the-Water, near Cheltenham, Gloucestershire after the Second World War.

James served in the Home Guard 15th July 1940–31st December 1944. He was briefly second in command of the local Home Guard under the Duke of Sutherland (also the Lord Lieutenant). He was granted the rank of lieutenant (colonel retired pay Reserve of Officers) on 1st February 1941 in 1st Sutherland Battalion Home Guard. On one occasion the Home Guard was called out to deal with reported enemy parachutists in a remote glen. Many of the soldiers were experienced stalkers and gillies and succeeded in shooting a number of suspects and capturing others before it was discovered that they were Norwegians training in the area. James was appointed Deputy Lieutenant for Sutherland on 3rd March 1942. He resigned on 7th July 1944, with all the other Deputy Lieutenants, in protest over the Lord Lieutenant's behaviour. The date coincides with James attaining the age limit of liability to recall and ceasing to belong to the Reserve of Officers. All the Deputy Lieutenants were reinstated by the King in 1946.

James attended the VC Garden Party at Buckingham Palace on 26th June 1920 and the VC Dinner at the Royal Gallery of the House of Lords, London on 9th November 1929. He died at his home at Chardwaw, Bourton-on-the-Water, Gloucestershire on 5th August 1955, leaving effects valued at £36,065/13/6. He is buried in Cheltenham Borough Cemetery, Bouncers Lane, Gloucestershire (Section E1, Grave 707). He is commemorated in a number of other places:

- Cheltenham College, Gloucestershire:
    - Classroom 9 of Anniversary Block was named in his honour in 1941.
    - Roll of Honour, Big Classical.
    - Memorial Book 'For Valour', Cheltenham College Library.
    - 'Honours Book', Archives Department.
- Border Regiment Victoria Cross Memorial, Carlisle Cathedral, Carlisle, Cumbria.
- Honours Board, Royal Military Academy, Sandhurst.
- A Department for Communities and Local Government commemorative paving stone was dedicated at Rydings Park, Halifax Road, Brighouse, West Yorkshire on 12th April 2018 to mark the centenary of his award.
- Candlestick at St Lawrence's Church, Bourton-on-the-Water, Gloucestershire.

In addition to the VC, DSO & Bar and MC he was awarded the 1914–15 Star, British War Medal 1914–20, Victory Medal 1914–19 with Mentioned-in-Despatches Oakleaf, Defence Medal 1939–45, George VI Coronation Medal 1937 and Elizabeth II Coronation Medal 1953. His medals were loaned to the Border Regiment Museum by the family in March 2006 on the proviso that the originals were displayed. This required significant alterations to be made to the security arrangements, which were in place by late September 2006. The VC is held by the Border Regiment Museum, Cumbria's Museum of Military Life, Alma Block, The Castle, Carlisle, Cumbria.

S/6522 SERGEANT WILLIAM GREGG
13th Battalion, The Rifle Brigade (The Prince Consort's Own)

William Gregg was born on 27th January 1890 at Mount Street, Heanor, Derbyshire. His father, also William Gregg (c.1863–29th February 1932) was a framework knitter living at 97 Yorke Street, Mansfield Woodhouse, Derbyshire. He married Harriet née Henshaw (c.1867–11th March 1956) on 25th December 1883 at St John's Church, Aldercar, Derbyshire. They were living at 32 Burnthouse Road,

Heanor in 1901 and at 9 Fair View, Heanor in 1911. William junior had twelve siblings but only ten survived infancy:

- Herbert Gregg (1884–16th January 1952), a coal miner hewer, married Mary Betsy Marriott (1887–12th March 1956) on 22nd September 1906 at St Lawrence, Heanor. They were living at 121 Derby Road, Heanor in 1911 and at 54 Thorpes Road, Heanor at the time of their deaths there. They had at least seven children:
    - William Gregg (18th December 1906–20th January 1971) is understood to have married Alice Hewitt (14th April 1906–November 2000) in 1935 at Basford. He was a celanese worker in 1952 and was living at 48 Ray Street, Heanor at the time of his death in Nottingham. They had a daughter, Beryl Gregg, in 1936.
    - Violet Gregg (11th April 1908–1984) married Thomas Weston (1901–10th September 1962) in 1934. They had three children – John B Weston 1939, Marion Weston 1940 and Barbara Weston 1942.
    - George Arthur Gregg (born 1909) married Minnie Hutchinson Straw (born 1916) in 1935. They had six children – Roy Gregg 1936, Joyce E Gregg 1937, Janet Gregg 1940, Ann Gregg 1945, Herbert Gregg 1946 and Paul Gregg 1956.
    - Evelyn Gregg (1912–24).
    - Thomas H Gregg (born 1916).
    - Clarice Gregg (born 1919) married Frank Jenkins in 1946. They had a son, Kevan M Jenkins, in 1946.
    - Iris Gregg (18th June 1927–November 1998) married Karl L Wambach in 1948. They had two children – Maria E Wambach 1956 and Helen T Wambach 1962.
- Thomas Gregg (1885–3rd February 1917), a coal miner loader, married Phoebe Ann Wilson (1887–1947) on 16th September 1905 at St Lawrence, Heanor. They were living at 51 Burnthouse Road, Heanor in 1911. Thomas enlisted at Ilkeston on 21st November 1914 and was described as 5′ 5½″ tall and weighing 142 lbs. He served as a stretcher-bearer in 1st King's Royal Rifle Corps (R17546). He was wounded on 15th/16th May 1915 and invalided for fourteen days as a result. He received a gunshot wound to the left hand on 27th July 1916 and was admitted to No.38 Casualty Clearing Station and transferred to 12th

St John's Church in Aldercar was built in 1871 as a Chapel of Ease and was extended in 1928–29.

General Hospital the following day. He was killed in action and is buried in Courcelette British Cemetery, France (I E 1). Phoebe was awarded a widows' pension of £1/2/1 on 20th August 1917. They had ten children, including two unknown who did not survive infancy:

- Joseph Edward Gregg (born and died 1906).
- Emily Gregg (14th February 1907–50) is believed to have married Frederick Cotton (1905–43) in 1933.
- Robert Gregg (29th December 1907–27th December 1914) died of post diphtheritic paralysis at 39 Nelson Street, Heanor.
- George Gregg (1909–10).
- Thomas Gregg (1909–11).
- Walter Gregg (10th December 1912–16th December 1914) died of membranus croup at 39 Nelson Street, Heanor.
- Harriet Gregg (7th November 1913–20th January 1915) died of acute gastritis and convulsions at 39 Nelson Street, Heanor.
- Rebecca Gregg (19th September 1914–August 1988) married Bernard Henshaw (28th July 1917–15th January 2008) in 1945 at Ilkeston. They had five children – Leonard Henshaw 1947, Joan Henshaw 1949, Geoffrey Henshaw c.1950, Ann Henshaw 1951 and Susan Henshaw 1956.

Phoebe married Arthur Parkins (6th June 1894–1968) in 1920 at Basford. They had a son, also Arthur Parkins, in 1923.

- Robert Gregg (1886–1939) was a coal miner hewer in 1911.
- Elizabeth Hannah Gregg (22nd June 1888–1976) married Joseph North (1883–1949), a coal miner hewer, on 26th March 1910 at St Lawrence, Heanor. He was born at Ruddington, Nottinghamshire. They were living at 44 High Street, Heanor in 1911 and at 139 Ray Street in 1939. They had six children:
    - James W North (1913–14).
    - Doris North (born 1915).
    - Wilfred North (1916–58) married Kitty Wright (21st July 1918–18th November 1997) in 1940. They had a daughter, Sandra North, in 1943. Kitty married Frank Ashton in 1959 at Ilkeston. She died in Derby.
    - William North (born 1918).
    - Annie M North (4th March 1920–1972) married Bernard Stone (12th September 1915–1973) in 1940. The marriage ended in divorce. Annie married Thomas Straw in 1944. Bernard married Audrey Morgan in 1945 and they had a son, Peter B Stone, in 1947.
    - Gladys North (27th October 1921–26th April 1989) was an ironer in a laundry works in 1939 and was living with her parents. She married Richard Charles Asher (17th November 1918–18th April 1985) in 1948. They had two children – Richard C Asher 1949 and Peter C Asher 1950. They were living at 132 Ray Street, Heanor at the time of their deaths there.
- Keziah Gregg (1892–1965) married John E Bullock in 1918.

- Elias Gregg (23rd September 1893–1969) was a coal miner in 1911. He married Eliza Banton (1892–1968), born at Hartshorne, Derbyshire, in 1913. They had six children:
  - Edna Gregg (born 1914).
  - Nora Gregg (28th June 1915–October 2001) married Ernest Davies in 1942. They had two children – Jean C Davies 1947 and Philip Davies 1952.
  - Jessie Gregg (born 1916).
  - Joyce Gregg (6th December 1919–22nd June 2008) married Douglas Meason (31st August 1914–March 1992) in 1939. He was born at Chesterfield, Derbyshire. They had a daughter, Merle Meason, in 1945. The marriage ended in divorce. Douglas married Pauline Taylor in 1973 at Southwell. Joyce married Leslie Crowe in 1974 at Basford.
  - Beryl (twin with Freda) (23rd April 1922–May 2000) married Albert Stanley Ball (23rd June 1921–22nd November 1983) in 1945. They were living at 197 Ladywood Road, Kirk Hallam, Ilkeston at the time of his death in Nottingham. They had three children – Stuart Ball 1947 and twins Brian and Ian Ball 1953.
  - Freda Gregg (twin with Beryl) (23rd April 1922–1923).
- Annie Gregg (1896–1968) married George A Farndon in 1920. They had four children:
  - Reginald Stanley Farndon (5th June 1921–19th March 1976) married Phyllis Thorpe (born 1924) in 1942 and they had three children – George J Farndon 1942, Patricia Farndon 1947 and Ann Farndon 1949.
  - Phyllis I Farndon (born 1923) married Harold Jackson in 1942. They had two children – Michael Jackson 1942 and Vanessa R Jackson 1953.
  - Betty Farndon (born 1929) married Ronald Aldred in 1953.
  - Christine M Farndon (born 1941) married Roy C Phillis (born 1941) in 1962. They had three children – Jane Phillis 1964, Kim Phillis 1967 and Mark Phillis 1975. Roy married Janet I Harris in 1980 at Grantham, Lincolnshire.
- Arthur Gregg (1899–1948) married Mary Ann Birkett (1900–58) in 1919 at Mansfield. They had a daughter, Jessie M Gregg, born and died in 1920. Arthur is understood to have served in the Royal Navy. That Arthur Gregg was born on 25th December 1898 at Derby and was a collier when he enlisted on 24th July 1917 (J74157), described as 5′ 4½″ tall, with light brown hair, hazel eyes and sallow complexion. He served on HMS *Victory I* 24th July 1917, *Brilliant* 27th November, *Ambitious* 26th January 1918, *Victory I* 24th April and *Malaga* 29th April until 1st March 1919.
- George Gregg (4th February 1900–1980) married Elizabeth Gill (21st April 1897–December 1991) in 1921 at Mansfield. They had four children:
  - Philip Gregg (21st November 1921–April 2006) married Jessie Mary Sheldon (28th February 1921–1983) in 1940 at Mansfield. They had four children – Brian Gregg 1942, Malcolm Gregg 1944, Barry Gregg 1950 and Stuart Gregg 1959.

William's paternal grandfather, Robert Gregg, was born at Gotham, Nottinghamshire about 1832. Its people feigned madness in the reign of King John to avoid a Royal highway being built through the village. The villagers would have been responsible for its maintenance. Madness was believed to be highly contagious and, when the King's men saw the villagers behaving insanely, they routed the highway to avoid it.

- Frank Gregg (1924–29).
- Lionel Gregg (15th January 1929–February 1993) married Iris Molly M Armstrong (2nd March 1933–November 1998) in 1957. They had five children – David Gregg 1958, Martin Gregg 1960, Paul Gregg 1961, Steven Gregg 1964 and Andrea Gregg 1967.
- William Gregg (born and died 1932).

- Sarah Betsy Gregg (3rd September 1905–11th August 1990) married Walter Carman (30th September 1902–September 1987) in 1924. They had three children:
  - Joan Carman (born 1925) married James P McMenemy (born 1927) in 1948. He was born at Prescot, Lancashire. They had a daughter, Margaret E McMenemy, in 1949.
  - Dorothy Carman (born 1928) married Robert Gregory in 1949. They had three children – Sharon Gregory 1950, Robert Gregory 1952 and Peter Gregory 1953.
  - Doreen Carman (1932–18th January 1991) never married and was living at 24 Ashforth Avenue, Marlpool, Heanor at the time of her death.

William's paternal grandfather, Robert Gregg (c.1832–79), born at Gotham, Nottinghamshire, was a framework knitter. He married Elizabeth née Perkins (c.1835–85), a seamstress, on 28th October 1855 at Gotham, where they were living in 1871. In 1881 Elizabeth was living at Nelson Street, Heanor. In addition to William they had four other children:

- Sarah Ann Gregg (1858–1932) married Thomas Brewin (1858–1936), a coal miner, in 1879. They were living at 17 Thorpes Road, Heanor in 1891 and 1901 and at 16 Booth Street, Mansfield Woodhouse, Nottinghamshire in 1911. They had four children:
  - Sarah Elizabeth Brewin (1881–1939) married Thomas Groves in 1900.
  - Robert Brewin (born 1884).
  - George Brewin (born 1887).
  - Harriet Brewin (born 1889).
- Mary Gregg (born 1867), a seamstress, married Charles Wright (1866–1938), born at Marlpool, near Heanor, on 23rd February 1889 at St Lawrence. In 1891 he was a coalminer loader and they were living at Burnthouse Road, Heanor. By 1901

they had moved to 85 Derby Road, Heanor. They had five children – Edward Arthur Wright 1889, John William Wright 1894, Clara Elizabeth Wright 1896, Laurence Wright 1899 and Nellie Wright 1902.

- Keziah Gregg (1870–1962), a seamstress, was boarding with her sister Sarah and family in 1891. She married Francis Albert Morton (1870–1939), a coal miner contractor, in 1892. They were living at 35 Elnor Street, Langley Mill, Nottinghamshire in 1911. They had four children including:
    - Harold Morton (born 1894).
    - Agnes Mabel Morton (born 1896).
    - Sabina Hilda Morton (born 1899) married James S Illingworth in 1924. They had two children – Leslie Illingworth 1926 and Frank Illingworth 1930.
- Rebecca Gregg (1873–1960), born at Gotham, was a seamstress, boarding with her sister Mary Wright and family in 1891. She married Joseph Bullock (born 1871), a lace hand, in 1896. They were living at 72 Bennett Street, Long Eaton, Derbyshire in 1911. They had three children:
    - Arnold Robert Bullock (1897–21st July 1918) was serving as a lance corporal (267630) with 6th Seaforth Highlanders when he was killed in action (Soissons Memorial, Aisne, France).
    - Joseph Bullock (born 1903).
    - Dorothy Bullock (born 1908).

His maternal grandfather, Thomas Henshaw (c.1833–1916), was a coal miner. He married Hannah 'Harriet' née Milner (c.1833–1915) in 1856. In 1881 they were living at Aldred's Lane, Heanor and they were still there in 1901 at No.26 and in 1911 at No.17. In addition to Harriet they had another five children:

- Edward Henshaw (1863–19th February 1943), a coal miner hewer, married Agnes Ellis (1867–12th September 1960) in 1885. They were living at 120 Westfield Lane, Mansfield in 1911. They were living at 86 Lynncroft (the author DH Lawrence once lived at No.97), Eastwood, Nottinghamshire at the time of his death. They had six children, three of whom did not survive infancy and are unknown – William Henshaw 1888, George Henshaw 1892 and Ethel Henshaw 1895.
- Emma Henshaw (1868–1929) married Francis Newton (1868–1941), a colliery deputy below ground, in 1888. They were living at 75 Cotmanhay Road, Ilkeston in 1911. They had six children – Mary Elizabeth Newton 1891, Alfred Newton 1894, Herbert Newton 1899, Beatrice Newton 1902, Doris Newton 1905 and John Newton 1908.
- Hannah Rebecca Henshaw (1870–1956) married William Eason (1869–3rd October 1936), a coal miner hewer, in 1890. He was born at Bingham, Nottinghamshire. They were living at 16 Sherwood Street, Mansfield in 1911 and at 4 Highfield Terrace, Mansfield at the time of his death there. They had five children:

  - William Henry Eason (27th December 1890–1978) married Edith NW Nicholson (25th March 1894–1979) in 1917.
  - Elizabeth Eason (17th March 1892–1975) married William Backen (9th June 1890–1971) in 1915. They had four children – John E Backen 1917, Joyce E Backen 1921, Gerald W Backen 1926 and Benjamin Backen 1934.
  - Elder Eason (born 1896) married Thomas Redmile in 1918 and they had a daughter, Irene E Redmile, in 1926.
  - Arthur Eason (born 1901).
  - Lilian Eason (born 1904) married Albert Dean in 1923 and they had two daughters – Lena E Dean 1924 and Jessie Dean 1926.
- Elizabeth Henshaw (born 1875).
- Arthur Henshaw (c.1878–1964), a coal miner contractor, married Ruth Hannah Brewin (1881–1960) in 1904. Her birth was registered as Brown. They were living at 20 Aldred's Lane, Heanor in 1911. They had three children:
  - Edith Henshaw (born 1905).
  - Lizzie Henshaw (born 1906).
  - Arthur Henshaw (10th February 1909–1970).

Mundy Street Boys' School opened on 2nd November 1891. In 1958 the school combined with Loscoe Road Girls' School to become Mundy Junior Mixed School.

William was educated at Mundy Street Boys' School, Heanor and then worked as a coal miner loader at Shipley Colliery. On 25th June 1910 he married Sarah Hardy (12th January 1892–25th June 1993), born at Fall Road, Heanor, at the Parish Church, Ilkeston. He was living at 9 Fair View, Heanor and she at 26 Park Street, Heanor at the time. They were living at 31 Park Street, Heanor in 1911 before moving to 6 Midland Road, Heanor. They had two children:

St Mary's, the parish church of Ilkeston, dates back to 1150. The spire on the tower was destroyed by lightning in 1714. The church was extensively restored between 1853 and 1855. The west end was enlarged in 1909–10 when the tower was rebuilt. The organ dates from 1831 and was originally used in St John the Evangelist, Paddington, London and is reputed to have been played by Mendelssohn.

- Nellie Gregg (19th September 1910–28th January 1978) married George Henry Mee (1905–15th November 1963) in 1934. They were living at 4 Midland Road, Heanor at the time of his death at the Memorial Hospital, Heanor. They had at least two children:

WAR SAVINGS ASSOCIATION

Affiliated to the

NATIONAL WAR SAVINGS COMMITTEE

Salisbury Square, Fleet Street, E.C.4.

Regd. No. of Association..................

Member's Number..................

Member's Name..................

Member's Address..................

Card Issued (Date).................. 191...

NOTE.—Any person finding this Card is requested to drop it into a Post Office Letter Box.

War Savings Certificates were introduced by the government in 1916 under the National Savings Committee. They were only available to individual buyers and holdings were limited to £500. Certificates were sold by war savings associations, post offices and banks. Each £1 certificate was sold for 15/6 and was guaranteed to be worth £1 after five years (29% interest). Not only was the return attractive but, being government sponsored, it was the most secure investment available and also made a contribution to the war effort. The government gained by attracting war finance and by the end of the Great War £207M of War Savings Certificates had been sold. After the war they were renamed National Savings Certificates and were used to fund house building, reconstruction and development projects. The National Savings Movement continued throughout the Second World War and grew to about seven million members. In 1976 the government announced that the 580 civil servants who supported the movement would be withdrawn over two years as part of public spending cuts. Without this support the movement was unable to function and the National Committee last met in February 1978. The swastika was abandoned when it was adopted by the German Nazi Party.

  - Roy Mee (born 1937) married Jennifer A Edwards (born 1939) in 1961. They had three children – David R Mee 1962, Susan Helen Mee 1966 and Richard Ian Mee 1973.
  - Brian Mee (born 1942).
- Kenneth William Gregg (14th March 1924–6th June 1982) married Barbara Shepherd (5th January 1931–31st March 1989) in 1952 and they lived at 3 Garnett Avenue, Heanor. They had a daughter, Lynne Gregg, in 1952. When he died his address was recorded as Town Hall, Market Place, Heanor.

William Gregg, on the right, and William Beesley look pleased with their VCs just after the investiture on 9th August 1918.

Sarah's father, William Hardy (born c.1862), an engineer in a coal pit, married Ruth née Aram (born c.1864) in 1883. In 1901 they were living at Fall Road, Heanor. He was a stationary engine driver by 1911 and they were living at 26 Park Street, Heanor. In addition to Sarah they had nine other children including:

- Henry Hardy (1883–3rd September 1916) was a coal miner hewer in 1901.
- Samuel Hardy (born 1887) was a coal miner hewer in 1901.
- Nelly Hardy (born 1889).
- Ruth Hardy (born 1894) was a winder in 1911.
- Ethel Hardy (born 1897) was a turner in 1911.
- Annie Hardy (born 1899).
- Eliza Hardy (born 1902).
- William Hardy (born 1907).

William enlisted in the Rifle Brigade on 24th November 1914 and went to France on 18th May 1915. He was wounded during the Somme offensive in 1916. Appointed acting corporal 7th January 1917. **Awarded the MM for his actions in the Hulluch Sector on 4th February 1917, when he volunteered to crawl across exposed ground between the opposing lines in daylight to establish the identity of a dead German soldier lying in a crater. He was under the view of an enemy sentry but returned with the soldier's shoulder straps, identity disc, pay book and personal letters, LG 26th March 1917.** Promoted corporal on 2nd March and appointed acting sergeant on 5th June. **Awarded the DCM for his actions south of the Menin Road on 30th November 1917 on a reconnaissance patrol. The enemy attacked and it was imperative that the battalion on the left should be informed so he volunteered to carry several messages across a road swept by machine gun fire. This enabled the other unit to cooperate in the defence. He also assisted in a successful counterattack, which killed many enemy and drove them off, 6th February 1918.** Promoted sergeant 12th December.

Awarded the VC for his actions at Bucquoy on 8th May 1918, LG 28th June 1918. He was the first of only eight men in the war to be awarded the VC, DCM and MM. The VC was presented by the King at HQ Third Army at the chateau at Frohen-le-Grand, France on 9th August 1918. He was presented with an illuminated address and £200 in War Savings Certificates by his home town in August 1918. A keen sportsman, with a passion for football, he was also very athletic and won a cross-country race organised by his CO in which 400 runners took part. His prize was a barrel of beer for A Company. William was later appointed company sergeant major and was discharged in March 1919.

There were about thirty pits at Shipley and the site produced coal for a total of 250 years. The mines there became uneconomical in the 1960s and were closed. The area in now a country park.

He returned to Shipley Colliery and worked there until forced to retire on 17th June 1949 due to osteoarthritis in the left knee and hip. He played for Heanor

Athletic FC as a fullback and helped to train the youth team. He served in the Sherwood Foresters, National Defence Company, during the Second World War as a warrant officer class II but was discharged in 1941. He reportedly then worked on a ferry that was involved in the Dieppe Raid in August 1942. William attended a number of VC Reunions – the VC Garden Party at Buckingham Palace on 26th June 1920, the VC Dinner at the Royal Gallery of the House of Lords, London on 9th November 1929, the Victory Day Celebration Dinner & Reception at The Dorchester, London on 8th June 1946, the VC Centenary Celebrations at Hyde Park, London on 26th June 1956 and the 1st VC Association Reunion at the Café Royal, London on 24th July 1958.

The War Medal 1939–1945 was instituted on 16th August 1945 to be awarded to those who served full-time in the armed forces or Merchant Navy for at least twenty-eight days between 3rd September 1939 and 2nd September 1945.

William Gregg died at Heanor Memorial Hospital, Derbyshire on 9th August 1969. The cause of death was cerebral thrombosis. He was cremated at Heanor Crematorium and his ashes were scattered in the Garden of Remembrance, where there is a memorial. He is commemorated in a number of other places:

- William Gregg VC Leisure Centre (formerly William Gregg VC Baths), Heanor, where there is a memorial plaque.
- Gregg Avenue, Heanor.
- The Gregg Cup, established before the Second World War, is competed for by school soccer teams in Derbyshire.
- Named on the Rifle Brigade Memorial at Winchester Cathedral, Winchester, Hampshire.
- A Department for Communities and Local Government commemorative paving stone was dedicated at Heanor Memorial Park on Ilkeston Road on 13th May 2018 to mark the centenary of his award.

On her 100th birthday in January 1992 his widow was visited by members of the Royal Green Jackets, who brought along her late husband's medals. Sarah had moved into Kidsley Grange Nursing Home, Heanor in 1991 and subsequently died there.

In addition to the VC, DCM and MM he was awarded the 1914–15 Star, British War Medal 1914–20, Victory Medal 1914–19, 1939–45 Star, War Medal 1939–45, George VI Coronation Medal 1937 and Elizabeth II Coronation Medal 1953. He kept his medals in a tin under his sideboard and questioned visitors wishing to see them, asking why they wanted to see 'those things'. The VC is held by the Royal Green Jackets (Rifles) Museum, Peninsula Barracks, Romsey Road, Winchester, Hampshire.

BRIGADIER-GENERAL GEORGE WILLIAM ST GEORGE GROGAN
The Worcestershire Regiment, commanding 23rd Infantry Brigade

George Grogan was born on 1st September 1875 at the Admiral Superintendent's House, Devonport, Devon, England. His father, Brigadier General Edward George Grogan CB CBE (21st June 1852–24th April 1944) was born in Dublin, Ireland. He was educated at Cheltenham College and was commissioned in 42nd Regiment (Black Watch) by purchase on 24th July 1869. He was promoted lieutenant on 28th October 1871 and served in the Gold Coast from 3rd December 1873 until 23rd March 1874 during the Third Anglo-Ashanti War, during which he was present at the Battle of Amoaful on 31st January, the capture and destruction of Becquah on 1st February and the capture of Coomassie on 4th February. At the latter he was slightly wounded by a gunshot to the neck. Edward married Margaret 'Meta' Anne Forman née King-Hall (1852–24th November 1881), born in Lancashire, on 19th October 1874 at Devonport. The Battalion moved to Malta on 14th November 1874. In 1881 they were living at Huntingtower Cottage, Tibbermore, Perth, Scotland, where she died later that year. Edward was promoted captain 19th June 1879, major 4th December 1885 and lieutenant colonel 24th May 1898. He married Ida Georgina Mary née Forman (11th November 1857–15th November 1943), born at Halifax, Nova Scotia, on 4th June 1883 at St Mary's Cathedral, Edinburgh, Midlothian. She was living with her children at 6 Bayshill Terrace, Cheltenham, Gloucestershire in 1901 and their address in July 1909 was 1 Gillespie Terrace, St Andrew's, Scotland. They were living at Torrevagh, St Andrews, Fife at the time of her death there. Edward commanded the 1st Battalion in South Africa during the Second Boer War for which he was mentioned in Lord Kitchener's final Despatch on 23rd June 1902. He was promoted brevet colonel on 24th May 1902, colonel on 3rd November 1902 and was awarded the CB (LG 31st October 1902). He commanded the 42nd Regiment District 1902–05 and was Colonel-in-Charge of the Highland Regiment District Records 1905–06. He was on half pay from 3rd November 1906 and retired pay from 22nd June 1907. In July 1909 they were living at 1 Gillespie Terrace, St Andrews. Edward was recalled and commanded 26th Brigade, 9th (Scottish)

Division from 16th November 1914 until 30th May 1915. Appointed temporary brigadier general on 19th July 1915 and retired as honorary brigadier general on 12th April 1917. He was awarded the CBE (LG 1st January 1919). Edward became a JP and was in charge of developing the dockyard at Devonport, Devon post-war. George had six siblings from his father's two marriages:

St Mary's Cathedral or the Cathedral Church of Saint Mary the Virgin of the Scottish Episcopal Church. It was built in the late 19th century in the Gothic style. It was designed by Sir George Gilbert Scott and the foundation stone was laid on 21st May 1874. The nave was opened on 25th January 1879 and the twin spires were begun in 1913 and completed in 1917. There is a memorial to Captain James Dundas VC (1842–79). Sir Walter Scott's pew was moved to the Cathedral in 2006, having been in St George's Church, York Place until 1932 and then in St Paul's Church across the road when the two congregations amalgamated.

- Edward Harry John Grogan (14th November 1876–14th July 1963) was born at Valetta, Malta and was known as Harry. He joined the Royal Navy, was appointed midshipman on 15th May 1893 and was commissioned as acting sub-lieutenant on 15th November 1896, later confirmed with the same date. During this part of his career he was appointed to a number of ships – HMS *Britannia* January 1891, HMS *Raleigh* January 1893, HMS *St George* December 1894, HMS *Penelope* May 1896, HMS *Swallow* May 1896, HMS *Vivid* July 1896, HMS *Wanderer* August 1896, HMS *Royal Sovereign* October 1896, HMS *Victory* for HMS *Hornet* January 1897, HMS *Lightning* January 1898, HMS *Volage* April 1898 and HMS *Victoria & Albert* July 1898. He was in action against Fodi Dilah in the Gambia in February 1894 and was slightly wounded in the attack on Mbarak stronghold in August 1895. On 30th April 1896 he was appointed ADC to C-in-C Cape. Promoted lieutenant 31st August 1898. He was serving in Malta when he met Beatrice 'Bee' Eleanor Farquharson (15th November 1869–22nd February 1912) in 1900 and they became engaged. Bee was born at Edinburgh, Midlothian, daughter of Frances Edward Henry Farquharson VC and Harriet Charlotte Henrietta Lowe. Harry's uncle, Captain George King Hall RN, gained the impression that Harry had drifted into the relationship and was not happy that he had done the right thing. He wrote to Sir John Fisher, C-in-C Mediterranean, requesting that Harry be posted out of Malta. This was approved but, before he could be moved, Harry married Bee by special licence on 28th March 1900. He served on HMS *Isis* September 1898, HMS *Caesar* December 1899, HMS *Tyne* March 1900 and HMS *Isis* again in May 1900. He was invalided home on HMS *Swallow* in April 1901 and retired unfit for service on 18th March 1902. He then joined the Egyptian

Government Survey Office, later the Coastguard Service and in May 1901 the Ports and Lighthouses Administration in Alexandria. In April 1911 he became its Chief Inspector. Bee died at Port House Arsenal, Alexandria, Egypt. He was employed on transport duties at Alexandria as a lieutenant commander (seniority from August 1906) from September 1914, as staff officer to the Principal Naval Transport Officer Egypt to assist with commercial shipping from 12th December 1917 and as unpaid Transport Officer 1st Grade from 7th February 1918. His appointments were paid for by the Egyptian Government. Edward was awarded the Egyptian Order of the Nile 4th Class (LG 29th December 1916) and OBE (LG 7th January 1918) for services as Chief Inspector of Ports and Lighthouses Administration in Egypt. He reverted to the Retired List on 8th August 1919 and was promoted commander (retired) in recognition of his war service with effect from 11th November 1918. Edward married Elizabeth Beckett Clayhills (4th February 1874–11th September 1958), born at Darlington, Co Durham, on 4th February 1920 at Dundee Cathedral, Angus and they had a child. He was living at Birnie, Alyth, Perthshire at the time of his death on Gibraltar.

- Meta Aileen Odette Grogan (12th December 1880–23rd September 1952) was born at Craig, Forfarshire, Scotland. She married Sir John Andrew Ogilvy-Wedderburn (16th September 1866–10th March 1956) on 4th October 1909. He was born at Oathlaw, Forfarshire and was educated at Bath College. He served in the Scottish Horse Yeomanry from 30th March 1903. He was serving with 3rd Line Scottish Horse Depot, Dunkeld when he lost the little finger on his left hand while exercising a charger. A medical board at Perth Military Hospital on 13th July 1915 found him fit for service. He was serving with 2/1st North Midland Heavy Brigade RGA in November 1917 when he developed emphysema bronchitis and was treated at No.20 Casualty Clearing Station and 20th General Hospital. He returned to Britain on 12th December from Calais to Dover. A medical board at the Scottish General Hospital, Aberdeen on 20th December granted him leave until 11th January 1918. On 11th February he informed his CO (3rd Cameron Highlanders) at Birr, Ireland, that he had changed his surname from Wedderburn Ogilvy to Ogilvy-Wedderburn. On 22nd February he was restored to the establishment of the Scottish Horse Yeomanry. On 3rd October he transferred to the TF Reserve as a major, on account of his age and medical category, having been promoted the previous day. He had also served previously in 2/1st Lovat Scouts. He retired with his rank, having reached the age limit, on 13th October 1921. They were living at Silvie, Alyth, Perthshire at the time of Meta's death at Meigle Cottage Hospital, Blairgowrie, Perthshire. He died at Silvie. They had four children:
    - Janet Meta Ogilvy-Wedderburn (1912–July 1995) was born at Ruthven, Scotland. She served as a junior commander in the Auxiliary Territorial Service during the Second World War. She married Francis William Alfred Fairfax-Cholmeley CBE (1904–7th April 1983) on 9th July 1940 at Chelsea,

London. They had three children – Caroline Ann Fairfax-Cholmeley 1941, Hugh Thomas Andrew Fairfax-Cholmeley 1946 and Mary Meta Fairfax-Cholmeley 1948.

- Elspeth Mary Ogilvy-Wedderburn (1913–21st August 2004) died unmarried at Rowan House, by Kirriemuir, Angus.
- Katherine Andrea Ogilvy-Wedderburn (1915–15th May 2007), born at St Andrews, Fife, Scotland, was a JP. She married George Macfarlan Sisson OBE (23rd February 1914–22nd October 2005) on 1st June 1940 at St Ninian's Episcopal Church, Alyth. He was born at Hexham, Northumberland and died at Wall, Northumberland. She died at Blackford, Somerset. They

Pall Mall Magazine was published monthly between 1893 and 1914. It included poetry, short stories, serialised fiction, general commentaries and extensive artwork. It was the first British magazine to publish numerous illustrations and the finish was comparable to American periodicals of the same class. Contributors included HG Wells, Rudyard Kipling, Jack London and Joseph Conrad. In 1914 it merged with *Nash's Magazine* as *Nash's Pall Mall* Magazine. From May 1927 the two magazines were published separately but merged again late in 1929. The final issue was in September 1937.

Gerald Forman Grogan's grave in Bard Cottage Cemetery, Boesinghe.

had four children – John Edward Sisson 1943, David George Sisson 1945, Alexander William Sisson 1949 and Julia Andrea Sisson 1952.

- ◦ John (later Sir John) Peter Ogilvy-Wedderburn (29th September 1917–13th August 1977) was educated at the Nautical College, Pangbourne, Berkshire. He was appointed midshipman in the Royal Navy on 1st September 1937 and acting and later substantive sub lieutenant on 1st September 1938. He served on HMS *York* August 1939 and was promoted lieutenant on 16th May 1940. He served on HMS *Urania* and on HMS *Queen Elizabeth* from 1st November 1945. Promoted lieutenant commander on 16th May 1948 and appointed to HMS *Victory* while an instructor at the School of Physical and Recreational Training on 9th July 1946. Joined HMS *St Angelo* in Malta in February 1953. Promoted commander 30th June 1955. He later served with Boom Defence Depot Clyde and at Woolwich and last appears in the Navy List in 1961. He married Elizabeth Catherine Cox (2nd December 1912–8th November 2003) on 16th March 1946. She died at Wester Strathgarry, Killiecrankie, Perthshire. They had four children – Henrietta Katharine Ogilvy-Wedderburn 1947, Jean Aileen Ogilvy-Wedderburn 1948, Elizabeth Helen Ogilvy-Wedderburn 1950 and Andrew John Alexander Ogilvy-Wedderburn 1952.

- Gerald Forman Grogan (15th or 18th May 1884–8th January 1918) born at Tibbermore, Perth. He was educated at Cheltenham and Edinburgh University, where he studied the sciences, intending to become a doctor. While there he served in No.4 (University) Company, Queen's Rifle Volunteer Battalion, Royal Scots. When he progressed to pathology his interest ceased and he went to Camborne Mining College to study mining engineering. He worked for a time in Arizona, USA and then Mexico until the Revolution in 1910, when conditions became too difficult for his work. He returned to England, had some poems published and got a job on the *Throne* and *Pall Mall Magazine*. He was also a novelist, publishing *A Drop in Infinity* 1915, *William Pollok and Other Tales* 1919 and *Poems* 1925, the latter illustrated by H Dorothy Foreman. Gerald served in the Honourable Artillery Company (358 later 1395) from 18th May 1914 as a driver and, from 9th August, as a private. He was mobilised on 5th August and went to France via Southampton on 17th September, spending the winter in the trenches with No.2 Company. On 3rd February 1915 he returned to Britain. He was commissioned in the Leicestershire Regiment on 10th February and subsequently returned to France. Gerald

George's brother, James Colin Grogan, was killed in action at Gallipoli.

left his unit on 1st December 1916 suffering from fever and on 7th December was evacuated from Le Havre to Southampton. A medical board at Yorkhill War Hospital, Glasgow on 21st December 1916 found him unfit for service for one month due to debility and he was sent on leave until 21st January 1917. A medical board at Dundee on 24th January found him fit for service. Gerald transferred to the Royal Engineers and was serving with 183rd Tunnelling Company when he was killed (Bard Cottage Cemetery, Boesinghe, Belgium – V C 44).

- Mary Ethel Esme Grogan (4th March 1887–1970), born in Malta, married Edmund George Hill Forman (1st July 1888–1954), born at Mankato, Minnesota, USA, in 1915 at St Andrews and St Leonards. They had a son, George E Forman (1916–24), born at Dover, Kent and died at St Andrews and St Leonards.
- James Colin Grogan (16 September 1889–4th June 1915) was born at Craig Park, Ratho, Scotland. He was educated at Cheltenham College from May 1903 and applied for the entrance examination for Sandhurst from there on 5th March 1908. He served as a lieutenant in 1st King's Own Scottish Borderers, embarked at Avonmouth on 18th March 1915 and landed at Cape Helles, Gallipoli on 25th April. He and 6654 CSM John Pearce were killed on 4th June by a hand grenade. In 1919 it was reported that James was buried in Church Farm Cemetery, Cape Helles but is now buried in Twelve Tree Copse Cemetery, near Krithia (II D 1). He was initially reported missing but the American Embassy in Constantinople ascertained from the Ottoman authorities in August 1915 that he had not been taken prisoner. He left effects valued at £201/5/6. Pearce's body was never recovered and he is commemorated on the Helles Memorial.
- Andrew Wauchope Grogan (6th May 1891–20th June 1978), born at Gibraltar, became a chartered accountant. He was commissioned in the Scottish Horse Yeomanry on 9th August 1909. 1/1st and 1/2nd Scottish Horse served in Gallipoli, Egypt, Salonika and France. On 1st October 1916 the two units formed 13th (Scottish Horse Yeomanry) Battalion, Black Watch. Andrew was promoted captain on 17th June 1915 and left 13th Black Watch on 17th September 1918. A medical board in France on 17th October found that he was suffering from debility resulting from recurring attacks of malaria contracted in Salonika. He was sent on three weeks leave in Britain until 11th November, embarking at Calais on 21st October. He suffered a severe attack of influenza and the leave was extended. Medical boards on 27th November and 27th December found he was still suffering from debility. The second board sent him to 3rd Black Watch at the Curragh, Ireland to recover from anaemia, as he was unfit for service for two months. Andrew was demobilised on 28th January 1919. On 3rd November 1920 he applied for transfer to the TF Reserve because he worked in Liverpool and could not reach his unit. Promoted captain on 24th January 1921. Andrew married Hilda Margaret Agmondisham Kirkland (14th June 1891–10th December 1968) in 1918 at Amersham, Buckinghamshire. She was born in Saskatchewan,

Canada. He was working with Baker & Nairns, Solicitors, 3 Laurence Pountney Hill, London in January 1946. They were living at 10A Crest Hill, Buckfastleigh, Devon at the time of their deaths.

His paternal grandfather, George Grogan (1816–20th November 1851), born at Seafield, Sutton, Dublin, Ireland, was the son of Colonel George Grogan and Elizabeth Phipps and the brother of Colonel Charles Edward Grogan. George was commissioned cornet by purchase in 6th Regiment of Dragoon Guards (Carabiniers) on 16th January 1835. Promoted lieutenant by purchase on 5th October 1838 and transferred to the 7th Regiment of Foot as a lieutenant vice Lieutenant Robert Francis Lord Gifford (father of Edric Frederick Gifford VC) on 1st February 1839. He married Mary Ann née MacKenzie (c.1826–11th August 1902), who was known as Marianne. In addition to Edward they are understood to have had two other children:

- Meta Aileen Odetta Grogan. No other details could be found about this girl, who has exactly the same name as the VC's eldest sister.
- Mary Elizabeth Esmé Grogan (c.1850–13th January 1925) married Andrew Scott Stevenson (29th May 1847–12th October 1892) on 19th October 1871 at St George's, Hanover Square, London. He was born at Carluke, Lanarkshire and was commissioned as an ensign by purchase in 42nd Royal Highlanders (Black Watch) on 17th March 1869. Promoted lieutenant on 28th October 1871 and appointed adjutant on 10th December 1873. He served in the Ashanti War on the Gold Coast 3rd December 1873–23rd March 1874 and was present at the Battle of Amoaful on 31st January, the capture and destruction of Becquah on 1st February and the capture of Coomassie on 4th February. At the former he was slightly wounded by a gunshot laceration to the neck and was MID. Andrew moved with the Battalion to Malta on 14th November 1874 and was Commander of Kyrenia 1878–83. He was appointed supernumerary captain on 19th June 1879 and was promoted captain on 14th March 1884. He served in the Egyptian Expedition 1884, at the Battle of Tamai and in the Nile Expedition 1884–85 (MID). He was promoted major on 1st July 1885 and brevet lieutenant colonel on 2nd July 1885 for services during operations in the Soudan. He was appointed Adjutant 9th Lanarkshire

Admiral Sir William King Hall.

Rifle Volunteers 4th December 1885–1890. Mary was the author of *Our Home in Cyprus* 1880, *Our Ride through Asia Minor* 1881 and *On Summer Seas* 1883. She was living at Esme, Mount Prospect, Newcastle, Natal, South Africa at the time of her death there. They had three children – Esmé Andrea Margaret Sybil Scott Stevenson (1872–1939), Andrew George Hamilton Scott Stevenson (1875–77) and Douglas Lorne Arthur Dormer Scott Stevenson (1888–93).

Mary Ann Grogan married Colonel Arthur St George Herbert Stepney CB (c.1816–23rd January 1867), 2nd Coldstream Guards on 15th May 1862 in Paris, France. He was commissioned as an ensign by purchase in the Coldstream Guards on 16th May 1834. Promoted lieutenant by purchase 10th November 1837 and captain by purchase 15th April 1842. He served with 29th Regiment in the Sutlej Campaign 1845–46 and assumed command during the night of 21st December 1845 during the Battle of Ferozeshuhur and was wounded. On 10th February 1846 he was severely wounded by grapeshot at the conclusion of the Battle of Sobraon. Appointed brevet major 3rd April 1846, promoted major by purchase 9th July 1850 and appointed brevet lieutenant colonel 20th June 1854. He served during the Siege of Sebastopol in the Crimea from January 1855 (CB 4th February 1856 and was also awarded the Order of the Medjidie 5th Class). Promoted colonel 26th October 1858 and was commanding 2nd Battalion, Coldstream Guards at the time of his marriage.

His maternal grandfather was Admiral Sir William King Hall KCB (11th March 1816–29th July 1886). King was included in his name from his godfather, Captain King, who had been his father's captain aboard HMS *Jason*. William King Hall's father, James Hall, was a Royal Navy surgeon who was at the bombardment of Algiers, saw Napoleon on St Helena and made three passages to Australia on convict ships. William joined the Royal Navy in 1829 as a volunteer 2nd class. He served on HMS *Rapid* 1829–34, then HMS *Barham* May 1833 and HMS *Childers* May 1834 as a master's assistant on the Mediterranean Station and in Britain. He transferred from the Master's to the Commissioned Branch and was appointed midshipman in November 1834. He then served on HMS *Talavera*, HMS *Viper* 1835–37 and HMS *Salamander* 1837–39 on the Lisbon Station, north coast of Spain and in England. He was on HMS *Benbow* 1839–41, on the Mediterranean and Lisbon Stations, and took part in operations off the coast of Syria in 1840 against the Egyptian ruler, Mehemmet Ali, and was in the landing at Tortosa. He served on HMS *Indus* 1841–44, on the Mediterranean and Lisbon Stations, and from 1845 to 1847 he was on HMS *Vindictive*, on the West Indies and North American Stations, flagship of Sir Francis Austen, brother of the authoress, Jane Austen. William served on HMS *Growler* 1847–48, during a Colonial Office trial to transport volunteer labour from West Africa to the West Indies. Yellow fever broke out, thirty emigrants and the captain died and William took command and had to restore morale amongst the crew. William married Louisa née Forman (c.1825–75) on 20th June 1848 at Halifax, Nova Scotia, where she was born. They became engaged while William was serving at Halifax on HMS *Royal Adelaide*. In addition to Meta they had nine other children:

- William Hall (1849–58) born at Weymouth, Dorset, died of brain fever there.
- George Fowler Hall (14th August 1850–10th September 1939), born at Weymouth, joined the Royal Navy as a cadet on 9th January 1864 on HMS *Britannia*. He was posted to HMS *Victory* for HMS *Narcissus* on 23rd March 1865 and was appointed midshipman on 21st September. He served aboard a number of ships thereafter – HMS *Challenger* 13th July 1866, HMS *Esk* 5th June 1867, HMS *Victory* 18th October 1867, HMS *Formidable* 26th December 1867 and HMS *Minotaur* 13th July 1868. He was promoted sub-lieutenant on 22nd March 1870 and then served on HMS *Excellent* 20th April 1870 and HMS *Lord Warden* 14th August 1870–21st September 1872. He was appointed acting lieutenant 22nd September–8th October 1872 and was promoted lieutenant on 8th April 1873. He was aboard HMS *Resistance* 29th July 1873–19th September 1874 and then HMS *Excellent* 29th September 1874–25th June 1875 for a gunnery course. On 21st October 1874 he added King to his surname. He was on half pay at his own request 26th June–30th September 1875 and joined HMS *Excellent* next day until 20th December 1876. He was at the RN College October 1874–June 1875 and then served aboard HMS *Lord Warden* 21st December 1876, HMS *Audacious* 7th February 1878 and HMS *Druid* 18th February 1879–6th March 1882. Appointed acting commander 7th March–3rd April 1882 and was then aboard HMS *Duncan* 2nd-4th September 1882 and HMS *Excellent* 3rd January–26th March 1883 to requalify in gunnery. Following this he served on HMS *Lord Warden* 27th March 1883 and HMS *Euryalus* 15th June 1884–18th April 1885. On 31st December 1884 he was promoted commander and served on HMS *Shannon* 11th August 1885–12th August 1887. A short period of half pay followed (13th August–19th September 1887), then he served aboard HMS *President* 20th September 1887. Half pay again, 15th October 1887–3rd January 1888, was followed by command of the sloop HMS *Penguin* 4th January 1888–16th July 1889. The ship was responsible for securing the Maldives as a British Protectorate and acted against slave traders in East African waters. Half pay for a day (17th July 1889) was followed by HMS *Racoon* 18th July 1889. Half pay 7th September–2nd October 1889 was followed by command of HMS *Melita* 3rd October 1889–20th February 1892. In May 1891 he was commended for supervising the salvaging of the French cruiser *Seignelay*, which had run aground off Jaffa. On 29th October 1891 the Egyptian Government thanked him for the assistance rendered during the stranding of the packet *Chibine*. He was again on half pay 21st February–29th September 1892 and on 31st December 1891 was promoted captain. George returned to HMS *President* 30th September 1892–30th June 1893 and was once again on half pay 1st-10th July 1893. He was on HMS *Andromeda* 11th July 1893 and then half pay 30th August 1893–17th July 1894, before joining HMS *Scylla* 18th July–29th August

George Fowler Hall commanded HMS *Melita* from 3rd October 1889 until 20th February 1892. In May 1891 the ship was involved in salvaging the French Cruiser *Seignelay* off Jaffa and later in assisting the stranded packet *Chibine*. *Melita* was a Mariner Class composite screw vessel carrying eight guns, later classified as a sloop. Uniquely she was the only significant Royal Navy warship built in Malta. Melita is the Latin name for the island. Her hull was composite, with an iron keel, frames, stem and sternposts and wooden planking. She was powered by a two-cylinder horizontal compound expansion steam engine driving a single screw and was also rigged with three masts. Her keel was laid down on 18th July 1883 but work was constantly interrupted when the Mediterranean Fleet's vessels needed attention in the dockyard. As a result, she was not launched until 20th March 1888 by Princess Victoria Melita, twelve-year-old daughter of the Duke of Edinburgh, C-in-C Mediterranean Fleet. *Melita* was commissioned on 27th October 1892. While serving aboard her, Lieutenant (later Rear Admiral) Edward Inglefield invented the Inglefield clip, enabling flags to be attached to each other quickly. They are still in use. *Melita* served in the Meditarranean until November 1901, when she was ordered to Devonport to be sold. However, she was retained and became a boom defence vessel at Southampton in May 1905 and a salvage vessel in December 1915, being renamed HMS *Ringdove*. She was sold as a salvage vessel to Falmouth Docks Board in 1920, when her name was changed to *Ringdove's Aid*. In 1927 she was sold to the Liverpool & Glasgow Salvage Association and her name was changed to *Restorer*. She was broken up in 1937.

1894. Half pay again 30th August–4th October 1894, then joined HMS *Volage* 5th October 1894–4th October 1896. Their Lordships displeasure was expressed when *Volage* grounded off Guernsey on 8th June 1896. Half pay 5th October 1896–20th October 1897 was followed by tours aboard HMS *Royal Arthur* 11th February–27th July 1897, HMS *Edgar* 21st October 1898, HMS *Narcissus* 7th March 1898 and HMS *Duke of Wellington* 24th June–14th July 1899. Half pay 15th July–19th December 1899, then to HMS *Renown* 12th April 1900–10th June 1902 as Chief of Staff to Sir John Fisher, C-in-C Mediterranean Station. Half pay 11th June–30th September 1902 then HMS *President* 1st October 1902–10th May 1904 as Assistant to Admiral Superintendent Naval Reserves and 11th May–14th October 1904 as Commander Coastguard and Reserves. Promoted rear admiral 11th May 1904 and was on half pay 15th October 1904–27th February 1906. He was appointed to HMS *Emerald* 28th February 1906–30th July 1908 as Senior Naval Officer Coast of Ireland at Queenstown. Half pay 15th October 1904–27th February 1906, including the Senior Officers' Signal Course 20th February 1905, Strategy Course 6th June 1905 and War Course 29th August–24th November 1905. Awarded the CVO (LG 19th July 1907). Promoted vice admiral 18th May 1908. Half pay 31st July 1908–30th December 1910 was followed by appointment as C-in-C Australia Station on 31st December 1910. He was aboard

HMS *Renown* (11,690 tons), a second-class pre-Dreadnought battleship, was laid down at Pembroke Dockyard on 1st February 1893, launched on 8th May 1895 and was commissioned on 8th June 1897. The design was innovative, being the first battleship to use Harvey armour, the first with a sloping armoured deck and the first with armoured shields over the main armament, which consisted of four Mark III 10″ guns. She also carried ten Mark II 6″ QF guns, twelve 12 Pounder QF guns, eight 3 Pounder Hotchkiss QF guns and five 18″ torpedo tubes. *Renown* was the flagship for the C-in-C, Vice Admiral Sir Nowell Salmon VC, on 26th June 1897 at the Spithead Fleet Review for Queen Victoria's Diamond Jubilee, with the Prince of Wales aboard. She became flagship on the North America and West Indies Station and later of the Mediterranean Fleet. In both instances Sir John Fisher was C-in-C. In 1902 she was fitted out at Portsmouth to carry the Duke and Duchess of Connaught on a royal tour of India, then rejoined the Mediterranean Fleet. *Renown* went into reserve on 15th May 1904 and the following February began a refit at Portsmouth to convert her into a royal yacht, which included removing the remainder of her armaments to increase space for accommodation. On 8th October 1905 she left Portsmouth for Genoa, Italy, where the Prince and Princess of Wales (future King George V and Queen Mary) embarked for a royal tour of India. She returned to Portsmouth on 7th May 1906 and went into reserve. From October to December 1907, *Renown* carried King Alfonso and Queen Victoria Eugenia of Spain on an official trip to Britain. She was transferred to 4th Division, Home Fleet at Portsmouth on 1st April 1909 and that September began a refit to convert her into a stoker's training ship. On 1st April 1914 she was sold for scrap and was broken up at Blyth.

HMS *Powerful* 31st December 1910–23rd February 1911 in transit. KCB (LG 9th June 1911). During this appointment he helped to generate public support for the fledgling Royal Australian Navy and to prepare it for the 1913 transfer of responsibility for Australia's naval defence. He incurred their Lordships displeasure for sending HMS *Torch* to sea in an unseaworthy condition. He was assigned to HMS *Encounter* 22nd December 1911–6th February 1912, HMS *Drake* (flagship of the Australia Station) 7th February 1912 and HMS *Cambrian* 3rd January–8th December 1913. Promoted admiral 19th May 1912 and returned to Britain aboard SS *Demosthenes* in December 1913. Half pay 9th December 1913–9th February 1914 and retired next day on a pension of £950 p.a. He was also granted a Good Service Pension of £300 p.a. from 28th June 1923. George married Mary Olga Felicia Dara Ker (c.1867–14th August 1950) on 5th April 1892 at St Paul's Church, London. She was a distant cousin of Winston Churchill and wrote a few novels, some in Italian. They had three children:

- William Stephen Richard King Hall (21st January 1893–2nd June 1966) was educated at Lausanne in Switzerland and at the Royal Naval College Dartmouth. He served during the Great War with the Grand Fleet on HMS *Southampton* and in 11th Submarine Flotilla. He was promoted commander in 1928 and resigned in 1929. William married Kathleen Amelia Spencer (c.1893–16th May 1963) on 15th April 1919 and they had three children – Edith J Ann King-Hall 1920, Frances Susan King-Hall 1927 and Amelia Jane King-Hall 1930. He wrote several plays between 1924 and 1940, including *Posterity*, which was accepted by Leonard Woolf for the Hogarth Essays. He joined the Royal Institute of International Affairs in 1929, having previously been awarded its Gold Medal for his 1920 thesis on submarine warfare. William entered Parliament unopposed in 1939 as the Labour MP for Ormskirk. He was later an independent and lost his seat to future Prime Minister Harold Wilson in 1945. During the Second World War he served in the Ministry of Aircraft Production under Lord Beaverbrook as Director of the Factory Defence Section. In 1944 he founded and chaired the Hansard Society to promote parliamentary democracy. He presented a programme for children on current affairs on both BBC radio and television. Created Knight Bachelor in 1954 and Baron King-Hall of Headley, Hampshire on 15th January 1966. They lived at Hartfield House, Headley. He was living at 162 Buckingham Palace Road, London at the time of his death at Westminster Hospital, London.

- Olga Louisa 'Lou' Elisabeth King Hall (22nd February 1897–7th January 1985) married Alastair MacLeod (12th November 1894–24th April 1982) in 1927 in Chelsea, London and they had a son, Michael J MacLeod, in 1943. Alastair was the son of Surgeon General Kenneth Macleod MD FRCS (1840–1922) and Jane Christie Aitken (1857–1939). He made his first-class debut as a batsman for Hampshire against Somerset in the 1914 County Championship and played five matches, scoring a career best of eighty-seven runs against Essex in a match that Hampshire won by an innings and nineteen runs. After the Great War he resumed his career with Hampshire and was appointed Secretary of Hampshire County Cricket Club 1936–39. Lou wrote *Fly Envious Times* in 1944. They were living at The Old Post House Flat, Pleshey, Chelmsford, Essex at the time of their deaths there.

Magdalen King Hall's novel, *Life And Death of the Wicked Lady Skelton*, was twice made into a film in 1945 and 1983.

- Magdalen 'Madge' King Hall (22nd July 1904–26th February 1971) was educated at Downe House School, Cold Ash, near Newbury, Berkshire and St Leonard's School, near St Andrews, Fife. She also spent some time in Switzerland and became a novelist (as Cleone Knox), journalist and children's fiction writer. Her novel *Life And Death of the Wicked Lady Skelton* was made into a film twice – *The Wicked Lady* 1945 with Margaret Lockwood and James Mason and the 1983 remake starring Faye Dunaway and Alan Bates. Magdalen married her distant cousin, Patrick Edward Perceval Maxwell (1900–18th August 1968), in 1929 in Chelsea, London. His father was Colonel Robert David Perceval Maxwell (1870–1932), who served in 13th Royal Irish Rifles and the Royal Munster Fusiliers during the Great War and was later an Ulster Unionist Party politician and member of the Senate of Northern Ireland. Patrick worked for the Sudan Cotton Plantation Syndicate before moving to London, then Co Down, where he farmed. He inherited Headborough House, Co Waterford in 1946. She was living at Langley Common House, Kings Langley, Hertfordshire at the time of her death there. They had three children – Richard Stephen Maxwell 1930, Alastair Patrick Maxwell 1937 and Brigid Louise Perceval-Maxwell 1940.

- Edmund Hobart Russell Hall (1854–7th July 1883), born at Weymouth, was known as Russell. He went to Australia, apparently in disgrace, after allegedly pawning a pair of diamond earrings and other jewellery belonging to an elderly lady calling herself Baroness Nelson and Bronté, who claimed to be the grand niece of Lord Nelson. On her return from Russia after thirty years she fell on hard times and decided to sell some jewellery. She claimed to have given the items to Russell to sell on her behalf but he pawned them and disappeared with the money. The case was reported in *The Times* on 31st May 1877 and 21st June 1877 but 'Baroness Nelson' proved to be unreliable and the outcome is not known. Russell met Elizabeth 'Buttercup' Gash in Australia but they are not believed to have married. He was proprietor of the *Ballarat Star* newspaper 1881–82 but became ill and was nursed by Buttercup's sister, Sarah, until he died at South Yarra, Victoria. Russell and Buttercup had a daughter, Violet Francis (sic) King Hall (1882–6th November 1947).
- Francis Robert Forman Hall (14th December 1856–6th June 1933), born in Nova Scotia, served during the Second Boer War in South Africa. He married Elizabeth Louisa Davies (born 1859) in 1901 at Westminster. She was the daughter of Reverend Canon Charles Davies. They lived at Fairholme, Emsworth, Hampshire. He was living at 22 Ovington Street, Chelsea at the time of his death there.
- Frances Mary Guildford Hall (1860–28th December 1925), born at Brompton, London, married Edward Banbury (15th August 1859–16th February 1933), a banker, on 15th December 1883 at Kensington. They were living at 60 Eaton Place, London by 1901. Both their deaths were registered at St George, Hanover Square, London. He left effects valued at £101,644/8/1 (£6.8M in 2018). They had four children:

- William Michael Victor Banbury (13th October 1884–17th August 1917) was educated at Eton 1898–1901 and served as a second lieutenant in the Norfolk Artillery (Militia) 1903–06. He was commissioned in the Rifle Brigade on 23rd May 1906 and served with the 4th Battalion in Malta and Egypt. Promoted lieutenant 24th March 1910 and resigned on 23rd November 1912. He was recalled from the Reserve of Officers on the outbreak of war, was appointed temporary captain in 11th Battalion on 14th September 1914 and went to France on 21st July 1915. He was admitted to 7th Stationary Hospital, Boulogne on 21st July 1916 with inflamed connective tissue of the leg. On 17th August 1917 at Hollebeke he was advancing with his company in 16th Rifle Brigade under a very heavy shellfire when he tried to place a wounded man into cover and was struck by a shell and killed instantly (Voormezeele Enclosures No.1 and No.2, Belgium – I E 7).
- Margaret Louise Banbury (born and died 1889).
- Francis Edward Banbury (12th February 1894–6th January 1956) was educated at Wellington College, Berkshire and Trinity College, Cambridge. He enlisted in 18th Royal Fusiliers (1234) on 12th November 1914 at Epsom, described as 5′ 11″ tall and weighing 160 lbs. He was discharged to a commission on 18th January 1915 but withdrew from RMA Woolwich in August 1915. He then applied for a Special Reserve commission in the Coldstream Guards on 21st July and was commissioned in the Coldstream Guards on 24th July, confirmed on 21st January 1916. However, he was sent home from France in March 1916 as unfit to command troops in the field and joined 5th (Reserve) Battalion, Coldstream Guards. His inability to lead men was also confirmed by his new CO and his application to transfer to the RFC on 6th June was approved. Francis reported to the RFC School of Instruction, Reading for preliminary instruction in aviation on 3rd July and subsequently went to France. His squadron commander decided that he was unlikely to become efficient as an observer and he was ordered to report to HQ Guards Division on 16th December. He was sent home, departing Le Havre on 31st December and arrived at Southampton on 1st January 1917. Francis was called upon to resign his commission due to unsuitability for the RFC and previous inefficiency as an infantry officer. HQ BEF confirmed that he was not to be sent to rejoin the forces in France. He applied to continue serving as an officer but with the Commission Internationale de Ravitaillement at Room 17, Empire House, Kingsway, London, which supported his request so that he could be employed to deal with the supply of munitions to allied governments. This was declined by the War Office and Army Council twice in March and April. He relinquished his commission on 23rd April 1917 and enlisted in the Royal Horse Artillery the following day at Woolwich. London (224033). He was posted as a gunner on 25th June but was again commissioned whilst employed as an interpreter on 1st August 1918. He returned to Britain from Russia in December 1918 with chronic prostatitis,

Herbert Goodenough Hall served on HMS *Sultan*. She was a broadside ironclad and carried her main armament in a central box battery. She was named for the Ottoman Sultan Abdülâziz, who was visiting Britain when she was laid down. She was commissioned at Chatham for the Channel Fleet but also served in the Mediterranean under the command of the Duke of Edinburgh. At the bombardment of Alexandria she lost two men killed and eight wounded. On 6th March 1889 she grounded in the Comino Channel between Malta and Gozo and ripped her bottom open. *Sultan* slowly flooded and in a gale on 14th March 1889 she sank. However, she was raised in August by the Italian firm of Baghino & Co, was brought into Malta and preliminary repairs were made. In December she moved back to Portsmouth under her own steam for further work in a dry dock. A major modernisation took place between October 1892 and March 1896. She then went into reserve but came out twice for the 1896 and 1900 annual manoeuvres. In 1906 she became an artificers' training ship and was renamed *Fisgard IV*. In 1931 she was converted into a mechanical repair ship and regained her original name. During the Second World War she was a depot ship for minesweepers at Portsmouth and was sold in 1947.

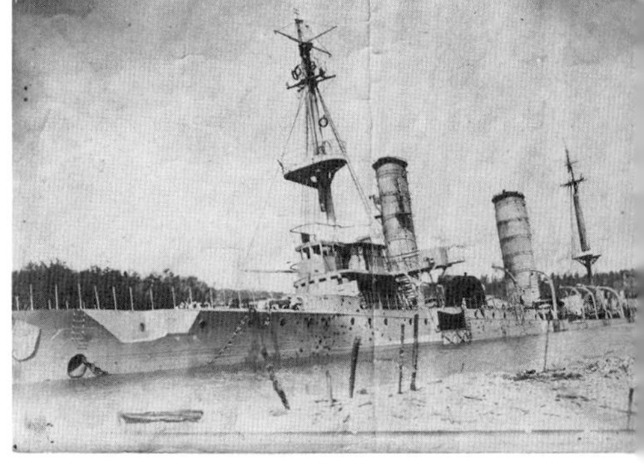

The wreck of SMS *Königsberg* (3,814 tons) on the Rufiji River in Tanzania. She was the lead ship of her class of light cruisers built for the German Imperial Navy. She was laid down in January 1905, launched that December and was completed in June 1906. Her main armament consisted of ten 10.5 cms (4.1″) guns and she had a top speed of 24.1 knots. *Königsberg* served with the High Seas Fleet in the reconnaissance force. She frequently escorted Kaiser Wilhelm II's yacht on visits to foreign countries. In April 1914 she was sent to German East Africa. When war broke out she attempted to intercept British and French commercial traffic but was hampered by a shortage of coal and only destroyed one merchant ship. On 20th September 1914 she surprised and sank HMS *Pegasus* and then retreated into the Rufiji River to repair her engines. She was discovered there and blockaded by British cruisers. Several attempts to sink her failed until on 11th July 1915 the monitors HMS *Mersey* and HMS *Severn* got close enough to severely damage *Königsberg*. The crew then scuttled the ship, salvaged all ten main guns and joined Lieutenant Colonel Paul von Lettow-Vorbeck's force. The wreck was partially broken up in 1963–65 for scrap and she rolled over in 1966 and sank into the mud.

which originated in June 1918, and was admitted to Grove Military Hospital, Tooting on 14th December. A medical board there on 18th December found him unfit for General Service but fit for Home Service and ordered him to report to the Military Intelligence Department, War Office next day. He was considered for an appointment there but was not taken up. However, he was employed by the Director of Military Intelligence in Paris for a short period and was discharged on 5th February 1919 from the Officers Dispersal Unit, London. Francis became a stockbroker and never married. He was residing at The International Sportsmen's Club, Upper Grosvenor Street, London at the time of his death at St Mary's Hospital, Praed Street, Paddington, London. He left effects valued at £51,419/18/1 (£1.3M in 2018).

  - Rose Mary Banbury (1896–1985).

- Herbert (later Sir Herbert) Goodenough Hall (15th March 1862–20th October 1936) joined the Royal Navy in 1875 and served on HMS *Sultan* in the bombardment of Alexandria and during the Egyptian War of 1882. He was promoted lieutenant on 18th November 1882 for services rendered during operations in Egypt. Herbert commanded HMS *Magpie* from 26th August 1893 during in the expedition against the Mandingoes in Gambia in 1894. He was Chief of Staff to Admiral Bedford and was awarded the DSO for his services during operations against Focley Silah in Combo, Gambia (LG 26th May 1894). Promoted commander 1st January 1895 and was posted to the Naval Intelligence Department 1895–96. He commanded HMS *Hearty* 26th January 1899–21st August 1900. Promoted captain 30th June 1900 and was the Naval Transport Officer, Natal during the Second Boer War. He commanded HMS *King Alfred* 22nd December 1903–18th April 1904, HMS *Endymion* 19th April–30th November 1904 and HMS *Cumberland* 1st December 1904–6th February 1906. Head of Foreign Division, Admiralty 20th March 1906–25th June 1908 (CB, LG 28th June 1907). Appointed Director of Naval Intelligence on 1st October 1907. He commanded HMS *Indomitable* 16th April 1908–26th July 1909 and took the Prince of Wales to Canada (CVO, LG 11th August 1908). Appointed ADC to the King 2nd July 1908–21st June 1909 and was promoted rear admiral on 22nd June 1909. Herbert was Director of Naval Mobilisation at the Admiralty 11th October 1909–8th January 1912. On 19th October 1911 he was appointed Rear Admiral Second Division, Home Fleet (Second Battle Squadron from 29th March 1912) until 29th October 1912. Appointed C-in-C Cape of Good Hope Station and West Africa Station 28th December 1912–20th December 1915. Promoted vice admiral 5th March 1915. He led the operation to destroy SMS *Königsberg* on the Rufiji River in Tanzania in July 1915. KCB, LG 1st January 1916. His last appointment was Flag Officer, Orkneys and Shetland 28th January 1918–1st March 1919. Promoted admiral on 25th August 1918 and retired at his own request on 1st May 1922. Herbert married Lady Mabel Emily Murray (23rd October 1866–18th July 1969) on 30th March 1905, daughter of William David Murray, Viscount Stormont, and Emily Louisa MacGregor. They lived at 7 and later 47 Sloane Gardens, London and did not have any children. He died there. She was living at 4 Wyndham House, Sloane Square at the time of her death.
- Edith Louisa Stewart Hall (1864–27th June 1933) was a spinster living at 28 Moore Street, Cadogan Square, Westminster at the time of her death at 60 Eaton Place, Westminster.

- Isabella 'Ella or Lel' Annette Hall (1866–21st November 1942), born at Sheppey, married Herbert Wotton/Wootton Westbrook (1881–22nd March 1959) in 1912 (no marriage record found). He was a teacher of Latin and Greek at Emsworth House Preparatory School, near Portsmouth, Hampshire, run by Ella's brother, Baldwin King-Hall. Herbert was also a journalist and an author, best known for working with PG Wodehouse (1881–1975), who called him 'Brook' or the 'Prince of Slackers', as his assistant during the writing of the *By the Way* column for *The Globe*. Herbert was the inspiration for Wodehouse's character, Stanley Featherstonehaugh Ukridge. Together they co-wrote some musicals and, under the pen name Basil Windham, a serial that appeared in *Chums: An Illustrated Paper for Boys* and was published as *The Luck Stone* in March 1997. Ella assisted them in writing a musical sketch, *The Bandit's Daughter*, which only played for a few days at the Bedford Theatre, Camden Town, London in 1907. Ella set up a literary agency and became Wodehouse's agent for his contracts in the UK until her retirement in 1935. Wodehouse wrote dedications to Herbert in *The Gold Bat* 1904 and *A Gentleman of Leisure* 1910. The latter read, *To Herbert Westbrook, without whose never-failing advice, help, and encouragement this book would have been finished in half the time*. Herbert collaborated with Wodehouse in 1911, adapting the latter's short story *Ahead of Schedule* into another musical sketch, *After the Show*. Herbert also published a few poems and short stories in *The Windsor Magazine*. Ella and Herbert were living at 53 Holland Road, London in 1935 and later at 58 Tidworth Gardens, London, where she died. He was living at 54 Flood Street, Chelsea at the time of his death at 21 South Park Hill Road, Croydon. There were no children.
- Baldwin Walker Hall (1868–15th November 1929), born at Sheppey and educated at Cambridge, was a schoolmaster in 1912. He later ran Emsworth House Preparatory School, Emsworth, Hampshire. PG Wodehouse wrote the dedication in *Indiscretions of Archie*, published on 14th February 1921, to Baldwin. He married Eleanor Kershaw Seppings-Wright (c.1887–25th November 1980) in 1927 at Havant, Hampshire. She was born in London, daughter of Henry Charles Seppings-Wright (1849–1937), an artist, and Maria Eliza Willows. Eleanor was living with her mother at 1 Cecil Court, Hollywood Road, Kensington, London in 1911. Her father, described as a war correspondent, was away at the time of the census. Henry was known for his artistic contributions to *Vanity Fair* under the pseudonym Stuff. He was living at Emsworth House, Emsworth, Hampshire at the time of his death there, leaving effects valued at £10,887/9/-. She was living at Trerose House, Mawnan, Cornwall at the time of her death. There were no children.

William King Hall's next appointment was HMS *Styx* 1851–53 in South Africa, East Indies and Hong Kong, including the latter part of the 8th Kaffir War. He was promoted captain in 1853 and was in action during the Crimean War, commanding HMS *Bulldog* during the bombardment and capture of Fort Bomarsund. He

A rather forlorn looking Stubbington House School soon after it closed in the 1960s. It was founded in 1841 by the Reverend William Foster in Stubbington, Hampshire, close to the Solent. It was known as 'the cradle of the Navy', at times educating up to forty percent of RN officer entrants. The original building was constructed around 1715 and was extended as the number of pupils increased. The school began with just ten pupils and by 1883 had increased to around 130. When the *Britannia* cadet training facility closed, pupils left Stubbington earlier to attend the Royal Naval College at Osbourne House on the Isle of Wight. As a result there were only seventy-seven pupils in 1913 but had risen to 130 again by 1930. Death duties and high maintainance costs forced the school to move to Ascot in 1962, where it merged with Earleywood School, which closed in 1997. A few of the Stubbington buildings remain but most were derelict within a year of being vacated. The main school building was demolished in 1967 and the site is now a community centre. In addition to George Grogan, a number of other VCs attended the school – Angus Falconer Douglas-Hamilton, Lanoe George Hawker, Anthony Cecil Capel Miers. Beachcroft Towse and Algernon Walker-Heneage-Vivian. Amongst its other famous alumni are:

- Admiral of the Fleet Andrew Browne Cunningham KT KCB OM DSO, 1st Viscount Cunningham of Hyndhope (1883–1963), who was C-in-C Mediterranean Fleet in the Second World War and later First Sea Lord.
- George Grogan's uncle, Herbert Goodenough Hall, C-in-C Cape of Good Hope Station.
- Robert Falcon Scott (1868–1912), the Antarctic explorer.
- Admiral Sir John Forster 'Sandy' Woodward GBE KCB (1932–2013), Commander of the Falklands Naval Task Force in 1982 and later C-in-C Naval Home Command.

The United Services College was a public school for the sons of military officers, founded to prepare them for military service. Many of its pupils went on to Sandhurst and Dartmouth. It was founded in 1874 and was absorbed by the Imperial Service College in 1906, which in turn merged with Haileybury College in 1942. Amongst the United Services College alumni are:

- Rudyard Kipling, who based his *Stalky & Co* stories on his experiences at the College and many of the characters appearing in them were at the College.
- Major General Lionel Dunsterville CB CSI, a contemporary of Kipling's, was the inspiration for Stalky.
- Bruce Bairnfather, the Great War cartoonist and author.
- Colonel Edward Douglas Browne-Synge-Hutchinson VC CB.
- Brigadier General The Honourable Alexander Gore Arkwright Hore-Ruthven VC GCMG CB DSO PC.
- Brigadier General Francis Aylmer Maxwell VC CSI DSO.
- Captain Anketell Mountary Read VC.

commanded HMS *Exmouth* 1855, flagship of Rear Admiral Sir Michael Seymour, during the attack on the Fortress of Sveaborg, near Helsinki. From 1856 until 1859 he commanded HMS *Calcutta*, flagship of Rear Admiral Seymour as C-in-C East Indies and China Station, during the Second China (Opium) War. William took part in the first attack on Canton in late 1856 and the assault on the Taku Forts in 1858. He commanded HMS *Indus* as Flag Captain to Sir Houston Stewart, C-in-C North America and West Indies Station. He also served on HMS *Royal Adelaide*, HMS *Russell* and HMS *Cumberland*. After the death of their son, William, in 1858, Louisa sailed to Canada to be with her parents as her husband, William, was once again at sea for an extended period. When William was appointed to command HMS *Indus* on the North America and West Indies Station, she decided to stay in Halifax. Appointed Superintendent of Sheerness Dockyard 1865 and was promoted rear admiral on 17th March 1869. The family was living at 32 Royal Crescent, Kensington in 1871. On 20th November 1871 he was appointed Superintendent of Devonport Dockyard and was promoted vice admiral on 30th July 1875. He was appointed C-in-C Nore in 1877 and was promoted admiral on 2nd August 1879. He retired voluntarily on 3rd January 1881 on a pension of £930 p.a. William married Charlotte Tillotson née Simpson (c.1828–2nd November 1912) in 1880 at St George's, Hanover Square, London. She was born at Brockton, Staffordshire. They lived at The Elms, Station Road, Sutton Bonington, Nottinghamshire. Charlotte had married Thomas Tillotson JP DL (1801–3rd January 1878) on 12th November 1850 at Brewood, near Chillington, Staffordshire. William died at 38 Jermyn Street, London. Charlotte married Sir Alexander Armstrong KCB LLD FRS (1818–5th July 1899) in 1894 at Westminster. They both died at The Elms.

Construction of Parkhurst Barracks was completed in September 1798 and shortly afterwards it was renamed Albany Barracks after Prince Frederick, Duke of York and Albany, who had been C-in-C of the Forces. In 1859 the Isle of Wight Rifles, raised as a defence force for the Island, was stationed there. The Barracks were decommissioned in the early 1960s and the site was redeveloped as Albany Prison.

George was educated at Stubbington House School, Hampshire, which had a strong tie with the Royal Navy, and the United Services College, Westward Ho!, Devon 1890–93. He trained at the Royal Military College, Sandhurst, Surrey and was commissioned on 5th September 1896 in the West India Regiment. Promoted lieutenant on 22nd December 1897 and served in Sierra Leone during 1898 and the Hut Tax War. He served in Lagos, Nigeria in 1898–9 and was also employed in the hinterland. Appointed acting captain on 5th November 1900 and was assigned to the Egyptian Army 9th May 1902–10th May 1907. He transferred to the King's Own Yorkshire Light Infantry on 23rd March 1907, was promoted captain four days later and qualified as a first class Arabic interpreter in July 1907. George transferred to the Worcestershire Regiment on 18th January 1908 and served with the 1st Battalion, returning with it from Egypt to Albany Barracks, Parkhurst, Carisbrooke, Isle of Wight, Hampshire. He was promoted major on 26th September 1914 and went to France with the 2nd Battalion on 9th November 1914. He took command in December 1914 and was wounded on 6th January 1915. On recovery he returned to France on 18th March, joined the 1st Battalion and was appointed CO on 22nd March 1915 and temporary lieutenant colonel 22nd April 1915–13th February 1920. **Awarded the CMG (LG 14th January 1916). Awarded the DSO for bold and capable leadership in command of his Battalion on 4th March 1917 in a successful attack to the east of Bouchavesnes. He visited the captured trenches and gave instructions regarding dispositions and consolidation. He kept Brigade HQ informed of the situation and his reports were of great value. The spirit of his Battalion owed much to his personal courage and cheerfulness (LG 11th May 1917).**

George was appointed temporary brigadier general and Commander 23rd Brigade (8th Division) 12th March 1917–12th May 1919. Promoted brevet lieutenant colonel 3rd June 1917. On 31st July 1917 he led the Brigade at Bellewaarde Ridge on the opening day of the Third Battle of Ypres, with Captain FC Roberts as the Brigade Major. Roberts was awarded the VC for his actions whilst commanding 1st Worcestershire on 23rd March 1918 at Pargny, France. **Awarded a Bar to the DSO for conspicuous gallantry and devotion to duty during a long period of active operations. On one occasion, on 29th March 1918 at Moreuil, when in command of the left of 8th Division, it was mainly due to his personal efforts that the line was maintained and extended when troops on the left were withdrawn. Whenever the position became critical he went forward himself to restore the situation and his splendid example of courage and endurance greatly inspired all ranks (LG 26th July 1918).**

Awarded the VC for his actions during the Second Battle of the Aisne on 27th-29th May 1918, LG 25th July 1918. Presented with the VC by the King at Headquarters First Army, Ranchicourt, France on 8th August 1918. George was mentioned in despatches nine times for his service during the war:

- Field Marshal Sir John French's Despatch of 30th November 1915 (LG 1st January 1916).
- Field Marshal Sir Douglas Haig's Despatches of 13th November 1916, 9th April 1917, 7th November 1917, 7th November 1917 (sic), 8th November 1918 and 16th March 1919 (LG 4th January 1917, 15th May 1917, 11th December 1917, 18th December 1917, 20th December 1918 and 5th July 1919 respectively).
- General Lord Rawlinson's Despatch of 11th November 1919 (LG 3rd February 1920).
- Major General Sir Edmund Ironside's Despatch of 1st November 1919 (LG 6th April 1920).

After the war he volunteered for the North Russia Relief Force in Archangel in 1919 with fellow VCs HEM Douglas, MSS Moore, J Sherwood-Kelly, AM Toye and WA White. He commanded 238th Infantry Brigade there under Lord Rawlinson 13th May–12th October 1919. **Awarded the CB (LG 3rd June 1919).** George relinquished the temporary rank of brigadier general on 13th October 1919. The CB was presented by the King in the ballroom at Buckingham Palace on 27th February 1920.

On 22nd January 1920 George married Ethel Gladys Elger (1885–11th December 1968), born at Kensington, London, at Holy Trinity Church, Sloane Street, London. They lived at Silverdene, Shrubbs Hill, Sunningdale, Berkshire. They had two sons:

George married Ethel Elger at Holy Trinity Church (The Church of the Holy and Undivided Trinity with St Jude), Sloane Street, London in January 1920. It was built in 1888–90 to an Arts & Crafts design by John Dando Sedding. It replaced an earlier building half its size. Its width exceeds that of St Paul's Cathedral by twenty-three centimetres. The Church was badly damaged by incendiary bombs in the Blitz but had been restored by the early 1960s. The church authorities wanted to demolish the building and replace it with something smaller but this was thwarted by a campaign led by John Betjeman and the Victorian Society. The Liberal Prime Minister Willian Ewart Gladstone (1808–98) attended the church.

- Gwyn St George Elger Grogan (7th August 1921–24th August 2005), born at Wandsworth, London, became a Special Entry Navy Cadet on 1st January 1939 and joined the Royal Navy as a cadet on 1st January 1940. Appointed midshipman 1st September 1940 and joined HMS *Warspite* the same day. He served on HMS *Jervis* from July 1941. He survived the sinking of HMS *Barham* on 25th November 1941, having joined her in October 1941. Promoted acting sub lieutenant on 1st May 1942 and lieutenant on 1st January 1943. Joined HMS *Queenborough* as First Lieutenant on 1st September 1942. He served on HMS *Berry Head* 11th October 1949, HMS *Ledbury* 19th June 1945, HMS *Vernon*, HMS *Charity* and HMS *Whirlwind* 8th March 1946. Promoted lieutenant commander 1st January 1951 and served on HMS *Unicorn* December 1951. He joined HMS *President* on 14th October 1953. Appointed to the staff of CinC Mediterranean and CinC Allied Forces Mediterranean at HMS *St Angelo*, Malta on 21st November 1955. He retired as a lieutenant commander in 1958. He married a lady named French, had a child and they lived at Sunningdale, Berkshire.

- George Edward Desmond Grogan (27th June 1924–5th October 1990), born at Wandsworth, was living at Silverdene, Shrubbs Hill, Sunningdale at the time of his death.

Ethel's father, John Elger (1858–28th May 1925), born at Westminster, London, married Ethel née Williams (1858–4th October 1940), born at Chelsea, London, in 1884 at Aylesbury, Buckinghamshire. They were living at Clayton Court, East Liss, Hampshire by 1891 and were still there in 1911. He was living at Priors Hatch, Godalming, Surrey at the time of his death, leaving effects valued at £87,606/10/8 (over £5M in 2018). She was still living there at the time of her death. In addition to Ethel they had three other children:

- Gwendoline/Gwendolen Katherine Elger (1887–17th November 1940), born at Kensington, London, married John Herbert Kerrich (14th March 1874–14th September 1914) on 24th September 1908 at Midhurst, Sussex. He was the son of General Walter D'Oyley Kerrich (c.1833–1911) and Louisa Jane née Cleveland. John was educated at St Paul's School and the Royal Military College, Sandhurst. He was commissioned on 10th October 1894 and promoted lieutenant on 23rd December 1896. He served in the Second Boer War as an intelligence officer 8th April–30th May 1901, taking part in operations in the Orange Free State April-May 1900 (including actions at Vet River (5th-6th May) and Zand River), the Transvaal May-June 1900 (including actions near Johannesburg, Pretoria and Diamond Hill (11th-12th June), in the Transvaal east of Pretoria July–29th November 1900 (including action at Belfast (26th-27th August), and in the Transvaal 30th November 1900–31st May 1902. Promoted captain 30th December 1900. He also served in India, Egypt and the Soudan, returning to Britain in March 1914. Promoted major on 24th March 1914 while stationed at Borden, Hampshire. He was a good cricketer and an excellent polo player; King Edward VII remarked on his skills as a horseman during a review at Aldershot, Hampshire. John was a member of the Army and Navy Club. He went to France commanding C Company, 2nd Welsh on 12th August 1914. During the Battle of the Aisne on 14th September, his men were lying prone in the open when he raised himself on his knees to direct their fire. A bullet hit him in the mouth, killing him instantly (Vendresse British Cemetery – II J 1). Gwendolen was living at Priors Hatch, Godalming, Surrey at the time of her death at High View Nursing Home, Nightingale Road, Godalming. They had two children:
  - Geoffrey John Kerrich (born 1909) married Marjorie Gray in 1938 and they had a daughter, Gwendolen M Kerrich, in 1946.
  - Rosemary KG Kerrich (born 1914) married Samuel H Bor (born 1912) in 1938 and they had a daughter, Ann M Bor in 1944.
- Cicely Margaret Gwyn Elger (1889–10th February 1919), born at Midhurst, was living as a spinster at Clayton Court, East Liss, Hampshire at the time of her death, leaving effects valued at £2,714/4/10.

- Phyllis Gwyn Elger (born 20th January 1892–24th July 1987), born at Midhurst, married William Lionel Eastwick-Field (1893–5th April 1962) there in 1917. He was commissioned in the Royal Garrison Artillery. He was awarded the MC – his battery was under heavy shellfire when a dump of ammunition blew up. He immediately organised a party to dig out the men who were buried and carried the wounded to safety (LG 16th August 1917). They were living at Eaton Brae, Blake Hill Crescent, Parkstone, Dorset at the time of his death there. She was living at 35 Blake Hill Crescent, Parkstone, Dorset at the time of her death there. They had a son, Gordon G Eastwick-Field, in 1921. Gordon married Elizabeth Battensby in 1958 and they had two children – Anne Eastwick-Field 1959 and Peter G Eastwick-Field 1961.

Fyzabad (now Faizabad), India was the capital of the princely state of Avadh, established in 1722, and was the scene of a battle during the Mutiny in 1857.

George was promoted lieutenant colonel and assumed command of 3rd Worcestershire on 14th February 1920 at Fyzabad, India. He brought the Battalion home for disbandment. He was appointed ADC to King George V on 8th April 1920 and was promoted brevet colonel the same day. Promoted colonel on 22nd October 1923 and was appointed Commander 5th Infantry Brigade (2nd Division) at Aldershot, Hampshire until 5th April 1925. He went onto half pay on 16th April 1925, retired as an honorary brigadier general on 26th June 1926 and was in the Reserve of Officers until 1930. He unveiled the War Memorial at St Jude's Cemetery, Egham, Surrey on 11th November 1929. George became a member of the King's Bodyguard of the Honorary Corps of Gentlemen-at-Arms on 23rd November 1933 until 1945. He succeeded Field Marshal Sir Claud W Jacob GCB GCSI KCMG as Honorary

The East and West Africa Medal, established in 1892, was awarded for minor campaigns between 1887 and 1900 to Royal Navy, West India Regiment and British led local forces, including locally recruited police. No units of the British Army qualified, although a number of officers and NCOs received the medal while seconded to local units. There are twenty-one clasps but the majority of recipients received only one. George had two clasps – '1898' was awarded for three separate expeditions in Northern Nigeria and 'Sierra Leone 1898–99' was awarded for two expeditions involving native troops and a naval brigade between 18th February 1898 and 9th March 1899.

Colonel of the Worcestershire Regiment on 21st November 1938 and served until 1st September 1945, when he reached the age limit for the appointment. He was a member of the United Services Club and his favourite pastimes were golf and reading.

George attended only two VC reunions – the VC Dinner at the Royal Gallery of the House of Lords, London on 9th November 1929 and the VC Centenary Celebrations at Hyde Park, London on 26th June 1956. He died at his home at Silverdene, Shrub Hill, Sunningdale, Berkshire on 3rd January 1962. He was cremated at Woking Crematorium in Surrey on 8th January and his ashes were scattered in the Tennyson Lake Garden of Remembrance. There is also an entry in the Book of Remembrance. He is commemorated in a number of other places:

- Memorial at Haileybury College Library, Westward Ho!, Devon.
- Named on the Honours Board, Royal Military Academy, Sandhurst, Surrey.
- A Department for Communities and Local Government commemorative paving stone was dedicated at the War Memorial, Plymouth Hoe, Devon on 29th May 2018 to mark the centenary of his award.

In addition to the VC, CB, CMG and DSO & Bar he was awarded the East & West Africa Medal 1887–1900 (clasps '1898' & 'Sierra Leone 1898–99'), 1914 Star with 'Mons' clasp, British War Medal 1914–20, Victory Medal 1914–19 with MID oakleaf, Defence Medal, George V Silver Jubilee Medal 1935, George VI Coronation Medal 1937 and Elizabeth II Coronation Medal 1953. His medals are on loan to the Imperial War Museum, Lambeth Road, London and are on display in the Lord Ashcroft VC Gallery.

9860 LANCE CORPORAL JOEL HALLIWELL
11th Battalion, The Lancashire Fusiliers

Joel Halliwell was born on 22nd September 1881 at 3 Parkfield, Middleton, near Manchester, Lancashire. His father, James Halliwell (19th January 1862–1925), born at High Barn, Middleton, was a cotton cloth dyer and silk winder. In early 1881 he was living with his grandfather, Joel Halliwell at 3 Parkfield, Middleton. James married Sarah née Spencer (1860–1923), born at Oldham, Lancashire, on 18th April 1881 at Holy Trinity Church, Archer Park, Middleton. In 1891 they were living at 8 Burton Street, Middleton and at 20 Parkfield, Middleton in 1901. By 1911 they had moved to 3 Parkfield and he was a labourer. The 1911 Census indicated that five children were born to the marriage, one of whom died in infancy and is not known. Joel's other three siblings were:

Holy Trinity Church, Middleton, where Joel's parents married in April 1881 and Joel married Sarah Greaves in 1920. His funeral took place there thirty-eight years later. The church was built in 1862 and the final service was held on 12th April 2015.

- Eliza 'Liza' Halliwell (1883–1955) was a cotton winder in 1901. She married Samuel Hilton (c.1885–1958) in 1907. Samuel served in the Lancashire Fusiliers (241424) and lost an arm and some fingers from his other hand at Passchendaele They had a daughter, Lena Hilton (27th March 1908–10th July 1981), who married James Smith (23rd May 1908–7th December 1978) in 1935. James' father, also James Smith (born 1880), was serving as a private in 2nd East Lancashire (7760) when he was killed during the Battle of Aubers Ridge, France on 9th May 1915 (Ploegsteert Memorial, Belgium). James died at Rochdale, Lancashire and

Samuel Hilton (Paul Smith).

Joel's sister Eliza with her daughter Lena (Paul Smith).

Lena died at Chelmsford, Essex. They had a son, Brian James Smith, on 30th May 1938. He married Elizabeth Anne Hardy (born 13th November 1937) in 1962 at Ashbourne, Derbyshire. She was born at Beckenham, Kent. Their eldest son, Paul Geoffrey Smith, was born on 20th January 1963.

- Herbert Halliwell (1885–1902) was a cotton cloth dyer in 1901.
- Thomas Halliwell (1887–2nd October 1916) was working at a calis print works in 1901. He married Ethel Fallows (18th August 1887–1974) at Holy Trinity Church, Parkfield, Middleton on 4th January 1908. Thomas enlisted in 6th Border (18014) at Manchester on 23rd November 1914, giving his address as 25 Parkfield Street, Middleton. He was described as a labourer, 5′ 6½″ tall and weighed 128 lbs. He joined at Carlisle on 25th November and was posted to the 10th Battalion on 28th November. He embarked for the 6th Battalion on 23rd September 1915 and joined it at Suvla, Gallipoli on 16th October. On 1st June 1916 at Ballah, Egypt he was changed 6¼d for the loss of his razor. He embarked at Alexandria for France on 28th June. He was wounded on 29th September and died at 2/1st South Midlands Casualty Clearing Station Special Hospital, Warloy (Warloy-Baillon Communal Cemetery Extension, France – VIII B 4). They had two children:
    - May Halliwell (20th May 1908–July 1997) married Henry Crompton (11th November 1904–December 1986) in 1928. He was born at Salford, Lancashire. They had four children – May Crompton 1929, Roy Crompton 1933, Barry Crompton 1942 and Dennis Crompton 1947.
    - Herbert Halliwell (28th December 1909–June 2003) married Marion Partington (14th July 1914–1969) in 1935. They had two children – Peter Halliwell 1938 and Leonard T Halliwell 1941.

  Ethel married Andrew Pryle (born 4th July 1889), a collier born at Wigan, in 1918 at Oldham. He enlisted in the Lancashire Fusiliers on 4th December 1907 (1341) and rose through the ranks to acting sergeant in the 1st Battalion during the Great War. They had a son, Harold Pryle, in 1920. He served in 2nd Loyal Regiment (North Lancashire) as a private during the Second World War (3856914) and died on 30th January 1942 in Singapore (Singapore Memorial – Column 74).

Thomas Halliwell's grave in Warloy-Baillon Communal Cemetery Extension. He was on the same draft to Gallipoli with 6th Border as the author's grandfather.

Joel's paternal grandfather, Thomas Halliwell (c.1836–1863/65), a labourer, married Ann née Smith (c.1841–1908), a reeler, on 3rd July 1859 at

Middleton Parish Church. They were living at Back Field, Middleton in 1861. In addition to James they also had a daughter, Sarah Halliwell (1861–66). Ann married Arthur Thornley (1841–83) in 1867. He was born at Preston, Lancashire. They were living at Burton Street, Middleton in 1871, when he was a labourer and she was a silk winder. They had moved to Little Green, Tonge, Middleton by 1881, by when he was a cotton mixer. Ann was living with her son James and family in 1901. Ann and Arthur had three children:

- Elizabeth Ann Thornley (1870–71).
- Elizabeth Annie Thornley (1874–1900).
- Herbert Thornley (born and died 1881).

His maternal grandfather, John Spencer (c.1831–70) married Eliza née Ogden (c.1832–78) on 12th January 1857 at Middleton Parish Church. She was living with her children at Boarshaw Clough, Middleton at the time of the 1871 Census. In addition to Sarah they had four other children:

Joel's nephew, Harold Pryle, is commemorated on the Singapore Memorial in Kranji War Cemetery, which was unveiled on 2nd March 1957 by Sir Robert Black, Governor of Singapore. It bears the names of 24,317 casualties of the land and air forces of the Commonwealth who died during the campaigns in Malaya and Indonesia or in captivity and have no known grave. The memorial also commemorates airmen who died in southern and eastern Asia and the surrounding seas and oceans. The Kranji area was used as a prisoner of war camp by the Japanese and in 1946 it was decided to expand the small cemetery there as Singapore's main war cemetery.

Middleton Parish Church (St Leonard's) is a Grade 1 listed building. The earliest church on the site was dedicated to St Cuthbert, whose remains were taken there around 880 to escape the attacks by pagan Danes. His decorated coffin is in Durham Cathedral. The Normans built a larger church dedicated to St Leonard. Much of the current building, which replaced the Norman church, was constructed in 1412 by Thomas Langley. He was born in Middleton in 1363 and became Bishop of Durham and Lord Chancellor of England. Parts of the old Norman church were used in the tower arch and the arch to the chantry chapel. The church was completed in 1524 by Sir Richard Assheton to celebrate his knighthood granted by Henry VIII for his part in the Battle of Flodden in 1513. The Flodden Window is believed to be the oldest war memorial in the country. The church also has an important collection of brasses. In 1666 the unusual wooden belfry was added to the tower to enable a new set of bells to be added. Various improvements were also carried out in Victorian times and the 20th century.

- James A Spencer (1858–1925) was an assistant in a chemical works in 1871.
- Mary Alice Spencer (born 1859).
- Amelia Spencer (1865–1936) was a boot fitter in 1881, living at 28 Lonsdale Street, Leicester with her unmarried aunt, Elizabeth Ogden (c1837–97), a cotton winder, and her two daughters, Elizabeth A Ogden (born 1860) and Emily Ogden (born c.1871) and a boarder, Samuel Stanning (1834–89), a glove hand. Amelia married Nathan Tansley (1867–1947), a street cleaner born at Kettering, Northamptonshire, in 1896 at Leicester. They were living at 89 Biddulph Street, Highfields, Leicester in 1911. They had six children:
    - Sidney James Tansley (1896–1960) married Ivy W Bolton in 1922.
    - Louisa Tansley (born 1898) married John E Harrison in 1920. They had a son, Nathan E, later that year.
    - Norah Tansley (born 1900) married Walter MW Bennett (born 1901) in 1925. They had a daughter, Noreen Bennett, in 1926.
    - Amy Alexandra Tansley (14th July 1902–1976) married Walter J Dunmore (1902–46) in 1923. They had two daughters – Norah G Dunmore 1923 and Sandra G Dunmore 1942.
    - Leslie Reginald Tansley (born 1904) married Winifred Phyllis N Spooner (14th February 1907–1976) in 1931.
    - Alice Hagar Tansley (1907) married Leonard T Cox in 1926. They had three children – Leonard E Cox 1926, Pauline I Cox 1930 and Lynn A Cox 1948.
- John Spencer (born 1868). By 1891 he was a labourer living with his stepfather. In 1911 he was still single, boarding at 6 Amy Street, Middleton.

Eliza married William Kent, a weaver, on 22nd September 1871 at Middleton Parish Church. He was living at 237 Oldham Road, Tonge, Lancashire in 1891. Joel was educated at Parkfield Church of England School, Middleton, where he was a keen footballer.

He worked at a Middleton cotton mill as a general labourer and by 1901 was a cotton cap packer. He became a foreman at the Rain and Forest Mill, Oldham. Joel enlisted in the Lancashire Fusiliers on 13th November 1914 at Bury, described as 5′ 5″ tall and weighing 134 lbs. He joined 11th Battalion on 17th November and was fined four days pay for being absent for thirteen hours on 16th January 1915. He was sentenced to three days detention for overstaying a pass by almost a day on 20th August and went to France with the Battalion on 25th September. He qualified for Class 2 Proficiency Pay at 3d per day on 13th November 1916. Joel was appointed unpaid lance corporal on 13th January 1917 and was promoted lance corporal on 16th June. He was granted leave in Britain 25th July–7th August 1917.

Awarded the VC for his actions near Muscourt, France on 27th May 1918, LG 25th July 1918. He was posted to the Base on 12th July and attached to HQ 151st Brigade on 4th August. The VC was presented by the King at Buckingham Palace on 11th September 1918. On his return to Middleton a few days later he was greeted by several thousand townsfolk at the railway station. He was presented with an illuminated address by the Mayor and Mayoress, Alderman and Mrs WM Wiggins, a large number of War Bonds, a gold pocket watch purchased by the Mayor and his wife (it was presented by Mrs Wiggins personally), and a chain from the Middleton Licensed Victuallers' Association. The pocket watch was purchased at auction by Rochdale Council's Arts and Heritage service and is held in Touchstones Museum, The Esplanade, Rochdale. Joel also visited his old school, where he was presented with a wallet containing four one-pound notes, three ten shilling notes and a gold sovereign. All the children were allowed to hold the VC. He was posted to 16th Battalion on 23rd December and to 10th Battalion on 18th January 1919, arriving two days later. He left France on 2nd March and was transferred to the Class Z Reserve on 30th April 1919.

Parkfield Church of England School, Middleton, where Joel was educated, opened on 28th June 1864. It is now Parkfield Junior School.

Joel Halliwell married Sarah Greaves (1886–1964) at Holy Trinity Church in 1920 and they lived in a terraced house at 24 Manchester New Road, Middleton. She was a cotton cardroom hand in 1901. They had three daughters:

- Vera Halliwell (27th August 1923–October 2000) married Harry Pickup in 1946. They lived at 18 Meadow Road, Middleton. Vera died at Rochdale, Lancashire. They had three children:
    - James F Pickup (born 1947).
    - Jennifer M Pickup (born 1950) married Nigel G Murray (born 1950) in 1972. He was born at Ormskirk, Lancashire. They had two children – Luke Joel Murray 1977 and Hannah Frances Murray 1981.
    - Robert I Pickup (born 1952).
- Nora Halliwell (born 1925) married Edward F Walling (born 1925), born at Mile End, London, in 1948 and they had a son, Russell.
- Dora Halliwell (born 1931) married Alan Holroyd Gartside (20th October 1928–July 1985) in 1969 and they had three children – Steven C Gartside 1956, Julie Gartside 1963 and Joanne Gartside 1971.

Sarah's father, James Greaves (1858–21st December 1934), married Emma née Mawdsley or Maudsley (1863–15th September 1918), born at Heywood, in 1884. Emma had a son, John William Mawdsley, in 1882 at Rochdale. He was a builder's labourer in 1901 living with his mother and stepfather. James was a woollen weaver in 1891 and they were living at 11 Back O'Barn, Castleton, Rochdale. By 1901 he was a platelayer and they were living at 118 Platting Lane, Rochdale and at 123 Vavasour Street, Rochdale by 1911. In addition to Sarah, James and Emma had a son, Frederick Greaves (1887–11th December 1932), who was a woollen piecer in 1901.

Joel ran The New Inn public house, Long Street, Middleton 1930–40 but tired of people asking him to recount his exploits. His miniature VC was stolen from the bar prior to 1939. He tried to rejoin the Army during the Second World War but was rejected through poor eyesight and a wound to his left leg. He became a foreman for Middleton Highways Department and finally worked for a firm of dyers. He attended four VC Reunions – the VC Garden Party at Buckingham Palace on 26th June 1920, the VC Dinner at the Royal Gallery of the House of Lords, London on 9th November 1929, the Victory Day Celebration Dinner & Reception at The Dorchester, London on 8th June 1946 and the VC Centenary Celebrations at Hyde Park, London on 26th June 1956. He also attended the coronations of King George VI in 1937 and Queen Elizabeth II in 1953.

Joel died at Oldham and District General Hospital on 14th June 1958. He had suffered from thrombosis and died of myocardial degeneration and arteriosclerosis. His funeral was held at Holy Trinity Church on 18th June. His medals were placed on a purple cushion on the coffin, which was draped with the Union Flag. He is buried in his wife's parents' grave (Plot D, Grave 1068) in Boarshaw New Cemetery, Middleton. A flat stone was erected over the grave and in 1991 a new headstone was funded by a charity run starting in Middleton town centre and finishing at Bury Barracks. Joel was a member of the British Legion, which provided financial support for his widow following his death. Joel is commemorated in a number of other places:

Joel Halliwell towards the end of his life.

Joel was the landlord of the New Inn on Long Street, Middleton 1930–40.

Oldham and District General Hospital, where Joel died. The hospital opened in 1872 as the infirmary to support the Oldham Union Workhouse on Rochdale Road. In 1913 the workhouse was renamed Westwood Park Poor Law Institution and by 1929 was Boundary Park Hospital. A number of other title changes followed – Oldham Municipal Hospital 1938, Boundary Park General Hospital 1943, Boundary Park Municipal Hospital 1948, Boundary Park General Hospital again 1950 and in 1955 Oldham and District General Hospital. This was the birthplace of Louise Brown, the world's first successful in vitro fertilised test tube baby on 25th July 1978. Large-scale demolition and reconstruction commenced in 1981 and the new Royal Oldham Hospital opened on the site in December 1989.

Joel Halliwell's grave in Boarshaw New Cemetery, Middleton.

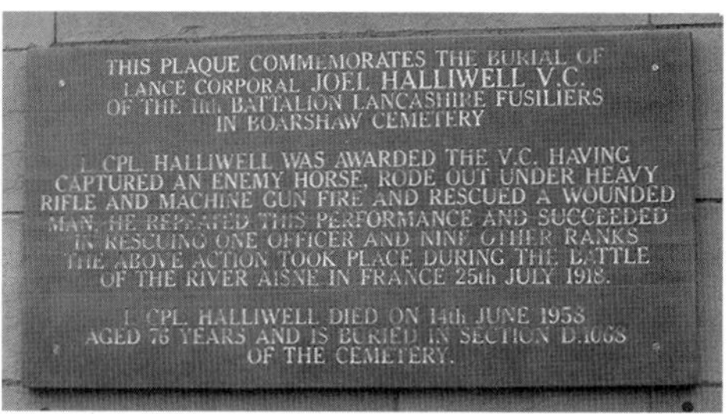

Memorial plaque on the exterior wall of Middleton Crematorium Chapel.

- LCpl Joel Halliwell VC Way, named in 2015, is the main internal road at Middleton Arena.
- Halliwell Park on a new housing estate at Langley, Middleton to be named in 2019.
- A Department of Communities and Local Government commemorative paving stone will be laid in his honour at Halliwell Park, Middleton in 2019.
- A plaque commemorating his burial on the exterior wall of Middleton Crematorium Chapel in Boarshaw New Cemetery. The date on the plaque is when the VC was gazetted (25th July 1918) rather than the date of the deed (27th May 1918).
- Memorial in Holy Trinity Church, Middleton, which closed in April 2015.

In addition to the VC he was awarded the 1914–15 Star, British War Medal 1914–20, Victory Medal 1914–19, George VI Coronation Medal 1937 and Elizabeth II Coronation Medal 1953. The VC is still owned by the family and is on loan to The

Fusiliers' Museum Lancashire, Moss Street, Bury, Lancashire. The Elizabeth II Coronation Medal is not with the medal group. The George VI Coronation Medal hangs from the Elizabeth II Coronation Medal ribbon.

TEMPORARY CHAPLAIN TO THE FORCES 4TH CLASS THEODORE BAYLEY HARDY
Army Chaplains' Department, attached 8th Battalion, The Lincolnshire Regiment

Theodore Hardy was born on 20th October 1863 at Barnfield House, Southernhay, Exeter, Devon. His father, George Hardy (1820–11th October 1870), born at Harberton, Devon, was a shopman living at Fore Street, Exeter in 1841. He married Elizabeth Carne Wilkinson (c.1824–53) in 1849. George was a commercial traveller in the wine, spirit and tea trade in 1851 and they were living at Castle Yard, Exeter and Precinct of Bradninch, near Exeter. Theodore's mother, Sarah Richards née Beedle (c.1826–99) married Henry Frederick Oliver Huntley (21st August 1822–1855), a surgeon dentist, on 12th January 1847 at Sherborne Parish Church, Dorset. They were living at 1 Barfield Place, Exeter in 1851. Theodore's parents married in Exeter in 1859. They were living at 16 Southernhay, St Sidwell, Exeter in 1861. George died at Wonford, near Exeter. In 1871 Sarah was a schoolmistress running a preparatory school for young gentlemen, living at 25 East Southernhay, Exeter. By 1881 she had moved to 124 Elgin Road, Paddington, London. She

Fore Street, Exeter, where George Hardy was living in 1841.

Harberton, Devon, where Theodore's father was born. Its croquet club is the only one in the country that plays by the Harberton Croquet Rules.

died at Thetford, Norfolk. Theodore had eight siblings from his parents' three marriages:

- Henry Gordon Huntley (1848–67).
- Possibly Frederick George Huntley (1849–52).
- Georgina Huntley (1850–1902) was a daily governess at her mother's preparatory school in 1871. She married George Trobridge (1851–8th April 1909) in 1879 at Kensington, London. They were living at 124 Elgin Road, Paddington, London in 1880 and moved to Co Antrim, Ireland by 1881. They were living at Mount Pleasant Street, Cromac, Co Antrim in 1901. After Georgina's death, George returned to England and was living at 10 Edgbaston Road, Smethwick, Staffordshire at the time of his death at Brunswick House, Brunswick Square, Gloucester. Georgina and George had six children:
    - Arthur Huntley Trobridge (born 1880).
    - Ethel Georgina Trobridge (September 1881–1959) was born in Belfast, Co Antrim. She married David Simms (1881–1962), born at Derrygarve, Co Derry, Ireland. They emigrated to New Zealand and both died at Gisborne, Poverty Bay. They had a son, Rowan Huntly Simms, in 1912.
    - Herbert Frank Trobridge (born c.1883).
    - Ernest George Trobridge (1884–14th June 1942) married Jennie Pulsford (1887–31st March 1961) in 1912 at Islington, London. Jennie was born in Scotland. They were living at Hayland, Kingsbury Road, Wembley, London at the time of his death at University College Hospital, London, leaving effects valued at £8,934/2/6. Jennie was still living at Hayland at the time of her death at Edgware General Hospital, Hendon, leaving effects valued at £1,267/11/9. They had six children – Mary J Trobridge 1915, Alan H Trobridge 1917, Ruth T Trobridge 1918, Thomas R Trobridge 1920, Dorothy H Trobridge 1923 and Edward John Brian Trobridge 1924.
    - Dorothy Helen Trobridge (27th January 1888–14th January 1971) married the Reverend John Rous Presland (c.1884–25th August 1958) in 1918 at Islington. They were living at 12 Southville Terrace, Lyncombe Vale, Bath, Somerset at the time of his death, leaving effects valued at £2,064/7/5. She was living at 19 Millbrook Lane, Eccleston, St Helens, Lancashire at the time of her death, leaving effects valued at £1,335. They had a son, Graham John Presland, in 1927.
    - Kathleen Mary Trobridge (23rd April 1891–22nd February 1980) never married and died at Meadowcroft Nursing Home, Towersey Road, Thame, Oxfordshire, leaving effects valued at £1,406.
- Frank Wilkinson Hardy (1851–55).
- Hubert Stobbs Huntley (1852–1929), birth registered as Herbert, was a cashier living with his mother in 1871. In 1881 he was a draper's clerk, still living with his mother in Paddington, London. He married Lucy Susanna Harley (1848–

1925) on 3rd February 1884 at St Augustine, Highbury, London. She was born at Windsor, Berkshire. Hubert was a clerk with the City Council in 1891 and they were living at 150 Albion Road, Hackney, London. By 1901 he was a commercial book keeper and they were living at 14 Burma Road, Stoke Newington, London. In 1911 they were living at 11 Compton Crescent, Chiswick, London. They had a son, Hubert Gordon Huntley, in 1889.

- Alfred George Hardy (1860–81) was a scholar at Pinner, Middlesex in 1871.
- Ernest William Hardy (28th July 1861–14th December 1946) was educated at Oundle School, London University 1882 and University College London College of Divinity 1887. In 1881 he was a tutor at 11 Park Crescent, Broadwater, Sussex. He was ordained in 1887 and made priest in 1888. Ernest was Curate of St Mark's, Birmingham 1887–90 and Euston, Norfolk 1891–95. He was also acting Chaplain to 4th Volunteer Battalion, Norfolk Regiment 23rd October 1895–31st March 1908 and was commissioned as Chaplain to the Forces 3rd Class on 1st April 1908, on the formation of the Territorial Force. Appointed temporary Chaplain to the Forces 4th Class on 4th March 1915 and relinquished his commission on reaching the age limit on 2nd November 1921 but remained an honorary chaplain to the TF. He was awarded the Territorial Decoration on 12th December 1916. Ernest was Vicar of St Mary's, Thetford, Norfolk 1895–1936 and was under the Diocese of Norfolk 1938–39. He married Mary 'Minnie' Sophia (c.1865–15th March 1952) in Ireland. She was born at Belfast, Ireland and was educated privately and in Germany. Her father was secretary of a Northern Ireland railway company and she was the niece of an Irish MP. Minnie became a novelist and her works include *Letters of a Grass Widow* in 1916, *Grounds for Divorce* in 1924, *Dr Mingay's Wife*, *Embroidery of Quiet* and *Nelson at Thetford*. They were living at 9 King Street, Thetford, Norfolk in 1901 and at St Mary's Vicarage, 22 Raymond Street, Thetford in 1911. Ernest died at Wayland, Norfolk and Mary died at home at 22 Raymond Street, Thetford. They had two sons:
    - Norman Evans Hardy (1890–1952) was a student in 1911. He became a Benedictine priest in Liverpool, Lancashire.
    - Cyril Ernest Hardy (1893–10th August 1952) was a pupil at St John's Foundation School For The Sons Of Poor Clergy (Church of England), Epsom Road, Leatherhead, Surrey in 1911. His studies at Durham University were interrupted by the outbreak of war. On 7th August 1914 he enlisted in 28th (County of London) Battalion, London Regiment (Artists' Rifles) (1708) and embarked at Southampton on 26th October. He was commissioned on 3rd March 1915 at Bailleul, France and posted to 1st King's Royal Rifle Corps. Cyril was severely wounded at Festubert on 15th May, resulting in a shortened femur by one and a half inches. He embarked at Boulogne on 11th June, disembarked at Southampton next day and was treated at Lady Mason's Hospital. A medical board at Caxton Hall on 27th July found him unfit for General Service for six months and

he was granted leave until 26th November, extended until 29th February 1916. A medical board at Newcastle-upon-Tyne on 7th March again found him unfit for General Service for six months. Medical boards on 16th March, 20th March and 2nd May found him unfit for General and Home Service permanently, but the latter expected he would be fit for light duties in four months and leave was extended to 1st September. Further medical boards at Norwich on 10th May, at Millbank on 17th June and at Norwich on 22nd August found him unfit for any service permanently. He was awarded a wound pension of £50 for the period 15th May 1916–14th May 1917. His leave was extended to 10th December in the hope that he may become fit enough for an office job. In contrast to previous predictions, a medical board on 11th December found him fit for General Service in two months and he joined 5th King's Royal Rifle Corps at Sheerness on 31st December on light duties. However, a medical board at the Military Hospital, Sheerness on 6th February 1917 found him unfit for any service permanently and he relinquished his commission due to ill health on 24th February. Cyril returned to Durham, St Chad's Hall and graduated BA in 1917. He was ordained in 1918 and made priest in 1919. He was curate of All Saints, Margaret Street, London 1918–19, St Barnabus, Pimlico 1919–21, St John's, Richmond, Surrey 1921–24, St Albans, Ventnor 1925–29 and St Mary, Slough 1929–31 before being appointed Vicar of St Alban's, Dale Street, Sneinton, Nottingham. Cyril married Mary Elizabeth Kirby (23rd September 1899–22nd September 1931) in 1929 at Thetford. She was born at Rangoon, Burma, daughter of Colonel Norborne Kirby CIE (1863–1922) (commissioned Royal Engineers 1886, India 1888, operations in Northern Chin Hills 1892–93, Commanding Royal Engineer 6th (Poona) Divisional Area during Great War, CIE LG 1st January 1917). They lived at St Alban's Vicarage, 8 Dale Street, Sneiton, Nottinghamshire. Mary died at Nottingham General Hospital, leaving £729/1/7 to her husband. They had a son, Paul Richard Hardy, in 1930. Cyril married Annie Severn (1902–26th June 1987) in 1942 at Basford, Nottinghamshire. They had a daughter, Pamela Hardy, in 1944. Cyril died at Nottingham General Hospital.

- Robert Jeffery Hardy (1865–73).

Nothing is known about Theodore's paternal grandparents. His maternal grandfather, Thomas George Beedle (c.1800–59) married Elizabeth née Salter (c.1798–1867). He was a retired chemist in 1851 and they were living at 50 Thrissell Street, Bristol. Elizabeth was a bank shareholder in 1861, living with her son-in-law and daughter, George and Sarah Hardy. In addition to Sarah they had four other children:

- George Charles Richard Beedle (c. 1831–1914), a chemist and druggist, married Ellen Amelia Morgan (c.1833–1918), a teacher, in 1853 at Frome, Somerset. They were living at Harton, Hartland, Devon in 1861, at Clifton, Bristol later in the 1860s and at Axbridge Hill, Axbridge, Somerset by 1869. They had eleven children – George Edward Beedle 1854, Arthur Thomas Morgan Beedle 1856, Charlotte Ellen Beedle 1858, Isabel Lucy Beedle 1860, Florence Amelia Beedle 1861, Charles Douglas Beedle 1862, Gertrude Amy Beedle c.1866, Lionel J Beedle 1867, Evelyn Jessie Beedle 1869, Mabel E Beedle 1870 and Ethel Cecilia Beedle 1871.
- Thomas Beedle (c.1833–1904), a bookseller, married Rebecca Charsley (c.1840–1910) on 13th October 1863 at Woodburn, Buckinghamshire. She was born at Clapton, Middlesex. They were living at 34 High Street, Weston-super-Mare, Somerset in 1871. By 1881 he was an inspector of life assurance agents and they were living at 54 Walton Street, Axford, Devon. By 1891 he was a commission agent and they had moved to 31 Queen Square, Bristol. They had six children – Robert W Beedle 1866, Alfred John Beedle 1868, Thomas George Edward Beedle 1869, Edith Rebecca Beedle 1871, Charles Herbert Beedle 1873 and Mary Elizabeth Beedle 1882.
- John Beedle (c.1837–86).
- Georgiana Beedle (1840–68) was a bank shareholder living with her brother-in-law and sister, George and Sarah Hardy, in 1861. She never married.

Theodore and his brother Ernest were educated at home by their mother initially. He played cricket and football but was hampered by poor eyesight. He was a boarder at the Commercial Travellers' School (Royal Commercial Travellers School from 1918), Uxbridge Road, Hatch End, Pinner, Middlesex 1872–79, then at the City

The Commercial Travellers' Schools were founded by John Robert Cuffley in 1845, to house, feed, clothe and educate necessitous children of brethren on the road who met untimely deaths or were unable to earn their livelihood. It opened in Wanstead with thirty-five boys and girls and had increased to 130 children by 1854. The following year Prince Albert opened the new Schools at Pinner, with accommodation for up to 300 children. In 1918 King George V authorised the Schools to be known as The Royal Commercial Travellers' Schools. The Schools closed in 1967.

The City of London School is partnered with the City of London School for Girls and the City of London Freemen's School. The City of London School traces its origins to a bequest of land by John Carpenter in 1442. The bequest was administered by the Corporation of London and around 1460 a small college was founded next to Guildhall Chapel. In 1823 a Charity Commission report revealed that income from the bequest vastly exceeded expenses and the City Lands Committee suggested that it be spent on educating a larger number of boys. In 1830 this resulted in the City of London Corporation School being established on the site of the disused London Workhouse. New facilities were constructed at Honey Lane Market on Milk Street and became the City of London School, which opened there in 1837. The School did not discriminate against pupils on grounds of religious persuasion and, unlike other independent schools, was a day school, with a few boarders, rather than vice versa. It was the first school in England to include science in the curriculum. It outgrew the Milk Street site and moved to a new site at Blackfriars on Victoria Embankment in 1883. In the Second World War the School was evacuated to Marlborough College in Wiltshire, returning to London in 1944. In 1986 the School moved to its present site in Queen Victoria Street and was opened officially by Princess Anne the following year. Famous alumni include:

Kingsley Amis, writer.
Herbert Asquith, Prime Minister 1908–16.
Bramwell Booth, founder of the Salvation Army.
Mike Brearley, England Cricket Captain 1977–81.
Daniel Radcliffe, actor in the *Harry Potter* films.

of London School, where he was captain of the rowing club. Theodore went on to London University (BA 1889).

On 13th September 1888 Theodore married Florence Elisabeth Hastings (c.1862–June 1914) at the Great Victoria Street Baptist Meeting House, Belfast, Ireland. They were living at 7 Yew Tree Avenue, Nottingham in 1901. They had two children:

- Mary Elizabeth Hardy (5th June 1889–3rd February 1972) was known as Elizabeth. She was an arts student

The congregation of Great Victoria Street Baptist Church met in King Street and later Academy Street before the building seen here was constructed on Great Victoria Street in 1866. Theodore married Florence Hastings there in 1888. That building was demolished in September 2014 due to structural problems and a new building has since replaced it.

in 1911. After graduating from London University (BA) she became a nurse and during the Great War worked at a Red Cross Hospital in Dunkirk, France for two years. She was living at Ivy House, Manea, Cambridgeshire in 1921. Elizabeth became headmistress of a school in Rangoon, Burma and, having escaped the Japanese in 1942, took over a school in Bangalore, India. She eventually returned to England and retired to Cornwall, where she died unmarried at Perran Bay Home for the Elderly, St Pirans Road, Perranporth.

- William Hastings Hardy (1892–24th March 1964) was a medical student in 1911. He studied at Queen's University, Belfast and became a doctor (MB, BCh 1915). On 14th May 1915 he was commissioned as a temporary lieutenant in the Royal Army Medical Corps and served in the Eastern Mediterranean, attaining the rank of captain on 14th May 1916 and served until June 1919. He married Eleanor Florence Parkes on 30th August 1919 at Howth Presbyterian Church, Dublin. Eleanore was the daughter of JJ Parkes of Winnipeg, Alberta, Canada. She was a senior nurse in the Queen Alexandra's Imperial Military Nursing Service during the Great War and they met on a troopship bound for the Middle East. They were living at 180 Brighton Road, South Croydon, Surrey in August 1944 and were still there in 1957. They were living at Riverglen, Delgany, Co Wicklow at the time of his death, leaving effects valued at £1,241. William and Eleanor's Great War medals were sold at Lockdales, 52 Barrack Square, Martlesham Heath, Ipswich, Suffolk on 15th March 2014 for an estimated value of £250–£300. They had a daughter, Patricia Florence Hastings Hardy, who lived at Delgany, Co Wicklow, Ireland. She died unmarried on 11th May 2005 at St John's House, Merrion Road, Dundrum, Dublin.

Florence's father, William Hastings (1814–92), a civil engineer and freelance architect, was born in Belfast, Ireland. He was Surveyor of Works for Belfast 1849–57 and his office was at 8 North Queen Street, Belfast in 1852. He was in private practice with offices on Victoria Street and Victoria Hall 1861–68. William was still working for Belfast Corporation in 1879. He designed the Villa, Dundela, Belfast in 1869, Glenravel House, Co Antrim in 1872 and 61 Donegall Street, Belfast and J Robb & Co Department Store, Castle Place, Belfast in 1874. William married Ellen née Rogers (died 1894). They were living at Mount Pottinger in 1861 and Academy Street, Belfast in 1870.

After graduating, Theodore became a teacher in London for two years before moving to Nottingham High School as an assistant schoolmaster in 1891. There he was form master to the Upper 2nd form and one of his pupils was the future novelist and poet, DH Lawrence. Theodore was a 3rd form master in 1902 and a 6th form master in 1905. He was ordained deacon at Southwell Minster, Nottingham on 18th December 1898 and was ordained priest at St George's Church, Nottingham the following year. In addition to his teaching career at Nottingham High School, he was curate of Burton Joyce-with-Bulcote, Nottinghamshire 1898–1902 and curate

David Herbert Lawrence (1885–1930), novelist, poet, playwright, critic and painter, was a controversial figure during his lifetime. His works explored many taboo issues and earned him many enemies and official persecution and censorship. When he died he was regarded by many as little more than a pornographer. However, EM Forster challenged this view and describing Lawrence as *the greatest imaginative novelist of our generation* (Lady Ottoline Morrell).

Nottingham High School is currently an independent day school for about 1,000 boys and girls. It was founded in 1513 as the Free School by Dame Agnes Mellers. Since 1868 the School has been on Waverley Mount, north of the city centre. Amongst its famous alumni are:

- Albert Ball VC DSO MC (1896–1917), a WW1 fighter pilot, who was at the School 1907–09 and after whom Ball's House is named.
- Ed Balls (born 1967), Labour politician and MP for Normanton 2005–10 and Morley and Outwood 2010–15.
- Geoff Hoon (born 1953), Labour politician and MP for Ashfield 1992–2010. He served as Defence Secretary, Transport Secretary, Leader of the House and Government Chief Whip.
- John Peake Knight (1828–86), a railway engineer credited with inventing the traffic light in 1868.
- Henry Garnet (1555–1606), Jesuit priest executed for his part in the Gunpowder Plot.
- Leslie Crowther CBE (1933–96), comedian, actor, TV presenter and game show host.
- Jesse Boot (1850–1931), 1st Baron Trent, transformed The Boots Company founded by his father into a national retailer.
- Kenneth Clarke (born 1940), Conservative politician and MP for Rushcliffe since 1970.

of St Augustine's, New Basford, Nottinghamshire 1902–07. In 1907 he became headmaster of Bentham Grammar School, Lancaster until 1913, when his wife became seriously ill and he resigned. He was appointed perpetual curate of St John's Church, Hutton Roof, near Kirkby Lonsdale, Westmoreland and curate-in-charge of Lupton. He was also scoutmaster at Hutton Roof. His wife died there and is buried in Hutton Roof Churchyard.

There may have been a church at Hutton Roof as early as the 13th century. Certainly churches were built there in 1616 and 1757. The current church was built in 1880–81.

Theodore volunteered for service in the Great War but was rejected initially due to his age. He persisted and undertook local ambulance classes and attempted to volunteer as a stretcher-bearer. He was commissioned in the Army Chaplains' Department as a temporary chaplain 4th class on 29th August 1916, aged fifty-three, and went to France soon afterwards. He was appointed temporary chaplain 4th class on 16th September. He underwent some basic military training at Étaples, near Boulogne, where he served with the Infantry Base Depots before being assigned to 8th Lincolnshire in December. He was also Padre to 8th Somerset Light Infantry, both battalions being in 63rd Brigade. However, his name does not appear on 63rd Brigade's nominal roll of officers at the end of March 1918, although another padre was shown under 4th Middlesex. Theodore was always about in the trenches, particularly at night, and adopted the catchphrase, *It's only me boys*. He filled a postman's sack with cigarettes, which he distributed to soldiers at the front.

Awarded the DSO for his actions at Oosttaverne, east of Wytschaete on 3rd August 1917, while under heavy fire and suffering a broken wrist. He volunteered to accompany a rescue party to release men trapped in mud the previous night in front of the enemy's outpost line. All the men were brought in except for one and he organised a party to rescue him. Hardy stayed with the wounded man, whom the stretcher-bearers could not release, for thirty-six hours in atrocious weather and under close range rifle fire, until he died. He collapsed with exhaustion shortly afterwards, LG 18th October 1917 and citation 7th March 1918.

Awarded the MC for his actions at Larch Wood, near Hill 60, Ypres in October 1917. He was passing on a light railway between Canada Street and Larch Wood tunnels when a gunner from an artillery battery shouted that they had a number of severely wounded men. Despite the enemy shelling, Theodore went to help with the aid of two stretcher-bearers (both awarded the MM), LG 17th December 1917 and citation 23rd April 1918. Theodore was also Mentioned in Sir Douglas Haig's Despatch dated 7th November 1917, LG 24th December 1917.

Awarded the VC for his actions on 5th April 1918 at Rossignol Wood and on 25th and 26th April 1918 at Bucquoy, LG 11th July 1918. There were four

The temporary bridge over the River Selle at Briastre where Theodore Hardy was wounded on 10th October 1918 and almost the same view today. Three buildings in the 1918 picture are arrowed in the modern picture. The original photograph was taken from an upstairs window in a house just out of shot on the right of the modern photograph.

No.2 Red Cross Hospital at Rouen.

Theodore Hardy's grave in St Sever Cemetery Extension.

separate recommendations for the VC. Theodore protested to his CO about them but was eventually persuaded to accept it. The VC was presented by the King at HQ Third Army at the chateau at Frohen-le-Grand, France on 9th August 1918. Theodore's daughter, Elizabeth, travelled to the ceremony in a car provided by General Byng, GOC Third Army. She was presented to the King, who spent several minutes speaking to her.

Theodore was appointed Honorary Chaplain to the King on 18th September and was offered the living of Caldbeck, near Carlisle; but he refused to leave the men until the war was over. On 10th October he was wounded by machine gun fire

Nottingham High School War Memorial.

The City of London School War Memorial.

Theodore's memorial plaque in St John's Church, Hutton Roof (Memorials to Valour).

in the thigh whilst crossing a temporary bridge over the River Selle at Briastre, exclaiming, *I've been hit, I'm sorry to be a nuisance*. He was evacuated to No.2 Red Cross Hospital, Rouen suffering from his wounds and severe fatigue. Pneumonia set in and he died on 18th October 1918. His daughter Elizabeth was at his side. He left effects valued at £739/16/0. He is buried in St Sever Cemetery Extension, Rouen (S V J 1). Six Rouen-based chaplains acted as pallbearers at his funeral, which was conducted by the Reverend Douglas Falkland Carey DSO. He is commemorated in a number of other places:

- A Green Plaque was dedicated at his birthplace on 27th June 2006 by Exeter City Council and Devon Armed Forces Charities. The plaque is on the corner of Barnfield and Southernhay East Roads, Exeter on the Southernhay side.
- Memorial plaque in Exeter Cathedral.
- Named on the City of London School War Memorial, Queen Victoria Street, London.
- Named on the Royal Commercial Travellers School War Memorial at Harrow Arts Centre (Elliott Hall), Uxbridge Road, Hatch End, Pinner, Middlesex.
- Named on the Nottingham High School War Memorial. The School also has Hardy's House in his memory.
- Plaque in the north aisle of Carlisle Cathedral, dedicated in August 1919.
- St John's Church, Hutton Roof, Kirby Lonsdale, Cumbria:

  - Memorial plaque in the Church.
  - Named on the Hutton Roof War Memorial in the churchyard.
  - Named on his wife's headstone in the churchyard.
- Named on a memorial to members of the Royal Army Chaplains' Department who died in the Great War (1914–20) in the chancel of the Royal Garrison Church of All Saints, Aldershot, Hampshire.
- A painting of Theodore's VC investiture by Terence Cuneo was unveiled at the Royal Army Chaplains' Department Depot at Bagshot, Surrey by Field Marshal Sir Richard Hull, Chief of the Defence Staff, on 31st May 1967.
- Department for Communities and Local Government commemorative paving stones were dedicated at the junction of Robin Lane and High Street, High Bentham, Yorkshire on 21st April 2018 and at Exeter War Memorial,

The Hutton Roof War Memorial in St John's Church churchyard (Memorials to Valour).

The Garrison Church of All Saints was built in 1863 in Gothic revival style. On 19th May 1914 King George V and Queen Mary attended Matins and in 1923 the King allowed 'Royal' to be added to the Church's name. In 1963 Queen Elizabeth II attended the centenary service. In the south porch is the 'Somme Cross', which commemorates members of 1st Division killed near High Wood in September 1916. 1st Division was based in Aldershot before the war. In 1927 it was brought back from France and was erected outside HQ 1st Division in Pennefather's Road, Aldershot. In January 1939 it was moved into the Royal Garrison Church to protect it from the elements.

The Military Cross was created on 28th December 1914 for officers of the rank of captain and below and warrant officers. In August 1916 bars were awarded for further acts of gallantry. In 1931 the MC was extended to majors and to members of the RAF for ground actions. In the 1993 honours review the Military Medal for other ranks was discontinued and the MC became the third level decoration for all ranks of the British Armed Forces for acts of gallantry on land.

Northernhay Gardens, Northernhay Gate, Exeter on 7th July 2018 to mark the centenary of his award.

In addition to the VC, DSO and MC he was awarded the British War Medal 1914–20 and Victory Medal 1914–19 with Mentioned-in-Despatches Oakleaf. The VC was presented on permanent loan to the Royal Army Chaplains' Department Museum in 1965 by his granddaughter, Miss Patricia Hastings Hardy. She bequeathed the VC to the Museum in her will in May 1995. The medals are held by The Museum of Army Chaplaincy, Amport House, Amport, Andover, Hampshire.

15883 LANCE CORPORAL JAMES HEWITSON
1/4th Battalion, The King's Own (Royal Lancaster Regiment)

James Hewitson was born on 15th October 1892 at Thwaite Farm, Coniston, Lancashire. His father, Matthew Hewitson (29th April 1855–28th July 1922), was born at New Hutton, near Kendal, Westmoreland. He married Margaret née Hayton (1855–29th July 1937), born at Kendal, Westmoreland, in 1883 at Kendal. She was a domestic cook at Hill Top, Hay & Hutton in Hay, Westmorland in 1881, working for the Brunskill family. He was a coach driver and farm labourer in 1881, working at Black Farm, Thursgill, Whinfell, Westmoreland for Richard Black. By 1891 they had moved to Thwaite Farm, Coniston and were still there in 1901 and 1911, by when he was a farm bailiff. He died at Waterhead, Coniston. Margaret was living at Boom Cragg, Coniston at the time of her death at Far End Farm, Coniston. James had two brothers:

- Harold Hewitson (15th June 1884–28th June 1958), born at Brathay Cottages, Brathay, Lancashire, was a farm labourer in 1901 living with his parents.

He married Helena Troughton (22nd September 1887–1956) on 23rd August 1909 at St George's, Kendal, Westmorland. He was a grocer's carter in 1911 and they were living at 10 Ash Street, Windermere, Westmorland. He died at 38 Limethwaite Road, Windermere. They had four children:

Mill Holme, New Hutton, where James' father was born in 1855.

- Horace Hewitson (1910–24th February 1956) married Frances Mamie Parker (born 1914) in 1935. She was born at Bootle, Cumberland. They were living at 7 Thornthwaite Road, Windermere at the time of his death there. They had four children – Alan Hewitson 1937, Derek Hewitson 1940, Ian Hewitson 1942 and JeGivan (sic) Hewitson 1947.
- Eric Hewitson (1912–28th January 1963) was a joiner in 1958. He was living at 38 Limethwaite Road, Windermere at the time of his death there.
- Cecil Hewitson (1914–15).
- Netta Hewitson (1924–5th April 2009) married Ivor Norman McLeod (2nd June 1925–5th December 1979) in 1945. He was born at West Derby, Lancashire. They were living at 35 Dale Avenue, Kendal at the time of his death. She died at Morecambe, Lancashire. They had three children – Malcolm McLeod 1948, Christine McLeod 1949 and Andrew McLeod 1965.

• Robert Hewitson (1887–90).

James' paternal grandfather, Robert Hewitson (c.1818–82), was an agricultural labourer. He married Mary née Winder (c.1829–1904) in 1850 at Kendal. They were living at Mill Holme, New Hutton in 1861 and 1871 and at North Lodge, Hay and Hutton in Hay in 1881. In addition to Matthew they had two other children:

- Elizabeth Hewitson (born October 1852).
- Robert Hewitson (1857–22nd July 1923) was a domestic servant living with his parents in 1881. Later he was a cattleman. He married Dorothy Wilson (1861–16th August 1946) in 1883. They were living at Undermillbeck, Westmorland in 1891 and at Low Fields, Barbon, Westmorland in 1901. They were living at Rose Cottage, Gawthorp, Dent, Yorkshire at their deaths. They had four children:
  - Robert Hewitson (1884–1966) married Mary E Fallowfield (c.1883–1954) in 1915.
  - George Arthur Hewitson (1888–1969) married Elizabeth A Nicholson (1890–1960) in 1913 and they had two children – Doris Hewitson 1915 and George A Hewitson 1923.

- ◦ Sarah Hewitson (born 1893) married Charles W Blenkhern at Sedburgh in 1918.
- ◦ Emily Hewitson (born 1896) married Robert H Johnson at Sedburgh in 1921 and they had two children – Norman J Hewitson 1921 and Dorothy M Hewitson 1924.

James' grandfather, James Hayton, was born at Brigsteer in 1822.

His maternal grandfather, James Hayton (October 1822–4th December 1913), born at Brigsteer, Westmorland, married Jane née Bell (c.1831–12th August 1911), born at Crosthwaite, Westmorland, on 9th May 1852 at Helsington, Westmorland. Jane had a daughter, Anne Bell, at Helsington in 1849. She was living with her grandparents, Leonard and Mary Clement, at Levens, Westmorland in 1851. James was an agricultural labourer and they were living at Helsington in 1861. They had moved to Brigsteer by 1881. Living with them at that time was a grandson, Ernest Hayton (born 1880), whose mother is unknown. Ernest was a carter in 1901 on the farm of William Dixon, Hayclose Lane, New Hutton, Westmorland. By 1891 James and Jane had moved to Fountain Head, Helsington. By 1901 he was a general labourer and they were living at Kell House Cottage, Brigsteer. In 1911 they were living at Plumtree Cottage, Brigsteer. In addition to Margaret they had four other children:

- Jane Hayton (1852–1922) had a son, Frank Hayton, in 1882. She married Joseph Lamb (c.1854–99), a woodcutter, who was born at Sawley, Lancashire. They had five children including – Anne Lamb 1884, James Lamb 1887, Edwin Lamb 1889 and Jessie Lamb 1893. Jane married John Cookson (1849–1906) in 1900. He was born at Threlkeld, Cumberland. John was a beer housekeeper in 1901 and they were living at 20 Summer Hill, Kendal. He died before 1911, by when she was a laundress living with her daughter, Jessie, at Storrs Cottage, Storrs Park, Undermillbeck, Westmorland.
- Mary Hayton (1858–1915) was a monthly nurse. In 1891 she was living with her parents. By 1901 she was employed by Joseph Altman at Boundary House Farm, Helsington and in 1911 by Thomas Leeming, a farmer, at High Chambers, Levens Helsington. She never married.
- Elizabeth Hayton (1863–1919) was living with her parents in 1911. She never married.
- James Hayton (1866–1944) married Jane Eccles (1866–1936) in 1889. He was an agricultural labourer and they were living at Plumtree Cottage, Brigsteer in 1891 and at Brow House, Brigsteer in 1901, by when he was a gamekeeper. They

Coniston was a farming village and expanded considerably to serve copper and slate mines. It became popular in Victorian times as a holiday destination. The poet John Ruskin (1819–1900) popularised the village and is buried in St Andrew's Churchyard there. The Ruskin Museum was established in 1901. In the 1950s Donald Campbell broke four world water speed records on Coniston Water. He was killed making another attempt in 1967, when *Bluebird K7* crashed at 470 kph. His body and *Bluebird* were recovered in 2001 and he was buried in the new graveyard at Coniston. A wing of the Ruskin Museum now houses the fully restored *Bluebird*. Most of the village is powered by a hydro-electric scheme.

were still there in 1911 but their daughters Margaret and Annie were living with his parents. They had eight children including – Winifred Hayton 1890, James Hayton 1892 (enlisted in the Royal Marines Light Infantry (Plymouth Division) on 28th August 1911 (15425)), Dorothy Mary Hayton 1896, Jane Eccles Hayton 1898, Margaret Hayton 1900, Annie Elizabeth Hayton 1903 and William Allen Hayton 1906.

James Hewitson receives his VC from the King at HQ First Army on 8th August 1918.

James was educated at Coniston Church of England School and then worked on the land as a timber feller around Coniston. He enlisted on 17th November 1914 in 8th King's Own and went to France on 27th September 1915. He was wounded three times, later transferred to 1/4th Battalion and was promoted lance corporal. **Awarded the VC for his actions at Givenchy on 26th April 1918, LG 28th June 1918.** Promoted corporal later in 1918. The VC was presented by the King at Headquarters First Army, Ranchicourt, France on 8th August 1918. He transferred to the Class Z Army Reserve on 2nd March 1919.

James Hewitson married Mary Elizabeth 'Liza' Dugdale (8th May 1890–2nd June 1971) on 11th June 1919 at Coniston Parish Church. She was born at Wray, Lancashire and was a general servant in a hotel at Coniston in 1911. They had a daughter:

- Dorothy May Hewitson (8th March 1920–28th July 1989) married Reginald Dodd (8th August 1919–October 1985) in 1938 at Ulverston. They had four children:
  - Richard J Dodd (born 1938).
  - Brian Dodd (1941–42).
  - Margaret E Dodd (born 1946).
  - Barbara Dodd (born 1951) is understood to have married George D Tarr (born 1951) in 1971 and they had three children – Anthony John Tarr 1972, Lee Jonathan Tarr 1974 and Deana Elizabeth Tarr 1977.

Mary's father, Lawrence/Laurance Dugdale (1853–6th June 1918) was born at Hawkshead, Lancashire. He married Grace Gilbanks née Clark (1862–1903), born at Langdale, Westmorland, in 1883 at Kendal. Lawrence was a farmer and they were living at Belle Grange Farm, Claife, Lancashire in 1891. By 1911 he was a labourer and they were living at Colthouse, Hawkshead, where he subsequently died. In addition to Mary they had another daughter:

James was treated at Tyrwhitt House on the outskirts of Leatherhead, Surrey. The house was taken over by the charity Combat Stress in 1946 and continues to treat ex-service personnel and rehabilitate them.

- Edith May Dugdale (11th October 1894–25th December 1974) married Herbert Grisedale (1893–1963) in 1932. She was living at 5 Lane End Cottages, Elterwater, Great Langdale, Cumbria at the time of her death there. They had a daughter, Mary E Grisedale (born 1934), who married Philip D Rice (20th November 1932–1973) in 1955 and they had two children – Elizabeth A Rice 1955 and David C Rice 1956. Mary married Harold Corr (born 1939) in 1978.

After the war James worked as a road repairer for ten years but he suffered from neurasthenia. He was treated in a hospital near Coniston 1931–33 and later at a nerve

The City of London Lunatic Asylum at Stone, Kent became the City of London Mental Hospital in 1924 and Stone House Hospital in 1948, when it was taken over by the National Health Service. It was built between 1862 and 1866 for the London Commissioners in Lunacy to provide for destitute mentally ill patients from the London area. It accommodated 220 patients initially and the grounds included a working farm. The Hospital was expanded in 1874, 1878 and 1885. The poet and composer, Ivor Gurney, spent the last fifteen years of his life there and died at the Hospital in 1937. It closed in 2007.

hospital at Tyrwhitt House, Leatherhead, Surrey, before being held at Stone House Mental Hospital, Dartford, Kent for over sixteen years. He had an operation to remove shrapnel from his spine and another in 1954 to remove shrapnel from his shoulder. He was then able to do simple work, earning 2/6d per hour cutting hedges, laying out rose gardens and cleaning out pigsties, but could only work a few hours per week. Mary lived without him for over eighteen years and made ends meet by taking in washing and selling garden produce.

Four King's Own (Royal Lancaster Regiment) VCs at a reunion at Bowerham Barracks, Lancaster in 1932. From the left – Albert Halton, James Hewitson and Tom Mayson with Harry Christian seated (King's Own Royal Regiment).

James attended a number of VC reunions – the VC Garden Party at Buckingham Palace on 26th June 1920, the VC Dinner at the Royal Gallery of the House of Lords, London on 9th November 1929, the VC Centenary Celebrations at Hyde Park, London on 26th June 1956 and the first three VC & GC Association Reunions at the Café Royal, London on 24th July 1958, 7th July 1960 and 18th July 1962.

James Hewitson died at Stanley Hospital, Ulverston, Lancashire on 2nd March 1963 and is buried in St Andrew's Churchyard, Coniston. He is commemorated in a number of other places:

James and Mary Hewitson are buried in St Andrew's Churchyard, Coniston.

- James Hewitson VC Memorial Shield was awarded annually by the Royal British Legion (Lancashire County) to a branch in the County but in 2008 it was gifted to the King's Own Royal Regiment Museum, where his tunic and cap are also held.
- Memorial plaque in St Andrew's Church, Coniston.
- A Department for Communities and Local Government commemorative paving stone was dedicated at St Andrew's Church, Coniston on 26th April 2018 to mark the centenary of his award.
- A Matchless 500 motorcycle that he bought in 1926 for £47/17/6 is displayed in the Ruskin Museum, Yewdale Road, Coniston.

In addition to the VC he was awarded the 1914–15 Star, British War Medal 1914–20, Victory Medal 1914–19, George VI Coronation Medal 1937 and Elizabeth II Coronation Medal 1953. His medals are owned privately.

SECOND LIEUTENANT BASIL ARTHUR HORSFALL
3rd, attached 11th Battalion, The East Lancashire Regiment

Basil Horsfall was born on 4th October 1887 at Kelvin Gerve, Colombo, Ceylon (now Sri Lanka). His father, Charles William Horsfall (4th February 1844–15th November 1921), was born in Stepney, Middlesex and went to Ceylon in the 1860s. He became one of the pioneers of the tea and coffee industry there. Charles married Maria Henrietta née Layard (18th July 1847–14th June 1935), of Florence, Kandy, Ceylon, on 16th April 1869. She was a niece of Sir Henry Austen Layard, the explorer and archaeologist who discovered the ruins of Nineveh. They were visitors in the home of Henry and Charlotte Frood, his brother-in-law and sister, at 11 Portsdown Road, Paddington, London in 1881. Charles returned to Ceylon and was living at Darlington, Polwatte Road, Colombo in 1918. He died in Ceylon, leaving effects valued at £3,428/1/6. Maria was living at 16 Princess Road, Branksome, Poole, Dorset at the time of her death, leaving effects valued at £364/3/3. Basil had seven siblings:

Colombo, near the harbour at around the turn of the 19th century (Lankapura.com).

- Harold Charles Horsfall (7th March 1871–5th November 1945) was living at 22 St Catherine's Road, Southbourne, Bournemouth at the time of his death at Boscombe Hospital, Bournemouth.
- Winifred Marie Horsfall (8th May 1875–1966) was living with her paternal grandparents in 1881 and with her uncle, Andrew Campbell Knox Lock, in 1891. She died unmarried at Christchurch, Hampshire.

Florence Villa at Kandy, Basil's mother's home before she married.

Sir Austen Henry Layard GCB PC (1817–94) was born in Paris, France. His father worked in the Ceylon Civil Service. His uncle, Benjamin Austen, a London solicitor and close friend of Benjamin Disraeli, employed Austen for six years. He left to seek an appointment in the Ceylon Civil Service and travelled through Asia but gave up the idea and was employed by the British Ambassador in Constantinople in various unofficial diplomatic missions in European Turkey. In 1845 he explored the ruins of Assyria, his curiosity having been aroused in his eastern travels by the ruins of Nimrud and other antiquities. He carried out excavations at Kuyunjik, which was identified as Ninevah, and Nimrud until 1847 then returned to England and published *Nineveh and Its Remains*. He returned to Constantinople as attaché to the embassy and in August 1849 commenced a second expedition to investigate the ruins of Babylon and the mounds of southern Mesopotamia. His record of this expedition, *Discoveries in the Ruins of Nineveh and Babylon*, was published in 1853. His finds form the majority of the Assyrian collection in the British Museum, of which he became a trustee in 1866. Austen was elected Liberal Member of Parliament for Aylesbury, Buckinghamshire in 1852. He went to the Crimea during the war and was a member of the committee appointed to inquire into its conduct. He was not re-elected in 1857 and went to India to investigate the causes of the Mutiny. He returned to contest York unsuccessfully in 1859 but was elected at Southwark in 1860. He was Under-Secretary for Foreign Affairs 1861–66. He resigned his seat in 1869 and was sent as envoy extraordinary to Madrid. In 1877 he was appointed Ambassador in Constantinople and retired in 1880 to Venice. He died in London and is buried in Dorset.

- John Edmund Bertram Layard Horsfall (born 1879), known as Bertram, was living with his paternal grandparents in 1881. He was a labour agent, living at Vryheid, KwaZulu-Natal, South Africa when he was initiated as a Freemason into St George Lodge on 13th October 1917. Bertram had at least one son, Peter Anthony Layard Horsfall (29th July 1926–21st July 1999), who was born in South Africa and was educated at Michaelhouse boarding school, Balgowan Valley, KwaZulu-Natal and Witwatersrand University, where he studied medicine. He completed his studies at Johannesburg Hospital and filled a number of appointments:

  House officer at Salisbury, Rhodesia 1950–51.

  Senior house officer, Cardiff, Glamorgan.

  Registrar at the Hospital for Tropical Diseases, University College Hospital, London.

  Tottenham Chest Clinic. London.

  Medical officer at the Jane Furse Memorial Hospital, Eastern Transvaal 1960–63.

  Senior chest physician, Grantham Hospital, Hong Kong, where he was also President of the British Medical Association.

  Peter married Edith in 1951 (she was also a doctor) and they had two children – David Horsfall and Monique Horsfall. He married Irene later. He retired in 1994 to Vancouver, Canada, occupying his time in ornithology and recorded over 1,100 species.

- Christabel Grace Horsfall (born 1882 in Ceylon).
- Edward Francis Horsfall (14th April 1883–1960) was a planter in Ceylon, where he served in the Ceylon Mounted Rifles 31st August 1909–2nd February 1915 as a trooper. He applied for a commission on 30th April 1915 and was commissioned in 3rd East Lancashire on probation on 21st May 1915, confirmed on 9th January 1916. Edward fell while training troops and damaged his knee. A medical board at the Military Hospital, Devonport on 4th September found he was unfit for service for two months and sent him on leave until 3rd November. A medical board at Colchester that day found he was unfit for General Service for three weeks but was fit for light duties. He was declared fit for service on 23rd November. Edward went to France on 12th July 1916. He suffered from trench fever and was wounded in the left thigh at Arras on 11th May 1917, while serving with 1st East Lancashire. He was evacuated from Calais to Dover on 15th May for treatment at Guy's Hospital, London. Medical boards at Caxton Hall, Westminster, London on 30th July and 13th September found him unfit for General Service for five and three-quarter months and four months respectively. He was sent to Peverell Park Convalescent Hospital, Plymouth on 20th September. A medical board on 20th October found him unfit for General Service for three months but fit for light duties and he was granted leave until 15th November. He was declared fit for General Service and return to 3rd East Lancashire at Saltburn, Yorkshire at Middlesborough on 24th December. Edward embarked at Southampton on 15th April 1918 and disembarked at Salonika on 3rd May, where he was attached to 9th South Staffordshire, joining in the field on 10th May. He suffered from diarrhoea from 15th June, reported sick on 27th June and was admitted to 86th Field Ambulance and 21st Stationary Hospital, where it was diagnosed as amoebic dysentery. He had suffered from it five times in Ceylon in the period 1902–15 and also had malaria in 1911 and dengue in 1913. He was admitted to 42nd General Hospital on 3rd July, where it was concluded that the recurrence of dysentery was not caused by his military service but acute field conditions had contributed towards it. He transferred to a convalescent home on 17th July and returned to his unit on 1st August. However, the dysentery returned on 4th August and he was admitted to 66th Field Ambulance and No.31 Casualty Clearing Station later the same day. He was transferred to 42nd General Hospital on 6th August and embarked on HMHS *Goorkha* on 28th September and disembarked in Malta for transfer to Imtarfa Hospital on 3rd October. A medical board there on 10th October 1918 found him unfit for service for three months and recommended he be transferred home. He embarked at Valletta on 25th December for Liverpool, arriving on 4th January 1919 and was admitted to 3rd London General Hospital, Wandsworth the same day. A medical board there on 27th January found him unfit for any service for one month and he transferred to the Dysentery Convalescent Hospital, Barton, New Milton, Hampshire on 4th February. A medical board there on 11th February found him fit for service after three weeks leave. He was posted

to the Officers Wing, Repatriation Camp, Winchester and sailed for Ceylon on SS *City of Exeter* on 13th July and was demobilised on arrival on 3rd August 1919, retaining the rank of lieutenant. Edward married May Olive Dempster (1st May 1891–1972) on 13th January 1919 at St Saviour, Alexandra Park, London. They were living at The Bungalow, Newton Ferrers, Devon in 1925. Their address in England, when sailing for Ceylon in 1939, was The Three Gables, West Mersea, Essex. He died at Aldershot, Hampshire and she at Richmond upon Thames, Surrey. They had three children – Elizabeth Horsfall 1921, Basil Charles Horsfall 1922 and a girl with initial S in 1926. Basil Charles Horsfall joined the Army on 29th December 1942 (295823) and transferred to the Army Air Corps on 22nd October 1943.

- Cuthbert William Horsfall (24th May 1884–12th July 1979) was a bank clerk. He married Mary Augusta Bown Jeneway (1889–1967) in 1923 at St Martin in the Fields, London. Cuthbert was appointed a clerk, special class at the Ministry of Labour (LG 9th May 1933). She died at Canterbury, Kent. He was living at 5 River Court, Chartham, Canterbury at the time of his death, leaving effects valued at £16,836. They had two children:
    - Dawn W Horsfall (born 1925) married Martinus H Slinger in 1946 at Brentford, Middlesex. He was possibly born on 23rd April 1910 at Rotterdam, Netherlands.
    - Marion SB Horsfall (born 1927) married Victor R Mayland (born 1918) in 1947. They had three children – Sarah D Mayland 1950, Andrew CL Mayland 1953 and James MW Mayland 1962.
- Godfrey Lock Horsfall (23rd November 1885–9th December 1967) was educated at Sir William Borlase School, Marlow, Buckinghamshire and became a tea and rubber planter in Ceylon. He served in the Ceylon Mounted Rifles as a trooper from 16th November 1914. He enlisted in 16th Lancers (GS 4691) on 13th December 1914, joined at the Curragh and was posted to 8th Reserve Cavalry Brigade on 31st December, described as 5′ 9½″ tall, weighing 153 lbs, with an enlarged left testicle. He applied for a commission in 2/1st Essex Yeomanry on 10th May 1915, giving his address as c/o Gordon Roberts, Eastdene, Halstead, Essex. He was commissioned in the Essex Yeomanry on 26th June 1915 and later transferred to 18th (Queen Mary's Own) Hussars. He was promoted lieutenant on 1st July 1917. Godfrey fractured a clavicle in France on 4th April 1917 and was evacuated from Calais on 9th April arriving at Dover next day on SS *Newhaven*. A medical board at Caxton Hall on 1st May found he would be fit for service after one month, recommended three weeks leave and then to rejoin at Aldershot. He received a leave of absence form until 22nd May and then reported back for onward passage to France. However, this conflicted with previous instructions given to him to return immediately and he was censured for the mistake. Godfrey married Muriel Gordon Roberts (born 1893) in 1917 at Halstead, Essex. He was a tea planter at Agratenna Estate, Badulla, Ceylon in 1924 and later at Oonoosalaya

Estate, Cotmale, Ceylon, where he subsequently died. They had two children – Michael B Horsfall 1919 and Helen R Horsfall 1923.

Basil's paternal grandfather, John Horsfall (c.1814–85), was born at Putney, Surrey, and worked for HM Customs. He married Charlotte née Vickress (c.1817–92), born at Hackney, London, on 16th April 1842 at Islington. They were living at 19 Cottage Grove, Mile End Old Town, London in 1844. By 1851 they had moved to 4 Medina Villas, Dalston Lane, Hackney, London and in 1881 they were living at St Agnes, Holdenhurst, near Christchurch, Hampshire. Charlotte was still living there in 1891. They both died at Christchurch. In addition to Charles they had eight other children:

- Charlotte Anne Horsfall (4th September 1845–27th March 1907) married Henry Thomas Frood (1845–9th April 1927) on 1st August 1872 at St Saviour's, Paddington. He was a Professor of Music in 1881 and they were living at 11 Portsdown Road, Paddington. She died at Horton Asylum, Epsom, Surrey. He died at 21 Willifield Way, Golders Green, Middlesex. They had three daughters – Dorothea Frood 1874, Sybil Frood 1876 and Phyllis Frood 1886.
- Maria Louisa Horsfall (1st June 1847–1931) married Hermann Friedrick Lorch (c.1849–6th December 1891) in 1868 at Lewisham, London. He was born in Germany and was a teacher of foreign languages in 1881, when they were living with his parents-in-law. He was a merchant's clerk in 1891 and they were living at 5 Queen's Road, Great Crosby, Liverpool, Lancashire, where he died later that

Horton Hospital, formerly Horton Asylum, a large psychiatric hospital built for London County Council, opened in 1902, the second of five mental institutions on the Horton Estate, known as the Epsom Cluster. During both two World Wars it was taken over as a military hospital. Horton was particularly noted for pioneering work on music therapy and the treatment of advanced syphilis and paedophilia. The hospital closed in 1997, although some elements remained open for longer. It was sold in 2002 and most of the buildings were demolished, although some were incorporated into a new village development on the site. By 2009 most of the site had been redeveloped into housing and apartments.

year. She died at Dartford, Kent. They had five children – Charles Hermann Lorch 1869, John H Lorch 1870, Theresa Maria Dorothea Lorch 1882, Bernard Sebastian Lorch 1885 and Joseph Anthony Lorch 1888.

- John Francis Rogers Horsfall (born 15th January 1849).
- Frederick James Horsfall (16th April 1851–1932) was a tea merchant in Ceylon. He married Susannah Rachel Packer (1849–1932). In 1891 they were living with his mother at St Agnes, Holdenhurst, near Christchurch. He was described as a tea merchant (retired Ceylon planter) and Susannah was her husband's assistant. By 1901 he was a tea and coffee dealer and they were living at Bournemouth, Hampshire. They both died at Dartford, Kent. They had a son, Wilfred J Horsfall, in 1877.
- Anne Elizabeth Horsfall (born and died 1853).
- Emily Augusta Horsfall (1854–84).
- Marian Frances Horsfall (3rd June 1856–16th June 1915) went to the West Indies, where she married Frederick Stephen Chesters (1845–1916) in c.1878. He was a Wesleyan Minister, born at Stoke on Trent, Staffordshire. They were living at 11 Barkham Street, Wainfleet St Mary, Lincolnshire in 1891 and at Chapel Street, Dawley Magna, Shropshire in 1901. She died at 71 Widmore Road, Bromley, London and he at Bromley, Kent. They had eight children – Walter Horsfall Chesters 1879, Frank Chesters 1882, Eric Horsfall Chesters 1883, Lilian H Chesters 1885, Albert Stephen Chesters 1887, May Chesters 1890, Hilda Chesters 1893 and Donald Frederick Chesters 1897.
- Ida Adelaide Horsfall (born c.1861 at Baden-Württemberg, Germany) was a governess in 1881.

His maternal grandfather, General William Twisleton Layard (4th August 1813–18th January 1891) was born at Kalutara, Ceylon. He was commissioned as an ensign by purchase in the Ceylon Rifles on 22nd February 1833 and was promoted lieutenant by purchase 22nd November 1836, captain 16th August 1839, major by purchase 28th September 1847, brevet lieutenant colonel 28th November 1854, lieutenant colonel 12th June 1859, colonel 1st March 1860, major general 6th March 1868, lieutenant general 1st October 1877 and retired as honorary general 1st July 1881. William married Catherine Anne née Sargent (1817–18th January 1898) on 11th August 1835 in Ceylon. She was born in Quebec, Canada. They were living at Oxford Street, Cheltenham, Gloucestershire in 1871 and at Highfield House, Tiverton, Devon in 1881. They also had a residence at Friedland, Southfields, Wandsworth, London, where he died, leaving effects valued at £5,207/5/8. She was living at 12 Wimbledon Park Road, Southfields, Wandsworth, London at the time of her death, leaving effects valued at £564/14/8. In addition to Maria they had eight other children:

- Matilda Layard (11th October 1836–4th October 1888) was born in England and married William Joseph Gorman (c.1826–1906) on 12th February 1856. His death was registered at St George, Hanover Square, London. They had at least four children – Kate MM Gorman 1859, Norah Gorman 1865, Sybil Gorman 1866 and Aileen Gorman c.1869.
- Charles Edmund Layard (18th September 1838–10th January 1920) was commissioned from the Royal Military College, Sandhurst in the 15th Regiment of Foot as an ensign, without purchase, on 8th July 1856. He was promoted lieutenant 28th May 1858, captain 3rd August 1866, major 15th August 1877, lieutenant colonel 6th September 1881, colonel 6th September 1885 and major general 6th September 1887. He married Euphemia 'Effie' EN Thomas (c.1845–8th March 1884) on 4th November 1871. She was born at Newtown Park, Black Rock, Dublin, Ireland and her death was registered at Ecclesall Bierlow, Yorkshire. They had two sons – William Layard 1873 and Edward Layard 1875. Charles married Jane 'Jennie' Hume Annesley née Anderson (c.1845–6th May 1901) on 9th April 1889 at All Saints, Paddington. She was the daughter of Sir George William Anderson KCB (1791–1867) and widow of Lieutenant Colonel Robert Michael Smith Annesley (1825–87), whom she married in 1866 at Kensington. Sir George entered the Bombay civil service in 1806, mainly on judicial duties until 1831, when he took administrative and political charge of the southern Mahratta districts. He framed the laws, known as the 'Bombay Code of 1827'. He was appointed to the Indian Law Commission 1835–38 and was then appointed to the Council of the Governor of Bombay. In April 1841 he became senior member of the Council to the Governor of Bombay until June 1842. He retired from the Indian Civil Service in February 1844. He was appointed Governor of Mauritius June 1849–October 1850 before transferring to the Government of Ceylon, carrying out reforms to the judicial system in both places. His health failed and he resigned in 1855. He married three times and had fifteen children. Jennie was living at Valentia Lodge, Bedford in 1887. She died at Bedford. Charles married Laura Susan Murray née Prestage (1869–1st May 1951) in 1914 at Bedford. She was the widow of Charles Stewart Murray (1858–4th May 1903), whom she married on 4th January 1892 at Barrackpore, India. They had three children – Archibald Alastair Stewart Murray 1892, Alastair Donald Stewart Murray 1898 and Charles Stewart Murray 1900. Charles was living at 16 Rothsay Place, Bedford at the time of his death, leaving effects valued at £4,004/7/11. Laura was living at St George's Retreat, Ditchling, Sussex when she died, leaving effects valued at £8,461/5/4.
- Catherine Anne Layard (5th March 1840–23rd February 1906) married Andrew Campbell Knox Lock (11th April 1827–16th April 1896). He was born in Scotland and was commissioned as an ensign in the Ceylon Rifle Regiment on 28th September 1847. He was promoted lieutenant on 8th June 1849, transferred to 3rd West India Regiment on 9th July 1850 and to 50th Regiment of Foot on

25th October 1850. He was promoted captain on 12th August 1853 and served in the Crimea 1854–55 at the Battles of Alma, Inkerman and the Siege of Sevastopol, including as Deputy Assistant Quartermaster General 8th November 1855–30th June 1856 (MID, Crimean Medal with three clasps, Knight of the Legion of Honour, Medjidie 5th Class and Turkish Medal). Appointed brevet major 2nd November 1855 and brevet lieutenant colonel 10th February 1865. He served in the New Zealand War 1864–66 in the Actions at Rangiawhia, Nukumara and Kakaramea (MID, LG 12th April 1865 and Medal). He was promoted major 10th November 1868, lieutenant colonel 12th August 1874 and brevet colonel 1st October 1877. On 21st June 1879 he was appointed Commander of Regimental District No.4, Lancaster and went onto half pay on 21st June 1884. He retired on 1st March 1888 as honorary major general. They were living at Over Hall, Colne Engain, Halstead, Essex in 1891. He died at 12 Wimbledon Park Road, Southfields, Wandsworth, leaving effects valued at £12,409/9/10. She was living at Park Gate, Castle Hedingham, Essex at the time of her death at Sudbury, Suffolk, leaving effects valued at £10,863/4/9.

- Emily Louisa Layard (15th May 1842–August 1894) married Dr William Carden Roe (30th November 1833–8th October 1922) on 1st March 1864. He was born at Loran Park, Roscrea, Co Tipperary, Ireland. They lived at Loran Park, Roscrea and at Shackenhurst, West Overcliffe Drive, Westbourne, Bournemouth, Hampshire. She died at Weymouth, Dorset. He died at Christchurch, Hampshire, leaving effects valued at £105,368/5/7 (£4.9M in 2018). They had four children – Annie Kathleen Roe 1865, Margaretta E Roe 1870, William Carden Robinson Robert Roe 1872 and Emily Georgina Roe 1875.
- Elizabeth Anna Layard (26th June 1845–6th March 1863).
- Frances Grace Layard (14th September 1846–1932) married Philip Arthur Templer (died 23rd August 1899) on 1st September 1866 in Ceylon. She died at Tonbridge, Kent. They had three children – Ethel Katherine Templer 1867, Cyril Frank Templer 1869 and Agnes Irene Templer 1871.
- Arthur Griffith Layard (1st September 1855–29th August 1941) was a tea planter in Ceylon. He married Margaret Capel Carnegie Arbuthnott (c.1858–1918) on 15th November 1894 at Balnamoon, Angus, Scotland. She died at Tonbridge, Kent. He was living at Lanka, Molyneux Park, Tunbridge Wells, Kent at the time of his death, leaving effects valued at £6,507/2/-. They had three children – twins Arthur Frank Capel Layard and Margaret Capel Layard 1895 and Katherine Mary Layard 1898.
- Edith Mary Layard (22nd June 1862–23rd October 1935) never married and was living at Kinniedon, Silverdale Road, Eastbourne, Sussex at the time of her death at 8 The Avenue, Eastbourne, leaving effects valued at £914/0/1.

Basil was educated at:

- St Thomas's College, Colombo, Ceylon.
- Sir William Borlase's Grammar School, Great Marlow, Buckinghamshire May 1903–July 1905. He was an all-round sportsman, excelling at cricket.

After school he worked for Barclay's Bank at 54 Lombard Street, London before returning to Ceylon, where he became a rubber planter on the Mundamani Estate. Later he was an accountant with the Public Works Department of Ceylon, rising to financial assistant by the outbreak of war. Basil became a Freemason, being Initiated into the Sphinx Lodge (No.107) of the Irish Constitution, on 19th April 1915, at 27 Pedris Road, Colombo, Ceylon.

Basil joined the Ceylon Engineer Volunteers on 2nd September 1912 and qualified in signalling and searchlights

St Thomas' College was founded by the first Bishop of Colombo, the Right Reverend James Chapman, an Old Etonian. His vision was to build a college and cathedral for the new Diocese of Colombo. It opened on 3rd February 1851 as the College of St Thomas the Apostle to train Christian clergy and to make children good Christian citizens. The College was originally at Mutwal, near Colombo harbour. In 1852 Bishop Chapman laid the foundation stone of the chapel, which became Christ Church Cathedral when it was dedicated on 21st September 1854. In 1918, the school moved from the dusty environs of Mutwal to Mount Lavinia. It is now a selective entry Anglican boy's school, one of the most prestigious in the country. It has educated four Sri Lankan Prime Ministers, including its first.

Barclay's Bank at 54 Lombard Street, London.

Sir William Borlase's Grammar School was founded in 1624 by Sir William Borlase in memory of his son, Henry Borlase MP, who died that year. The free school was to teach twenty-four poor children to write, read and cast accounts. Part of the School still occupies the original flint building seen here. There have been various building additions to cater for expansion over the centuries.

No.7 Officer Cadet Battalion was established at Fermoy, Ireland. East Barracks was established there in 1806 and in 1809 West Barracks was built. In total they accommodated 183 officers, 2,816 men and 152 horses. By the 1830s Fermoy was the largest military establishment in Ireland. The town of Fermoy gained significant economic benefit from the expansion.

for coastal defence. When war broke out the unit was mobilised. He travelled to England on leave but was unable to gain clearance to join the Army because of the important work carried out by the unit in Ceylon. In February 1915 he was admitted to hospital to have his appendix removed. On 8th July 1916 he resigned and returned to England, where he applied for a commission on 15th August and enlisted in 5th London Regiment (London Rifle Brigade) at Whitehall, London on 4th September (5962 and 303887), described as 5′ 11″ tall and weighing 146 lbs. Next day he was posted to No.7 Officer Cadet Battalion at Fermoy, Co Cork, Ireland and was commissioned in 3rd East Lancashire on 19th December 1916. He joined the unit at Efford Camp, Plymouth and from 13th January 1917 he was attached to 11th Battalion in France.

On 11th May 1917 he received gunshot wounds to the right arm and buttock at Roeux, near Arras and was treated at St John's Ambulance Brigade Hospital, Étaples from 13th May. On 16th May he was evacuated to Britain, where he was treated at the Royal Free Hospital, London. A medical board at Caxton Hall on 25th June found him unfit for General Service for three months but fit for light duties after three weeks leave, which was granted until 16th July. He then joined 3rd East Lancashire at Saltburn and Marske-by-the-Sea, Yorkshire. A medical board at Furness Auxiliary Hospital, Harrogate (JRR Tolkien was also treated there) on 18th August found him fit for General Service and he rejoined 3rd East Lancashire. He returned to France on 24th October. **Awarded the VC for his actions on 27th March 1918 between Moyenneville and Ablainzevelle, France, LG 22nd May 1918.** Basil was killed during his VC action and is commemorated on Bay 6 of the Arras Memorial, France. He left effects valued at £156/9/5. The VC was presented to his parents by the acting Governor of Ceylon at the Galle Face in Colombo, Ceylon on 16th August 1918. Basil is commemorated in a number of other places:

- The Department for Communities and Local Government decided to provide a commemorative paving stone at the birthplace of every Great War Victoria Cross recipient in the United Kingdom. For the 145 born overseas, including Australia, Belgium, Canada, China, Denmark, Egypt, France, Germany, India, Iraq, Japan, Nepal, Netherlands, New Zealand, Pakistan, South Africa, Sri Lanka, Ukraine and United States of America, there are individual commemorative stones at the National Memorial Arboretum, Alrewas, Staffordshire. They were unveiled by the British Prime Minister, David Cameron MP, and Sergeant Johnson Beharry VC on 5th March 2015.
- Regimental Victoria Cross Memorial, Blackburn Cathedral, Lancashire.

Basil was treated at the St John's Ambulance Brigade Hospital, Étaples after being wounded on 11th May 1917.

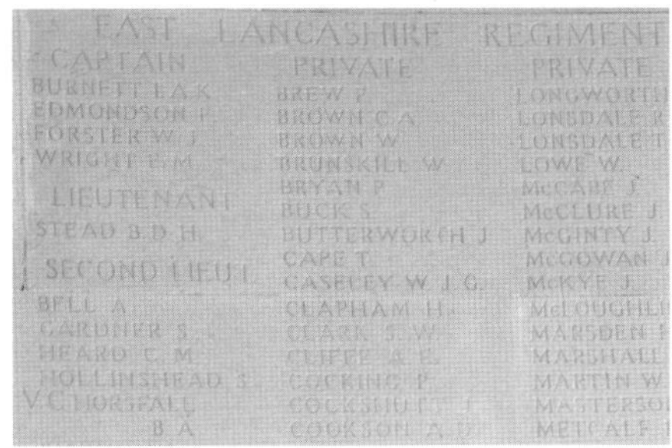

Basil's name (bottom left) on the East Lancashire Regiment panel of the Arras Memorial.

The London General Institution for the Gratuitous Cure of Malignant Diseases opened on 17th April 1828 at 16 Greville Street, Hatton Garden. Initially it was a dispensary but soon had thirty beds with free treatment for all. Queen Victoria became its patroness in 1837 and in recognition of its work during the cholera epidemic it became the Royal Free Hospital. In 1844 it moved to Grays' Inn Road and became a teaching hospital in 1877. It was the only hospital to accept female medical students before 1947. A new Helena Building, completed in 1915, was immediately requisitioned by the War Office and became the Royal Free Military Hospital for Officers. The military section had 150 beds, each with a down quilt covered in plain green or blue silk. On 5th July 1944 the Victoria Wing was severely damaged by a V1 flying bomb. There were few casualties but 120 beds were lost and 140 patients had to be evacuated. On 9th February 1945 a V2 rocket destroyed the end of the Laboratory Wing in Hunter Street. The Hospital closed in 1974. In 1978 a new Royal Free Hospital, in Pond Street, was opened by the Queen on its 150th anniversary.

The memorial plaque outside Sir William Borlase's Grammar School.

The East Lancashire Regiment Victoria Cross Memorial in Blackburn Cathedral.

- Named on the war memorial in the chapel at Sir William Borlase's Grammar School, West Street, Marlow, Berkshire. There is also a memorial plaque outside.
- A Department for Communities and Local Government commemorative VC paving stone was dedicated at the Accrington Pals Memorial, Church of St James, Cannon Street on 27th March 2018 to mark the centenary of his award.

In addition to the VC he was awarded the British War Medal 1914–20 and Victory Medal 1914–19. The VC and medals were offered for sale by Spink's on 1st March 1982 for £9,750, together with a wealth of documentation. The VC group was loaned to Blackburn Museum for a period for a display of artefacts relating of Basil Horsfall VC and Harold Ervine-Andrews VC. The group was returned to the Queen's Lancashire Regiment Museum about 2002. His medals are held by the Lancashire Infantry Museum, Fulwood Barracks, Watling Street Road, Preston, Lancashire.

889958 CORPORAL JOSEPH THOMAS KAEBLE
22nd Battalion, (French Canadians), Canadian Expeditionary Force

Joseph Kaeble was born on 5th May 1893 at St Moïse, Matane County, Quebec, Canada. He was born Keable but a clerical error, possibly when he enlisted, changed this to Kaeble and it stuck. His father, also Joseph Keable (1862–29th December 1900), married Marie née Ducas (c.1864–3rd October 1934) on 19th August 1890 at St Moïse. Marie married Damase Neveu (14th December 1869–6th October 1941), born at St

Robert, Pierre-De Saurel, Montérégie, on 2nd August 1904. They were living at Sayabec Station, Quebec in 1918. Damase had married Marie Labrie (10th February 1870–23rd April 1903) about 1893 and they had three children – Antoine Neveu 1894 (served in 1st Depot Battalion, 2nd Quebec Regiment during the Great War (3289659)), Annie Neveu 1897 and Clara Neveu 1899. Marie died at Longueil, Quebec and Damase at Edmundston, New Brunswick. Joseph had three siblings:

- Wilbrod Keable (4th May 1896–1941) enlisted in Quebec on 20th July 1918 as Kaible, described as a mechanic, 5′ 5″ tall, weighing 135 lbs, with medium complexion, brown eyes, brown hair and his religious denomination was Roman Catholic. He was assigned to 5th Military District, 1st Depot Battalion, Second Quebec Regiment (3289591). He was discharged on 6th August 1918, probably on medical grounds as he had a scar on the back of a hand resulting in loss of power and also varicose veins in his legs.
- Ursule Keable (25th January 1899–1976) was a teacher in 1923.
- Alfred Adrien Neveu-Keable (25th April 1905–27th November 1967), known as Adrien, married Marie Marguerite Gertrude Rioux (27th June 1913–19th December 1977) on 22nd November 1938 at St Jacques Cathedral, St Denis Street, Montreal, Quebec. She was known as Gertrude. Alfred died at Longueil, Quebec. Gertrude married Converse Burdette (10th May 1903–November 1970). Alfred and Gertrude had three children, including Claude Neveu-Keable in 1939.

Joseph's paternal grandfather, another Joseph Keable (20th January 1838–17th May 1903), was born at Rimouski, Quebec of German origin. Joseph's grandfather, Theodore Keable (1756–13th August 1823), arrived in Canada at the time of the American Revolution in 1776. He was born at Mainz, Rhineland Palatinate and married Marie Louise Cameron (1763–15th November 1835) on 4th October 1787. She was born in Aberdeenshire, Scotland. Joseph married Ursule née LeClerc (6th February 1845–23rd June 1890), born at Ste Luce, Rimouski, Quebec, on 25th November 1861 at Ste Anne Des Monts, Gaspésie, Matane County, Quebec. Joseph was a cultivator in 1871 and they were living at Gaspésie West, Quebec. Ursule died at St Moïse de Matapédia, Matane County. Joseph married Caroline Desjardins Levesque (born 2nd July 1855), born at Rimouski, on 30th October 1891 at Ste Octave des Metis, Matane County, Quebec. They had a son, Francois Keable (25th October 1893–18th February 1933) at Amqui, who married Albertine Vaillancourt (born c.1895) on 18th January 1916 at Sayabec, Quebec. Caroline had married Thomas Aubin (1838–26th April 1890) on 29th July 1874 at Ste Germain, Rimouski, and had three children – Marie-Madeleine Aubin c.1877, Marie-Pauline Aubin 1880) and Apolline Aubin. Thomas died at Grande-Vallée, Gaspé, Quebec. In addition to Joseph, Ursule and Joseph had eleven other children, all born at Ste Anne Des Monts, Gaspésie, except Alphee:

- Francois Xavier Keable (16th February 1865–15th January 1880).
- Jean Baptiste Keable (23rd January 1867–25th June 1869).
- Philibert 'Felix' Keable (9th May 1869–19th December 1930) married Marie-Oliva Gagné (born c.1870) on 7th January 1891 at St Moise de Matapedia, Matane County, Quebec. He married Marie-Oliva-Clothilde Simoneau on 14th August 1894 at Amqui, Matapedia, Quebec. He is understood to have had seven children.
- Joachim Keable (born 23rd April 1871), a carpenter, married Marie Roy (born c.1875) on 8th May 1894 at Amqui. They had five children – Joseph Keable 1896, Maria Keable 1899, Suedevie Keable 1900, Ernest Keable 1902 and Marie Luce Keable 1903.
- Zozime Keable (26th March 1873–16th May 1874).
- Alphonse-Alphée Keable (born 16th April 1875), born at Cap Chat, Gaspésie, Quebec, married Apolline Aubin (daughter of his grandfather's second wife, from her first marriage) on 5th October 1897 at Amqui, Matapedia. He married Marie-Philomene Coulombe (born 1st June 1882) on 15th January 1901 at Amqui. He married his sister-in-law, Emma Kaeble née Coulombe, widow of his brother Honoré, on 6th November 1922, also at Amqui.
- Honoré Keable (30th August 1877–24th February 1916) married Marie-Louise Emma Coulombe (born 27th August 1877) on 13th June 1899 at Amqui. They had six children including – Marie-Anna Keable 1900 and Marie-Jeanne Keable.
- Marcel Keable (born 25th July 1879), also seen as Odina.
- Tharcicius Keable (born 16th March 1883), also seen as Narcissus, married Carolina Ouellet (born c.1884) on 26th February 1906.
- Marie-Anne Keable (born 8th September 1884) married Elzear Coulombe (born 29th June 1877) on 23rd February 1903. He was born at Ste Cécille, Cloridorme.
- Marie-Anne Ursule Keable (born 23rd November 1886).

His maternal grandfather, Denis Ducas, married Marie née Labrie. Denis' family emigrated to Canada from Normandy, France.

Joseph was educated at Les Frères de la Croix Village School, Sayabec, Matane County, Quebec. He was employed as a driver-mechanic with a lumber firm in Princeville, Quebec from 1910. He enlisted in 189th Battalion CEF at Sayabec, Matane County, Quebec on 20th March 1916 (889958), described as 5′ 7″ tall, with dark complexion, black eyes, black hair and his religious denomination was Roman Catholic. He gave his occupation as machinist. Joseph embarked on SS *Lapland* at Halifax, Nova Scotia on 27th September 1916 and arrived in England on 6th October. The 189th Battalion personnel were absorbed into 69th Battalion at Dibgate Camp, Shorncliffe, Kent. Joseph transferred to the strength of 22nd Battalion on 12th November and joined the Canadian Base Depot in France next day. He left the Depot on 2nd December, joined 2nd Canadian Entrenching Battalion on 6th December and did not arrive in 22nd Battalion until 3rd March 1917. On 30th April he was admitted to 13th General Hospital, Boulogne with a gunshot wound to his

SS *Lapland* (18,565 tons), built by Harland & Wolff for the Red Star Line, was launched on 27th June 1908. Her maiden voyage was on 10th April 1909 from Antwerp to New York via Dover. She plied the same route until January 1914 when she switched to the Liverpool – New York route. In April 1912 she was hired by the White Star Line to bring back the surviving RMS *Titanic* crew, arriving in England on 28th April. In October 1914 she commenced crossings from Liverpool to New York under charter to Cunard Line. In April 1917 she was mined off the Mersey but reached Liverpool and in June was requisitioned and converted into a troopship. In August 1917 she carried 1st Aero Squadron, the first US Army Air Service unit, to France. On 24th November 1918 she reverted to civilian use on the Liverpool – New York route for White Star Line. In September 1919 she transferred to the Southampton – New York route. A refit followed and she resumed service with the Red Star Line on 3rd January 1920 from Antwerp and Southampton to New York. Hollywood actors Douglas Fairbanks and Mary Pickford honeymooned aboard her in June 1920. In April 1927 she was altered to carry cabin, tourist and 3rd class passengers and on 29th April 1932 started her last voyage. In 1932–33 *Lapland* was used on Mediterranean cruises and was then sold for scrap at Osaka, Japan.

right shoulder. On 2nd May he transferred to No.1 Convalescent Depot, Boulogne and was discharged on 25th May. He joined the Canadian Base Depot, Le Havre on 29th May and the same day forfeited three days pay for being drunk. He rejoined 22nd Battalion on 12th June and was sentenced to twenty-eight days Field Punishment No.1 on 5th September for leaving his billeting area on 29th August without a pass while on active service. He was granted fourteen days leave from 1st December and rejoined his unit on 18th December.

The Salvation Army hut at Dibgate Camp.

Awarded the VC for his actions at Neuville-Vitasse, France on 8th/9th June 1918, LG 16th September 1918. Joseph was admitted to 2/1st London Field Ambulance (56th Division) with compound fractures of legs and wounds in both arms, left hand and neck. He died there on 9th June and is buried in Wanquentin Communal Cemetery Extension, near Arras, France (II A 8). **Awarded the MM, LG 7th October 1918.** The VC was presented to his mother by the Duke of Devonshire, Governor General of Canada, at Rimouski, Quebec on

13th General in the casino at Boulogne.

CCGS *Caporal Kaeble V.C.* entered service on 22nd September 2014.

Joseph's grave in Wanquentin Communal Cemetery Extension.

16th December 1918. Joseph is commemorated in a number of other places:

- Quebec:
    - CCGS *Caporal Kaeble V.C.* (253 tons), one of nine *Hero* class mid-shore patrol vessels for the Canadian Coast Guard, built in 2012 by Halifax Shipyards Ltd at Halifax, Nova Scotia. She entered service on 22nd September 2014. Based at Quebec, she patrols the St Lawrence River between the river mouth and Cornwall.

Victor Christian William Cavendish, 9th Duke of Devonshire KG GCMG GCVO TD KStJ PC JP FRS (1868–1938), while Governor General of Canada. He served in the Derbyshire Yeomanry 1890–1911 and in 1891 became the youngest MP in Parliament at the time, winning his father's former seat of West Derbyshire. Numerous parliamentary positions followed, including appointment to the Privy Council in 1905. In 1892 he married Lady Evelyn MitzMaurice, daughter of the Viceroy of India. In 1907 he became a deputy lieutenant of Derbyshire and the following year Lord Lieutenant and also Honorary Colonel of 5th Sherwood Foresters (TF). Cavendish inherited his uncle's dukedom in 1908 and took his place in the House of Lords. In 1916 he was appointed Governor General of Canada to replace Prince Arthur and was succeeded by Lord Byng in 1921. Devonshire was Secretary of State for the Colonies 1922–24. He is buried in St Peter's Churchyard, Edensor. In the church are the colours of 16th (Chatsworth Rifles) Battalion, The Sherwood Foresters in which served Corporal Ernest Albert Egerton VC. Also buried in the Churchyard is Kathleen Cavendish (1920–48), sister of US President John F Kennedy (1917–63), who married William Cavendish (1917–44), Marquess of Hartington, who was killed in action in Belgium on 9th September 1944 serving with the Coldstream Guards (Dupras & Colas).

  - Joseph Kaeble VC MM Branch No.36, Royal Canadian Legion, 175 Rue Dumais, Rimouski opened on 4th July 1931.
  - Rue Kaeble, Sayabec.
  - Memorial plaque in Sayabec Parish Church and on the Cenotaph at Municipal Park, Sayabec.
  - Bronze bust at The Citadel, Quebec City and a plaque at Le Musée, Royal 22e Regiment Museum there.
  - Mont Kaeble near Valcartier, the base of the Royal 22nd Regiment.
- Ontario
  - Joseph Kaeble Building, L'Academie La Pinede, 116 Waterloo Road East, CFB Borden, Ontario, is a Francophone public elementary school. It was opened in October 1948 as Joseph Kaeble School for Anglophone dependants of Department of National Defense personnel. In September 1973 it became École Joseph Kaeble for Francophone dependents. It closed in 1995 and was absorbed into Frederick Campbell Elementary School.
  - Named on a Victoria Cross obelisk to all Canadian VCs at Military Heritage Park, Barrie, Ontario dedicated by The Princess Royal on 22nd October 2013.
- Ottawa
  - Named on one of eleven plaques honouring 175 men from overseas awarded the VC for the Great War. The plaques were unveiled by the Senior Minister of State at the Foreign & Commonwealth Office and Minister for Faith and Communities, Baroness Warsi, at a reception at Lancaster House, London on 26th June 2014 attended by The Duke of Kent and relatives of the VC recipients. The Canadian plaque was unveiled outside the British High Commission in Elgin Street, Ottawa on 10th November 2014 by The Princess Royal in the presence of British High Commissioner Howard Drake, Canadian Minister of Veterans Affairs Julian Fantino and Canadian Chief of the Defence Staff General Thomas J Lawson.
  - A bronze bust at Valiants Memorial near Sappers Staircase, Confederation Square, adjacent to the National War Memorial, Ottawa.

Joseph's bust at Valiants Memorial, Ottawa.

- Toronto
  - Named on Plaque No.71 on the York Cemetery VC Memorial, West Don River Valley, Toronto, Canada unveiled on 25th June 2017.

  - ◦ A wooden plaque bearing fifty-six maple leaves each inscribed with the name of a Canadian-born VC holder was dedicated at the Canadian Forces College, Toronto on Remembrance Day 1999.
- Two 49 cents postage stamps in honour of the ninety-four Canadian VC winners were issued by Canada Post on 21st October 2004 on the 150th Anniversary of the first Canadian VC's action, Alexander Roberts Dunn VC.
- Communities and Local Government commemorative paving stones for the 145 VCs born in Australia, Belgium, Canada, China, Denmark, Egypt, France, Germany, India, Iraq, Japan, Nepal, Netherlands, Newfoundland, New Zealand, Pakistan, South Africa, Sri Lanka, Ukraine and United States of America were unveiled at the National Memorial Arboretum, Alrewas, Staffordshire by Prime Minister David Cameron MP and Sergeant Johnson Beharry VC on 5th March 2015.

The entrance to the Citadelle of Quebec, HQ of the Royal 22nd Regiment and home of its Museum. It is the oldest military building in Canada and is also the secondary official residence of the monarch and Governor General of Canada. The strategic value of the site was identified by Samuel de Champlain in 1608 and Quebec City was founded below. The defences were first developed by the French and later by the British. The Quebec Conferences in 1943 and 1944 were held at the Citadelle and were attended by Canadian PM William Lyon Mackenzie King, British PM Winston Churchill and US President Franklin D Roosevelt. It was designated a World Heritage Site in 1985.

In addition to the VC and MM he was awarded the British War Medal 1914–20 and Victory Medal 1914–19. As he died on operational duty, his next-of-kin is eligible to receive the Canadian Memorial Cross GRI. His VC is held by the Royal 22nd Regiment Museum, La Citadelle, Quebec City, Quebec.

PRIVATE RICHARD GEORGE MASTERS
Army Service Corps (Motor Transport) attached 141st Field Ambulance

Richard Masters was born on 23rd March 1877 at 61a Everton Road, Birkdale, Lancashire. His father, David Brown Masters (1841–29th August 1926), was born at Biggleswade, Bedfordshire. He married Elizabeth Ann Endersby (also seen as Insby and Ensby) (born 15th October 1843) on 19th November 1864 at Dunton, Bedfordshire. She was born at Wrestlingworth, Bedfordshire. In 1871 he was a housekeeper and they were living at the stables attached to 101 Linaker Street, Southport, Lancashire. David was later a carter for Townends of Southport and

by 1911 was a labourer. It is not known what became of Elizabeth. David married Margaret Harris Vittle née Doney (also seen as Dony and Downey) (7th May 1850–8th February 1928) on 16th April 1876 at Stoke Newington Parish Church, London. Margaret was born at Tywardreath, near St Austell, Cornwall. They were living at 61a Everton Road, Birkdale in 1881 and had moved to 4 Bury Road, Birkdale by 1901. Richard had ten siblings from his father's two marriages:

- Mary Jane Masters (born 1865), born at Biggleswade, Bedfordshire, was a servant in the home of Elias Bloomfield and family at 61 Everton Road, Everton, Birkdale, Lancashire in 1881.
- Jesse Brown Masters (8th March 1868–1869), born at Lewisham, baptised at St Mary Magdalene, Woolwich, Kent and died at Woolwich.
- Catherine Mary Elizabeth Masters (1878–2nd December 1952) died unmarried.
- Alice Amelia Masters, born and died 1879.
- Louisa Mary Ann Masters (1881–1964) was a domestic servant in 1901. She married William Fowden/Foden Whitlock (1884–1951), a labourer, in 1908 at Bucklow, Cheshire. They had four children:
    - William Whitlock (1908–25th January 1959) married Doris Booth in 1935 and they had a daughter, Elizabeth A Whitlock, in 1936. They were living at 8 Spring Street, Wilmslow, Cheshire at the time of his death at Baguley Hospital, Wythenshawe, Lancashire.
    - Bessie Whitlock (19th November 1910–1981) married Percy Hall Messenger (3rd March 1909–9th January 1990) in 1930. He was living at 66 South Oak Lane, Wilmslow at the time of his death there. They had four children – William A Messenger 1931, David Messenger 1933, Percy H Messenger 1936 and Rodney S Messenger 1944.
    - Margaret Eliza Whitlock (3rd August 1912–1993) married Joseph Henry Pell (16th August 1910–1986) in 1935. They had three children – Muriel A Pell 1935, Joseph H Pell 1936 and Margaret E Pell 1955.
    - Louisa Whitlock (10th November 1916–1997) married Sydney Holland Steele (10th May 1911–1976) in 1941.
- William Masters, born and died 1883, registered at Ormskirk, Lancashire.
- David William Masters (1885–10th March 1918) was born at Southport, Lancashire. He was a plumber's apprentice in 1901 and a nurseryman by 1911. He married Maria Mayo (27th July 1887–6th December 1977) in 1907. They were living at 3 Bedford Road, Birkdale in 1911. David served as a private in 2/5th Loyal North Lancashire Regiment (29046) and was killed in action on 10th March 1918 (Anzac Cemetery, Sailly-sur-la-Lys, France – III B 5). David and Maria had two children – Annie Masters 1908 and Ronald Masters 1911. Maria married James

Howard in 1923 and they lived at 3 Bedford Road, Birkdale. James and Maria had two sons – James Howard 1925 and Alan Howard 1927. She was living at 134 Stamford Road, Southport at the time of her death there.

David Masters' grave in Anzac Cemetery, Sailly-sur-la-Lys.

- Matthew Masters (1887–17th January 1955) was an assistant pork butcher living with his parents in 1911. He enlisted and was embodied in 1/1st Welsh Division Cyclist Company (59) at Stockport on 10th May 1915, described as 5′ 3″ tall and weighing 123 lbs. The unit became 53rd (Welsh) Division Cyclist Company. He was working for Llewellyn Roberts & Co, wine and spirits merchants in Wilmslow, as a carter at the time and was living at Lacy Green, Wilmslow. His next of kin was his sister, Louisa Whitlock. Matthew served with the Mediterranean Expeditionary Force from 17th July and was attached to 53rd Division Signal Company RE at Gallipoli on 11th October. He transferred to the Army Cyclist Corps (20073) on 1st November 1916. One of his functions was post orderly. He was absent from roll call at Tineh on 4th December 1916 but the award is missing in his service record. He was granted Class II Proficiency Pay on 11th May 1917, War Pay at 3d per day on 10th May 1918 and Class I Proficiency Pay on 1st July 1918. He joined the Demobilisation Camp, Kantara on 15th February 1919 and was admitted to 44th Stationary Hospital with scabies 19th February–9th March. Matthew embarked on HT *Kaisar-i-Hind* at Port Said for Britain via Marseille, France on 15th March. He was demobilised on 2nd April 1919 from No.1 Dispersal Unit, Prees Heath and was discharged on 31st March 1920. He married Margaret Caroline Seavert (20th October 1888–1974) on 4th June 1921. Her birth was registered as Sievert. They had two daughters:
    - Marjorie G Masters (born 1923) married Kenneth C Lloyd in 1944 and they had a daughter, Susan D Lloyd, in 1948.
    - Kathleen M Masters (born 1925) married Peter W Kearsley (born 1926) in 1951 and they had a daughter, Rosalind J Kearsley, in 1953.
- Bessie Masters (27th September 1890–1981) was a shop assistant living with her parents in 1911. Her birth was registered as Brownmasters at Ormskirk. She married Arthur Rose (1897–21st December 1972), a plumber, on 1st August 1921 at St Peter's Church, Birkdale. They had a daughter, Edna Rose (1923–2005), who served in the Women's Royal Naval Service during the Second World War. She married Samuel Bagley (1920–2011) in 1947. He served in the RAF during

Richard's paternal grandfather was born at Baldock, Hertfordshire, a town that has been occupied since prehistoric times. In the Iron Age Baldock was the site of possibly the largest oppidum in Britain, which later became a Roman settlement. However, the settlement appears to have died out later as it does not appear in the Domesday Book. The Knights Templar established Baldock as a market town in the 1140s. They built a church, which was largely rebuilt about 1330 and is now the parish church of St Mary the Virgin. Due to its location, the town was a staging post between London and the north with many coaching inns. A shutter telegraph station was located there 1808–14 in the chain that connected the Admiralty to Great Yarmouth. Malting and brewing were the major industries but nothing of it remains. An annual music festival raises money for charity.

the Second World War. Edna and Samuel had three children – Susan Bagley 1948, David B Bagley 1950 and Graeme I Bagley 1960.

- John Masters (14th September 1892–23rd November 1985) was an apprentice joiner living with his parents in 1911. He served with the Army Service Corps as a wheeler in France. He married Sarah Hughes (16th September 1890–16th July 1975) in 1915. He was living at 111 Forest Road, Southport at the time of his death there. They had two children:
    - Gladys Masters (born 1918) married Frederick H Jenkins in 1940.
    - John A Masters (born 1920).

Richard's paternal grandfather, David Brown Masters (c.1814–1888), was born at Baldock, Hertfordshire. He married Catherine née Brown (1814–1906) on 12th October 1836 at Dunton, Bedfordshire. In 1851 he was a visitor in the home of Foster and Jemina Rogers at 122 Warwick Street, Westminster, London. Jemima was David's sister and Foster was an assistant chaplain at the House of Correction in Westminster. Catherine was living with her children in Dunton village at that time and has not been located in a census after 1851. David appeared in court on 29th June 1852 charged with threatened assault on James Gregory at Dunton, Bedfordshire on 4th June (outcome not known). David married Louisa Strange (c.1837–1872) on 13th August 1871 at St Margaret, Plumstead, London. He was a general labourer and

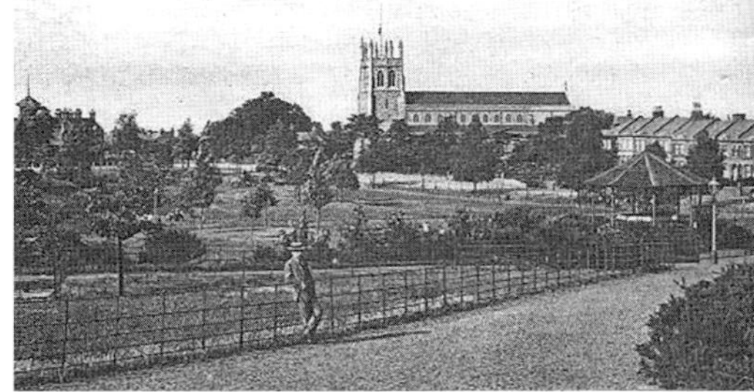

Richard's parents married at St Margaret, Plumstead in 1871. The church was consecrated on 25th April 1859. In 1864 St Margaret became the parish church of Plumstead. By 1966 the church fabric was in such poor state that it had to be closed. Services transferred to St Mark's, which was built in 1901 and demolished in 1974. A new church of St Mark and St Margaret was built on the site of St Mark's on Old Mill Road.

they were living at 5 Crawley Cottages, Greenwich, London in 1881. In addition to David they had six other children, all births registered at Biggleswade, Bedfordshire:

- Mary Elizabeth Masters (1839–1929), whose birth was registered unnamed, married William Thornley (c.1828–1924), a domestic gardener, on 7th March 1864 at Woolwich Parish Church. He was born at Boston, Lincolnshire. They were living at 115 Loampit Vale, Lewisham in 1881 and 1891 and at 15 Courthill Road, Lewisham in 1901 and 1911. They had ten children – John Thornley 1864, Catherine Thornley 1866, Elizabeth Thornley 1868, Annie Thornley 1870, Hannah Alice Thornley 1872, Penelope Thornley 1874, Penelope Thornley 1876, Florence Emily Thornley 1878 and twins William and Thomas Thornley 1881.
- Jesse Masters (born c.1842), whose birth was registered unnamed and who died in infancy.
- Louisa Masters (twin with Jemima) (born 1847). The twins were living with their aunt, Jemima E Rogers, at Pope's Grove, Twickenham in 1861. In 1881 Louisa was living with a man named Daniel (born c.1844) at Wolverhampton, Staffordshire, an unemployed hammer man, as his wife, at 9 Queen Street, Greenwich, although no marriage record has been found. Louisa had two daughters – Louisa Catherine Masters 1876 and Susan Daniel 1880.
- Jemima Masters (twin with Louisa) (1847–94) married Henry Doe (1844–82) on 24th June 1869 at St Albans. He was a general labourer, born at Takeley, Essex. They were living at 37 Elswick Road, Lewisham, London in 1881. They had three children – Julia Doe 1870, David Doe 1872 and Albert Edward Doe 1880. Jemima married John Alfred Wood (born c.1852), a general labourer, in 1883 at Lewisham and they had a daughter, Eliza Wood, in 1884. They were living at 66 Roan Street, Greenwich in 1891.
- Jesse Masters (1852–1932) was a blacksmith striker, working at Beckton Gas Works. He married Catherine Hankinson (1848–1922) in 1870 at Woolwich, London. They were living at 17a High Street, East Ham in 1881, at 10 Crosby Row, East Ham in 1901 and at 36 Gascoigne Road, Barking, Essex in 1911. They had ten children, including Richard David Masters 1875 and Albert William Masters 1880. Only three children were living in 1911.
- Eliza Brown (1855–57).

His maternal grandfather, William Dony (6th June 1824–1891), was born at Dobwalls, Liskeard, Cornwall. He married Mary Ann née Vittle (c.1824–19th March 1913), born at Tywardreath, near St Austell, Cornwall, in 1850. She was working as a servant in the home of William Pearse, clerk of works, at St Blazey, near St Austell, in 1841. William Dony was a blacksmith in 1851 and they were living at Albert Place, Beaumaris, Anglesey. They were living at Stantonbury, Buckinghamshire by 1861, at 109 Middle Street, New Bradwell, Buckinghamshire by 1871 and at 16 Newdigate Street, Crewe, Cheshire in 1881. In 1911 Mary was living with her daughter, Margaret Masters and family. She died at Southport, Lancashire registered as Downey. In addition to Margaret they had six other children:

- Joseph Henry Dony (1852–8th May 1926), born at Holyhead, Anglesey, was an apprentice turner in 1871 and by 1891 was an engine fitter. He married Mary Ann Gear (1852–1939), a straw hat and bonnet maker, in 1874 at Luton, Bedfordshire. They were living at 41 Chobham Street, Luton in 1891. They had eight children – John Richard G Dony 1875, Mary Elizabeth Dony 1877, William Dony 1879, Joseph Henry Dony 1882, Alfred Francis Dony 1884, May Dony 1886, Frederick Llewellyn Dony 1891 and Elizabeth Mary Dony 1893.
- William Dony (1856–1935), born at Bradwell, Buckinghamshire, was a boilermaker in 1881. He married Eliza Clarice Goulder (c.1862–1898) in 1883 at Nantwich, Cheshire. They had a daughter, Bessie Dony, in 1895. William married Margaret Elizabeth Lane née Vittle (1862–1915) in 1901 at Pembroke, Pembrokeshire. She was a dressmaker in 1891 living with her mother and siblings at 42 Llanreath, Pembroke. She married John Lane (c.1851–99) in 1895 and they had three children – Agnes Matilda Lane 1896, Francis John Henry Lane 1897 and Bessie Lane 1898. William and Margaret had a son, William David Dony, in 1905, and were living at 12 Ford Lane, Crewe, Cheshire in 1911.
- Mary Elizabeth Doney (1859–1922) married Edward Moseley (1860–1912), a straw hat blocker, in 1889 at Luton, Bedfordshire. They were living at 46 Tavistock Street, Luton in 1891 and were still there in 1901.
- Richard George Dony (1861–75).
- Matthew Dony (1864–1951) was an apprentice boilermaker in 1881. He married Sophia Eynon (1865–1927) in 1888 at Pembroke. By 1901 he was a ship's fitter and they were living at 12 Nelson Street, Pembroke. They had seven children – Mary Ann Dony 1889, Elizabeth Dony 1890, William Parker Dony 1891, Millicent Sarah Dony 1894, Margaret Ellen Dony 1896 and James Henry Dony 1899 and Ruth Dony 1906. James enlisted in 4th Reserve Battalion, Welsh Regiment (82420) at Carmarthen on 9th July 1918, described as 5′ 4¾″ tall. He worked for the Chief Engineer, HM Dockyard Pembroke as an engine fitter. He suffered a septic leg caused by marching on 10th August and was treated at the Military Hospital, Pembroke Dock. He transferred to the Class Z Reserve on 17th February 1919 and was living at 18 Castle Street, Pennar, Pembroke Dock at the time.
- John Dony (1868–1942) was an electrical fitter. He married Gertrude Henrietta Madeline Savage (1881–1944) in 1909 at Portsmouth, Hampshire. They were living at 159 Wingfield Street, Landport, Hampshire in 1911. They had eight children – John Dony 1910, William Dony 1911, Arthur Dony 1913, Matthew Dony 1915, Gertrude M Dony 1918, Henrietta Dony 1919, Mary Dony 1923 and Frederick Dony 1924.

Richard was educated at St Peter's School, Birkdale, Birkdale Council School and Bury Road School, Southport until 1891. He was employed delivering wines and spirits and food from a shop in Everton Road, Southport. Later he was an assistant in the cycle trade for Messrs Timberlake and by 1901 was a cycle fitter. He was also employed at Bamber's Cycles in Hall Street and Kensington Road, Southport and became a foreman cycle mechanic. From 1898 until he enlisted he was a chauffeur for Mr Pennington of Lancaster Road, Birkdale. Richard was a champion cyclist, winning several trophies, including the North of England Champion 1898–1900. He held world records for the tandem quarter and half mile with W Birtwhistle. He was also the Liverpool District National Cycling Union Champion on four occasions and also won the Centenary Shield four times. During the winter he ran in cross-country championships.

On 9th November 1901 Richard Masters married Alice Johnson (c.1878–17th June 1943) at Ormskirk, Lancashire. She was a laundry maid in 1901, living with her parents at 110 Meols Cop Road, Southport. They lived at 102 Norwood Road, Southport and later at 35 Palmerston Road, Southport. They had three children:

- Bessie Masters (11th September 1902–7th September 1982) married John Terence Shea (12th February 1905–26th April 1988) in 1931. He was born at Cambridge. She was living at 35 Palmerston Road, Southport, Lancashire at the time of her death there. He died at 12 Haigh Court, Peel Street, Southport.
- Constance Masters (born 27th January 1907) married Leslie Wilson in 1937. She was living at Red Stacks, Black Moss Lane, Aughton, near Ormskirk in 1963.
- Douglas Masters (born 19th January 1911) married, as Douglas F Masters, Winifred S Bootle (born 1911) in 1935.

Alice's father, Richard Johnson (c.1839–15th April 1918), was born at Blowick, Southport. He married Elizabeth née Wright (c.1839–1913), born at Birkdale, c.1859. Richard was a carter in 1881, a green grocer in 1891, a road labourer in 1901 and a gardener in 1911. They were living at 110 Meols Cop Road, Southport in 1881 and had moved to 11 Norwood Road, Southport by 1911. He died at 15 Market Street, Southport. In addition to Alice they had nine other children, three of whom had died by 1911. The following are known:

- Jane Anne Johnson (1860–1913) was a laundress in 1881, living with her parents. She had a daughter, Elizabeth Johnson, in 1883. She married William Johnson (born c.1856), a corporation carter, in 1885. They were living at 124 North Meols Road, Southport in 1891. By 1901 they had moved to 110a Norwood Road, Southport.
- Nicholas Johnson (1864–17th August 1928) married Ann Rimmer (c.1866–29th December 1943) in 1884. He was a coal dealer in 1891 and they were living at 179 Meols Cop Road, Southport. By 1901 he was a general labourer and they

were living at 4 Clifton Road, Southport. In 1911 they were living at 99 Clifton Road, Blowick, by when he was an engineer's labourer. They were living at 110a Norwood Road, Southport at the time of his death there. She was living at 34 Salford Road, Ainsdale, Southport at the time of her death there. They had five children, three of whom were deceased by 1911, including – Nancy Johnson 1887, Elizabeth Johnson 1888, Richard Johnson 1890, Hannah Johnson 1890.

- Peter Johnson (born 1867) married Jane Rimmer (born c.1875) in 1888. He was a general labourer in 1901 and a bricklayer in 1911. They were living at 16 Joseph Street, Bolton, Lancashire in 1901. He was living with his family at 20 Morris Green Lane, Bolton in 1911. They had six children – Mary Johnson 1890, Richard Johnson 1891, Elizabeth Johnson 1894, James Johnson 1896, Joseph Johnson 1898 and Alice Johnson 1901.
- John Johnson (born 1869) married Margaret Howard (c.1868–before 1911) in 1890. He was a carter in 1891 and a municipal labourer in 1901. They were living at 219 Hart Street, Southport in 1891 and by 1901 had moved to 110 Old Park Lane, Southport. They had four children – Isabella Johnson 1891, Nathan Johnson 1892, Margaret Johnson c.1897 and Alice Johnson 1900. By 1911 John was living with his sister, Jane, and her husband.
- Nathan Johnson (1870–1916) was a carter in 1891 and a laundry man in 1901, living with his parents. He married Mary Ellen Johnson (1874–1932), a charwoman, in 1904 at Bury, Lancashire. Mary had a son, Richard Henry Johnson, in 1898, and they were living with her cousins, William and Jane Anne Johnson, at 110a Norwood Road, Southport in 1901. By 1911 Nathan was an assistant in a public house and they were living at 5 Water Side, Heap Bridge, Bury. They had at least one daughter, Elizabeth Johnson, in 1910.
- Richard Johnson (born c.1875) was a greengrocer's assistant in 1891 and a bricklayer's labourer in 1901, living with his parents. He married Mary Jane Whitley/Whiteley (born c.1872) in 1903. She was born at Warrington, Lancashire and had a son, Albert Edward Whitley, in 1897, who was living with his grandparents at 113 Church Street, Warrington in 1901. Richard was a plaster's labourer in 1911 and they were living at 7 Church Street, Bell Lane, Bury. They had a son, Richard Johnson, in 1904.

Richard enlisted as a driver in the Army Service Corps in London on 8th February 1915 and joined at Grove Park, Greenwich the following day (S/110292 later M/2048544.). He was described as 5′ 6¼″ tall and his religious denomination was Church of England. He trained at Grove Park Motor Transport Reserve Depot from 16th February and embarked on SS *St Pancras* on 12th March, landing at Rouen, France on 15th March. He was attached to the Heavy Motor Transport Depot on 21st March until posted to 3rd Field Ambulance RAMC, 1st Division for specialist training. On 3rd September he was posted to 141st Field Ambulance RAMC and was awarded the Good Conduct Badge on 8th February 1917.

Grove Park Hospital on Marvels Lane was originally a workhouse built 1899–1902, with accommodation for 815 inmates. At the beginning of the war it was requisitioned by the Army and became a major training centre for the Army Service Corps. In 1919 the hospital was sold to the Metropolitan Asylums Board for use as a tuberculosis hospital but due to the remoteness of the site it remained empty until 1926, when it was finally adapted, with 299 beds. A nurses' home was built in 1938. During the Blitz in November 1940 the Hospital was damaged by a bomb and two nurses, Mary Fleming and Aileen Turner, crawled through an upper window and across the swaying floor of a ward to reach trapped patients. The floor collapsed a few minutes after the rescue and they were both awarded the George Medal. By 1945 the Hospital had become a centre for thoracic surgery. In December 1957 the Hospital helped treat the victims of the St John's railway station crash in which ninety-two people were killed and 173 injured. In 1977 it was redesignated for mentally handicapped patients and closed in 1994. The site has been redeveloped for housing and many of the original buildings were demolished; but some of the workhouse buildings along Marvels Lane have survived.

Field sign used by 141st Field Ambulance RAMC.

The French Croix de Guerre was first awarded in 1915 to individuals or units distinguishing themselves by acts of heroism. Some notable recipients include:

- Josephine Baker – American born French dancer, singer and actress for her work in the Resistance.
- Jacques Cousteau – pioneer diver and underwater filmmaker.
- General Dwight D Eisenhower – Supreme Allied Commander during Operation OVERLORD.
- Noor Inayat Khan and Violette Szabo – British SOE agents awarded the George Cross and executed by the Nazis.
- Audie Murphy – actor and the most decorated US soldier of WW2, including the Medal of Honor.
- General George S Patton – commander of US Third Army in the Second World War.
- Theodore Roosevelt – son of President Theodore Roosevelt, awarded the Medal of Honor for 6th June 1944 on Utah Beach.
- James Stewart – actor for his role in the liberation of France as a USAAF Colonel.
- Major Richard D Winters – Easy Company, 506th Parachute Infantry Regiment, made famous by the TV series and book *Band of Brothers*.
- Sergeant Alvin C York – American First World War Medal of Honor winner and subject of a film in 1941 starring Gary Cooper.

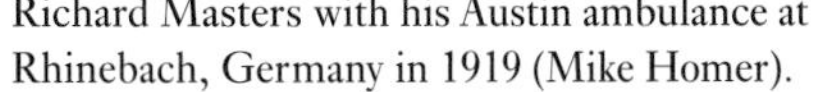

Richard Masters with his Austin ambulance at Rhinebach, Germany in 1919 (Mike Homer).

Southport Town Hall, where Richard received the Croix de Guerre.

Awarded the French Croix de Guerre for his actions on the Somme on 7th March 1917 – following a bombing raid he drove his ambulance to an advanced dressing station located in a quarry four times under heavy artillery fire in order to clear the wounded who were trapped there, LG 14th July 1917. He was granted leave 15th-25th May. He was wounded by shrapnel in his knee at Passchendaele and returned to duty on 9th November.

Sir William Pickles Hartley (1846–1922) was born in Colne, the only surviving child of John Hartley, a tinsmith, and Margaret Pickles. He started the jam business in 1871 when a supplier failed to deliver a batch. William made his own, which proved to be popular. In 1874 he moved the business to Bootle, in 1880 to Southport and in 1886 to Aintree. Hartley became an influential benefactor and entrepreneur and was also an active member of the Methodist Church. In 1888 he built a model village at Aintree and the following year introduced a profit-sharing scheme. He provided free medical treatment to his workforce. Hartley usually donated only part of any sum requested, in order to encourage others to give. He endowed a number of hospitals in Colne, Liverpool and London and financed departments at Liverpool and Manchester universities. Within Primitive Methodism, he supported the building of chapels, acted as treasurer of its missionary society and converted the old Holborn Town Hall into its national headquarters. In 1896 the Primitive Methodists created the Hartley Lectures in recognition of his work. They continue to this day as the Fernley-Hartley Lectures, created following the amalgamation of the Primitive and Wesleyan Methodist Churches. In 1906 the Manchester theological college for Primitive Methodist ministers was renamed Hartley College, later Hartley Victoria College. William was a member of Liverpool City Council 1895–98 and was knighted in 1908. One of his daughters, Christiana, became Southport's first woman mayor in 1921.

The Croix de Guerre was presented by Brigadier General Richard Fielding Edwards CMG (1866–1942), Commander Mersey Defences, at the Town Hall, Southport, Lancashire on 24th January 1918. Richard was granted leave 13th-27th February 1918. **Awarded the VC for his actions near Béthune, France on 9th April 1918, LG 8th May 1918.** The VC was presented by the King at HQ First Army, Ranchicourt, France on 8th August. Richard was granted leave 20th August–10th September. A public subscription was set up in Southport and £500 was invested in War Bonds for him. His wife and daughter were presented with jewellery. He was also presented with a gold signet ring by Bury Road School, Southport. Richard had his discharge medical at No.1 Driver Motor Transport Company ASC at Bonn, Germany on 20th April 1919 and was transferred to the Reserve on 24th May.

Post war he continued working as a chauffeur for Sir George Stephenson, owner of the *Southport Visitor* newspaper, and later for Sir William Pickles Hartley, of Hartley's Jams. Later he became a van driver with Southport Corporation Gas Department.

Richard attended a number of VC Reunions – the VC Garden Party at Buckingham Palace on 26th June 1920, the VC Dinner at the Royal Gallery of the House of Lords, London on 9th November 1929 and the VC Centenary Celebrations at Hyde Park, London on 26th June 1956. He was an enthusiastic supporter of the RASC and was appointed Life President of the Southport Branch. He also became a member of the Royal Society of St George in 1956, being proposed by the Duke of Devonshire and seconded by Brigadier Sir John Smythe VC MC.

Richard died at his home at 35 Palmerston Road, Southport on 4th April 1963 after a few months' illness. He was buried with his wife at St Cuthbert's Parish

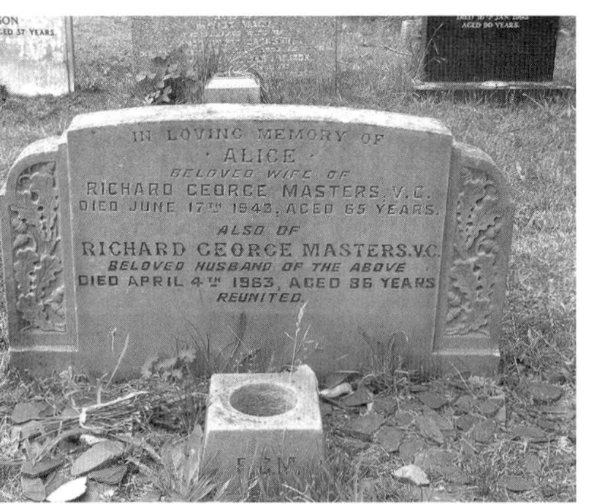

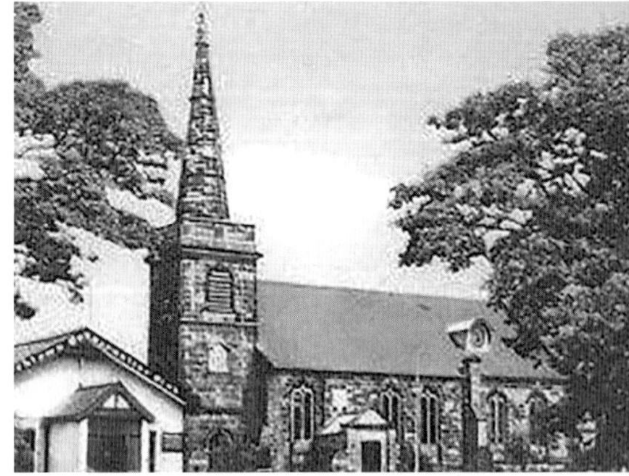

Richard and Alice are buried in St Cuthbert's Parish Churchyard, Churchtown, Southport. St Cuthbert's Church is in the Diocese of Liverpool and is a Grade II listed building. There has been a church on the site since at least the time of King Stephen, who died in 1154. The current church was built 1730–39 to replace the original, which burned down. Alterations were made in 1806 and it was extensively restored in 1908–09. The church contains a number of memorials to the Fleetwood and Hesketh families, who owned most of the local area, including the family seats of Meols Hall and Greaves Hall.

Churchyard, Churchtown, Southport, Lancashire on 8th April (Section II). Richard is commemorated in a number of other places:

- *R.G. Masters VC* (167 tons) was built by Jones' Buckie Shipyard at Buckie, Banff in 1953 and was completed on 9th July 1954 as HMS *Halsham*, a Royal Navy Ham Class inshore minesweeper (Pennant M2633 later IMS35). She was in reserve at Gosport 1955–57 and was seconded to the Air Ministry in 1966 for the RAF Marine Branch as *Interim Recovery Vessel* 5002 (renumbered 5012 in 1967). In 1968 she was loaned to the Royal Aircraft Establishment, Farnborough as a research vessel crewed by the RAF Marine Branch and operated by 1107 Marine Craft Unit, Newhaven for Ministry of Technology sea trials of RAF scientific equipment. She returned to the Royal Navy on 17th October 1972 and transferred to the Royal Corps of Transport as *R.G. Masters VC* in February 1973 at Gun Wharf, Portsmouth and was operated for RAE Farnborough by 20 Maritime Regiment RCT at Gosport. She was withdrawn from service in 1981 and stored at Portsmouth Naval Dockyard until sold in 1982 to Ionian Cruises, Corfu, Greece, for conversion to a passenger ferry and renamed *Sotirakis*.
- *Richard Masters V.C.*, an Honours Class range safety craft (32.7 tons) built in 1980 by Anderson, Rigden & Perkins Ltd at Whitstable for the Royal Corps of Transport. She was operated in UK coastal waters by 18 Maritime Squadron RCT and transferred to the Royal Maritime Auxiliary Service (Pennant 7820) on 1st October 1988. She was managed and operated by Smit International (Scotland) as a range safety craft under MOD contract from 1995 and renamed *RSC 7820*, based at Portland. She was transferred to the MOD Police in the early-2000s as *Police Launch Richard Masters*, based at Portsmouth.
- Masters accommodation block, Royal Military Academy Sandhurst, opened by Johnson Beharry VC on 26th January 2006.
- RG Masters VC Army Reserve Centre, 30 Pelham Drive, off Netherton Way, Bootle, Lancashire opened on 1st May 2009 by the Duke of Gloucester. The

The original Southport VC memorial in Southport Garden of Remembrance was replaced in 2013 with this version.

The former range safety craft, *Richard Masters V.C.*, now operated by the MOD Police as *Police Launch Richard Masters* at Portsmouth.

Centre is home to 238 (Sefton) Transport Squadron, Royal Logistic Corps (V) and two cadet organisations.
- Masters Troop, 96 (The Duke of Gloucester) Squadron RLC, Army Training Regiment, Pirbright, Surrey.
- Named on a memorial in Southport Garden of Remembrance, dedicated to Southport men awarded the VC. Also commemorated are Sergeant WE Heaton, King's Liverpool, Captain H Ackroyd RAMC, Sergeant AHL Richardson, Lord Strathcona's Horse, and Lieutenant WA Sandys-Clare, Loyal North Lancashire.
- A Department for Communities and Local Government commemorative paving stone was dedicated at Southport War Memorial, Lord Street, Southport on 21st April 2018 to mark the centenary of his award.

In addition to the VC he was awarded the 1914–15 Star, British War Medal 1914–20, Victory Medal 1914–19, George VI Coronation Medal 1937, Elizabeth II Coronation Medal 1953 and the French Croix de Guerre 1914–18 with Bronze Palm. The medal group was presented to the RASC at a ceremony on 30th July 1963 by his son Douglas and daughter Bessie. They were received by Major General Sir William Gordon Roe KBE CB. The VC is held by the Royal Logistic Corps Officers' Mess, Princess Royal Barracks, Deepcut, Camberley, Surrey.

4061 SERGEANT STANLEY ROBERT MCDOUGALL
47th Australian Infantry Battalion AIF

Stanley McDougall was born on 23rd July 1889 at Recherche, Tasmania, Australia. His father, John Henry McDougall (21st May 1853–27th March 1910), a saw miller, was born at Cygnet, Tasmania. He married Susannah Ann née Cate (26th December 1856–28th February 1919), born at Nelson, Marlborough, New Zealand, on 13th February 1884 at Esperance, Tasmania. She was living at Catamaran, Recherche, Tasmania in 1911, at 13 Melifort Street, West Hobart, Tasmania in 1915, at Ramsgate, Recherche in 1917 and at Murray Street, Hobart in 1918. Stanley had six siblings:

- John 'Jock' Henry McDougall (1st May 1885–20th November 1952) married Elsie Gertrude Hay (28th April 1883–19th February 1955) on 27th December 1906 at Hastings Congregational Church. He died at Ranelagh and she at Sandy Bay, Tasmania. They had six children:

Port Cygnet, where Stanley's father was born.

Stanley's mother was born at Nelson, New Zealand.

HMAS *Sydney*, was ordered for the Royal Navy as HMS *Phaeton*, a *Leander* Class light cruiser, but was purchased by the Australian government and renamed prior to being launched in 1934. She helped to enforce sanctions during the Abyssinian Crisis and, when war broke out, was assigned to convoy escort and patrol duties in Australian waters. In May 1940 she joined the British Mediterranean Fleet and sank two Italian warships, participated in a number of shore bombardments and supported the Malta convoys before returning to Australia in February 1941. On 19th November 1941, *Sydney* was involved in an engagement with the German auxiliary cruiser *Kormoran*, as a result of which both vessels were lost. The two wrecks were discovered in March 2008. Sydney's loss came as a major blow to Australia and her company made up 35% of the Royal Australian Navy's wartime fatalities. Internationally the loss had less impact, coming as it did just before Pearl Harbor on 7th December and the loss of HMS *Repulse* and *Prince of Wales* on 10th December.

- John Henry McDougall (29th August 1909–13th October 1962) served during the Second World War and was at Tobruk. He died in New Zealand.
- Elda McDougall (1912–7th October 2009) married and had six children. She died at Launceston.
- Keith McDougall (1915–1st December 1918) was born at Hawthorn, Victoria, Australia. He died at Castle Hill, Victoria.
- Wallace McDougall (24th October 1918–20th November 1941), born at Hawthorn, Victoria, enlisted in the Royal Australian Navy on 4th June

1935 (20816). He was promoted able seaman on 5th November 1938 and leading seaman on 1st October 1941. He married Vivienne Monteith (born 1923), of Strathfield, New South Wales, at Auburn in November 1941 and reported for duty aboard HMAS *Sydney* immediately after the reception. On 19th November 1941 *Sydney* was lost with all 645 hands. Wallace is commemorated on the Plymouth Naval Memorial, Devon (Panel 56, Column 3).

Murray Street, Hobart.

- ◦ Ailsa McDougall (1921–3rd June 1996), born at Bairnsdale, Victoria, died at Hobart, Tasmania.
- ◦ Donald McDougall (15th December 1923–7th January 1975), born at Sorell, Tasmania, married Valma May Parsons (1927–65) on 1st October 1943 at Brisbane, Queensland. She was born in Queensland and died in Brisbane. He died at Launceston, Tasmania. They had three children – Marion Dale McDougall 1947, Raymond McDougall 1949 and Anthony Wayne McDougall 1949.

- William George McDougall (12th July 1886–15th March 1905) was born at Ringarooma, Tasmania. His name has also been seen as Willmott. He was killed in an accident when a rolling log fractured his skull at Clayton's Hill, near Scottsdale, Tasmania.
- Holly Marion McDougall (11th March 1888–8th June 1922), born at Dover, Tasmania, married Percy Enoch Grubb (8th June 1884–c.1959), a telegraph linesman, on 27th December 1911 at Catamaran, Recherche and they had

Plymouth Naval Memorial is one of three memorials to the Royal Navy's missing. The other identical memorials are at Chatham and Portsmouth. They were designed by Sir Robert Lorimer with sculpture by Henry Poole. The Plymouth Naval memorial commemorates more than 7,200 sailors of the First World War and nearly 16,000 of the Second World War who have no known grave. It was unveiled by Prince George in July 1924 (as seen in this picture) and the Second World War extension by Princess Margaret on 20th May 1954. More than a quarter of the men commemorated were lost at The Battle of Jutland in May/June 1916. The governments of most Commonwealth nations chose to commemorate their naval dead elsewhere, but sailors from Australia and South Africa are commemorated here.

a child. They were living at Hobart North, Denison, Tasmania in 1919. Percy served during the Second World War (TI5003), enlisting at Hobart and recording his next-of-kin as Frances McCormack.

- Malcolm Samuel McDougall (7th April 1891–19th March 1969), born at Southport, Tasmania, married Eva Gladys Grubb (8th August 1892–24th May 1950) on 30th October 1918 at St Raphael's, Fern Tree, Tasmania. She was born at Hobart, sister of Percy Enoch Grubb, who married Malcolm's sister Holly. Their address in 1923 was Main Road, Glenorchy, Hobart.
- Wallace Carlyle McDougall (29th December 1893–7th June 1917), born at Recherche, Tasmania, was an engine driver when he enlisted in 40th Australian Infantry Battalion AIF at Claremont on 29th February 1916 (682). He was described as 5′ 9″ tall, weighing 152 lbs, with medium complexion, blue eyes, light brown hair and his religious denomination was Church of England. He was absent from parade on 2nd April, resulting in him being confined to camp for three days and fined 5/-. He was absent without leave from Claremont from reveille on 29th May until reveille on 10th June, for which he forfeited twelve days pay and was fined £2. Wallace sailed for Devonport, Devon from Hobart aboard HMAT A35 *Berrima* on 1st July 1916, arriving on 22nd August. He went to France on 23rd November and was admitted to 10th Field Ambulance and No.1 Canadian Casualty Clearing Station with mumps on 18th December. Having transferred to 7th General Hospital, St Omer next day, he was discharged to the Base Depot on 9th January 1917 and rejoined 40th Battalion on the 10th. He was admitted to 9th Field Ambulance with influenza 2nd-4th February 1917. Wallace was killed in action on 7th June 1917 and is buried in Messines Ridge British Cemetery, Belgium (I D 18). His brother, Stanley, applied for his medals in 1935 and received them in July 1936.
- Ivy Susann McDougall (3rd September 1894–28th July 1972), born at Southport, Tasmania, married Colin Isaac Hay (13th November 1892–17th March 1961), a carpenter, on 22nd December 1919 at Chalmers Free Church, Harrington Street, Hobart. Colin enlisted in 40th Battalion AIF on 29th February 1916 at Claremont, Tasmania (672), described as 5′ 6″ tall, weighing 147 lbs, with fair complexion, hazel eyes, brown hair and his religious denomination was Church of England. He was absent from Claremont 30th May–10th June 1916 and forfeited eleven days' pay. He sailed for Britain aboard HMAT A35 *Berrima* from Hobart on 1st July, arriving at Devonport, Devon on 22nd August. He was stationed at Perham Down, Wiltshire and was admitted to 10th Australian Field Ambulance at Larkhill, Wiltshire with follicular tonsillitis 1st-4th October. Colin was also admitted to Beaufort War Hospital, Stapleton, Gloucestershire on 8th February 1917. He went to France on 9th May and received gunshot wounds to the back and right thigh. Having been evacuated to England, he was admitted to Edmonton Military Hospital, London 23rd June–9th July and returned to France on 19th September. Having been promoted lance corporal on 20th

November, he was admitted to 9th Australian Field Ambulance with asthma on 3rd December. He was evacuated to England on 8th December and was treated at 3rd Southern General Hospital, Oxford 9th-23rd December. He was granted leave 31st December 1917–14th January 1918, from when he was transferred to No.2 Command Depot, Weymouth, Dorset for convalescence. Colin returned to Australia aboard RMS *Osterley*, arriving at 3rd Military District on 4th April. He was discharged in Tasmania on 21st May 1918 and was awarded an incapacity pension of 30/- per fortnight. They were living at Princess Street, Sandy Bay, Tasmania and moved to Adam Street, Sandy Bay in May 1924. Ivy and Colin had two daughters:

  - Phyllis Susannah Hay (27th October 1920–3rd January 2007) married John 'Jack' McMullen (2nd November 1904–1994) and they had three children.
  - Dulcie Hay.

Stanley's paternal grandfather, William Parker McDougall (26th February 1822–19th April 1907), born at Glasgow, Lanarkshire, Scotland, emigrated to Tasmania. He married Mary née Coulter (14th May 1825–28th June 1898) on 1st April 1850 at Port Cygnet, Tasmania. She was also born in Glasgow and emigrated to Tasmania on 11th February 1848. They both died at Franklin, Tasmania. In addition to John they had four other children:

- William Charles McDougall (March 1852–22nd March 1939), born at Port Cygnet, married Hannah Jane Archer (17th October 1853–24th June 1930) on 8th July 1877 at Hobart. She was born at Stowmarket, Suffolk, England. He was living at 154 Melville Street, Hobart when he died. They had seven children – Edith Jane McDougall 1880, twins Charles William McDougall and Mabel Eva McDougall 1883, Sydney Hilmor McDougall 1886, Percy Milford McDougall 1888, Linda Daisy McDougall 1891 and Allen Benson McDougall 1895.
- Sarah Ann McDougall (10th November 1856–9th November 1933), born at Port Cygnet, married John Hay (26th April 1832–15th May 1902) on 23rd November 1881 at the Congregational Church, Port Esperance, Tasmania. John was born at Seaton, Angus, Scotland and emigrated to Tasmania (Van Diemen's Land), arriving at Hobart Town on 26th January 1841. He married Ann Matilda Meredith (27th December 1834–29th August 1880) on 23rd May 1849 at the Independent Chapel, Brisbane Street, Hobart and they had eleven children – John Hay 1854, Mary Hay 1856, Robert Hay 1858, Annie Hay 1860, Charles William Hay 1862, Margaret Hay 1865, William Hay 1866, Mary Margaret Hay 1869, Nathaniel Hay 1872, James Hay 1873 and Herbert Hay 1876. Sarah and John lived at Arbroath Cottage, Franklin. They had ten children – Jessie Hay 1882, James McDougall Hay 1884, Leslie Seaton Hay 1885, Henry George Hay 1887, Horace Coulter Hay 1887, Hilda Sarah Hay 1888, Ralph Emerson Hay 1889, Maud Mabel Hay 1892, Gladys May Hay 1893 and Emerson Hay 1896.

- Mary Agnes McDougall (23rd July 1857–15th October 1917), born at Port Cygnet, married Edward Stride (1861–13th January 1908) on 7th December 1887 at Hobart. He was born Edwin 1861 at Portsea, Hampshire and was living with his mother, a laundress, and siblings at 52 Frederick Street, Portsea in 1871. He was riding a bicycle in Queen's Domain, Hobart on 13th January 1908 when he collided with a cab and was rushed to the General Hospital, where he died of haemorrhage and shock.
- George Parker McDougall (5th October 1860–28th May 1933), a draper, married Eliza and they had two daughters, Sheila, who married as Jeffreys, and Edith Florence, who married as Knapp.

His maternal grandfather, William Cate (c.1822–27th September 1870), born in Hampshire, England, was an agricultural labourer when he emigrated to New Zealand aboard SV *Bolton*, departing Gravesend, Kent on 29th October 1841. *Bolton* was dismasted in a storm, lost her sails and much of the upper deck. Fortunately a French ship chanced upon her and supplied timber to effect repairs that allowed *Bolton* to continue the journey to Nelson, New Zealand, arriving on 15th March 1842. He married Susannah L née Higgs (c.1832–7th March 1911), born in Warwickshire, England, on 26th November 1851 at Richmond, New Zealand. They are believed to have separated by 1870. He died at Waimea, Nelson. In addition to Susannah they had three other children:

- Henry Cate (born 1853).
- Eliza Cate (30th November 1853–29th July 1931), born at Nelson, married William Henry Barlow (22nd November 1824–10th June 1912) there on 6th June 1874. He was born in Gloucestershire, England and died at Waingaro, Motueka, New Zealand. She died at Nelson. They had seven children – Annie Kate Barlow 1874, Lily Alceine Barlow 1877, William Henry Barlow 1878, Samuel Artemas Barlow 1881, Rita Ethel Barlow 1889, Edward Lawrence Barlow 1891 and Minnie Alberta Barlow 1893.
- Samuel Cate (26th September 1858–20th September 1943), born at Nelson, married Alicena Ellen Fauchelle (22nd October 1864–31st January 1884) on 18th April 1883 at East Takaka. They had a son, Ernest Samuel Cate, born on 26th January 1884. Samuel married Clara Emily Talbot (28th May 1868–12th November 1899) on 11th July 1889 and they had two children – Samuel Henry Cate 1891 and Ellen Margaret Cate 1894. He married Dorothea Margaret Matilda Schroder (1873–2nd June 1946) on 12th May 1903 at Motueka. They had two children – Graci Cate 1905 and Alicena Doris Cate 1907.

Susannah married Robert George Tilt (c.1820–21st October 1891) on 30th October 1877 at Chalmers Free Presbyterian Church, Hobart, Tasmania. They had five children – Mary Ann Tilt 18th July 1865, Susannah Tilt 3rd February 1867, Ellen

Tilt 15th August 1868, Charlotte Tilt 17th May 1870 and Robert Joseph Tilt 11th May 1874.

Stanley was educated locally in the Recherche area and became a blacksmith. He was an excellent horseman, marksman and bushman and also took up amateur boxing. He enlisted in the Australian Imperial Force on 31st August 1915, described as 5′ 5½″ tall, weighing 179 lbs, with fair complexion, blue eyes, light brown hair and his religious denomination was Presbyterian. He was posted to Claremont, Tasmania. His experience as a farrier was wanted by a light horse unit but Stanley chose to stay with the infantry. He embarked for the Middle East with 12th Reinforcement Group, 15th Battalion at Melbourne on RMS *Orontes* on 24th November and disembarked at Alexandria, Egypt. On 3rd March 1916 he moved to Heliopolis and Tel-el-Kebir and transferred to 47th Battalion on 9th March 1916.

Stanley's grandmother, Susannah, married for the second time at Chalmers Free Presbyterian Church, Hobart, Tasmania. It was built in 1859 as a Free Church of Scotland and became a Presbyterian Church in 1896. It was deconsecrated in 1981.

Stanley embarked on HMT *Caledonia* at Alexandria for Marseille, France on 2nd September 1916. He reported sick on 2nd January 1917 and was treated at 8th Field Ambulance and the New Zealand Stationary Hospital, Amiens for myalgia on 10th January. From there he was moved to 10th General Hospital, Rouen on 13th January and 2nd Convalescent Depot on 15th January. He rejoined his unit on 6th February from 4th Australian Division Base Depot. He was treated at 3rd Australian Field Ambulance for staphylococcus aureus (generally known as Staph) of the foot on 27th February and returned to

HMAT A38 *Ulysses* (14,499 tons), owned by the China Mutual Steam Navigation Co of London, was leased by the Commonwealth until 15th August 1917, making six journeys from Australia carrying troops and general goods. She was then taken over by the Admiralty. On 11th April 1942, en route from Sydney to Liverpool, she was hit in the stern by a torpedo from U-*160* south of Cape Hatteras, North Carolina. While the crew abandoned ship, the U-boat fired another torpedo amidships and the ship sank in thirty minutes. All aboard (190 crew, five gunners and ninety-five passengers) were picked up by USS *Manley* and landed at Charleston, South Carolina.

RMS *Orontes*, built for the Orient Steam Navigation Co, made her maiden voyage on 24th October 1902, carrying mail and passengers from London to Melbourne and Sydney via Suez, which became her regular route. In October 1916 she was requisitioned as a troopship, HMAT *Orontes*. In 1917 she was relinquished by the Admiralty as her refrigerated hold was more useful for transporting produce from Australia to Britain, rather than troops. In 1919 she resumed the Australia service but in 1921 was laid up in the Thames. She resumed service with the Orient Line in 1923 but was scrapped several years later (State Library of Queensland).

his unit on 5th March. On 21st March he was ill with mumps and was treated at 2nd Stationary Hospital, Abbeville. He transferred to 16th General Hospital, Le Tréport on 23rd March, to 4th Australian Division Base Depot on 11th April and rejoined the unit on 19th April.

Stanley was promoted lance corporal 5th May, corporal 19th June, temporary sergeant 2nd November and sergeant on 23rd January 1918. He was granted leave in England 3rd–16th July 1917 and in Paris, France 20th February–8th March 1918. **Awarded the VC for his actions at Dernancourt, France on 28th March 1918, LG 3rd May 1918. Awarded the MM for his actions at Dernancourt, France on 5th April 1918, when another heavy enemy attack took place, he managed to get a Lewis gun to an exposed position and enfiladed the Germans from as close as thirty metres. Enemy fire damaged the gun, forcing him to crawl about 275m under fire to obtain a replacement. During a counterattack the platoon commander was killed and he commanded the platoon for the remainder of the action, LG 16th July 1918.**

Having been attached to the Lewis Gun School at Le Touquet from 8th May, he transferred to 48th Battalion on 28th May when 47th Battalion disbanded. On 5th August he was posted to the AIF's London Headquarters for leave. The VC and MM were presented by the King at Windsor Castle on 19th August. On 22nd August he reported to No.2 Command Depot, Weymouth. Two days later he embarked on HMAT D21 *Medic* to return to Australia to support recruiting. Aboard were fellow VCs John Carroll, John James Dwyer, Reginald Inwood, Joergen Jensen, Thomas Kenny, Leonard Keysor,

2nd Stationary Hospital, Abbeville.

HMAT D21 *Medic* (11,985 tons) was built in 1899 by Harland & Wolff in Belfast for the Oceanic Steam Navigation Co. In 1928 she was renamed *Hektoria* by her new owners of the same name and was converted to a whale factory. She was sunk by U-*211* and U-*608* on 11th September 1942 en route from Liverpool to New York.

The Warwick Street/Murray Street area of Hobart.

Walter Peeler, William Ruthven and John Whittle. They arrived on 11th October. Stanley was discharged from the 6th Military District, Tasmania on 15th December 1918.

He joined the Tasmanian Forestry Commission and in 1923 his address was c/o Mrs Goschman, Boarding House, Warwick Street, Hobart. In the early 1930s he became an inspector in charge of all forests in the northwest of Tasmania. On several occasions he performed outstanding organisational and rescue work during bushfires, particularly those around Fitzgerald in 1934. On one occasion his vehicle was burned under him while he attempted to shift a family's belongings from the path of a fire.

Stanley married Martha 'Matty' Florence Anderson-Harrison (27th June 1888–1974) in 1926 and they settled at 10 Christopher Street, Scottsdale, Tasmania. They were living at 9A Ferndene Avenue, South Hobart, Tasmania in April 1935.

Matty and Stanley initially settled at 10 Christopher Street, Scottsdale (realestate).

Matty and Stanley later lived at 42 Lochner Street, West Hobart.

John Harrison is named on the 26th Infantry Battalion panel of the Villers-Bretonneux Memorial Australian National Memorial, which commemorates 10,773 soldiers of the Australian Imperial Force who died in France and Belgium in the Great War and who have no known grave. The location was chosen due to the important role played by the AIF in the Second Battle of Villers-Bretonneux in April 1918. It was designed by Sir Edwin Lutyens after previous designs proved too expensive. The memorial was unveiled on 22nd July 1938 by King George VI, whose speech was broadcast directly to Australia.

There were no children. Matty's father, John Anderson-Harrison (c.1843–22nd November 1931) married Martha née Anderson (c.1860–30th December 1947) on 21st October 1884. They lived at 42 Lochner Street, West Hobart. She was living at 68 Lochner Street, West Hobart at the time of her death. In addition to Martha they had two other children:

- Eleanor 'Elsie' Harrison married WG Oakes.
- John Harrison (24th October 1890–29th July 1916) enlisted in 26th Australian Infantry Battalion AIF (154G). He was killed in action on 29th July 1916 and is commemorated on the Villers-Bretonneux Memorial, France.

Stanley was at the Anzac Commemoration Service on 25th April 1927 at the Exhibition Building, Melbourne, Victoria in the presence of the Duke of York (future King George VI). In the march past the twenty-six VCs conceded pride of place to blinded soldiers who insisted on marching. An Anzac Dinner was held two nights before, hosted by Lieutenant General Sir John Monash GCMG KCB VD, and was attended by twenty-three VCs. For an unknown reason The Duke of York was not invited. In 1937 Stanley lost his MM. The police found it but it was destroyed before he could reclaim it and he therefore applied for a replacement on repayment. At an ANZAC Day parade in Sydney in 1938 he lost his Coronation Medal and applied for a replacement. Stanley attended the VC Centenary Celebrations at Hyde Park, London on 26th June 1956, travelling on SS *Orcades* with other Australian VCs. In 1964 he was one of seventeen Australian VCs present at the opening of the

SS *Orcades* was the Orient Line's third ship of that name. Her maiden voyage from Tilbury to Australia commenced on 14th December 1948. In 1955 she began a world service westwards, departing London to New Zealand and Australia via the Panama Canal and returning to Britain via the Suez Canal. During the November 1956 Olympic Games in Melbourne she was used as an accommodation ship. She sailed her last cruises in 1972 and was broken up in 1973.

VC Corner at the Australian War Memorial by the Governor General, Lord De L'Isle VC.

Stanley died at the North East Soldiers' Memorial Hospital, Scottsdale on 7th July 1968. He was given a funeral with full military honours on 10th July at Holy Trinity Church, followed by cremation at Cornelian Bay Cemetery. It is not known what became of his ashes. He is commemorated in a number of other places:

- Display in the Hall of Valour, Australian War Memorial, Canberra, Australian Capital Territory. The uniform he wore and the Lewis gun he used at Dernancourt are displayed together with his VC and a portrait by Frank Crozier.
- Named on one of eleven plaques honouring 175 men from overseas awarded the VC for the Great War. The plaques were unveiled by the Senior Minister of State

The North East Soldiers' Memorial Hospital, Scottsdale, where Stanley died on 7th July 1968.

Stanley's memorial at Norwood Crematorium, Canberra.

Victoria Cross Memorial, Queen Victoria Building, George Street, Sydney (MaritimeQuest.com).

The Military Medal was awarded to other ranks of the British Army (later extended to other services) and Commonwealth countries for bravery on land. It was established on 25th March 1916 as the other ranks equivalent of the Military Cross, which was awarded to commissioned officers and warrant officers. It was the third level gallantry award, ranking below the Distinguished Conduct Medal. Over 115,000 MMs were awarded during the Great War, as well as 5,700 bars and 180 second bars. Private Ernest Corey, a stretcher-bearer with 55th Australian Infantry Battalion, was awarded three bars. Over 15,000 MMs were awarded during the Second World War. It was discontinued in 1993, since when the Military Cross has been awarded to all ranks within the British honours system. Most Commonwealth nations established their own honours systems after the Second World War and award their own gallantry decorations.

at the Foreign & Commonwealth Office and Minister for Faith and Communities, Baroness Warsi, at a reception at Lancaster House, London on 26th June 2014 attended by The Duke of Kent and relatives of the VC recipients. The Australian plaque is at the Australian War Memorial.

- Australian Victoria Cross Recipients plaque on the Victoria Cross Memorial, Campbell, Canberra, Australian Capital Territory, dedicated on 24th July 2000.
- Bronze plaque at Norwood Crematorium, Sandford Street, Mitchell, Canberra, Australia Capital Territory, although his ashes are not located there.
- Victoria Cross Memorial, Hobart Cenotaph, Tasmania, dedicated on 11th May 2003.
- Memorial at Dover RSL Club, 1 Chapman Avenue, Dover, Tasmania.
- The Stanley Robert McDougall VC Premium Benchmark 78 Handicap, a Tasmanian Turf Club horse race (2100m) held annually on Anzac Day at Launceston Racecourse, Mowbray. It is one of four Anzac Day races at Launceston named after Tasmanian-born VCs. The others are John Dwyer, Harry Murray and Percy Statton.
- McDougall Street, Wodonga, Victoria, on White Box Rise estate, built on land formerly part of Bandiana Army Camp.

- Victoria Cross Memorial, Queen Victoria Building, George Street, Sydney, New South Wales dedicated on 23rd February 1992 to commemorate the visit of Queen Elizabeth II and Prince Phillip on the occasion of the Sesquicentenary of the City of Sydney. Sir Roden Cutler VC, Edward Kenna VC and Keith Payne VC were in attendance.
- Victoria Cross Recipients Wall, North Bondi War Memorial, New South Wales donated to the community of Waverley on 27th November 2011 by The Returned & Services League of Australia.
- Communities and Local Government commemorative paving stones for the 145 VCs born in Australia, Belgium, Canada, China, Denmark, Egypt, France, Germany, India, Iraq, Japan, Nepal, Netherlands, Newfoundland, New Zealand, Pakistan, South Africa, Sri Lanka, Ukraine and United States of America were unveiled at the National Memorial Arboretum, Alrewas, Staffordshire by Prime Minister David Cameron MP and Sergeant Johnson Beharry VC on 5th March 2015.

In addition to the VC and MM he was awarded the 1914–15 Star, British War Medal 1914–20, Victory Medal 1914–19, George VI Coronation Medal 1937 and Elizabeth II Coronation Medal 1953. The VC is held by the 'Hall of Valour' at the Australian War Memorial, Treloar Crescent, Campbell, Australian Capital Territory, Australia.

LIEUTENANT GEORGE BURDON McKEAN
14th Battalion (Royal Montreal Regiment) CEF

George McKean was born on 4th July 1888 at 102 High Street, Willington, Bishop Auckland, Co Durham. His father, James McKean (c.1840–13th November 1891) was born in Scotland. He married Jane Ann née Henderson (1849–6th May 1905), born at Evenwood, Co Durham, in 1865 at Durham. He was a coal miner and they were living at 6 Katherine Street, Willington in 1881. By 1888 he was a furniture broker. They were living at 71 High Street, Durham in 1891. Their son, George, was living next door at 72 High Street with William and Jane Rutherford's family. James died at 71 High Street. Jane was living at Armstrong Cottages, 28 North Bondgate, Bishop Auckland in 1901. She died at 21 Oxford Terrace, Bishop Auckland. George had seven siblings:

The family was living on North Bondgate, Bishop Auckland in 1901.

George McKean was born on High Street, Willington, Bishop Auckland.

- Jessie Ann McKean (1867–1947) married John Westgarth (1865–1940) in 1887. He was an underground mason in 1911 and they were living at 14 High Bridge Street, Bishop Auckland. They had eleven children:
    - James Westgarth (1887–91).
    - Jane Ann Westgarth (1889–1954) married John William Catchpole (1886–1954) in 1909. He was a coal miner hewer in 1911 and they were living at 3 Stone Row, Leasingthorne, Bishop Auckland. They had three children – Margaret Elsie Catchpole 1910, Elizabeth Catchpole 1914 and Jessie Catchpole 1928.
    - Margaret Westgarth (1891–1965) was working at the Hippodrome, Bishop Auckland in 1911. She married Thomas Cleminson (1890–1962) on 24th August 1912. They had nine children – John Hedley Cleminson 1913, Alfred Hedley Cleminson 1915, Alice E Cleminson 1920, Thomas Cleminson 1921, Eleanor Cleminson 1923, Jessie Cleminson 1924, Edith Cleminson 1926, George Cleminson 1929 and Ronald Cleminson 1932. Thomas enlisted in the Army Service Corps (RTS 6561) on 15th March 1915 and joined at Woolwich on 19th March, described as a cartman, 5′ 5″ tall and his address was 5 Margaret Terrace, Coronation, near Bishop Auckland. Thomas went to France on 1st April 1915 and was appointed unpaid acting lance corporal on 22nd July 1916 but reverted to private for misconduct in November 1916. He transferred to 9th King's Royal Rifle Corps (a/202430) on 22nd August 1917, retaining ASC rates of pay of 3/- per day. On 4th April 1918 he was taken prisoner of war at Hamel and was held at Lamsdorf. He returned to the Depot on 6th January 1919 and transferred to the Class Z Reserve on 6th April suffering from rheumatism attributable to military service. He was assessed as being twenty percent disabled and was granted a conditional pension of 8/- per week from 18th September. Thomas was demobilised from the Reserve on 31st March 1920. They were living at 1 Oxford Street, Eldon Lane, Bishop Auckland in January 1921.

- ° Robert Newton Westgarth (1892–1938).
- ° Elizabeth Newton Westgarth (1895–1963) was an assistant printer in 1911. She married Robert Thomson (29th April 1892–1974) in 1919.
- ° John Westgarth (1898–1948) married Annie Brown Vickers (1894–1969) in 1919. They had three children – Irene E Westgarth 1925, Mary Westgarth 1931 and Jessie A Westgarth 1933.
- ° Alice Eva Westgarth (1901–19).
- ° Thomas Newton Westgarth (30th July 1903–1972) married Nora Gilbey (1908–47) in 1928. They had three children – Allan Westgarth 1929, Clive Westgarth 1930 and Olwen Westgarth 1934.
- ° Mary Gertrude Westgarth (born 1905) married John Wilson in 1932 and they had a son, John C Wilson, in 1933.
- ° Edith Westgarth (born 1907) married James H Jackson in 1932. They had four children – Keith Jackson 1933, Margaret E Jackson 1935, Enid Jackson 1936 and Alan Jackson 1941.
- ° Annie Westgarth (born 1910) married Andrew Baister (1908–68) in 1932. They had a son, Andrew Baister, in 1934.

• John William McKean (1869–29th November 1958) was a coalminer living with his parents in 1891. He married Mary Jane Hill (c.1868–20th September 1947) in 1896. She was born in Manchester, Lancashire. He was a science teacher and superintendent in 1901 and they were living at 63 Cumberland Street, Darlington, Co Durham. They emigrated to Canada on 30th May 1904, disembarking at

Lethbridge grew from a population of 2,072 in 1901 to almost 93,000 by 2016, to become Alberta's fourth largest city. The city's economy was based upon drift mining, which began in 1874. Indeed the city is named after William Lethbridge, president of North Western Coal and Navigation Company. The last mine closed in 1957. The years between 1907 and 1913 were a boom time as Lethbridge grew into the main marketing, distribution and service centre of southern Alberta. Agriculture also played an important part in local economic life but after the Great War a drought drove farmers from their farms. Post Second World War irrigation did much to rebalance this.

Medicine Hat is approximately 170 kms east of Lethbridge. Its population of just 1,570 in 1901 had grown to 63,260 by 2016, the sixth largest city in Alberta. The Canadian Pacific Railway reached Medicine Hat in 1883. The area is rich in resources, including natural gas, coal, clay and agriculture. Industries were attracted there by cheap energy resources, including coal, brick, pottery, glass and flour mills. Similar to Lethbridge, there was an economic boom in the years 1909 to 1914. During the Second World War one of the largest prisoner of war camps in Canada was established there.

Montreal before moving to Lethbridge, Alberta. They had moved to Medicine Hat by 1911, where he became a farmer. She died at Saanich, British Columbia. He died at Victoria, British Columbia.

- James McKean (1873–1905).
- Mary Jane McKean (1875–1921) was a domestic servant living with his parents in 1891. She married Morgan Francis Shea (1869–1921), a carpet weaver, in 1894. His birth was registered as Michael MF Shay. By 1911 he was a coal miner hewer and they were living at 14 Claypath, Durham. Their deaths were registered consecutively in the 2nd quarter of 1921 at Durham. They had nine children:
    - Morgan Francis Shea (1894–95).
    - James William Shea (27th February 1896–1974) married Jane 'Jean' Falconer/Faulkner Mitchell (8th March 1897–January 1985) in 1918. She was living with her spinster aunt, Jean Falconer Mitchell (1855–1917), at Acorn Villa, Daisy Hill, Chester le Street, Co Durham in 1901 and 1911. They had a daughter, Mary A Shea, in 1922.
    - George Henry Shea (20th December 1897–1970) married Jennie Coulthard (1st June 1903–December 1986) in 1923. She was living with her parents at 6 Allergate, Durham in 1911.
    - Joseph Ernest Shea (1903–04).
    - Cecilia Mary Shea (1901–07).
    - Walter Shea (13th July 1905–May 1995) married Annie Allan (5th January 1908–June 2000) in 1928. They had two children – Dorothy Shea 1931 and Alan Shea 1933.
    - Gladys Shea (1907–39) married James Leonard Hick (18th November 1908–1979) in 1931 at Scarborough, Yorkshire, where he was born. They had two children – Mary M Hick 1932 and Ronald J Hick 1937. James married

Jessie Smith (2nd June 1916–February 1995) in 1942 at Birmingham, Warwickshire.
  - Marian Kate Shea (27th January 1911–November 1994) married Thomas Richard Hart (18th December 1904–July 1997) in 1931 at Scarborough, where he was born. They had two children – Raymond Hart 1935 and Thomas R Hart 1938.
  - Mary Shea, born and died 1914.
- Sarah McKean (1878–1957) married Arthur Wade (1875–1954) on 16th June 1900 at St Anne's Church, Bishop Auckland. He was a railway porter, born at North Cowton, Richmond, Yorkshire. They were living at 4 Grey Street, Bishop Auckland in 1911. They had seven children:
  - Elizabeth Jane Wade (1900–17).
  - Arthur Wade (1903–26).
  - Elsie Wade (1905–April 1988) married Norman Ward (1904–69) in 1926. They had a daughter, Dorothy Ward, in 1928. It is assumed that the marriage ended in divorce. Elsie married Robert Frederick Frankish (1906–23rd January 1983) in 1949. He was living at 10 Rosewood Grange, Chilton, Ferryhill, Co Durham at the time of his death.
  - George William Wade (18th September 1907–31st March 1958) married Winifred Tweddle (24th May 1909–9th February 2008) on 12th September 1936 at Northallerton, Yorkshire.
  - Jonas Wade (1910–2001) married Mary Elizabeth Watson (1909–71) in 1936 at Northallerton. She was born at Bedale, Yorkshire. Her death was registered at Northallerton. He died at Melbourne, Victoria, Australia.
  - William Henry Wade (31st May 1916–18th July 1996) married Irene Margaret Ludlam Wilson (15th March 1917–September 1995) in 1939. They had a son, Peter Wade, in 1941.
  - Edna Wade (1918–43) married George Bellwood (born 1915) in 1939.
- Frances Wilson McKean (23rd December 1879–6th April 1951) married Christopher Rutherford (30th September 1878–1947), a railway porter, on 21st March 1901 at St Anne's Church, Bishop Auckland. By 1939 he was a road worker for Durham County Council and they were living at 12 Bell Street, Bishop Auckland, where she subsequently died. They had ten children:
  - Jane Rutherford (29th March 1901–3rd September 1980) married Ernest Craddock (1894–8th December 1961) in 1920. He was living at Claveresk, Durham Road, Bishop Auckland at the time of his death at the General Hospital, Bishop Auckland. She was living at 17 Teesdale Avenue, Darlington at the time of her death there. They had three children – Ronald Craddock 1922, Cecil Craddock 1923 and Keith Craddock 1932.
  - Doris Rutherford (4th January 1903–December 1979) was an assistant at the Cooperative Tobacco factory in 1939, living with her parents.
  - Evelyn Rutherford (1905–08).

  - Frances Rutherford (1906–08).
  - Olive Rutherford (20th January 1909–20th July 1975) was a shop assistant in 1939, living with her parents. She married John Henry Cummins (1899–1958) in 1947. She was living at 8 Tivoli Place, Bishop Auckland at the time of her death there.
  - Thomas Rutherford (12th March 1911–1978).
  - John Middlewood Rutherford (3rd June 1912–1974) was an inspector working for the United Bus Company in 1939. He married Joycelynne Calvert in 1941 and they had two children – Peter C Rutherford 1943 and Richard Rutherford 1946.
  - Mildred Rutherford (6th October 1914–1998) was a shop assistant in 1939, living with her parents. She married Thomas Bell in 1945.
  - George Rutherford (10th November 1917–14th March 1990) was living at 13 Marden Road, South Whitley Bay, Tyne & Wear when he died.
  - Vera Rutherford (1st July 1920–21st November 1991) was a shop assistant in 1939, living with her parents. She married John Reginald Beckett (1917–11th May 1963) in 1941. He was born at Driffield, Yorkshire. They were living at 12 St Mary's Road, Belmont, Co Durham at the time of his death at Dryburn Hospital, Durham. She was living at 39 Bell Street, Bishop Auckland at the time of her death there. They had two children – John M Beckett 1950 and Gillian Beckett 1961.
- Kate McKean (1885–1949) was a print compositor in 1901. She married Jonas Laight (1884–1932), a coal miner hewer, in 1907. Jonas had married Mildred Blanche Landick (1883–1906) in 1906. Jonas and Kate were living at 21 Albion Street, Middlestone Moor, Co Durham in 1911. They emigrated to Canada, departing Liverpool and arriving at Halifax, Nova Scotia on 18th October 1911. He was appointed acting Chief of Police at Medicine Hat, Alberta in 1919.

George's paternal grandfather, John McKean (15th November 1817–10th September 1880), was born at Barony, Lanarkshire, Scotland. He married Janet 'Jessie' née Cassells (9th December 1812–28th October 1880), born at Glasgow, Lanarkshire, on 17th November 1836 at Glasgow. He was a coal miner and they were living at 92 Rose Street, Gorbals, Lanarkshire in 1851, at Trimdon Colliery Village, Co Durham in 1861 and at 10 Katherine Street, Willington, Co Durham in 1871. In addition to James they had seven other children:

- Janet McKean (born c.1837).
- John McKean (born c.1837).
- Robert McKean (born 17th August 1838–1908) married Jessie Ross (c.1841–1903) in 1869 at Anderston. They had five children – William McKean 1869, Robert McKean 1871, Andrew McKean 1873, Isabella McKean 1878 and Jessie McKean 1879.

- William McKean (born c.1843–1915) was a coal miner living with his parents in 1861. He married Anne Maria Fox in 1867 and they had a daughter, Annie McKean, in 1870. He married Catherine Halliday (1853–c.1929), born at Easington, in 1878. They emigrated to the USA c.1880 and both died in Clay County, Indiana. They had five children – John McKean 1882, James McKean 1887, Catherine McKean 1889, William McKean 1892 and Mary Adeline McKean 1895.
- Daniel McKean (c.1846–1900) married Mary Maddison (1851–93) in 1870 at Durham. She died at Portland, Jay, Indiana, USA. He died in Clay County, Indiana. They had eight children – John McKean 1871, George McKean 1874, Elizabeth Maddison McKean 1876, Daniel McKean 1878, Jessie McKean 1881, Mary McKean 1883, Sarah McKean 1884 and Jasper McKean 1887.
- Edward McKean (c.1848–1909) was recorded as Ewart in the 1861 Census. He married Mary Ann Henderson (c.1852–94) in 1871 at Durham. She was born at Brampton, Carlisle, Cumberland. He was a peddler and they were living on Main Road, Shincliffe, Co Durham in 1881. By 1891 he was a traveller in hosiery and they were living at 75 Commercial Street, Willington. They had seven children – Annie McKean 1872, Janet McKean 1876, Mary Jane McKean 1878, Edward McKean 1880, Joseph Henderson McKean 1882, Sarah McKean 1884 and Emily McKean 1891. Edward married Anne 'Annie' Brown (born 1857) in 1897 at Sunderland, Co Durham. They had two children – Grace Blanche McKean 1898 and Rebecca McKean 1901. Annie had another daughter, Florence 'Florrie' Brown, born at Willington in 1884, who married Clifford Kirkham in 1905 at Prestwich, Lancashire. In 1911 Annie was living with Florrie and her husband at 72 Firwood Avenue, Urmston, Lancashire. In 1911 Mary Jane McKean was a boarding house keeper at 25 Stanley Street, Blyth, Northumberland and her siblings Joseph, Emily, Grace and Rebecca were living with her.
- Sarah McKean (born c.1852) married George Parkinson Burdon (1851–19th September 1906), a tailor, in 1872 at Durham. They were living at Commercial Street, Willington in 1881 and at 51 High Street, Brandon, Co Durham in 1891. They emigrated to the USA, arriving at New York on 2nd September 1904. He died in Clay County, Indiana. They had eight children – John Burdon 1873, Janet Burdon 1875, William Burdon 1877, Mary Burdon 1882, Sarah Burdon 1884, Annie Burdon 1887, Beatrice Burdon 1895 and George Parkinson Burdon 1898.

His maternal grandfather, David Henderson (c.1821–90), born at Hamsterley, Co Durham, was a blacksmith. He married Frances 'Fanny' née Wilson (c.1825–1st May 1878), born at Potters Cross, Co Durham, on 25th December 1844 at Hamsterley. They were living at 12 Oaks, Evenwood, Co Durham in 1851, at New Row, Willington in 1861, at 30 Katherine Street, Willington, Co Durham in 1871 and at 21 Katherine Street in 1881. In addition to Jane they had four other children:

- Joseph Henderson (1846–1913), a blacksmith, married Mary Dixon (1851–1930), born at Hurworth, Co Durham. They were living at Post Office Square, West Auckland in 1911. They had nine children – Robert D Henderson 1871, Sarah Henderson 1873, John Henderson 1876, George Henderson 1878, Fanny Henderson 1879, Josephine Henderson 1884, Albert E Henderson 1886, Beatrice Henderson 1888 and Joseph Henderson 1891.
- Ralph Henderson (1850–29th June 1911) was a pick carrier in 1861 and a blacksmith in 1871. He married Jane Forster (born c.1850) on 30th May 1875 at Willington. She was born at West Moor, Northumberland and had a daughter prior to the marriage, Mary Jane Forster, in 1869. He was a fireman at a pit boiler in 1881 and they were living at 18 Victoria Street, Willington. He was a colliery engineman and they were living at Fan Cottages, Oakenshaw, Willington at the time of his death at County Hospital, Durham. They had eleven children including – Frances Annie Henderson 1876, David Henderson 1877, Elizabeth Hannah Henderson 1880, Sarah Henderson 1883, Martha Henderson 1889 and William Henderson 1891.
- Luke Wilson Henderson (1853–1927) was a blacksmith in 1871. He married Mary Jane Pearse (1859–1936) in 1886. Her birth was registered as Pierce at Durham. He was a stationary engineman and they were living at 1 Elliott's Yard, Willington in 1891 and at 16 Catherine Street, Willington in 1911. They had five children – David William Henderson 1886, Robert Wilson Henderson 1889, Frances 'Fanny' Henderson 1891, Sarah Jane Henderson 1893 and Walter Henderson 1896.
- David Henderson (1855–18th August 1938) was a labourer in a colliery in 1871. He married Jane Heron (1862–1939) on 27th September 1880 at Brancepeth, Co Durham. They were living with his father in 1881, by when he was a boiler minder. By 1891 he was a stationary engine driver and they were living at 6 Park Street, Stockley, Co Durham. He was living at 14 Carville Terrace, Willington at the time of his death there. They had four children – Phyllis J Henderson 1882, Robert W Henderson 1885, Frances A Henderson 1887 and Richard H Henderson 1889.

George was educated at Bishop Barrington School, Bishop Auckland, Co Durham and served an apprenticeship as a cabinetmaker with Messrs T Thompson's Exors, of Newgate Street, Bishop Auckland. He emigrated to Canada alone, possibly as early as 1902 but it may have been after the death of his mother in 1905. He worked on a cattle ranch and later on a farm owned by his brother, John William McKean. In 1912 he entered Alberta College South, the Faculty of Theology at the University of Alberta, Edmonton, Canada, where he trained for the Presbyterian ministry but enlisted prior to completing his studies. While there he was a keen sportsman, playing football for the University, and was editor of *The Gateway* magazine. During the summers he was a student missionary at Hardieville and Athabasca Landing and was also an assistant to the minister at Robertson Presbyterian (later Robertson-

Robertson Presbyterian Church formed in 1909 and the first meetings were held in the basement of First Presbyterian Church until a new building was built in 1910. It was named after Presbyterian Missionary Superintendent James Robertson. It outgrew its original building and the new building seen here was constructed on the corner of 123rd Street and 102nd Avenue, with the first service being held there early in 1914. In 1971 Robertson merged with Wesley United Church to form Robertson-Wesley United Church.

Bishop Barrington School, Bishop Auckland was originally in the Barrington Building. It was built on the site of Pollard's Hall in the Market Place and the School opened on 26th May 1810. In 1974 it moved to Woodhouse Lane. The Barrington Building and its neighbour, a former bank, are being converted into an art gallery, opening in 2019.

George was apprenticed to Messrs T Thompson's in Newgate Street, Bishop Auckland.

Wesley United) Church in Edmonton. In 1913 he organized the first Boy Scout troop at the Church, Robertson Troop.

George enlisted at Edmonton on 23rd January 1915, having been previously turned down on medical grounds on three occasions (436568). He was described as a schoolteacher, 5′ 6″ tall, with medium complexion, dark blue eyes, dark brown hair and his religious denomination was Presbyterian. George married Isa/Isobella Hall Mckay (born 21st January 1888) on 6th December 1915 at Calgary, Alberta. She was born in Scotland and was most commonly named Isobel in her husband's service documents. During the war she was living at various times at 697, 23rd Street, Edmonton, Alberta, at 121, 13th Avenue West, Calgary, Alberta and at 211 Anderson Apartments, Calgary, Alberta. On 15th May 1916 he made a will leaving everything to her in the event of his death.

Isobella's father, John McKay (5th April 1865–22nd August 1906), married Helen Brunton née Stalker (born 9th July 1861) in 1887 at Galashiels, Selkirkshire. In addition to Isabella they had another daughter, Jennie/Jeanie McKay, born in 1892 in Scotland. They emigrated to Montreal, Quebec, Canada. Helen married

David Leighton Ruthven Donaldson (26th June 1874–19th May 1954) on 7th April 1908 at Montreal, Quebec. He was born at Coupar Angus, Perthshire and died at Edinburgh, Midlothian.

George sailed from Halifax, Nova Scotia with 51st Battalion CEF on 18th April 1916, arriving at Liverpool, Lancashire on 28th April and was appointed provisional sergeant. He went to Bramshott, Hampshire with 51st Battalion. On 8th June George went to France and reverted to the ranks. He arrived at the Canadian Base Depot, Le Havre on 9th June and joined 14th Battalion on 11th June.

George was promoted corporal and appointed lance sergeant on 22nd June and attended a Stokes Gun Course 26th June–2nd July. He reverted to the ranks at his own request on 24th July. On 4th October he was appointed acting corporal without pay. He was wounded by a gunshot to the scalp on 27th November and was admitted to 2nd Canadian Field Ambulance and to No.23 Casualty Clearing Station next day. On 30th November he was admitted to 8th Stationary Hospital, Wimereux via No.31 Ambulance Train and was transferred to

Anderson Apartments on 18th Avenue South West in Calgary is the last address in George's service record for his wife, Isobel.

Bramshott Camp on Bramshott Common was a major Canadian base in both world wars. This road is now the main A3.

The Convalescent Depot at Boulogne, where George was declared fit on 6th December 1916 (Wellcome).

The Canadian Base Depot at Le Havre.

No.1 Convalescent Depot, Boulogne on 3rd December, where he was declared fit on 6th December. He joined the Canadian Base Depot on 11th December and rejoined his unit on 17th December. Promoted corporal on 12th December.

Awarded the Military Medal in March 1917 for leading scouting patrols at Bully-Grenay, near Lens, during which he was wounded, LG 26th April 1917. George was recommended for a commission and joined the Canadian Base Depot on 5th March 1917 for transfer to England to attend officer training at the Cadet School, while on the strength of 1st Quebec Regiment, Shoreham. He was commissioned as a temporary lieutenant in 23rd Reserve Battalion on 28th April. He attended an Anti-Gas Course at Eastern Command Gas School and qualified 1st Class on 30th June. On 20th October he was posted to 14th Battalion and joined the Canadian Base Depot the following day. He departed for the Canadian Corps Reinforcement Camp on 24th October and joined 14th Battalion on 6th November. He was granted leave in Britain 17th February–5th March 1918.

Awarded the VC for his actions in the Gavrelle Sector, near Arras, France on 27th/28th April 1918, LG 28 June 1918. Appointed Scout Officer on 29th April and attended a course at the Canadian Corps Intelligence School 7th–15th June. On 15th July he was granted fourteen days' leave in Britain. The VC and MM were presented by the King in the quadrangle at Buckingham Palace on 17th July 1918. At a ceremony at King's Hall, Bishop Auckland he was presented with an illuminated address and a gold watch by members of the town council. He was reported absent without leave on 29th July but his leave appears to have been extended and he rejoining the unit on 18th August. **Awarded the MC for leading scouting patrols for two days during an attack near Cagnicourt, France on 1st/2nd September. He was wounded by a gunshot to his right leg but pressed on with his mission, sent in accurate reports and rallied men who had lost their officers. He entered Cagnicourt with three men and spotted one hundred enemy soldiers leaving the village, so he dashed to their flank to head them off and waved his arms and yelled orders to an imaginary force. The Germans were fooled and surrendered. Had they gained the high ground east of the village, they would have inflicted heavy casualties on the attacking troops. He continued sending valuable information to headquarters until exhausted by loss of blood, LG 1st February 1919.**

George was admitted to No.1 Casualty Clearing Station before being transferred to No.10 British Red Cross Hospital, Le Tréport on 4th September. He was on the held strength of 1st Quebec Regimental Depot, Bramshott, Hampshire from 7th September. On 8th September he was evacuated to Prince of Wales's Hospital, Marylebone Road, London and transferred to Kitchener Indian General Hospital, Brighton, Sussex on 21st October. On 15th January 1919 he transferred to the Canadian Convalescent Officers' Hospital, Matlock Bath, Derbyshire, where a medical board on 17th January found him fit for General Service. He was taken on strength of 23rd Canadian Reserve Battalion, Ripon on 23rd January and was

George after his investiture at Buckingham Palace. He is holding one of the medal boxes in his left hand.

The King's Hall, opened in 1902 in Newgate Street, was where George was an apprentice before going to Canada. At Christmas 1914 it became the King's Café and Cinema, which also included a ballroom, bookshop and tearoom. The cinema seated 1,028. It was taken over by the Newcastle based Essoldo cinema chain in 1947 and closed in 1960 to become one of the first supermarkets in Bishop Auckland. Much of the building has since been demolished but the front, less the upper floors, is still there and is used as a shop.

appointed acting captain on 27th January. He was posted to the strength of 1st Quebec Regimental Depot at Ripon, Yorkshire and detached to the Khaki University in London on 14th February. He was appointed temporary captain on 15th June and retired from the Canadian Forces on 26th July, remaining in Britain. His address was 2 Russell Street, Brighton, home of his future second father-in-law. The account making payments to his wife in Canada was closed on 31st July 1919. It is not known what became of her.

In the British Army he was promoted captain and transferred to the Corps of Military Accountants as accounts officer 6th class on 19th November. He served in Egypt until September 1925, following the disbandment of the Corps of Military Accountants in July. He returned to Britain aboard SS *City of Marseilles* and was discharged from the Army on 17th March 1926.

The Prince of Wales Hospital at 222 Marylebone Road, London opened in 1916 in the 700-bed Great Central Hotel and closed in July 1919. During its time as an officers' hospital it had a bad reputation. The food was poor and patients were not allowed to leave the hospital before 1 p.m. nor attend theatre matinées without permission. The Commandant required those fit enough to attend military lectures for two hours on alternate mornings or afternoons. The hotel was a convalescent hospital during the Second World War and later became headquarters of the British Railways Board; the staff knew it as the Kremlin. In the 1980s the building became a hotel again.

The Canadian Convalescent Officers' Hospital at Matlock Bath was based on the Royal Hotel. It suffered a disastrous fire in 1929 and had to be demolished.

There were a number of military hospitals in Brighton during the Great War. More than 12,000 Indian soldiers were treated there, mainly at the Royal Pavilion, Corn Exchange (Dome) and the Kitchener. When the bulk of the Indian forces in France transferred to the Middle East, the Pavilion then cared for limbless soldiers and the Kitchener Indian Hospital treated Canadian casualties. The Kitchener, a former workhouse, is now Brighton General Hospital, the Dome is a concert venue and the Royal Pavilion is once again a major tourist attraction.

The Khaki University (also known as the Khaki College or University of Vimy Ridge) was set up for the Canadian Army in 1917–19 by Colonel Henry Marshall Tory and Edmund Henry Oliver, supported by the YMCA. Initially the scheme was run in France by Oliver and in England by Tory. Tory was on leave as the first president of the University of Alberta 1908–29. The makeshift colleges (there were eleven in Britain by May 1918) provided education on a wide range of subjects to more than 50,000 soldiers. The certificates issued were accepted by Canadian universities. George was recruited by Tory, his old university president, to run the London Bureau of the Canadian Khaki University in London. A similar educational programme was set up for Canadian service personnel in 1945–46.

SS *City of Marseilles* (8,317 tons) was launched at Jarrow on 26th October 1912 for Ellerman's Hall Line and departed Liverpool on 26th January 1913 on her maiden voyage. On 23rd November 1915 she was attacked by a U-boat and was hit by gunfire. After the war she ran the New York - Port Said – Bombay route for Ellerman Bucknall's American & Indian Line and made regular trooping voyages to India 1923–30. On 6th January 1940, she hit a mine off the River Tay laid by U-*13* but was repaired. On 22nd January 1943 she was stranded off Batticaloa, Ceylon and refloated but was scrapped in 1947.

Russell Street in Brighton has since been demolished and is now covered by a shopping centre.

George married Constance Hilton Slaughter (12th December 1892–14th October 1982) in 1923 at Brighton, Sussex. She was born at 59 Archway Street, Barnes, Surrey and was admitted to Holy Trinity School, Lewisham, London on 13th April 1896. They were living at 8 Dove Lane, Potters Bar, London in late 1926. They had a daughter, Constance Patricia McKean (born 2nd March 1920) at Steyning, Sussex. She was a shorthand typist with Kodak in 1939 living with her mother. She married Frederick Stanley (born 1919) in 1947 at Christchurch, Hampshire.

Constance's father, Edward Hilton Slaughter (c.1859–1st January 1937), was a grocer's porter in 1881, lodging at 3 Catherine Street, Lambeth. He married Mary Ann Freeman (c.1857–89) on 12th June 1881 at St Andrew's Church, Lambeth, London. She died at Edmonton following complications with the birth of her daughter Ethel. Edward and Mary had three children:

- Florence Mary Slaughter (1882–31st January 1964) married Arthur Forty (1858–1936), a domestic servant, c.1904. He was born at Tetbury, Gloucestershire. They were living at 1 Howell Street, Edgware, Middlesex in 1911. He died at Paddington, London. She was living at 27 Paddington Green at the time of her death at 4 Devon Close, Perivale, Greenford, London. They had seven children – Arthur Forty 1905, Eileen Forty 1908, Winifred F Forty 1910, Geoffrey R Forty 1912, Hilda HE Forty 1916, Edith J Forty 1918 and Elsie M Forty 1920. The births from Hilda onwards were registered with Hilton as the mother's maiden name and not Slaughter.

- Edward Hilton Slaughter (1886–1900) was working as a page at the Grand Hotel, Northumberland Avenue, London, when he died after falling down a lift shaft.
- Ethel Mary Slaughter (1889–2nd November 1939) never married and was living at 30 Acme Road, Watford, Hertfordshire at the time of her death at 60 Vicarage Road, Watford.

Edward married Blanche Hilton née Tasker (1867–1938), born at Henry Street, Tottenham Court Road, London, on 30th August 1889 at the new Parish Church of Emmanuel, West Hampstead, London. Edward was superintendent of an insurance company and they were living at Waltham Lane, Cheshunt in 1891. The following year they moved to 59 Archway Street, Barnes, Surrey and to Dacres Cottage, Forest Hill, London by 1896. By 1901 he was a photographer and they were living at 2 Beetonian House, New Hunstanton, Norfolk. She was living with four of her daughters at 32 Perowne Road, Cambridge in 1911. Her husband was a patient at Addenbrooke's Hospital, Cambridge at the time. They changed their surname to Hilton and were living at 2 Russell Street, Brighton, Sussex during the period 1914–20, where he published picture postcards of military camps and training exercises in central and southern Sussex. The marriage failed and he was known to have lived in London and travelled overseas without his wife. Edward died at Kensington, London. In addition to Constance they had eight other children:

- Blanche Hilda Slaughter (1890–4th January 1969), born at Waltham Abbey, Hertfordshire, was boarding with her future husband, Geoffrey Richard Leyland (12th December 1888–3rd May 1941), at Chestney House, New Hunstanton, Norfolk at the time of the 1911 Census. Her maiden name was recorded as Hilton. They married on 21st October 1911 at St Mary's Church, Paddington, London. He was born at Prescot, Lancashire. Blanche was living with her son, Frederick, at 40 Charleville Road, Fulham, London in 1939. Geoffrey was living at All Saints Hall, Creeting St Mary, Suffolk at the time of his death there. She was living at Flat 5, 45 Cheapside, Brighton at the time of her death there. They had two children – Frederick Derek Leyland 1912 and Geoffrey Douglas Leyland 1915.

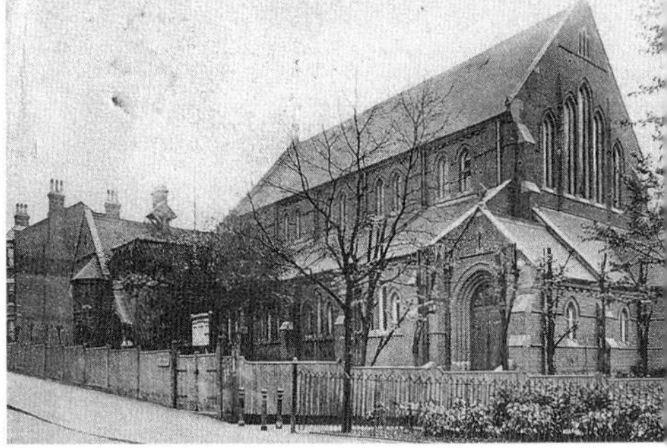

In 1874 the vicar of Holy Trinity, Hampstead arranged for a small mission church to serve the people of West End. The congregation outgrew the church and in 1884 it was doubled in size. However, the continuing increase in the population led to the decision to separate it from Holy Trinity and create a new parish. On 9th May 1885 Emmanuel became the parish church of the new parish of West End, Hampstead. The congregation continued to grow and land was acquired at the junction of the main crossroads of the parish. The foundation stone for a new church was laid on 19th June 1897 and the partly built church was consecrated on 8th October 1898.

- Henry 'Harry' Hilton Slaughter (12th April 1896–18th May 1965), born at Dacres Cottage, Forest Hill, London was a domestic servant in 1911 living with his half sister Florence and her family. By 1920 he was back with his parents at 2 Russell Street, Brighton. He married Rosina Louvain Fox (13th July 1918–27th January 2002) in 1938 at Dover, Kent. He was a butcher, grocer and provision retail dealer in 1939 and they were living at 22 Upper Rooms, Market Square, Dover. They were living at 6 Albany Place, Dover at the time of his death at Buckland Hospital, Dover. Her death was registered at Thanet with Dover.
- Elsie Hilton Slaughter (born 23rd June 1899) was born at 2 Beetonian Villa, New Hunstanton, Norfolk. She married Isaac James Dent (20th September 1895–1977) in 1916 at Smallburgh, Norfolk. He was born at Maldon, Essex. They divorced and Elsie married Clifford EW Rogers (16th October 1902–1975) in 1933 at Blofield, Norfolk. Isaac married Lucy Ellen D Cracknell (30th November 1895–1972) in 1935 at Epping and they had a daughter, Edna M Dent, in 1936. Isaac married Ethel C Hayward in 1973 at Epping.
- Naomi Hilton Slaughter (19th June 1901–17th February 1963), born at 2 Beetonian Villa, married Frederick James Greenfield (3rd March 1893–31st January 1980), a postman, in 1921 at Brighton, where he was born. They were living at 31 Mafeking Road, Brighton in 1939 and were still there when she died at the Sussex Throat and Ear Hospital, Brighton. He was living at 83 Victoria Road, West Prestatyn, Clwyd when he died. They had a son, David F Greenfield, in 1934.
- Josephine 'Jessie' Hilton Slaughter (born 23rd March 1903), born at 2 Beetonian Villa.
- Zena Hilton Slaughter (1906–07), born at Docking.
- Vera Hilda Slaughter (10th June 1909–1st November 1983), born at 32 Perowne Street, Cambridge, married Bernard Frederick Elkins (7th March 1910–21st November 1993), a police constable, in 1932 at Brighton. He was born at Whitchurch, Oxfordshire. They were living at the Police Station, Beckley, Battle, Sussex in 1939. They were living at 17 Eridge Road, Eastbourne at the time of Vera's death there. Bernard was living at 36 The Crescent, Crynant, Neath, West Glamorgan at the time of his death. They had six children – Frank G Elkins 1933, Brian G Elkins 1934, Leonard M Elkins 1936, Gerald B Elkins 1937, Pamela VL Elkins 1940 and Valerie B Elkins 1947.
- Derrick Hilton Slaughter (born 25th May 1911) was born at 166 East Road, Cambridge. He married Mary F Lyons in 1940 at Hendon, Middlesex. His surname was registered as Hilton. They had three children – Naomi E Hilton 1941, Jack Hilton 1942 and James M Hilton 1944.

George settled at Cuffley, Hertfordshire, where he ran a sawmill. He attended the VC Garden Party at Buckingham Palace on 26th June 1920. He wrote two books – *Scouting Thrills* 1919 and *Making Good* 1920, which dealt with his emigration

George's headstone inexplicably shows the incorrect date of death and age (Memorials to Valour).

George settled at Cuffley, where on 3rd September 1916 the first German airship (SL 11) was shot down over Britain by Lieutenant W Leefe Robinson, who was awarded the Victoria Cross for this deed.

Mount McKean in Jasper National Park is named after George McKean, one of five mountains named after Great War Victoria Cross recipients with Alberta connections in 1951. The others are John Chipman Kerr, Cecil John Kinross, John George Pattison and Raphael Louis Zengel (Mountain Nerd).

The memorial to George Burdon McKean at Cagnicourt, France (Memorials to Valour).

to Canada. On 26th November 1926 a circular saw at his sawmill burst and a piece struck him on the head. He was rushed to Potters Bar Cottage Hospital, South Mimms, Hertfordshire but never regained consciousness and died later that day. An inquest on 30th November, chaired by Dr George Cohen, Coroner for Middlesex, recorded a verdict of death by misadventure. He was cremated at Golders Green Crematorium, Hoop Lane, London on 2nd December. His ashes were buried at Brighton Extra-Mural Cemetery, Lewes Road (Grave XM 41624) on 3rd December. He left effects valued at £1,134/17/9, resworn £850/14/8, probate to his widow and his sister, Frances Rutherford. George is commemorated in a number of other places:

- Mount McKean, Jasper National Park, Alberta.
- La Place de George Burdon McKean, Cagnicourt, France was dedicated on 6th September 2003 following a plea from Michel Gravel, an amateur historian from Ontario, Canada. The Mayor of Cagnicourt unveiled the memorial. George's daughter, Pat Stanley, other family members and Michel Gravel attended.
- Lt G.B. McKean, VC MC MM RMR Pistol Shooting Trophy – awarded to the Royal Montreal Regiment officer achieving the highest score in the Regiment's annual pistol competition.
- Named on one of eleven plaques honouring 175 men from overseas awarded the VC for the Great War. The plaques were unveiled by the Senior Minister of State at the Foreign & Commonwealth Office and Minister for Faith and Communities, Baroness Warsi, at a reception at Lancaster House, London on 26th June 2014 attended by The Duke of Kent and relatives of the VC recipients. The Canadian plaque was unveiled outside the British High Commission in Elgin Street, Ottawa on 10th November 2014 by The Princess Royal in the presence of British High Commissioner Howard Drake, Canadian Minister of Veterans Affairs Julian Fantino and Canadian Chief of the Defence Staff General Thomas J Lawson.
- Named on a Victoria Cross obelisk to all Canadian VCs at Military Heritage Park, Barrie, Ontario dedicated by The Princess Royal on 22nd October 2013.
- Plaque on the York Cemetery VC Memorial, West Don River Valley, Toronto, Ontario dedicated on 25th June 2017.
- A Department for Communities and Local Government commemorative paving stone was dedicated at Willington, Bishop Auckland, Co Durham on 28th April 2018 to mark the centenary of his award.
- His VC action featured in Issue No.1096 of the Victor Comic entitled *A True Story of Men at War* dated 20th February 1982.
- Two 49 cents postage stamps in honour of the ninety-four Canadian VC winners were issued by Canada Post on 21st October 2004 on the 150th Anniversary of the first Canadian VC's action, Alexander Roberts Dunn VC.
- There is a painting of him at the Canadian War Museum.

George's untimely death left Constance in severe financial difficulties. She married George W Raby in 1928 at Brighton. They were living at 45 Sherington Avenue, Harrow, London in 1939. She was living at 41 Seaward Tower, Trinity Green, Gosport, Hampshire at the time of her death there.

In addition to the VC, MC and MM he was also awarded the British War Medal 1914–20 and Victory Medal 1914–19. His medals were sold by his widow on 21st March 1979 to JB Hayward & Son of London at Sotheby's for £17,000. They were purchased by Jack Stenabaugh, a medal collector from Huntsville, Ontario. They were later owned by a British collector in Colchester, Essex before being purchased by the Canadian War Museum for an undisclosed sum. They are held by the Canadian War Museum, 1 Vimy Place, Ottawa, Ontario.

200854 SERGEANT JOHN MEIKLE
1/4th Battalion, Seaforth Highlanders (Ross-Shire Buffs, The Duke of Albany's)

John Meikle was born on 11th September 1898 at 34 Freeland Place, Kirkintilloch, Dunbartonshire, Scotland. His father, also John Meikle (1st December 1858–18th July 1931), born at Linlithgow, West Lothian, was a carter, of West Port, Linlithgow. He married Elizabeth Ballantine (6th September 1861–28th May 1881), a domestic servant born at Gogar, Currie, Midlothian, on 31st December 1880. They were living at 153 High Street, Linlithgow, West Lothian at the time of Elizabeth's death there of *debility due to confinement*, only three weeks after the birth of her daughter Jane. John senior served as a gunner (32593) in Burma with No.8 Battery, 1st Battalion, 2nd Division, Royal Artillery 1885–87 (India General Service Medal 1854–95). He married Anna 'Annie' née Hollywood (26th May 1872–9th May 1953), a domestic servant born at Cross, Kirkintilloch, Dunbartonshire, on 11th April 1890 at the Wesleyan Methodist Church, Cowgate Street, Kirkintilloch. At the time he was living at Townhead

John Meikle was born at Kirkintilloch, Dunbartonshire.

Linlithgow High Street, where John's father was living when his first wife died there in 1881.

John's father was living at Townhead, Kirkintilloch when he married John's mother in 1890.

John's mother was living on Cowgate Street, Kirkintilloch when she married John Meikle senior.

and she at 19 Cowgate Street, both in Kirkintilloch. In 1901 he was a general labourer and they were living at 42 Freeland Place, Kirkintilloch. They moved to Nitshill, Renfrewshire after the 1901 Census, when John accepted the post of section chargehand at Perry & Hope Co's new chemical works there. They were living at Dunlop Street, Nitshill by 1903 and later at 1 Office Row, Nitshill. Anne died at 452 Nitshill Road, Pollokshaws. John junior had eleven siblings from his fathers two marriages:

- Jane 'Jeanie' Ballantine Meikle (born 9th May 1881), born at Linlithgow, West Lothian, married Archibald Fullarton (born c.1877), a shale miner born at Armadale, West Lothian, on 28th December 1900. They had a son, Donald McKillop Fullarton, born on 17th July 1901 at Larkhall, Lanarkshire.
- Jane 'Jean'/'Jeannie'/'Janie' Hollywood Meikle (9th December 1890–5th December 1918) born at Cross, Kirkintilloch, was a threadmill worker.
- Jessie Hollywood Meikle (12th June 1892–2nd May 1923) born at West Highgate, Kirkintilloch, was a threadmill worker. She dies of tuberculosis.
- Robert Meikle (17th-20th December 1894).
- Margaret 'Maggie' Banks Meikle (5th May 1896–18th February 1915), born at 40 Townhead, Kirkintilloch, was a threadmill worker.
- William Meikle (twin with Annie) (22nd–25th February 1901).
- Annie Meikle (twin with William) (22nd–25th February 1901).
- Job Meikle (born and died 14th August 1902).
- Annie Hollywood Meikle (31st July 1903–22nd October 1920), born at Dunlop Street, Nitshill, Renfrewshire, was an ironmonger's assistant.
- Mary Hollywood Meikle (14th August 1905–1992), born at 1 Office Row, Nitshill. Married James Stuart in 1928 at Barrhead, Renfrewshire.
- Job Hollywood Archibald Meikle (born 1st October 1908–27th May 1981) married Janet Stoddart Weir (27th May 1912–9th October 2012) on 16th July 1937 at The Church of Scotland, Leadhills, Lanarkshire. They lived at 77b Bruce House,

Braeface Road, Cumbernauld, Lanarkshire and had two sons – John Meikle 1943 and Alan Job Meikle 1950.
- Janet Henderson Meikle (20th November 1911–24th July 2008) married William McQuat Salkeld (19th January 1904–8th November 1995) on 9th September 1941. They were living at Crookfur Home, Crookfur Road, Newton-Mearns, Renfrewshire at the time of his death there. They had two sons – William McQuat Salkeld 1946 and John Hollywood Salkeld 1949.

John's paternal grandfather, Robert Meikle (6th November 1831–5th December 1902), born at Abercorn, Linlithgow, West Lothian, was a journeyman maltman in 1851, living with his parents at Strawberry Bank, Linlithgow. He married Janet née Henderson (1834–20th September 1922), a domestic servant born at Dalkeith, Edinburgh, Midlothian on 8th February 1856. They were living at 380 High Street, Linlithgow, West Lothian in 1871. He died at his home at 358 High Street, Linlithgow and she at 4 High Street, Linlithgow. In addition to John they had six other children:

- Archibald Henderson Meikle (28th August 1856–2nd October 1942), a master baker, married Elizabeth Peascod (28th December 1856–14th January 1942), a lady's maid born at Carlisle, Cumberland, on 16th June 1884 at Linlithgow. Elizabeth had a son, Joseph Prescott Peascod (9th May 1881–20th January 1955). Archibald and Elizabeth had two sons – William Archibald Meikle (22nd October 1887–12th October 1960) and John Robert 'Robin' Meikle (18th September 1892–24th December 1963). The marriage ended in divorce on 23rd March 1903. Elizabeth married Sinclair McLeod (20th September 1863–26th May 1947), born at Prestonpans, East Lothian, on 13th April 1912 at Dunfermline, Fife. Sinclair was a coalminer living at 7 Forthill, Prestonpans when he married Mary Jane Matthews, a dressmaker, on 24th April 1885 at Tranent, East Lothian. Sinclair and Mary Jane had eight children – Mary Jane Angwin McLeod 1888, Elizabeth McLeod 1890, Maria Matthews McLeod 1891, Priscilla McLeod 1895, Annie McLeod 1899, Alice McLeod 1903, Pauline McLeod 1908 and Archibald McLeod 1909. Elizabeth was living at 126 Moss Side Road, Cowdenbeath, Fife at the time of her death there. Archibald married Jane Stewart Kay (25th August 1869–16th August 1913), born at St Quivox and Newton-on-Ayr, Ayrshire, on 17th July 1903 in Glasgow. They were living at 135 Townhead, Kirkintilloch in 1903 and at 16 Milton Street, Partick in 1911. Jane died at 59 Hopeful Road, Glasgow. Archibald married Margaret Eleanor Ranson (11th February 1866–25th August 1943) on 10th January 1933 at Gateshead, Co Durham. Margaret was a confectioner's assistant in 1901 boarding at 39 Brunswick Street, Gateshead. They were living at 119 Park Road, Newcastle-upon-Tyne. Northumberland at the time of his death at 416 Westgate Road, Newcastle-upon-Tyne.

- Walter Henderson Meikle (25th January 1861–14th June 1947), birth registered as Mickel, a marine stoker, married Jane Alexander Campbell (23rd May 1865–27th August 1951) on 13th August 1883 at Govan, Lanarkshire. She was born at Bathgate, West Lothian. He died at Ann Arbor, Washtenaw, Michigan, USA. She died at Lodi Township, Washtenaw. They had two children – Euphemia Gourlay Campbell Meikle (17th April 1887–November 1973) and Janet Henderson Meikle (14th December 1888–1st October 1973).
- Margaret Henderson Meikle (born 27th July 1865 and died soon afterwards).
- Robert Meikle (21st June 1863–28th January 1929) married Margaret Helen Makinson (8th September 1871–3rd December 1942) on 27th September 1894 at South Ronaldsay and Burray, Orkney, where she was born. He died at Edinburgh, Midlothian. She was living there at 5 West Crosscauseway at the time of her death at George Square, Edinburgh.
- Janet Henderson Meikle (22nd October 1866–12th December 1937) married William Anderson Richardson (born 27th July 1870), a brakeman of 328 High Street, Linlithgow, on 20th December 1893 at 358 High Street, Linlithgow. She died in hospital at Brooklyn, Kings County, New York, USA. They had a daughter, Janet 'Nettie' Sanderson Richardson (12th June 1897–September 1977).
- Margaret Banks Meikle (born 27th June 1872).

His maternal grandfather, Job Hollywood (27th September 1844–17th November 1908), born at Campsie, Stirlingshire, married Jane née Lockhart (c.1845–c.1914), born at Belfast, Ireland, on 5th February 1867. In 1881 he was a clock and watchmaker and they were

Maryhill Barracks opened as Garrioch Barracks in 1872 to accommodate an infantry regiment, a squadron of cavalry and a battery of field artillery. It resulted from Glasgow City Corporation's perceived need for military protection against 'riot and tumult' in the growing city. Married quarters were added in 1911. Maryhill Barracks became the Highland Light Infantry Depot in 1921 and was also home to the Royal Scots Greys and Royal Highland Fusiliers. In 1941 Rudolf Hess was held there for a while, when the barracks was being used as a prisoner of war camp. In 1942 General Charles de Gaulle visited Free French troops there. Most of the Barracks were demolished in the 1960s to make way for Wyndford housing estate. The guardroom and boundary walls remain.

Levern Public School, Nitshill, attended by John Meikle was built in 1875 and demolished in the 1960s.

John's grave (bottom right) in Marfaux British Cemetery. In the distance is the Bullin spur where his VC action and death took place.

Lieutenant General Sir Frederick William Nicholas McCracken KCB DSO (1859–1949) was commissioned in the 49th Regiment of Foot (later 1st Royal Berkshire) in 1879 and served in the Anglo-Egyptian War 1882, Mahdist War 1885 and the Second Boer War, during which he commanded 2nd Royal Berkshires (DSO & MID). In 1912 he took command of 7th Infantry Brigade, went with it to France in August 1914 and was wounded at Le Cateau. In October 1914 he was promoted major general and appointed Inspector of Infantry. In 1915 he took command of 15th (Scottish) Division and led it through the Battles of Loos, Somme and Arras. In June 1917 he was promoted to command XIII Corps but was removed in March 1918 and sent home to take over Scottish Command, in which capacity he presented John Meikle's VC to his father in October 1918. During the Great War he was MID seven times and made KCB. He retired in 1922.

living at 7 Cowgate, Kirkintilloch. They moved to Larbert, Stirlingshire by 1901. Job died of apoplexy at Hillhead Institution, Balfron, Stirlingshire. Jane was with her son, Job, in New York, USA in 1916. In addition to Anna they had six other children:

- Job Hollywood (3rd February 1868–28th September 1955), a jeweller, emigrated to New York, USA, arriving on 26th April 1896. He ran his own jewellery store in Brooklyn. Job married Sarah Denham on 3rd March 1913 (20th July 1887–14th May 1981). She was born at Amsterdam, Montgomery County, New York. He died at Aurora, Adams County, Colorado, USA and she at Wolfforth, Lubbock, Texas. They had four children – Job Hollywood (1914–93), Herbert Ross Hollywood (1916–75), Alfred Denham Hollywood (1917–63) and Edward James Hollywood (1924–95).
- Jessie Hollywood (26th January 1870–1940) married William Crean (c.1858–1937) in 1897. She died at Pollock, Glasgow, Lanarkshire. They had four children – Andrew Crean (born c.1898), Jane Crean (born c.1900), John Crean (1907–84) and James Crean (c.1918–c.2000).

The memorial in Station Square, Dingwall, where it was moved in 1971 from Nitshill Station (Iain Stewart).

The Town House in Dingwall, which houses Dingwall Museum, where John Meikle's VC is held.

The plaque at Nitshill Station.

Nitshill War Memorial.

- Jane Hollywood (11th February 1875–8th April 1955) married George Nelson (11th June 1867–23rd June 1955), a house carpenter, on 20th August 1895 at 5 Cowgate Street, Kirkintilloch. He was born at Carrickfergus, Co Antrim, Ireland and was the son of a military bandmaster. They were living in 115 Alexander Park Avenue, Duncairn Ward, Co Antrim, Ireland in 1901 and at 88 Alexander Park Avenue in 1911. They had four children – Mary Nelson (born 8th December 1897), Georgina Nelson (born c.1901), Robert Nelson (born 31st October 1905) and George Arthur Nelson (9th July 1908–13th November 1979). George and Jane were found unconscious in the kitchen of their home at 189 Merville Garden Village, Drumnadrough, Co Antrim, Northern Ireland after being exposed to a coal gas leak on 8th April 1955. Jane could not be resuscitated and her cause of death was registered as misadventure. George was living at 167 Belmont Road, Belfast at the time of his death there ten weeks later.
- Robert Hollywood (24th January–14th September 1879).
- James Ross Hollywood (19th July 1881–September 1976) was a driver when he emigrated to New York, arriving on 9th August 1903. He became a shipping clerk and married Mary B Beecham (born c.1888) on 21st January 1905 at Brooklyn. She was born in Kirkintilloch. In 1917 he was a shipping clerk working for Stowell Engineering Company, living at 296 Duncan Avenue, Hudson, New Jersey when he registered for the US Army. He was of medium height and build with grey eyes and dark hair. By 1920 he was a manager in a silk house in Hudson, New Jersey. They were living at 148 St Paul's Place, Brooklyn in 1942 when he registered for service in the Second World War (No.2083). At the time he was working for Morris Mandell & Co, Bingo equipment suppliers, 131 West Street 14 Street, New York. They had eight children – May M Hollywood 1905, Jennie Hollywood 1907, James Eugene Hollywood 1909, John P Hollywood 1911, Emma Hollywood 1913, Jessie J Hollywood 1917, Robert Hollywood 1919 and Blanche Hollywood 1920.
- Mary Hollywood (1st May 1885–c.1980) married William Johnston Forsyth (1880–1940), an irondresser, on 3rd June 1904 at the Wesleyan Methodist Church, Kirkintilloch. He was born at Cumbernauld. They had four children – Alexander Forsyth 1912, Mary Forsyth 1915 and twins John Meikle Forsyth and James Forsyth 1918.

John was educated at Levern Public School, Nitshill, Glasgow. He worked as a clerk with Glasgow, Barrhead and Kilmarnock Joint Railway Co at Nitshill for 7/6 per week. John played or watched soccer at any opportunity and was a strong supporter of Nitshill Victoria Football Club. He enlisted in 4th Seaforth Highlanders on 7th February 1915 (3156 later 200854) aged sixteen and lied about his age. He ate extra portions of porridge to broaden his chest. John reported to Maryhill Barracks, Glasgow. As he was too young to go abroad he served in Scotland, possibly at Dingwall, Ross-shire. John went to France on 31st July 1916, still under eighteen years old, when the legal minimum for service overseas at that time was nineteen. **Awarded the MM for bravery and leadership on 20th September 1917 in the Battle of the Menin Road Ridge during the Third Battle of Ypres, when his Battalion was in the line between White House and Pheasant Farm. He was wounded by a bayonet in this action, LG 12th December 1917.**

John Meikle's memorial in its original location at Nitshill Station, Glasgow.

John was promoted corporal on 21st September. He returned home for a short leave after winning the MM and was presented with a gold watch by the people of Nitshill at Hurley & Nitshill Public Hall. He was promoted sergeant on 12th April 1918. **Awarded the VC for his actions at Marfaux on 20th July 1918, LG 16th September 1918.** He was the youngest Scottish recipient of the VC. The VC was presented to John's father by Lieutenant General Sir Frederick William Nicholas McCracken KCB DSO at Maryhill Barracks, Glasgow on 28th October 1918.

John was killed during his VC action and is buried at Marfaux British Cemetery, Marne, France (VIII C 1). After his death his mother presented some of the money she had been saving for his return to two local churches at Nitshill for the installation of electric light, a new pulpit, bible and scarf, and towards a new organ for the Methodist Church at Pollokshaws. John was fond of writing poetry and sent some verses home to his mother. He is commemorated in a number of other places:

- A rough-hewn granite memorial was erected by his railway colleagues at Nitshill Station, Glasgow and was dedicated in January 1920 by Lady Lorimer. The memorial was moved to Station Square, Dingwall on 12th March 1971 by 4th Seaforth Club and was unveiled by Colonel HAC Mackenzie, who introduced Simon Calder, who had fought alongside John during his VC action.
- Plaque at Nitshill Station dedicated in October 2016.
- Plaque at Nitshill Public Hall, where John received his gold watch in 1917. The plaque was later moved to Levern Primary School and after it closed was rescued by his sister, Janet Salkeld, who presented it to Dingwall Museum in 1996.
- Named on the War Memorial, Nitshill, Glasgow.
- Named on the war memorials at Edinburgh Castle, Midlothian and at St Enoch's Railway Station, Glasgow.
- Rolls of Honour at Pollokshaws Methodist Church, United Free Church, Nitshill and Nitshill Rechabite Society.

- Department for Communities and Local Government commemorative paving stones were dedicated at Nitshill Railway Station, Glasgow and at Barleybank, near St Mary's Church, Kirkintilloch, East Dunbartonshire on 20th July 2018 to mark the centenary of his award.

John's mother was invited to the VC Garden Party at Buckingham Palace in 1920 and his brother, Job, and one of his sisters attended the 1956 VC Centenary Celebrations at Hyde Park, London. In addition to the VC and MM he was awarded the British War Medal 1914–20 and Victory Medal 1914–19. When his father died, the VC passed to Job. He presented his brother's medals to the 4th Seaforth Highlanders Reunion Club at their Annual General Meeting in the National Hotel, Dingwall on 11th November 1972. Baillie Roderick McNab accepted the medals and citation from Job Meikle. The medals are held by Dingwall Museum, Town House, High Street, Dingwall, Ross-shire.

19/11 SERGEANT ALBERT MOUNTAIN
15th/17th Battalion, The Prince of Wales's Own (West Yorkshire Regiment)

Albert Mountain was born on 19th April 1896 at 151 York Road, Leeds, Yorkshire. His father, James Mountain (1859–1929), married Mary Ann née Swales (1864–1910), born at Ripon, Yorkshire, on 14th June 1891 at St Simon, Leeds. At the time of the 1881 Census she was a visitor at 25 Peel Street, Leeds and he was a tobacconist living with his parents. Mary had married John William Cowling (1848–90) in 1890. In 1881 John was an iron-moulder lodging in the home of Hugh and Rachel Whitehead at 12 Hollis Street, Leeds. James and Mary were living at 151 York Road, Leeds by 1896. By 1901 James was a hotel keeper and they were living at the Alexandra Hotel, 2 Westgate, Ripon. In 1911 Mary was living at 34 Sutherland Mount, Hudson Road, Leeds. Albert had five siblings from his mother's two marriages:

- John William Cowling (born 1890) was a general labourer in 1911.
- Charles Harold Mountain (1892–4th August 1945) was a printer's clerk in 1911. He enlisted in the Army Service Corps on 11th March 1915 (S/4/07034G) described as 5′ 6″ tall and weighing 106 lbs. He served in the Adriatic Mission, Mediterranean Expeditionary Force 31st December 1915–6th November 1916. He returned to Britain on 9th November and was treated at 3rd Western General Hospital, Newport until 25th January 1917 for a duodenal ulcer and then at

2nd Northern General Hospital, Leeds until 12th March for dyspepsia. He was discharged on medical grounds on 9th May 1917 at Southport, Lancashire. The condition was not caused, but was aggravated, by military service. He was described as 5′ 8″ tall, with fresh complexion, blue eyes, brown hair and his address was 55 Belle Vue Avenue, North Lane, Roundhay, Leeds. Charles married Marie Esther Ribbons (1890–27th May 1981) in 1915 at Wharfedale, Yorkshire. They were living at 51 Belle Vue Avenue, Leeds in 1939 and at 10 Gainsborough Drive, Adel, Leeds at the time of his death, leaving effects valued at £498/3/3. They had three children – John Eric Mountain 1919, Dennis William James Mountain 1920 and Barbara Elizabeth Mountain 1922.

- Eliza Mountain (born 27th October 1893) was a gas burner maker in 1911. She married Albert Simmons in 1948 and they had a son, Kenneth Drake, in 1933.
- Lily Mountain (born 19th August 1898).
- Elsie Mountain (born 1901).

Albert's paternal grandfather, William Mountain (c.1834–1915), born at Tong, Yorkshire, married Eliza née Pearson (8th May 1837–1888), born at Cleckheaton, Yorkshire, a worsted spinner, in 1858 at Dewsbury, Yorkshire. William was a carpenter in 1861 and they were living at Windmill, Farnley, Leeds. By 1871 he was a tobacconist and they were living at 4 Freehold Street, Leeds. By 1881 they were at 161 York Road, Leeds. He was retired and living on his own at 151 York Road in 1891. By 1911 he was boarding at 18 Station Road, Barwick-in-Elmet, Yorkshire. In addition to James they had a daughter, Ann Mountain, born at Tong in 1858.

Albert's paternal grandparents were living at 4 Freehold Street, Leeds in 1871, seen here on the right of the centre block.

His maternal grandfather, Robert Swales (born c.1834), born at Brompton on Swale, Yorkshire, was a hawker. He married Esther née Wilson (c.1833–1903), born at Kirkbymoorside, Yorkshire, in 1855 at Beverley, Yorkshire. They were living at 3 Chancery Street, Darlington, Co Durham in 1871. By 1881 they had moved to Wilsons Yard, Layerthorpe, Yorkshire. Esther was living with her daughter, Elizabeth and family, in 1901. In addition to Mary they had six other children:

Albert's maternal grandmother, Esther Wilson, was born at Kirkbymoorside, Yorkshire c.1833.

- Elizabeth Swales (1860–1923) married Robert Warrior (1855–1911), a bricklayer's labourer born at Ripon, in 1879 at Bedale, Yorkshire. She was a hawker in 1881. By 1891 he was a hawker and they were living at Quarry Yard, Knaresborough. They were living at 21 Church Street, Darlington, Co Durham in 1901. They had five children – Selina Warrior 1880, Esther Ann Warrior 1885, Elizabeth Warrior 1890, William Warrior 1892 and George Warrior 1894.
- John Thomas Swales (born 1862) was a general dealer in 1881.
- James Swales (born 1863).
- Esther Swales (1865–1933) was a general dealer in 1881. She married John Moore (born 1863) in 1882 at York. He was a hawker selling hardware in 1901 and they were living at 15 Church Street, Darlington. By 1911 they were living at 48 Park Place, Darlington. They had nine children including, Jane Elizabeth N Moore 1892, Margaret Moore 1893, Mary Ann Moore 1896, John Moore 1898, Elizabeth Moore 1901, Benjamin Moore 1904 and Robert Moore 1908.
- William Swales (born 1868).
- Jane Swales (born 1870).

The French Médaille Militaire, established in 1852, is awarded for meritorious service or bravery in action and is the third highest award of the French Republic. During the First World War 230,000 medals were awarded. Foreign recipients include the black American fighter pilot Eugene Jacques Bullard, Winston Churchill, Dwight D Eisenhower, Field Marshal Bernard Montgomery, President Franklin D Roosevelt and President Josip Broz Tito (Fdutil).

Albert was educated at Saville Green School, York Road, Leeds. He was a coal miner hewer in 1911. He enlisted in 17th Battalion (2nd Leeds), West Yorkshire, a bantam unit, and went with the Battalion to France on 1st February 1916. Later he transferred to 15th Battalion (1st Leeds). The 15th and 17th Battalions amalgamated on 7th December 1917 to form 15th/17th Battalion. **Awarded the VC for his actions at Hamelincourt, France on 26th-27th March 1918, LG 7th June 1918.** Albert was presented with the VC ribbon by Major TC Gibson, commanding 15th/17th West Yorkshire, at a parade on 10th June. The VC was presented by the King in the quadrangle of Buckingham Palace on 29th June 1918. Albert was discharged to the Class Z Reserve on 15th January 1919. **Awarded the French Médaille Militaire, LG 29th January 1919.**

15th (1st Leeds) and 17th (2nd Leeds) Battalion, West Yorkshire Regiment used the Leeds coat of arms as their cap badge, rather than the usual White Horse of Hanover.

Albert Mountain married Ethel Smith (17th January 1895–April 1976) on 27th September 1919 at St Agnes

Albert's son, Jack, was licensee of the Britannia Hotel, Holbeck, Leeds. In June 1967 he presented his father's VC to the West Yorkshire Regiment Museum there.

and St Stephen Church, Burmantofts, Yorkshire. He was living at 34 Sutherland Mount and she at 36 Bromhill Avenue, Leeds at the time. They lived at The Miners Arms, Aberford Road, Garforth, Yorkshire from 1953. They had four children:

- Jean Mountain (born 26th July 1921–1977) married John Cliff (1919–48) in 1945. They had a son, Shaun Michael Cliff (2nd August 1947–11th October 2004), who married Christine V Dudding (born 1943) in 1968. He is understood to have been an aerial photographer working for Hambleton Aviation. They had at least a daughter, Rebecca Margaret J Cliff, in 1979. Jean married Kenneth Cave (1921–2007) in 1955 and they had two children – Nigel P Cave 1956 and Marna D Cave 1958.
- Jack 'Sonny' Mountain (1st August 1923–28th September 1998) married Violet Legg (born 1924) in 1947. Jack became licensee of the Britannia Hotel, Holbeck, Leeds. They had three children – Gail Mountain 1951, Craig Albert Mountain 1966 and Penelope Mountain 1967.
- Mavis Mountain (22nd May 1926–December 2002) married Dennis Gannon (1926–18th December 2003) in 1950.
- Wendy Mountain (born 17th February 1935) married Thomas B Lindley (born 1929) in March 1956. They had four children – Kevin B Lindley 1957, Darrel R Lindley 1963 (served in the REME 1980–86), Antony Lindley 1964 and Carl Albert Lindley 1969.

Ethel's father, Tom Smith (1849–1920), a paper stainer, married Charlotte née Hope (1854–1927) in 1874 at Leeds, Yorkshire. They were living at 51 Acorn Street in 1881, at 4 Boston Street in 1891, at 4 Lincoln Field in 1901 and 49 Sutherland Mount in 1911, all in Leeds. In addition to Ethel they had another eleven children, including:

- John Smith (born c.1875) was a mechanic's labourer in 1891. He married Annie Theobald (born 1875) in 1896. They were living at 4 Napoleon Street, Leeds in 1901, by when he was a stationary engine stoker. In 1911 he was a stoker on the railways and was living with his parents. Annie was not with him. They had three children including – Amy Smith 1901 and Doris Smith 1903.
- Thomas Smith (born c.1876).

- Ada Smith (born c.1879) was an assistant in a clothing warehouse in 1901.
- James Smith (born c1881) was a stable groom in 1901.
- William Smith (born c.1883) was a machine fitter in 1901.
- Arthur Smith (born c.1888) was an errand boy in 1901.
- Lily Smith (born c.1891).
- Tom Smith (born c.1893) was a warehouse assistant in 1911.
- George Smith (born c.1897) was an apprentice engineer in 1911.
- Walter Smith (born c.1901).

Post-war Albert worked as the chauffeur for the Lord Mayor of Leeds. Later he was a timekeeper at Burton's clothing factory in Leeds. From 1953 he was landlord of The Miners Arms, Aberford Road, Garforth, Yorkshire. Ethel was still living there at the time of her death in 1976. Albert attended a number of VC Reunions – the VC Garden Party at Buckingham Palace on 26th June 1920, the VC Dinner at the Royal Gallery of the House of Lords, London on 9th November 1929, the Victory Day Celebration Dinner & Reception at The Dorchester, London on 8th June 1946 and the VC Centenary Celebrations at Hyde Park, London on 26th June 1956.

He attended the funeral of John Crawshaw Raynes VC on 16th November 1929 with fellow VCs George Sanders, Wilfrid Edwards, Fred McNess, Charles Hull, Frederick Dobson, Arthur Poulter, William Butler, Samuel Meekosha, Albert Shepherd and John Ormsby. He was also at the funeral of George Sanders VC in 1950 with fellow VCs Wilfrid Edwards and Charles Hull.

Albert died after a long illness at his home at The Miners Arms, Aberford Road, Garforth, Leeds on 7th January 1967. The funeral service, at St Mary's Parish Church, Garforth on 12th January was attended by Major WTA Brooks, representing the Colonel of the Regiment, Lieutenant Colonel W Harris MBE, representing the West Yorkshire and Prince of Wales's Own Regimental Association and VCs William B Butler and Wilfrid Edwards. He was cremated at Lawnswood Crematorium, Leeds and his ashes were scattered in New Adel Lane Avenue, Plot K2–380 in the Garden of Remembrance. Albert is commemorated in a number of other places:

Albert's funeral was conducted at the Church of St Mary the Blessed Virgin in Garforth. The church is the third (possibly fourth) on this site and the foundation stone was laid in July 1844. It was consecrated on 14th November 1845 by the first Bishop of Ripon, Dr Charles Thomas Longley.

- Leeds Victoria Cross Memorial, outside Leeds City Art Gallery, Victoria Square, The Headrow, Leeds, West Yorkshire commemorating seventeen Leeds VCs – AL

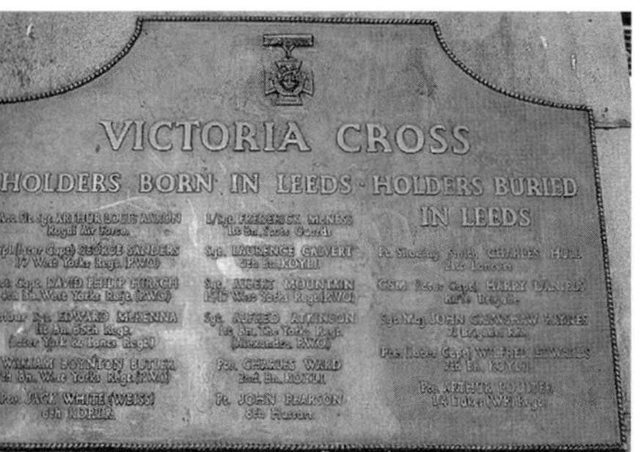

The commemorative plaque commemorating seventeen Leeds VCs, including Albert Mountain, outside the City Art Gallery in Victoria Square.

Albert was landlord of the Miners Arms, Aberford Road, Garforth from 1953. He died there on 7th January 1967. A Garforth Historical Society Blue Plaque was subsequently placed on the left side of the ground floor (Memorials to Valour).

Aaron, A Atkinson, WB Butler, L Calvert, H Daniels, W Edwards, DP Hirsch, C Hull, E McKenna, F McNess, A Mountain, J Pearson, A Poulter, JC Raynes, G Sanders, C Ward and J White.

- Memorial plaque at St Mary the Virgin Church, Church Lane, Garforth, Yorkshire.
- Garforth Historical Society Blue Plaque on his former home at The Miners Arms, Aberford Road, Garforth dedicated in April 2007.
- A Department for Communities and Local Government commemorative VC paving stone was dedicated at The Miners Bar & Kitchen, Aberford Road, Garforth on 26th March 2018 to mark the centenary of his award.

In addition to the VC he was awarded the British War Medal 1914–20, Victory Medal 1914–19, George VI Coronation Medal 1937, Elizabeth II Coronation Medal 1953 and the French Médaille Militaire. He is reputed to have also been awarded the French Croix de Guerre 1914–18 but no record of it has been found in the London Gazette. The VC was presented to the curator of the West Yorkshire Regiment Museum, Major HAV Spencer, at a ceremony at the Britannia Hotel, Holbeck, Leeds, by his son Jack in June 1967. It is held by the Prince of Wales's Own Regiment of Yorkshire Museum, 3A Tower Street, York, Yorkshire.

24066 PRIVATE ARTHUR POULTER
1/4th Battalion, The Duke of Wellington's (West Riding Regiment)

Arthur Poulter was born on 16th December 1893 at Kilgram Bridge, near East Witton, North Yorkshire. His father, Robert Poulter (10th January 1848–January 1906) was a farm labourer. He married Jane née Todd (1851–April 1920), born at Nosterfield, Yorkshire, on 23rd November 1870 at West Tanfield, Yorkshire. She was living with her grandmother, Jane Lancaster, at Nosterfield in 1861. They were living at Ward Gunner Cottage, West Tanfield in 1871, at Quarry House, North Stainley cum Sleningford in 1881 and at Squirrel Bank, East Witton, Yorkshire in 1891. By 1901 he was a shepherd and they were living at Kilgram Grange, East Witton Without, Richmond, Yorkshire. Also living with the family in 1901 was a grandson, Ernest Poulter (28th December 1891–1936), who was a platelayer (railway) at the time of his enlistment into the Royal Navy on 14th January 1916. He was described as 5′ 7½″ tall, with brown hair, blue eyes and fresh complexion. He served on HMS *Victory II* as a stoker class II 14th January–8th July 1916, on HMS *Woolwich* 9th July 1916–30th June 1918 and on HMS *Columbine* as a stoker class I 1st July 1918–29th September 1919. Jane was living with her son Frederick in 1911. Arthur had ten siblings:

- Frederick Poulter (1st August 1873–3rd May 1951) was a rabbit catcher/game keeper in 1901. He married Grace Eliza Boynton (1884–28th October 1904) on 16th February 1904 at East Witton Church, Leyburn, Yorkshire. He was living at East Witton, Middleham, Yorkshire in 1911. He married Ann Hardy (31st July

Kilgram Bridge (Dave Rodgers).

Arthur Poulter's family was living at Squirrel Bank, East Witton, Yorkshire in 1891 (Dave Rodgers).

1884–28th June 1957) on 26th April 1913 at Leyburn. They were living at 18 East Witton, near Leyburn at the time of his death there on 3rd May 1951. She was living there at the time of her death at Rookwith, Ripon, Yorkshire. Frederick and Ann had six children:

  - Margaret Poulter (born and died 1914).
  - Margaret Evelyn Poulter (28th February 1915–1976) married William Davy (1914–90) in 1945 at Wensleydale. They had two children – Ann Davy 1948 and Joan M Davy 1954.
  - Laura Poulter (born 1916) married Dennis Charles Flack (1921–98) in 1945 at Wensleydale. He was born at Warwick. They had two children – Gillian Flack 1948 and Peter Flack 1951.
  - Phyllis Poulter (1st January 1918–14th November 1995) married Bertie Hanslip Laing (1919–8th July 1979) in 1945 at Wensleydale. They were living at South Lodge, Jervaulx, Ripon at the time of his death at Northallerton. She was living at 20 The Springs, Middleham at the time of her death there. They had a son, Ian Laing, in 1946.
  - Robert William Poulter (21st October 1920–2nd October 1979) married Edna Johnson on 17th October 1942 at Scunthorpe. He was a gamekeeper in 1957. They were living at North Lodge, Blenheim Park, Woodstock, Oxfordshire at the time of his death there. They had three children – Frederick M Poulter 1944, Robert G Poulter 1947 and Alison E Poulter 1954.
  - Thomas Stanley Poulter (6th December 1922–February 1998) married Margaret Wilson (born 1928) in 1953.

- John Poulter (5th March 1875–13th December 1957), a corn miller, married Margaret Pearson (1874–December 1905) on 24th June 1899 at North Stainley, They lived at Sleningford Mill, West Tanfield. He married Annie Fossick (22nd January 1874–September 1964) in 1907 at Bedale. John died at Sleningford Mill, leaving effects valued at £2,120/17/2. They had four children:
  - Margery Poulter (22nd April 1908–2nd December 1993) died unmarried.
  - Cathlyn Poulter (born 20th February 1910–12th April 1975) married John William Bootland (c.1911–90) in 1936. They were living at 1 South View Street, West Tanfield at the time of her death. He was living at 4 The Row, West Tanfield at the time of his death. They had a daughter, Jacqualyn Bootland, in 1943.
  - Robert Poulter (1912–August 1915).
  - Miles Fossick Poulter (1913–February 1914).
- Alfred Poulter (15th March 1879–1964), a coal miner hewer, married Annie Plaxton (14th December 1880–1966) in 1903 at Knaresborough. She was born at Allerston, Yorkshire. They were living at Chapel Lane, Barwick-in-Elmet in 1911. They had ten children:
  - Dorothy Poulter (1903–September 1905).

  - Alice Poulter (27th October 1904–1977) married Henry 'Harry' West (1904–49) on 22nd December 1928 at St John's Church, Roundhay, Leeds. He was born at Lotherton cum Aberford, Yorkshire.
  - Emily Poulter (born 6th May 1906).
  - Margaret Poulter (1907–September 1937) died unmarried.
  - Herbert Poulter (30th July 1909–16th October 1955) married Lily Glover née Mavir (1901–89) in 1949 at Whitehaven, Cumberland. Herbert was living at 6 Smithfield, Egremont, Cumberland at the time of his death there. Lily had previously married Joseph Barnes Glover (1900–35) in 1933.
  - Freda Poulter (16th September 1912–2003) married Frederick Richard Ball (1899–1982) in 1939. They were living at 24 Luxor Road, Leeds at the time of his death on 29th August 1982. They had a daughter, Brenda A Ball, in 1940.
  - Ethel Vera Poulter (1914–October 1925).
  - Alfred Poulter (2nd June 1917–4th March 1994).
  - Frederick H Poulter (1922–92).
  - William Leslie Poulter (8th May 1924–11th August 1990) married Edna Dyer (1927–99) in 1949. They had three children – Malcolm L Poulter 1949, Margaret Poulter 1954 and Ann Poulter 1961.
- Henry 'Harry' Poulter (30th March 1884–27th July 1945) was a colliery horse keeper below ground. He married Sarah Jane Bodman (28th March 1886–29th December 1947) in 1911 at Sedgefield, Co Durham. She was born at Chilton, Co Durham and was living with her family at 1 Linden Terrace, Ferryhill, Co Durham in 1911. They were living at 7 Firwood Terrace, Ferryhill Station at the time of their deaths there. They had seven children:
  - Robert Samuel Poulter (1912–15).
  - Harry Poulter (19th March 1914–1970) married Argent Hannah Appleby (26th June 1918–2006) in 1935. They had seven children – Alan Poulter 1936, Fred Poulter 1940, Irene Poulter 1941, Harry Poulter 1943, Joan Poulter 1948, Eric Poulter 1952 and Julie Poulter 1960. Argent married John Hogg in 1979, registered as Argent N Poulter.
  - Jane Cowans Poulter (1st May 1915–1973) married Edwin Morgan (26th March 1912–July 1986) in 1936. They had two children – Raymond Morgan 1938 and Robert W Morgan 1940.
  - Fred Poulter (16th May 1917–26th May 1983), a coal miner, was living at 22 Haig Street, Ferryhill Station, Co Durham at the time of his death there.
  - Robert William Poulter (2nd February 1920–4th March 1978), a colliery putter, married Catherine Isabel Jackson née Crossan (22nd May 1927–1966) in 1956. She was born at Tynemouth, Northumberland. Catherine had previously married Sidney Jackson in 1948 and they had a daughter, Angela Jackson, in 1949. It is assumed that the marriage failed and that Catherine started a relationship with Robert Poulter c.1953. Robert and

Catherine had two children registered as Jackson and Poulter – Robert M in 1953 and Kevin P in 1955. They had two other sons – Edwin Poulter 1956 and Shaun H Poulter 1963. Robert was living at 15 Firwood Terrace, Ferryhill Station at the time of his death there.
  - Louisa Poulter (27th June 1922–1945) died unmarried.
  - Annie Poulter (11th March 1925–10th June 1988) married Arthur Willoughby (27th January 1917–3rd March 1996) in 1947. They had two children – Arthur Willoughby 1948 and Jennifer A Willoughby 1950.
- Robert William Poulter (13th January 1887–1953) was a farm labourer in 1911, living at Park Grange, Harmby, Leyburn, Yorkshire.
- Frank Poulter (29th August 1888–1958), a farm labourer, was working for George Atkinson Hamilton in Bedale, Yorkshire in 1911. He married Elizabeth Thorpe (3rd November 1901–1925) on 31st March 1923 at Wath, Yorkshire. They were living at The Bungalow, Studley Roger, Ripon, Yorkshire in 1939.
- Thomas Herbert Poulter (26th October 1889–1964) was a coalminer/stoneman in 1911, boarding at 3 Bob Gins, Causey, Co Durham.
- Elizabeth Poulter (1871–10th September 1951) was a domestic servant in the home of William Greensit, a farmer, at West Tanfield, Yorkshire in 1891. She married Charles Thomas Sly (11th March 1872–1950), a brewer's labourer, on 25th November 1893 at Leyburn, Yorkshire. She was living at Leeming, near Northallerton, Yorkshire at the time of her death there. They had eight children:
  - Emily Sly (born and died 1894).
  - Ethel Sly (born 25th March 1895) married Fred Allinson (born 26th April 1890) in 1914 at Bedale. He was born at Morton-on-Swale, Yorkshire and was a horseman on a farm at Scruton, Yorkshire in 1911. They had seven children – Harold Allinson 1914, George F Allinson 1916, William A Allinson 1918, Freda M Allinson 1923, Charles Derrick Allinson 1926, Grace E Allinson 1929 and Raymond Allinson 1932.
  - William Harold Sly (1897–9th January 1980), an engineer's slinger, married Cicely Jane Beck (29th January 1901–7th March 1954) in 1922 at Guisborough, Yorkshire. They were living at 20 Southam Road, Dunchurch, Rugby, Warwickshire at the time of her death at the Hospital of St Cross, Rugby. He was living at 6 Bartholomews Close, Cresswell, Morpeth, Northumberland at the time of his death. They had two children – William Harold Sly 1923 and Rita Sly 1931.
  - Unnamed male child (born and died 1899).
  - Mabel Sly (born and died 1900).
  - May Sly (19th May 1903–1986) married Albert W Floyd (10th July 1899–1968) in 1927 at Richmond, Yorkshire.
  - Grace Sly (22nd April 1905–February 2002) married William Draper (8th August 1901–July 1996) in 1932. They had two children – Brian Draper 1935 and Joyce Draper 1940.

  - Nora Sly (5th October 1907–February 2003) married Wilfred Abbott (8th August 1905–March 1995) in 1927. They had two children – Clifford William Abbott 1927 and Elizabeth Abbott 1937.
- Annie Poulter (3rd March 1877–8th January 1958) married John Henry Tarren (18th December 1880–24th July 1969), a railway shunter, on 19th January 1901 at Leyburn, Yorkshire. They were living at 3 White Street, Thornaby-on-Tees, Yorkshire in 1911. They were living at 16 Wilson Street, Thornaby-on-Tees at the time of her death there. He was living at 453 Thornaby Road, Stockton-on-Tees at the time of his death there. They had five children:
  - Violet Beatrice Tarren (28th April 1901–20th April 1981) was a spinster living at 21 Ridge Green, Scalby, Scarborough, Yorkshire at the time of her death there.
  - George Henry Tarren (1902–09).
  - Ernest Tarren (1905–September 1950) married Emily Warburton (1906–December 1937) in 1926 at Auckland, Co Durham. They had four children – Ernest J Tarren 1926, Olive Margaret Tarren 1929, John Tarren 1932 and Joan V Tarren 1937.
  - David Tarren (13th February 1909–23rd August 1963), a haulage contractor, married Joan Picken (26th December 1918–2000) in 1941. She was born at Stockton-on-Tees, Co Durham. They were living at Maltby House, Maltby, Cleveland at the time of his death there. They had five children – Ann Tarren 1942, Roger Tarren 1944, David Tarren 1947, Robert W Tarren 1955 and Linda E Tarren 1959.
  - Olive J Tarren (1916–19).
- Rhoda Poulter (28th February 1881–2nd May 1950) was a spinster living at 16 Wilson Street, Thornaby-on-Tees, Yorkshire at the time of her death.

Arthur's paternal grandfather, John Poulter (c.1817–27th December 1881), an agricultural labourer, was born at Dishforth, Yorkshire. He married Eliza Ann née Carr (c.1818–5th February 1893) on 24th November 1845 at Malton, Yorkshire. She was born at Settrington, near Lamton, Yorkshire. They were living at 55 New Inn, Tholthorpe, Yorkshire in 1851. John developed a clot on his brain, which compressed the right side and, as a result, he spent many years in and out of the North Riding Asylum from about 1854. They were living at Smiths Ford, Easingwold, Yorkshire in 1871. She was living at Smith's Yard, Easingwold, Yorkshire with her son, Tom, and granddaughter, Anne, in 1881. She was living at Little Lane Alms Houses, Easingwold at the time of her death there. In addition to Robert they had seven other children:

- William Poulter (1847–1904), an agricultural labourer, was living at Raskelf, Yorkshire in 1861 and was boarding at Long Street, Easingwold in 1871. He married Mary (c.1837–1904) and was a labourer in an iron works by 1881, when they were living at 7 Cargo Fleet Road, Middlesbrough, Yorkshire. By 1891 they were living at 30 Cargo Fleet Road and he was a bricklayer's labourer. They had a son, John William Poulter, in 1875.

- Tom Poulter (1850–2nd January 1913) married Mary Hannah Young (1858–October 1919), a dressmaker, on 29th November 1881 at Easingwold. They emigrated to New York, USA aboard SS *City of Richmond*, arriving on 3rd April 1885. Mary had returned to England with her two children by 1891 and was living with her mother Hannah Young at Long Street, Easingwold and was still there in 1911. Tom was living at Church Lane, Boroughbridge, Yorkshire at the time of his death at Leeds General Infirmary. Mary was living at Long Street at the time of her death. They had two children – John William Poulter 1882 and Arthur Poulter 1886.
- Mary Jane Poulter (born 1851) had a daughter, Annie Poulter, in 1871.
- John Poulter (20th June 1853–26th April 1933) married Frances 'Fanny' Johnson (28th April 1859–19th July 1942) on 27th October 1877. They emigrated to New York, USA, arriving on 16th February 1882. He was a farm labourer on 4th June 1900 and they were living at Prophetstown, Whiteside, Illinois. They had eleven children – Robert William Poulter 1877, John Thomas Poulter 1879, Elizabeth Poulter 1881, George Poulter 1882, Jennie Poulter 1884, Harry Poulter 1887, Ralph Poulter 1890, Jay Johnson Poulter 1892, William Almon Poulter 1896, Madge Poulter 1898 and Lloyd Oliver Poulter 1901.
- Susanna Thornton Poulter (1855–5th April 1912) had three children – Annie Elizabeth Thompson Poulter 1877, Kate Poulter 1880 and John Herbert Poulter 1883. She was housekeeper for William Thompson (8th May 1809–1892), a shoemaker, at Helperby, Yorkshire in 1881. William had married Isabella Boynton (1803–75) on 24th December 1831 at Crayke, Co Durham and they had seven children – Mary Thompson 1833, Catherine Thompson 1834, Edmund/Edward Thompson 1836, Frances Thompson 1838, Elizabeth Thompson 1840, John Thompson 1843 and Jane Thompson 1846. William was a groom in 1841, living with his family at Philip's Square, Easingwold. By 1851 he was a cordwainer, living with his children at High Street, Easingwold. Susanna married William on 24th December 1883 at Brafferton, Yorkshire. They were living at Boat Street, Helperby in 1891. They had two children – Edith Thompson 1886 and Charles Thompson 1890. Susanna had another son after her husband's death, William Thompson, on 12th September 1894. She was admitted to High Royds Psychiatric Hospital, Menston, Yorkshire on 3rd August 1909 and subsequently died there.
- Margaret Poulter (4th March 1857–January 1921) married Ezekiel Potter (1855–April 1920), a farm labourer, on 17th July 1876 at Malton, Yorkshire. They were living at Mill House, Foston, Yorkshire in 1891 and at Sutton-on-the-Forest, Yorkshire in 1911. She died at Easingwold Infirmary. They had thirteen children – Richard Potter 1877, John William Potter 1879, Eliza Ellen Potter 1880, Sarah Potter 1882, Martha Potter 1883, Tom Potter 1885, Henry Potter 1887, James

Potter 1889, Margaret Potter 1890, Frank Potter 1892, Annie Potter 1893, Lily Potter 1895 and Mary Jane Potter 1897.

- Eliza Esther Poulter (12th February 1859–8th May 1946) had a daughter, Maggie Poulter, in 1875. She married Thomas Robert Stainton (14th March 1855–6th April 1915) on 28th October 1879. He was born at Great Ouseburn, Yorkshire. In 1881 he was a wagoner at a malt kilns and they were living at Tollerton, Yorkshire. Thomas followed his father James to Australia some time after 1885 and settled at Armadale, Victoria. His father had emigrated there in 1863. Eliza remained and moved to Easingwold without passing her address to her husband. He tried to re-establish contact through an article in *Empire News* but they were never reunited. Eliza was living as head of household at Smith's Yard, Easingwold in 1891, working as a laundress. By 1911 she was registered as a widow, while employed as a grocer and general dealer, living at Stockton-on-Tees, Co Durham. Eliza died at Thornaby, Yorkshire. She and Thomas had two children – Henry 'Harry' Stainton on 6th March 1880 and Jane Stainton on 23rd December 1884. Harry Stainton married Mary Jane Teasdale on 30th April 1908 and they had three children – Alan Stainton 1903, Cora Stainton 1908 and Edna Stainton 1910. He was a laundry van/drayman/horseman living at 20 George Street, Thornaby, when he attested in the King's Own Yorkshire Light Infantry (31442) on 9th December 1915 and transferred to the Reserve next day. He was mobilised on 5th June 1916 and enlisted at Richmond, Yorkshire next day, described as 5′ 6½″ tall and his religious denomination was Church of England. He was posted to 1st (Reserve) Garrison Battalion on 10th June and transferred to 25th (Works) Battalion, Durham Light Infantry on 14th April 1917. He transferred to 356th (Home Service) Labour Company, 7th Labour Battalion (185514 later 238366) at Belton Park, Grantham on 28th April 1917, to 3rd Agricultural Company, Durham Light Infantry on 8th June, to 410th Agricultural Company, Labour Corps at Glen Parva Barracks, Leicester on 30th June and to 482nd Agricultural Company, Labour Corps at Leicester on 1st June 1918. He was posted to the Labour Centre, Ripon on 23rd January 1919 and was demobilised on 15th February 1919 from Clipstone.

His maternal grandfather, Thomas Todd (c.1825–April 1895), an agricultural labourer, married Elizabeth née Lancaster (c.1831–March 1855) in 1850 at Ripon, Yorkshire. She was born at Thornborough, Yorkshire. Thomas was living at Ebenezer Chapel, Nosterfield in 1861. He married Margaret Gill (born c.1837) in 1862 at Ripon. She was born in Jersey, Channel Islands, daughter of John Gill (1795–1869), an army pensioner in 1861, and Ann Huggett (1809–72). Margaret had a son, Thomas Gill born in 1860, prior to her marriage to Thomas Todd. Thomas and Margaret had five children:

Ripon, North Yorkshire.

Thomas Todd's name (bottom right) on the Pozières Memorial.

- Ambrose Todd (1863–1916), a general labourer, married Sarah Ann Hardcastle (1864–1953) on 29th November 1884. They were living at 7 Garbutt's Court, Stonebridge Gate, Ripon in 1891 and were still there in 1911. They had twelve children – Margaret Jane Todd 1886, Annie Todd 1888, Eliza Todd 1890, Zetta Todd 1892 Mabel Todd 1894, Sidney Todd 1896, Violetta Todd 1898, Clara Todd 1900, Ambrose Todd 1902, Laurence Todd 1905, Stanley Todd 1907 and Alice Todd 1909.
- Sidney Todd (26th September 1865–1943), was registered as Signee Todd at birth. He married Mary Jane Simpson (c.1865–1901) in 1883. They had five sons – John William Todd 1885, Thomas Todd 1887, Ambrose Todd 1889, Miles Sidney Todd 1890 and Walter Todd 1892. Thomas served as a private in 2nd West Yorkshire (200980) and was killed in action on 24th April 1918 (Pozières Memorial, France – Panels 26 and 27).
- Alice Todd (1869–74).
- Eliza Todd (1872–1927) married Herbert Harpham (also seen as Harphum) (born 1869), a builder's labourer, in 1891. They were living at Dunham, Nottinghamshire in 1901 and at Ragnall Dunham, Nottingham in 1911. They had six children – John Tomas Harpham 1892, Rose Harpham 1895, Herbert Harpham 1899, Alice Harpham 1904, Edith Harpham 1908 and Margaret Harpham 1912.
- Zetta Todd (1875–October 1926) married John Hudson (c.1874–3rd January 1947) on 26th October 1898 at Bedale, Yorkshire. He was at Marton cum Grafton, Yorkshire and was a labourer on an estate in 1901. They both died at Darlington, Co Durham. They had six children – Margaret Ann Hudson 1898, Alice Hudson 1900, Oliver Hudson 1901, Albert Hudson 1904, Hilda Hudson 1905 and Harold Hudson 1907.

Little is known about Arthur's early life. After school he worked on his father's farm until 1908, when he left home. He became a farm servant and was working at the farm of Thomas Richmond, his mother-in-law's second husband, at Spring House, Grewelthorpe, Ripon, Yorkshire in 1911. He moved to Leeds in 1912 and became a drayman with Messrs Timothy Taylor at their maltings at the Gelderd Road Depot. He then took up firewood delivery with a horse and cart in the New Wortley district for Thomas Rochford, his mother-in-law's second husband.

Arthur Poulter married Ada Briggs (15th June 1899–12th March 1954) on 12th August 1916 at St Mary of Bethany, New Wortley, Leeds. Her birth was registered at Hunslet, Yorkshire. They lived at 5–13th Avenue, Wortley before moving to 18–14th Avenue, Wortley. Ada and Arthur had thirteen children:

- Edward Poulter (22nd September 1916–6th February 1978), a clerk, married Nellie Tong (31st March 1918–25th October 1985) in 1937. She was born at Bramley. He was a warehouseman in 1956 and they were living at 71 Silver Royd Hill, Wortley at the time of his death there. She was living at 8 Fearnley Place, Leeds at the time of her death there. They had a daughter, Sandra R Poulter, in 1942. She married Sydney Wilson in 1961 and they ran the Poulter Hotel, 20 West Square, Scarborough for a number of years. Sandra and Sydney had four children – Dean Wilson 1962, Gary Wilson 1963, Julie Wilson 1965 and Mark Wilson 1968.
- Harry Poulter (16th June 1918–15th April 1975) was an engineer in 1956. He was living at Shaftesbury House, Beeston Road, Leeds at the time of his death.
- Arthur Poulter (25th July 1919–7th January 1947) served during the Second World War in the King's Own Royal Regiment (Lancaster) (4540872). He was taken prisoner by the Germans in France and was imprisoned at Stalag XX-B, Malbork, Poland (Prisoner 19712). He was repatriated after the war in very poor health and was admitted to Middleton Sanatorium, Ilkley, Yorkshire, where he subsequently died.
- Joseph Poulter (born and died 1920).
- Irene Poulter (19th July 1921–16th November 1997) married James W Greenfield in 1945. They had two sons – Brian Poulter Greenfield 1948 and David A Greenfield 1951.
- John Poulter (28th August 1922–24th January 2009) is believed to have served in the Royal Navy during the Second World War. He married Margaret Cunnington (28th November 1920–1999) in 1945. She was born at Hunslet, Yorkshire. They had two children – Carol A Poulter 1947 and Robert A Poulter 1949.
- Fred Poulter (1923–24).
- Dennis Poulter (born and died 1925).
- Thomas Poulter (7th December 1925–December 1995) served in the Army during the Second World War. He married Roma Chambers (born 1931) in 1953 at Hartlepool, Co Durham. Her birth was registered at Stockton-on-Tees, Co Durham. They had two sons – Thomas F Poulter 1954 and Barry Poulter 1958. When aged eleven he swapped his father's VC, which was kept in a drawer, with a friend for a bag of marbles. Ada learned of this and marched her son down the road to retrieve the medal and return the marbles.

- Ivy Poulter (15th April 1927–22nd November 2004) was known as Pat. She married Harold Harrison (5th January 1924–2004) in 1946 at Leeds. They had four children – Patricia A Harrison 1948, Larrain Harrison 1950, Jennifer Harrison 1951 and John S Harrison 1960.
- Leslie Poulter (4th November 1928–25th May 2010) married Sheila Lee in 1952 at Wharfedale, Yorkshire. Her sister, Violet, married Leslie's brother, Raymond. They had two children – Lesley Poulter 1953 and Christopher E Poulter 1959.
- Ronald Poulter (5th May 1931–April 1993) married Sheila White in 1959 at Barkston Ash, Yorkshire. They had three children – Stephen Poulter 1963, Antony Poulter 1967 and Amanda Jane Poulter 1968.
- Raymond Poulter (17th October 1933–16th June 1980) married Violet Lee in 1956. Her sister, Sheila, married Raymond's brother, Leslie. He was living at 12 Acres Hall Crescent, Pudsey, near Leeds at the time of his death. They had a son, Dennis Poulter, in 1958.

Ada's father, Joe Jackson Briggs (1867–1901), a brewer, married Adelaide née Rawling (27th December 1868–April 1939) on 6th July 1893 at Hunslet Register Office, both giving their address as 1 Charlotte Street, Hunslet. She was born at Collingham, Yorkshire. They were living at 16 Silsbury Street, Hunslet in 1901. In addition to Ada they had a son, Edward Briggs, in 1897. He served as a bugler in 1st Rifle Brigade (S/11375) and was killed in action on 1st July 1916 (Thiepval Memorial, France – Pier and Face 16B and 16C). Adelaide married Thomas Rochford (c.1873–January 1931), a bricklayer's labourer, on 27th September 1902 at Holbeck Church, Leeds. In 1901 he was boarding at 33 Chatham Street, Leeds. They moved to 39 Recreation Street, Holbeck after their marriage. He was a firewood dealer in 1911 and they were living at 18 Strawberry Mount, Bramley and later at 5–13th Avenue, Bramley. She moved to 8 Gloucester Lane, Bramley. Adelaide and Thomas had four children:

Arthur's brother-in-law, Edward Briggs, is commemorated on the Thiepval Memorial.

Ada Poulter's family was living on Silsbury Street, Hunslet in 1901.

- John Rochford (8th August 1904–22nd August 1976) married Vera Alice Wilkinson (24th December 1903–2nd June 1985) on 11th April 1925. She was living at 45 Manston Grove, Leeds at the time of her death there. They had a daughter, Peggy Rochford, in 1926.

- Lily Rochford (3rd January 1907–1979) married Richard Mark Tasker (30th August 1903–20th April 1986), born at Malton, Yorkshire, in 1926. He was living at 13 Greenthorpe Road, Bramley at the time of his death there. They had two children – Betty Tasker 1931 and Fred Tasker 1934.
- Joe Rochford (1909–10).
- Doris Rochford (18th April 1911–21st February 1988) married Joseph Foster (3rd January 1908–1971) in 1934. She was living at 24 Hartley Grove, Leeds at the time of her death there. They had two children – Joan Foster 1935 and Shirley Foster 1937.

Arthur enlisted in 1/4th Duke of Wellington's on 1st March 1916. **Awarded the VC for his actions at Erquinghem-Lys on 10th April 1918, LG 28th June 1918.** Initially he was sent to a French hospital and was transferred to Stanford Road Military Hospital, Norbury, London, part of Croydon War Hospital. While

Stanford Road Military Hospital, based on Stanford Road School, Norbury, was one of five complexes that made up Croydon War Hospital. The others were school buildings in Davidson Road, Ecclesbourne Road, Ingram Road and The Crescent. Having been requisitioned by the War Office, the Hospital opened under Eastern Command on 30th June 1915. Eventually there were 1,070 beds. Doctors were provided by the RAMC, supplemented with local general practitioners, and many of the nursing staff were provided by Voluntary Aid Detachments. At one time all the nursing staff came from Australia. The facilities were originally intended to treat troops in Eastern Command for nerve, joint or jaw injuries, diseases of the ear, or for general medical care. However, as the war progressed, ear and nerve cases were treated elsewhere, freeing beds for the wounded and sick from overseas. The King and Queen visited in October 1916. Stanford Road School had only just been built when war broke out and it was requisitioned before being used. There were 165 beds. It was used to treat mandibular fractures caused by shrapnel and gunshot wounds. Croydon War Hospital closed on 9th May 1919, having treated 19,182 patients, of whom 4,153 were discharged as invalids. Most of the original school buildings have survived except for Stanford Road School (later Norbury Manor Secondary School), which was demolished in 1987. The site is now Freeman Court, sheltered housing for the elderly.

Arthur was a pallbearer at the funeral of John Crawshaw Raynes VC in November 1929.

recovering there, Mr HT Kemp KC, Recorder of Hull and Chairman of the Society of Yorkshiremen in London, presented him with a silver watch on behalf of the Society. Arthur was discharged from the Army on 7th October 1918 and received the Silver War Badge. The VC was presented by the King in the Ballroom at Buckingham Palace on 13th December 1918. A testimonial fund by the people of Leeds raised £556, of which £500 was invested in War Bonds. The balance was transferred to Arthur's account following a civic reception at Leeds on 19th December 1918. He was also presented with an engraved pocket watch by the citizens of Leeds. The watch was donated to the Duke of Wellington's Regiment (West Riding) Museum, Bankfield Museum, Boothtown Road, Halifax, West Yorkshire in May 2001. Arthur was one of the Honour Guard at the burial of the Unknown Warrior at Westminster Abbey on 11th November 1920. He attended the funeral of John Crawshaw Raynes VC on 16th November 1929 with ten other VCs. Eight acted as pallbearers (G Sanders, W Edwards, F McNess, C Hull, A Mountain, F Dobson, A Poulter and W Butler). The other three were S Meekosha, AE Shepherd and JW Ormsby.

Arthur found employment with the Leeds Transport Depot as a tram conductor before being employed by Price (Tailors) Ltd. He was hit by a police car in April 1953 and, although he recovered, was forced to retire through ill health in February 1956. He and Ada retired to 4 Back, Florence Road, Armley, Yorkshire. Arthur attended a number of VC reunions – the VC Garden Party at Buckingham Palace on 26th June 1920, the VC Dinner at the Royal Gallery of the House of Lords, London on 9th November 1929 and the VC Centenary Celebrations at Hyde Park, London on 26th June 1956.

Arthur's grave in New Wortley Cemetery.

Arthur died on 29th August 1956 at 10 Back, Florence Road, Armley, Yorkshire. He is buried in New Wortley Cemetery (Grave 2500), Middle Cross Street, Leeds, where his parents, wife and five of his sons also lay. A new headstone was erected over his grave in August 2010. He left effects valued at £990/2/2. Arthur is commemorated in a number of other places:

Arthur Poulter's medals are held by the Duke of Wellington's Regiment Museum in Halifax (Dave Rodgers).

The memorial to Arthur Poulter at Erquinghem-Lys. The railway runs across the photograph behind the hedge, with Rue Delpierre crossing it on the right. The building in the right background is the former Erquinghem-Lys railway station.

- Memorial by the railway crossing on Rue Delpierre, Erquinghem-Lys, dedicated on 9th April 1998.
- The Leeds Victoria Cross Memorial, outside Leeds City Art Gallery, Victoria Square, The Headrow, Leeds, West Yorkshire with sixteen other Leeds VCs – AL Aaron, A Atkinson, WB Butler, L Calvert, H Daniels, W Edwards, DP Hirsch, C Hull, E McKenna, F McNess, A Mountain, J Pearson, JC Raynes, G Sanders, C Ward and J White.
- A Department of Communities and Local Government commemorative paving stone was dedicated at East Witton War Memorial, Church of St John the Evangelist, East Witton, North Yorkshire on 10th April 2018 to mark the centenary of his award.

In addition to the VC he was awarded the British War Medal 1914–20, Victory Medal 1914–19, George VI Coronation Medal 1937 and Elizabeth II Coronation Medal 1953. The VC was loaned to Leeds City Museum by the family in December 1956 before being donated to the Duke of Wellington's (West Riding) Regiment on 11th June 1999. The VC is held by the Duke of Wellington's Regiment (West Riding) Museum, Bankfield Museum, Boothtown Road, Halifax, West Yorkshire.

CAPTAIN THOMAS TANNATT PRYCE
4th Battalion, Grenadier Guards

Thomas Pryce was born on 17th January 1886 at Javastraat, The Hague, Netherlands. His father, also Thomas Pryce (5th September 1833–23rd June 1904), born at Trederwen Hall, Llansantffraid, Montgomeryshire, was a landowner and a merchant for John Pryce & Co of Lombard Street, London and The Hague, trading in tea,

coffee and snakeskins. The family had extensive interests in the Dutch East Indies. He lived in Java for twenty-eight years, where he served as a captain in the Batavia Regiment of Yeomanry Cavalry and was a member of the Batavian Board of Trade.

Thomas married Rosalie Susannah née Van Motman (1st January 1843–6th December 1915), born at Dramaga, Buitenzorg, Java, on 28th November 1863 in Java. They lived there until 1884 and then moved to the Netherlands before returning to Britain, where he was a JP and a county councillor for Montgomeryshire. He leased Pentrehylin Hall, Llandysilio, Montgomeryshire from James Turner, grandfather of Llewelyn Alberic Emilius Price-Davies VC. They also had a home at 25 Cleveland Square, Hyde Park, London. Thomas was a member of the council of the Powysland Club and a keen local historian, publishing *The History of the Parish of Llandysilio*. He died at Llanfyllin, Montgomeryshire, leaving effects valued at £18,749 4s 8d (£2.17M in 2018). Rosalie died at 25 Cleveland Square, Hyde Park, London, leaving effects valued at £17,558 7s 5d (£1.93M in 2018). Thomas junior had four siblings:

- Mary Aldouse Rosalie Pryce (29th June 1869–16th June 1947) married the Reverend John Ellis Cardigan Williams (1864–3rd December 1935) on 18th September 1906 at Christ Church, Lancaster Gate, London. He died at 11 Carlton Road, Ealing, London. She was living at 36 Victoria Park, Hafod-y-Bryn, Colwyn Bay, Denbighshire with Jane Ann Edwards (born 17th December 1868) in 1939. She was living at 16 Welsby Court, Ealing at the time of her death at 28 Kenilworth Road, Ealing, leaving effects valued at £63,570/2/11 (£2.5M in 2018).

Javastraat in The Hague, where Thomas Pryce was born in 1886 (Mapio).

Thomas' father was born at Trederwen Hall, Llansantffraid.

Pentrehylin Hall, Llandysilio, Montgomeryshire, where the Pryce family lived after returning from Java and the Netherlands.

Thomas' mother, Rosalie, was living in Cleveland Square, London when she died in 1915.

- Ann Rosalie Tannatt Pryce (17th May 1871–14th May 1958) married the Reverend Robert Stephen Edwards (1864–13th January 1927) in 1897 at Llanfyllin, Montgomeryshire. He was born at Brymbo, Denbighshire. They were living at Rectory House, Westcott Barton, Oxfordshire in 1901 and at 25 St Margaret's Road, Oxford in 1911. They were living at The Vicarage, Northmoor, Oxfordshire at the time of his death there. She died at 56 Elsham Road, Kensington, London. They had six children:
    - David Augustine Pryce Edwards (1898–17th October 1903).
    - Thomas James Edwards (1899–17th July 1914).
    - Mary Rosalie Jane 'Mona' Edwards (12th October 1902–22nd July 1994) was appointed Guide Lecturer at the British Museum of Natural History on 17th September 1931 and became a leading expert on whales. She was appointed governor of an internment camp on the Isle of Man during the Second World War. She was eventually appointed Chief Exhibition Officer at the British Museum of Natural History (MBE, LG 1st January 1963). Mona was living at Raikes, Loders, Bridport, Dorset at the time of her death there.
    - Edward Cecil Theodore Edwards (5th August 1905–31st August 1940) was known as 'Sphinx'. He was educated at Oxford University (MA) and was a rowing Blue, taking part in the 1925, 1926 and 1927 Oxford/Cambridge Boat Races. He also joined the Oxford Air Squadron, becoming its first member to qualify as a pilot. He was living at 56 Elsham Road, Kensington, London when he qualified for the Royal Aero Club Aviator's Certificate on 30th November 1927, flying a De Haviland Moth 30hp Cirrus at the London Aeroplane Club. In 1930 he and Winifred Spooner attempted to fly to Cape Town, South Africa in a Desoutter. They had to ditch in the sea off Italy and swim a mile to shore. Edward took part in the King's Cup Air Race round Britain in 1931, 1932, 1933, 1935, 1937 and 1938. He won

the event at Heston on 25th July 1931 in a field of forty competitors in a Blackburn Bluebird IV (G-AACC) at an average speed of 117.8 mph. He joined the RAF and was granted a permanent commission as a pilot officer in the General Duties Branch on 30th April 1928, with seniority from 30th April 1927 (05146). He was promoted flying officer 30th October 1928, flight lieutenant 1st December 1932, squadron leader 1st June 1937 and temporary wing commander 1st June 1940. He was posted to No.53 Squadron and was flying a Bristol Blenheim on a sortie over the Netherlands on 31st August 1940 when he was shot down. All three of the crew were killed and are buried in Rotterdam (Crooswijk) General Cemetery, Netherlands in Plot LL. Edward is buried in Row 1, Grave 5, 552175 Sergeant (Wireless Operator/Air Gunner) John Thomas Beesley in Row 1, Grave 6 and 751790 Sergeant (Observer) Lionel Louis Benjamin in Row 2, Grave 5. The crews of the other four aircraft on the raid reported heavy flak and searchlights over the target.

The Blackburn Bluebird IV (G-AACC) in which Thomas' cousin, Edward Cecil Theodore Edwards, won the King's Cup Air Race in 1931.

◦ Hugh 'Jumbo' Robert Arthur Edwards (17th November 1906–21st December 1972) was educated at Westminster School and Christ Church, Oxford 1925–27, where he was the only freshman to row in the 1926 Oxford and Cambridge Boat Race, in which he competed with his brother Edward. Hugh collapsed halfway along Chiswick Eyot and was later diagnosed with a hypertrophied heart. He failed his examinations, left Oxford to become a schoolteacher and took up rowing with London Rowing Club, competing at Henley Royal Regatta in 1928–30 and winning the Grand Challenge Cup in 1930. The Club was selected to represent England in the Empire Games in Canada in 1930 and won the eights and coxed fours. Hugh returned to Oxford in 1930 to complete his degree and rowed in that year's Boat Race. He also took part in the 1931 Henley Regatta, winning three finals on the same day, a feat never repeated – Grand Challenge Cup, Stewards' Challenge Cup and, with Lewis Clive, the Silver Goblets and Nickalls Cup. He was selected for the Los Angeles Olympic Games in 1932, winning gold in the coxless pairs with Lewis Clive and gold in the Great Britain coxless four, after replacing a sick team member. Hugh took part in the King's Cup Air Race around Britain in 1932, 1934, 1935 and 1937, finishing second in 1935. He was commissioned as a pilot officer on probation in the RAF General Duties Branch on 15th April 1929 and was granted a permanent commission as pilot officer on 15th April 1930. He was promoted flying officer 24th October

1931, flight lieutenant 1st April 1936, squadron leader 1st December 1938 and temporary wing commander (05203) on 1st March 1941. Hugh married Michael (sic) Lydia Rosemary Williams (14th February 1908–1984) in 1934 at Salisbury, Wiltshire. She was the daughter of Major John Williams, Royal Fusiliers. Michele and Hugh had two sons – John Hugh Michael Edwards 1935 and David CR Edwards. They were living at Wroughton Cottages, Abingdon, Berkshire in 1935 and at Windmill, Abingdon in 1955. He was in charge of flying operations at the RAF training centre at Jurby, Isle of Man, when he brought five Hampden bombers to Syerston, near Nottingham to take part in the first Thousand Bomber Raid on Cologne on 30th/31st May 1942. They were found to be not up to operational standards and did not take part. However, two nights later they took part in the second Thousand Bomber Raid against Essen. He flew a Hampden during a raid over Cologne, Germany that was badly damaged and managed to fly it safely back to Britain, for which he was awarded the Air Force Cross (LG 1st January 1943). It is not known if this refers to the 30th/31st May 1942 raid or a separate mission. He commanded No.53 Squadron February–November 1943, previously commanded by his brother, in Coastal Command. He was on convoy escort duty on 20th November 1943 flying Liberator GV.5 (BZ 819) when three engines failed. He was forced to ditch in the sea four miles off the Cornish coast and was the only survivor. He sculled his rubber dinghy to safety through shipping lanes and a minefield. Awarded the Distinguished Flying Cross (LG 28th March 1944). Appointed temporary group captain on 1st July 1944 and was promoted group captain on 1st July 1947. Appointed to the Air Staff (Navigation), HQ Coastal Command, Northwood, Middlesex on 6th July 1953 and retired on 18th November 1956. Hugh was appointed to the Oxford University coaching team in 1949 until he resigned in 1957 after a disagreement with the President, Roderick Carnegie. He was invited back in 1959 by President Ronnie Howard, but provoked a rebellion and resignation by certain members of the crew, who considered him overly demanding. Notwithstanding the resignations, Oxford beat Cambridge, with his son David in the team. In total Hugh coached Oxford nineteen times between 1949 and 1972. His sons, David and John,

The gold medal winning Great Britain coxless fours team at the 1932 Los Angeles Olympic Games. This was Jumbo Edwards (second from the right) second gold medal on the same day, a feat not equaled until gymnast Max Whitlock, won two golds on the same day in 2016 at Rio de Janeiro (River & Rowing Museum).

The Air Force Cross awarded for acts of valour, courage or devotion to duty whilst not on active flying operations against the enemy. It was established on 3rd June 1918 and originally it was awarded to officers and warrant officers of the RAF. After the Second World War this was expanded to include Royal Navy and Army aviation officers. In 1993 it was expanded to other ranks when the Air Force Medal was discontinued. During the Second World War, 2,001 were awarded, with twenty-six bars and one second bar.

The Distinguished Flying Cross is a third tier gallantry award for acts of valour, courage or devotion to duty whilst on active flying operations against the enemy. In common with the AFC, it was established on 3rd June 1918, originally for officers and warrant officers of the RAF. During the Second World War, Royal Artillery officers serving as air observation posts were added and after the war Royal Navy and Army aviation officers. In 1993 it was expanded to other ranks when the Distinguished Flying Medal was discontinued. During the Second World War, 20,354 DFCs were awarded, more than any other gallantry award. In addition there were 1,550 bars and forty-five second bars. Notable recipients include Flight Lieutenant Michelle Goodman, who in 2008 became the first woman to be awarded the DFC. Another was Group Captain Peter Townsend CVO DSO DFC & Bar, a flying ace, Equerry to George VI 1944–52 and Elizabeth II 1952–53, who had a romance with Princess Margaret.

were members of the Welsh coxless four that won medals at the 1958 (bronze) and 1962 (silver) Commonwealth Games. In the latter year Hugh coached the crew in Perth, Australia. In 1960 he coached the Great Britain crew in the Olympic Games. A coxed four boat belonging to Christ Church Boat Club is named *Jumbo Edwards* in his honour. He wrote a book on rowing technique in 1963, *The Way of a Man with a Blade* and took part in the first Round Britain

and Ireland Yacht Race in 1966. Following retirement, Hugh spent a great deal of time teaching sailing and navigation. He collapsed aboard his yacht off Hamble-le-Rice, Hampshire and died at Southampton Hospital.
  - John Oswald Valentine Edwards (1912–10th April 1942) was educated at Keble College, Oxford (MA). He was commissioned as a university candidate on the General List Territorial Army on 6th July 1931. He transferred to the East Surrey Regiment with seniority from 28th January 1932 and was promoted lieutenant 28th January 1935 and captain 28th January 1940. On 11th July 1938 he was seconded to the Burma Defence Force and was reported missing in action at Paungde on 10th April 1942 (Rangoon Memorial – Face 13).

Jumbo Edwards' book on rowing technique, *The Way of a Man with a Blade*.

- James David Tannatt Pryce (28th June 1874–28th September 1875).
- Jane Esther Pryce (17th April 1884–31st October 1909) married Gerard Hero Omko Geertsema (24th February 1883–21st February 1958) on 9th June 1908 at Christ Church, Lancaster Gate, London. She died at Driebergen, Utrecht, Netherlands.

Thomas' paternal grandfather, David Pryce (8th January 1788–4th September 1846) was born at Llandrinio, Montgomeryshire. He married Ann née Tannatt (31st January 1790–2nd June 1834), born at Rhysnant, Montgomeryshire, on 22nd June 1813 at Llandysilio, Montgomeryshire. They lived at Trederwen Hall, Llansantffraid, Montgomeryshire. She died at Llandrinio and he died at Llandysilio. In addition to Thomas they had seven other children:

- David Tannatt Pryce (3rd November 1815–29th March 1892) married Jane Jones (c.1829–1st March 1887) in 1849 at Montgomery. They both died at Bala, Merionethshire. They had a son, Edward Montgomery Tannatt Pryce (1850–2nd May 1881).
- Edward Pryce (May 1818–9th January 1822).
- John Montgomery Tannatt Pryce (11th September 1819–12th April 1891) was a merchant. He married Augusta Elisabeth du Puy (1st December 1823–29th April 1855) on 3rd January 1850 in Java. She was born at Padang, Sumatra. They had three children – John Edwin Pryce 1850, David Tannatt Montgomery Pryce 1853 and James Tannatt Pryce 1854. Augusta died at Jamestown, St Helena. John

married Margaret Maxwell Maclaine (c.1832–5th February 1861) on 30th January 1858 in Java. She was born at Lochbuie, Argyllshire, daughter of Donald Maclaine, proprietor of the Lochbuie Estate on the Isle of Mull. She died at 117 Princes Street, Edinburgh, Midlothian giving birth to a stillborn daughter. John married Ellen Jane Rankine (13th August 1848–1st May 1872) in 1867 at Steyning, Sussex. She was born at Kilmarnock, Ayrshire. They had three children – a stillborn son 1869, Emelie Elizabeth Pryce 1870 and Ellen Anna Maria Pryce 1872. They were living at Llwyngroes Hall, Llwyntidman, Llanymynech, Montgomeryshire in 1871, by when he was retired. Ellen died there following complications with the birth of her daughter Ellen. John married Eleanor Rogers (c.1829–4th February 1903) on 15th June 1872 at Helsington, Westmoreland. She was born at Oswestry, Shropshire. John died at his home, Belmont, Milverton Terrace, Milverton, Warwickshire. Eleanor died at Leamington Spa, Warwickshire.

- Elijah Pryce (21st March 1821–1st March 1896) married Jane Thompson Edmond Balfour (12th February 1827–30th April 1898) on 3rd November 1858 at St Mary, St Denys and St George (Manchester Cathedral), Manchester, Lancashire. She was born at Stirling, Stirlingshire. He died at Trederwen House, Llansantffraid, Montgomeryshire. Jane also died there, leaving effects valued at £20,148 (£2.5M in 2018).
- Edward David Pryce (29th April 1825–4th December 1902) married Margaret Miles (born c.1822) on 1st November 1844 at Newtown, Montgomeryshire. They emigrated to South Africa, where she died between 1850 and 1852. Edward married Sarah Haysom (c.1832–3rd October 1911) in 1858 in Sydney, New South Wales, Australia. She was born at Swanage, Dorset and arrived in Australia aboard the *Herefordshire* on 27th May 1857. Edward and Sarah had seven children – Sarah Elizabeth Pryce 1858, Alice Jane Pryce 1860, David Charles Pryce 1861, Mary Tannatt Pryce 1866, Ellen Louise Pryce 1867, Edward Samuel Pryce 1869 and John Thomas Pryce 1873. Edward died at Guildford, New South Wales and Sarah died at Granville, New South Wales.
- Samuel Pryce (1826–54) was educated at Upper Brook Street School, Oswestry, Shropshire. He died at sea aboard the *Richard Thornton*.
- Mary Pryce (1829–94) married Guillaume Louis Jacques van der Hucht (20th December 1812–5th March 1874) on 17th August 1848 in Java. He was born at Bergen op Zoom, Noord-Brabant, Netherlands and was a partner in the firm John Pryce & Co. He died at Santpoort, Netherlands. She also died in the Netherlands.

His maternal grandfather, Jacob Gerrit Theodoor van Motman (19th November 1816–20th September 1890) was born at Ni Wanajassa Krawang, Java, son of Gerrit Willem Casimir van Motman (1773–1821), who purchased the family estate, Groot Dramaga, there around 1813, and Reinieara Jacoba Bangemann (1778–1860). Jacob cultivated tea and coffee on his plantation until it was hit by a plague of black flies. Thereafter he planted rubber trees and sugar cane. He married Petronella Rosalie Aldouse née van Swieten (20th November 1815–3rd July 1888) on 21st August 1839.

She was born at Amsterdam, Netherlands. Jacob died in Java and is buried at Ni Bogor Buana Minggu. In addition to Rosalie they had four other children, two of whom did not survive infancy:

Thomas' maternal grandfather, Jacob Gerrit Theodoor van Motman.

- Constantijn Jacob van Motman (10th October 1848–6th July 1923) was physically very strong and was known as 'le tigre de Java' (the tiger of Java) by fellow students at the Polytechnicum in Zürich, Switzerland. He married Constance Louise van Oosterhoudt (28th December 1852–15th October 1920) on 17th December 1872 at Buitenzorg, Java. She was born at Pondok Gedeh, Java. They ran a plantation at Djasinga, Java. She died at Weltevreden, Java and he died at Penang, Malaya. They had twelve children, of whom one died young, including, Aldonse Louise Catherine van Motman 1873, Ferdinand Theodoor van Motman 1874, Constance Helene van Motman 1875, Richard Pieter Constantijn van Motman 1876, Rosalie Adelaide van Motman 1877, Jacob Gerrit Theodoor van Motman 1878, Augusta Maria van Motman 1881, Jenny Claresse van Motman 1885, Henriette Constance Louise van Motman 1887, Petronella Reiniera Pauline van Motman 1888 and Piet Hein van Motman 1890.

Shrewsbury School was founded in 1552 and moved to its present site, a former workhouse, in 1882. It is one of the original seven public schools defined in the Public Schools Act 1868. Old Salopians include naturalist Charles Darwin, the novelist Nevil Shute, the actor and TV presenter Michael Palin and the politician Lord Michael Heseltine. In addition to Thomas Pryce, the school had another Great War VC, Harold Ackroyd VC MC RAMC.

The Royal Agricultural College (University from 2013) was founded in 1842 and the first twenty-five students were admitted in 1845, when Queen Victoria granted a Royal Charter. There has been a royal patron ever since, currently Prince Charles since 1982. Amongst its many notable alumni are:

- Jonathan Dimbleby, television presenter.
- Edward John, 8th Earl Spencer MVO, father of Diana, Princess of Wales.
- Mark Phillips, former husband of the Princess Royal and Great Britain equestrian rider.

Alexander Pigott Wernher's grave in Citadel New Military Cemetery, Fricourt.

The High Street in Ashwell, Hertfordshire, where Thomas' wife, Margaret, was born and where they married.

• Pieter van Motman (1850–1911) ran Dramaga very successfully. He married Pauline Kleyn and they had four sons, one named Alphonse. Of the others one died young, another aged nineteen and the third aged twenty-seven.

Thomas was educated at Mr Deede's Preparatory School in Shrewsbury, Shropshire and Shrewsbury School 1900–04, where he was a member of the OTC. He was at the Royal Agricultural College, Cirencester, Wiltshire for two terms in 1905. In a class of nine he came first in Practical Agriculture and Mensuration, third in Veterinary Medicine & Surgery, fifth in Bookkeeping, Zoology and Mechanics and Physics, eighth in Chemistry and Practical Chemistry, ninth in Architectural Drawing, was highly commended in Farm Journal & College Farm and commended in Hospital Practice, Dentition and Stable Work. He won both the three-mile race

Craufurd Lodge, Maidenhead, where Thomas and Margaret lived from 1912.

(sixteen minutes and fifty-three seconds) and the mile race (five minutes and eleven seconds). He then worked as a clerk for Henry Tudor & Son in London, applied for admission to the London Stock Exchange and was elected a member on 21st April 1913. Thomas was a member of the Ashwell Cricket Club, Hertfordshire and competed in long-distance running and shooting. Despite his war service he applied for re-election to the Stock Exchange for 1915, 1917 and 1918.

Thomas Pryce married Margaret Sybil Fordham (13th December 1886–13th January 1967) at Ashwell, Hertfordshire, where she was born, on 11th March 1908. They moved to Craufurd Lodge, Grynger Hill (later Gringer Hill), Maidenhead, Berkshire in 1912. Second Lieutenant Alexander Pigott Wernher (18th January 1897–10th September 1916), 1st Welsh Guards, who was killed in action at Givenchy (Citadel New Military Cemetery, Fricourt – II A 5), left £50,000 (£4.9M in 2018) to Margaret. His relationship to Margaret is not known. Alexander was the son of Sir Julius Wernher and brother of Major General Sir Harold Wernher, who played a vital role in coordinating logistic resources in preparation for Operation Overlord in 1944, including production of the Mulberry harbours. Thomas and Margaret had three daughters:

- Rosalie Doreen Margaret Pryce (27th May 1910–6th May 1949), born at Paddington, London, married Douglas Osborne May (3rd May 1904–July 1993) on 10th September 1941 in New York, USA. Douglas had married Rhona Alice Karklinnis (1906–19th April 1941), at All Souls, Langham Place, Marylebone, London in 1935. She was born at Croydon, Surrey and was manageress of Elizabeth Arden, Bond Street, London. Douglas was commissioned in the Royal Engineers on 5th February 1940 (118732) and served at Dunkirk and in Cairo, Egypt. He was promoted war substantive captain on 4th March 1943 and was demobilised in 1945 as a lieutenant colonel. Douglas and Rhona were living at Pinehill, Aspenden, Buntingford, Hertfordshire in 1941. She was visiting her mother-in-law, Ethel May, at Elm Lawn, Woodhall Avenue, Pinner, Middlesex on 19th April 1941 when a German bomb hit the house, killing them both. Douglas and Rosalie lived at New House, Bolney, Sussex and they had a son:
    - Michael Osborne Pryce May FRSA (born 1942) was Chairman of Kilby & Gayford (Building) Ltd for twenty years. The company was founded by his great grandfather in 1860. He was Master of The Worshipful Company of Constructors and later The Worshipful Company of Carpenters. He married Sarah Jane Attridge (born 1944) on 4th May 1967 at Cuckfield, where she was born. The marriage ended in divorce. He married Zanta Maria Dexter née French (born 1944) on 1st May 1984 at Haywards Heath, Sussex. She was born in the New Forest, Hampshire. She had married John Richard Lambert Dexter in 1965 at Christchurch, Hampshire and had two daughters – Sophie Jane Dexter 1967 and Rachel Maria Dexter 1970.

Lady Myra Idina Sackville.

- Violet Rita May Pryce (26th February 1912–October 1986), born at Maidenhead, Berkshire, married Vincent William Soltau (22nd April 1903–1st August 1964) and they had two children – Thomas Soltau and Ann Soltau. Vincent was born at Heathfield, Crown Hill, Plymouth, Devon. He was commissioned as a RAF pilot officer (18185) on probation on 14th January 1924 and was known as Lynx because he had *the eyes of a lynx when flying*. He was promoted flying officer on 14th September 1925 and transferred to the Reserve on 14th January 1929. The marriage ended in divorce. Lynx married Lady Myra Idina Sackville (1893–1955) in 1939, her fifth husband. They divorced in 1946 without issue. Lynx was recalled to the RAF as a flight lieutenant on 3rd September 1939. He was promoted squadron leader on 3rd September 1942 and wing commander on 1st July 1944. Idina was a member of the notorious Happy Valley set in Kenya, whose exploits were the subject of the film *White Mischief*. Lynx married Grace (born 1926) in 1946, probably in Kenya. He died at 68 Kensington High Street, London. Violet married Geoffrey Ashlin Wood (29th November 1908–15th February 1942) on 7th February 1940 at Penang, Malaya and they had a daughter, Shirley Wood, on 11th December 1940. He was working for Shell Oil Co and was stationed at Penang, Malaya when the Japanese invaded on 8th December 1941. Violet and her daughter were evacuated on one of the last boats for Australia before returning to Britain in 1944. Geoffrey served as 13946 Company Quartermaster Sergeant GA Wood, 2nd (Selangor) Battalion, Federated Malay States Volunteer Force and died on 15th February 1942 (Singapore Memorial – Column 390). Violet married Douglas Osborne May, her brother-in-law, in 1949 at Westminster, London. They had two children:
    - George Osborne May (born 1950) married Amanda Dunlop and they had four children.
    - Patricia Ethel Julia May (born 1952) married Anthony S Minns (born 1947) in 1980 at London City. They had two children – Nicholas Minns and Elizabeth Minns.
- Pauline Leonora Evelyn Pryce (8th August 1915–26th December 1984) married Denis Erskine Hughes (29th July 1908–8th November 1975), a chartered accountant, in 1936. They were living at Twiggs, 40 College Road, Maidenhead at the time of his death. They had two children:
    - Valerie Hughes (1939–c.2005).
    - Elizabeth Hughes (born 1943) married Anthony Stevens in 1964 and they had two children – Christopher Stevens 1966 and Emma Stevens.

An advertisement for Forham's Ashwell Brewery.

Margaret's father, Edward Snow Fordham MA LLM (15th January 1858–28th January 1919), born at Ashwell, Hertfordshire, was a barrister (Inner Temple 1883). He practiced on the Midland Circuit and was also a Metropolitan Police Magistrate in North London 1898–1910, West London 1910, was Chairman of the Quarter Sessions for Cambridgeshire 1901–1912 and retired in 1917. He also owned Ashwell Brewery and about a hundred public houses. His brother, Wolverley Attwood Fordham (9th September 1859–24th February 1921), was the husband of Phyllis Gribble (1882–24th February 1958), sister of Julian Royds Gribble VC. Edward married Annie née CarrJackson (c.1855–16th February 1931), born at St Pancras, London, in 1880 at Wandsworth, London. He was appointed JP and DL Hertfordshire, Cambridgeshire and Bedfordshire and JP Kent, Surrey, London, Middlesex and Essex. They were living at Elbrook House, Ashwell, Hertfordshire in 1911. He died there leaving effects valued at £40,159/13/8 (£2.2M in 2018). She died there, leaving effects valued at £6,446/3/7. In addition to Margaret they had four other children:

- Edward King Fordham (1881–27th July 1922) was living at Elbrook House, Ashwell, Hertfordshire at the time of his death at Stewards Court, Weymouth, Dorset.
- Mabel Evelyn Fordham (1883–29th August 1945) married Arthur Frederick Grundy (1874–27th June 1949) in 1907 at Royston. He was an assistant manager at a brewery bottling store in 1911 and they were living at 2 Kensington Court Gardens, London. They were living at 3 West Terrace, Folkestone, Kent at the time of her death at Royal Victoria Hospital, Folkestone. He was living at 53 Kneesworth Road, Royston at the time of his death at St George's Hospital, Royston. They had two children – Clive Arthur Fordham Grundy 1908 and Richard Fordham Grundy 1910.
- Oswald Fordham (1889–29th November 1962) was living at 16 Cadogan Square, Chelsea, London at the time of his death at The Aldwych Theatre, London.
- Hugh Alexander Fordham (4th March 1894–11th November 1986) was at university in 1911 and at the Royal Military College in 1914. He was commissioned in the Northumberland Fusiliers on 11th November 1914. He was promoted temporary captain 12th June 1915, temporary lieutenant 25th July and lieutenant 20th August. He qualified for the Royal Aero Club Aviator's Certificate (No.2744) flying a Maurice Farman biplane at the Military School, Brooklands, Surrey on 7th April 1916. He transferred to the Royal Flying Corps and was appointed

Thomas Pryce's name on the Ploegsteert Memorial.

flying officer on 22nd June and temporary captain and flight commander with the Military Wing on 14th June 1917. On 7th August he was appointed GSO3 and was appointed acting major on 1st November 1918. Promoted captain 30th July 1919 and resigned his commission the same day, retaining the rank of major. He was residing at Sandhurst Hotel, Grand Parade, Eastbourne, Sussex at the time of his death there.

Thomas enlisted in No.2 Company, Honourable Artillery Company on 25th August 1914 (1559) and went to France on 29th December. He was promoted acting lance corporal on 7th May 1915 and corporal on 1st August 1915. He was commissioned in 1/6th Gloucestershire on 3rd October 1915. **Awarded the MC for his actions on the night of 25th/26th November 1915, when C Company mounted a raid near the southeast corner of Gommecourt Wood. Thomas commanded the right assault party. The barrage fell at 1.03 a.m. The right party found only low wire and got into the German trenches without alerting the enemy. A number of shelters were bombed and a block was formed. In the withdrawal Thomas was wounded by a German officer but he killed him with his revolver (LG 23rd December 1915).**

Thomas was evacuated to Britain and returned to France in May 1916 with 2/6th Gloucestershire. He was promoted temporary lieutenant on 21st June 1916. **Awarded a Bar to the MC for his actions at Ovillers on 19th July 1916, when he commanded the leading platoon in an assault with great dash and determination right up to the enemy's trenches, under very heavy fire of all kinds (LG 9th September 1916).** He was promoted lieutenant on 9th September and transferred to 4th Grenadier Guards on 13th September, reverting to second lieutenant with seniority from 23rd December 1915. He returned to Britain in September 1916 and was promoted lieutenant on 14th September. He returned to France in February 1917 and was appointed acting captain on 10th April 1918 while

The War Memorial, Four Crosses, Llandysilio (Memorials to Valour).

The dedication of the Shrewsbury School War Memorial.

The memorial that Margaret erected to her husband in the Church of St Tysilio, Llandysilio (Memorials to Valour).

commanding a company. **Mentioned in Field Marshal Sir Douglas Haig's Despatch dated 7th April 1918, LG 23rd May 1918. Awarded the VC for his actions at Vieux Berquin, France on 11th-13th April 1918, LG 21st May 1918.** He was killed during the VC action on 13th April 1918 and is commemorated on the Ploegsteert Memorial, Hainaut, Belgium (Panel 1). Thomas was listed as missing until 28996 Private WH Warburton, 4th Grenadier Guards, confirmed his death by letter from a POW Camp at Soltau in Germany on 5th September 1918. This was also confirmed by Private SR Rowbotham. Thomas left effects valued at £19,281/6/10 (£1.27M in 2018). The VC was presented to his widow by the King in the ballroom at Buckingham Palace on 12th April 1919. He is commemorated in a number of other places:

- War Memorial, Four Crosses, Llandysilio, Montgomeryshire.
- War Memorial, St Ives Road, Maidenhead, Berkshire.
- Plaque in the Church of St Tysilio, Llandysilio and also on the Roll of Honour.
- Shrewsbury School War Memorial.
- Plaque in St Giles Church, Shrewsbury.
- Stock Exchange War Memorial in the City of London. The original deteriorated and was replaced with a bronze panel on the exterior of the Stock Exchange offices at Paternoster Square.
- The Household Division (Foot Guards) Honour Roll for the Victoria Cross in the Sergeants' Mess, Wellington Barracks, London.
- The Royal Borough of Windsor & Maidenhead created a Remembrance Garden in Kidwells Park, Maidenhead, which included a display board giving information about the part played by the town during the First World War and brief details of the seven VC recipients connected with Maidenhead, including Thomas Pryce. It was dedicated on 25th August 2015 by the Mayor of Windsor and Maidenhead, Councillor Eileen Quick. In attendance was Michael May, grandson of Thomas Pryce, plus other members of the Pryce family.

- The Royal Borough of Windsor & Maidenhead VC Memorial Garden, Bachelor's Acre, Windsor was opened by the Deputy Mayor, Councillor John Lenton, on 25th November 2016. The seven VCs connected to the Royal Borough are named on two panels – Harry Greenwood, Charles Doughty-Wylie, William Forshaw, Francis Grenfell, Thomas Pryce, Oliver Brooks and Ferdinand West.
- Department for Communities and Local Government commemorative paving stones dedicated to the 145 VC recipients of the First World War who were born overseas (Australia, Belgium, Canada, China, Denmark, Egypt, France, Germany, India, Iraq, Japan, Nepal, Netherlands, New Zealand, Pakistan, South Africa, Sri Lanka, Ukraine and United States of America), were unveiled at the National Memorial Arboretum, Alrewas, Staffordshire by Prime Minister David Cameron MP and Sergeant Johnson Beharry VC on 5th March 2015.
- A Department for Communities and Local Government commemorative paving stone was dedicated at Kidwells Park, The Royal Borough of Windsor & Maidenhead on 13th April 2018 to mark the centenary of his award. It was unveiled by Prime Minister Theresa May, MP for Maidenhead. Many members of Thomas' family were present, including Michael May, who made a speech.

Margaret married Leonard Saxton Waterall (20th October 1884–25th February 1951) on 7th November 1921 at St Augustine's Church, Tanga, Tanganyika Territory. He was born at Islington, London and was educated at St Paul's School and Cambridge University before being employed as a Native Commissioner in the Northern Rhodesia Civil Service from February 1908. He served as an officer in the Congo-Belge Volunteers August-November 1914 and was living at 40 Holland Road, Kensington when he applied for a commission on 24th December 1914. He was commissioned on 14th January 1915 in 13th Rifle Brigade and went to France on 29th July. Leonard was very seriously wounded by two gunshots to the right lung at Contalmaison, France on 10th July 1916. He was evacuated from Boulogne to Dover to the Hall-Walker Hospital for Officers, Regent's Park, London on 16th July and transferred to the held strength of 5th Reserve Battalion. Medical boards at Caxton Hall, London on 26th July, 27th September, 27th October and 17th November found him unfit for General Service for periods of four months down to two months, Home Service for periods of three months down to one month and light duties for two months until he was fit for office work on the last date. Medical boards at Northampton on 2nd January and 9th April 1917 found him unfit for General Service for two months and fit for Home Service. He was considered fit for General Service in a warm climate. Leonard transferred to 1st Reserve Garrison Battalion, Suffolk Regiment and then to 19th Training Reserve Battalion, Eastern Command. He was ordered to Egypt, departing Southampton on SS *Princess Clementine* on 18th April 1917, having been appointed Assistant Political Officer, Maliniji District, Civil Administration, Occupied Territory, German East Africa on 24th March. He did not relinquish his commission until 1st February 1921. Margaret and Leonard

HM Submarine *Triumph* (N18), a T-Class, launched by Vickers at Barrow-in Furness in September 1938. Her bow was damaged by a mine on 26th December 1939 and she underwent repairs at Chatham until 27th September 1940. From early 1941 *Triumph* operated in the Mediterranean, where she sank a number of merchant vessels, tankers and patrol craft. She also damaged the Italian armed merchant cruiser *Ramb III* and in June 1941 sank the Italian submarine *Salpa*. *Triumph* was also used for covert operations and, in December 1941, she landed agents in Greece. However, she did not return for the arranged pick up rendezvous on 9th January 1942 and no trace of her has been found since. All fifty-nine crewmen were lost, including George Waterall.

continued living at Craufurd Lodge. He died at The Hospital, Maidenhead. She died at her home at Craufurd Lodge, leaving effects valued at £118,828 (£2.1M in 2018). Leonard and Margaret had a son:

- George Desmond Waterall (1923–January 1942), born at Wandsworth, London, joined Dartmouth Naval College and was appointed midshipman on 1st May 1941. He was appointed to HM Submarine *Triumph*. She was lost with all hands in early January 1942 and his date of death is registered as 20th January 1942 (Portsmouth Naval Memorial – Panel 62, Column 1).

In addition to the VC and MC & Bar he was awarded the 1914–15 Star, British War Medal 1914–20 and Victory Medal 1914–19 with Mentioned-in-Despatches Oakleaf. The VC is held on loan by HQ Grenadier Guards, Guards Museum, Wellington Barracks, Birdcage Walk, London.

1946 SERGEANT WILLIAM RUTHVEN
22nd Australian Infantry Battalion AIF

William Ruthven was born on 21st May 1893 at Collingwood, Melbourne, Victoria, Australia. He was known as Rusty. His father, Peter Ruthven (1860–1930), a carpenter born at Collingwood, married Catherine Charlotte 'Shawl' née Bedwell (1859–18th July 1940) in 1883. She was born at Moorabool, Victoria and lived at 48 Francis Street, Collingwood. She died at Northcote, Victoria. William had six siblings:

Johnstone Street, Collingwood.

The Charles Brownlow Trophy, known as the Brownlow Medal or just 'Charlie' is awarded annually to the 'best and fairest' player in the Australian Football League. The award is decided by votes cast by the field umpires and is the most prestigious award for individual players. The Brownlow Medal was first awarded by the Victorian Football League (VFL) to honour Charles Brownlow, who played for Geelong 1880–91, was club secretary 1885–1923 and VFL President 1918–19.

- James John Ruthven (1884–1954) married Amy Marion Blair (1884–1965) in 1905. She was born at Fitzroy, Victoria. They had six children including:
    - Irene Florence Ruthven (born 1906) married William Joseph Foote in 1933.
    - George Albert Ruthven (1908–21st July 1989) was living at 129 Hawke Street, Melbourne West in 1924. He married Elsie Jane Pretoria Bromley (21st June 1900–25th October 1994) in 1928. She was born at Harrietville, Victoria. They both died in Melbourne. They had three children – Allan Gordon Ruthven 1922, George Bromley Ruthven 1930 and Peter Kenneth Ruthven 1937. Allan Gordon Ruthven (17th April 1922–14th March 2003) was known as The Baron, either because of his dapper dress or after Australian Governor General, Baron Hore-Ruthven. Allan played Australian Rules Football for Fitzroy Lions in Melbourne 1940–54 and was the Brownlow Medal winner for 1950. He played in 222 games and was the captain in 1948 and 1950–54 and the captain coach 1952–54. He also played seventeen games for the Victorian representative team, scoring forty-seven goals. He was a member of the premiership team of 1944 when Fitzroy defeated Richmond by fifteen points at Junction Oval, Melbourne. After his playing career he was a regular panellist on Channel 7's World of Sport. Allan married Shirley Ida Holland (1925–3rd Augsut 2006) in 1947.

  - Herbert William Ruthven (1914–79) married Phyllis Edna Sanders (1916–62) in 1937. She was born at Carlton, Victoria. They had a son, Barry Ruthven, who was born and died in 1940.
  - Reginald James Ruthven (1917–18).
- George Ruthven (1886–1957) married Minnie Elizabeth Gilder (1899–1981) in 1936 in Victoria, She was born at Collingwood and was a tailoress in 1921, living with her parents at 8 Bower Street, Northcote, Victoria. George was a brewery worker in 1937 and they were living at 6 Albert Street, Batman, Victoria. George died at Fairfield, Victoria. Minnie was still living at 6 Albert Street in 1980.
- Jessie Ruthven (1888–1962) married Louis Bloom (possibly Louisa Paul Bloom born c.1884–88 and died 1962) in 1916. She died at Box Hill, Victoria.
- Charles Henry Ruthven (1890–1902) died at Carlton Hospital, Melbourne.
- Unnamed female born and died in 1892. Her death was recorded as an unnamed male.
- May Ruthven (1895–1966) married Joseph Henry Williams (1887–1970) in 1920. She died at Montrose, Victoria. They had a son, Joseph Henry Williams (1922–79).

William's paternal grandfather, John Ruthven (1830–19th May 1900), born in Midlothian, Scotland, was living with his parents, Peter Ruthven and Margaret Johnston, at Lasswade Village, Midlothian in 1841. He married Janet née Carnegie (1830–30th August 1902) on 27th July 1852 at St Cuthbert's, Edinburgh, Midlothian. She was born at Leith, Midlothian, daughter of William Carnegie and Janet Aitken, who were living at 2 Almada Street, Hamilton, Lanarkshire in 1851. John and Janet emigrated to Australia and settled in Melbourne, Victoria. He died at Heidelberg, Melbourne and she died at Clifton Hill, Victoria. In addition to Peter they had six other children:

- Janet Aitken Ruthven (1854–79) married Charles Minn (2nd June 1841–5th September 1933) in 1879. He was born at Mecklenburg, Germany. Charles had married Emma Bowman (1854–27th November 1876) on 19th October 1874 at Collingwood, Victoria. She was born at Strand, London and died at Adelaide, South Australia. Charles and Emma had a son, Charles William Minn (1876–76). Charles married Rosetta Jane Dalgleish (16th March 1860–3rd August 1941) in 1880. She was born at Newtown, Geelong, Victoria. Charles died at Castlemaine and she died at Preston, Darebin, Victoria.
- Margaret Johnstone Ruthven (1857–1902) married Charles Henry Tattersall (1855–23rd June 1903) in 1879. Margaret had a daughter, Margaret Ethel Tattersall (1877–1957), who married John O'Shannessy (1876–1930) in 1903. John was born in North Melbourne and died after accidentally falling from his horse. They had four children – John Patrick O'Shannessy 1903, Walter David O'Shannessy 1904, Margaret Veronica O'Shannessy 1906 and Joseph Edward O'Shannessy 1909.

William's grandfather, James Bedwell, was born in the cathedral city of Canterbury in Kent c.1828. This is the Butter Market area.

William's grandmother, Ann 'Hannah' Stephenson was born in Newcastle upon Tyne but married James Bedwell in Canterbury. This is Northumberland Street about the time of the Great War.

- William Ruthven born and died 1866.
- Annie Carnegie Ruthven (1867–1952) married Harry Nash (1863–19th April 1931) in 1888. He was born at Wycombe, Buckinghamshire, England. He died at Hotham and she died at Fairfield, both in Victoria. They had four children:
    - Edward John Nash (1889–1964).
    - Herbert Harry Nash (1902–1966) married Ethel Zerepha Smith (died 1970) in 1926.
    - Jessie Edith Nash (1905–1906).
    - Lily Nash (born and died 1907).
- Jane Spencer Ruthven (1869–1955) married George Edward Treverton (1862–20th November 1913), a medical commission agent born at Smythesdale, Victoria, in 1894. He died at Watchupga, near Woomelang, Victoria and she died at Moonee Ponds. They had a daughter, Myrtle Treverton (1895–1896).
- John Ruthven (1871–1938) died at Heidelberg.

William's maternal grandparents were living at North Lane, Westgate Without, Canterbury in 1851.

His maternal grandfather, James Bedwell (c.1827–21st April 1894), was born at Canterbury, Kent. He married Ann 'Hannah' née Stephenson (1834–24th October 1895) there in 1850. She was born at Newcastle upon Tyne, Northumberland. He was a bricklayer's labourer and they were living at North Lane, Westgate Without, Canterbury, Kent in 1851. They emigrated to Australia, arriving on 23rd July 1854, and settled in Victoria. He died at Collingwood, Victoria and she died at Newport, Melbourne. In addition to Catherine they had seven other children:

- Eliza Bedwell (16th November 1850–1913) born at Bridge, Kent. She married Thomas Lowe (c.1842–1919) in 1873 in Victoria. He was born in Guernsey, Channel Islands. She died at Carlton, Victoria and he died at Northcote, Victoria. They had seven children:
  - Caroline Charlotte 'Carrie' Lowe (1874–1948) married Charles Seaberg in 1900 at Fremantle, Western Australia. They had a daughter, Irene Seaberg.
  - Susan Ann Lowe (1876–1934) married John George McKay (1876–1944) in 1901. They had two children – George Bruce McKay 1903 and Cath Myrtle Jean McKay 1910.
  - Alice May Lowe (1878–1948) married Walter James Spurr (1874–1955) on 18th October 1899. He was born at Maryborough and died at Northcote. They had four children – Alice May Spurr 1901, Doris Rose Spurr 1903, Thelma Irene Spurr 1906 and Walter James Spurr 1917.
  - George Thomas Lowe (1881–1959), born at Northcote and died at Thornbury, married Mary Esther Evelyn Field (1884–1967) in 1907. They had two children – Esther Dorothy Lowe 1908 and Allen George Frederick Lowe 1911.
  - Eliza Elsie Lowe (1884–1928), born at Northcote and died at Prahran, married John Francis Wilkinson (1884–1954) in 1904. They had two children – John 'Jack' Thomas Wilkinson 1905 and George Walter Wilkinson 1908.
  - Lillian Louisa Lowe (1887–1963), born at Northcote and died at Heidelberg, married Martin Schon (died 1911), born in Germany, in 1909. She married James Francis MacKay (1887–1960) in 1913. They had four children – Agnes Steele MacKay 1913, Jean, Marjorie and Jack.
  - Irene Rose Lowe (1891–1972), born at Northcote and died at Parkville, married Christian Schon in 1913. They had two daughters – Irene Merle Schon 1915 and Edna. Irene married William Bradford Torrens (1893–1950) in 1920. They had three sons – William, Robert and John.
- Hannah Alice Bedwell (10th April 1853–8th August 1949) married John Bedford (8th March 1852–24th March 1883) on 21st June 1873 at Emerald Hill, Victoria. He was born at Northchurch, Hertfordshire. Hannah died at Burnley and John at Eldorado. They had six children:
  - Elizabeth Anne Bedford (1874–1949) born in Melbourne and died at Euroa.
  - John James Bedford (1875–1884) born at Collingwood and died at Northcote.
  - Louisa Grace Bedford (1876–1956) married Charles Rees Turner (died 1948) in 1898. She died at Parkville.
  - Sarah Ann Bedford (1878–1973), born at Eldorado, married Edmund Kerr McComb (1874–1957) in 1901. They had seven children – William Edmund

McComb 1903, Myra McComb 1905, unnamed male and unnamed female 1907, Harold Bedford McComb 1911, Bruce Richardson McComb 1913 and Ernest Nevin McComb 1917. She died at Frankston.
  - William Henry Bedford (1880–1957) was born at Eldorado and died in Melbourne.
  - Alice May Bedford (1882–1884), born at Wangaratta and died at Collingwood.

Hannah married John Brown (1847–2nd March 1935) in 1888. He was born at Wisbech, Cambridgeshire. Hannah died at Burnley, Victoria. They had three children – Frederick Brown 1889, Edith May Brown 1891 and Ruby Myrtle Brown 1895.

- Matilda Maria Bedwell (26th June 1855–15th February 1897), born at Kildare, married Angus McConnell (1853–1905) in 1877. He was born in Glasgow, Lanarkshire, Scotland. She died at Brunswick and he at Heidelberg, both in Victoria. They had eight children:
  - Unnamed born and died 1878 at Collingwood.
  - Ann Marion McConnell (1879–1967) married Robert Roderick Mitchell (1880–1959) in 1906. She died at Heidelberg. They had three children – Donald Edward Angus Mitchell 1911, Elsie Janet Mitchell 1907 and Robert Keith Mitchell 1913.
  - George Edward McConnell (1881–1921).
  - Elsie May McConnell (1884–1964), born at Collingwood, married Walter Henry Isaac Parsons (died 1959) in 1910. They had a son, Walter Angus McConnell, in 1911. Elsie died at Parkville.
  - David Charles McConnell (born and died 1887).
  - William Angus McConnell (1888–1968).
  - David James McConnell (1891–92), born and died at Brunswick.
  - Stella McConnell, born and died 1894. He died at Carlton Children's Hospital.
- George Bedwell (31st October 1861–1923), born at Lethbridge, married Isabella Christina Thomson (1867–1944) in 1891. He died at Heidelberg and she at Prahran. They had three children:
  - George Leslie Bedwell (1892–1954), born at Richmond, married Florence Elinor Newton Watson in 1920. They had a daughter, Nancy Florence Bedwell.
  - Lindus Bedwell (1892–1976), born at North Carlton and died at Bundoora.
  - Simon Bedwell (1895–1981), born at North Fitzroy and died at Fitzroy.
- Elizabeth Bedwell (1865–1942), born at Lethbridge, married William Cadzow (7th September 1859–6th January 1943) on 2nd April 1885 at St Philip's Church, Collingwood. She died at Malvern and he at Williamstown, both in Victoria. They had three children:
  - William James Cadzow (1895–1953).

Vere Street National School (No.2462) was established in 1882. Cromwell Street State School joined it in 1912 and in 1915 Collingwood Domestic Arts School was established. In 1975 it became Collingwood Education Centre and was renamed Collingwood College in 1990 (Public Records Office of Victoria).

The Australian Voluntary Hospital was staffed by Australian expatriates in Britain and served on the Western Front 1914–16. In August 1914, Lady Rachel Dudley, wife of the former Governor-General of Australia, Lord Dudley, created a hospital using Australian doctors and nurses in the United Kingdom. Lady Dudley discussed the idea with the King, Lord Kitchener and Sir Arthur Sloggett, Director General of the British Army's Medical Services. The hospital was formally offered to the British government by the Australian High Commissioner on 15th August 1914. It was commanded by Lieutenant Colonel William L'Estrange Eames, Australian Army Medical Corps, who had served in South Africa in the Second Boer War and happened to be holidaying in England at the time. Unable to join the AIF because enlistments outside Australia were not being accepted, he was commissioned in the RAMC instead. Ida Greaves from the Royal Newcastle Hospital became the matron. The staff grew to 120, including thirty-six nurses. It assembled in the grounds of the Ranelagh Club and departed for France on 29th August 1914. It arrived at Le Havre but moved to St Nazaire on the French west coast on 2nd September. The one hundred-bed hospital moved to Wimereux on 26th October and the capacity increased to two hundred beds. Until April 1916 the Hospital was the only Australian presence on the Western Front. The Australian Voluntary Hospital site in Wimereux was taken over by No.3 Australian General Hospital in June 1916 and its personnel were absorbed into the British 32nd Stationary Hospital, with Eames remaining in command. By the time it closed on 1st May 1919, the Hospital had treated 73,868 patients (Australian War Memorial).

    - Doris Elizabeth Cadzow (1900–82) married Stanley Atkinson Twist (1898–1960) in 1923.
    - Allen Cadzow born and died 1906.
- John James Bedwell (21st October 1868–1929), born at Lethbridge, married Marion Alice Ryan (born 1867) in 1898. They both died at Fitzroy. They had two sons – John Frederick Bedwell 1905 and Francis Vermont Bedwell 1908.
- Isaac Bedwell (21st May 1871–4th March 1904) died at Bulong, Kalgoorlie-Boulder, Western Australia.

William was educated at Vere Street State School, Collingwood, Victoria. He worked as a mechanical engineer and a clerk in the timber industry. On 19th April 1915 he enlisted in the Australian Imperial Force in Melbourne and was posted as a reinforcement to 22nd Battalion (1946). He was described as

Camp Heliopolis, Cairo.

5′ 6″ tall, weighing 146 lbs, with fresh complexion, brown eyes, dark brown hair and his religious denomination was Methodist (later Church of England). He embarked at Melbourne for the Middle East with B Company aboard HMAT A38 *Ulysses* on 10th May, disembarked at Alexandria, Egypt and moved to Camp Heliopolis. He served at Gallipoli from 25th October and was evacuated to Camp Tel-el-Kebir, Egypt from Mudros on 27th December. William embarked at Alexandria for Marseille, France on 18th March 1916 and was involved in operations from 7th April. He was wounded by a gunshot to the left leg at Fleurbaix on 17th April 1916 and was admitted to 8th Stationary Hospital on 20th April, before being transferred to the Australian Voluntary Hospital, Wimereux on 25th April.

William was promoted lance corporal on 12th August, temporary corporal two days later, corporal on 2nd October, temporary sergeant 13th December and sergeant 26th January 1917. On 2nd March he joined 6th Training Battalion at Larkhill on Salisbury Plain. He attended No.36 Physical and Bayonet Training Course at Aldershot, Hampshire 6th August–1st September and was posted to Longbridge Deverill, Wiltshire prior to embarking at Southampton for France on 18th November. He rejoined his unit on 22nd November. On 11th June 1918 he was wounded but remained on duty.

Awarded the VC for his actions at Ville-sur-Ancre on 18th May 1918, LG 11th July 1918. William was wounded at Méricourt on 11th June but remained on duty. He was commissioned on 1st July and transferred to AIF Headquarters in London on 2nd August. The VC was presented by the King at Buckingham Palace on 16th August. On 24th August he embarked on HMAT D21 *Medic* to return to Australia on leave and to support recruiting. On board were fellow VCs John Carroll, John James Dwyer, Reginald Inwood, Joergen Jensen, Thomas Kenny, Leonard Keysor, Stanley McDougall, Walter Peeler and John Whittle. William was

The YMCA at Longbridge Deverill Camp.

The ten Australian VCs aboard HMAT D21 *Medic* on their way home. William Ruthven is sitting behind the ship's officers on the right.

A soldier settler in the Werrimull area. It was opened up to farming in the 1920s, with the railway reaching it in 1923. Most of the Soldier Settlements were of one square-mile, which was found to be too small and many men were unable to make a living from them.

William's wife, Irene May White, was born at South Yarra, Victoria.

St Philip's Anglican Church, Collingwood started as a church-run school in 1855. The parish was declared in 1863, prior to that being part of St Mark's, Fitzroy, and the church was consecrated in 1867.

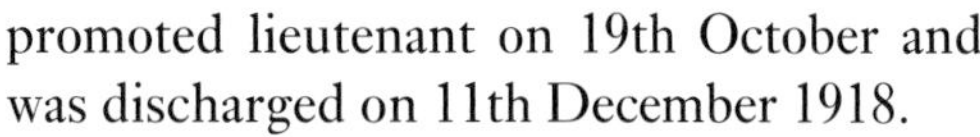

promoted lieutenant on 19th October and was discharged on 11th December 1918.

William worked as a wood machinist in Melbourne but left in 1923 and took over an 800–acre property at Werrimull in the Victorian Mallee, as a soldier settler. A number of bad seasons and poor health forced him to return to Collingwood in 1931. He worked as a master carrier and later with the State Rivers and Water Supply Commission. In 1931 he was elected Councillor on Collingwood Council and become Mayor in 1945. On 10th November 1945 he was elected to the Victorian Legislative Assembly as the Labor Member for Preston, Victoria. He held the Reservoir seat from 28th May 1955 until retirement on 15th July 1961. William was President of the Werrimull and Collingwood Returned Sailors' and Soldiers' Imperial League of Australia sub-branches, a life member of the Preston sub-branch and a trustee of Melbourne's Shrine of Remembrance and St Kilda Memorial Hall.

William Ruthven married Irene May White (20th March 1896–6th June 1983), born at South Yarra, Victoria, on 20th December 1919 at St Philip's Anglican Church, Abbotsford, Victoria. They lived at 22 The Esplanade, Clifton Hill, Victoria. By 1961 they had moved to 104 Regent Street, Preston, and by 1969 to Namur Street, East Kew, Melbourne. Irene died at Brunswick, Victoria and her ashes were interred with those of her husband. William and Irene had a daughter and a son:

- Ailsa Irene Ruthven (9th September 1921–1st September 2012), born in Melbourne, Victoria, married Victor Albert Woolcock (27th February 1920–20th March 2014) in 1948. He was born at Northcote, Victoria. He enlisted in the Australian Army on 28th August 1942 at Mount Martha, Victoria (VX112286). He was discharged as a captain from 151 General Transport Company on 11th December 1946, listing his next of kin as Frederick Woolcock. Victor was a public servant with the Tax Office. They lived at 32 Knott Street, Balwyn, Victoria and later at 10 Thompsons Road, Balwyn. Victor was awarded the OAM for service to the welfare of ex-service personnel (Australia Gazette 26th January 1980). They are understood to have had two daughters – Ethel Mary Woolcock (died 1986) and Cheryl Susanne Woolcock.
- Noel William Ruthven (born 22nd November 1926) was born at Clifton Hill, Victoria. He served as an ordinary seaman class II in the Royal Australian Navy (PM7896) 9th January 1945–24th October 1946), having enlisted at Port Melbourne, Victoria. He was discharged from HMAS *Cerberus*. Noel was later Health Inspector of Preston City Council, Victoria.

Irene's father, Frederick William Thomas White (1871–11th January 1960), married Caroline Jessie Wicks (1866–1935) in 1893. In addition to Irene they had another daughter, Beryl Louisa White (18th October 1904–21st April 1987), born at Clifton Hill. She married Eric Francis Cock (1st July 1902–24th May 1965), also born at Clifton Hill, on 11th February 1928. Eric enlisted in the Australian Citizen Military Force on 13th July 1942 at Westgarth, Northcote, Victoria (V335976). He was serving with 2nd Battalion, Volunteer Defence Corps at the time of his discharge as a private on 9th October 1945. They had three children, including Desma Louise Cock (born and died 1930).

William attended the Anzac Commemoration Service on 25th April 1927 at the Exhibition Building, Melbourne, Victoria in the presence of the Duke of York (future King George VI) and took part in the march past. The other VCs who attended were: TL Axford, A Borella, WE Brown, J Carroll, G Cartwright, WM Currey, H Dalziel, BS Gordon, RC Grieve, JP Hamilton, GJ Howell, GM Ingram, JWA Jackson, WD Joynt, TJB Kenny, AD Lowerson, SR McDougall, RV Moon, JE Newland, W Peeler, W Ruthven, I Smith, PC Statton, AP Sullivan, ET Towner and J Woods. Two nights before an Anzac Dinner was hosted by Lieutenant General Sir John Monash GCMG KCB VD and was attended by twenty-three VCs – Axford, Borella, Brown,

Victoria Barracks on St Kilda Road in Melbourne, built in the 19th century for British garrison troops, housed the Department of Defence for the Commonwealth of Australia (Federation) from 1901 until 1958, when it moved to Canberra. During the Second World War the Barracks housed the Australian War Cabinet. It was also the HQ of General Sir Thomas Blamey as C-in-C Australian Military Forces and C-in-C Allied Land Forces in the South-West Pacific Area, under US General Douglas MacArthur. Victoria Barracks now accommodates a variety of defence organisations.

A prisoner of war camp in the Murchison area of Victoria (Australian War Museum).

William while serving during the Second World War.

Cartwright, Currey, Dalziel, Dwyer, Hamilton, Howell, Ingram, Joynt, Bede Kenny, Lowerson, McCarthy, McDougall, Moon, Peeler, Ruthven, Statton, Sullivan, Towner, Whittle and Woods. For an unknown reason the Duke of York was not invited. William was one of the pallbearer's at the funeral of Albert Jacka VC MC at St Kilda Cemetery, Melbourne, Victoria on 19th January 1932.

In 1938 he was in Russell Street, Melbourne, when he heard two boys calling for help from a lift that had broken down. He immediately grabbed the rope, which was travelling so fast that it burned his hands, and managed to arrest it. He was the official timekeeper for Collingwood Football Club 1939–46, although he had to be substituted 1942–45 while he was on war service. He was also a foundation member of its social club.

William was commissioned as a lieutenant in the Australian Military Forces at St Kilda Barracks, Melbourne on 11th December 1941 and was posted to 3rd Australian Garrison Battalion (V144509). He was appointed acting OC D Company on 10th February 1942. On 1st March he was appointed temporary captain and was detached to Southern Command Training School, Course No.57 at Seymour, Victoria on 7th March. He was detached to Course No.15 at Wolloomanata, near Lara, Victoria on 23rd March. On 25th July he was appointed temporary major and on 21st August was posted to 9th Garrison Battalion at Portsea, Victoria. He was treated in hospital for furunculosis of the ear 8th-14th September. On 28th September he was detached to 23rd Garrison Battalion and returned to 9th Garrison Battalion on 25th January 1943. William was promoted captain on 30th June. He spent short spells in 58 Camp Hospital, Queenscliff from 21st June until 14th July before rejoining his unit again. On 1st September he transferred to 23rd Garrison Battalion, Prisoner of War Group, Murchison, Victoria and was appointed Camp Commandant, C Camp on 27th October. He was promoted major on 1st March 1944 and relinquished his appointment on 30th August 1944. He was posted to 50th Garrison Company, where he ceased full-time duty and was placed on the Retired List on 11th June 1945. He marched out to the General Detail Depot, Royal Park, Melbourne on 25th June and was placed on the Retired List (Victoria) on 6th July.

William in 1940.

William attended the funeral of William Currey VC at St Stephen's Church, Macquarie Street, Sydney on 3rd May 1948 with fellow VCs George Cartwright, Thomas Bede Kenny and Snowy Howell. He was also present at the funeral of Richard Kelliher VC at Springvale Cemetery, Melbourne on 30th January 1963.

William was presented to Queen Elizabeth II at Melbourne Cricket Ground in February 1954. He attended three VC Reunions. On 26th June 1956 he was at the

William Ruthven died at Heidelberg Repatriation Hospital, Melbourne in January 1970.

All Saints' Church, where William's funeral was held.

VC Centenary Celebrations at Hyde Park, London. He travelled on SS *Orcades* with other Australian VCs, who were part of the 301 Victoria Cross recipients from across the Commonwealth to attend. He also attended the third and sixth VC & GC Association Reunions at the Café Royal, London on 18th July 1962 and 19th July 1968.

In 1964 he was one of eighteen Australian VCs at the opening of VC Corner at the Australian War Memorial by the Governor General, Lord De L'Isle VC. On 25th April 1965 he was one of seventy-seven veterans to visit Anzac Cove, Gallipoli. During the visit they met thirty-four Turkish veterans.

William Ruthven had a heart condition for many years and died at Heidelberg Repatriation Hospital, Melbourne on 12th January 1970. He was given a full military funeral at All Saints' Church, Preston, Melbourne and was cremated at Fawkner Crematorium on 14th January 1970, where his ashes are interred. He is commemorated in a number of other places:

- Melbourne
  - Memorial in 4th Avenue Wall Niches (North Side), Section 1, Compartment X, Niche 127 at Fawkner Crematorium & Memorial Park.
  - Ruthven Soldiers' Club, Broadmeadows Camp opened in 1959.
  - Named on the Victoria Cross Memorial at Springvale Botanical Cemetery, Melbourne, Victoria unveiled on 10th November 2013.
- Reservoir, Victoria
  - Ruthven Railway Station, High Street named on 5th August 1963.
  - Ruthven Primary School, Glasgow Avenue opened in 1968. In 2010 it absorbed the primary component of Merrilands P-12 College and was renamed William Ruthven Primary School. It relocated to Merrilands Road Campus on 2nd February 2012. The William Ruthven VC Memorial House Shield is awarded annually to the house judged to be the best of the year.
  - William Ruthven Secondary College, Merrilands Road Campus established in 2010 by the merger of Lakeside Secondary College and Years 7–12 of Merrilands P-12 College. It is co-located with William Ruthven Primary School.
- Wodonga, Victoria
  - Ruthven Avenue on White Box Rise estate, built on the former Bandiana Army Camp.
  - W. Ruthven V.C. Cup was presented to the winning unit in the 8th Division (Victorian Units) Football Competition held at Wodonga during the Second World War. The first presentation was on 26th October 1940.
- Canberra, Australian Capital Territory
  - Ruthven Street named on 8th February 1978.
  - Australian Victoria Cross Recipients plaque on the Victoria Cross Memorial, Campbell, dedicated on 24th July 2000.

   - Named on one of eleven plaques honouring 175 men from overseas awarded the VC for the Great War. The plaques were unveiled by the Senior Minister of State at the Foreign & Commonwealth Office and Minister for Faith and Communities, Baroness Warsi, at a reception at Lancaster House, London on 26th June 2014 attended by the Duke of Kent and relatives of the VC recipients. The Australian plaque is at the Australian War Memorial.
   - A portrait by George Bell at the Australian War Memorial.
   - Display in the Hall of Valour, Australian War Memorial.
- Named on the Victoria Cross Monument, Esplanade & Albert Street, Alfred Square, St Kilda, Victoria, dedicated on 21st April 1985.
- Victoria Cross Memorial, Queen Victoria Building, George Street, Sydney, New South Wales dedicated on 23rd February 1992 to commemorate the visit of Queen Elizabeth II and Prince Phillip on the occasion of the Sesquicentenary of the City of Sydney. Sir Roden Cutler VC AK KCMG, Edward Kenna VC and Keith Payne VC were in attendance.
- Victoria Cross Recipients Wall, North Bondi War Memorial, New South Wales, donated to the community of Waverley on 27th November 2011 by The Returned & Services League of Australia.
- Communities and Local Government commemorative paving stones for the 145 VCs born in Australia, Belgium, Canada, China, Denmark, Egypt, France, Germany, India, Iraq, Japan, Nepal, Netherlands, Newfoundland, New Zealand, Pakistan, South Africa, Sri Lanka, Ukraine and United States of America were unveiled at the National Memorial Arboretum, Alrewas, Staffordshire by Prime Minister David Cameron MP and Sergeant Johnson Beharry VC on 5th March 2015.

The Australia Service Medal 1939–1945 was awarded to members of the Australian armed forces, Mercantile Marine and Volunteer Defence Corps during the Second World War. The qualifying period was eighteen months full-time service at home or overseas or three years part-time service between 3rd September 1939 and 2nd September 1945. There was no minimum qualifying period for those killed, wounded or disabled due to service. In August 1996 the qualifying period was reduced to thirty days for full-time service and ninety days for part-time service.

In addition to the VC he was awarded the 1914–15 Star, British War Medal 1914–20, Victory Medal 1914–19, War Medal 1939–45, Australia Service Medal 1939–45, George VI Coronation Medal 1937, Elizabeth II Coronation Medal 1953 and the Efficiency Decoration with 'Australia' clasp. His medals are held in the Hall of Valour, Australian War Memorial, Treloar Crescent, Campbell, Australian Capital Territory.

LIEUTENANT CLIFFORD WILLIAM KING SADLIER
51st Australian Infantry Battalion AIF

Clifford Sadlier was born on 11th June 1892 at Camberwell, Melbourne, Victoria, Australia. His father, Thomas George Sadlier (25th June 1865–1951), was born at Tallow, Co Waterford, Ireland. He emigrated to Victoria, Australia, where he became a salesman. He married Mary Ann née Roberts (31st March 1863–1930), born at Mount Barker, near Adelaide, South Australia, on 3rd October 1887 at St Phillip's, Collingwood, Melbourne. They were living at Barkly Ward, Yarra, Melbourne in 1903. He became a manager and was also an indent agent at one time. They moved to Adelaide, South Australia, where he worked for Messrs Goode Durrant & Co Ltd, Grenfell Street. Mary was living with her son Egbert and daughter Estella at 27 Barker Road, Subiaco, Perth, Western Australia in 1913–14. She was living at Braemar, Percy Street, Goodwood, South Australia in September 1915. He lived at various addresses in Adelaide – 7 Bowers Building, Charles Street by March 1925, Room 23, Haigh's Building, 41 Rundle Street by May 1929 and at 49 East Street at some other time. They also lived at 98 Hamersley Road, Subiaco, Perth, Western Australia. Mary died at Northcote, Melbourne, Victoria. Thomas was living at St Kilda West, Balaclava, Melbourne in 1936 and died at Hawthorn, Melbourne. Clifford had four siblings:

Camberwell, Melbourne, where Clifford was born in 1892.

- Egbert 'Bert' George Harold Sadlier (c.1888–6th January 1927) was manager for Messrs S Smith & Sons Ltd. He travelled to Liverpool, departing from there for the United States on the return journey on SS *Carmania* on 16th August 1919. While in Britain he stayed with his aunt, Mrs Dr Gibson at 41 Spottiswood Street, Edinburgh, Midlothian. Bert married Daisy Constance Foster (1887–3rd July

Clifford's parents married at St Philip's, Collingwood, Melbourne (Collingwood Library).

1953) at Newtown, New South Wales in 1912. She was born at Perth, Western Australia. They lived at Bedford Avenue, Subiaco, Western Australia, at 67 Hay Street, Subiaco by 1925 and at 3 Bedford Avenue, Subiaco in 1931. They had three children:

- Marjorie Sadlier (September 1913–16th January 1998) married Cecil Lancelot 'Lance' Howard (12th January 1913–26th December 1989) on 14th February 1941 at St Clement's Anglican Church, Mosman, New South Wales. Lance was a clerk 1933–37 and had become a commercial traveller by 1940. He was born at Everleigh, Rose Street, Fremantle, Western Australia. Lance enlisted at No.4 Royal Australian Air Force Recruiting Centre, Perth, Western Australia on 7th October 1940. He was described as 5′ 10″ tall, weighing 193 lbs, with medium complexion, brown eyes, black hair and his religious denomination was Church of England. His wife was living at 3 Bedford Avenue, Subiaco with her parents. He commenced aircrew training and was promoted leading aircraftsman on 7th December. He transferred from pilot to observer training on 12th January 1941 and completed flying training at No.1 Air Navigation School (awarded Air Observers Badge 23rd August 1941). Lance was promoted sergeant on 19th September 1941 and was posted to 5 Embarkation Depot the same day. He was posted to 2 Embarkation Depot on 11th October 1941 and embarked at Sydney on 16th October 1941, arriving in Britain on 23rd November via Canada (embarked 12th November). He was posted to 3 Personnel Reception Centre on 23rd November 1941 and then to 14 Operational Training Unit, Cottesmore on 9th December. Lance was promoted flight sergeant on 19th March 1942 and on 7th May was posted to 49 Squadron. He remustered as a navigator on 23rd July, was posted to 49 Conversion Flight on 10th August and returned to 49 Squadron on 7th September. He was commissioned as a pilot officer (406248) on 21st January 1943. He was posted to 617 Squadron on 25th March 1943, with the experience of twenty-five operations behind him, and took part in Operation Chastise, the Dams Raid, led by Wing Commander Guy Gibson, who was awarded the VC for his part in that action, on 16th/17th May 1943. Lance was the navigator with 656738 Flight Sergeant William Clifford Townsend DFM, flying Lancaster ED886/G (AJ-O 'Orange') against the Ennepe Dam, the only aircraft to engage this target. In his own account in *Australia's Dambusters* by Colin Burgess – *It was a clear night with a full moon and we flew at 60 to 100 feet to keep under German radar. On the way in we received a radio message to attack the Ennepe dam, which indicated that the main target, the Möhne, had been breached. This we saw for ourselves shortly afterwards as we used this for a turning point on the way to the Ennepe..... We attacked the Ennepe at sixty feet height and a speed of 240 miles per hour. There were no defences and the bomb was accurate. But no breach was observed and it was obvious that two or more bombs would be needed. Unfortunately there were no*

Lance Howard was flying under the command of Wing Commander Guy Gibson, who was awarded the VC for his part in the Dams Raid on 16th/17th May 1943.

Lance Howard on the left in November 1943 with his brother, 427327 Sergeant Godfrey Denzil Vaughan Howard RAAF. Godfrey was lost on an operation over Italy on 25th February 1944, serving in 104 Squadron. He is buried in Bari War Cemetery (XV D 33) (Australian War Memorial).

other aircraft ... Lance was awarded the DFC (LG 25th May 1943). He was one of eight Australians amongst the 133 aircrew who took part in the raid. He was promoted flying officer on 21st July 1943 and was posted to 1654 Heavy Conversion Unit, RAF Wigsley, Nottinghamshire on 5th October 1943. On 21st February 1944 he was posted to 11 Personnel Despatch and Receiving Centre, Brighton, Sussex and sailed to the USA, disembarking in New York on 9th March. He travelled by train from New York to San Francisco 19th-25th March and returned to Australia, disembarking at Sydney on 12th May. He was posted to 5 Personnel Depot, RAAF Bradfield Park, New South Wales on 24th May 1944, to General Reconnaissance School, RAAF

One of the Lancaster bombers that was modified to carry the Upkeep bomb used on the Dams Raid.

The target for Lancaster ED886/G (AJ-O 'Orange') was the Ennepe Dam which, although hit, was not breached.

Station Bairnsdale, Victoria 8th July–15th September and to HQ 1 Training Group on 12th September. Promoted flight lieutenant on 21st January 1945 and was posted to 5 Personnel Depot on 31st January 1945. His appointment was terminated on 19th March 1945. Marjorie and Lance lived at various addresses around Perth – 3 Bedford Avenue, Subiaco, then 268 Newcastle Street, North Perth, at Scampton, Urch Road, Roleystone, Canning by 1949, at 94 Alderbury Street, Floreat Park, Fremantle in 1954, at 84 Alderbury Street, Floreat in 1958 and at 1 Harris House, Air Force Homes, Leach Highway, Bull Creek from 1977.

    - Geoffrey Sadlier (born 7th March 1915) enlisted in the Australian Army on 28th May 1940 (WX3516) at Perth and served as a private in 2/16th Battalion, 7th Division until being discharged on 27th September 1945.
    - Clifford Sadlier (1st December 1917–8th April 1986) enlisted in the Australian Army on 30th July 1941 (WX15472) at Claremont, Western Australia and served as a private in 2/7th Australian Infantry Battalion until discharged on 23rd March 1945.

- Estella Lorrette Myrtle Sadlier (1889–1974) married Charles Wilson Iredale (c.1887–1955) at Subiaco in 1913. He died at Cambrian Hill, Victoria and she died at Macleod, Melbourne, Victoria.
- Thomas Edward Reginald Sadlier (21st February 1890–26th July 1960), a librarian and a lecturer, lived at Palmra, East Terrace, Adelaide, South Australia. He was a member of the Junior Cadets, Melbourne University Volunteer Corps for five years. Thomas was engaged to Miss RS Taylor when he enlisted in 3rd Light Horse Regiment (77) at Morphetville, South Australia on 19th August 1914. He was described as 5′ 8¾″ tall, weighing 145 lbs, with fresh complexion, blue eyes, brown hair and his religious denomination was Church of England. He was promoted corporal in the pay office on 20th August and local sergeant on 28th October. He joined the Mediterranean Expeditionary Force at Gallipoli on 9th May 1915 and was appointed squadron quartermaster sergeant on 24th May. He suffered from diarrhoea on 1st July and was treated at the Australian Casualty Clearing Station before being evacuated to 2nd Stationary Hospital, Mudros next day. He was evacuated to St Andrew Hospital, Malta on HMHS *Devanha* on 14th July with rheumatism and debility. Declared fit for service on 23rd August, he was transferred to the Overseas Base Mustapha and sailed for Mudros and Gallipoli aboard HMAT A10 *Karoo* on 30th August. He rejoined the unit on 27th September but was taken sick again on 25th October. He was treated at 1st Australian Field Ambulance and transferred to No.13 Casualty Clearing Station, Mudros next day with rheumatism and myalgia. He was evacuated to Malta on HMHS *Rewa* with acute rheumatism and peritoneal adhesions on 2nd November. He was treated for enteric fever at Floriana Hospital from 18th November. On 24th November he left Malta aboard HMHS *Grenart Castle* and transferred to RMS *Aquitania* on 25th November for onward travel to Britain, where he was

admitted to Brook War Hospital, Woolwich on 4th December 1915. He was transferred to the Supernumerary List on 26th January 1916. On 24th October he was discharged from Woodcote Park Hospital, Epsom, Surrey and granted leave until 6th December, when he was to report to Perham Down. He went to No.1 Australian Convalescent Depot, Harefield on 11th December. On 23rd March 1917 he transferred to 69th Battalion and to 65th Battalion at Wareham as regimental quartermaster sergeant on 29th March. On 19th September he transferred to 5th Battalion on marching out to 63rd Draft Battalion and went to France from Southampton on 17th October to join 1st Australian Division Base Depot, Le Havre next day. He was taken on strength 5th Battalion on 1st November 1917. On 15th November he was commissioned and transferred to 6th Battalion. However, on 22nd January 1918 he was invalided with trench nephritis to 2nd Australian Casualty Clearing Station and to 24th General Hospital, Étaples on 23rd January. He embarked aboard HMHS *Stad Antwerpen* for Britain

The Canadian Convalescent Hospital was established at Woodcote Park, Epsom, Surrey, which had been purchased by the Royal Automobile Club in 1913 and was requisitioned by the War Office in 1914 to train new recruits. Work began in November to build a camp for 5,400 men and 200 officers but in 1915 it was decided that the camp should be a convalescent hospital, mainly for Canadian troops. It opened on 5th September 1915, initially with 500 beds, but growing rapidly so that by 10th November 1918 there were 4,142 patients. The first patients were ANZACs wounded at Gallipoli, who were soon joined by British and Canadian servicemen. The whole complex, which was divided into two sections - Farm Camp and Woodcote Park Camp - became known as 'Tin City'. In July 1916 the King and Queen visited. The Hospital closed on 30th June 1919 and became Queen Mary's Convalescent Centre for the treatment and training of ex-servicemen. In 1923 the estate was returned to the RAC. In the Second World War the house was used as a training centre and the estate was used for agriculture. The estate is still run by the RAC as a country club and golf course.

7 Palliser Road, Barons Court, London, where Thomas Sadlier's wife, Edna, was living in November 1917.

on 3rd February and was admitted to 3rd London General Hospital the same day. A medical board on 4th March granted him leave in Australia until recalled. He returned to Australia aboard SS *Kenilworth Castle*, departing England on 12th March and Durban, South Africa on 23rd April. Thomas married Edna Mary Foy (1894–1940) on 7th February 1917 at Kensington, London. She was living at 7 Palliser Road, Barons Court, London in November 1917 and at 24 Russell Road, Kensington on 7th January 1918. She lived at other addresses during his service – Blue Lion Hotel, Collingbourne and 29 Craven Street, Charing Cross, London. His father wrote to the Officer-in-Charge Base Depot in March 1925 and May 1929 trying to find his son's address as letters posted to Trundel, New South Wales went unanswered. Thomas joined the Civil Construction Corps (CV122545) as a clerk in the Second World War, working with the Allied Works Council, Lonsdale Street, Melbourne and Lewis Construction Co, Mangalore, India. He was a widower, living at 17 Ebden Avenue, Black Rock, described as 5′ 9″ tall and weighing 175 lbs. His employment with AWC was terminated on 5th February 1944 and he was discharged on 12th February. Thomas and Edna had a son:

  ◦ Thomas Geoffrey Cornelius Edward Sadlier (23rd March 1917–10th February 2005). He was born at Kensington, London and died at Bentleigh, Victoria.

- Clarence Andrew James Sadlier (1895–28th March 1978) was a warehouseman and had served in the Naval Reserve for four and a half years when he enlisted in 21st Regiment, 2nd Field Artillery Brigade on 31st May 1915 (28286). He was described as 5′ 8½″ tall, weighing 157 lbs, with dark complexion, brown eyes, black hair and his religious denomination was Church of England. His address was 98 Hamersley Road, Subiaco, Perth, Western Australia. He was admitted to 1st Australian General Hospital, Heliopolis, Egypt on 9th January 1916 with influenza, transferred to Al Hayat on 18th January and the Convalescent Depot, Helouan the same day. He was discharged to duty on 21st January. On 9th February he returned to Australia on nursing duty aboard HMAT A71 *Nestor* from Suez, as did his brother, Clifford. On 25th October he embarked on HMAT A38 *Ulysses* at Melbourne and was appointed acting sergeant. On arriving at Plymouth, Devon on 28th December he reverted to gunner and was posted to No.21 Camp, Larkhill, Wiltshire next day. He was attached to the Permanent Staff of Reserve Brigade Australian Artillery and appointed temporary sergeant on 17th February 1917 but reverted to gunner on 23rd February and ceased duty with the Permanent Staff on 20th July. Clarence went to France on 23rd July from Southampton and joined the Australian General Base Depot at Rouelles next day. He was attached to 8th Light Trench Mortar Battery from Artillery Details on 1st August and was taken on strength on 30th September. He was attached to 1st Anzac Corps School 7th-27th August and was promoted corporal on 1st October. On 9th November he transferred to 5th Divisional Ammunition Column and was attached to 1st Anzac

Gas School 16th-27th December. On 15th January 1918 he was attached to 5th Divisional Salvage Company and was granted leave in Paris 28th February–9th March. Clarence was admitted to 14th Australian Field Ambulance with tonsillitis on 30th April, transferred to No.30 Casualty Clearing Station on 8th May, to No.61 Casualty Clearing Station on 9th May, No.10 Ambulance Train on 10th May and 9th General Hospital on 11th May. He was evacuated to England next day and sent to Magdalen Camp Hospital, Winchester on 13th May. He was transferred to No.1 Australian Auxiliary Hospital, Harefield Park on 1st June, to No.3 Convalescent Depot, Hurdcott on 4th June and the Military Hospital at Fovant on 14th June. He transferred to the Training Depot on 17th July, to No.3 Convalescent Depot on 17th July, the Reserve Brigade Australian Artillery, Heytesbury on 13th September and the Overseas Training Brigade on 28th December. Clarence returned to Australia on HMAT A40 *Ceramic* on 25th January 1919 and was discharged on 30th April. He married Daphne Youle Dean (1894–1986) in 1919 at Perth. During the Second World War, Clarence served as a sergeant (W237374) in HQ Western Australia Line of Communication Area, Australian Military Forces. He was tried by court martial on 13th February 1943 but for what offence and the outcome are not known. Daphne and Clarence had a son:

  ◦ Terence Charles Youle Sadlier (15th January 1925–1996) enlisted in the Royal Australian Air Force on 27th February 1943 at Perth (436667). He was promoted through the ranks to warrant officer by the time of his discharge on 1st February 1946. He married Patricia Mary Smart (8th September 1928–1972) on 1st December 1951 at Mount Lawley, Western Australia. She died at Kalgoorlie and he at Bassendean.

Clifford's paternal grandfather, Christopher Townsend Sadlier (1838–78), was born in Ireland. He married Elizabeth née Latham (1840–1st February 1892), born at Douglas, Co Cork, in 1862. He was a schoolmaster at St Mary, Yorkshire before emigrating to Australia, settling at Hawthorn, Victoria. Elizabeth was a schoolteacher and later a journalist in Victoria. She died at Pyramid Hill, Victoria. In addition to Thomas they had four other children:

Clifford's paternal grandmother, Elizabeth Latham, was born at Douglas, Co Cork, Ireland.

- John Henry Sadlier (born and died 1863 in Ireland).
- William Charles Sadlier (29th May 1867–1st February 1935), born at Bandon, Co Cork, was a clergyman. He married Edith Ellen Lievesley (1st November 1870–1971) on 16th April 1895 at St Paul's, Bendigo, Victoria, where he was curate. They moved to New Zealand, where he

was appointed Bishop of Nelson. William travelled to England from Wellington with his son, Arthur, on 18th August 1926. William died at Wrays House Nursing Home, Warblington, Hampshire and Edith died at Cheltenham, Gloucestershire. They had four children – Horace William Augustine Sadlier 1896, Dorothy Emma Elizabeth Sadlier 1901, Sheelah Mary Vera Sadlier 1905 and Arthur 'Pat' John Latham Sadlier 1907.

- James Latham Sadlier (7th May 1869–10th August 1926) married Emma (also seen as Ellen) Lillian Nelson (1880–9th October 1933) on 28th August 1902 at Tallangatta, Victoria. She was born at Pleasant Creek, near Stawell, Victoria. They were living at Rutherglen, Victoria in 1909 and at Hutt, Wellington, New Zealand in 1911. They had four children, the first two in Victoria and the others in New Zealand:
    - Alma Ellen Elizabeth Sadlier (1904–died before 1913).
    - James Edward Henry Sadlier (1905–06).
    - Frank Sadlier (born 1909).
    - Alma Sadlier (born 1913).

  Emma married Alfred Ernest Brownhill (October 1885–17th November 1963) in 1928. Alfred married Ismay Nadine Humberstone (née Bechervaise) (1888–17th July 1974) in 1935. She was born at West Ham, London and had married Harold Bertram Humberstone (12th May 1896–6th May 1956) there in 1923. They had a daughter, Rose M Humberstone later that year. Harold enlisted in the Royal Navy on 14th December 1914 (PC 349047) described as 5′ 3¾″ tall with fair hair, hazel eyes and fresh complexion. He served on HMS *Dido* 19th December, HMS *Pembroke I* 20th June 1915, HMS *Cyclops* 30th June, HMS *Pembroke* 7th December 1918–29th September 1919. Harold and Ismay emigrated to New Zealand, where he became an orchardist living at Kaipara. Their marriage ended in divorce and he was a ship's steward in 1935. Harold married Dorothy Alice Norah Norton (1910–87) in 1954 at Southend-on-Sea, Essex.
- Elizabeth Christina Anne Sadlier (9th July 1878–1920) married Frederick Edwin Sawtell (28th August 1881–20th May 1943) in 1908 at Perth, Western Australia. The marriage ended in divorce. Elizabeth married Dr Arthur Horace Gibson (born 21st October 1880) in 1912 at Perth. He was commissioned as a captain (medical officer) on 1st May 1915, described as 5′ 11½″ tall and weighing 163 lbs. He embarked at Fremantle aboard RMS *Mooltan* on 24th May for Mudros. Admitted to 3rd Australian General Hospital, Mudros with jaundice on 1st October. Evacuated to Alexandria, Egypt on 27th January 1916. Promoted major 25th February and transferred to 5th Field Ambulance, Abbassia on 4th March, which moved to France soon afterwards. On 30th July 1917 he was posted to 2nd Australian Casualty Clearing Station and was granted leave in Paris 4th-14th October and special leave in Britain 21st October–24th November. Transferred to 15th Australian Field Ambulance on 26th November. Appointed temporary lieutenant colonel with 12th Australian Field Ambulance on 15th February 1918.

> Granted leave to Britain 13th–28th March. Promoted lieutenant colonel 2nd May 1918. Mentioned in Sir Douglas Haig's Despatch of 8th November 1918. Transferred to England 16th March 1919. Elizabeth was living at Pier Street, East Fremantle in June 1919.

His maternal grandfather, Edward Roberts, married Rhoda née Appleton in Adelaide in 1852. In addition to Mary they had five other children – Lydia Roberts 1855, Edward Henry Roberts 1856, Thomas Roberts 1859, Rhoda Roberts 1860 and Priscilla Roberts 1865.

Clifford was educated at University High School, Melbourne, Victoria and worked as a commercial traveller after moving to Western Australia, where he lived at 98 Hamersley Road, Subiaco, Perth. He enlisted in Perth, Western Australia on 26th May 1915 and was posted to Blackboy Hill Camp, Northam with the Australian Army Medical Corps (4871 later 2858). He was described as 5′ 9″ tall, weighing 126 lbs, with fair complexion, blue eyes, fair hair and his religious denomination was Church of England. He embarked at Fremantle as a reinforcement for the Hospital and Convalescent Home aboard HMAT A62 *Wandilla* on 25th June and disembarked at Suez, Egypt on 18th July. He joined 1st Australian General Hospital, Heliopolis, Cairo and was admitted to it 22nd December 1915–27th January 1916. Clifford returned to Australia on nursing duty on 9th February 1916 aboard HMAT A71 *Nestor* from Suez, arriving on 13th March. He was appointed acting sergeant and embarked for Britain

SS *Wandilla* was operated by the Adelaide Steamship Co on the Fremantle to Sydney route from 1912. In 1915 she became a military transport and in 1916 a hospital ship. She was attacked by a U-boat in February 1918, but the torpedo failed to explode. In 1921 she was sold to the Bermuda & West Indies Steam Ship Co and was renamed *Fort St George* in 1921. In 1924 she collided with RMS *Olympic* at New York. In 1935 she was sold to Lloyd Triestino and renamed *Cesarea* and *Arno* in 1938. In the Second World War she was used by the Italian Regia Marina as a hospital ship, but was sunk by British aircraft on 10th September 1942. The British claimed a decoded German radio message indicated that the ship was carrying supplies to Benghazi and this justified the attack. Allegations that the attack was a war crime were not investigated after the war.

Blackboy Hill Camp, Bellevue, Western Australia in 1914 (Australian War Memorial).

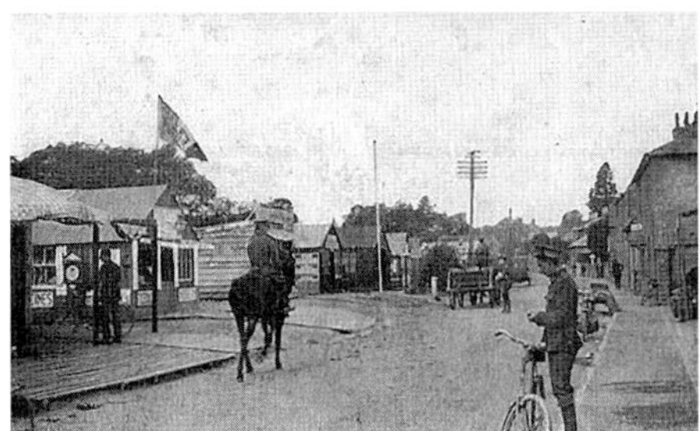

Codford Camp, Wiltshire was used by ANZAC forces as a training and transit depot to and from France. The AIF badge was carved into the chalk on the hillside above the camp (53m x 45m) in 1916. The soldiers of 13th Training Battalion, who had to maintain the badge, named it 'Misery Hill'. The nearby CWGC cemetery contains the graves of sixty-six New Zealanders and thirty-one Australians. The local community still feels a strong bond with the ANZAC troops and hold a remembrance ceremony on Anzac Day, 25th April, every year. A similar bond exists at nearby Sutton Veny.

Clifford was on the staff of 1st Australian General Hospital at Heliopolis, Egypt and later was a patient. The Hospital was raised in August 1914 and departed Brisbane on 21st November for Egypt aboard HMAT A55 *Kyarra*, part of the first convoy from Albany to Alexandria. On arrival, on 14th January 1915, it was established in buildings and tents at Heliopolis and opened for patients ten days later. In March 1916 the hospital closed and moved to France. It opened at Rouen on 29th April 1916. The last patients were admitted on 30th November 1918 and it closed on 7th December. The staff joined the hospital at Sutton Veny, Wiltshire.

with 51st Battalion, 7th Reinforcement Group from Fremantle aboard HMAT A8 *Argyllshire* on 9th November. He reported sick with venereal disease on 11th November and was admitted to the isolation hospital aboard until 28th November. He disembarked at Devonport on 10th January 1917, reverted to private next day and was posted to 13th Training Battalion, Codford, Wiltshire on 21st January. Clifford attended a cadre course for NCOs at Candahar Barracks, Tidworth, Wiltshire 13th-25th February. He embarked at Folkestone, Kent for Étaples, France on 9th May, reverting to private again next day and joined 4th Australian Division Base Depot. He joined 10 Platoon, C Company, 51st Battalion on 13th May and was promoted corporal on 18th May.

Candahar Barracks, Tidworth. The War Office acquired Tedworth House and land to the north in 1897. Southern Command was established there in 1905, the same year that Lucknow and Mooltan Barracks were completed. Tidworth Military Hospital was finished in 1907 and six other barracks followed - Aliwal, Assaye, Bhurtpore, Candahar, Delhi and Jellalabad. Tidworth Military Cemetery contains 417 graves from the First World War and another 106 from the Second World War. Tidworth remains a major garrison for the British Army.

Clifford was commissioned on 14th July and was granted leave in England 6th-24th November 1917 and 20th March–4th April 1918. He was promoted lieutenant on 1st April 1918. **Awarded the VC for**

his actions near Villers-Bretonneux on 24th April 1918, LG 11th July 1918 and Commonwealth of Australia Gazette 27th November 1918.

SS *City of Karachi* (5,547 tons) was owned by Ellerman & Bucknall Steamship Co of London. She was scrapped in 1934 in Japan.

Clifford was treated at 2/3rd Anzac Corps Field Ambulance for a gunshot wound to the right arm and was transferred to 8th General Hospital, Rouen on 26th April. He was evacuated to Britain on HMHS *Guildford Castle* on 27th April and was admitted to 3rd London General Hospital next day. After a medical board on 6th June he was transferred to 6th Australian Auxiliary Hospital, Moreton Gardens, South Kensington next day. Leave was recommended until 25th June. A medical board on 10th July resulted in him being readmitted to 6th Australian Auxiliary Hospital. The VC was presented by the King George V at Buckingham Palace on 17th July 1918. Clifford was transferred to the Supernumary List on 16th August. He embarked on SS *City of Karachi* on 24th August, disembarking at Fremantle on 24th October and then travelled overland to 5th Military District, from where he was discharged from the Army on 4th March 1919. He was appointed lieutenant in the Australian Military Forces on 1st January 1920 and placed on the Retired List on 1st September 1927.

Clifford was State Secretary of the Returned Soldiers, Sailors and Airmen's Imperial League for a short time and in 1919 he set up the Subiaco sub-branch, serving as its first President. He was a manufacturer's agent in the 1920s, running his own indent agency briefly in 1929. Clifford and fellow VCs John Carroll, Hugo Throssell and James Woods attended a lunch to honour those VCs who could not attend the VC Reunion at the House of Lords in London, hosted by Colonel Sir William Campion KCMG DSO TD, Governor of Western Australia, at Government House, Perth on Armistice Day 1929. The following year he unsuccessfully contested the State seat of Nedlands, Perth as a Nationalist. In 1936 he was appointed as a clerk in the Repatriation Department in Perth and was invalided out of the public service in 1949.

Clifford married Maude Victoria Moore (born 1892) on 23rd August 1922 at St Mary's Anglican Church, Perth. She was the daughter of James Eames Moore and Emily Ann née Roe. The marriage ended in divorce in 1934 and she was living at 19 Finlayson Street, Subiaco in 1936. He married Alice Edith Smart on 17th July 1936 at the Presbyterian Manse, Subiaco, Perth. They were living at 4 Campbell Street, Subiaco later in 1936 before moving to 155 Bussell Highway, Busselton, near Perth. Clifford attended the VC Centenary Celebrations at Hyde Park, London on 26th June 1956. He travelled on SS *Orcades* with other Australian VCs, part of the 301 Victoria Cross recipients from across the Commonwealth to attend.

Clifford suffered from emphysematic bronchitis for ten years and died at Busselton District Hospital, Perth on 28th April 1964. A full military funeral was attended by over seventy former soldiers from 51st Battalion and a bearer party from 22nd Construction Squadron, Royal Australian Engineers. He was cremated at Karrakatta Crematorium, Perth and a commemorative plaque was placed on the Western Australian Garden of Remembrance Memorial (Wall 4 Row C). His ashes were scattered in the Indian Ocean on 17th May 1990. He is commemorated in a number of other places:

The Australian War Memorial, Canberra, is the nation's national memorial to members of the armed forces and supporting organisations. It was dedicated in November 1941. The Memorial has three parts. The Commemorative Area includes the Hall of Memory and the Tomb of the Unknown Australian Soldier. The other parts are the Galleries (museum) and Research Centre (records). There is also a Sculpture Garden. Although separate, Anzac Parade leads to the Memorial.

- Sadlier-Stokes Memorial Scholarship established by the Australian Federal Government in 1990 and awarded annually on Anzac Day to French students from the Somme or Nord Pas-de-Calais regions of France to further their knowledge of Australia, particularly tertiary study in Australia.
- Australian Capital Territory
    - Sadlier Street.
    - Victoria Cross Memorial, Campbell dedicated on 24th July 2000.
    - Display in the Hall of Valour, Australian War Memorial.
    - Named on one of eleven plaques honouring 175 men from overseas awarded the VC for the Great War. The plaques were unveiled by the Senior Minister of State at the Foreign & Commonwealth Office and Minister for Faith and Communities, Baroness Warsi, at a reception at Lancaster House, London on 26th June 2014 attended by The Duke of Kent and relatives of the VC recipients. The Australian plaque is at the Australian War Memorial.
- Melbourne, Victoria
    - Sadlier Court, Crib Point.
    - Victoria Cross Memorial, Springvale Botanical Cemetery unveiled on 10th November 2013.
- Victoria Cross Memorial, Queen Victoria Building, George Street, Sydney, New South Wales commemorates the visit of Queen Elizabeth II and Prince Phillip on the occasion of the Sesquicentenary of the City of Sydney on 23rd February 1992. Sir Roden Cutler VC, Edward Kenna VC and Keith Payne VC were in attendance.
- Sadlier Street, Wodonga, on White Box Rise estate built on land formerly part of Bandiana Army Camp.

- Perth
  - Sylvia Perry MBE Wing, Hollywood Private Hospital, opened on 24th July 2002 by Danna Vale MP Minister for Veterans' Affairs, has nineteen wards named after Australian VC/GCs. The two in the new Wing are named after John Carroll and Clifford Sadlier.
  - Cliff Sadlier VC Mixed Fours – a lawn bowls event sponsored by Osborne Park Returned & Services League Sub-Branch played annually at Osborne Park Bowling Club, Tuart Hill.
  - Cliff Sadlier Reserve, Daglish, a dog exercise area.
  - Sadlier Street, Subiaco.
  - Memorial plaque at the State War Memorial, King's Park dedicated on 26th January 1996.
- Victoria Cross Recipients Wall at the North Bondi War Memorial, New South Wales donated to the community of Waverley on 27th November 2011 by The Returned & Services League of Australia.
- Communities and Local Government commemorative paving stones for the 145 VCs born in Australia, Belgium, Canada, China, Denmark, Egypt, France, Germany, India, Iraq, Japan, Nepal, Netherlands, Newfoundland, New Zealand, Pakistan, South Africa, Sri Lanka, Ukraine and United States of America were unveiled at the National Memorial Arboretum, Alrewas, Staffordshire by Prime Minister David Cameron MP and Sergeant Johnson Beharry VC on 5th March 2015.

In addition to the VC he was awarded the 1914–15 Star, British War Medal 1914–20, Victory Medal 1914–19, George VI Coronation Medal 1937 and Elizabeth II Coronation Medal 1953. He bequeathed his VC to the Cathedral of St George, 38 St George's Terrace, Perth. His other medals were reunited with it, having been at the Army Museum of Western Australia, at a ceremony on Anzac Day 2009.

SECOND LIEUTENANT JOHN SCHOFIELD
2/5th Battalion, The Lancashire Fusiliers

John Schofield was born on 4th March 1892 at 17 Artillery Street, Blackburn, Lancashire. His father, also John Schofield (1863–24th May 1917), was born at Withnell, Lancashire and his surname was registered as Scholfield. He was a fishmonger's apprentice in 1881, living with his sisters, Martha and May at 52 Ordnance Street, Blackburn. He married Martha née Haworth (1863/64–3rd June 1931) in 1886. John became a well-known fish and game dealer. They were living at 17 Artillery Street, Blackburn in 1891 and at Balnagall, 16 Wycollar Road in 1901 and 1911. When he died there, he left effects valued at £13,162/8/6 (£1.1M in 2018). Martha was living at Sunny Bank House, Torver, Coniston, Lancashire at the time of her death, leaving effects valued at £11,851/19/1. John junior had four siblings:

John Schofield's family lived at 16 Wycollar Road in Blackburn for a considerable number of years. It is only a few hundred metres from Blackburn Golf Club, where John was a member.

- Martha Schofield (16th April 1887–8th August 1935) was a clerk, working for her father in 1911. She married John William Charnley (born 1884–28th February 1956), a timber merchant born at Ulverston, Lancashire, in 1923. They were living at Sunny Bank House, Torver, Coniston, Lancashire at the time of her death, leaving effects valued at £4,569/4/0. They had a son:
    - Richard John Schofield Charnley (1925–21st June 2002), who married Violet Gladstone Creasey (1928–75). They had two sons – Richard John Schofield Charnley 1950 and Kenneth John William Charnley 1955. Richard married again in 1986. He was a director of the family freight transport business of R Charnley & Grandsons Ltd at 7 Sandysike Industrial Estate, Longtown, Cumbria.

Sunny Bank Mill House at Torver, Coniston, where John's mother lived, is now self-catering holiday accommodation (HomeAway).

John married Elsie Mildred Mester née Clark (1890–28th February 1956) in 1938. She had married Richard W Mester (1878–1926), a grocer, in 1912 and they had two children – Richard R Mester 1914 and Elizabeth Mester 1923. Richard's father, Carl Hendrich Louis Mester (1850–1930) was born in Prussia. John and Elsie were living at Flosh Park, Cummertrees, Annan, Dumfriesshire at the time of his death, leaving effects valued at £7,958/3/1.

- Elizabeth Schofield (16th November 1888–12th February 1963) married George Barker Jeffery FRS (9th May 1891–27th April 1957) in 1915. George and Elizabeth were living at Balnagall, Potter Street, Pinner, Middlesex at the time of his death at Great North Road, near Woomer Green, Hertfordshire, leaving effects valued

George Barker Jeffery was educated at Strand School, Wilson's School and King's College London. In 1909 he qualified as a teacher at the London Day Training College and graduated from University College London in 1911. He was Assistant Lecturer in Applied Mathematics at University College, London 1912–21. George was a Quaker and was imprisoned in 1916 as a conscientious objector. Instead of military service he worked at the Home Office Work Centre in Wakefield, Yorkshire. In 1921 he became University Reader in Mathematics at University College and was appointed Professor of Mathematics at King's College. He published a paper describing the motion of ellipsoidal particles in a viscous fluid in 1922 and setting out Jeffery's equations. In 1923, with W Perrett, he published the definitive English translation of the papers on relativity by Einstein, Lorenz, Weyl and Minkowski. In 1924 he returned to University College as Astor Professor of Pure Mathematics. He was elected as a Fellow of the Royal Society in 1926 and served as Vice President 1938–40. In 1934 he gave the Swarthmore Lecture to the Yearly Meeting of Quakers, entitled *Christ, Yesterday and Today*. In 1945 he was appointed Director of the University of London Institute of Education and was also involved in the Secondary School Examinations Council, the National Advisory Council on the Training and Supply of Teachers, the National Foundation for Educational Research, the New Education Fellowship, the Advisory Council on Education in the Colonies and the Association of Teachers in Colleges and Departments of Education. In October 1949 he was invited by the Secretary of State for the Colonies to advise on a West African School Examinations Council. He visited the Gambia, Sierra Leone, Gold Coast and Nigeria from December 1949 until March 1950 and his findings and recommendations in the Jeffery Report were adopted in full.

at £5,416/4/11. She was living at Malet House, 101 Dorridge Road, Dorridge, Solihull, Warwickshire at the time of her death at 2 Clarendon Place, Leamington, Warwickshire, leaving effects valued at £28,237/1/-. They had three children:

- ° Janet Elizabeth Jeffery (1916–92) married David J Pratt in 1953. They were living at 3 Thames Reach, Lower Teddington Road, Hampton Wick, Kingston-upon-Thames, Surrey at the time of her death.
- ° David Schofield Jeffery (1921–22nd August 2012) studied engineering but deferred his studies during the Second World War to work with the Friends Relief Service, equipping evacuation hostels in Birmingham. He became a medical practitioner in general practice. He married Marion K Mackenzie (born 1923) in 1952 at Wood Green, Middlesex.
- ° Barbara Joyce Jeffery (1925–2004) married Dr Gordon Robert James Moodie (born 1925) in 1949 and they had a daughter, Jane C Moodie, in 1955. They lived at Worksop, Nottinghamshire, where he had a medical practice at Bardwell, Sparken Hill.

- Ellen Schofield (9th September 1890–8th February 1966) married David Charles McIntyre (1888–1968), a schoolmaster, in 1920 at Cockermouth, Cumberland. They were living at Seadown, Furze Road, High Salvington, Worthing, Sussex at the time of her death at 42 Shelley Road, Worthing. They had three children:

Fred Schofield's grave, front row left, in Péronne Road Cemetery, Maricourt. Also buried there is William Anderson, whose VC action was close by.

- Dorothy Winifred McIntyre (12th-16th April 1924).
- Nancie May McIntyre (1926–1st March 2015) married Raymond John Hanks (died 1st August 2009) in 1956 at Worthing, Sussex. They were living at Norwich, Norfolk in 2002 and also lived at Torquay, Devon. They had two children – Julia S Hanks 1958 and Denise E Hanks 1960.
- John S McIntyre (born 1928) married Patricia F Simms in 1957 at Harrow, Middlesex.

- Fred Schofield (6th September 1894–14th July 1916) enlisted in the Royal Field Artillery (L/8561) and was serving in 150th Brigade RFA as a corporal when he was killed in action (Péronne Road Cemetery, Maricourt, France – I F I). He left effects valued at £1,334/0/4.

John's paternal grandfather, William Schofield (c.1831–94), married Judith née Lucas (born c.1828) at Withnell, Lancashire. They were living at Mount Pleasant, Withnell in 1861 but thereafter she does not appear in any census returns with the family. He was a labourer at a cotton mill in 1871, living with a Mary Schofield (born c.1823) and his children at 52 Ordnance Street, Blackburn. By 1891 he was living with his daughter, Martha, at 15 Ordnance Street. In addition to John, William had five other children:

- Simeon Schofield (1852–4th March 1890) was a cotton spinner in 1871. He married Ellen Waterworth (1851–1st March 1927) on 24th December 1873 at Blackburn. She was born at Stainburn, Yorkshire. They were living at 198 Audley Range, Blackburn in 1881, by when he was a fish and fruit dealer and she was a grocer. He died at his home at 208 Audley Range, Blackburn, leaving effects valued at £278/1/2. Ellen married James Marsden (c.1850–1918), a grocer, on 12th January 1892. They were living at 207 Whalley Back Road, Blackburn in 1901 and at 10 Barley Bank Street, Darwen at the time of his death, leaving effects valued at £628/8/1. She was living at 1 Hall Street, Blackburn at the time of her death there, leaving effects valued at £293/7/6.

Audley Range in Blackburn.

- Martha Schofield (1854–23rd January 1907) was a cotton weaver, living as head of household at 52 Ordnance Street, Blackburn in 1881. She was a greengrocer in 1891, living at 15 Ordnance Street. In 1901 she was still living there, with two of her sister Mary Hindle's children, Martha and Harry. She never married and died there, leaving effects valued at £384/3/4.
- Ann Schofield (c.1856–1891) was a cotton weaver in 1871. She married John Hindle (born 1856) on 27th March 1875 at St Thomas', Blackburn. John was a cotton overlooker in 1881 and they were living at 67 Whalley Street, Blackburn. He was living with his children at 53 Whalley Street in 1891. They had three children – Martha Alice Hindle 1879, Robert Hindle 1881 and Harry Hindle 1888.
- Mary Schofield (born 1858) was a cotton weaver in 1871 and 1881. She married Charles Henry Harrison (1862–1940) on 24th May 1885 at St Thomas, Blackburn. In 1891 they were living at 21 Ordnance Street, Blackburn and he was a fishmonger and she was a cotton operative. By 1901 he was a fish and fruit hawker and they were living at 17 Ordnance Street, next door to Mary's sister, Martha. By 1911 he was a greengrocer and they were living at 15 Ordnance Street. They had five children – William Harrison 1886, Fred Harrison 1887, Herbert Harrison 1890, Martha Ann Harrison 1891 and Bertha Harrison 1898.
- James Schofield (born 1859) was a cotton spinner in 1881.

John was educated at Blackburn Church of England Higher Grade School and at Arnold School, Lytham Road, Blackpool, Lancashire 1904–09. He was a sergeant in the school's Officer Training Corps and won the Form IV Mathematics Prize in 1905. John was a talented sportsman and captained the Cricket XI in 1909. In 1911

Arnold School, founded on 4th May 1896 as South Shore Collegiate School, moved to Lytham Road and gradually expanded on the site of an earlier Victorian public school, whose name, Arnold House School, was adopted and was later shortened to Arnold School. In 2013 Arnold merged with King Edward VII and Queen Mary School, Lytham, not without considerable opposition, to become AKS Lytham Independent School. The old Arnold School buildings have since been demolished. Notable alumni include:

- Sir William Lyons (1901–85), co-founder of Jaguar Cars.
- Jimmy Armfield CBE (1935–2018), the Blackpool FC player, was capped forty-three times for England and captained the team on fifteen occasions. He was a member of the 1966 World Cup squad but did not play due to an injury.
- Tom Graveney (1927–2015) played in seventy-nine cricket Test matches for England, including once as captain.
- Peter Purves (born 1939) co-presented the BBC children's programme *Blue Peter* for eleven years in the 1960s and 70s.

he was a fish salesman at Brighton Hydro, Blackpool. He joined the family firm as a wholesale fish and game salesman at Blackburn fish market. John was a member of the East Lancashire Tennis Club and Blackburn Golf Club. He was engaged to Ethel Hargreaves, who lived at 33 Duke's Brow, Blackburn, Lancashire.

John attempted to enlist on two occasions but was rejected due to defective eyesight. He persisted and was accepted into the Army Service Corps as a clerk at Blackburn on 21st October 1915 (S4/143820). He joined at Aldershot on 25th October, described as 5′ 9½″ tall and weighing 146 lbs. He departed Devonport aboard HT *Corsican* on 30th December 1915 and arrived at Alexandria, Egypt on 14th January 1916. He embarked on HT *Minneapolis* on 18th January and disembarked on 27th January in Salonika to join 598th (Mechanical Transport) Company, Base Motor Transport Depot. He was appointed acting corporal on 8th June 1916 and was promoted corporal on 23rd February 1917. He departed Salonika on 8th March, reverting to private the same day, arrived in England on 24th March and commenced training at No.20 Officer Cadet Battalion, Crookham, Aldershot, Hampshire on 7th June. John was commissioned in 4th (Extra Reserve) Battalion, Lancashire Fusiliers, based at Barry, South Wales, on 26th September 1917. On 7th December he returned to France to join 2/5th Lancashire Fusiliers. John was wounded on 22nd March 1918 but not seriously.

John Schofield's grave in Vielle-Chapelle New Military Cemetery.

Awarded the VC for his actions at Givenchy, France on 9th April 1918, LG 28th June 1918. He died of wounds sustained during the VC action later the same day and was originally buried in King's Liverpool Graveyard Extension, near Cuinchy and was moved after the war to Vielle-Chapelle New Military Cemetery (Ill C 8). He left effects valued at £615/8/6. The VC was presented to his mother by the King at Buckingham Palace on 4th September 1918. John is commemorated in a number of other places:

The Arnold School memorial plaque (Mike Coyle).

The memorial in Blackburn Town Hall, one of four to local VCs (Memorials to Valour).

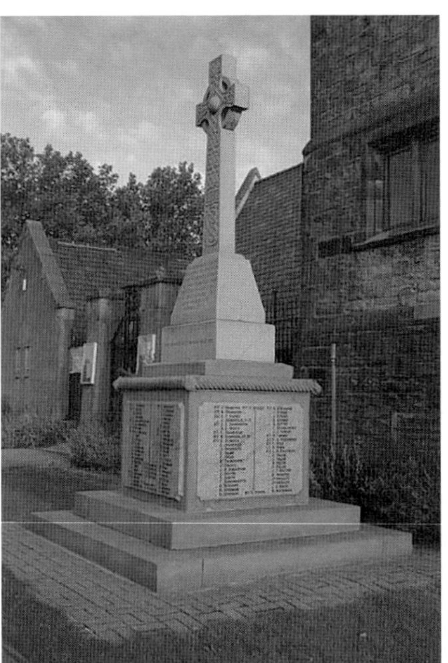

St Jude's Church war memorial. John Schofield's name is in the left column on this face of the memorial (Memorials to Valour).

- The family headstone in St Peter's Churchyard, Ribchester Road, Salesbury, Lancashire.
- Named on a memorial plaque and on the war memorial at AKS Lytham Independent School, successor to Arnold School, unveiled in 1922 by the Bishop of Manchester.
- Victoria Cross memorial in Blackburn Town Hall.
- He and his brother Fred were named on the war memorial that stood outside St Thomas's Church, Blackburn until the church was demolished. The memorial was salvaged and it now stands outside St Jude's Church, Accrington Road, Blackburn.
- Blackburn Golf Club war memorial, Revidge Road, Blackburn.
- A Department for Communities and Local Government commemorative VC paving stone was dedicated at Blackburn Town Hall on 23rd April 2018 to mark the centenary of his award. A duplicate black granite stone was dedicated at Blackburn Town Hall, King William Street in October 2018.

In addition to the VC he was awarded the British War Medal 1914–20 and Victory Medal 1914–19. The VC was presented to the Lancashire Fusiliers in 1989 by his niece, Mrs Janet Pratt, of Kingston upon Thames, Surrey. It is held by The Fusiliers' Museum Lancashire, Moss Street, Bury, Lancashire.

LIEUTENANT PERCY VALENTINE STORKEY
19th Australian Infantry Battalion AIF

Percy Storkey was born on 9th September 1893 at Napier, Hawke's Bay, New Zealand. His father, Samuel James Storkey (29th January 1865–1st June 1955) was born at Norwood, Surrey, England. He was living with his grandparents, James and Elizabeth Brazier, at Cameron Place, Warlingham, Surrey in 1871. He moved to New Zealand with his father and married Sarah Edith née Dean (20th January 1866–29th December 1941) on 22nd January 1890 at Napier, Hawke's Bay. They lived at Nelson Crescent, Napier, Hawke's Bay. Later Samuel lived at 45 Village High Road, Vaucluse, New South Wales, Australia but he died at Napier. Percy had four siblings:

- Marvel Edna Storkey (9th September 1891–17th April 1960) married Eric James Gilberd (12th June 1883–24th May 1952) on 18th September 1908. His father, James Gatland Gilberd (1851–1912) was born at San Juan, California. Marvel and Eric had at least two sons – Sydney James Gilberd 1910 and Frank Eric Gilberd 1912.
- Gertrude Annie Storkey (12th November 1896–January 1973) married Charles John Armstrong (1890–1925) on 8th April 1913. They had at least three children – Stanley Charles Armstrong 1914, Cecil Ernest Armstrong 1916 and Alma Elizabeth Armstrong 1917.
- Horace Charles Storkey (29th December 1898–1953) married Frances Adelaide Goullet (born 21st April 1901) in 1919. They had a son, Eric Morgan Storkey, on 13th June 1923.

Hastings Street, Napier, which is on the east coast of North Island in Hawke's Bay. It has a long Maori history. Captain James Cook passed by in October 1769 and it was subsequently settled by European traders, whalers and missionaries. Farmers and hotel keepers followed. The Crown purchased the area in 1851 and a few years later a planned town was laid out named after Sir Charles Napier. It was the administrative centre for Hawke's Bay Province 1858–76 and became a borough in 1874. On 3rd February 1931 most of the town was destroyed by an earthquake, which killed 256 people. Much of the rebuild was in Art Deco style and the town is considered to be one of the best-preserved Art Deco towns in the world and is an UNESCO World Heritage Site.

- Alba Victrix Fellowes (3rd March 1900–1970s) married Cyril Ernest Hounsell (24th April 1898–17th July 1963). Cyril had married Isobel Poole (born 15th August 1900) on 26th April 1927 at Napier.

Percy's paternal grandfather, William Storkey (13th May 1837–19th March 1882), was a shoemaker, living with his parents at Earsham, Norfolk in 1851. He had moved to Lambeth St Mary the Less, Norwood, Surrey by 1861. He married Amy Elizabeth née Brazier (11th April 1840–30th July 1869) at Warlingham, Surrey on 25th December 1861. She died at Norwood, probably due to complications with the birth of Ebenezer. In addition to Samuel they had two other children:

- Annie Elizabeth Storkey (born 24th December 1862) married Charles Goddart in New Zealand 1881.
- Ebenezer William Storkey (9th June 1869–25th August 1870).

William married Mary Ann Luetchford (11th October 1845–6th November 1931) on 23rd August 1870 at Norwood. They moved to New Zealand in 1874 and settled at Napier, Hawke's Bay. They had five children:

- Edith Martha Storkey (22nd July 1873–16th August 1874) was born at Croydon, Surrey and died at Cape St Vincent, Spain on the journey to New Zealand.
- Kate Mary Ann Storkey (23rd June 1875–8th February 1936) married Walter Leonard Spackman (26th September 1877–2nd February 1954) on 31st October 1901. He was the brother of Rupert Spackman, who married Kate's sister, Florence. Walter was born at Wairarapa, New Zealand. She died at Napier and he at Rotorua, Bay of Plenty. They had five sons – Leonard Storkey Spackman 1902, Clifford Tanner Spackman 1904, Bernard Clarence Walter Spackman 1907, Edric Ian Spackman 1909 and Malcolm Lawry Spackman 1910.
- Ernest William Storkey (29th January 1878–2nd August 1930) married Florence Barbara Sandy (12th November 1884–28th June 1970) on 19th May 1915. She was born at Streatham, London. They had a son, Leslie Ernest Storkey, on 27th July 1924.
- Florence Emily Storkey (30th August 1880–31st December 1949) married Rupert Howard Spackman (24th September 1882–13th June 1949), born at Masterton, Wairarapa, in 1903. He was the brother of Walter Spackman, who married Florence's sister, Kate. They had four children – Edna Florence Spackman 1903, Howard Storkey Spackman 1905, Freda Marjorie Spackman 1912 and Sydney John Rupert Spackman 1917.
- William Edwin (23rd November 1882–16th August 1932) married Margaret Elsie Thomson (25th September 1890–11th November 1977) in 1913. They had twins, Douglas William Storkey and Geoffrey Ernest Storkey, in 1917.

His maternal grandfather, John Thomas Dean (c.1834–17th March 1905), born at Bilston, Staffordshire, was a pawnbroker. He married Sarah née Fellows (c.1834–

23rd September 1897), also born at Bilston, on 9th May 1854 at St Luke's Church, Bilston. They were living at 47 & 48 Temple Lane, Bilston in 1861 and moved to New Zealand later. In addition to Sarah they had seven other children:

- Horace Dean (1855–1929).
- Clara Anita Dean (23rd November 1857–14th October 1929) married John Robert Redstone (16th January 1850–21 October 1932) on 26th January 1875 in New Zealand. He was born at Tavistock, Devon. They had six children – Florence Clara Annette Redstone 1886, Bernard Edwin Redstone 1888, Louis Hilton Russel Redstone 1891, Ronald Redstone 1893, Galene Innes Una Redstone 1894 and Godfrey Redstone 1896. Bernard, born on 1st July 1888, was a motor salesman working for his father when he enlisted in 3rd Battalion, Wellington Regiment, New Zealand Expeditionary Force (41891) at Gisborne on 1st November 1916. He had previously served in the school and city cadets. He was described as 5′ 7½″ tall, weighing 157 lbs, with fresh complexion, brown eyes, dark hair and his religious denomination was Church of England. Bernard was posted to B Company, 24th Battalion on 2nd January 1917, transferred to Details on 5th April and to B Company, 25th Battalion on 17th April. On 21st April he was promoted corporal. He served in New Zealand until embarking at Wellington on 26th April 1917, disembarking at Devonport, England on 20th July and was posted to 4th Reserve Battalion at Sling Camp, Bulford, Wiltshire the same day. He reverted to lance corporal. On 5th September he went to France and joined the Base Depot at Étaples on 9th September. When he joined 3rd Wellington on 20th September, he reverted to private. Bernard was killed in action on 4th October 1917 and is commemorated on the Tyne Cot Memorial (New Zealand Apse, Panel 6).
- Florence Maud Dean (1860–91) married Alfred William Luckes Cottrell (1853–1942) in 1878 at Napier. He was born at Greenwich, London and became an insurance canvasser. They lived at Wairarapa, New Zealand and she died at Melbourne South Homeopathic Hospital, Victoria, Australia. They had three children – Maud Florence Cottrell 1879, Ruby Pearl Cottrell 1883 and Elsie Dean Cottrell 1890. Alfred married Sarah Lees (1855–1926) on 2nd May 1892 at

Percy's cousin, Bernard Edwin Redstone (bottom right), is commemorated in the New Zealand Apse of the Tyne Cot Memorial, Belgium.

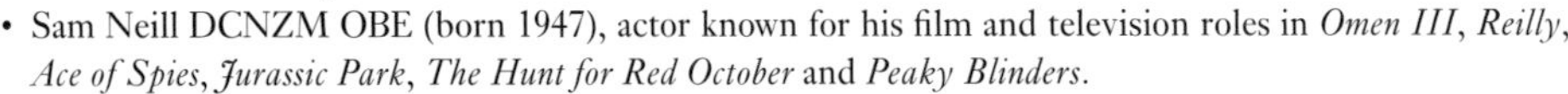

The Hunter Building, the original part of Victoria University College, was built in 1904–05 and was expanded later. On the dissolution of the University of New Zealand in 1961, Victoria became Victoria University of Wellington. The original campus was in Kelburn with other campuses being added in Te Aro and Pipitea. Famous alumni include:

- Sir Michael Hardie Boys GNZM GCMG QSO KStJ PC (born 1931), New Zealand jurist and the country's 17th Governor-General 1996–2001.
- Sir John Ross Marshall GBE CH ED PC (1912–88), New Zealand National Party politician, Deputy Prime Minister for twelve years and the 28th Prime Minister in 1972.
- Sam Neill DCNZM OBE (born 1947), actor known for his film and television roles in *Omen III*, *Reilly, Ace of Spies*, *Jurassic Park*, *The Hunt for Red October* and *Peaky Blinders*.
- Sir Paul Alfred Reeves ONZ GCMG GCVO QSO KStJ (1932–2011), clergyman and civil servant, Archbishop and Primate of New Zealand 1980–85 and 15th Governor-General 1985–90.
- Frances Rosemary Walsh, Lady Jackson MNZM (born 1959), screenwriter, film producer and lyricist. She is the long-time partner of filmmaker Peter Jackson and has worked on all of his productions since 1989, including *The Lord of the Rings*. She won three Academy Awards in 2003 for Best Picture, Best Adapted Screenplay and Best Original Song.

198 Park Street, Fitzroy, Victoria. She was born in Staffordshire, England. Alfred became a private detective and Sarah was a nurse.

- Elizabeth 'Lizzy' Laura Dean (born 1863 at Auckland, New Zealand).
- Mary Ann Dean (born 1868 at Tahiti, French Polynesia).
- Julia Eleanor Dean (1871–21st March 1924) was born in Tahiti. She married Stephen Tilly (1862–1927) in 1888 in New Zealand. He was born at Islington, London. They had two children – Horace Percy Stephen Tilly 1890 and Melva Grace Tilly 1892. The marriage ended in divorce. Stephen married Maud Haggerty (1879–1964) in 1916 and they had three children – Doris Amelia Tilly 1903, Harold Leonard Tilly 1904 and Cyril Ridgeway Tilly 1906. Julia married Christopher Frederick Naden (29th August 1867–19th November 1955) in 1900. He was born at Slinfold, Sussex. They had six sons – William Morton Naden 1901, Joseph Morton Naden 1902, Cyril Phillip George Naden 1904, Laurence Christopher Naden 1906 and twins Thomas James Naden and Claude Harold Naden 1907. After Stephen died, Maud married Thomas William Allen in 1930.
- John Edwin Dean (1875–8th November 1941) died at Moonee Ponds, Victoria.

Percy was educated at:

- Napier Boys High School, where he was a Dux student in 1910 and won an essay competition in New Zealand on *Why Britain must command the sea* in 1911. He was awarded the Board of Governors' Gold Medal for general excellence.

- Victoria University College, Wellington, where he undertook the first year of an arts course, then moved to Sydney, New South Wales with his father late in 1911.
- Sydney University, New South Wales, Australia 1913–15, where he studied law, completing his studies and graduating after the Great War (LL.B 1921).

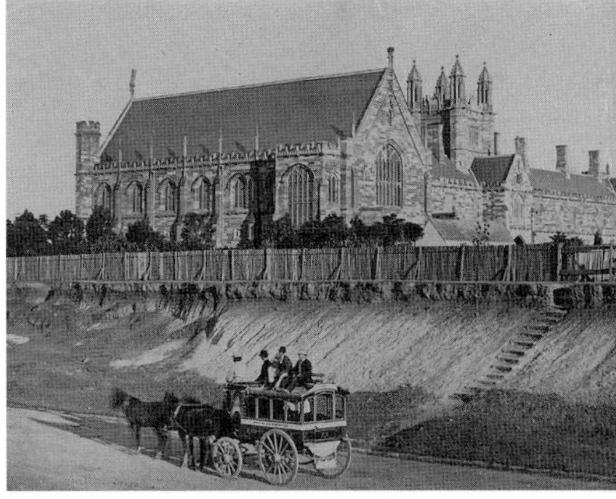

Sydney University grew from a plan in 1848 to expand Sydney College. It was established on 24th September 1850 and received its Royal Charter on 27th February 1858. By 1859 it had moved to its current site in Camperdown. Famous alumni include:

- Two Governor-Generals – Sir John Kerr (1974–77) and Sir William Deane (1996–2001).
- Seven Prime Ministers including Gough Whitlam 1972–75, John Howard 1996–2007, Tony Abbott 2013–15 and Malcolm Turnbull 2015–18.
- Germaine Greer (born 1939), writer and feminist.
- Dame Joan Sutherland (1926–2010), opera singer.
- Roden Cutler VC (1916–2002).

While studying, Percy also worked in the office of the Orient Steamship Co in 1911. He then worked for the Teachers' College, Blackfriars, Sydney before joining the administrative staff of the University of Sydney in 1912. Percy also served for five years with the Wellington Infantry (Militia) in New Zealand, reaching the rank of colour sergeant, including two months with F Battery.

Percy enlisted in the Australian Imperial Force (576) on 10th May 1915 and was posted to Liverpool, New South Wales. His date of birth was recorded as 9th September 1891. He was described as 5′ 7½″ tall, weighing 136 lbs, with dark complexion, blue eyes, black hair and his religious denomination was Church of England. Percy passed NCOs Depot School and No.1 Officers' School and was attached to C Company, 30th Battalion on 1st August 1915 as a platoon sergeant. He transferred to 7th Reinforcements, 19th Battalion on 7th September. He was commissioned on 24th September and embarked at Sydney on HMAT A29 *Suevic* on 23rd December, disembarking at Plymouth, Devon. He was posted to the Administrative Headquarters in London until embarking at Southampton, Hampshire for Le Havre, France on 7th November 1916. He reported to the Reinforcement Camp at Étaples on 9th November, joined 5th Training Battalion on 12th November and 19th Battalion on 14th November. On the same day he was in action at Gird Trenches, near Flers on the Somme front and received a gunshot wound to the thigh. He was admitted to No.36 Casualty Clearing Station at Heilly, near Méricourt-l'Abbé, next day and was moved by ambulance train on 16th November to 2nd Red Cross Hospital, Rouen on 16th November. He embarked on HMHS *St George* at Rouen for England on 20th November and was transferred to 3rd London General Hospital next day.

SS *Suevic* (12,531 tons) was built for the White Star Line for the Liverpool–Cape Town–Sydney route. She was launched on 8th December 1900 and her maiden voyage commenced on 23rd March 1901. She transported troops during the Second Boer War. In 1903 Charles Lightoller served aboard her for one trip, met his future wife during the voyage and married her in Sydney. Lightoller was second officer aboard RMS *Titanic* when she sank in 1912. On 17th March 1907 *Suevic* was inbound to Liverpool in thick fog when she ran aground at full speed about 400m off the Lizard, Cornwall. All aboard were saved and the rescue was the largest ever by the RNLI. Although the bow was badly damaged, the rest of the ship was not. Over three days the cargo was unloaded to lighten her, with the intention of refloating the ship. This failed and storms pushed *Suevic* further onto the rocks. The bow could not be saved but carefully placed explosive charges separated the damaged section from the undamaged stern and on 4th April the aft half floated free. *Suevic* steamed under her own power in reverse to Southampton. The bow broke up on the rocks. A new 212' bow section was built by Harland & Wolff in Belfast. When it was launched in October 1907 *Suevic* was said to be the longest ship in the world, with her bow in Belfast and her stern in Southampton. The new bow was towed to Southampton and was joined to the rest of the ship. On 14th January 1908, *Suevic* returned to service. In March 1915 she carried troops to Mudros for the Gallipoli campaign. For the rest of the war she operated under the Liner Requisition Scheme, as HMAT A29, as well as continuing her commercial route to Australia. In 1928 she was sold, renamed *Skytteren* and converted to a whaling factory ship. When Germany invaded Norway in April 1940, *Skytteren* was interned in neutral Gothenburg, Sweden, with other Norwegian ships. On 1st April 1942 ten Norwegian ships there attempted to escape. Sweden would not allow them to use their neutral waters and Swedish ships steered them towards waiting German warships. Only two made it through to the British, six were sunk or scuttled by their crew, including *Skytteren*, and two returned to Gothenburg. *Skytteren*'s crew was taken prisoner.

3rd London General Hospital started life in 1859 as the Victoria Patriotic Asylum for orphan daughters of soldiers, sailors and marines. It was renamed the Royal Patriotic School and in 1914 became a Territorial Force hospital with the staff being provided by the Middlesex, St Mary's and University College Hospitals. It originally only had 200 beds, but was eventually expanded to almost 2,000. A temporary railway enabled wounded to be brought from the south coast ports. The Hospital had its own newspaper, *The Gazette*, run by RAMC orderlies drawn from the Chelsea Arts Club. It closed in August 1920, having treated almost 63,000 patients. In recent times the Royal Victoria Patriotic Building was converted into apartments, studios, workshops, a drama school and a restaurant.

No.3 Australian Casualty Clearing Station formed on 17th March 1916 and sailed from Port Melbourne on 20th May. It landed at Le Havre on 26th September and in early October relieved the British No.11 Casualty Clearing Station at Gezaincourt in the Somme valley. In February 1917 it moved to Dernancourt near Albert and in April to Grévilliers near Bapaume. In July it moved to Brandhoek near Ypres and next month to Nine Elms at Poperinghe, where it was when Percy passed through it in October. In April 1918 it moved back to Esquelbecq during the German spring offensive, where it remained until September. A series of quick moves forward followed to Bandaghem, Dadizeele and Oudenarde, where it was when the war ended. On 21st December it took over from No.1 Canadian Casualty Clearing Station at Euskirchen, where it remained until late April 1919 and then disbanded.

Digswell House was built c.1805–07 for the Honourable Edward Spencer Cowper. A manor house existed nearby from the early 15th century and Capability Brown created some of the landscape work 1771–73. During the Great War the house was used by 5th Australian Auxiliary Hospital, staffed by the Red Cross. Some wounded Belgian and British were also treated there. The house was a conference centre 1928–39 and guests included Mahatma Gandhi, George Bernard Shaw and Hugh Gaitskell. After the Second World War it became a boarding house and artists' retreat until 1985, when it was sold and converted into private dwellings.

Percy was promoted lieutenant on 18th December 1916. A medical board at 3rd London General Hospital on 3rd January 1917 found him unfit for General Service for three weeks. He transferred to 5th Australian Auxiliary Hospital, Digswell House, Welwyn on 6th January. A medical board at the Australian Military Offices, London on 29th January found him unfit for General Service for seven days. He was discharged to No.1 Command Depot, Perham Down, Wiltshire next day and was posted to the Infantry Draft Depot there as an instructor on 5th February. He was held on the Supernumerary List from 14th February. On 5th July he embarked at Southampton for France from Tidworth and joined 2nd Australian Division Base Depot at Le Havre next day. He departed on 12th July and was restored to the establishment of his unit from the Supernumerary List on 13th July.

Percy was wounded during the Third Battle of Ypres, with a crushed/bruised ankle on 10th October 1917. He was treated at No.3 Australian Casualty Clearing

The YMCA at Greenhill House used by Australian troops while training at Sutton Veny.

Headquarters of the Overseas Training Brigade at Longbridge Deverill.

Station and 7th Stationary Hospital at Boulogne, before embarking on HMHS *Jan Breydel* for England on 13th October and arrived at 3rd London General Hospital, Wandsworth later that day. A medical board at the Australian Military Offices, London on 25th October found him unfit for General Service for three weeks. He was discharged to No.1 Command Depot, Sutton Veny, Wiltshire on 8th November. A medical board at Bhurtpore Barracks,

Percy with a friend following his investiture at Buckingham Palace on 22nd June 1918.

SS *Runic* (12,490 tons) was constructed by Harland & Wolff for the White Star Line in Belfast and launched on 25th October 1900. Her maiden voyage to Cape Town commenced on 3rd January 1901. She had an eventful life. On 25th November 1901 she towed the cripped Union Castle liner *Dunattor Castle* into Dakar. She was leased as a troopship (HMAT A54 *Runic*) during the Great War until 27th November 1917, when she operated under the Liner Requisition Scheme for the rest of the conflict. On 3rd November 1920 she collided with HMS *London* at Gourock on the Clyde. She was sold to Christian Salveson Whaling Co in 1930 and converted to a whaling factory ship, renamed *New Sevilla*. She was torpedoed and sunk on 20th September 1940 off Islay, Scotland by U-*138* with the loss of two crewmen.

Tidworth on 12th November found him fit for General Service and he transferred to the Overseas Training Brigade, Longbridge Deverill near Sutton Veny on 16th November.

On 3rd December 1917 Percy embarked at Southampton for France. He joined 2nd Australian Division Base Depot at Le Havre on 5th December, 1st Australian Reinforcement Company on 9th December and rejoined his unit on 11th December. He attended Second Army Central School 28th December 1917–2nd February 1918. **Awarded the VC for his actions at Hangard Wood, France on 7th April 1918, LG 7th June 1918.**

Percy was appointed temporary captain while commanding a company on 16th May 1918 and was promoted captain on 10th June. The VC was presented by the King in the quadrangle at Buckingham Palace on 22nd June 1918. He was granted leave in England 3rd–27th July and remained there from 28th July. He sailed for Australia aboard HMAT A54 *Runic* on 23rd September. He was granted leave on 26th November and afterwards joined 2nd Military District, from where his appointment with the AIF was terminated on 31st January 1919.

In the 1850s there were four separate groups of Presbyterians in New South Wales. By 1865 there was increasing pressure for unification, which resulted in the formation of the Presbyterian Church of New South Wales. The Iron Church (a prefabricated structure) in Macquarie Street became St Stephen's but, by 1872, was too small for the growing congregation. It merged with the Phillip Street congregation, also called St Stephen's (seen here), which was built in the 1870s. This church was demolished in the early 1930s to make way for the extension of Martin Place and a new St Stephen's opened in 1935 on Macquarie Street.

Percy was an associate to Justice of the Supreme Court of New South Wales Sir Charles Wade, who was previously Premier of New South Wales, whilst completing his law degree. He was admitted to the Bar on 8th June 1921. After a period of private practice, he became Crown Prosecutor of the South-Western Circuit in 1922. On 1st May 1939 he was appointed District Court Judge and Chairman of Quarter Sessions in the Northern District of New South Wales, a position he held until retirement in 1955.

Percy married Minnie 'Molly' Mary née Burnett (1880–28th August 1973) on 15th April 1922 at St Stephen's Presbyterian Church, Sydney, New South Wales. She was born at Cheddar, Somerset. They lived at Vaucluse, Sydney. Minnie had married a man named Gordon, who was a railway construction engineer, and they spent eight years in Africa. They had two sons who stayed with their natural father when the marriage failed. Percy and Minnie had no children and moved to England after he retired. They lived at 20 Trowlock Avenue, Teddington, London. She died at 1 Barons Court, Broom Road, Teddington, leaving effects valued at £15,645.

Minnie's father, George Burnett (born 23rd August 1853), was born at Warrington, Lancashire. He married Sarah Betty late Cox née Green (1843–1923) in 1876 at Shepton Mallet, Somerset. She was born at Stoke St Michael, Somerset. Sarah had married William Cox (died 1869) in 1865 at Bath, Somerset and had three children – William Cox 1865, Martha Cox 1868 and Janet Harriet G Cox 1869. In 1871 Sarah and her children were living at Withybrook, Stoke Lane, Stoke St Michael, Somerset. George was a teacher in an elementary school in 1891 and they were living at Bullmire Street, Cheddar, Somerset. In addition to Minnie, George and Sarah had two other children:

- Emily Martha 'Poppy' Burnett (10th January 1877–30th August 1974) married Edwin Richard Brown (1875–13th August 1947) in 1903 at Axbridge. She was living as head of household at 25 Victoria Road, Salisbury, Wiltshire in 1911. They had three children – Roger Burnett Brown 1906, Barbara Mary Brown 1908 and Anthony R Brown 1912.
- George Herbert Burnett (2nd November 1882–1st December 1973) married Dorothy Franklin in 1917 at Lambeth, London. He was living at Flat 2, 36 Whickham Avenue, Bexhill-on-Sea, Sussex at the time of his death. They had two children – George Franklin Burnett 1921 and Mary Sally Burnett 1924.

By 1911 George Burnett was living with his daughter, Emily Brown, at Salisbury, Wiltshire. Sarah was living alone at North Street, Cheddar in 1911.

Percy and six fellow VCs attended the first Australian Imperial Force Reunion Dinner at Sydney Town Hall on 8th August 1928 to celebrate the 10th anniversary of the commencement of 'The Big Push'. He and thirteen other VCs were entertained at a luncheon at Government House in November 1929 by the Governor of New South Wales, Sir Dudley de Chair. Within the Reserve of Officers, Percy transferred as a captain to the Australian Legal Department

Cheddar, which gives its name to Cheddar cheese, is on the southern edge of the Mendip Hills. On its northern edge is Cheddar Gorge, the largest in the United Kingdom, which contains several show caves. It has been inhabited since Neolithic times and the oldest complete skeleton found in the country, c.9,000 years old, was discovered there in 1903.

Sir Dudley Rawson Stratford de Chair KCB KCMG MVO (1864–1958) outside Government House in 1925. He was born in Quebec, Canada and the family returned to England in 1870. In 1878 he joined the Royal Navy and was held captive by Arabi Pasha for six weeks in 1882. In 1915–16 as a rear admiral he commanded the 10th Cruiser Squadron in the North Sea blockade of Germany. He was promoted to vice admiral to command 3rd Battle Squadron in 1917 but was relieved and placed on half pay when he refused a post on the Board of Admiralty and for criticising the treatment of Lord Jellicoe. In July 1918 he took command of Coastguard and Reserves and was President of the Inter-Allied Commission on enemy warships 1921–23 as an admiral. In October 1923 he was appointed Governor of New South Wales, arriving in Sydney with his wife on 28th February 1924. He retired on 8th April 1930 to London. His autobiography, *The Sea is Strong*, was published posthumously in 1961.

Government House, overlooking Sydney Harbour, was constructed between 1837 and 1843. It was temporarily the residence of the Governor-General of Australia 1901–14, until that office moved to Admiralty House, and it reverted to the residence of the Governor of New South Wales. From 1996 the Governor lived and worked elsewhere nearby, as the result of a political decision by the Premier of New South Wales, However, it was realised that it was more expensive than using Government House and the Governor returned there in 2011. On 13th December that year the building, its grounds and furnishings were listed on the New South Wales State Heritage Register.

on 1st September 1938. He was appointed a legal staff officer in HQ 2nd Division but relinquished the appointment in May 1939 when he became District Court Judge and Chairman of Quarter Sessions on the Northern Circuit, New South Wales. Percy also served as President of the Vaucluse Returned Services League Branch. He attended the funeral of Thomas Bede Kenny VC at Mary Immaculate Church, Waverley, New South Wales on 17th April 1953 with fellow VCs George Cartwright, Snowy Howell and John Jackson. He attended the VC Centenary Celebrations at Hyde Park, London on 26th June 1956, travelling on SS *Orcades* with other Australian VCs. He also attended the first three VC & GC Association Reunions at the Café Royal, London on 24th July 1958, 7th July 1960 and 18th July 1962.

Percy Storkey died of bronchial pneumonia and arteriosclerosis at his home at 20 Trowlock Avenue, Teddington, Middlesex on 3rd October 1969. He was cremated at the South-West Middlesex Crematorium, Hounslow Road, Hanworth, London on 9th October and his ashes were scattered at Lawn 3–B3. He is recorded in the Book of Remembrance and there is also a memorial plaque at the Crematorium. Percy is commemorated in a number of other places:

- New Zealand
    - Storkey Barracks, Linton Military Camp, near Palmerston North, New Zealand.

- ◦ Storkey Street, Marewa, Napier, New Zealand.
- ◦ Napier High School:
  - ❑ Storkey VC Prize – awarded annually to a Year 13 student for excellence in mathematics and science.
  - ❑ Storkey Award for Citizenship – awarded annually to one student in each of Years 9, 10, 11, 12 and 13.
  - ❑ Storkey VC Medallion – presented annually as a special award to five senior students.

South-West Middlesex Crematorium, Hounslow Road, Hanworth, London, where Percy was cremated and his ashes were scattered.

The Australian VC plaque at the Australian War Memorial, unveiled at Lancaster House, London on 26th June 2014.

- ◦ Named on two of eleven plaques honouring 175 men from overseas awarded the VC for the Great War. The plaques were unveiled by the Senior Minister of State at the Foreign & Commonwealth Office and Minister for Faith and Communities, Baroness Warsi, at a reception at Lancaster House, London on 26th June 2014 attended by The Duke of Kent and relatives of the VC recipients. The Australian plaque is at the Australian War Memorial. The New Zealand plaque is mounted on a wall between the Parliament and the Cenotaph in Wellington.

- Australian Capital Territory
  - ◦ Storkey Place, Canberra, gazetted on 8 February 1978.
  - ◦ Display in the Hall of Valour, Australian War Memorial, Canberra, including a replica VC and a portrait by Max Meldrum.
  - ◦ Australian Victoria Cross Recipients plaque on the Victoria Cross Memorial, Campbell, Canberra, dedicated on 24th July 2000.
- New South Wales
  - ◦ New South Wales Garden of Remembrance, Rookwood Cemetery and Necropolis, Hawthorne Avenue, Rookwood on Memorial Wall 26 Panel A.
  - ◦ Victoria Cross Memorial, Queen Victoria Building, George Street, Sydney dedicated on 23rd February 1992 to commemorate the visit of Queen Elizabeth II and Prince Phillip on the occasion of the Sesquicentenary of the

The National Army Museum, State Highway One, Waiouru, New Zealand, where Percy's VC is on long-loan.

The 145 overseas centenary commemorative VC paving stones at the National Memorial Arboretum, Alrewas, Staffordshire dedicated on 5th March 2015 (Memorials to Valour).

City of Sydney. Sir Roden Cutler VC, Edward Kenna VC and Keith Payne VC were in attendance.

- ° Victoria Cross Recipients Wall, North Bondi War Memorial donated to the community of Waverley on 27th November 2011 by The Returned & Services League of Australia.

- Communities and Local Government commemorative paving stones for the 145 VCs born in Australia, Belgium, Canada, China, Denmark, Egypt, France, Germany, India, Iraq, Japan, Nepal, Netherlands, Newfoundland, New Zealand, Pakistan, South Africa, Sri Lanka, Ukraine and United States of America were unveiled at the National Memorial Arboretum, Alrewas, Staffordshire by Prime Minister David Cameron MP and Sergeant Johnson Beharry VC on 5th March 2015.

The Queen Elizabeth II Coronation Medal 1953 was awarded immediately after the coronation on 2nd June 1953 as a personal souvenir from the Queen to members of the Royal Family, selected officers of state, members of the Royal Household, government and local government officials, mayors, public servants, members of the armed forces, and police in Britain, the colonies and Dominions. It was also awarded to members of the Mount Everest expedition, two of whom reached the summit for the first time four days before the coronation. A total of 129,051 medals were awarded, including 11,561 to Australians.

In addition to the VC he was awarded the British War Medal 1914–20, Victory Medal 1914–19, George VI Coronation Medal 1937 and Elizabeth II Coronation Medal 1953. He left his medals to Napier Boys High. In 1983 the Parents' League of the school decided to sell the VC to establish a scholarship fund in his memory, but the public was outraged and the sale did not proceed. The medals are on long-term loan to the National Army Museum, State Highway One, Waiouru, New Zealand and a replica VC is on display in the school's memorial library.

CAPTAIN ALFRED MAURICE TOYE
2nd Battalion, The Duke of Cambridge's Own (Middlesex Regiment)

Alfred Maurice Toye, known as Maurice, was born on 15th April 1897 at D Terrace, Stanhope Lines, Aldershot, Hampshire. His father, James Robert Toye (9th November 1854–27th June 1943), was born at City Road, Shoreditch, London. He was a clerk when he enlisted in 1/25th Regiment of Foot, 6th Brigade (429) at Westminster, London on 12th February 1875, described as 5′ 5¼″ tall, with fresh complexion, grey eyes, brown hair and his religious denomination was Church of England. James was promoted corporal 12th October 1875, sergeant 6th September 1878 and colour sergeant 4th October 1881. He gained the Second Class Certificate of Education on 8th May 1875 and First Class on 5th October 1888. He was granted Good Conduct Pay at 1d per day on 13th February 1877 and at 3d per day on 13th February 1887. James travelled to the East Indies aboard HMS *Malabar* 12th October–15th November 1875 and served at Deolali, Fyzabad, Naini Tal and Peshawar. He took part in the Afghanistan Campaign 1878–80 (Afghanistan Medal 1878–80). Having returned to Britain on 20th March 1880, he served at the New Infantry Barracks, Fulford Road, York from 19th May, which was then the Depot of the 25th Regiment, and extended his service to complete twelve years on 21st February 1881. He was posted to Berwick-upon-Tweed, Northumberland on 29th July 1881, when the Depot moved there and the Regiment became the King's Own Scottish Borderers. He returned to York on 30th July 1885 and became a sergeant Instructor of Musketry. On 1st April 1886 he transferred to the Corps of Military Staff Clerks on appointment to quartermaster sergeant and was granted increased pay of 6d per day on 1st April 1889. He was posted to Portsmouth, Hampshire on 27th April 1892, transferred to the Army Service Corps on 1st April 1893 and re-engaged for twenty-one years' service on 13th April 1893. He was permitted to serve beyond twenty-one years on 14th August 1895 and

The infantry barracks at Fulford were built in 1877–78 initially as Depots of the 14th and 25th (Sussex) Regiments. The latter became the King's Own Scottish Borderers and moved to Berwick in 1881. The barracks were named Imphal in 1950, one of the West Yorkshire Regiment's Second World War battle honours. In 1958 HQ Northern Command was established there and it was also the home of the Prince of Wales's Own Regiment of Yorkshire (amalgamation of West and East Yorkshire Regiments). Since then the HQs of North East District, 2nd Infantry Division, 6th Division, 15th Infantry Brigade, 4th Infantry Brigade and 1st (UK) Division have been based there at various times. The barracks are scheduled to close in 2031.

The Stanhope Lines Post Office, close to where Maurice Toye was born.

HMS *Malabar*, one of five Euphrates Class troopships, was launched in 1866, to carry up to 1,200 persons between Britain and India. She became the base ship in Bermuda in 1897, was renamed HMS *Terror* in 1905 and was sold in 1918. In 1873 her single-expansion steam engine was replaced with a two-cylinder compound-expansion engine.

travelled to the Gold Coast, Africa aboard SS *Bathurst*, departing on 23rd November 1895, where he took part in the Ashanti Expedition (Ashanti Star 1895–96). He returned to Britain aboard the *Cape Coast Castle* on 14th December 1896 and was posted to Aldershot, Hampshire. James was discharged at his own request after three months' notice on 18th February 1898, having been awarded the Long Service & Good Conduct Medal. He was appointed Chief Clerk of the General Registry, Aldershot Command.

James married Mary Spelling (1861–7th August 1890) on 24th March 1883 at Stepney Green, London. Mary was living with her father, four brothers and sister at 1 Peel Grove, Bethnal Green, London in 1871 and with her mother and two brothers at 30 Cambridge Road, Bethnal Green in 1881. She died at York in 1890. James married Elizabeth Charlotte née Dodds (1862–3rd November 1947), born at Newcastle upon Tyne, Northumberland, on 22nd August 1891 at St Saviourgate, York. Elizabeth was a pupil at the Convent of Notre Dame, Mount Pleasant, Liverpool, Lancashire with her sister, Frances, in 1881. They were living

James and Elizabeth Toye.

Alfred's mother, Elizabeth, and her sister, Frances, were pupils at Notre Dame, Mount Pleasant, Liverpool in 1881. The Sisters of Notre Dame de Namur was founded in 1805 in France and Belgium for the education of the poor and to train nuns to teach in schools. The Sisters came to England in 1845, first to Penryn, Cornwall and to Clapham, London a few years later. Liverpool was one of the first communities outside Cornwall and London. In the 19th century it was common for young people to be apprenticed as pupil teachers and the Sisters began training laywomen at Mount Pleasant, Liverpool in 1855. From age thirteen girls were boarded, educated and prepared for the teaching profession there. They were apprenticed for five years and were on the staff of schools during the day and in the evenings were taught by the Sisters. In 1980 the college joined two others in an ecumenical federation that became Liverpool Hope University.

at 13 St Michael's Road, Aldershot in 1901 and at Inglesant, 50 St George's Road, Aldershot by 1911. James was a Christian Scientist and ran the 2nd Aldershot Troop, Boy Scouts 1909–13 located in Wellington Lines, Aldershot. He died in 1943 at his home at Lynwood, Heath End, Farnham, Surrey, leaving effects valued at £653/5/5. Elizabeth died there in 1947, leaving effects valued at £144/18/5. Maurice had four siblings from his father's two marriages:

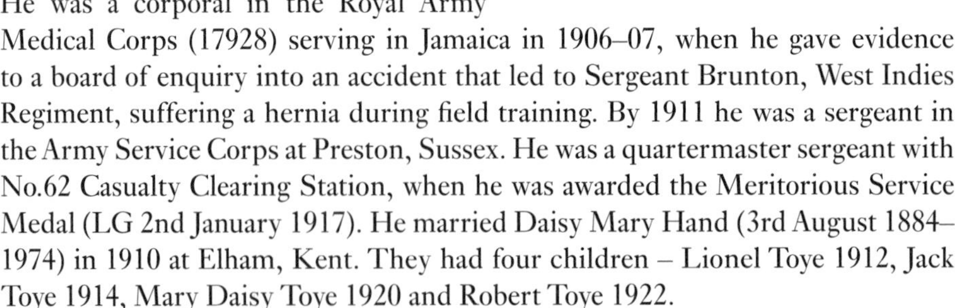

- George Herbert Toye (1884–85).
- William Spelling Toye (11th February 1885–1964) was a pupil teacher in 1901. He was a corporal in the Royal Army Medical Corps (17928) serving in Jamaica in 1906–07, when he gave evidence to a board of enquiry into an accident that led to Sergeant Brunton, West Indies Regiment, suffering a hernia during field training. By 1911 he was a sergeant in the Army Service Corps at Preston, Sussex. He was a quartermaster sergeant with No.62 Casualty Clearing Station, when he was awarded the Meritorious Service Medal (LG 2nd January 1917). He married Daisy Mary Hand (3rd August 1884–1974) in 1910 at Elham, Kent. They had four children – Lionel Toye 1912, Jack Toye 1914, Mary Daisy Toye 1920 and Robert Toye 1922.
- Ethel Dora Toye (20th June 1892–19th October 1982) married John Norman Chandler (25th October 1889–11th May 1959), a nurseryman and florist, on 3rd January 1918 at St John the Evangelist, Hale, Surrey. John was living at The Laurels, Heath End, Farnham when he attested on 25th January 1916 at Stoughton Barracks, Guildford, Surrey (42534) and transferred to the Reserve next day. He was 5′ 6½″ tall. He enlisted in 6th Royal Fusiliers on 20th July 1916 and went to

France on 23rd November. On 8th December he transferred to 2nd Battalion. John was wounded in the forehead in an accident about 20th February 1917 and was admitted to No.13 Stationary Hospital, Boulogne around 29th February. He was transferred to No.1 Convalescent Camp, Boulogne around 5th March. A medical board at 39th Infantry Base Depot in May/June 1917 classified him B II and on 19th August he returned to Britain as part of an agricultural draft. He reported to Hounslow Regimental Depot, Royal Fusiliers and transferred to 425th Agricultural Company at Stoughton Barracks on 29th August (435121). John then worked for his father at Heatherfield Nursery, Heath End, Farnham, Surrey and was demobilised on 13th February 1919 at No.2 Dispersal Unit, Crystal Palace, London. He was living at 148 Farnborough Road, Heath End, Farnham at the time of his death, leaving effects valued at £1,235/18/11 to his widow. She died at Sunways Nursing Home, Manor Road, Aldershot, leaving effects valued at £45,921. Ethel and John had three sons – Norman Alan Chandler 1919, Ronald John Chandler 1922 and Kenneth J Chandler 1927.

- Henry Julian Toye (26th June 1899–1926) was an engineer when he enlisted in the RAF on 8th May 1918 (176137). He was described as 5′ 5″ tall with dark brown hair, hazel eyes, fresh complexion and his religious denomination was Christian Scientist. He was posted to the Cadet Distribution Depot at Hampstead, the Cadet Wing at Denham in Buckinghamshire, No.2 School of Aeronautics at Oxford on 12th July, the Armament School on 31st August and Hill Cadet Wing, where he was promoted sergeant on 28th September. He qualified as a pilot in an Avro Biplane at the Military School, Baldonnel Aerodrome, Co Dublin, Ireland on 7th January 1919 (Certificate 6628). Posted to 141 Squadron on 11th December 1919 and later to 100 Squadron, both at Baldonnel. He re-enlisted on 22nd March 1920 (340961) and was deemed to have been discharged on 30th April 1920. Henry married Florence J Viner (1900–75) in 1918 at Uxbridge. There were no children. She was living at 13 Cutler Street, Aldershot after they married. Florence married Siddle Nicholson (1899–1975) in 1951 at Aldershot. Siddle served during the Great War as a private in the Tank Corps (315596). They were living at 13 Arthur Street, Aldershot at the time of his death in January 1975, leaving effects valued at £2,672. Florence died there in December 1975, leaving effects valued at £5,478.

Three Colt Street, Bethnal Green, close to where Alfred's paternal grandfather, Alfred Toye, was born in 1817.

Maurice's paternal grandfather, Alfred Toye (24th April 1817–20th November

1896), a silk weaver, was born at Three Colt Corner, Bethnal Green, London. He married Jane née Rozee (8th November 1822–28th May 1903), born at Bethnal Green, in 1841 at Stepney, London. Her name was recorded as Royce. They were living at Luke Street, Stepney in 1841, at King Edward Yard in 1844 and at 17 Dunnings Alley in 1849. Jane was living with her daughter, Jane Hoskins, in 1901. In addition to James they had seven other children:

- Eliza Toye (23rd May 1841–22nd January 1920) married Alfred Cox (1841–22nd October 1920), a cork cutter, on 25th December 1863 at Tower Hamlets, London. They migrated to Canada before 1871 and settled at Hamilton City, Ontario. They both died at Wentworth, Ontario. They had four children – Lydia Jane Cox 1871, Florence Clara Cox 1874, Bertha Eliza Cox 1882 and Algar Roland Cox 1884.
- Alfred Toye (born and died 1843).
- Jane Toye (born 8th July 1844) is understood to have died in infancy although no record of her death has been found. She does not appear with the family in the 1851 Census and another Jane was born into the family in 1856.
- John Samuel Toye (5th December 1846–28th January 1934), a coal agent, married Adelaide Bartlett (1853–5th April 1949) in 1875. They were living at 156 Stepney Green, Mile End Old Town by 1881. By 1891 he was a missionary preacher and a Unitarian Minister by 1901. They had moved to 23 Church Crescent, South Hackney by 1911. John was living at 6 Primrose Avenue, Barley Lane, Chadwell Heath, Essex at the time of his death, leaving effects valued at £1,828/16/1. Adelaide was living at 15 Castleton Road, Goodmayes, Essex at the time of her death, leaving effects valued at £434/19/3 to her daughter, Annie Marguerite Newton. They had six children, including Eleanor Jane Toye 1876, Maud Toye 1878, Roland John Toye 1881, Annie Marguerite Toye 1883 and Henry Estlin Toye 1885.
- Alfred Thomas Rozee Toye (17th March 1849–1889) married Mary Ann Theresa Ferguson (1850–93) on 17th May 1869 at St Mary's, Spitalfields, London. Mary was a domestic servant living at Shoreditch Union Workhouse on Kingsland Road in 1871 after giving birth to her second son. Alfred and Mary had two sons – Alfred Charles Toye (born and died 1870) and Alfred Charles Toye (28th March 1871–1956). Alfred married Hannah Jane Lashbrook Barber née Hawkins (1842–91) on 26th July 1893 at All Hallows, Bromley-by-Bow, London. His name was registered as Alfred Rosee Toye. She was born at Bristol, Gloucestershire and had married James Barber (died 1889) in 1860 at St George in the East, London. Mary married John Bannister on 2nd August 1875 at St Thomas, Bethnal Green and was recorded on the marriage certificate as a widow, aged 23, living at 4 Luke Street, Mile End. John Bannister was living at 7 Friars Bank, Mile End. In 1891 they were living at 333 Cable Street, St George in the East and he was a dock labourer and she was a stay maker. Mary and John had four children – Albert Bannister 1874, Grace Theresa Bannister 1880, Theresa 'Freisa' Bannister 1886 and Maud Bannister 1891.

- Walter Charles Toye (1851–16th January 1925) married Hannah Burge (1849–20th October 1929) in 1878 at Edmonton, Middlesex. They had migrated to Hamilton, Ontario by 1891, where he was a drug clerk. They both died at Wentworth, Ontario. They had ten children – Walter Thomas Toye 1879, James Robert Toye 1880, Hannah Burge Toye 1882, Henry John Toye 1884, Mary Lilian Toye 1885, Charles W Toye 1887, Arnold Richard Toye 1888, Gilbert Ernest Toye 1890, Annie Beatrice Irene Toye 1893 and Thomas Burge Toye.
- Jane Toye (born 1856) was a visitor at the home of Elizabeth Spelling in 1881. She married Roland St George Hoskins (1856–6th February 1905) in 1882 at Mile End. He was a wharf clerk in 1901 and they were living at 64 Latimer Road, West Ham, London. He died there leaving effects valued at £133/15/7. They had three children – twins Constance Grace and Edwin Darlison Hoskins 1886 and Olive Dora Thurston Hoskins 1896.

His maternal grandfather, George Dodds (August 1829–19th December 1897), married Elizabeth Charlotte née Cardwell (c.1833–1915), on 1st February 1855 at Brunswick Place Chapel, Newcastle upon Tyne. She was living there at Rye Hill and he at Liverpool Street. In 1861 he was a coach spring maker and they were living at 10 Chapel Lane, Westgate St John, Northumberland. By 1871 he was a wagon inspector and they were living at 8 Oxford Street, Micklegate, York. In 1911 Elizabeth was living with her daughter, Georgina, at 46 Moorland Road, Scarborough, Yorkshire. In addition to Elizabeth they had another eleven children including:

Brunswick Place Wesleyan Methodist Chapel, Newcastle upon Tyne, where Alfred's maternal grandparents married in 1855, opened in 1821. It replaced Orphan House in Northumberland Street, built in the early 1740s, which was only the second Methodist chapel built in England. However, Orphan House proved too small for the congregation and the first stone of the present chapel was laid on 5th May 1820. It has a capacity of 2,300 people. A major refurbishment was carried out in 1981.

- George William Dodds (1855–14th June 1933) was a coach body maker in 1871. He married Eleanor Braithwaite (1857–1943) in 1881 at York. They were living at 69 Thorpe Street, York in 1911 by when he was a timber clerk with a railway company. He was living at 14 Rosedale Avenue, Acomb, Yorkshire at the time of his death, leaving effects valued at £824/0/8. They had four children, including Alice Maud Dodds 1881, Arthur Basil Dodds 1882 and Sydney Herbert Dodds 1887.

- Margaret Ann Dodds (1857–30th November 1932) married Mathew Mayson (born c.1843), a master butcher, in 1882. He was born at Birtley, Co Durham. They were living at 3 Buslingthorpe Lane, Leeds, Yorkshire in 1891. She married Thomas Mountain (c.1853–7th June 1923), a railway ticket examiner, in 1899. They were living at 32 Scott Street, Scarcroft Road, York at the time of his death, leaving effects valued at £438/19/4. She died there leaving effects valued at £470/3/2.
- James Frederick Dodds (1859–31st October 1918) married Edith Hare (1868–31st May 1950) in 1889. In 1901 he was an engineer with the North Eastern Railway and they were living at 24 Wentworth Road, Micklegate, York. He was living there at the time of his death, leaving effects valued at £1,440/12/9 to his sons. She was living at 100 Stainburn Crescent, Harrogate Road, Leeds at the time of her death, leaving effects valued at £1,037/13/7 to her daughter, Mary. They had three children – Eric Dodds 1890, Harold Dodds 1892 and Mary Dodds 1905.
- Georgina Maria Dodds (1861–25th October 1938) was a spinster living at 59 Clarendon Road, Putney, London at the time of her death at St Stephen's Hospital, Fulham Road, London, leaving effects valued at £300/19/-.
- Mary Amelia Dodds (1866–1923), a dressmaker, married William Shepherd (born 1864) in 1887. She was head of household, living with her children at 19 North Eastern Terrace, Dringhouses, York in 1911. They had two children – Eleanor Shepherd 1888 and George William Shepherd 1891.
- Rosanna Matilda Dodds (1867–28th April 1956) married George Young (1860–3rd October 1933), a railway carriage builder, in 1888. They were living at 20 Beaconsfield Street, Acomb, Yorkshire in 1911. They were living at Penhale, 13 Mayfield Avenue, Burniston Road, Scarborough at the time of his death, leaving effects valued at £1,175/12/3. They had eight children, including Lilian Beatrice Young 1890, Charles Rowland Young 1891, Arthur Ernest Young 1895, Elsie Phoebe Young 1899, George Edwin Young 1901 and Eric Young 1905.
- Charles John Dodds (1869–1935).
- Alfred Edward Dodds (born and died 1871).

Maurice was educated at the Garrison School, Aldershot, Hampshire. He was a First Patrol Leader with 2nd Aldershot Scout Troop, which was run by his father, and became a King's Scout. He enlisted as a boy trumpeter in the Royal Engineers on 15th December 1911 (22355) and was posted to The Curragh, Co Kildare, Ireland in December 1912. He went to France on 3rd August 1915 and was promoted acting corporal in 1916. Towards the end of the year he applied for a commission and attended the Cadet School at Blendecques, near St Omer, France. He was commissioned into 2nd Middlesex on 15th February 1917. **Awarded the MC for his actions during the Third Battle of Ypres, when in charge of communications he went to a most forward position and carried out his duties under heavy and continuous fire of every kind. It was due to him that the situation was**

Maurice receives his VC from the King on Queen's Parade, Aldershot on 8th June 1918.

A Venture Scout unit was later named after Maurice in Aldershot.

The Curragh's history as a military assembly area goes back to before Elizabethan times. Training camps were set up there during the 19th century and the first wooden camp was built in 1855 during the Crimean War. Brick built structures started in 1879 with Beresford Barracks and six more barracks followed. The Home Rule Act of 1914 led to a number of officers threatening to resign in the Curragh Incident rather than enforcing Home Rule against the will of the Unionists. On 16th May 1922 the camp was handed over to the Irish Free State Army on the formation of the Irish Republic. Since then it has continued as a military camp, but has also been used as a detention centre on a number of occasions, including during the civil war, the Emergency 1939–46 and the 1950s. During the Second World War separate sections of the camp were occupied by Allied, Axis and IRA personnel. The Curragh is now the Defence Forces Training Centre.

cleared up and communications maintained, LG 26th September 1917, citation 9th January 1918. It is not clear in which action this took place. There appear to be two options – the attack northeast of Westhoek on 31st July or the attack on Westhoek Ridge, south of the railway and north of Westhoek, on 16th August.

Maurice was appointed acting captain 15th August 1917–26th September 1918 while in command of a company. **Awarded the VC for his actions at Éterpigny and other locations in France on 25th and 31st March and 24th April 1918, LG 8th May 1918.** Maurice is understood to be the only VC born and raised in Aldershot, Home of the British Army. He was evacuated to Britain on 24th April. The VC was presented by the King on Queen's Parade, Aldershot, Hampshire on 8th June 1918.

Maurice Toye married Flora Robertson (29th January 1896–16th January 1979), an Army schoolteacher, on 15th June 1918 at the Old Parish Church of St Michael the Archangel, Aldershot, Hampshire. She was born at Ahmednagar, India. The best man was Captain Evans MC, 2nd Middlesex and Flora was given away by her brother Gordon. They had two daughters:

Flora and Maurice on their wedding day.

St Michael's, Aldershot stands on land owned by Alfred the Great, who left it to the monks of Winchester Cathedral. The church was built between 1120 and 1150. By 1400 it was in a state of collapse and, despite repairs being ordered, the church was still in a poor condition eighty years later. In 1481 John Awbrey pledged £126 to restore it. Local legend has it that in 1678 Nell Gwyne stopped in the area, while travelling from Portsmouth to London, and gave birth to a stillborn child of Charles II. The child is reputed to have been buried under a tree in the churchyard. In the 1850s, when the Army came to Aldershot, St Michael's was expanded, a process that went on until 1912.

- Joan Flora Toye (26th August 1920–8th February 2017) born in Cologne, Germany, was a Registered Nurse at The Middlesex Hospital, London 1939–42 (No.118656), living at 519 Croydon Road, Beckenham, Kent. She married Frederick J Maher (1912–50) in 1943 at Salisbury, Wiltshire. Frederick was born at Naas, Ireland. He was living at 25 Barton Road, Dover, Kent at the time of his death there on 27th September 1950. They had two daughters – Penelope Maher 1944 and Melissa M Maher 1946.

The gateway to Ahmednagar Fort, India in 1882. Alfred's wife, Flora, was born in the town in 1896.

- Enid Audrey Toye (14th August 1925–10th August 2000) was also born at Cologne. She married James Craig Jenkins (11th November 1928–February 2003) on 21st June 1957 (possibly 1958) at Miami, Florida. He was born in Ohio, USA. They both died at Johnson City, Washington, Tennessee, USA. They had three sons – Darrell Lynn Jenkins, Todd Allan Jenkins and Kerry Scott Jenkins.

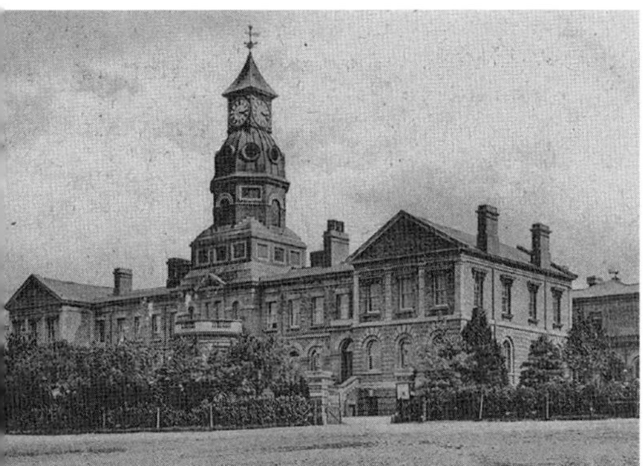

Cambridge Military Hospital, Aldershot, named after Prince George, Duke of Cambridge, opened on 18th July 1879. It was the first base hospital to receive casualties directly from the Western Front in the Great War. The first plastic surgery in the British Empire was performed there in 1915 by Captain (later Sir Harold) Gillies. After the Second World War civilians were also admitted to the hospital. It closed on 2nd February 1996.

Broad Street, Stirling, where Flora's father was born in 1860.

Flora's father, George Pringle Robertson (1st May 1860–5th February 1912), was born at 42 Broad Street, Stirling, Scotland, the son of James Dixon Robertson, a musician. George enlisted as a boy in 55th Brigade in Dublin, Ireland on 23rd June 1874 (1686), described as 4′ 11⅝″ tall, with fresh complexion, hazel eyes, brown hair and his religious denomination was Church of England. He joined at Fort George, Ardersier, Inverness, Scotland and gained the Second Class Certificate of Education on 17th July 1875. George was appointed private in 71st (Highland) Regiment of Foot (Light Infantry) (1st Highland Light Infantry in 1881) on 24th June 1877 and was posted to the Mediterranean on 1st October. He was promoted lance corporal 19th March 1879, corporal 10th August 1881, lance sergeant 8th January 1883, sergeant bugler 16th April 1883 and sergeant 17th

Flora's father, George Robertson, joined for duty at Fort George, Ardersier in 1874. The first Fort George, built in 1727 in Inverness, was blown up by the Jacobites in 1746. When the uprising had been put down, a new site was selected on a spit of land at Ardersier, about eighteen kilometres northeast of Inverness, which dominated the sea approach to the town. Work began in 1748 and by 1757 the main defences were in place, although it took until 1769 to complete construction. The Fort became the Depot of the Seaforth Highlanders following the Childers Reforms in 1881. In 1961 the Seaforths amalgamated with the Queen's Own Cameron Highlanders to form the Queen's Own Highlanders, with its Depot at Fort George. In 2007 the Fort became the home of 3rd Battalion, Royal Regiment of Scotland. In 2016 the MOD announced that the site would close in 2032. Part of the Fort is open to the public, including the Highlanders' Museum (Queen's Own Highlanders and Lovat Scouts) (Press & Journal).

May 1884. He received Good Conduct Pay at 1d per day from 24th June 1879 and returned to Britain on 8th March 1880. On 28th April 1885 he gained the First Class Certificate of Education and transferred to 1st Middlesex on appointment to Bandmaster (warrant officer) on 24th February 1886. On 6th October 1887 he was posted to the 2nd Battalion in the East Indies and re-engaged to complete twenty-one years' service on 23rd November at Kamplee, India. He gave notice of continuing service beyond twenty-one years on 17th August 1894 and returned to Britain on 13th February 1898. He was discharged on 13th February 1908 at Guernsey, Channel Islands, described as 5′ 11″ tall, with medium complexion, hazel eyes and dark brown hair. He had served for thirty-three years and 235 days and was awarded the Long Service & Good Conduct Medal in 1902. George married Ada Amelia née Pentelow (April 1868–1953) on 4th January 1887 at St Stephen's, Hounslow. They lived at Clinthills, 11 Church Lane East, Aldershot before moving to 62 Heathwood Gardens, Charlton, London by 1901. George died at Cambridge Hospital, Aldershot and is buried in Aldershot Military Cemetery. He left £143/2/4 to his widow. In addition to Flora they had three sons:

- George Lewis Robertson (10th October 1888–28th December 1952) was born in India. He served five years and 196 days in the ranks and three years and 156 days as a WO2 (promoted 29th January 1915) before being appointed 2nd Class Army Schoolmaster as a WO1 on 4th July 1918 in India. He married Aileen Eltrude Browne (c.1889–22nd April 1952) on 17th October 1913 at Bellary, Madras, India. He last appears in the Army List in July 1931. They were living at Lindfield, 9 Palfrey Road, Ensbury, Bournemouth, Hampshire at the time of their deaths. She left effects valued at £3,612/11/8.
- Gordon Pentelow Robertson (8th August 1891–24th February 1984) was born at Mhow, India. He enlisted in the Corps of Army Schoolmasters on 11th July 1911 and served three years and 181 days in the ranks and five years and 154 days as a WO2 (promoted 29th January 1915). He served at Home until 13th March 1919, when he went to India and transferred to the Army Educational Corps on its formation on 15th June 1920. While in India he served at Army HQ in Dehli and Simla on cipher duties May 1919–March 1920, then with 8th Hussars at Lucknow as a schoolmaster until June 1920. On promotion to WO1 on 1st July 1920 he was an educational instructor with 16/5th Lancers at Lucknow until June 1923 and with the Queen's Bays until 3rd November 1923, when he returned to Britain. He was employed at Queen Victoria School, Dunblane, Scotland and went back to India on 7th March 1928, where he served as an educational instructor with 23rd Field Brigade RA at Nowshera until March 1929 and 25th Field Brigade RA at Nowshera until April 1932. He was appointed Intelligence Officer, HQ Nowshera Indian Infantry Brigade and accompanied the Nowshera Column to Peshawar and the Khajuri Plain during operations on the North West Frontier in 1930 (India General Service Medal with clasp 'NW Frontier 1930–31' and Long Service & Good Conduct

Medal). He served with 1st Hampshire at Nowshera and Cherat from April 1932. On returning to Britain on 29th November 1932 he was appointed headmaster of the Garrison Elder Children's School at Shorncliffe. He retired on 10th July 1933 (7720645), described as 5′ 5½″ tall, with fair complexion, grey eyes and light brown hair. Gordon received a Regular Army Emergency Commission in the Royal Army Service Corps (23189) as a lieutenant on 7th October 1940. He was an instructor at the Tregantle Wing of the Army Gas School, while Maurice Toye was Commandant of the whole Army Gas School organisation. Promoted war substantive captain on 6th April 1942 and had transferred to the Reserve by October 1945 as an honorary major. Gordon married Florence Alder (14th May 1907–19th March 1994) on 31st December 1938 at Hendon, Middlesex. She was born at Front Street, Guide Post, Bedlington, Northumberland, daughter of George Alder (1885–1941), a coal miner (stonemason) and Rose Thompson (1888–1946), of Sheepwash Bank, Choppington, Co Durham. They were living at 53A Church Road, Aldershot, Hampshire at the time of his death there. She was living at 25 Bourne Court, Manor Road, Aldershot at the time of her death there. They had two sons:

- Ian Gordon Robertson (born 1943) was Director of the National Army Museum 1988–2003. During this time he introduced a proactive public relations department, increased the size of the education department and brought modern management techniques to the museum.
- Brian Robertson (born 1947) OStJ TD MICPEM LRCP MRCS served in 167th (City of London) Field Ambulance RAMC TA and then the University of London Officer Training Corps while training to be a doctor at the Royal Free Hospital School of Medicine. On 26th May 1970 he was commissioned in the Royal Army Medical Corps (489651) and served In Germany, Aldershot and Woolwich until January 1979 when he left the Regular Army as a captain (11th January 1974) and continued service in the TA. He was promoted major 26th April 1979, lieutenant colonel 1st November 1985 and colonel 1st September 1995. Brian was involved with ambulance trains 1979–94 in Germany, the last nine years of that period as commander of the Ambulance Train Squadron RAMC(V) and was CO 306th Field Hospital (V) 1995–December 1999. He was awarded the TD (LG 30th May 1989) and OStJ in 1992. Brian was awarded the Churchill Travelling Fellowship in 1992, the Haywood Medal by the British Association for Immediate Care (BASICS) in 1997 and the Asmund Laerdal Award. From 1996 he was Medical Director of the Farnborough International Air Show. On 9th April 2002 he was Tactical Medical Commander (Silver Doctor) for the funeral of Queen Elizabeth, the Queen Mother in London. Brian was a member of the Board of the Football Licensing Authority 2002–08, National Chairman of BASICS from September 2002 and Medical Co-ordinator (Civil) for the events commemorating the 200th anniversary of the Battle of Trafalgar held in Portsmouth, Hampshire January–July 2005. He retired in 2006.

- Rollo Robertson (13th August 1898–1988) AMIMechE was commissioned in the Army Service Corps on 1st May 1917 and served in France from 1st September until 1st February 1918. He married Lilian May Broach (born 1897) on 9th April 1919 at Farnham, Surrey. Rollo was promoted lieutenant on 2nd July 1919 and served in Malta. Promoted captain on 21st December 1928 and was a TA adjutant 1st November 1932–31st October 1936. Promoted major 1st August 1938, acting lieutenant colonel 20th September 1940 and temporary lieutenant colonel on 20th December 1940. He appears in the Reserve in the Army List from April 1945.

HQ Nowshera Column near Peshawar on 11th August 1930. WO1 Gordon Pentelow Robertson is second from the right. The commander, Brigadier CA Milward, is in the left foreground (Brian Robertson).

Maurice was promoted lieutenant on 15th August 1918. He was granted the Freedom of Aldershot, with the document being placed in a silver casket accompanied by a large portrait. His wife was presented with a diamond pendant. The ceremony had been planned for 21st August but he was unexpectedly recalled to active service. The Council arranged a hurried reception on the evening of 20th August, thus denying the public a

Lieutenant George Roupell VC (1892–1974), was the son of Colonel Francis Frederick Fyler Roupell (1848–1916), who presented the Roupell Cup to the Army Rifle Association, which is still competed for each year at Bisley. George was commissioned in 1st East Surrey in March 1912. He was awarded the VC for his actions at Hill 60, near Ypres, Belgium on 20th April 1915. He served throughout the war on the Western Front and afterwards in North Russia. He was held in Butyrka Prison, Moscow and was not released until May 1920, when he continued his military career. Tours of duty included the Canadian Royal Military College, Kingston, Ontario 1929–31, commanding the East Surrey Depot at Kingston-upon-Thames 1931–34 and China Command 1934–35. George commanded 1st East Surrey 1935–38 and 36th Brigade 1939–40. On 19/20th May 1940, 36th Brigade was surrounded and George gave orders for the men to split up and escape independently. He and two other officers avoided capture and worked on a farm near Rouen until the Resistance got them out through Spain in 1942. He was appointed to command 105th Infantry Brigade, the same formation in which he had been Brigade Major 1916–18. He retired as honorary brigadier in February 1946.

spectacle worthy of the town's only VC winner. Maurice arrived in France on 23rd August. He was appointed acting major 27th September 1918–21st July 1919 while second-in-command. He was wounded three times during the war.

Maurice volunteered for the North Russia Relief Force in Archangel on 9th April 1919 and served with a number of fellow VCs – HEM Douglas, GWStG Grogan, MSS Moore, J Sherwood-Kelly. GRP Roupell and WA White. He served in 238th Infantry Brigade, commanded by Brigadier GWStG Grogan VC, as the Staff Lieutenant 1st Class working in intelligence 23rd May–21st July. On 22nd July he was appointed GSO3 as a temporary captain until 5th October, replacing Lieutenant GRP Roupell VC, who had been taken prisoner while visiting a White Russian unit that had mutinied. Maurice returned to Britain on 21st October 1919. **Mentioned in General Lord Rawlinson's Despatch dated 11th November 1919, LG 3rd February 1920.** He attended the VC Garden Party at Buckingham Palace on 26th June 1920.

Maurice joined the General Staff of HQ 54th East Anglia Division 9th April–12th May 1921. He was posted to a specialist appointment (Class FF) with Rhine Army 1st March 1923–8th June 1924, based in Cologne. On 26th April 1924 he was promoted captain and transferred to the Oxford and Buckinghamshire Light Infantry. He was employed with the Egyptian Army as Assistant Commandant and Chief Instructor of the Royal Egyptian Military College in Cairo 18th November 1925–17th November 1935 and was also Director General of Aviation in Egypt. **Appointed Commander of the Egyptian Order of the Nile, LG 31st March 1936.**

The Order of the Nile, Egypt's highest state honour, was instituted in 1915 for exceptional services to the nation. It was reconstituted under the Republic in June 1953. There were originally five grades - Grand Cordon, Grand Officer, Commander, Officer and Knight, although only the highest level is awarded today. Famous appointees include the Soviet astronaut, Yuri Gagarin, Emperor Haile Selassie of Ethiopia, President Nelson Mandela of South Africa, Earl Mountbatten of Burma, Marshal Josip Tito of Yugoslavia and Queen Elizabeth II.

On returning to the UK, he lived in married quarters at 11 Ypres Road, Reed Hall, Colchester and was promoted major on 5th March 1938. On 12th April 1939 he was appointed Chief Instructor, Army Gas School. On 1st July he was appointed brevet lieutenant colonel and on 17th August was appointed Assistant Commandant & Chief Instructor, Passive Air Defence and Anti-Gas School, Tregantle Fort, Cornwall (under the Army Gas School). He was appointed Commandant Army Gas School, Winterbourne Gunner, Wiltshire 9th September 1940–30th December 1942. During this period he received a number of promotions – acting lieutenant colonel 18th

GHQ Middle East Land Forces at Fayid, near Ismailia, Egypt after the Second World War.

The Civilian Anti Gas School was set up at Eastwood Park, an 18th century mansion, in 1936 and during the war it became the Ministry of Home Security Air Raid Precautions School. A Civil Defence training site was built there. After the war it became a police training school until the Home Office resumed control in 1949 to run civil defence courses in the event of nuclear war. 'The Range', a mock semi-ruined village, was built to resemble the aftermath on the outskirts of a nuclear explosion. Exercises were held in search and rescue and first aid. In 1969 the site passed to the Department of Health and Social Security as a National Training Centre. Healthcare courses continue to be run there and the main house is also a conference and wedding centre.

'The Range' at Eastwood Park.

October 1939, temporary lieutenant colonel 18th January 1940, acting colonel 9th September 1940, war substantive lieutenant colonel 9th March 1941 (substantive 27th October 1942), temporary colonel 9th March 1941–30th June 1943 and colonel 1st July 1943, backdated to 1st July 1942. He was appointed an instructor at the Staff College, Camberley in 1943 and a deputy brigade commander Home Forces on 14th May 1943. Later in 1943 he was appointed within 6th Airborne Division and GSO1 Home Forces 18th February 1944–16th September 1945.

Maurice's and Flora's grave in Tiverton Cemetery. Thomas Sage VC is also buried there (Memorials to Valour).

Maurice in 1950 (Elliott & Fry).

Maurice was appointed to GHQ Middle East Land Forces as Assistant Adjutant General 5th-26th October 1945 and, as an acting brigadier, was Adjutant General 27th October–2nd December 1945, then reverted to Assistant Adjutant General until 3rd November 1946. He was appointed acting brigadier 4th November 1946, temporary brigadier 29th March 1947 and was promoted brigadier on 1st July 1948. Maurice retired on 19th January 1949. He became Commandant of the Home Office Civil Defence School at Eastwood

The British War Medal was instituted on 26th July 1919 for all ranks who served for twenty-eight days in an operational theatre between 5th August 1914 and 11th November 1918, or died on active service before the completion of this period. Eligibility was extended in 1919–20 to mine-clearing at sea and operations in North and South Russia, eastern Baltic, Siberia, Black Sea and Caspian Sea. Many veterans were awarded the 1914–15 Star, British War Medal and Victory Medal. They became known as Pip, Squeak and Wilfred after a strip cartoon published in the *Daily Mirror* from 1919 to 1956.

Park, Falfield, Gloucestershire until 1955. During this time he and Flora lived at Eastwood Park, Falfield.

Maurice was diagnosed with cancer and was almost paralysed during the last six months of his life. He died at the Madame Curie Memorial Foundation, Tidcombe Hall, Tiverton, Devon on 6th September 1955 and is buried in Tiverton Cemetery, Devon (Section XF, Grave 31). He left effects valued at £804/4/6 to his widow. Flora was living at 4 Nutbourne, Weybourne, Farnham, Surrey at the time of her death and is buried with her husband. Maurice is commemorated in a number of other places:

- 2nd Aldershot (Toye's Own) Venture Scout Unit, Hampshire.
- Maurice Toye House, Middle Hill, Aldershot, a purpose-built Army Welfare Service Centre opened in February 2010.
- A Department for Communities and Local Government commemorative paving stone was dedicated at Municipal Gardens, Aldershot on 25th March 2018 to mark the centenary of his award.
- His VC action featured in Issue 1081 of the Victor Comic entitled *A True Story of Men at War* dated 7th November 1981.

In addition to the VC and MC he was awarded the 1914–15 Star, British War Medal 1914–20, Victory Medal 1914–19 with Mentioned-in-Despatches Oakleaf, Defence Medal, War Medal 1939–45, General Service Medal 1918–62 with clasp 'Palestine 1945–48', George VI Coronation Medal 1937, Elizabeth II Coronation Medal 1953 and the Egyptian Commander of the Order of the Nile. Maurice left his VC and MC to a named beneficiary. They were sold at Sotheby's on 17th September 1992 to the National Army Museum for £25,000. At the time the Museum Director was Maurice's nephew, Ian Robertson. The VC is held by the National Army Museum on Royal Hospital Road, Chelsea, London.

9/523 SERGEANT RICHARD CHARLES TRAVIS (DICKSON CORNELIUS SAVAGE)
2nd Battalion, Otago Regiment, New Zealand Expeditionary Force

Richard Travis was born Dickson Cornelius Savage on 6th April 1884 at Otara, Opotiki, Southland, New Zealand but will be referred to as Richard. His father, James Whitford Savage (c.1835–7th January 1918), born at Island Magee, Co Antrim, Ireland, migrated to New Zealand c.1858 and settled as a farmer at Melrose Farm, Otara, Opotiki, Bay of Plenty. He also served in the New Zealand Armed Constabulary. He married Frances 'Fanny' Theresa née O'Keefe (c.1853–24th

March 1922), born at Sydney, New South Wales, Australia, in 1875 at Opotiki. Richard had eight siblings:

- Mary Susannah Savage (29th January 1876–20th February 1945) married Edward Ogilvie Ross (4th December 1867–28th February 1934), born at Tapatahi, Gisborne, on 13th July 1898. They were living at Karamu, Auckland in 1941. They had nine children:
  - Frances Margaret Ross (20th August 1899–30th August 1963) married Hector MacFarlane Hodges (1887–25th March 1954) on 11th June 1919. They had four children, including William Hector Hodges 1920 and Margaret Rose Hodges 1935.
  - Richard Kennedy Ross (24th May 1901–12th February 1964) married Dorothy Katherine Louisa Pevreal (9th November 1911–2001) in 1929. They had three children, including Richard 'John' Ross (1935–94).
  - Jessie Ross (30th March 1907–31st May 1966) married Jack Walters and they had a child.
  - Donald Whitford/Whiteford Ross (9th April 1910–24th August 1972) married Frances May Ostberg (2nd May 1915–14th February 1978), born at Pirongia to a Swedish father, on 29th September 1936 at Te Awamutu. They had 11 children, including Colin Barry Ross (1943–69) and a stillborn child in 1950.
  - Violet Myrtle Ross (21st April 1912–14th June 1993) married William Ivo John Watson (1913–30th March 1961) in 1934. They had three children, including Heather Kathleen Watson (1941–92) and Jennifer Watson.
  - Jean Winifred/Winifred Jean Ross (3rd May 1915–28th February 1986) married Leonard Giles Hoglund Mashlan (9th July 1914–28th February 1986), a marine engineer, in 1938. They had four children, including Leonard Ross Ogilvie Mashlan (1941–30th November 2004). Leonard was a labourer in 1932, working for Ralph Townsend Fullerton Smith, a farmer of Okahukurra, when he obtained a cheque for £2/9/-. He altered the value to £20/9/- and purchased a motorcycle for £17/10/-. He was charged at Auckland on 14th November 1932 and sentenced to two years' probation. He was charged with a breach of probation on 31st March 1934 and sentenced to two years in Waikeria Borstal Institution, described as 6′ tall, with pale complexion, light brown hair, grey eyes and medium build. Leonard was released on 13th March 1936. They were living at Central Hotel, Putaruru, Waikato in 1946. By 1957 he was a caterer and they were living at 29 Ferryhill Road, Auckland. Jean was a caterer in 1963 living with her son Leonard, a salesman, at 8 Gorrie Avenue, Auckland. Her husband's whereabouts are not known. She had moved to 24 Rewa Street, Auckland by 1969, to 43 Grange Road, Auckland by 1972 and to 2/55 Pleasant Street, Onehunuga by 1978.

    - Charles Edward Ross (1917–17th October 1941) served in the New Zealand Army Service Corps as a driver (9868) and was killed in action in Egypt (El Alamein War Cemetery – XXX B 4).
    - Dorothy Mary Ross (11th April 1920–1993).
    - Ivy Ross (30th June 1923–1994).
- Frances Helena Savage (1st January 1878–6th September 1936) married Walter Maxwell (1873–11th July 1942), born at Canonbie, Dumfriesshire, Scotland, in 1899. They had four children:
    - Walter Charles Maxwell (13th June 1900–28th January 1985) died at Waipa, Waikato.
    - Dixon Bernard Maxwell (3rd May 1903–21st April 1984) died at Waipa.
    - Edward Howard Maxwell (27th September 1905–19th June 1983) married Rita Alice Hart (13th July 1913–1st April 2010) in 1936.
    - Violet Hazelena Maxwell (born 29th March 1908).
- Matilda Mary 'May' Savage (24th May 1880–20th January 1881).
- Flora Savage (1st January 1882–21st September 1946) married her brother-in-law, Louis Dunlop Ross (1874–14th September 1953), a farmer, on 20th June 1905. They had five children:
    - Mary Ross (10th February 1906–1985) married and had two children.
    - John Louis Ross (15th November 1908–20th August 1995) married Jean Capon Johnstone (1911–84) in 1931.
    - James Edward Ross (1911–80) married Eileen Charlotte Spanhake (16th August 1911–7th June 1995) in 1934 and they had three children.
    - Malcolm Trevor Ross (30th May 1916–16th December 1976) married in 1940 and had a son. He was a farmer at Waiawa in 1946. He married Mary in 1951 and they had two sons and a daughter.
    - Leslie Walter Ross (1921–25th May 1985) married in 1946 and they had a daughter.
- Charles James Savage (21st November 1886–8th June 1967), a farmer, married Emily Annie Clarke (11th November 1896–30th December 1955), born at Irvington-on-Hudson, Westchester County, New York, USA, on 16th May 1917 at Opotiki. They had a son:
    - James Dickson Thomas Savage (4th August 1922–18th July 2003) married Anne Mary McGivern (2nd January 1927–10th June 1981) and they lived at Opotiki. They had three children – Des Savage, Maureen Savage (1953–73) and Patricia Savage. James married Nola Ladds Wordlaw Menzies (12th May 1926–4th September 2006), born at Waimana, Whakatane, Bay of Plenty.
- Margaret Jane May Savage (10th August 1889–19th February 1956).
- Clara Agnes Josephine Savage (19th June 1892–11th January 1959) married Percival Brockett (4th March 1879–9th November 1971) on 23rd October 1915. He was a pipe worker when he enlisted in the New Zealand Army during the Great War (81591). He was a farmer in 1919 living with his wife and his sister-

in-law, Mrs Lilian 'Dolly' Mary Bockett (née Bridger) at Otara Road, Opotiki. By 1928 he was a labourer and they were living at Otara Road and were still there in 1969. They had a son, Percival Daniel Bockett (1st September 1917–26th August 1983), who married and had two sons and a daughter, including Noel Bockett, who moved to Australia.

- Winifred Evelyn Savage (3rd December 1895–13th July 1975) married Angus McKay MacDonald (1889–18th July 1966), born at Halkirk, Caithness, Scotland in 1916. He was a farmer and they were living at Box 63, Otara Road, Opotiki in 1941. They had at least two children – John Angus MacDonald 1917 and James Richard MacDonald 1918.

Opotiki School, Bay of Plenty, North Island.

The Limehills area of Southland.

Winton Main Street.

Richard's paternal grandparents were John E Savage, a weaver, and Margaret née Thompson. His maternal grandparents were William Manus O'Keefe and Susan née McCloskey.

Richard was educated at Opotiki School, Bay of Plenty, North Island until 7th February 1899 and at Otara Schools, Auckland, leaving on 6th September 1901. He worked for his father on the family farm. It is understood that after an argument with his father, when aged nineteen, he rode off. His movements thereafter are not known accurately. At Gisborne he worked as a horse breaker and may have 'got a young lady into trouble there'. In 1906 he may have been a member of O'Neill's Buckjumpers. He was a drover for Mr M Roe, followed by maize picking for Charles Tietjen of Bushmere in the summer of 1906–07. He was taken on as a general farmhand after the season finished and stayed for two years. Then he moved to South Island and worked for William Christie at Limehills, Southland, then at Win Burdon's threshing mill at Winton under Arthur Clark, of Wright's Bush, Southland from February 1910, before working with Tom Murray at Ryal Bush. He appeared at country fairs in Winton in 1910 under the name of Richard Charles Travis. He claimed to come from Poverty Bay on North Island and even the United States but never mentioned his family, with whom he last had contact in 1909. At other times he also worked for Ward & Co at Invercargill, J Christie, a farmer of Centre Bush, and at several flax mills.

Richard joined the Royal St George Oddfellows Lodge and became engaged to Evelyn Letitia 'Lettie' Murray (23rd October 1891–20th September 1960), daughter of his boss at Ryal Bush. He enlisted in the 1st New Zealand Expeditionary Force at Ryal Bush on 11th August 1914, described as 5′ 6″ tall, weighing 133 lbs, with fair hair, blue eyes and slim build. He was assigned to 7th (Southland) Squadron, Otago Mounted Rifles as a trooper on 20th August and was billeted at Tahuna Park, Dunedin. He embarked at Port Chalmers aboard HMNZT No.9 *Hawke's Bay* on 22nd September 1914 and reached Wellington on 24th September, where he disembarked and was camped at Miramar. He sailed on 16th October via Fremantle, Colombo and Aden, disembarking at Alexandria, Egypt on 2nd December.

SS *Hawkes Bay* (8,418 tons) was built in 1912 by Workman, Clark & Co at Belfast, Ireland for the Tyser Line. She could accommodate 1,000 emigrants and was immediately employed on the Victoria Government's emigrant service. On 23rd January 1914 she transferred to the Commonwealth & Dominion Line and later that year became a troopship. In April 1916 she was renamed *Port Napier*. In 1932 she was laid up at Tollesbury on the River Blackwater and remained there until 1936, when she was transferred to T & J Brocklebank Ltd and renamed *Martand*. She was sold to A Zanchi of Genoa in 1938 and was renamed *Martano* and later that year, *Mar Blanco*. On 8th September 1943 she was taken over by the Germans at Ancona when the Italians capitulated and was used as a supply ship. On 7th December she was bombed and sunk by Allied aircraft off Zara.

In early April 1915 the dismounted members of the Regiment embarked for Gallipoli as reinforcements. Richard remained with the Transport. However, he turned up at Gallipoli with the Australians in May, was promptly returned to Egypt under escort and was sentenced to fourteen days detention at Sidi Bishr Barracks. He returned to Gallipoli in October 1915 and took part in the evacuation on 20th December, embarking on HMAT A68 *Anchises*. During the night she and another ship collided. *Anchises* dropped anchor and the damage was inspected the following morning but was found to be superficial and she got underway again. Back in Egypt he was billeted at Zeitoun Camp, Alexandria.

On 21st January 1916 he was trying to break a horse when it reared and fell over backwards, striking its head on the ground and dying instantly. Richard jumped clear but his knee was injured and he was admitted to the New Zealand General Hospital, Pont-de-Koubbeh, Cairo. He was discharged on 10th March and transferred to 8th (Southland) Company, 2nd Battalion, Otago Infantry Regiment on 27th March.

Zeitoun Camp.

New Zealand sick and wounded were admitted to British and Australian hospitals until April 1915, when the Egyptian Army Hospital at Pont de Koubbeh, Cairo was offered for the use of the New Zealand force. It was based around a two-storey stone building, with deep verandas. There was accommodation for about 250 patients but a large quadrangle was covered with marquees when the facility was taken over by No.2 New Zealand Stationary Hospital when it arrived in July 1915. The whole facility was enlarged to 500 beds but with more and more casualties arriving in August the capacity was increased. It was eventually transformed into a base hospital with 1,040 beds and its name changed to No.1 New Zealand General Hospital. In June 1916 the staff and much of the equipment were transferred to Brockenhurst, England (Major Cyprian Brereton).

On 8th April 1916 Richard entrained at Moascar for Alexandria where he boarded SS *Llandovery Castle* and disembarked at Marseille, France on 16th April. He quickly built a reputation as an aggressive observer, who would crawl into no man's land and entice the enemy into declaring their positions by bombing them or rattling barbed wire. As soon as they opened fire he would note their positions and report back to his Battalion HQ. On one occasion he took three men with him and all returned visibly shaken by the audacity of his methods. In mid-May he accurately mapped the enemy positions prior to an attack by 2nd Otago on 16th June. **Mentioned in 2nd New Zealand Brigade Routine Orders on 5th July 1916 for carrying out a daylight search for wounded soldiers and recovering a large quantity of abandoned equipment.** He was also mentioned in orders for excellent services during the previous six weeks when on patrol in no man's land for forty nights in succession, gathering vital intelligence. As a result he became known as *Prince of Scouts*, *King of No Man's Land* and the *greatest raiding sergeant on the Western Front*. Not satisfied with operating at night, he repeatedly led daylight patrols. **For his devotion to duty he was commended in Routine Orders on 20th July 1916.**

Richard was wounded on 23rd July and returned to duty on 29th August. **Awarded the DCM for his actions on 13th September at High Wood on the Somme. He went out alone in daylight and stalked and killed several snipers between the lines, who were firing at a working party, LG 25th November 1916.** On another occasion he went out with Scottie Nicholson and VP Hislop. They managed to get behind a German pillbox and blew up the occupants

In April 1912 the Royal Mail Line took control of Union-Castle Mail Steamship Co and the first new Union Castle ships were ordered, including *Llandovery Castle* (11,423 tons). She was built by Barclay Curle & Co in Glasgow and was launched on 3rd September 1913. He maiden voyage commenced in January 1914 from London on the East Africa service. In August 1914 she was transferred to the West Africa service. On 26th July 1916 she became a hospital ship, equipped with 622 beds and 102 medical staff to transport wounded Canadians from Europe to Nova Scotia. On 27th June 1918, HMHS *Llandovery Castle* was torpedoed by U-*86*, 116 miles southwest of Fastnet, Ireland. She was clearly marked as a hospital ship, as seen here, and the German captain, Helmut Brümmer-Panzig committed one of the worst ever atrocities at sea in contravention of international law and the standing orders of the Imperial German Navy. Fortunately there were no patients on board but there was a large group of medical staff and crew. When they took to the lifeboats, U-*86* surfaced and ran down every lifeboat except one that managed to get away. The survivors in the water were machine-gunned and killed to hide the evidence of the atrocity. There were only twenty-four survivors, all in the lifeboat that managed to escape, which was the last to leave the sinking ship. The U-boat crew somehow missed them. They were rescued a little later by HMS *Lysander*. A total of 234 doctors, nurses, CAMC soldiers and seamen died in the sinking and subsequent actions by the U-boat crew. After the war, *Llandovery Castle* was one of six British cases presented at the Leipzig trials. Helmut Brümmer-Panzig and two of his lieutenants, Ludwig Dithmar and John Boldt, were arraigned for trial. Panzig avoided prosecution by fleeing the country. On 21st July 1921 Dithmar and Boldt were tried, convicted and sentenced to four years in prison but on appeal both were acquitted on the grounds that the captain was solely responsible.

with grenades. Richard was promoted lance corporal on 26th September, corporal on 7th October and sergeant on 17th October. At the end of 1916 he was granted leave and went to Scotland.

Richard was appointed leader of the Snipers & Observers Section under Captain MA Watt, the Intelligence Officer. His Section comprised Sergeant Alex 'Sandy' D Swainson (later MM & Bar), 9/1801 Private ADD 'Shorty' Clydesdale, 35686 Private Roley V Conway (a former Auckland jockey), 8/3006 Private Harry Melville (later DCM) and 5119 Private N Thompson. Richard continually harassed the enemy by crawling up to their trenches in the dead of night, attaching the end of a roll of wire to the German barbed wire and returning to his own lines. At irregular intervals he would tug the wire and cause alarm amongst the Germans, who would lob grenades into their own wire. He would wait for some time, allowing the enemy to settle down, before tugging the wire again. By such methods he was able to wear his opponents down.

On 14th February 1917, Richard was sent to the rear for three weeks recreation and training. On 10th-11th October he led a patrol to ascertain the new wire defences around the enemy pillboxes and front trenches on Bellevue Ridge, Passchendaele, which assisted the subsequent attack by the New Zealand Division. He was sent to the Base on 12th November for a tour of duty in England, arriving at the beginning of December. He rejoined the Battalion on 17th January 1918.

Awarded the MM for his actions while commanding a patrol of four men (Privates Melville, Conway, Clydesdale and Thompson) near Owl Trench, east of Hébuterne on 14th May 1918. Although the Battalion was in support, they volunteered to go out and secure identification, which was urgently required. They left the front line about 7.15 p.m, in broad daylight and, by skilful use of ground, crept up to an enemy post unobserved and completely surprised it. The officer had to be shot but the other six Germans surrendered. Alerted by the commotion, a neighbouring post rushed to the aid of their comrades. The patrol came under heavy machine gun fire on withdrawing and was sniped at from all sides as they rushed back, covered by Richard with his revolver. Two of the prisoners were shot by their own comrades. The operation was a complete success, without any casualties to the raiders, LG 13th September 1918. Richard's four comrades were also awarded the MM.

On 31st May Richard crawled out with Sergeant Swainson and Privates Billy Ballantyne and Roley Conway to surprise an enemy post. They captured two prisoners before the enemy in the rear counterattacked. Richard shot three with his revolver and captured another three Germans, including two officers. However, he only managed to bring one soldier and one officer back. Richard was granted leave to England on 21st June and returned

The Belgian Croix de Guerre was established by Royal Decree on 25th October 1915, primarily for bravery or other military virtue on the battlefield. It was re-established on 20th July 1940 by the Belgian government in exile to recognise bravery and military virtue but could also be awarded collectively to units. It was re-established again on 3rd April 1954, but only for individuals. The Croix de Guerre in the Great War was also awarded for three years service on the front line and for good conduct on the battlefield. It was also awarded to volunteers aged forty or more or younger than sixteen after a minimum of eighteen months service, to escaped prisoners of war and to military personnel placed on inactive duty because of injury.

to the Battalion on 10th July. **Awarded the Belgian Croix de Guerre, LG 12th July 1918.**

Awarded the VC for his actions at Hawk Trench, Rossignol Wood, north of Hébuterne, France on 24th July 1918, LG 27th September 1918. Next day he accompanied Second Lieutenant Charles Allanton Kerse on an inspection of the trenches during an enemy bombardment. They encouraged the men and between 8.00 and 9.00 a.m. sat down for a rest on a fire step in a bay close to Hawk Trench. A shell landed close by, killing both men. Richard's loss was felt throughout the Battalion and beyond. Their bodies were buried in falling rain on the evening of 26th July in what is now Couin New British Cemetery – Richard in Grave G 5 and Kerse in G 6. A large number of men attended, including the brigade commander. When the men of 2nd Otago returned from the cemetery they were cheered by the same British soldiers who had earlier stood to salute Richard Travis.

Richard Travis' grave in Couin New British Cemetery.

The VC, DCM and MM were sent to the Governor General of New Zealand, Lord Liverpool, on 21st November 1918 to be presented to Travis' next of kin. Under the Royal Warrant of 11th May 1917 the VC would have been sent to the VC's mother as next of kin regardless of any testamentary disposition. However, this was cancelled by the Royal Warrant of 30th May 1918 and thereafter medals were disposed of in accordance with any will left by the deceased. It was not until December 1919 that Travis' real name was established and that his mother lived at Opotiki. His brother, Charles, was informed of the alias and that he had been killed, but responded that he did not wish that to be communicated to his mother. Travis' fiancée, Lettie Murray, had no knowledge of his previous life, always knew him as Travis and asked for a family photograph of him as Savage to ensure it was the same man. However, Charles Savage declined to supply a photograph to the Officer-in-Charge of Base Records. Colonel Gerald Arnold Ward CBE visited Charles Savage and Jane Savage (sister) and became aware that they were acquainted with Travis' exploits and death but had kept the latter from his mother, who believed her son was still travelling. Ward was convinced by them, and the local Roman Catholic priest, that telling her the news may prove fatal. On 20th September 1920 Lord Milner wrote to the Governor General from Downing Street in reply to his letter of 28th May. The Army Council had considered the matter and ruled that the VC, DCM and MM should go Miss Murray in accordance with the will. The King's letter of sympathy, if still held, should not be sent to Travis' mother until she was in a condition to receive it. On 22nd February 1921 Colonel Ward again visited Charles and Jane Savage at Opotiki. He informed them that the Governor General, by then Viscount Jellicoe, had written to Miss Murray asking her if she would prefer to have the Cross as Travis' sole beneficiary, or should it be sent to the VC's mother, who was in very poor health and was not aware that her son had been killed. Miss Murray replied that she wished to have the Cross, as that was Travis' wish. Ward handed the Savages a copy of the official account of the VC action. They were grateful for the Governor General's consideration and expressed their sincere appreciation. Once the Savages had been made aware of the situation, the Governor General sent the VC to Miss Murray by registered post on 28th February 1921. This was to avoid a public presentation, which would probably have become known to Travis' mother. Although Richard's possessions passed to Lettie, in accordance with his will, his prized possession, a Zeiss binocular-periscope, which he obtained from a dead German, was buried with his mother. Lettie married John Wilson (1897–24th March 1983) on 3rd January 1923. He was a farmer and they were living at Tussock

The Dick Travis VC National .303 Target Rifle Competition, organised by the Wellington Rifle Association, is shot over 300, 500 and 600 yards. The inaugural competition, hosted by Karori Rifle Club, was held at Trentham Rifle Range on 18th/19th February 2012.

The memorial sundial at Caroline Bay, Timaru.

Creek, Awarua, Southland in 1928. By 1957 he was a wool classer and they were living at 101 Metzger Street, Invercargill.

Richard Travis is commemorated in a number of other places:

The war memorial at Ryal Bush. Ryal Bush is twelve miles from Invercargill in the Wallacetown riding of the county of Southland. In 1901 it had a population of just 218.

- Travis Barracks, Linton Military Camp, near Palmerston North.
- Travis Street, Taradale, Napier.
- Dick Travis VC Trophy – awarded to the winner of the annual Dick Travis VC National .303 Target Rifle Competition.
- Plaque at Travis Memorial Car Park, Dunedin.
- An obelisk surmounted with a sundial in the centre of the War Memorial Wall, Caroline Bay, Timaru bears the names of eleven New Zealand VCs, including Richard Travis.
- Victoria Cross winners' memorial dedicated by the Reverend Keith Elliott VC outside the Headquarters of the Dunedin Branch of the Returned Services Association and unveiled by Governor General Sir Charles Willoughby Moke Norrie GCMG GCVO CB DSO MC on 29th January 1956, the centenary of the institution of the VC by Queen Victoria. The memorial was transferred to Anzac Square in front of the railway station. It was moved to near Dunedin Cenotaph in Queen's Gardens and rededicated on 11th November 2001.
- Named on the war memorial at Ryal Bush.
- Named on a panel at the Auckland War Memorial Museum.
- Dick Travis Memorial Wall dedicated at Pukerau School, Southland on 25th April 2018, by David MacDonald (great nephew) on behalf of the Travis family. The ceremony was also attended by Noel Bockett (great nephew), who travelled from Australia.

The Richard Travis 60c stamp issued by New Zealand Post on 14th April 2011.

- Named on one of eleven plaques honouring 175 men from overseas awarded the VC for the Great War. The plaques were unveiled by the Senior Minister of State at the Foreign & Commonwealth Office and Minister for Faith and Communities,

Southland Museum, where Richard's medals are held.

Baroness Warsi, at a reception at Lancaster House, London on 26th June 2014 attended by the Duke of Kent and relatives of the VC recipients. The New Zealand plaque was unveiled on 7th May 2015 at a ceremony attended by Defence Minister Gerry Brownlee and Defence Force Chief Lieutenant General Tim Keating. Corporal Willie Apiata VC read the names of the sixteen men on the plaque, which is displayed in the grounds of Parliament in Wellington.

- An issue of twenty-two 60c stamps by New Zealand Post entitled 'Victoria Cross – the New Zealand Story' honouring New Zealand's twenty-two Victoria Cross holders was issued on 14th April 2011.
- Communities and Local Government commemorative paving stones for the 145 VCs born in Australia, Belgium, Canada, China, Denmark, Egypt, France, Germany, India, Iraq, Japan, Nepal, Netherlands, Newfoundland, New Zealand, Pakistan, South Africa, Sri Lanka, Ukraine and United States of America were unveiled at the National Memorial Arboretum, Alrewas, Staffordshire by Prime Minister David Cameron MP and Sergeant Johnson Beharry VC on 5th March 2015.

In addition to the VC, DCM and MM he was awarded the 1914–15 Star, British War Medal 1914–20, Victory Medal 1914–19 with MID Oakleaf and Belgian Croix de Guerre. When Lettie died, the medals passed to John Wilson, who presented them to Southland Museum, Gala Street, Queens Park, Invercargill, Otago in September 1972, where they are held.

LIEUTENANT COLONEL OLIVER CYRIL SPENCER WATSON
1st County of London Yeomanry (Middlesex, Duke of Cambridge's Hussars), attached 5th Battalion, The King's Own (Yorkshire Light Infantry)

Oliver Watson was born at Cavendish Square, London on 7th September 1876. His father, William Spencer Watson MB FRCS (2nd March 1836–17th September 1906), was a surgeon (MRCS) in 1861, living with his parents. He married Georgine Mary Jane née Mair (July 1841–11th March 1878) on 23rd January 1866 at Bloomsbury St George, London. In 1871 William was a surgeon and occulist, living with his family at 15 Henrietta Street, Cavendish Square, Marylebone. Georgine died at their home at 7 Henrietta Street, Cavendish Square. In 1881 William was living there with his family. His sister-in-law, Jane Isabella Mary Mair, was his housekeeper. By 1902 he had moved to 61 Bedford Square, Kensington, London. He died at 44 Chepstow Place, Bayswater, London, leaving effects valued at £17,656/1/5 (£2M in 2018). Oliver had seven siblings:

- John Mair Watson (26th December 1866–1885).
- Emma Jane Watson (born 3rd January 1868).
- George Spencer Watson (8th March 1869–11th April 1934) was educated at Merchant Taylors' School and became an artist, studying at the Royal Academy from 1889 and exhibited there from 1891. He was awarded Royal Academy Schools Silver Medals in 1889 and 1891 and the Landseer Scholarship in 1892. In 1901 he was living with his siblings, Mary, Alice and Spencer, at 61 Bedford Gardens, Kensington. George married Hilda Mary Gardiner (1880–4th September 1952), a dancer and mime artist, on 4th August 1909 at East Grinstead Parish Church, Sussex. He was elected to the Royal Institute of Oil Painters in 1900, the Royal Society of Portrait Painters in 1904, became an associate of the Royal Academy in 1923 and a Member of the Royal Academy in 1932. In 1911 they were living at 17 Melbury Road, Kensington. In 1923 he bought Dunshay Manor, Isle of Purbeck, Dorset. He was living at 20 Holland Park Road, Kensington at the time of his death, leaving effects valued at £11,772/9/9. A memorial exhibition was held at the Fine Art Society the same year. There is a memorial to him in the north vestibule of St James's Church, Piccadilly, London. Examples of his works are held by Tate Britain, the Harris Art Gallery in Preston and in collections in Bournemouth, Liverpool, Plymouth and the National Gallery of Canada. Hilda died at Wenlock Lodge, Uppingham, Rutland, leaving effects valued at

Oliver was born at Cavendish Square.

£5,299/13/4. They had a daughter, Mary Spencer Watson (7th May 1913–7th March 2006), who became a sculptor.

- Georgine Florence Watson (21st September 1870–12th January 1901) died unmarried at 61 Bedford Gardens, Kensington, leaving effects valued at £1,295/18/5.
- Mary Anne Grace Watson (24th December 1871–29th March 1911) was living with her brother, George, in 1901. She died unmarried at The Retreat, Fairford, Gloucestershire, leaving effects valued at £1,392/14/11.
- Alice Cradock Watson (1873–31st May 1948) was living with her brother, George, in 1901. She married Dr John McCrea (c.1872–23rd October 1950) on 30th July 1907 at St Mary's Church, Wargrave, Berkshire. He was born in Belfast, Co Antrim, Ireland. They were living at Lisna, School Lane, Wargrave, Berkshire when she claimed her brother's Great War medals on 18th March 1922. Her death was registered at Wokingham, Berkshire and she left effects valued at £3,385/8/5. He died at Lisna, School Lane, Wargrave, leaving effects valued at £14,778/7/10. They had three children:
    - Mary Florence McCrea (5th March 1910–17th March 2001) married Sidney Thomas Twemlow (born 1911) in 1936 at Hitchin, Hertfordshire. He was born at Prestwich, Lancashire. Mary died at Norwich, Norfolk. They had two children – Joanna Twemlow 1938 and Sarah Twemlow 1944.
    - John Mair McCrea (1912–16th October 1952) was a solicitor, residing or working at 109 Blackheath Park, London in 1947. He was living at Hillcrest, The Heads, Keswick, Cumberland at the time of his death at the Infirmary, Workington, Cumberland. He left effects valued at £9,226/0/8.

  - Alice Catherine Houghton McCrea (1913–4th January 1992), known as Catherine, married Gerald Saumarez Whittuck (13th October 1912–1997) on 23rd July 1938 at St Mary's Church, Wargrave. He was born at Keynsham, Somerset. He was appointed to the Air Ministry, London as a junior grade of the Administrative Class on 18th October 1935. Later he became Assistant Under-Secretary of State in the Air Ministry (CB, LG 1st January 1959) and was a member of the Royal Patriotic Fund Corporation September 1971–May 1974. Catherine inherited her uncle's VC. She died at 15A Greenaway Gardens, Hampstead, London. His death was registered at Camden, London. They had two children – William Whittuck 1942 and Andrew Whittuck 1944.
- Spencer Burton Watson (11th August 1874–28th December 1950) was commissioned from the Royal Military College, Sandhurst on 10th October 1894, with a view to being appointed to the Indian Staff Corps. He joined the Indian Army as a second lieutenant with seniority from 10th October 1894 from the Unattached List on 20th December 1895. He served in 64th Pioneers and was promoted lieutenant on 10th January 1897, captain 10th October 1903 and major 10th October 1912. At the time of the 1901 Census he was recorded as a lieutenant Indian Staff Corps and was living (probably home on leave from India) with his brother, George, in Kensington. He married Aline Undine Frederica Breithaupt (21st June 1874–11th October 1967) on 27th August 1913 at St Stephen's Church, Ootacamund (Ooty), Madras, India. She was born at Ootacamund, Madras, daughter of George Avenal Breithaupt (c.1848–1935), a banker, and Elle Charlotte Dry née West (1852–1949). Spencer served in France and Belgium 6th February–10th November 1915, in Mesopotamia 4th December 1915–4th October 1916, 5th March 1917–5th April 1918 and 13th May–28th June 1918, with the Egyptian Expeditionary Force 11th July–31st October 1918 and in North West Persia 2nd October 1920–16th May 1921. He was appointed acting lieutenant colonel 27th November 1915–25th March 1916 and was promoted lieutenant colonel on 3rd June 1916. Spencer was appointed second in command of 1/155th Pioneers on 22nd September 1916 and CO on 27th May 1918. He was twice Mentioned in Despatches (LG 19th October 1916 and 5th June 1919) and was awarded the Order of the Nile, 3rd Class while serving as a brevet and acting lieutenant colonel of 64th Pioneers attached to 1/155th Pioneers, Indian Army (LG 16th January 1920). He was promoted substantive lieutenant colonel Indian Army on 20th August 1920 and appointed CO of 1st Madras Pioneers. He was granted leave outside India for eight months from 29th March 1923 and relinquished command on 19th August 1924. Spencer and Aline were living at Mineown, Mixtow, Lanteglos by Fowey, Cornwall at the time of his death at Ghota Ghar, Eastcliffe Road, St Austell, Cornwall, leaving effects valued at £9,509/14/8. She died at 19 Alexandra Road, St Austell, leaving effects valued at £16,335.

The Order of the Nile, established in 1915 by Sultan Hussein Kamel, was one of Egypt's principal orders until the monarchy was abolished in 1953. It was then reconstituted as the Republic's highest state honour. It is awarded to those who had rendered useful service to the country. Originally there were five classes - Grand Cordon, Grand Officer, Commander (3rd Class), Officer and Knight. Today there are just two - Collar of the Nile and Order of the Nile. During the monarchy, another recipient of the 3rd Class was Howard Carter, archaeologist and Egyptologist, in 1926.

Ootacamund is usually known as Ooty. At 2,267m (7,440′) it became popular with Europeans escaping the summer heat of the plains of India. Many typically English houses were built on narrow lanes bordered by imported English shrubs and flowers. From 1861 Ooty became the summer headquarters for the Madras government. St Stephen's Church was designed by Captain John James Underwood and was built in 1830. The original teak timbers were from Tipu Sultan's Palace at Seringapatam. The foundation stone was laid by Stephen Rumbold Lushington, Governor of Madras, on 23rd April 1829, the birthday of King George IV. The church was consecrated by John Matthias Turner, Bishop of Calcutta, on 5th November 1830.

Oliver's paternal grandfather, Dr John Watson MRCS (20th April 1814–28th March 1898), was born at St Mary Magdalene, Bermondsey, London. He was educated at St Andrews, Fife. John married Emia Cradock née Burton (1813–22nd June 1888), born at Bloomsbury, London, on 28th March 1835 at St Mary's Church, Islington, London. They were living at 13 Southampton Street, Bloomsbury in 1851, at 6 Southampton Street in 1861 and at 23 Woburn Square, Bloomsbury by 1888. Emie died there, leaving effects valued at £1,143/15/-. John later moved to 9 Leonard Place, Kensington and died there, leaving effects valued at £3,400/8/9 (resworn £4,198/2/4). In addition to William they had five other children:

- Henry George Burton Watson (1st November 1837–2nd April 1929) was educated at St John's College, Oxford (BA 1860, MA 1863). He married Lucy Eleanor Ann Gillman (4th July 1838–20th February 1929) on 19th May 1863 at St George, Wandsworth, London. She was born at Barfrestone, Barston, Kent, daughter of the Reverend James Gillman (1808–77) and Sophia née Riley (1816–62). Henry was Curate of Tring 1861–69, Vicar of Long Marston, Hertfordshire 1868–69, Vicar of St Leonard's, Aston Clinton, Aylesbury, Buckinghamshire 1869–95 and Vicar of Great Staughton, Cambridgeshire 1895–1909. They were living at The Wilderness, Aspley Heath, Woburn Sands, Bedfordshire in 1911. Lucy and Henry both died at St Leonard's, Woburn Sands. Henry left effects valued at £3,266/14/6. They had twelve children including, Henry James John Cradock Watson 1864, William Stephen S Watson 1866, Fredrick Harvey Watson 1867, Lucy Eleanor A Watson 1868, Rosalie Amelia St Leo Watson 1870, Florence Cawardine Watson 1871, Clement A Watson 1872, Leonard Burton Watson 1875, Edward Gillman Watson 1877, Arthur Spencer Watson 1878 and Herbert Coleridge Watson 1880. Herbert was a barrister of the Inner Temple and Literary Critic of *The Daily Telegraph*. He was serving as a lance corporal in 1st King's Royal Rifle Corps (R/21218) when he died on 5th March 1917 (Étaples Military Cemetery, France – XXI N 3A).
- Charles Cradock Watson (5th July 1839–22nd November 1917) married Amelia Caroline Steinbach (1847–80) on 11th November 1872. Her birth was registered as Amalia Carolina Steinbach. Her death was registered at Brighton, Sussex. They had three children, all born at Karlsruhe, Germany – Ludwig Henry Cradock Watson 1873, Florence Emia Cradock Watson 1874 and Violet Watson 1877. In 1891 Charles was living at Eling, Hampshire, looking after his niece, Alice Cradock Watson, and nephews, Spencer Burton Watson and Oliver Cyril Spencer Watson. He married Ann Sorel Cole née Laverty (7th February 1849–9th June 1930) in 1899 at Steyning, Sussex. Ann was born in St Helier, Jersey, Channel Islands, daughter of John Nicholas Laverty, a naval instructor, and Ann Tracy Le Gros. Ann had married Alfred Benjamin Cole (1840–93) in 1885 at Hampstead. They had a daughter, Violet Maud Mary Vicat Cole, in 1886. Charles and Ann were living at Copythorne, Cadnam, New Forest in 1901. He was living at Poonah Lodge, Cadnam, Hampshire at the time of his death, leaving effects valued at £11,360/5/11. Ann was living at L'Abri, 1 Princess Road, St Leonards-on-Sea, Sussex at the time of her death, leaving effects valued at £2,712/19/9.
- Emia Ann Watson (1845–12th August 1901) was living at 9 Leonard Place, Kensington as Eunice A Watson, looking after her nephews, Ludwig Henry Cradock Watson and Arthur Spencer Watson, and her niece, Florence Emia Cradock Watson. Emie never married and was still living there at the time of her death at 45 Sylvan Road, Upper Norwood, London, leaving effects valued at £14,448/13/2 (£1.7M in 2018).

- Edward John Watson (3rd November 1846–23rd November 1929) was educated at Merchant Taylors' School and Christ's College, Cambridge (BA 1869, MA 1872). He was admitted to Lincoln's Inn on 22nd January 1868 and was called to the Bar on 26th January 1871. He married Florence Aldridge (1849–72) on 12th July 1870 at St George, Bloomsbury and they were living at 31 Bristol Gardens, Paddington in 1871. Edward was ordained deacon (Bath and Wells) in 1872 and priest 1874. He was employed at Selwood Academy, Frome, Somerset 1872–75 and College of Christ Church, St Leonards-on-Sea, Sussex 1875–76. Edward was received into the Roman Catholic Church by Cardinal Newman on 21st December 1876. He was an assistant master at St Edmund's College, Standon St Mary, Hertfordshire and at Oscott College, Birmingham, Warwickshire in 1877. He was ordained in 1879 and was rector of St Mary's Presbytery, Hertford 1880–83. After curacies in London, he became parish priest of St Edmund's, Ware and chaplain at St Charles, Brentwood, Essex 1902–13. Edward was one of the founders of Westminster Cathedral and was Domestic Prelate to the Pope 1907. He was appointed Right Reverend Monsignor by 1911, living at St Charles' House, Brentwood, Essex. He was an expert in the matter of Lapidary Latin inscriptions. He was living at Westward House, 41 Kneesworth Road, New London Road, Royston, Hertfordshire at the time of his death there, leaving effects valued at £674/0/5.
- Thomas Cradock Watson (19th October 1848–17th November 1917) was educated at the Merchant Taylors' School and Trinity College, Cambridge from 28th January 1867 (BA 1871, MA 1874). He was admitted to the Bar in 1875 and had a practice at 59 Lincoln's Inn Fields. Thomas married Emily Mary Hastings Patten (1861–30th December 1923) in 1885 at Paddington, London. He lost the use of his legs about 1892. They were living at 5 East Cliff, Dover, Kent in 1911. He died at The Haven, New Road, Richmond, Surrey. She lived at Denton, near Canterbury, Kent and died at Canterbury Hospital, leaving effects valued at £820/11/5. They had three children – Mary Winifred Emily Cradock Watson 1887, Emia Gwendolen Cradock Watson 1889 and Arthur Vivian Cradock Watson 1890. In 1911 Mary was a jobbing gardener and Emia was a masseuse.

His maternal grandfather, George James John Mair (c.1810–17th July 1889), was an architect. He married Jane née Rumley (c.1813–10th March 1889), born at Portsmouth, Hampshire, on 18th April 1839 at Bloomsbury, London. They were living at 18 Charlotte Street, Bloomsbury, London in 1851 and at 41 Upper Bedford Place, Russell Square, London in 1881. Jane and George both died there. She left effects valued at £639/11/7 and he left £25,158/11/5 (£3.1M in 2018). In addition to Georgine they had five other children:

- John George Valentine Mair (5th September 1843–20th December 1920), a civil engineer, later changed his name to Mair-Rumley. He married Louisa Helena

Pascoe (1854–8th March 1919) in 1875 at Westminster, London. She was born at Edmonton, Middlesex. They were living at 12 Carlyle Square, Chelsea, London in 1881. She died at Brighton, Sussex. He was living at The Hammonds, Udimore, Sussex at the time of his death, leaving effects valued at £49,953/18/2 (£2.5M in 2018). They had four children – George Pascoe Mair 1876, Ida Florence Mair 1878, Elsie Jane Nelly Mair 1881 and Robert Pascoe Mair 1886.

- Henry George Mair (1846–51).
- Jane Isabella Mary Mair (1848–7th November 1922) died unmarried while living at Wargrave Lodge, Wargrave-on-Thames, Berkshire, leaving effects valued at £5,616/14/3.
- Florence Mary Jane Mair (13th June 1850–23rd November 1930) married Frederick Freeman Allen (18th March 1825–29th December 1888) on 11th June 1887 at Hastings, Sussex. He was born at Long Buckby, Northamptonshire. Frederick was a surgeon (MRCS 1846, LSA 1847) and was appointed assistant surgeon in the Royal Navy 4th July 1847–6th September 1848. He then served in the Bengal Medical Service as an assistant surgeon in Bengal from 20th November 1848, surgeon 13th November 1862, surgeon major 20th November 1868 and deputy surgeon general 6th December 1876. Frederick gained a great deal of operational experience:

  Central India 1851.

  Indian Mutiny 1857–58–siege and capture of Delhi with 4th Regiment Irregular Cavalry and the hospital of 2nd Bengal Fusiliers.

  Brigadier Shower's column into Mewatee on 2nd October 1857 and was present at the capture of Forts Rewaree, Jhojjur and Kamound.

  Oudh with 2nd Goorkhas October 1858.

  Cold weather operations with Brigadier Barker's column 1858–59.

  Peshawur frontier with 2nd Goorkhas 1863–64 and was present at the action by the Doaba Field Force under Colonel Macdonnel on 2nd January 1864 at Shubkuddur against the Momunds.

  Huzara campaign on the Black Mountain 7th August–12th November 1868 with 2nd Goorkhas.

  Principal Medical Officer right column Lushai Field Force, North East Frontier 1871–2 (CB, LG 10th September 1872).

  Deputy Surgeon General with the Kooram Field Force, Afghanistan 1878–9 and was Mentioned in Despatches by Sir Frederick Roberts for the efficient manner in which the hospitals were maintained.

  Frederick retired on 31st August 1880 and was appointed an honorary physician to Queen Victoria on 27th October. He died at The Hermitage, Frant Road, Tunbridge Wells, Kent, leaving effects valued at £5,056/10/1. Florence received a widow's pension of £250/6/4 p.a. from 30th December 1888. In 1891 she was living at The Hermitage with her sister Jane. Florence married James William Groves (1848–16th May 1902) on 24th March 1892 at The Strand, London. He was a Professor of Botany, born at Putney, London. They were lodging at 4 Lennox Road, Portsmouth, Hampshire in 1901. He died at Welwyn, Hertfordshire, leaving effects valued at £46,874/6/11 (£5.4M in 2018). When James died, Florence's pension of £264/6/4 from the Bengal Military Fund was reinstated, having lost it when she remarried. In 1911 she was the head of household, living with her sister, Jane, at Wargrave Lodge, Wargrave, Berkshire. Florence died there, leaving effects valued at £18,702/15/10.

- Mary Martha Anne Jane Mair (17th April 1852–15th February 1932) married Alfred James Emberson (1855–5th January 1924), a stockbroker, in 1887 at Holborn, London. They were living at 66 Eversfield Place, Hastings in 1901 before moving to 9 Pine Tree Glen, Bournemouth, Hampshire. Alfred died at Wargrave Lodge, Wargrave-on-Thames, leaving effects valued at £2,446/1/1. Mary lived at 39 Empress Road, Derby before bring admitted to Marley Nursing Home, Southbourne, Hampshire, where she died, leaving effects valued at £560/17/-. They had a daughter, Mary Alfreda Emberson, in 1888.

Oliver was educated at St Paul's School, Hammersmith, London from September 1888. He was a member of the OTC and the future novelist, GK Chesterton, was a fellow form member. Oliver started well as a pupil but his performance deteriorated in later years. For example in the summer term of 1889 in the Upper 3rd Form he was first out of seventeen. The following term in the Lower 4th Form he was first out of twenty-one. However, by the Christmas term of 1894 he was twelfth out of twenty-two and in the summer term of 1895 was twentieth out of twenty. He was intelligent but inclined to be idle in academic work. Nonetheless Oliver was popular and modest. His main strengths were in sports (boxing, cricket, rugby, football and rowing), where he exhibited cheery and indomitable courage, never sparing himself. He also rode to hounds.

Oliver entered the Royal Military College, Sandhurst in June 1895. He was commissioned in The Princess of Wales's Own (Yorkshire Regiment) on 20th February 1897 and was posted to the 2nd Battalion in India. He served in the Tirah Campaign 1897–98 on the North West Frontier, where he took part in the capture of the Sampagha and Arhanga Passes, reconnaissance of the Saran Sar and the action of 9th November 1897. On 24th November he was involved in operations around the Dwatoi Defile. The Battalion took the heights on the right flank and then moved along them. Lieutenant David Edward Osborne Jones (1870–97) went down the hill with three men in an attempt to turn the enemy behind the crest of the hill. However, they were well concealed. Jones spotted one of them and fired his revolver before being hit in the heart. Oliver Watson brought a section to his rescue under very heavy fire. He managed to extract Jones on a stretcher, using his own coat as a pillow, but was seriously wounded by a bullet, which just missed his lung. Lance Corporal F Brunton was killed and Lieutenant Jones later died of his wounds. Oliver later took part in operations against the Khani Khel Chamkhannis.

St Paul's School takes its name from St Paul's Cathedral, which had a cathedral school from 1103. By the 16th century it had declined and in 1509 a new school for 153 pupils was founded to the north of the Cathedral by John Colet. Colet was an outspoken critic of the Church and ensured that the School was managed by the Mercer's Company, the premier livery company in the City of London. The original school was destroyed in the Great Fire of 1666. It was rebuilt in 1670 and again in Cheapside in 1822. Towards the end of the 19th century it was decided to move to larger premises in Hammersmith in 1884 designed by Alfred Waterhouse. In September 1939 the School was evacuated to Easthampstead Park, near Crowthorne, Berkshire. The Hammersmith buildings became HQ Home Forces in July 1940 and HQ 21st Army Group in July 1943. It was commanded by General (later Field Marshal) Bernard Law Montgomery, coincidentally an Old Pauline, in the planning and execution of the invasion of Europe. The school returned in September 1945. By 1961 it become clear that the old school buildings were unsuited to modern needs. A new school was built at Barnes, close to Hammersmith Bridge. It opened in September 1968 and by 2009 had 856 boys. Amongst its numerous famous alumni are:

- Thomas Gresham (1519–79), founder of the Royal Exchange.
- John Milton (1608–74), poet.
- Samuel Pepys (1633–1703), civil servant and diarist.
- John Churchill (1650–1722), 1st Duke of Marlborough.
- Henry Baden-Powell KC (1847–1921), older brother of Robert Baden-Powell, founder of the Sea Scouts.
- Randolph Cosby Nesbitt VC (1867–1956).
- Laurence Binyon (1869–1943), poet.
- GK Chesterton (1874–1936), writer.
- Cuthbert Bromley VC (1878–1915).
- Compton Mackenzie (1883–1972), writer.
- Philip Clayton (1885–1972), founder of Toc H.
- Paul Nash (1889–1946), artist.
- Basil Liddell Hart (1895–1970), military strategist.
- Pete Murray (born 1925), disc jockey and broadcaster.
- Nicholas Parsons (born 1923), actor and television presenter.
- Robert Winston (born 1940), biologist and television presenter.
- John Simpson (born 1944), journalist.
- George Osborne (born 1971), Conservative MP and Chancellor 2010–16.
- Dan Snow (born 1978), journalist & television presenter.

He was promoted lieutenant on 17th August 1898 and was appointed Transport Officer of 4th Brigade in China during the Boxer Rebellion in 1900. He subsequently returned to India and was invalided home in 1903 with a serious illness. He transferred to the Reserve of Officers on 16th January 1904.

Troops in the Sampagha Pass.

Oliver ran the Parkwood Estate for Sir Charles Henry Bt MP at Parkwood and Crazies Hill, near Henley-on-Thames 1904–14. In 1911 he was living at Home Farm, Parkwood, Henley-on-Thames. He was a Freemason, Initiated into Loddon Lodge No.3427, 7 Reading Road, Wokingham, Berkshire on 21st January 1911 and was Passed on 18th March and Raised on 22nd April.

The Parkwood Estate at Parkwood and Crazies Hill, near Henley-on-Thames, was owned by Sir Charles Henry.

He was commissioned in 1st County of London Yeomanry on 8th September 1909 and was promoted lieutenant on 24th November 1911 and captain on 12th November 1913. When war broke out Oliver was embodied. Several sources state that he sailed for Egypt on 27th April 1915 and was appointed to command C Company/Squadron before landing at Suvla Bay, Gallipoli on 18th August 1915. However, his Medal Index Card does not support this, recording his first overseas theatre as France with no date given. Also he was not awarded the 1914–15 Star, which would be the case if he had served at Gallipoli. 1st County of London Yeomanry did serve there and perhaps it has been assumed in the past that he was with the unit. He is mentioned in the war diary of 1st County of London Yeomanry in Sinai, Egypt in April and May 1916.

Whatever his previous service entailed, Oliver had returned to Britain before 19th July 1916 and was attached to 2/5th King's Own Yorkshire Light Infantry as a major and second-in-command with seniority from 28th July 1915. He went to France with 2/5th Battalion, landing at Le Havre on 15th January 1917. **Awarded the DSO for his actions on 3rd May at Bullecourt. His CO, Lieutenant Colonel William Watson, was killed in the initial attack. Oliver found most of the men sheltering in a railway cutting. He reorganised and inspired them to go forward in a second attack, which he led. The attack failed but he pressed on, trying to contact survivors from the first attack until he was badly wounded, LG 26th July 1917. Mentioned in Sir Douglas Haig's**

Oliver's memorial paving stone outside Freemason's Hall, Covent Garden.

The Distinguished Service Order is awarded for meritorious or distinguished service by officers of the armed forces during wartime. It was instituted on 6th September 1886 by Queen Victoria. It is usually awarded to majors (or equivalent) or higher, particularly those in command. However, it has been awarded to especially valorous junior officers. In such cases it is usually an acknowledgement that the recipient just missed out on a VC. 8,981 DSOs were awarded during the Great War. Prior to 1943 the DSO could only be given to someone also Mentioned in Despatches. Since 1993 the DSO has been restricted to distinguished service, such as leadership and command by any rank, but has yet to be awarded to a non-commissioned rank.

Despatch dated 7th November 1917, LG 21st December 1917.

Oliver was hospitalised for a period and returned to active service in January 1918, although not fully fit. On 2nd February 1918, 2/5th and 1/5th Battalions joined to form 5th Battalion. **Awarded the VC for his actions near Rossignol Wood on 28th March 1918, LG 8th May 1918.** Oliver was killed during the VC action and is commemorated on the Arras Memorial, France under the Middlesex Yeomanry (Bay 7). He left effects valued at £513/3/4. At the time of his death he appears in the Army List under the Reserve of Officers (Yorkshire Regiment) as a major 5th Yorkshire Light Infantry and captain 1st County of London Yeomanry. As Oliver never married the posthumous VC was sent to GOC Home Forces on 12th June 1918 for onward transmission to his sister Alice McCrea. Oliver is commemorated in a number of other places:

- War Memorial, St Mary's Church, Wargrave, Berkshire and on a memorial plaque inside the church.
- Middlesex Yeomanry Memorial, The Crypt, St Paul's Cathedral, London.

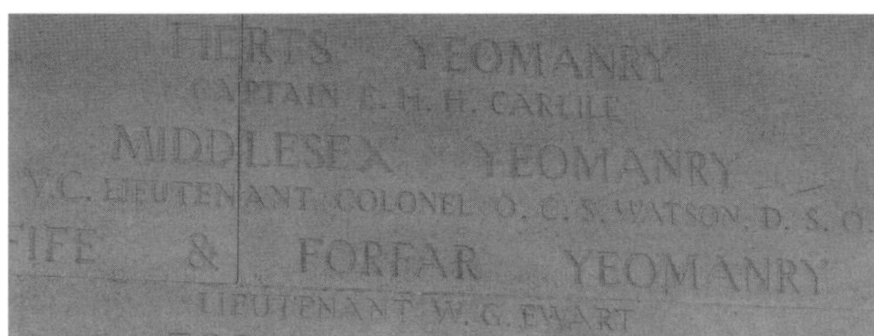

Oliver Watson's name on the Middlesex Yeomanry panel of the Arras Memorial.

- Named on the Yorkshire Regiment (later Green Howards) panel in the Royal Memorial Chapel, Royal Military Academy, Sandhurst. He appears under 1916, although at the time of his death in 1918 he was 1st County of London Yeomanry, attached to the King's Own Yorkshire Light Infantry. The regimental panels only carry the names of those officers trained at Sandhurst and, at that time, Territorial Force officers were not trained there. When he died he was only attached to the King's Own Yorkshire Light Infantry, so regardless of the unit he was serving with when he died, he was first and foremost a Green Howard when it came to commemorating him at Sandhurst.

The China War Medal 1900 was approved in 1901 for those who served in the Boxer Rebellion 11th June - 3rd December 1900. It could be issued without a clasp, or with one of the three – 'Taku Forts', 'Defence of Legations' and 'Relief of Pekin'.

The India Medal 1895–1902 was approved in 1896 for officers and men of the British and Indian armies and replaced the India General Service Medal 1854. It was awarded for various minor campaigns in India, mainly for the North-West Frontier, with each campaign represented by a clasp, of which there were seven.

- St Paul's School War Memorial, Lonsdale Road, Barnes, London.
- Memorial paving stone dedicated outside Freemason's Hall, Covent Garden, London on 25th April 2017 by The Duke of Kent KG.
- A Department for Communities and Local Government commemorative VC paving stone was dedicated at Victoria Embankment Gardens, London on 22nd March 2018 to mark the centenary of his award.

In addition to the VC and DSO he was awarded the India Medal 1895–1902 with two clasps ('Punjab Frontier 1897–98' and 'Tirah 1897–98'), China War Medal 1900, British War Medal 1914–20 and Victory Medal 1914–19 with Mentioned-in-Despatches Oakleaf. The medals were loaned to the Green Howards Regimental Museum in 1956 and were subsequently donated in 1992 by Gerald Whittuck, husband of Oliver's niece, Mrs Catherine Whittuck, who died in 1991. They are held by the Green Howards Regimental Museum, Trinity Church Square, Richmond, Yorkshire.

Wargrave War Memorial, St Mary's Church, Berkshire.

Z1030 LANCE SERGEANT JOSEPH EDWARD WOODALL
1st Battalion, The Rifle Brigade (The Prince Consort's Own)

Joseph Woodall was born on 1st June 1896 at Robinson Street, off Regent Road, Salford, Lancashire. His father, Thomas Woodall (27th November 1868–1935), born at Pendleton, Lancashire, worked for the London and North Western Railway as a train driver. He married Hannah née Valentine (20th March 1876–1925), a calico weaver born at Hulme, Lancashire, on 6th August 1894 at St Bartholomew's Church, Salford, Lancashire. They lived at Beech Street, Patricroft, Eccles, Manchester. By 1901 they had moved to 8 Commission Street, Salford and he was a railway engine stoker. By 1903 they had moved to 39 Bridgewater Street, Winton, Eccles. They were still living there in 1911, by when he was employed on general work in the engine sheds. Joseph had ten siblings:

- Believed to be Thomas Woodall (born and died 1895).
- Mary Alice Woodall (4th April 1899–1977) married William Howarth in 1922. They had two children:
    - Maud M Howarth (born 1922) married Robert W Gerrard (c.1910–59) in 1947. They had two children – Jean Gerrard 1948 and Alan Gerrard 1949.

Maud married Henry A Irving (born 1924) in 1963. They had a son, Neil H Irving, in 1964.
    - Clarence Howarth (born 1925).
- Ada Woodall (2nd September 1900–December 1984) married Harold Mayne (1904–17th July 1961) in 1926. They were living at 39 Bridgewater Street, Winton, Eccles at the time of his death at Hope Hospital, Salford. They had a son, Harold G Mayne, in 1927.
- May Woodall (born 1903) married Robert William Sutcliffe (17th September 1904–1979) in 1928. They had a daughter, May Sutcliffe (18th February 1929–1977), who married Charles Tarbrook (13th June 1925–2005) in 1949 and they had a son, Philip C Tarbrook, in 1955. Charles married Ellen Steele in 1981.
- Emily Woodall (19th December 1905–April 1992) married Joseph Ellis (11th July 1904–30th July 1976) in 1933. He was living at 9 Wycliffe Street, Patricroft, Eccles at the time of his death there. They had two children:
    - Doris Ellis (born and died 1934).
    - Derek Ellis (born 1942).
- Arthur Woodall (born 1907) moved to Canada about 1929 and served in the Royal Canadian Artillery during the Second World War. He married in Canada and had three children.
- Charles Henry Woodall (8th January 1910–19th October 1973) married Winifred Ashurst (1911–25th July 2007) in 1945. He was living at 143 Cromwell Road, Eccles at the time of his death.
- William Woodall (28th January 1913–1981) served in the South Lancashire Regiment during the Second World War. He lived at Park Street, Peel Green.
- Harry Woodall (5th August 1915–January 1996) married Alice Hood

Regent Road, Salford, close to where Joseph Woodall was born.

Joseph's parents married at St Bartholomew's Church, Salford, which was founded in 1842 and closed in 1975. It has since been demolished.

(24th April 1914–1980) in 1937. Harry served in the King's Own Royal Regiment during the Second World War. He lived at Bridgewater Street, Winton. They had a daughter, Doreen Woodall, in 1938, who married James Rimmer in 1957 and they had three children – Vivienne G Woodall 1958, Adrian J Woodall 1959 and Joanne Woodall 1963.

- George Woodall (15th November 1916–October 1984) served in the Lancashire Fusiliers during the Second World War. He lived at Eccles Road, Eccles. He married Ruby Barnett (27th September 1918–August 1986) in 1944 and they had two children:
    - Brian G Woodall (born 1949) married Beverley Willock (born 1955), birth registered as Wellock, in 1976.
    - David T Woodall (born 1954) married Denise Cawley (born 1957) in 1977 and they had a son, Daniel Woodall in 1980.

Joseph's paternal grandfather, William Henry Woodall (16th September 1849–6th February 1892), a plumber, was born at Snaith, Yorkshire. He married Mary née Bowring (1844–8th March 1912) in 1868. She was born at Pendleton, Salford, Lancashire. They were living at 24 Freehold Terrace, Pendleton, Salford in 1871 and at 16 Wheat Street, Scarborough, Yorkshire in 1881. They were living at 13 Albion Place, Pendleton at the time of his death there. Mary married Arthur Warburton (1858–13th November 1934), a brick setter, in 1893. They were living at 13 Albion Place, Pendleton at the time of her death there. He was living at 62 Park Street, Swinton, Lancashire at the time of his death at Green Lane Institution, Patricroft, Lancashire. In addition to Thomas, William and Mary had another son:

- Charles Henry Woodall (18th August 1870–1936), a copper roller engraver, married Elizabeth Alice Barlow (23rd April 1872–1946) on 27th May 1893 at St George's Church, Charlestown, Lancashire. They were living at 14 Marsland Street, Broughton in 1911. Charles enlisted in 8th Lancashire Fusiliers at Lower Broughton, Lancashire on 13th October 1915 (306501), described as 5′ 1¾″ tall. He served in the Mediterranean Expeditionary Force from 27th March 1916 and in France from 23rd February 1917. He was evacuated to England and admitted to the Royal Pavilion Hospital, Brighton, Sussex on 13th May 1918. On 13th August he was discharged as no longer fit for war service. They lived at 33 Broomfield Street, Cheetham, Lancashire and had eight children – Mary Alice Bowring Woodall 1893, Henry/Harry Woodall 1894, William Arthur Woodall 1896, Charles Woodall 1898, Rose Woodall 1900, George Woodall 1901, Elsie Woodall 1905 and Dorothy Woodall 1909.

His maternal grandfather, Joseph Valentine (1853–1905), born at Chorlton, Lancashire, married Mary Ann née Hannah (1854–1927), born in Manchester, Lancashire, at the Cathedral Parish Church there on 2nd January 1871. They were

Joseph's paternal grandfather came from Snaith in the East Riding of Yorkshire. It was the site of a Bomber Command airfield in the Second World War.

Joseph's maternal grandparents married in Manchester Cathedral, seat of the Bishop of Manchester, and also the city's parish church. The medieval church was refaced, restored and extended in the Victorian period and also following bomb damage in the Second World War. There is evidence of a church on the site as early as 700 AD and a collegiate church was established in 1421. The new Manchester Diocese came into effect in 1847. The Cathedral was damaged again in the 1996 IRA terrorist bombing. The building has been granted Grade I listing status.

living at 12 Hampton Place, Stretford Road, Manchester at the time. In 1876 he was a packer and they were living at 10 Pine Street, Hulme, Lancashire. By 1881 they had moved to 312 City Road, Hulme and by 1891 he was a stationary engine driver and they were living at 4 Winchester Place, Salford. He was a railway porter by 1901. Mary was lodging as a housekeeper at 77 James's Street, Salford in 1911. In addition to Hannah they had three other children:

- Joseph Valentine (1873–1956) was an iron turner in 1891. He married Elizabeth Shaw James (1877–1957) in 1899. She was born at Crewe, Cheshire. They were living at 21 Derwent Street, Salford in 1911. They had five children including – Elizabeth Valentine 1900, Gladys Valentine 1903, Alfred Egerton Valentine 1908 and Florence Valentine 1915.
- Jane Valentine (1878–1966) married Joseph Warrender (1875–23rd March 1957) in 1901. He was a tea and coffee dealer in 1911 and they were living at 15 Gee Lane, Winton, Lancashire. They were living at Winton House, Gee Lane, Winton at the time of his death at Park Hospital, Davyhulme, Lancashire. They had a son, Joseph Warrender, in 1906, who married Mavis Higgins (born 1907) in 1935 and they had two daughters – Patricia Warrender 1939 and Brenda M Higgins 1945.
- Thomas Valentine (1880–1967) was a brass finisher. He married Maria Russell (1884–1927) in 1904. They were living at 78 Derg Street, Pendleton in 1911. They

had four children including – Thomas Valentine 1904, Mary Margaret Valentine 1908 and Alan Valentine 1913.

Joseph was educated at:

- St Ambrose Infants' School, Salford.
- St Michael's Junior School, Eccles.
- Beech Street School, Patricroft, Eccles.

When he applied for a commission in 1918, he specified Peel Green British Elementary School, Manchester. Joseph worked for a local newsagent in Eccles before being employed at Ermen & Roby's Mill, Cawdor Street, Patricroft, Lancashire as a mill jobber. Later he was employed by George Mort's Quilt Manufacturers, Leigh Street as a cotton operative. Joseph enlisted in 1st Rifle Brigade on 2nd September 1914. He went to France on 29th July 1915 and was promoted lance corporal, corporal and acting lance sergeant. **Awarded the VC for his actions at La Pannerie, near Hinges, France, on 22nd April 1918, LG 28th June 1918.** He applied for a commission on 28th May 1918, described as 5′ 6″ tall and weighing 126 lbs. He commenced training at No.8 Officer Cadet Battalion, Lichfield on 20th September. The VC was presented by the King at Buckingham Palace on 23rd November 1918. Later that day he was escorted to the Palladium Cinema in Eccles by the Mayor and presented with an illuminated address and a sum of money. He was commissioned into the Regiment's service battalions on 17th March 1919 and transferred to the Class Z Reserve on 1st September 1920. He relinquished his commission on 1st September 1921, retaining the rank of second lieutenant.

One of the schools attended by Joseph Woodall was Beech Street School, Patricroft, Eccles now Beech Street Primary School.

After the war George Mort offered him a bicycle in recognition of his gallantry but did not offer him his old job back. He found employment at Royton Mill in Oldham. Joseph was severely injured in 1920, losing part of his arm in an accident involving an unfenced scutching machine. He attended a course in textiles at Salford Technical School and became a grey buyer in 1925 for the United Turkey Red Company in Manchester.

Joseph Woodall married Rosannah Lighton (also seen as Leighton) (born 28th January 1902) in 1923 at Salford. They lived at Edale, Lumb Lane, Bramhall, Cheshire before moving to Dun Laoghaire, Ireland in 1955. They had two children:

- Patricia Woodall (born 1926) married as Mahoney and had at least one son, Michael Mahoney, who travelled from Australia for the dedication of the commemorative paving stone in April 2018. Michael Mahoney lived at Manly Beach, Sydney and was a chartered accountant.
- David Woodall (6th April 1929–14th April 1996).

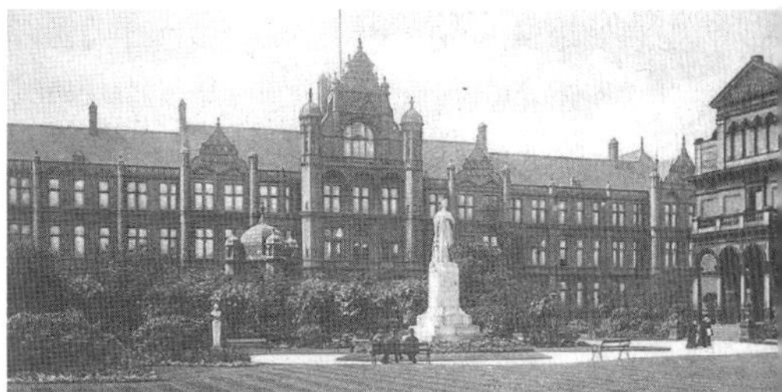

Salford Technical School, more correctly the Salford Royal Technical Institute, was renamed the Royal Technical College in 1921. In 1958 it split into The Royal College of Advanced Technology and the Peel Park Technical College, the latter becoming the Peel Park Technical Institute in 1961, the Salford College of Technology in 1970, and University College Salford in 1992. Meanwhile in 1967 the Royal College of Advanced Technology became the University of Salford, which merged with University College Salford into a single institution in 1996.

Rosannah's father, David Lighton (1860–1906), married Elizabeth née Tully (15th January 1867–1908) on 28th August 1886 at Mother of God and St James Church, Pendleton Way, Pendleton, Salford. She was born in Dublin, Ireland. He was a bricklayer's labourer in 1901 and they were living at 7 Newton Street, Pendleton, Salford. In addition to Rosannah they had five other children:

- John Joseph Lighton (1887–1954) married Louisa Jarrett (1886–1962) in 1906. In 1911 he was a coalminer hewer and they were living at 26 Rossall Street, Pendleton. They had seven children – Elizabeth Ann Lighton 1906, John Joseph Lighton 1907, Julia Ann Lighton 1908, James H Lighton 1911, Catherine Leighton 1915, Richard E Leighton 1917 and David Leighton 1927.
- David Lighton (born 1889) was a collier in 1911. He married Gertrude Keane (born 1899) in 1921.
- James Lighton (10th March 1892–1977) was a printer's labourer with Letterpress Printing in 1911. He is understood to have married Ruth Loxley (13th November 1887–1976) in 1915. She was born at Hadfield, Derbyshire, daughter of Edward and Annie Loxley. The Loxley family moved to Essex, Massachusetts, USA prior to 1891 and appeared there in the 1900 United States Federal Census. Ruth returned to England and was a cotton winder boarding with John and Jane Morris at 2 Maud Street, Pendleton in 1911. They had a daughter, Ruth Leighton, in 1915.
- Mary Catherine Lighton (born 1894) was a blouse machinist in 1911.
- Margaret Mary Lighton (born 1896) was a bobbin doffer in a cotton mill in 1911. She is understood to have married John Daniels (born 1895) in 1931 at Barton upon Irwell, her name being registered as Leighton. They had a daughter, Patricia Daniels, in 1934.

David, James, Mary, Margaret and Rosannah were living with their grandparents, James and Mary Tully, at 1 Newton Street, Salford in 1911, all recorded as Leighton.

St Michael's Hospital, Newtownsmith, Dún Laoghaire, where Joseph died in 1962.

Joseph attended a number of VC Reunions – the VC Garden Party at Buckingham Palace on 26th June 1920, the VC Dinner at the Royal Gallery of the House of Lords, London on 9th November 1929 and the Victory Day Celebration Dinner & Reception at The Dorchester, London on 8th June 1946. He did not attend the VC Centenary celebrations in 1956, but was present at Dublin's Festival of Remembrance in November 1956 with fellow VCs Sir Adrian Carton de Wiart, James Duffy and John Moyney, accompanied by Sir A Clutterbuck, the British Ambassador.

Joseph's headstone in Dean's Grange Cemetery, Dún Laoghaire, with the reference to the actual burial site at the bottom (Frank O'Neill).

Joseph suffered a fit in his flat at Sandycove, Dublin and fell over a live electric fire. He was discovered by Joseph King, a neighbour, and rushed to St Michael's Hospital, Newtownsmith, Dún Laoghaire. He developed bronchial pneumonia and died there on 2nd January 1962. He is buried in Dean's Grange Cemetery, Dún Laoghaire (St Patrick's Plot, Block H, Grave 173). The plot was purchased by the King family and Joseph King was buried there when he died on 30th April 1993.

The King family would not allow a marker on the grave but the cemetery authorities agreed to a headstone in another part of the cemetery bearing the grave reference. The headstone was dedicated on 2nd January 2010. The ceremony was attended by David The O'Morohoe, two mayors from Northern Ireland, the Cathaoireleach (Chair) of Dún Laoghaire-Rathdown County Council, representatives of The Connaught Rangers Association and the Royal Munster Fusiliers Association. The headstone was funded by the Ulster Defence Regimental Associations, the Medal Society of Ireland, Mid-Antrim Friends of the Somme, Antrim Community Church, Air Cadets (Northern Ireland Command), Antrim Ulster Unionist Party and Larne businessman, Kenny Hogg. Joseph is commemorated in a number of other places:

Part of the Rifle Brigade Memorial in Winchester Cathedral. Joseph Woodall's name is towards the bottom of the left panel. At the bottom of the same panel are the names of William Gregg and William Beesley, who also appear in this book (Paul Goodwin).

- On the Rifle Brigade Memorial, Winchester Cathedral, Hampshire.
- A Department for Communities and Local Government commemorative paving stone was dedicated at Regent Square Park War Memorial, Ordsall, Salford, Lancashire on 22nd April 2018 to mark the centenary of his award.

In addition to the VC he was awarded the 1914–15 Star, British War Medal 1914–20, Victory Medal 1914–19, George VI Coronation Medal 1937 and Elizabeth II Coronation Medal 1953. The medals were on loan to the Royal Green Jackets Museum, Peninsular Barracks, Romsey Road, Winchester, Hampshire for a period before being moved to the Imperial War Museum, again on loan, in November 2007. They are displayed in the Lord Ashcroft VC Gallery of the Imperial War Museum, Lambeth Road, London.

203590 PRIVATE THOMAS YOUNG
1/9th Battalion, The Durham Light Infantry (Pioneers)

Thomas Young was born on 28th January 1895 at 2 Hedworth Lane, High Spen, Boldon, Co Durham, registered as Thomas Murrell. His father, also Thomas Murrell (1857–21st August 1896), was a bricklayer's labourer in 1871. His surname has also been seen as Morrell. He married Mary née Walker (21st May 1875–2nd July 1925) in 1890 at South Shields, Co Durham. He was a coach trimmer and they were living at 84 Marsden Street, Westoe, South Shields in 1891. Mary married Surtees Young (3rd October 1875–18th May 1939) in 1899. Surtees was an apprentice mason in 1891, living with his parents at Elders Buildings, Whitburn, South Shields. In 1901 he was a mason and they were living at Cliff Terrace, Ryhope, Houghton le Spring, Co Durham. By 1911 he was a coal miner and they were living at The Square, Willington on Tyne, Northumberland. Thomas had twelve siblings from his mother's two marriages, including:

- Thomas Murrell (born and died 1892), birth registered as Morrell.
- Surtees Young (23rd March 1900–1964) married Alice Welsh (born April 1897) in 1928, the VC's sister-in-law. Surtees served during the Second World War and may have served underage in the Great War. They had two children – Surtees Young 1930 and Norma Young 1931.
- Preston Young (1902–50) served during the Second World War.
- John William Young (born 1903) served during the Second World War.
- Maud Young (8th November 1905–2001) married Matthew Hetherington (1890–1956) in 1928. They had a daughter, Mary W Hetherington, in 1929.
- Sarah Walker Young (16th May 1906–5th May 1969) married John Robert Bone (23rd July 1906–11th January 1994) in 1933. They had three children – Brian Bone 1937, Margaret Bone 1939 and Stella Bone 1947.
- Mary Ellen Young (9th January 1908–February 1999) married Leonard Barham in 1932 at Croydon, Surrey. They had two children – Heather Barham 1934 and George Barham 1936.
- Francis John Peat Young (1909–May 1985) married Hilda Elizabeth Waller (30th October 1916–6th September 2006) in 1939 at Woolwich, Kent. They had a daughter, Frances J Young, in 1940. She is understood to have died at Lismore, New South Wales, Australia.
- James Young (1911–20th July 1945) married Jennie Ward Lee (born 1916) in 1940. He served as a gunner (805122) in 6th Heavy Anti-Aircraft Regiment, Royal Artillery and died as a prisoner in Brunei, possibly during the final Sandakan Death March. He is buried in Labuan War Cemetery, Sabah, Malaysia (F A 16).

Willington High Street.

Westoe village, South Shields.

- William Edward Young (7th August 1912–15th February 1989) married Evelyn Beck (born 1904) in 1933. They had two children – Lavinia Young 1934 and William Young 1938.

Thomas' paternal grandfather, Thomas Murrell (c.1832–2nd May 1887), was a colliery engineman. He married Jane née Parker (25th July 1826–1895) on 23rd November 1856 at Flag Lane Chapel, Sunderland. They were living at Ivy Cottage, Wagonway Side, Long Benton, Northumberland in 1871. She was living with her son Thomas and family at 84 Marsden Street, Westoe in 1891. In addition to Thomas they had four other children:

Thomas's brother, James, is buried in Labuan War Cemetery. Labuan, a small island in Brunei Bay off the coast of northwest Borneo, is part of Sabah, Malaysia. He served in 6th Heavy Anti-Aircraft Regiment, Royal Artillery. The Regiment formed before the Second World War and was evacuated from Dunkirk prior to helping to defend London and the West Midlands during the Battle of Britain and the Blitz. The Regiment was sent to the Middle East but was diverted to the Far East, when the Japanese invaded Malaya in December 1941. Almost all of the Regiment was captured at Singapore, Java and Sumatra by 12th March 1942. The men worked on the Burma Railway and elsewhere for their captors in appalling conditions. Several thousand British and Australian prisoners were sent to the Sandakan area in Borneo, where they were employed on airfield construction. They were starved, beaten and overworked. In February 1945 the Japanese decided to move the prisoners westwards to Ranau, over 260 kms inland. Almost 2,000 took part in three death marches from Sandakan. Any who fell on the journey were shot. Only 260 men arrived at Ranau. Of these only six survived the war by escaping to live with the natives. After the war the bodies of the victims of the Sandakan death marches, and from scattered graves throughout Borneo, were taken to Sandakan, where a large number of prisoners were already buried. However, the area was subject to severe flooding and a permanent cemetery there was impracticable. The remains of 2,700 men, more than half unknown, were transferred to Labuan War Cemetery, which was specially constructed to receive graves from all over Borneo. Given the date of his death, in late July 1945, it seems likely that James died on the last of the Sandarkan death marches. His Regiment suffered 495 fatal casualties during the war. Of these, twenty-nine were in France and Belgium in 1940 and nineteen were in Britain but the vast majority, 447, were in the Far East, mainly as prisoners of war. Two VCs are buried at Labuan - Jack Mackey and Tom Derrick.

- John 'Jack' Murrell (born c.1858).
- William Murrell (born 1st July 1859) was a farm labourer in 1871 and later a coal miner. He married Barbara Walker (1863–1922) on 1st January 1887 at Hedworth, Co Durham. Barbara was the VC's maternal aunt. They were living at 6 Imeary Street, Westoe, Co Durham in 1891. She and her children were living with her parents at Rectory Bank, Boldon Colliery, Co Durham in 1901 and at 78 Arnold Street, Boldon Colliery with sons, James and William, both coal miners, in 1911. They had six children including – Jane Murrell 1887, John Thomas Murrell 1888, James Walker Murrell 1889 and William Murrell 1894. James Walker Murrell enlisted in the Yorkshire Regiment (7/13817) at Bolden Colliery on 31st August 1914. He was described as a miner, 5′ 10½″ tall, weighing 157 lbs, with dark complexion, blue eyes, brown hair and his religious denomination was Church of England. He was promoted lance corporal 16th October 1914, corporal 3rd November, lance sergeant 21st November and sergeant 16th January 1915. He went to France on 13th July 1915 with 7th Battalion and received a severe gunshot wound to the head on 17th February 1916. He was evacuated to Britain on the strength of the Depot on 5th March and admitted to King George Hospital, Stamford Street, London on the same day. A medical board on 17th April noted that he had a depressed fracture of the skull, which resulted in immediate paralysis of the right arm and leg. His speech had almost returned to normal but his brain was still visible through a large oval gap in the left parietal region. He was discharged no longer fit for war service on 16th May 1916, with a pension of 29/- per week. His address was 17 Cooperative Buildings, Bolden Colliery, Co Durham but he received further treatment at Gifford House Auxiliary Hospital, Roehampton, Surrey. A medical board on 29th September noted that he was totally incapacitated. Silver War Badge No.92864 was forwarded to him on 15th December. A medical board on 23rd March 1917 noted that he had no earnings and his pension was raised to 32/- per week. He died on 26th March 1917 according to his service record, although CWGC records give his date of death as 6th April 1917. James is buried in Bolden Cemetery (A C 154).
- Martha Murrell (1861–1932) married Joseph Crawford Moore (1859–1935), a coalminer, in 1886. They had a son, Joseph Moore, in 1886 and were living at Holly Street, Heworth, Co Durham in 1891.
- Margaret Murrell (6th April 1865–1st November 1949) married Robert Moralee (10th May 1861–22nd August 1939), a coalminer hewer, on 1st July 1882. They were living at 45 West Terrace, Boldon in 1891, at 4 Fir Street, Hebburn, Co Durham in 1901 and at 27 Clyde Street, Ebchester, Co Durham in 1911. They had thirteen children including, Robert William Moralee 1884, Henry Moralee 1886, Thomas Murrell Moralee 1888, Andrew Moralee 1890, Margaret Murrell Moralee 1891, Jane Moralee 1895, Ruth Moralee 1898, Martha Moralee 1902 and John Moralee 1905. Thomas Murrell Moralee (12th February 1888–13th

November 1918) was serving as a lance corporal in 25th Squadron, Machine Gun Corps (51207) when he died on active service (North Gate War Cemetery, Baghdad, Iraq – VI L 4).

His maternal grandfather, John Walker (c.1832–16th November 1907), a coal miner, married Sarah née Robson (c.1835–13th December 1905) in 1856. They were living at Colliery Stock Yard, Westoe, Co Durham in 1861. By 1871 he was a brakeman and they had moved to Boldon, Co Durham. They were living at 13 Burns Street, Bolden in 1881 and at Rectory Bank, South Shields by 1901. In addition to Mary they had nine other children:

- George Walker (born 1857) was a coal miner in 1871.
- Mary Ann Walker (born 1858) was a domestic servant in 1871.
- William Robson Walker (1860–1935) was a coal miner in 1871.
- Sarah Jane Walker (born 1861).
- Barbara Walker (1863–1922) married William Murrell, the VC's paternal uncle – see above.
- Elizabeth Robson Walker (born 1864).
- Catherine Walker (born 1866).
- James Walker (born 1868) was a butcher's assistant in 1881.
- Thomas Walker (born 1870).

Thomas was educated at High Spen Primary School, Co Durham and became a miner at Garesfield Colliery, High Spen. He enlisted in 9th Durham Light Infantry in 1913 (1975 later 203590) and went to France on 20th April 1915. He was gassed the following month and spent ten weeks in hospital in early 1916. **Awarded the VC for his actions at Bucquoy, France 25th-31st March 1918, LG 4th June 1918.** The VC was presented by the King in the quadrangle of Buckingham Palace on 29th June 1918.

He was greeted at Newcastle Central Station by five coal mining officials, who took him home in a pony and trap via Scotswood Road to Blaydon and High Spen. He was living in East Street at the time. The Earl of Durham welcomed him and he was presented with a watch, War Bonds and a silver cigarette case. Local pit owners subsequently presented him with a gold watch and chain and more presentations followed from Blaydon Council. At Saltwell Park, Gateshead 15,000 people greeted him and Colonel Francis John Cheverton, a former curate, conducted a drumhead service.

After the war Thomas returned to the mines as a hewer, but ill health forced him to quit and he was then employed as a bath attendant at the mine on £9 per week. Thomas Young married Rachel née Welsh (1894–21st April 1940) in 1919 at Gateshead, Co Durham. She was a farm worker in 1911. He was recorded as

Thomas was a miner at Garesfield Colliery, High Spen. It consisted of a number of pits, the first of which was in production in 1801. Ten others followed and the last closed in January 1960. It was owned by the Marquis of Bute until the 1890s, when the Consett Iron Co took it over. It 1947 it came under the National Coal Board. The coal was particularly suitable for making coke for iron manufacture.

High Spen Primary School (Chronicle Live).

Thomas M Young, probably for Murrell. They are understood to have had five children:

- Marian Morrell (born 1920) married George Charlton (she was registered as Young) in 1945.
- Isabel Morrell (born 1921) married Basil Milner (born 1923) in 1947. They had a son, John Milner, the same year.
- Rita Murrell (born 1924) married Philip Grant (born 1919) in 1958.
- Thomas Murrell (born 1927).
- John Walker Morrell (born 1929) married Elizabeth 'Betty' Brooks (born 1928) in 1950. She was the cousin of Edward Colquhoun Charlton VC. They had a son, John W Morrell, in 1951.

Rachel's father, James Welsh (6th April 1855–1929), a coal miner hewer, was born at St Ninian's, Stirlingshire, Scotland. He married Isabella née Hedley (1863–1937), born at North Cramlington, Northumberland, on 18th April 1885 at the Register Office, Tynemouth, Co Durham. They were living at Storbys Blags, Weetslade, Northumberland in 1901 and at 13 Townley Terrace, High Spen in 1911. In addition to Rachel, Isabella and James had thirteen other children, including:

Thomas at his investiture at Buckingham Palace on 29th June 1918. On the left is Sergeant Albert Mountain VC, whose story is told elsewhere in this book.

- William Hedley (1884–1930), a coal miner hewer, changed his name to William Hedley Welsh. He married Sarah Ann Fletcher (1887–1944) in 1907 at Lanchester, Co Durham. They

John George Lambton, 3rd Earl of Durham KG GCVO PC VD (1855–1928), was the great-grandson of Prime Minister Charles Grey, 2nd Earl Grey. He served in the Coldstream Guards and was later Honorary Colonel of the Durham Heavy Brigade RA, 6th Northumberland Fusiliers and 8th Durham light Infantry. He was Lord Lieutenant of Durham 1884–1928 and Lord High Steward to King George V during his visit to India 1911–12. Lord Durham married Ethel Elizabeth Louisa Milner in 1882 but the marriage was childless and she was committed to a mental institution for most of her life. He had a child, John RH Rudge, with the dancer Letty Lind, with whom he was with for many years until her death in 1923. Durham was a member of the Jockey Club and ensured that racing continued during the First World War. He was also responsible for abolishing the flag start in favour of the starting gate. He bred most of his own horses but a classic win eluded him until *Beam* won the 1927 Epsom Oaks. Having waited almost a lifetime for this win, it is rather suitable that the family motto is *The Day will Come*.

were living with his mother and family in 1911. They had nine children – James Welsh 1909, William Welsh 1912, John McG Welsh 1914, Isabella Welsh 1915, Robert Welsh 1916, Mary Welsh 1919, Joseph Welsh 1920, Ralph Welsh 1921 and Thomas Welsh 1923.

- James Welsh (born 1887) was a coal miner (underground engine plane).
- Robert Welsh (c.1888–19th July 1916) was a coal mine pony driver. He was serving as a lance corporal (5718) in 2/7th Royal Warwickshire when he was killed in action. He is commemorated on the Loos Memorial, France (Panel 22–25).
- John 'Jack' Welsh (born c.1890) was a coal miner hewer.
- Minnie Welsh (1892–1951) was a dressmaker in 1911.
- Alice Welsh (born 1897) was a farm worker in 1911. She married her brother-in-law, Surtees Young, in 1928.
- Joseph Welsh (born 1899).
- Ralph Welsh (1901–51) married Minnie Ward (13th July 1910–1974) in 1929. They had six children, including James Welsh 1929, Marion Welsh 1930, Norma Welsh 1933, Robert Welsh 1935 and Eva A Welsh 1941.
- Isabella Welsh (born c.1903).
- Thomas Welsh (born c.1907).

Robert Welsh's name on the Loos Memorial.

Thomas appeared in court on 30th August 1923 with Samuel Cutter, charged with stealing four hens from a poultry house. His lawyer based the defence on Thomas being so drunk after visiting a flower show that he did not know what he was doing. He passed out in his kitchen to find the chickens beside him when he awoke next day. He was put on probation.

Thomas attended a number of VC reunions – the VC Garden Party at Buckingham Palace on 26th June 1920, the VC Dinner at the Royal Gallery of the House of Lords, London on 9th November 1929, the Victory Day Celebration Dinner & Reception at The Dorchester, London on 8th June 1946, the VC Centenary Celebrations at Hyde Park, London on 26th June 1956 and the 3rd and 4th VC & GC Association Reunions at the Café Royal, London on 18th July 1962 and 16th July 1964.

The Empire Palace Theatre on Newgate Street, Newcastle was known simply as The Empire. It opened as the Empire Variety Theatre on 1st December 1890, with a capacity of 2,000 people. It was rebuilt in 1903 and in 1913 the Empire Cinema opened alongside. The Empire was demolished in 1963.

In 1939 Thomas re-enlisted in the Durham Light Infantry but, when his wife died in April 1940, he was discharged in order to be able to look after his young family. He then served in the Home Guard. His life was marred by ill health, drink and financial troubles. He is reputed to have marched on stage at the Empire Palace Theatre, Newcastle and encouraged people to throw money at him. While on Home Guard duty on one of the Tyne bridges he is said to have had a tin box between his feet, begging for contributions. Whether these stories are true or not, the fact that they are attributed to him is a sad epitaph for a soldier who displayed great gallantry in the face of the enemy in the service of his country.

Thomas Young died at Whickham Council Men's Hostel, The Hermitage, Front Street, Whickham, Co Durham on 15th October 1966. His medals were displayed at his funeral at which the Last Post was sounded. He is buried with his wife in St Patrick's Cemetery, High Spen, Co Durham. Thomas is commemorated in a number of other places:

- High Spen Primary School, Co Durham memorial to the two VC holders associated with the village, Thomas Young VC buried in St Patrick's Cemetery and Frederick Dobson VC, who lived there prior to WWI. The memorial was unveiled on 8th July 2007, funded by Gateshead Council and local veterans' associations but the school alone raised £32,000.

- Thomas Young VC Class, High Spen Primary School, Hugar Road, High Spen, Rowlands Gill, Tyne and Weir. The other five classes are named St George, Florence Nightingale, Grace Darling, Martin Luther and Frederick William Dobson VC.
- A commemorative stone to honour eleven Durham Light Infantry VCs was dedicated in the grounds of the Durham Light Infantry Museum, Aykley Heads, Durham on 8th September 2001 by Brigadier Robin MacGregor-Oakford MC. The memorial was funded by the Durham Light Infantry veterans' group 'The Faithful Inkerman Dinner Club'. An honour guard was provided by the 68th Foot Re-Enactment Society in red tunics. The ceremony was attended by the Regiment's sole surviving VC, Captain Richard Annand.
- Bronze statue on Shields Town Hall staircase, dedicated in 2007.
- Named on the Honours Board, Gateshead Library, Prince Consort Road, Gateshead, Tyne & Wear.
- A Department for Communities and Local Government commemorative VC paving stone was dedicated at Boldon Colliery War Memorial, Cotswold Lane

The Hermitage at Whickham, where Thomas Young died in October 1966. It was built around 1790 for a Quaker family, the Taylors, who establish a brewery in nearby Swalwell and owned the Hermitage until 1910. Thereafter it was used as the village library and a care home. In 2014 it was converted into apartments (Rightmove).

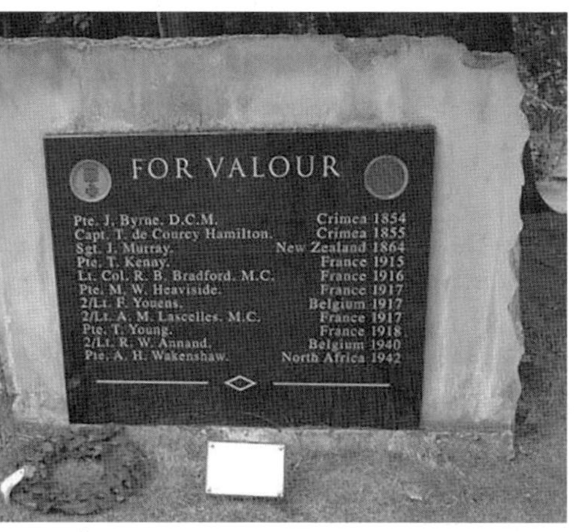

The commemorative stone honouring the eleven Durham Light Infantry soldiers awarded the VC in the grounds of the former Durham Light Infantry Museum at Aykley Heads, Durham (Memorials to Valour).

Thomas Young's grave in St Patrick's Cemetery at High Spen (Memorials to Valour).

The King George VI Coronation Medal was awarded to the Royal Family, selected officers of state, officials, servants of the Royal Household, ministers, government and local government officials, mayors, public servants, members of the armed forces and police in Britain, the colonies and Dominions. A total of 90,279 medals were awarded.

on 27th March 2018 to mark the centenary of his award.

In addition to the VC he was awarded the 1914–15 Star, British War Medal 1914–20, Victory Medal 1914–19, George VI Coronation Medal 1937 and Elizabeth II Coronation Medal 1953. Thomas had to pawn his gold watch and VC in 1936. They were spotted by a former 9th Durham Light Infantry officer and were bought by the Regiment for £50 and £60 respectively. The medals were held by the Durham Light Infantry Museum, Aykley Heads, Framwell Gate, Durham until it closed due to funding difficulties. The Durham Light Infantry Medal Collection is on loan to the Palace Green Library, Durham University, Stockton Road, Durham and is not on display but can be accessed by appointment.

Sources

The following institutions, individuals and publications were consulted:

Regimental Museums

King's Own Royal Lancaster Regiment Museum, Lancaster; Light Infantry Office (Yorkshire), Pontefract; Blackburn Museum and Art Gallery; Lancashire County and Regimental Museum, Preston; The Royal Army Chaplain's Department Association; RHQ Worcestershire and Sherwood Foresters, Beeston; The Worcestershire Regiment Museum Trust, Worcester; Green Howards Museum, Richmond, Yorkshire; RHQ Queen's Lancashire Regiment, Preston; RHQ Prince of Wales's Own Regiment of Yorkshire, York; Border Regiment and Kings Own Royal Border Regiment Museum, Carlisle; Canadian War Museum, Ottawa; Royal Artillery Historical Trust; Lancashire HQ Royal Regiment of Fusiliers.

Individuals

Heather & Raymond Allen, Doug and Richard Arman, Rosemary Barnett, Tony Barnett, Ken Beesley, Rosemary Beharrell, David Blanchard, Roger Capewell, John Charnley, Maj John Cotterill, HF Counter, Peter Donnolly, Maj (Ret'd) MA Easey, Kenneth Forbes-Robertson, Lynne Gregg-Boot, Lt Cdr (Ret'd) Gwyn St G E Grogan, Terry Hissey, Mike Homer, Andy Johnson, Tom Johnson, Alan Jordan, Judith Lappin, Steve Lee, Darrell Lindley, Alasdair Macintyre, Michael May, Mark McGiffin, Isobel Osmont, Doug Porter, David Pratt, Brian Robertson, David Rodgers, Mike Shaw, Paul Smith, Iain Stewart, Vic Tambling, David Wilson, Lt Col Les Wilson MBE, Jane & Ian Yonge.

Newspapers

Jersey Evening Post.

Divisional Histories

The History of the Second Division 1914–18. E Wyrell. Nelson 1921. Two volumes.
The Eighth Division in War 1914–18. Lt Col J H Boraston and Capt C E O Bax. Medici Society 1926.

The History of the 19th Division 1914–18. E Wyrell. Arnold 1932.
A Short History of the 19th (Western) Division 1914–18. Anon. John Murray 1919.
The 25th Division in France and Flanders. Lt Col M Kincaid-Smith. Harrison 1919.
The Story of the 29th Division – A Record of Gallant Deeds. Capt S Gillon. Nelson 1925.
The 33rd Division in France and Flanders 1915–19. Lt Col G S Hutchinson. Waterlow 1921.
The History of the 40th Division. Lt Col F E Whitton. Gale & Polden 1926.
A Short History of the 49th West Riding and Midlands Infantry Division (TA). Lt Col F K Hughes. Stellar 1958.
The History of the 51st (Highland) Division 1914–18. Maj F W Bewsher. Blackwood 1921.
The Story of the 55th (West Lancashire) Division. Rev'd J O Coop. Liverpool Daily Post 1919.
The Royal Naval Division. D Jerrold. Hutchinson 1923. (63rd Division).

Regimental/Unit Histories

Royal Artillery
The Royal Artillery War Commemoration Book. Anon. G Bell 1970.
History of the Royal Regiment of Artillery, Western Front, 1914–18. Gen Sir M Farndale. Dorset Press 1986.
ARTYVICS – The Victoria Cross and The Royal Regiment of Artillery. Marc J Sherriff. Witherbys, Aylesbury St, London.

Grenadier Guards
The Grenadier Guards in the Great War of 1914–18. Lt Col Sir F Ponsonby. Macmillan 1920. Three volumes.

The King's Own (Royal Lancaster Regiment)
The King's Own, The Story of a Royal Regiment, Volume III 1914–50. Compiler Col J M Cowper. Gale & Polden 1957.
The King's (Liverpool Regiment)
The History of the King's Regiment (Liverpool) 1914–19. E Wyrell. Arnold 1928–35. Three volumes.

The Lincolnshire Regiment
History of the Lincolnshire Regiment 1914–18. Editor Maj Gen C R Simpson. Medici Society 1931.

The Prince of Wales's Own (West Yorkshire Regiment)
The West Yorkshire Regiment in the Great War 1914–18. E Wyrell. The Bodley Head 1924–27. Two volumes.

The Bedfordshire Regiment

The 16th Foot, A History of the Bedfordshire and Hertfordshire Regiment. Maj Gen Sir F Maurice. Constable 1931.

The Story of the Bedfordshire and Hertfordshire Regiment Volume II – 1914–58. Compiled by Lt Col T J Barrow DSO, Maj V A French and J Seabrook Esq. Published privately 1986.

Alexandra, Princess of Wales's Own (Yorkshire Regiment)

The Green Howards in the Great War 1914–19. Col H C Wylly. Butler & Tanner 1926.

The Green Howards – For Valour 1914–18. Anon. Published 1964.

The History of the Green Howards – 300 Years of Service. G Powell. Arms and Armour 1992.

The Lancashire Fusiliers

The History of the Lancashire Fusiliers 1914–18, Volumes I and II. Maj Gen J C Latter. Gale & Polden 1949.

The Lancashire Fusiliers Annual. No 26–1916 and No 28–1918. Editor Major B Smyth. Sackville Press 1917 and 1919

The Worcestershire Regiment

The Worcestershire Regiment in the Great War. Capt H Fitzm Stacke. G T Cheshire 1929.

The East Lancashire Regiment

History of the East Lancashire Regiment in the Great War 1914–18. Edited by Maj Gen Sir N Nicholson and Maj H T McMullen. Littlebury 1936.

The Duke of Wellington's (West Riding Regiment)

History of the Duke of Wellington's Regiment (West Riding) 1702–1992. J M Brereton and A C S Savoury. Amadeus 1993.

The Border Regiment

The Border Regiment in the Great War. Col H C Wylly. Gale & Polden 1924.

Tried and Valiant, The History of the Border Regiment 1702–1959. D Sutherland. Leo Cooper 1972.

The Prince of Wales's Volunteers (South Lancashire Regiment)

The South Lancashire Regiment. Col B R Mullaly. White Swan Press.

Ich Dien, The Prince of Wales's Volunteers (South Lancashire) 1914–34. Capt H Whalley-Kelly. Gale & Polden 1935.

The King's Own (Yorkshire Light Infantry)

History of the King's Own Yorkshire Light Infantry in the Great War, Volume III 1914–18. Lt Col R C Bond. Percy Lund, Humphries 1930.

The King's Own Yorkshire Light Infantry, Register of Officers 1755–1945. CP Deedes.

The Duke of Cambridge's Own (Middlesex Regiment)

The Die Hards in the Great War, A History of the Duke of Cambridge's Own (Middlesex Regiment). E Wyrall. Harrison 1926–30. Two volumes (1914–16 and 1916–19).

The Durham Light Infantry

Faithful, The Story of the Durham Light Infantry. S G P Ward. Nelson 1962.

The Durham Forces in the Field 1914–18, Volume II The Service Battalions of the Durham Light Infantry. Capt W Miles. Cassell 1920.

Officers of the Durham Light Infantry 1758–1968 (Volume 1–Regulars). M McGregor. Published privately 1989.

The Highland Light Infantry

Proud Heritage, The Story of the Highland Light Infantry, Volume III 1882–1918. Lt Col L B Oates. House of Grant 1961.

Seaforth Highlanders (Ross-shire Buffs, The Duke of Albany's)

Seaforth Highlanders. Editor Col J Sym. Gale & Polden 1962.

The Rifle Brigade (The Prince Consort's Own)

The History of the Rifle Brigade in the War 1914–18. Volume II, January 1917–June 1919. W W Seymour. Rifle Brigade Club 1936.

As above. Appendix – List of Officers and Other Ranks of the Rifle Brigade awarded Decorations or MID for services during the Great War. Compiled by Lt Col T R Eastwood and Maj H G Parkyn. Rifle Brigade Club 1936.

Rifle Brigade Chronicles 1915–1920. Editor Col W Verner. John Bale 1916–1921.

A Rifle Brigade Register 1905–63, Part 1–A Roll of Officers who have served in the Regiment. Compiled by Col W P S Curtis. Culverlands Press 1964.

Machine Gun Corps

Machine Guns, Their History and Tactical Employment (Being also a History of the Machine Gun Corps 1916–22). Lt Col G S Hutchinson. MacMillan 1938.

Royal Army Chaplains Department

In This Sign Conquer, The Story of the Army Chaplains. Brig Sir J Smyth. Mowbray 1968.

Australian Imperial Force
Official History of Australia in the War of 1914–1918, Volume IV – The Australian Imperial Force in France, 1917. 11th Edition 1941.
They Dared Mightily. Lionel Wigmore, Jeff Williams & Anthony Staunton 1963 & 1986.
Battle Scared: the 47th Battalion in the First World War. Craig Deayton 2011.
Fighting Nineteenth: History of the 19th Infantry Battalion AIF 1915–1918. David Wilson and Wayne Matthews 2011.

Canadian Expeditionary Force
Official History of the Canadian Army in the First World War – Canadian Expeditionary Force 1914–19. Col GWL Nicholson 1962.
Canada in Flanders. Sir Max Aitken 1916.

New Zealand
The New Zealand Division 1916–1919. A Popular History Based on Official Records. Col H Stewart CMG DSO MC. Whitcombe & Tombs Ltd, Auckland 1921.

General Works

A Bibliography of Regimental Histories of the British Army. Compiler A S White. Society for Army Historical Research 1965.
A Military Atlas of the First World War. A Banks & A Palmer. Purnell 1975.
The Times History of the Great War.
Topography of Armageddon, A British Trench Map Atlas of the Western Front 1914–18. P Chasseaud. Mapbooks 1991.
Before Endeavours Fade. R E B Coombs. Battle of Britain Prints 1976.
British Regiments 1914–18. Brig E A James. Samson 1978.

Biographical/Autobiographical

The Dictionary of National Biography 1901–85. Various volumes. Oxford University Press.
The Cross of Sacrifice, Officers Who Died in the Service of the British, Indian and East African Regiments and Corps 1914–19. S D and D B Jarvis. Roberts Medals 1993.
Australian Dictionary of Biography.
Whitaker's Peerage, Baronetage, Knightage & Companionage 1915.
Our Heroes – Containing Photographs with Biographical Notes of Officers of Irish Regiments and of Irish Officers of British Regiments who have fallen or who have been mentioned for distinguished conduct from August 1914 to July 1916. Printed as supplements to Irish Life from 1914 to 1916.
The Bond of Sacrifice, A Biographical Record of all British Officers Who Fell in the Great War. Volume I Aug–Dec 1915, Volume II Jan–Jun 1915. Editor Col L A Clutterbuck. Pulman 1916 and 1919.

The Roll of Honour Parts 1–5, A Biographical Record of Members of His Majesty's Naval and Military Forces who fell in the Great War 1914–18. Marquis de Ruvigny. Standard Art Book Co 1917–19.

The Dictionary of Edwardian Biography – various volumes. Printed 1904–08, reprinted 1985–87 Peter Bell Edinburgh.

Dictionary of Canadian Biography.

Valiant Hearts. Atlantic Canada and the Victoria Cross. John Boileau. Nimbus Publishing, Halifax, Nova Scotia 2005.

It's Only Me. David Raw (Theodore Hardy VC DSO MC)

The Military Exploits of Captain John James Crowe V.C. Doreen & Robin Pannett. Reveille Press 2013.

Specific Works on the Victoria Cross

The Register of the Victoria Cross. This England 1981 and 1988.

The Story of the Victoria Cross 1856–1963. Brig Sir J Smyth. Frederick Muller 1963.

The Evolution of the Victoria Cross, A Study in Administrative History. M J Crook. Midas 1975.

The Victoria Cross and the George Cross. IWM 1970.

The Victoria Cross, The Empire's Roll of Valour. Lt Col R Stewart. Hutchinson 1928.

The Victoria Cross 1856–1920. Sir O'Moore Creagh and E M Humphris. Standard Art Book Company, London 1920.

Victoria Cross – Awards to Irish Servicemen. B Clark. Published in The Irish Sword summer 1986.

Heart of a Dragon, VC's of Wales and the Welsh Regiments 1914–82. W Alister Williams. Bridge Books 2006.

Brave Railwaymen. A Stanistreet. Telen Publishing 1989.

Devotion to Duty, Tributes to a Region's VCs. J W Bancroft. Aim High 1990.

For Conspicuous Gallantry, A Brief History of the recipients of the VC from Nottinghamshire and Derbyshire. N McCrery. J H Hall 1990.

For Valour, The Victoria Cross, Courage in Action. J Percival. Thames Methuen 1985.

The Four Blackburn VCs. H L Kirby and R R Walsh. THCL 1986.

VC Locator. D Pillinger and A Staunton. Highland Press, Queanbeyan, New South Wales, Australia 1991.

Black Country VCs. B Harry. Black Country Society 1985.

The VC Roll of Honour. J W Bancroft. Aim High 1989.

A Bibliography of the Victoria Cross. W James McDonald. W J Mcdonald, Nova Scotia 1994.

Canon Lummis VC Files held in the National Army Museum, Chelsea.

Recipients of the Victoria Cross in the Care of the Commonwealth War Graves Commission. CWGC 1997.

Victoria Cross Heroes. Michael Ashcroft. Headline Review 2006

Monuments to Courage. David Harvey. 1999.

Liverpool Heroes – Book 1. Ann Clayton. Noel Chavasse VC Memorial Association.

Beyond the Five Points – Masonic Winners of The Victoria Cross and The George Cross. Phillip May GC, edited by Richard Cowley. Twin Pillars Books, Northamptonshire 2001.
Irish Winners of the Victoria Cross. Richard Doherty & David Truesdale. Four Courts Press, Dublin, Ireland 2000.
Our Bravest and Our Best: The Stories of Canada's Victoria Cross Winners. Arthur Bishop 1995.
A Breed Apart. Richard Leake. Great Northern Publishing 2008.
Beyond Their Duty – Heroes of the Green Howards. Roger Chapman. Green Howards Museum 2001.

Other Honours and Awards

Recipients of Bars to the Military Cross 1916–20. J V Webb 1988.
Distinguished Conduct Medal 1914–18, Citations of Recipients. London Stamp Exchange 1983.
Recipients of the Distinguished Conduct Medal 1914–1920. RW Walker.
The Distinguished Service Order 1886–1923 (in 2 volumes). Sir O'Moore Creagh and E M Humphris. J B Hayward 1978 (originally published 1924).
Orders and Medals Society Journal (various articles).
The Old Contemptibles Honours and Awards. First published 1915. Reprinted by J B Hayward & Son 1971.
Burke's Handbook to the Most Excellent Order of the British Empire. A Winton Thorpe (Editor). Burke Publishing Co Ltd, London 1921.
South African War – Honours and Awards 1899–1902.
Honours and Awards of the Indian Army: August 1914–August 1921. 1931.
The New Zealand Distinguished Service Order. J Bryant Haigh & Alan J Polaschek. 1993.

University and Schools Publications

The OTC Roll – A Roll of Members and Ex-members of the OTC Gazetted to Commissions in the Army August 1914–March 1915. Tim Donovan 1989.

Official Publications and Sources

History of the Great War, Order of Battle of Divisions. Compiler Maj A F Becke. HMSO.
History of the Great War, Military Operations, France and Belgium. Compiler Brig Gen Sir J E Edmonds. HMSO. Published in 14 volumes of text, with 7 map volumes and 2 separate Appendices between 1923 and 1948.
Location of Hospitals and Casualty Clearing Stations, BEF 1914–19. Ministry of Pensions 1923.

List of British Officers taken Prisoner in the Various Theatres of War between August 1914 and November 1918. Compiled from Official Records by Messrs Cox & Co, Charing Cross, London 1919.
London Gazettes.
Census returns, particularly for 1881, 1891, 1901 and 1911.
Officers and Soldiers Died in the Great War.
Australian service records in the National Archives of Australia.
Service records from the Library and Archives of Canada.
Service records in Archives New Zealand.

National Archives

Unit War Diaries under WO 95
Imperial Yeomanry Attestation Papers under WO 128/13
Military maps under WO 297.
Medal Cards and Medal Rolls under WO 329 and ADM 171.
Soldier's Service Records under WO 97, 363 and 364.
Officer's Records WO 25, 76, 339 and 374.
RAF Officer's Records under Air 76.
Births, Marriages and Deaths records.

Official Lists

Navy Lists.
Army Lists – including Graduation Lists and Record of War Service.
Air Force Lists.
Home Guard Lists 1942–44.
Indian Army Lists 1897–1940.
India List 1923–40.

Reference Publications

Who's Who and Who Was Who.
The Times 1914 onwards.
The Daily Telegraph 1914 onwards.
Kelly's Handbook to the Titled, Landed and Official Classes.
Burke's Peerage.

Internet Websites

History of the Victoria Cross – www2.prestel.co.uk/stewart – Iain Stewart.
Commonwealth War Graves Commission – www.yard.ccta.gov.uk/cwgc.

Scottish General Registry Office – www.origins.net/GRO.
Free Births, Marriages and Deaths – www.freebmd.com
Memorials to Valour – http://www.memorialstovalour.co.uk

Periodicals

This England magazine – various editions.
Coin and Medal News – various editions.
Journal of The Victoria Cross Society
Gun Fire – A Journal of First World War History. Edited by AJ Peacock, but no longer published
Stand To! – journal of the Western Front Association.

Useful Information

(Some details may be affected by Brexit)

Accommodation – there is a wide variety of accommodation available in France. Search on-line for your requirements. There are also numerous campsites, but many close for the winter from late September.

Clothing and Kit – consider taking:

Waterproofs.
Headwear and gloves.
Walking shoes/boots.
Shades and sunscreen.
Binoculars and camera.
Snacks and drinks.

Customs/Behaviour – local people are generally tolerant of battlefield visitors but please respect their property and address them respectfully. The French are less inclined to switch to English than other Europeans. If you try some basic French it will be appreciated.

Driving – rules of the road are similar to UK, apart from having to drive on the right. If in doubt about priorities, give way to the right, particularly in France. Obey laws and road signs – police impose harsh on-the-spot fines. Penalties for drinking and driving are heavy and the legal limit is lower than UK (50mg rather than 80mg). Most autoroutes in France are toll roads.

Fuel – petrol stations are usually only open 24 hours on major routes. Some accept credit cards in automatic tellers. The cheapest fuel is at hypermarkets.

Mandatory Requirements – if taking your own car you need:

Full driving licence (an International Driving Permit may also be required post-Brexit).
Vehicle registration document.
Comprehensive motor insurance valid in Europe (Green Card).
European breakdown and recovery cover.
Letter of authorisation from the owner if the vehicle is not yours.
Spare set of bulbs, headlight beam adjusters, warning triangle, GB sticker, high visibility vest and breathalyzer.

Emergency – keep details required in an emergency separate from wallet or handbag:
Photocopy passport, insurance documents and EHIC (see Health below).
Mobile phone details.
Credit/debit card numbers and cancellation telephone contacts.
Travel insurance company contact number.

Ferries – the closest ports are Boulogne, Calais and Dunkirk. The Shuttle is quicker, but usually more expensive.

Health

European Health Insurance Card – entitles the holder to medical treatment at local rates. Apply online at www.ehic.org.uk/Internet/startApplication.do. Issued free and valid for five years but Brexit may affect this. You are only covered if you have the EHIC with you when you go for treatment.

Travel Insurance – you are also strongly advised to have full travel insurance. If you receive treatment get a statement by the doctor (*feuille de soins*) and a receipt to make a claim on return.

Personal Medical Kit – treating minor ailments saves time and money. Pack sufficient prescription medicine for the trip.

Chemist (*Pharmacie*) – look for the green cross. They provide some treatment and if unable to help will direct you to a doctor. Most open 0900–1900 except Sunday. Out of hours services (*pharmacie de garde*) are advertised in Pharmacie windows.

Doctor and Dentist – hotel receptions have details of local practices. Beware private doctors/hospitals, as extra charges cannot be reclaimed – the French national health service is known as *conventionné*.

Rabies – contact with infected animals is very rare, but if bitten by any animal, get the wound examined professionally immediately.

Money

ATMs – at most banks and post offices with instructions in English. Check your card can be used in France and what charges apply. Some banks limit how much can be withdrawn. Let your bank know you will be away, as some block cards if transactions take place unexpectedly.

Credit/Debit Cards – major cards are usually accepted, but some have different names – Visa is Carte Bleue and Mastercard is Eurocard.

Exchange – beware 0% commission, as the rate may be poor. The Post Office takes back unused currency at the same rate, which may or may not be advantageous. Since the Euro, currency exchange facilities are scarce.

Local Taxes – if you buy high value items you can reclaim tax. Get the forms completed by the shop, have them stamped by Customs, post them to the shop and they will refund about 12%.

Passport – a valid passport is required.

Post – postcard stamps are available from vendors, newsagents and tabacs.

Public Holidays – just about everything closes and banks can close early the day before. Transport may be affected, but tourist attractions in high season are unlikely to be. The following dates/days are public holidays:

1 January
Easter Monday
1 May
8 May
Ascension Day
Whit Monday
14 July
15 August
1 & 11 November
25 December

In France many businesses and restaurants close for the majority of August.

Radio – if you want to pick up the news from home try BBC Radio 4 on 198 kHz long wave. BBC Five Live on 909 kHz medium wave can sometimes be received. There are numerous internet options for keeping up with the news.

Shops – in large towns and tourist areas they tend to open all day. In more remote places they may close for lunch. Some bakers open Sunday a.m. and during the week take later lunch breaks. In general shops do not open on Sundays.

Telephone

To UK – 0044, delete initial 0 then dial the rest of the number.

Local Calls – dial the full number even if within the same zone.

Mobiles – check yours will work in France and the charges.
Emergencies – dial 112 for medical, fire and police anywhere in Europe from any landline, pay phone or mobile. Calls are free

British Embassy (Paris) – 01 44 51 31 00.

Time Zone – one hour ahead of UK.

Tipping – a small tip is expected by cloakroom and lavatory attendants and porters. Not required in restaurants, when a service charge is included.

Toilets – the best are in museums and the main tourist attractions. Towns usually have public toilets where markets are held; some are coin operated. Otherwise on the battlefields facilities are sparse. Finding a local café may be the best option, although they are closing as rapidly as British pubs.

Index

Notes:
1. Not every person or location is included. Most family members named in the Biographies are not.
2. Armed forces units, establishments, etc are grouped under the respective country, except for Britain's, which appear under the three services – British Army, Royal Air Force and Royal Navy. Royal Naval Division units appear under British Army for convenience.
3. Newfoundland appears under Canada although not part of it at the time.
4. Cemeteries/Crematoria, Cathedrals, Churches, Hospitals, Schools, Trenches, Universities and Commonwealth War Graves Commission appear under those group headings.
5. All orders, medals and decorations appear under Orders.
6. Belgium, Britain, France and Germany are not indexed in the accounts of the VC actions as there are too many mentions. Similarly England, Britain and United Kingdom are not indexed in the biographies.